T0304452

Introduction to Algorithms

Fourth Edition

Thomas H. Cormen
Charles E. Leiserson
Ronald L. Rivest
Clifford Stein

Introduction to Algorithms
Fourth Edition

The MIT Press
Cambridge, Massachusetts   London, England

The MIT Press would like to thank the anonymous peer reviewers who provided comments on drafts of this book. The generous work of academic experts is essential for establishing the authority and quality of our publications. We acknowledge with gratitude the contributions of these otherwise uncredited readers.

This book was set in Times Roman and MathTime Professional II by the authors.

Printed and bound in China.

Names: Cormen, Thomas H., author. | Leiserson, Charles Eric, author. |
  Rivest, Ronald L., author. | Stein, Clifford, author.
Title: Introduction to algorithms / Thomas H. Cormen, Charles E. Leiserson,
  Ronald L. Rivest, Clifford Stein.
Description: Fourth edition. | Cambridge, Massachusetts : The MIT Press,
  [2022] | Includes bibliographical references and index.
Identifiers: LCCN 2021037260 | ISBN 9780262046305
Subjects: LCSH: Computer programming. | Computer algorithms.
Classification: LCC QA76.6 .C662 2022 | DDC 005.13--dc23
LC record available at http://lccn.loc.gov/2021037260

10 9 8 7 6 5 4 3

Contents

IV   Advanced Design and Analysis Techniques

VII   *Selected Topics*

Preface

Not so long ago, anyone who had heard the word "algorithm" was almost certainly a computer scientist or mathematician. With computers having become prevalent in our modern lives, however, the term is no longer esoteric. If you look around your home, you'll find algorithms running in the most mundane places: your microwave oven, your washing machine, and, of course, your computer. You ask algorithms to make recommendations to you: what music you might like or what route to take when driving. Our society, for better or for worse, asks algorithms to suggest sentences for convicted criminals. You even rely on algorithms to keep you alive, or at least not to kill you: the control systems in your car or in medical equipment.[1] The word "algorithm" appears somewhere in the news seemingly every day.

Therefore, it behooves you to understand algorithms not just as a student or practitioner of computer science, but as a citizen of the world. Once you understand algorithms, you can educate others about what algorithms are, how they operate, and what their limitations are.

This book provides a comprehensive introduction to the modern study of computer algorithms. It presents many algorithms and covers them in considerable depth, yet makes their design accessible to all levels of readers. All the analyses are laid out, some simple, some more involved. We have tried to keep explanations clear without sacrificing depth of coverage or mathematical rigor.

Each chapter presents an algorithm, a design technique, an application area, or a related topic. Algorithms are described in English and in a pseudocode designed to be readable by anyone who has done a little programming. The book contains 231 figures—many with multiple parts—illustrating how the algorithms work. Since we emphasize *efficiency* as a design criterion, we include careful analyses of the running times of the algorithms.

---

[1] To understand many of the ways in which algorithms influence our daily lives, see the book by Fry [162].

The text is intended primarily for use in undergraduate or graduate courses in algorithms or data structures. Because it discusses engineering issues in algorithm design, as well as mathematical aspects, it is equally well suited for self-study by technical professionals.

In this, the fourth edition, we have once again updated the entire book. The changes cover a broad spectrum, including new chapters and sections, color illustrations, and what we hope you'll find to be a more engaging writing style.

To the teacher

We have designed this book to be both versatile and complete. You should find it useful for a variety of courses, from an undergraduate course in data structures up through a graduate course in algorithms. Because we have provided considerably more material than can fit in a typical one-term course, you can select the material that best supports the course you wish to teach.

You should find it easy to organize your course around just the chapters you need. We have made chapters relatively self-contained, so that you need not worry about an unexpected and unnecessary dependence of one chapter on another. Whereas in an undergraduate course, you might use only some sections from a chapter, in a graduate course, you might cover the entire chapter.

We have included 931 exercises and 162 problems. Each section ends with exercises, and each chapter ends with problems. The exercises are generally short questions that test basic mastery of the material. Some are simple self-check thought exercises, but many are substantial and suitable as assigned homework. The problems include more elaborate case studies which often introduce new material. They often consist of several parts that lead the student through the steps required to arrive at a solution.

As with the third edition of this book, we have made publicly available solutions to some, but by no means all, of the problems and exercises. You can find these solutions on our website, http://mitpress.mit.edu/algorithms/. You will want to check this site to see whether it contains the solution to an exercise or problem that you plan to assign. Since the set of solutions that we post might grow over time, we recommend that you check the site each time you teach the course.

We have starred ($\star$) the sections and exercises that are more suitable for graduate students than for undergraduates. A starred section is not necessarily more difficult than an unstarred one, but it may require an understanding of more advanced mathematics. Likewise, starred exercises may require an advanced background or more than average creativity.

To the student

We hope that this textbook provides you with an enjoyable introduction to the field of algorithms. We have attempted to make every algorithm accessible and interesting. To help you when you encounter unfamiliar or difficult algorithms, we describe each one in a step-by-step manner. We also provide careful explanations of the mathematics needed to understand the analysis of the algorithms and supporting figures to help you visualize what is going on.

Since this book is large, your class will probably cover only a portion of its material. Although we hope that you will find this book helpful to you as a course textbook now, we have also tried to make it comprehensive enough to warrant space on your future professional bookshelf.

What are the prerequisites for reading this book?

- You need some programming experience. In particular, you should understand recursive procedures and simple data structures, such as arrays and linked lists (although Section 10.2 covers linked lists and a variant that you may find new).

- You should have some facility with mathematical proofs, and especially proofs by mathematical induction. A few portions of the book rely on some knowledge of elementary calculus. Although this book uses mathematics throughout, Part I and Appendices A–D teach you all the mathematical techniques you will need.

Our website, http://mitpress.mit.edu/algorithms/, links to solutions for some of the problems and exercises. Feel free to check your solutions against ours. We ask, however, that you not send your solutions to us.

To the professional

The wide range of topics in this book makes it an excellent handbook on algorithms. Because each chapter is relatively self-contained, you can focus on the topics most relevant to you.

Since most of the algorithms we discuss have great practical utility, we address implementation concerns and other engineering issues. We often provide practical alternatives to the few algorithms that are primarily of theoretical interest.

If you wish to implement any of the algorithms, you should find the translation of our pseudocode into your favorite programming language to be a fairly straightforward task. We have designed the pseudocode to present each algorithm clearly and succinctly. Consequently, we do not address error handling and other software-engineering issues that require specific assumptions about your programming environment. We attempt to present each algorithm simply and directly without allowing the idiosyncrasies of a particular programming language to obscure its essence. If you are used to 0-origin arrays, you might find our frequent practice of indexing arrays from 1 a minor stumbling block. You can always either subtract 1 from our indices or just overallocate the array and leave position 0 unused.

We understand that if you are using this book outside of a course, then you might be unable to check your solutions to problems and exercises against solutions provided by an instructor. Our website, http://mitpress.mit.edu/algorithms/, links to solutions for some of the problems and exercises so that you can check your work. Please do not send your solutions to us.

To our colleagues

We have supplied an extensive bibliography and pointers to the current literature. Each chapter ends with a set of chapter notes that give historical details and references. The chapter notes do not provide a complete reference to the whole field of algorithms, however. Though it may be hard to believe for a book of this size, space constraints prevented us from including many interesting algorithms.

Despite myriad requests from students for solutions to problems and exercises, we have adopted the policy of not citing references for them, removing the temptation for students to look up a solution rather than to discover it themselves.

Changes for the fourth edition

As we said about the changes for the second and third editions, depending on how you look at it, the book changed either not much or quite a bit. A quick look at the table of contents shows that most of the third-edition chapters and sections appear in the fourth edition. We removed three chapters and several sections, but we have added three new chapters and several new sections apart from these new chapters.

We kept the hybrid organization from the first three editions. Rather than organizing chapters only by problem domains or only according to techniques, this book incorporates elements of both. It contains technique-based chapters on divide-and-conquer, dynamic programming, greedy algorithms, amortized analysis, augmenting data structures, NP-completeness, and approximation algorithms. But it also has entire parts on sorting, on data structures for dynamic sets, and on algorithms for graph problems. We find that although you need to know how to apply techniques for designing and analyzing algorithms, problems seldom announce to you which techniques are most amenable to solving them.

Some of the changes in the fourth edition apply generally across the book, and some are specific to particular chapters or sections. Here is a summary of the most significant general changes:

- We added 140 new exercises and 22 new problems. We also improved many of the old exercises and problems, often as the result of reader feedback. (Thanks to all readers who made suggestions.)

- We have color! With designers from the MIT Press, we selected a limited palette, devised to convey information and to be pleasing to the eye. (We are delighted to display red-black trees in—get this—red and black!) To enhance readability, defined terms, pseudocode comments, and page numbers in the index are in color.

- Pseudocode procedures appear on a tan background to make them easier to spot, and they do not necessarily appear on the page of their first reference. When they don't, the text directs you to the relevant page. In the same vein, nonlocal references to numbered equations, theorems, lemmas, and corollaries include the page number.

- We removed topics that were rarely taught. We dropped in their entirety the chapters on Fibonacci heaps, van Emde Boas trees, and computational geometry. In addition, the following material was excised: the maximum-subarray problem, implementing pointers and objects, perfect hashing, randomly built binary search trees, matroids, push-relabel algorithms for maximum flow, the iterative fast Fourier transform method, the details of the simplex algorithm for linear programming, and integer factorization. You can find all the removed material on our website, http://mitpress.mit.edu/algorithms/.

- We reviewed the entire book and rewrote sentences, paragraphs, and sections to make the writing clearer, more personal, and gender neutral. For example, the "traveling-salesman problem" in the previous editions is now called the "traveling-salesperson problem." We believe that it is critically important for engineering and science, including our own field of computer science, to be welcoming to everyone. (The one place that stumped us is in Chapter 13, which requires a term for a parent's sibling. Because the English language has no such gender-neutral term, we regretfully stuck with "uncle.")

- The chapter notes, bibliography, and index were updated, reflecting the dramatic growth of the field of algorithms since the third edition.

- We corrected errors, posting most corrections on our website of third-edition errata. Those that were reported while we were in full swing preparing this edition were not posted, but were corrected in this edition. (Thanks again to all readers who helped us identify issues.)

The specific changes for the fourth edition include the following:

- We renamed Chapter 3 and added a section giving an overview of asymptotic notation before delving into the formal definitions.

- Chapter 4 underwent substantial changes to improve its mathematical foundation and make it more robust and intuitive. The notion of an algorithmic recurrence was introduced, and the topic of ignoring floors and ceilings in recurrences was addressed more rigorously. The second case of the master theorem incorporates polylogarithmic factors, and a rigorous proof of a "continuous" version of the master theorem is now provided. We also present the powerful and general Akra-Bazzi method (without proof).

- The deterministic order-statistic algorithm in Chapter 9 is slightly different, and the analyses of both the randomized and deterministic order-statistic algorithms have been revamped.

- In addition to stacks and queues, Section 10.1 discusses ways to store arrays and matrices.

- Chapter 11 on hash tables includes a modern treatment of hash functions. It also emphasizes linear probing as an efficient method for resolving collisions when the underlying hardware implements caching to favor local searches.

- To replace the sections on matroids in Chapter 15, we converted a problem in the third edition about offline caching into a full section.

- Section 16.4 now contains a more intuitive explanation of the potential functions to analyze table doubling and halving.

- Chapter 17 on augmenting data structures was relocated from Part III to Part V, reflecting our view that this technique goes beyond basic material.

- Chapter 25 is a new chapter about matchings in bipartite graphs. It presents algorithms to find a matching of maximum cardinality, to solve the stable-marriage problem, and to find a maximum-weight matching (known as the "assignment problem").

- Chapter 26, on task-parallel computing, has been updated with modern terminology, including the name of the chapter.

- Chapter 27, which covers online algorithms, is another new chapter. In an online algorithm, the input arrives over time, rather than being available in its entirety at the start of the algorithm. The chapter describes several examples of online algorithms, including determining how long to wait for an elevator before taking the stairs, maintaining a linked list via the move-to-front heuristic, and evaluating replacement policies for caches.

- In Chapter 29, we removed the detailed presentation of the simplex algorithm, as it was math heavy without really conveying many algorithmic ideas. The chapter now focuses on the key aspect of how to model problems as linear programs, along with the essential duality property of linear programming.

- Section 32.5 adds to the chapter on string matching the simple, yet powerful, structure of suffix arrays.

- Chapter 33, on machine learning, is the third new chapter. It introduces several basic methods used in machine learning: clustering to group similar items together, weighted-majority algorithms, and gradient descent to find the minimizer of a function.

- Section 34.5.6 summarizes strategies for polynomial-time reductions to show that problems are NP-hard.

- The proof of the approximation algorithm for the set-covering problem in Section 35.3 has been revised.

Website

You can use our website, http://mitpress.mit.edu/algorithms/, to obtain supplementary information and to communicate with us. The website links to a list of known errors, material from the third edition that is not included in the fourth edition, solutions to selected exercises and problems, Python implementations of many of the algorithms in this book, a list explaining the corny professor jokes (of course), as well as other content, which we may add to. The website also tells you how to report errors or make suggestions.

How we produced this book

Like the previous three editions, the fourth edition was produced in LaTeX 2_ε. We used the Times font with mathematics typeset using the MathTime Professional II fonts. As in all previous editions, we compiled the index using Windex, a C program that we wrote, and produced the bibliography using BIBTeX. The PDF files for this book were created on a MacBook Pro running macOS 10.14.

Our plea to Apple in the preface of the third edition to update MacDraw Pro for macOS 10 went for naught, and so we continued to draw illustrations on pre-Intel Macs running MacDraw Pro under the Classic environment of older versions of macOS 10. Many of the mathematical expressions appearing in illustrations were laid in with the psfrag package for LaTeX 2_ε.

Acknowledgments for the fourth edition

We have been working with the MIT Press since we started writing the first edition in 1987, collaborating with several directors, editors, and production staff. Throughout our association with the MIT Press, their support has always been outstanding. Special thanks to our editors Marie Lee, who put up with us for far too long, and Elizabeth Swayze, who pushed us over the finish line. Thanks also to Director Amy Brand and to Alex Hoopes.

As in the third edition, we were geographically distributed while producing the fourth edition, working in the Dartmouth College Department of Computer Science; the MIT Computer Science and Artificial Intelligence Laboratory and the MIT Department of Electrical Engineering and Computer Science; and the Columbia University Department of Industrial Engineering and Operations Research, Department of Computer Science, and Data Science Institute. During the COVID-19 pandemic, we worked largely from home. We thank our respective universities and colleagues for providing such supportive and stimulating environments. As we complete this book, those of us who are not retired are eager to return to our respective universities now that the pandemic seems to be abating.

Julie Sussman, P.P.A., came to our rescue once again with her technical copy-editing under tremendous time pressure. If not for Julie, this book would be riddled with errors (or, let's say, many more errors than it has) and would be far less readable. Julie, we will be forever indebted to you. Errors that remain are the responsibility of the authors (and probably were inserted after Julie read the material).

Dozens of errors in previous editions were corrected in the process of creating this edition. We thank our readers—too many to list them all—who have reported errors and suggested improvements over the years.

We received considerable help in preparing some of the new material in this edition. Neville Campbell (unaffiliated), Bill Kuszmaul of MIT, and Chee Yap of NYU provided valuable advice regarding the treatment of recurrences in Chapter 4. Yan Gu of the University of California, Riverside, provided feedback on parallel algorithms in Chapter 26. Rob Shapire of Microsoft Research altered our approach to the material on machine learning with his detailed comments on Chapter 33. Qi Qi of MIT helped with the analysis of the Monty Hall problem (Problem C-1).

Molly Seaman and Mary Reilly of the MIT Press helped us select the color palette in the illustrations, and Wojciech Jarosz of Dartmouth College suggested design improvements to our newly colored figures. Yichen (Annie) Ke and Linda Xiao, who have since graduated from Dartmouth, aided in colorizing the illustrations, and Linda also produced many of the Python implementations that are available on the book's website.

Finally, we thank our wives—Wendy Leiserson, Gail Rivest, Rebecca Ivry, and the late Nicole Cormen—and our families. The patience and encouragement of those who love us made this project possible. We affectionately dedicate this book to them.

THOMAS H. CORMEN   *Lebanon, New Hampshire*
CHARLES E. LEISERSON   *Cambridge, Massachusetts*
RONALD L. RIVEST   *Cambridge, Massachusetts*
CLIFFORD STEIN   *New York, New York*

June, 2021

Part I   Foundations

Introduction

When you design and analyze algorithms, you need to be able to describe how they operate and how to design them. You also need some mathematical tools to show that your algorithms do the right thing and do it efficiently. This part will get you started. Later parts of this book will build upon this base.

Chapter 1 provides an overview of algorithms and their place in modern computing systems. This chapter defines what an algorithm is and lists some examples. It also makes a case for considering algorithms as a technology, alongside technologies such as fast hardware, graphical user interfaces, object-oriented systems, and networks.

In Chapter 2, we see our first algorithms, which solve the problem of sorting a sequence of n numbers. They are written in a pseudocode which, although not directly translatable to any conventional programming language, conveys the structure of the algorithm clearly enough that you should be able to implement it in the language of your choice. The sorting algorithms we examine are insertion sort, which uses an incremental approach, and merge sort, which uses a recursive technique known as "divide-and-conquer." Although the time each requires increases with the value of n, the rate of increase differs between the two algorithms. We determine these running times in Chapter 2, and we develop a useful "asymptotic" notation to express them.

Chapter 3 precisely defines asymptotic notation. We'll use asymptotic notation to bound the growth of functions—most often, functions that describe the running time of algorithms—from above and below. The chapter starts by informally defining the most commonly used asymptotic notations and giving an example of how to apply them. It then formally defines five asymptotic notations and presents conventions for how to put them together. The rest of Chapter 3 is primarily a presentation of mathematical notation, more to ensure that your use of notation matches that in this book than to teach you new mathematical concepts.

Chapter 4 delves further into the divide-and-conquer method introduced in Chapter 2. It provides two additional examples of divide-and-conquer algorithms for multiplying square matrices, including Strassen's surprising method. Chapter 4 contains methods for solving recurrences, which are useful for describing the running times of recursive algorithms. In the substitution method, you guess an answer and prove it correct. Recursion trees provide one way to generate a guess. Chapter 4 also presents the powerful technique of the "master method," which you can often use to solve recurrences that arise from divide-and-conquer algorithms. Although the chapter provides a proof of a foundational theorem on which the master theorem depends, you should feel free to employ the master method without delving into the proof. Chapter 4 concludes with some advanced topics.

Chapter 5 introduces probabilistic analysis and randomized algorithms. You typically use probabilistic analysis to determine the running time of an algorithm in cases in which, due to the presence of an inherent probability distribution, the running time may differ on different inputs of the same size. In some cases, you might assume that the inputs conform to a known probability distribution, so that you are averaging the running time over all possible inputs. In other cases, the probability distribution comes not from the inputs but from random choices made during the course of the algorithm. An algorithm whose behavior is determined not only by its input but by the values produced by a random-number generator is a randomized algorithm. You can use randomized algorithms to enforce a probability distribution on the inputs—thereby ensuring that no particular input always causes poor performance—or even to bound the error rate of algorithms that are allowed to produce incorrect results on a limited basis.

Appendices A–D contain other mathematical material that you will find helpful as you read this book. You might have seen much of the material in the appendix chapters before having read this book (although the specific definitions and notational conventions we use may differ in some cases from what you have seen in the past), and so you should think of the appendices as reference material. On the other hand, you probably have not already seen most of the material in Part I. All the chapters in Part I and the appendices are written with a tutorial flavor.

1   The Role of Algorithms in Computing

What are algorithms? Why is the study of algorithms worthwhile? What is the role of algorithms relative to other technologies used in computers? This chapter will answer these questions.

1.1   Algorithms

Informally, an *algorithm* is any well-defined computational procedure that takes some value, or set of values, as *input* and produces some value, or set of values, as *output* in a finite amount of time. An algorithm is thus a sequence of computational steps that transform the input into the output.

You can also view an algorithm as a tool for solving a well-specified *computational problem*. The statement of the problem specifies in general terms the desired input/output relationship for problem instances, typically of arbitrarily large size. The algorithm describes a specific computational procedure for achieving that input/output relationship for all problem instances.

As an example, suppose that you need to sort a sequence of numbers into monotonically increasing order. This problem arises frequently in practice and provides fertile ground for introducing many standard design techniques and analysis tools. Here is how we formally define the *sorting problem*:

Input: A sequence of n numbers $\langle a_1, a_2, \ldots, a_n \rangle$.

Output: A permutation (reordering) $\langle a'_1, a'_2, \ldots, a'_n \rangle$ of the input sequence such that $a'_1 \leq a'_2 \leq \cdots \leq a'_n$.

Thus, given the input sequence $\langle 31, 41, 59, 26, 41, 58 \rangle$, a correct sorting algorithm returns as output the sequence $\langle 26, 31, 41, 41, 58, 59 \rangle$. Such an input sequence is called an *instance* of the sorting problem. In general, an *instance of a problem*[1] consists of the input (satisfying whatever constraints are imposed in the problem statement) needed to compute a solution to the problem.

Because many programs use it as an intermediate step, sorting is a fundamental operation in computer science. As a result, you have a large number of good sorting algorithms at your disposal. Which algorithm is best for a given application depends on—among other factors—the number of items to be sorted, the extent to which the items are already somewhat sorted, possible restrictions on the item values, the architecture of the computer, and the kind of storage devices to be used: main memory, disks, or even—archaically—tapes.

An algorithm for a computational problem is *correct* if, for every problem instance provided as input, it *halts*—finishes its computing in finite time—and outputs the correct solution to the problem instance. A correct algorithm *solves* the given computational problem. An incorrect algorithm might not halt at all on some input instances, or it might halt with an incorrect answer. Contrary to what you might expect, incorrect algorithms can sometimes be useful, if you can control their error rate. We'll see an example of an algorithm with a controllable error rate in Chapter 31 when we study algorithms for finding large prime numbers. Ordinarily, however, we'll concern ourselves only with correct algorithms.

An algorithm can be specified in English, as a computer program, or even as a hardware design. The only requirement is that the specification must provide a precise description of the computational procedure to be followed.

What kinds of problems are solved by algorithms?

Sorting is by no means the only computational problem for which algorithms have been developed. (You probably suspected as much when you saw the size of this book.) Practical applications of algorithms are ubiquitous and include the following examples:

- The Human Genome Project has made great progress toward the goals of identifying all the roughly 30,000 genes in human DNA, determining the sequences of the roughly 3 billion chemical base pairs that make up human DNA, storing this information in databases, and developing tools for data analysis. Each of these steps requires sophisticated algorithms. Although the solutions to the various problems involved are beyond the scope of this book, many methods to solve these biological problems use ideas presented here, enabling scientists to accomplish tasks while using resources efficiently. Dynamic programming, as

---

[1] Sometimes, when the problem context is known, problem instances are themselves simply called "problems."

in Chapter 14, is an important technique for solving several of these biological problems, particularly ones that involve determining similarity between DNA sequences. The savings realized are in time, both human and machine, and in money, as more information can be extracted by laboratory techniques.

- The internet enables people all around the world to quickly access and retrieve large amounts of information. With the aid of clever algorithms, sites on the internet are able to manage and manipulate this large volume of data. Examples of problems that make essential use of algorithms include finding good routes on which the data travels (techniques for solving such problems appear in Chapter 22), and using a search engine to quickly find pages on which particular information resides (related techniques are in Chapters 11 and 32).

- Electronic commerce enables goods and services to be negotiated and exchanged electronically, and it depends on the privacy of personal information such as credit card numbers, passwords, and bank statements. The core technologies used in electronic commerce include public-key cryptography and digital signatures (covered in Chapter 31), which are based on numerical algorithms and number theory.

- Manufacturing and other commercial enterprises often need to allocate scarce resources in the most beneficial way. An oil company might wish to know where to place its wells in order to maximize its expected profit. A political candidate might want to determine where to spend money buying campaign advertising in order to maximize the chances of winning an election. An airline might wish to assign crews to flights in the least expensive way possible, making sure that each flight is covered and that government regulations regarding crew scheduling are met. An internet service provider might wish to determine where to place additional resources in order to serve its customers more effectively. All of these are examples of problems that can be solved by modeling them as linear programs, which Chapter 29 explores.

Although some of the details of these examples are beyond the scope of this book, we do give underlying techniques that apply to these problems and problem areas. We also show how to solve many specific problems, including the following:

- You have a road map on which the distance between each pair of adjacent intersections is marked, and you wish to determine the shortest route from one intersection to another. The number of possible routes can be huge, even if you disallow routes that cross over themselves. How can you choose which of all possible routes is the shortest? You can start by modeling the road map (which is itself a model of the actual roads) as a graph (which we will meet in Part VI and Appendix B). In this graph, you wish to find the shortest path from one vertex to another. Chapter 22 shows how to solve this problem efficiently.

- Given a mechanical design in terms of a library of parts, where each part may include instances of other parts, list the parts in order so that each part appears before any part that uses it. If the design comprises n parts, then there are $n!$ possible orders, where $n!$ denotes the factorial function. Because the factorial function grows faster than even an exponential function, you cannot feasibly generate each possible order and then verify that, within that order, each part appears before the parts using it (unless you have only a few parts). This problem is an instance of topological sorting, and Chapter 20 shows how to solve this problem efficiently.

- A doctor needs to determine whether an image represents a cancerous tumor or a benign one. The doctor has available images of many other tumors, some of which are known to be cancerous and some of which are known to be benign. A cancerous tumor is likely to be more similar to other cancerous tumors than to benign tumors, and a benign tumor is more likely to be similar to other benign tumors. By using a clustering algorithm, as in Chapter 33, the doctor can identify which outcome is more likely.

- You need to compress a large file containing text so that it occupies less space. Many ways to do so are known, including "LZW compression," which looks for repeating character sequences. Chapter 15 studies a different approach, "Huffman coding," which encodes characters by bit sequences of various lengths, with characters occurring more frequently encoded by shorter bit sequences.

These lists are far from exhaustive (as you again have probably surmised from this book's heft), but they exhibit two characteristics common to many interesting algorithmic problems:

1. They have many candidate solutions, the overwhelming majority of which do not solve the problem at hand. Finding one that does, or one that is "best," without explicitly examining each possible solution, can present quite a challenge.

2. They have practical applications. Of the problems in the above list, finding the shortest path provides the easiest examples. A transportation firm, such as a trucking or railroad company, has a financial interest in finding shortest paths through a road or rail network because taking shorter paths results in lower labor and fuel costs. Or a routing node on the internet might need to find the shortest path through the network in order to route a message quickly. Or a person wishing to drive from New York to Boston might want to find driving directions using a navigation app.

Not every problem solved by algorithms has an easily identified set of candidate solutions. For example, given a set of numerical values representing samples of a signal taken at regular time intervals, the discrete Fourier transform converts the time domain to the frequency domain. That is, it approximates the signal as a weighted sum of sinusoids, producing the strength of various frequencies which, when summed, approximate the sampled signal. In addition to lying at the heart of signal processing, discrete Fourier transforms have applications in data compression and multiplying large polynomials and integers. Chapter 30 gives an efficient algorithm, the fast Fourier transform (commonly called the FFT), for this problem. The chapter also sketches out the design of a hardware FFT circuit.

Data structures

This book also presents several data structures. A *data structure* is a way to store and organize data in order to facilitate access and modifications. Using the appropriate data structure or structures is an important part of algorithm design. No single data structure works well for all purposes, and so you should know the strengths and limitations of several of them.

Technique

Although you can use this book as a "cookbook" for algorithms, you might someday encounter a problem for which you cannot readily find a published algorithm (many of the exercises and problems in this book, for example). This book will teach you techniques of algorithm design and analysis so that you can develop algorithms on your own, show that they give the correct answer, and analyze their efficiency. Different chapters address different aspects of algorithmic problem solving. Some chapters address specific problems, such as finding medians and order statistics in Chapter 9, computing minimum spanning trees in Chapter 21, and determining a maximum flow in a network in Chapter 24. Other chapters introduce techniques, such as divide-and-conquer in Chapters 2 and 4, dynamic programming in Chapter 14, and amortized analysis in Chapter 16.

Hard problems

Most of this book is about efficient algorithms. Our usual measure of efficiency is speed: how long does an algorithm take to produce its result? There are some problems, however, for which we know of no algorithm that runs in a reasonable amount of time. Chapter 34 studies an interesting subset of these problems, which are known as NP-complete.

Why are NP-complete problems interesting? First, although no efficient algorithm for an NP-complete problem has ever been found, nobody has ever proven that an efficient algorithm for one cannot exist. In other words, no one knows whether efficient algorithms exist for NP-complete problems. Second, the set of

NP-complete problems has the remarkable property that if an efficient algorithm exists for any one of them, then efficient algorithms exist for all of them. This relationship among the NP-complete problems makes the lack of efficient solutions all the more tantalizing. Third, several NP-complete problems are similar, but not identical, to problems for which we do know of efficient algorithms. Computer scientists are intrigued by how a small change to the problem statement can cause a big change to the efficiency of the best known algorithm.

You should know about NP-complete problems because some of them arise surprisingly often in real applications. If you are called upon to produce an efficient algorithm for an NP-complete problem, you are likely to spend a lot of time in a fruitless search. If, instead, you can show that the problem is NP-complete, you can spend your time developing an efficient approximation algorithm, that is, an algorithm that gives a good, but not necessarily the best possible, solution.

As a concrete example, consider a delivery company with a central depot. Each day, it loads up delivery trucks at the depot and sends them around to deliver goods to several addresses. At the end of the day, each truck must end up back at the depot so that it is ready to be loaded for the next day. To reduce costs, the company wants to select an order of delivery stops that yields the lowest overall distance traveled by each truck. This problem is the well-known "traveling-salesperson problem," and it is NP-complete.[2] It has no known efficient algorithm. Under certain assumptions, however, we know of efficient algorithms that compute overall distances close to the smallest possible. Chapter 35 discusses such "approximation algorithms."

Alternative computing models

For many years, we could count on processor clock speeds increasing at a steady rate. Physical limitations present a fundamental roadblock to ever-increasing clock speeds, however: because power density increases superlinearly with clock speed, chips run the risk of melting once their clock speeds become high enough. In order to perform more computations per second, therefore, chips are being designed to contain not just one but several processing "cores." We can liken these multicore computers to several sequential computers on a single chip. In other words, they are a type of "parallel computer." In order to elicit the best performance from multicore computers, we need to design algorithms with parallelism in mind. Chapter 26 presents a model for "task-parallel" algorithms, which take advantage of multiple processing cores. This model has advantages from both theoretical and

---

[2] To be precise, only decision problems—those with a "yes/no" answer—can be NP-complete. The decision version of the traveling salesperson problem asks whether there exists an order of stops whose distance totals at most a given amount.

practical standpoints, and many modern parallel-programming platforms embrace something similar to this model of parallelism.

Most of the examples in this book assume that all of the input data are available when an algorithm begins running. Much of the work in algorithm design makes the same assumption. For many important real-world examples, however, the input actually arrives over time, and the algorithm must decide how to proceed without knowing what data will arrive in the future. In a data center, jobs are constantly arriving and departing, and a scheduling algorithm must decide when and where to run a job, without knowing what jobs will be arriving in the future. Traffic must be routed in the internet based on the current state, without knowing about where traffic will arrive in the future. Hospital emergency rooms make triage decisions about which patients to treat first without knowing when other patients will be arriving in the future and what treatments they will need. Algorithms that receive their input over time, rather than having all the input present at the start, are *online algorithms*, which Chapter 27 examines.

Exercises

1.1-1
Describe your own real-world example that requires sorting. Describe one that requires finding the shortest distance between two points.

1.1-2
Other than speed, what other measures of efficiency might you need to consider in a real-world setting?

1.1-3
Select a data structure that you have seen, and discuss its strengths and limitations.

1.1-4
How are the shortest-path and traveling-salesperson problems given above similar? How are they different?

1.1-5
Suggest a real-world problem in which only the best solution will do. Then come up with one in which "approximately" the best solution is good enough.

1.1-6
Describe a real-world problem in which sometimes the entire input is available before you need to solve the problem, but other times the input is not entirely available in advance and arrives over time.

1.2   Algorithms as a technology

If computers were infinitely fast and computer memory were free, would you have any reason to study algorithms? The answer is yes, if for no other reason than that you would still like to be certain that your solution method terminates and does so with the correct answer.

If computers were infinitely fast, any correct method for solving a problem would do. You would probably want your implementation to be within the bounds of good software engineering practice (for example, your implementation should be well designed and documented), but you would most often use whichever method was the easiest to implement.

Of course, computers may be fast, but they are not infinitely fast. Computing time is therefore a bounded resource, which makes it precious. Although the saying goes, "Time is money," time is even more valuable than money: you can get back money after you spend it, but once time is spent, you can never get it back. Memory may be inexpensive, but it is neither infinite nor free. You should choose algorithms that use the resources of time and space efficiently.

Efficiency

Different algorithms devised to solve the same problem often differ dramatically in their efficiency. These differences can be much more significant than differences due to hardware and software.

As an example, Chapter 2 introduces two algorithms for sorting. The first, known as *insertion sort*, takes time roughly equal to $c_1 n^2$ to sort n items, where c_1 is a constant that does not depend on n. That is, it takes time roughly proportional to n^2. The second, *merge sort*, takes time roughly equal to $c_2 n \lg n$, where $\lg n$ stands for $\log_2 n$ and c_2 is another constant that also does not depend on n. Insertion sort typically has a smaller constant factor than merge sort, so that $c_1 < c_2$. We'll see that the constant factors can have far less of an impact on the running time than the dependence on the input size n. Let's write insertion sort's running time as $c_1 n \cdot n$ and merge sort's running time as $c_2 n \cdot \lg n$. Then we see that where insertion sort has a factor of n in its running time, merge sort has a factor of $\lg n$, which is much smaller. For example, when n is 1000, $\lg n$ is approximately 10, and when n is 1,000,000, $\lg n$ is approximately only 20. Although insertion sort usually runs faster than merge sort for small input sizes, once the input size n becomes large enough, merge sort's advantage of $\lg n$ versus n more than compensates for the difference in constant factors. No matter how much smaller c_1 is than c_2, there is always a crossover point beyond which merge sort is faster.

For a concrete example, let us pit a faster computer (computer A) running insertion sort against a slower computer (computer B) running merge sort. They each must sort an array of 10 million numbers. (Although 10 million numbers might seem like a lot, if the numbers are eight-byte integers, then the input occupies about 80 megabytes, which fits in the memory of even an inexpensive laptop computer many times over.) Suppose that computer A executes 10 billion instructions per second (faster than any single sequential computer at the time of this writing) and computer B executes only 10 million instructions per second (much slower than most contemporary computers), so that computer A is 1000 times faster than computer B in raw computing power. To make the difference even more dramatic, suppose that the world's craftiest programmer codes insertion sort in machine language for computer A, and the resulting code requires $2n^2$ instructions to sort n numbers. Suppose further that just an average programmer implements merge sort, using a high-level language with an inefficient compiler, with the resulting code taking $50 n \lg n$ instructions. To sort 10 million numbers, computer A takes

$$\frac{2 \cdot (10^7)^2 \text{ instructions}}{10^{10} \text{ instructions/second}} = 20{,}000 \text{ seconds (more than 5.5 hours)} ,$$

while computer B takes

$$\frac{50 \cdot 10^7 \lg 10^7 \text{ instructions}}{10^7 \text{ instructions/second}} \approx 1163 \text{ seconds (under 20 minutes)} .$$

By using an algorithm whose running time grows more slowly, even with a poor compiler, computer B runs more than 17 times faster than computer A! The advantage of merge sort is even more pronounced when sorting 100 million numbers: where insertion sort takes more than 23 days, merge sort takes under four hours. Although 100 million might seem like a large number, there are more than 100 million web searches every half hour, more than 100 million emails sent every minute, and some of the smallest galaxies (known as ultra-compact dwarf galaxies) contain about 100 million stars. In general, as the problem size increases, so does the relative advantage of merge sort.

Algorithms and other technologies

The example above shows that you should consider algorithms, like computer hardware, as a *technology*. Total system performance depends on choosing efficient algorithms as much as on choosing fast hardware. Just as rapid advances are being made in other computer technologies, they are being made in algorithms as well.

You might wonder whether algorithms are truly that important on contemporary computers in light of other advanced technologies, such as

- advanced computer architectures and fabrication technologies,

- easy-to-use, intuitive, graphical user interfaces (GUIs),

- object-oriented systems,

- integrated web technologies,

- fast networking, both wired and wireless,

- machine learning,

- and mobile devices.

The answer is yes. Although some applications do not explicitly require algorithmic content at the application level (such as some simple, web-based applications), many do. For example, consider a web-based service that determines how to travel from one location to another. Its implementation would rely on fast hardware, a graphical user interface, wide-area networking, and also possibly on object orientation. It would also require algorithms for operations such as finding routes (probably using a shortest-path algorithm), rendering maps, and interpolating addresses.

Moreover, even an application that does not require algorithmic content at the application level relies heavily upon algorithms. Does the application rely on fast hardware? The hardware design used algorithms. Does the application rely on graphical user interfaces? The design of any GUI relies on algorithms. Does the application rely on networking? Routing in networks relies heavily on algorithms. Was the application written in a language other than machine code? Then it was processed by a compiler, interpreter, or assembler, all of which make extensive use of algorithms. Algorithms are at the core of most technologies used in contemporary computers.

Machine learning can be thought of as a method for performing algorithmic tasks without explicitly designing an algorithm, but instead inferring patterns from data and thereby automatically learning a solution. At first glance, machine learning, which automates the process of algorithmic design, may seem to make learning about algorithms obsolete. The opposite is true, however. Machine learning is itself a collection of algorithms, just under a different name. Furthermore, it currently seems that the successes of machine learning are mainly for problems for which we, as humans, do not really understand what the right algorithm is. Prominent examples include computer vision and automatic language translation. For algorithmic problems that humans understand well, such as most of the problems in this book, efficient algorithms designed to solve a specific problem are typically more successful than machine-learning approaches.

Data science is an interdisciplinary field with the goal of extracting knowledge and insights from structured and unstructured data. Data science uses methods from statistics, computer science, and optimization. The design and analysis of algorithms is fundamental to the field. The core techniques of data science, which overlap significantly with those in machine learning, include many of the algorithms in this book.

Furthermore, with the ever-increasing capacities of computers, we use them to solve larger problems than ever before. As we saw in the above comparison between insertion sort and merge sort, it is at larger problem sizes that the differences in efficiency between algorithms become particularly prominent.

Having a solid base of algorithmic knowledge and technique is one characteristic that defines the truly skilled programmer. With modern computing technology, you can accomplish some tasks without knowing much about algorithms, but with a good background in algorithms, you can do much, much more.

Exercises

1.2-1
Give an example of an application that requires algorithmic content at the application level, and discuss the function of the algorithms involved.

1.2-2
Suppose that for inputs of size n on a particular computer, insertion sort runs in $8n^2$ steps and merge sort runs in $64n \lg n$ steps. For which values of n does insertion sort beat merge sort?

1.2-3
What is the smallest value of n such that an algorithm whose running time is $100n^2$ runs faster than an algorithm whose running time is 2^n on the same machine?

Problems

1-1 Comparison of running times
For each function $f(n)$ and time t in the following table, determine the largest size n of a problem that can be solved in time t, assuming that the algorithm to solve the problem takes $f(n)$ microseconds.

	1 second	1 minute	1 hour	1 day	1 month	1 year	1 century
$\lg n$							
$\sqrt{n}$							
n							
$n \lg n$							
n^2							
n^3							
2^n							
$n!$							

Chapter notes

There are many excellent texts on the general topic of algorithms, including those by Aho, Hopcroft, and Ullman [5, 6], Dasgupta, Papadimitriou, and Vazirani [107], Edmonds [133], Erickson [135], Goodrich and Tamassia [195, 196], Kleinberg and Tardos [257], Knuth [259, 260, 261, 262, 263], Levitin [298], Louridas [305], Mehlhorn and Sanders [325], Mitzenmacher and Upfal [331], Neapolitan [342], Roughgarden [385, 386, 387, 388], Sanders, Mehlhorn, Dietzfelbinger, and Dementiev [393], Sedgewick and Wayne [402], Skiena [414], Soltys-Kulinicz [419], Wilf [455], and Williamson and Shmoys [459]. Some of the more practical aspects of algorithm design are discussed by Bentley [49, 50, 51], Bhargava [54], Kochenderfer and Wheeler [268], and McGeoch [321]. Surveys of the field of algorithms can also be found in books by Atallah and Blanton [27, 28] and Mehta and Sahni [326]. For less technical material, see the books by Christian and Griffiths [92], Cormen [104], Erwig [136], MacCormick [307], and Vöcking et al. [448]. Overviews of the algorithms used in computational biology can be found in books by Jones and Pevzner [240], Elloumi and Zomaya [134], and Marchisio [315].

2 Getting Started

This chapter will familiarize you with the framework we'll use throughout the book to think about the design and analysis of algorithms. It is self-contained, but it does include several references to material that will be introduced in Chapters 3 and 4. (It also contains several summations, which Appendix A shows how to solve.)

We'll begin by examining the insertion sort algorithm to solve the sorting problem introduced in Chapter 1. We'll specify algorithms using a pseudocode that should be understandable to you if you have done computer programming. We'll see why insertion sort correctly sorts and analyze its running time. The analysis introduces a notation that describes how running time increases with the number of items to be sorted. Following a discussion of insertion sort, we'll use a method called divide-and-conquer to develop a sorting algorithm called merge sort. We'll end with an analysis of merge sort's running time.

2.1 Insertion sort

Our first algorithm, insertion sort, solves the *sorting problem* introduced in Chapter 1:

Input: A sequence of n numbers $\langle a_1, a_2, \ldots, a_n \rangle$.

Output: A permutation (reordering) $\langle a_1', a_2', \ldots, a_n' \rangle$ of the input sequence such that $a_1' \leq a_2' \leq \cdots \leq a_n'$.

The numbers to be sorted are also known as the *keys*. Although the problem is conceptually about sorting a sequence, the input comes in the form of an array with n elements. When we want to sort numbers, it's often because they are the keys associated with other data, which we call *satellite data*. Together, a key and satellite data form a *record*. For example, consider a spreadsheet containing student records with many associated pieces of data such as age, grade-point average, and number of courses taken. Any one of these quantities could be a key, but when the spreadsheet sorts, it moves the associated record (the satellite data) with the key. When describing a sorting algorithm, we focus on the keys, but it is important to remember that there usually is associated satellite data.

In this book, we'll typically describe algorithms as procedures written in a *pseudocode* that is similar in many respects to C, C++, Java, Python,[1] or JavaScript. (Apologies if we've omitted your favorite programming language. We can't list them all.) If you have been introduced to any of these languages, you should have little trouble understanding algorithms "coded" in pseudocode. What separates pseudocode from real code is that in pseudocode, we employ whatever expressive method is most clear and concise to specify a given algorithm. Sometimes the clearest method is English, so do not be surprised if you come across an English phrase or sentence embedded within a section that looks more like real code. Another difference between pseudocode and real code is that pseudocode often ignores aspects of software engineering—such as data abstraction, modularity, and error handling—in order to convey the essence of the algorithm more concisely.

We start with *insertion sort*, which is an efficient algorithm for sorting a small number of elements. Insertion sort works the way you might sort a hand of playing cards. Start with an empty left hand and the cards in a pile on the table. Pick up the first card in the pile and hold it with your left hand. Then, with your right hand, remove one card at a time from the pile, and insert it into the correct position in your left hand. As Figure 2.1 illustrates, you find the correct position for a card by comparing it with each of the cards already in your left hand, starting at the right and moving left. As soon as you see a card in your left hand whose value is less than or equal to the card you're holding in your right hand, insert the card that you're holding in your right hand just to the right of this card in your left hand. If all the cards in your left hand have values greater than the card in your right hand, then place this card as the leftmost card in your left hand. At all times, the cards held in your left hand are sorted, and these cards were originally the top cards of the pile on the table.

The pseudocode for insertion sort is given as the procedure INSERTION-SORT on the facing page. It takes two parameters: an array A containing the values to be sorted and the number n of values of sort. The values occupy positions $A[1]$ through $A[n]$ of the array, which we denote by $A[1:n]$. When the INSERTION-SORT procedure is finished, array $A[1:n]$ contains the original values, but in sorted order.

---

[1] If you're familiar with only Python, you can think of arrays as similar to Python lists.

Figure 2.1 Sorting a hand of cards using insertion sort.

INSERTION-SORT(A, n)

```
1  for i = 2 to n
2      key = A[i]
3      // Insert A[i] into the sorted subarray A[1 : i − 1].
4      j = i − 1
5      while j > 0 and A[j] > key
6          A[j + 1] = A[j]
7          j = j − 1
8      A[j + 1] = key
```

Loop invariants and the correctness of insertion sort

Figure 2.2 shows how this algorithm works for an array A that starts out with the sequence $\langle 5, 2, 4, 6, 1, 3 \rangle$. The index i indicates the "current card" being inserted into the hand. At the beginning of each iteration of the **for** loop, which is indexed by i, the *subarray* (a contiguous portion of the array) consisting of elements $A[1 : i − 1]$ (that is, $A[1]$ through $A[i − 1]$) constitutes the currently sorted hand, and the remaining subarray $A[i + 1 : n]$ (elements $A[i + 1]$ through $A[n]$) corresponds to the pile of cards still on the table. In fact, elements $A[1 : i − 1]$ are the elements *originally* in positions 1 through $i − 1$, but now in sorted order. We state these properties of $A[1 : i − 1]$ formally as a *loop invariant*:

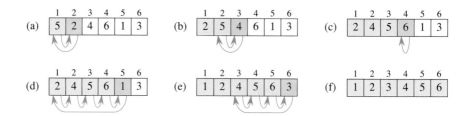

Figure 2.2 The operation of INSERTION-SORT(A, n), where A initially contains the sequence $\langle 5, 2, 4, 6, 1, 3 \rangle$ and $n = 6$. Array indices appear above the rectangles, and values stored in the array positions appear within the rectangles. **(a)–(e)** The iterations of the **for** loop of lines 1–8. In each iteration, the blue rectangle holds the key taken from $A[i]$, which is compared with the values in tan rectangles to its left in the test of line 5. Orange arrows show array values moved one position to the right in line 6, and blue arrows indicate where the key moves to in line 8. **(f)** The final sorted array.

At the start of each iteration of the **for** loop of lines 1–8, the subarray $A[1 : i - 1]$ consists of the elements originally in $A[1 : i - 1]$, but in sorted order.

Loop invariants help us understand why an algorithm is correct. When you're using a loop invariant, you need to show three things:

Initialization: It is true prior to the first iteration of the loop.

Maintenance: If it is true before an iteration of the loop, it remains true before the next iteration.

Termination: The loop terminates, and when it terminates, the invariant—usually along with the reason that the loop terminated—gives us a useful property that helps show that the algorithm is correct.

When the first two properties hold, the loop invariant is true prior to every iteration of the loop. (Of course, you are free to use established facts other than the loop invariant itself to prove that the loop invariant remains true before each iteration.) A loop-invariant proof is a form of mathematical induction, where to prove that a property holds, you prove a base case and an inductive step. Here, showing that the invariant holds before the first iteration corresponds to the base case, and showing that the invariant holds from iteration to iteration corresponds to the inductive step.

The third property is perhaps the most important one, since you are using the loop invariant to show correctness. Typically, you use the loop invariant along with the condition that caused the loop to terminate. Mathematical induction typically applies the inductive step infinitely, but in a loop invariant the "induction" stops when the loop terminates.

Let's see how these properties hold for insertion sort.

Initialization: We start by showing that the loop invariant holds before the first loop iteration, when $i = 2$.[2] The subarray $A[1:i-1]$ consists of just the single element $A[1]$, which is in fact the original element in $A[1]$. Moreover, this subarray is sorted (after all, how could a subarray with just one value not be sorted?), which shows that the loop invariant holds prior to the first iteration of the loop.

Maintenance: Next, we tackle the second property: showing that each iteration maintains the loop invariant. Informally, the body of the **for** loop works by moving the values in $A[i-1]$, $A[i-2]$, $A[i-3]$, and so on by one position to the right until it finds the proper position for $A[i]$ (lines 4–7), at which point it inserts the value of $A[i]$ (line 8). The subarray $A[1:i]$ then consists of the elements originally in $A[1:i]$, but in sorted order. *Incrementing i* (increasing its value by 1) for the next iteration of the **for** loop then preserves the loop invariant.

A more formal treatment of the second property would require us to state and show a loop invariant for the **while** loop of lines 5–7. Let's not get bogged down in such formalism just yet. Instead, we'll rely on our informal analysis to show that the second property holds for the outer loop.

Termination: Finally, we examine loop termination. The loop variable i starts at 2 and increases by 1 in each iteration. Once i's value exceeds n in line 1, the loop terminates. That is, the loop terminates once i equals $n + 1$. Substituting $n + 1$ for i in the wording of the loop invariant yields that the subarray $A[1:n]$ consists of the elements originally in $A[1:n]$, but in sorted order. Hence, the algorithm is correct.

This method of loop invariants is used to show correctness in various places throughout this book.

Pseudocode conventions

We use the following conventions in our pseudocode.

- Indentation indicates block structure. For example, the body of the **for** loop that begins on line 1 consists of lines 2–8, and the body of the **while** loop that

---

[2] When the loop is a **for** loop, the loop-invariant check just prior to the first iteration occurs immediately after the initial assignment to the loop-counter variable and just before the first test in the loop header. In the case of INSERTION-SORT, this time is after assigning 2 to the variable i but before the first test of whether $i \leq n$.

begins on line 5 contains lines 6–7 but not line 8. Our indentation style applies to **if**-**else** statements[3] as well. Using indentation instead of textual indicators of block structure, such as **begin** and **end** statements or curly braces, reduces clutter while preserving, or even enhancing, clarity.[4]

- The looping constructs **while**, **for**, and **repeat**-**until** and the **if**-**else** conditional construct have interpretations similar to those in C, C++, Java, Python, and JavaScript.[5] In this book, the loop counter retains its value after the loop is exited, unlike some situations that arise in C++ and Java. Thus, immediately after a **for** loop, the loop counter's value is the value that first exceeded the **for** loop bound.[6] We used this property in our correctness argument for insertion sort. The **for** loop header in line 1 is **for** $i = 2$ **to** n, and so when this loop terminates, i equals $n+1$. We use the keyword **to** when a **for** loop increments its loop counter in each iteration, and we use the keyword **downto** when a **for** loop *decrements* its loop counter (reduces its value by 1 in each iteration). When the loop counter changes by an amount greater than 1, the amount of change follows the optional keyword **by**.

- The symbol "**//**" indicates that the remainder of the line is a comment.

- Variables (such as i, j, and *key*) are local to the given procedure. We won't use global variables without explicit indication.

- We access array elements by specifying the array name followed by the index in square brackets. For example, $A[i]$ indicates the ith element of the array A.

  Although many programming languages enforce 0-origin indexing for arrays (0 is the smallest valid index), we choose whichever indexing scheme is clearest for human readers to understand. Because people usually start counting at 1, not 0, most—but not all—of the arrays in this book use 1-origin indexing. To be

---

[3] In an **if**-**else** statement, we indent **else** at the same level as its matching **if**. The first executable line of an **else** clause appears on the same line as the keyword **else**. For multiway tests, we use **elseif** for tests after the first one. When it is the first line in an **else** clause, an **if** statement appears on the line following **else** so that you do not misconstrue it as **elseif**.

[4] Each pseudocode procedure in this book appears on one page so that you do not need to discern levels of indentation in pseudocode that is split across pages.

[5] Most block-structured languages have equivalent constructs, though the exact syntax may differ. Python lacks **repeat**-**until** loops, and its **for** loops operate differently from the **for** loops in this book. Think of the pseudocode line "**for** $i = 1$ **to** n" as equivalent to "for i in range(1, n+1)" in Python.

[6] In Python, the loop counter retains its value after the loop is exited, but the value it retains is the value it had during the final iteration of the **for** loop, rather than the value that exceeded the loop bound. That is because a Python **for** loop iterates through a list, which may contain nonnumeric values.

clear about whether a particular algorithm assumes 0-origin or 1-origin index-ing, we'll specify the bounds of the arrays explicitly. If you are implementing an algorithm that we specify using 1-origin indexing, but you're writing in a programming language that enforces 0-origin indexing (such as C, C++, Java, Python, or JavaScript), then give yourself credit for being able to adjust. You can either always subtract 1 from each index or allocate each array with one extra position and just ignore position 0.

The notation ":" denotes a subarray. Thus, $A[i : j]$ indicates the subarray of A consisting of the elements $A[i], A[i + 1], \ldots, A[j]$.[7] We also use this notation to indicate the bounds of an array, as we did earlier when discussing the array $A[1 : n]$.

- We typically organize compound data into *objects*, which are composed of *attributes*. We access a particular attribute using the syntax found in many object-oriented programming languages: the object name, followed by a dot, followed by the attribute name. For example, if an object x has attribute f, we denote this attribute by $x.f$.

  We treat a variable representing an array or object as a pointer (known as a reference in some programming languages) to the data representing the array or object. For all attributes f of an object x, setting $y = x$ causes $y.f$ to equal $x.f$. Moreover, if we now set $x.f = 3$, then afterward not only does $x.f$ equal 3, but $y.f$ equals 3 as well. In other words, x and y point to the same object after the assignment $y = x$. This way of treating arrays and objects is consistent with most contemporary programming languages.

  Our attribute notation can "cascade." For example, suppose that the attribute f is itself a pointer to some type of object that has an attribute g. Then the notation $x.f.g$ is implicitly parenthesized as $(x.f).g$. In other words, if we had assigned $y = x.f$, then $x.f.g$ is the same as $y.g$.

  Sometimes a pointer refers to no object at all. In this case, we give it the special value NIL.

- We pass parameters to a procedure *by value*: the called procedure receives its own copy of the parameters, and if it assigns a value to a parameter, the change is *not* seen by the calling procedure. When objects are passed, the pointer to the data representing the object is copied, but the object's attributes are not. For example, if x is a parameter of a called procedure, the assignment $x = y$ within

---

[7] If you're used to programming in Python, bear in mind that in this book, the subarray $A[i : j]$ includes the element $A[j]$. In Python, the last element of $A[i : j]$ is $A[j - 1]$. Python allows negative indices, which count from the back end of the list. This book does not use negative array indices.

the called procedure is not visible to the calling procedure. The assignment $x.f = 3$, however, is visible if the calling procedure has a pointer to the same object as x. Similarly, arrays are passed by pointer, so that a pointer to the array is passed, rather than the entire array, and changes to individual array elements are visible to the calling procedure. Again, most contemporary programming languages work this way.

- A **return** statement immediately transfers control back to the point of call in the calling procedure. Most **return** statements also take a value to pass back to the caller. Our pseudocode differs from many programming languages in that we allow multiple values to be returned in a single **return** statement without having to create objects to package them together.[8]

- The boolean operators "and" and "or" are *short circuiting*. That is, evaluate the expression "x and y" by first evaluating x. If x evaluates to FALSE, then the entire expression cannot evaluate to TRUE, and therefore y is not evaluated. If, on the other hand, x evaluates to TRUE, y must be evaluated to determine the value of the entire expression. Similarly, in the expression "x or y" the expression y is evaluated only if x evaluates to FALSE. Short-circuiting operators allow us to write boolean expressions such as "$x \neq$ NIL and $x.f = y$" without worrying about what happens upon evaluating $x.f$ when x is NIL.

- The keyword **error** indicates that an error occurred because conditions were wrong for the procedure to have been called, and the procedure immediately terminates. The calling procedure is responsible for handling the error, and so we do not specify what action to take.

Exercises

2.1-1
Using Figure 2.2 as a model, illustrate the operation of INSERTION-SORT on an array initially containing the sequence $\langle 31, 41, 59, 26, 41, 58 \rangle$.

2.1-2
Consider the procedure SUM-ARRAY on the facing page. It computes the sum of the n numbers in array $A[1 : n]$. State a loop invariant for this procedure, and use its initialization, maintenance, and termination properties to show that the SUM-ARRAY procedure returns the sum of the numbers in $A[1 : n]$.

---

[8] Python's tuple notation allows **return** statements to return multiple values without creating objects from a programmer-defined class.

```
SUM-ARRAY(A, n)
1   sum = 0
2   for i = 1 to n
3       sum = sum + A[i]
4   return sum
```

2.1-3

Rewrite the INSERTION-SORT procedure to sort into monotonically decreasing instead of monotonically increasing order.

2.1-4

Consider the *searching problem*:

Input: A sequence of n numbers $\langle a_1, a_2, \ldots, a_n \rangle$ stored in array $A[1:n]$ and a value x.

Output: An index i such that x equals $A[i]$ or the special value NIL if x does not appear in A.

Write pseudocode for *linear search*, which scans through the array from beginning to end, looking for x. Using a loop invariant, prove that your algorithm is correct. Make sure that your loop invariant fulfills the three necessary properties.

2.1-5

Consider the problem of adding two n-bit binary integers a and b, stored in two n-element arrays $A[0:n-1]$ and $B[0:n-1]$, where each element is either 0 or 1, $a = \sum_{i=0}^{n-1} A[i] \cdot 2^i$, and $b = \sum_{i=0}^{n-1} B[i] \cdot 2^i$. The sum $c = a + b$ of the two integers should be stored in binary form in an $(n+1)$-element array $C[0:n]$, where $c = \sum_{i=0}^{n} C[i] \cdot 2^i$. Write a procedure ADD-BINARY-INTEGERS that takes as input arrays A and B, along with the length n, and returns array C holding the sum.

2.2   Analyzing algorithms

Analyzing an algorithm has come to mean predicting the resources that the algorithm requires. You might consider resources such as memory, communication bandwidth, or energy consumption. Most often, however, you'll want to measure computational time. If you analyze several candidate algorithms for a problem, you can identify the most efficient one. There might be more than just one viable candidate, but you can often rule out several inferior algorithms in the process.

Before you can analyze an algorithm, you need a model of the technology that it runs on, including the resources of that technology and a way to express their costs. Most of this book assumes a generic one-processor, *random-access machine (RAM)* model of computation as the implementation technology, with the understanding that algorithms are implemented as computer programs. In the RAM model, instructions execute one after another, with no concurrent operations. The RAM model assumes that each instruction takes the same amount of time as any other instruction and that each data access—using the value of a variable or storing into a variable—takes the same amount of time as any other data access. In other words, in the RAM model each instruction or data access takes a constant amount of time—even indexing into an array.[9]

Strictly speaking, we should precisely define the instructions of the RAM model and their costs. To do so, however, would be tedious and yield little insight into algorithm design and analysis. Yet we must be careful not to abuse the RAM model. For example, what if a RAM had an instruction that sorts? Then you could sort in just one step. Such a RAM would be unrealistic, since such instructions do not appear in real computers. Our guide, therefore, is how real computers are designed. The RAM model contains instructions commonly found in real computers: arithmetic (such as add, subtract, multiply, divide, remainder, floor, ceiling), data movement (load, store, copy), and control (conditional and unconditional branch, subroutine call and return).

The data types in the RAM model are integer, floating point (for storing real-number approximations), and character. Real computers do not usually have a separate data type for the boolean values TRUE and FALSE. Instead, they often test whether an integer value is 0 (FALSE) or nonzero (TRUE), as in C. Although we typically do not concern ourselves with precision for floating-point values in this book (many numbers cannot be represented exactly in floating point), precision is crucial for most applications. We also assume that each word of data has a limit on the number of bits. For example, when working with inputs of size n, we typically

---

[9] We assume that each element of a given array occupies the same number of bytes and that the elements of a given array are stored in contiguous memory locations. For example, if array $A[1:n]$ starts at memory address 1000 and each element occupies four bytes, then element $A[i]$ is at address $1000 + 4(i - 1)$. In general, computing the address in memory of a particular array element requires at most one subtraction (no subtraction for a 0-origin array), one multiplication (often implemented as a shift operation if the element size is an exact power of 2), and one addition. Furthermore, for code that iterates through the elements of an array in order, an optimizing compiler can generate the address of each element using just one addition, by adding the element size to the address of the preceding element.

assume that integers are represented by $c \log_2 n$ bits for some constant $c \geq 1$. We require $c \geq 1$ so that each word can hold the value of n, enabling us to index the individual input elements, and we restrict c to be a constant so that the word size does not grow arbitrarily. (If the word size could grow arbitrarily, we could store huge amounts of data in one word and operate on it all in constant time—an unrealistic scenario.)

Real computers contain instructions not listed above, and such instructions represent a gray area in the RAM model. For example, is exponentiation a constant-time instruction? In the general case, no: to compute x^n when x and n are general integers typically takes time logarithmic in n (see equation (31.34) on page 934), and you must worry about whether the result fits into a computer word. If n is an exact power of 2, however, exponentiation can usually be viewed as a constant-time operation. Many computers have a "shift left" instruction, which in constant time shifts the bits of an integer by n positions to the left. In most computers, shifting the bits of an integer by 1 position to the left is equivalent to multiplying by 2, so that shifting the bits by n positions to the left is equivalent to multiplying by 2^n. Therefore, such computers can compute 2^n in 1 constant-time instruction by shifting the integer 1 by n positions to the left, as long as n is no more than the number of bits in a computer word. We'll try to avoid such gray areas in the RAM model and treat computing 2^n and multiplying by 2^n as constant-time operations when the result is small enough to fit in a computer word.

The RAM model does not account for the memory hierarchy that is common in contemporary computers. It models neither caches nor virtual memory. Several other computational models attempt to account for memory-hierarchy effects, which are sometimes significant in real programs on real machines. Section 11.5 and a handful of problems in this book examine memory-hierarchy effects, but for the most part, the analyses in this book do not consider them. Models that include the memory hierarchy are quite a bit more complex than the RAM model, and so they can be difficult to work with. Moreover, RAM-model analyses are usually excellent predictors of performance on actual machines.

Although it is often straightforward to analyze an algorithm in the RAM model, sometimes it can be quite a challenge. You might need to employ mathematical tools such as combinatorics, probability theory, algebraic dexterity, and the ability to identify the most significant terms in a formula. Because an algorithm might behave differently for each possible input, we need a means for summarizing that behavior in simple, easily understood formulas.

Analysis of insertion sort

How long does the INSERTION-SORT procedure take? One way to tell would be for you to run it on your computer and time how long it takes to run. Of course, you'd first have to implement it in a real programming language, since you cannot run our pseudocode directly. What would such a timing test tell you? You would find out how long insertion sort takes to run on your particular computer, on that particular input, under the particular implementation that you created, with the particular compiler or interpreter that you ran, with the particular libraries that you linked in, and with the particular background tasks that were running on your computer concurrently with your timing test (such as checking for incoming information over a network). If you run insertion sort again on your computer with the same input, you might even get a different timing result. From running just one implementation of insertion sort on just one computer and on just one input, what would you be able to determine about insertion sort's running time if you were to give it a different input, if you were to run it on a different computer, or if you were to implement it in a different programming language? Not much. We need a way to predict, given a new input, how long insertion sort will take.

Instead of timing a run, or even several runs, of insertion sort, we can determine how long it takes by analyzing the algorithm itself. We'll examine how many times it executes each line of pseudocode and how long each line of pseudocode takes to run. We'll first come up with a precise but complicated formula for the running time. Then, we'll distill the important part of the formula using a convenient notation that can help us compare the running times of different algorithms for the same problem.

How do we analyze insertion sort? First, let's acknowledge that the running time depends on the input. You shouldn't be terribly surprised that sorting a thousand numbers takes longer than sorting three numbers. Moreover, insertion sort can take different amounts of time to sort two input arrays of the same size, depending on how nearly sorted they already are. Even though the running time can depend on many features of the input, we'll focus on the one that has been shown to have the greatest effect, namely the size of the input, and describe the running time of a program as a function of the size of its input. To do so, we need to define the terms "running time" and "input size" more carefully. We also need to be clear about whether we are discussing the running time for an input that elicits the worst-case behavior, the best-case behavior, or some other case.

The best notion for *input size* depends on the problem being studied. For many problems, such as sorting or computing discrete Fourier transforms, the most natural measure is the *number of items in the input*—for example, the number n of items being sorted. For many other problems, such as multiplying two integers, the best measure of input size is the *total number of bits* needed to represent the input in ordinary binary notation. Sometimes it is more appropriate to describe the size of the input with more than just one number. For example, if the input to an algorithm is a graph, we usually characterize the input size by both the number of vertices and the number of edges in the graph. We'll indicate which input size measure is being used with each problem we study.

The *running time* of an algorithm on a particular input is the number of instructions and data accesses executed. How we account for these costs should be independent of any particular computer, but within the framework of the RAM model. For the moment, let us adopt the following view. A constant amount of time is required to execute each line of our pseudocode. One line might take more or less time than another line, but we'll assume that each execution of the kth line takes c_k time, where c_k is a constant. This viewpoint is in keeping with the RAM model, and it also reflects how the pseudocode would be implemented on most actual computers.[10]

Let's analyze the INSERTION-SORT procedure. As promised, we'll start by devising a precise formula that uses the input size and all the statement costs c_k. This formula turns out to be messy, however. We'll then switch to a simpler notation that is more concise and easier to use. This simpler notation makes clear how to compare the running times of algorithms, especially as the size of the input increases.

To analyze the INSERTION-SORT procedure, let's view it on the following page with the time cost of each statement and the number of times each statement is executed. For each $i = 2, 3, \ldots, n$, let t_i denote the number of times the **while** loop test in line 5 is executed for that value of i. When a **for** or **while** loop exits in the usual way—because the test in the loop header comes up FALSE—the test is executed one time more than the loop body. Because comments are not executable statements, assume that they take no time.

The running time of the algorithm is the sum of running times for each statement executed. A statement that takes c_k steps to execute and executes m times contributes $c_k m$ to the total running time.[11] We usually denote the running time of an algorithm on an input of size n by $T(n)$. To compute $T(n)$, the running time of INSERTION-SORT on an input of n values, we sum the products of the *cost* and *times* columns, obtaining

---

[10] There are some subtleties here. Computational steps that we specify in English are often variants of a procedure that requires more than just a constant amount of time. For example, in the RADIX-SORT procedure on page 213, one line reads "use a stable sort to sort array A on digit i," which, as we shall see, takes more than a constant amount of time. Also, although a statement that calls a subroutine takes only constant time, the subroutine itself, once invoked, may take more. That is, we separate the process of *calling* the subroutine—passing parameters to it, etc.—from the process of *executing* the subroutine.

[11] This characteristic does not necessarily hold for a resource such as memory. A statement that references m words of memory and is executed n times does not necessarily reference mn distinct words of memory.

INSERTION-SORT(A, n)	cost	times
1 **for** $i = 2$ **to** n	c_1	n
2 $key = A[i]$	c_2	$n - 1$
3 // Insert $A[i]$ into the sorted subarray $A[1 : i - 1]$.	0	$n - 1$
4 $j = i - 1$	c_4	$n - 1$
5 **while** $j > 0$ and $A[j] > key$	c_5	$\sum_{i=2}^{n} t_i$
6 $A[j + 1] = A[j]$	c_6	$\sum_{i=2}^{n} (t_i - 1)$
7 $j = j - 1$	c_7	$\sum_{i=2}^{n} (t_i - 1)$
8 $A[j + 1] = key$	c_8	$n - 1$

$$T(n) = c_1 n + c_2(n - 1) + c_4(n - 1) + c_5 \sum_{i=2}^{n} t_i + c_6 \sum_{i=2}^{n} (t_i - 1)$$

$$+ c_7 \sum_{i=2}^{n} (t_i - 1) + c_8(n - 1) \, .$$

Even for inputs of a given size, an algorithm's running time may depend on *which* input of that size is given. For example, in INSERTION-SORT, the best case occurs when the array is already sorted. In this case, each time that line 5 executes, the value of *key*—the value originally in $A[i]$—is already greater than or equal to all values in $A[1 : i - 1]$, so that the **while** loop of lines 5–7 always exits upon the first test in line 5. Therefore, we have that $t_i = 1$ for $i = 2, 3, \ldots, n$, and the best-case running time is given by

$$T(n) = c_1 n + c_2(n - 1) + c_4(n - 1) + c_5(n - 1) + c_8(n - 1)$$
$$= (c_1 + c_2 + c_4 + c_5 + c_8)n - (c_2 + c_4 + c_5 + c_8) \, . \qquad (2.1)$$

We can express this running time as $an + b$ for *constants* a and b that depend on the statement costs c_k (where $a = c_1 + c_2 + c_4 + c_5 + c_8$ and $b = -(c_2 + c_4 + c_5 + c_8)$). The running time is thus a *linear function* of n.

The worst case arises when the array is in reverse sorted order—that is, it starts out in decreasing order. The procedure must compare each element $A[i]$ with each element in the entire sorted subarray $A[1 : i - 1]$, and so $t_i = i$ for $i = 2, 3, \ldots, n$. (The procedure finds that $A[j] > key$ every time in line 5, and the **while** loop exits only when j reaches 0.) Noting that

$$\sum_{i=2}^{n} i = \left(\sum_{i=1}^{n} i \right) - 1$$

$$= \frac{n(n + 1)}{2} - 1 \quad \text{(by equation (A.2) on page 1141)}$$

and

$$\sum_{i=2}^{n} (i - 1) = \sum_{i=1}^{n-1} i$$

$$= \frac{n(n - 1)}{2} \quad \text{(again, by equation (A.2))},$$

we find that in the worst case, the running time of INSERTION-SORT is

$$T(n) = c_1 n + c_2(n - 1) + c_4(n - 1) + c_5 \left(\frac{n(n + 1)}{2} - 1 \right)$$

$$+ c_6 \left(\frac{n(n - 1)}{2} \right) + c_7 \left(\frac{n(n - 1)}{2} \right) + c_8(n - 1)$$

$$= \left(\frac{c_5}{2} + \frac{c_6}{2} + \frac{c_7}{2} \right) n^2 + \left(c_1 + c_2 + c_4 + \frac{c_5}{2} - \frac{c_6}{2} - \frac{c_7}{2} + c_8 \right) n$$

$$- (c_2 + c_4 + c_5 + c_8) . \tag{2.2}$$

We can express this worst-case running time as $an^2 + bn + c$ for constants a, b, and c that again depend on the statement costs c_k (now, $a = c_5/2 + c_6/2 + c_7/2$, $b = c_1 + c_2 + c_4 + c_5/2 - c_6/2 - c_7/2 + c_8$, and $c = -(c_2 + c_4 + c_5 + c_8)$). The running time is thus a *quadratic function* of n.

Typically, as in insertion sort, the running time of an algorithm is fixed for a given input, although we'll also see some interesting "randomized" algorithms whose behavior can vary even for a fixed input.

Worst-case and average-case analysis

Our analysis of insertion sort looked at both the best case, in which the input array was already sorted, and the worst case, in which the input array was reverse sorted. For the remainder of this book, though, we'll usually (but not always) concentrate on finding only the *worst-case running time*, that is, the longest running time for *any* input of size n. Why? Here are three reasons:

- The worst-case running time of an algorithm gives an upper bound on the running time for *any* input. If you know it, then you have a guarantee that the algorithm never takes any longer. You need not make some educated guess about the running time and hope that it never gets much worse. This feature is especially important for real-time computing, in which operations must complete by a deadline.

- For some algorithms, the worst case occurs fairly often. For example, in searching a database for a particular piece of information, the searching algorithm's worst case often occurs when the information is not present in the database. In some applications, searches for absent information may be frequent.

- The "average case" is often roughly as bad as the worst case. Suppose that you run insertion sort on an array of n randomly chosen numbers. How long does it take to determine where in subarray $A[1 : i - 1]$ to insert element $A[i]$? On average, half the elements in $A[1 : i - 1]$ are less than $A[i]$, and half the elements are greater. On average, therefore, $A[i]$ is compared with just half of the subarray $A[1 : i - 1]$, and so t_i is about $i/2$. The resulting average-case running time turns out to be a quadratic function of the input size, just like the worst-case running time.

In some particular cases, we'll be interested in the *average-case* running time of an algorithm. We'll see the technique of *probabilistic analysis* applied to various algorithms throughout this book. The scope of average-case analysis is limited, because it may not be apparent what constitutes an "average" input for a particular problem. Often, we'll assume that all inputs of a given size are equally likely. In practice, this assumption may be violated, but we can sometimes use a *randomized algorithm*, which makes random choices, to allow a probabilistic analysis and yield an *expected* running time. We explore randomized algorithms more in Chapter 5 and in several other subsequent chapters.

Order of growth

In order to ease our analysis of the INSERTION-SORT procedure, we used some simplifying abstractions. First, we ignored the actual cost of each statement, using the constants c_k to represent these costs. Still, the best-case and worst-case running times in equations (2.1) and (2.2) are rather unwieldy. The constants in these expressions give us more detail than we really need. That's why we also expressed the best-case running time as $an + b$ for constants a and b that depend on the statement costs c_k and why we expressed the worst-case running time as $an^2 + bn + c$ for constants a, b, and c that depend on the statement costs. We thus ignored not only the actual statement costs, but also the abstract costs c_k.

Let's now make one more simplifying abstraction: it is the *rate of growth*, or *order of growth*, of the running time that really interests us. We therefore consider only the leading term of a formula (e.g., an^2), since the lower-order terms are relatively insignificant for large values of n. We also ignore the leading term's constant coefficient, since constant factors are less significant than the rate of growth in determining computational efficiency for large inputs. For insertion sort's worst-case running time, when we ignore the lower-order terms and the leading term's constant coefficient, only the factor of n^2 from the leading term remains. That factor, n^2, is by far the most important part of the running time. For example, suppose that an algorithm implemented on a particular machine takes $n^2/100 + 100n + 17$ microseconds on an input of size n. Although the coefficients of $1/100$ for the n^2 term and 100 for the n term differ by four orders of magnitude, the $n^2/100$ term dominates the $100n$ term once n exceeds 10,000. Although 10,000 might seem large, it is smaller than the population of an average town. Many real-world problems have much larger input sizes.

To highlight the order of growth of the running time, we have a special notation that uses the Greek letter Θ (theta). We write that insertion sort has a worst-case running time of $\Theta(n^2)$ (pronounced "theta of n-squared" or just "theta n-squared"). We also write that insertion sort has a best-case running time of $\Theta(n)$ ("theta of n" or "theta n"). For now, think of Θ-notation as saying "roughly proportional when n is large," so that $\Theta(n^2)$ means "roughly proportional to n^2 when n is large" and $\Theta(n)$ means "roughly proportional to n when n is large" We'll use Θ-notation informally in this chapter and define it precisely in Chapter 3.

We usually consider one algorithm to be more efficient than another if its worst-case running time has a lower order of growth. Due to constant factors and lower-order terms, an algorithm whose running time has a higher order of growth might take less time for small inputs than an algorithm whose running time has a lower order of growth. But on large enough inputs, an algorithm whose worst-case running time is $\Theta(n^2)$, for example, takes less time in the worst case than an algorithm whose worst-case running time is $\Theta(n^3)$. Regardless of the constants hidden by the Θ-notation, there is always some number, say n_0, such that for all input sizes $n \geq n_0$, the $\Theta(n^2)$ algorithm beats the $\Theta(n^3)$ algorithm in the worst case.

Exercises

2.2-1
Express the function $n^3/1000 + 100n^2 - 100n + 3$ in terms of Θ-notation.

2.2-2
Consider sorting n numbers stored in array $A[1:n]$ by first finding the smallest element of $A[1:n]$ and exchanging it with the element in $A[1]$. Then find the smallest element of $A[2:n]$, and exchange it with $A[2]$. Then find the smallest element of $A[3:n]$, and exchange it with $A[3]$. Continue in this manner for the first $n-1$ elements of A. Write pseudocode for this algorithm, which is known as *selection sort*. What loop invariant does this algorithm maintain? Why does it need to run for only the first $n-1$ elements, rather than for all n elements? Give the worst-case running time of selection sort in Θ-notation. Is the best-case running time any better?

2.2-3
Consider linear search again (see Exercise 2.1-4). How many elements of the input array need to be checked on the average, assuming that the element being searched for is equally likely to be any element in the array? How about in the worst case?

Using Θ-notation, give the average-case and worst-case running times of linear search. Justify your answers.

2.2-4
How can you modify any sorting algorithm to have a good best-case running time?

2.3   Designing algorithms

You can choose from a wide range of algorithm design techniques. Insertion sort uses the *incremental* method: for each element $A[i]$, insert it into its proper place in the subarray $A[1:i]$, having already sorted the subarray $A[1:i-1]$.

This section examines another design method, known as "divide-and-conquer," which we explore in more detail in Chapter 4. We'll use divide-and-conquer to design a sorting algorithm whose worst-case running time is much less than that of insertion sort. One advantage of using an algorithm that follows the divide-and-conquer method is that analyzing its running time is often straightforward, using techniques that we'll explore in Chapter 4.

2.3.1   The divide-and-conquer method

Many useful algorithms are *recursive* in structure: to solve a given problem, they *recurse* (call themselves) one or more times to handle closely related subproblems. These algorithms typically follow the *divide-and-conquer* method: they break the problem into several subproblems that are similar to the original problem but smaller in size, solve the subproblems recursively, and then combine these solutions to create a solution to the original problem.

In the divide-and-conquer method, if the problem is small enough—the *base case*—you just solve it directly without recursing. Otherwise—the *recursive case*—you perform three characteristic steps:

Divide the problem into one or more subproblems that are smaller instances of the same problem.

Conquer the subproblems by solving them recursively.

Combine the subproblem solutions to form a solution to the original problem.

The *merge sort* algorithm closely follows the divide-and-conquer method. In each step, it sorts a subarray $A[p:r]$, starting with the entire array $A[1:n]$ and recursing down to smaller and smaller subarrays. Here is how merge sort operates:

Divide the subarray $A[p:r]$ to be sorted into two adjacent subarrays, each of half the size. To do so, compute the midpoint q of $A[p:r]$ (taking the average of p and r), and divide $A[p:r]$ into subarrays $A[p:q]$ and $A[q+1:r]$.

Conquer by sorting each of the two subarrays $A[p:q]$ and $A[q+1:r]$ recursively using merge sort.

Combine by merging the two sorted subarrays $A[p:q]$ and $A[q+1:r]$ back into $A[p:r]$, producing the sorted answer.

The recursion "bottoms out"—it reaches the base case—when the subarray $A[p:r]$ to be sorted has just 1 element, that is, when p equals r. As we noted in the initialization argument for INSERTION-SORT's loop invariant, a subarray comprising just a single element is always sorted.

The key operation of the merge sort algorithm occurs in the "combine" step, which merges two adjacent, sorted subarrays. The merge operation is performed by the auxiliary procedure MERGE(A, p, q, r) on the following page, where A is an array and p, q, and r are indices into the array such that $p \leq q < r$. The procedure assumes that the adjacent subarrays $A[p:q]$ and $A[q+1:r]$ were already recursively sorted. It *merges* the two sorted subarrays to form a single sorted subarray that replaces the current subarray $A[p:r]$.

To understand how the MERGE procedure works, let's return to our card-playing motif. Suppose that you have two piles of cards face up on a table. Each pile is sorted, with the smallest-value cards on top. You wish to merge the two piles into a single sorted output pile, which is to be face down on the table. The basic step consists of choosing the smaller of the two cards on top of the face-up piles, removing it from its pile—which exposes a new top card—and placing this card face down onto the output pile. Repeat this step until one input pile is empty, at which time you can just take the remaining input pile and flip over the entire pile, placing it face down onto the output pile.

Let's think about how long it takes to merge two sorted piles of cards. Each basic step takes constant time, since you are comparing just the two top cards. If the two sorted piles that you start with each have $n/2$ cards, then the number of basic steps is at least $n/2$ (since in whichever pile was emptied, every card was found to be smaller than some card from the other pile) and at most n (actually, at most $n-1$, since after $n-1$ basic steps, one of the piles must be empty). With each basic step taking constant time and the total number of basic steps being between $n/2$ and n, we can say that merging takes time roughly proportional to n. That is, merging takes $\Theta(n)$ time.

In detail, the MERGE procedure works as follows. It copies the two subarrays $A[p:q]$ and $A[q+1:r]$ into temporary arrays L and R ("left" and "right"), and then it merges the values in L and R back into $A[p:r]$. Lines 1 and 2 compute the lengths n_L and n_R of the subarrays $A[p:q]$ and $A[q+1:r]$, respectively. Then

MERGE(A, p, q, r)

```
 1  n_L = q − p + 1      // length of A[p : q]
 2  n_R = r − q          // length of A[q + 1 : r]
 3  let L[0 : n_L − 1] and R[0 : n_R − 1] be new arrays
 4  for i = 0 to n_L − 1    // copy A[p : q] into L[0 : n_L − 1]
 5      L[i] = A[p + i]
 6  for j = 0 to n_R − 1   // copy A[q + 1 : r] into R[0 : n_R − 1]
 7      R[j] = A[q + j + 1]
 8  i = 0                // i indexes the smallest remaining element in L
 9  j = 0                // j indexes the smallest remaining element in R
10  k = p                // k indexes the location in A to fill
11  // As long as each of the arrays L and R contains an unmerged element,
    //     copy the smallest unmerged element back into A[p : r].
12  while i < n_L and j < n_R
13      if L[i] ≤ R[j]
14          A[k] = L[i]
15          i = i + 1
16      else A[k] = R[j]
17          j = j + 1
18      k = k + 1
19  // Having gone through one of L and R entirely, copy the
    //     remainder of the other to the end of A[p : r].
20  while i < n_L
21      A[k] = L[i]
22      i = i + 1
23      k = k + 1
24  while j < n_R
25      A[k] = R[j]
26      j = j + 1
27      k = k + 1
```

line 3 creates arrays $L[0 : n_L − 1]$ and $R[0 : n_R − 1]$ with respective lengths n_L and n_R.[12] The **for** loop of lines 4–5 copies the subarray $A[p : q]$ into L, and the **for** loop of lines 6–7 copies the subarray $A[q + 1 : r]$ into R.

Lines 8–18, illustrated in Figure 2.3, perform the basic steps. The **while** loop of lines 12–18 repeatedly identifies the smallest value in L and R that has yet to

---

[12] This procedure is the rare case that uses both 1-origin indexing (for array A) and 0-origin indexing (for arrays L and R). Using 0-origin indexing for L and R makes for a simpler loop invariant in Exercise 2.3-3.

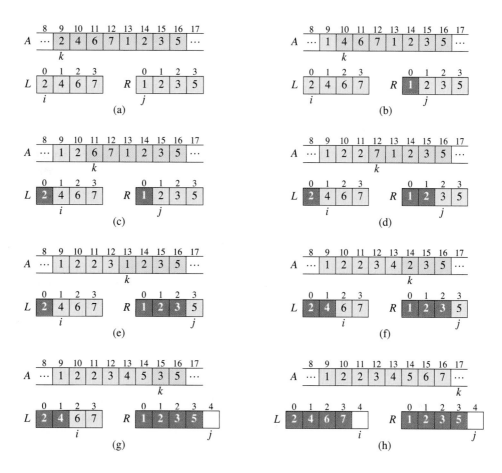

Figure 2.3 The operation of the **while** loop in lines 8–18 in the call Merge(*A*, 9, 12, 16), when the subarray *A*[9 : 16] contains the values ⟨2, 4, 6, 7, 1, 2, 3, 5⟩. After allocating and copying into the arrays *L* and *R*, the array *L* contains ⟨2, 4, 6, 7⟩, and the array *R* contains ⟨1, 2, 3, 5⟩. Tan positions in *A* contain their final values, and tan positions in *L* and *R* contain values that have yet to be copied back into *A*. Taken together, the tan positions always comprise the values originally in *A*[9 : 16]. Blue positions in *A* contain values that will be copied over, and dark positions in *L* and *R* contain values that have already been copied back into *A*. **(a)–(g)** The arrays *A*, *L*, and *R*, and their respective indices *k*, *i*, and *j* prior to each iteration of the loop of lines 12–18. At the point in part (g), all values in *R* have been copied back into *A* (indicated by *j* equaling the length of *R*), and so the **while** loop in lines 12–18 terminates. **(h)** The arrays and indices at termination. The **while** loops of lines 20–23 and 24–27 copied back into *A* the remaining values in *L* and *R*, which are the largest values originally in *A*[9 : 16]. Here, lines 20–23 copied *L*[2 : 3] into *A*[15 : 16], and because all values in *R* had already been copied back into *A*, the **while** loop of lines 24–27 iterated 0 times. At this point, the subarray in *A*[9 : 16] is sorted.

be copied back into $A[p:r]$ and copies it back in. As the comments indicate, the index k gives the position of A that is being filled in, and the indices i and j give the positions in L and R, respectively, of the smallest remaining values. Eventually, either all of L or all of R is copied back into $A[p:r]$, and this loop terminates. If the loop terminates because all of R has been copied back, that is, because j equals n_R, then i is still less than n_L, so that some of L has yet to be copied back, and these values are the greatest in both L and R. In this case, the **while** loop of lines 20–23 copies these remaining values of L into the last few positions of $A[p:r]$. Because j equals n_R, the **while** loop of lines 24–27 iterates 0 times. If instead the **while** loop of lines 12–18 terminates because i equals n_L, then all of L has already been copied back into $A[p:r]$, and the **while** loop of lines 24–27 copies the remaining values of R back into the end of $A[p:r]$.

To see that the MERGE procedure runs in $\Theta(n)$ time, where $n = r - p + 1$,[13] observe that each of lines 1–3 and 8–10 takes constant time, and the **for** loops of lines 4–7 take $\Theta(n_L + n_R) = \Theta(n)$ time.[14] To account for the three **while** loops of lines 12–18, 20–23, and 24–27, observe that each iteration of these loops copies exactly one value from L or R back into A and that every value is copied back into A exactly once. Therefore, these three loops together make a total of n iterations. Since each iteration of each of the three loops takes constant time, the total time spent in these three loops is $\Theta(n)$.

We can now use the MERGE procedure as a subroutine in the merge sort algorithm. The procedure MERGE-SORT(A, p, r) on the facing page sorts the elements in the subarray $A[p:r]$. If p equals r, the subarray has just 1 element and is therefore already sorted. Otherwise, we must have $p < r$, and MERGE-SORT runs the divide, conquer, and combine steps. The divide step simply computes an index q that partitions $A[p:r]$ into two adjacent subarrays: $A[p:q]$, containing $\lceil n/2 \rceil$ elements, and $A[q + 1:r]$, containing $\lfloor n/2 \rfloor$ elements.[15] The initial call MERGE-SORT$(A, 1, n)$ sorts the entire array $A[1:n]$.

Figure 2.4 illustrates the operation of the procedure for $n = 8$, showing also the sequence of divide and merge steps. The algorithm recursively divides the array down to 1-element subarrays. The combine steps merge pairs of 1-element subar-

---

[13] If you're wondering where the "+1" comes from, imagine that $r = p + 1$. Then the subarray $A[p:r]$ consists of two elements, and $r - p + 1 = 2$.

[14] Chapter 3 shows how to formally interpret equations containing Θ-notation.

[15] The expression $\lceil x \rceil$ denotes the least integer greater than or equal to x, and $\lfloor x \rfloor$ denotes the greatest integer less than or equal to x. These notations are defined in Section 3.3. The easiest way to verify that setting q to $\lfloor (p + r)/2 \rfloor$ yields subarrays $A[p:q]$ and $A[q + 1:r]$ of sizes $\lceil n/2 \rceil$ and $\lfloor n/2 \rfloor$, respectively, is to examine the four cases that arise depending on whether each of p and r is odd or even.

MERGE-SORT(A, p, r)

```
1   if p ≥ r                        // zero or one element?
2       return
3   q = ⌊(p + r)/2⌋                 // midpoint of A[p : r]
4   MERGE-SORT(A, p, q)             // recursively sort A[p : q]
5   MERGE-SORT(A, q + 1, r)         // recursively sort A[q + 1 : r]
6   // Merge A[p : q] and A[q + 1 : r] into A[p : r].
7   MERGE(A, p, q, r)
```

rays to form sorted subarrays of length 2, merges those to form sorted subarrays of length 4, and merges those to form the final sorted subarray of length 8. If n is not an exact power of 2, then some divide steps create subarrays whose lengths differ by 1. (For example, when dividing a subarray of length 7, one subarray has length 4 and the other has length 3.) Regardless of the lengths of the two subarrays being merged, the time to merge a total of n items is $\Theta(n)$.

2.3.2 Analyzing divide-and-conquer algorithms

When an algorithm contains a recursive call, you can often describe its running time by a *recurrence equation* or *recurrence*, which describes the overall running time on a problem of size n in terms of the running time of the same algorithm on smaller inputs. You can then use mathematical tools to solve the recurrence and provide bounds on the performance of the algorithm.

A recurrence for the running time of a divide-and-conquer algorithm falls out from the three steps of the basic method. As we did for insertion sort, let $T(n)$ be the worst-case running time on a problem of size n. If the problem size is small enough, say $n < n_0$ for some constant $n_0 > 0$, the straightforward solution takes constant time, which we write as $\Theta(1)$.[16] Suppose that the division of the problem yields a subproblems, each with size n/b, that is, $1/b$ the size of the original. For merge sort, both a and b are 2, but we'll see other divide-and-conquer algorithms in which $a \neq b$. It takes $T(n/b)$ time to solve one subproblem of size n/b, and so it takes $aT(n/b)$ time to solve all a of them. If it takes $D(n)$ time to divide the problem into subproblems and $C(n)$ time to combine the solutions to the subproblems into the solution to the original problem, we get the recurrence

---

[16] If you're wondering where $\Theta(1)$ comes from, think of it this way. When we say that $n^2/100$ is $\Theta(n^2)$, we are ignoring the coefficient $1/100$ of the factor n^2. Likewise, when we say that a constant c is $\Theta(1)$, we are ignoring the coefficient c of the factor 1 (which you can also think of as n^0).

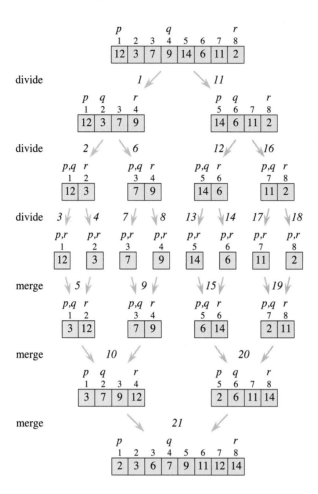

Figure 2.4 The operation of merge sort on the array A with length 8 that initially contains the sequence $\langle 12, 3, 7, 9, 14, 6, 11, 2 \rangle$. The indices p, q, and r into each subarray appear above their values. Numbers in italics indicate the order in which the MERGE-SORT and MERGE procedures are called following the initial call of MERGE-SORT($A, 1, 8$).

$$T(n) = \begin{cases} \Theta(1) & \text{if } n < n_0 \,, \\ D(n) + aT(n/b) + C(n) & \text{otherwise} \,. \end{cases}$$

Chapter 4 shows how to solve common recurrences of this form.

Sometimes, the n/b size of the divide step isn't an integer. For example, the MERGE-SORT procedure divides a problem of size n into subproblems of sizes $\lceil n/2 \rceil$ and $\lfloor n/2 \rfloor$. Since the difference between $\lceil n/2 \rceil$ and $\lfloor n/2 \rfloor$ is at most 1, which for large n is much smaller than the effect of dividing n by 2, we'll squint a little and just call them both size $n/2$. As Chapter 4 will discuss, this simplification of ignoring floors and ceilings does not generally affect the order of growth of a solution to a divide-and-conquer recurrence.

Another convention we'll adopt is to omit a statement of the base cases of the recurrence, which we'll also discuss in more detail in Chapter 4. The reason is that the base cases are pretty much always $T(n) = \Theta(1)$ if $n < n_0$ for some constant $n_0 > 0$. That's because the running time of an algorithm on an input of constant size is constant. We save ourselves a lot of extra writing by adopting this convention.

Analysis of merge sort

Here's how to set up the recurrence for $T(n)$, the worst-case running time of merge sort on n numbers.

Divide: The divide step just computes the middle of the subarray, which takes constant time. Thus, $D(n) = \Theta(1)$.

Conquer: Recursively solving two subproblems, each of size $n/2$, contributes $2T(n/2)$ to the running time (ignoring the floors and ceilings, as we discussed).

Combine: Since the MERGE procedure on an n-element subarray takes $\Theta(n)$ time, we have $C(n) = \Theta(n)$.

When we add the functions $D(n)$ and $C(n)$ for the merge sort analysis, we are adding a function that is $\Theta(n)$ and a function that is $\Theta(1)$. This sum is a linear function of n. That is, it is roughly proportional to n when n is large, and so merge sort's dividing and combining times together are $\Theta(n)$. Adding $\Theta(n)$ to the $2T(n/2)$ term from the conquer step gives the recurrence for the worst-case running time $T(n)$ of merge sort:

$$T(n) = 2T(n/2) + \Theta(n) \,. \tag{2.3}$$

Chapter 4 presents the "master theorem," which shows that $T(n) = \Theta(n \lg n)$.[17] Compared with insertion sort, whose worst-case running time is $\Theta(n^2)$, merge sort trades away a factor of n for a factor of $\lg n$. Because the logarithm function grows more slowly than any linear function, that's a good trade. For large enough inputs, merge sort, with its $\Theta(n \lg n)$ worst-case running time, outperforms insertion sort, whose worst-case running time is $\Theta(n^2)$.

---

[17] The notation $\lg n$ stands for $\log_2 n$, although the base of the logarithm doesn't matter here, but as computer scientists, we like logarithms base 2. Section 3.3 discusses other standard notation.

We do not need the master theorem, however, to understand intuitively why the solution to recurrence (2.3) is $T(n) = \Theta(n \lg n)$. For simplicity, assume that n is an exact power of 2 and that the implicit base case is $n = 1$. Then recurrence (2.3) is essentially

$$T(n) = \begin{cases} c_1 & \text{if } n = 1 \text{,} \\ 2T(n/2) + c_2 n & \text{if } n > 1 \text{,} \end{cases} \tag{2.4}$$

where the constant $c_1 > 0$ represents the time required to solve a problem of size 1, and $c_2 > 0$ is the time per array element of the divide and combine steps.[18]

Figure 2.5 illustrates one way of figuring out the solution to recurrence (2.4). Part (a) of the figure shows $T(n)$, which part (b) expands into an equivalent tree representing the recurrence. The $c_2 n$ term denotes the cost of dividing and combining at the top level of recursion, and the two subtrees of the root are the two smaller recurrences $T(n/2)$. Part (c) shows this process carried one step further by expanding $T(n/2)$. The cost for dividing and combining at each of the two nodes at the second level of recursion is $c_2 n/2$. Continue to expand each node in the tree by breaking it into its constituent parts as determined by the recurrence, until the problem sizes get down to 1, each with a cost of c_1. Part (d) shows the resulting *recursion tree*.

Next, add the costs across each level of the tree. The top level has total cost $c_2 n$, the next level down has total cost $c_2(n/2) + c_2(n/2) = c_2 n$, the level after that has total cost $c_2(n/4) + c_2(n/4) + c_2(n/4) + c_2(n/4) = c_2 n$, and so on. Each level has twice as many nodes as the level above, but each node contributes only half the cost of a node from the level above. From one level to the next, doubling and halving cancel each other out, so that the cost across each level is the same: $c_2 n$. In general, the level that is i levels below the top has 2^i nodes, each contributing a cost of $c_2(n/2^i)$, so that the ith level below the top has total cost $2^i \cdot c_2(n/2^i) = c_2 n$. The bottom level has n nodes, each contributing a cost of c_1, for a total cost of $c_1 n$.

The total number of levels of the recursion tree in Figure 2.5 is $\lg n + 1$, where n is the number of leaves, corresponding to the input size. An informal inductive argument justifies this claim. The base case occurs when $n = 1$, in which case the tree has only 1 level. Since $\lg 1 = 0$, we have that $\lg n + 1$ gives the correct number of levels. Now assume as an inductive hypothesis that the number of levels of a recursion tree with 2^i leaves is $\lg 2^i + 1 = i + 1$ (since for any value of i, we have that $\lg 2^i = i$). Because we assume that the input size is an exact power of 2, the next input size to consider is 2^{i+1}. A tree with $n = 2^{i+1}$ leaves has 1 more

---

[18] It is unlikely that c_1 is exactly the time to solve problems of size 1 and that $c_2 n$ is exactly the time of the divide and combine steps. We'll look more closely at bounding recurrences in Chapter 4, where we'll be more careful about this kind of detail.

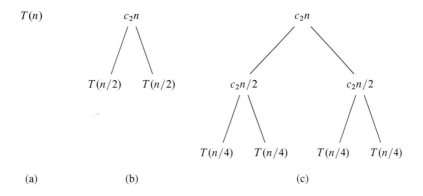

(a)   (b)   (c)

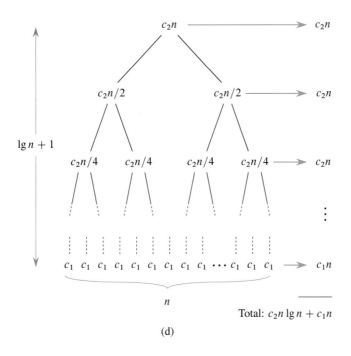

(d)

Figure 2.5 How to construct a recursion tree for the recurrence (2.4). Part **(a)** shows $T(n)$, which progressively expands in **(b)–(d)** to form the recursion tree. The fully expanded tree in part (d) has $\lg n + 1$ levels. Each level above the leaves contributes a total cost of $c_2 n$, and the leaf level contributes $c_1 n$. The total cost, therefore, is $c_2 n \lg n + c_1 n = \Theta(n \lg n)$.

level than a tree with 2^i leaves, and so the total number of levels is $(i + 1) + 1 = \lg 2^{i+1} + 1$.

To compute the total cost represented by the recurrence (2.4), simply add up the costs of all the levels. The recursion tree has $\lg n + 1$ levels. The levels above the leaves each cost $c_2 n$, and the leaf level costs $c_1 n$, for a total cost of $c_2 n \lg n + c_1 n = \Theta(n \lg n)$.

Exercises

2.3-1
Using Figure 2.4 as a model, illustrate the operation of merge sort on an array initially containing the sequence $\langle 3, 41, 52, 26, 38, 57, 9, 49 \rangle$.

2.3-2
The test in line 1 of the MERGE-SORT procedure reads "**if** $p \geq r$" rather than "**if** $p \neq r$." If MERGE-SORT is called with $p > r$, then the subarray $A[p:r]$ is empty. Argue that as long as the initial call of MERGE-SORT$(A, 1, n)$ has $n \geq 1$, the test "**if** $p \neq r$" suffices to ensure that no recursive call has $p > r$.

2.3-3
State a loop invariant for the **while** loop of lines 12–18 of the MERGE procedure. Show how to use it, along with the **while** loops of lines 20–23 and 24–27, to prove that the MERGE procedure is correct.

2.3-4
Use mathematical induction to show that when $n \geq 2$ is an exact power of 2, the solution of the recurrence

$$T(n) = \begin{cases} 2 & \text{if } n = 2, \\ 2T(n/2) + n & \text{if } n > 2 \end{cases}$$

is $T(n) = n \lg n$.

2.3-5
You can also think of insertion sort as a recursive algorithm. In order to sort $A[1:n]$, recursively sort the subarray $A[1:n-1]$ and then insert $A[n]$ into the sorted subarray $A[1:n-1]$. Write pseudocode for this recursive version of insertion sort. Give a recurrence for its worst-case running time.

2.3-6
Referring back to the searching problem (see Exercise 2.1-4), observe that if the subarray being searched is already sorted, the searching algorithm can check the midpoint of the subarray against x and eliminate half of the subarray from further

consideration. The *binary search* algorithm repeats this procedure, halving the size of the remaining portion of the subarray each time. Write pseudocode, either iterative or recursive, for binary search. Argue that the worst-case running time of binary search is $\Theta(\lg n)$.

2.3-7

The **while** loop of lines 5–7 of the INSERTION-SORT procedure in Section 2.1 uses a linear search to scan (backward) through the sorted subarray $A[1:i-1]$. What if insertion sort used a binary search (see Exercise 2.3-6) instead of a linear search? Would that improve the overall worst-case running time of insertion sort to $\Theta(n \lg n)$?

2.3-8

Describe an algorithm that, given a set S of n integers and another integer x, determines whether S contains two elements that sum to exactly x. Your algorithm should take $\Theta(n \lg n)$ time in the worst case.

Problems

2-1 *Insertion sort on small arrays in merge sort*

Although merge sort runs in $\Theta(n \lg n)$ worst-case time and insertion sort runs in $\Theta(n^2)$ worst-case time, the constant factors in insertion sort can make it faster in practice for small problem sizes on many machines. Thus it makes sense to *coarsen* the leaves of the recursion by using insertion sort within merge sort when subproblems become sufficiently small. Consider a modification to merge sort in which n/k sublists of length k are sorted using insertion sort and then merged using the standard merging mechanism, where k is a value to be determined.

a. Show that insertion sort can sort the n/k sublists, each of length k, in $\Theta(nk)$ worst-case time.

b. Show how to merge the sublists in $\Theta(n \lg(n/k))$ worst-case time.

c. Given that the modified algorithm runs in $\Theta(nk + n \lg(n/k))$ worst-case time, what is the largest value of k as a function of n for which the modified algorithm has the same running time as standard merge sort, in terms of Θ-notation?

d. How should you choose k in practice?

2-2   *Correctness of bubblesort*

Bubblesort is a popular, but inefficient, sorting algorithm. It works by repeatedly swapping adjacent elements that are out of order. The procedure BUBBLESORT sorts array $A[1:n]$.

BUBBLESORT(A, n)

1 **for** $i = 1$ **to** $n - 1$
2   **for** $j = n$ **downto** $i + 1$
3   **if** $A[j] < A[j - 1]$
4   exchange $A[j]$ with $A[j - 1]$

---

a. Let A' denote the array A after BUBBLESORT(A, n) is executed. To prove that BUBBLESORT is correct, you need to prove that it terminates and that

$$A'[1] \le A'[2] \le \cdots \le A'[n] \; . \tag{2.5}$$

In order to show that BUBBLESORT actually sorts, what else do you need to prove?

The next two parts prove inequality (2.5).

b. State precisely a loop invariant for the **for** loop in lines 2–4, and prove that this loop invariant holds. Your proof should use the structure of the loop-invariant proof presented in this chapter.

c. Using the termination condition of the loop invariant proved in part (b), state a loop invariant for the **for** loop in lines 1–4 that allows you to prove inequality (2.5). Your proof should use the structure of the loop-invariant proof presented in this chapter.

d. What is the worst-case running time of BUBBLESORT? How does it compare with the running time of INSERTION-SORT?

2-3   *Correctness of Horner's rule*

You are given the coefficents $a_0, a_1, a_2, \ldots, a_n$ of a polynomial

$$P(x) = \sum_{k=0}^{n} a_k x^k$$
$$= a_0 + a_1 x + a_2 x^2 + \cdots + a_{n-1} x^{n-1} + a_n x^n \; ,$$

and you want to evaluate this polynomial for a given value of x. *Horner's rule* says to evaluate the polynomial according to this parenthesization:

$$P(x) = a_0 + x\left(a_1 + x\left(a_2 + \cdots + x(a_{n-1} + xa_n)\cdots\right)\right).$$

The procedure HORNER implements Horner's rule to evaluate $P(x)$, given the coefficients $a_0, a_1, a_2, \ldots, a_n$ in an array $A[0:n]$ and the value of x.

HORNER(A, n, x)

```
1  p = 0
2  for i = n downto 0
3      p = A[i] + x · p
4  return p
```

a. In terms of Θ-notation, what is the running time of this procedure?

b. Write pseudocode to implement the naive polynomial-evaluation algorithm that computes each term of the polynomial from scratch. What is the running time of this algorithm? How does it compare with HORNER?

c. Consider the following loop invariant for the procedure HORNER:

> At the start of each iteration of the **for** loop of lines 2–3,
> $$p = \sum_{k=0}^{n-(i+1)} A[k+i+1] \cdot x^k.$$

Interpret a summation with no terms as equaling 0. Following the structure of the loop-invariant proof presented in this chapter, use this loop invariant to show that, at termination, $p = \sum_{k=0}^{n} A[k] \cdot x^k$.

2-4 *Inversions*

Let $A[1:n]$ be an array of n distinct numbers. If $i < j$ and $A[i] > A[j]$, then the pair (i, j) is called an *inversion* of A.

a. List the five inversions of the array $\langle 2, 3, 8, 6, 1 \rangle$.

b. What array with elements from the set $\{1, 2, \ldots, n\}$ has the most inversions? How many does it have?

c. What is the relationship between the running time of insertion sort and the number of inversions in the input array? Justify your answer.

d. Give an algorithm that determines the number of inversions in any permutation on n elements in $\Theta(n \lg n)$ worst-case time. (*Hint:* Modify merge sort.)

Chapter notes

In 1968, Knuth published the first of three volumes with the general title *The Art of Computer Programming* [259, 260, 261]. The first volume ushered in the modern study of computer algorithms with a focus on the analysis of running time. The full series remains an engaging and worthwhile reference for many of the topics presented here. According to Knuth, the word "algorithm" is derived from the name "al-Khowârizmî," a ninth-century Persian mathematician.

Aho, Hopcroft, and Ullman [5] advocated the asymptotic analysis of algorithms —using notations that Chapter 3 introduces, including Θ-notation—as a means of comparing relative performance. They also popularized the use of recurrence relations to describe the running times of recursive algorithms.

Knuth [261] provides an encyclopedic treatment of many sorting algorithms. His comparison of sorting algorithms (page 381) includes exact step-counting analyses, like the one we performed here for insertion sort. Knuth's discussion of insertion sort encompasses several variations of the algorithm. The most important of these is Shell's sort, introduced by D. L. Shell, which uses insertion sort on periodic subarrays of the input to produce a faster sorting algorithm.

Merge sort is also described by Knuth. He mentions that a mechanical collator capable of merging two decks of punched cards in a single pass was invented in 1938. J. von Neumann, one of the pioneers of computer science, apparently wrote a program for merge sort on the EDVAC computer in 1945.

The early history of proving programs correct is described by Gries [200], who credits P. Naur with the first article in this field. Gries attributes loop invariants to R. W. Floyd. The textbook by Mitchell [329] is a good reference on how to prove programs correct.

3 Characterizing Running Times

The order of growth of the running time of an algorithm, defined in Chapter 2, gives a simple way to characterize the algorithm's efficiency and also allows us to compare it with alternative algorithms. Once the input size n becomes large enough, merge sort, with its $\Theta(n \lg n)$ worst-case running time, beats insertion sort, whose worst-case running time is $\Theta(n^2)$. Although we can sometimes determine the exact running time of an algorithm, as we did for insertion sort in Chapter 2, the extra precision is rarely worth the effort of computing it. For large enough inputs, the multiplicative constants and lower-order terms of an exact running time are dominated by the effects of the input size itself.

When we look at input sizes large enough to make relevant only the order of growth of the running time, we are studying the *asymptotic* efficiency of algorithms. That is, we are concerned with how the running time of an algorithm increases with the size of the input *in the limit*, as the size of the input increases without bound. Usually, an algorithm that is asymptotically more efficient is the best choice for all but very small inputs.

This chapter gives several standard methods for simplifying the asymptotic analysis of algorithms. The next section presents informally the three most commonly used types of "asymptotic notation," of which we have already seen an example in Θ-notation. It also shows one way to use these asymptotic notations to reason about the worst-case running time of insertion sort. Then we look at asymptotic notations more formally and present several notational conventions used throughout this book. The last section reviews the behavior of functions that commonly arise when analyzing algorithms.

3.1   *O*-notation, Ω-notation, and Θ-notation

When we analyzed the worst-case running time of insertion sort in Chapter 2, we started with the complicated expression

$$\left(\frac{c_5}{2} + \frac{c_6}{2} + \frac{c_7}{2}\right) n^2 + \left(c_1 + c_2 + c_4 + \frac{c_5}{2} - \frac{c_6}{2} - \frac{c_7}{2} + c_8\right) n$$
$$- (c_2 + c_4 + c_5 + c_8) .$$

We then discarded the lower-order terms $(c_1 + c_2 + c_4 + c_5/2 - c_6/2 - c_7/2 + c_8)n$ and $c_2 + c_4 + c_5 + c_8$, and we also ignored the coefficient $c_5/2 + c_6/2 + c_7/2$ of n^2. That left just the factor n^2, which we put into Θ-notation as $\Theta(n^2)$. We use this style to characterize running times of algorithms: discard the lower-order terms and the coefficient of the leading term, and use a notation that focuses on the rate of growth of the running time.

Θ-notation is not the only such "asymptotic notation." In this section, we'll see other forms of asymptotic notation as well. We start with intuitive looks at these notations, revisiting insertion sort to see how we can apply them. In the next section, we'll see the formal definitions of our asymptotic notations, along with conventions for using them.

Before we get into specifics, bear in mind that the asymptotic notations we'll see are designed so that they characterize functions in general. It so happens that the functions we are most interested in denote the running times of algorithms. But asymptotic notation can apply to functions that characterize some other aspect of algorithms (the amount of space they use, for example), or even to functions that have nothing whatsoever to do with algorithms.

O-notation

O-notation characterizes an *upper bound* on the asymptotic behavior of a function. In other words, it says that a function grows *no faster* than a certain rate, based on the highest-order term. Consider, for example, the function $7n^3 + 100n^2 - 20n + 6$. Its highest-order term is $7n^3$, and so we say that this function's rate of growth is n^3. Because this function grows no faster than n^3, we can write that it is $O(n^3)$. You might be surprised that we can also write that the function $7n^3 + 100n^2 - 20n + 6$ is $O(n^4)$. Why? Because the function grows more slowly than n^4, we are correct in saying that it grows no faster. As you might have guessed, this function is also $O(n^5)$, $O(n^6)$, and so on. More generally, it is $O(n^c)$ for any constant $c \geq 3$.

Ω-notation

Ω-notation characterizes a *lower bound* on the asymptotic behavior of a function. In other words, it says that a function grows *at least as fast* as a certain rate, based —as in *O*-notation—on the highest-order term. Because the highest-order term in the function $7n^3 + 100n^2 - 20n + 6$ grows at least as fast as n^3, this function is $\Omega(n^3)$. This function is also $\Omega(n^2)$ and $\Omega(n)$. More generally, it is $\Omega(n^c)$ for any constant $c \leq 3$.

Θ-notation

Θ-notation characterizes a *tight bound* on the asymptotic behavior of a function. It says that a function grows *precisely* at a certain rate, based—once again—on the highest-order term. Put another way, Θ-notation characterizes the rate of growth of the function to within a constant factor from above and to within a constant factor from below. These two constant factors need not be equal.

If you can show that a function is both $O(f(n))$ and $\Omega(f(n))$ for some function $f(n)$, then you have shown that the function is $\Theta(f(n))$. (The next section states this fact as a theorem.) For example, since the function $7n^3 + 100n^2 - 20n + 6$ is both $O(n^3)$ and $\Omega(n^3)$, it is also $\Theta(n^3)$.

Example: Insertion sort

Let's revisit insertion sort and see how to work with asymptotic notation to characterize its $\Theta(n^2)$ worst-case running time without evaluating summations as we did in Chapter 2. Here is the INSERTION-SORT procedure once again:

```
INSERTION-SORT(A, n)
1   for i = 2 to n
2       key = A[i]
3       // Insert A[i] into the sorted subarray A[1 : i − 1].
4       j = i − 1
5       while j > 0 and A[j] > key
6           A[j + 1] = A[j]
7           j = j − 1
8       A[j + 1] = key
```

What can we observe about how the pseudocode operates? The procedure has nested loops. The outer loop is a **for** loop that runs $n - 1$ times, regardless of the values being sorted. The inner loop is a **while** loop, but the number of iterations it makes depends on the values being sorted. The loop variable j starts at $i - 1$

$A[1:n/3]$	$A[n/3 + 1 : 2n/3]$	$A[2n/3 + 1 : n]$
each of the $n/3$ largest values moves	through each of these $n/3$ positions	to somewhere in these $n/3$ positions

Figure 3.1 The $\Omega(n^2)$ lower bound for insertion sort. If the first $n/3$ positions contain the $n/3$ largest values, each of these values must move through each of the middle $n/3$ positions, one position at a time, to end up somewhere in the last $n/3$ positions. Since each of $n/3$ values moves through at least each of $n/3$ positions, the time taken in this case is at least proportional to $(n/3)(n/3) = n^2/9$, or $\Omega(n^2)$.

and decreases by 1 in each iteration until either it reaches 0 or $A[j] \leq key$. For a given value of i, the **while** loop might iterate 0 times, $i - 1$ times, or anywhere in between. The body of the **while** loop (lines 6–7) takes constant time per iteration of the **while** loop.

These observations suffice to deduce an $O(n^2)$ running time for any case of INSERTION-SORT, giving us a blanket statement that covers all inputs. The running time is dominated by the inner loop. Because each of the $n - 1$ iterations of the outer loop causes the inner loop to iterate at most $i - 1$ times, and because i is at most n, the total number of iterations of the inner loop is at most $(n - 1)(n - 1)$, which is less than n^2. Since each iteration of the inner loop takes constant time, the total time spent in the inner loop is at most a constant times n^2, or $O(n^2)$.

With a little creativity, we can also see that the worst-case running time of INSERTION-SORT is $\Omega(n^2)$. By saying that the worst-case running time of an algorithm is $\Omega(n^2)$, we mean that for every input size n above a certain threshold, there is at least one input of size n for which the algorithm takes at least cn^2 time, for some positive constant c. It does not necessarily mean that the algorithm takes at least cn^2 time for all inputs.

Let's now see why the worst-case running time of INSERTION-SORT is $\Omega(n^2)$. For a value to end up to the right of where it started, it must have been moved in line 6. In fact, for a value to end up k positions to the right of where it started, line 6 must have executed k times. As Figure 3.1 shows, let's assume that n is a multiple of 3 so that we can divide the array A into groups of $n/3$ positions. Suppose that in the input to INSERTION-SORT, the $n/3$ largest values occupy the first $n/3$ array positions $A[1:n/3]$. (It does not matter what relative order they have within the first $n/3$ positions.) Once the array has been sorted, each of these $n/3$ values ends up somewhere in the last $n/3$ positions $A[2n/3 + 1 : n]$. For that to happen, each of these $n/3$ values must pass through each of the middle $n/3$ positions $A[n/3 + 1 : 2n/3]$. Each of these $n/3$ values passes through these middle

$n/3$ positions one position at a time, by at least $n/3$ executions of line 6. Because at least $n/3$ values have to pass through at least $n/3$ positions, the time taken by INSERTION-SORT in the worst case is at least proportional to $(n/3)(n/3) = n^2/9$, which is $\Omega(n^2)$.

Because we have shown that INSERTION-SORT runs in $O(n^2)$ time in all cases and that there is an input that makes it take $\Omega(n^2)$ time, we can conclude that the worst-case running time of INSERTION-SORT is $\Theta(n^2)$. It does not matter that the constant factors for upper and lower bounds might differ. What matters is that we have characterized the worst-case running time to within constant factors (discounting lower-order terms). This argument does not show that INSERTION-SORT runs in $\Theta(n^2)$ time in *all* cases. Indeed, we saw in Chapter 2 that the best-case running time is $\Theta(n)$.

Exercises

3.1-1
Modify the lower-bound argument for insertion sort to handle input sizes that are not necessarily a multiple of 3.

3.1-2
Using reasoning similar to what we used for insertion sort, analyze the running time of the selection sort algorithm from Exercise 2.2-2.

3.1-3
Suppose that α is a fraction in the range $0 < \alpha < 1$. Show how to generalize the lower-bound argument for insertion sort to consider an input in which the αn largest values start in the first αn positions. What additional restriction do you need to put on α? What value of α maximizes the number of times that the αn largest values must pass through each of the middle $(1 - 2\alpha)n$ array positions?

3.2 Asymptotic notation: formal definitions

Having seen asymptotic notation informally, let's get more formal. The notations we use to describe the asymptotic running time of an algorithm are defined in terms of functions whose domains are typically the set $\mathbb{N}$ of natural numbers or the set $\mathbb{R}$ of real numbers. Such notations are convenient for describing a running-time function $T(n)$. This section defines the basic asymptotic notations and also introduces some common "proper" notational abuses.

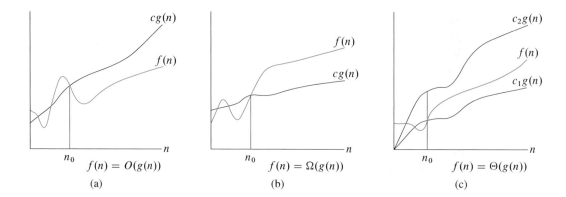

Figure 3.2 Graphic examples of the O, Ω, and Θ notations. In each part, the value of n_0 shown is the minimum possible value, but any greater value also works. **(a)** O-notation gives an upper bound for a function to within a constant factor. We write $f(n) = O(g(n))$ if there are positive constants n_0 and c such that at and to the right of n_0, the value of $f(n)$ always lies on or below $cg(n)$. **(b)** Ω-notation gives a lower bound for a function to within a constant factor. We write $f(n) = \Omega(g(n))$ if there are positive constants n_0 and c such that at and to the right of n_0, the value of $f(n)$ always lies on or above $cg(n)$. **(c)** Θ-notation bounds a function to within constant factors. We write $f(n) = \Theta(g(n))$ if there exist positive constants n_0, c_1, and c_2 such that at and to the right of n_0, the value of $f(n)$ always lies between $c_1g(n)$ and $c_2g(n)$ inclusive.

O-notation

As we saw in Section 3.1, O-notation describes an ***asymptotic upper bound***. We use O-notation to give an upper bound on a function, to within a constant factor.

Here is the formal definition of O-notation. For a given function $g(n)$, we denote by $O(g(n))$ (pronounced "big-oh of g of n" or sometimes just "oh of g of n") the *set of functions*

$$O(g(n)) = \{f(n) : \text{there exist positive constants } c \text{ and } n_0 \text{ such that}$$
$$0 \le f(n) \le cg(n) \text{ for all } n \ge n_0\} \,.^{[1]}$$

A function $f(n)$ belongs to the set $O(g(n))$ if there exists a positive constant c such that $f(n) \le cg(n)$ for sufficiently large n. Figure 3.2(a) shows the intuition behind O-notation. For all values n at and to the right of n_0, the value of the function $f(n)$ is on or below $cg(n)$.

The definition of $O(g(n))$ requires that every function $f(n)$ in the set $O(g(n))$ be ***asymptotically nonnegative***: $f(n)$ must be nonnegative whenever n is sufficiently large. (An ***asymptotically positive*** function is one that is positive for all

---

[1] Within set notation, a colon means "such that."

sufficiently large n.) Consequently, the function $g(n)$ itself must be asymptotically nonnegative, or else the set $O(g(n))$ is empty. We therefore assume that every function used within O-notation is asymptotically nonnegative. This assumption holds for the other asymptotic notations defined in this chapter as well.

You might be surprised that we define O-notation in terms of sets. Indeed, you might expect that we would write "$f(n) \in O(g(n))$" to indicate that $f(n)$ belongs to the set $O(g(n))$. Instead, we usually write "$f(n) = O(g(n))$" and say "$f(n)$ is big-oh of $g(n)$" to express the same notion. Although it may seem confusing at first to abuse equality in this way, we'll see later in this section that doing so has its advantages.

Let's explore an example of how to use the formal definition of O-notation to justify our practice of discarding lower-order terms and ignoring the constant coefficient of the highest-order term. We'll show that $4n^2 + 100n + 500 = O(n^2)$, even though the lower-order terms have much larger coefficients than the leading term. We need to find positive constants c and n_0 such that $4n^2 + 100n + 500 \leq cn^2$ for all $n \geq n_0$. Dividing both sides by n^2 gives $4 + 100/n + 500/n^2 \leq c$. This inequality is satisfied for many choices of c and n_0. For example, if we choose $n_0 = 1$, then this inequality holds for $c = 604$. If we choose $n_0 = 10$, then $c = 19$ works, and choosing $n_0 = 100$ allows us to use $c = 5.05$.

We can also use the formal definition of O-notation to show that the function $n^3 - 100n^2$ does not belong to the set $O(n^2)$, even though the coefficient of n^2 is a large negative number. If we had $n^3 - 100n^2 = O(n^2)$, then there would be positive constants c and n_0 such that $n^3 - 100n^2 \leq cn^2$ for all $n \geq n_0$. Again, we divide both sides by n^2, giving $n - 100 \leq c$. Regardless of what value we choose for the constant c, this inequality does not hold for any value of $n > c + 100$.

Ω-notation

Just as O-notation provides an asymptotic *upper* bound on a function, Ω-notation provides an ***asymptotic lower bound***. For a given function $g(n)$, we denote by $\Omega(g(n))$ (pronounced "big-omega of g of n" or sometimes just "omega of g of n") the set of functions

$$\Omega(g(n)) = \{f(n) : \text{there exist positive constants } c \text{ and } n_0 \text{ such that}$$
$$0 \leq cg(n) \leq f(n) \text{ for all } n \geq n_0\} \,.$$

Figure 3.2(b) shows the intuition behind Ω-notation. For all values n at or to the right of n_0, the value of $f(n)$ is on or above $cg(n)$.

We've already shown that $4n^2 + 100n + 500 = O(n^2)$. Now let's show that $4n^2 + 100n + 500 = \Omega(n^2)$. We need to find positive constants c and n_0 such that $4n^2 + 100n + 500 \geq cn^2$ for all $n \geq n_0$. As before, we divide both sides by n^2, giving $4 + 100/n + 500/n^2 \geq c$. This inequality holds when n_0 is any positive integer and $c = 4$.

What if we had subtracted the lower-order terms from the $4n^2$ term instead of adding them? What if we had a small coefficient for the n^2 term? The function would still be $\Omega(n^2)$. For example, let's show that $n^2/100 - 100n - 500 = \Omega(n^2)$. Dividing by n^2 gives $1/100 - 100/n - 500/n^2 \geq c$. We can choose any value for n_0 that is at least 10,005 and find a positive value for c. For example, when $n_0 = 10,005$, we can choose $c = 2.49 \times 10^{-9}$. Yes, that's a tiny value for c, but it is positive. If we select a larger value for n_0, we can also increase c. For example, if $n_0 = 100,000$, then we can choose $c = 0.0089$. The higher the value of n_0, the closer to the coefficient $1/100$ we can choose c.

Θ-notation

We use Θ-notation for *asymptotically tight bounds*. For a given function $g(n)$, we denote by $\Theta(g(n))$ ("theta of g of n") the set of functions

$$\Theta(g(n)) = \{f(n) : \text{there exist positive constants } c_1, c_2, \text{and } n_0 \text{ such that}$$
$$0 \leq c_1 g(n) \leq f(n) \leq c_2 g(n) \text{ for all } n \geq n_0\} .$$

Figure 3.2(c) shows the intuition behind Θ-notation. For all values of n at and to the right of n_0, the value of $f(n)$ lies at or above $c_1 g(n)$ and at or below $c_2 g(n)$. In other words, for all $n \geq n_0$, the function $f(n)$ is equal to $g(n)$ to within constant factors.

The definitions of O-, Ω-, and Θ-notations lead to the following theorem, whose proof we leave as Exercise 3.2-4.

Theorem 3.1
For any two functions $f(n)$ and $g(n)$, we have $f(n) = \Theta(g(n))$ if and only if $f(n) = O(g(n))$ and $f(n) = \Omega(g(n))$. ∎

We typically apply Theorem 3.1 to prove asymptotically tight bounds from asymptotic upper and lower bounds.

Asymptotic notation and running times

When you use asymptotic notation to characterize an algorithm's running time, make sure that the asymptotic notation you use is as precise as possible without overstating which running time it applies to. Here are some examples of using asymptotic notation properly and improperly to characterize running times.

Let's start with insertion sort. We can correctly say that insertion sort's worst-case running time is $O(n^2)$, $\Omega(n^2)$, and—due to Theorem 3.1—$\Theta(n^2)$. Although all three ways to characterize the worst-case running times are correct, the $\Theta(n^2)$ bound is the most precise and hence the most preferred. We can also correctly say that insertion sort's best-case running time is $O(n)$, $\Omega(n)$, and $\Theta(n)$, again with $\Theta(n)$ the most precise and therefore the most preferred.

Here is what we *cannot* correctly say: insertion sort's running time is $\Theta(n^2)$. That is an overstatement because by omitting "worst-case" from the statement, we're left with a blanket statement covering all cases. The error here is that insertion sort does not run in $\Theta(n^2)$ time in all cases since, as we've seen, it runs in $\Theta(n)$ time in the best case. We can correctly say that insertion sort's running time is $O(n^2)$, however, because in all cases, its running time grows no faster than n^2. When we say $O(n^2)$ instead of $\Theta(n^2)$, there is no problem in having cases whose running time grows more slowly than n^2. Likewise, we cannot correctly say that insertion sort's running time is $\Theta(n)$, but we can say that its running time is $\Omega(n)$.

How about merge sort? Since merge sort runs in $\Theta(n \lg n)$ time in all cases, we can just say that its running time is $\Theta(n \lg n)$ without specifying worst-case, best-case, or any other case.

People occasionally conflate O-notation with Θ-notation by mistakenly using O-notation to indicate an asymptotically tight bound. They say things like "an $O(n \lg n)$-time algorithm runs faster than an $O(n^2)$-time algorithm." Maybe it does, maybe it doesn't. Since O-notation denotes only an asymptotic upper bound, that so-called $O(n^2)$-time algorithm might actually run in $\Theta(n)$ time. You should be careful to choose the appropriate asymptotic notation. If you want to indicate an asymptotically tight bound, use Θ-notation.

We typically use asymptotic notation to provide the simplest and most precise bounds possible. For example, if an algorithm has a running time of $3n^2 + 20n$ in all cases, we use asymptotic notation to write that its running time is $\Theta(n^2)$. Strictly speaking, we are also correct in writing that the running time is $O(n^3)$ or $\Theta(3n^2 + 20n)$. Neither of these expressions is as useful as writing $\Theta(n^2)$ in this case, however: $O(n^3)$ is less precise than $\Theta(n^2)$ if the running time is $3n^2 + 20n$, and $\Theta(3n^2 + 20n)$ introduces complexity that obscures the order of growth. By writing the simplest and most precise bound, such as $\Theta(n^2)$, we can categorize and compare different algorithms. Throughout the book, you will see asymptotic running times that are almost always based on polynomials and logarithms: functions such as n, $n \lg^2 n$, $n^2 \lg n$, or $n^{1/2}$. You will also see some other functions, such as exponentials, $\lg \lg n$, and $\lg^* n$ (see Section 3.3). It is usually fairly easy to compare the rates of growth of these functions. Problem 3-3 gives you good practice.

Asymptotic notation in equations and inequalities

Although we formally define asymptotic notation in terms of sets, we use the equal sign ($=$) instead of the set membership sign ($\in$) within formulas. For example, we wrote that $4n^2 + 100n + 500 = O(n^2)$. We might also write $2n^2 + 3n + 1 = 2n^2 + \Theta(n)$. How do we interpret such formulas?

When the asymptotic notation stands alone (that is, not within a larger formula) on the right-hand side of an equation (or inequality), as in $4n^2 + 100n + 500 = O(n^2)$, the equal sign means set membership: $4n^2 + 100n + 500 \in O(n^2)$. In general, however, when asymptotic notation appears in a formula, we interpret it as standing for some anonymous function that we do not care to name. For example, the formula $2n^2 + 3n + 1 = 2n^2 + \Theta(n)$ means that $2n^2 + 3n + 1 = 2n^2 + f(n)$, where $f(n) \in \Theta(n)$. In this case, we let $f(n) = 3n + 1$, which indeed belongs to $\Theta(n)$.

Using asymptotic notation in this manner can help eliminate inessential detail and clutter in an equation. For example, in Chapter 2 we expressed the worst-case running time of merge sort as the recurrence

$$T(n) = 2T(n/2) + \Theta(n) .$$

If we are interested only in the asymptotic behavior of $T(n)$, there is no point in specifying all the lower-order terms exactly, because they are all understood to be included in the anonymous function denoted by the term $\Theta(n)$.

The number of anonymous functions in an expression is understood to be equal to the number of times the asymptotic notation appears. For example, in the expression

$$\sum_{i=1}^{n} O(i) ,$$

there is only a single anonymous function (a function of i). This expression is thus *not* the same as $O(1) + O(2) + \cdots + O(n)$, which doesn't really have a clean interpretation.

In some cases, asymptotic notation appears on the left-hand side of an equation, as in

$$2n^2 + \Theta(n) = \Theta(n^2) .$$

Interpret such equations using the following rule: *No matter how the anonymous functions are chosen on the left of the equal sign, there is a way to choose the anonymous functions on the right of the equal sign to make the equation valid.* Thus, our example means that for *any* function $f(n) \in \Theta(n)$, there is *some* function $g(n) \in \Theta(n^2)$ such that $2n^2 + f(n) = g(n)$ for all n. In other words, the right-hand side of an equation provides a coarser level of detail than the left-hand side.

We can chain together a number of such relationships, as in

$$2n^2 + 3n + 1 = 2n^2 + \Theta(n)$$
$$= \Theta(n^2) .$$

By the rules above, interpret each equation separately. The first equation says that there is *some* function $f(n) \in \Theta(n)$ such that $2n^2 + 3n + 1 = 2n^2 + f(n)$ for all n. The second equation says that for *any* function $g(n) \in \Theta(n)$ (such as the $f(n)$ just mentioned), there is *some* function $h(n) \in \Theta(n^2)$ such that $2n^2 + g(n) = h(n)$ for all n. This interpretation implies that $2n^2 + 3n + 1 = \Theta(n^2)$, which is what the chaining of equations intuitively says.

Proper abuses of asymptotic notation

Besides the abuse of equality to mean set membership, which we now see has a precise mathematical interpretation, another abuse of asymptotic notation occurs when the variable tending toward ∞ must be inferred from context. For example, when we say $O(g(n))$, we can assume that we're interested in the growth of $g(n)$ as n grows, and if we say $O(g(m))$ we're talking about the growth of $g(m)$ as m grows. The free variable in the expression indicates what variable is going to ∞.

The most common situation requiring contextual knowledge of which variable tends to ∞ occurs when the function inside the asymptotic notation is a constant, as in the expression $O(1)$. We cannot infer from the expression which variable is going to ∞, because no variable appears there. The context must disambiguate. For example, if the equation using asymptotic notation is $f(n) = O(1)$, it's apparent that the variable we're interested in is n. Knowing from context that the variable of interest is n, however, allows us to make perfect sense of the expression by using the formal definition of O-notation: the expression $f(n) = O(1)$ means that the function $f(n)$ is bounded from above by a constant as n goes to ∞. Technically, it might be less ambiguous if we explicitly indicated the variable tending to ∞ in the asymptotic notation itself, but that would clutter the notation. Instead, we simply ensure that the context makes it clear which variable (or variables) tend to ∞.

When the function inside the asymptotic notation is bounded by a positive constant, as in $T(n) = O(1)$, we often abuse asymptotic notation in yet another way, especially when stating recurrences. We may write something like $T(n) = O(1)$ for $n < 3$. According to the formal definition of O-notation, this statement is meaningless, because the definition only says that $T(n)$ is bounded above by a positive constant c for $n \geq n_0$ for some $n_0 > 0$. The value of $T(n)$ for $n < n_0$ need not be so bounded. Thus, in the example $T(n) = O(1)$ for $n < 3$, we cannot infer any constraint on $T(n)$ when $n < 3$, because it might be that $n_0 > 3$.

What is conventionally meant when we say $T(n) = O(1)$ for $n < 3$ is that there exists a positive constant c such that $T(n) \leq c$ for $n < 3$. This convention saves us the trouble of naming the bounding constant, allowing it to remain anonymous while we focus on more important variables in an analysis. Similar abuses occur with the other asymptotic notations. For example, $T(n) = \Theta(1)$ for $n < 3$ means that $T(n)$ is bounded above and below by positive constants when $n < 3$.

Occasionally, the function describing an algorithm's running time may not be defined for certain input sizes, for example, when an algorithm assumes that the input size is an exact power of 2. We still use asymptotic notation to describe the growth of the running time, understanding that any constraints apply only when the function is defined. For example, suppose that $f(n)$ is defined only on a subset of the natural or nonnegative real numbers. Then $f(n) = O(g(n))$ means that the bound $0 \leq T(n) \leq cg(n)$ in the definition of O-notation holds for all $n \geq n_0$ over the domain of $f(n)$, that is, where $f(n)$ is defined. This abuse is rarely pointed out, since what is meant is generally clear from context.

In mathematics, it's okay—and often desirable—to abuse a notation, as long as we don't misuse it. If we understand precisely what is meant by the abuse and don't draw incorrect conclusions, it can simplify our mathematical language, contribute to our higher-level understanding, and help us focus on what really matters.

o-notation

The asymptotic upper bound provided by O-notation may or may not be asymptotically tight. The bound $2n^2 = O(n^2)$ is asymptotically tight, but the bound $2n = O(n^2)$ is not. We use o-notation to denote an upper bound that is not asymptotically tight. We formally define $o(g(n))$ ("little-oh of g of n") as the set

$$o(g(n)) = \{f(n) : \text{for any positive constant } c > 0, \text{ there exists a constant} \\ n_0 > 0 \text{ such that } 0 \leq f(n) < cg(n) \text{ for all } n \geq n_0\}\ .$$

For example, $2n = o(n^2)$, but $2n^2 \neq o(n^2)$.

The definitions of O-notation and o-notation are similar. The main difference is that in $f(n) = O(g(n))$, the bound $0 \leq f(n) \leq cg(n)$ holds for *some* constant $c > 0$, but in $f(n) = o(g(n))$, the bound $0 \leq f(n) < cg(n)$ holds for *all* constants $c > 0$. Intuitively, in o-notation, the function $f(n)$ becomes insignificant relative to $g(n)$ as n gets large:

$$\lim_{n \to \infty} \frac{f(n)}{g(n)} = 0\ .$$

Some authors use this limit as a definition of the o-notation, but the definition in this book also restricts the anonymous functions to be asymptotically nonnegative.

ω-notation

By analogy, ω-notation is to Ω-notation as o-notation is to O-notation. We use ω-notation to denote a lower bound that is not asymptotically tight. One way to define it is by

$f(n) \in \omega(g(n))$ if and only if $g(n) \in o(f(n))$.

Formally, however, we define $\omega(g(n))$ ("little-omega of g of n") as the set

$$\omega(g(n)) = \{f(n) : \text{for any positive constant } c > 0, \text{ there exists a constant}$$
$$n_0 > 0 \text{ such that } 0 \le cg(n) < f(n) \text{ for all } n \ge n_0\} \ .$$

Where the definition of o-notation says that $f(n) < cg(n)$, the definition of ω-notation says the opposite: that $cg(n) < f(n)$. For examples of ω-notation, we have $n^2/2 = \omega(n)$, but $n^2/2 \ne \omega(n^2)$. The relation $f(n) = \omega(g(n))$ implies that

$$\lim_{n \to \infty} \frac{f(n)}{g(n)} = \infty \ ,$$

if the limit exists. That is, $f(n)$ becomes arbitrarily large relative to $g(n)$ as n gets large.

Comparing functions

Many of the relational properties of real numbers apply to asymptotic comparisons as well. For the following, assume that $f(n)$ and $g(n)$ are asymptotically positive.

Transitivity:

$$f(n) = \Theta(g(n)) \ \text{ and } \ g(n) = \Theta(h(n)) \quad \text{imply} \quad f(n) = \Theta(h(n)) \ ,$$
$$f(n) = O(g(n)) \ \text{ and } \ g(n) = O(h(n)) \quad \text{imply} \quad f(n) = O(h(n)) \ ,$$
$$f(n) = \Omega(g(n)) \ \text{ and } \ g(n) = \Omega(h(n)) \quad \text{imply} \quad f(n) = \Omega(h(n)) \ ,$$
$$f(n) = o(g(n)) \ \text{ and } \ g(n) = o(h(n)) \quad \text{imply} \quad f(n) = o(h(n)) \ ,$$
$$f(n) = \omega(g(n)) \ \text{ and } \ g(n) = \omega(h(n)) \quad \text{imply} \quad f(n) = \omega(h(n)) \ .$$

Reflexivity:

$$f(n) = \Theta(f(n)) \ ,$$
$$f(n) = O(f(n)) \ ,$$
$$f(n) = \Omega(f(n)) \ .$$

Symmetry:

$$f(n) = \Theta(g(n)) \ \text{ if and only if } \ g(n) = \Theta(f(n)) \ .$$

Transpose symmetry:

$$f(n) = O(g(n)) \quad \text{if and only if} \quad g(n) = \Omega(f(n)) \, ,$$
$$f(n) = o(g(n)) \quad \text{if and only if} \quad g(n) = \omega(f(n)) \, .$$

Because these properties hold for asymptotic notations, we can draw an analogy between the asymptotic comparison of two functions f and g and the comparison of two real numbers a and b:

$f(n) = O(g(n))$ is like $a \leq b$,
$f(n) = \Omega(g(n))$ is like $a \geq b$,
$f(n) = \Theta(g(n))$ is like $a = b$,
$f(n) = o(g(n))$ is like $a < b$,
$f(n) = \omega(g(n))$ is like $a > b$.

We say that $f(n)$ is *asymptotically smaller* than $g(n)$ if $f(n) = o(g(n))$, and $f(n)$ is *asymptotically larger* than $g(n)$ if $f(n) = \omega(g(n))$.

One property of real numbers, however, does not carry over to asymptotic notation:

Trichotomy: For any two real numbers a and b, exactly one of the following must hold: $a < b$, $a = b$, or $a > b$.

Although any two real numbers can be compared, not all functions are asymptotically comparable. That is, for two functions $f(n)$ and $g(n)$, it may be the case that neither $f(n) = O(g(n))$ nor $f(n) = \Omega(g(n))$ holds. For example, we cannot compare the functions n and $n^{1+\sin n}$ using asymptotic notation, since the value of the exponent in $n^{1+\sin n}$ oscillates between 0 and 2, taking on all values in between.

Exercises

3.2-1
Let $f(n)$ and $g(n)$ be asymptotically nonnegative functions. Using the basic definition of Θ-notation, prove that $\max \{f(n), g(n)\} = \Theta(f(n) + g(n))$.

3.2-2
Explain why the statement, "The running time of algorithm A is at least $O(n^2)$," is meaningless.

3.2-3
Is $2^{n+1} = O(2^n)$? Is $2^{2n} = O(2^n)$?

3.2-4
Prove Theorem 3.1.

3.2-5

Prove that the running time of an algorithm is $\Theta(g(n))$ if and only if its worst-case running time is $O(g(n))$ and its best-case running time is $\Omega(g(n))$.

3.2-6

Prove that $o(g(n)) \cap \omega(g(n))$ is the empty set.

3.2-7

We can extend our notation to the case of two parameters n and m that can go to ∞ independently at different rates. For a given function $g(n, m)$, we denote by $O(g(n, m))$ the set of functions

$$O(g(n, m)) = \{ f(n, m) : \text{ there exist positive constants } c, n_0, \text{ and } m_0$$
$$\text{such that } 0 \le f(n, m) \le cg(n, m)$$
$$\text{for all } n \ge n_0 \text{ or } m \ge m_0 \} .$$

Give corresponding definitions for $\Omega(g(n, m))$ and $\Theta(g(n, m))$.

3.3   Standard notations and common functions

This section reviews some standard mathematical functions and notations and explores the relationships among them. It also illustrates the use of the asymptotic notations.

Monotonicity

A function $f(n)$ is *monotonically increasing* if $m \le n$ implies $f(m) \le f(n)$. Similarly, it is *monotonically decreasing* if $m \le n$ implies $f(m) \ge f(n)$. A function $f(n)$ is *strictly increasing* if $m < n$ implies $f(m) < f(n)$ and *strictly decreasing* if $m < n$ implies $f(m) > f(n)$.

Floors and ceilings

For any real number x, we denote the greatest integer less than or equal to x by $\lfloor x \rfloor$ (read "the floor of x") and the least integer greater than or equal to x by $\lceil x \rceil$ (read "the ceiling of x"). The floor function is monotonically increasing, as is the ceiling function.

Floors and ceilings obey the following properties. For any integer n, we have

$$\lfloor n \rfloor = n = \lceil n \rceil . \tag{3.1}$$

For all real x, we have

$$x - 1 < \lfloor x \rfloor \le x \le \lceil x \rceil < x + 1 . \tag{3.2}$$

We also have

$$- \lfloor x \rfloor = \lceil -x \rceil , \tag{3.3}$$

or equivalently,

$$- \lceil x \rceil = \lfloor -x \rfloor . \tag{3.4}$$

For any real number $x \ge 0$ and integers $a, b > 0$, we have

$$\left\lceil \frac{\lceil x/a \rceil}{b} \right\rceil = \left\lceil \frac{x}{ab} \right\rceil , \tag{3.5}$$

$$\left\lfloor \frac{\lfloor x/a \rfloor}{b} \right\rfloor = \left\lfloor \frac{x}{ab} \right\rfloor , \tag{3.6}$$

$$\left\lceil \frac{a}{b} \right\rceil \le \frac{a + (b - 1)}{b} , \tag{3.7}$$

$$\left\lfloor \frac{a}{b} \right\rfloor \ge \frac{a - (b - 1)}{b} . \tag{3.8}$$

For any integer n and real number x, we have

$$\lfloor n + x \rfloor = n + \lfloor x \rfloor , \tag{3.9}$$

$$\lceil n + x \rceil = n + \lceil x \rceil . \tag{3.10}$$

Modular arithmetic

For any integer a and any positive integer n, the value $a \bmod n$ is the *remainder* (or *residue*) of the quotient a/n:

$$a \bmod n = a - n \lfloor a/n \rfloor . \tag{3.11}$$

It follows that

$$0 \le a \bmod n < n , \tag{3.12}$$

even when a is negative.

Given a well-defined notion of the remainder of one integer when divided by another, it is convenient to provide special notation to indicate equality of remainders. If $(a \bmod n) = (b \bmod n)$, we write $a = b \pmod{n}$ and say that a is *equivalent* to b, modulo n. In other words, $a = b \pmod{n}$ if a and b have the same remainder when divided by n. Equivalently, $a = b \pmod{n}$ if and only if n is a divisor of $b - a$. We write $a \ne b \pmod{n}$ if a is not equivalent to b, modulo n.

Polynomials

Given a nonnegative integer d, a *polynomial in n of degree d* is a function $p(n)$ of the form

$$p(n) = \sum_{i=0}^{d} a_i n^i \ ,$$

where the constants $a_0, a_1, \ldots, a_d$ are the *coefficients* of the polynomial and $a_d \neq 0$. A polynomial is asymptotically positive if and only if $a_d > 0$. For an asymptotically positive polynomial $p(n)$ of degree d, we have $p(n) = \Theta(n^d)$. For any real constant $a \geq 0$, the function n^a is monotonically increasing, and for any real constant $a \leq 0$, the function n^a is monotonically decreasing. We say that a function $f(n)$ is *polynomially bounded* if $f(n) = O(n^k)$ for some constant k.

Exponentials

For all real $a > 0, m$, and n, we have the following identities:

$$\begin{aligned}
a^0 &= 1 \ , \\
a^1 &= a \ , \\
a^{-1} &= 1/a \ , \\
(a^m)^n &= a^{mn} \ , \\
(a^m)^n &= (a^n)^m \ , \\
a^m a^n &= a^{m+n} \ .
\end{aligned}$$

For all n and $a \geq 1$, the function a^n is monotonically increasing in n. When convenient, we assume that $0^0 = 1$.

We can relate the rates of growth of polynomials and exponentials by the following fact. For all real constants $a > 1$ and b, we have

$$\lim_{n \to \infty} \frac{n^b}{a^n} = 0 \ ,$$

from which we can conclude that

$$n^b = o(a^n) \ . \tag{3.13}$$

Thus, any exponential function with a base strictly greater than 1 grows faster than any polynomial function.

Using e to denote $2.71828\ldots$, the base of the natural-logarithm function, we have for all real x,

$$e^x = 1 + x + \frac{x^2}{2!} + \frac{x^3}{3!} + \cdots = \sum_{i=0}^{\infty} \frac{x^i}{i!} \ ,$$

where "!" denotes the factorial function defined later in this section. For all real x, we have the inequality

$$1 + x \le e^x \,, \tag{3.14}$$

where equality holds only when $x = 0$. When $|x| \le 1$, we have the approximation

$$1 + x \le e^x \le 1 + x + x^2 \,. \tag{3.15}$$

When $x \to 0$, the approximation of e^x by $1 + x$ is quite good:

$$e^x = 1 + x + \Theta(x^2) \,.$$

(In this equation, the asymptotic notation is used to describe the limiting behavior as $x \to 0$ rather than as $x \to \infty$.) We have for all x,

$$\lim_{n \to \infty} \left(1 + \frac{x}{n}\right)^n = e^x \,. \tag{3.16}$$

Logarithms

We use the following notations:

$$
\begin{aligned}
\lg n &= \log_2 n &&\text{(binary logarithm)}\,, \\
\ln n &= \log_e n &&\text{(natural logarithm)}\,, \\
\lg^k n &= (\lg n)^k &&\text{(exponentiation)}\,, \\
\lg \lg n &= \lg(\lg n) &&\text{(composition)}\,.
\end{aligned}
$$

We adopt the following notational convention: in the absence of parentheses, *a logarithm function applies only to the next term in the formula*, so that $\lg n + 1$ means $(\lg n) + 1$ and not $\lg(n + 1)$.

For any constant $b > 1$, the function $\log_b n$ is undefined if $n \le 0$, strictly increasing if $n > 0$, negative if $0 < n < 1$, positive if $n > 1$, and 0 if $n = 1$. For all real $a > 0, b > 0, c > 0$, and n, we have

$$a = b^{\log_b a} \,, \tag{3.17}$$

$$\log_c(ab) = \log_c a + \log_c b \,, \tag{3.18}$$

$$\log_b a^n = n \log_b a \,,$$

$$\log_b a = \frac{\log_c a}{\log_c b} \,, \tag{3.19}$$

$$\log_b(1/a) = -\log_b a \,, \tag{3.20}$$

$$\log_b a = \frac{1}{\log_a b} \,,$$

$$a^{\log_b c} = c^{\log_b a} \,, \tag{3.21}$$

where, in each equation above, logarithm bases are not 1.

By equation (3.19), changing the base of a logarithm from one constant to another changes the value of the logarithm by only a constant factor. Consequently, we often use the notation "lg n" when we don't care about constant factors, such as in O-notation. Computer scientists find 2 to be the most natural base for logarithms because so many algorithms and data structures involve splitting a problem into two parts.

There is a simple series expansion for $\ln(1 + x)$ when $|x| < 1$:

$$\ln(1 + x) = x - \frac{x^2}{2} + \frac{x^3}{3} - \frac{x^4}{4} + \frac{x^5}{5} - \cdots . \tag{3.22}$$

We also have the following inequalities for $x > -1$:

$$\frac{x}{1 + x} \leq \ln(1 + x) \leq x , \tag{3.23}$$

where equality holds only for $x = 0$.

We say that a function $f(n)$ is *polylogarithmically bounded* if $f(n) = O(\lg^k n)$ for some constant k. We can relate the growth of polynomials and polylogarithms by substituting $\lg n$ for n and 2^a for a in equation (3.13). For all real constants $a > 0$ and b, we have

$$\lg^b n = o(n^a) . \tag{3.24}$$

Thus, any positive polynomial function grows faster than any polylogarithmic function.

Factorials

The notation $n!$ (read "n factorial") is defined for integers $n \geq 0$ as

$$n! = \begin{cases} 1 & \text{if } n = 0 , \\ n \cdot (n-1)! & \text{if } n > 0 . \end{cases}$$

Thus, $n! = 1 \cdot 2 \cdot 3 \cdots n$.

A weak upper bound on the factorial function is $n! \leq n^n$, since each of the n terms in the factorial product is at most n. *Stirling's approximation*,

$$n! = \sqrt{2\pi n} \left(\frac{n}{e}\right)^n \left(1 + \Theta\left(\frac{1}{n}\right)\right) , \tag{3.25}$$

where e is the base of the natural logarithm, gives us a tighter upper bound, and a lower bound as well. Exercise 3.3-4 asks you to prove the three facts

$$n! = o(n^n) , \tag{3.26}$$

$$n! = \omega(2^n) , \tag{3.27}$$

$$\lg(n!) = \Theta(n \lg n) , \tag{3.28}$$

where Stirling's approximation is helpful in proving equation (3.28). The following equation also holds for all $n \geq 1$:

$$n! = \sqrt{2\pi n} \left(\frac{n}{e}\right)^n e^{\alpha_n} \tag{3.29}$$

where

$$\frac{1}{12n + 1} < \alpha_n < \frac{1}{12n} \ .$$

Functional iteration

We use the notation $f^{(i)}(n)$ to denote the function $f(n)$ iteratively applied i times to an initial value of n. Formally, let $f(n)$ be a function over the reals. For non-negative integers i, we recursively define

$$f^{(i)}(n) = \begin{cases} n & \text{if } i = 0, \\ f(f^{(i-1)}(n)) & \text{if } i > 0. \end{cases} \tag{3.30}$$

For example, if $f(n) = 2n$, then $f^{(i)}(n) = 2^i n$.

The iterated logarithm function

We use the notation $\lg^* n$ (read "log star of n") to denote the iterated logarithm, defined as follows. Let $\lg^{(i)} n$ be as defined above, with $f(n) = \lg n$. Because the logarithm of a nonpositive number is undefined, $\lg^{(i)} n$ is defined only if $\lg^{(i-1)} n > 0$. Be sure to distinguish $\lg^{(i)} n$ (the logarithm function applied i times in succession, starting with argument n) from $\lg^i n$ (the logarithm of n raised to the ith power). Then we define the iterated logarithm function as

$$\lg^* n = \min \left\{ i \geq 0 : \lg^{(i)} n \leq 1 \right\} \ .$$

The iterated logarithm is a *very* slowly growing function:

$$\begin{aligned} \lg^* 2 &= 1 \ , \\ \lg^* 4 &= 2 \ , \\ \lg^* 16 &= 3 \ , \\ \lg^* 65536 &= 4 \ , \\ \lg^* (2^{65536}) &= 5 \ . \end{aligned}$$

Since the number of atoms in the observable universe is estimated to be about 10^{80}, which is much less than $2^{65536} = 10^{65536/\lg 10} \approx 10^{19,728}$, we rarely encounter an input size n for which $\lg^* n > 5$.

Fibonacci numbers

We define the *Fibonacci numbers* F_i, for $i \geq 0$, as follows:

$$F_i = \begin{cases} 0 & \text{if } i = 0, \\ 1 & \text{if } i = 1, \\ F_{i-1} + F_{i-2} & \text{if } i \geq 2. \end{cases} \tag{3.31}$$

Thus, after the first two, each Fibonacci number is the sum of the two previous ones, yielding the sequence

$$0, 1, 1, 2, 3, 5, 8, 13, 21, 34, 55, \ldots.$$

Fibonacci numbers are related to the *golden ratio* ϕ and its conjugate $\hat{\phi}$, which are the two roots of the equation

$$x^2 = x + 1.$$

As Exercise 3.3-7 asks you to prove, the golden ratio is given by

$$\begin{aligned} \phi &= \frac{1 + \sqrt{5}}{2} \\ &= 1.61803\ldots, \end{aligned} \tag{3.32}$$

and its conjugate, by

$$\begin{aligned} \hat{\phi} &= \frac{1 - \sqrt{5}}{2} \\ &= -.61803\ldots. \end{aligned} \tag{3.33}$$

Specifically, we have

$$F_i = \frac{\phi^i - \hat{\phi}^i}{\sqrt{5}},$$

which can be proved by induction (Exercise 3.3-8). Since $\left| \hat{\phi} \right| < 1$, we have

$$\begin{aligned} \frac{\left| \hat{\phi}^i \right|}{\sqrt{5}} &< \frac{1}{\sqrt{5}} \\ &< \frac{1}{2}, \end{aligned}$$

which implies that

$$F_i = \left\lfloor \frac{\phi^i}{\sqrt{5}} + \frac{1}{2} \right\rfloor, \tag{3.34}$$

which is to say that the ith Fibonacci number F_i is equal to $\phi^i / \sqrt{5}$ rounded to the nearest integer. Thus, Fibonacci numbers grow exponentially.

Exercises

3.3-1
Show that if $f(n)$ and $g(n)$ are monotonically increasing functions, then so are the functions $f(n) + g(n)$ and $f(g(n))$, and if $f(n)$ and $g(n)$ are in addition nonnegative, then $f(n) \cdot g(n)$ is monotonically increasing.

3.3-2
Prove that $\lfloor \alpha n \rfloor + \lceil (1 - \alpha)n \rceil = n$ for any integer n and real number α in the range $0 \leq \alpha \leq 1$.

3.3-3
Use equation (3.14) or other means to show that $(n + o(n))^k = \Theta(n^k)$ for any real constant k. Conclude that $\lceil n \rceil^k = \Theta(n^k)$ and $\lfloor n \rfloor^k = \Theta(n^k)$.

3.3-4
Prove the following:

a. Equation (3.21).

b. Equations (3.26)–(3.28).

c. $\lg(\Theta(n)) = \Theta(\lg n)$.

★ ***3.3-5***
Is the function $\lceil \lg n \rceil!$ polynomially bounded? Is the function $\lceil \lg \lg n \rceil!$ polynomially bounded?

★ ***3.3-6***
Which is asymptotically larger: $\lg(\lg^* n)$ or $\lg^*(\lg n)$?

3.3-7
Show that the golden ratio ϕ and its conjugate $\hat{\phi}$ both satisfy the equation $x^2 = x + 1$.

3.3-8
Prove by induction that the ith Fibonacci number satisfies the equation

$$F_i = (\phi^i - \hat{\phi}^i)/\sqrt{5},$$

where ϕ is the golden ratio and $\hat{\phi}$ is its conjugate.

3.3-9
Show that $k \lg k = \Theta(n)$ implies $k = \Theta(n/\lg n)$.

Problems

3-1 Asymptotic behavior of polynomials
Let

$$p(n) = \sum_{i=0}^{d} a_i n^i ,$$

where $a_d > 0$, be a degree-d polynomial in n, and let k be a constant. Use the definitions of the asymptotic notations to prove the following properties.

a. If $k \geq d$, then $p(n) = O(n^k)$.

b. If $k \leq d$, then $p(n) = \Omega(n^k)$.

c. If $k = d$, then $p(n) = \Theta(n^k)$.

d. If $k > d$, then $p(n) = o(n^k)$.

e. If $k < d$, then $p(n) = \omega(n^k)$.

3-2 Relative asymptotic growths
Indicate, for each pair of expressions (A, B) in the table below whether A is $O, o,$ $\Omega, \omega,$ or Θ of B. Assume that $k \geq 1, \epsilon > 0$, and $c > 1$ are constants. Write your answer in the form of the table with "yes" or "no" written in each box.

	A	B	O	o	Ω	ω	Θ
a.	$\lg^k n$	n^ϵ					
b.	n^k	c^n					
c.	$\sqrt{n}$	$n^{\sin n}$					
d.	2^n	$2^{n/2}$					
e.	$n^{\lg c}$	$c^{\lg n}$					
f.	$\lg(n!)$	$\lg(n^n)$					

3-3 Ordering by asymptotic growth rates
a. Rank the following functions by order of growth. That is, find an arrangement $g_1, g_2, \ldots, g_{30}$ of the functions satisfying $g_1 = \Omega(g_2), g_2 = \Omega(g_3), \ldots,$ $g_{29} = \Omega(g_{30})$. Partition your list into equivalence classes such that functions $f(n)$ and $g(n)$ belong to the same class if and only if $f(n) = \Theta(g(n))$.

$$\lg(\lg^* n) \quad 2^{\lg^* n} \quad (\sqrt{2})^{\lg n} \quad n^2 \quad n! \quad (\lg n)!$$

$$(3/2)^n \quad n^3 \quad \lg^2 n \quad \lg(n!) \quad 2^{2^n} \quad n^{1/\lg n}$$

$$\ln \ln n \quad \lg^* n \quad n \cdot 2^n \quad n^{\lg \lg n} \quad \ln n \quad 1$$

$$2^{\lg n} \quad (\lg n)^{\lg n} \quad e^n \quad 4^{\lg n} \quad (n+1)! \quad \sqrt{\lg n}$$

$$\lg^*(\lg n) \quad 2^{\sqrt{2 \lg n}} \quad n \quad 2^n \quad n \lg n \quad 2^{2^{n+1}}$$

b. Give an example of a single nonnegative function $f(n)$ such that for all functions $g_i(n)$ in part (a), $f(n)$ is neither $O(g_i(n))$ nor $\Omega(g_i(n))$.

3-4 *Asymptotic notation properties*
Let $f(n)$ and $g(n)$ be asymptotically positive functions. Prove or disprove each of the following conjectures.

a. $f(n) = O(g(n))$ implies $g(n) = O(f(n))$.

b. $f(n) + g(n) = \Theta(\min\{f(n), g(n)\})$.

c. $f(n) = O(g(n))$ implies $\lg f(n) = O(\lg g(n))$, where $\lg g(n) \geq 1$ and $f(n) \geq 1$ for all sufficiently large n.

d. $f(n) = O(g(n))$ implies $2^{f(n)} = O\left(2^{g(n)}\right)$.

e. $f(n) = O\left((f(n))^2\right)$.

f. $f(n) = O(g(n))$ implies $g(n) = \Omega(f(n))$.

g. $f(n) = \Theta(f(n/2))$.

h. $f(n) + o(f(n)) = \Theta(f(n))$.

3-5 *Manipulating asymptotic notation*
Let $f(n)$ and $g(n)$ be asymptotically positive functions. Prove the following identities:

a. $\Theta(\Theta(f(n))) = \Theta(f(n))$.

b. $\Theta(f(n)) + O(f(n)) = \Theta(f(n))$.

c. $\Theta(f(n)) + \Theta(g(n)) = \Theta(f(n) + g(n))$.

d. $\Theta(f(n)) \cdot \Theta(g(n)) = \Theta(f(n) \cdot g(n))$.

e. Argue that for any real constants $a_1, b_1 > 0$ and integer constants k_1, k_2, the following asymptotic bound holds:

$$(a_1 n)^{k_1} \lg^{k_2}(a_2 n) = \Theta(n^{k_1} \lg^{k_2} n) \, .$$

★ *f.* Prove that for $S \subseteq \mathbb{Z}$, we have

$$\sum_{k \in S} \Theta(f(k)) = \Theta\left(\sum_{k \in S} f(k) \right) ,$$

assuming that both sums converge.

★ *g.* Show that for $S \subseteq \mathbb{Z}$, the following asymptotic bound does not necessarily hold, even assuming that both products converge, by giving a counterexample:

$$\prod_{k \in S} \Theta(f(k)) = \Theta\left(\prod_{k \in S} f(k) \right) .$$

3-6 *Variations on O and Ω*

Some authors define Ω-notation in a slightly different way than this textbook does. We'll use the nomenclature $\overset{\infty}{\Omega}$ (read "omega infinity") for this alternative definition. We say that $f(n) = \overset{\infty}{\Omega}(g(n))$ if there exists a positive constant c such that $f(n) \geq cg(n) \geq 0$ for infinitely many integers n.

a. Show that for any two asymptotically nonnegative functions $f(n)$ and $g(n)$, we have $f(n) = O(g(n))$ or $f(n) = \overset{\infty}{\Omega}(g(n))$ (or both).

b. Show that there exist two asymptotically nonnegative functions $f(n)$ and $g(n)$ for which neither $f(n) = O(g(n))$ nor $f(n) = \Omega(g(n))$ holds.

c. Describe the potential advantages and disadvantages of using $\overset{\infty}{\Omega}$-notation instead of Ω-notation to characterize the running times of programs.

Some authors also define O in a slightly different manner. We'll use O' for the alternative definition: $f(n) = O'(g(n))$ if and only if $|f(n)| = O(g(n))$.

d. What happens to each direction of the "if and only if" in Theorem 3.1 on page 56 if we substitute O' for O but still use Ω?

Some authors define $\widetilde{O}$ (read "soft-oh") to mean O with logarithmic factors ignored:

$$\widetilde{O}(g(n)) = \{f(n) : \text{there exist positive constants } c, k, \text{ and } n_0 \text{ such that}$$
$$0 \le f(n) \le cg(n)\lg^k(n) \text{ for all } n \ge n_0\} \,.$$

e. Define $\widetilde{\Omega}$ and $\widetilde{\Theta}$ in a similar manner. Prove the corresponding analog to Theorem 3.1.

3-7   *Iterated functions*

We can apply the iteration operator $*$ used in the $\lg^*$ function to any monotonically increasing function $f(n)$ over the reals. For a given constant $c \in \mathbb{R}$, we define the iterated function f_c^* by

$$f_c^*(n) = \min\left\{i \ge 0 : f^{(i)}(n) \le c\right\},$$

which need not be well defined in all cases. In other words, the quantity $f_c^*(n)$ is the minimum number of iterated applications of the function f required to reduce its argument down to c or less.

For each of the functions $f(n)$ and constants c in the table below, give as tight a bound as possible on $f_c^*(n)$. If there is no i such that $f^{(i)}(n) \le c$, write "undefined" as your answer.

	$f(n)$	c	$f_c^*(n)$
a.	$n-1$	0	
b.	$\lg n$	1	
c.	$n/2$	1	
d.	$n/2$	2	
e.	$\sqrt{n}$	2	
f.	$\sqrt{n}$	1	
g.	$n^{1/3}$	2	

Chapter notes

Knuth [259] traces the origin of the O-notation to a number-theory text by P. Bachmann in 1892. The o-notation was invented by E. Landau in 1909 for his discussion of the distribution of prime numbers. The Ω and Θ notations were advocated by Knuth [265] to correct the popular, but technically sloppy, practice in the literature of using O-notation for both upper and lower bounds. As noted earlier in this chapter, many people continue to use the O-notation where the Θ-notation is more technically precise. The soft-oh notation $\widetilde{O}$ in Problem 3-6 was introduced by Babai, Luks, and Seress [31], although it was originally written as $O\sim$. Some authors now define $\widetilde{O}(g(n))$ as ignoring factors that are logarithmic in $g(n)$, rather than in n. With this definition, we can say that $n2^n = \widetilde{O}(2^n)$, but with the definition in Problem 3-6, this statement is not true. Further discussion of the history and development of asymptotic notations appears in works by Knuth [259, 265] and Brassard and Bratley [70].

Not all authors define the asymptotic notations in the same way, although the various definitions agree in most common situations. Some of the alternative definitions encompass functions that are not asymptotically nonnegative, as long as their absolute values are appropriately bounded.

Equation (3.29) is due to Robbins [381]. Other properties of elementary mathematical functions can be found in any good mathematical reference, such as Abramowitz and Stegun [1] or Zwillinger [468], or in a calculus book, such as Apostol [19] or Thomas et al. [433]. Knuth [259] and Graham, Knuth, and Patashnik [199] contain a wealth of material on discrete mathematics as used in computer science.

4 Divide-and-Conquer

The divide-and-conquer method is a powerful strategy for designing asymptotically efficient algorithms. We saw an example of divide-and-conquer in Section 2.3.1 when learning about merge sort. In this chapter, we'll explore applications of the divide-and-conquer method and acquire valuable mathematical tools that you can use to solve the recurrences that arise when analyzing divide-and-conquer algorithms.

Recall that for divide-and-conquer, you solve a given problem (instance) recursively. If the problem is small enough—the *base case*—you just solve it directly without recursing. Otherwise—the *recursive case*—you perform three characteristic steps:

Divide the problem into one or more subproblems that are smaller instances of the same problem.

Conquer the subproblems by solving them recursively.

Combine the subproblem solutions to form a solution to the original problem.

A divide-and-conquer algorithm breaks down a large problem into smaller subproblems, which themselves may be broken down into even smaller subproblems, and so forth. The recursion *bottoms out* when it reaches a base case and the subproblem is small enough to solve directly without further recursing.

Recurrences

To analyze recursive divide-and-conquer algorithms, we'll need some mathematical tools. A *recurrence* is an equation that describes a function in terms of its value on other, typically smaller, arguments. Recurrences go hand in hand with the divide-and-conquer method because they give us a natural way to characterize the running times of recursive algorithms mathematically. You saw an example of a recurrence in Section 2.3.2 when we analyzed the worst-case running time of merge sort.

For the divide-and-conquer matrix-multiplication algorithms presented in Sections 4.1 and 4.2, we'll derive recurrences that describe their worst-case running times. To understand why these two divide-and-conquer algorithms perform the way they do, you'll need to learn how to solve the recurrences that describe their running times. Sections 4.3–4.7 teach several methods for solving recurrences. These sections also explore the mathematics behind recurrences, which can give you stronger intuition for designing your own divide-and-conquer algorithms.

We want to get to the algorithms as soon as possible. So, let's just cover a few recurrence basics now, and then we'll look more deeply at recurrences, especially how to solve them, after we see the matrix-multiplication examples.

The general form of a recurrence is an equation or inequality that describes a function over the integers or reals using the function itself. It contains two or more cases, depending on the argument. If a case involves the recursive invocation of the function on different (usually smaller) inputs, it is a *recursive case*. If a case does not involve a recursive invocation, it is a *base case*. There may be zero, one, or many functions that satisfy the statement of the recurrence. The recurrence is *well defined* if there is at least one function that satisfies it, and *ill defined* otherwise.

Algorithmic recurrences

We'll be particularly interested in recurrences that describe the running times of divide-and-conquer algorithms. A recurrence $T(n)$ is *algorithmic* if, for every sufficiently large *threshold* constant $n_0 > 0$, the following two properties hold:

1. For all $n < n_0$, we have $T(n) = \Theta(1)$.

2. For all $n \geq n_0$, every path of recursion terminates in a defined base case within a finite number of recursive invocations.

Similar to how we sometimes abuse asymptotic notation (see page 60), when a function is not defined for all arguments, we understand that this definition is constrained to values of n for which $T(n)$ is defined.

Why would a recurrence $T(n)$ that represents a (correct) divide-and-conquer algorithm's worst-case running time satisfy these properties for all sufficiently large threshold constants? The first property says that there exist constants c_1, c_2 such that $0 < c_1 \leq T(n) \leq c_2$ for $n < n_0$. For every legal input, the algorithm must output the solution to the problem it's solving in finite time (see Section 1.1). Thus we can let c_1 be the minimum amount of time to call and return from a procedure, which must be positive, because machine instructions need to be executed to invoke a procedure. The running time of the algorithm may not be defined for some values of n if there are no legal inputs of that size, but it must be defined for at least one, or else the "algorithm" doesn't solve any problem. Thus we can let c_2 be the algorithm's maximum running time on any input of size $n < n_0$, where n_0 is sufficiently large that the algorithm solves at least one problem of size less than n_0. The maximum is well defined, since there are at most a finite number of inputs of size less than n_0, and there is at least one if n_0 is sufficiently large. Consequently, $T(n)$ satisfies the first property. If the second property fails to hold for $T(n)$, then the algorithm isn't correct, because it would end up in an infinite recursive loop or otherwise fail to compute a solution. Thus, it stands to reason that a recurrence for the worst-case running time of a correct divide-and-conquer algorithm would be algorithmic.

Conventions for recurrences

We adopt the following convention:

> *Whenever a recurrence is stated without an explicit base case, we assume that the recurrence is algorithmic.*

That means you're free to pick any sufficiently large threshold constant n_0 for the range of base cases where $T(n) = \Theta(1)$. Interestingly, the asymptotic solutions of most algorithmic recurrences you're likely to see when analyzing algorithms don't depend on the choice of threshold constant, as long as it's large enough to make the recurrence well defined.

Asymptotic solutions of algorithmic divide-and-conquer recurrences also don't tend to change when we drop any floors or ceilings in a recurrence defined on the integers to convert it to a recurrence defined on the reals. Section 4.7 gives a sufficient condition for ignoring floors and ceilings that applies to most of the divide-and-conquer recurrences you're likely to see. Consequently, we'll frequently state algorithmic recurrences without floors and ceilings. Doing so generally simplifies the statement of the recurrences, as well as any math that we do with them.

You may sometimes see recurrences that are not equations, but rather inequalities, such as $T(n) \leq 2T(n/2) + \Theta(n)$. Because such a recurrence states only an upper bound on $T(n)$, we express its solution using O-notation rather than Θ-notation. Similarly, if the inequality is reversed to $T(n) \geq 2T(n/2) + \Theta(n)$, then, because the recurrence gives only a lower bound on $T(n)$, we use Ω-notation in its solution.

Divide-and-conquer and recurrences

This chapter illustrates the divide-and-conquer method by presenting and using recurrences to analyze two divide-and-conquer algorithms for multiplying $n \times n$ matrices. Section 4.1 presents a simple divide-and-conquer algorithm that solves a matrix-multiplication problem of size n by breaking it into eight subproblems of size $n/2$, which it then solves recursively. The running time of the algorithm can be characterized by the recurrence

$$T(n) = 8T(n/2) + \Theta(1) \,,$$

which turns out to have the solution $T(n) = \Theta(n^3)$. Although this divide-and-conquer algorithm is no faster than the straightforward method that uses a triply nested loop, it leads to an asymptotically faster divide-and-conquer algorithm due to V. Strassen, which we'll explore in Section 4.2. Strassen's remarkable algorithm divides a problem of size n into seven subproblems of size $n/2$ which it solves recursively. The running time of Strassen's algorithm can be described by the recurrence

$$T(n) = 7T(n/2) + \Theta(n^2) \,,$$

which has the solution $T(n) = \Theta(n^{\lg 7}) = O(n^{2.81})$. Strassen's algorithm beats the straightforward looping method asymptotically.

These two divide-and-conquer algorithms both break a problem of size n into several subproblems of size $n/2$. Although it is common when using divide-and-conquer for all the subproblems to have the same size, that isn't always the case. Sometimes it's productive to divide a problem of size n into subproblems of different sizes, and then the recurrence describing the running time reflects the irregularity. For example, consider a divide-and-conquer algorithm that divides a problem of size n into one subproblem of size $n/3$ and another of size $2n/3$, taking $\Theta(n)$ time to divide the problem and combine the solutions to the subproblems. Then the algorithm's running time can be described by the recurrence

$$T(n) = T(n/3) + T(2n/3) + \Theta(n) \,,$$

which turns out to have solution $T(n) = \Theta(n \lg n)$. We'll even see an algorithm in Chapter 9 that solves a problem of size n by recursively solving a subproblem of size $n/5$ and another of size $7n/10$, taking $\Theta(n)$ time for the divide and combine steps. Its performance satisfies the recurrence

$$T(n) = T(n/5) + T(7n/10) + \Theta(n) \,,$$

which has solution $T(n) = \Theta(n)$.

Although divide-and-conquer algorithms usually create subproblems with sizes a constant fraction of the original problem size, that's not always the case. For example, a recursive version of linear search (see Exercise 2.1-4) creates just one subproblem, with one element less than the original problem. Each recursive call takes constant time plus the time to recursively solve a subproblem with one less element, leading to the recurrence

$$T(n) = T(n-1) + \Theta(1) \,,$$

which has solution $T(n) = \Theta(n)$. Nevertheless, the vast majority of efficient divide-and-conquer algorithms solve subproblems that are a constant fraction of the size of the original problem, which is where we'll focus our efforts.

Solving recurrences

After learning about divide-and-conquer algorithms for matrix multiplication in Sections 4.1 and 4.2, we'll explore several mathematical tools for solving recurrences—that is, for obtaining asymptotic Θ-, O-, or Ω-bounds on their solutions. We want simple-to-use tools that can handle the most commonly occurring situations. But we also want general tools that work, perhaps with a little more effort, for less common cases. This chapter offers four methods for solving recurrences:

- In the *substitution method* (Section 4.3), you guess the form of a bound and then use mathematical induction to prove your guess correct and solve for constants. This method is perhaps the most robust method for solving recurrences, but it also requires you to make a good guess and to produce an inductive proof.

- The *recursion-tree method* (Section 4.4) models the recurrence as a tree whose nodes represent the costs incurred at various levels of the recursion. To solve the recurrence, you determine the costs at each level and add them up, perhaps using techniques for bounding summations from Section A.2. Even if you don't use this method to formally prove a bound, it can be helpful in guessing the form of the bound for use in the substitution method.

- The *master method* (Sections 4.5 and 4.6) is the easiest method, when it applies. It provides bounds for recurrences of the form

$$T(n) = aT(n/b) + f(n) \,,$$

where $a > 0$ and $b > 1$ are constants and $f(n)$ is a given "driving" function. This type of recurrence tends to arise more frequently in the study of algorithms than any other. It characterizes a divide-and-conquer algorithm that creates a subproblems, each of which is $1/b$ times the size of the original problem, using $f(n)$ time for the divide and combine steps. To apply the master method, you need to memorize three cases, but once you do, you can easily determine asymptotic bounds on running times for many divide-and-conquer algorithms.

- The *Akra-Bazzi method* (Section 4.7) is a general method for solving divide-and-conquer recurrences. Although it involves calculus, it can be used to attack more complicated recurrences than those addressed by the master method.

4.1   Multiplying square matrices

We can use the divide-and-conquer method to multiply square matrices. If you've seen matrices before, then you probably know how to multiply them. (Otherwise, you should read Section D.1.) Let $A = (a_{ik})$ and $B = (b_{kj})$ be square $n \times n$ matrices. The matrix product $C = A \cdot B$ is also an $n \times n$ matrix, where for $i, j = 1, 2, \ldots, n$, the (i, j) entry of C is given by

$$c_{ij} = \sum_{k=1}^{n} a_{ik} \cdot b_{kj} \ . \tag{4.1}$$

Generally, we'll assume that the matrices are *dense*, meaning that most of the n^2 entries are not 0, as opposed to *sparse*, where most of the n^2 entries are 0 and the nonzero entries can be stored more compactly than in an $n \times n$ array.

Computing the matrix C requires computing n^2 matrix entries, each of which is the sum of n pairwise products of input elements from A and B. The MATRIX-MULTIPLY procedure implements this strategy in a straightforward manner, and it generalizes the problem slightly. It takes as input three $n \times n$ matrices A, B, and C, and it adds the matrix product $A \cdot B$ to C, storing the result in C. Thus, it computes $C = C + A \cdot B$, instead of just $C = A \cdot B$. If only the product $A \cdot B$ is needed, just initialize all n^2 entries of C to 0 before calling the procedure, which takes an additional $\Theta(n^2)$ time. We'll see that the cost of matrix multiplication asymptotically dominates this initialization cost.

MATRIX-MULTIPLY(A, B, C, n)

```
1  for i = 1 to n              // compute entries in each of n rows
2      for j = 1 to n          // compute n entries in row i
3          for k = 1 to n
4              c_ij = c_ij + a_ik · b_kj   // add in another term of equation (4.1)
```

The pseudocode for MATRIX-MULTIPLY works as follows. The **for** loop of lines 1–4 computes the entries of each row i, and within a given row i, the **for** loop of lines 2–4 computes each of the entries c_{ij} for each column j. Each iteration of the **for** loop of lines 3–4 adds in one more term of equation (4.1).

Because each of the triply nested **for** loops runs for exactly n iterations, and each execution of line 4 takes constant time, the MATRIX-MULTIPLY procedure operates in $\Theta(n^3)$ time. Even if we add in the $\Theta(n^2)$ time for initializing C to 0, the running time is still $\Theta(n^3)$.

A simple divide-and-conquer algorithm

Let's see how to compute the matrix product $A \cdot B$ using divide-and-conquer. For $n > 1$, the divide step partitions the $n \times n$ matrices into four $n/2 \times n/2$ submatrices. We'll assume that n is an exact power of 2, so that as the algorithm recurses, we are guaranteed that the submatrix dimensions are integer. (Exercise 4.1-1 asks you to relax this assumption.) As with MATRIX-MULTIPLY, we'll actually compute $C = C + A \cdot B$. But to simplify the math behind the algorithm, let's assume that C has been initialized to the zero matrix, so that we are indeed computing $C = A \cdot B$.

The divide step views each of the $n \times n$ matrices A, B, and C as four $n/2 \times n/2$ submatrices:

$$A = \begin{pmatrix} A_{11} & A_{12} \\ A_{21} & A_{22} \end{pmatrix}, \quad B = \begin{pmatrix} B_{11} & B_{12} \\ B_{21} & B_{22} \end{pmatrix}, \quad C = \begin{pmatrix} C_{11} & C_{12} \\ C_{21} & C_{22} \end{pmatrix}. \tag{4.2}$$

Then we can write the matrix product as

$$\begin{pmatrix} C_{11} & C_{12} \\ C_{21} & C_{22} \end{pmatrix} = \begin{pmatrix} A_{11} & A_{12} \\ A_{21} & A_{22} \end{pmatrix}\begin{pmatrix} B_{11} & B_{12} \\ B_{21} & B_{22} \end{pmatrix} \tag{4.3}$$

$$= \begin{pmatrix} A_{11} \cdot B_{11} + A_{12} \cdot B_{21} & A_{11} \cdot B_{12} + A_{12} \cdot B_{22} \\ A_{21} \cdot B_{11} + A_{22} \cdot B_{21} & A_{21} \cdot B_{12} + A_{22} \cdot B_{22} \end{pmatrix}, \tag{4.4}$$

which corresponds to the equations

$$C_{11} = A_{11} \cdot B_{11} + A_{12} \cdot B_{21} , \tag{4.5}$$

$$C_{12} = A_{11} \cdot B_{12} + A_{12} \cdot B_{22} , \tag{4.6}$$

$$C_{21} = A_{21} \cdot B_{11} + A_{22} \cdot B_{21} , \tag{4.7}$$

$$C_{22} = A_{21} \cdot B_{12} + A_{22} \cdot B_{22} . \tag{4.8}$$

Equations (4.5)–(4.8) involve eight $n/2 \times n/2$ multiplications and four additions of $n/2 \times n/2$ submatrices.

As we look to transform these equations to an algorithm that can be described with pseudocode, or even implemented for real, there are two common approaches for implementing the matrix partitioning.

One strategy is to allocate temporary storage to hold A's four submatrices A_{11}, A_{12}, A_{21}, and A_{22} and B's four submatrices B_{11}, B_{12}, B_{21}, and B_{22}. Then copy each element in A and B to its corresponding location in the appropriate submatrix. After the recursive conquer step, copy the elements in each of C's four submatrices C_{11}, C_{12}, C_{21}, and C_{22} to their corresponding locations in C. This approach takes $\Theta(n^2)$ time, since $3n^2$ elements are copied.

The second approach uses index calculations and is faster and more practical. A submatrix can be specified within a matrix by indicating where within the matrix the submatrix lies without touching any matrix elements. Partitioning a matrix (or recursively, a submatrix) only involves arithmetic on this location information, which has constant size independent of the size of the matrix. Changes to the submatrix elements update the original matrix, since they occupy the same storage.

Going forward, we'll assume that index calculations are used and that partitioning can be performed in $\Theta(1)$ time. Exercise 4.1-3 asks you to show that it makes no difference to the overall asymptotic running time of matrix multiplication, however, whether the partitioning of matrices uses the first method of copying or the second method of index calculation. But for other divide-and-conquer matrix calculations, such as matrix addition, it can make a difference, as Exercise 4.1-4 asks you to show.

The procedure MATRIX-MULTIPLY-RECURSIVE uses equations (4.5)–(4.8) to implement a divide-and-conquer strategy for square-matrix multiplication. Like MATRIX-MULTIPLY, the procedure MATRIX-MULTIPLY-RECURSIVE computes $C = C + A \cdot B$ since, if necessary, C can be initialized to 0 before the procedure is called in order to compute only $C = A \cdot B$.

MATRIX-MULTIPLY-RECURSIVE(A, B, C, n)

```
 1  if n == 1
 2      // Base case.
 3      c₁₁ = c₁₁ + a₁₁ · b₁₁
 4      return
 5  // Divide.
 6  partition A, B, and C into n/2 × n/2 submatrices
          A₁₁, A₁₂, A₂₁, A₂₂; B₁₁, B₁₂, B₂₁, B₂₂;
          and C₁₁, C₁₂, C₂₁, C₂₂; respectively
 7  // Conquer.
 8  MATRIX-MULTIPLY-RECURSIVE(A₁₁, B₁₁, C₁₁, n/2)
 9  MATRIX-MULTIPLY-RECURSIVE(A₁₁, B₁₂, C₁₂, n/2)
10  MATRIX-MULTIPLY-RECURSIVE(A₂₁, B₁₁, C₂₁, n/2)
11  MATRIX-MULTIPLY-RECURSIVE(A₂₁, B₁₂, C₂₂, n/2)
12  MATRIX-MULTIPLY-RECURSIVE(A₁₂, B₂₁, C₁₁, n/2)
13  MATRIX-MULTIPLY-RECURSIVE(A₁₂, B₂₂, C₁₂, n/2)
14  MATRIX-MULTIPLY-RECURSIVE(A₂₂, B₂₁, C₂₁, n/2)
15  MATRIX-MULTIPLY-RECURSIVE(A₂₂, B₂₂, C₂₂, n/2)
```

As we walk through the pseudocode, we'll derive a recurrence to characterize its running time. Let $T(n)$ be the worst-case time to multiply two $n \times n$ matrices using this procedure.

In the base case, when $n = 1$, line 3 performs just the one scalar multiplication and one addition, which means that $T(1) = \Theta(1)$. As is our convention for constant base cases, we can omit this base case in the statement of the recurrence.

The recursive case occurs when $n > 1$. As discussed, we'll use index calculations to partition the matrices in line 6, taking $\Theta(1)$ time. Lines 8–15 recursively call MATRIX-MULTIPLY-RECURSIVE a total of eight times. The first four recursive calls compute the first terms of equations (4.5)–(4.8), and the subsequent four recursive calls compute and add in the second terms. Each recursive call adds the product of a submatrix of A and a submatrix of B to the appropriate submatrix of C in place, thanks to index calculations. Because each recursive call multiplies two $n/2 \times n/2$ matrices, thereby contributing $T(n/2)$ to the overall running time, the time taken by all eight recursive calls is $8T(n/2)$. There is no combine step, because the matrix C is updated in place. The total time for the recursive case, therefore, is the sum of the partitioning time and the time for all the recursive calls, or $\Theta(1) + 8T(n/2)$.

Thus, omitting the statement of the base case, our recurrence for the running time of MATRIX-MULTIPLY-RECURSIVE is

$$T(n) = 8T(n/2) + \Theta(1) . \tag{4.9}$$

As we'll see from the master method in Section 4.5, recurrence (4.9) has the solution $T(n) = \Theta(n^3)$, which means that it has the same asymptotic running time as the straightforward MATRIX-MULTIPLY procedure.

Why is the $\Theta(n^3)$ solution to this recurrence so much larger than the $\Theta(n \lg n)$ solution to the merge-sort recurrence (2.3) on page 41? After all, the recurrence for merge sort contains a $\Theta(n)$ term, whereas the recurrence for recursive matrix multiplication contains only a $\Theta(1)$ term.

Let's think about what the recursion tree for recurrence (4.9) would look like as compared with the recursion tree for merge sort, illustrated in Figure 2.5 on page 43. The factor of 2 in the merge-sort recurrence determines how many children each tree node has, which in turn determines how many terms contribute to the sum at each level of the tree. In comparison, for the recurrence (4.9) for MATRIX-MULTIPLY-RECURSIVE, each internal node in the recursion tree has eight children, not two, leading to a "bushier" recursion tree with many more leaves, despite the fact that the internal nodes are each much smaller. Consequently, the solution to recurrence (4.9) grows much more quickly than the solution to recurrence (2.3), which is borne out in the actual solutions: $\Theta(n^3)$ versus $\Theta(n \lg n)$.

Exercises

Note: You may wish to read Section 4.5 before attempting some of these exercises.

4.1-1
Generalize MATRIX-MULTIPLY-RECURSIVE to multiply $n \times n$ matrices for which n is not necessarily an exact power of 2. Give a recurrence describing its running time. Argue that it runs in $\Theta(n^3)$ time in the worst case.

4.1-2
How quickly can you multiply a $kn \times n$ matrix (kn rows and n columns) by an $n \times kn$ matrix, where $k \geq 1$, using MATRIX-MULTIPLY-RECURSIVE as a subroutine? Answer the same question for multiplying an $n \times kn$ matrix by a $kn \times n$ matrix. Which is asymptotically faster, and by how much?

4.1-3

Suppose that instead of partitioning matrices by index calculation in MATRIX-MULTIPLY-RECURSIVE, you copy the appropriate elements of A, B, and C into separate $n/2 \times n/2$ submatrices $A_{11}, A_{12}, A_{21}, A_{22}$; $B_{11}, B_{12}, B_{21}, B_{22}$; and $C_{11}, C_{12}, C_{21}, C_{22}$, respectively. After the recursive calls, you copy the results from C_{11}, C_{12}, C_{21}, and C_{22} back into the appropriate places in C. How does recurrence (4.9) change, and what is its solution?

4.1-4

Write pseudocode for a divide-and-conquer algorithm MATRIX-ADD-RECURSIVE that sums two $n \times n$ matrices A and B by partitioning each of them into four $n/2 \times n/2$ submatrices and then recursively summing corresponding pairs of submatrices. Assume that matrix partitioning uses $\Theta(1)$-time index calculations. Write a recurrence for the worst-case running time of MATRIX-ADD-RECURSIVE, and solve your recurrence. What happens if you use $\Theta(n^2)$-time copying to implement the partitioning instead of index calculations?

4.2 Strassen's algorithm for matrix multiplication

You might find it hard to imagine that any matrix multiplication algorithm could take less than $\Theta(n^3)$ time, since the natural definition of matrix multiplication requires n^3 scalar multiplications. Indeed, many mathematicians presumed that it was not possible to multiply matrices in $o(n^3)$ time until 1969, when V. Strassen [424] published a remarkable recursive algorithm for multiplying $n \times n$ matrices. Strassen's algorithm runs in $\Theta(n^{\lg 7})$ time. Since $\lg 7 = 2.8073549\ldots$, Strassen's algorithm runs in $O(n^{2.81})$ time, which is asymptotically better than the $\Theta(n^3)$ MATRIX-MULTIPLY and MATRIX-MULTIPLY-RECURSIVE procedures.

The key to Strassen's method is to use the divide-and-conquer idea from the MATRIX-MULTIPLY-RECURSIVE procedure, but make the recursion tree less bushy. We'll actually increase the work for each divide and combine step by a constant factor, but the reduction in bushiness will pay off. We won't reduce the bushiness from the eight-way branching of recurrence (4.9) all the way down to the two-way branching of recurrence (2.3), but we'll improve it just a little, and that will make a big difference. Instead of performing eight recursive multiplications of $n/2 \times n/2$ matrices, Strassen's algorithm performs only seven. The cost of eliminating one matrix multiplication is several new additions and subtractions of $n/2 \times n/2$ matrices, but still only a constant number. Rather than saying "additions and subtractions" everywhere, we'll adopt the common terminology of calling them both "additions" because subtraction is structurally the same computation as addition, except for a change of sign.

To get an inkling how the number of multiplications might be reduced, as well as why reducing the number of multiplications might be desirable for matrix calculations, suppose that you have two numbers x and y, and you want to calculate the quantity $x^2 - y^2$. The straightforward calculation requires two multiplications to square x and y, followed by one subtraction (which you can think of as a "negative addition"). But let's recall the old algebra trick $x^2 - y^2 = x^2 - xy + xy - y^2 = x(x - y) + y(x - y) = (x + y)(x - y)$. Using this formulation of the desired quantity, you could instead compute the sum $x + y$ and the difference $x - y$ and then multiply them, requiring only a single multiplication and two additions. At the cost of an extra addition, only one multiplication is needed to compute an expression that looks as if it requires two. If x and y are scalars, there's not much difference: both approaches require three scalar operations. If x and y are large matrices, however, the cost of multiplying outweighs the cost of adding, in which case the second method outperforms the first, although not asymptotically.

Strassen's strategy for reducing the number of matrix multiplications at the expense of more matrix additions is not at all obvious—perhaps the biggest understatement in this book! As with MATRIX-MULTIPLY-RECURSIVE, Strassen's algorithm uses the divide-and-conquer method to compute $C = C + A \cdot B$, where A, B, and C are all $n \times n$ matrices and n is an exact power of 2. Strassen's algorithm computes the four submatrices C_{11}, C_{12}, C_{21}, and C_{22} of C from equations (4.5)–(4.8) on page 82 in four steps. We'll analyze costs as we go along to develop a recurrence $T(n)$ for the overall running time. Let's see how it works:

1. If $n = 1$, the matrices each contain a single element. Perform a single scalar multiplication and a single scalar addition, as in line 3 of MATRIX-MULTIPLY-RECURSIVE, taking $\Theta(1)$ time, and return. Otherwise, partition the input matrices A and B and output matrix C into $n/2 \times n/2$ submatrices, as in equation (4.2). This step takes $\Theta(1)$ time by index calculation, just as in MATRIX-MULTIPLY-RECURSIVE.

2. Create $n/2 \times n/2$ matrices $S_1, S_2, \ldots, S_{10}$, each of which is the sum or difference of two submatrices from step 1. Create and zero the entries of seven $n/2 \times n/2$ matrices $P_1, P_2, \ldots, P_7$ to hold seven $n/2 \times n/2$ matrix products. All 17 matrices can be created, and the P_i initialized, in $\Theta(n^2)$ time.

3. Using the submatrices from step 1 and the matrices $S_1, S_2, \ldots, S_{10}$ created in step 2, recursively compute each of the seven matrix products $P_1, P_2, \ldots, P_7$, taking $7T(n/2)$ time.

4. Update the four submatrices $C_{11}, C_{12}, C_{21}, C_{22}$ of the result matrix C by adding or subtracting various P_i matrices, which takes $\Theta(n^2)$ time.

We'll see the details of steps 2–4 in a moment, but we already have enough information to set up a recurrence for the running time of Strassen's method. As is common, the base case in step 1 takes $\Theta(1)$ time, which we'll omit when stating the recurrence. When $n > 1$, steps 1, 2, and 4 take a total of $\Theta(n^2)$ time, and step 3 requires seven multiplications of $n/2 \times n/2$ matrices. Hence, we obtain the following recurrence for the running time of Strassen's algorithm:

$$T(n) = 7T(n/2) + \Theta(n^2) \,. \tag{4.10}$$

Compared with MATRIX-MULTIPLY-RECURSIVE, we have traded off one recursive submatrix multiplication for a constant number of submatrix additions. Once you understand recurrences and their solutions, you'll be able to see why this trade-off actually leads to a lower asymptotic running time. By the master method in Section 4.5, recurrence (4.10) has the solution $T(n) = \Theta(n^{\lg 7}) = O(n^{2.81})$, beating the $\Theta(n^3)$-time algorithms.

Now, let's delve into the details. Step 2 creates the following 10 matrices:

$$
\begin{aligned}
S_1 &= B_{12} - B_{22} \,, \\
S_2 &= A_{11} + A_{12} \,, \\
S_3 &= A_{21} + A_{22} \,, \\
S_4 &= B_{21} - B_{11} \,, \\
S_5 &= A_{11} + A_{22} \,, \\
S_6 &= B_{11} + B_{22} \,, \\
S_7 &= A_{12} - A_{22} \,, \\
S_8 &= B_{21} + B_{22} \,, \\
S_9 &= A_{11} - A_{21} \,, \\
S_{10} &= B_{11} + B_{12} \,.
\end{aligned}
$$

This step adds or subtracts $n/2 \times n/2$ matrices 10 times, taking $\Theta(n^2)$ time.

Step 3 recursively multiplies $n/2 \times n/2$ matrices 7 times to compute the following $n/2 \times n/2$ matrices, each of which is the sum or difference of products of A and B submatrices:

$$
\begin{aligned}
P_1 &= A_{11} \cdot S_1 \ (= A_{11} \cdot B_{12} - A_{11} \cdot B_{22}) \,, \\
P_2 &= S_2 \cdot B_{22} \ (= A_{11} \cdot B_{22} + A_{12} \cdot B_{22}) \,, \\
P_3 &= S_3 \cdot B_{11} \ (= A_{21} \cdot B_{11} + A_{22} \cdot B_{11}) \,, \\
P_4 &= A_{22} \cdot S_4 \ (= A_{22} \cdot B_{21} - A_{22} \cdot B_{11}) \,, \\
P_5 &= S_5 \cdot S_6 \ (= A_{11} \cdot B_{11} + A_{11} \cdot B_{22} + A_{22} \cdot B_{11} + A_{22} \cdot B_{22}) \,, \\
P_6 &= S_7 \cdot S_8 \ (= A_{12} \cdot B_{21} + A_{12} \cdot B_{22} - A_{22} \cdot B_{21} - A_{22} \cdot B_{22}) \,, \\
P_7 &= S_9 \cdot S_{10} \ (= A_{11} \cdot B_{11} + A_{11} \cdot B_{12} - A_{21} \cdot B_{11} - A_{21} \cdot B_{12}) \,.
\end{aligned}
$$

The only multiplications that the algorithm performs are those in the middle column of these equations. The right-hand column just shows what these products equal in terms of the original submatrices created in step 1, but the terms are never explicitly calculated by the algorithm.

Step 4 adds to and subtracts from the four $n/2 \times n/2$ submatrices of the product C the various P_i matrices created in step 3. We start with

$$C_{11} = C_{11} + P_5 + P_4 - P_2 + P_6 .$$

Expanding the calculation on the right-hand side, with the expansion of each P_i on its own line and vertically aligning terms that cancel out, we see that the update to C_{11} equals

$$
\begin{array}{l}
A_{11} \cdot B_{11} + A_{11} \cdot B_{22} + A_{22} \cdot B_{11} + A_{22} \cdot B_{22} \\
\qquad\qquad\qquad - A_{22} \cdot B_{11} \qquad\qquad\quad + A_{22} \cdot B_{21} \\
\qquad - A_{11} \cdot B_{22} \qquad\qquad\qquad\qquad\qquad\qquad - A_{12} \cdot B_{22} \\
\qquad\qquad\qquad\qquad - A_{22} \cdot B_{22} - A_{22} \cdot B_{21} + A_{12} \cdot B_{22} + A_{12} \cdot B_{21} \\
\hline
A_{11} \cdot B_{11} \qquad\qquad\qquad\qquad\qquad\qquad\qquad\qquad\quad + A_{12} \cdot B_{21} ,
\end{array}
$$

which corresponds to equation (4.5). Similarly, setting

$$C_{12} = C_{12} + P_1 + P_2$$

means that the update to C_{12} equals

$$
\begin{array}{l}
A_{11} \cdot B_{12} - A_{11} \cdot B_{22} \\
\qquad\quad + A_{11} \cdot B_{22} + A_{12} \cdot B_{22} \\
\hline
A_{11} \cdot B_{12} \qquad\quad + A_{12} \cdot B_{22} ,
\end{array}
$$

corresponding to equation (4.6). Setting

$$C_{21} = C_{21} + P_3 + P_4$$

means that the update to C_{21} equals

$$
\begin{array}{l}
A_{21} \cdot B_{11} + A_{22} \cdot B_{11} \\
\qquad\quad - A_{22} \cdot B_{11} + A_{22} \cdot B_{21} \\
\hline
A_{21} \cdot B_{11} \qquad\quad + A_{22} \cdot B_{21} ,
\end{array}
$$

corresponding to equation (4.7). Finally, setting

$$C_{22} = C_{22} + P_5 + P_1 - P_3 - P_7$$

means that the update to C_{22} equals

$$
\begin{array}{ll}
A_{11} \cdot B_{11} + A_{11} \cdot B_{22} + A_{22} \cdot B_{11} + A_{22} \cdot B_{22} & \\
\qquad - A_{11} \cdot B_{22} & + A_{11} \cdot B_{12} \\
\qquad\qquad - A_{22} \cdot B_{11} & - A_{21} \cdot B_{11} \\
- A_{11} \cdot B_{11} & - A_{11} \cdot B_{12} + A_{21} \cdot B_{11} + A_{21} \cdot B_{12} \\
\hline
\qquad\qquad A_{22} \cdot B_{22} & + A_{21} \cdot B_{12} \ ,
\end{array}
$$

which corresponds to equation (4.8). Altogether, since we add or subtract $n/2 \times n/2$ matrices 12 times in step 4, this step indeed takes $\Theta(n^2)$ time.

We can see that Strassen's remarkable algorithm, comprising steps 1–4, produces the correct matrix product using 7 submatrix multiplications and 18 submatrix additions. We can also see that recurrence (4.10) characterizes its running time. Since Section 4.5 shows that this recurrence has the solution $T(n) = \Theta(n^{\lg 7}) = o(n^3)$, Strassen's method asymptotically beats the $\Theta(n^3)$ MATRIX-MULTIPLY and MATRIX-MULTIPLY-RECURSIVE procedures.

Exercises

Note: You may wish to read Section 4.5 before attempting some of these exercises.

4.2-1
Use Strassen's algorithm to compute the matrix product

$$
\begin{pmatrix} 1 & 3 \\ 7 & 5 \end{pmatrix} \begin{pmatrix} 6 & 8 \\ 4 & 2 \end{pmatrix} .
$$

Show your work.

4.2-2
Write pseudocode for Strassen's algorithm.

4.2-3
What is the largest k such that if you can multiply 3×3 matrices using k multiplications (not assuming commutativity of multiplication), then you can multiply $n \times n$ matrices in $o(n^{\lg 7})$ time? What is the running time of this algorithm?

4.2-4
V. Pan discovered a way of multiplying 68×68 matrices using 132,464 multiplications, a way of multiplying 70×70 matrices using 143,640 multiplications, and a way of multiplying 72×72 matrices using 155,424 multiplications. Which method yields the best asymptotic running time when used in a divide-and-conquer matrix-multiplication algorithm? How does it compare with Strassen's algorithm?

4.2-5

Show how to multiply the complex numbers $a + bi$ and $c + di$ using only three multiplications of real numbers. The algorithm should take a, b, c, and d as input and produce the real component $ac - bd$ and the imaginary component $ad + bc$ separately.

4.2-6

Suppose that you have a $\Theta(n^{\alpha})$-time algorithm for squaring $n \times n$ matrices, where $\alpha \geq 2$. Show how to use that algorithm to multiply two different $n \times n$ matrices in $\Theta(n^{\alpha})$ time.

4.3   The substitution method for solving recurrences

Now that you have seen how recurrences characterize the running times of divide-and-conquer algorithms, let's learn how to solve them. We start in this section with the *substitution method*, which is the most general of the four methods in this chapter. The substitution method comprises two steps:

1. Guess the form of the solution using symbolic constants.

2. Use mathematical induction to show that the solution works, and find the constants.

To apply the inductive hypothesis, you substitute the guessed solution for the function on smaller values—hence the name "substitution method." This method is powerful, but you must guess the form of the answer. Although generating a good guess might seem difficult, a little practice can quickly improve your intuition.

You can use the substitution method to establish either an upper or a lower bound on a recurrence. It's usually best not to try to do both at the same time. That is, rather than trying to prove a Θ-bound directly, first prove an O-bound, and then prove an Ω-bound. Together, they give you a Θ-bound (Theorem 3.1 on page 56).

As an example of the substitution method, let's determine an asymptotic upper bound on the recurrence:

$$T(n) = 2T(\lfloor n/2 \rfloor) + \Theta(n) . \tag{4.11}$$

This recurrence is similar to recurrence (2.3) on page 41 for merge sort, except for the floor function, which ensures that $T(n)$ is defined over the integers. Let's guess that the asymptotic upper bound is the same—$T(n) = O(n \lg n)$—and use the substitution method to prove it.

We'll adopt the inductive hypothesis that $T(n) \leq cn \lg n$ for all $n \geq n_0$, where we'll choose the specific constants $c > 0$ and $n_0 > 0$ later, after we see what constraints they need to obey. If we can establish this inductive hypothesis, we can conclude that $T(n) = O(n \lg n)$. It would be dangerous to use $T(n) = O(n \lg n)$ as the inductive hypothesis because the constants matter, as we'll see in a moment in our discussion of pitfalls.

Assume by induction that this bound holds for all numbers at least as big as n_0 and less than n. In particular, therefore, if $n \geq 2n_0$, it holds for $\lfloor n/2 \rfloor$, yielding $T(\lfloor n/2 \rfloor) \leq c \lfloor n/2 \rfloor \lg(\lfloor n/2 \rfloor)$. Substituting into recurrence (4.11)—hence the name "substitution" method—yields

$$
\begin{aligned}
T(n) &\leq 2(c \lfloor n/2 \rfloor \lg(\lfloor n/2 \rfloor)) + \Theta(n) \\
&\leq 2(c(n/2) \lg(n/2)) + \Theta(n) \\
&= cn \lg(n/2) + \Theta(n) \\
&= cn \lg n - cn \lg 2 + \Theta(n) \\
&= cn \lg n - cn + \Theta(n) \\
&\leq cn \lg n \,,
\end{aligned}
$$

where the last step holds if we constrain the constants n_0 and c to be sufficiently large that for $n \geq 2n_0$, the quantity cn dominates the anonymous function hidden by the $\Theta(n)$ term.

We've shown that the inductive hypothesis holds for the inductive case, but we also need to prove that the inductive hypothesis holds for the base cases of the induction, that is, that $T(n) \leq cn \lg n$ when $n_0 \leq n < 2n_0$. As long as $n_0 > 1$ (a new constraint on n_0), we have $\lg n > 0$, which implies that $n \lg n > 0$. So let's pick $n_0 = 2$. Since the base case of recurrence (4.11) is not stated explicitly, by our convention, $T(n)$ is algorithmic, which means that $T(2)$ and $T(3)$ are constant (as they should be if they describe the worst-case running time of any real program on inputs of size 2 or 3). Picking $c = \max \{T(2), T(3)\}$ yields $T(2) \leq c < (2 \lg 2)c$ and $T(3) \leq c < (3 \lg 3)c$, establishing the inductive hypothesis for the base cases.

Thus, we have $T(n) \leq cn \lg n$ for all $n \geq 2$, which implies that the solution to recurrence (4.11) is $T(n) = O(n \lg n)$.

In the algorithms literature, people rarely carry out their substitution proofs to this level of detail, especially in their treatment of base cases. The reason is that for most algorithmic divide-and-conquer recurrences, the base cases are all handled in pretty much the same way. You ground the induction on a range of values from a convenient positive constant n_0 up to some constant $n_0' > n_0$ such that for $n \geq n_0'$, the recurrence always bottoms out in a constant-sized base case between n_0 and n_0'. (This example used $n_0' = 2n_0$.) Then, it's usually apparent, without spelling out the details, that with a suitably large choice of the leading constant (such as c for this example), the inductive hypothesis can be made to hold for all the values in the range from n_0 to n_0'.

Making a good guess

Unfortunately, there is no general way to correctly guess the tightest asymptotic solution to an arbitrary recurrence. Making a good guess takes experience and, occasionally, creativity. Fortunately, learning some recurrence-solving heuristics, as well as playing around with recurrences to gain experience, can help you become a good guesser. You can also use recursion trees, which we'll see in Section 4.4, to help generate good guesses.

If a recurrence is similar to one you've seen before, then guessing a similar solution is reasonable. As an example, consider the recurrence

$$T(n) = 2T(n/2 + 17) + \Theta(n) ,$$

defined on the reals. This recurrence looks somewhat like the merge-sort recurrence (2.3), but it's more complicated because of the added "17" in the argument to T on the right-hand side. Intuitively, however, this additional term shouldn't substantially affect the solution to the recurrence. When n is large, the relative difference between $n/2$ and $n/2 + 17$ is not that large: both cut n nearly in half. Consequently, it makes sense to guess that $T(n) = O(n \lg n)$, which you can verify is correct using the substitution method (see Exercise 4.3-1).

Another way to make a good guess is to determine loose upper and lower bounds on the recurrence and then reduce your range of uncertainty. For example, you might start with a lower bound of $T(n) = \Omega(n)$ for recurrence (4.11), since the recurrence includes the term $\Theta(n)$, and you can prove an initial upper bound of $T(n) = O(n^2)$. Then split your time between trying to lower the upper bound and trying to raise the lower bound until you converge on the correct, asymptotically tight solution, which in this case is $T(n) = \Theta(n \lg n)$.

A trick of the trade: subtracting a low-order term

Sometimes, you might correctly guess a tight asymptotic bound on the solution of a recurrence, but somehow the math fails to work out in the induction proof. The problem frequently turns out to be that the inductive assumption is not strong enough. The trick to resolving this problem is to revise your guess by *subtracting* a lower-order term when you hit such a snag. The math then often goes through.

Consider the recurrence

$$T(n) = 2T(n/2) + \Theta(1) \tag{4.12}$$

defined on the reals. Let's guess that the solution is $T(n) = O(n)$ and try to show that $T(n) \leq cn$ for $n \geq n_0$, where we choose the constants $c, n_0 > 0$ suitably. Substituting our guess into the recurrence, we obtain

$$T(n) \leq 2(c(n/2)) + \Theta(1)$$
$$= cn + \Theta(1) ,$$

which, unfortunately, does not imply that $T(n) \leq cn$ for *any* choice of c. We might be tempted to try a larger guess, say $T(n) = O(n^2)$. Although this larger guess works, it provides only a loose upper bound. It turns out that our original guess of $T(n) = O(n)$ is correct and tight. In order to show that it is correct, however, we must strengthen our inductive hypothesis.

Intuitively, our guess is nearly right: we are off only by $\Theta(1)$, a lower-order term. Nevertheless, mathematical induction requires us to prove the *exact* form of the inductive hypothesis. Let's try our trick of subtracting a lower-order term from our previous guess: $T(n) \leq cn - d$, where $d \geq 0$ is a constant. We now have

$$
\begin{aligned}
T(n) &\leq 2(c(n/2) - d) + \Theta(1) \\
&= cn - 2d + \Theta(1) \\
&\leq cn - d - (d - \Theta(1)) \\
&\leq cn - d
\end{aligned}
$$

as long as we choose d to be larger than the anonymous upper-bound constant hidden by the Θ-notation. Subtracting a lower-order term works! Of course, we must not forget to handle the base case, which is to choose the constant c large enough that $cn - d$ dominates the implicit base cases.

You might find the idea of subtracting a lower-order term to be counterintuitive. After all, if the math doesn't work out, shouldn't you increase your guess? Not necessarily! When the recurrence contains more than one recursive invocation (recurrence (4.12) contains two), if you add a lower-order term to the guess, then you end up adding it once for each of the recursive invocations. Doing so takes you even further away from the inductive hypothesis. On the other hand, if you subtract a lower-order term from the guess, then you get to subtract it once for each of the recursive invocations. In the above example, we subtracted the constant d twice because the coefficient of $T(n/2)$ is 2. We ended up with the inequality $T(n) \leq cn - d - (d - \Theta(1))$, and we readily found a suitable value for d.

Avoiding pitfalls

Avoid using asymptotic notation in the inductive hypothesis for the substitution method because it's error prone. For example, for recurrence (4.11), we can falsely "prove" that $T(n) = O(n)$ if we unwisely adopt $T(n) = O(n)$ as our inductive hypothesis:

$$
\begin{aligned}
T(n) &\leq 2 \cdot O(\lfloor n/2 \rfloor) + \Theta(n) \\
&= 2 \cdot O(n) + \Theta(n) \\
&= O(n) . \qquad \Longleftarrow \textit{wrong!}
\end{aligned}
$$

The problem with this reasoning is that the constant hidden by the O-notation changes. We can expose the fallacy by repeating the "proof" using an explicit constant. For the inductive hypothesis, assume that $T(n) \leq cn$ for all $n \geq n_0$, where $c, n_0 > 0$ are constants. Repeating the first two steps in the inequality chain yields

$$T(n) \leq 2(c \lfloor n/2 \rfloor) + \Theta(n)$$
$$\leq cn + \Theta(n) .$$

Now, indeed $cn + \Theta(n) = O(n)$, but the constant hidden by the O-notation must be larger than c because the anonymous function hidden by the $\Theta(n)$ is asymptotically positive. We cannot take the third step to conclude that $cn + \Theta(n) \leq cn$, thus exposing the fallacy.

When using the substitution method, or more generally mathematical induction, you must be careful that the constants hidden by any asymptotic notation are the same constants throughout the proof. Consequently, it's best to avoid asymptotic notation in your inductive hypothesis and to name constants explicitly.

Here's another fallacious use of the substitution method to show that the solution to recurrence (4.11) is $T(n) = O(n)$. We guess $T(n) \leq cn$ and then argue

$$T(n) \leq 2(c \lfloor n/2 \rfloor) + \Theta(n)$$
$$\leq cn + \Theta(n)$$
$$= O(n) , \qquad \Longleftarrow wrong!$$

since c is a positive constant. The mistake stems from the difference between our goal—to prove that $T(n) = O(n)$—and our inductive hypothesis—to prove that $T(n) \leq cn$. When using the substitution method, or in any inductive proof, you must prove the *exact* statement of the inductive hypothesis. In this case, we must explicitly prove that $T(n) \leq cn$ to show that $T(n) = O(n)$.

Exercises

4.3-1
Use the substitution method to show that each of the following recurrences defined on the reals has the asymptotic solution specified:

a. $T(n) = T(n - 1) + n$ has solution $T(n) = O(n^2)$.

b. $T(n) = T(n/2) + \Theta(1)$ has solution $T(n) = O(\lg n)$.

c. $T(n) = 2T(n/2) + n$ has solution $T(n) = \Theta(n \lg n)$.

d. $T(n) = 2T(n/2 + 17) + n$ has solution $T(n) = O(n \lg n)$.

e. $T(n) = 2T(n/3) + \Theta(n)$ has solution $T(n) = \Theta(n)$.

f. $T(n) = 4T(n/2) + \Theta(n)$ has solution $T(n) = \Theta(n^2)$.

4.3-2

The solution to the recurrence $T(n) = 4T(n/2) + n$ turns out to be $T(n) = \Theta(n^2)$. Show that a substitution proof with the assumption $T(n) \leq cn^2$ fails. Then show how to subtract a lower-order term to make a substitution proof work.

4.3-3

The recurrence $T(n) = 2T(n-1) + 1$ has the solution $T(n) = O(2^n)$. Show that a substitution proof fails with the assumption $T(n) \leq c2^n$, where $c > 0$ is constant. Then show how to subtract a lower-order term to make a substitution proof work.

4.4 The recursion-tree method for solving recurrences

Although you can use the substitution method to prove that a solution to a recurrence is correct, you might have trouble coming up with a good guess. Drawing out a recursion tree, as we did in our analysis of the merge-sort recurrence in Section 2.3.2, can help. In a *recursion tree*, each node represents the cost of a single subproblem somewhere in the set of recursive function invocations. You typically sum the costs within each level of the tree to obtain the per-level costs, and then you sum all the per-level costs to determine the total cost of all levels of the recursion. Sometimes, however, adding up the total cost takes more creativity.

A recursion tree is best used to generate intuition for a good guess, which you can then verify by the substitution method. If you are meticulous when drawing out a recursion tree and summing the costs, however, you can use a recursion tree as a direct proof of a solution to a recurrence. But if you use it only to generate a good guess, you can often tolerate a small amount of "sloppiness," which can simplify the math. When you verify your guess with the substitution method later on, your math should be precise. This section demonstrates how you can use recursion trees to solve recurrences, generate good guesses, and gain intuition for recurrences.

An illustrative example

Let's see how a recursion tree can provide a good guess for an upper-bound solution to the recurrence

$$T(n) = 3T(n/4) + \Theta(n^2) . \tag{4.13}$$

Figure 4.1 shows how to derive the recursion tree for $T(n) = 3T(n/4) + cn^2$, where the constant $c > 0$ is the upper-bound constant in the $\Theta(n^2)$ term. Part (a) of the figure shows $T(n)$, which part (b) expands into an equivalent tree representing the recurrence. The cn^2 term at the root represents the cost at the top level of recursion, and the three subtrees of the root represent the costs incurred by the

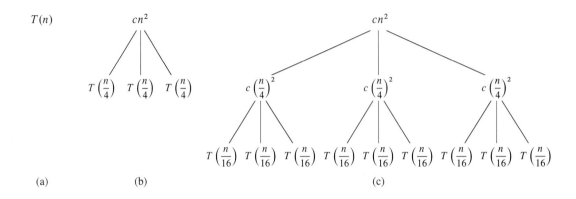

(a)   (b)   (c)

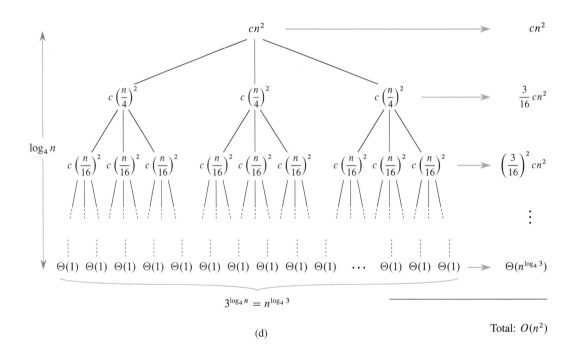

(d)

Figure 4.1 Constructing a recursion tree for the recurrence $T(n) = 3T(n/4) + cn^2$. Part **(a)** shows $T(n)$, which progressively expands in **(b)–(d)** to form the recursion tree. The fully expanded tree in **(d)** has height $\log_4 n$.

subproblems of size $n/4$. Part (c) shows this process carried one step further by expanding each node with cost $T(n/4)$ from part (b). The cost for each of the three children of the root is $c(n/4)^2$. We continue expanding each node in the tree by breaking it into its constituent parts as determined by the recurrence.

Because subproblem sizes decrease by a factor of 4 every time we go down one level, the recursion must eventually bottom out in a base case where $n < n_0$. By convention, the base case is $T(n) = \Theta(1)$ for $n < n_0$, where $n_0 > 0$ is any threshold constant sufficiently large that the recurrence is well defined. For the purpose of intuition, however, let's simplify the math a little. Let's assume that n is an exact power of 4 and that the base case is $T(1) = \Theta(1)$. As it turns out, these assumptions don't affect the asymptotic solution.

What's the height of the recursion tree? The subproblem size for a node at depth i is $n/4^i$. As we descend the tree from the root, the subproblem size hits $n = 1$ when $n/4^i = 1$ or, equivalently, when $i = \log_4 n$. Thus, the tree has internal nodes at depths $0, 1, 2, \ldots, \log_4 n - 1$ and leaves at depth $\log_4 n$.

Part (d) of Figure 4.1 shows the cost at each level of the tree. Each level has three times as many nodes as the level above, and so the number of nodes at depth i is 3^i. Because subproblem sizes reduce by a factor of 4 for each level further from the root, each internal node at depth $i = 0, 1, 2, \ldots, \log_4 n - 1$ has a cost of $c(n/4^i)^2$. Multiplying, we see that the total cost of all nodes at a given depth i is $3^i c(n/4^i)^2 = (3/16)^i cn^2$. The bottom level, at depth $\log_4 n$, contains $3^{\log_4 n} = n^{\log_4 3}$ leaves (using equation (3.21) on page 66). Each leaf contributes $\Theta(1)$, leading to a total leaf cost of $\Theta(n^{\log_4 3})$.

Now we add up the costs over all levels to determine the cost for the entire tree:

$$
\begin{aligned}
T(n) &= cn^2 + \frac{3}{16}cn^2 + \left(\frac{3}{16}\right)^2 cn^2 + \cdots + \left(\frac{3}{16}\right)^{\log_4 n} cn^2 + \Theta(n^{\log_4 3}) \\
&= \sum_{i=0}^{\log_4 n} \left(\frac{3}{16}\right)^i cn^2 + \Theta(n^{\log_4 3}) \\
&< \sum_{i=0}^{\infty} \left(\frac{3}{16}\right)^i cn^2 + \Theta(n^{\log_4 3}) \\
&= \frac{1}{1 - (3/16)} cn^2 + \Theta(n^{\log_4 3}) \qquad \text{(by equation (A.7) on page 1142)} \\
&= \frac{16}{13} cn^2 + \Theta(n^{\log_4 3}) \\
&= O(n^2) \qquad\qquad\qquad (\Theta(n^{\log_4 3}) = O(n^{0.8}) = O(n^2)) \,.
\end{aligned}
$$

We've derived the guess of $T(n) = O(n^2)$ for the original recurrence. In this example, the coefficients of cn^2 form a decreasing geometric series. By equation (A.7), the sum of these coefficients is bounded from above by the constant 16/13. Since the root's contribution to the total cost is cn^2, the cost of the root dominates the total cost of the tree.

In fact, if $O(n^2)$ is indeed an upper bound for the recurrence (as we'll verify in a moment), then it must be a tight bound. Why? The first recursive call contributes a cost of $\Theta(n^2)$, and so $\Omega(n^2)$ must be a lower bound for the recurrence.

Let's now use the substitution method to verify that our guess is correct, namely, that $T(n) = O(n^2)$ is an upper bound for the recurrence $T(n) = 3T(n/4) + \Theta(n^2)$. We want to show that $T(n) \leq dn^2$ for some constant $d > 0$. Using the same constant $c > 0$ as before, we have

$$
\begin{aligned}
T(n) &\leq 3T(n/4) + cn^2 \\
&\leq 3d(n/4)^2 + cn^2 \\
&= \frac{3}{16}dn^2 + cn^2 \\
&\leq dn^2 ,
\end{aligned}
$$

where the last step holds if we choose $d \geq (16/13)c$.

For the base case of the induction, let $n_0 > 0$ be a sufficiently large threshold constant that the recurrence is well defined when $T(n) = \Theta(1)$ for $n < n_0$. We can pick d large enough that d dominates the constant hidden by the Θ, in which case $dn^2 \geq d \geq T(n)$ for $1 \leq n < n_0$, completing the proof of the base case.

The substitution proof we just saw involves two named constants, c and d. We named c and used it to stand for the upper-bound constant hidden and guaranteed to exist by the Θ-notation. We cannot pick c arbitrarily—it's given to us—although, for any such c, any constant $c' \geq c$ also suffices. We also named d, but we were free to choose any value for it that fit our needs. In this example, the value of d happened to depend on the value of c, which is fine, since d is constant if c is constant.

An irregular example

Let's find an asymptotic upper bound for another, more irregular, example. Figure 4.2 shows the recursion tree for the recurrence

$$
T(n) = T(n/3) + T(2n/3) + \Theta(n) . \tag{4.14}
$$

This recursion tree is unbalanced, with different root-to-leaf paths having different lengths. Going left at any node produces a subproblem of one-third the size, and going right produces a subproblem of two-thirds the size. Let $n_0 > 0$ be the implicit threshold constant such that $T(n) = \Theta(1)$ for $0 < n < n_0$, and let c represent the upper-bound constant hidden by the $\Theta(n)$ term for $n \geq n_0$. There are actually two n_0 constants here—one for the threshold in the recurrence, and the other for the threshold in the Θ-notation, so we'll let n_0 be the larger of the two constants.

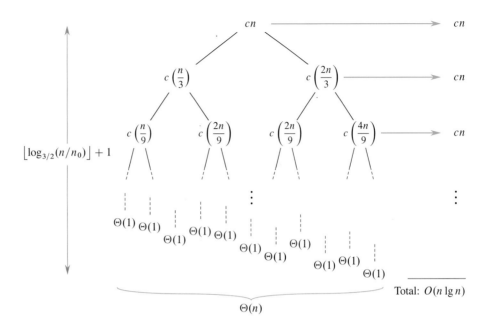

Figure 4.2   A recursion tree for the recurrence $T(n) = T(n/3) + T(2n/3) + cn$.

The height of the tree runs down the right edge of the tree, corresponding to subproblems of sizes n, $(2/3)n$, $(4/9)n, \ldots, \Theta(1)$ with costs bounded by cn, $c(2n/3)$, $c(4n/9), \ldots, \Theta(1)$, respectively. We hit the rightmost leaf when $(2/3)^h n < n_0 \leq (2/3)^{h-1}n$, which happens when $h = \lfloor \log_{3/2}(n/n_0) \rfloor + 1$ since, applying the floor bounds in equation (3.2) on page 64 with $x = \log_{3/2}(n/n_0)$, we have $(2/3)^h n = (2/3)^{\lfloor x \rfloor + 1}n < (2/3)^x n = (n_0/n)n = n_0$ and $(2/3)^{h-1}n = (2/3)^{\lfloor x \rfloor}n \geq (2/3)^x n = (n_0/n)n = n_0$. Thus, the height of the tree is $h = \Theta(\lg n)$.

We're now in a position to understand the upper bound. Let's postpone dealing with the leaves for a moment. Summing the costs of internal nodes across each level, we have at most cn per level times the $\Theta(\lg n)$ tree height for a total cost of $O(n \lg n)$ for all internal nodes.

It remains to deal with the leaves of the recursion tree, which represent base cases, each costing $\Theta(1)$. How many leaves are there? It's tempting to upperbound their number by the number of leaves in a complete binary tree of height $h = \lfloor \log_{3/2}(n/n_0) \rfloor + 1$, since the recursion tree is contained within such a complete binary tree. But this approach turns out to give us a poor bound. The complete binary tree has 1 node at the root, 2 nodes at depth 1, and generally 2^k nodes at depth k. Since the height is $h = \lfloor \log_{3/2} n \rfloor + 1$, there are

$2^h = 2^{\lfloor \log_{3/2} n \rfloor + 1} \leq 2n^{\log_{3/2} 2}$ leaves in the complete binary tree, which is an upper bound on the number of leaves in the recursion tree. Because the cost of each leaf is $\Theta(1)$, this analysis says that the total cost of all leaves in the recursion tree is $O(n^{\log_{3/2} 2}) = O(n^{1.71})$, which is an asymptotically greater bound than the $O(n \lg n)$ cost of all internal nodes. In fact, as we're about to see, this bound is not tight. The cost of all leaves in the recursion tree is $O(n)$—asymptotically *less* than $O(n \lg n)$. In other words, the cost of the internal nodes dominates the cost of the leaves, not vice versa.

Rather than analyzing the leaves, we could quit right now and prove by substitution that $T(n) = \Theta(n \lg n)$. This approach works (see Exercise 4.4-3), but it's instructive to understand how many leaves this recursion tree has. You may see recurrences for which the cost of leaves dominates the cost of internal nodes, and then you'll be in better shape if you've had some experience analyzing the number of leaves.

To figure out how many leaves there really are, let's write a recurrence $L(n)$ for the number of leaves in the recursion tree for $T(n)$. Since all the leaves in $T(n)$ belong either to the left subtree or the right subtree of the root, we have

$$L(n) = \begin{cases} 1 & \text{if } n < n_0 , \\ L(n/3) + L(2n/3) & \text{if } n \geq n_0 . \end{cases} \tag{4.15}$$

This recurrence is similar to recurrence (4.14), but it's missing the $\Theta(n)$ term, and it contains an explicit base case. Because this recurrence omits the $\Theta(n)$ term, it is much easier to solve. Let's apply the substitution method to show that it has solution $L(n) = O(n)$. Using the inductive hypothesis $L(n) \leq dn$ for some constant $d > 0$, and assuming that the inductive hypothesis holds for all values less than n, we have

$$\begin{aligned} L(n) &= L(n/3) + L(2n/3) \\ &\leq dn/3 + 2(dn)/3 \\ &\leq dn , \end{aligned}$$

which holds for any $d > 0$. We can now choose d large enough to handle the base case $L(n) = 1$ for $0 < n < n_0$, for which $d = 1$ suffices, thereby completing the substitution method for the upper bound on leaves. (Exercise 4.4-2 asks you to prove that $L(n) = \Theta(n)$.)

Returning to recurrence (4.14) for $T(n)$, it now becomes apparent that the total cost of leaves over all levels must be $L(n) \cdot \Theta(1) = \Theta(n)$. Since we have derived the bound of $O(n \lg n)$ on the cost of the internal nodes, it follows that the solution to recurrence (4.14) is $T(n) = O(n \lg n) + \Theta(n) = O(n \lg n)$. (Exercise 4.4-3 asks you to prove that $T(n) = \Theta(n \lg n)$.)

It's wise to verify any bound obtained with a recursion tree by using the substitution method, especially if you've made simplifying assumptions. But another strategy altogether is to use more-powerful mathematics, typically in the form of the master method in the next section (which unfortunately doesn't apply to recurrence (4.14)) or the Akra-Bazzi method (which does, but requires calculus). Even if you use a powerful method, a recursion tree can improve your intuition for what's going on beneath the heavy math.

Exercises

4.4-1
For each of the following recurrences, sketch its recursion tree, and guess a good asymptotic upper bound on its solution. Then use the substitution method to verify your answer.

a. $T(n) = T(n/2) + n^3$.

b. $T(n) = 4T(n/3) + n$.

c. $T(n) = 4T(n/2) + n$.

d. $T(n) = 3T(n-1) + 1$.

4.4-2
Use the substitution method to prove that recurrence (4.15) has the asymptotic lower bound $L(n) = \Omega(n)$. Conclude that $L(n) = \Theta(n)$.

4.4-3
Use the substitution method to prove that recurrence (4.14) has the solution $T(n) = \Omega(n \lg n)$. Conclude that $T(n) = \Theta(n \lg n)$.

4.4-4
Use a recursion tree to justify a good guess for the solution to the recurrence $T(n) = T(\alpha n) + T((1-\alpha)n) + \Theta(n)$, where α is a constant in the range $0 < \alpha < 1$.

4.5   The master method for solving recurrences

The master method provides a "cookbook" method for solving algorithmic recurrences of the form

$$T(n) = aT(n/b) + f(n), \tag{4.16}$$

where $a > 0$ and $b > 1$ are constants. We call $f(n)$ a *driving function*, and we call a recurrence of this general form a *master recurrence*. To use the master method, you need to memorize three cases, but then you'll be able to solve many master recurrences quite easily.

A master recurrence describes the running time of a divide-and-conquer algorithm that divides a problem of size n into a subproblems, each of size $n/b < n$. The algorithm solves the a subproblems recursively, each in $T(n/b)$ time. The driving function $f(n)$ encompasses the cost of dividing the problem before the recursion, as well as the cost of combining the results of the recursive solutions to subproblems. For example, the recurrence arising from Strassen's algorithm is a master recurrence with $a = 7, b = 2$, and driving function $f(n) = \Theta(n^2)$.

As we have mentioned, in solving a recurrence that describes the running time of an algorithm, one technicality that we'd often prefer to ignore is the requirement that the input size n be an integer. For example, we saw that the running time of merge sort can be described by recurrence (2.3), $T(n) = 2T(n/2) + \Theta(n)$, on page 41. But if n is an odd number, we really don't have two problems of exactly half the size. Rather, to ensure that the problem sizes are integers, we round one subproblem down to size $\lfloor n/2 \rfloor$ and the other up to size $\lceil n/2 \rceil$, so the true recurrence is $T(n) = T(\lceil n/2 \rceil) + T(\lfloor n/2 \rfloor) + \Theta(n)$. But this floors-and-ceilings recurrence is longer to write and messier to deal with than recurrence (2.3), which is defined on the reals. We'd rather not worry about floors and ceilings, if we don't have to, especially since the two recurrences have the same $\Theta(n \lg n)$ solution.

The master method allows you to state a master recurrence without floors and ceilings and implicitly infer them. No matter how the arguments are rounded up or down to the nearest integer, the asymptotic bounds that it provides remain the same. Moreover, as we'll see in Section 4.6, if you define your master recurrence on the reals, without implicit floors and ceilings, the asymptotic bounds still don't change. Thus you can ignore floors and ceilings for master recurrences. Section 4.7 gives sufficient conditions for ignoring floors and ceilings in more general divide-and-conquer recurrences.

The master theorem

The master method depends upon the following theorem.

Theorem 4.1 (Master theorem)
Let $a > 0$ and $b > 1$ be constants, and let $f(n)$ be a driving function that is defined and nonnegative on all sufficiently large reals. Define the recurrence $T(n)$ on $n \in \mathbb{N}$ by

$$T(n) = aT(n/b) + f(n) , \tag{4.17}$$

where $aT(n/b)$ actually means $a'T(\lfloor n/b \rfloor) + a''T(\lceil n/b \rceil)$ for some constants $a' \geq 0$ and $a'' \geq 0$ satisfying $a = a' + a''$. Then the asymptotic behavior of $T(n)$ can be characterized as follows:

1. If there exists a constant $\epsilon > 0$ such that $f(n) = O(n^{\log_b a - \epsilon})$, then $T(n) = \Theta(n^{\log_b a})$.

2. If there exists a constant $k \geq 0$ such that $f(n) = \Theta(n^{\log_b a} \lg^k n)$, then $T(n) = \Theta(n^{\log_b a} \lg^{k+1} n)$.

3. If there exists a constant $\epsilon > 0$ such that $f(n) = \Omega(n^{\log_b a + \epsilon})$, and if $f(n)$ additionally satisfies the *regularity condition* $af(n/b) \leq cf(n)$ for some constant $c < 1$ and all sufficiently large n, then $T(n) = \Theta(f(n))$. ∎

Before applying the master theorem to some examples, let's spend a few moments to understand broadly what it says. The function $n^{\log_b a}$ is called the *watershed function*. In each of the three cases, we compare the driving function $f(n)$ to the watershed function $n^{\log_b a}$. Intuitively, if the watershed function grows asymptotically faster than the driving function, then case 1 applies. Case 2 applies if the two functions grow at nearly the same asymptotic rate. Case 3 is the "opposite" of case 1, where the driving function grows asymptotically faster than the watershed function. But the technical details matter.

In case 1, not only must the watershed function grow asymptotically faster than the driving function, it must grow *polynomially* faster. That is, the watershed function $n^{\log_b a}$ must be asymptotically larger than the driving function $f(n)$ by at least a factor of $\Theta(n^{\epsilon})$ for some constant $\epsilon > 0$. The master theorem then says that the solution is $T(n) = \Theta(n^{\log_b a})$. In this case, if we look at the recursion tree for the recurrence, the cost per level grows at least geometrically from root to leaves, and the total cost of leaves dominates the total cost of the internal nodes.

In case 2, the watershed and driving functions grow at nearly the same asymptotic rate. But more specifically, the driving function grows faster than the watershed function by a factor of $\Theta(\lg^k n)$, where $k \geq 0$. The master theorem says that we tack on an extra $\lg n$ factor to $f(n)$, yielding the solution $T(n) = \Theta(n^{\log_b a} \lg^{k+1} n)$. In this case, each level of the recursion tree costs approximately the same—$\Theta(n^{\log_b a} \lg^k n)$—and there are $\Theta(\lg n)$ levels. In practice, the most common situation for case 2 occurs when $k = 0$, in which case the watershed and driving functions have the same asymptotic growth, and the solution is $T(n) = \Theta(n^{\log_b a} \lg n)$.

Case 3 mirrors case 1. Not only must the driving function grow asymptotically faster than the watershed function, it must grow *polynomially* faster. That is, the driving function $f(n)$ must be asymptotically larger than the watershed function $n^{\log_b a}$ by at least a factor of $\Theta(n^{\epsilon})$ for some constant $\epsilon > 0$. Moreover, the driving function must satisfy the regularity condition that $af(n/b) \leq cf(n)$. This condition is satisfied by most of the polynomially bounded functions that you're likely to encounter when applying case 3. The regularity condition might not be satisfied if the driving function grows slowly in local areas, yet relatively quickly overall. (Exercise 4.5-5 gives an example of such a function.) For case 3, the master theorem says that the solution is $T(n) = \Theta(f(n))$. If we look at the recursion tree, the cost per level drops at least geometrically from the root to the leaves, and the root cost dominates the cost of all other nodes.

It's worth looking again at the requirement that there be polynomial separation between the watershed function and the driving function for either case 1 or case 3 to apply. The separation doesn't need to be much, but it must be there, and it must grow polynomially. For example, for the recurrence $T(n) = 4T(n/2) + n^{1.99}$ (admittedly not a recurrence you're likely to see when analyzing an algorithm), the watershed function is $n^{\log_b a} = n^2$. Hence the driving function $f(n) = n^{1.99}$ is polynomially smaller by a factor of $n^{0.01}$. Thus case 1 applies with $\epsilon = 0.01$.

Using the master method

To use the master method, you determine which case (if any) of the master theorem applies and write down the answer.

As a first example, consider the recurrence $T(n) = 9T(n/3) + n$. For this recurrence, we have $a = 9$ and $b = 3$, which implies that $n^{\log_b a} = n^{\log_3 9} = \Theta(n^2)$. Since $f(n) = n = O(n^{2-\epsilon})$ for any constant $\epsilon \le 1$, we can apply case 1 of the master theorem to conclude that the solution is $T(n) = \Theta(n^2)$.

Now consider the recurrence $T(n) = T(2n/3) + 1$, which has $a = 1$ and $b = 3/2$, which means that the watershed function is $n^{\log_b a} = n^{\log_{3/2} 1} = n^0 = 1$. Case 2 applies since $f(n) = 1 = \Theta(n^{\log_b a} \lg^0 n) = \Theta(1)$. The solution to the recurrence is $T(n) = \Theta(\lg n)$.

For the recurrence $T(n) = 3T(n/4) + n \lg n$, we have $a = 3$ and $b = 4$, which means that $n^{\log_b a} = n^{\log_4 3} = O(n^{0.793})$. Since $f(n) = n \lg n = \Omega(n^{\log_4 3 + \epsilon})$, where ϵ can be as large as approximately 0.2, case 3 applies as long as the regularity condition holds for $f(n)$. It does, because for sufficiently large n, we have that $af(n/b) = 3(n/4) \lg(n/4) \le (3/4)n \lg n = cf(n)$ for $c = 3/4$. By case 3, the solution to the recurrence is $T(n) = \Theta(n \lg n)$.

Next, let's look at the recurrence $T(n) = 2T(n/2) + n \lg n$, where we have $a = 2$, $b = 2$, and $n^{\log_b a} = n^{\log_2 2} = n$. Case 2 applies since $f(n) = n \lg n = \Theta(n^{\log_b a} \lg^1 n)$. We conclude that the solution is $T(n) = \Theta(n \lg^2 n)$.

We can use the master method to solve the recurrences we saw in Sections 2.3.2, 4.1, and 4.2.

Recurrence (2.3), $T(n) = 2T(n/2) + \Theta(n)$, on page 41, characterizes the running time of merge sort. Since $a = 2$ and $b = 2$, the watershed function is $n^{\log_b a} = n^{\log_2 2} = n$. Case 2 applies because $f(n) = \Theta(n)$, and the solution is $T(n) = \Theta(n \lg n)$.

Recurrence (4.9), $T(n) = 8T(n/2) + \Theta(1)$, on page 84, describes the running time of the simple recursive algorithm for matrix multiplication. We have $a = 8$ and $b = 2$, which means that the watershed function is $n^{\log_b a} = n^{\log_2 8} = n^3$. Since n^3 is polynomially larger than the driving function $f(n) = \Theta(1)$—indeed, we have $f(n) = O(n^{3-\epsilon})$ for any positive $\epsilon < 3$—case 1 applies. We conclude that $T(n) = \Theta(n^3)$.

Finally, recurrence (4.10), $T(n) = 7T(n/2) + \Theta(n^2)$, on page 87, arose from the analysis of Strassen's algorithm for matrix multiplication. For this recurrence, we have $a = 7$ and $b = 2$, and the watershed function is $n^{\log_b a} = n^{\lg 7}$. Observing that $\lg 7 = 2.807355\ldots$, we can let $\epsilon = 0.8$ and bound the driving function $f(n) = \Theta(n^2) = O(n^{\lg 7 - \epsilon})$. Case 1 applies with solution $T(n) = \Theta(n^{\lg 7})$.

When the master method doesn't apply

There are situations where you can't use the master theorem. For example, it can be that the watershed function and the driving function cannot be asymptotically compared. We might have that $f(n) \gg n^{\log_b a}$ for an infinite number of values of n but also that $f(n) \ll n^{\log_b a}$ for an infinite number of different values of n. As a practical matter, however, most of the driving functions that arise in the study of algorithms can be meaningfully compared with the watershed function. If you encounter a master recurrence for which that's not the case, you'll have to resort to substitution or other methods.

Even when the relative growths of the driving and watershed functions can be compared, the master theorem does not cover all the possibilities. There is a gap between cases 1 and 2 when $f(n) = o(n^{\log_b a})$, yet the watershed function does not grow polynomially faster than the driving function. Similarly, there is a gap between cases 2 and 3 when $f(n) = \omega(n^{\log_b a})$ and the driving function grows more than polylogarithmically faster than the watershed function, but it does not grow polynomially faster. If the driving function falls into one of these gaps, or if the regularity condition in case 3 fails to hold, you'll need to use something other than the master method to solve the recurrence.

As an example of a driving function falling into a gap, consider the recurrence $T(n) = 2T(n/2) + n/\lg n$. Since $a = 2$ and $b = 2$, the watershed function is $n^{\log_b a} = n^{\log_2 2} = n^1 = n$. The driving function is $n/\lg n = o(n)$, which means that it grows asymptotically more slowly than the watershed function n. But $n/\lg n$ grows only *logarithmically* slower than n, not *polynomially* slower. More precisely, equation (3.24) on page 67 says that $\lg n = o(n^\epsilon)$ for any constant $\epsilon > 0$, which means that $1/\lg n = \omega(n^{-\epsilon})$ and $n/\lg n = \omega(n^{1-\epsilon}) = \omega(n^{\log_b a - \epsilon})$. Thus no constant $\epsilon > 0$ exists such that $n/\lg n = O(n^{\log_b a - \epsilon})$, which is required for case 1 to apply. Case 2 fails to apply as well, since $n/\lg n = \Theta(n^{\log_b a} \lg^k n)$, where $k = -1$, but k must be nonnegative for case 2 to apply.

To solve this kind of recurrence, you must use another method, such as the substitution method (Section 4.3) or the Akra-Bazzi method (Section 4.7). (Exercise 4.6-3 asks you to show that the answer is $\Theta(n \lg \lg n)$.) Although the master theorem doesn't handle this particular recurrence, it does handle the overwhelming majority of recurrences that tend to arise in practice.

Exercises

4.5-1
Use the master method to give tight asymptotic bounds for the following recurrences.

a. $T(n) = 2T(n/4) + 1$.

b. $T(n) = 2T(n/4) + \sqrt{n}$.

c. $T(n) = 2T(n/4) + \sqrt{n} \lg^2 n$.

d. $T(n) = 2T(n/4) + n$.

e. $T(n) = 2T(n/4) + n^2$.

4.5-2
Professor Caesar wants to develop a matrix-multiplication algorithm that is asymptotically faster than Strassen's algorithm. His algorithm will use the divide-and-conquer method, dividing each matrix into $n/4 \times n/4$ submatrices, and the divide and combine steps together will take $\Theta(n^2)$ time. Suppose that the professor's algorithm creates a recursive subproblems of size $n/4$. What is the largest integer value of a for which his algorithm could possibly run asymptotically faster than Strassen's?

4.5-3
Use the master method to show that the solution to the binary-search recurrence $T(n) = T(n/2) + \Theta(1)$ is $T(n) = \Theta(\lg n)$. (See Exercise 2.3-6 for a description of binary search.)

4.5-4
Consider the function $f(n) = \lg n$. Argue that although $f(n/2) < f(n)$, the regularity condition $af(n/b) \le cf(n)$ with $a = 1$ and $b = 2$ does not hold for any constant $c < 1$. Argue further that for any $\epsilon > 0$, the condition in case 3 that $f(n) = \Omega(n^{\log_b a + \epsilon})$ does not hold.

4.5-5
Show that for suitable constants a, b, and ϵ, the function $f(n) = 2^{\lceil \lg n \rceil}$ satisfies all the conditions in case 3 of the master theorem except the regularity condition.

★ 4.6 Proof of the continuous master theorem

Proving the master theorem (Theorem 4.1) in its full generality, especially dealing with the knotty technical issue of floors and ceilings, is beyond the scope of this book. This section, however, states and proves a variant of the master theorem, called the *continuous master theorem*[1] in which the master recurrence (4.17) is defined over sufficiently large positive real numbers. The proof of this version, uncomplicated by floors and ceilings, contains the main ideas needed to understand how master recurrences behave. Section 4.7 discusses floors and ceilings in divide-and-conquer recurrences at greater length, presenting sufficient conditions for them not to affect the asymptotic solutions.

Of course, since you need not understand the proof of the master theorem in order to apply the master method, you may choose to skip this section. But if you wish to study more-advanced algorithms beyond the scope of this textbook, you may appreciate a better understanding of the underlying mathematics, which the proof of the continuous master theorem provides.

Although we usually assume that recurrences are algorithmic and don't require an explicit statement of a base case, we must be much more careful for proofs that justify the practice. The lemmas and theorem in this section explicitly state the base cases, because the inductive proofs require mathematical grounding. It is common in the world of mathematics to be extraordinarily careful proving theorems that justify acting more casually in practice.

The proof of the continuous master theorem involves two lemmas. Lemma 4.2 uses a slightly simplified master recurrence with a threshold constant of $n_0 = 1$, rather than the more general $n_0 > 0$ threshold constant implied by the unstated base case. The lemma employs a recursion tree to reduce the solution of the simplified master recurrence to that of evaluating a summation. Lemma 4.3 then provides asymptotic bounds for the summation, mirroring the three cases of the master theorem. Finally, the continuous master theorem itself (Theorem 4.4) gives asymptotic bounds for master recurrences, while generalizing to an arbitrary threshold constant $n_0 > 0$ as implied by the unstated base case.

---

[1] This terminology does not mean that either $T(n)$ or $f(n)$ need be continuous, only that the domain of $T(n)$ is the real numbers, as opposed to integers.

Some of the proofs use the properties described in Problem 3-5 on pages 72–73 to combine and simplify complicated asymptotic expressions. Although Problem 3-5 addresses only Θ-notation, the properties enumerated there can be extended to O-notation and Ω-notation as well.

Here's the first lemma.

Lemma 4.2

Let $a > 0$ and $b > 1$ be constants, and let $f(n)$ be a function defined over real numbers $n \geq 1$. Then the recurrence

$$T(n) = \begin{cases} \Theta(1) & \text{if } 0 \leq n < 1, \\ aT(n/b) + f(n) & \text{if } n \geq 1 \end{cases}$$

has solution

$$T(n) = \Theta(n^{\log_b a}) + \sum_{j=0}^{\lfloor \log_b n \rfloor} a^j f(n/b^j) . \tag{4.18}$$

Proof   Consider the recursion tree in Figure 4.3. Let's look first at its internal nodes. The root of the tree has cost $f(n)$, and it has a children, each with cost $f(n/b)$. (It is convenient to think of a as being an integer, especially when visualizing the recursion tree, but the mathematics does not require it.) Each of these children has a children, making a^2 nodes at depth 2, and each of the a children has cost $f(n/b^2)$. In general, there are a^j nodes at depth j, and each node has cost $f(n/b^j)$.

Now, let's move on to understanding the leaves. The tree grows downward until n/b^j becomes less than 1. Thus, the tree has height $\lfloor \log_b n \rfloor + 1$, because $n/b^{\lfloor \log_b n \rfloor} \geq n/b^{\log_b n} = 1$ and $n/b^{\lfloor \log_b n \rfloor + 1} < n/b^{\log_b n} = 1$. Since, as we have observed, the number of nodes at depth j is a^j and all the leaves are at depth $\lfloor \log_b n \rfloor + 1$, the tree contains $a^{\lfloor \log_b n \rfloor + 1}$ leaves. Using the identity (3.21) on page 66, we have $a^{\lfloor \log_b n \rfloor + 1} \leq a^{\log_b n + 1} = a n^{\log_b a} = O(n^{\log_b a})$, since a is constant, and $a^{\lfloor \log_b n \rfloor + 1} \geq a^{\log_b n} = n^{\log_b a} = \Omega(n^{\log_b a})$. Consequently, the total number of leaves is $\Theta(n^{\log_b a})$—asymptotically, the watershed function.

We are now in a position to derive equation (4.18) by summing the costs of the nodes at each depth in the tree, as shown in the figure. The first term in the equation is the total costs of the leaves. Since each leaf is at depth $\lfloor \log_b n \rfloor + 1$ and $n/b^{\lfloor \log_b n \rfloor + 1} < 1$, the base case of the recurrence gives the cost of a leaf: $T(n/b^{\lfloor \log_b n \rfloor + 1}) = \Theta(1)$. Hence the cost of all $\Theta(n^{\log_b a})$ leaves is $\Theta(n^{\log_b a}) \cdot \Theta(1) = \Theta(n^{\log_b a})$ by Problem 3-5(d). The second term in equation (4.18) is the cost of the internal nodes, which, in the underlying divide-and-conquer algorithm, represents the costs of dividing problems into subproblems and

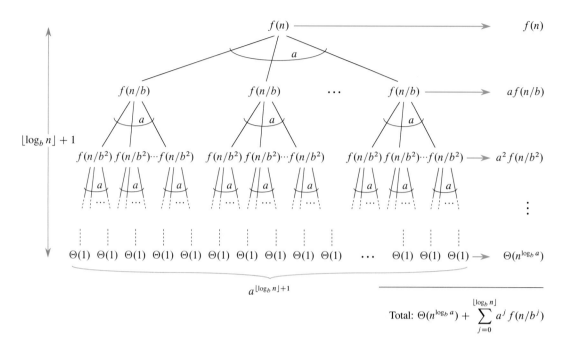

Figure 4.3   The recursion tree generated by $T(n) = aT(n/b) + f(n)$. The tree is a complete a-ary tree with $a^{\lfloor \log_b n \rfloor + 1}$ leaves and height $\lfloor \log_b n \rfloor + 1$. The cost of the nodes at each depth is shown at the right, and their sum is given in equation (4.18).

then recombining the subproblems. Since the cost for all the internal nodes at depth j is $a^j f(n/b^j)$, the total cost of all internal nodes is

$$\sum_{j=0}^{\lfloor \log_b n \rfloor} a^j f(n/b^j) \,.$$ ∎

As we'll see, the three cases of the master theorem depend on the distribution of the total cost across levels of the recursion tree:

Case 1:   The costs increase geometrically from the root to the leaves, growing by a constant factor with each level.

Case 2:   The costs depend on the value of k in the theorem. With $k = 0$, the costs are equal for each level; with $k = 1$, the costs grow linearly from the root to the leaves; with $k = 2$, the growth is quadratic; and in general, the costs grow polynomially in k.

Case 3:   The costs decrease geometrically from the root to the leaves, shrinking by a constant factor with each level.

The summation in equation (4.18) describes the cost of the dividing and combining steps in the underlying divide-and-conquer algorithm. The next lemma provides asymptotic bounds on the summation's growth.

Lemma 4.3

Let $a > 0$ and $b > 1$ be constants, and let $f(n)$ be a function defined over real numbers $n \geq 1$. Then the asymptotic behavior of the function

$$g(n) = \sum_{j=0}^{\lfloor \log_b n \rfloor} a^j f(n/b^j) , \tag{4.19}$$

defined for $n \geq 1$, can be characterized as follows:

1. If there exists a constant $\epsilon > 0$ such that $f(n) = O(n^{\log_b a - \epsilon})$, then $g(n) = O(n^{\log_b a})$.

2. If there exists a constant $k \geq 0$ such that $f(n) = \Theta(n^{\log_b a} \lg^k n)$, then $g(n) = \Theta(n^{\log_b a} \lg^{k+1} n)$.

3. If there exists a constant c in the range $0 < c < 1$ such that $0 < af(n/b) \leq cf(n)$ for all $n \geq 1$, then $g(n) = \Theta(f(n))$.

Proof For case 1, we have $f(n) = O(n^{\log_b a - \epsilon})$, which implies that $f(n/b^j) = O((n/b^j)^{\log_b a - \epsilon})$. Substituting into equation (4.19) yields

$$g(n) = \sum_{j=0}^{\lfloor \log_b n \rfloor} a^j O\left(\left(\frac{n}{b^j} \right)^{\log_b a - \epsilon} \right)$$

$$= O\left(\sum_{j=0}^{\lfloor \log_b n \rfloor} a^j \left(\frac{n}{b^j} \right)^{\log_b a - \epsilon} \right) \qquad \text{(by Problem 3-5(c), repeatedly)}$$

$$= O\left(n^{\log_b a - \epsilon} \sum_{j=0}^{\lfloor \log_b n \rfloor} \left(\frac{ab^\epsilon}{b^{\log_b a}} \right)^j \right)$$

$$= O\left(n^{\log_b a - \epsilon} \sum_{j=0}^{\lfloor \log_b n \rfloor} (b^\epsilon)^j \right) \qquad \text{(by equation (3.17) on page 66)}$$

$$= O\left(n^{\log_b a - \epsilon} \left(\frac{b^{\epsilon(\lfloor \log_b n \rfloor + 1)} - 1}{b^\epsilon - 1} \right) \right) \qquad \text{(by equation (A.6) on page 1142) ,}$$

the last series being geometric. Since b and ϵ are constants, the $b^\epsilon - 1$ denominator doesn't affect the asymptotic growth of $g(n)$, and neither does the -1 in the numerator. Since $b^{\epsilon(\lfloor \log_b n \rfloor + 1)} \le (b^{\log_b n + 1})^{\epsilon} = b^{\epsilon} n^{\epsilon} = O(n^{\epsilon})$, we obtain $g(n) = O(n^{\log_b a - \epsilon} \cdot O(n^{\epsilon})) = O(n^{\log_b a})$, thereby proving case 1.

Case 2 assumes that $f(n) = \Theta(n^{\log_b a} \lg^k n)$, from which we can conclude that $f(n/b^j) = \Theta((n/b^j)^{\log_b a} \lg^k (n/b^j))$. Substituting into equation (4.19) and repeatedly applying Problem 3-5(c) yields

$$
\begin{aligned}
g(n) &= \Theta \left(\sum_{j=0}^{\lfloor \log_b n \rfloor} a^j \left(\frac{n}{b^j} \right)^{\log_b a} \lg^k \left(\frac{n}{b^j} \right) \right) \\
&= \Theta \left(n^{\log_b a} \sum_{j=0}^{\lfloor \log_b n \rfloor} \frac{a^j}{b^{j \log_b a}} \lg^k \left(\frac{n}{b^j} \right) \right) \\
&= \Theta \left(n^{\log_b a} \sum_{j=0}^{\lfloor \log_b n \rfloor} \lg^k \left(\frac{n}{b^j} \right) \right) \\
&= \Theta \left(n^{\log_b a} \sum_{j=0}^{\lfloor \log_b n \rfloor} \left(\frac{\log_b (n/b^j)}{\log_b 2} \right)^k \right) && \text{(by equation (3.19) on page 66)} \\
&= \Theta \left(n^{\log_b a} \sum_{j=0}^{\lfloor \log_b n \rfloor} \left(\frac{\log_b n - j}{\log_b 2} \right)^k \right) && \begin{array}{l}\text{(by equations (3.17), (3.18),} \\ \text{and (3.20))}\end{array} \\
&= \Theta \left(\frac{n^{\log_b a}}{\log_b^k 2} \sum_{j=0}^{\lfloor \log_b n \rfloor} (\log_b n - j)^k \right) \\
&= \Theta \left(n^{\log_b a} \sum_{j=0}^{\lfloor \log_b n \rfloor} (\log_b n - j)^k \right) && \text{($b > 1$ and k are constants) .}
\end{aligned}
$$

The summation within the Θ-notation can be bounded from above as follows:

$$
\begin{aligned}
\sum_{j=0}^{\lfloor \log_b n \rfloor} (\log_b n - j)^k &\le \sum_{j=0}^{\lfloor \log_b n \rfloor} (\lfloor \log_b n \rfloor + 1 - j)^k \\
&= \sum_{j=1}^{\lfloor \log_b n \rfloor + 1} j^k && \text{(reindexing—pages 1143–1144)} \\
&= O((\lfloor \log_b n \rfloor + 1)^{k+1}) && \text{(by Exercise A.1-5 on page 1144)} \\
&= O(\log_b^{k+1} n) && \text{(by Exercise 3.3-3 on page 70) .}
\end{aligned}
$$

Exercise 4.6-1 asks you to show that the summation can similarly be bounded from below by $\Omega(\log_b^{k+1} n)$. Since we have tight upper and lower bounds, the summation is $\Theta(\log_b^{k+1} n)$, from which we can conclude that $g(n) = \Theta\left(n^{\log_b a} \log_b^{k+1} n\right)$, thereby completing the proof of case 2.

For case 3, observe that $f(n)$ appears in the definition (4.19) of $g(n)$ (when $j = 0$) and that all terms of $g(n)$ are positive. Therefore, we must have $g(n) = \Omega(f(n))$, and it only remains to prove that $g(n) = O(f(n))$. Performing j iterations of the inequality $af(n/b) \le cf(n)$ yields $a^j f(n/b^j) \le c^j f(n)$. Substituting into equation (4.19), we obtain

$$
\begin{aligned}
g(n) &= \sum_{j=0}^{\lfloor \log_b n \rfloor} a^j f(n/b^j) \\
&\le \sum_{j=0}^{\lfloor \log_b n \rfloor} c^j f(n) \\
&\le f(n) \sum_{j=0}^{\infty} c^j \\
&= f(n) \left(\frac{1}{1-c} \right) \qquad \text{(by equation (A.7) on page 1142 since } |c| < 1) \\
&= O(f(n)) .
\end{aligned}
$$

Thus, we can conclude that $g(n) = \Theta(f(n))$. With case 3 proved, the entire proof of the lemma is complete.   ∎

We can now state and prove the continuous master theorem.

Theorem 4.4 (Continuous master theorem)

Let $a > 0$ and $b > 1$ be constants, and let $f(n)$ be a driving function that is defined and nonnegative on all sufficiently large reals. Define the algorithmic recurrence $T(n)$ on the positive real numbers by

$$ T(n) = aT(n/b) + f(n) . $$

Then the asymptotic behavior of $T(n)$ can be characterized as follows:

1. If there exists a constant $\epsilon > 0$ such that $f(n) = O(n^{\log_b a - \epsilon})$, then $T(n) = \Theta(n^{\log_b a})$.

2. If there exists a constant $k \ge 0$ such that $f(n) = \Theta(n^{\log_b a} \lg^k n)$, then $T(n) = \Theta(n^{\log_b a} \lg^{k+1} n)$.

3. If there exists a constant $\epsilon > 0$ such that $f(n) = \Omega(n^{\log_b a + \epsilon})$, and if $f(n)$ additionally satisfies the regularity condition $af(n/b) \le cf(n)$ for some constant $c < 1$ and all sufficiently large n, then $T(n) = \Theta(f(n))$.

Proof   The idea is to bound the summation (4.18) from Lemma 4.2 by applying Lemma 4.3. But we must account for Lemma 4.2 using a base case for $0 < n < 1$, whereas this theorem uses an implicit base case for $0 < n < n_0$, where $n_0 > 0$ is an arbitrary threshold constant. Since the recurrence is algorithmic, we can assume that $f(n)$ is defined for $n \geq n_0$.

For $n > 0$, let us define two auxiliary functions $T'(n) = T(n_0 n)$ and $f'(n) = f(n_0 n)$. We have

$$
\begin{aligned}
T'(n) &= T(n_0 n) \\
&= \begin{cases} \Theta(1) & \text{if } n_0 n < n_0 , \\ aT(n_0 n/b) + f(n_0 n) & \text{if } n_0 n \geq n_0 \end{cases} \\
&= \begin{cases} \Theta(1) & \text{if } n < 1 , \\ aT'(n/b) + f'(n) & \text{if } n \geq 1 . \end{cases}
\end{aligned}
\tag{4.20}
$$

We have obtained a recurrence for $T'(n)$ that satisfies the conditions of Lemma 4.2, and by that lemma, the solution is

$$
T'(n) = \Theta(n^{\log_b a}) + \sum_{j=0}^{\lfloor \log_b n \rfloor} a^j f'(n/b^j) .
\tag{4.21}
$$

To solve $T'(n)$, we first need to bound $f'(n)$. Let's examine the individual cases in the theorem.

The condition for case 1 is $f(n) = O(n^{\log_b a - \epsilon})$ for some constant $\epsilon > 0$. We have

$$
\begin{aligned}
f'(n) &= f(n_0 n) \\
&= O((n_0 n)^{\log_b a - \epsilon}) \\
&= O(n^{\log_b a - \epsilon}) ,
\end{aligned}
$$

since a, b, n_0, and ϵ are all constant. The function $f'(n)$ satisfies the conditions of case 1 of Lemma 4.3, and the summation in equation (4.18) of Lemma 4.2 evaluates to $O(n^{\log_b a})$. Because a, b and n_0 are all constants, we have

$$
\begin{aligned}
T(n) &= T'(n/n_0) \\
&= \Theta((n/n_0)^{\log_b a}) + O((n/n_0)^{\log_b a}) \\
&= \Theta(n^{\log_b a}) + O(n^{\log_b a}) \\
&= \Theta(n^{\log_b a}) \qquad \text{(by Problem 3-5(b))} ,
\end{aligned}
$$

thereby completing case 1 of the theorem.

The condition for case 2 is $f(n) = \Theta(n^{\log_b a} \lg^k n)$ for some constant $k \geq 0$. We have

$$
\begin{aligned}
f'(n) &= f(n_0 n) \\
&= \Theta((n_0 n)^{\log_b a} \lg^k (n_0 n)) \\
&= \Theta(n^{\log_b a} \lg^k n) \qquad \text{(by eliminating the constant terms)} .
\end{aligned}
$$

Similar to the proof of case 1, the function $f'(n)$ satisfies the conditions of case 2 of Lemma 4.3. The summation in equation (4.18) of Lemma 4.2 is therefore $\Theta(n^{\log_b a} \lg^{k+1} n)$, which implies that

$$
\begin{aligned}
T(n) &= T'(n/n_0) \\
&= \Theta((n/n_0)^{\log_b a}) + \Theta((n/n_0)^{\log_b a} \lg^{k+1}(n/n_0)) \\
&= \Theta(n^{\log_b a}) + \Theta(n^{\log_b a} \lg^{k+1} n) \\
&= \Theta(n^{\log_b a} \lg^{k+1} n) \qquad \text{(by Problem 3-5(c))} ,
\end{aligned}
$$

which proves case 2 of the theorem.

Finally, the condition for case 3 is $f(n) = \Omega(n^{\log_b a + \epsilon})$ for some constant $\epsilon > 0$ and $f(n)$ additionally satisfies the regularity condition $af(n/b) \leq cf(n)$ for all $n \geq n_0$ and some constants $c < 1$ and $n_0 > 1$. The first part of case 3 is like case 1:

$$
\begin{aligned}
f'(n) &= f(n_0 n) \\
&= \Omega((n_0 n)^{\log_b a + \epsilon}) \\
&= \Omega(n^{\log_b a + \epsilon}) .
\end{aligned}
$$

Using the definition of $f'(n)$ and the fact that $n_0 n \geq n_0$ for all $n \geq 1$, we have for $n \geq 1$ that

$$
\begin{aligned}
af'(n/b) &= af(n_0 n/b) \\
&\leq cf(n_0 n) \\
&= cf'(n) .
\end{aligned}
$$

Thus $f'(n)$ satisfies the requirements for case 3 of Lemma 4.3, and the summation in equation (4.18) of Lemma 4.2 evaluates to $\Theta(f'(n))$, yielding

$$
\begin{aligned}
T(n) &= T'(n/n_0) \\
&= \Theta((n/n_0)^{\log_b a}) + \Theta(f'(n/n_0)) \\
&= \Theta(f'(n/n_0)) \\
&= \Theta(f(n)) ,
\end{aligned}
$$

which completes the proof of case 3 of the theorem and thus the whole theorem. ∎

Exercises

4.6-1
Show that $\sum_{j=0}^{\lfloor \log_b n \rfloor}(\log_b n - j)^k = \Omega(\log_b^{k+1} n)$.

★ **4.6-2**
Show that case 3 of the master theorem is overstated (which is also why case 3 of Lemma 4.3 does not require that $f(n) = \Omega(n^{\log_b a + \epsilon})$) in the sense that the

regularity condition $af(n/b) \leq cf(n)$ for some constant $c < 1$ implies that there exists a constant $\epsilon > 0$ such that $f(n) = \Omega(n^{\log_b a + \epsilon})$.

★ *4.6-3*
For $f(n) = \Theta(n^{\log_b a} / \lg n)$, prove that the summation in equation (4.19) has solution $g(n) = \Theta(n^{\log_b a} \lg \lg n)$. Conclude that a master recurrence $T(n)$ using $f(n)$ as its driving function has solution $T(n) = \Theta(n^{\log_b a} \lg \lg n)$.

★ 4.7 Akra-Bazzi recurrences

This section provides an overview of two advanced topics related to divide-and-conquer recurrences. The first deals with technicalities arising from the use of floors and ceilings, and the second discusses the Akra-Bazzi method, which involves a little calculus, for solving complicated divide-and-conquer recurrences.

In particular, we'll look at the class of algorithmic divide-and-conquer recurrences originally studied by M. Akra and L. Bazzi [13]. These *Akra-Bazzi* recurrences take the form

$$T(n) = f(n) + \sum_{i=1}^{k} a_i T(n/b_i) , \qquad (4.22)$$

where k is a positive integer; all the constants $a_1, a_2, \ldots, a_k \in \mathbb{R}$ are strictly positive; all the constants $b_1, b_2, \ldots, b_k \in \mathbb{R}$ are strictly greater than 1; and the driving function $f(n)$ is defined on sufficiently large nonnegative reals and is itself nonnegative.

Akra-Bazzi recurrences generalize the class of recurrences addressed by the master theorem. Whereas master recurrences characterize the running times of divide-and-conquer algorithms that break a problem into equal-sized subproblems (modulo floors and ceilings), Akra-Bazzi recurrences can describe the running time of divide-and-conquer algorithms that break a problem into different-sized subproblems. The master theorem, however, allows you to ignore floors and ceilings, but the Akra-Bazzi method for solving Akra-Bazzi recurrences needs an additional requirement to deal with floors and ceilings.

But before diving into the Akra-Bazzi method itself, let's understand the limitations involved in ignoring floors and ceilings in Akra-Bazzi recurrences. As you're aware, algorithms generally deal with integer-sized inputs. The mathematics for recurrences is often easier with real numbers, however, than with integers, where we must cope with floors and ceilings to ensure that terms are well defined. The difference may not seem to be much—especially because that's often the truth with recurrences—but to be mathematically correct, we must be careful with our assumptions. Since our end goal is to understand algorithms and not the vagaries of mathematical corner cases, we'd like to be casual yet rigorous. How can we treat floors and ceilings casually while still ensuring rigor?

From a mathematical point of view, the difficulty in dealing with floors and ceilings is that some driving functions can be really, really weird. So it's not okay in general to ignore floors and ceilings in Akra-Bazzi recurrences. Fortunately, most of the driving functions we encounter in the study of algorithms behave nicely, and floors and ceilings don't make a difference.

The polynomial-growth condition

If the driving function $f(n)$ in equation (4.22) is well behaved in the following sense, it's okay to drop floors and ceilings.

> A function $f(n)$ defined on all sufficiently large positive reals satisfies the *polynomial-growth condition* if there exists a constant $\hat{n} > 0$ such that the following holds: for every constant $\phi \geq 1$, there exists a constant $d > 1$ (depending on ϕ) such that $f(n)/d \leq f(\psi n) \leq df(n)$ for all $1 \leq \psi \leq \phi$ and $n \geq \hat{n}$.

This definition may be one of the hardest in this textbook to get your head around. To a first order, it says that $f(n)$ satisfies the property that $f(\Theta(n)) = \Theta(f(n))$, although the polynomial-growth condition is actually somewhat stronger (see Exercise 4.7-4). The definition also implies that $f(n)$ is asymptotically positive (see Exercise 4.7-3).

Examples of functions that satisfy the polynomial-growth condition include any function of the form $f(n) = \Theta(n^{\alpha} \lg^{\beta} n \lg \lg^{\gamma} n)$, where α, β, and γ are constants. Most of the polynomially bounded functions used in this book satisfy the condition. Exponentials and superexponentials do not (see Exercise 4.7-2, for example), and there also exist polynomially bounded functions that do not.

Floors and ceilings in "nice" recurrences

When the driving function in an Akra-Bazzi recurrence satisfies the polynomial-growth condition, floors and ceilings don't change the asymptotic behavior of the solution. The following theorem, which is presented without proof, formalizes this notion.

Theorem 4.5

Let $T(n)$ be a function defined on the nonnegative reals that satisfies recurrence (4.22), where $f(n)$ satisfies the polynomial-growth condition. Let $T'(n)$ be another function defined on the natural numbers also satisfying recurrence (4.22), except that each $T(n/b_i)$ is replaced either with $T(\lceil n/b_i \rceil)$ or with $T(\lfloor n/b_i \rfloor)$. Then we have $T'(n) = \Theta(T(n))$. ∎

Floors and ceilings represent a minor perturbation to the arguments in the recursion. By inequality (3.2) on page 64, they perturb an argument by at most 1. But much larger perturbations are tolerable. As long as the driving function $f(n)$ in recurrence (4.22) satisfies the polynomial-growth condition, it turns out that replacing any term $T(n/b_i)$ with $T(n/b_i + h_i(n))$, where $|h_i(n)| = O(n/\lg^{1+\epsilon} n)$ for some constant $\epsilon > 0$ and sufficiently large n, leaves the asymptotic solution unaffected. Thus, the divide step in a divide-and-conquer algorithm can be moderately coarse without affecting the solution to its running-time recurrence.

The Akra-Bazzi method

The Akra-Bazzi method, not surprisingly, was developed to solve Akra-Bazzi recurrences (4.22), which by dint of Theorem 4.5, applies in the presence of floors and ceilings or even larger perturbations, as just discussed. The method involves first determining the unique real number p such that $\sum_{i=1}^{k} a_i/b_i^p = 1$. Such a p always exists, because when $p \to -\infty$, the sum goes to ∞; it decreases as p increases; and when $p \to \infty$, it goes to 0. The Akra-Bazzi method then gives the solution to the recurrence as

$$T(n) = \Theta\left(n^p \left(1 + \int_1^n \frac{f(x)}{x^{p+1}}\, dx \right) \right) . \tag{4.23}$$

As an example, consider the recurrence

$$T(n) = T(n/5) + T(7n/10) + n . \tag{4.24}$$

We'll see the similar recurrence (9.1) on page 240 when we study an algorithm for selecting the ith smallest element from a set of n numbers. This recurrence has the form of equation (4.22), where $a_1 = a_2 = 1, b_1 = 5, b_2 = 10/7$, and $f(n) = n$. To solve it, the Akra-Bazzi method says that we should determine the unique p satisfying

$$\left(\frac{1}{5}\right)^p + \left(\frac{7}{10}\right)^p = 1 .$$

Solving for p is kind of messy—it turns out that $p = 0.83978\ldots$—but we can solve the recurrence without actually knowing the exact value for p. Observe that $(1/5)^0 + (7/10)^0 = 2$ and $(1/5)^1 + (7/10)^1 = 9/10$, and thus p lies in the range $0 < p < 1$. That turns out to be sufficient for the Akra-Bazzi method to give us the solution. We'll use the fact from calculus that if $k \neq -1$, then $\int x^k dx = x^{k+1}/(k+1)$, which we'll apply with $k = -p \neq -1$. The Akra-Bazzi solution (4.23) gives us

$$
\begin{aligned}
T(n) &= \Theta\left(n^p \left(1 + \int_1^n \frac{f(x)}{x^{p+1}}\, dx\right)\right) \\
&= \Theta\left(n^p \left(1 + \int_1^n x^{-p}\, dx\right)\right) \\
&= \Theta\left(n^p \left(1 + \left[\frac{x^{1-p}}{1-p}\right]_1^n\right)\right) \\
&= \Theta\left(n^p \left(1 + \left(\frac{n^{1-p}}{1-p} - \frac{1}{1-p}\right)\right)\right) \\
&= \Theta\left(n^p \cdot \Theta(n^{1-p})\right) \qquad\quad \text{(because } 1 - p \text{ is a positive constant)} \\
&= \Theta(n) \qquad\qquad\qquad\qquad \text{(by Problem 3-5(d))} \ .
\end{aligned}
$$

Although the Akra-Bazzi method is more general than the master theorem, it requires calculus and sometimes a bit more reasoning. You also must ensure that your driving function satisfies the polynomial-growth condition if you want to ignore floors and ceilings, although that's rarely a problem. When it applies, the master method is much simpler to use, but only when subproblem sizes are more or less equal. They are both good tools for your algorithmic toolkit.

Exercises

★ ***4.7-1***
Consider an Akra-Bazzi recurrence $T(n)$ on the reals as given in recurrence (4.22), and define $T'(n)$ as

$$
T'(n) = cf(n) + \sum_{i=1}^k a_i T'(n/b_i) \ ,
$$

where $c > 0$ is constant. Prove that whatever the implicit initial conditions for $T(n)$ might be, there exist initial conditions for $T'(n)$ such that $T'(n) = cT(n)$ for all $n > 0$. Conclude that we can drop the asymptotics on a driving function in any Akra-Bazzi recurrence without affecting its asymptotic solution.

4.7-2
Show that $f(n) = n^2$ satisfies the polynomial-growth condition but that $f(n) = 2^n$ does not.

4.7-3
Let $f(n)$ be a function that satisfies the polynomial-growth condition. Prove that $f(n)$ is asymptotically positive, that is, there exists a constant $n_0 \geq 0$ such that $f(n) \geq 0$ for all $n \geq n_0$.

★ **4.7-4**

Give an example of a function $f(n)$ that does not satisfy the polynomial-growth condition but for which $f(\Theta(n)) = \Theta(f(n))$.

4.7-5

Use the Akra-Bazzi method to solve the following recurrences.

a. $T(n) = T(n/2) + T(n/3) + T(n/6) + n \lg n$.

b. $T(n) = 3T(n/3) + 8T(n/4) + n^2/\lg n$.

c. $T(n) = (2/3)T(n/3) + (1/3)T(2n/3) + \lg n$.

d. $T(n) = (1/3)T(n/3) + 1/n$.

e. $T(n) = 3T(n/3) + 3T(2n/3) + n^2$.

★ **4.7-6**

Use the Akra-Bazzi method to prove the continuous master theorem.

Problems

4-1 *Recurrence examples*

Give asymptotically tight upper and lower bounds for $T(n)$ in each of the following algorithmic recurrences. Justify your answers.

a. $T(n) = 2T(n/2) + n^3$.

b. $T(n) = T(8n/11) + n$.

c. $T(n) = 16T(n/4) + n^2$.

d. $T(n) = 4T(n/2) + n^2 \lg n$.

e. $T(n) = 8T(n/3) + n^2$.

f. $T(n) = 7T(n/2) + n^2 \lg n$.

g. $T(n) = 2T(n/4) + \sqrt{n}$.

h. $T(n) = T(n-2) + n^2$.

4-2   *Parameter-passing costs*

Throughout this book, we assume that parameter passing during procedure calls takes constant time, even if an N-element array is being passed. This assumption is valid in most systems because a pointer to the array is passed, not the array itself. This problem examines the implications of three parameter-passing strategies:

1. Arrays are passed by pointer. Time $= \Theta(1)$.

2. Arrays are passed by copying. Time $= \Theta(N)$, where N is the size of the array.

3. Arrays are passed by copying only the subrange that might be accessed by the called procedure. Time $= \Theta(n)$ if the subarray contains n elements.

Consider the following three algorithms:

a. The recursive binary-search algorithm for finding a number in a sorted array (see Exercise 2.3-6).

b. The MERGE-SORT procedure from Section 2.3.1.

c. The MATRIX-MULTIPLY-RECURSIVE procedure from Section 4.1.

Give nine recurrences $T_{a1}(N,n), T_{a2}(N,n), \ldots, T_{c3}(N,n)$ for the worst-case running times of each of the three algorithms above when arrays and matrices are passed using each of the three parameter-passing strategies above. Solve your recurrences, giving tight asymptotic bounds.

4-3   *Solving recurrences with a change of variables*

Sometimes, a little algebraic manipulation can make an unknown recurrence similar to one you have seen before. Let's solve the recurrence

$$T(n) = 2T\left(\sqrt{n}\right) + \Theta(\lg n) \tag{4.25}$$

by using the change-of-variables method.

a. Define $m = \lg n$ and $S(m) = T(2^m)$. Rewrite recurrence (4.25) in terms of m and $S(m)$.

b. Solve your recurrence for $S(m)$.

c. Use your solution for $S(m)$ to conclude that $T(n) = \Theta(\lg n \lg \lg n)$.

d. Sketch the recursion tree for recurrence (4.25), and use it to explain intuitively why the solution is $T(n) = \Theta(\lg n \lg \lg n)$.

Solve the following recurrences by changing variables:

e. $T(n) = 2T(\sqrt{n}) + \Theta(1)$.

f. $T(n) = 3T(\sqrt[3]{n}) + \Theta(n)$.

4-4 More recurrence examples

Give asymptotically tight upper and lower bounds for $T(n)$ in each of the following recurrences. Justify your answers.

a. $T(n) = 5T(n/3) + n \lg n$.

b. $T(n) = 3T(n/3) + n/\lg n$.

c. $T(n) = 8T(n/2) + n^3 \sqrt{n}$.

d. $T(n) = 2T(n/2 - 2) + n/2$.

e. $T(n) = 2T(n/2) + n/\lg n$.

f. $T(n) = T(n/2) + T(n/4) + T(n/8) + n$.

g. $T(n) = T(n-1) + 1/n$.

h. $T(n) = T(n-1) + \lg n$.

i. $T(n) = T(n-2) + 1/\lg n$.

j. $T(n) = \sqrt{n}\, T(\sqrt{n}) + n$.

4-5 Fibonacci numbers

This problem develops properties of the Fibonacci numbers, which are defined by recurrence (3.31) on page 69. We'll explore the technique of generating functions to solve the Fibonacci recurrence. Define the *generating function* (or *formal power series*) $\mathcal{F}$ as

$$\mathcal{F}(z) = \sum_{i=0}^{\infty} F_i z^i$$
$$= 0 + z + z^2 + 2z^3 + 3z^4 + 5z^5 + 8z^6 + 13z^7 + 21z^8 + \cdots,$$

where F_i is the ith Fibonacci number.

a. Show that $\mathcal{F}(z) = z + z\mathcal{F}(z) + z^2\mathcal{F}(z)$.

b. Show that

$$\mathcal{F}(z) = \frac{z}{1 - z - z^2}$$

$$= \frac{z}{(1 - \phi z)(1 - \hat{\phi} z)}$$

$$= \frac{1}{\sqrt{5}} \left(\frac{1}{1 - \phi z} - \frac{1}{1 - \hat{\phi} z} \right) ,$$

where ϕ is the golden ratio, and $\hat{\phi}$ is its conjugate (see page 69).

c. Show that

$$\mathcal{F}(z) = \sum_{i=0}^{\infty} \frac{1}{\sqrt{5}} (\phi^i - \hat{\phi}^i) z^i .$$

You may use without proof the generating-function version of equation (A.7) on page 1142, $\sum_{k=0}^{\infty} x^k = 1/(1 - x)$. Because this equation involves a generating function, x is a formal variable, not a real-valued variable, so that you don't have to worry about convergence of the summation or about the requirement in equation (A.7) that $|x| < 1$, which doesn't make sense here.

d. Use part (c) to prove that $F_i = \phi^i / \sqrt{5}$ for $i > 0$, rounded to the nearest integer. (*Hint:* Observe that $|\hat{\phi}| < 1$.)

e. Prove that $F_{i+2} \geq \phi^i$ for $i \geq 0$.

4-6   *Chip testing*

Professor Diogenes has n supposedly identical integrated-circuit chips that in principle are capable of testing each other. The professor's test jig accommodates two chips at a time. When the jig is loaded, each chip tests the other and reports whether it is good or bad. A good chip always reports accurately whether the other chip is good or bad, but the professor cannot trust the answer of a bad chip. Thus, the four possible outcomes of a test are as follows:

Chip A says	Chip B says	Conclusion
B is good	A is good	both are good, or both are bad
B is good	A is bad	at least one is bad
B is bad	A is good	at least one is bad
B is bad	A is bad	at least one is bad

a. Show that if at least $n/2$ chips are bad, the professor cannot necessarily determine which chips are good using any strategy based on this kind of pairwise test. Assume that the bad chips can conspire to fool the professor.

Now you will design an algorithm to identify which chips are good and which are bad, assuming that more than $n/2$ of the chips are good. First, you will determine how to identify one good chip.

b. Show that $\lfloor n/2 \rfloor$ pairwise tests are sufficient to reduce the problem to one of nearly half the size. That is, show how to use $\lfloor n/2 \rfloor$ pairwise tests to obtain a set with at most $\lceil n/2 \rceil$ chips that still has the property that more than half of the chips are good.

c. Show how to apply the solution to part (b) recursively to identify one good chip. Give and solve the recurrence that describes the number of tests needed to identify one good chip.

You have now determined how to identify one good chip.

d. Show how to identify all the good chips with an additional $\Theta(n)$ pairwise tests.

4-7 *Monge arrays*

An $m \times n$ array A of real numbers is a *Monge array* if for all i, j, k, and l such that $1 \le i < k \le m$ and $1 \le j < l \le n$, we have

$$A[i, j] + A[k, l] \le A[i, l] + A[k, j] \,.$$

In other words, whenever we pick two rows and two columns of a Monge array and consider the four elements at the intersections of the rows and the columns, the sum of the upper-left and lower-right elements is less than or equal to the sum of the lower-left and upper-right elements. For example, the following array is Monge:

```
10  17  13  28  23
17  22  16  29  23
24  28  22  34  24
11  13   6  17   7
45  44  32  37  23
36  33  19  21   6
75  66  51  53  34
```

a. Prove that an array is Monge if and only if for all $i = 1, 2, ..., m - 1$ and $j = 1, 2, ..., n - 1$, we have

$$A[i, j] + A[i + 1, j + 1] \le A[i, j + 1] + A[i + 1, j] \,.$$

(*Hint:* For the "if" part, use induction separately on rows and columns.)

b. The following array is not Monge. Change one element in order to make it Monge. (*Hint:* Use part (a).)

$$
\begin{array}{cccc}
37 & 23 & 22 & 32 \\
21 & 6 & 7 & 10 \\
53 & 34 & 30 & 31 \\
32 & 13 & 9 & 6 \\
43 & 21 & 15 & 8
\end{array}
$$

c. Let $f(i)$ be the index of the column containing the leftmost minimum element of row i. Prove that $f(1) \leq f(2) \leq \cdots \leq f(m)$ for any $m \times n$ Monge array.

d. Here is a description of a divide-and-conquer algorithm that computes the leftmost minimum element in each row of an $m \times n$ Monge array A:

Construct a submatrix A' of A consisting of the even-numbered rows of A. Recursively determine the leftmost minimum for each row of A'. Then compute the leftmost minimum in the odd-numbered rows of A.

Explain how to compute the leftmost minimum in the odd-numbered rows of A (given that the leftmost minimum of the even-numbered rows is known) in $O(m + n)$ time.

e. Write the recurrence for the running time of the algorithm in part (d). Show that its solution is $O(m + n \log m)$.

Chapter notes

Divide-and-conquer as a technique for designing algorithms dates back at least to 1962 in an article by Karatsuba and Ofman [242], but it might have been used well before then. According to Heideman, Johnson, and Burrus [211], C. F. Gauss devised the first fast Fourier transform algorithm in 1805, and Gauss's formulation breaks the problem into smaller subproblems whose solutions are combined.

Strassen's algorithm [424] caused much excitement when it appeared in 1969. Before then, few imagined the possibility of an algorithm asymptotically faster than the basic MATRIX-MULTIPLY procedure. Shortly thereafter, S. Winograd reduced the number of submatrix additions from 18 to 15 while still using seven submatrix multiplications. This improvement, which Winograd apparently never published (and which is frequently miscited in the literature), may enhance the practicality of the method, but it does not affect its asymptotic performance. Probert [368] described Winograd's algorithm and showed that with seven multiplications, 15 additions is the minimum possible.

Strassen's $\Theta(n^{\lg 7}) = O(n^{2.81})$ bound for matrix multiplication held until 1987, when Coppersmith and Winograd [103] made a significant advance, improving the bound to $O(n^{2.376})$ time with a mathematically sophisticated but wildly impractical algorithm based on tensor products. It took approximately 25 years before the asymptotic upper bound was again improved. In 2012 Vassilevska Williams [445] improved it to $O(n^{2.37287})$, and two years later Le Gall [278] achieved $O(n^{2.37286})$, both of them using mathematically fascinating but impractical algorithms. The best lower bound to date is just the obvious $\Omega(n^2)$ bound (obvious because any algorithm for matrix multiplication must fill in the n^2 elements of the product matrix).

The performance of MATRIX-MULTIPLY-RECURSIVE can be improved in practice by coarsening the leaves of the recursion. It also exhibits better cache behavior than MATRIX-MULTIPLY, although MATRIX-MULTIPLY can be improved by "tiling." Leiserson et al. [293] conducted a performance-engineering study of matrix multiplication in which a parallel and vectorized divide-and-conquer algorithm achieved the highest performance. Strassen's algorithm can be practical for large dense matrices, although large matrices tend to be sparse, and sparse methods can be much faster. When using limited-precision floating-point values, Strassen's algorithm produces larger numerical errors than the $\Theta(n^3)$ algorithms do, although Higham [215] demonstrated that Strassen's algorithm is amply accurate for some applications.

Recurrences were studied as early as 1202 by Leonardo Bonacci [66], also known as Fibonacci, for whom the Fibonacci numbers are named, although Indian mathematicians had discovered Fibonacci numbers centuries before. The French mathematician De Moivre [108] introduced the method of generating functions with which he studied Fibonacci numbers (see Problem 4-5). Knuth [259] and Liu [302] are good resources for learning the method of generating functions.

Aho, Hopcroft, and Ullman [5, 6] offered one of the first general methods for solving recurrences arising from the analysis of divide-and-conquer algorithms. The master method was adapted from Bentley, Haken, and Saxe [52]. The Akra-Bazzi method is due (unsurprisingly) to Akra and Bazzi [13]. Divide-and-conquer recurrences have been studied by many researchers, including Campbell [79], Graham, Knuth, and Patashnik [199], Kuszmaul and Leiserson [274], Leighton [287], Purdom and Brown [371], Roura [389], Verma [447], and Yap [462].

The issue of floors and ceilings in divide-and-conquer recurrences, including a theorem similar to Theorem 4.5, was studied by Leighton [287]. Leighton proposed a version of the polynomial-growth condition. Campbell [79] removed several limitations in Leighton's statement of it and showed that there were polynomially bounded functions that do not satisfy Leighton's condition. Campbell also carefully studied many other technical issues, including the well-definedness of divide-and-conquer recurrences. Kuszmaul and Leiserson [274] provided a proof of Theorem 4.5 that does not involve calculus or other higher math. Both Campbell and Leighton explored the perturbations of arguments beyond simple floors and ceilings.

5   Probabilistic Analysis and Randomized Algorithms

This chapter introduces probabilistic analysis and randomized algorithms. If you are unfamiliar with the basics of probability theory, you should read Sections C.1–C.4 of Appendix C, which review this material. We'll revisit probabilistic analysis and randomized algorithms several times throughout this book.

5.1   The hiring problem

Suppose that you need to hire a new office assistant. Your previous attempts at hiring have been unsuccessful, and you decide to use an employment agency. The employment agency sends you one candidate each day. You interview that person and then decide either to hire that person or not. You must pay the employment agency a small fee to interview an applicant. To actually hire an applicant is more costly, however, since you must fire your current office assistant and also pay a substantial hiring fee to the employment agency. You are committed to having, at all times, the best possible person for the job. Therefore, you decide that, after interviewing each applicant, if that applicant is better qualified than the current office assistant, you will fire the current office assistant and hire the new applicant. You are willing to pay the resulting price of this strategy, but you wish to estimate what that price will be.

The procedure HIRE-ASSISTANT on the facing page expresses this strategy for hiring in pseudocode. The candidates for the office assistant job are numbered 1 through n and interviewed in that order. The procedure assumes that after interviewing candidate i, you can determine whether candidate i is the best candidate you have seen so far. It starts by creating a dummy candidate, numbered 0, who is less qualified than each of the other candidates.

The cost model for this problem differs from the model described in Chapter 2. We focus not on the running time of HIRE-ASSISTANT, but instead on the fees paid for interviewing and hiring. On the surface, analyzing the cost of this algorithm

HIRE-ASSISTANT(n)

1   $best = 0$ **//** candidate 0 is a least-qualified dummy candidate
2   **for** $i = 1$ **to** n
3   interview candidate i
4   **if** candidate i is better than candidate *best*
5           $best = i$
6   hire candidate i

may seem very different from analyzing the running time of, say, merge sort. The analytical techniques used, however, are identical whether we are analyzing cost or running time. In either case, we are counting the number of times certain basic operations are executed.

Interviewing has a low cost, say c_i, whereas hiring is expensive, costing c_h. Letting m be the number of people hired, the total cost associated with this algorithm is $O(c_i n + c_h m)$. No matter how many people you hire, you always interview n candidates and thus always incur the cost $c_i n$ associated with interviewing. We therefore concentrate on analyzing $c_h m$, the hiring cost. This quantity depends on the order in which you interview candidates.

This scenario serves as a model for a common computational paradigm. Algorithms often need to find the maximum or minimum value in a sequence by examining each element of the sequence and maintaining a current "winner." The hiring problem models how often a procedure updates its notion of which element is currently winning.

Worst-case analysis

In the worst case, you actually hire every candidate that you interview. This situation occurs if the candidates come in strictly increasing order of quality, in which case you hire n times, for a total hiring cost of $O(c_h n)$.

Of course, the candidates do not always come in increasing order of quality. In fact, you have no idea about the order in which they arrive, nor do you have any control over this order. Therefore, it is natural to ask what we expect to happen in a typical or average case.

Probabilistic analysis

Probabilistic analysis is the use of probability in the analysis of problems. Most commonly, we use probabilistic analysis to analyze the running time of an algorithm. Sometimes we use it to analyze other quantities, such as the hiring cost in procedure HIRE-ASSISTANT. In order to perform a probabilistic analysis, we must use knowledge of, or make assumptions about, the distribution of the inputs. Then we analyze our algorithm, computing an average-case running time, where we take the average, or expected value, over the distribution of the possible inputs. When reporting such a running time, we refer to it as the ***average-case running time***.

You must be careful in deciding on the distribution of inputs. For some problems, you may reasonably assume something about the set of all possible inputs, and then you can use probabilistic analysis as a technique for designing an efficient algorithm and as a means for gaining insight into a problem. For other problems, you cannot characterize a reasonable input distribution, and in these cases you cannot use probabilistic analysis.

For the hiring problem, we can assume that the applicants come in a random order. What does that mean for this problem? We assume that you can compare any two candidates and decide which one is better qualified, which is to say that there is a total order on the candidates. (See Section B.2 for the definition of a total order.) Thus, you can rank each candidate with a unique number from 1 through n, using $rank(i)$ to denote the rank of applicant i, and adopt the convention that a higher rank corresponds to a better qualified applicant. The ordered list $\langle rank(1), rank(2), \ldots, rank(n) \rangle$ is a permutation of the list $\langle 1, 2, \ldots, n \rangle$. Saying that the applicants come in a random order is equivalent to saying that this list of ranks is equally likely to be any one of the $n!$ permutations of the numbers 1 through n. Alternatively, we say that the ranks form a ***uniform random permutation***, that is, each of the possible $n!$ permutations appears with equal probability.

Section 5.2 contains a probabilistic analysis of the hiring problem.

Randomized algorithms

In order to use probabilistic analysis, you need to know something about the distribution of the inputs. In many cases, you know little about the input distribution. Even if you do know something about the distribution, you might not be able to model this knowledge computationally. Yet, probability and randomness often serve as tools for algorithm design and analysis, by making part of the algorithm behave randomly.

In the hiring problem, it may seem as if the candidates are being presented to you in a random order, but you have no way of knowing whether they really are. Thus, in order to develop a randomized algorithm for the hiring problem, you need greater control over the order in which you'll interview the candidates. We will, therefore, change the model slightly. The employment agency sends you a list of the n candidates in advance. On each day, you choose, randomly, which candidate to interview. Although you know nothing about the candidates (besides their names), we have made a significant change. Instead of accepting the order given to you by the employment agency and hoping that it's random, you have instead gained control of the process and enforced a random order.

More generally, we call an algorithm *randomized* if its behavior is determined not only by its input but also by values produced by a *random-number generator*. We assume that we have at our disposal a random-number generator RANDOM. A call to RANDOM(a, b) returns an integer between a and b, inclusive, with each such integer being equally likely. For example, RANDOM($0, 1$) produces 0 with probability $1/2$, and it produces 1 with probability $1/2$. A call to RANDOM($3, 7$) returns any one of 3, 4, 5, 6, or 7, each with probability $1/5$. Each integer returned by RANDOM is independent of the integers returned on previous calls. You may imagine RANDOM as rolling a $(b - a + 1)$-sided die to obtain its output. (In practice, most programming environments offer a *pseudorandom-number generator*: a deterministic algorithm returning numbers that "look" statistically random.)

When analyzing the running time of a randomized algorithm, we take the expectation of the running time over the distribution of values returned by the random number generator. We distinguish these algorithms from those in which the input is random by referring to the running time of a randomized algorithm as an *expected running time*. In general, we discuss the average-case running time when the probability distribution is over the inputs to the algorithm, and we discuss the expected running time when the algorithm itself makes random choices.

Exercises

5.1-1
Show that the assumption that you are always able to determine which candidate is best, in line 4 of procedure HIRE-ASSISTANT, implies that you know a total order on the ranks of the candidates.

★ **5.1-2**
Describe an implementation of the procedure RANDOM(a, b) that makes calls only to RANDOM($0, 1$). What is the expected running time of your procedure, as a function of a and b?

★ **5.1-3**
You wish to implement a program that outputs 0 with probability $1/2$ and 1 with probability $1/2$. At your disposal is a procedure BIASED-RANDOM that outputs either 0 or 1, but it outputs 1 with some probability p and 0 with probability $1 - p$, where $0 < p < 1$. You do not know what p is. Give an algorithm that uses BIASED-RANDOM as a subroutine, and returns an unbiased answer, returning 0 with probability $1/2$ and 1 with probability $1/2$. What is the expected running time of your algorithm as a function of p?

5.2   Indicator random variables

In order to analyze many algorithms, including the hiring problem, we use indicator random variables. Indicator random variables provide a convenient method for converting between probabilities and expectations. Given a sample space S and an event A, the *indicator random variable* $I\{A\}$ associated with event A is defined as

$$I\{A\} = \begin{cases} 1 & \text{if } A \text{ occurs}, \\ 0 & \text{if } A \text{ does not occur}. \end{cases} \tag{5.1}$$

As a simple example, let us determine the expected number of heads obtained when flipping a fair coin. The sample space for a single coin flip is $S = \{H, T\}$, with $\Pr\{H\} = \Pr\{T\} = 1/2$. We can then define an indicator random variable X_H, associated with the coin coming up heads, which is the event H. This variable counts the number of heads obtained in this flip, and it is 1 if the coin comes up heads and 0 otherwise. We write

$$X_H = I\{H\}$$
$$= \begin{cases} 1 & \text{if } H \text{ occurs}, \\ 0 & \text{if } T \text{ occurs}. \end{cases}$$

The expected number of heads obtained in one flip of the coin is simply the expected value of our indicator variable X_H:

$$\begin{aligned} E[X_H] &= E[I\{H\}] \\ &= 1 \cdot \Pr\{H\} + 0 \cdot \Pr\{T\} \\ &= 1 \cdot (1/2) + 0 \cdot (1/2) \\ &= 1/2. \end{aligned}$$

Thus the expected number of heads obtained by one flip of a fair coin is $1/2$. As the following lemma shows, the expected value of an indicator random variable associated with an event A is equal to the probability that A occurs.

Lemma 5.1
Given a sample space S and an event A in the sample space S, let $X_A = I\{A\}$. Then $E[X_A] = \Pr\{A\}$.

Proof   By the definition of an indicator random variable from equation (5.1) and the definition of expected value, we have

$$\begin{aligned} E[X_A] &= E[I\{A\}] \\ &= 1 \cdot \Pr\{A\} + 0 \cdot \Pr\{\overline{A}\} \\ &= \Pr\{A\}, \end{aligned}$$

where $\overline{A}$ denotes $S - A$, the complement of A.   ∎

Although indicator random variables may seem cumbersome for an application such as counting the expected number of heads on a flip of a single coin, they are useful for analyzing situations that perform repeated random trials. In Appendix C, for example, indicator random variables provide a simple way to determine the expected number of heads in n coin flips. One option is to consider separately the probability of obtaining 0 heads, 1 head, 2 heads, etc. to arrive at the result of equation (C.41) on page 1199. Alternatively, we can employ the simpler method proposed in equation (C.42), which uses indicator random variables implicitly. Making this argument more explicit, let X_i be the indicator random variable associated with the event in which the ith flip comes up heads: $X_i = I\{$the ith flip results in the event $H\}$. Let X be the random variable denoting the total number of heads in the n coin flips, so that

$$X = \sum_{i=1}^{n} X_i \; .$$

In order to compute the expected number of heads, take the expectation of both sides of the above equation to obtain

$$\mathrm{E}\,[X] = \mathrm{E}\left[\sum_{i=1}^{n} X_i\right] \; . \tag{5.2}$$

By Lemma 5.1, the expectation of each of the random variables is $\mathrm{E}\,[X_i] = 1/2$ for $i = 1, 2, \ldots, n$. Then we can compute the sum of the expectations: $\sum_{i=1}^{n} \mathrm{E}\,[X_i] = n/2$. But equation (5.2) calls for the expectation of the sum, not the sum of the expectations. How can we resolve this conundrum? Linearity of expectation, equation (C.24) on page 1192, to the rescue: *the expectation of the sum always equals the sum of the expectations*. Linearity of expectation applies even when there is dependence among the random variables. Combining indicator random variables with linearity of expectation gives us a powerful technique to compute expected values when multiple events occur. We now can compute the expected number of heads:

$$\mathrm{E}\,[X] = \mathrm{E}\left[\sum_{i=1}^{n} X_i\right]$$
$$= \sum_{i=1}^{n} \mathrm{E}\,[X_i]$$
$$= \sum_{i=1}^{n} 1/2$$
$$= n/2 \; .$$

Thus, compared with the method used in equation (C.41), indicator random variables greatly simplify the calculation. We use indicator random variables throughout this book.

Analysis of the hiring problem using indicator random variables

Returning to the hiring problem, we now wish to compute the expected number of times that you hire a new office assistant. In order to use a probabilistic analysis, let's assume that the candidates arrive in a random order, as discussed in Section 5.1. (We'll see in Section 5.3 how to remove this assumption.) Let X be the random variable whose value equals the number of times you hire a new office assistant. We could then apply the definition of expected value from equation (C.23) on page 1192 to obtain

$$\mathrm{E}\,[X] = \sum_{x=1}^{n} x \, \Pr\{X = x\}\,,$$

but this calculation would be cumbersome. Instead, let's simplify the calculation by using indicator random variables.

To use indicator random variables, instead of computing $\mathrm{E}\,[X]$ by defining just one variable denoting the number of times you hire a new office assistant, think of the process of hiring as repeated random trials and define n variables indicating whether each particular candidate is hired. In particular, let X_i be the indicator random variable associated with the event in which the ith candidate is hired. Thus,

$$
\begin{aligned}
X_i &= \mathrm{I}\{\text{candidate } i \text{ is hired}\} \\
&= \begin{cases} 1 & \text{if candidate } i \text{ is hired}\,, \\ 0 & \text{if candidate } i \text{ is not hired}\,, \end{cases}
\end{aligned}
$$

and

$$X = X_1 + X_2 + \cdots + X_n\,. \tag{5.3}$$

Lemma 5.1 gives

$$\mathrm{E}\,[X_i] = \Pr\{\text{candidate } i \text{ is hired}\}\,,$$

and we must therefore compute the probability that lines 5–6 of HIRE-ASSISTANT are executed.

Candidate i is hired, in line 6, exactly when candidate i is better than each of candidates 1 through $i - 1$. Because we have assumed that the candidates arrive in a random order, the first i candidates have appeared in a random order. Any one of these first i candidates is equally likely to be the best qualified so far. Candidate i has a probability of $1/i$ of being better qualified than candidates 1 through $i - 1$ and thus a probability of $1/i$ of being hired. By Lemma 5.1, we conclude that

$$\mathrm{E}[X_i] = 1/i \ . \tag{5.4}$$

Now we can compute $\mathrm{E}[X]$:

$$
\begin{aligned}
\mathrm{E}[X] &= \mathrm{E}\left[\sum_{i=1}^{n} X_i\right] \quad \text{(by equation (5.3))} \tag{5.5}\\
&= \sum_{i=1}^{n} \mathrm{E}[X_i] \quad \text{(by equation (C.24), linearity of expectation)}\\
&= \sum_{i=1}^{n} \frac{1}{i} \quad \text{(by equation (5.4))}\\
&= \ln n + O(1) \quad \text{(by equation (A.9), the harmonic series) .} \tag{5.6}
\end{aligned}
$$

Even though you interview n people, you actually hire only approximately $\ln n$ of them, on average. We summarize this result in the following lemma.

Lemma 5.2
Assuming that the candidates are presented in a random order, algorithm HIRE-ASSISTANT has an average-case total hiring cost of $O(c_h \ln n)$.

Proof   The bound follows immediately from our definition of the hiring cost and equation (5.6), which shows that the expected number of hires is approximately $\ln n$. ∎

The average-case hiring cost is a significant improvement over the worst-case hiring cost of $O(c_h n)$.

Exercises

5.2-1
In HIRE-ASSISTANT, assuming that the candidates are presented in a random order, what is the probability that you hire exactly one time? What is the probability that you hire exactly n times?

5.2-2
In HIRE-ASSISTANT, assuming that the candidates are presented in a random order, what is the probability that you hire exactly twice?

5.2-3
Use indicator random variables to compute the expected value of the sum of n dice.

5.2-4

This exercise asks you to (partly) verify that linearity of expectation holds even if the random variables are not independent. Consider two 6-sided dice that are rolled independently. What is the expected value of the sum? Now consider the case where the first die is rolled normally and then the second die is set equal to the value shown on the first die. What is the expected value of the sum? Now consider the case where the first die is rolled normally and the second die is set equal to 7 minus the value of the first die. What is the expected value of the sum?

5.2-5

Use indicator random variables to solve the following problem, which is known as the *hat-check problem*. Each of n customers gives a hat to a hat-check person at a restaurant. The hat-check person gives the hats back to the customers in a random order. What is the expected number of customers who get back their own hat?

5.2-6

Let $A[1:n]$ be an array of n distinct numbers. If $i < j$ and $A[i] > A[j]$, then the pair (i, j) is called an *inversion* of A. (See Problem 2-4 on page 47 for more on inversions.) Suppose that the elements of A form a uniform random permutation of $\langle 1, 2, \ldots, n \rangle$. Use indicator random variables to compute the expected number of inversions.

5.3   Randomized algorithms

In the previous section, we showed how knowing a distribution on the inputs can help us to analyze the average-case behavior of an algorithm. What if you do not know the distribution? Then you cannot perform an average-case analysis. As mentioned in Section 5.1, however, you might be able to use a randomized algorithm.

For a problem such as the hiring problem, in which it is helpful to assume that all permutations of the input are equally likely, a probabilistic analysis can guide us when developing a randomized algorithm. Instead of *assuming* a distribution of inputs, we *impose* a distribution. In particular, before running the algorithm, let's randomly permute the candidates in order to enforce the property that every permutation is equally likely. Although we have modified the algorithm, we still expect to hire a new office assistant approximately $\ln n$ times. But now we expect this to be the case for *any* input, rather than for inputs drawn from a particular distribution.

Let us further explore the distinction between probabilistic analysis and randomized algorithms. In Section 5.2, we claimed that, assuming that the candidates arrive in a random order, the expected number of times you hire a new office assistant is about $\ln n$. This algorithm is deterministic: for any particular input, the number of times a new office assistant is hired is always the same. Furthermore, the number of times you hire a new office assistant differs for different inputs, and it depends on the ranks of the various candidates. Since this number depends only on the ranks of the candidates, to represent a particular input, we can just list, in order, the ranks $\langle rank(1), rank(2), \ldots, rank(n) \rangle$ of the candidates. Given the rank list $A_1 = \langle 1, 2, 3, 4, 5, 6, 7, 8, 9, 10 \rangle$, a new office assistant is always hired 10 times, since each successive candidate is better than the previous one, and lines 5–6 of HIRE-ASSISTANT are executed in each iteration. Given the list of ranks $A_2 = \langle 10, 9, 8, 7, 6, 5, 4, 3, 2, 1 \rangle$, a new office assistant is hired only once, in the first iteration. Given a list of ranks $A_3 = \langle 5, 2, 1, 8, 4, 7, 10, 9, 3, 6 \rangle$, a new office assistant is hired three times, upon interviewing the candidates with ranks 5, 8, and 10. Recalling that the cost of our algorithm depends on how many times you hire a new office assistant, we see that there are expensive inputs such as A_1, inexpensive inputs such as A_2, and moderately expensive inputs such as A_3.

Consider, on the other hand, the randomized algorithm that first permutes the list of candidates and then determines the best candidate. In this case, we randomize in the algorithm, not in the input distribution. Given a particular input, say A_3 above, we cannot say how many times the maximum is updated, because this quantity differs with each run of the algorithm. The first time you run the algorithm on A_3, it might produce the permutation A_1 and perform 10 updates. But the second time you run the algorithm, it might produce the permutation A_2 and perform only one update. The third time you run the algorithm, it might perform some other number of updates. Each time you run the algorithm, its execution depends on the random choices made and is likely to differ from the previous execution of the algorithm. For this algorithm and many other randomized algorithms, *no particular input elicits its worst-case behavior*. Even your worst enemy cannot produce a bad input array, since the random permutation makes the input order irrelevant. The randomized algorithm performs badly only if the random-number generator produces an "unlucky" permutation.

For the hiring problem, the only change needed in the code is to randomly permute the array, as done in the RANDOMIZED-HIRE-ASSISTANT procedure. This simple change creates a randomized algorithm whose performance matches that obtained by assuming that the candidates were presented in a random order.

RANDOMIZED-HIRE-ASSISTANT(n)

1   randomly permute the list of candidates
2   HIRE-ASSISTANT(n)

Lemma 5.3
The expected hiring cost of the procedure Randomized-Hire-Assistant is $O(c_h \ln n)$.

Proof Permuting the input array achieves a situation identical to that of the probabilistic analysis of Hire-Assistant in Section 5.2. ∎

By carefully comparing Lemmas 5.2 and 5.3, you can see the difference between probabilistic analysis and randomized algorithms. Lemma 5.2 makes an assumption about the input. Lemma 5.3 makes no such assumption, although randomizing the input takes some additional time. To remain consistent with our terminology, we couched Lemma 5.2 in terms of the average-case hiring cost and Lemma 5.3 in terms of the expected hiring cost. In the remainder of this section, we discuss some issues involved in randomly permuting inputs.

Randomly permuting arrays

Many randomized algorithms randomize the input by permuting a given input array. We'll see elsewhere in this book other ways to randomize an algorithm, but now, let's see how we can randomly permute an array of n elements. The goal is to produce a *uniform random permutation*, that is, a permutation that is as likely as any other permutation. Since there are $n!$ possible permutations, we want the probability that any particular permutation is produced to be $1/n!$.

You might think that to prove that a permutation is a uniform random permutation, it suffices to show that, for each element $A[i]$, the probability that the element winds up in position j is $1/n$. Exercise 5.3-4 shows that this weaker condition is, in fact, insufficient.

Our method to generate a random permutation permutes the array *in place*: at most a constant number of elements of the input array are ever stored outside the array. The procedure Randomly-Permute permutes an array $A[1:n]$ in place in $\Theta(n)$ time. In its ith iteration, it chooses the element $A[i]$ randomly from among elements $A[i]$ through $A[n]$. After the ith iteration, $A[i]$ is never altered.

Randomly-Permute(A, n)

```
1   for i = 1 to n
2       swap A[i] with A[Random(i, n)]
```

We use a loop invariant to show that procedure Randomly-Permute produces a uniform random permutation. A *k-permutation* on a set of n elements is a sequence containing k of the n elements, with no repetitions. (See page 1180 in Appendix C.) There are $n!/(n-k)!$ such possible k-permutations.

Lemma 5.4
Procedure RANDOMLY-PERMUTE computes a uniform random permutation.

Proof We use the following loop invariant:

> Just prior to the ith iteration of the **for** loop of lines 1–2, for each possible $(i-1)$-permutation of the n elements, the subarray $A[1:i-1]$ contains this $(i-1)$-permutation with probability $(n-i+1)!/n!$.

We need to show that this invariant is true prior to the first loop iteration, that each iteration of the loop maintains the invariant, that the loop terminates, and that the invariant provides a useful property to show correctness when the loop terminates.

Initialization: Consider the situation just before the first loop iteration, so that $i = 1$. The loop invariant says that for each possible 0-permutation, the subarray $A[1:0]$ contains this 0-permutation with probability $(n-i+1)!/n! = n!/n! = 1$. The subarray $A[1:0]$ is an empty subarray, and a 0-permutation has no elements. Thus, $A[1:0]$ contains any 0-permutation with probability 1, and the loop invariant holds prior to the first iteration.

Maintenance: By the loop invariant, we assume that just before the ith iteration, each possible $(i-1)$-permutation appears in the subarray $A[1:i-1]$ with probability $(n-i+1)!/n!$. We shall show that after the ith iteration, each possible i-permutation appears in the subarray $A[1:i]$ with probability $(n-i)!/n!$. Incrementing i for the next iteration then maintains the loop invariant.

Let us examine the ith iteration. Consider a particular i-permutation, and denote the elements in it by $\langle x_1, x_2, \ldots, x_i \rangle$. This permutation consists of an $(i-1)$-permutation $\langle x_1, \ldots, x_{i-1} \rangle$ followed by the value x_i that the algorithm places in $A[i]$. Let E_1 denote the event in which the first $i-1$ iterations have created the particular $(i-1)$-permutation $\langle x_1, \ldots, x_{i-1} \rangle$ in $A[1:i-1]$. By the loop invariant, $\Pr\{E_1\} = (n-i+1)!/n!$. Let E_2 be the event that the ith iteration puts x_i in position $A[i]$. The i-permutation $\langle x_1, \ldots, x_i \rangle$ appears in $A[1:i]$ precisely when both E_1 and E_2 occur, and so we wish to compute $\Pr\{E_2 \cap E_1\}$. Using equation (C.16) on page 1187, we have

$$\Pr\{E_2 \cap E_1\} = \Pr\{E_2 \mid E_1\}\Pr\{E_1\} \ .$$

The probability $\Pr\{E_2 \mid E_1\}$ equals $1/(n-i+1)$ because in line 2 the algorithm chooses x_i randomly from the $n-i+1$ values in positions $A[i:n]$. Thus, we have

$$\begin{aligned}
\Pr\{E_2 \cap E_1\} &= \Pr\{E_2 \mid E_1\}\Pr\{E_1\} \\
&= \frac{1}{n-i+1} \cdot \frac{(n-i+1)!}{n!} \\
&= \frac{(n-i)!}{n!} .
\end{aligned}$$

Termination: The loop terminates, since it is a **for** loop iterating n times. At termination, $i = n + 1$, and we have that the subarray $A[1:n]$ is a given n-permutation with probability $(n - (n + 1) + 1)!/n! = 0!/n! = 1/n!$.

Thus, RANDOMLY-PERMUTE produces a uniform random permutation.   ∎

A randomized algorithm is often the simplest and most efficient way to solve a problem.

Exercises

5.3-1
Professor Marceau objects to the loop invariant used in the proof of Lemma 5.4. He questions whether it holds prior to the first iteration. He reasons that we could just as easily declare that an empty subarray contains no 0-permutations. Therefore, the probability that an empty subarray contains a 0-permutation should be 0, thus invalidating the loop invariant prior to the first iteration. Rewrite the procedure RANDOMLY-PERMUTE so that its associated loop invariant applies to a nonempty subarray prior to the first iteration, and modify the proof of Lemma 5.4 for your procedure.

5.3-2
Professor Kelp decides to write a procedure that produces at random any permutation except the ***identity permutation***, in which every element ends up where it started. He proposes the procedure PERMUTE-WITHOUT-IDENTITY. Does this procedure do what Professor Kelp intends?

```
PERMUTE-WITHOUT-IDENTITY(A, n)
1  for i = 1 to n − 1
2      swap A[i] with A[RANDOM(i + 1, n)]
```

5.3-3
Consider the PERMUTE-WITH-ALL procedure on the facing page, which instead of swapping element $A[i]$ with a random element from the subarray $A[i:n]$, swaps it with a random element from anywhere in the array. Does PERMUTE-WITH-ALL produce a uniform random permutation? Why or why not?

PERMUTE-WITH-ALL(A, n)

1   **for** $i = 1$ **to** n
2   swap $A[i]$ with $A[\text{RANDOM}(1, n)]$

5.3-4

Professor Knievel suggests the procedure PERMUTE-BY-CYCLE to generate a uniform random permutation. Show that each element $A[i]$ has a $1/n$ probability of winding up in any particular position in B. Then show that Professor Knievel is mistaken by showing that the resulting permutation is not uniformly random.

PERMUTE-BY-CYCLE(A, n)

1   let $B[1:n]$ be a new array
2   *offset* $= \text{RANDOM}(1, n)$
3   **for** $i = 1$ **to** n
4   *dest* $= i + \textit{offset}$
5   **if** *dest* $> n$
6   *dest* $= \textit{dest} - n$
7       $B[\textit{dest}] = A[i]$
8   **return** B

5.3-5

Professor Gallup wants to create a *random sample* of the set $\{1, 2, 3, \ldots, n\}$, that is, an m-element subset S, where $0 \leq m \leq n$, such that each m-subset is equally likely to be created. One way is to set $A[i] = i$, for $i = 1, 2, 3, \ldots, n$, call RANDOMLY-PERMUTE(A), and then take just the first m array elements. This method makes n calls to the RANDOM procedure. In Professor Gallup's application, n is much larger than m, and so the professor wants to create a random sample with fewer calls to RANDOM.

RANDOM-SAMPLE(m, n)

1   $S = \emptyset$
2   **for** $k = n - m + 1$ **to** n // iterates m times
3       $i = \text{RANDOM}(1, k)$
4   **if** $i \in S$
5           $S = S \cup \{k\}$
6   **else** $S = S \cup \{i\}$
7   **return** S

Show that the procedure RANDOM-SAMPLE on the previous page returns a random m-subset S of $\{1, 2, 3, \ldots, n\}$, in which each m-subset is equally likely, while making only m calls to RANDOM.

★ 5.4   Probabilistic analysis and further uses of indicator random variables

This advanced section further illustrates probabilistic analysis by way of four examples. The first determines the probability that in a room of k people, two of them share the same birthday. The second example examines what happens when randomly tossing balls into bins. The third investigates "streaks" of consecutive heads when flipping coins. The final example analyzes a variant of the hiring problem in which you have to make decisions without actually interviewing all the candidates.

5.4.1   The birthday paradox

Our first example is the *birthday paradox*. How many people must there be in a room before there is a 50% chance that two of them were born on the same day of the year? The answer is surprisingly few. The paradox is that it is in fact far fewer than the number of days in a year, or even half the number of days in a year, as we shall see.

To answer this question, we index the people in the room with the integers $1, 2, \ldots, k$, where k is the number of people in the room. We ignore the issue of leap years and assume that all years have $n = 365$ days. For $i = 1, 2, \ldots, k$, let b_i be the day of the year on which person i's birthday falls, where $1 \leq b_i \leq n$. We also assume that birthdays are uniformly distributed across the n days of the year, so that $\Pr\{b_i = r\} = 1/n$ for $i = 1, 2, \ldots, k$ and $r = 1, 2, \ldots, n$.

The probability that two given people, say i and j, have matching birthdays depends on whether the random selection of birthdays is independent. We assume from now on that birthdays are independent, so that the probability that i's birthday and j's birthday both fall on day r is

$$\Pr\{b_i = r \text{ and } b_j = r\} = \Pr\{b_i = r\} \Pr\{b_j = r\}$$
$$= \frac{1}{n^2} \, .$$

Thus, the probability that they both fall on the same day is

$$\Pr\{b_i = b_j\} = \sum_{r=1}^{n} \Pr\{b_i = r \text{ and } b_j = r\}$$

$$= \sum_{r=1}^{n} \frac{1}{n^2}$$
$$= \frac{1}{n} .\tag{5.7}$$

More intuitively, once b_i is chosen, the probability that b_j is chosen to be the same day is $1/n$. As long as the birthdays are independent, the probability that i and j have the same birthday is the same as the probability that the birthday of one of them falls on a given day.

We can analyze the probability of at least 2 out of k people having matching birthdays by looking at the complementary event. The probability that at least two of the birthdays match is 1 minus the probability that all the birthdays are different. The event B_k that k people have distinct birthdays is

$$B_k = \bigcap_{i=1}^{k} A_i ,$$

where A_i is the event that person i's birthday is different from person j's for all $j < i$. Since we can write $B_k = A_k \cap B_{k-1}$, we obtain from equation (C.18) on page 1189 the recurrence

$$\Pr\{B_k\} = \Pr\{B_{k-1}\} \Pr\{A_k \mid B_{k-1}\} ,\tag{5.8}$$

where we take $\Pr\{B_1\} = \Pr\{A_1\} = 1$ as an initial condition. In other words, the probability that $b_1, b_2, \ldots, b_k$ are distinct birthdays equals the probability that $b_1, b_2, \ldots, b_{k-1}$ are distinct birthdays multiplied by the probability that $b_k \neq b_i$ for $i = 1, 2, \ldots, k - 1$, given that $b_1, b_2, \ldots, b_{k-1}$ are distinct.

If $b_1, b_2, \ldots, b_{k-1}$ are distinct, the conditional probability that $b_k \neq b_i$ for $i = 1, 2, \ldots, k - 1$ is $\Pr\{A_k \mid B_{k-1}\} = (n - k + 1)/n$, since out of the n days, $n - (k - 1)$ days are not taken. We iteratively apply the recurrence (5.8) to obtain

$$\begin{aligned}
\Pr\{B_k\} &= \Pr\{B_{k-1}\} \Pr\{A_k \mid B_{k-1}\} \\
&= \Pr\{B_{k-2}\} \Pr\{A_{k-1} \mid B_{k-2}\} \Pr\{A_k \mid B_{k-1}\} \\
&\ \ \vdots \\
&= \Pr\{B_1\} \Pr\{A_2 \mid B_1\} \Pr\{A_3 \mid B_2\} \cdots \Pr\{A_k \mid B_{k-1}\} \\
&= 1 \cdot \left(\frac{n-1}{n}\right) \left(\frac{n-2}{n}\right) \cdots \left(\frac{n-k+1}{n}\right) \\
&= 1 \cdot \left(1 - \frac{1}{n}\right) \left(1 - \frac{2}{n}\right) \cdots \left(1 - \frac{k-1}{n}\right) .
\end{aligned}$$

Inequality (3.14) on page 66, $1 + x \leq e^x$, gives us

$$\Pr\{B_k\} \leq e^{-1/n}e^{-2/n}\cdots e^{-(k-1)/n}$$
$$= e^{-\sum_{i=1}^{k-1} i/n}$$
$$= e^{-k(k-1)/2n}$$
$$\leq \frac{1}{2}$$

when $-k(k-1)/2n \leq \ln(1/2)$. The probability that all k birthdays are distinct is at most $1/2$ when $k(k-1) \geq 2n \ln 2$ or, solving the quadratic equation, when $k \geq (1 + \sqrt{1 + (8\ln 2)n})/2$. For $n = 365$, we must have $k \geq 23$. Thus, if at least 23 people are in a room, the probability is at least $1/2$ that at least two people have the same birthday. Since a year on Mars is 669 Martian days long, it takes 31 Martians to get the same effect.

An analysis using indicator random variables

Indicator random variables afford a simpler but approximate analysis of the birthday paradox. For each pair (i, j) of the k people in the room, define the indicator random variable X_{ij}, for $1 \leq i < j \leq k$, by

$$X_{ij} = I\{\text{person } i \text{ and person } j \text{ have the same birthday}\}$$
$$= \begin{cases} 1 & \text{if person } i \text{ and person } j \text{ have the same birthday}, \\ 0 & \text{otherwise}. \end{cases}$$

By equation (5.7), the probability that two people have matching birthdays is $1/n$, and thus by Lemma 5.1 on page 130, we have

$$E[X_{ij}] = \Pr\{\text{person } i \text{ and person } j \text{ have the same birthday}\}$$
$$= 1/n.$$

Letting X be the random variable that counts the number of pairs of individuals having the same birthday, we have

$$X = \sum_{i=1}^{k-1} \sum_{j=i+1}^{k} X_{ij}.$$

Taking expectations of both sides and applying linearity of expectation, we obtain

$$E[X] = E\left[\sum_{i=1}^{k-1} \sum_{j=i+1}^{k} X_{ij}\right]$$
$$= \sum_{i=1}^{k-1} \sum_{j=i+1}^{k} E[X_{ij}]$$

$$= \binom{k}{2} \frac{1}{n}$$
$$= \frac{k(k-1)}{2n} .$$

When $k(k-1) \geq 2n$, therefore, the expected number of pairs of people with the same birthday is at least 1. Thus, if we have at least $\sqrt{2n}+1$ individuals in a room, we can expect at least two to have the same birthday. For $n = 365$, if $k = 28$, the expected number of pairs with the same birthday is $(28 \cdot 27)/(2 \cdot 365) \approx 1.0356$. Thus, with at least 28 people, we expect to find at least one matching pair of birthdays. On Mars, with 669 days per year, we need at least 38 Martians.

The first analysis, which used only probabilities, determined the number of people required for the probability to exceed $1/2$ that a matching pair of birthdays exists, and the second analysis, which used indicator random variables, determined the number such that the expected number of matching birthdays is 1. Although the exact numbers of people differ for the two situations, they are the same asymptotically: $\Theta(\sqrt{n})$.

5.4.2 Balls and bins

Consider a process in which you randomly toss identical balls into b bins, numbered $1, 2, \ldots, b$. The tosses are independent, and on each toss the ball is equally likely to end up in any bin. The probability that a tossed ball lands in any given bin is $1/b$. If we view the ball-tossing process as a sequence of Bernoulli trials (see Appendix C.4), where success means that the ball falls in the given bin, then each trial has a probability $1/b$ of success. This model is particularly useful for analyzing hashing (see Chapter 11), and we can answer a variety of interesting questions about the ball-tossing process. (Problem C-2 asks additional questions about balls and bins.)

- *How many balls fall in a given bin?* The number of balls that fall in a given bin follows the binomial distribution $b(k; n, 1/b)$. If you toss n balls, equation (C.41) on page 1199 tells us that the expected number of balls that fall in the given bin is n/b.

- *How many balls must you toss, on the average, until a given bin contains a ball?* The number of tosses until the given bin receives a ball follows the geometric distribution with probability $1/b$ and, by equation (C.36) on page 1197, the expected number of tosses until success is $1/(1/b) = b$.

- *How many balls must you toss until every bin contains at least one ball?* Let us call a toss in which a ball falls into an empty bin a "hit." We want to know the expected number n of tosses required to get b hits.

Using the hits, we can partition the n tosses into stages. The ith stage consists of the tosses after the $(i-1)$st hit up to and including the ith hit. The first stage consists of the first toss, since you are guaranteed to have a hit when all bins are empty. For each toss during the ith stage, $i-1$ bins contain balls and $b-i+1$ bins are empty. Thus, for each toss in the ith stage, the probability of obtaining a hit is $(b-i+1)/b$.

Let n_i denote the number of tosses in the ith stage. The number of tosses required to get b hits is $n = \sum_{i=1}^{b} n_i$. Each random variable n_i has a geometric distribution with probability of success $(b-i+1)/b$ and thus, by equation (C.36), we have

$$\mathrm{E}[n_i] = \frac{b}{b-i+1} \ .$$

By linearity of expectation, we have

$$\mathrm{E}[n] = \mathrm{E}\left[\sum_{i=1}^{b} n_i\right]$$

$$= \sum_{i=1}^{b} \mathrm{E}[n_i]$$

$$= \sum_{i=1}^{b} \frac{b}{b-i+1}$$

$$= b \sum_{i=1}^{b} \frac{1}{i} \qquad \text{(by equation (A.14) on page 1144)}$$

$$= b(\ln b + O(1)) \quad \text{(by equation (A.9) on page 1142)} \ .$$

It therefore takes approximately $b \ln b$ tosses before we can expect that every bin has a ball. This problem is also known as the *coupon collector's problem*, which says that if you are trying to collect each of b different coupons, then you should expect to acquire approximately $b \ln b$ randomly obtained coupons in order to succeed.

5.4.3   Streaks

Suppose that you flip a fair coin n times. What is the longest streak of consecutive heads that you expect to see? We'll prove upper and lower bounds separately to show that the answer is $\Theta(\lg n)$.

We first prove that the expected length of the longest streak of heads is $O(\lg n)$. The probability that each coin flip is a head is $1/2$. Let A_{ik} be the event that a streak of heads of length at least k begins with the ith coin flip or, more precisely, the event that the k consecutive coin flips $i, i + 1, \ldots, i + k - 1$ yield only heads, where $1 \leq k \leq n$ and $1 \leq i \leq n - k + 1$. Since coin flips are mutually independent, for any given event A_{ik}, the probability that all k flips are heads is

$$\Pr\{A_{ik}\} = \frac{1}{2^k} \, . \tag{5.9}$$

For $k = 2\lceil \lg n \rceil$,

$$
\begin{aligned}
\Pr\{A_{i,2\lceil \lg n \rceil}\} &= \frac{1}{2^{2\lceil \lg n \rceil}} \\
&\leq \frac{1}{2^{2\lg n}} \\
&= \frac{1}{n^2} \, ,
\end{aligned}
$$

and thus the probability that a streak of heads of length at least $2\lceil \lg n \rceil$ begins in position i is quite small. There are at most $n - 2\lceil \lg n \rceil + 1$ positions where such a streak can begin. The probability that a streak of heads of length at least $2\lceil \lg n \rceil$ begins anywhere is therefore

$$
\begin{aligned}
\Pr\left\{ \bigcup_{i=1}^{n-2\lceil \lg n \rceil + 1} A_{i,2\lceil \lg n \rceil} \right\} \\
\leq \sum_{i=1}^{n-2\lceil \lg n \rceil + 1} \Pr\{A_{i,2\lceil \lg n \rceil}\} \quad \text{(by Boole's inequality (C.21) on page 1190)} \\
\leq \sum_{i=1}^{n-2\lceil \lg n \rceil + 1} \frac{1}{n^2} \\
< \sum_{i=1}^{n} \frac{1}{n^2} \\
= \frac{1}{n} \, . \tag{5.10}
\end{aligned}
$$

We can use inequality (5.10) to bound the length of the longest streak. For $j = 0, 1, 2, \ldots, n$, let L_j be the event that the longest streak of heads has length exactly j, and let L be the length of the longest streak. By the definition of expected value, we have

$$\mathrm{E}[L] = \sum_{j=0}^{n} j \Pr\{L_j\} \, . \tag{5.11}$$

We could try to evaluate this sum using upper bounds on each $\Pr\{L_j\}$ similar to those computed in inequality (5.10). Unfortunately, this method yields weak bounds. We can use some intuition gained by the above analysis to obtain a good bound, however. For no individual term in the summation in equation (5.11) are both the factors j and $\Pr\{L_j\}$ large. Why? When $j \geq 2\lceil \lg n \rceil$, then $\Pr\{L_j\}$ is very small, and when $j < 2\lceil \lg n \rceil$, then j is fairly small. More precisely, since the events L_j for $j = 0, 1, \ldots, n$ are disjoint, the probability that a streak of heads of length at least $2\lceil \lg n \rceil$ begins anywhere is $\sum_{j=2\lceil \lg n \rceil}^{n} \Pr\{L_j\}$. Inequality (5.10) tells us that the probability that a streak of heads of length at least $2\lceil \lg n \rceil$ begins anywhere is less than $1/n$, which means that $\sum_{j=2\lceil \lg n \rceil}^{n} \Pr\{L_j\} < 1/n$. Also, noting that $\sum_{j=0}^{n} \Pr\{L_j\} = 1$, we have that $\sum_{j=0}^{2\lceil \lg n \rceil -1} \Pr\{L_j\} \leq 1$. Thus, we obtain

$$
\begin{aligned}
\mathrm{E}\,[L] &= \sum_{j=0}^{n} j \Pr\{L_j\} \\
&= \sum_{j=0}^{2\lceil \lg n \rceil -1} j \Pr\{L_j\} + \sum_{j=2\lceil \lg n \rceil}^{n} j \Pr\{L_j\} \\
&< \sum_{j=0}^{2\lceil \lg n \rceil -1} (2\lceil \lg n \rceil) \Pr\{L_j\} + \sum_{j=2\lceil \lg n \rceil}^{n} n \Pr\{L_j\} \\
&= 2\lceil \lg n \rceil \sum_{j=0}^{2\lceil \lg n \rceil -1} \Pr\{L_j\} + n \sum_{j=2\lceil \lg n \rceil}^{n} \Pr\{L_j\} \\
&< 2\lceil \lg n \rceil \cdot 1 + n \cdot \frac{1}{n} \\
&= O(\lg n)\, .
\end{aligned}
$$

The probability that a streak of heads exceeds $r\lceil \lg n \rceil$ flips diminishes quickly with r. Let's get a rough bound on the probability that a streak of at least $r\lceil \lg n \rceil$ heads occurs, for $r \geq 1$. The probability that a streak of at least $r\lceil \lg n \rceil$ heads starts in position i is

$$
\begin{aligned}
\Pr\{A_{i,r\lceil \lg n \rceil}\} &= \frac{1}{2^{r\lceil \lg n \rceil}} \\
&\leq \frac{1}{n^r}\, .
\end{aligned}
$$

A streak of at least $r\lceil \lg n \rceil$ heads cannot start in the last $n - r\lceil \lg n \rceil + 1$ flips, but let's overestimate the probability of such a streak by allowing it to start anywhere within the n coin flips. Then the probability that a streak of at least $r\lceil \lg n \rceil$ heads occurs is at most

$$\Pr\left\{\bigcup_{i=1}^{n} A_{i,r\lceil \lg n\rceil}\right\} \leq \sum_{i=1}^{n} \Pr\{A_{i,r\lceil \lg n\rceil}\} \qquad \text{(by Boole's inequality (C.21))}$$
$$\leq \sum_{i=1}^{n} \frac{1}{n^r}$$
$$= \frac{1}{n^{r-1}}\ .$$

Equivalently, the probability is at least $1 - 1/n^{r-1}$ that the longest streak has length less than $r\lceil \lg n\rceil$.

As an example, during $n = 1000$ coin flips, the probability of encountering a streak of at least $2\lceil \lg n\rceil = 20$ heads is at most $1/n = 1/1000$. The chance of a streak of at least $3\lceil \lg n\rceil = 30$ heads is at most $1/n^2 = 1/1{,}000{,}000$.

Let's now prove a complementary lower bound: the expected length of the longest streak of heads in n coin flips is $\Omega(\lg n)$. To prove this bound, we look for streaks of length s by partitioning the n flips into approximately n/s groups of s flips each. If we choose $s = \lfloor(\lg n)/2\rfloor$, we'll see that it is likely that at least one of these groups comes up all heads, which means that it's likely that the longest streak has length at least $s = \Omega(\lg n)$. We'll then show that the longest streak has expected length $\Omega(\lg n)$.

Let's partition the n coin flips into at least $\lfloor n/\lfloor(\lg n)/2\rfloor\rfloor$ groups of $\lfloor(\lg n)/2\rfloor$ consecutive flips and bound the probability that no group comes up all heads. By equation (5.9), the probability that the group starting in position i comes up all heads is

$$\Pr\{A_{i,\lfloor(\lg n)/2\rfloor}\} = \frac{1}{2^{\lfloor(\lg n)/2\rfloor}}$$
$$\geq \frac{1}{\sqrt{n}}\ .$$

The probability that a streak of heads of length at least $\lfloor(\lg n)/2\rfloor$ does not begin in position i is therefore at most $1 - 1/\sqrt{n}$. Since the $\lfloor n/\lfloor(\lg n)/2\rfloor\rfloor$ groups are formed from mutually exclusive, independent coin flips, the probability that every one of these groups *fails* to be a streak of length $\lfloor(\lg n)/2\rfloor$ is at most

$$\left(1 - 1/\sqrt{n}\right)^{\lfloor n/\lfloor(\lg n)/2\rfloor\rfloor} \leq \left(1 - 1/\sqrt{n}\right)^{n/\lfloor(\lg n)/2\rfloor - 1}$$
$$\leq \left(1 - 1/\sqrt{n}\right)^{2n/\lg n - 1}$$
$$\leq e^{-(2n/\lg n - 1)/\sqrt{n}}$$
$$= O(e^{-\ln n})$$
$$= O(1/n)\ . \tag{5.12}$$

For this argument, we used inequality (3.14), $1 + x \leq e^x$, on page 66 and the fact, which you may verify, that $(2n/\lg n - 1)/\sqrt{n} \geq \ln n$ for sufficiently large n.

We want to bound the probability that the longest streak equals or exceeds $\lfloor (\lg n)/2 \rfloor$. To do so, let L be the event that the longest streak of heads equals or exceeds $s = \lfloor (\lg n)/2 \rfloor$. Let $\overline{L}$ be the complementary event, that the longest streak of heads is strictly less than s, so that $\Pr\{L\} + \Pr\{\overline{L}\} = 1$. Let F be the event that every group of s flips fails to be a streak of s heads. By inequality (5.12), we have $\Pr\{F\} = O(1/n)$. If the longest streak of heads is less than s, then certainly every group of s flips fails to be a streak of s heads, which means that event $\overline{L}$ implies event F. Of course, event F could occur even if event $\overline{L}$ does not (for example, if a streak of s or more heads crosses over the boundary between two groups), and so we have $\Pr\{\overline{L}\} \leq \Pr\{F\} = O(1/n)$. Since $\Pr\{L\} + \Pr\{\overline{L}\} = 1$, we have that

$$
\begin{aligned}
\Pr\{L\} &= 1 - \Pr\{\overline{L}\} \\
&\geq 1 - \Pr\{F\} \\
&= 1 - O(1/n) \ .
\end{aligned}
$$

That is, the probability that the longest streak equals or exceeds $\lfloor (\lg n)/2 \rfloor$ is

$$
\sum_{j=\lfloor (\lg n)/2 \rfloor}^{n} \Pr\{L_j\} \geq 1 - O(1/n) \ . \tag{5.13}
$$

We can now calculate a lower bound on the expected length of the longest streak, beginning with equation (5.11) and proceeding in a manner similar to our analysis of the upper bound:

$$
\begin{aligned}
\mathrm{E}[L] &= \sum_{j=0}^{n} j \Pr\{L_j\} \\
&= \sum_{j=0}^{\lfloor (\lg n)/2 \rfloor - 1} j \Pr\{L_j\} + \sum_{j=\lfloor (\lg n)/2 \rfloor}^{n} j \Pr\{L_j\} \\
&\geq \sum_{j=0}^{\lfloor (\lg n)/2 \rfloor - 1} 0 \cdot \Pr\{L_j\} + \sum_{j=\lfloor (\lg n)/2 \rfloor}^{n} \lfloor (\lg n)/2 \rfloor \Pr\{L_j\} \\
&= 0 \cdot \sum_{j=0}^{\lfloor (\lg n)/2 \rfloor - 1} \Pr\{L_j\} + \lfloor (\lg n)/2 \rfloor \sum_{j=\lfloor (\lg n)/2 \rfloor}^{n} \Pr\{L_j\} \\
&\geq 0 + \lfloor (\lg n)/2 \rfloor \, (1 - O(1/n)) \qquad \text{(by inequality (5.13))} \\
&= \Omega(\lg n) \ .
\end{aligned}
$$

As with the birthday paradox, we can obtain a simpler, but approximate, analysis using indicator random variables. Instead of determining the expected length of the longest streak, we'll find the expected number of streaks with at least a given length. Let $X_{ik} = I\{A_{ik}\}$ be the indicator random variable associated with a streak of heads of length at least k beginning with the ith coin flip. To count the total number of such streaks, define

$$X_k = \sum_{i=1}^{n-k+1} X_{ik} \, .$$

Taking expectations and using linearity of expectation, we have

$$
\begin{aligned}
E[X_k] &= E\left[\sum_{i=1}^{n-k+1} X_{ik} \right] \\
&= \sum_{i=1}^{n-k+1} E[X_{ik}] \\
&= \sum_{i=1}^{n-k+1} Pr\{A_{ik}\} \\
&= \sum_{i=1}^{n-k+1} \frac{1}{2^k} \\
&= \frac{n-k+1}{2^k} \, .
\end{aligned}
$$

By plugging in various values for k, we can calculate the expected number of streaks of length at least k. If this expected number is large (much greater than 1), then we expect many streaks of length k to occur, and the probability that one occurs is high. If this expected number is small (much less than 1), then we expect to see few streaks of length k, and the probability that one occurs is low. If $k = c \lg n$, for some positive constant c, we obtain

$$
\begin{aligned}
E[X_{c \lg n}] &= \frac{n - c \lg n + 1}{2^{c \lg n}} \\
&= \frac{n - c \lg n + 1}{n^c} \\
&= \frac{1}{n^{c-1}} - \frac{(c \lg n - 1)/n}{n^{c-1}} \\
&= \Theta(1/n^{c-1}) \, .
\end{aligned}
$$

If c is large, the expected number of streaks of length $c \lg n$ is small, and we conclude that they are unlikely to occur. On the other hand, if $c = 1/2$, then we obtain $E[X_{(1/2)\lg n}] = \Theta(1/n^{1/2-1}) = \Theta(n^{1/2})$, and we expect there to be numerous streaks of length $(1/2)\lg n$. Therefore, one streak of such a length is likely to occur. We can conclude that the expected length of the longest streak is $\Theta(\lg n)$.

5.4.4   The online hiring problem

As a final example, let's consider a variant of the hiring problem. Suppose now that you do not wish to interview all the candidates in order to find the best one. You also want to avoid hiring and firing as you find better and better applicants. Instead, you are willing to settle for a candidate who is close to the best, in exchange for hiring exactly once. You must obey one company requirement: after each interview you must either immediately offer the position to the applicant or immediately reject the applicant. What is the trade-off between minimizing the amount of interviewing and maximizing the quality of the candidate hired?

We can model this problem in the following way. After meeting an applicant, you are able to give each one a score. Let $score(i)$ denote the score you give to the ith applicant, and assume that no two applicants receive the same score. After you have seen j applicants, you know which of the j has the highest score, but you do not know whether any of the remaining $n - j$ applicants will receive a higher score. You decide to adopt the strategy of selecting a positive integer $k < n$, interviewing and then rejecting the first k applicants, and hiring the first applicant thereafter who has a higher score than all preceding applicants. If it turns out that the best-qualified applicant was among the first k interviewed, then you hire the nth applicant—the last one interviewed. We formalize this strategy in the procedure ONLINE-MAXIMUM(k, n), which returns the index of the candidate you wish to hire.

```
ONLINE-MAXIMUM(k, n)
1   best-score = −∞
2   for i = 1 to k
3       if score(i) > best-score
4           best-score = score(i)
5   for i = k + 1 to n
6       if score(i) > best-score
7           return i
8   return n
```

If we determine, for each possible value of k, the probability that you hire the most qualified applicant, then you can choose the best possible k and implement the strategy with that value. For the moment, assume that k is fixed. Let

$M(j) = \max\{score(i) : 1 \leq i \leq j\}$ denote the maximum score among applicants 1 through j. Let S be the event that you succeed in choosing the best-qualified applicant, and let S_i be the event that you succeed when the best-qualified applicant is the ith one interviewed. Since the various S_i are disjoint, we have that $\Pr\{S\} = \sum_{i=1}^{n} \Pr\{S_i\}$. Noting that you never succeed when the best-qualified applicant is one of the first k, we have that $\Pr\{S_i\} = 0$ for $i = 1, 2, \ldots, k$. Thus, we obtain

$$\Pr\{S\} = \sum_{i=k+1}^{n} \Pr\{S_i\} . \tag{5.14}$$

We now compute $\Pr\{S_i\}$. In order to succeed when the best-qualified applicant is the ith one, two things must happen. First, the best-qualified applicant must be in position i, an event which we denote by B_i. Second, the algorithm must not select any of the applicants in positions $k + 1$ through $i - 1$, which happens only if, for each j such that $k + 1 \leq j \leq i - 1$, line 6 finds that $score(j) < best\text{-}score$. (Because scores are unique, we can ignore the possibility of $score(j) = best\text{-}score$.) In other words, all of the values $score(k + 1)$ through $score(i - 1)$ must be less than $M(k)$. If any are greater than $M(k)$, the algorithm instead returns the index of the first one that is greater. We use O_i to denote the event that none of the applicants in position $k + 1$ through $i - 1$ are chosen. Fortunately, the two events B_i and O_i are independent. The event O_i depends only on the relative ordering of the values in positions 1 through $i - 1$, whereas B_i depends only on whether the value in position i is greater than the values in all other positions. The ordering of the values in positions 1 through $i - 1$ does not affect whether the value in position i is greater than all of them, and the value in position i does not affect the ordering of the values in positions 1 through $i - 1$. Thus, we can apply equation (C.17) on page 1188 to obtain

$$\Pr\{S_i\} = \Pr\{B_i \cap O_i\} = \Pr\{B_i\}\Pr\{O_i\} .$$

We have $\Pr\{B_i\} = 1/n$ since the maximum is equally likely to be in any one of the n positions. For event O_i to occur, the maximum value in positions 1 through $i - 1$, which is equally likely to be in any of these $i - 1$ positions, must be in one of the first k positions. Consequently, $\Pr\{O_i\} = k/(i - 1)$ and $\Pr\{S_i\} = k/(n(i - 1))$. Using equation (5.14), we have

$$\Pr\{S\} = \sum_{i=k+1}^{n} \Pr\{S_i\}$$
$$= \sum_{i=k+1}^{n} \frac{k}{n(i - 1)}$$

$$= \frac{k}{n} \sum_{i=k+1}^{n} \frac{1}{i-1}$$

$$= \frac{k}{n} \sum_{i=k}^{n-1} \frac{1}{i} .$$

We approximate by integrals to bound this summation from above and below. By the inequalities (A.19) on page 1150, we have

$$\int_{k}^{n} \frac{1}{x} \, dx \le \sum_{i=k}^{n-1} \frac{1}{i} \le \int_{k-1}^{n-1} \frac{1}{x} \, dx .$$

Evaluating these definite integrals gives us the bounds

$$\frac{k}{n}(\ln n - \ln k) \le \Pr\{S\} \le \frac{k}{n}(\ln(n-1) - \ln(k-1)) ,$$

which provide a rather tight bound for $\Pr\{S\}$. Because you wish to maximize your probability of success, let us focus on choosing the value of k that maximizes the lower bound on $\Pr\{S\}$. (Besides, the lower-bound expression is easier to maximize than the upper-bound expression.) Differentiating the expression $(k/n)(\ln n - \ln k)$ with respect to k, we obtain

$$\frac{1}{n}(\ln n - \ln k - 1) .$$

Setting this derivative equal to 0, we see that you maximize the lower bound on the probability when $\ln k = \ln n - 1 = \ln(n/e)$ or, equivalently, when $k = n/e$. Thus, if you implement our strategy with $k = n/e$, you succeed in hiring the best-qualified applicant with probability at least $1/e$.

Exercises

5.4-1
How many people must there be in a room before the probability that someone has the same birthday as you do is at least $1/2$? How many people must there be before the probability that at least two people have a birthday on July 4 is greater than $1/2$?

5.4-2
How many people must there be in a room before the probability that two people have the same birthday is at least 0.99? For that many people, what is the expected number of pairs of people who have the same birthday?

5.4-3

You toss balls into b bins until some bin contains two balls. Each toss is independent, and each ball is equally likely to end up in any bin. What is the expected number of ball tosses?

★ 5.4-4

For the analysis of the birthday paradox, is it important that the birthdays be mutually independent, or is pairwise independence sufficient? Justify your answer.

★ 5.4-5

How many people should be invited to a party in order to make it likely that there are *three* people with the same birthday?

★ 5.4-6

What is the probability that a k-string (defined on page 1179) over a set of size n forms a k-permutation? How does this question relate to the birthday paradox?

★ 5.4-7

You toss n balls into n bins, where each toss is independent and the ball is equally likely to end up in any bin. What is the expected number of empty bins? What is the expected number of bins with exactly one ball?

★ 5.4-8

Sharpen the lower bound on streak length by showing that in n flips of a fair coin, the probability is at least $1 - 1/n$ that a streak of length $\lg n - 2 \lg \lg n$ consecutive heads occurs.

Problems

5-1 *Probabilistic counting*

With a b-bit counter, we can ordinarily only count up to $2^b - 1$. With R. Morris's *probabilistic counting*, we can count up to a much larger value at the expense of some loss of precision.

We let a counter value of i represent a count of n_i for $i = 0, 1, \ldots, 2^b - 1$, where the n_i form an increasing sequence of nonnegative values. We assume that the initial value of the counter is 0, representing a count of $n_0 = 0$. The INCREMENT operation works on a counter containing the value i in a probabilistic manner. If $i = 2^b - 1$, then the operation reports an overflow error. Otherwise, the INCREMENT operation increases the counter by 1 with probability $1/(n_{i+1} - n_i)$, and it leaves the counter unchanged with probability $1 - 1/(n_{i+1} - n_i)$.

If we select $n_i = i$ for all $i \geq 0$, then the counter is an ordinary one. More interesting situations arise if we select, say, $n_i = 2^{i-1}$ for $i > 0$ or $n_i = F_i$ (the ith Fibonacci number—see equation (3.31) on page 69).

For this problem, assume that n_{2^b-1} is large enough that the probability of an overflow error is negligible.

a. Show that the expected value represented by the counter after n INCREMENT operations have been performed is exactly n.

b. The analysis of the variance of the count represented by the counter depends on the sequence of the n_i. Let us consider a simple case: $n_i = 100i$ for all $i \geq 0$. Estimate the variance in the value represented by the register after n INCREMENT operations have been performed.

5-2   *Searching an unsorted array*

This problem examines three algorithms for searching for a value x in an unsorted array A consisting of n elements.

Consider the following randomized strategy: pick a random index i into A. If $A[i] = x$, then terminate; otherwise, continue the search by picking a new random index into A. Continue picking random indices into A until you find an index j such that $A[j] = x$ or until every element of A has been checked. This strategy may examine a given element more than once, because it picks from the whole set of indices each time.

a. Write pseudocode for a procedure RANDOM-SEARCH to implement the strategy above. Be sure that your algorithm terminates when all indices into A have been picked.

b. Suppose that there is exactly one index i such that $A[i] = x$. What is the expected number of indices into A that must be picked before x is found and RANDOM-SEARCH terminates?

c. Generalizing your solution to part (b), suppose that there are $k \geq 1$ indices i such that $A[i] = x$. What is the expected number of indices into A that must be picked before x is found and RANDOM-SEARCH terminates? Your answer should be a function of n and k.

d. Suppose that there are no indices i such that $A[i] = x$. What is the expected number of indices into A that must be picked before all elements of A have been checked and RANDOM-SEARCH terminates?

Now consider a deterministic linear search algorithm. The algorithm, which we call DETERMINISTIC-SEARCH, searches A for x in order, considering $A[1]$, $A[2]$,

$A[3], \ldots, A[n]$ until either it finds $A[i] = x$ or it reaches the end of the array. Assume that all possible permutations of the input array are equally likely.

e. Suppose that there is exactly one index i such that $A[i] = x$. What is the average-case running time of DETERMINISTIC-SEARCH? What is the worst-case running time of DETERMINISTIC-SEARCH?

f. Generalizing your solution to part (e), suppose that there are $k \geq 1$ indices i such that $A[i] = x$. What is the average-case running time of DETERMINISTIC-SEARCH? What is the worst-case running time of DETERMINISTIC-SEARCH? Your answer should be a function of n and k.

g. Suppose that there are no indices i such that $A[i] = x$. What is the average-case running time of DETERMINISTIC-SEARCH? What is the worst-case running time of DETERMINISTIC-SEARCH?

Finally, consider a randomized algorithm SCRAMBLE-SEARCH that first randomly permutes the input array and then runs the deterministic linear search given above on the resulting permuted array.

h. Letting k be the number of indices i such that $A[i] = x$, give the worst-case and expected running times of SCRAMBLE-SEARCH for the cases in which $k = 0$ and $k = 1$. Generalize your solution to handle the case in which $k \geq 1$.

i. Which of the three searching algorithms would you use? Explain your answer.

Chapter notes

Bollobás [65], Hofri [223], and Spencer [420] contain a wealth of advanced probabilistic techniques. The advantages of randomized algorithms are discussed and surveyed by Karp [249] and Rabin [372]. The textbook by Motwani and Raghavan [336] gives an extensive treatment of randomized algorithms.

The RANDOMLY-PERMUTE procedure is by Durstenfeld [128], based on an earlier procedure by Fisher and Yates [143, p. 34].

Several variants of the hiring problem have been widely studied. These problems are more commonly referred to as "secretary problems." Examples of work in this area are the paper by Ajtai, Meggido, and Waarts [11] and another by Kleinberg [258], which ties the secretary problem to online ad auctions.

Part II   Sorting and Order Statistics

Introduction

This part presents several algorithms that solve the following *sorting problem*:

Input: A sequence of n numbers $\langle a_1, a_2, \ldots, a_n \rangle$.

Output: A permutation (reordering) $\langle a'_1, a'_2, \ldots, a'_n \rangle$ of the input sequence such that $a'_1 \leq a'_2 \leq \cdots \leq a'_n$.

The input sequence is usually an n-element array, although it may be represented in some other fashion, such as a linked list.

The structure of the data

In practice, the numbers to be sorted are rarely isolated values. Each is usually part of a collection of data called a *record*. Each record contains a *key*, which is the value to be sorted. The remainder of the record consists of *satellite data*, which are usually carried around with the key. In practice, when a sorting algorithm permutes the keys, it must permute the satellite data as well. If each record includes a large amount of satellite data, it often pays to permute an array of pointers to the records rather than the records themselves in order to minimize data movement.

In a sense, it is these implementation details that distinguish an algorithm from a full-blown program. A sorting algorithm describes the *method* to determine the sorted order, regardless of whether what's being sorted are individual numbers or large records containing many bytes of satellite data. Thus, when focusing on the problem of sorting, we typically assume that the input consists only of numbers. Translating an algorithm for sorting numbers into a program for sorting records is conceptually straightforward, although in a given engineering situation other subtleties may make the actual programming task a challenge.

Why sorting?

Many computer scientists consider sorting to be the most fundamental problem in the study of algorithms. There are several reasons:

- Sometimes an application inherently needs to sort information. For example, in order to prepare customer statements, banks need to sort checks by check number.

- Algorithms often use sorting as a key subroutine. For example, a program that renders graphical objects which are layered on top of each other might have to sort the objects according to an "above" relation so that it can draw these objects from bottom to top. We will see numerous algorithms in this text that use sorting as a subroutine.

- We can draw from among a wide variety of sorting algorithms, and they employ a rich set of techniques. In fact, many important techniques used throughout algorithm design appear in sorting algorithms that have been developed over the years. In this way, sorting is also a problem of historical interest.

- We can prove a nontrivial lower bound for sorting (as we'll do in Chapter 8). Since the best upper bounds match the lower bound asymptotically, we can conclude that certain of our sorting algorithms are asymptotically optimal. Moreover, we can use the lower bound for sorting to prove lower bounds for various other problems.

- Many engineering issues come to the fore when implementing sorting algorithms. The fastest sorting program for a particular situation may depend on many factors, such as prior knowledge about the keys and satellite data, the memory hierarchy (caches and virtual memory) of the host computer, and the software environment. Many of these issues are best dealt with at the algorithmic level, rather than by "tweaking" the code.

Sorting algorithms

We introduced two algorithms that sort n real numbers in Chapter 2. Insertion sort takes $\Theta(n^2)$ time in the worst case. Because its inner loops are tight, however, it is a fast sorting algorithm for small input sizes. Moreover, unlike merge sort, it sorts *in place*, meaning that at most a constant number of elements of the input array are ever stored outside the array, which can be advantageous for space efficiency. Merge sort has a better asymptotic running time, $\Theta(n \lg n)$, but the MERGE procedure it uses does not operate in place. (We'll see a parallelized version of merge sort in Section 26.3.)

This part introduces two more algorithms that sort arbitrary real numbers. Heapsort, presented in Chapter 6, sorts n numbers in place in $O(n \lg n)$ time. It uses an important data structure, called a heap, which can also implement a priority queue.

Quicksort, in Chapter 7, also sorts n numbers in place, but its worst-case running time is $\Theta(n^2)$. Its expected running time is $\Theta(n \lg n)$, however, and it generally outperforms heapsort in practice. Like insertion sort, quicksort has tight code, and so the hidden constant factor in its running time is small. It is a popular algorithm for sorting large arrays.

Insertion sort, merge sort, heapsort, and quicksort are all comparison sorts: they determine the sorted order of an input array by comparing elements. Chapter 8 begins by introducing the decision-tree model in order to study the performance limitations of comparison sorts. Using this model, we prove a lower bound of $\Omega(n \lg n)$ on the worst-case running time of any comparison sort on n inputs, thus showing that heapsort and merge sort are asymptotically optimal comparison sorts.

Chapter 8 then goes on to show that we might be able to beat this lower bound of $\Omega(n \lg n)$ if an algorithm can gather information about the sorted order of the input by means other than comparing elements. The counting sort algorithm, for example, assumes that the input numbers belong to the set $\{0, 1, \ldots, k\}$. By using array indexing as a tool for determining relative order, counting sort can sort n numbers in $\Theta(k + n)$ time. Thus, when $k = O(n)$, counting sort runs in time that is linear in the size of the input array. A related algorithm, radix sort, can be used to extend the range of counting sort. If there are n integers to sort, each integer has d digits, and each digit can take on up to k possible values, then radix sort can sort the numbers in $\Theta(d(n + k))$ time. When d is a constant and k is $O(n)$, radix sort runs in linear time. A third algorithm, bucket sort, requires knowledge of the probabilistic distribution of numbers in the input array. It can sort n real numbers uniformly distributed in the half-open interval $[0, 1)$ in average-case $O(n)$ time.

The table on the following page summarizes the running times of the sorting algorithms from Chapters 2 and 6–8. As usual, n denotes the number of items to sort. For counting sort, the items to sort are integers in the set $\{0, 1, \ldots, k\}$. For radix sort, each item is a d-digit number, where each digit takes on k possible values. For bucket sort, we assume that the keys are real numbers uniformly distributed in the half-open interval $[0, 1)$. The rightmost column gives the average-case or expected running time, indicating which one it gives when it differs from the worst-case running time. We omit the average-case running time of heapsort because we do not analyze it in this book.

Algorithm	Worst-case running time	Average-case/expected running time
Insertion sort	$\Theta(n^2)$	$\Theta(n^2)$
Merge sort	$\Theta(n \lg n)$	$\Theta(n \lg n)$
Heapsort	$O(n \lg n)$	—
Quicksort	$\Theta(n^2)$	$\Theta(n \lg n)$ (expected)
Counting sort	$\Theta(k + n)$	$\Theta(k + n)$
Radix sort	$\Theta(d(n + k))$	$\Theta(d(n + k))$
Bucket sort	$\Theta(n^2)$	$\Theta(n)$ (average-case)

Order statistics

The ith order statistic of a set of n numbers is the ith smallest number in the set. You can, of course, select the ith order statistic by sorting the input and indexing the ith element of the output. With no assumptions about the input distribution, this method runs in $\Omega(n \lg n)$ time, as the lower bound proved in Chapter 8 shows.

Chapter 9 shows how to find the ith smallest element in $O(n)$ time, even when the elements are arbitrary real numbers. We present a randomized algorithm with tight pseudocode that runs in $\Theta(n^2)$ time in the worst case, but whose expected running time is $O(n)$. We also give a more complicated algorithm that runs in $O(n)$ worst-case time.

Background

Although most of this part does not rely on difficult mathematics, some sections do require mathematical sophistication. In particular, analyses of quicksort, bucket sort, and the order-statistic algorithm use probability, which is reviewed in Appendix C, and the material on probabilistic analysis and randomized algorithms in Chapter 5.

6 Heapsort

This chapter introduces another sorting algorithm: heapsort. Like merge sort, but unlike insertion sort, heapsort's running time is $O(n \lg n)$. Like insertion sort, but unlike merge sort, heapsort sorts in place: only a constant number of array elements are stored outside the input array at any time. Thus, heapsort combines the better attributes of the two sorting algorithms we have already discussed.

Heapsort also introduces another algorithm design technique: using a data structure, in this case one we call a "heap," to manage information. Not only is the heap data structure useful for heapsort, but it also makes an efficient priority queue. The heap data structure will reappear in algorithms in later chapters.

The term "heap" was originally coined in the context of heapsort, but it has since come to refer to "garbage-collected storage," such as the programming languages Java and Python provide. Please don't be confused. The heap data structure is *not* garbage-collected storage. This book is consistent in using the term "heap" to refer to the data structure, not the storage class.

6.1 Heaps

The *(binary) heap* data structure is an array object that we can view as a nearly complete binary tree (see Section B.5.3), as shown in Figure 6.1. Each node of the tree corresponds to an element of the array. The tree is completely filled on all levels except possibly the lowest, which is filled from the left up to a point. An array $A[1:n]$ that represents a heap is an object with an attribute $A.heap\text{-}size$, which represents how many elements in the heap are stored within array A. That is, although $A[1:n]$ may contain numbers, only the elements in $A[1:A.heap\text{-}size]$, where $0 \le A.heap\text{-}size \le n$, are valid elements of the heap. If $A.heap\text{-}size = 0$, then the heap is empty. The root of the tree is $A[1]$, and given the index i of a node,

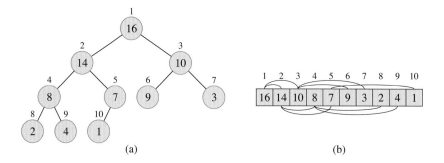

Figure 6.1 A max-heap viewed as **(a)** a binary tree and **(b)** an array. The number within the circle at each node in the tree is the value stored at that node. The number above a node is the corresponding index in the array. Above and below the array are lines showing parent-child relationships, with parents always to the left of their children. The tree has height 3, and the node at index 4 (with value 8) has height 1.

there's a simple way to compute the indices of its parent, left child, and right child with the one-line procedures PARENT, LEFT, and RIGHT.

PARENT(i)
1   **return** $\lfloor i/2 \rfloor$

LEFT(i)
1   **return** $2i$

RIGHT(i)
1   **return** $2i + 1$

On most computers, the LEFT procedure can compute $2i$ in one instruction by simply shifting the binary representation of i left by one bit position. Similarly, the RIGHT procedure can quickly compute $2i + 1$ by shifting the binary representation of i left by one bit position and then adding 1. The PARENT procedure can compute $\lfloor i/2 \rfloor$ by shifting i right one bit position. Good implementations of heapsort often implement these procedures as macros or inline procedures.

There are two kinds of binary heaps: max-heaps and min-heaps. In both kinds, the values in the nodes satisfy a *heap property*, the specifics of which depend on the kind of heap. In a *max-heap*, the *max-heap property* is that for every node i other than the root,

$$A[\text{PARENT}(i)] \geq A[i] \,,$$

that is, the value of a node is at most the value of its parent. Thus, the largest element in a max-heap is stored at the root, and the subtree rooted at a node contains values no larger than that contained at the node itself. A *min-heap* is organized in the opposite way: the *min-heap property* is that for every node i other than the root,

$$A[\text{PARENT}(i)] \leq A[i] .$$

The smallest element in a min-heap is at the root.

The heapsort algorithm uses max-heaps. Min-heaps commonly implement priority queues, which we discuss in Section 6.5. We'll be precise in specifying whether we need a max-heap or a min-heap for any particular application, and when properties apply to either max-heaps or min-heaps, we just use the term "heap."

Viewing a heap as a tree, we define the *height* of a node in a heap to be the number of edges on the longest simple downward path from the node to a leaf, and we define the height of the heap to be the height of its root. Since a heap of n elements is based on a complete binary tree, its height is $\Theta(\lg n)$ (see Exercise 6.1-2). As we'll see, the basic operations on heaps run in time at most proportional to the height of the tree and thus take $O(\lg n)$ time. The remainder of this chapter presents some basic procedures and shows how they are used in a sorting algorithm and a priority-queue data structure.

- The MAX-HEAPIFY procedure, which runs in $O(\lg n)$ time, is the key to maintaining the max-heap property.

- The BUILD-MAX-HEAP procedure, which runs in linear time, produces a max-heap from an unordered input array.

- The HEAPSORT procedure, which runs in $O(n \lg n)$ time, sorts an array in place.

- The procedures MAX-HEAP-INSERT, MAX-HEAP-EXTRACT-MAX, MAX-HEAP-INCREASE-KEY, and MAX-HEAP-MAXIMUM allow the heap data structure to implement a priority queue. They run in $O(\lg n)$ time plus the time for mapping between objects being inserted into the priority queue and indices in the heap.

Exercises

6.1-1
What are the minimum and maximum numbers of elements in a heap of height h?

6.1-2
Show that an n-element heap has height $\lfloor \lg n \rfloor$.

6.1-3
Show that in any subtree of a max-heap, the root of the subtree contains the largest value occurring anywhere in that subtree.

6.1-4
Where in a max-heap might the smallest element reside, assuming that all elements are distinct?

6.1-5
At which levels in a max-heap might the kth largest element reside, for $2 \leq k \leq \lfloor n/2 \rfloor$, assuming that all elements are distinct?

6.1-6
Is an array that is in sorted order a min-heap?

6.1-7
Is the array with values $\langle 33, 19, 20, 15, 13, 10, 2, 13, 16, 12 \rangle$ a max-heap?

6.1-8
Show that, with the array representation for storing an n-element heap, the leaves are the nodes indexed by $\lfloor n/2 \rfloor + 1, \lfloor n/2 \rfloor + 2, \ldots, n$.

6.2   Maintaining the heap property

The procedure MAX-HEAPIFY on the facing page maintains the max-heap property. Its inputs are an array A with the *heap-size* attribute and an index i into the array. When it is called, MAX-HEAPIFY assumes that the binary trees rooted at LEFT(i) and RIGHT(i) are max-heaps, but that $A[i]$ might be smaller than its children, thus violating the max-heap property. MAX-HEAPIFY lets the value at $A[i]$ "float down" in the max-heap so that the subtree rooted at index i obeys the max-heap property.

Figure 6.2 illustrates the action of MAX-HEAPIFY. Each step determines the largest of the elements $A[i]$, $A[\text{LEFT}(i)]$, and $A[\text{RIGHT}(i)]$ and stores the index of the largest element in *largest*. If $A[i]$ is largest, then the subtree rooted at node i is already a max-heap and nothing else needs to be done. Otherwise, one of the two children contains the largest element. Positions i and *largest* swap their contents, which causes node i and its children to satisfy the max-heap property. The node indexed by *largest*, however, just had its value decreased, and thus the subtree rooted at *largest* might violate the max-heap property. Consequently, MAX-HEAPIFY calls itself recursively on that subtree.

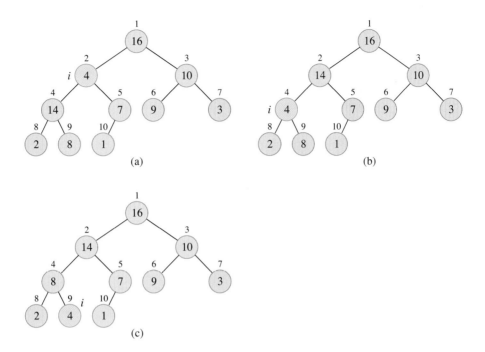

Figure 6.2   The action of MAX-HEAPIFY($A, 2$), where $A.\textit{heap-size} = 10$. The node that potentially violates the max-heap property is shown in blue. **(a)** The initial configuration, with $A[2]$ at node $i = 2$ violating the max-heap property since it is not larger than both children. The max-heap property is restored for node 2 in **(b)** by exchanging $A[2]$ with $A[4]$, which destroys the max-heap property for node 4. The recursive call MAX-HEAPIFY($A, 4$) now has $i = 4$. After $A[4]$ and $A[9]$ are swapped, as shown in **(c)**, node 4 is fixed up, and the recursive call MAX-HEAPIFY($A, 9$) yields no further change to the data structure.

MAX-HEAPIFY(A, i)

```
1   l = LEFT(i)
2   r = RIGHT(i)
3   if l ≤ A.heap-size and A[l] > A[i]
4       largest = l
5   else largest = i
6   if r ≤ A.heap-size and A[r] > A[largest]
7       largest = r
8   if largest ≠ i
9       exchange A[i] with A[largest]
10      MAX-HEAPIFY(A, largest)
```

To analyze MAX-HEAPIFY, let $T(n)$ be the worst-case running time that the procedure takes on a subtree of size at most n. For a tree rooted at a given node i, the running time is the $\Theta(1)$ time to fix up the relationships among the elements $A[i]$, $A[\text{LEFT}(i)]$, and $A[\text{RIGHT}(i)]$, plus the time to run MAX-HEAPIFY on a subtree rooted at one of the children of node i (assuming that the recursive call occurs). The children's subtrees each have size at most $2n/3$ (see Exercise 6.2-2), and therefore we can describe the running time of MAX-HEAPIFY by the recurrence

$$T(n) \leq T(2n/3) + \Theta(1) . \tag{6.1}$$

The solution to this recurrence, by case 2 of the master theorem (Theorem 4.1 on page 102), is $T(n) = O(\lg n)$. Alternatively, we can characterize the running time of MAX-HEAPIFY on a node of height h as $O(h)$.

Exercises

6.2-1
Using Figure 6.2 as a model, illustrate the operation of MAX-HEAPIFY$(A, 3)$ on the array $A = \langle 27, 17, 3, 16, 13, 10, 1, 5, 7, 12, 4, 8, 9, 0 \rangle$.

6.2-2
Show that each child of the root of an n-node heap is the root of a subtree containing at most $2n/3$ nodes. What is the smallest constant α such that each subtree has at most αn nodes? How does that affect the recurrence (6.1) and its solution?

6.2-3
Starting with the procedure MAX-HEAPIFY, write pseudocode for the procedure MIN-HEAPIFY(A, i), which performs the corresponding manipulation on a min-heap. How does the running time of MIN-HEAPIFY compare with that of MAX-HEAPIFY?

6.2-4
What is the effect of calling MAX-HEAPIFY(A, i) when the element $A[i]$ is larger than its children?

6.2-5
What is the effect of calling MAX-HEAPIFY(A, i) for $i > A.heap\text{-}size/2$?

6.2-6
The code for MAX-HEAPIFY is quite efficient in terms of constant factors, except possibly for the recursive call in line 10, for which some compilers might produce inefficient code. Write an efficient MAX-HEAPIFY that uses an iterative control construct (a loop) instead of recursion.

6.2-7

Show that the worst-case running time of MAX-HEAPIFY on a heap of size n is $\Omega(\lg n)$. (*Hint:* For a heap with n nodes, give node values that cause MAX-HEAPIFY to be called recursively at every node on a simple path from the root down to a leaf.)

6.3   Building a heap

The procedure BUILD-MAX-HEAP converts an array $A[1:n]$ into a max-heap by calling MAX-HEAPIFY in a bottom-up manner. Exercise 6.1-8 says that the elements in the subarray $A[\lfloor n/2 \rfloor + 1 : n]$ are all leaves of the tree, and so each is a 1-element heap to begin with. BUILD-MAX-HEAP goes through the remaining nodes of the tree and runs MAX-HEAPIFY on each one. Figure 6.3 shows an example of the action of BUILD-MAX-HEAP.

```
BUILD-MAX-HEAP(A, n)

1   A.heap-size = n
2   for i = ⌊n/2⌋ downto 1
3       MAX-HEAPIFY(A, i)
```

To show why BUILD-MAX-HEAP works correctly, we use the following loop invariant:

> At the start of each iteration of the **for** loop of lines 2–3, each node $i + 1$, $i + 2, \ldots, n$ is the root of a max-heap.

We need to show that this invariant is true prior to the first loop iteration, that each iteration of the loop maintains the invariant, that the loop terminates, and that the invariant provides a useful property to show correctness when the loop terminates.

Initialization: Prior to the first iteration of the loop, $i = \lfloor n/2 \rfloor$. Each node $\lfloor n/2 \rfloor + 1, \lfloor n/2 \rfloor + 2, \ldots, n$ is a leaf and is thus the root of a trivial max-heap.

Maintenance: To see that each iteration maintains the loop invariant, observe that the children of node i are numbered higher than i. By the loop invariant, therefore, they are both roots of max-heaps. This is precisely the condition required for the call MAX-HEAPIFY(A, i) to make node i a max-heap root. Moreover, the MAX-HEAPIFY call preserves the property that nodes $i + 1$, $i + 2, \ldots, n$ are all roots of max-heaps. Decrementing i in the **for** loop update reestablishes the loop invariant for the next iteration.

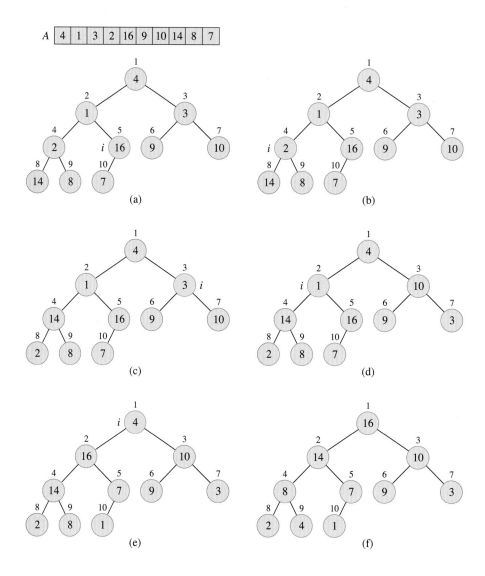

Figure 6.3 The operation of BUILD-MAX-HEAP, showing the data structure before the call to MAX-HEAPIFY in line 3 of BUILD-MAX-HEAP. The node indexed by i in each iteration is shown in blue. **(a)** A 10-element input array A and the binary tree it represents. The loop index i refers to node 5 before the call MAX-HEAPIFY(A, i). **(b)** The data structure that results. The loop index i for the next iteration refers to node 4. **(c)–(e)** Subsequent iterations of the **for** loop in BUILD-MAX-HEAP. Observe that whenever MAX-HEAPIFY is called on a node, the two subtrees of that node are both max-heaps. **(f)** The max-heap after BUILD-MAX-HEAP finishes.

Termination: The loop makes exactly $\lfloor n/2 \rfloor$ iterations, and so it terminates. At
termination, $i = 0$. By the loop invariant, each node $1, 2, \ldots, n$ is the root of a
max-heap. In particular, node 1 is.

We can compute a simple upper bound on the running time of BUILD-MAX-
HEAP as follows. Each call to MAX-HEAPIFY costs $O(\lg n)$ time, and BUILD-
MAX-HEAP makes $O(n)$ such calls. Thus, the running time is $O(n \lg n)$. This
upper bound, though correct, is not as tight as it can be.

We can derive a tighter asymptotic bound by observing that the time for MAX-
HEAPIFY to run at a node varies with the height of the node in the tree, and that the
heights of most nodes are small. Our tighter analysis relies on the properties that
an n-element heap has height $\lfloor \lg n \rfloor$ (see Exercise 6.1-2) and at most $\lceil n/2^{h+1} \rceil$
nodes of any height h (see Exercise 6.3-4).

The time required by MAX-HEAPIFY when called on a node of height h
is $O(h)$. Letting c be the constant implicit in the asymptotic notation, we can
express the total cost of BUILD-MAX-HEAP as being bounded from above by
$\sum_{h=0}^{\lfloor \lg n \rfloor} \lceil n/2^{h+1} \rceil ch$. As Exercise 6.3-2 shows, we have $\lceil n/2^{h+1} \rceil \geq 1/2$ for
$0 \leq h \leq \lfloor \lg n \rfloor$. Since $\lceil x \rceil \leq 2x$ for any $x \geq 1/2$, we have $\lceil n/2^{h+1} \rceil \leq n/2^h$. We
thus obtain

$$
\sum_{h=0}^{\lfloor \lg n \rfloor} \left\lceil \frac{n}{2^{h+1}} \right\rceil ch
$$

$$
\leq \sum_{h=0}^{\lfloor \lg n \rfloor} \frac{n}{2^h} ch
$$

$$
= cn \sum_{h=0}^{\lfloor \lg n \rfloor} \frac{h}{2^h}
$$

$$
\leq cn \sum_{h=0}^{\infty} \frac{h}{2^h}
$$

$$
\leq cn \cdot \frac{1/2}{(1 - 1/2)^2} \quad \text{(by equation (A.11) on page 1142 with } x = 1/2)
$$

$$
= O(n) \, .
$$

Hence, we can build a max-heap from an unordered array in linear time.

To build a min-heap, use the procedure BUILD-MIN-HEAP, which is the same as
BUILD-MAX-HEAP but with the call to MAX-HEAPIFY in line 3 replaced by a call
to MIN-HEAPIFY (see Exercise 6.2-3). BUILD-MIN-HEAP produces a min-heap
from an unordered linear array in linear time.

Exercises

6.3-1
Using Figure 6.3 as a model, illustrate the operation of BUILD-MAX-HEAP on the array $A = \langle 5, 3, 17, 10, 84, 19, 6, 22, 9 \rangle$.

6.3-2
Show that $\lceil n/2^{h+1} \rceil \geq 1/2$ for $0 \leq h \leq \lfloor \lg n \rfloor$.

6.3-3
Why does the loop index i in line 2 of BUILD-MAX-HEAP decrease from $\lfloor n/2 \rfloor$ to 1 rather than increase from 1 to $\lfloor n/2 \rfloor$?

6.3-4
Show that there are at most $\lceil n/2^{h+1} \rceil$ nodes of height h in any n-element heap.

6.4   The heapsort algorithm

The heapsort algorithm, given by the procedure HEAPSORT, starts by calling the BUILD-MAX-HEAP procedure to build a max-heap on the input array $A[1:n]$. Since the maximum element of the array is stored at the root $A[1]$, HEAPSORT can place it into its correct final position by exchanging it with $A[n]$. If the procedure then discards node n from the heap—and it can do so by simply decrementing *A.heap-size*—the children of the root remain max-heaps, but the new root element might violate the max-heap property. To restore the max-heap property, the procedure just calls MAX-HEAPIFY$(A, 1)$, which leaves a max-heap in $A[1:n-1]$. The HEAPSORT procedure then repeats this process for the max-heap of size $n - 1$ down to a heap of size 2. (See Exercise 6.4-2 for a precise loop invariant.)

HEAPSORT(A, n)

1   BUILD-MAX-HEAP(A, n)
2   **for** $i = n$ **downto** 2
3   exchange $A[1]$ with $A[i]$
4      $A.heap\text{-}size = A.heap\text{-}size - 1$
5   MAX-HEAPIFY$(A, 1)$

Figure 6.4 shows an example of the operation of HEAPSORT after line 1 has built the initial max-heap. The figure shows the max-heap before the first iteration of the **for** loop of lines 2–5 and after each iteration.

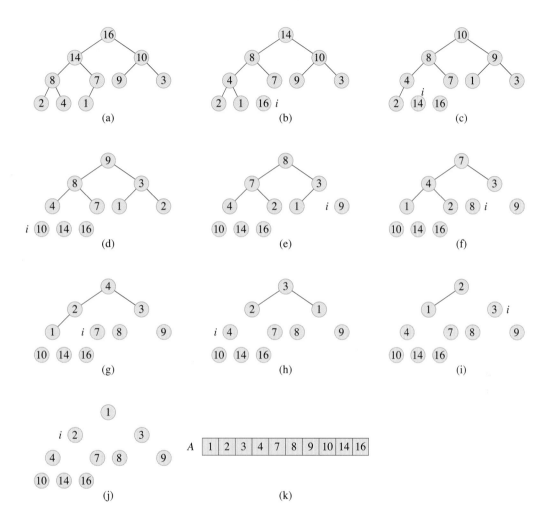

Figure 6.4   The operation of HEAPSORT. **(a)** The max-heap data structure just after BUILD-MAX-HEAP has built it in line 1. **(b)–(j)** The max-heap just after each call of MAX-HEAPIFY in line 5, showing the value of i at that time. Only blue nodes remain in the heap. Tan nodes contain the largest values in the array, in sorted order. **(k)** The resulting sorted array A.

The HEAPSORT procedure takes $O(n \lg n)$ time, since the call to BUILD-MAX-HEAP takes $O(n)$ time and each of the $n-1$ calls to MAX-HEAPIFY takes $O(\lg n)$ time.

Exercises

6.4-1
Using Figure 6.4 as a model, illustrate the operation of HEAPSORT on the array $A = \langle 5, 13, 2, 25, 7, 17, 20, 8, 4 \rangle$.

6.4-2
Argue the correctness of HEAPSORT using the following loop invariant:

> At the start of each iteration of the **for** loop of lines 2–5, the subarray $A[1:i]$ is a max-heap containing the i smallest elements of $A[1:n]$, and the subarray $A[i+1:n]$ contains the $n-i$ largest elements of $A[1:n]$, sorted.

6.4-3
What is the running time of HEAPSORT on an array A of length n that is already sorted in increasing order? How about if the array is already sorted in decreasing order?

6.4-4
Show that the worst-case running time of HEAPSORT is $\Omega(n \lg n)$.

★ ***6.4-5***
Show that when all the elements of A are distinct, the best-case running time of HEAPSORT is $\Omega(n \lg n)$.

6.5   Priority queues

In Chapter 8, we will see that any comparison-based sorting algorithm requires $\Omega(n \lg n)$ comparisons and hence $\Omega(n \lg n)$ time. Therefore, heapsort is asymptotically optimal among comparison-based sorting algorithms. Yet, a good implementation of quicksort, presented in Chapter 7, usually beats it in practice. Nevertheless, the heap data structure itself has many uses. In this section, we present one of the most popular applications of a heap: as an efficient priority queue. As with heaps, priority queues come in two forms: max-priority queues and min-priority queues. We'll focus here on how to implement max-priority queues, which are in turn based on max-heaps. Exercise 6.5-3 asks you to write the procedures for min-priority queues.

A *priority queue* is a data structure for maintaining a set S of elements, each with an associated value called a *key*. A *max-priority queue* supports the following operations:

INSERT(S, x, k) inserts the element x with key k into the set S, which is equivalent to the operation $S = S \cup \{x\}$.

MAXIMUM(S) returns the element of S with the largest key.

EXTRACT-MAX(S) removes and returns the element of S with the largest key.

INCREASE-KEY(S, x, k) increases the value of element x's key to the new value k, which is assumed to be at least as large as x's current key value.

Among their other applications, you can use max-priority queues to schedule jobs on a computer shared among multiple users. The max-priority queue keeps track of the jobs to be performed and their relative priorities. When a job is finished or interrupted, the scheduler selects the highest-priority job from among those pending by calling EXTRACT-MAX. The scheduler can add a new job to the queue at any time by calling INSERT.

Alternatively, a *min-priority queue* supports the operations INSERT, MINIMUM, EXTRACT-MIN, and DECREASE-KEY. A min-priority queue can be used in an event-driven simulator. The items in the queue are events to be simulated, each with an associated time of occurrence that serves as its key. The events must be simulated in order of their time of occurrence, because the simulation of an event can cause other events to be simulated in the future. The simulation program calls EXTRACT-MIN at each step to choose the next event to simulate. As new events are produced, the simulator inserts them into the min-priority queue by calling INSERT. We'll see other uses for min-priority queues, highlighting the DECREASE-KEY operation, in Chapters 21 and 22.

When you use a heap to implement a priority queue within a given application, elements of the priority queue correspond to objects in the application. Each object contains a key. If the priority queue is implemented by a heap, you need to determine which application object corresponds to a given heap element, and vice versa. Because the heap elements are stored in an array, you need a way to map application objects to and from array indices.

One way to map between application objects and heap elements uses *handles*, which are additional information stored in the objects and heap elements that give enough information to perform the mapping. Handles are often implemented to be opaque to the surrounding code, thereby maintaining an abstraction barrier between the application and the priority queue. For example, the handle within an application object might contain the corresponding index into the heap array. But since only the code for the priority queue accesses this index, the index is entirely hidden from the application code. Because heap elements change locations within the array during heap operations, an actual implementation of the priority queue, upon relocating a heap element, must also update the array indices in the corresponding handles. Conversely, each element in the heap might contain a pointer to the corresponding application object, but the heap element knows this pointer as only an opaque handle and the application maps this handle to an application object. Typically, the worst-case overhead for maintaining handles is $O(1)$ per access.

As an alternative to incorporating handles in application objects, you can store within the priority queue a mapping from application objects to array indices in the heap. The advantage of doing so is that the mapping is contained entirely within the priority queue, so that the application objects need no further embellishment. The disadvantage lies in the additional cost of establishing and maintaining the mapping. One option for the mapping is a hash table (see Chapter 11).[1] The added expected time for a hash table to map an object to an array index is just $O(1)$, though the worst-case time can be as bad as $\Theta(n)$.

Let's see how to implement the operations of a max-priority queue using a max-heap. In the previous sections, we treated the array elements as the keys to be sorted, implicitly assuming that any satellite data moved with the corresponding keys. When a heap implements a priority queue, we instead treat each array element as a pointer to an object in the priority queue, so that the object is analogous to the satellite data when sorting. We further assume that each such object has an attribute *key*, which determines where in the heap the object belongs. For a heap implemented by an array A, we refer to $A[i].key$.

The procedure MAX-HEAP-MAXIMUM on the facing page implements the MAXIMUM operation in $\Theta(1)$ time, and MAX-HEAP-EXTRACT-MAX implements the operation EXTRACT-MAX. MAX-HEAP-EXTRACT-MAX is similar to the **for** loop body (lines 3–5) of the HEAPSORT procedure. We implicitly assume that MAX-HEAPIFY compares priority-queue objects based on their *key* attributes. We also assume that when MAX-HEAPIFY exchanges elements in the array, it is exchanging pointers and also that it updates the mapping between objects and array indices. The running time of MAX-HEAP-EXTRACT-MAX is $O(\lg n)$, since it performs only a constant amount of work on top of the $O(\lg n)$ time for MAX-HEAPIFY, plus whatever overhead is incurred within MAX-HEAPIFY for mapping priority-queue objects to array indices.

The procedure MAX-HEAP-INCREASE-KEY on page 176 implements the INCREASE-KEY operation. It first verifies that the new key k will not cause the key in the object x to decrease, and if there is no problem, it gives x the new key value. The procedure then finds the index i in the array corresponding to object x,

---

[1] In Python, dictionaries are implemented with hash tables.

MAX-HEAP-MAXIMUM(*A*)

1 **if** *A.heap-size* < 1
2   **error** "heap underflow"
3 **return** *A*[1]

MAX-HEAP-EXTRACT-MAX(*A*)

1 *max* = MAX-HEAP-MAXIMUM(*A*)
2 *A*[1] = *A*[*A.heap-size*]
3 *A.heap-size* = *A.heap-size* − 1
4 MAX-HEAPIFY(*A*, 1)
5 **return** *max*

so that $A[i]$ is x. Because increasing the key of $A[i]$ might violate the max-heap property, the procedure then, in a manner reminiscent of the insertion loop (lines 5–7) of INSERTION-SORT on page 19, traverses a simple path from this node toward the root to find a proper place for the newly increased key. As MAX-HEAP-INCREASE-KEY traverses this path, it repeatedly compares an element's key to that of its parent, exchanging pointers and continuing if the element's key is larger, and terminating if the element's key is smaller, since the max-heap property now holds. (See Exercise 6.5-7 for a precise loop invariant.) Like MAX-HEAPIFY when used in a priority queue, MAX-HEAP-INCREASE-KEY updates the information that maps objects to array indices when array elements are exchanged. Figure 6.5 shows an example of a MAX-HEAP-INCREASE-KEY operation. In addition to the overhead for mapping priority queue objects to array indices, the running time of MAX-HEAP-INCREASE-KEY on an n-element heap is $O(\lg n)$, since the path traced from the node updated in line 3 to the root has length $O(\lg n)$.

The procedure MAX-HEAP-INSERT on the next page implements the INSERT operation. It takes as inputs the array A implementing the max-heap, the new object x to be inserted into the max-heap, and the size n of array A. The procedure first verifies that the array has room for the new element. It then expands the max-heap by adding to the tree a new leaf whose key is $-\infty$. Then it calls MAX-HEAP-INCREASE-KEY to set the key of this new element to its correct value and maintain the max-heap property. The running time of MAX-HEAP-INSERT on an n-element heap is $O(\lg n)$ plus the overhead for mapping priority queue objects to indices.

In summary, a heap can support any priority-queue operation on a set of size n in $O(\lg n)$ time, plus the overhead for mapping priority queue objects to array indices.

MAX-HEAP-INCREASE-KEY(A, x, k)

1 **if** $k < x.key$
2   **error** "new key is smaller than current key"
3 $x.key = k$
4 find the index i in array A where object x occurs
5 **while** $i > 1$ and $A[\text{PARENT}(i)].key < A[i].key$
6   exchange $A[i]$ with $A[\text{PARENT}(i)]$, updating the information that maps priority queue objects to array indices
7      $i = \text{PARENT}(i)$

MAX-HEAP-INSERT(A, x, n)

1 **if** $A.heap\text{-}size == n$
2   **error** "heap overflow"
3 $A.heap\text{-}size = A.heap\text{-}size + 1$
4 $k = x.key$
5 $x.key = -\infty$
6 $A[A.heap\text{-}size] = x$
7 map x to index $heap\text{-}size$ in the array
8 MAX-HEAP-INCREASE-KEY(A, x, k)

Exercises

6.5-1
Suppose that the objects in a max-priority queue are just keys. Illustrate the operation of MAX-HEAP-EXTRACT-MAX on the heap $A = \langle 15, 13, 9, 5, 12, 8, 7, 4, 0, 6, 2, 1 \rangle$.

6.5-2
Suppose that the objects in a max-priority queue are just keys. Illustrate the operation of MAX-HEAP-INSERT$(A, 10)$ on the heap $A = \langle 15, 13, 9, 5, 12, 8, 7, 4, 0, 6, 2, 1 \rangle$.

6.5-3
Write pseudocode to implement a min-priority queue with a min-heap by writing the procedures MIN-HEAP-MINIMUM, MIN-HEAP-EXTRACT-MIN, MIN-HEAP-DECREASE-KEY, and MIN-HEAP-INSERT.

6.5-4
Write pseudocode for the procedure MAX-HEAP-DECREASE-KEY(A, x, k) in a max-heap. What is the running time of your procedure?

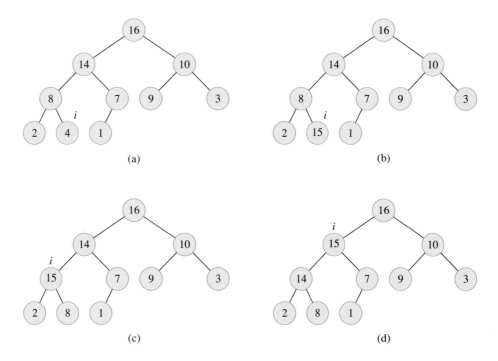

Figure 6.5 The operation of MAX-HEAP-INCREASE-KEY. Only the key of each element in the priority queue is shown. The node indexed by i in each iteration is shown in blue. **(a)** The max-heap of Figure 6.4(a) with i indexing the node whose key is about to be increased. **(b)** This node has its key increased to 15. **(c)** After one iteration of the **while** loop of lines 5–7, the node and its parent have exchanged keys, and the index i moves up to the parent. **(d)** The max-heap after one more iteration of the **while** loop. At this point, $A[\text{PARENT}(i)] \geq A[i]$. The max-heap property now holds and the procedure terminates.

6.5-5
Why does MAX-HEAP-INSERT bother setting the key of the inserted object to $-\infty$ in line 5 given that line 8 will set the object's key to the desired value?

6.5-6
Professor Uriah suggests replacing the **while** loop of lines 5–7 in MAX-HEAP-INCREASE-KEY by a call to MAX-HEAPIFY. Explain the flaw in the professor's idea.

6.5-7
Argue the correctness of MAX-HEAP-INCREASE-KEY using the following loop invariant:

At the start of each iteration of the **while** loop of lines 5–7:

a. If both nodes PARENT(i) and LEFT(i) exist, then $A[\text{PARENT}(i)].key \geq A[\text{LEFT}(i)].key$.

b. If both nodes PARENT(i) and RIGHT(i) exist, then $A[\text{PARENT}(i)].key \geq A[\text{RIGHT}(i)].key$.

c. The subarray $A[1 : A.\textit{heap-size}]$ satisfies the max-heap property, except that there may be one violation, which is that $A[i].key$ may be greater than $A[\text{PARENT}(i)].key$.

You may assume that the subarray $A[1 : A.\textit{heap-size}]$ satisfies the max-heap property at the time MAX-HEAP-INCREASE-KEY is called.

6.5-8

Each exchange operation on line 6 of MAX-HEAP-INCREASE-KEY typically requires three assignments, not counting the updating of the mapping from objects to array indices. Show how to use the idea of the inner loop of INSERTION-SORT to reduce the three assignments to just one assignment.

6.5-9

Show how to implement a first-in, first-out queue with a priority queue. Show how to implement a stack with a priority queue. (Queues and stacks are defined in Section 10.1.3.)

6.5-10

The operation MAX-HEAP-DELETE(A, x) deletes the object x from max-heap A. Give an implementation of MAX-HEAP-DELETE for an n-element max-heap that runs in $O(\lg n)$ time plus the overhead for mapping priority queue objects to array indices.

6.5-11

Give an $O(n \lg k)$-time algorithm to merge k sorted lists into one sorted list, where n is the total number of elements in all the input lists. (*Hint:* Use a min-heap for k-way merging.)

Problems

6-1   *Building a heap using insertion*

One way to build a heap is by repeatedly calling MAX-HEAP-INSERT to insert the elements into the heap. Consider the procedure BUILD-MAX-HEAP' on the facing page. It assumes that the objects being inserted are just the heap elements.

```
BUILD-MAX-HEAP'(A, n)
1   A.heap-size = 1
2   for i = 2 to n
3       MAX-HEAP-INSERT(A, A[i], n)
```

a. Do the procedures BUILD-MAX-HEAP and BUILD-MAX-HEAP' always create the same heap when run on the same input array? Prove that they do, or provide a counterexample.

b. Show that in the worst case, BUILD-MAX-HEAP' requires $\Theta(n \lg n)$ time to build an n-element heap.

6-2   *Analysis of d-ary heaps*

A *d-ary heap* is like a binary heap, but (with one possible exception) nonleaf nodes have d children instead of two children. In all parts of this problem, assume that the time to maintain the mapping between objects and heap elements is $O(1)$ per operation.

a. Describe how to represent a d-ary heap in an array.

b. Using Θ-notation, express the height of a d-ary heap of n elements in terms of n and d.

c. Give an efficient implementation of EXTRACT-MAX in a d-ary max-heap. Analyze its running time in terms of d and n.

d. Give an efficient implementation of INCREASE-KEY in a d-ary max-heap. Analyze its running time in terms of d and n.

e. Give an efficient implementation of INSERT in a d-ary max-heap. Analyze its running time in terms of d and n.

6-3   *Young tableaus*

An $m \times n$ *Young tableau* is an $m \times n$ matrix such that the entries of each row are in sorted order from left to right and the entries of each column are in sorted order from top to bottom. Some of the entries of a Young tableau may be ∞, which we treat as nonexistent elements. Thus, a Young tableau can be used to hold $r \leq mn$ finite numbers.

a. Draw a 4×4 Young tableau containing the elements $\{9, 16, 3, 2, 4, 8, 5, 14, 12\}$.

b. Argue that an $m \times n$ Young tableau Y is empty if $Y[1, 1] = \infty$. Argue that Y is full (contains mn elements) if $Y[m, n] < \infty$.

c. Give an algorithm to implement EXTRACT-MIN on a nonempty $m \times n$ Young tableau that runs in $O(m + n)$ time. Your algorithm should use a recursive subroutine that solves an $m \times n$ problem by recursively solving either an $(m - 1) \times n$ or an $m \times (n - 1)$ subproblem. (*Hint:* Think about MAX-HEAPIFY.) Explain why your implementation of EXTRACT-MIN runs in $O(m + n)$ time.

d. Show how to insert a new element into a nonfull $m \times n$ Young tableau in $O(m + n)$ time.

e. Using no other sorting method as a subroutine, show how to use an $n \times n$ Young tableau to sort n^2 numbers in $O(n^3)$ time.

f. Give an $O(m + n)$-time algorithm to determine whether a given number is stored in a given $m \times n$ Young tableau.

Chapter notes

The heapsort algorithm was invented by Williams [456], who also described how to implement a priority queue with a heap. The BUILD-MAX-HEAP procedure was suggested by Floyd [145]. Schaffer and Sedgewick [395] showed that in the best case, the number of times elements move in the heap during heapsort is approximately $(n/2) \lg n$ and that the average number of moves is approximately $n \lg n$.

We use min-heaps to implement min-priority queues in Chapters 15, 21, and 22. Other, more complicated, data structures give better time bounds for certain min-priority queue operations. Fredman and Tarjan [156] developed Fibonacci heaps, which support INSERT and DECREASE-KEY in $O(1)$ amortized time (see Chapter 16). That is, the average worst-case running time for these operations is $O(1)$. Brodal, Lagogiannis, and Tarjan [73] subsequently devised strict Fibonacci heaps, which make these time bounds the actual running times. If the keys are unique and drawn from the set $\{0, 1, \ldots, n - 1\}$ of nonnegative integers, van Emde Boas trees [440, 441] support the operations INSERT, DELETE, SEARCH, MINIMUM, MAXIMUM, PREDECESSOR, and SUCCESSOR in $O(\lg \lg n)$ time.

If the data are b-bit integers, and the computer memory consists of addressable b-bit words, Fredman and Willard [157] showed how to implement MINIMUM in $O(1)$ time and INSERT and EXTRACT-MIN in $O(\sqrt{\lg n})$ time. Thorup [436] has improved the $O(\sqrt{\lg n})$ bound to $O(\lg \lg n)$ time by using randomized hashing, requiring only linear space.

An important special case of priority queues occurs when the sequence of EXTRACT-MIN operations is *monotone*, that is, the values returned by successive EXTRACT-MIN operations are monotonically increasing over time. This case arises in several important applications, such as Dijkstra's single-source shortest-paths algorithm, which we discuss in Chapter 22, and in discrete-event simulation. For Dijkstra's algorithm it is particularly important that the DECREASE-KEY operation be implemented efficiently. For the monotone case, if the data are integers in the range $1, 2, \ldots, C$, Ahuja, Mehlhorn, Orlin, and Tarjan [8] describe how to implement EXTRACT-MIN and INSERT in $O(\lg C)$ amortized time (Chapter 16 presents amortized analysis) and DECREASE-KEY in $O(1)$ time, using a data structure called a radix heap. The $O(\lg C)$ bound can be improved to $O(\sqrt{\lg C})$ using Fibonacci heaps in conjunction with radix heaps. Cherkassky, Goldberg, and Silverstein [90] further improved the bound to $O(\lg^{1/3+\epsilon} C)$ expected time by combining the multilevel bucketing structure of Denardo and Fox [112] with the heap of Thorup mentioned earlier. Raman [375] further improved these results to obtain a bound of $O\left(\min\left\{\lg^{1/4+\epsilon} C, \lg^{1/3+\epsilon} n\right\}\right)$, for any fixed $\epsilon > 0$.

Many other variants of heaps have been proposed. Brodal [72] surveys some of these developments.

7   Quicksort

The quicksort algorithm has a worst-case running time of $\Theta(n^2)$ on an input array of n numbers. Despite this slow worst-case running time, quicksort is often the best practical choice for sorting because it is remarkably efficient on average: its expected running time is $\Theta(n \lg n)$ when all numbers are distinct, and the constant factors hidden in the $\Theta(n \lg n)$ notation are small. Unlike merge sort, it also has the advantage of sorting in place (see page 158), and it works well even in virtual-memory environments.

Our study of quicksort is broken into four sections. Section 7.1 describes the algorithm and an important subroutine used by quicksort for partitioning. Because the behavior of quicksort is complex, we'll start with an intuitive discussion of its performance in Section 7.2 and analyze it precisely at the end of the chapter. Section 7.3 presents a randomized version of quicksort. When all elements are distinct,[1] this randomized algorithm has a good expected running time and no particular input elicits its worst-case behavior. (See Problem 7-2 for the case in which elements may be equal.) Section 7.4 analyzes the randomized algorithm, showing that it runs in $\Theta(n^2)$ time in the worst case and, assuming distinct elements, in expected $O(n \lg n)$ time.

---

[1] You can enforce the assumption that the values in an array A are distinct at the cost of $\Theta(n)$ additional space and only constant overhead in running time by converting each input value $A[i]$ to an ordered pair $(A[i], i)$ with $(A[i], i) < (A[j], j)$ if $A[i] < A[j]$ or if $A[i] = A[j]$ and $i < j$. There are also more practical variants of quicksort that work well when elements are not distinct.

7.1   Description of quicksort

Quicksort, like merge sort, applies the divide-and-conquer method introduced in Section 2.3.1. Here is the three-step divide-and-conquer process for sorting a subarray $A[p:r]$:

Divide by partitioning (rearranging) the array $A[p:r]$ into two (possibly empty) subarrays $A[p:q-1]$ (the *low side*) and $A[q+1:r]$ (the *high side*) such that each element in the low side of the partition is less than or equal to the *pivot* $A[q]$, which is, in turn, less than or equal to each element in the high side. Compute the index q of the pivot as part of this partitioning procedure.

Conquer by calling quicksort recursively to sort each of the subarrays $A[p:q-1]$ and $A[q+1:r]$.

Combine by doing nothing: because the two subarrays are already sorted, no work is needed to combine them. All elements in $A[p:q-1]$ are sorted and less than or equal to $A[q]$, and all elements in $A[q+1:r]$ are sorted and greater than or equal to the pivot $A[q]$. The entire subarray $A[p:r]$ cannot help but be sorted!

The QUICKSORT procedure implements quicksort. To sort an entire n-element array $A[1:n]$, the initial call is QUICKSORT($A, 1, n$).

QUICKSORT(A, p, r)

```
1  if p < r
2      // Partition the subarray around the pivot, which ends up in A[q].
3      q = PARTITION(A, p, r)
4      QUICKSORT(A, p, q - 1)  // recursively sort the low side
5      QUICKSORT(A, q + 1, r)  // recursively sort the high side
```

Partitioning the array

The key to the algorithm is the PARTITION procedure on the next page, which rearranges the subarray $A[p:r]$ in place, returning the index of the dividing point between the two sides of the partition.

Figure 7.1 shows how PARTITION works on an 8-element array. PARTITION always selects the element $x = A[r]$ as the pivot. As the procedure runs, each element falls into exactly one of four regions, some of which may be empty. At the start of each iteration of the **for** loop in lines 3–6, the regions satisfy certain properties, shown in Figure 7.2. We state these properties as a loop invariant:

PARTITION(A, p, r)

```
1   x = A[r]                          // the pivot
2   i = p − 1                         // highest index into the low side
3   for j = p to r − 1                // process each element other than the pivot
4       if A[j] ≤ x                   // does this element belong on the low side?
5           i = i + 1                 // index of a new slot in the low side
6           exchange A[i] with A[j]   // put this element there
7   exchange A[i + 1] with A[r]       // pivot goes just to the right of the low side
8   return i + 1                      // new index of the pivot
```

At the beginning of each iteration of the loop of lines 3–6, for any array index k, the following conditions hold:

1. if $p \leq k \leq i$, then $A[k] \leq x$ (the tan region of Figure 7.2);
2. if $i + 1 \leq k \leq j - 1$, then $A[k] > x$ (the blue region);
3. if $k = r$, then $A[k] = x$ (the yellow region).

We need to show that this loop invariant is true prior to the first iteration, that each iteration of the loop maintains the invariant, that the loop terminates, and that correctness follows from the invariant when the loop terminates.

Initialization: Prior to the first iteration of the loop, we have $i = p - 1$ and $j = p$. Because no values lie between p and i and no values lie between $i + 1$ and $j - 1$, the first two conditions of the loop invariant are trivially satisfied. The assignment in line 1 satisfies the third condition.

Maintenance: As Figure 7.3 shows, we consider two cases, depending on the outcome of the test in line 4. Figure 7.3(a) shows what happens when $A[j] > x$: the only action in the loop is to increment j. After j has been incremented, the second condition holds for $A[j - 1]$ and all other entries remain unchanged. Figure 7.3(b) shows what happens when $A[j] \leq x$: the loop increments i, swaps $A[i]$ and $A[j]$, and then increments j. Because of the swap, we now have that $A[i] \leq x$, and condition 1 is satisfied. Similarly, we also have that $A[j - 1] > x$, since the item that was swapped into $A[j - 1]$ is, by the loop invariant, greater than x.

Termination: Since the loop makes exactly $r - p$ iterations, it terminates, whereupon $j = r$. At that point, the unexamined subarray $A[j : r - 1]$ is empty, and every entry in the array belongs to one of the other three sets described by the invariant. Thus, the values in the array have been partitioned into three sets: those less than or equal to x (the low side), those greater than x (the high side), and a singleton set containing x (the pivot).

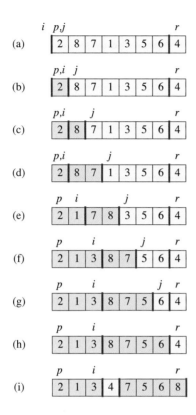

Figure 7.1   The operation of PARTITION on a sample array. Array entry $A[r]$ becomes the pivot element x. Tan array elements all belong to the low side of the partition, with values at most x. Blue elements belong to the high side, with values greater than x. White elements have not yet been put into either side of the partition, and the yellow element is the pivot x. **(a)** The initial array and variable settings. None of the elements have been placed into either side of the partition. **(b)** The value 2 is "swapped with itself" and put into the low side. **(c)–(d)** The values 8 and 7 are placed into to high side. **(e)** The values 1 and 8 are swapped, and the low side grows. **(f)** The values 3 and 7 are swapped, and the low side grows. **(g)–(h)** The high side of the partition grows to include 5 and 6, and the loop terminates. **(i)** Line 7 swaps the pivot element so that it lies between the two sides of the partition, and line 8 returns the pivot's new index.

The final two lines of PARTITION finish up by swapping the pivot with the leftmost element greater than x, thereby moving the pivot into its correct place in the partitioned array, and then returning the pivot's new index. The output of PARTITION now satisfies the specifications given for the divide step. In fact, it satisfies a slightly stronger condition: after line 3 of QUICKSORT, $A[q]$ is strictly less than every element of $A[q + 1 : r]$.

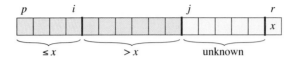

Figure 7.2   The four regions maintained by the procedure PARTITION on a subarray $A[p:r]$. The tan values in $A[p:i]$ are all less than or equal to x, the blue values in $A[i+1:j-1]$ are all greater than x, the white values in $A[j:r-1]$ have unknown relationships to x, and $A[r] = x$.

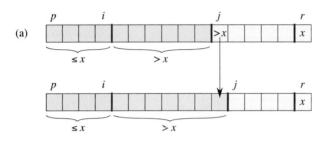

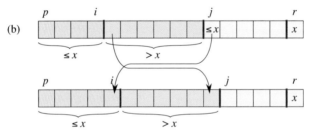

Figure 7.3   The two cases for one iteration of procedure PARTITION. **(a)** If $A[j] > x$, the only action is to increment j, which maintains the loop invariant. **(b)** If $A[j] \leq x$, index i is incremented, $A[i]$ and $A[j]$ are swapped, and then j is incremented. Again, the loop invariant is maintained.

Exercise 7.1-3 asks you to show that the running time of PARTITION on a subarray $A[p:r]$ of $n = r - p + 1$ elements is $\Theta(n)$.

Exercises

7.1-1
Using Figure 7.1 as a model, illustrate the operation of PARTITION on the array $A = \langle 13, 19, 9, 5, 12, 8, 7, 4, 21, 2, 6, 11 \rangle$.

7.1-2

What value of q does PARTITION return when all elements in the subarray $A[p:r]$ have the same value? Modify PARTITION so that $q = \lfloor (p+r)/2 \rfloor$ when all elements in the subarray $A[p:r]$ have the same value.

7.1-3

Give a brief argument that the running time of PARTITION on a subarray of size n is $\Theta(n)$.

7.1-4

Modify QUICKSORT to sort into monotonically decreasing order.

7.2 Performance of quicksort

The running time of quicksort depends on how balanced each partitioning is, which in turn depends on which elements are used as pivots. If the two sides of a partition are about the same size—the partitioning is balanced—then the algorithm runs asymptotically as fast as merge sort. If the partitioning is unbalanced, however, it can run asymptotically as slowly as insertion sort. To allow you to gain some intuition before diving into a formal analysis, this section informally investigates how quicksort performs under the assumptions of balanced versus unbalanced partitioning.

But first, let's briefly look at the maximum amount of memory that quicksort requires. Although quicksort sorts in place according to the definition on page 158, the amount of memory it uses—aside from the array being sorted—is not constant. Since each recursive call requires a constant amount of space on the runtime stack, outside of the array being sorted, quicksort requires space proportional to the maximum depth of the recursion. As we'll see now, that could be as bad as $\Theta(n)$ in the worst case.

Worst-case partitioning

The worst-case behavior for quicksort occurs when the partitioning produces one subproblem with $n-1$ elements and one with 0 elements. (See Section 7.4.1.) Let us assume that this unbalanced partitioning arises in each recursive call. The partitioning costs $\Theta(n)$ time. Since the recursive call on an array of size 0 just returns without doing anything, $T(0) = \Theta(1)$, and the recurrence for the running time is

$$T(n) = T(n-1) + T(0) + \Theta(n)$$
$$= T(n-1) + \Theta(n) .$$

By summing the costs incurred at each level of the recursion, we obtain an arithmetic series (equation (A.3) on page 1141), which evaluates to $\Theta(n^2)$. Indeed, the substitution method can be used to prove that the recurrence $T(n) = T(n-1) + \Theta(n)$ has the solution $T(n) = \Theta(n^2)$. (See Exercise 7.2-1.)

Thus, if the partitioning is maximally unbalanced at every recursive level of the algorithm, the running time is $\Theta(n^2)$. The worst-case running time of quicksort is therefore no better than that of insertion sort. Moreover, the $\Theta(n^2)$ running time occurs when the input array is already completely sorted—a situation in which insertion sort runs in $O(n)$ time.

Best-case partitioning

In the most even possible split, PARTITION produces two subproblems, each of size no more than $n/2$, since one is of size $\lfloor(n-1)/2\rfloor \leq n/2$ and one of size $\lceil(n-1)/2\rceil - 1 \leq n/2$. In this case, quicksort runs much faster. An upper bound on the running time can then be described by the recurrence

$$T(n) = 2T(n/2) + \Theta(n) .$$

By case 2 of the master theorem (Theorem 4.1 on page 102), this recurrence has the solution $T(n) = \Theta(n \lg n)$. Thus, if the partitioning is equally balanced at every level of the recursion, an asymptotically faster algorithm results.

Balanced partitioning

As the analyses in Section 7.4 will show, the average-case running time of quicksort is much closer to the best case than to the worst case. By appreciating how the balance of the partitioning affects the recurrence describing the running time, we can gain an understanding of why.

Suppose, for example, that the partitioning algorithm always produces a 9-to-1 proportional split, which at first blush seems quite unbalanced. We then obtain the recurrence

$$T(n) = T(9n/10) + T(n/10) + \Theta(n) ,$$

on the running time of quicksort. Figure 7.4 shows the recursion tree for this recurrence, where for simplicity the $\Theta(n)$ driving function has been replaced by n, which won't affect the asymptotic solution of the recurrence (as Exercise 4.7-1 on page 118 justifies). Every level of the tree has cost n, until the recursion bottoms out in a base case at depth $\log_{10} n = \Theta(\lg n)$, and then the levels have cost

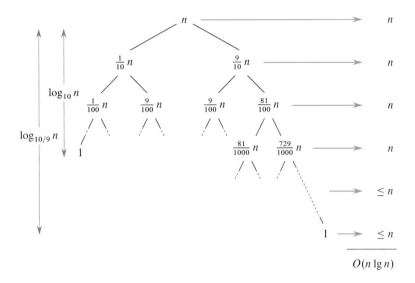

Figure 7.4 A recursion tree for QUICKSORT in which PARTITION always produces a 9-to-1 split, yielding a running time of $O(n \lg n)$. Nodes show subproblem sizes, with per-level costs on the right.

at most n. The recursion terminates at depth $\log_{10/9} n = \Theta(\lg n)$. Thus, with a 9-to-1 proportional split at every level of recursion, which intuitively seems highly unbalanced, quicksort runs in $O(n \lg n)$ time—asymptotically the same as if the split were right down the middle. Indeed, even a 99-to-1 split yields an $O(n \lg n)$ running time. In fact, any split of *constant* proportionality yields a recursion tree of depth $\Theta(\lg n)$, where the cost at each level is $O(n)$. The running time is therefore $O(n \lg n)$ whenever the split has constant proportionality. The ratio of the split affects only the constant hidden in the O-notation.

Intuition for the average case

To develop a clear notion of the expected behavior of quicksort, we must assume something about how its inputs are distributed. Because quicksort determines the sorted order using only comparisons between input elements, its behavior depends on the relative ordering of the values in the array elements given as the input, not on the particular values in the array. As in the probabilistic analysis of the hiring problem in Section 5.2, assume that all permutations of the input numbers are equally likely and that the elements are distinct.

When quicksort runs on a random input array, the partitioning is highly unlikely to happen in the same way at every level, as our informal analysis has assumed.

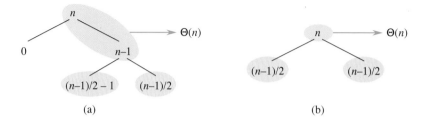

(a)   (b)

Figure 7.5 **(a)** Two levels of a recursion tree for quicksort. The partitioning at the root costs n and produces a "bad" split: two subarrays of sizes 0 and $n - 1$. The partitioning of the subarray of size $n - 1$ costs $n - 1$ and produces a "good" split: subarrays of size $(n - 1)/2 - 1$ and $(n - 1)/2$. **(b)** A single level of a recursion tree that is well balanced. In both parts, the partitioning cost for the subproblems shown with blue shading is $\Theta(n)$. Yet the subproblems remaining to be solved in (a), shown with tan shading, are no larger than the corresponding subproblems remaining to be solved in (b).

We expect that some of the splits will be reasonably well balanced and that some will be fairly unbalanced. For example, Exercise 7.2-6 asks you to show that about 80% of the time PARTITION produces a split that is at least as balanced as 9 to 1, and about 20% of the time it produces a split that is less balanced than 9 to 1.

In the average case, PARTITION produces a mix of "good" and "bad" splits. In a recursion tree for an average-case execution of PARTITION, the good and bad splits are distributed randomly throughout the tree. Suppose for the sake of intuition that the good and bad splits alternate levels in the tree, and that the good splits are best-case splits and the bad splits are worst-case splits. Figure 7.5(a) shows the splits at two consecutive levels in the recursion tree. At the root of the tree, the cost is n for partitioning, and the subarrays produced have sizes $n - 1$ and 0: the worst case. At the next level, the subarray of size $n - 1$ undergoes best-case partitioning into subarrays of size $(n - 1)/2 - 1$ and $(n - 1)/2$. Let's assume that the base-case cost is 1 for the subarray of size 0.

The combination of the bad split followed by the good split produces three subarrays of sizes 0, $(n - 1)/2 - 1$, and $(n - 1)/2$ at a combined partitioning cost of $\Theta(n) + \Theta(n - 1) = \Theta(n)$. This situation is at most a constant factor worse than that in Figure 7.5(b), namely, where a single level of partitioning produces two subarrays of size $(n - 1)/2$, at a cost of $\Theta(n)$. Yet this latter situation is balanced! Intuitively, the $\Theta(n - 1)$ cost of the bad split in Figure 7.5(a) can be absorbed into the $\Theta(n)$ cost of the good split, and the resulting split is good. Thus, the running time of quicksort, when levels alternate between good and bad splits, is like the running time for good splits alone: still $O(n \lg n)$, but with a slightly larger constant hidden by the O-notation. We'll analyze the expected running time of a randomized version of quicksort rigorously in Section 7.4.2.

Exercises

7.2-1
Use the substitution method to prove that the recurrence $T(n) = T(n-1) + \Theta(n)$
has the solution $T(n) = \Theta(n^2)$, as claimed at the beginning of Section 7.2.

7.2-2
What is the running time of QUICKSORT when all elements of array A have the
same value?

7.2-3
Show that the running time of QUICKSORT is $\Theta(n^2)$ when the array A contains
distinct elements and is sorted in decreasing order.

7.2-4
Banks often record transactions on an account in order of the times of the transactions, but many people like to receive their bank statements with checks listed
in order by check number. People usually write checks in order by check number, and merchants usually cash them with reasonable dispatch. The problem of
converting time-of-transaction ordering to check-number ordering is therefore the
problem of sorting almost-sorted input. Explain persuasively why the procedure
INSERTION-SORT might tend to beat the procedure QUICKSORT on this problem.

7.2-5
Suppose that the splits at every level of quicksort are in the constant proportion α
to β, where $\alpha + \beta = 1$ and $0 < \alpha \leq \beta < 1$. Show that the minimum depth of a
leaf in the recursion tree is approximately $\log_{1/\alpha} n$ and that the maximum depth is
approximately $\log_{1/\beta} n$. (Don't worry about integer round-off.)

7.2-6
Consider an array with distinct elements and for which all permutations of the elements are equally likely. Argue that for any constant $0 < \alpha \leq 1/2$, the probability
is approximately $1 - 2\alpha$ that PARTITION produces a split at least as balanced as
$1 - \alpha$ to α.

7.3   A randomized version of quicksort

In exploring the average-case behavior of quicksort, we have assumed that all permutations of the input numbers are equally likely. This assumption does not always hold, however, as, for example, in the situation laid out in the premise for

Exercise 7.2-4. Section 5.3 showed that judicious randomization can sometimes be added to an algorithm to obtain good expected performance over all inputs. For quicksort, randomization yields a fast and practical algorithm. Many software libraries provide a randomized version of quicksort as their algorithm of choice for sorting large data sets.

In Section 5.3, the RANDOMIZED-HIRE-ASSISTANT procedure explicitly permutes its input and then runs the deterministic HIRE-ASSISTANT procedure. We could do the same for quicksort as well, but a different randomization technique yields a simpler analysis. Instead of always using $A[r]$ as the pivot, a randomized version randomly chooses the pivot from the subarray $A[p:r]$, where each element in $A[p:r]$ has an equal probability of being chosen. It then exchanges that element with $A[r]$ before partitioning. Because the pivot is chosen randomly, we expect the split of the input array to be reasonably well balanced on average.

The changes to PARTITION and QUICKSORT are small. The new partitioning procedure, RANDOMIZED-PARTITION, simply swaps before performing the partitioning. The new quicksort procedure, RANDOMIZED-QUICKSORT, calls RANDOMIZED-PARTITION instead of PARTITION. We'll analyze this algorithm in the next section.

```
RANDOMIZED-PARTITION(A, p, r)

1   i = RANDOM(p, r)
2   exchange A[r] with A[i]
3   return PARTITION(A, p, r)


RANDOMIZED-QUICKSORT(A, p, r)

1   if p < r
2       q = RANDOMIZED-PARTITION(A, p, r)
3       RANDOMIZED-QUICKSORT(A, p, q − 1)
4       RANDOMIZED-QUICKSORT(A, q + 1, r)
```

Exercises

7.3-1
Why do we analyze the expected running time of a randomized algorithm and not its worst-case running time?

7.3-2
When RANDOMIZED-QUICKSORT runs, how many calls are made to the random-number generator RANDOM in the worst case? How about in the best case? Give your answer in terms of Θ-notation.

7.4 Analysis of quicksort

Section 7.2 gave some intuition for the worst-case behavior of quicksort and for why we expect the algorithm to run quickly. This section analyzes the behavior of quicksort more rigorously. We begin with a worst-case analysis, which applies to either QUICKSORT or RANDOMIZED-QUICKSORT, and conclude with an analysis of the expected running time of RANDOMIZED-QUICKSORT.

7.4.1 Worst-case analysis

We saw in Section 7.2 that a worst-case split at every level of recursion in quicksort produces a $\Theta(n^2)$ running time, which, intuitively, is the worst-case running time of the algorithm. We now prove this assertion.

We'll use the substitution method (see Section 4.3) to show that the running time of quicksort is $O(n^2)$. Let $T(n)$ be the worst-case time for the procedure QUICKSORT on an input of size n. Because the procedure PARTITION produces two subproblems with total size $n - 1$, we obtain the recurrence

$$T(n) = \max \{T(q) + T(n - 1 - q) : 0 \le q \le n - 1\} + \Theta(n) , \qquad (7.1)$$

We guess that $T(n) \le cn^2$ for some constant $c > 0$. Substituting this guess into recurrence (7.1) yields

$$
\begin{aligned}
T(n) &\le \max \{cq^2 + c(n - 1 - q)^2 : 0 \le q \le n - 1\} + \Theta(n) \\
&= c \cdot \max \{q^2 + (n - 1 - q)^2 : 0 \le q \le n - 1\} + \Theta(n) .
\end{aligned}
$$

Let's focus our attention on the maximization. For $q = 0, 1, \ldots, n - 1$, we have

$$
\begin{aligned}
q^2 + (n - 1 - q)^2 &= q^2 + (n - 1)^2 - 2q(n - 1) + q^2 \\
&= (n - 1)^2 + 2q(q - (n - 1)) \\
&\le (n - 1)^2
\end{aligned}
$$

because $q \le n - 1$ implies that $2q(q - (n - 1)) \le 0$. Thus every term in the maximization is bounded by $(n - 1)^2$.

Continuing with our analysis of $T(n)$, we obtain

$$T(n) \leq c(n-1)^2 + \Theta(n)$$
$$\leq cn^2 - c(2n-1) + \Theta(n)$$
$$\leq cn^2,$$

by picking the constant c large enough that the $c(2n-1)$ term dominates the $\Theta(n)$ term. Thus $T(n) = O(n^2)$. Section 7.2 showed a specific case where quicksort takes $\Omega(n^2)$ time: when partitioning is maximally unbalanced. Thus, the worst-case running time of quicksort is $\Theta(n^2)$.

7.4.2 Expected running time

We have already seen the intuition behind why the expected running time of RANDOMIZED-QUICKSORT is $O(n \lg n)$: if, in each level of recursion, the split induced by RANDOMIZED-PARTITION puts any constant fraction of the elements on one side of the partition, then the recursion tree has depth $\Theta(\lg n)$ and $O(n)$ work is performed at each level. Even if we add a few new levels with the most unbalanced split possible between these levels, the total time remains $O(n \lg n)$. We can analyze the expected running time of RANDOMIZED-QUICKSORT precisely by first understanding how the partitioning procedure operates and then using this understanding to derive an $O(n \lg n)$ bound on the expected running time. This upper bound on the expected running time, combined with the $\Theta(n \lg n)$ best-case bound we saw in Section 7.2, yields a $\Theta(n \lg n)$ expected running time. We assume throughout that the values of the elements being sorted are distinct.

Running time and comparisons

The QUICKSORT and RANDOMIZED-QUICKSORT procedures differ only in how they select pivot elements. They are the same in all other respects. We can therefore analyze RANDOMIZED-QUICKSORT by considering the QUICKSORT and PARTITION procedures, but with the assumption that pivot elements are selected randomly from the subarray passed to RANDOMIZED-PARTITION. Let's start by relating the asymptotic running time of QUICKSORT to the number of times elements are compared (all in line 4 of PARTITION), understanding that this analysis also applies to RANDOMIZED-QUICKSORT. Note that we are counting the number of times that *array elements* are compared, not comparisons of indices.

Lemma 7.1
The running time of QUICKSORT on an n-element array is $O(n + X)$, where X is the number of element comparisons performed.

Proof The running time of QUICKSORT is dominated by the time spent in the PARTITION procedure. Each time PARTITION is called, it selects a pivot element, which is never included in any future recursive calls to QUICKSORT and PARTITION. Thus, there can be at most n calls to PARTITION over the entire execution of the quicksort algorithm. Each time QUICKSORT calls PARTITION, it also recursively calls itself twice, so there are at most $2n$ calls to the QUICKSORT procedure itself.

One call to PARTITION takes $O(1)$ time plus an amount of time that is proportional to the number of iterations of the **for** loop in lines 3–6. Each iteration of this **for** loop performs one comparison in line 4, comparing the pivot element to another element of the array A. Therefore, the total time spent in the **for** loop across all executions is proportional to X. Since there are at most n calls to PARTITION and the time spent outside the **for** loop is $O(1)$ for each call, the total time spent in PARTITION outside of the **for** loop is $O(n)$. Thus the total time for quicksort is $O(n + X)$. ∎

Our goal for analyzing RANDOMIZED-QUICKSORT, therefore, is to compute the expected value $\mathrm{E}[X]$ of the random variable X denoting the total number of comparisons performed in all calls to PARTITION. To do so, we must understand when the quicksort algorithm compares two elements of the array and when it does not. For ease of analysis, let's index the elements of the array A by their position in the sorted output, rather than their position in the input. That is, although the elements in A may start out in any order, we'll refer to them by $z_1, z_2, \ldots, z_n$, where $z_1 < z_2 < \cdots < z_n$, with strict inequality because we assume that all elements are distinct. We denote the set $\{z_i, z_{i+1}, \ldots, z_j\}$ by Z_{ij}.

The next lemma characterizes when two elements are compared.

Lemma 7.2

During the execution of RANDOMIZED-QUICKSORT on an array of n distinct elements $z_1 < z_2 < \cdots < z_n$, an element z_i is compared with an element z_j, where $i < j$, if and only if one of them is chosen as a pivot before any other element in the set Z_{ij}. Moreover, no two elements are ever compared twice.

Proof Let's look at the first time that an element $x \in Z_{ij}$ is chosen as a pivot during the execution of the algorithm. There are three cases to consider. If x is neither z_i nor z_j—that is, $z_i < x < z_j$—then z_i and z_j are not compared at any subsequent time, because they fall into different sides of the partition around x. If $x = z_i$, then PARTITION compares z_i with every other item in Z_{ij}. Similarly, if $x = z_j$, then PARTITION compares z_j with every other item in Z_{ij}. Thus, z_i and z_j are compared if and only if the first element to be chosen as a pivot from Z_{ij} is either z_i or z_j. In the latter two cases, where one of z_i and z_j is chosen as a pivot, since the pivot is removed from future comparisons, it is never compared again with the other element.   ∎

As an example of this lemma, consider an input to quicksort of the numbers 1 through 10 in some arbitrary order. Suppose that the first pivot element is 7. Then the first call to PARTITION separates the numbers into two sets: $\{1, 2, 3, 4, 5, 6\}$ and $\{8, 9, 10\}$. In the process, the pivot element 7 is compared with all other elements, but no number from the first set (e.g., 2) is or ever will be compared with any number from the second set (e.g., 9). The values 7 and 9 are compared because 7 is the first item from $Z_{7,9}$ to be chosen as a pivot. In contrast, 2 and 9 are never compared because the first pivot element chosen from $Z_{2,9}$ is 7.

The next lemma gives the probability that two elements are compared.

Lemma 7.3
Consider an execution of the procedure RANDOMIZED-QUICKSORT on an array of n distinct elements $z_1 < z_2 < \cdots < z_n$. Given two arbitrary elements z_i and z_j where $i < j$, the probability that they are compared is $2/(j - i + 1)$.

Proof Let's look at the tree of recursive calls that RANDOMIZED-QUICKSORT makes, and consider the sets of elements provided as input to each call. Initially, the root set contains all the elements of Z_{ij}, since the root set contains every element in A. The elements belonging to Z_{ij} all stay together for each recursive call of RANDOMIZED-QUICKSORT until PARTITION chooses some element $x \in Z_{ij}$ as a pivot. From that point on, the pivot x appears in no subsequent input set. The first time that RANDOMIZED-SELECT chooses a pivot $x \in Z_{ij}$ from a set containing all the elements of Z_{ij}, each element in Z_{ij} is equally likely to be x because the pivot is chosen uniformly at random. Since $|Z_{ij}| = j - i + 1$, the probability is $1/(j - i + 1)$ that any given element in Z_{ij} is the first pivot chosen from Z_{ij}. Thus, by Lemma 7.2, we have

$$
\begin{aligned}
\Pr\{z_i \text{ is compared with } z_j\} &= \Pr\{z_i \text{ or } z_j \text{ is the first pivot chosen from } Z_{ij}\} \\
&= \Pr\{z_i \text{ is the first pivot chosen from } Z_{ij}\} \\
&\quad + \Pr\{z_j \text{ is the first pivot chosen from } Z_{ij}\} \\
&= \frac{2}{j - i + 1},
\end{aligned}
$$

where the second line follows from the first because the two events are mutually exclusive.   ∎

We can now complete the analysis of randomized quicksort.

Theorem 7.4
The expected running time of RANDOMIZED-QUICKSORT on an input of n distinct elements is $O(n \lg n)$.

Proof The analysis uses indicator random variables (see Section 5.2). Let the n distinct elements be $z_1 < z_2 < \cdots < z_n$, and for $1 \le i < j \le n$, define the indicator random variable $X_{ij} = I\{z_i$ is compared with $z_j\}$. From Lemma 7.2, each pair is compared at most once, and so we can express X as follows:

$$X = \sum_{i=1}^{n-1} \sum_{j=i+1}^{n} X_{ij} .$$

By taking expectations of both sides and using linearity of expectation (equation (C.24) on page 1192) and Lemma 5.1 on page 130, we obtain

$$\begin{aligned}
E[X] &= E\left[\sum_{i=1}^{n-1} \sum_{j=i+1}^{n} X_{ij}\right] \\
&= \sum_{i=1}^{n-1} \sum_{j=i+1}^{n} E[X_{ij}] && \text{(by linearity of expectation)} \\
&= \sum_{i=1}^{n-1} \sum_{j=i+1}^{n} \Pr\{z_i \text{ is compared with } z_j\} && \text{(by Lemma 5.1)} \\
&= \sum_{i=1}^{n-1} \sum_{j=i+1}^{n} \frac{2}{j-i+1} && \text{(by Lemma 7.3)} .
\end{aligned}$$

We can evaluate this sum using a change of variables $(k = j - i)$ and the bound on the harmonic series in equation (A.9) on page 1142:

$$\begin{aligned}
E[X] &= \sum_{i=1}^{n-1} \sum_{j=i+1}^{n} \frac{2}{j-i+1} \\
&= \sum_{i=1}^{n-1} \sum_{k=1}^{n-i} \frac{2}{k+1} \\
&< \sum_{i=1}^{n-1} \sum_{k=1}^{n} \frac{2}{k} \\
&= \sum_{i=1}^{n-1} O(\lg n) \\
&= O(n \lg n) .
\end{aligned}$$

This bound and Lemma 7.1 allow us to conclude that the expected running time of RANDOMIZED-QUICKSORT is $O(n \lg n)$ (assuming that the element values are distinct). ∎

Exercises

7.4-1
Show that the recurrence

$$T(n) = \max \{T(q) + T(n - q - 1) : 0 \le q \le n - 1\} + \Theta(n)$$

has a lower bound of $T(n) = \Omega(n^2)$.

7.4-2
Show that quicksort's best-case running time is $\Omega(n \lg n)$.

7.4-3
Show that the expression $q^2 + (n - q - 1)^2$ achieves its maximum value over $q = 0, 1, \ldots, n - 1$ when $q = 0$ or $q = n - 1$.

7.4-4
Show that RANDOMIZED-QUICKSORT's expected running time is $\Omega(n \lg n)$.

7.4-5
Coarsening the recursion, as we did in Problem 2-1 for merge sort, is a common way to improve the running time of quicksort in practice. We modify the base case of the recursion so that if the array has fewer than k elements, the subarray is sorted by insertion sort, rather than by continued recursive calls to quicksort. Argue that the randomized version of this sorting algorithm runs in $O(nk + n \lg(n/k))$ expected time. How should you pick k, both in theory and in practice?

★ ***7.4-6***
Consider modifying the PARTITION procedure by randomly picking three elements from subarray $A[p:r]$ and partitioning about their median (the middle value of the three elements). Approximate the probability of getting worse than an α-to-$(1 - \alpha)$ split, as a function of α in the range $0 < \alpha < 1/2$.

Problems

7-1   *Hoare partition correctness*

The version of PARTITION given in this chapter is not the original partitioning algorithm. Here is the original partitioning algorithm, which is due to C. A. R. Hoare.

HOARE-PARTITION(A, p, r)

```
1   x = A[p]
2   i = p − 1
3   j = r + 1
4   while TRUE
5       repeat
6           j = j − 1
7       until A[j] ≤ x
8       repeat
9           i = i + 1
10      until A[i] ≥ x
11      if i < j
12          exchange A[i] with A[j]
13      else return j
```

a. Demonstrate the operation of HOARE-PARTITION on the array $A = \langle 13, 19, 9, 5, 12, 8, 7, 4, 11, 2, 6, 21 \rangle$, showing the values of the array and the indices i and j after each iteration of the **while** loop in lines 4–13.

b. Describe how the PARTITION procedure in Section 7.1 differs from HOARE-PARTITION when all elements in $A[p:r]$ are equal. Describe a practical advantage of HOARE-PARTITION over PARTITION for use in quicksort.

The next three questions ask you to give a careful argument that the procedure HOARE-PARTITION is correct. Assuming that the subarray $A[p:r]$ contains at least two elements, prove the following:

c. The indices i and j are such that the procedure never accesses an element of A outside the subarray $A[p:r]$.

d. When HOARE-PARTITION terminates, it returns a value j such that $p \leq j < r$.

e. Every element of $A[p:j]$ is less than or equal to every element of $A[j+1:r]$ when HOARE-PARTITION terminates.

The PARTITION procedure in Section 7.1 separates the pivot value (originally in $A[r]$) from the two partitions it forms. The HOARE-PARTITION procedure, on the other hand, always places the pivot value (originally in $A[p]$) into one of the two partitions $A[p:j]$ and $A[j+1:r]$. Since $p \leq j < r$, neither partition is empty.

f. Rewrite the QUICKSORT procedure to use HOARE-PARTITION.

7-2   Quicksort with equal element values

The analysis of the expected running time of randomized quicksort in Section 7.4.2 assumes that all element values are distinct. This problem examines what happens when they are not.

a. Suppose that all element values are equal. What is randomized quicksort's running time in this case?

b. The PARTITION procedure returns an index q such that each element of $A[p:q-1]$ is less than or equal to $A[q]$ and each element of $A[q+1:r]$ is greater than $A[q]$. Modify the PARTITION procedure to produce a procedure PARTITION$'(A, p, r)$, which permutes the elements of $A[p:r]$ and returns two indices q and t, where $p \leq q \leq t \leq r$, such that

- all elements of $A[q:t]$ are equal,
- each element of $A[p:q-1]$ is less than $A[q]$, and
- each element of $A[t+1:r]$ is greater than $A[q]$.

Like PARTITION, your PARTITION$'$ procedure should take $\Theta(r-p)$ time.

c. Modify the RANDOMIZED-PARTITION procedure to call PARTITION$'$, and name the new procedure RANDOMIZED-PARTITION$'$. Then modify the QUICKSORT procedure to produce a procedure QUICKSORT$'(A, p, r)$ that calls RANDOMIZED-PARTITION$'$ and recurses only on partitions where elements are not known to be equal to each other.

d. Using QUICKSORT$'$, adjust the analysis in Section 7.4.2 to avoid the assumption that all elements are distinct.

7-3   Alternative quicksort analysis

An alternative analysis of the running time of randomized quicksort focuses on the expected running time of each individual recursive call to RANDOMIZED-QUICKSORT, rather than on the number of comparisons performed. As in the analysis of Section 7.4.2, assume that the values of the elements are distinct.

a. Argue that, given an array of size n, the probability that any particular element is chosen as the pivot is $1/n$. Use this probability to define indicator random variables $X_i = I\{i\text{th smallest element is chosen as the pivot}\}$. What is $E[X_i]$?

b. Let $T(n)$ be a random variable denoting the running time of quicksort on an array of size n. Argue that

$$E[T(n)] = E\left[\sum_{q=1}^{n} X_q \left(T(q-1) + T(n-q) + \Theta(n)\right)\right].\tag{7.2}$$

c. Show how to rewrite equation (7.2) as

$$E[T(n)] = \frac{2}{n} \sum_{q=1}^{n-1} E[T(q)] + \Theta(n).\tag{7.3}$$

d. Show that

$$\sum_{q=1}^{n-1} q \lg q \leq \frac{n^2}{2} \lg n - \frac{n^2}{8}\tag{7.4}$$

for $n \geq 2$. (*Hint:* Split the summation into two parts, one summation for $q = 1, 2, \ldots, \lceil n/2 \rceil - 1$ and one summation for $q = \lceil n/2 \rceil, \ldots, n-1$.)

e. Using the bound from equation (7.4), show that the recurrence in equation (7.3) has the solution $E[T(n)] = O(n \lg n)$. (*Hint:* Show, by substitution, that $E[T(n)] \leq an \lg n$ for sufficiently large n and for some positive constant a.)

7-4 Stooge sort

Professors Howard, Fine, and Howard have proposed a deceptively simple sorting algorithm, named stooge sort in their honor, appearing on the following page.

a. Argue that the call STOOGE-SORT($A, 1, n$) correctly sorts the array $A[1:n]$.

b. Give a recurrence for the worst-case running time of STOOGE-SORT and a tight asymptotic (Θ-notation) bound on the worst-case running time.

c. Compare the worst-case running time of STOOGE-SORT with that of insertion sort, merge sort, heapsort, and quicksort. Do the professors deserve tenure?

STOOGE-SORT(A, p, r)

1 **if** $A[p] > A[r]$
2   exchange $A[p]$ with $A[r]$
3 **if** $p + 1 < r$
4      $k = \lfloor (r - p + 1)/3 \rfloor$ // round down
5   STOOGE-SORT($A, p, r - k$)   // first two-thirds
6   STOOGE-SORT($A, p + k, r$)   // last two-thirds
7   STOOGE-SORT($A, p, r - k$)   // first two-thirds again

7-5   *Stack depth for quicksort*

The QUICKSORT procedure of Section 7.1 makes two recursive calls to itself. After QUICKSORT calls PARTITION, it recursively sorts the low side of the partition and then it recursively sorts the high side of the partition. The second recursive call in QUICKSORT is not really necessary, because the procedure can instead use an iterative control structure. This transformation technique, called *tail-recursion elimination*, is provided automatically by good compilers. Applying tail-recursion elimination transforms QUICKSORT into the TRE-QUICKSORT procedure.

TRE-QUICKSORT(A, p, r)

1 **while** $p < r$
2   // Partition and then sort the low side.
3      $q = $ PARTITION(A, p, r)
4   TRE-QUICKSORT($A, p, q - 1$)
5      $p = q + 1$

a. Argue that TRE-QUICKSORT($A, 1, n$) correctly sorts the array $A[1:n]$.

Compilers usually execute recursive procedures by using a *stack* that contains pertinent information, including the parameter values, for each recursive call. The information for the most recent call is at the top of the stack, and the information for the initial call is at the bottom. When a procedure is called, its information is *pushed* onto the stack, and when it terminates, its information is *popped*. Since we assume that array parameters are represented by pointers, the information for each procedure call on the stack requires $O(1)$ stack space. The *stack depth* is the maximum amount of stack space used at any time during a computation.

b. Describe a scenario in which TRE-QUICKSORT's stack depth is $\Theta(n)$ on an n-element input array.

c. Modify TRE-QUICKSORT so that the worst-case stack depth is $\Theta(\lg n)$. Maintain the $O(n \lg n)$ expected running time of the algorithm.

7-6 Median-of-3 partition

One way to improve the RANDOMIZED-QUICKSORT procedure is to partition around a pivot that is chosen more carefully than by picking a random element from the subarray. A common approach is the *median-of-3* method: choose the pivot as the median (middle element) of a set of 3 elements randomly selected from the subarray. (See Exercise 7.4-6.) For this problem, assume that the n elements in the input subarray $A[p:r]$ are distinct and that $n \geq 3$. Denote the sorted version of $A[p:r]$ by $z_1, z_2, \ldots, z_n$. Using the median-of-3 method to choose the pivot element x, define $p_i = \Pr\{x = z_i\}$.

a. Give an exact formula for p_i as a function of n and i for $i = 2, 3, \ldots, n - 1$. (Observe that $p_1 = p_n = 0$.)

b. By what amount does the median-of-3 method increase the likelihood of choosing the pivot to be $x = z_{\lfloor(n+1)/2\rfloor}$, the median of $A[p:r]$, compared with the ordinary implementation? Assume that $n \to \infty$, and give the limiting ratio of these probabilities.

c. Suppose that we define a "good" split to mean choosing the pivot as $x = z_i$, where $n/3 \leq i \leq 2n/3$. By what amount does the median-of-3 method increase the likelihood of getting a good split compared with the ordinary implementation? (*Hint:* Approximate the sum by an integral.)

d. Argue that in the $\Omega(n \lg n)$ running time of quicksort, the median-of-3 method affects only the constant factor.

7-7 Fuzzy sorting of intervals

Consider a sorting problem in which you do not know the numbers exactly. Instead, for each number, you know an interval on the real line to which it belongs. That is, you are given n closed intervals of the form $[a_i, b_i]$, where $a_i \leq b_i$. The goal is to *fuzzy-sort* these intervals: to produce a permutation $\langle i_1, i_2, \ldots, i_n \rangle$ of the intervals such that for $j = 1, 2, \ldots, n$, there exist $c_j \in [a_{i_j}, b_{i_j}]$ satisfying $c_1 \leq c_2 \leq \cdots \leq c_n$.

a. Design a randomized algorithm for fuzzy-sorting n intervals. Your algorithm should have the general structure of an algorithm that quicksorts the left endpoints (the a_i values), but it should take advantage of overlapping intervals to improve the running time. (As the intervals overlap more and more, the problem of fuzzy-sorting the intervals becomes progressively easier. Your algorithm should take advantage of such overlapping, to the extent that it exists.)

b. Argue that your algorithm runs in $\Theta(n \lg n)$ expected time in general, but runs in $\Theta(n)$ expected time when all of the intervals overlap (i.e., when there exists a value x such that $x \in [a_i, b_i]$ for all i). Your algorithm should not be checking for this case explicitly, but rather, its performance should naturally improve as the amount of overlap increases.

Chapter notes

Quicksort was invented by Hoare [219], and his version of PARTITION appears in Problem 7-1. Bentley [51, p. 117] attributes the PARTITION procedure given in Section 7.1 to N. Lomuto. The analysis in Section 7.4 based on an analysis due to Motwani and Raghavan [336]. Sedgewick [401] and Bentley [51] provide good references on the details of implementation and how they matter.

McIlroy [323] shows how to engineer a "killer adversary" that produces an array on which virtually any implementation of quicksort takes $\Theta(n^2)$ time.

8 Sorting in Linear Time

We have now seen a handful of algorithms that can sort n numbers in $O(n \lg n)$ time. Whereas merge sort and heapsort achieve this upper bound in the worst case, quicksort achieves it on average. Moreover, for each of these algorithms, we can produce a sequence of n input numbers that causes the algorithm to run in $\Omega(n \lg n)$ time.

These algorithms share an interesting property: *the sorted order they determine is based only on comparisons between the input elements.* We call such sorting algorithms *comparison sorts*. All the sorting algorithms introduced thus far are comparison sorts.

In Section 8.1, we'll prove that any comparison sort must make $\Omega(n \lg n)$ comparisons in the worst case to sort n elements. Thus, merge sort and heapsort are asymptotically optimal, and no comparison sort exists that is faster by more than a constant factor.

Sections 8.2, 8.3, and 8.4 examine three sorting algorithms—counting sort, radix sort, and bucket sort—that run in linear time on certain types of inputs. Of course, these algorithms use operations other than comparisons to determine the sorted order. Consequently, the $\Omega(n \lg n)$ lower bound does not apply to them.

8.1 Lower bounds for sorting

A comparison sort uses only comparisons between elements to gain order information about an input sequence $\langle a_1, a_2, \ldots, a_n \rangle$. That is, given two elements a_i and a_j, it performs one of the tests $a_i < a_j, a_i \le a_j, a_i = a_j, a_i \ge a_j,$ or $a_i > a_j$ to determine their relative order. It may not inspect the values of the elements or gain order information about them in any other way.

Since we are proving a lower bound, we assume without loss of generality in this section that all the input elements are distinct. After all, a lower bound for distinct elements applies when elements may or may not be distinct. Consequently,

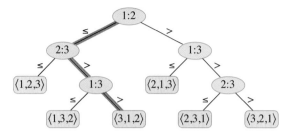

Figure 8.1 The decision tree for insertion sort operating on three elements. An internal node (shown in blue) annotated by $i:j$ indicates a comparison between a_i and a_j. A leaf annotated by the permutation $\langle \pi(1), \pi(2), \ldots, \pi(n) \rangle$ indicates the ordering $a_{\pi(1)} \leq a_{\pi(2)} \leq \cdots \leq a_{\pi(n)}$. The highlighted path indicates the decisions made when sorting the input sequence $\langle a_1 = 6, a_2 = 8, a_3 = 5 \rangle$. Going left from the root node, labeled 1:2, indicates that $a_1 \leq a_2$. Going right from the node labeled 2:3 indicates that $a_2 > a_3$. Going right from the node labeled 1:3 indicates that $a_1 > a_3$. Therefore, we have the ordering $a_3 \leq a_1 \leq a_2$, as indicated in the leaf labeled $\langle 3, 1, 2 \rangle$. Because the three input elements have $3! = 6$ possible permutations, the decision tree must have at least 6 leaves.

comparisons of the form $a_i = a_j$ are useless, which means that we can assume that no comparisons for exact equality occur. Moreover, the comparisons $a_i \leq a_j$, $a_i \geq a_j$, $a_i > a_j$, and $a_i < a_j$ are all equivalent in that they yield identical information about the relative order of a_i and a_j. We therefore assume that all comparisons have the form $a_i \leq a_j$.

The decision-tree model

We can view comparison sorts abstractly in terms of decision trees. A *decision tree* is a full binary tree (each node is either a leaf or has both children) that represents the comparisons between elements that are performed by a particular sorting algorithm operating on an input of a given size. Control, data movement, and all other aspects of the algorithm are ignored. Figure 8.1 shows the decision tree corresponding to the insertion sort algorithm from Section 2.1 operating on an input sequence of three elements.

A decision tree has each internal node annotated by $i:j$ for some i and j in the range $1 \leq i, j \leq n$, where n is the number of elements in the input sequence. We also annotate each leaf by a permutation $\langle \pi(1), \pi(2), \ldots, \pi(n) \rangle$. (See Section C.1 for background on permutations.) Indices in the internal nodes and the leaves always refer to the original positions of the array elements at the start of the sorting algorithm. The execution of the comparison sorting algorithm corresponds to tracing a simple path from the root of the decision tree down to a leaf. Each internal node indicates a comparison $a_i \leq a_j$. The left subtree then dictates subsequent comparisons once we know that $a_i \leq a_j$, and the right subtree dictates subsequent comparisons when $a_i > a_j$. Arriving at a leaf, the sorting algorithm has established the ordering $a_{\pi(1)} \leq a_{\pi(2)} \leq \cdots \leq a_{\pi(n)}$. Because any correct sorting algorithm must be able to produce each permutation of its input, each of the $n!$ permutations on n elements must appear as at least one of the leaves of the decision tree for a comparison sort to be correct. Furthermore, each of these leaves must be reachable from the root by a downward path corresponding to an actual execution of the comparison sort. (We call such leaves "reachable.") Thus, we consider only decision trees in which each permutation appears as a reachable leaf.

A lower bound for the worst case

The length of the longest simple path from the root of a decision tree to any of its reachable leaves represents the worst-case number of comparisons that the corresponding sorting algorithm performs. Consequently, the worst-case number of comparisons for a given comparison sort algorithm equals the height of its decision tree. A lower bound on the heights of all decision trees in which each permutation appears as a reachable leaf is therefore a lower bound on the running time of any comparison sort algorithm. The following theorem establishes such a lower bound.

Theorem 8.1
Any comparison sort algorithm requires $\Omega(n \lg n)$ comparisons in the worst case.

Proof   From the preceding discussion, it suffices to determine the height of a decision tree in which each permutation appears as a reachable leaf. Consider a decision tree of height h with l reachable leaves corresponding to a comparison sort on n elements. Because each of the $n!$ permutations of the input appears as one or more leaves, we have $n! \leq l$. Since a binary tree of height h has no more than 2^h leaves, we have

$$n! \leq l \leq 2^h ,$$

which, by taking logarithms, implies

$h \geq \lg(n!)$ (since the lg function is monotonically increasing)

$\quad = \Omega(n \lg n)$ (by equation (3.28) on page 67) .   ∎

Corollary 8.2
Heapsort and merge sort are asymptotically optimal comparison sorts.

Proof   The $O(n \lg n)$ upper bounds on the running times for heapsort and merge sort match the $\Omega(n \lg n)$ worst-case lower bound from Theorem 8.1.   ∎

Exercises

8.1-1
What is the smallest possible depth of a leaf in a decision tree for a comparison sort?

8.1-2
Obtain asymptotically tight bounds on $\lg(n!)$ without using Stirling's approximation. Instead, evaluate the summation $\sum_{k=1}^{n} \lg k$ using techniques from Section A.2.

8.1-3
Show that there is no comparison sort whose running time is linear for at least half of the $n!$ inputs of length n. What about a fraction of $1/n$ of the inputs of length n? What about a fraction $1/2^n$?

8.1-4
You are given an n-element input sequence, and you know in advance that it is partly sorted in the following sense. Each element initially in position i such that $i \bmod 4 = 0$ is either already in its correct position, or it is one place away from its correct position. For example, you know that after sorting, the element initially in position 12 belongs in position 11, 12, or 13. You have no advance information about the other elements, in positions i where $i \bmod 4 \neq 0$. Show that an $\Omega(n \lg n)$ lower bound on comparison-based sorting still holds in this case.

8.2   Counting sort

Counting sort assumes that each of the n input elements is an integer in the range 0 to k, for some integer k. It runs in $\Theta(n + k)$ time, so that when $k = O(n)$, counting sort runs in $\Theta(n)$ time.

Counting sort first determines, for each input element x, the number of elements less than or equal to x. It then uses this information to place element x directly into its position in the output array. For example, if 17 elements are less than or equal to x, then x belongs in output position 17. We must modify this scheme slightly to handle the situation in which several elements have the same value, since we do not want them all to end up in the same position.

The COUNTING-SORT procedure on the facing page takes as input an array $A[1:n]$, the size n of this array, and the limit k on the nonnegative integer values in A. It returns its sorted output in the array $B[1:n]$ and uses an array $C[0:k]$ for temporary working storage.

COUNTING-SORT(A, n, k)

```
 1   let B[1:n] and C[0:k] be new arrays
 2   for i = 0 to k
 3        C[i] = 0
 4   for j = 1 to n
 5        C[A[j]] = C[A[j]] + 1
 6   // C[i] now contains the number of elements equal to i.
 7   for i = 1 to k
 8        C[i] = C[i] + C[i − 1]
 9   // C[i] now contains the number of elements less than or equal to i.
10   // Copy A to B, starting from the end of A.
11   for j = n downto 1
12        B[C[A[j]]] = A[j]
13        C[A[j]] = C[A[j]] − 1   // to handle duplicate values
14   return B
```

Figure 8.2 illustrates counting sort. After the **for** loop of lines 2–3 initializes the array C to all zeros, the **for** loop of lines 4–5 makes a pass over the array A to inspect each input element. Each time it finds an input element whose value is i, it increments $C[i]$. Thus, after line 5, $C[i]$ holds the number of input elements equal to i for each integer $i = 0, 1, \ldots, k$. Lines 7–8 determine for each $i = 0, 1, \ldots, k$ how many input elements are less than or equal to i by keeping a running sum of the array C.

Finally, the **for** loop of lines 11–13 makes another pass over A, but in reverse, to place each element $A[j]$ into its correct sorted position in the output array B. If all n elements are distinct, then when line 11 is first entered, for each $A[j]$, the value $C[A[j]]$ is the correct final position of $A[j]$ in the output array, since there are $C[A[j]]$ elements less than or equal to $A[j]$. Because the elements might not be distinct, the loop decrements $C[A[j]]$ each time it places a value $A[j]$ into B. Decrementing $C[A[j]]$ causes the previous element in A with a value equal to $A[j]$, if one exists, to go to the position immediately before $A[j]$ in the output array B.

How much time does counting sort require? The **for** loop of lines 2–3 takes $\Theta(k)$ time, the **for** loop of lines 4–5 takes $\Theta(n)$ time, the **for** loop of lines 7–8 takes $\Theta(k)$ time, and the **for** loop of lines 11–13 takes $\Theta(n)$ time. Thus, the overall time is $\Theta(k + n)$. In practice, we usually use counting sort when we have $k = O(n)$, in which case the running time is $\Theta(n)$.

Counting sort can beat the lower bound of $\Omega(n \lg n)$ proved in Section 8.1 because it is not a comparison sort. In fact, no comparisons between input elements occur anywhere in the code. Instead, counting sort uses the actual values of the

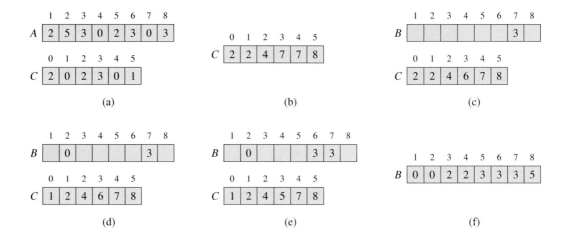

Figure 8.2   The operation of COUNTING-SORT on an input array $A[1:8]$, where each element of A is a nonnegative integer no larger than $k = 5$. **(a)** The array A and the auxiliary array C after line 5. **(b)** The array C after line 8. **(c)–(e)** The output array B and the auxiliary array C after one, two, and three iterations of the loop in lines 11–13, respectively. Only the tan elements of array B have been filled in. **(f)** The final sorted output array B.

elements to index into an array. The $\Omega(n \lg n)$ lower bound for sorting does not apply when we depart from the comparison sort model.

An important property of counting sort is that it is *stable*: elements with the same value appear in the output array in the same order as they do in the input array. That is, it breaks ties between two elements by the rule that whichever element appears first in the input array appears first in the output array. Normally, the property of stability is important only when satellite data are carried around with the element being sorted. Counting sort's stability is important for another reason: counting sort is often used as a subroutine in radix sort. As we shall see in the next section, in order for radix sort to work correctly, counting sort must be stable.

Exercises

8.2-1
Using Figure 8.2 as a model, illustrate the operation of COUNTING-SORT on the array $A = \langle 6, 0, 2, 0, 1, 3, 4, 6, 1, 3, 2 \rangle$.

8.2-2
Prove that COUNTING-SORT is stable.

8.2-3
Suppose that we were to rewrite the **for** loop header in line 11 of the COUNTING-SORT as

11 **for** $j = 1$ **to** n

Show that the algorithm still works properly, but that it is not stable. Then rewrite the pseudocode for counting sort so that elements with the same value are written into the output array in order of increasing index and the algorithm is stable.

8.2-4
Prove the following loop invariant for COUNTING-SORT:

At the start of each iteration of the **for** loop of lines 11–13, the last element in A with value i that has not yet been copied into B belongs in $B[C[i]]$.

8.2-5
Suppose that the array being sorted contains only integers in the range 0 to k and that there are no satellite data to move with those keys. Modify counting sort to use just the arrays A and C, putting the sorted result back into array A instead of into a new array B.

8.2-6
Describe an algorithm that, given n integers in the range 0 to k, preprocesses its input and then answers any query about how many of the n integers fall into a range $[a:b]$ in $O(1)$ time. Your algorithm should use $\Theta(n + k)$ preprocessing time.

8.2-7
Counting sort can also work efficiently if the input values have fractional parts, but the number of digits in the fractional part is small. Suppose that you are given n numbers in the range 0 to k, each with at most d decimal (base 10) digits to the right of the decimal point. Modify counting sort to run in $\Theta(n + 10^d k)$ time.

8.3 Radix sort

Radix sort is the algorithm used by the card-sorting machines you now find only in computer museums. The cards have 80 columns, and in each column a machine can punch a hole in one of 12 places. The sorter can be mechanically "programmed" to examine a given column of each card in a deck and distribute the card into one

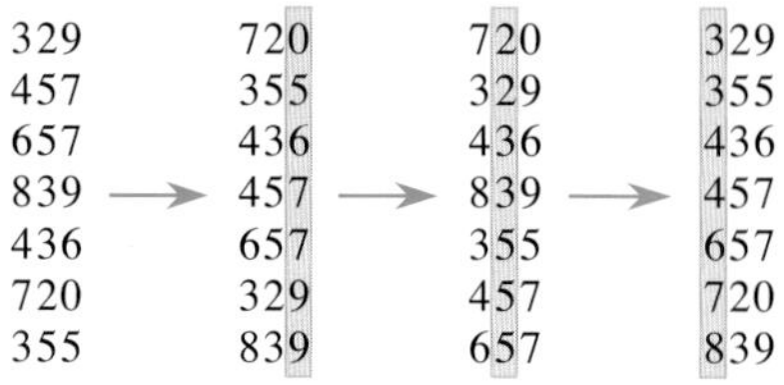

```
329       720       720       329
457       355       329       355
657       436       436       436
839  ───►  457  ───►  839  ───►  457
436       657       355       657
720       329       457       720
355       839       657       839
```

Figure 8.3 The operation of radix sort on seven 3-digit numbers. The leftmost column is the input. The remaining columns show the numbers after successive sorts on increasingly significant digit positions. Tan shading indicates the digit position sorted on to produce each list from the previous one.

of 12 bins depending on which place has been punched. An operator can then gather the cards bin by bin, so that cards with the first place punched are on top of cards with the second place punched, and so on.

For decimal digits, each column uses only 10 places. (The other two places are reserved for encoding nonnumeric characters.) A d-digit number occupies a field of d columns. Since the card sorter can look at only one column at a time, the problem of sorting n cards on a d-digit number requires a sorting algorithm.

Intuitively, you might sort numbers on their *most significant* (leftmost) digit, sort each of the resulting bins recursively, and then combine the decks in order. Unfortunately, since the cards in 9 of the 10 bins must be put aside to sort each of the bins, this procedure generates many intermediate piles of cards that you would have to keep track of. (See Exercise 8.3-6.)

Radix sort solves the problem of card sorting—counterintuitively—by sorting on the *least significant* digit first. The algorithm then combines the cards into a single deck, with the cards in the 0 bin preceding the cards in the 1 bin preceding the cards in the 2 bin, and so on. Then it sorts the entire deck again on the second-least significant digit and recombines the deck in a like manner. The process continues until the cards have been sorted on all d digits. Remarkably, at that point the cards are fully sorted on the d-digit number. Thus, only d passes through the deck are required to sort. Figure 8.3 shows how radix sort operates on a "deck" of seven 3-digit numbers.

In order for radix sort to work correctly, the digit sorts must be stable. The sort performed by a card sorter is stable, but the operator must be careful not to change the order of the cards as they come out of a bin, even though all the cards in a bin have the same digit in the chosen column.

In a typical computer, which is a sequential random-access machine, we sometimes use radix sort to sort records of information that are keyed by multiple fields. For example, we might wish to sort dates by three keys: year, month, and day. We could run a sorting algorithm with a comparison function that, given two dates, compares years, and if there is a tie, compares months, and if another tie occurs, compares days. Alternatively, we could sort the information three times with a stable sort: first on day (the "least significant" part), next on month, and finally on year.

The code for radix sort is straightforward. The RADIX-SORT procedure assumes that each element in array $A[1:n]$ has d digits, where digit 1 is the lowest-order digit and digit d is the highest-order digit.

RADIX-SORT(A, n, d)

1 **for** $i = 1$ **to** d
2   use a stable sort to sort array $A[1:n]$ on digit i

Although the pseudocode for RADIX-SORT does not specify which stable sort to use, COUNTING-SORT is commonly used. If you use COUNTING-SORT as the stable sort, you can make RADIX-SORT a little more efficient by revising COUNTING-SORT to take a pointer to the output array as a parameter, having RADIX-SORT preallocate this array, and alternating input and output between the two arrays in successive iterations of the **for** loop in RADIX-SORT.

Lemma 8.3
Given n d-digit numbers in which each digit can take on up to k possible values, RADIX-SORT correctly sorts these numbers in $\Theta(d(n + k))$ time if the stable sort it uses takes $\Theta(n + k)$ time.

Proof The correctness of radix sort follows by induction on the column being sorted (see Exercise 8.3-3). The analysis of the running time depends on the stable sort used as the intermediate sorting algorithm. When each digit lies in the range 0 to $k - 1$ (so that it can take on k possible values), and k is not too large, counting sort is the obvious choice. Each pass over n d-digit numbers then takes $\Theta(n + k)$ time. There are d passes, and so the total time for radix sort is $\Theta(d(n + k))$. ∎

When d is constant and $k = O(n)$, we can make radix sort run in linear time. More generally, we have some flexibility in how to break each key into digits.

Lemma 8.4
Given n b-bit numbers and any positive integer $r \le b$, RADIX-SORT correctly sorts these numbers in $\Theta((b/r)(n + 2^r))$ time if the stable sort it uses takes $\Theta(n + k)$ time for inputs in the range 0 to k.

Proof For a value $r \leq b$, view each key as having $d = \lceil b/r \rceil$ digits of r bits each. Each digit is an integer in the range 0 to $2^r - 1$, so that we can use counting sort with $k = 2^r - 1$. (For example, we can view a 32-bit word as having four 8-bit digits, so that $b = 32, r = 8, k = 2^r - 1 = 255$, and $d = b/r = 4$.) Each pass of counting sort takes $\Theta(n + k) = \Theta(n + 2^r)$ time and there are d passes, for a total running time of $\Theta(d(n + 2^r)) = \Theta((b/r)(n + 2^r))$. ∎

Given n and b, what value of $r \leq b$ minimizes the expression $(b/r)(n + 2^r)$? As r decreases, the factor b/r increases, but as r increases so does 2^r. The answer depends on whether $b < \lfloor \lg n \rfloor$. If $b < \lfloor \lg n \rfloor$, then $r \leq b$ implies $(n + 2^r) = \Theta(n)$. Thus, choosing $r = b$ yields a running time of $(b/b)(n + 2^b) = \Theta(n)$, which is asymptotically optimal. If $b \geq \lfloor \lg n \rfloor$, then choosing $r = \lfloor \lg n \rfloor$ gives the best running time to within a constant factor, which we can see as follows.[1] Choosing $r = \lfloor \lg n \rfloor$ yields a running time of $\Theta(bn / \lg n)$. As r increases above $\lfloor \lg n \rfloor$, the 2^r term in the numerator increases faster than the r term in the denominator, and so increasing r above $\lfloor \lg n \rfloor$ yields a running time of $\Omega(bn / \lg n)$. If instead r were to decrease below $\lfloor \lg n \rfloor$, then the b/r term increases and the $n + 2^r$ term remains at $\Theta(n)$.

Is radix sort preferable to a comparison-based sorting algorithm, such as quicksort? If $b = O(\lg n)$, as is often the case, and $r \approx \lg n$, then radix sort's running time is $\Theta(n)$, which appears to be better than quicksort's expected running time of $\Theta(n \lg n)$. The constant factors hidden in the Θ-notation differ, however. Although radix sort may make fewer passes than quicksort over the n keys, each pass of radix sort may take significantly longer. Which sorting algorithm to prefer depends on the characteristics of the implementations, of the underlying machine (e.g., quicksort often uses hardware caches more effectively than radix sort), and of the input data. Moreover, the version of radix sort that uses counting sort as the intermediate stable sort does not sort in place, which many of the $\Theta(n \lg n)$-time comparison sorts do. Thus, when primary memory storage is at a premium, an in-place algorithm such as quicksort could be the better choice.

Exercises

8.3-1
Using Figure 8.3 as a model, illustrate the operation of RADIX-SORT on the following list of English words: COW, DOG, SEA, RUG, ROW, MOB, BOX, TAB, BAR, EAR, TAR, DIG, BIG, TEA, NOW, FOX.

---

[1] The choice of $r = \lfloor \lg n \rfloor$ assumes that $n > 1$. If $n \leq 1$, there is nothing to sort.

8.3-2
Which of the following sorting algorithms are stable: insertion sort, merge sort, heapsort, and quicksort? Give a simple scheme that makes any comparison sort stable. How much additional time and space does your scheme entail?

8.3-3
Use induction to prove that radix sort works. Where does your proof need the assumption that the intermediate sort is stable?

8.3-4
Suppose that COUNTING-SORT is used as the stable sort within RADIX-SORT. If RADIX-SORT calls COUNTING-SORT d times, then since each call of COUNTING-SORT makes two passes over the data (lines 4–5 and 11–13), altogether $2d$ passes over the data occur. Describe how to reduce the total number of passes to $d + 1$.

8.3-5
Show how to sort n integers in the range 0 to $n^3 - 1$ in $O(n)$ time.

★ ***8.3-6***
In the first card-sorting algorithm in this section, which sorts on the most significant digit first, exactly how many sorting passes are needed to sort d-digit decimal numbers in the worst case? How many piles of cards does an operator need to keep track of in the worst case?

8.4   Bucket sort

Bucket sort assumes that the input is drawn from a uniform distribution and has an average-case running time of $O(n)$. Like counting sort, bucket sort is fast because it assumes something about the input. Whereas counting sort assumes that the input consists of integers in a small range, bucket sort assumes that the input is generated by a random process that distributes elements uniformly and independently over the interval $[0, 1)$. (See Section C.2 for a definition of a uniform distribution.)

Bucket sort divides the interval $[0, 1)$ into n equal-sized subintervals, or *buckets*, and then distributes the n input numbers into the buckets. Since the inputs are uniformly and independently distributed over $[0, 1)$, we do not expect many numbers to fall into each bucket. To produce the output, we simply sort the numbers in each bucket and then go through the buckets in order, listing the elements in each.

The BUCKET-SORT procedure on the next page assumes that the input is an array $A[1 : n]$ and that each element $A[i]$ in the array satisfies $0 \leq A[i] < 1$. The code requires an auxiliary array $B[0 : n - 1]$ of linked lists (buckets) and assumes

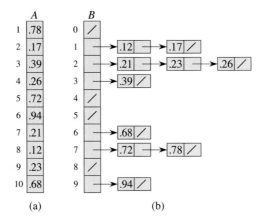

Figure 8.4   The operation of BUCKET-SORT for $n = 10$. **(a)** The input array $A[1:10]$. **(b)** The array $B[0:9]$ of sorted lists (buckets) after line 7 of the algorithm, with slashes indicating the end of each bucket. Bucket i holds values in the half-open interval $[i/10, (i+1)/10)$. The sorted output consists of a concatenation of the lists $B[0], B[1], \dots, B[9]$ in order.

that there is a mechanism for maintaining such lists. (Section 10.2 describes how to implement basic operations on linked lists.) Figure 8.4 shows the operation of bucket sort on an input array of 10 numbers.

BUCKET-SORT(A, n)

```
1   let B[0:n-1] be a new array
2   for i = 0 to n-1
3       make B[i] an empty list
4   for i = 1 to n
5       insert A[i] into list B[⌊n · A[i]⌋]
6   for i = 0 to n-1
7       sort list B[i] with insertion sort
8   concatenate the lists B[0], B[1], ..., B[n-1] together in order
9   return the concatenated lists
```

To see that this algorithm works, consider two elements $A[i]$ and $A[j]$. Assume without loss of generality that $A[i] \leq A[j]$. Since $\lfloor n \cdot A[i] \rfloor \leq \lfloor n \cdot A[j] \rfloor$, either element $A[i]$ goes into the same bucket as $A[j]$ or it goes into a bucket with a lower index. If $A[i]$ and $A[j]$ go into the same bucket, then the **for** loop of lines 6–7 puts them into the proper order. If $A[i]$ and $A[j]$ go into different buckets, then line 8 puts them into the proper order. Therefore, bucket sort works correctly.

To analyze the running time, observe that, together, all lines except line 7 take $O(n)$ time in the worst case. We need to analyze the total time taken by the n calls to insertion sort in line 7.

To analyze the cost of the calls to insertion sort, let n_i be the random variable denoting the number of elements placed in bucket $B[i]$. Since insertion sort runs in quadratic time (see Section 2.2), the running time of bucket sort is

$$T(n) = \Theta(n) + \sum_{i=0}^{n-1} O(n_i^2) \, . \tag{8.1}$$

We now analyze the average-case running time of bucket sort, by computing the expected value of the running time, where we take the expectation over the input distribution. Taking expectations of both sides and using linearity of expectation (equation (C.24) on page 1192), we have

$$
\begin{aligned}
\mathrm{E}\left[T(n)\right] &= \mathrm{E}\left[\Theta(n) + \sum_{i=0}^{n-1} O(n_i^2)\right] \\
&= \Theta(n) + \sum_{i=0}^{n-1} \mathrm{E}\left[O(n_i^2)\right] \quad \text{(by linearity of expectation)} \\
&= \Theta(n) + \sum_{i=0}^{n-1} O\left(\mathrm{E}\left[n_i^2\right]\right) \quad \text{(by equation (C.25) on page 1193)} \, . \tag{8.2}
\end{aligned}
$$

We claim that

$$\mathrm{E}\left[n_i^2\right] = 2 - 1/n \tag{8.3}$$

for $i = 0, 1, \ldots, n-1$. It is no surprise that each bucket i has the same value of $\mathrm{E}[n_i^2]$, since each value in the input array A is equally likely to fall in any bucket.

To prove equation (8.3), view each random variable n_i as the number of successes in n Bernoulli trials (see Section C.4). Success in a trial occurs when an element goes into bucket $B[i]$, with a probability $p = 1/n$ of success and $q = 1 - 1/n$ of failure. A binomial distribution counts n_i, the number of successes, in the n trials. By equations (C.41) and (C.44) on pages 1199–1200, we have $\mathrm{E}[n_i] = np = n(1/n) = 1$ and $\mathrm{Var}[n_i] = npq = 1 - 1/n$. Equation (C.31) on page 1194 gives

$$
\begin{aligned}
\mathrm{E}\left[n_i^2\right] &= \mathrm{Var}\left[n_i\right] + \mathrm{E}^2\left[n_i\right] \\
&= (1 - 1/n) + 1^2 \\
&= 2 - 1/n \, ,
\end{aligned}
$$

which proves equation (8.3). Using this expected value in equation (8.2), we get that the average-case running time for bucket sort is $\Theta(n) + n \cdot O(2 - 1/n) = \Theta(n)$.

Even if the input is not drawn from a uniform distribution, bucket sort may still run in linear time. As long as the input has the property that the sum of the squares of the bucket sizes is linear in the total number of elements, equation (8.1) tells us that bucket sort runs in linear time.

Exercises

8.4-1
Using Figure 8.4 as a model, illustrate the operation of BUCKET-SORT on the array $A = \langle .79, .13, .16, .64, .39, .20, .89, .53, .71, .42 \rangle$.

8.4-2
Explain why the worst-case running time for bucket sort is $\Theta(n^2)$. What simple change to the algorithm preserves its linear average-case running time and makes its worst-case running time $O(n \lg n)$?

8.4-3
Let X be a random variable that is equal to the number of heads in two flips of a fair coin. What is $E[X^2]$? What is $E^2[X]$?

8.4-4
An array A of size $n > 10$ is filled in the following way. For each element $A[i]$, choose two random variables x_i and y_i uniformly and independently from $[0, 1)$. Then set

$$A[i] = \frac{\lfloor 10x_i \rfloor}{10} + \frac{y_i}{n} \,.$$

Modify bucket sort so that it sorts the array A in $O(n)$ expected time.

★ 8.4-5
You are given n points in the unit disk, $p_i = (x_i, y_i)$, such that $0 < x_i^2 + y_i^2 \leq 1$ for $i = 1, 2, \ldots, n$. Suppose that the points are uniformly distributed, that is, the probability of finding a point in any region of the disk is proportional to the area of that region. Design an algorithm with an average-case running time of $\Theta(n)$ to sort the n points by their distances $d_i = \sqrt{x_i^2 + y_i^2}$ from the origin. (*Hint:* Design the bucket sizes in BUCKET-SORT to reflect the uniform distribution of the points in the unit disk.)

★ 8.4-6
A *probability distribution function* $P(x)$ for a random variable X is defined by $P(x) = \Pr\{X \leq x\}$. Suppose that you draw a list of n random variables

$X_1, X_2, \ldots, X_n$ from a continuous probability distribution function P that is computable in $O(1)$ time (given y you can find x such that $P(x) = y$ in $O(1)$ time). Give an algorithm that sorts these numbers in linear average-case time.

Problems

8-1 Probabilistic lower bounds on comparison sorting

In this problem, you will prove a probabilistic $\Omega(n \lg n)$ lower bound on the running time of any deterministic or randomized comparison sort on n distinct input elements. You'll begin by examining a deterministic comparison sort A with decision tree T_A. Assume that every permutation of A's inputs is equally likely.

a. Suppose that each leaf of T_A is labeled with the probability that it is reached given a random input. Prove that exactly $n!$ leaves are labeled $1/n!$ and that the rest are labeled 0.

b. Let $D(T)$ denote the external path length of a decision tree T — the sum of the depths of all the leaves of T. Let T be a decision tree with $k > 1$ leaves, and let LT and RT be the left and right subtrees of T. Show that $D(T) = D(LT) + D(RT) + k$.

c. Let $d(k)$ be the minimum value of $D(T)$ over all decision trees T with $k > 1$ leaves. Show that $d(k) = \min\{d(i) + d(k - i) + k : 1 \le i \le k - 1\}$. (*Hint:* Consider a decision tree T with k leaves that achieves the minimum. Let i_0 be the number of leaves in LT and $k - i_0$ the number of leaves in RT.)

d. Prove that for a given value of $k > 1$ and i in the range $1 \le i \le k - 1$, the function $i \lg i + (k - i) \lg(k - i)$ is minimized at $i = k/2$. Conclude that $d(k) = \Omega(k \lg k)$.

e. Prove that $D(T_A) = \Omega(n! \lg(n!))$, and conclude that the average-case time to sort n elements is $\Omega(n \lg n)$.

Now consider a *randomized* comparison sort B. We can extend the decision-tree model to handle randomization by incorporating two kinds of nodes: ordinary comparison nodes and "randomization" nodes. A randomization node models a random choice of the form RANDOM$(1, r)$ made by algorithm B. The node has r children, each of which is equally likely to be chosen during an execution of the algorithm.

f. Show that for any randomized comparison sort B, there exists a deterministic comparison sort A whose expected number of comparisons is no more than those made by B.

8-2   *Sorting in place in linear time*

You have an array of n data records to sort, each with a key of 0 or 1. An algorithm for sorting such a set of records might possess some subset of the following three desirable characteristics:

1. The algorithm runs in $O(n)$ time.

2. The algorithm is stable.

3. The algorithm sorts in place, using no more than a constant amount of storage space in addition to the original array.

a. Give an algorithm that satisfies criteria 1 and 2 above.

b. Give an algorithm that satisfies criteria 1 and 3 above.

c. Give an algorithm that satisfies criteria 2 and 3 above.

d. Can you use any of your sorting algorithms from parts (a)–(c) as the sorting method used in line 2 of RADIX-SORT, so that RADIX-SORT sorts n records with b-bit keys in $O(bn)$ time? Explain how or why not.

e. Suppose that the n records have keys in the range from 1 to k. Show how to modify counting sort so that it sorts the records in place in $O(n + k)$ time. You may use $O(k)$ storage outside the input array. Is your algorithm stable?

8-3   *Sorting variable-length items*

a. You are given an array of integers, where different integers may have different numbers of digits, but the total number of digits over *all* the integers in the array is n. Show how to sort the array in $O(n)$ time.

b. You are given an array of strings, where different strings may have different numbers of characters, but the total number of characters over all the strings is n. Show how to sort the strings in $O(n)$ time. (The desired order is the standard alphabetical order: for example, a $<$ ab $<$ b.)

8-4   *Water jugs*

You are given n red and n blue water jugs, all of different shapes and sizes. All the red jugs hold different amounts of water, as do all the blue jugs, and you cannot tell from the size of a jug how much water it holds. Moreover, for every jug of one color, there is a jug of the other color that holds the same amount of water.

Your task is to group the jugs into pairs of red and blue jugs that hold the same amount of water. To do so, you may perform the following operation: pick a pair of jugs in which one is red and one is blue, fill the red jug with water, and then pour the water into the blue jug. This operation tells you whether the red jug or the blue jug can hold more water, or that they have the same volume. Assume that such a comparison takes one time unit. Your goal is to find an algorithm that makes a minimum number of comparisons to determine the grouping. Remember that you may not directly compare two red jugs or two blue jugs.

a. Describe a deterministic algorithm that uses $\Theta(n^2)$ comparisons to group the jugs into pairs.

b. Prove a lower bound of $\Omega(n \lg n)$ for the number of comparisons that an algorithm solving this problem must make.

c. Give a randomized algorithm whose expected number of comparisons is $O(n \lg n)$, and prove that this bound is correct. What is the worst-case number of comparisons for your algorithm?

8-5 *Average sorting*

Suppose that, instead of sorting an array, we just require that the elements increase on average. More precisely, we call an n-element array A *k-sorted* if, for all $i = 1, 2, \ldots, n - k$, the following holds:

$$\frac{\sum_{j=i}^{i+k-1} A[j]}{k} \leq \frac{\sum_{j=i+1}^{i+k} A[j]}{k} .$$

a. What does it mean for an array to be 1-sorted?

b. Give a permutation of the numbers $1, 2, \ldots, 10$ that is 2-sorted, but not sorted.

c. Prove that an n-element array is k-sorted if and only if $A[i] \leq A[i + k]$ for all $i = 1, 2, \ldots, n - k$.

d. Give an algorithm that k-sorts an n-element array in $O(n \lg(n/k))$ time.

We can also show a lower bound on the time to produce a k-sorted array, when k is a constant.

e. Show how to sort a k-sorted array of length n in $O(n \lg k)$ time. (*Hint:* Use the solution to Exercise 6.5-11.)

f. Show that when k is a constant, k-sorting an n-element array requires $\Omega(n \lg n)$ time. (*Hint:* Use the solution to part (e) along with the lower bound on comparison sorts.)

8-6   *Lower bound on merging sorted lists*

The problem of merging two sorted lists arises frequently. We have seen a procedure for it as the subroutine MERGE in Section 2.3.1. In this problem, you will prove a lower bound of $2n - 1$ on the worst-case number of comparisons required to merge two sorted lists, each containing n items. First, you will show a lower bound of $2n - o(n)$ comparisons by using a decision tree.

a. Given $2n$ numbers, compute the number of possible ways to divide them into two sorted lists, each with n numbers.

b. Using a decision tree and your answer to part (a), show that any algorithm that correctly merges two sorted lists must perform at least $2n - o(n)$ comparisons.

Now you will show a slightly tighter $2n - 1$ bound.

c. Show that if two elements are consecutive in the sorted order and from different lists, then they must be compared.

d. Use your answer to part (c) to show a lower bound of $2n - 1$ comparisons for merging two sorted lists.

8-7   *The 0-1 sorting lemma and columnsort*

A *compare-exchange* operation on two array elements $A[i]$ and $A[j]$, where $i < j$, has the form

```
COMPARE-EXCHANGE(A, i, j)
1   if A[i] > A[j]
2       exchange A[i] with A[j]
```

After the compare-exchange operation, we know that $A[i] \le A[j]$.

An *oblivious compare-exchange algorithm* operates solely by a sequence of prespecified compare-exchange operations. The indices of the positions compared in the sequence must be determined in advance, and although they can depend on the number of elements being sorted, they cannot depend on the values being sorted, nor can they depend on the result of any prior compare-exchange operation. For example, the COMPARE-EXCHANGE-INSERTION-SORT procedure on the facing page shows a variation of insertion sort as an oblivious compare-exchange algorithm. (Unlike the INSERTION-SORT procedure on page 19, the oblivious version runs in $\Theta(n^2)$ time in all cases.)

The *0-1 sorting lemma* provides a powerful way to prove that an oblivious compare-exchange algorithm produces a sorted result. It states that if an oblivious compare-exchange algorithm correctly sorts all input sequences consisting of only 0s and 1s, then it correctly sorts all inputs containing arbitrary values.

COMPARE-EXCHANGE-INSERTION-SORT(A, n)

```
1  for i = 2 to n
2      for j = i − 1 downto 1
3          COMPARE-EXCHANGE(A, j, j + 1)
```

You will prove the 0-1 sorting lemma by proving its contrapositive: if an oblivious compare-exchange algorithm fails to sort an input containing arbitrary values, then it fails to sort some 0-1 input. Assume that an oblivious compare-exchange algorithm X fails to correctly sort the array $A[1 : n]$. Let $A[p]$ be the smallest value in A that algorithm X puts into the wrong location, and let $A[q]$ be the value that algorithm X moves to the location into which $A[p]$ should have gone. Define an array $B[1 : n]$ of 0s and 1s as follows:

$$B[i] = \begin{cases} 0 & \text{if } A[i] \leq A[p] , \\ 1 & \text{if } A[i] > A[p] . \end{cases}$$

a. Argue that $A[q] > A[p]$, so that $B[p] = 0$ and $B[q] = 1$.

b. To complete the proof of the 0-1 sorting lemma, prove that algorithm X fails to sort array B correctly.

Now you will use the 0-1 sorting lemma to prove that a particular sorting algorithm works correctly. The algorithm, *columnsort*, works on a rectangular array of n elements. The array has r rows and s columns (so that $n = rs$), subject to three restrictions:

- r must be even,

- s must be a divisor of r, and

- $r \geq 2s^2$.

When columnsort completes, the array is sorted in *column-major order*: reading down each column in turn, from left to right, the elements monotonically increase.

Columnsort operates in eight steps, regardless of the value of n. The odd steps are all the same: sort each column individually. Each even step is a fixed permutation. Here are the steps:

1. Sort each column.

2. Transpose the array, but reshape it back to r rows and s columns. In other words, turn the leftmost column into the top r/s rows, in order; turn the next column into the next r/s rows, in order; and so on.

10	14	5
8	7	17
12	1	6
16	9	11
4	15	2
18	3	13

(a)

4	1	2
8	3	5
10	7	6
12	9	11
16	14	13
18	15	17

(b)

4	8	10
12	16	18
1	3	7
9	14	15
2	5	6
11	13	17

(c)

1	3	6
2	5	7
4	8	10
9	13	15
11	14	17
12	16	18

(d)

1	4	11
3	8	14
6	10	17
2	9	12
5	13	16
7	15	18

(e)

1	4	11
2	8	12
3	9	14
5	10	16
6	13	17
7	15	18

(f)

	5	10	16
	6	13	17
	7	15	18
1	4	11	
2	8	12	
3	9	14	

(g)

4	10	16
5	11	17
6	12	18
1	7	13
2	8	14
3	9	15

(h)

1	7	13
2	8	14
3	9	15
4	10	16
5	11	17
6	12	18

(i)

Figure 8.5 The steps of columnsort. **(a)** The input array with 6 rows and 3 columns. (This example does not obey the $r \geq 2s^2$ requirement, but it works.) **(b)** After sorting each column in step 1. **(c)** After transposing and reshaping in step 2. **(d)** After sorting each column in step 3. **(e)** After performing step 4, which inverts the permutation from step 2. **(f)** After sorting each column in step 5. **(g)** After shifting by half a column in step 6. **(h)** After sorting each column in step 7. **(i)** After performing step 8, which inverts the permutation from step 6. Steps 6–8 sort the bottom half of each column with the top half of the next column. After step 8, the array is sorted in column-major order.

3. Sort each column.

4. Perform the inverse of the permutation performed in step 2.

5. Sort each column.

6. Shift the top half of each column into the bottom half of the same column, and shift the bottom half of each column into the top half of the next column to the right. Leave the top half of the leftmost column empty. Shift the bottom half of the last column into the top half of a new rightmost column, and leave the bottom half of this new column empty.

7. Sort each column.

8. Perform the inverse of the permutation performed in step 6.

You can think of steps 6–8 as a single step that sorts the bottom half of each column and the top half of the next column. Figure 8.5 shows an example of the steps of columnsort with $r = 6$ and $s = 3$. (Even though this example violates the requirement that $r \geq 2s^2$, it happens to work.)

c. Argue that we can treat columnsort as an oblivious compare-exchange algorithm, even if we do not know what sorting method the odd steps use.

Although it might seem hard to believe that columnsort actually sorts, you will use the 0-1 sorting lemma to prove that it does. The 0-1 sorting lemma applies because we can treat columnsort as an oblivious compare-exchange algorithm. A couple of definitions will help you apply the 0-1 sorting lemma. We say that an area of an array is *clean* if we know that it contains either all 0s or all 1s or if it is empty. Otherwise, the area might contain mixed 0s and 1s, and it is *dirty*. From here on, assume that the input array contains only 0s and 1s, and that we can treat it as an array with r rows and s columns.

d. Prove that after steps 1–3, the array consists of clean rows of 0s at the top, clean rows of 1s at the bottom, and at most s dirty rows between them. (One of the clean rows could be empty.)

e. Prove that after step 4, the array, read in column-major order, starts with a clean area of 0s, ends with a clean area of 1s, and has a dirty area of at most s^2 elements in the middle. (Again, one of the clean areas could be empty.)

f. Prove that steps 5–8 produce a fully sorted 0-1 output. Conclude that column-sort correctly sorts all inputs containing arbitrary values.

g. Now suppose that s does not divide r. Prove that after steps 1–3, the array consists of clean rows of 0s at the top, clean rows of 1s at the bottom, and at most $2s - 1$ dirty rows between them. (Once again, one of the clean areas could be empty.) How large must r be, compared with s, for columnsort to correctly sort when s does not divide r?

h. Suggest a simple change to step 1 that allows us to maintain the requirement that $r \geq 2s^2$ even when s does not divide r, and prove that with your change, columnsort correctly sorts.

Chapter notes

The decision-tree model for studying comparison sorts was introduced by Ford and Johnson [150]. Knuth's comprehensive treatise on sorting [261] covers many variations on the sorting problem, including the information-theoretic lower bound on the complexity of sorting given here. Ben-Or [46] studied lower bounds for sorting using generalizations of the decision-tree model.

Knuth credits H. H. Seward with inventing counting sort in 1954, as well as with the idea of combining counting sort with radix sort. Radix sorting starting with the least significant digit appears to be a folk algorithm widely used by operators of mechanical card-sorting machines. According to Knuth, the first published reference to the method is a 1929 document by L. J. Comrie describing punched-card equipment. Bucket sorting has been in use since 1956, when the basic idea was proposed by Isaac and Singleton [235].

Munro and Raman [338] give a stable sorting algorithm that performs $O(n^{1+\epsilon})$ comparisons in the worst case, where $0 < \epsilon \leq 1$ is any fixed constant. Although any of the $O(n \lg n)$-time algorithms make fewer comparisons, the algorithm by Munro and Raman moves data only $O(n)$ times and operates in place.

The case of sorting n b-bit integers in $o(n \lg n)$ time has been considered by many researchers. Several positive results have been obtained, each under slightly different assumptions about the model of computation and the restrictions placed on the algorithm. All the results assume that the computer memory is divided into addressable b-bit words. Fredman and Willard [157] introduced the fusion tree data structure and used it to sort n integers in $O(n \lg n / \lg \lg n)$ time. This bound was later improved to $O(n \sqrt{\lg n})$ time by Andersson [17]. These algorithms require the use of multiplication and several precomputed constants. Andersson, Hagerup, Nilsson, and Raman [18] have shown how to sort n integers in $O(n \lg \lg n)$ time without using multiplication, but their method requires storage that can be unbounded in terms of n. Using multiplicative hashing, we can reduce the storage needed to $O(n)$, but then the $O(n \lg \lg n)$ worst-case bound on the running time becomes an expected-time bound. Generalizing the exponential search trees of Andersson [17], Thorup [434] gave an $O(n(\lg \lg n)^2)$-time sorting algorithm that does not use multiplication or randomization, and it uses linear space. Combining these techniques with some new ideas, Han [207] improved the bound for sorting to $O(n \lg \lg n \lg \lg \lg n)$ time. Although these algorithms are important theoretical breakthroughs, they are all fairly complicated and at the present time seem unlikely to compete with existing sorting algorithms in practice.

The columnsort algorithm in Problem 8-7 is by Leighton [286].

9   Medians and Order Statistics

The ith *order statistic* of a set of n elements is the ith smallest element. For example, the *minimum* of a set of elements is the first order statistic ($i = 1$), and the *maximum* is the nth order statistic ($i = n$). A *median*, informally, is the "halfway point" of the set. When n is odd, the median is unique, occurring at $i = (n+1)/2$. When n is even, there are two medians, the *lower median* occurring at $i = n/2$ and the *upper median* occurring at $i = n/2 + 1$. Thus, regardless of the parity of n, medians occur at $i = \lfloor (n + 1)/2 \rfloor$ and $i = \lceil (n + 1)/2 \rceil$. For simplicity in this text, however, we consistently use the phrase "the median" to refer to the lower median.

This chapter addresses the problem of selecting the ith order statistic from a set of n distinct numbers. We assume for convenience that the set contains distinct numbers, although virtually everything that we do extends to the situation in which a set contains repeated values. We formally specify the *selection problem* as follows:

Input: A set A of n distinct numbers[1] and an integer i, with $1 \leq i \leq n$.

Output: The element $x \in A$ that is larger than exactly $i - 1$ other elements of A.

We can solve the selection problem in $O(n \lg n)$ time simply by sorting the numbers using heapsort or merge sort and then outputting the ith element in the sorted array. This chapter presents asymptotically faster algorithms.

Section 9.1 examines the problem of selecting the minimum and maximum of a set of elements. More interesting is the general selection problem, which we investigate in the subsequent two sections. Section 9.2 analyzes a practical randomized algorithm that achieves an $O(n)$ expected running time, assuming dis-

---

[1] As in the footnote on page 182, you can enforce the assumption that the numbers are distinct by converting each input value $A[i]$ to an ordered pair $(A[i], i)$ with $(A[i], i) < (A[j], j)$ if either $A[i] < A[j]$ or $A[i] = A[j]$ and $i < j$.

tinct elements. Section 9.3 contains an algorithm of more theoretical interest that achieves the $O(n)$ running time in the worst case.

9.1   Minimum and maximum

How many comparisons are necessary to determine the minimum of a set of n elements? To obtain an upper bound of $n - 1$ comparisons, just examine each element of the set in turn and keep track of the smallest element seen so far. The MINIMUM procedure assumes that the set resides in array $A[1:n]$.

```
MINIMUM(A, n)
1   min = A[1]
2   for i = 2 to n
3       if min > A[i]
4           min = A[i]
5   return min
```

It's no more difficult to find the maximum with $n - 1$ comparisons.

Is this algorithm for minimum the best we can do? Yes, because it turns out that there's a lower bound of $n - 1$ comparisons for the problem of determining the minimum. Think of any algorithm that determines the minimum as a tournament among the elements. Each comparison is a match in the tournament in which the smaller of the two elements wins. Since every element except the winner must lose at least one match, we can conclude that $n - 1$ comparisons are necessary to determine the minimum. Hence the algorithm MINIMUM is optimal with respect to the number of comparisons performed.

Simultaneous minimum and maximum

Some applications need to find both the minimum and the maximum of a set of n elements. For example, a graphics program may need to scale a set of (x, y) data to fit onto a rectangular display screen or other graphical output device. To do so, the program must first determine the minimum and maximum value of each coordinate.

Of course, we can determine both the minimum and the maximum of n elements using $\Theta(n)$ comparisons. We simply find the minimum and maximum independently, using $n - 1$ comparisons for each, for a total of $2n - 2 = \Theta(n)$ comparisons.

Although $2n - 2$ comparisons is asymptotically optimal, it is possible to improve the leading constant. We can find both the minimum and the maximum using at most $3 \lfloor n/2 \rfloor$ comparisons. The trick is to maintain both the minimum and maximum elements seen thus far. Rather than processing each element of the input by comparing it against the current minimum and maximum, at a cost of 2 comparisons per element, process elements in pairs. Compare pairs of elements from the input first *with each other*, and then compare the smaller with the current minimum and the larger to the current maximum, at a cost of 3 comparisons for every 2 elements.

How you set up initial values for the current minimum and maximum depends on whether n is odd or even. If n is odd, set both the minimum and maximum to the value of the first element, and then process the rest of the elements in pairs. If n is even, perform 1 comparison on the first 2 elements to determine the initial values of the minimum and maximum, and then process the rest of the elements in pairs as in the case for odd n.

Let's count the total number of comparisons. If n is odd, then $3 \lfloor n/2 \rfloor$ comparisons occur. If n is even, 1 initial comparison occurs, followed by another $3(n - 2)/2$ comparisons, for a total of $3n/2 - 2$. Thus, in either case, the total number of comparisons is at most $3 \lfloor n/2 \rfloor$.

Exercises

9.1-1
Show that the second smallest of n elements can be found with $n + \lceil \lg n \rceil - 2$ comparisons in the worst case. (*Hint:* Also find the smallest element.)

9.1-2
Given $n > 2$ distinct numbers, you want to find a number that is neither the minimum nor the maximum. What is the smallest number of comparisons that you need to perform?

9.1-3
A racetrack can run races with five horses at a time to determine their relative speeds. For 25 horses, it takes six races to determine the fastest horse, assuming transitivity (see page 1159). What's the minimum number of races it takes to determine the fastest three horses out of 25?

★ ***9.1-4***
Prove the lower bound of $\lceil 3n/2 \rceil - 2$ comparisons in the worst case to find both the maximum and minimum of n numbers. (*Hint:* Consider how many numbers are potentially either the maximum or minimum, and investigate how a comparison affects these counts.)

9.2   Selection in expected linear time

The general selection problem—finding the ith order statistic for any value of i—appears more difficult than the simple problem of finding a minimum. Yet, surprisingly, the asymptotic running time for both problems is the same: $\Theta(n)$. This section presents a divide-and-conquer algorithm for the selection problem. The algorithm RANDOMIZED-SELECT is modeled after the quicksort algorithm of Chapter 7. Like quicksort it partitions the input array recursively. But unlike quicksort, which recursively processes both sides of the partition, RANDOMIZED-SELECT works on only one side of the partition. This difference shows up in the analysis: whereas quicksort has an expected running time of $\Theta(n \lg n)$, the expected running time of RANDOMIZED-SELECT is $\Theta(n)$, assuming that the elements are distinct.

RANDOMIZED-SELECT uses the procedure RANDOMIZED-PARTITION introduced in Section 7.3. Like RANDOMIZED-QUICKSORT, it is a randomized algorithm, since its behavior is determined in part by the output of a random-number generator. The RANDOMIZED-SELECT procedure returns the ith smallest element of the array $A[p:r]$, where $1 \leq i \leq r - p + 1$.

RANDOMIZED-SELECT(A, p, r, i)

1 **if** $p == r$
2   **return** $A[p]$ **//** $1 \leq i \leq r - p + 1$ when $p == r$ means that $i = 1$
3 $q = $ RANDOMIZED-PARTITION(A, p, r)
4 $k = q - p + 1$
5 **if** $i == k$
6   **return** $A[q]$ **//** the pivot value is the answer
7 **elseif** $i < k$
8   **return** RANDOMIZED-SELECT$(A, p, q - 1, i)$
9 **else return** RANDOMIZED-SELECT$(A, q + 1, r, i - k)$

Figure 9.1 illustrates how the RANDOMIZED-SELECT procedure works. Line 1 checks for the base case of the recursion, in which the subarray $A[p:r]$ consists of just one element. In this case, i must equal 1, and line 2 simply returns $A[p]$ as the ith smallest element. Otherwise, the call to RANDOMIZED-PARTITION in line 3 partitions the array $A[p:r]$ into two (possibly empty) subarrays $A[p:q-1]$ and $A[q+1:r]$ such that each element of $A[p:q-1]$ is less than or equal to $A[q]$, which in turn is less than each element of $A[q+1:r]$. (Although our analysis assumes that the elements are distinct, the procedure still yields the correct result even if equal elements are present.) As in quicksort, we'll refer to $A[q]$ as the *pivot* element. Line 4 computes the number k of elements in the subarray $A[p:q]$, that is,

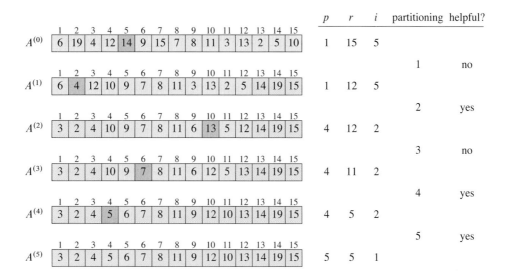

Figure 9.1 The action of RANDOMIZED-SELECT as successive partitionings narrow the subarray $A[p:r]$, showing the values of the parameters p, r, and i at each recursive call. The subarray $A[p:r]$ in each recursive step is shown in tan, with the dark tan element selected as the pivot for the next partitioning. Blue elements are outside $A[p:r]$. The answer is the tan element in the bottom array, where $p = r = 5$ and $i = 1$. The array designations $A^{(0)}, A^{(1)}, \ldots, A^{(5)}$, the partitioning numbers, and whether the partitioning is helpful are explained on the following page.

the number of elements in the low side of the partition, plus 1 for the pivot element. Line 5 then checks whether $A[q]$ is the ith smallest element. If it is, then line 6 returns $A[q]$. Otherwise, the algorithm determines in which of the two subarrays $A[p:q-1]$ and $A[q+1:r]$ the ith smallest element lies. If $i < k$, then the desired element lies on the low side of the partition, and line 8 recursively selects it from the subarray. If $i > k$, however, then the desired element lies on the high side of the partition. Since we already know k values that are smaller than the ith smallest element of $A[p:r]$—namely, the elements of $A[p:q]$—the desired element is the $(i-k)$th smallest element of $A[q+1:r]$, which line 9 finds recursively. The code appears to allow recursive calls to subarrays with 0 elements, but Exercise 9.2-1 asks you to show that this situation cannot happen.

The worst-case running time for RANDOMIZED-SELECT is $\Theta(n^2)$, even to find the minimum, because it could be extremely unlucky and always partition around the largest remaining element before identifying the ith smallest when only one element remains. In this worst case, each recursive step removes only the pivot from consideration. Because partitioning n elements takes $\Theta(n)$ time, the recurrence for the worst-case running time is the same as for QUICKSORT:

$T(n) = T(n-1) + \Theta(n)$, with the solution $T(n) = \Theta(n^2)$. We'll see that the algorithm has a linear expected running time, however, and because it is randomized, no particular input elicits the worst-case behavior.

To see the intuition behind the linear expected running time, suppose that each time the algorithm randomly selects a pivot element, the pivot lies somewhere within the second and third quartiles—the "middle half"—of the remaining elements in sorted order. If the ith smallest element is less than the pivot, then all the elements greater than the pivot are ignored in all future recursive calls. These ignored elements include at least the uppermost quartile, and possibly more. Likewise, if the ith smallest element is greater than the pivot, then all the elements less than the pivot—at least the first quartile—are ignored in all future recursive calls. Either way, therefore, at least $1/4$ of the remaining elements are ignored in all future recursive calls, leaving at most $3/4$ of the remaining elements *in play*: residing in the subarray $A[p:r]$. Since RANDOMIZED-PARTITION takes $\Theta(n)$ time on a subarray of n elements, the recurrence for the worst-case running time is $T(n) = T(3n/4) + \Theta(n)$. By case 3 of the master method (Theorem 4.1 on page 102), this recurrence has solution $T(n) = \Theta(n)$.

Of course, the pivot does not necessarily fall into the middle half every time. Since the pivot is selected at random, the probability that it falls into the middle half is about $1/2$ each time. We can view the process of selecting the pivot as a Bernoulli trial (see Section C.4) with success equating to the pivot residing in the middle half. Thus the expected number of trials needed for success is given by a geometric distribution: just two trials on average (equation (C.36) on page 1197). In other words, we expect that half of the partitionings reduce the number of elements still in play by at least $3/4$ and that half of the partitionings do not help as much. Consequently, the expected number of partitionings at most doubles from the case when the pivot always falls into the middle half. The cost of each extra partitioning is less than the one that preceded it, so that the expected running time is still $\Theta(n)$.

To make the above argument rigorous, we start by defining the random variable $A^{(j)}$ as the set of elements of A that are still in play after j partitionings (that is, within the subarray $A[p:r]$ after j calls of RANDOMIZED-SELECT), so that $A^{(0)}$ consists of all the elements in A. Since each partitioning removes at least one element—the pivot—from being in play, the sequence $|A^{(0)}|, |A^{(1)}|, |A^{(2)}|, \ldots$ strictly decreases. Set $A^{(j-1)}$ is in play before the jth partitioning, and set $A^{(j)}$ remains in play afterward. For convenience, assume that the initial set $A^{(0)}$ is the result of a 0th "dummy" partitioning.

Let's call the jth partitioning *helpful* if $|A^{(j)}| \leq (3/4)|A^{(j-1)}|$. Figure 9.1 shows the sets $A^{(j)}$ and whether partitionings are helpful for an example array. A helpful partitioning corresponds to a successful Bernoulli trial. The following lemma shows that a partitioning is at least as likely to be helpful as not.

Lemma 9.1
A partitioning is helpful with probability at least $1/2$.

Proof   Whether a partitioning is helpful depends on the randomly chosen pivot.
We discussed the "middle half" in the informal argument above. Let's more precisely define the middle half of an n-element subarray as all but the smallest
$\lceil n/4 \rceil - 1$ and greatest $\lceil n/4 \rceil - 1$ elements (that is, all but the first $\lceil n/4 \rceil - 1$
and last $\lceil n/4 \rceil - 1$ elements if the subarray were sorted). We'll prove that if the
pivot falls into the middle half, then the pivot leads to a helpful partitioning, and
we'll also prove that the probability of the pivot falling into the middle half is at
least $1/2$.

Regardless of where the pivot falls, either all the elements greater than it or all
the elements less than it, along with the pivot itself, will no longer be in play after
partitioning. If the pivot falls into the middle half, therefore, at least $\lceil n/4 \rceil - 1$
elements less than the pivot or $\lceil n/4 \rceil - 1$ elements greater than the pivot, plus
the pivot, will no longer be in play after partitioning. That is, at least $\lceil n/4 \rceil$ elements will no longer be in play. The number of elements remaining in play will
be at most $n - \lceil n/4 \rceil$, which equals $\lfloor 3n/4 \rfloor$ by Exercise 3.3-2 on page 70. Since
$\lfloor 3n/4 \rfloor \leq 3n/4$, the partitioning is helpful.

To determine a lower bound on the probability that a randomly chosen pivot falls
into the middle half, we determine an upper bound on the probability that it does
not. That probability is

$$\frac{2(\lceil n/4 \rceil - 1)}{n} \leq \frac{2((n/4 + 1) - 1)}{n} \quad \text{(by inequality (3.2) on page 64)}$$

$$= \frac{n/2}{n}$$

$$= 1/2 .$$

Thus, the pivot has a probability of at least $1/2$ of falling into the middle half, and
so the probability is at least $1/2$ that a partitioning is helpful.   ■

We can now bound the expected running time of RANDOMIZED-SELECT.

Theorem 9.2
The procedure RANDOMIZED-SELECT on an input array of n distinct elements has
an expected running time of $\Theta(n)$.

Proof   Since not every partitioning is necessarily helpful, let's give each partitioning an index starting at 0 and denote by $\langle h_0, h_1, h_2, \ldots, h_m \rangle$ the sequence
of partitionings that are helpful, so that the h_kth partitioning is helpful for $k =
0, 1, 2, \ldots, m$. Although the number m of helpful partitionings is a random vari-

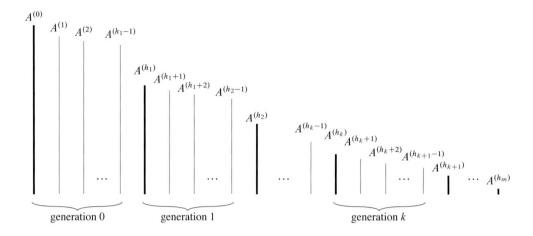

Figure 9.2 The sets within each generation in the proof of Theorem 9.2. Vertical lines represent the sets, with the height of each line indicating the size of the set, which equals the number of elements in play. Each generation starts with a set $A^{(h_k)}$, which is the result of a helpful partitioning. These sets are drawn in black and are at most $3/4$ the size of the sets to their immediate left. Sets drawn in orange are not the first within a generation. A generation may contain just one set. The sets in generation k are $A^{(h_k)}, A^{(h_k+1)}, \ldots, A^{(h_{k+1}-1)}$. The sets $A^{(h_k)}$ are defined so that $|A^{(h_k)}| \leq (3/4)|A^{(h_k-1)}|$. If the partitioning gets all the way to generation h_m, set $A^{(h_m)}$ has at most one element in play.

able, we can bound it, since after at most $\lceil \log_{4/3} n \rceil$ helpful partitionings, only one element remains in play. Consider the dummy 0th partitioning as helpful, so that $h_0 = 0$. Denote $|A^{(h_k)}|$ by n_k, where $n_0 = |A^{(0)}|$ is the original problem size. Since the h_kth partitioning is helpful and the sizes of the sets $A^{(j)}$ strictly decrease, we have $n_k = |A^{(h_k)}| \leq (3/4)|A^{(h_k-1)}| = (3/4)\,n_{k-1}$ for $k = 1, 2, \ldots, m$. By iterating $n_k \leq (3/4)\,n_{k-1}$, we have that $n_k \leq (3/4)^k n_0$ for $k = 0, 1, 2, \ldots, m$.

As Figure 9.2 depicts, we break up the sequence of sets $A^{(j)}$ into m *generations* consisting of consecutively partitioned sets, starting with the result $A^{(h_k)}$ of a helpful partitioning and ending with the last set $A^{(h_{k+1}-1)}$ before the next helpful partitioning, so that the sets in generation k are $A^{(h_k)}, A^{(h_k+1)}, \ldots, A^{(h_{k+1}-1)}$. Then for each set of elements $A^{(j)}$ in the kth generation, we have that $|A^{(j)}| \leq |A^{(h_k)}| = n_k \leq (3/4)^k n_0$.

Next, we define the random variable

$$X_k = h_{k+1} - h_k$$

for $k = 0, 1, 2, \ldots, m - 1$. That is, X_k is the number of sets in the kth generation, so that the sets in the kth generation are $A^{(h_k)}, A^{(h_k+1)}, \ldots, A^{(h_k+X_k-1)}$.

By Lemma 9.1, the probability that a partitioning is helpful is at least $1/2$. The probability is actually even higher, since a partitioning is helpful even if the pivot does not fall into the middle half but the ith smallest element happens to lie in the smaller side of the partitioning. We'll just use the lower bound of $1/2$, however, and then equation (C.36) gives that $\mathrm{E}[X_k] \leq 2$ for $k = 0, 1, 2, \ldots, m - 1$.

Let's derive an upper bound on how many comparisons are made altogether during partitioning, since the running time is dominated by the comparisons. Since we are calculating an upper bound, assume that the recursion goes all the way until only one element remains in play. The jth partitioning takes the set $A^{(j-1)}$ of elements in play, and it compares the randomly chosen pivot with all the other $|A^{(j-1)}| - 1$ elements, so that the jth partitioning makes fewer than $|A^{(j-1)}|$ comparisons. The sets in the kth generation have sizes $|A^{(h_k)}|, |A^{(h_k+1)}|, \ldots,$ $|A^{(h_k+X_k-1)}|$. Thus, the total number of comparisons during partitioning is less than

$$\sum_{k=0}^{m-1} \sum_{j=h_k}^{h_k+X_k-1} |A^{(j)}| \leq \sum_{k=0}^{m-1} \sum_{j=h_k}^{h_k+X_k-1} |A^{(h_k)}|$$

$$= \sum_{k=0}^{m-1} X_k \, |A^{(h_k)}|$$

$$\leq \sum_{k=0}^{m-1} X_k \left(\frac{3}{4}\right)^k n_0 \, .$$

Since $\mathrm{E}[X_k] \leq 2$, we have that the expected total number of comparisons during partitioning is less than

$$\mathrm{E}\left[\sum_{k=0}^{m-1} X_k \left(\frac{3}{4}\right)^k n_0\right] = \sum_{k=0}^{m-1} \mathrm{E}\left[X_k \left(\frac{3}{4}\right)^k n_0\right] \quad \text{(by linearity of expectation)}$$

$$= n_0 \sum_{k=0}^{m-1} \left(\frac{3}{4}\right)^k \mathrm{E}[X_k]$$

$$\leq 2n_0 \sum_{k=0}^{m-1} \left(\frac{3}{4}\right)^k$$

$$< 2n_0 \sum_{k=0}^{\infty} \left(\frac{3}{4}\right)^k$$

$$= 8n_0 \quad \text{(by equation (A.7) on page 1142)} \, .$$

Since n_0 is the size of the original array A, we conclude that the expected number of comparisons, and thus the expected running time, for RANDOMIZED-SELECT is $O(n)$. All n elements are examined in the first call of RANDOMIZED-

PARTITION, giving a lower bound of $\Omega(n)$. Hence the expected running time is $\Theta(n)$. ∎

Exercises

9.2-1
Show that RANDOMIZED-SELECT never makes a recursive call to a 0-length array.

9.2-2
Write an iterative version of RANDOMIZED-SELECT.

9.2-3
Suppose that RANDOMIZED-SELECT is used to select the minimum element of the array $A = \langle 2, 3, 0, 5, 7, 9, 1, 8, 6, 4 \rangle$. Describe a sequence of partitions that results in a worst-case performance of RANDOMIZED-SELECT.

9.2-4
Argue that the expected running time of RANDOMIZED-SELECT does not depend on the order of the elements in its input array $A[p:r]$. That is, the expected running time is the same for any permutation of the input array $A[p:r]$. (*Hint:* Argue by induction on the length n of the input array.)

9.3   Selection in worst-case linear time

We'll now examine a remarkable and theoretically interesting selection algorithm whose running time is $\Theta(n)$ in the worst case. Although the RANDOMIZED-SELECT algorithm from Section 9.2 achieves linear expected time, we saw that its running time in the worst case was quadratic. The selection algorithm presented in this section achieves linear time in the worst case, but it is not nearly as practical as RANDOMIZED-SELECT. It is mostly of theoretical interest.

Like the expected linear-time RANDOMIZED-SELECT, the worst-case linear-time algorithm SELECT finds the desired element by recursively partitioning the input array. Unlike RANDOMIZED-SELECT, however, SELECT *guarantees* a good split by choosing a provably good pivot when partitioning the array. The cleverness in the algorithm is that it finds the pivot recursively. Thus, there are two invocations of SELECT: one to find a good pivot, and a second to recursively find the desired order statistic.

The partitioning algorithm used by SELECT is like the deterministic partitioning algorithm PARTITION from quicksort (see Section 7.1), but modified to take the element to partition around as an additional input parameter. Like PARTITION, the

PARTITION-AROUND algorithm returns the index of the pivot. Since it's so similar to PARTITION, the pseudocode for PARTITION-AROUND is omitted.

The SELECT procedure takes as input a subarray $A[p : r]$ of $n = r - p + 1$ elements and an integer i in the range $1 \leq i \leq n$. It returns the ith smallest element of A. The pseudocode is actually more understandable than it might appear at first.

```
SELECT(A, p, r, i)
1   while (r − p + 1) mod 5 ≠ 0
2       for j = p + 1 to r                    // put the minimum into A[p]
3           if A[p] > A[j]
4               exchange A[p] with A[j]
5       // If we want the minimum of A[p : r], we're done.
6       if i == 1
7           return A[p]
8       // Otherwise, we want the (i − 1)st element of A[p + 1 : r].
9       p = p + 1
10      i = i − 1
11  g = (r − p + 1)/5                          // number of 5-element groups
12  for j = p to p + g − 1                     // sort each group
13      sort ⟨A[j], A[j + g], A[j + 2g], A[j + 3g], A[j + 4g]⟩ in place
14  // All group medians now lie in the middle fifth of A[p : r].
15  // Find the pivot x recursively as the median of the group medians.
16  x = SELECT(A, p + 2g, p + 3g − 1, ⌈g/2⌉)
17  q = PARTITION-AROUND(A, p, r, x)           // partition around the pivot
18  // The rest is just like lines 3–9 of RANDOMIZED-SELECT.
19  k = q − p + 1
20  if i == k
21      return A[q]                            // the pivot value is the answer
22  elseif i < k
23      return SELECT(A, p, q − 1, i)
24  else return SELECT(A, q + 1, r, i − k)
```

The pseudocode starts by executing the **while** loop in lines 1–10 to reduce the number $r - p + 1$ of elements in the subarray until it is divisible by 5. The **while** loop executes 0 to 4 times, each time rearranging the elements of $A[p : r]$ so that $A[p]$ contains the minimum element. If $i = 1$, which means that we actually want the minimum element, then the procedure simply returns it in line 7. Otherwise, SELECT eliminates the minimum from the subarray $A[p : r]$ and iterates to find the $(i - 1)$st element in $A[p + 1 : r]$. Lines 9–10 do so by incrementing p and decrementing i. If the **while** loop completes all of its iterations without returning a

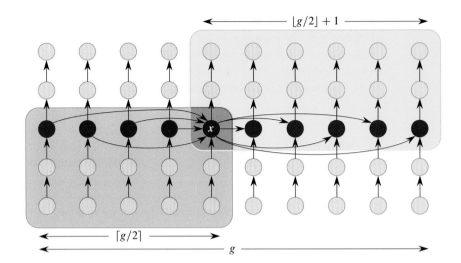

Figure 9.3 The relationships between elements (shown as circles) immediately after line 17 of the selection algorithm SELECT. There are $g = (r - p + 1)/5$ groups of 5 elements, each of which occupies a column. For example, the leftmost column contains elements $A[p]$, $A[p + g]$, $A[p + 2g]$, $A[p + 3g]$, $A[p + 4g]$, and the next column contains $A[p + 1]$, $A[p + g + 1]$, $A[p + 2g + 1]$, $A[p + 3g + 1]$, $A[p + 4g + 1]$. The medians of the groups are red, and the pivot x is labeled. Arrows go from smaller elements to larger. The elements on the blue background are all known to be less than or equal to x and cannot fall into the high side of the partition around x. The elements on the yellow background are known to be greater than or equal to x and cannot fall into the low side of the partition around x. The pivot x belongs to both the blue and yellow regions and is shown on a green background. The elements on the white background could lie on either side of the partition.

result, the procedure executes the core of the algorithm in lines 11–24, assured that the number $r - p + 1$ of elements in $A[p : r]$ is evenly divisible by 5.

The next part of the algorithm implements the following idea, illustrated in Figure 9.3. Divide the elements in $A[p : r]$ into $g = (r - p + 1)/5$ groups of 5 elements each. The first 5-element group is

$$\langle A[p], A[p + g], A[p + 2g], A[p + 3g], A[p + 4g] \rangle \,,$$

the second is

$$\langle A[p + 1], A[p + g + 1], A[p + 2g + 1], A[p + 3g + 1], A[p + 4g + 1] \rangle \,,$$

and so forth until the last, which is

$$\langle A[p + g - 1], A[p + 2g - 1], A[p + 3g - 1], A[p + 4g - 1], A[r] \rangle \,.$$

(Note that $r = p + 5g - 1$.) Line 13 puts each group in order using, for example, insertion sort (Section 2.1), so that for $j = p, p + 1, \ldots, p + g - 1$, we have

$$A[j] \leq A[j + g] \leq A[j + 2g] \leq A[j + 3g] \leq A[j + 4g] \ .$$

Each vertical column in Figure 9.3 depicts a sorted group of 5 elements. The median of each 5-element group is $A[j + 2g]$, and thus all the 5-element medians, shown in red, lie in the range $A[p + 2g : p + 3g - 1]$.

Next, line 16 determines the pivot x by recursively calling SELECT to find the median (specifically, the $\lceil g/2 \rceil$th smallest) of the g group medians. Line 17 uses the modified PARTITION-AROUND algorithm to partition the elements of $A[p : r]$ around x, returning the index q of x, so that $A[q] = x$, elements in $A[p : q]$ are all at most x, and elements in $A[q : r]$ are greater than or equal to x.

The remainder of the code mirrors that of RANDOMIZED-SELECT. If the pivot x is the ith largest, the procedure returns it. Otherwise, the procedure recursively calls itself on either $A[p : q - 1]$ or $A[q + 1 : r]$, depending on the value of i.

Let's analyze the running time of SELECT and see how the judicious choice of the pivot x plays into a guarantee on its worst-case running time.

Theorem 9.3
The running time of SELECT on an input of n elements is $\Theta(n)$.

Proof   Define $T(n)$ as the worst-case time to run SELECT on any input subarray $A[p : r]$ of size at most n, that is, for which $r - p + 1 \leq n$. By this definition, $T(n)$ is monotonically increasing.

We first determine an upper bound on the time spent outside the recursive calls in lines 16, 23, and 24. The **while** loop in lines 1–10 executes 0 to 4 times, which is $O(1)$ times. Since the dominant time within the loop is the computation of the minimum in lines 2–4, which takes $\Theta(n)$ time, lines 1–10 execute in $O(1) \cdot \Theta(n) = O(n)$ time. The sorting of the 5-element groups in lines 12–13 takes $\Theta(n)$ time because each 5-element group takes $\Theta(1)$ time to sort (even using an asymptotically inefficient sorting algorithm such as insertion sort), and there are g elements to sort, where $n/5 - 1 < g \leq n/5$. Finally, the time to partition in line 17 is $\Theta(n)$, as Exercise 7.1-3 on page 187 asks you to show. Because the remaining bookkeeping only costs $\Theta(1)$ time, the total amount of time spent outside of the recursive calls is $O(n) + \Theta(n) + \Theta(n) + \Theta(1) = \Theta(n)$.

Now let's determine the running time for the recursive calls. The recursive call to find the pivot in line 16 takes $T(g) \leq T(n/5)$ time, since $g \leq n/5$ and $T(n)$ monotonically increases. Of the two recursive calls in lines 23 and 24, at most one is executed. But we'll see that no matter which of these two recursive calls to SELECT actually executes, the number of elements in the recursive call turns out to be at most $7n/10$, and hence the worst-case cost for lines 23 and 24 is at most $T(7n/10)$. Let's now show that the machinations with group medians and the choice of the pivot x as the median of the group medians guarantees this property.

Figure 9.3 helps to visualize what's going on. There are $g \leq n/5$ groups of 5 elements, with each group shown as a column sorted from bottom to top. The arrows show the ordering of elements within the columns. The columns are ordered from left to right with groups to the left of x's group having a group median less than x and those to the right of x's group having a group median greater than x. Although the relative order within each group matters, the relative order among groups to the left of x's column doesn't really matter, and neither does the relative order among groups to the right of x's column. The important thing is that the groups to the left have group medians less than x (shown by the horizontal arrows entering x), and that the groups to the right have group medians greater than x (shown by the horizontal arrows leaving x). Thus, the yellow region contains elements that we know are greater than or equal to x, and the blue region contains elements that we know are less than or equal to x.

These two regions each contain at least $3g/2$ elements. The number of group medians in the yellow region is $\lfloor g/2 \rfloor + 1$, and for each group median, two additional elements are greater than it, making a total of $3(\lfloor g/2 \rfloor + 1) \geq 3g/2$ elements. Similarly, the number of group medians in the blue region is $\lceil g/2 \rceil$, and for each group median, two additional elements are less than it, making a total of $3 \lceil g/2 \rceil \geq 3g/2$.

The elements in the yellow region cannot fall into the low side of the partition around x, and those in the blue region cannot fall into the high side. The elements in neither region—those lying on a white background—could fall into either side of the partition. But since the low side of the partition excludes the elements in the yellow region, and there are a total of $5g$ elements, we know that the low side of the partition can contain at most $5g - 3g/2 = 7g/2 \leq 7n/10$ elements. Likewise, the high side of the partition excludes the elements in the blue region, and a similar calculation shows that it also contains at most $7n/10$ elements.

All of which leads to the following recurrence for the worst-case running time of SELECT:

$$T(n) \leq T(n/5) + T(7n/10) + \Theta(n) \ . \tag{9.1}$$

We can show that $T(n) = O(n)$ by substitution.[2] More specifically, we'll prove that $T(n) \leq cn$ for some suitably large constant $c > 0$ and all $n > 0$. Substituting this inductive hypothesis into the right-hand side of recurrence (9.1) and assuming that $n \geq 5$ yields

---

[2] We could also use the Akra-Bazzi method from Section 4.7, which involves calculus, to solve this recurrence. Indeed, a similar recurrence (4.24) on page 117 was used to illustrate that method.

$$
\begin{aligned}
T(n) &\leq c(n/5) + c(7n/10) + \Theta(n) \\
&\leq 9cn/10 + \Theta(n) \\
&= cn - cn/10 + \Theta(n) \\
&\leq cn
\end{aligned}
$$

if c is chosen large enough that $c/10$ dominates the upper-bound constant hidden by the $\Theta(n)$. In addition to this constraint, we can pick c large enough that $T(n) \leq cn$ for all $n \leq 4$, which is the base case of the recursion within SELECT. The running time of SELECT is therefore $O(n)$ in the worst case, and because line 13 alone takes $\Theta(n)$ time, the total time is $\Theta(n)$. ∎

As in a comparison sort (see Section 8.1), SELECT and RANDOMIZED-SELECT determine information about the relative order of elements only by comparing elements. Recall from Chapter 8 that sorting requires $\Omega(n \lg n)$ time in the comparison model, even on average (see Problem 8-1). The linear-time sorting algorithms in Chapter 8 make assumptions about the type of the input. In contrast, the linear-time selection algorithms in this chapter do not require any assumptions about the input's type, only that the elements are distinct and can be pairwise compared according to a linear order. The algorithms in this chapter are not subject to the $\Omega(n \lg n)$ lower bound, because they manage to solve the selection problem without sorting all the elements. Thus, solving the selection problem by sorting and indexing, as presented in the introduction to this chapter, is asymptotically inefficient in the comparison model.

Exercises

9.3-1
In the algorithm SELECT, the input elements are divided into groups of 5. Show that the algorithm works in linear time if the input elements are divided into groups of 7 instead of 5.

9.3-2
Suppose that the preprocessing in lines 1–10 of SELECT is replaced by a base case for $n \geq n_0$, where n_0 is a suitable constant; that g is chosen as $\lfloor r - p + 1)/5 \rfloor$; and that the elements in $A[5g:n]$ belong to no group. Show that although the recurrence for the running time becomes messier, it still solves to $\Theta(n)$.

9.3-3
Show how to use SELECT as a subroutine to make quicksort run in $O(n \lg n)$ time in the worst case, assuming that all elements are distinct.

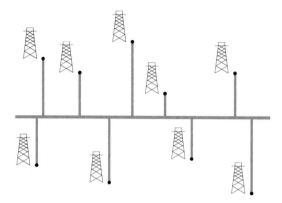

Figure 9.4   Professor Olay needs to determine the position of the east-west oil pipeline that minimizes the total length of the north-south spurs.

★ *9.3-4*

Suppose that an algorithm uses only comparisons to find the ith smallest element in a set of n elements. Show that it can also find the $i - 1$ smaller elements and the $n - i$ larger elements without performing any additional comparisons.

9.3-5

Show how to determine the median of a 5-element set using only 6 comparisons.

9.3-6

You have a "black-box" worst-case linear-time median subroutine. Give a simple, linear-time algorithm that solves the selection problem for an arbitrary order statistic.

9.3-7

Professor Olay is consulting for an oil company, which is planning a large pipeline running east to west through an oil field of n wells. The company wants to connect a spur pipeline from each well directly to the main pipeline along a shortest route (either north or south), as shown in Figure 9.4. Given the x- and y-coordinates of the wells, how should the professor pick an optimal location of the main pipeline to minimize the total length of the spurs? Show how to determine an optimal location in linear time.

9.3-8

The kth *quantiles* of an n-element set are the $k - 1$ order statistics that divide the sorted set into k equal-sized sets (to within 1). Give an $O(n \lg k)$-time algorithm to list the kth quantiles of a set.

9.3-9
Describe an $O(n)$-time algorithm that, given a set S of n distinct numbers and a positive integer $k \leq n$, determines the k numbers in S that are closest to the median of S.

9.3-10
Let $X[1:n]$ and $Y[1:n]$ be two arrays, each containing n numbers already in sorted order. Give an $O(\lg n)$-time algorithm to find the median of all $2n$ elements in arrays X and Y. Assume that all $2n$ numbers are distinct.

Problems

9-1 Largest i numbers in sorted order
You are given a set of n numbers, and you wish to find the i largest in sorted order using a comparison-based algorithm. Describe the algorithm that implements each of the following methods with the best asymptotic worst-case running time, and analyze the running times of the algorithms in terms of n and i.

a. Sort the numbers, and list the i largest.

b. Build a max-priority queue from the numbers, and call EXTRACT-MAX i times.

c. Use an order-statistic algorithm to find the ith largest number, partition around that number, and sort the i largest numbers.

9-2 Variant of randomized selection
Professor Mendel has proposed simplifying RANDOMIZED-SELECT by eliminating the check for whether i and k are equal. The simplified procedure is SIMPLER-RANDOMIZED-SELECT.

```
SIMPLER-RANDOMIZED-SELECT(A, p, r, i)

1  if p == r
2      return A[p]        // 1 ≤ i ≤ r − p + 1 means that i = 1
3  q = RANDOMIZED-PARTITION(A, p, r)
4  k = q − p + 1
5  if i ≤ k
6      return SIMPLER-RANDOMIZED-SELECT(A, p, q, i)
7  else return SIMPLER-RANDOMIZED-SELECT(A, q + 1, r, i − k)
```

a. Argue that in the worst case, SIMPLER-RANDOMIZED-SELECT never terminates.

b. Prove that the expected running time of SIMPLER-RANDOMIZED-SELECT is still $O(n)$.

9-3 *Weighted median*

Consider n elements $x_1, x_2, \ldots, x_n$ with positive weights $w_1, w_2, \ldots, w_n$ such that $\sum_{i=1}^n w_i = 1$. The *weighted (lower) median* is an element x_k satisfying

$$\sum_{x_i < x_k} w_i < \frac{1}{2}$$

and

$$\sum_{x_i > x_k} w_i \leq \frac{1}{2}.$$

For example, consider the following elements x_i and weights w_i:

i	1	2	3	4	5	6	7
x_i	3	8	2	5	4	1	6
w_i	0.12	0.35	0.025	0.08	0.15	0.075	0.2

For these elements, the median is $x_5 = 4$, but the weighted median is $x_7 = 6$. To see why the weighted median is x_7, observe that the elements less than x_7 are x_1, x_3, x_4, x_5, and x_6, and the sum $w_1 + w_3 + w_4 + w_5 + w_6 = 0.45$, which is less than $1/2$. Furthermore, only element x_2 is greater than x_7, and $w_2 = 0.35$, which is no greater than $1/2$.

a. Argue that the median of $x_1, x_2, \ldots, x_n$ is the weighted median of the x_i with weights $w_i = 1/n$ for $i = 1, 2, \ldots, n$.

b. Show how to compute the weighted median of n elements in $O(n \lg n)$ worst-case time using sorting.

c. Show how to compute the weighted median in $\Theta(n)$ worst-case time using a linear-time median algorithm such as SELECT from Section 9.3.

The *post-office location problem* is defined as follows. The input is n points $p_1, p_2, \ldots, p_n$ with associated weights $w_1, w_2, \ldots, w_n$. A solution is a point p (not necessarily one of the input points) that minimizes the sum $\sum_{i=1}^n w_i \, d(p, p_i)$, where $d(a, b)$ is the distance between points a and b.

d. Argue that the weighted median is a best solution for the one-dimensional post-office location problem, in which points are simply real numbers and the distance between points a and b is $d(a, b) = |a - b|$.

e. Find the best solution for the two-dimensional post-office location problem, in which the points are (x, y) coordinate pairs and the distance between points $a = (x_1, y_1)$ and $b = (x_2, y_2)$ is ***Manhattan distance*** given by $d(a, b) = |x_1 - x_2| + |y_1 - y_2|$.

9-4   *Small order statistics*

Let's denote by $S(n)$ the worst-case number of comparisons used by SELECT to select the ith order statistic from n numbers. Although $S(n) = \Theta(n)$, the constant hidden by the Θ-notation is rather large. When i is small relative to n, there is an algorithm that uses SELECT as a subroutine but makes fewer comparisons in the worst case.

a. Describe an algorithm that uses $U_i(n)$ comparisons to find the ith smallest of n elements, where

$$U_i(n) = \begin{cases} S(n) & \text{if } i \geq n/2, \\ \lfloor n/2 \rfloor + U_i(\lceil n/2 \rceil) + S(2i) & \text{otherwise} . \end{cases}$$

(*Hint:* Begin with $\lfloor n/2 \rfloor$ disjoint pairwise comparisons, and recurse on the set containing the smaller element from each pair.)

b. Show that, if $i < n/2$, then $U_i(n) = n + O(S(2i) \lg(n/i))$.

c. Show that if i is a constant less than $n/2$, then $U_i(n) = n + O(\lg n)$.

d. Show that if $i = n/k$ for $k \geq 2$, then $U_i(n) = n + O(S(2n/k) \lg k)$.

9-5   *Alternative analysis of randomized selection*

In this problem, you will use indicator random variables to analyze the procedure RANDOMIZED-SELECT in a manner akin to our analysis of RANDOMIZED-QUICKSORT in Section 7.4.2.

As in the quicksort analysis, we assume that all elements are distinct, and we rename the elements of the input array A as $z_1, z_2, \ldots, z_n$, where z_i is the ith smallest element. Thus the call RANDOMIZED-SELECT$(A, 1, n, i)$ returns z_i.

For $1 \leq j < k \leq n$, let

$$X_{ijk} = \text{I}\{z_j \text{ is compared with } z_k \text{ sometime during the execution of the algorithm to find } z_i\} .$$

a. Give an exact expression for $\mathrm{E}[X_{ijk}]$. (*Hint:* Your expression may have different values, depending on the values of i, j, and k.)

b. Let X_i denote the total number of comparisons between elements of array A when finding z_i. Show that

$$\mathrm{E}[X_i] \leq 2 \left(\sum_{j=1}^{i} \sum_{k=i}^{n} \frac{1}{k-j+1} + \sum_{k=i+1}^{n} \frac{k-i-1}{k-i+1} + \sum_{j=1}^{i-2} \frac{i-j-1}{i-j+1} \right).$$

c. Show that $\mathrm{E}[X_i] \leq 4n$.

d. Conclude that, assuming all elements of array A are distinct, RANDOMIZED-SELECT runs in $O(n)$ expected time.

9-6   *Select with groups of 3*

Exercise 9.3-1 asks you to show that the SELECT algorithm still runs in linear time if the elements are divided into groups of 7. This problem asks about dividing into groups of 3.

a. Show that SELECT runs in linear time if you divide the elements into groups whose size is any odd constant greater than 3.

b. Show that SELECT runs in $O(n \lg n)$ time if you divide the elements into groups of size 3.

Because the bound in part (b) is just an upper bound, we do not know whether the groups-of-3 strategy actually runs in $O(n)$ time. But by repeating the groups-of-3 idea on the middle group of medians, we can pick a pivot that guarantees $O(n)$ time. The SELECT3 algorithm on the next page determines the ith smallest of an input array of $n > 1$ distinct elements.

c. Describe in English how the SELECT3 algorithm works. Include in your description one or more suitable diagrams.

d. Show that SELECT3 runs in $O(n)$ time in the worst case.

Chapter notes

The worst-case linear-time median-finding algorithm was devised by Blum, Floyd, Pratt, Rivest, and Tarjan [62]. The fast randomized version is due to Hoare [218]. Floyd and Rivest [147] have developed an improved randomized version that partitions around an element recursively selected from a small sample of the elements.

SELECT3(A, p, r, i)

```
 1  while (r − p + 1) mod 9 ≠ 0
 2      for j = p + 1 to r                    // put the minimum into A[p]
 3          if A[p] > A[j]
 4              exchange A[p] with A[j]
 5      // If we want the minimum of A[p : r], we're done.
 6      if i == 1
 7          return A[p]
 8      // Otherwise, we want the (i − 1)st element of A[p + 1 : r].
 9      p = p + 1
10      i = i − 1
11  g = (r − p + 1)/3                          // number of 3-element groups
12  for j = p to p + g − 1                     // run through the groups
13      sort ⟨A[j], A[j + g], A[j + 2g]⟩ in place
14  // All group medians now lie in the middle third of A[p : r].
15  g' = g/3                                   // number of 3-element subgroups
16  for j = p + g to p + g + g' − 1            // sort the subgroups
17      sort ⟨A[j], A[j + g'], A[j + 2g']⟩ in place
18  // All subgroup medians now lie in the middle ninth of A[p : r].
19  // Find the pivot x recursively as the median of the subgroup medians.
20  x = SELECT3(A, p + 4g', p + 5g' − 1, ⌈g'/2⌉)
21  q = PARTITION-AROUND(A, p, r, x)          // partition around the pivot
22  // The rest is just like lines 19–24 of SELECT.
23  k = q − p + 1
24  if i == k
25      return A[q]                           // the pivot value is the answer
26  elseif i < k
27      return SELECT3(A, p, q − 1, i)
28  else return SELECT3(A, q + 1, r, i − k)
```

It is still unknown exactly how many comparisons are needed to determine the median. Bent and John [48] gave a lower bound of $2n$ comparisons for median finding, and Schönhage, Paterson, and Pippenger [397] gave an upper bound of $3n$. Dor and Zwick have improved on both of these bounds. Their upper bound [123] is slightly less than $2.95n$, and their lower bound [124] is $(2 + \epsilon)n$, for a small positive constant ϵ, thereby improving slightly on related work by Dor et al. [122]. Paterson [354] describes some of these results along with other related work.

Problem 9-6 was inspired by a paper by Chen and Dumitrescu [84].

Part III   Data Structures

Introduction

Sets are as fundamental to computer science as they are to mathematics. Whereas mathematical sets are unchanging, the sets manipulated by algorithms can grow, shrink, or otherwise change over time. We call such sets *dynamic*. The next four chapters present some basic techniques for representing finite dynamic sets and manipulating them on a computer.

Algorithms may require several types of operations to be performed on sets. For example, many algorithms need only the ability to insert elements into, delete elements from, and test membership in a set. We call a dynamic set that supports these operations a *dictionary*. Other algorithms require more complicated operations. For example, min-priority queues, which Chapter 6 introduced in the context of the heap data structure, support the operations of inserting an element into and extracting the smallest element from a set. The best way to implement a dynamic set depends upon the operations that you need to support.

Elements of a dynamic set

In a typical implementation of a dynamic set, each element is represented by an object whose attributes can be examined and manipulated given a pointer to the object. Some kinds of dynamic sets assume that one of the object's attributes is an identifying *key*. If the keys are all different, we can think of the dynamic set as being a set of key values. The object may contain *satellite data*, which are carried around in other object attributes but are otherwise unused by the set implementation. It may also have attributes that are manipulated by the set operations. These attributes may contain data or pointers to other objects in the set.

Some dynamic sets presuppose that the keys are drawn from a totally ordered set, such as the real numbers, or the set of all words under the usual alphabetic ordering. A total ordering allows us to define the minimum element of the set, for example, or to speak of the next element larger than a given element in a set.

Operations on dynamic sets

Operations on a dynamic set can be grouped into two categories: *queries*, which simply return information about the set, and *modifying operations*, which change the set. Here is a list of typical operations. Any specific application will usually require only a few of these to be implemented.

SEARCH(S, k)
> A query that, given a set S and a key value k, returns a pointer x to an element in S such that $x.key = k$, or NIL if no such element belongs to S.

INSERT(S, x)
> A modifying operation that adds the element pointed to by x to the set S. We usually assume that any attributes in element x needed by the set implementation have already been initialized.

DELETE(S, x)
> A modifying operation that, given a pointer x to an element in the set S, removes x from S. (Note that this operation takes a pointer to an element x, not a key value.)

MINIMUM(S) and MAXIMUM(S)
> Queries on a totally ordered set S that return a pointer to the element of S with the smallest (for MINIMUM) or largest (for MAXIMUM) key.

SUCCESSOR(S, x)
> A query that, given an element x whose key is from a totally ordered set S, returns a pointer to the next larger element in S, or NIL if x is the maximum element.

PREDECESSOR(S, x)
> A query that, given an element x whose key is from a totally ordered set S, returns a pointer to the next smaller element in S, or NIL if x is the minimum element.

In some situations, we can extend the queries SUCCESSOR and PREDECESSOR so that they apply to sets with nondistinct keys. For a set on n keys, the normal presumption is that a call to MINIMUM followed by $n - 1$ calls to SUCCESSOR enumerates the elements in the set in sorted order.

We usually measure the time taken to execute a set operation in terms of the size of the set. For example, Chapter 13 describes a data structure that can support any of the operations listed above on a set of size n in $O(\lg n)$ time.

Of course, you can always choose to implement a dynamic set with an array. The advantage of doing so is that the algorithms for the dynamic-set operations are simple. The downside, however, is that many of these operations have a worst-case running time of $\Theta(n)$. If the array is not sorted, INSERT and DELETE can take $\Theta(1)$ time, but the remaining operations take $\Theta(n)$ time. If instead the array is maintained in sorted order, then MINIMUM, MAXIMUM, SUCCESSOR, and PREDECESSOR take $\Theta(1)$ time; SEARCH takes $O(\lg n)$ time if implemented with binary search; but INSERT and DELETE take $\Theta(n)$ time in the worst case. The data structures studied in this part improve on the array implementation for many of the dynamic-set operations.

Overview of Part III

Chapters 10–13 describe several data structures that we can use to implement dynamic sets. We'll use many of these data structures later to construct efficient algorithms for a variety of problems. We already saw another important data structure —the heap—in Chapter 6.

Chapter 10 presents the essentials of working with simple data structures such as arrays, matrices, stacks, queues, linked lists, and rooted trees. If you have taken an introductory programming course, then much of this material should be familiar to you.

Chapter 11 introduces hash tables, a widely used data structure supporting the dictionary operations INSERT, DELETE, and SEARCH. In the worst case, hash tables require $\Theta(n)$ time to perform a SEARCH operation, but the expected time for hash-table operations is $O(1)$. We rely on probability to analyze hash-table operations, but you can understand how the operations work even without probability.

Binary search trees, which are covered in Chapter 12, support all the dynamic-set operations listed above. In the worst case, each operation takes $\Theta(n)$ time on a tree with n elements. Binary search trees serve as the basis for many other data structures.

Chapter 13 introduces red-black trees, which are a variant of binary search trees. Unlike ordinary binary search trees, red-black trees are guaranteed to perform well: operations take $O(\lg n)$ time in the worst case. A red-black tree is a balanced search tree. Chapter 18 in Part V presents another kind of balanced search tree, called a B-tree. Although the mechanics of red-black trees are somewhat intricate, you can glean most of their properties from the chapter without studying the mechanics in detail. Nevertheless, you probably will find walking through the code to be instructive.

10 Elementary Data Structures

In this chapter, we examine the representation of dynamic sets by simple data structures that use pointers. Although you can construct many complex data structures using pointers, we present only the rudimentary ones: arrays, matrices, stacks, queues, linked lists, and rooted trees.

10.1 Simple array-based data structures: arrays, matrices, stacks, queues

10.1.1 Arrays

We assume that, as in most programming languages, an array is stored as a contiguous sequence of bytes in memory. If the first element of an array has index s (for example, in an array with 1-origin indexing, $s = 1$), the array starts at memory address a, and each array element occupies b bytes, then the ith element occupies bytes $a + b(i - s)$ through $a + b(i - s + 1) - 1$. Since most of the arrays in this book are indexed starting at 1, and a few starting at 0, we can simplify these formulas a little. When $s = 1$, the ith element occupies bytes $a + b(i - 1)$ through $a + bi - 1$, and when $s = 0$, the ith element occupies bytes $a + bi$ through $a + b(i + 1) - 1$. Assuming that the computer can access all memory locations in the same amount of time (as in the RAM model described in Section 2.2), it takes constant time to access any array element, regardless of the index.

Most programming languages require each element of a particular array to be the same size. If the elements of a given array might occupy different numbers of bytes, then the above formulas fail to apply, since the element size b is not a constant. In such cases, the array elements are usually objects of varying sizes, and what actually appears in each array element is a pointer to the object. The number of bytes occupied by a pointer is typically the same, no matter what the pointer references, so that to access an object in an array, the above formulas give the address of the pointer to the object and then the pointer must be followed to access the object itself.

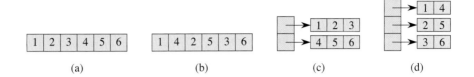

(a)   (b)   (c)   (d)

Figure 10.1   Four ways to store the 2×3 matrix M from equation (10.1). **(a)** In row-major order, in a single array. **(b)** In column-major order, in a single array. **(c)** In row-major order, with one array per row (tan) and a single array (blue) of pointers to the row arrays. **(d)** In column-major order, with one array per column (tan) and a single array (blue) of pointers to the column arrays.

10.1.2   Matrices

We typically represent a matrix or two-dimensional array by one or more one-dimensional arrays. The two most common ways to store a matrix are row-major and column-major order. Let's consider an $m \times n$ matrix—a matrix with m rows and n columns. In *row-major order*, the matrix is stored row by row, and in *column-major order*, the matrix is stored column by column. For example, consider the 2×3 matrix

$$M = \begin{pmatrix} 1 & 2 & 3 \\ 4 & 5 & 6 \end{pmatrix}. \tag{10.1}$$

Row-major order stores the two rows 1 2 3 and 4 5 6, whereas column-major order stores the three columns 1 4; 2 5; and 3 6.

Parts (a) and (b) of Figure 10.1 show how to store this matrix using a single one-dimensional array. It's stored in row-major order in part (a) and in column-major order in part (b). If the rows, columns, and the single array all are indexed starting at s, then $M[i, j]$—the element in row i and column j—is at array index $s + (n(i - s)) + (j - s)$ with row-major order and $s + (m(j - s)) + (i - s)$ with column-major order. When $s = 1$, the single-array indices are $n(i - 1) + j$ with row-major order and $i + m(j - 1)$ with column-major order. When $s = 0$, the single-array indices are simpler: $ni + j$ with row-major order and $i + mj$ with column-major order. For the example matrix M with 1-origin indexing, element $M[2, 1]$ is stored at index $3(2-1)+1 = 4$ in the single array using row-major order and at index $2 + 2(1 - 1) = 2$ using column-major order.

Parts (c) and (d) of Figure 10.1 show multiple-array strategies for storing the example matrix. In part (c), each row is stored in its own array of length n, shown in tan. Another array, with m elements, shown in blue, points to the m row arrays. If we call the blue array A, then $A[i]$ points to the array storing the entries for row i of M, and array element $A[i][j]$ stores matrix element $M[i, j]$. Part (d) shows the column-major version of the multiple-array representation, with n arrays, each of length m, representing the n columns. Matrix element $M[i, j]$ is stored in array element $A[j][i]$.

Single-array representations are typically more efficient on modern machines than multiple-array representations. But multiple-array representations can sometimes be more flexible, for example, allowing for "ragged arrays," in which the rows in the row-major version may have different lengths, or symmetrically for the column-major version, where columns may have different lengths.

Occasionally, other schemes are used to store matrices. In the *block representation*, the matrix is divided into blocks, and each block is stored contiguously. For example, a 4×4 matrix that is divided into 2×2 blocks, such as

$$\begin{pmatrix} 1 & 2 & 3 & 4 \\ 5 & 6 & 7 & 8 \\ 9 & 10 & 11 & 12 \\ 13 & 14 & 15 & 16 \end{pmatrix}$$

might be stored in a single array in the order $\langle 1, 2, 5, 6, 3, 4, 7, 8, 9, 10, 13, 14, 11, 12, 15, 16 \rangle$.

10.1.3   Stacks and queues

Stacks and queues are dynamic sets in which the element removed from the set by the DELETE operation is prespecified. In a *stack*, the element deleted from the set is the one most recently inserted: the stack implements a *last-in, first-out*, or *LIFO*, policy. Similarly, in a *queue*, the element deleted is always the one that has been in the set for the longest time: the queue implements a *first-in, first-out*, or *FIFO*, policy. There are several efficient ways to implement stacks and queues on a computer. Here, you will see how to use an array with attributes to store them.

Stacks

The INSERT operation on a stack is often called PUSH, and the DELETE operation, which does not take an element argument, is often called POP. These names are allusions to physical stacks, such as the spring-loaded stacks of plates used in cafeterias. The order in which plates are popped from the stack is the reverse of the order in which they were pushed onto the stack, since only the top plate is accessible.

Figure 10.2 shows how to implement a stack of at most n elements with an array $S[1:n]$. The stack has attributes $S.top$, indexing the most recently inserted element, and $S.size$, equaling the size n of the array. The stack consists of elements $S[1 : S.top]$, where $S[1]$ is the element at the bottom of the stack and $S[S.top]$ is the element at the top.

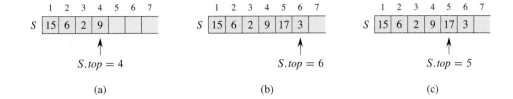

Figure 10.2 An array implementation of a stack S. Stack elements appear only in the tan positions. **(a)** Stack S has 4 elements. The top element is 9. **(b)** Stack S after the calls PUSH$(S, 17)$ and PUSH$(S, 3)$. **(c)** Stack S after the call POP(S) has returned the element 3, which is the one most recently pushed. Although element 3 still appears in the array, it is no longer in the stack. The top is element 17.

When $S.top = 0$, the stack contains no elements and is *empty*. We can test whether the stack is empty with the query operation STACK-EMPTY. Upon an attempt to pop an empty stack, the stack *underflows*, which is normally an error. If $S.top$ exceeds $S.size$, the stack *overflows*.

The procedures STACK-EMPTY, PUSH, and POP implement each of the stack operations with just a few lines of code. Figure 10.2 shows the effects of the modifying operations PUSH and POP. Each of the three stack operations takes $O(1)$ time.

STACK-EMPTY(S)

1 **if** $S.top == 0$
2   **return** TRUE
3 **else return** FALSE

PUSH(S, x)

1 **if** $S.top == S.size$
2   **error** "overflow"
3 **else** $S.top = S.top + 1$
4      $S[S.top] = x$

POP(S)

1 **if** STACK-EMPTY(S)
2   **error** "underflow"
3 **else** $S.top = S.top - 1$
4   **return** $S[S.top + 1]$

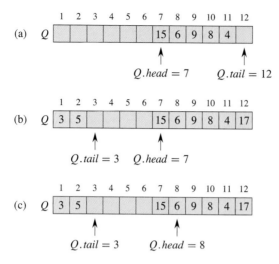

Figure 10.3 A queue implemented using an array $Q[1:12]$. Queue elements appear only in the tan positions. **(a)** The queue has 5 elements, in locations $Q[7:11]$. **(b)** The configuration of the queue after the calls ENQUEUE$(Q, 17)$, ENQUEUE$(Q, 3)$, and ENQUEUE$(Q, 5)$. **(c)** The configuration of the queue after the call DEQUEUE(Q) returns the key value 15 formerly at the head of the queue. The new head has key 6.

Queues

We call the INSERT operation on a queue ENQUEUE, and we call the DELETE operation DEQUEUE. Like the stack operation POP, DEQUEUE takes no element argument. The FIFO property of a queue causes it to operate like a line of customers waiting for service. The queue has a *head* and a *tail*. When an element is enqueued, it takes its place at the tail of the queue, just as a newly arriving customer takes a place at the end of the line. The element dequeued is always the one at the head of the queue, like the customer at the head of the line, who has waited the longest.

Figure 10.3 shows one way to implement a queue of at most $n - 1$ elements using an array $Q[1:n]$, with the attribute $Q.size$ equaling the size n of the array. The queue has an attribute $Q.head$ that indexes, or points to, its head. The attribute $Q.tail$ indexes the next location at which a newly arriving element will be inserted into the queue. The elements in the queue reside in locations $Q.head, Q.head + 1,$ $\ldots, Q.tail - 1$, where we "wrap around" in the sense that location 1 immediately follows location n in a circular order. When $Q.head = Q.tail$, the queue is empty. Initially, we have $Q.head = Q.tail = 1$. An attempt to dequeue an element from an empty queue causes the queue to underflow. When $Q.head = Q.tail + 1$ or both

$Q.head = 1$ and $Q.tail = Q.size$, the queue is full, and an attempt to enqueue an element causes the queue to overflow.

In the procedures ENQUEUE and DEQUEUE, we have omitted the error checking for underflow and overflow. (Exercise 10.1-5 asks you to supply these checks.) Figure 10.3 shows the effects of the ENQUEUE and DEQUEUE operations. Each operation takes $O(1)$ time.

ENQUEUE(Q, x)

1 $Q[Q.tail] = x$
2 **if** $Q.tail == Q.size$
3      $Q.tail = 1$
4 **else** $Q.tail = Q.tail + 1$

DEQUEUE(Q)

1 $x = Q[Q.head]$
2 **if** $Q.head == Q.size$
3      $Q.head = 1$
4 **else** $Q.head = Q.head + 1$
5 **return** x

Exercises

10.1-1
Consider an $m \times n$ matrix in row-major order, where both m and n are powers of 2 and rows and columns are indexed from 0. We can represent a row index i in binary by the $\lg m$ bits $\langle i_{\lg m-1}, i_{\lg m-2}, \ldots, i_0 \rangle$ and a column index j in binary by the $\lg n$ bits $\langle j_{\lg n-1}, j_{\lg n-2}, \ldots, j_0 \rangle$. Suppose that this matrix is a 2×2 block matrix, where each block has $m/2$ rows and $n/2$ columns, and it is to be represented by a single array with 0-origin indexing. Show how to construct the binary representation of the $(\lg m + \lg n)$-bit index into the single array from the binary representations of i and j.

10.1-2
Using Figure 10.2 as a model, illustrate the result of each operation in the sequence PUSH$(S, 4)$, PUSH$(S, 1)$, PUSH$(S, 3)$, POP(S), PUSH$(S, 8)$, and POP(S) on an initially empty stack S stored in array $S[1:6]$

10.1-3

Explain how to implement two stacks in one array $A[1:n]$ in such a way that neither stack overflows unless the total number of elements in both stacks together is n. The PUSH and POP operations should run in $O(1)$ time.

10.1-4

Using Figure 10.3 as a model, illustrate the result of each operation in the sequence ENQUEUE$(Q, 4)$, ENQUEUE$(Q, 1)$, ENQUEUE$(Q, 3)$, DEQUEUE(Q), ENQUEUE$(Q, 8)$, and DEQUEUE(Q) on an initially empty queue Q stored in array $Q[1:6]$.

10.1-5

Rewrite ENQUEUE and DEQUEUE to detect underflow and overflow of a queue.

10.1-6

Whereas a stack allows insertion and deletion of elements at only one end, and a queue allows insertion at one end and deletion at the other end, a *deque* (double-ended queue, pronounced like "deck") allows insertion and deletion at both ends. Write four $O(1)$-time procedures to insert elements into and delete elements from both ends of a deque implemented by an array.

10.1-7

Show how to implement a queue using two stacks. Analyze the running time of the queue operations.

10.1-8

Show how to implement a stack using two queues. Analyze the running time of the stack operations.

10.2   Linked lists

A *linked list* is a data structure in which the objects are arranged in a linear order. Unlike an array, however, in which the linear order is determined by the array indices, the order in a linked list is determined by a pointer in each object. Since the elements of linked lists often contain keys that can be searched for, linked lists are sometimes called *search lists*. Linked lists provide a simple, flexible representation for dynamic sets, supporting (though not necessarily efficiently) all the operations listed on page 250.

As shown in Figure 10.4, each element of a *doubly linked list L* is an object with an attribute *key* and two pointer attributes: *next* and *prev*. The object may

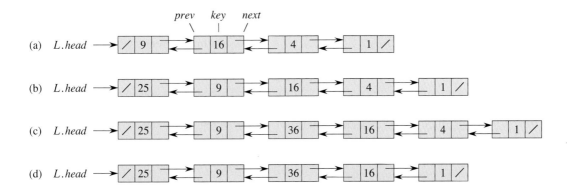

Figure 10.4 **(a)** A doubly linked list L representing the dynamic set $\{1, 4, 9, 16\}$. Each element in the list is an object with attributes for the key and pointers (shown by arrows) to the next and previous objects. The *next* attribute of the tail and the *prev* attribute of the head are NIL, indicated by a diagonal slash. The attribute $L.head$ points to the head. **(b)** Following the execution of LIST-PREPEND(L, x), where $x.key = 25$, the linked list has an object with key 25 as the new head. This new object points to the old head with key 9. **(c)** The result of calling LIST-INSERT(x, y), where $x.key = 36$ and y points to the object with key 9. **(d)** The result of the subsequent call LIST-DELETE(L, x), where x points to the object with key 4.

also contain other satellite data. Given an element x in the list, $x.next$ points to its successor in the linked list, and $x.prev$ points to its predecessor. If $x.prev = $ NIL, the element x has no predecessor and is therefore the first element, or **head**, of the list. If $x.next = $ NIL, the element x has no successor and is therefore the last element, or **tail**, of the list. An attribute $L.head$ points to the first element of the list. If $L.head = $ NIL, the list is empty.

A list may have one of several forms. It may be either singly linked or doubly linked, it may be sorted or not, and it may be circular or not. If a list is *singly linked*, each element has a *next* pointer but not a *prev* pointer. If a list is *sorted*, the linear order of the list corresponds to the linear order of keys stored in elements of the list. The minimum element is then the head of the list, and the maximum element is the tail. If the list is *unsorted*, the elements can appear in any order. In a *circular list*, the *prev* pointer of the head of the list points to the tail, and the *next* pointer of the tail of the list points to the head. You can think of a circular list as a ring of elements. In the remainder of this section, we assume that the lists we are working with are unsorted and doubly linked.

Searching a linked list

The procedure LIST-SEARCH(L, k) finds the first element with key k in list L by a simple linear search, returning a pointer to this element. If no object with key k appears in the list, then the procedure returns NIL. For the linked list in Figure 10.4(a), the call LIST-SEARCH($L, 4$) returns a pointer to the third element, and the call LIST-SEARCH($L, 7$) returns NIL. To search a list of n objects, the LIST-SEARCH procedure takes $\Theta(n)$ time in the worst case, since it may have to search the entire list.

LIST-SEARCH(L, k)

1 $x = L.head$
2 **while** $x \neq$ NIL and $x.key \neq k$
3      $x = x.next$
4 **return** x

Inserting into a linked list

Given an element x whose *key* attribute has already been set, the LIST-PREPEND procedure adds x to the front of the linked list, as shown in Figure 10.4(b). (Recall that our attribute notation can cascade, so that $L.head.prev$ denotes the *prev* attribute of the object that $L.head$ points to.) The running time for LIST-PREPEND on a list of n elements is $O(1)$.

LIST-PREPEND(L, x)

1 $x.next = L.head$
2 $x.prev =$ NIL
3 **if** $L.head \neq$ NIL
4      $L.head.prev = x$
5 $L.head = x$

You can insert anywhere within a linked list. As Figure 10.4(c) shows, if you have a pointer y to an object in the list, the LIST-INSERT procedure on the facing page "splices" a new element x into the list, immediately following y, in $O(1)$ time. Since LIST-INSERT never references the list object L, it is not supplied as a parameter.

```
LIST-INSERT(x, y)
1   x.next = y.next
2   x.prev = y
3   if y.next ≠ NIL
4        y.next.prev = x
5   y.next = x
```

Deleting from a linked list

The procedure LIST-DELETE removes an element x from a linked list L. It must
be given a pointer to x, and it then "'splices" x out of the list by updating pointers.
To delete an element with a given key, first call LIST-SEARCH to retrieve a pointer
to the element. Figure 10.4(d) shows how an element is deleted from a linked list.
LIST-DELETE runs in $O(1)$ time, but to delete an element with a given key, the call
to LIST-SEARCH makes the worst-case running time be $\Theta(n)$.

```
LIST-DELETE(L, x)
1   if x.prev ≠ NIL
2        x.prev.next = x.next
3   else L.head = x.next
4   if x.next ≠ NIL
5        x.next.prev = x.prev
```

Insertion and deletion are faster operations on doubly linked lists than on arrays.
If you want to insert a new first element into an array or delete the first element in
an array, maintaining the relative order of all the existing elements, then each of the
existing elements needs to be moved by one position. In the worst case, therefore,
insertion and deletion take $\Theta(n)$ time in an array, compared with $O(1)$ time for a
doubly linked list. (Exercise 10.2-1 asks you to show that deleting an element from
a singly linked list takes $\Theta(n)$ time in the worst case.) If, however, you want to find
the kth element in the linear order, it takes just $O(1)$ time in an array regardless
of k, but in a linked list, you'd have to traverse k elements, taking $\Theta(k)$ time.

Sentinels

The code for LIST-DELETE is simpler if you ignore the boundary conditions at the
head and tail of the list:

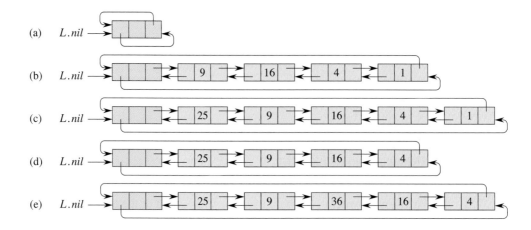

Figure 10.5 A circular, doubly linked list with a sentinel. The sentinel $L.nil$, in blue, appears between the head and tail. The attribute $L.head$ is no longer needed, since the head of the list is $L.nil.next$. **(a)** An empty list. **(b)** The linked list from Figure 10.4(a), with key 9 at the head and key 1 at the tail. **(c)** The list after executing LIST-INSERT$'(x, L.nil)$, where $x.key = 25$. The new object becomes the head of the list. **(d)** The list after deleting the object with key 1. The new tail is the object with key 4. **(e)** The list after executing LIST-INSERT$'(x, y)$, where $x.key = 36$ and y points to the object with key 9.

LIST-DELETE$'(x)$

1   $x.prev.next = x.next$
2   $x.next.prev = x.prev$

A *sentinel* is a dummy object that allows us to simplify boundary conditions. In a linked list L, the sentinel is an object $L.nil$ that represents NIL but has all the attributes of the other objects in the list. References to NIL are replaced by references to the sentinel $L.nil$. As shown in Figure 10.5, this change turns a regular doubly linked list into a *circular, doubly linked list with a sentinel*, in which the sentinel $L.nil$ lies between the head and tail. The attribute $L.nil.next$ points to the head of the list, and $L.nil.prev$ points to the tail. Similarly, both the *next* attribute of the tail and the *prev* attribute of the head point to $L.nil$. Since $L.nil.next$ points to the head, the attribute $L.head$ is eliminated altogether, with references to it replaced by references to $L.nil.next$. Figure 10.5(a) shows that an empty list consists of just the sentinel, and both $L.nil.next$ and $L.nil.prev$ point to $L.nil$.

To delete an element from the list, just use the two-line procedure LIST-DELETE$'$ from before. Just as LIST-INSERT never references the list object L, neither does

LIST-DELETE$'$. You should never delete the sentinel $L.nil$ unless you are deleting the entire list!

The LIST-INSERT$'$ procedure inserts an element x into the list following object y. No separate procedure for prepending is necessary: to insert at the head of the list, let y be $L.nil$; and to insert at the tail, let y be $L.nil.prev$. Figure 10.5 shows the effects of LIST-INSERT$'$ and LIST-DELETE$'$ on a sample list.

LIST-INSERT$'(x, y)$

1   $x.next = y.next$
2   $x.prev = y$
3   $y.next.prev = x$
4   $y.next = x$

Searching a circular, doubly linked list with a sentinel has the same asymptotic running time as without a sentinel, but it is possible to decrease the constant factor. The test in line 2 of LIST-SEARCH makes two comparisons: one to check whether the search has run off the end of the list and, if not, one to check whether the key resides in the current element x. Suppose that you *know* that the key is somewhere in the list. Then you do not need to check whether the search runs off the end of the list, thereby eliminating one comparison in each iteration of the **while** loop.

The sentinel provides a place to put the key before starting the search. The search starts at the head $L.nil.next$ of list L, and it stops if it finds the key somewhere in the list. Now the search is guaranteed to find the key, either in the sentinel or before reaching the sentinel. If the key is found before reaching the sentinel, then it really is in the element where the search stops. If, however, the search goes through all the elements in the list and finds the key only in the sentinel, then the key is not really in the list, and the search returns NIL. The procedure LIST-SEARCH$'$ embodies this idea. (If your sentinel requires its *key* attribute to be NIL, then you might want to assign $L.nil.key =$ NIL before line 5.)

LIST-SEARCH$'(L, k)$

1   $L.nil.key = k$ **//** store the key in the sentinel to guarantee it is in list
2   $x = L.nil.next$ **//** start at the head of the list
3   **while** $x.key \neq k$
4        $x = x.next$
5   **if** $x == L.nil$ **//** found k in the sentinel
6   **return** NIL   **//** k was not really in the list
7   **else return** x **//** found k in element x

Sentinels often simplify code and, as in searching a linked list, they might speed up code by a small constant factor, but they don't typically improve the asymptotic running time. Use them judiciously. When there are many small lists, the extra storage used by their sentinels can represent significant wasted memory. In this book, we use sentinels only when they significantly simplify the code.

Exercises

10.2-1
Explain why the dynamic-set operation INSERT on a singly linked list can be implemented in $O(1)$ time, but the worst-case time for DELETE is $\Theta(n)$.

10.2-2
Implement a stack using a singly linked list. The operations PUSH and POP should still take $O(1)$ time. Do you need to add any attributes to the list?

10.2-3
Implement a queue using a singly linked list. The operations ENQUEUE and DEQUEUE should still take $O(1)$ time. Do you need to add any attributes to the list?

10.2-4
The dynamic-set operation UNION takes two disjoint sets S_1 and S_2 as input, and it returns a set $S = S_1 \cup S_2$ consisting of all the elements of S_1 and S_2. The sets S_1 and S_2 are usually destroyed by the operation. Show how to support UNION in $O(1)$ time using a suitable list data structure.

10.2-5
Give a $\Theta(n)$-time nonrecursive procedure that reverses a singly linked list of n elements. The procedure should use no more than constant storage beyond that needed for the list itself.

★ 10.2-6
Explain how to implement doubly linked lists using only one pointer value $x.np$ per item instead of the usual two (*next* and *prev*). Assume that all pointer values can be interpreted as k-bit integers, and define $x.np = x.next$ XOR $x.prev$, the k-bit "exclusive-or" of $x.next$ and $x.prev$. The value NIL is represented by 0. Be sure to describe what information you need to access the head of the list. Show how to implement the SEARCH, INSERT, and DELETE operations on such a list. Also show how to reverse such a list in $O(1)$ time.

10.3   Representing rooted trees

Linked lists work well for representing linear relationships, but not all relationships are linear. In this section, we look specifically at the problem of representing rooted trees by linked data structures. We first look at binary trees, and then we present a method for rooted trees in which nodes can have an arbitrary number of children.

We represent each node of a tree by an object. As with linked lists, we assume that each node contains a *key* attribute. The remaining attributes of interest are pointers to other nodes, and they vary according to the type of tree.

Binary trees

Figure 10.6 shows how to use the attributes p, *left*, and *right* to store pointers to the parent, left child, and right child of each node in a binary tree T. If $x.p = $ NIL, then x is the root. If node x has no left child, then $x.left = $ NIL, and similarly for the right child. The root of the entire tree T is pointed to by the attribute $T.root$. If $T.root = $ NIL, then the tree is empty.

Rooted trees with unbounded branching

It's simple to extend the scheme for representing a binary tree to any class of trees in which the number of children of each node is at most some constant k: replace the *left* and *right* attributes by $child_1, child_2, \ldots, child_k$. This scheme no longer works when the number of children of a node is unbounded, however, since we do not know how many attributes to allocate in advance. Moreover, if k, the number of children, is bounded by a large constant but most nodes have a small number of children, we may waste a lot of memory.

Fortunately, there is a clever scheme to represent trees with arbitrary numbers of children. It has the advantage of using only $O(n)$ space for any n-node rooted tree. The *left-child, right-sibling representation* appears in Figure 10.7. As before, each node contains a parent pointer p, and $T.root$ points to the root of tree T. Instead of having a pointer to each of its children, however, each node x has only two pointers:

1. $x.left\text{-}child$ points to the leftmost child of node x, and

2. $x.right\text{-}sibling$ points to the sibling of x immediately to its right.

If node x has no children, then $x.left\text{-}child = $ NIL, and if node x is the rightmost child of its parent, then $x.right\text{-}sibling = $ NIL.

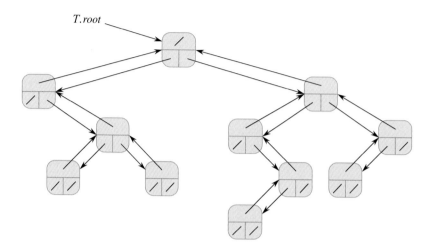

Figure 10.6   The representation of a binary tree T. Each node x has the attributes $x.p$ (top), $x.left$ (lower left), and $x.right$ (lower right). The *key* attributes are not shown.

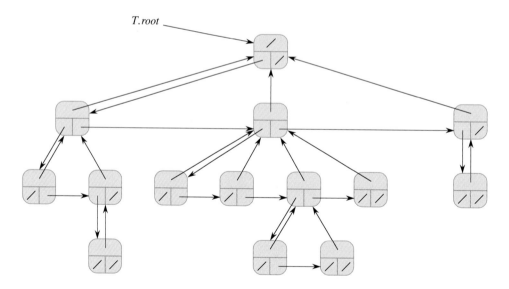

Figure 10.7   The left-child, right-sibling representation of a tree T. Each node x has attributes $x.p$ (top), $x.left\text{-}child$ (lower left), and $x.right\text{-}sibling$ (lower right). The *key* attributes are not shown.

Other tree representations

We sometimes represent rooted trees in other ways. In Chapter 6, for example, we represented a heap, which is based on a complete binary tree, by a single array along with an attribute giving the index of the last node in the heap. The trees that appear in Chapter 19 are traversed only toward the root, and so only the parent pointers are present: there are no pointers to children. Many other schemes are possible. Which scheme is best depends on the application.

Exercises

10.3-1

Draw the binary tree rooted at index 6 that is represented by the following attributes:

index	key	left	right
1	17	8	9
2	14	NIL	NIL
3	12	NIL	NIL
4	20	10	NIL
5	33	2	NIL
6	15	1	4
7	28	NIL	NIL
8	22	NIL	NIL
9	13	3	7
10	25	NIL	5

10.3-2

Write an $O(n)$-time recursive procedure that, given an n-node binary tree, prints out the key of each node in the tree.

10.3-3

Write an $O(n)$-time nonrecursive procedure that, given an n-node binary tree, prints out the key of each node in the tree. Use a stack as an auxiliary data structure.

10.3-4

Write an $O(n)$-time procedure that prints out all the keys of an arbitrary rooted tree with n nodes, where the tree is stored using the left-child, right-sibling representation.

★ *10.3-5*

Write an $O(n)$-time nonrecursive procedure that, given an n-node binary tree, prints out the key of each node. Use no more than constant extra space outside of the tree itself and do not modify the tree, even temporarily, during the procedure.

★ *10.3-6*

The left-child, right-sibling representation of an arbitrary rooted tree uses three pointers in each node: *left-child*, *right-sibling*, and *parent*. From any node, its parent can be accessed in constant time and all its children can be accessed in time linear in the number of children. Show how to use only two pointers and one boolean value in each node x so that x's parent or all of x's children can be accessed in time linear in the number of x's children.

Problems

10-1   *Comparisons among lists*

For each of the four types of lists in the following table, what is the asymptotic worst-case running time for each dynamic-set operation listed?

	unsorted, singly linked	sorted, singly linked	unsorted, doubly linked	sorted, doubly linked
SEARCH				
INSERT				
DELETE				
SUCCESSOR				
PREDECESSOR				
MINIMUM				
MAXIMUM				

10-2   *Mergeable heaps using linked lists*

A *mergeable heap* supports the following operations: MAKE-HEAP (which creates an empty mergeable heap), INSERT, MINIMUM, EXTRACT-MIN, and UNION.[1]

---

[1] Because we have defined a mergeable heap to support MINIMUM and EXTRACT-MIN, we can also refer to it as a *mergeable min-heap*. Alternatively, if it supports MAXIMUM and EXTRACT-MAX, it is a *mergeable max-heap*.

Show how to implement mergeable heaps using linked lists in each of the following cases. Try to make each operation as efficient as possible. Analyze the running time of each operation in terms of the size of the dynamic set(s) being operated on.

a. Lists are sorted.

b. Lists are unsorted.

c. Lists are unsorted, and dynamic sets to be merged are disjoint.

10-3 *Searching a sorted compact list*

We can represent a singly linked list with two arrays, *key* and *next*. Given the index i of an element, its value is stored in $key[i]$, and the index of its successor is given by $next[i]$, where $next[i] = $ NIL for the last element. We also need the index *head* of the first element in the list. An n-element list stored in this way is ***compact*** if it is stored only in positions 1 through n of the *key* and *next* arrays.

Let's assume that all keys are distinct and that the compact list is also sorted, that is, $key[i] < key[next[i]]$ for all $i = 1, 2, \ldots, n$ such that $next[i] \neq$ NIL. Under these assumptions, you will show that the randomized algorithm COMPACT-LIST-SEARCH searches the list for key k in $O(\sqrt{n})$ expected time.

```
COMPACT-LIST-SEARCH(key, next, head, n, k)
1   i = head
2   while i ≠ NIL and key[i] < k
3       j = RANDOM(1, n)
4       if key[i] < key[j] and key[j] ≤ k
5           i = j
6           if key[i] == k
7               return i
8       i = next[i]
9   if i == NIL or key[i] > k
10      return NIL
11  else return i
```

If you ignore lines 3–7 of the procedure, you can see that it's an ordinary algorithm for searching a sorted linked list, in which index i points to each position of the list in turn. The search terminates once the index i "falls off" the end of the list or once $key[i] \geq k$. In the latter case, if $key[i] = k$, the procedure has found a key with the value k. If, however, $key[i] > k$, then the search will never find a key with the value k, so that terminating the search was the correct action.

Lines 3–7 attempt to skip ahead to a randomly chosen position j. Such a skip helps if $key[j]$ is larger than $key[i]$ and no larger than k. In such a case, j marks a position in the list that i would reach during an ordinary list search. Because the list is compact, we know that any choice of j between 1 and n indexes some element in the list.

Instead of analyzing the performance of COMPACT-LIST-SEARCH directly, you will analyze a related algorithm, COMPACT-LIST-SEARCH$'$, which executes two separate loops. This algorithm takes an additional parameter t, which specifies an upper bound on the number of iterations of the first loop.

COMPACT-LIST-SEARCH$'$(*key, next, head, n, k, t*)

```
1   i = head
2   for q = 1 to t
3       j = RANDOM(1, n)
4       if key[i] < key[j] and key[j] ≤ k
5           i = j
6           if key[i] == k
7               return i
8   while i ≠ NIL and key[i] < k
9       i = next[i]
10  if i == NIL or key[i] > k
11      return NIL
12  else return i
```

To compare the execution of the two algorithms, assume that the sequence of calls of RANDOM$(1, n)$ yields the same sequence of integers for both algorithms.

a. Argue that for any value of t, COMPACT-LIST-SEARCH(*key, next, head, n, k*) and COMPACT-LIST-SEARCH$'$(*key, next, head, n, k, t*) return the same result and that the number of iterations of the **while** loop of lines 2–8 in COMPACT-LIST-SEARCH is at most the total number of iterations of both the **for** and **while** loops in COMPACT-LIST-SEARCH$'$.

In the call COMPACT-LIST-SEARCH$'$(*key, next, head, n, k, t*), let X_t be the random variable that describes the distance in the linked list (that is, through the chain of *next* pointers) from position i to the desired key k after t iterations of the **for** loop of lines 2–7 have occurred.

b. Argue that COMPACT-LIST-SEARCH$'$(*key, next, head, n, k, t*) has an expected running time of $O(t + \mathrm{E}[X_t])$.

c. Show that $\mathrm{E}[X_t] = \sum_{r=1}^{n}(1 - r/n)^t$. (*Hint:* Use equation (C.28) on page 1193.)

d. Show that $\sum_{r=0}^{n-1} r^t \le n^{t+1}/(t+1)$. (*Hint:* Use inequality (A.18) on page 1150.)

e. Prove that $\mathrm{E}[X_t] \le n/(t+1)$.

f. Show that COMPACT-LIST-SEARCH$'(key, next, head, n, k, t)$ has an expected running time of $O(t + n/t)$.

g. Conclude that COMPACT-LIST-SEARCH runs in $O(\sqrt{n})$ expected time.

h. Why do we assume that all keys are distinct in COMPACT-LIST-SEARCH? Argue that random skips do not necessarily help asymptotically when the list contains repeated key values.

Chapter notes

Aho, Hopcroft, and Ullman [6] and Knuth [259] are excellent references for elementary data structures. Many other texts cover both basic data structures and their implementation in a particular programming language. Examples of these types of textbooks include Goodrich and Tamassia [196], Main [311], Shaffer [406], and Weiss [452, 453, 454]. The book by Gonnet and Baeza-Yates [193] provides experimental data on the performance of many data-structure operations.

The origin of stacks and queues as data structures in computer science is unclear, since corresponding notions already existed in mathematics and paper-based business practices before the introduction of digital computers. Knuth [259] cites A. M. Turing for the development of stacks for subroutine linkage in 1947.

Pointer-based data structures also seem to be a folk invention. According to Knuth, pointers were apparently used in early computers with drum memories. The A-1 language developed by G. M. Hopper in 1951 represented algebraic formulas as binary trees. Knuth credits the IPL-II language, developed in 1956 by A. Newell, J. C. Shaw, and H. A. Simon, for recognizing the importance and promoting the use of pointers. Their IPL-III language, developed in 1957, included explicit stack operations.

11 Hash Tables

Many applications require a dynamic set that supports only the dictionary operations INSERT, SEARCH, and DELETE. For example, a compiler that translates a programming language maintains a symbol table, in which the keys of elements are arbitrary character strings corresponding to identifiers in the language. A hash table is an effective data structure for implementing dictionaries. Although searching for an element in a hash table can take as long as searching for an element in a linked list — $\Theta(n)$ time in the worst case — in practice, hashing performs extremely well. Under reasonable assumptions, the average time to search for an element in a hash table is $O(1)$. Indeed, the built-in dictionaries of Python are implemented with hash tables.

A hash table generalizes the simpler notion of an ordinary array. Directly addressing into an ordinary array takes advantage of the $O(1)$ access time for any array element. Section 11.1 discusses direct addressing in more detail. To use direct addressing, you must be able to allocate an array that contains a position for every possible key.

When the number of keys actually stored is small relative to the total number of possible keys, hash tables become an effective alternative to directly addressing an array, since a hash table typically uses an array of size proportional to the number of keys actually stored. Instead of using the key as an array index directly, we *compute* the array index from the key. Section 11.2 presents the main ideas, focusing on "chaining" as a way to handle "collisions," in which more than one key maps to the same array index. Section 11.3 describes how to compute array indices from keys using hash functions. We present and analyze several variations on the basic theme. Section 11.4 looks at "open addressing," which is another way to deal with collisions. The bottom line is that hashing is an extremely effective and practical technique: the basic dictionary operations require only $O(1)$ time on the average. Section 11.5 discusses the hierarchical memory systems of modern computer systems have and illustrates how to design hash tables that work well in such systems.

11.1   Direct-address tables

Direct addressing is a simple technique that works well when the universe U of keys is reasonably small. Suppose that an application needs a dynamic set in which each element has a distinct key drawn from the universe $U = \{0, 1, \ldots, m-1\}$, where m is not too large.

To represent the dynamic set, you can use an array, or *direct-address table*, denoted by $T[0:m-1]$, in which each position, or *slot*, corresponds to a key in the universe U. Figure 11.1 illustrates this approach. Slot k points to an element in the set with key k. If the set contains no element with key k, then $T[k] = \text{NIL}$.

The dictionary operations DIRECT-ADDRESS-SEARCH, DIRECT-ADDRESS-INSERT, and DIRECT-ADDRESS-DELETE on the following page are trivial to implement. Each takes only $O(1)$ time.

For some applications, the direct-address table itself can hold the elements in the dynamic set. That is, rather than storing an element's key and satellite data in an object external to the direct-address table, with a pointer from a slot in the table to the object, save space by storing the object directly in the slot. To indicate an empty slot, use a special key. Then again, why store the key of the object at all? The index of the object *is* its key! Of course, then you'd need some way to tell whether slots are empty.

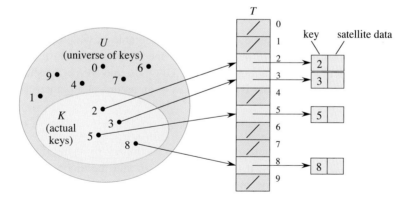

Figure 11.1   How to implement a dynamic set by a direct-address table T. Each key in the universe $U = \{0, 1, \ldots, 9\}$ corresponds to an index into the table. The set $K = \{2, 3, 5, 8\}$ of actual keys determines the slots in the table that contain pointers to elements. The other slots, in blue, contain NIL.

DIRECT-ADDRESS-SEARCH(T, k)

1 **return** $T[k]$

DIRECT-ADDRESS-INSERT(T, x)

1 $T[x.key] = x$

DIRECT-ADDRESS-DELETE(T, x)

1 $T[x.key] = \text{NIL}$

Exercises

11.1-1
A dynamic set S is represented by a direct-address table T of length m. Describe a procedure that finds the maximum element of S. What is the worst-case performance of your procedure?

11.1-2
A *bit vector* is simply an array of bits (each either 0 or 1). A bit vector of length m takes much less space than an array of m pointers. Describe how to use a bit vector to represent a dynamic set of distinct elements drawn from the set $\{0, 1, \dots, m - 1\}$ and with no satellite data. Dictionary operations should run in $O(1)$ time.

11.1-3
Suggest how to implement a direct-address table in which the keys of stored elements do not need to be distinct and the elements can have satellite data. All three dictionary operations (INSERT, DELETE, and SEARCH) should run in $O(1)$ time. (Don't forget that DELETE takes as an argument a pointer to an object to be deleted, not a key.)

★ ***11.1-4***
Suppose that you want to implement a dictionary by using direct addressing on a *huge* array. That is, if the array size is m and the dictionary contains at most n elements at any one time, then $m \gg n$. At the start, the array entries may contain garbage, and initializing the entire array is impractical because of its size. Describe a scheme for implementing a direct-address dictionary on a huge array. Each stored object should use $O(1)$ space; the operations SEARCH, INSERT, and DELETE should take $O(1)$ time each; and initializing the data structure should take $O(1)$ time. (*Hint:* Use an additional array, treated somewhat like a stack whose size is the number of keys actually stored in the dictionary, to help determine whether a given entry in the huge array is valid or not.)

11.2 Hash tables

The downside of direct addressing is apparent: if the universe U is large or infinite, storing a table T of size $|U|$ may be impractical, or even impossible, given the memory available on a typical computer. Furthermore, the set K of keys *actually stored* may be so small relative to U that most of the space allocated for T would be wasted.

When the set K of keys stored in a dictionary is much smaller than the universe U of all possible keys, a hash table requires much less storage than a direct-address table. Specifically, the storage requirement reduces to $\Theta(|K|)$ while maintaining the benefit that searching for an element in the hash table still requires only $O(1)$ time. The catch is that this bound is for the *average-case time*,[1] whereas for direct addressing it holds for the *worst-case time*.

With direct addressing, an element with key k is stored in slot k, but with hashing, we use a *hash function* h to compute the slot number from the key k, so that the element goes into slot $h(k)$. The hash function h maps the universe U of keys into the slots of a *hash table* $T[0:m-1]$:

$$h : U \to \{0, 1, \ldots, m-1\}\ ,$$

where the size m of the hash table is typically much less than $|U|$. We say that an element with key k *hashes* to slot $h(k)$, and we also say that $h(k)$ is the *hash value* of key k. Figure 11.2 illustrates the basic idea. The hash function reduces the range of array indices and hence the size of the array. Instead of a size of $|U|$, the array can have size m. An example of a simple, but not particularly good, hash function is $h(k) = k \bmod m$.

There is one hitch, namely that two keys may hash to the same slot. We call this situation a *collision*. Fortunately, there are effective techniques for resolving the conflict created by collisions.

Of course, the ideal solution is to avoid collisions altogether. We might try to achieve this goal by choosing a suitable hash function h. One idea is to make h appear to be "random," thus avoiding collisions or at least minimizing their number. The very term "to hash," evoking images of random mixing and chopping, captures the spirit of this approach. (Of course, a hash function h must be deterministic in that a given input k must always produce the same output $h(k)$.) Because $|U| > m$, however, there must be at least two keys that have the same hash value,

---

[1] The definition of "average-case" requires care—are we assuming an input distribution over the keys, or are we randomizing the choice of hash function itself? We'll consider both approaches, but with an emphasis on the use of a randomly chosen hash function.

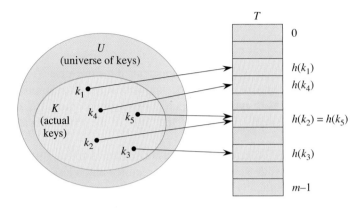

Figure 11.2 Using a hash function h to map keys to hash-table slots. Because keys k_2 and k_5 map to the same slot, they collide.

and avoiding collisions altogether is impossible. Thus, although a well-designed, "random"-looking hash function can reduce the number of collisions, we still need a method for resolving the collisions that do occur.

The remainder of this section first presents a definition of "independent uniform hashing," which captures the simplest notion of what it means for a hash function to be "random." It then presents and analyzes the simplest collision resolution technique, called chaining. Section 11.4 introduces an alternative method for resolving collisions, called open addressing.

Independent uniform hashing

An "ideal" hashing function h would have, for each possible input k in the domain U, an output $h(k)$ that is an element randomly and independently chosen uniformly from the range $\{0, 1, \ldots, m-1\}$. Once a value $h(k)$ is randomly chosen, each subsequent call to h with the same input k yields the same output $h(k)$.

We call such an ideal hash function an *independent uniform hash function*. Such a function is also often called a *random oracle* [43]. When hash tables are implemented with an independent uniform hash function, we say we are using *independent uniform hashing*.

Independent uniform hashing is an ideal theoretical abstraction, but it is not something that can reasonably be implemented in practice. Nonetheless, we'll analyze the efficiency of hashing under the assumption of independent uniform hashing and then present ways of achieving useful practical approximations to this ideal.

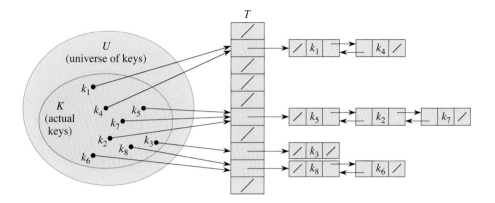

Figure 11.3 Collision resolution by chaining. Each nonempty hash-table slot $T[j]$ points to a linked list of all the keys whose hash value is j. For example, $h(k_1) = h(k_4)$ and $h(k_5) = h(k_2) = h(k_7)$. The list can be either singly or doubly linked. We show it as doubly linked because deletion may be faster that way when the deletion procedure knows which list element (not just which key) is to be deleted.

Collision resolution by chaining

At a high level, you can think of hashing with chaining as a nonrecursive form of divide-and-conquer: the input set of n elements is divided randomly into m subsets, each of approximate size n/m. A hash function determines which subset an element belongs to. Each subset is managed independently as a list.

Figure 11.3 shows the idea behind *chaining*: each nonempty slot points to a linked list, and all the elements that hash to the same slot go into that slot's linked list. Slot j contains a pointer to the head of the list of all stored elements with hash value j. If there are no such elements, then slot j contains NIL.

When collisions are resolved by chaining, the dictionary operations are straightforward to implement. They appear on the next page and use the linked-list procedures from Section 10.2. The worst-case running time for insertion is $O(1)$. The insertion procedure is fast in part because it assumes that the element x being inserted is not already present in the table. To enforce this assumption, you can search (at additional cost) for an element whose key is $x.key$ before inserting. For searching, the worst-case running time is proportional to the length of the list. (We'll analyze this operation more closely below.) Deletion takes $O(1)$ time if the lists are doubly linked, as in Figure 11.3. (Since CHAINED-HASH-DELETE takes as input an element x and not its key k, no search is needed. If the hash table supports deletion, then its linked lists should be doubly linked in order to delete an item quickly. If the lists were only singly linked, then by Exercise 10.2-1, deletion

CHAINED-HASH-INSERT(T, x)

1   LIST-PREPEND($T[h(x.key)], x$)

CHAINED-HASH-SEARCH(T, k)

1   **return** LIST-SEARCH($T[h(k)], k$)

CHAINED-HASH-DELETE(T, x)

1   LIST-DELETE($T[h(x.key)], x$)

could take time proportional to the length of the list. With singly linked lists, both deletion and searching would have the same asymptotic running times.)

Analysis of hashing with chaining

How well does hashing with chaining perform? In particular, how long does it take to search for an element with a given key?

Given a hash table T with m slots that stores n elements, we define the *load factor* α for T as n/m, that is, the average number of elements stored in a chain. Our analysis will be in terms of α, which can be less than, equal to, or greater than 1.

The worst-case behavior of hashing with chaining is terrible: all n keys hash to the same slot, creating a list of length n. The worst-case time for searching is thus $\Theta(n)$ plus the time to compute the hash function—no better than using one linked list for all the elements. We clearly don't use hash tables for their worst-case performance.

The average-case performance of hashing depends on how well the hash function h distributes the set of keys to be stored among the m slots, on the average (meaning with respect to the distribution of keys to be hashed and with respect to the choice of hash function, if this choice is randomized). Section 11.3 discusses these issues, but for now we assume that any given element is equally likely to hash into any of the m slots. That is, the hash function is *uniform*. We further assume that where a given element hashes to is *independent* of where any other elements hash to. In other words, we assume that we are using *independent uniform hashing*.

Because hashes of distinct keys are assumed to be independent, independent uniform hashing is *universal*: the chance that any two distinct keys k_1 and k_2 collide is at most $1/m$. Universality is important in our analysis and also in the specification of universal families of hash functions, which we'll see in Section 11.3.2.

For $j = 0, 1, \ldots, m - 1$, denote the length of the list $T[j]$ by n_j, so that

$$n = n_0 + n_1 + \cdots + n_{m-1} \, , \tag{11.1}$$

and the expected value of n_j is $\mathrm{E}\,[n_j] = \alpha = n/m$.

We assume that $O(1)$ time suffices to compute the hash value $h(k)$, so that the time required to search for an element with key k depends linearly on the length $n_{h(k)}$ of the list $T[h(k)]$. Setting aside the $O(1)$ time required to compute the hash function and to access slot $h(k)$, we'll consider the expected number of elements examined by the search algorithm, that is, the number of elements in the list $T[h(k)]$ that the algorithm checks to see whether any have a key equal to k. We consider two cases. In the first, the search is unsuccessful: no element in the table has key k. In the second, the search successfully finds an element with key k.

Theorem 11.1
In a hash table in which collisions are resolved by chaining, an unsuccessful search takes $\Theta(1 + \alpha)$ time on average, under the assumption of independent uniform hashing.

Proof   Under the assumption of independent uniform hashing, any key k not already stored in the table is equally likely to hash to any of the m slots. The expected time to search unsuccessfully for a key k is the expected time to search to the end of list $T[h(k)]$, which has expected length $\mathrm{E}\,[n_{h(k)}] = \alpha$. Thus, the expected number of elements examined in an unsuccessful search is α, and the total time required (including the time for computing $h(k)$) is $\Theta(1 + \alpha)$.   ∎

The situation for a successful search is slightly different. An unsuccessful search is equally likely to go to any slot of the hash table. A successful search, however, cannot go to an empty slot, since it is for an element that is present in one of the linked lists. We assume that the element searched for is equally likely to be any one of the elements in the table, so the longer the list, the more likely that the search is for one of its elements. Even so, the expected search time still turns out to be $\Theta(1 + \alpha)$.

Theorem 11.2
In a hash table in which collisions are resolved by chaining, a successful search takes $\Theta(1 + \alpha)$ time on average, under the assumption of independent uniform hashing.

Proof   We assume that the element being searched for is equally likely to be any of the n elements stored in the table. The number of elements examined during a successful search for an element x is 1 more than the number of elements that appear before x in x's list. Because new elements are placed at the front of the list, elements before x in the list were all inserted after x was inserted. Let x_i denote the ith element inserted into the table, for $i = 1, 2, \ldots, n$, and let $k_i = x_i.key$.

Our analysis uses indicator random variables extensively. For each slot q in the table and for each pair of distinct keys k_i and k_j, we define the indicator random variable

$$X_{ijq} = I\{\text{the search is for } x_i, h(k_i) = q, \text{ and } h(k_j) = q\} \ .$$

That is, $X_{ijq} = 1$ when keys k_i and k_j collide at slot q and the search is for element x_i. Because $\Pr\{\text{the search is for } x_i\} = 1/n$, $\Pr\{h(k_i) = q\} = 1/m$, $\Pr\{h(k_j) = q\} = 1/m$, and these events are all independent, we have that $\Pr\{X_{ijq} = 1\} = 1/nm^2$. Lemma 5.1 on page 130 gives $E[X_{ijq}] = 1/nm^2$.

Next, we define, for each element x_j, the indicator random variable

$$
\begin{aligned}
Y_j &= I\{x_j \text{ appears in a list prior to the element being searched for}\} \\
&= \sum_{q=0}^{m-1} \sum_{i=1}^{j-1} X_{ijq} \ ,
\end{aligned}
$$

since at most one of the X_{ijq} equals 1, namely when the element x_i being searched for belongs to the same list as x_j (pointed to by slot q), and $i < j$ (so that x_i appears after x_j in the list).

Our final random variable is Z, which counts how many elements appear in the list prior to the element being searched for:

$$Z = \sum_{j=1}^{n} Y_j \ .$$

Because we must count the element being searched for as well as all those preceding it in its list, we wish to compute $E[Z + 1]$. Using linearity of expectation (equation (C.24) on page 1192), we have

$$
\begin{aligned}
E[Z + 1] &= E\left[1 + \sum_{j=1}^{n} Y_j\right] \\
&= 1 + E\left[\sum_{j=1}^{n} \sum_{q=0}^{m-1} \sum_{i=1}^{j-1} X_{ijq}\right] \\
&= 1 + E\left[\sum_{q=0}^{m-1} \sum_{j=1}^{n} \sum_{i=1}^{j-1} X_{ijq}\right] \\
&= 1 + \sum_{q=0}^{m-1} \sum_{j=1}^{n} \sum_{i=1}^{j-1} E[X_{ijq}] \qquad \text{(by linearity of expectation)}
\end{aligned}
$$

$$= 1 + \sum_{q=0}^{m-1} \sum_{j=1}^{n} \sum_{i=1}^{j-1} \frac{1}{nm^2}$$

$$= 1 + m \cdot \frac{n(n-1)}{2} \cdot \frac{1}{nm^2} \qquad \text{(by equation (A.2) on page 1141)}$$

$$= 1 + \frac{n-1}{2m}$$

$$= 1 + \frac{n}{2m} - \frac{1}{2m}$$

$$= 1 + \frac{\alpha}{2} - \frac{\alpha}{2n} .$$

Thus, the total time required for a successful search (including the time for computing the hash function) is $\Theta(2 + \alpha/2 - \alpha/2n) = \Theta(1 + \alpha)$. ∎

What does this analysis mean? If the number of elements in the table is at most proportional to the number of hash-table slots, we have $n = O(m)$ and, consequently, $\alpha = n/m = O(m)/m = O(1)$. Thus, searching takes constant time on average. Since insertion takes $O(1)$ worst-case time and deletion takes $O(1)$ worst-case time when the lists are doubly linked (assuming that the list element to be deleted is known, and not just its key), we can support all dictionary operations in $O(1)$ time on average.

The analysis in the preceding two theorems depends only on two essential properties of independent uniform hashing: uniformity (each key is equally likely to hash to any one of the m slots), and independence (so any two distinct keys collide with probability $1/m$).

Exercises

11.2-1
You use a hash function h to hash n distinct keys into an array T of length m. Assuming independent uniform hashing, what is the expected number of collisions? More precisely, what is the expected cardinality of $\{\{k_1, k_2\} : k_1 \neq k_2 \text{ and } h(k_1) = h(k_2)\}$?

11.2-2
Consider a hash table with 9 slots and the hash function $h(k) = k \bmod 9$. Demonstrate what happens upon inserting the keys $5, 28, 19, 15, 20, 33, 12, 17, 10$ with collisions resolved by chaining.

11.2-3

Professor Marley hypothesizes that he can obtain substantial performance gains by modifying the chaining scheme to keep each list in sorted order. How does the professor's modification affect the running time for successful searches, unsuccessful searches, insertions, and deletions?

11.2-4

Suggest how to allocate and deallocate storage for elements within the hash table itself by creating a "free list": a linked list of all the unused slots. Assume that one slot can store a flag and either one element plus a pointer or two pointers. All dictionary and free-list operations should run in $O(1)$ expected time. Does the free list need to be doubly linked, or does a singly linked free list suffice?

11.2-5

You need to store a set of n keys in a hash table of size m. Show that if the keys are drawn from a universe U with $|U| > (n-1)m$, then U has a subset of size n consisting of keys that all hash to the same slot, so that the worst-case searching time for hashing with chaining is $\Theta(n)$.

11.2-6

You have stored n keys in a hash table of size m, with collisions resolved by chaining, and you know the length of each chain, including the length L of the longest chain. Describe a procedure that selects a key uniformly at random from among the keys in the hash table and returns it in expected time $O(L \cdot (1 + 1/\alpha))$.

11.3   Hash functions

For hashing to work well, it needs a good hash function. Along with being efficiently computable, what properties does a good hash function have? How do you design good hash functions?

This section first attempts to answer these questions based on two ad hoc approaches for creating hash functions: hashing by division and hashing by multiplication. Although these methods work well for some sets of input keys, they are limited because they try to provide a single fixed hash function that works well on any data—an approach called *static hashing*.

We then see that provably good average-case performance for *any* data can be obtained by designing a suitable *family* of hash functions and choosing a hash function at random from this family at runtime, independent of the data to be hashed. The approach we examine is called random hashing. A particular kind of random hashing, universal hashing, works well. As we saw with quicksort in Chapter 7, randomization is a powerful algorithmic design tool.

What makes a good hash function?

A good hash function satisfies (approximately) the assumption of independent uniform hashing: each key is equally likely to hash to any of the m slots, independently of where any other keys have hashed to. What does "equally likely" mean here? If the hash function is fixed, any probabilities would have to be based on the probability distribution of the input keys.

Unfortunately, you typically have no way to check this condition, unless you happen to know the probability distribution from which the keys are drawn. Moreover, the keys might not be drawn independently.

Occasionally you might know the distribution. For example, if you know that the keys are random real numbers k independently and uniformly distributed in the range $0 \leq k < 1$, then the hash function

$$h(k) = \lfloor km \rfloor$$

satisfies the condition of independent uniform hashing.

A good static hashing approach derives the hash value in a way that you expect to be independent of any patterns that might exist in the data. For example, the "division method" (discussed in Section 11.3.1) computes the hash value as the remainder when the key is divided by a specified prime number. This method may give good results, if you (somehow) choose a prime number that is unrelated to any patterns in the distribution of keys.

Random hashing, described in Section 11.3.2, picks the hash function to be used at random from a suitable family of hashing functions. This approach removes any need to know anything about the probability distribution of the input keys, as the randomization necessary for good average-case behavior then comes from the (known) random process used to pick the hash function from the family of hash functions, rather than from the (unknown) process used to create the input keys. We recommend that you use random hashing.

Keys are integers, vectors, or strings

In practice, a hash function is designed to handle keys that are one of the following two types:

- A short nonnegative integer that fits in a w-bit machine word. Typical values for w would be 32 or 64.

- A short vector of nonnegative integers, each of bounded size. For example, each element might be an 8-bit byte, in which case the vector is often called a (byte) string. The vector might be of variable length.

To begin, we assume that keys are short nonnegative integers. Handling vector keys is more complicated and discussed in Sections 11.3.5 and 11.5.2.

11.3.1   Static hashing

Static hashing uses a single, fixed hash function. The only randomization available is through the (usually unknown) distribution of input keys. This section discusses two standard approaches for static hashing: the division method and the multiplication method. Although static hashing is no longer recommended, the multiplication method also provides a good foundation for "nonstatic" hashing—better known as random hashing—where the hash function is chosen at random from a suitable family of hash functions.

The division method

The *division method* for creating hash functions maps a key k into one of m slots by taking the remainder of k divided by m. That is, the hash function is

$$h(k) = k \bmod m .$$

For example, if the hash table has size $m = 12$ and the key is $k = 100$, then $h(k) = 4$. Since it requires only a single division operation, hashing by division is quite fast.

The division method may work well when m is a prime not too close to an exact power of 2. There is no guarantee that this method provides good average-case performance, however, and it may complicate applications since it constrains the size of the hash tables to be prime.

The multiplication method

The general *multiplication method* for creating hash functions operates in two steps. First, multiply the key k by a constant A in the range $0 < A < 1$ and extract the fractional part of kA. Then, multiply this value by m and take the floor of the result. That is, the hash function is

$$h(k) = \lfloor m \, (kA \bmod 1) \rfloor ,$$

where "$kA \bmod 1$" means the fractional part of kA, that is, $kA - \lfloor kA \rfloor$. The general multiplication method has the advantage that the value of m is not critical and you can choose it independently of how you choose the multiplicative constant A.

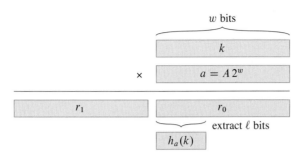

Figure 11.4   The multiply-shift method to compute a hash function. The w-bit representation of the key k is multiplied by the w-bit value $a = A \cdot 2^w$. The ℓ highest-order bits of the lower w-bit half of the product form the desired hash value $h_a(k)$.

The multiply-shift method

In practice, the multiplication method is best in the special case where the number m of hash-table slots is an exact power of 2, so that $m = 2^\ell$ for some integer ℓ, where $\ell \le w$ and w is the number of bits in a machine word. If you choose a fixed w-bit positive integer $a = A \, 2^w$, where $0 < A < 1$ as in the multiplication method so that a is in the range $0 < a < 2^w$, you can implement the function on most computers as follows. We assume that a key k fits into a single w-bit word.

Referring to Figure 11.4, first multiply k by the w-bit integer a. The result is a $2w$-bit value $r_1 2^w + r_0$, where r_1 is the high-order w-bit word of the product and r_0 is the low-order w-bit word of the product. The desired ℓ-bit hash value consists of the ℓ most significant bits of r_0. (Since r_1 is ignored, the hash function can be implemented on a computer that produces only a w-bit product given two w-bit inputs, that is, where the multiplication operation computes modulo 2^w.)

In other words, you define the hash function $h = h_a$, where

$$h_a(k) = (ka \bmod 2^w) \ggg (w - \ell) \tag{11.2}$$

for a fixed nonzero w-bit value a. Since the product ka of two w-bit words occupies $2w$ bits, taking this product modulo 2^w zeroes out the high-order w bits (r_1), leaving only the low-order w bits (r_0). The $\ggg$ operator performs a logical right shift by $w - \ell$ bits, shifting zeros into the vacated positions on the left, so that the ℓ most significant bits of r_0 move into the ℓ rightmost positions. (It's the same as dividing by $2^{w-\ell}$ and taking the floor of the result.) The resulting value equals the ℓ most significant bits of r_0. The hash function h_a can be implemented with three machine instructions: multiplication, subtraction, and logical right shift.

As an example, suppose that $k = 123456$, $\ell = 14$, $m = 2^{14} = 16384$, and $w = 32$. Suppose further that we choose $a = 2654435769$ (following a suggestion of Knuth [261]). Then $ka = 327706022297664 = (76300 \cdot 2^{32}) + 17612864$, and so $r_1 = 76300$ and $r_0 = 17612864$. The 14 most significant bits of r_0 yield the value $h_a(k) = 67$.

Even though the multiply-shift method is fast, it doesn't provide any guarantee of good average-case performance. The universal hashing approach presented in the next section provides such a guarantee. A simple randomized variant of the multiply-shift method works well on the average, when the program begins by picking a as a randomly chosen odd integer.

11.3.2   Random hashing

Suppose that a malicious adversary chooses the keys to be hashed by some fixed hash function. Then the adversary can choose n keys that all hash to the same slot, yielding an average retrieval time of $\Theta(n)$. Any static hash function is vulnerable to such terrible worst-case behavior. The only effective way to improve the situation is to choose the hash function *randomly* in a way that is *independent* of the keys that are actually going to be stored. This approach is called *random hashing*. A special case of this approach, called *universal hashing*, can yield provably good performance on average when collisions are handled by chaining, no matter which keys the adversary chooses.

To use random hashing, at the beginning of program execution you select the hash function at random from a suitable family of functions. As in the case of quicksort, randomization guarantees that no single input always evokes worst-case behavior. Because you randomly select the hash function, the algorithm can behave differently on each execution, even for the same set of keys to be hashed, guaranteeing good average-case performance.

Let $\mathcal{H}$ be a finite family of hash functions that map a given universe U of keys into the range $\{0, 1, \ldots, m-1\}$. Such a family is said to be *universal* if for each pair of distinct keys $k_1, k_2 \in U$, the number of hash functions $h \in \mathcal{H}$ for which $h(k_1) = h(k_2)$ is at most $|\mathcal{H}|/m$. In other words, with a hash function randomly chosen from $\mathcal{H}$, the chance of a collision between distinct keys k_1 and k_2 is no more than the chance $1/m$ of a collision if $h(k_1)$ and $h(k_2)$ were randomly and independently chosen from the set $\{0, 1, \ldots, m-1\}$.

Independent uniform hashing is the same as picking a hash function uniformly at random from a family of m^n hash functions, each member of that family mapping the n keys to the m hash values in a different way.

Every independent uniform random family of hash function is universal, but the converse need not be true: consider the case where $U = \{0, 1, \ldots, m-1\}$ and the only hash function in the family is the identity function. The probability that two distinct keys collide is zero, even though each key is hashes to a fixed value.

The following corollary to Theorem 11.2 on page 279 says that universal hashing provides the desired payoff: it becomes impossible for an adversary to pick a sequence of operations that forces the worst-case running time.

Corollary 11.3

Using universal hashing and collision resolution by chaining in an initially empty table with m slots, it takes $\Theta(s)$ expected time to handle any sequence of s INSERT, SEARCH, and DELETE operations containing $n = O(m)$ INSERT operations.

Proof The INSERT and DELETE operations take constant time. Since the number n of insertions is $O(m)$, we have that $\alpha = O(1)$. Furthermore, the expected time for each SEARCH operation is $O(1)$, which can be seen by examining the proof of Theorem 11.2. That analysis depends only on collision probabilities, which are $1/m$ for any pair k_1, k_2 of keys by the choice of an independent uniform hash function in that theorem. Using a universal family of hash functions here instead of using independent uniform hashing changes the probability of collision from $1/m$ to at most $1/m$. By linearity of expectation, therefore, the expected time for the entire sequence of s operations is $O(s)$. Since each operation takes $\Omega(1)$ time, the $\Theta(s)$ bound follows.   ∎

11.3.3 Achievable properties of random hashing

There is a rich literature on the properties a family $\mathcal{H}$ of hash functions can have, and how they relate to the efficiency of hashing. We summarize a few of the most interesting ones here.

Let $\mathcal{H}$ be a family of hash functions, each with domain U and range $\{0, 1, \dots, m-1\}$, and let h be any hash function that is picked uniformly at random from $\mathcal{H}$. The probabilities mentioned are probabilities over the picks of h.

- The family $\mathcal{H}$ is *uniform* if for any key k in U and any slot q in the range $\{0, 1, \dots, m-1\}$, the probability that $h(k) = q$ is $1/m$.

- The family $\mathcal{H}$ is *universal* if for any distinct keys k_1 and k_2 in U, the probability that $h(k_1) = h(k_2)$ is at most $1/m$.

- The family $\mathcal{H}$ of hash functions is ϵ-*universal* if for any distinct keys k_1 and k_2 in U, the probability that $h(k_1) = h(k_2)$ is at most ϵ. Therefore, a universal family of hash functions is also $1/m$-universal.[2]

---

[2] In the literature, a (c/m)-universal hash function is sometimes called c-universal or c-approximately universal. We'll stick with the notation (c/m)-universal.

- The family $\mathcal{H}$ is **d-independent** if for any distinct keys $k_1, k_2, \ldots, k_d$ in U and any slots $q_1, q_2, \ldots, q_d$, not necessarily distinct, in $\{0, 1, \ldots, m-1\}$ the probability that $h(k_i) = q_i$ for $i = 1, 2, \ldots, d$ is $1/m^d$.

Universal hash-function families are of particular interest, as they are the simplest type supporting provably efficient hash-table operations for any input data set. Many other interesting and desirable properties, such as those noted above, are also possible and allow for efficient specialized hash-table operations.

11.3.4 Designing a universal family of hash functions

This section presents two ways to design a universal (or ϵ-universal) family of hash functions: one based on number theory and another based on a randomized variant of the multiply-shift method presented in Section 11.3.1. The first method is a bit easier to prove universal, but the second method is newer and faster in practice.

A universal family of hash functions based on number theory

We can design a universal family of hash functions using a little number theory. You may wish to refer to Chapter 31 if you are unfamiliar with basic concepts in number theory.

Begin by choosing a prime number p large enough so that every possible key k lies in the range 0 to $p - 1$, inclusive. We assume here that p has a "reasonable" length. (See Section 11.3.5 for a discussion of methods for handling long input keys, such as variable-length strings.) Let $\mathbb{Z}_p$ denote the set $\{0, 1, \ldots, p-1\}$, and let $\mathbb{Z}_p^*$ denote the set $\{1, 2, \ldots, p-1\}$. Since p is prime, we can solve equations modulo p with the methods given in Chapter 31. Because the size of the universe of keys is greater than the number of slots in the hash table (otherwise, just use direct addressing), we have $p > m$.

Given any $a \in \mathbb{Z}_p^*$ and any $b \in \mathbb{Z}_p$, define the hash function h_{ab} as a linear transformation followed by reductions modulo p and then modulo m:

$$h_{ab}(k) = ((ak + b) \bmod p) \bmod m \,. \tag{11.3}$$

For example, with $p = 17$ and $m = 6$, we have

$$
\begin{aligned}
h_{3,4}(8) &= ((3 \cdot 8 + 4) \bmod 17) \bmod 6 \\
&= (28 \bmod 17) \bmod 6 \\
&= 11 \bmod 6 \\
&= 5 \,.
\end{aligned}
$$

Given p and m, the family of all such hash functions is

$$\mathcal{H}_{pm} = \{h_{ab} : a \in \mathbb{Z}_p^* \text{ and } b \in \mathbb{Z}_p\} \,. \tag{11.4}$$

Each hash function h_{ab} maps $\mathbb{Z}_p$ to $\mathbb{Z}_m$. This family of hash functions has the nice property that the size m of the output range (which is the size of the hash table) is arbitrary—it need not be prime. Since you can choose from among $p - 1$ values for a and p values for b, the family $\mathscr{H}_{pm}$ contains $p(p - 1)$ hash functions.

Theorem 11.4
The family $\mathscr{H}_{pm}$ of hash functions defined by equations (11.3) and (11.4) is universal.

Proof   Consider two distinct keys k_1 and k_2 from $\mathbb{Z}_p$, so that $k_1 \neq k_2$. For a given hash function h_{ab}, let

$$r_1 = (ak_1 + b) \bmod p \,,$$
$$r_2 = (ak_2 + b) \bmod p \,.$$

We first note that $r_1 \neq r_2$. Why? Since we have $r_1 - r_2 = a(k_1 - k_2) \pmod{p}$, it follows that $r_1 \neq r_2$ because p is prime and both a and $(k_1 - k_2)$ are nonzero modulo p. By Theorem 31.6 on page 908, their product must also be nonzero modulo p. Therefore, when computing any $h_{ab} \in \mathscr{H}_{pm}$, distinct inputs k_1 and k_2 map to distinct values r_1 and r_2 modulo p, and there are no collisions yet at the "mod p level." Moreover, each of the possible $p(p - 1)$ choices for the pair (a, b) with $a \neq 0$ yields a *different* resulting pair (r_1, r_2) with $r_1 \neq r_2$, since we can solve for a and b given r_1 and r_2:

$$a = \big((r_1 - r_2)((k_1 - k_2)^{-1} \bmod p)\big) \bmod p \,,$$
$$b = (r_1 - ak_1) \bmod p \,,$$

where $((k_1 - k_2)^{-1} \bmod p)$ denotes the unique multiplicative inverse, modulo p, of $k_1 - k_2$. For each of the p possible values of r_1, there are only $p - 1$ possible values of r_2 that do not equal r_1, making only $p(p - 1)$ possible pairs (r_1, r_2) with $r_1 \neq r_2$. Therefore, there is a one-to-one correspondence between pairs (a, b) with $a \neq 0$ and pairs (r_1, r_2) with $r_1 \neq r_2$. Thus, for any given pair of distinct inputs k_1 and k_2, if we pick (a, b) uniformly at random from $\mathbb{Z}_p^* \times \mathbb{Z}_p$, the resulting pair (r_1, r_2) is equally likely to be any pair of distinct values modulo p.

Therefore, the probability that distinct keys k_1 and k_2 collide is equal to the probability that $r_1 = r_2 \pmod{m}$ when r_1 and r_2 are randomly chosen as distinct values modulo p. For a given value of r_1, of the $p - 1$ possible remaining values for r_2, the number of values r_2 such that $r_2 \neq r_1$ and $r_2 = r_1 \pmod{m}$ is at most

$$\left\lceil \frac{p}{m} \right\rceil - 1 \leq \frac{p + m - 1}{m} - 1 \quad \text{(by inequality (3.7) on page 64)}$$
$$= \frac{p - 1}{m} \,.$$

The probability that r_2 collides with r_1 when reduced modulo m is at most $((p-1)/m)/(p-1) = 1/m$, since r_2 is equally likely to be any of the $p-1$ values in Z_p that are different from r_1, but at most $(p-1)/m$ of those values are equivalent to r_1 modulo m.

Therefore, for any pair of distinct values $k_1, k_2 \in \mathbb{Z}_p$,

$$\Pr\{h_{ab}(k_1) = h_{ab}(k_2)\} \leq 1/m ,$$

so that $\mathcal{H}_{pm}$ is indeed universal.   ∎

A 2/m-universal family of hash functions based on the multiply-shift method

We recommend that in practice you use the following hash-function family based on the multiply-shift method. It is exceptionally efficient and (although we omit the proof) provably $2/m$-universal. Define $\mathcal{H}$ to be the family of multiply-shift hash functions with odd constants a:

$$\mathcal{H} = \{h_a : a \text{ is odd}, 1 \leq a < m, \text{ and } h_a \text{ is defined by equation (11.2)}\} . \quad (11.5)$$

Theorem 11.5
The family of hash functions $\mathcal{H}$ given by equation (11.5) is $2/m$-universal.   ∎

That is, the probability that any two distinct keys collide is at most $2/m$. In many practical situations, the speed of computing the hash function more than compensates for the higher upper bound on the probability that two distinct keys collide when compared with a universal hash function.

11.3.5   Hashing long inputs such as vectors or strings

Sometimes hash function inputs are so long that they cannot be easily encoded modulo a reasonably sized prime number p or encoded within a single word of, say, 64 bits. As an example, consider the class of vectors, such as vectors of 8-bit bytes (which is how strings in many programming languages are stored). A vector might have an arbitrary nonnegative length, in which case the length of the input to the hash function may vary from input to input.

Number-theoretic approaches

One way to design good hash functions for variable-length inputs is to extend the ideas used in Section 11.3.4 to design universal hash functions. Exercise 11.3-6 explores one such approach.

Cryptographic hashing

Another way to design a good hash function for variable-length inputs is to use a hash function designed for cryptographic applications. *Cryptographic hash functions* are complex pseudorandom functions, designed for applications requiring properties beyond those needed here, but are robust, widely implemented, and usable as hash functions for hash tables.

A cryptographic hash function takes as input an arbitrary byte string and returns a fixed-length output. For example, the NIST standard deterministic cryptographic hash function SHA-256 [346] produces a 256-bit (32-byte) output for any input.

Some chip manufacturers include instructions in their CPU architectures to provide fast implementations of some cryptographic functions. Of particular interest are instructions that efficiently implement rounds of the Advanced Encryption Standard (AES), the "AES-NI" instructions. These instructions execute in a few tens of nanoseconds, which is generally fast enough for use with hash tables. A message authentication code such as CBC-MAC based on AES and the use of the AES-NI instructions could be a useful and efficient hash function. We don't pursue the potential use of specialized instruction sets further here.

Cryptographic hash functions are useful because they provide a way of implementing an approximate version of a random oracle. As noted earlier, a random oracle is equivalent to an independent uniform hash function family. From a theoretical point of view, a random oracle is an unachievable ideal: a deterministic function that provides a randomly selected output for each input. Because it is deterministic, it provides the same output if queried again for the same input. From a practical point of view, constructions of hash function families based on cryptographic hash functions are sensible substitutes for random oracles.

There are many ways to use a cryptographic hash function as a hash function. For example, we could define

$$h(k) = \text{SHA-256}(k) \bmod m \ .$$

To define a family of such hash functions one may prepend a "salt" string a to the input before hashing it, as in

$$h_a(k) = \text{SHA-256}(a \parallel k) \bmod m \ ,$$

where $a \parallel k$ denotes the string formed by concatenating the strings a and k. The literature on message authentication codes (MACs) provides additional approaches.

Cryptographic approaches to hash-function design are becoming more practical as computers arrange their memories in hierarchies of differing capacities and speeds. Section 11.5 discusses one hash-function design based on the RC6 encryption method.

Exercises

11.3-1
You wish to search a linked list of length n, where each element contains a key k along with a hash value $h(k)$. Each key is a long character string. How might you take advantage of the hash values when searching the list for an element with a given key?

11.3-2
You hash a string of r characters into m slots by treating it as a radix-128 number and then using the division method. You can represent the number m as a 32-bit computer word, but the string of r characters, treated as a radix-128 number, takes many words. How can you apply the division method to compute the hash value of the character string without using more than a constant number of words of storage outside the string itself?

11.3-3
Consider a version of the division method in which $h(k) = k \bmod m$, where $m = 2^p - 1$ and k is a character string interpreted in radix 2^p. Show that if string x can be converted to string y by permuting its characters, then x and y hash to the same value. Give an example of an application in which this property would be undesirable in a hash function.

11.3-4
Consider a hash table of size $m = 1000$ and a corresponding hash function $h(k) = \lfloor m (kA \bmod 1) \rfloor$ for $A = (\sqrt{5} - 1)/2$. Compute the locations to which the keys $61, 62, 63, 64$, and 65 are mapped.

★ *11.3-5*
Show that any ϵ-universal family $\mathcal{H}$ of hash functions from a finite set U to a finite set Q has $\epsilon \geq 1/|Q| - 1/|U|$.

★ *11.3-6*
Let U be the set of d-tuples of values drawn from $\mathbb{Z}_p$, and let $Q = \mathbb{Z}_p$, where p is prime. Define the hash function $h_b : U \to Q$ for $b \in \mathbb{Z}_p$ on an input d-tuple $\langle a_0, a_1, \ldots, a_{d-1} \rangle$ from U as

$$h_b(\langle a_0, a_1, \ldots, a_{d-1} \rangle) = \left(\sum_{j=0}^{d-1} a_j b^j \right) \bmod p \, ,$$

and let $\mathcal{H} = \{h_b : b \in \mathbb{Z}_p\}$. Argue that $\mathcal{H}$ is ϵ-universal for $\epsilon = (d-1)/p$. (*Hint:* See Exercise 31.4-4.)

11.4   Open addressing

This section describes open addressing, a method for collision resolution that, unlike chaining, does not make use of storage outside of the hash table itself. In *open addressing*, all elements occupy the hash table itself. That is, each table entry contains either an element of the dynamic set or NIL. No lists or elements are stored outside the table, unlike in chaining. Thus, in open addressing, the hash table can "fill up" so that no further insertions can be made. One consequence is that the load factor α can never exceed 1.

Collisions are handled as follows: when a new element is to be inserted into the table, it is placed in its "first-choice" location if possible. If that location is already occupied, the new element is placed in its "second-choice" location. The process continues until an empty slot is found in which to place the new element. Different elements have different preference orders for the locations.

To search for an element, systematically examine the preferred table slots for that element, in order of decreasing preference, until either you find the desired element or you find an empty slot and thus verify that the element is not in the table.

Of course, you could use chaining and store the linked lists inside the hash table, in the otherwise unused hash-table slots (see Exercise 11.2-4), but the advantage of open addressing is that it avoids pointers altogether. Instead of following pointers, you compute the sequence of slots to be examined. The memory freed by not storing pointers provides the hash table with a larger number of slots in the same amount of memory, potentially yielding fewer collisions and faster retrieval.

To perform insertion using open addressing, successively examine, or *probe*, the hash table until you find an empty slot in which to put the key. Instead of being fixed in the order $0, 1, \ldots, m - 1$ (which implies a $\Theta(n)$ search time), the sequence of positions probed depends upon the key being inserted. To determine which slots to probe, the hash function includes the probe number (starting from 0) as a second input. Thus, the hash function becomes

$$h : U \times \{0, 1, \ldots, m - 1\} \rightarrow \{0, 1, \ldots, m - 1\} \ .$$

Open addressing requires that for every key k, the *probe sequence* $\langle h(k, 0), h(k, 1), \ldots, h(k, m - 1) \rangle$ be a permutation of $\langle 0, 1, \ldots, m - 1 \rangle$, so that every hash-table position is eventually considered as a slot for a new key as the table fills up. The HASH-INSERT procedure on the following page assumes that the elements in the hash table T are keys with no satellite information: the key k is identical to the element containing key k. Each slot contains either a key or NIL (if the slot is empty). The HASH-INSERT procedure takes as input a hash table T and a key k

that is assumed to be not already present in the hash table. It either returns the slot number where it stores key k or flags an error because the hash table is already full.

HASH-INSERT(T, k)

```
1  i = 0
2  repeat
3      q = h(k, i)
4      if T[q] == NIL
5          T[q] = k
6          return q
7      else i = i + 1
8  until i == m
9  error "hash table overflow"
```

HASH-SEARCH(T, k)

```
1  i = 0
2  repeat
3      q = h(k, i)
4      if T[q] == k
5          return q
6      i = i + 1
7  until T[q] == NIL or i == m
8  return NIL
```

The algorithm for searching for key k probes the same sequence of slots that the insertion algorithm examined when key k was inserted. Therefore, the search can terminate (unsuccessfully) when it finds an empty slot, since k would have been inserted there and not later in its probe sequence. The procedure HASH-SEARCH takes as input a hash table T and a key k, returning q if it finds that slot q contains key k, or NIL if key k is not present in table T.

Deletion from an open-address hash table is tricky. When you delete a key from slot q, it would be a mistake to mark that slot as empty by simply storing NIL in it. If you did, you might be unable to retrieve any key k for which slot q was probed and found occupied when k was inserted. One way to solve this problem is by marking the slot, storing in it the special value DELETED instead of NIL. The HASH-INSERT procedure then has to treat such a slot as empty so that it can insert a new key there. The HASH-SEARCH procedure passes over DELETED values while searching, since slots containing DELETED were filled when the key being searched for was inserted. Using the special value DELETED, however, means that search times no longer depend on the load factor α, and for this reason chaining is frequently selected as a collision resolution technique when keys must be deleted. There is a simple special case of open addressing, linear probing, that avoids the need to mark slots with DELETED. Section 11.5.1 shows how to delete from a hash table when using linear probing.

In our analysis, we assume *independent uniform permutation hashing* (also confusingly known as *uniform hashing* in the literature): the probe sequence of each key is equally likely to be any of the $m!$ permutations of $\langle 0, 1, \ldots, m - 1 \rangle$. Independent uniform permutation hashing generalizes the notion of independent uniform hashing defined earlier to a hash function that produces not just a single slot number, but a whole probe sequence. True independent uniform permutation hashing is difficult to implement, however, and in practice suitable approximations (such as double hashing, defined below) are used.

We'll examine both double hashing and its special case, linear probing. These techniques guarantee that $\langle h(k, 0), h(k, 1), \ldots, h(k, m - 1) \rangle$ is a permutation of $\langle 0, 1, \ldots, m - 1 \rangle$ for each key k. (Recall that the second parameter to the hash function h is the probe number.) Neither double hashing nor linear probing meets the assumption of independent uniform permutation hashing, however. Double hashing cannot generate more than m^2 different probe sequences (instead of the $m!$ that independent uniform permutation hashing requires). Nonetheless, double hashing has a large number of possible probe sequences and, as you might expect, seems to give good results. Linear probing is even more restricted, capable of generating only m different probe sequences.

Double hashing

Double hashing offers one of the best methods available for open addressing because the permutations produced have many of the characteristics of randomly chosen permutations. *Double hashing* uses a hash function of the form

$$h(k, i) = (h_1(k) + i h_2(k)) \bmod m ,$$

where both h_1 and h_2 are *auxiliary hash functions*. The initial probe goes to position $T[h_1(k)]$, and successive probe positions are offset from previous positions by the amount $h_2(k)$, modulo m. Thus, the probe sequence here depends in two ways upon the key k, since the initial probe position $h_1(k)$, the step size $h_2(k)$, or both, may vary. Figure 11.5 gives an example of insertion by double hashing.

In order for the entire hash table to be searched, the value $h_2(k)$ must be relatively prime to the hash-table size m. (See Exercise 11.4-5.) A convenient way to ensure this condition is to let m be an exact power of 2 and to design h_2 so that it always produces an odd number. Another way is to let m be prime and to design h_2 so that it always returns a positive integer less than m. For example, you

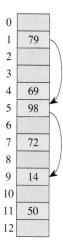

Figure 11.5 Insertion by double hashing. The hash table has size 13 with $h_1(k) = k$ mod 13 and $h_2(k) = 1 + (k \bmod 11)$. Since $14 = 1 \pmod{13}$ and $14 = 3 \pmod{11}$, the key 14 goes into empty slot 9, after slots 1 and 5 are examined and found to be occupied.

could choose m prime and let

$$h_1(k) = k \bmod m ,$$
$$h_2(k) = 1 + (k \bmod m') ,$$

where m' is chosen to be slightly less than m (say, $m - 1$). For example, if $k = 123456$, $m = 701$, and $m' = 700$, then $h_1(k) = 80$ and $h_2(k) = 257$, so that the first probe goes to position 80, and successive probes examine every 257th slot (modulo m) until the key has been found or every slot has been examined.

Although values of m other than primes or exact powers of 2 can in principle be used with double hashing, in practice it becomes more difficult to efficiently generate $h_2(k)$ (other than choosing $h_2(k) = 1$, which gives linear probing) in a way that ensures that it is relatively prime to m, in part because the relative density $\phi(m)/m$ of such numbers for general m may be small (see equation (31.25) on page 921).

When m is prime or an exact power of 2, double hashing produces $\Theta(m^2)$ probe sequences, since each possible $(h_1(k), h_2(k))$ pair yields a distinct probe sequence. As a result, for such values of m, double hashing appears to perform close to the "ideal" scheme of independent uniform permutation hashing.

Linear probing

Linear probing, a special case of double hashing, is the simplest open-addressing approach to resolving collisions. As with double hashing, an auxiliary hash function h_1 determines the first probe position $h_1(k)$ for inserting an element. If slot $T[h_1(k)]$ is already occupied, probe the next position $T[h_1(k)+1]$. Keep going as necessary, on up to slot $T[m-1]$, and then wrap around to slots $T[0]$, $T[1]$, and so on, but never going past slot $T[h_1(k)-1]$. To view linear probing as a special case of double hashing, just set the double-hashing step function h_2 to be fixed at 1: $h_2(k) = 1$ for all k. That is, the hash function is

$$h(k,i) = (h_1(k) + i) \bmod m \tag{11.6}$$

for $i = 0, 1, \ldots, m-1$. The value of $h_1(k)$ determines the entire probe sequence, and so assuming that $h_1(k)$ can take on any value in $\{0, 1, \ldots, m-1\}$, linear probing allows only m distinct probe sequences.

We'll revisit linear probing in Section 11.5.1.

Analysis of open-address hashing

As in our analysis of chaining in Section 11.2, we analyze open addressing in terms of the load factor $\alpha = n/m$ of the hash table. With open addressing, at most one element occupies each slot, and thus $n \leq m$, which implies $\alpha \leq 1$. The analysis below requires α to be strictly less than 1, and so we assume that at least one slot is empty. Because deleting from an open-address hash table does not really free up a slot, we assume as well that no deletions occur.

For the hash function, we assume independent uniform permutation hashing. In this idealized scheme, the probe sequence $\langle h(k,0), h(k,1), \ldots, h(k,m-1) \rangle$ used to insert or search for each key k is equally likely to be any permutation of $\langle 0, 1, \ldots, m-1 \rangle$. Of course, any given key has a unique fixed probe sequence associated with it. What we mean here is that, considering the probability distribution on the space of keys and the operation of the hash function on the keys, each possible probe sequence is equally likely.

We now analyze the expected number of probes for hashing with open addressing under the assumption of independent uniform permutation hashing, beginning with the expected number of probes made in an unsuccessful search (assuming, as stated above, that $\alpha < 1$).

The bound proven, of $1/(1 - \alpha) = 1 + \alpha + \alpha^2 + \alpha^3 + \cdots$, has an intuitive interpretation. The first probe always occurs. With probability approximately α, the first probe finds an occupied slot, so that a second probe happens. With probability approximately α^2, the first two slots are occupied so that a third probe ensues, and so on.

Theorem 11.6

Given an open-address hash table with load factor $\alpha = n/m < 1$, the expected number of probes in an unsuccessful search is at most $1/(1 - \alpha)$, assuming independent uniform permutation hashing and no deletions.

Proof   In an unsuccessful search, every probe but the last accesses an occupied slot that does not contain the desired key, and the last slot probed is empty. Let the random variable X denote the number of probes made in an unsuccessful search, and define the event A_i, for $i = 1, 2, \ldots$, as the event that an ith probe occurs and it is to an occupied slot. Then the event $\{X \geq i\}$ is the intersection of events $A_1 \cap A_2 \cap \cdots \cap A_{i-1}$. We bound $\Pr\{X \geq i\}$ by bounding $\Pr\{A_1 \cap A_2 \cap \cdots \cap A_{i-1}\}$. By Exercise C.2-5 on page 1190,

$$\Pr\{A_1 \cap A_2 \cap \cdots \cap A_{i-1}\} = \Pr\{A_1\} \cdot \Pr\{A_2 \mid A_1\} \cdot \Pr\{A_3 \mid A_1 \cap A_2\} \cdots$$
$$\Pr\{A_{i-1} \mid A_1 \cap A_2 \cap \cdots \cap A_{i-2}\} \ .$$

Since there are n elements and m slots, $\Pr\{A_1\} = n/m$. For $j > 1$, the probability that there is a jth probe and it is to an occupied slot, given that the first $j - 1$ probes were to occupied slots, is $(n - j + 1)/(m - j + 1)$. This probability follows because the jth probe would be finding one of the remaining $(n - (j - 1))$ elements in one of the $(m - (j - 1))$ unexamined slots, and by the assumption of independent uniform permutation hashing, the probability is the ratio of these quantities. Since $n < m$ implies that $(n - j)/(m - j) \leq n/m$ for all j in the range $0 \leq j < m$, it follows that for all i in the range $1 \leq i \leq m$, we have

$$\begin{aligned}
\Pr\{X \geq i\} &= \frac{n}{m} \cdot \frac{n-1}{m-1} \cdot \frac{n-2}{m-2} \cdots \frac{n-i+2}{m-i+2} \\
&\leq \left(\frac{n}{m}\right)^{i-1} \\
&= \alpha^{i-1} \ .
\end{aligned}$$

The product in the first line has $i - 1$ factors. When $i = 1$, the product is 1, the identity for multiplication, and we get $\Pr\{X \geq 1\} = 1$, which makes sense, since there must always be at least 1 probe. If each of the first n probes is to an occupied slot, then all occupied slots have been probed. Then, the $(n + 1)$st probe must be to an empty slot, which gives $\Pr\{X \geq i\} = 0$ for $i > n + 1$. Now, we use equation (C.28) on page 1193 to bound the expected number of probes:

$$\begin{aligned}
\mathrm{E}[X] &= \sum_{i=1}^{\infty} \Pr\{X \geq i\} \\
&= \sum_{i=1}^{n+1} \Pr\{X \geq i\} + \sum_{i > n+1} \Pr\{X \geq i\}
\end{aligned}$$

$$\leq \sum_{i=1}^{\infty} \alpha^{i-1} + 0$$

$$= \sum_{i=0}^{\infty} \alpha^{i}$$

$$= \frac{1}{1-\alpha} \qquad \text{(by equation (A.7) on page 1142 because } 0 \leq \alpha < 1\text{)} . \qquad \blacksquare$$

If α is a constant, Theorem 11.6 predicts that an unsuccessful search runs in $O(1)$ time. For example, if the hash table is half full, the average number of probes in an unsuccessful search is at most $1/(1-.5) = 2$. If it is 90% full, the average number of probes is at most $1/(1-.9) = 10$.

Theorem 11.6 yields almost immediately how well the HASH-INSERT procedure performs.

Corollary 11.7
Inserting an element into an open-address hash table with load factor α, where $\alpha < 1$, requires at most $1/(1-\alpha)$ probes on average, assuming independent uniform permutation hashing and no deletions.

Proof An element is inserted only if there is room in the table, and thus $\alpha < 1$. Inserting a key requires an unsuccessful search followed by placing the key into the first empty slot found. Thus, the expected number of probes is at most $1/(1-\alpha)$. $\blacksquare$

It takes a little more work to compute the expected number of probes for a successful search.

Theorem 11.8
Given an open-address hash table with load factor $\alpha < 1$, the expected number of probes in a successful search is at most

$$\frac{1}{\alpha} \ln \frac{1}{1-\alpha} ,$$

assuming independent uniform permutation hashing with no deletions and assuming that each key in the table is equally likely to be searched for.

Proof A search for a key k reproduces the same probe sequence as when the element with key k was inserted. If k was the $(i + 1)$st key inserted into the hash table, then the load factor at the time it was inserted was i/m, and so by Corollary 11.7, the expected number of probes made in a search for k is at most $1/(1 - i/m) = m/(m - i)$. Averaging over all n keys in the hash table gives us the expected number of probes in a successful search:

$$\frac{1}{n} \sum_{i=0}^{n-1} \frac{m}{m-i} = \frac{m}{n} \sum_{i=0}^{n-1} \frac{1}{m-i}$$

$$= \frac{1}{\alpha} \sum_{k=m-n+1}^{m} \frac{1}{k}$$

$$\leq \frac{1}{\alpha} \int_{m-n}^{m} \frac{1}{x} \, dx \qquad \text{(by inequality (A.19) on page 1150)}$$

$$= \frac{1}{\alpha} (\ln m - \ln(m-n))$$

$$= \frac{1}{\alpha} \ln \frac{m}{m-n}$$

$$= \frac{1}{\alpha} \ln \frac{1}{1-\alpha} \,. \qquad \blacksquare$$

If the hash table is half full, the expected number of probes in a successful search is less than 1.387. If the hash table is 90% full, the expected number of probes is less than 2.559. If $\alpha = 1$, then in an unsuccessful search, all m slots must be probed. Exercise 11.4-4 asks you to analyze a successful search when $\alpha = 1$.

Exercises

11.4-1
Consider inserting the keys $10, 22, 31, 4, 15, 28, 17, 88, 59$ into a hash table of length $m = 11$ using open addressing. Illustrate the result of inserting these keys using linear probing with $h(k, i) = (k + i) \bmod m$ and using double hashing with $h_1(k) = k$ and $h_2(k) = 1 + (k \bmod (m - 1))$.

11.4-2
Write pseudocode for HASH-DELETE that fills the deleted key's slot with the special value DELETED, and modify HASH-SEARCH and HASH-INSERT as needed to handle DELETED.

11.4-3
Consider an open-address hash table with independent uniform permutation hashing and no deletions. Give upper bounds on the expected number of probes in an unsuccessful search and on the expected number of probes in a successful search when the load factor is $3/4$ and when it is $7/8$.

11.4-4

Show that the expected number of probes required for a successful search when $\alpha = 1$ (that is, when $n = m$), is H_m, the mth harmonic number.

★ **11.4-5**

Show that, with double hashing, if m and $h_2(k)$ have greatest common divisor $d \geq 1$ for some key k, then an unsuccessful search for key k examines $(1/d)$th of the hash table before returning to slot $h_1(k)$. Thus, when $d = 1$, so that m and $h_2(k)$ are relatively prime, the search may examine the entire hash table. (*Hint:* See Chapter 31.)

★ **11.4-6**

Consider an open-address hash table with a load factor α. Approximate the nonzero value α for which the expected number of probes in an unsuccessful search equals twice the expected number of probes in a successful search. Use the upper bounds given by Theorems 11.6 and 11.8 for these expected numbers of probes.

11.5 Practical considerations

Efficient hash table algorithms are not only of theoretical interest, but also of immense practical importance. Constant factors can matter. For this reason, this section discusses two aspects of modern CPUs that are not included in the standard RAM model presented in Section 2.2:

Memory hierarchies: The memory of modern CPUs has a number of levels, from the fast registers, through one or more levels of *cache memory*, to the main-memory level. Each successive level stores more data than the previous level, but access is slower. As a consequence, a complex computation (such as a complicated hash function) that works entirely within the fast registers can take less time than a single read operation from main memory. Furthermore, cache memory is organized in *cache blocks* of (say) 64 bytes each, which are always fetched together from main memory. There is a substantial benefit for ensuring that memory usage is local: reusing the same cache block is much more efficient than fetching a different cache block from main memory.

The standard RAM model measures efficiency of a hash-table operation by counting the number of hash-table slots probed. In practice, this metric is only a crude approximation to the truth, since once a cache block is in the cache, successive probes to that cache block are much faster than probes that must access main memory.

Advanced instruction sets: Modern CPUs may have sophisticated instruction sets that implement advanced primitives useful for encryption or other forms of cryptography. These instructions may be useful in the design of exceptionally efficient hash functions.

Section 11.5.1 discusses linear probing, which becomes the collision-resolution method of choice in the presence of a memory hierarchy. Section 11.5.2 suggests how to construct "advanced" hash functions based on cryptographic primitives, suitable for use on computers with hierarchical memory models.

11.5.1   Linear probing

Linear probing is often disparaged because of its poor performance in the standard RAM model. But linear probing excels for hierarchical memory models, because successive probes are usually to the same cache block of memory.

Deletion with linear probing

Another reason why linear probing is often not used in practice is that deletion seems complicated or impossible without using the special DELETED value. Yet we'll now see that deletion from a hash table based on linear probing is not all that difficult, even without the DELETED marker. The deletion procedure works for linear probing, but not for open-address probing in general, because with linear probing keys all follow the same simple cyclic probing sequence (albeit with different starting points).

The deletion procedure relies on an "inverse" function to the linear-probing hash function $h(k, i) = (h_1(k) + i) \bmod m$, which maps a key k and a probe number i to a slot number in the hash table. The inverse function g maps a key k and a slot number q, where $0 \le q < m$, to the probe number that reaches slot q:

$$g(k, q) = (q - h_1(k)) \bmod m \ .$$

If $h(k, i) = q$, then $g(k, q) = i$, and so $h(k, g(k, q)) = q$.

The procedure LINEAR-PROBING-HASH-DELETE on the facing page deletes the key stored in position q from hash table T. Figure 11.6 shows how it works. The procedure first deletes the key in position q by setting $T[q]$ to NIL in line 2. It then searches for a slot q' (if any) that contains a key that should be moved to the slot q just vacated by key k. Line 9 asks the critical question: does the key k' in slot q' need to be moved to the vacated slot q in order to preserve the accessibility of k'? If $g(k', q) < g(k', q')$, then during the insertion of k' into the table, slot q was examined but found to be already occupied. But now slot q, where a search will look for k', is empty. In this case, key k' moves to slot q in line 10, and the

	(a)			(b)	
0			0		
1			1		
2	82		2	82	
3	43		3	93	
4	74		4	74	
5	93		5	92	
6	92		6		
7			7		
8	18		8	18	
9	38		9	38	

Figure 11.6 Deletion in a hash table that uses linear probing. The hash table has size 10 with $h_1(k) = k \bmod 10$. **(a)** The hash table after inserting keys in the order 74, 43, 93, 18, 82, 38, 92. **(b)** The hash table after deleting the key 43 from slot 3. Key 93 moves up to slot 3 to keep it accessible, and then key 92 moves up to slot 5 just vacated by key 93. No other keys need to be moved.

search continues, to see whether any later key also needs to be moved to the slot q' that was just freed up when k' moved.

LINEAR-PROBING-HASH-DELETE(T, q)

```
1   while TRUE
2       T[q] = NIL                    // make slot q empty
3       q' = q                        // starting point for search
4       repeat
5           q' = (q' + 1) mod m       // next slot number with linear probing
6           k' = T[q']                // next key to try to move
7           if k' == NIL
8               return                // return when an empty slot is found
9       until g(k', q) < g(k', q')    // was empty slot q probed before q'?
10      T[q] = k'                     // move k' into slot q
11      q = q'                        // free up slot q'
```

Analysis of linear probing

Linear probing is popular to implement, but it exhibits a phenomenon known as *primary clustering*. Long runs of occupied slots build up, increasing the average search time. Clusters arise because an empty slot preceded by i full slots gets filled next with probability $(i + 1)/m$. Long runs of occupied slots tend to get longer, and the average search time increases.

In the standard RAM model, primary clustering is a problem, and general double hashing usually performs better than linear probing. By contrast, in a hierarchical memory model, primary clustering is a beneficial property, as elements are often stored together in the same cache block. Searching proceeds through one cache block before advancing to search the next cache block. With linear probing, the running time for a key k of HASH-INSERT, HASH-SEARCH, or LINEAR-PROBING-HASH-DELETE is at most proportional to the distance from $h_1(k)$ to the next empty slot.

The following theorem is due to Pagh et al. [351]. A more recent proof is given by Thorup [438]. We omit the proof here. The need for 5-independence is by no means obvious; see the cited proofs.

Theorem 11.9
If h_1 is 5-independent and $\alpha \leq 2/3$, then it takes expected constant time to search for, insert, or delete a key in a hash table using linear probing. ∎

(Indeed, the expected operation time is $O(1/\epsilon^2)$ for $\alpha = 1 - \epsilon$.)

★   ### 11.5.2   Hash functions for hierarchical memory models

This section illustrates an approach for designing efficient hash tables in a modern computer system having a memory hierarchy.

Because of the memory hierarchy, linear probing is a good choice for resolving collisions, as probe sequences are sequential and tend to stay within cache blocks. But linear probing is most efficient when the hash function is complex (for example, 5-independent as in Theorem 11.9). Fortunately, having a memory hierarchy means that complex hash functions can be implemented efficiently.

As noted in Section 11.3.5, one approach is to use a cryptographic hash function such as SHA-256. Such functions are complex and sufficiently random for hash table applications. On machines with specialized instructions, cryptographic functions can be quite efficient.

Instead, we present here a simple hash function based only on addition, multiplication, and swapping the halves of a word. This function can be implemented entirely within the fast registers, and on a machine with a memory hierarchy, its latency is small compared with the time taken to access a random slot of the hash table. It is related to the RC6 encryption algorithm and can for practical purposes be considered a "random oracle."

The wee hash function

Let w denote the word size of the machine (e.g., $w = 64$), assumed to be even, and let a and b be w-bit unsigned (nonnegative) integers such that a is odd. Let $\text{swap}(x)$ denote the w-bit result of swapping the two $w/2$-bit halves of w-bit input x. That is,

$$\text{swap}(x) = (x \ggg (w/2)) + (x \lll (w/2))$$

where "$\ggg$" is "logical right shift" (as in equation (11.2)) and "$\lll$ is "left shift." Define

$$f_a(k) = \text{swap}((2k^2 + ak) \bmod 2^w) .$$

Thus, to compute $f_a(k)$, evaluate the quadratic function $2k^2 + ak$ modulo 2^w and then swap the left and right halves of the result.

Let r denote a desired number of "rounds" for the computation of the hash function. We'll use $r = 4$, but the hash function is well defined for any nonnegative r. Denote by $f_a^{(r)}(k)$ the result of iterating f_a a total of r times (that is, r rounds) starting with input value k. For any odd a and any $r \geq 0$, the function $f_a^{(r)}$, although complicated, is one-to-one (see Exercise 11.5-1). A cryptographer would view $f_a^{(r)}$ as a simple block cipher operating on w-bit input blocks, with r rounds and key a.

We first define the wee hash function h for short inputs, where by "short" we means "whose length t is at most w-bits," so that the input fits within one computer word. We would like inputs of different lengths to be hashed differently. The *wee hash function* $h_{a,b,t,r}(k)$ for parameters a, b, and r on t-bit input k is defined as

$$h_{a,b,t,r}(k) = \left(f_{a+2t}^{(r)}(k + b) \right) \bmod m . \tag{11.7}$$

That is, the hash value for t-bit input k is obtained by applying $f_{a+2t}^{(r)}$ to $k + b$, then taking the final result modulo m. Adding the value b provides hash-dependent randomization of the input, in a way that ensures that for variable-length inputs the 0-length input does not have a fixed hash value. Adding the value $2t$ to a ensures that the hash function acts differently for inputs of different lengths. (We use $2t$ rather than t to ensure that the key $a + 2t$ is odd if a is odd.) We call this hash function "wee" because it uses a tiny amount of memory—more precisely, it can be implemented efficiently using only the computer's fast registers. (This hash function does not have a name in the literature; it is a variant we developed for this textbook.)

Speed of the wee hash function

It is surprising how much efficiency can be bought with locality. Experiments (unpublished, by the authors) suggest that evaluating the wee hash function takes less time than probing a *single* randomly chosen slot in a hash table. These experiments were run on a laptop (2019 MacBook Pro) with $w = 64$ and $a = 123$. For large hash tables, evaluating the wee hash function was 2 to 10 times faster than performing a single probe of the hash table.

The wee hash function for variable-length inputs

Sometimes inputs are long—more than one w-bit word in length—or have variable length, as discussed in Section 11.3.5. We can extend the wee hash function, defined above for inputs that are at most single w-bit word in length, to handle long or variable-length inputs. Here is one method for doing so.

Suppose that an input k has length t (measured in bits). Break k into a sequence $\langle k_1, k_2, \ldots, k_u \rangle$ of w-bit words, where $u = \lceil t/w \rceil$, k_1 contains the least-significant w bits of k, and k_u contains the most significant bits. If t is not a multiple of w, then k_u contains fewer than w bits, in which case, pad out the unused high-order bits of k_u with 0-bits. Define the function chop to return a sequence of the w-bit words in k:

$$\text{chop}(k) = \langle k_1, k_2, \ldots, k_u \rangle .$$

The most important property of the chop operation is that it is one-to-one, given t: for any two t-bit keys k and k', if $k \neq k'$ then $\text{chop}(k) \neq \text{chop}(k')$, and k can be derived from $\text{chop}(k)$ and t. The chop operation also has the useful property that a single-word input key yields a single-word output sequence: $\text{chop}(k) = \langle k \rangle$.

With the chop function in hand, we specify the wee hash function $h_{a,b,t,r}(k)$ for an input k of length t bits as follows:

$$h_{a,b,t,r}(k) = \text{WEE}(k, a, b, t, r, m) ,$$

where the procedure WEE defined on the facing page iterates through the elements of the w-bit words returned by $\text{chop}(k)$, applying f_a^r to the sum of the current word k_i and the previously computed hash value so far, finally returning the result obtained modulo m. This definition for variable-length and long (multiple-word) inputs is a consistent extension of the definition in equation (11.7) for short (single-word) inputs. For practical use, we recommend that a be a randomly chosen odd w-bit word, b be a randomly chosen w-bit word, and that $r = 4$.

Note that the wee hash function is really a hash function family, with individual hash functions determined by parameters $a, b, t, r,$ and m. The (approximate) 5-independence of the wee hash function family for variable-length inputs can be argued based on the assumption that the 1-word wee hash function is a random oracle and on the security of the cipher-block-chaining message authentication code (CBC-MAC), as studied by Bellare et al. [42]. The case here is actually simpler than that studied in the literature, since if two messages have different lengths t and t', then their "keys" are different: $a + 2t \neq a + 2t'$. We omit the details.

$\text{WEE}(k, a, b, t, r, m)$

1 $u = \lceil t/w \rceil$
2 $\langle k_1, k_2, \ldots, k_u \rangle = \text{chop}(k)$
3 $q = b$
4 **for** $i = 1$ **to** u
5      $q = f_{a+2t}^{(r)}(k_i + q)$
6 **return** $q \bmod m$

This definition of a cryptographically inspired hash-function family is meant to be realistic, yet only illustrative, and many variations and improvements are possible. See the chapter notes for suggestions.

In summary, we see that when the memory system is hierarchical, it becomes advantageous to use linear probing (a special case of double hashing), since successive probes tend to stay in the same cache block. Furthermore, hash functions that can be implemented using only the computer's fast registers are exceptionally efficient, so they can be quite complex and even cryptographically inspired, providing the high degree of independence needed for linear probing to work most efficiently.

Exercises

★ *11.5-1*
Complete the argument that for any odd positive integer a and any integer $r \geq 0$, the function $f_a^{(r)}$ is one-to-one. Use a proof by contradiction and make use of the fact that the function f_a works modulo 2^w.

★ *11.5-2*
Argue that a random oracle is 5-independent.

★ *11.5-3*
Consider what happens to the value $f_a^{(r)}(k)$ as we flip a single bit k_i of the input value k, for various values of r. Let $k = \sum_{i=0}^{w-1} k_i 2^i$ and $g_a(k) = \sum_{j=0}^{w-1} b_j 2^j$ define the bit values k_i in the input (with k_0 the least-significant bit) and the bit values b_j in $g_a(k) = (2k^2 + ak) \bmod 2^w$ (where $g_a(k)$ is the value that, when its halves are swapped, becomes $f_a(k)$). Suppose that flipping a single bit k_i of the input k may cause any bit b_j of $g_a(k)$ to flip, for $j \geq i$. What is the least value of r for which flipping the value of any single bit k_i may cause *any* bit of the output $f_a^{(r)}(k)$ to flip? Explain.

Problems

11-1   Longest-probe bound for hashing

Suppose you are using an open-addressed hash table of size m to store $n \leq m/2$ items.

a. Assuming independent uniform permutation hashing, show that for $i = 1, 2, \ldots, n$, the probability is at most 2^{-p} that the ith insertion requires strictly more than p probes.

b. Show that for $i = 1, 2, \ldots, n$, the probability is $O(1/n^2)$ that the ith insertion requires more than $2 \lg n$ probes.

Let the random variable X_i denote the number of probes required by the ith insertion. You have shown in part (b) that $\Pr \{X_i > 2 \lg n\} = O(1/n^2)$. Let the random variable $X = \max \{X_i : 1 \leq i \leq n\}$ denote the maximum number of probes required by any of the n insertions.

c. Show that $\Pr \{X > 2 \lg n\} = O(1/n)$.

d. Show that the expected length $\mathrm{E}[X]$ of the longest probe sequence is $O(\lg n)$.

11-2   Searching a static set

You are asked to implement a searchable set of n elements in which the keys are numbers. The set is static (no INSERT or DELETE operations), and the only operation required is SEARCH. You are given an arbitrary amount of time to preprocess the n elements so that SEARCH operations run quickly.

a. Show how to implement SEARCH in $O(\lg n)$ worst-case time using no extra storage beyond what is needed to store the elements of the set themselves.

b. Consider implementing the set by open-address hashing on m slots, and assume independent uniform permutation hashing. What is the minimum amount of extra storage $m - n$ required to make the average performance of an unsuccessful SEARCH operation be at least as good as the bound in part (a)? Your answer should be an asymptotic bound on $m - n$ in terms of n.

11-3   Slot-size bound for chaining

Given a hash table with n slots, with collisions resolved by chaining, suppose that n keys are inserted into the table. Each key is equally likely to be hashed to each slot. Let M be the maximum number of keys in any slot after all the keys have been inserted. Your mission is to prove an $O(\lg n / \lg \lg n)$ upper bound on $\mathrm{E}[M]$, the expected value of M.

a. Argue that the probability Q_k that exactly k keys hash to a particular slot is given by

$$Q_k = \left(\frac{1}{n}\right)^k \left(1 - \frac{1}{n}\right)^{n-k} \binom{n}{k} .$$

b. Let P_k be the probability that $M = k$, that is, the probability that the slot containing the most keys contains k keys. Show that $P_k \leq n Q_k$.

c. Show that $Q_k < e^k / k^k$. *Hint:* Use Stirling's approximation, equation (3.25) on page 67.

d. Show that there exists a constant $c > 1$ such that $Q_{k_0} < 1/n^3$ for $k_0 = c \lg n / \lg \lg n$. Conclude that $P_k < 1/n^2$ for $k \geq k_0 = c \lg n / \lg \lg n$.

e. Argue that

$$\mathrm{E}[M] \leq \Pr\left\{M > \frac{c \lg n}{\lg \lg n}\right\} \cdot n + \Pr\left\{M \leq \frac{c \lg n}{\lg \lg n}\right\} \cdot \frac{c \lg n}{\lg \lg n} .$$

Conclude that $\mathrm{E}[M] = O(\lg n / \lg \lg n)$.

11-4 *Hashing and authentication*
Let $\mathcal{H}$ be a family of hash functions in which each hash function $h \in \mathcal{H}$ maps the universe U of keys to $\{0, 1, \ldots, m - 1\}$.

a. Show that if the family $\mathcal{H}$ of hash functions is 2-independent, then it is universal.

b. Suppose that the universe U is the set of n-tuples of values drawn from $\mathbb{Z}_p = \{0, 1, \ldots, p - 1\}$, where p is prime. Consider an element $x = \langle x_0, x_1, \ldots, x_{n-1} \rangle \in U$. For any n-tuple $a = \langle a_0, a_1, \ldots, a_{n-1} \rangle \in U$, define the hash function h_a by

$$h_a(x) = \left(\sum_{j=0}^{n-1} a_j x_j\right) \bmod p .$$

Let $\mathcal{H} = \{h_a : a \in U\}$. Show that $\mathcal{H}$ is universal, but not 2-independent. (*Hint:* Find a key for which all hash functions in $\mathcal{H}$ produce the same value.)

c. Suppose that we modify $\mathcal{H}$ slightly from part (b): for any $a \in U$ and for any $b \in \mathbb{Z}_p$, define

$$h'_{ab}(x) = \left(\sum_{j=0}^{n-1} a_j x_j + b \right) \bmod p$$

and $\mathcal{H}' = \{ h'_{ab} : a \in U \text{ and } b \in \mathbb{Z}_p \}$. Argue that $\mathcal{H}'$ is 2-independent. (*Hint:* Consider fixed n-tuples $x \in U$ and $y \in U$, with $x_i \neq y_i$ for some i. What happens to $h'_{ab}(x)$ and $h'_{ab}(y)$ as a_i and b range over $\mathbb{Z}_p$?)

d. Alice and Bob secretly agree on a hash function h from a 2-independent family $\mathcal{H}$ of hash functions. Each $h \in \mathcal{H}$ maps from a universe of keys U to $\mathbb{Z}_p$, where p is prime. Later, Alice sends a message m to Bob over the internet, where $m \in U$. She authenticates this message to Bob by also sending an authentication tag $t = h(m)$, and Bob checks that the pair (m, t) he receives indeed satisfies $t = h(m)$. Suppose that an adversary intercepts (m, t) en route and tries to fool Bob by replacing the pair (m, t) with a different pair (m', t'). Argue that the probability that the adversary succeeds in fooling Bob into accepting (m', t') is at most $1/p$, no matter how much computing power the adversary has, even if the adversary knows the family $\mathcal{H}$ of hash functions used.

Chapter notes

The books by Knuth [261] and Gonnet and Baeza-Yates [193] are excellent references for the analysis of hashing algorithms. Knuth credits H. P. Luhn (1953) for inventing hash tables, along with the chaining method for resolving collisions. At about the same time, G. M. Amdahl originated the idea of open addressing. The notion of a random oracle was introduced by Bellare et al. [43]. Carter and Wegman [80] introduced the notion of universal families of hash functions in 1979.

Dietzfelbinger et al. [113] invented the multiply-shift hash function and gave a proof of Theorem 11.5. Thorup [437] provides extensions and additional analysis. Thorup [438] gives a simple proof that linear probing with 5-independent hashing takes constant expected time per operation. Thorup also describes the method for deletion in a hash table using linear probing.

Fredman, Komlós, and Szemerédi [154] developed a perfect hashing scheme for static sets—"perfect" because all collisions are avoided. An extension of their method to dynamic sets, handling insertions and deletions in amortized expected time $O(1)$, has been given by Dietzfelbinger et al. [114].

The wee hash function is based on the RC6 encryption algorithm [379]. Leiserson et al. [292] propose an "RC6MIX" function that is essentially the same as the wee hash function. They give experimental evidence that it has good randomness, and they also give a "DOTMIX" function for dealing with variable-length inputs. Bellare et al. [42] provide an analysis of the security of the cipher-block-chaining message authentication code. This analysis implies that the wee hash function has the desired pseudorandomness properties.

12   Binary Search Trees

The search tree data structure supports each of the dynamic-set operations listed on page 250: SEARCH, MINIMUM, MAXIMUM, PREDECESSOR, SUCCESSOR, INSERT, and DELETE. Thus, you can use a search tree both as a dictionary and as a priority queue.

Basic operations on a binary search tree take time proportional to the height of the tree. For a complete binary tree with n nodes, such operations run in $\Theta(\lg n)$ worst-case time. If the tree is a linear chain of n nodes, however, the same operations take $\Theta(n)$ worst-case time. In Chapter 13, we'll see a variation of binary search trees, red-black trees, whose operations guarantee a height of $O(\lg n)$. We won't prove it here, but if you build a binary search tree on a random set of n keys, its expected height is $O(\lg n)$ even if you don't try to limit its height.

After presenting the basic properties of binary search trees, the following sections show how to walk a binary search tree to print its values in sorted order, how to search for a value in a binary search tree, how to find the minimum or maximum element, how to find the predecessor or successor of an element, and how to insert into or delete from a binary search tree. The basic mathematical properties of trees appear in Appendix B.

12.1   What is a binary search tree?

A binary search tree is organized, as the name suggests, in a binary tree, as shown in Figure 12.1. You can represent such a tree with a linked data structure, as in Section 10.3. In addition to a *key* and satellite data, each node object contains attributes *left*, *right*, and *p* that point to the nodes corresponding to its left child, its right child, and its parent, respectively. If a child or the parent is missing, the appropriate attribute contains the value NIL. The tree itself has an attribute *root*

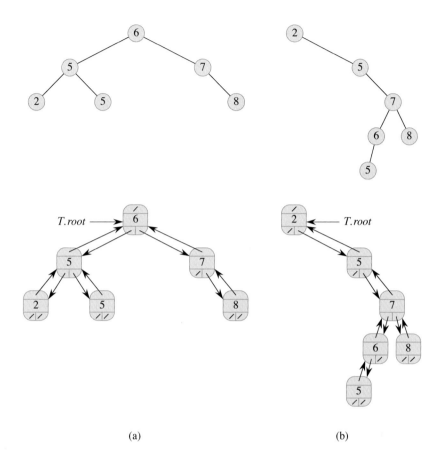

(a)   (b)

Figure 12.1 Binary search trees. For any node x, the keys in the left subtree of x are at most $x.key$, and the keys in the right subtree of x are at least $x.key$. Different binary search trees can represent the same set of values. The worst-case running time for most search-tree operations is proportional to the height of the tree. **(a)** A binary search tree on 6 nodes with height 2. The top figure shows how to view the tree conceptually, and the bottom figure shows the *left*, *right*, and *p* attributes in each node, in the style of Figure 10.6 on page 266. **(b)** A less efficient binary search tree, with height 4, that contains the same keys.

that points to the root node, or NIL if the tree is empty. The root node $T.root$ is the only node in a tree T whose parent is NIL.

The keys in a binary search tree are always stored in such a way as to satisfy the *binary-search-tree property*:

Let x be a node in a binary search tree. If y is a node in the left subtree of x, then $y.key \leq x.key$. If y is a node in the right subtree of x, then $y.key \geq x.key$.

Thus, in Figure 12.1(a), the key of the root is 6, the keys 2, 5, and 5 in its left subtree are no larger than 6, and the keys 7 and 8 in its right subtree are no smaller than 6. The same property holds for every node in the tree. For example, looking at the root's left child as the root of a subtree, this subtree root has the key 5, the key 2 in its left subtree is no larger than 5, and the key 5 in its right subtree is no smaller than 5.

Because of the binary-search-tree property, you can print out all the keys in a binary search tree in sorted order by a simple recursive algorithm, called an *inorder tree walk*, given by the procedure INORDER-TREE-WALK. This algorithm is so named because it prints the key of the root of a subtree between printing the values in its left subtree and printing those in its right subtree. (Similarly, a *preorder tree walk* prints the root before the values in either subtree, and a *postorder tree walk* prints the root after the values in its subtrees.) To print all the elements in a binary search tree T, call INORDER-TREE-WALK($T.root$). For example, the inorder tree walk prints the keys in each of the two binary search trees from Figure 12.1 in the order $2, 5, 5, 6, 7, 8$. The correctness of the algorithm follows by induction directly from the binary-search-tree property.

INORDER-TREE-WALK(x)

1 **if** $x \neq$ NIL
2   INORDER-TREE-WALK($x.left$)
3   print $x.key$
4   INORDER-TREE-WALK($x.right$)

It takes $\Theta(n)$ time to walk an n-node binary search tree, since after the initial call, the procedure calls itself recursively exactly twice for each node in the tree—once for its left child and once for its right child. The following theorem gives a formal proof that it takes linear time to perform an inorder tree walk.

Theorem 12.1
If x is the root of an n-node subtree, then the call INORDER-TREE-WALK(x) takes $\Theta(n)$ time.

Proof Let $T(n)$ denote the time taken by INORDER-TREE-WALK when it is called on the root of an n-node subtree. Since INORDER-TREE-WALK visits all n nodes of the subtree, we have $T(n) = \Omega(n)$. It remains to show that $T(n) = O(n)$.

Since INORDER-TREE-WALK takes a small, constant amount of time on an empty subtree (for the test $x \neq$ NIL), we have $T(0) = c$ for some constant $c > 0$.

For $n > 0$, suppose that INORDER-TREE-WALK is called on a node x whose left subtree has k nodes and whose right subtree has $n - k - 1$ nodes. The time to perform INORDER-TREE-WALK(x) is bounded by $T(n) \leq T(k) + T(n-k-1) + d$ for some constant $d > 0$ that reflects an upper bound on the time to execute the body of INORDER-TREE-WALK(x), exclusive of the time spent in recursive calls.

We use the substitution method to show that $T(n) = O(n)$ by proving that $T(n) \leq (c+d)n + c$. For $n = 0$, we have $(c+d) \cdot 0 + c = c = T(0)$. For $n > 0$, we have

$$
\begin{aligned}
T(n) &\leq T(k) + T(n - k - 1) + d \\
&\leq ((c + d)k + c) + ((c + d)(n - k - 1) + c) + d \\
&= (c + d)n + c - (c + d) + c + d \\
&= (c + d)n + c ,
\end{aligned}
$$

which completes the proof. ∎

Exercises

12.1-1
For the set $\{1, 4, 5, 10, 16, 17, 21\}$ of keys, draw binary search trees of heights 2, 3, 4, 5, and 6.

12.1-2
What is the difference between the binary-search-tree property and the min-heap property on page 163? Can the min-heap property be used to print out the keys of an n-node tree in sorted order in $O(n)$ time? Show how, or explain why not.

12.1-3
Give a nonrecursive algorithm that performs an inorder tree walk. (*Hint:* An easy solution uses a stack as an auxiliary data structure. A more complicated, but elegant, solution uses no stack but assumes that you can test two pointers for equality.)

12.1-4
Give recursive algorithms that perform preorder and postorder tree walks in $\Theta(n)$ time on a tree of n nodes.

12.1-5
Argue that since sorting n elements takes $\Omega(n \lg n)$ time in the worst case in the comparison model, any comparison-based algorithm for constructing a binary search tree from an arbitrary list of n elements takes $\Omega(n \lg n)$ time in the worst case.

12.2   Querying a binary search tree

Binary search trees can support the queries MINIMUM, MAXIMUM, SUCCESSOR, and PREDECESSOR, as well as SEARCH. This section examines these operations and shows how to support each one in $O(h)$ time on any binary search tree of height h.

Searching

To search for a node with a given key in a binary search tree, call the TREE-SEARCH procedure. Given a pointer x to the root of a subtree and a key k, TREE-SEARCH(x, k) returns a pointer to a node with key k if one exists in the subtree; otherwise, it returns NIL. To search for key k in the entire binary search tree T, call TREE-SEARCH$(T.root, k)$.

TREE-SEARCH(x, k)

1 **if** x == NIL or k == $x.key$
2   **return** x
3 **if** $k < x.key$
4   **return** TREE-SEARCH$(x.left, k)$
5 **else return** TREE-SEARCH$(x.right, k)$

ITERATIVE-TREE-SEARCH(x, k)

1 **while** $x \neq$ NIL and $k \neq x.key$
2   **if** $k < x.key$
3          $x = x.left$
4   **else** $x = x.right$
5 **return** x

The TREE-SEARCH procedure begins its search at the root and traces a simple path downward in the tree, as shown in Figure 12.2(a). For each node x it encounters, it compares the key k with $x.key$. If the two keys are equal, the search terminates. If k is smaller than $x.key$, the search continues in the left subtree of x, since the binary-search-tree property implies that k cannot reside in the right subtree. Symmetrically, if k is larger than $x.key$, the search continues in the right subtree. The nodes encountered during the recursion form a simple path downward from the root of the tree, and thus the running time of TREE-SEARCH is $O(h)$, where h is the height of the tree.

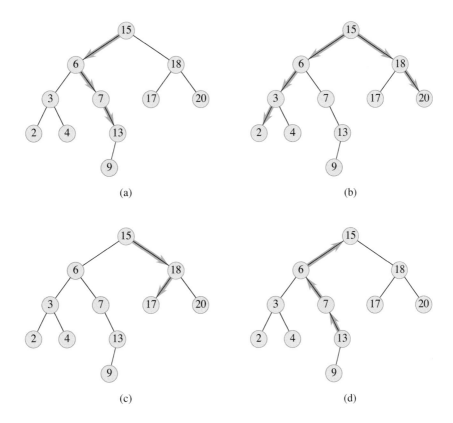

(a)   (b)

(c)   (d)

Figure 12.2   Queries on a binary search tree. Nodes and paths followed in each query are colored blue. **(a)** A search for the key 13 in the tree follows the path $15 \rightarrow 6 \rightarrow 7 \rightarrow 13$ from the root. **(b)** The minimum key in the tree is 2, which is found by following *left* pointers from the root. The maximum key 20 is found by following *right* pointers from the root. **(c)** The successor of the node with key 15 is the node with key 17, since it is the minimum key in the right subtree of 15. **(d)** The node with key 13 has no right subtree, and thus its successor is its lowest ancestor whose left child is also an ancestor. In this case, the node with key 15 is its successor.

Since the Tree-Search procedure recurses on either the left subtree or the right subtree, but not both, we can rewrite the algorithm to "unroll" the recursion into a **while** loop. On most computers, the Iterative-Tree-Search procedure on the facing page is more efficient.

Minimum and maximum

To find an element in a binary search tree whose key is a minimum, just follow *left* child pointers from the root until you encounter a NIL, as shown in Figure 12.2(b).

The TREE-MINIMUM procedure returns a pointer to the minimum element in the subtree rooted at a given node x, which we assume to be non-NIL.

TREE-MINIMUM(x)

1 **while** $x.left \neq$ NIL
2      $x = x.left$
3 **return** x

TREE-MAXIMUM(x)

1 **while** $x.right \neq$ NIL
2      $x = x.right$
3 **return** x

The binary-search-tree property guarantees that TREE-MINIMUM is correct. If node x has no left subtree, then since every key in the right subtree of x is at least as large as $x.key$, the minimum key in the subtree rooted at x is $x.key$. If node x has a left subtree, then since no key in the right subtree is smaller than $x.key$ and every key in the left subtree is not larger than $x.key$, the minimum key in the subtree rooted at x resides in the subtree rooted at $x.left$.

The pseudocode for TREE-MAXIMUM is symmetric. Both TREE-MINIMUM and TREE-MAXIMUM run in $O(h)$ time on a tree of height h since, as in TREE-SEARCH, the sequence of nodes encountered forms a simple path downward from the root.

Successor and predecessor

Given a node in a binary search tree, how can you find its successor in the sorted order determined by an inorder tree walk? If all keys are distinct, the successor of a node x is the node with the smallest key greater than $x.key$. Regardless of whether the keys are distinct, we define the *successor* of a node as the next node visited in an inorder tree walk. The structure of a binary search tree allows you to determine the successor of a node without comparing keys. The TREE-SUCCESSOR procedure on the facing page returns the successor of a node x in a binary search tree if it exists, or NIL if x is the last node that would be visited during an inorder walk.

The code for TREE-SUCCESSOR has two cases. If the right subtree of node x is nonempty, then the successor of x is just the leftmost node in x's right subtree, which line 2 finds by calling TREE-MINIMUM($x.right$). For example, the successor of the node with key 15 in Figure 12.2(c) is the node with key 17.

On the other hand, as Exercise 12.2-6 asks you to show, if the right subtree of node x is empty and x has a successor y, then y is the lowest ancestor of x whose

TREE-SUCCESSOR(x)

1 **if** x.right ≠ NIL
2   **return** TREE-MINIMUM(x.right)   // leftmost node in right subtree
3 **else** // find the lowest ancestor of x whose left child is an ancestor of x
4   y = x.p
5   **while** y ≠ NIL and x == y.right
6   x = y
7   y = y.p
8   **return** y

left child is also an ancestor of x. In Figure 12.2(d), the successor of the node with key 13 is the node with key 15. To find y, go up the tree from x until you encounter either the root or a node that is the left child of its parent. Lines 4–8 of TREE-SUCCESSOR handle this case.

The running time of TREE-SUCCESSOR on a tree of height h is $O(h)$, since it either follows a simple path up the tree or follows a simple path down the tree. The procedure TREE-PREDECESSOR, which is symmetric to TREE-SUCCESSOR, also runs in $O(h)$ time.

In summary, we have proved the following theorem.

Theorem 12.2
The dynamic-set operations SEARCH, MINIMUM, MAXIMUM, SUCCESSOR, and PREDECESSOR can be implemented so that each one runs in $O(h)$ time on a binary search tree of height h.   ∎

Exercises

12.2-1
You are searching for the number 363 in a binary search tree containing numbers between 1 and 1000. Which of the following sequences *cannot* be the sequence of nodes examined?

a. 2, 252, 401, 398, 330, 344, 397, 363.

b. 924, 220, 911, 244, 898, 258, 362, 363.

c. 925, 202, 911, 240, 912, 245, 363.

d. 2, 399, 387, 219, 266, 382, 381, 278, 363.

e. 935, 278, 347, 621, 299, 392, 358, 363.

12.2-2

Write recursive versions of TREE-MINIMUM and TREE-MAXIMUM.

12.2-3

Write the TREE-PREDECESSOR procedure.

12.2-4

Professor Kilmer claims to have discovered a remarkable property of binary search trees. Suppose that the search for key k in a binary search tree ends up at a leaf. Consider three sets: A, the keys to the left of the search path; B, the keys on the search path; and C, the keys to the right of the search path. Professor Kilmer claims that any three keys $a \in A$, $b \in B$, and $c \in C$ must satisfy $a \leq b \leq c$. Give a smallest possible counterexample to the professor's claim.

12.2-5

Show that if a node in a binary search tree has two children, then its successor has no left child and its predecessor has no right child.

12.2-6

Consider a binary search tree T whose keys are distinct. Show that if the right subtree of a node x in T is empty and x has a successor y, then y is the lowest ancestor of x whose left child is also an ancestor of x. (Recall that every node is its own ancestor.)

12.2-7

An alternative method of performing an inorder tree walk of an n-node binary search tree finds the minimum element in the tree by calling TREE-MINIMUM and then making $n - 1$ calls to TREE-SUCCESSOR. Prove that this algorithm runs in $\Theta(n)$ time.

12.2-8

Prove that no matter what node you start at in a height-h binary search tree, k successive calls to TREE-SUCCESSOR take $O(k + h)$ time.

12.2-9

Let T be a binary search tree whose keys are distinct, let x be a leaf node, and let y be its parent. Show that $y.key$ is either the smallest key in T larger than $x.key$ or the largest key in T smaller than $x.key$.

12.3 Insertion and deletion

The operations of insertion and deletion cause the dynamic set represented by a binary search tree to change. The data structure must be modified to reflect this change, but in such a way that the binary-search-tree property continues to hold. We'll see that modifying the tree to insert a new element is relatively straightforward, but deleting a node from a binary search tree is more complicated.

Insertion

The TREE-INSERT procedure inserts a new node into a binary search tree. The procedure takes a binary search tree T and a node z for which $z.key$ has already been filled in, $z.left =$ NIL, and $z.right =$ NIL. It modifies T and some of the attributes of z so as to insert z into an appropriate position in the tree.

```
TREE-INSERT(T, z)
1   x = T.root          // node being compared with z
2   y = NIL             // y will be parent of z
3   while x ≠ NIL       // descend until reaching a leaf
4       y = x
5       if z.key < x.key
6           x = x.left
7       else x = x.right
8   z.p = y             // found the location—insert z with parent y
9   if y == NIL
10      T.root = z      // tree T was empty
11  elseif z.key < y.key
12      y.left = z
13  else y.right = z
```

Figure 12.3 shows how TREE-INSERT works. Just like the procedures TREE-SEARCH and ITERATIVE-TREE-SEARCH, TREE-INSERT begins at the root of the tree and the pointer x traces a simple path downward looking for a NIL to replace with the input node z. The procedure maintains the *trailing pointer* y as the parent of x. After initialization, the **while** loop in lines 3–7 causes these two pointers to move down the tree, going left or right depending on the comparison of $z.key$ with $x.key$, until x becomes NIL. This NIL occupies the position where node z will go. More precisely, this NIL is a *left* or *right* attribute of the node that will become z's parent, or it is $T.root$ if tree T is currently empty. The procedure needs the

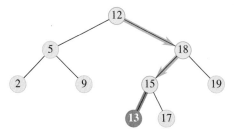

Figure 12.3 Inserting a node with key 13 into a binary search tree. The simple path from the root down to the position where the node is inserted is shown in blue. The new node and the link to its parent are highlighted in orange.

trailing pointer y, because by the time it finds the NIL where z belongs, the search has proceeded one step beyond the node that needs to be changed. Lines 8–13 set the pointers that cause z to be inserted.

Like the other primitive operations on search trees, the procedure TREE-INSERT runs in $O(h)$ time on a tree of height h.

Deletion

The overall strategy for deleting a node z from a binary search tree T has three basic cases and, as we'll see, one of the cases is a bit tricky.

- If z has no children, then simply remove it by modifying its parent to replace z with NIL as its child.

- If z has just one child, then elevate that child to take z's position in the tree by modifying z's parent to replace z by z's child.

- If z has two children, find z's successor y—which must belong to z's right subtree—and move y to take z's position in the tree. The rest of z's original right subtree becomes y's new right subtree, and z's left subtree becomes y's new left subtree. Because y is z's successor, it cannot have a left child, and y's original right child moves into y's original position, with the rest of y's original right subtree following automatically. This case is the tricky one because, as we'll see, it matters whether y is z's right child.

The procedure for deleting a given node z from a binary search tree T takes as arguments pointers to T and z. It organizes its cases a bit differently from the three cases outlined previously by considering the four cases shown in Figure 12.4.

- If z has no left child, then as in part (a) of the figure, replace z by its right child, which may or may not be NIL. When z's right child is NIL, this case deals with

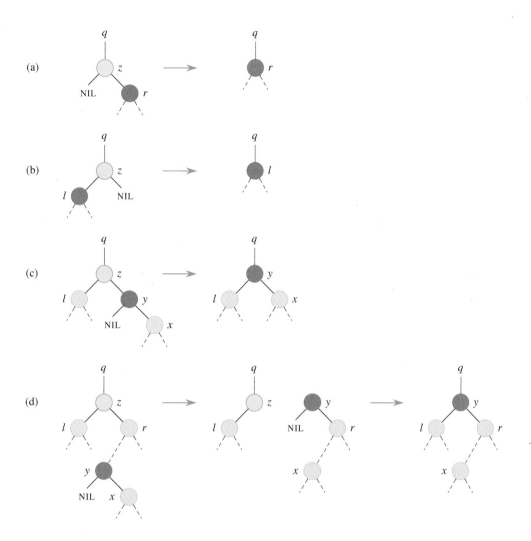

Figure 12.4 Deleting a node z, in blue, from a binary search tree. Node z may be the root, a left child of node q, or a right child of q. The node that will replace node z in its position in the tree is colored orange. **(a)** Node z has no left child. Replace z by its right child r, which may or may not be NIL. **(b)** Node z has a left child l but no right child. Replace z by l. **(c)** Node z has two children. Its left child is node l, its right child is its successor y (which has no left child), and y's right child is node x. Replace z by y, updating y's left child to become l, but leaving x as y's right child. **(d)** Node z has two children (left child l and right child r), and its successor $y \neq r$ lies within the subtree rooted at r. First replace y by its own right child x, and set y to be r's parent. Then set y to be q's child and the parent of l.

the situation in which z has no children. When z's right child is non-NIL, this case handles the situation in which z has just one child, which is its right child.

- Otherwise, if z has just one child, then that child is a left child. As in part (b) of the figure, replace z by its left child.

- Otherwise, z has both a left and a right child. Find z's successor y, which lies in z's right subtree and has no left child (see Exercise 12.2-5). Splice node y out of its current location and replace z by y in the tree. How to do so depends on whether y is z's right child:

  ○ If y is z's right child, then as in part (c) of the figure, replace z by y, leaving y's right child alone.

  ○ Otherwise, y lies within z's right subtree but is not z's right child. In this case, as in part (d) of the figure, first replace y by its own right child, and then replace z by y.

As part of the process of deleting a node, subtrees need to move around within the binary search tree. The subroutine TRANSPLANT replaces one subtree as a child of its parent with another subtree. When TRANSPLANT replaces the subtree rooted at node u with the subtree rooted at node v, node u's parent becomes node v's parent, and u's parent ends up having v as its appropriate child. TRANSPLANT allows v to be NIL instead of a pointer to a node.

TRANSPLANT(T, u, v)

```
1  if u.p == NIL
2      T.root = v
3  elseif u == u.p.left
4      u.p.left = v
5  else u.p.right = v
6  if v ≠ NIL
7      v.p = u.p
```

Here is how TRANSPLANT works. Lines 1–2 handle the case in which u is the root of T. Otherwise, u is either a left child or a right child of its parent. Lines 3–4 take care of updating $u.p.left$ if u is a left child, and line 5 updates $u.p.right$ if u is a right child. Because v may be NIL, lines 6–7 update $v.p$ only if v is non-NIL. The procedure TRANSPLANT does not attempt to update $v.left$ and $v.right$. Doing so, or not doing so, is the responsibility of TRANSPLANT's caller.

The procedure TREE-DELETE on the facing page uses TRANSPLANT to delete node z from binary search tree T. It executes the four cases as follows. Lines 1–2 handle the case in which node z has no left child (Figure 12.4(a)), and lines 3–4 handle the case in which z has a left child but no right child (Figure 12.4(b)). Lines 5–12 deal with the remaining two cases, in which z has two children. Line 5 finds node y, which is the successor of z. Because z has a nonempty right subtree, its successor must be the node in that subtree with the smallest key; hence the call to TREE-MINIMUM($z.right$). As we noted before, y has no left child. The procedure needs to splice y out of its current location and replace z by y in the tree. If y is z's right child (Figure 12.4(c)), then lines 10–12 replace z as a child of its parent by y and replace y's left child by z's left child. Node y retains its right child (x in Figure 12.4(c)), and so no change to $y.right$ needs to occur. If y is not z's right child (Figure 12.4(d)), then two nodes have to move. Lines 7–9 replace y as a child of its parent by y's right child (x in Figure 12.4(c)) and make z's right child (r in the figure) become y's right child instead. Finally, lines 10–12 replace z as a child of its parent by y and replace y's left child by z's left child.

TREE-DELETE(T, z)

```
 1  if z.left == NIL
 2      TRANSPLANT(T, z, z.right)        // replace z by its right child
 3  elseif z.right == NIL
 4      TRANSPLANT(T, z, z.left)         // replace z by its left child
 5  else y = TREE-MINIMUM(z.right)       // y is z's successor
 6      if y ≠ z.right                   // is y farther down the tree?
 7          TRANSPLANT(T, y, y.right)    // replace y by its right child
 8          y.right = z.right            // z's right child becomes
 9          y.right.p = y                //      y's right child
10      TRANSPLANT(T, z, y)              // replace z by its successor y
11      y.left = z.left                  // and give z's left child to y,
12      y.left.p = y                     //      which had no left child
```

Each line of TREE-DELETE, including the calls to TRANSPLANT, takes constant time, except for the call to TREE-MINIMUM in line 5. Thus, TREE-DELETE runs in $O(h)$ time on a tree of height h.

In summary, we have proved the following theorem.

Theorem 12.3

The dynamic-set operations INSERT and DELETE can be implemented so that each one runs in $O(h)$ time on a binary search tree of height h. ∎

Exercises

12.3-1
Give a recursive version of the TREE-INSERT procedure.

12.3-2
Suppose that you construct a binary search tree by repeatedly inserting distinct values into the tree. Argue that the number of nodes examined in searching for a value in the tree is 1 plus the number of nodes examined when the value was first inserted into the tree.

12.3-3
You can sort a given set of n numbers by first building a binary search tree containing these numbers (using TREE-INSERT repeatedly to insert the numbers one by one) and then printing the numbers by an inorder tree walk. What are the worst-case and best-case running times for this sorting algorithm?

12.3-4
When TREE-DELETE calls TRANSPLANT, under what circumstances can the parameter v of TRANSPLANT be NIL?

12.3-5
Is the operation of deletion "commutative" in the sense that deleting x and then y from a binary search tree leaves the same tree as deleting y and then x? Argue why it is or give a counterexample.

12.3-6
Suppose that instead of each node x keeping the attribute $x.p$, pointing to x's parent, it keeps $x.succ$, pointing to x's successor. Give pseudocode for TREE-SEARCH, TREE-INSERT, and TREE-DELETE on a binary search tree T using this representation. These procedures should operate in $O(h)$ time, where h is the height of the tree T. You may assume that all keys in the binary search tree are distinct. (*Hint:* You might wish to implement a subroutine that returns the parent of a node.)

12.3-7
When node z in TREE-DELETE has two children, you can choose node y to be its predecessor rather than its successor. What other changes to TREE-DELETE are necessary if you do so? Some have argued that a fair strategy, giving equal priority to predecessor and successor, yields better empirical performance. How might TREE-DELETE be minimally changed to implement such a fair strategy?

Problems

12-1 *Binary search trees with equal keys*
Equal keys pose a problem for the implementation of binary search trees.

a. What is the asymptotic performance of TREE-INSERT when used to insert n items with identical keys into an initially empty binary search tree?

Consider changing TREE-INSERT to test whether $z.key = x.key$ before line 5 and to test whether $z.key = y.key$ before line 11. If equality holds, implement one of the following strategies. For each strategy, find the asymptotic performance of inserting n items with identical keys into an initially empty binary search tree. (The strategies are described for line 5, which compares the keys of z and x. Substitute y for x to arrive at the strategies for line 11.)

b. Keep a boolean flag $x.b$ at node x, and set x to either $x.left$ or $x.right$ based on the value of $x.b$, which alternates between FALSE and TRUE each time TREE-INSERT visits x while inserting a node with the same key as x.

c. Keep a list of nodes with equal keys at x, and insert z into the list.

d. Randomly set x to either $x.left$ or $x.right$. (Give the worst-case performance and informally derive the expected running time.)

12-2 *Radix trees*
Given two strings $a = a_0 a_1 \ldots a_p$ and $b = b_0 b_1 \ldots b_q$, where each a_i and each b_j belongs to some ordered set of characters, we say that string a is *lexicographically less than* string b if either

1. there exists an integer j, where $0 \le j \le \min\{p, q\}$, such that $a_i = b_i$ for all $i = 0, 1, \ldots, j - 1$ and $a_j < b_j$, or

2. $p < q$ and $a_i = b_i$ for all $i = 0, 1, \ldots, p$.

For example, if a and b are bit strings, then $10100 < 10110$ by rule 1 (letting $j = 3$) and $10100 < 101000$ by rule 2. This ordering is similar to that used in English-language dictionaries.

   The *radix tree* data structure shown in Figure 12.5 (also known as a *trie*) stores the bit strings $1011, 10, 011, 100$, and 0. When searching for a key $a = a_0 a_1 \ldots a_p$, go left at a node of depth i if $a_i = 0$ and right if $a_i = 1$. Let S be a set of distinct bit strings whose lengths sum to n. Show how to use a radix tree to sort S lexicographically in $\Theta(n)$ time. For the example in Figure 12.5, the output of the sort should be the sequence $0, 011, 10, 100, 1011$.

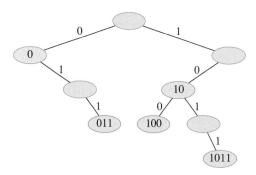

Figure 12.5   A radix tree storing the bit strings $1011, 10, 011, 100$, and 0. To determine each node's key, traverse the simple path from the root to that node. There is no need, therefore, to store the keys in the nodes. The keys appear here for illustrative purposes only. Keys corresponding to blue nodes are not in the tree. Such nodes are present only to establish a path to other nodes.

12-3   *Average node depth in a randomly built binary search tree*

A *randomly built binary search tree* on n keys is a binary search tree created by starting with an empty tree and inserting the keys in random order, where each of the $n!$ permutations of the keys is equally likely. In this problem, you will prove that the average depth of a node in a randomly built binary search tree with n nodes is $O(\lg n)$. The technique reveals a surprising similarity between the building of a binary search tree and the execution of RANDOMIZED-QUICKSORT from Section 7.3.

Denote the depth of any node x in tree T by $d(x, T)$. Then the *total path length* $P(T)$ of a tree T is the sum, over all nodes x in T, of $d(x, T)$.

a. Argue that the average depth of a node in T is

$$\frac{1}{n} \sum_{x \in T} d(x, T) = \frac{1}{n} P(T) .$$

Thus, you need to show that the expected value of $P(T)$ is $O(n \lg n)$.

b. Let T_L and T_R denote the left and right subtrees of tree T, respectively. Argue that if T has n nodes, then

$$P(T) = P(T_L) + P(T_R) + n - 1 .$$

c. Let $P(n)$ denote the average total path length of a randomly built binary search tree with n nodes. Show that

$$P(n) = \frac{1}{n} \sum_{i=0}^{n-1} (P(i) + P(n-i-1) + n - 1) \, .$$

d. Show how to rewrite $P(n)$ as

$$P(n) = \frac{2}{n} \sum_{k=1}^{n-1} P(k) + \Theta(n) \, .$$

e. Recalling the alternative analysis of the randomized version of quicksort given in Problem 7-3, conclude that $P(n) = O(n \lg n)$.

Each recursive invocation of randomized quicksort chooses a random pivot element to partition the set of elements being sorted. Each node of a binary search tree partitions the set of elements that fall into the subtree rooted at that node.

f. Describe an implementation of quicksort in which the comparisons to sort a set of elements are exactly the same as the comparisons to insert the elements into a binary search tree. (The order in which comparisons are made may differ, but the same comparisons must occur.)

12-4 *Number of different binary trees*

Let b_n denote the number of different binary trees with n nodes. In this problem, you will find a formula for b_n, as well as an asymptotic estimate.

a. Show that $b_0 = 1$ and that, for $n \geq 1$,

$$b_n = \sum_{k=0}^{n-1} b_k b_{n-1-k} \, .$$

b. Referring to Problem 4-5 on page 121 for the definition of a generating function, let $B(x)$ be the generating function

$$B(x) = \sum_{n=0}^{\infty} b_n x^n \, .$$

Show that $B(x) = xB(x)^2 + 1$, and hence one way to express $B(x)$ in closed form is

$$B(x) = \frac{1}{2x} \left(1 - \sqrt{1 - 4x} \right) \, .$$

The *Taylor expansion* of $f(x)$ around the point $x = a$ is given by

$$f(x) = \sum_{k=0}^{\infty} \frac{f^{(k)}(a)}{k!}(x-a)^k \,,$$

where $f^{(k)}(x)$ is the kth derivative of f evaluated at x.

c. Show that

$$b_n = \frac{1}{n+1}\binom{2n}{n}$$

(the nth *Catalan number*) by using the Taylor expansion of $\sqrt{1-4x}$ around $x = 0$. (If you wish, instead of using the Taylor expansion, you may use the generalization of the binomial theorem, equation (C.4) on page 1181, to noninteger exponents n, where for any real number n and for any integer k, you can interpret $\binom{n}{k}$ to be $n(n-1)\cdots(n-k+1)/k!$ if $k \geq 0$, and 0 otherwise.)

d. Show that

$$b_n = \frac{4^n}{\sqrt{\pi}n^{3/2}}(1 + O(1/n)) \,.$$

Chapter notes

Knuth [261] contains a good discussion of simple binary search trees as well as many variations. Binary search trees seem to have been independently discovered by a number of people in the late 1950s. Radix trees are often called "tries," which comes from the middle letters in the word *retrieval*. Knuth [261] also discusses them.

Many texts, including the first two editions of this book, describe a somewhat simpler method of deleting a node from a binary search tree when both of its children are present. Instead of replacing node z by its successor y, delete node y but copy its key and satellite data into node z. The downside of this approach is that the node actually deleted might not be the node passed to the delete procedure. If other components of a program maintain pointers to nodes in the tree, they could mistakenly end up with "stale" pointers to nodes that have been deleted. Although the deletion method presented in this edition of this book is a bit more complicated, it guarantees that a call to delete node z deletes node z and only node z.

Section 14.5 will show how to construct an optimal binary search tree when you know the search frequencies before constructing the tree. That is, given the frequencies of searching for each key and the frequencies of searching for values that fall between keys in the tree, a set of searches in the constructed binary search tree examines the minimum number of nodes.

13   Red-Black Trees

Chapter 12 showed that a binary search tree of height h can support any of the basic dynamic-set operations—such as SEARCH, PREDECESSOR, SUCCESSOR, MINIMUM, MAXIMUM, INSERT, and DELETE—in $O(h)$ time. Thus, the set operations are fast if the height of the search tree is small. If its height is large, however, the set operations may run no faster than with a linked list. Red-black trees are one of many search-tree schemes that are "balanced" in order to guarantee that basic dynamic-set operations take $O(\lg n)$ time in the worst case.

13.1   Properties of red-black trees

A *red-black tree* is a binary search tree with one extra bit of storage per node: its *color*, which can be either RED or BLACK. By constraining the node colors on any simple path from the root to a leaf, red-black trees ensure that no such path is more than twice as long as any other, so that the tree is approximately *balanced*. Indeed, as we're about to see, the height of a red-black tree with n keys is at most $2\lg(n + 1)$, which is $O(\lg n)$.

Each node of the tree now contains the attributes *color*, *key*, *left*, *right*, and *p*. If a child or the parent of a node does not exist, the corresponding pointer attribute of the node contains the value NIL. Think of these NILs as pointers to leaves (external nodes) of the binary search tree and the normal, key-bearing nodes as internal nodes of the tree.

A red-black tree is a binary search tree that satisfies the following *red-black properties*:

1. Every node is either red or black.

2. The root is black.

3. Every leaf (NIL) is black.

4. If a node is red, then both its children are black.

5. For each node, all simple paths from the node to descendant leaves contain the same number of black nodes.

Figure 13.1(a) shows an example of a red-black tree.

As a matter of convenience in dealing with boundary conditions in red-black tree code, we use a single sentinel to represent NIL (see page 262). For a red-black tree T, the sentinel $T.nil$ is an object with the same attributes as an ordinary node in the tree. Its *color* attribute is BLACK, and its other attributes—p, *left*, *right*, and *key*—can take on arbitrary values. As Figure 13.1(b) shows, all pointers to NIL are replaced by pointers to the sentinel $T.nil$.

Why use the sentinel? The sentinel makes it possible to treat a NIL child of a node x as an ordinary node whose parent is x. An alternative design would use a distinct sentinel node for each NIL in the tree, so that the parent of each NIL is well defined. That approach needlessly wastes space, however. Instead, just the one sentinel $T.nil$ represents all the NILs—all leaves and the root's parent. The values of the attributes p, *left*, *right*, and *key* of the sentinel are immaterial. The red-black tree procedures can place whatever values in the sentinel that yield simpler code.

We generally confine our interest to the internal nodes of a red-black tree, since they hold the key values. The remainder of this chapter omits the leaves in drawings of red-black trees, as shown in Figure 13.1(c).

We call the number of black nodes on any simple path from, but not including, a node x down to a leaf the ***black-height*** of the node, denoted bh(x). By property 5, the notion of black-height is well defined, since all descending simple paths from the node have the same number of black nodes. The black-height of a red-black tree is the black-height of its root.

The following lemma shows why red-black trees make good search trees.

Lemma 13.1
A red-black tree with n internal nodes has height at most $2\lg(n + 1)$.

Proof We start by showing that the subtree rooted at any node x contains at least $2^{\text{bh}(x)} - 1$ internal nodes. We prove this claim by induction on the height of x. If the height of x is 0, then x must be a leaf ($T.nil$), and the subtree rooted at x indeed contains at least $2^{\text{bh}(x)} - 1 = 2^0 - 1 = 0$ internal nodes. For the inductive step, consider a node x that has positive height and is an internal node. Then node x has two children, either or both of which may be a leaf. If a child is black, then it contributes 1 to x's black-height but not to its own. If a child is red, then it contributes to neither x's black-height nor its own. Therefore, each child has a black-height of either bh(x) $- 1$ (if it's black) or bh(x) (if it's red). Since the height of a child of x is less than the height of x itself, we can apply the inductive

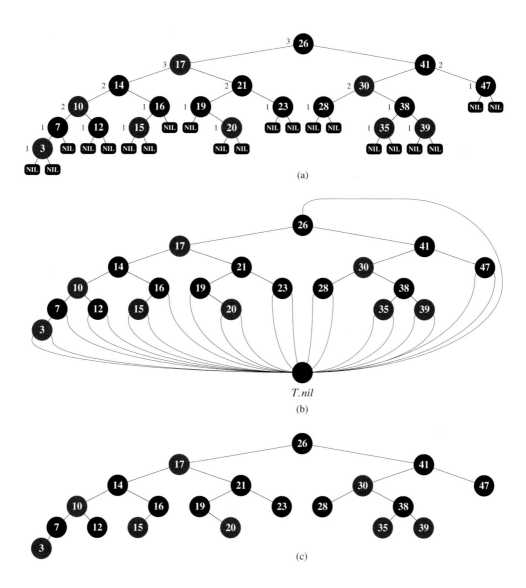

Figure 13.1 A red-black tree. Every node in a red-black tree is either red or black, the children of a red node are both black, and every simple path from a node to a descendant leaf contains the same number of black nodes. **(a)** Every leaf, shown as a NIL, is black. Each non-NIL node is marked with its black-height, where NILs have black-height 0. **(b)** The same red-black tree but with each NIL replaced by the single sentinel *T.nil*, which is always black, and with black-heights omitted. The root's parent is also the sentinel. **(c)** The same red-black tree but with leaves and the root's parent omitted entirely. The remainder of this chapter uses this drawing style.

hypothesis to conclude that each child has at least $2^{bh(x)-1} - 1$ internal nodes. Thus, the subtree rooted at x contains at least $(2^{bh(x)-1} - 1) + (2^{bh(x)-1} - 1) + 1 = 2^{bh(x)} - 1$ internal nodes, which proves the claim.

To complete the proof of the lemma, let h be the height of the tree. According to property 4, at least half the nodes on any simple path from the root to a leaf, not including the root, must be black. Consequently, the black-height of the root must be at least $h/2$, and thus,

$$n \geq 2^{h/2} - 1 .$$

Moving the 1 to the left-hand side and taking logarithms on both sides yields $\lg(n + 1) \geq h/2$, or $h \leq 2\lg(n + 1)$. ∎

As an immediate consequence of this lemma, each of the dynamic-set operations SEARCH, MINIMUM, MAXIMUM, SUCCESSOR, and PREDECESSOR runs in $O(\lg n)$ time on a red-black tree, since each can run in $O(h)$ time on a binary search tree of height h (as shown in Chapter 12) and any red-black tree on n nodes is a binary search tree with height $O(\lg n)$. (Of course, references to NIL in the algorithms of Chapter 12 have to be replaced by *T.nil*.) Although the procedures TREE-INSERT and TREE-DELETE from Chapter 12 run in $O(\lg n)$ time when given a red-black tree as input, you cannot just use them to implement the dynamic-set operations INSERT and DELETE. They do not necessarily maintain the red-black properties, so you might not end up with a legal red-black tree. The remainder of this chapter shows how to insert into and delete from a red-black tree in $O(\lg n)$ time.

Exercises

13.1-1
In the style of Figure 13.1(a), draw the complete binary search tree of height 3 on the keys $\{1, 2, \ldots, 15\}$. Add the NIL leaves and color the nodes in three different ways such that the black-heights of the resulting red-black trees are 2, 3, and 4.

13.1-2
Draw the red-black tree that results after TREE-INSERT is called on the tree in Figure 13.1 with key 36. If the inserted node is colored red, is the resulting tree a red-black tree? What if it is colored black?

13.1-3
Define a *relaxed red-black tree* as a binary search tree that satisfies red-black properties 1, 3, 4, and 5, but whose root may be either red or black. Consider a relaxed red-black tree T whose root is red. If the root of T is changed to black but no other changes occur, is the resulting tree a red-black tree?

13.1-4

Suppose that every black node in a red-black tree "absorbs" all of its red children, so that the children of any red node become children of the black parent. (Ignore what happens to the keys.) What are the possible degrees of a black node after all its red children are absorbed? What can you say about the depths of the leaves of the resulting tree?

13.1-5

Show that the longest simple path from a node x in a red-black tree to a descendant leaf has length at most twice that of the shortest simple path from node x to a descendant leaf.

13.1-6

What is the largest possible number of internal nodes in a red-black tree with black-height k? What is the smallest possible number?

13.1-7

Describe a red-black tree on n keys that realizes the largest possible ratio of red internal nodes to black internal nodes. What is this ratio? What tree has the smallest possible ratio, and what is the ratio?

13.1-8

Argue that in a red-black tree, a red node cannot have exactly one non-NIL child.

13.2   Rotations

The search-tree operations TREE-INSERT and TREE-DELETE, when run on a red-black tree with n keys, take $O(\lg n)$ time. Because they modify the tree, the result may violate the red-black properties enumerated in Section 13.1. To restore these properties, colors and pointers within nodes need to change.

The pointer structure changes through *rotation*, which is a local operation in a search tree that preserves the binary-search-tree property. Figure 13.2 shows the two kinds of rotations: left rotations and right rotations. Let's look at a left rotation on a node x, which transforms the structure on the right side of the figure to the structure on the left. Node x has a right child y, which must not be $T.nil$. The left rotation changes the subtree originally rooted at x by "twisting" the link between x and y to the left. The new root of the subtree is node y, with x as y's left child and y's original left child (the subtree represented by β in the figure) as x's right child.

The pseudocode for LEFT-ROTATE appearing on the following page assumes that $x.right \neq T.nil$ and that the root's parent is $T.nil$. Figure 13.3 shows an

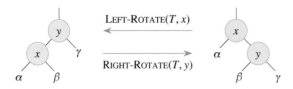

Figure 13.2 The rotation operations on a binary search tree. The operation LEFT-ROTATE(T, x) transforms the configuration of the two nodes on the right into the configuration on the left by changing a constant number of pointers. The inverse operation RIGHT-ROTATE(T, y) transforms the configuration on the left into the configuration on the right. The letters α, β, and γ represent arbitrary subtrees. A rotation operation preserves the binary-search-tree property: the keys in α precede $x.key$, which precedes the keys in β, which precede $y.key$, which precedes the keys in γ.

example of how LEFT-ROTATE modifies a binary search tree. The code for RIGHT-ROTATE is symmetric. Both LEFT-ROTATE and RIGHT-ROTATE run in $O(1)$ time. Only pointers are changed by a rotation, and all other attributes in a node remain the same.

LEFT-ROTATE(T, x)

```
 1  y = x.right
 2  x.right = y.left        // turn y's left subtree into x's right subtree
 3  if y.left ≠ T.nil       // if y's left subtree is not empty . . .
 4      y.left.p = x        // . . . then x becomes the parent of the subtree's root
 5  y.p = x.p               // x's parent becomes y's parent
 6  if x.p == T.nil         // if x was the root . . .
 7      T.root = y          // . . . then y becomes the root
 8  elseif x == x.p.left    // otherwise, if x was a left child . . .
 9      x.p.left = y        // . . . then y becomes a left child
10  else x.p.right = y      // otherwise, x was a right child, and now y is
11  y.left = x             // make x become y's left child
12  x.p = y
```

Exercises

13.2-1
Write pseudocode for RIGHT-ROTATE.

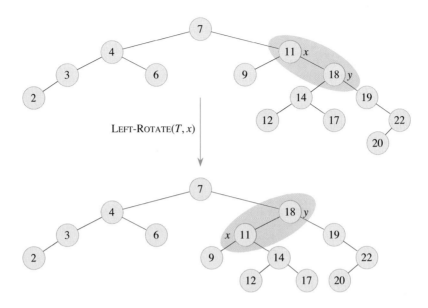

Figure 13.3   An example of how the procedure LEFT-ROTATE(T, x) modifies a binary search tree. Inorder tree walks of the input tree and the modified tree produce the same listing of key values.

13.2-2
Argue that in every n-node binary search tree, there are exactly $n - 1$ possible rotations.

13.2-3
Let a, b, and c be arbitrary nodes in subtrees α, β, and γ, respectively, in the right tree of Figure 13.2. How do the depths of a, b, and c change when a left rotation is performed on node x in the figure?

13.2-4
Show that any arbitrary n-node binary search tree can be transformed into any other arbitrary n-node binary search tree using $O(n)$ rotations. (*Hint:* First show that at most $n - 1$ right rotations suffice to transform the tree into a right-going chain.)

★ ***13.2-5***
We say that a binary search tree T_1 can be ***right-converted*** to binary search tree T_2 if it is possible to obtain T_2 from T_1 via a series of calls to RIGHT-ROTATE. Give an example of two trees T_1 and T_2 such that T_1 cannot be right-converted to T_2. Then, show that if a tree T_1 can be right-converted to T_2, it can be right-converted using $O(n^2)$ calls to RIGHT-ROTATE.

13.3   Insertion

In order to insert a node into a red-black tree with n internal nodes in $O(\lg n)$ time and maintain the red-black properties, we'll need to slightly modify the TREE-INSERT procedure on page 321. The procedure RB-INSERT starts by inserting node z into the tree T as if it were an ordinary binary search tree, and then it colors z red. (Exercise 13.3-1 asks you to explain why to make node z red rather than black.) To guarantee that the red-black properties are preserved, an auxiliary procedure RB-INSERT-FIXUP on the facing page recolors nodes and performs rotations. The call RB-INSERT(T, z) inserts node z, whose *key* is assumed to have already been filled in, into the red-black tree T.

RB-INSERT(T, z)

```
 1   x = T.root              // node being compared with z
 2   y = T.nil               // y will be parent of z
 3   while x ≠ T.nil         // descend until reaching the sentinel
 4       y = x
 5       if z.key < x.key
 6           x = x.left
 7       else x = x.right
 8   z.p = y                 // found the location—insert z with parent y
 9   if y == T.nil
10       T.root = z          // tree T was empty
11   elseif z.key < y.key
12       y.left = z
13   else y.right = z
14   z.left = T.nil          // both of z's children are the sentinel
15   z.right = T.nil
16   z.color = RED           // the new node starts out red
17   RB-INSERT-FIXUP(T, z)   // correct any violations of red-black properties
```

The procedures TREE-INSERT and RB-INSERT differ in four ways. First, all instances of NIL in TREE-INSERT are replaced by $T.nil$. Second, lines 14–15 of RB-INSERT set $z.left$ and $z.right$ to $T.nil$, in order to maintain the proper tree structure. (TREE-INSERT assumed that z's children were already NIL.) Third, line 16 colors z red. Fourth, because coloring z red may cause a violation of one of the red-black properties, line 17 of RB-INSERT calls RB-INSERT-FIXUP(T, z) in order to restore the red-black properties.

RB-INSERT-FIXUP(T, z)

```
 1  while z.p.color == RED
 2      if z.p == z.p.p.left              // is z's parent a left child?
 3          y = z.p.p.right               // y is z's uncle
 4          if y.color == RED             // are z's parent and uncle both red?
 5              z.p.color = BLACK         ⎫
 6              y.color = BLACK           ⎬ case 1
 7              z.p.p.color = RED         ⎪
 8              z = z.p.p                 ⎭
 9          else
10              if z == z.p.right
11                  z = z.p              ⎫ case 2
12                  LEFT-ROTATE(T, z)    ⎭
13              z.p.color = BLACK         ⎫
14              z.p.p.color = RED         ⎬ case 3
15              RIGHT-ROTATE(T, z.p.p)    ⎭
16      else // same as lines 3–15, but with "right" and "left" exchanged
17          y = z.p.p.left
18          if y.color == RED
19              z.p.color = BLACK
20              y.color = BLACK
21              z.p.p.color = RED
22              z = z.p.p
23          else
24              if z == z.p.left
25                  z = z.p
26                  RIGHT-ROTATE(T, z)
27              z.p.color = BLACK
28              z.p.p.color = RED
29              LEFT-ROTATE(T, z.p.p)
30  T.root.color = BLACK
```

To understand how RB-INSERT-FIXUP works, let's examine the code in three major steps. First, we'll determine which violations of the red-black properties might arise in RB-INSERT upon inserting node z and coloring it red. Second, we'll consider the overall goal of the **while** loop in lines 1–29. Finally, we'll explore each of the three cases within the **while** loop's body (case 2 falls through into case 3, so these two cases are not mutually exclusive) and see how they accomplish the goal.

In describing the structure of a red-black tree, we'll often need to refer to the sibling of a node's parent. We use the term *uncle* for such a node.[1] Figure 13.4 shows how RB-INSERT-FIXUP operates on a sample red-black tree, with cases depending in part on the colors of a node, its parent, and its uncle.

What violations of the red-black properties might occur upon the call to RB-INSERT-FIXUP? Property 1 certainly continues to hold (every node is either red or black), as does property 3 (every leaf is black), since both children of the newly inserted red node are the sentinel $T.nil$. Property 5, which says that the number of black nodes is the same on every simple path from a given node, is satisfied as well, because node z replaces the (black) sentinel, and node z is red with sentinel children. Thus, the only properties that might be violated are property 2, which requires the root to be black, and property 4, which says that a red node cannot have a red child. Both possible violations may arise because z is colored red. Property 2 is violated if z is the root, and property 4 is violated if z's parent is red. Figure 13.4(a) shows a violation of property 4 after the node z has been inserted.

The **while** loop of lines 1–29 has two symmetric possibilities: lines 3–15 deal with the situation in which node z's parent $z.p$ is a left child of z's grandparent $z.p.p$, and lines 17–29 apply when z's parent is a right child. Our proof will focus only on lines 3–15, relying on the symmetry in lines 17–29.

We'll show that the **while** loop maintains the following three-part invariant at the start of each iteration of the loop:

a. Node z is red.

b. If $z.p$ is the root, then $z.p$ is black.

c. If the tree violates any of the red-black properties, then it violates at most one of them, and the violation is of either property 2 or property 4, but not both. If the tree violates property 2, it is because z is the root and is red. If the tree violates property 4, it is because both z and $z.p$ are red.

Part (c), which deals with violations of red-black properties, is more central to showing that RB-INSERT-FIXUP restores the red-black properties than parts (a) and (b), which we'll use along the way to understand situations in the code. Because we'll be focusing on node z and nodes near it in the tree, it helps to know from part (a) that z is red. Part (b) will help show that z's grandparent $z.p.p$ exists when it's referenced in lines 2, 3, 7, 8, 14, and 15 (recall that we're focusing only on lines 3–15).

---

[1] Although we try to avoid gendered language in this book, the English language lacks a gender-neutral word for a parent's sibling.

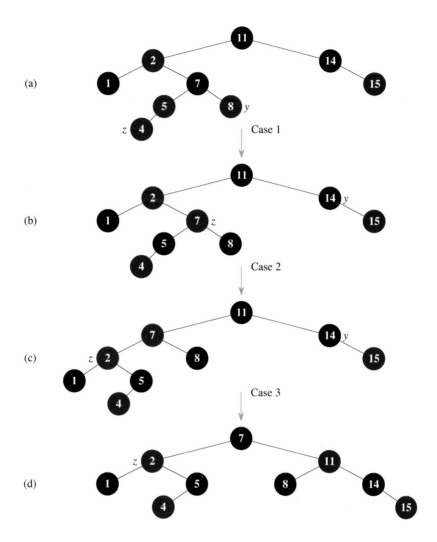

Figure 13.4 The operation of RB-INSERT-FIXUP. **(a)** A node z after insertion. Because both z and its parent $z.p$ are red, a violation of property 4 occurs. Since z's uncle y is red, case 1 in the code applies. Node z's grandparent $z.p.p$ must be black, and its blackness transfers down one level to z's parent and uncle. Once the pointer z moves up two levels in the tree, the tree shown in **(b)** results. Once again, z and its parent are both red, but this time z's uncle y is black. Since z is the right child of $z.p$, case 2 applies. Performing a left rotation results in the tree in **(c)**. Now z is the left child of its parent, and case 3 applies. Recoloring and right rotation yield the tree in **(d)**, which is a legal red-black tree.

Recall that to use a loop invariant, we need to show that the invariant is true upon entering the first iteration of the loop, that each iteration maintains it, that the loop terminates, and that the loop invariant gives us a useful property at loop termination. We'll see that each iteration of the loop has two possible outcomes: either the pointer z moves up the tree, or some rotations occur and then the loop terminates.

Initialization: Before RB-INSERT is called, the red-black tree has no violations. RB-INSERT adds a red node z and calls RB-INSERT-FIXUP. We'll show that each part of the invariant holds at the time RB-INSERT-FIXUP is called:

a. When RB-INSERT-FIXUP is called, z is the red node that was added.

b. If $z.p$ is the root, then $z.p$ started out black and did not change before the call of RB-INSERT-FIXUP.

c. We have already seen that properties 1, 3, and 5 hold when RB-INSERT-FIXUP is called.

If the tree violates property 2 (the root must be black), then the red root must be the newly added node z, which is the only internal node in the tree. Because the parent and both children of z are the sentinel, which is black, the tree does not also violate property 4 (both children of a red node are black). Thus this violation of property 2 is the only violation of red-black properties in the entire tree.

If the tree violates property 4, then, because the children of node z are black sentinels and the tree had no other violations prior to z being added, the violation must be because both z and $z.p$ are red. Moreover, the tree violates no other red-black properties.

Maintenance: There are six cases within the **while** loop, but we'll examine only the three cases in lines 3–15, when node z's parent $z.p$ is a left child of z's grandparent $z.p.p$. The proof for lines 17–29 is symmetric. The node $z.p.p$ exists, since by part (b) of the loop invariant, if $z.p$ is the root, then $z.p$ is black. Since RB-INSERT-FIXUP enters a loop iteration only if $z.p$ is red, we know that $z.p$ cannot be the root. Hence, $z.p.p$ exists.

Case 1 differs from cases 2 and 3 by the color of z's uncle y. Line 3 makes y point to z's uncle $z.p.p.right$, and line 4 tests y's color. If y is red, then case 1 executes. Otherwise, control passes to cases 2 and 3. In all three cases, z's grandparent $z.p.p$ is black, since its parent $z.p$ is red, and property 4 is violated only between z and $z.p$.

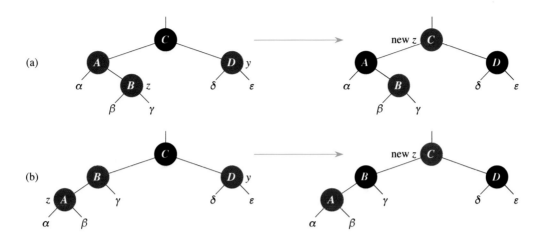

Figure 13.5   Case 1 of the procedure RB-INSERT-FIXUP. Both z and its parent $z.p$ are red, violating property 4. In case 1, z's uncle y is red. The same action occurs regardless of whether **(a)** z is a right child or **(b)** z is a left child. Each of the subtrees α, β, γ, δ, and ε has a black root—possibly the sentinel—and each has the same black-height. The code for case 1 moves the blackness of z's grandparent down to z's parent and uncle, preserving property 5: all downward simple paths from a node to a leaf have the same number of blacks. The **while** loop continues with node z's grandparent $z.p.p$ as the new z. If the action of case 1 causes a new violation of property 4 to occur, it must be only between the new z, which is red, and its parent, if it is red as well.

Case 1: z's uncle y is red

Figure 13.5 shows the situation for case 1 (lines 5–8), which occurs when both $z.p$ and y are red. Because z's grandparent $z.p.p$ is black, its blackness can transfer down one level to both $z.p$ and y, thereby fixing the problem of z and $z.p$ both being red. Having had its blackness transferred down one level, z's grandparent becomes red, thereby maintaining property 5. The **while** loop repeats with $z.p.p$ as the new node z, so that the pointer z moves up two levels in the tree.

Now, we show that case 1 maintains the loop invariant at the start of the next iteration. We use z to denote node z in the current iteration, and $z' = z.p.p$ to denote the node that will be called node z at the test in line 1 upon the next iteration.

a. Because this iteration colors $z.p.p$ red, node z' is red at the start of the next iteration.

b. The node $z'.p$ is $z.p.p.p$ in this iteration, and the color of this node does not change. If this node is the root, it was black prior to this iteration, and it remains black at the start of the next iteration.

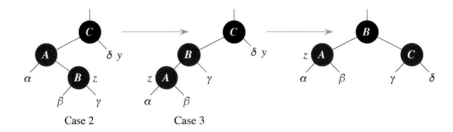

Figure 13.6 Cases 2 and 3 of the procedure RB-INSERT-FIXUP. As in case 1, property 4 is violated in either case 2 or case 3 because z and its parent $z.p$ are both red. Each of the subtrees α, β, γ, and δ has a black root (α, β, and γ from property 4, and δ because otherwise case 1 would apply), and each has the same black-height. Case 2 transforms into case 3 by a left rotation, which preserves property 5: all downward simple paths from a node to a leaf have the same number of blacks. Case 3 causes some color changes and a right rotation, which also preserve property 5. The **while** loop then terminates, because property 4 is satisfied: there are no longer two red nodes in a row.

c. We have already argued that case 1 maintains property 5, and it does not introduce a violation of properties 1 or 3.

If node z' is the root at the start of the next iteration, then case 1 corrected the lone violation of property 4 in this iteration. Since z' is red and it is the root, property 2 becomes the only one that is violated, and this violation is due to z'.

If node z' is not the root at the start of the next iteration, then case 1 has not created a violation of property 2. Case 1 corrected the lone violation of property 4 that existed at the start of this iteration. It then made z' red and left $z'.p$ alone. If $z'.p$ was black, there is no violation of property 4. If $z'.p$ was red, coloring z' red created one violation of property 4, between z' and $z'.p$.

Case 2: *z's uncle y is black and z is a right child*
Case 3: *z's uncle y is black and z is a left child*

In cases 2 and 3, the color of z's uncle y is black. We distinguish the two cases, which assume that z's parent $z.p$ is red and a left child, according to whether z is a right or left child of $z.p$. Lines 11–12 constitute case 2, which is shown in Figure 13.6 together with case 3. In case 2, node z is a right child of its parent. A left rotation immediately transforms the situation into case 3 (lines 13–15), in which node z is a left child. Because both z and $z.p$ are red, the rotation affects neither the black-heights of nodes nor property 5. Whether case 3 executes directly or through case 2, z's uncle y is black, since otherwise case 1 would have run. Additionally, the node $z.p.p$ exists, since we have argued that this node existed at the time that lines 2 and 3 were executed, and after moving z up one level in line 11 and then down one level in line 12, the identity of $z.p.p$ remains unchanged. Case 3 performs some color changes and a right rotation, which preserve property 5. At this point, there are no longer two red nodes in a row. The **while** loop terminates upon the next test in line 1, since $z.p$ is now black.

We now show that cases 2 and 3 maintain the loop invariant. (As we have just argued, $z.p$ will be black upon the next test in line 1, and the loop body will not execute again.)

a. Case 2 makes z point to $z.p$, which is red. No further change to z or its color occurs in cases 2 and 3.

b. Case 3 makes $z.p$ black, so that if $z.p$ is the root at the start of the next iteration, it is black.

c. As in case 1, properties 1, 3, and 5 are maintained in cases 2 and 3.

Since node z is not the root in cases 2 and 3, we know that there is no violation of property 2. Cases 2 and 3 do not introduce a violation of property 2, since the only node that is made red becomes a child of a black node by the rotation in case 3.

Cases 2 and 3 correct the lone violation of property 4, and they do not introduce another violation.

Termination: To see that the loop terminates, observe that if only case 1 occurs, then the node pointer z moves toward the root in each iteration, so that eventually $z.p$ is black. (If z is the root, then $z.p$ is the sentinel $T.nil$, which is black.) If either case 2 or case 3 occurs, then we've seen that the loop terminates. Since the loop terminates because $z.p$ is black, the tree does not violate property 4 at loop termination. By the loop invariant, the only property that might fail to hold is property 2. Line 30 restores this property by coloring the root black, so that when RB-INSERT-FIXUP terminates, all the red-black properties hold.

Thus, we have shown that RB-INSERT-FIXUP correctly restores the red-black properties.

Analysis

What is the running time of RB-INSERT? Since the height of a red-black tree on n nodes is $O(\lg n)$, lines 1–16 of RB-INSERT take $O(\lg n)$ time. In RB-INSERT-FIXUP, the **while** loop repeats only if case 1 occurs, and then the pointer z moves two levels up the tree. The total number of times the **while** loop can be executed is therefore $O(\lg n)$. Thus, RB-INSERT takes a total of $O(\lg n)$ time. Moreover, it never performs more than two rotations, since the **while** loop terminates if case 2 or case 3 is executed.

Exercises

13.3-1
Line 16 of RB-INSERT sets the color of the newly inserted node z to red. If instead z's color were set to black, then property 4 of a red-black tree would not be violated. Why not set z's color to black?

13.3-2
Show the red-black trees that result after successively inserting the keys $41, 38, 31, 12, 19, 8$ into an initially empty red-black tree.

13.3-3
Suppose that the black-height of each of the subtrees $\alpha, \beta, \gamma, \delta, \varepsilon$ in Figures 13.5 and 13.6 is k. Label each node in each figure with its black-height to verify that the indicated transformation preserves property 5.

13.3-4
Professor Teach is concerned that RB-INSERT-FIXUP might set $T.nil.color$ to RED, in which case the test in line 1 would not cause the loop to terminate when z is the root. Show that the professor's concern is unfounded by arguing that RB-INSERT-FIXUP never sets $T.nil.color$ to RED.

13.3-5
Consider a red-black tree formed by inserting n nodes with RB-INSERT. Argue that if $n > 1$, the tree has at least one red node.

13.3-6
Suggest how to implement RB-INSERT efficiently if the representation for red-black trees includes no storage for parent pointers.

13.4 Deletion

Like the other basic operations on an n-node red-black tree, deletion of a node takes $O(\lg n)$ time. Deleting a node from a red-black tree is more complicated than inserting a node.

The procedure for deleting a node from a red-black tree is based on the TREE-DELETE procedure on page 325. First, we need to customize the TRANSPLANT subroutine on page 324 that TREE-DELETE calls so that it applies to a red-black tree. Like TRANSPLANT, the new procedure RB-TRANSPLANT replaces the subtree rooted at node u by the subtree rooted at node v. The RB-TRANSPLANT procedure differs from TRANSPLANT in two ways. First, line 1 references the sentinel $T.nil$ instead of NIL. Second, the assignment to $v.p$ in line 6 occurs unconditionally: the procedure can assign to $v.p$ even if v points to the sentinel. We'll take advantage of the ability to assign to $v.p$ when $v = T.nil$.

RB-TRANSPLANT(T, u, v)

```
1  if u.p == T.nil
2      T.root = v
3  elseif u == u.p.left
4      u.p.left = v
5  else u.p.right = v
6  v.p = u.p
```

The procedure RB-DELETE on the next page is like the TREE-DELETE procedure, but with additional lines of pseudocode. The additional lines deal with nodes x and y that may be involved in violations of the red-black properties. When the node z being deleted has at most one child, then y will be z. When z has two children, then, as in TREE-DELETE, y will be z's successor, which has no left child and moves into z's position in the tree. Additionally, y takes on z's color. In either case, node y has at most one child: node x, which takes y's place in the tree. (Node x will be the sentinel $T.nil$ if y has no children.) Since node y will be either removed from the tree or moved within the tree, the procedure needs to keep track of y's original color. If the red-black properties might be violated after deleting node z, RB-DELETE calls the auxiliary procedure RB-DELETE-FIXUP, which changes colors and performs rotations to restore the red-black properties.

Although RB-DELETE contains almost twice as many lines of pseudocode as TREE-DELETE, the two procedures have the same basic structure. You can find each line of TREE-DELETE within RB-DELETE (with the changes of replacing NIL by $T.nil$ and replacing calls to TRANSPLANT by calls to RB-TRANSPLANT), executed under the same conditions.

In detail, here are the other differences between the two procedures:

- Lines 1 and 9 set node y as described above: line 1 when node z has at most one child and line 9 when z has two children.

- Because node y's color might change, the variable *y-original-color* stores y's color before any changes occur. Lines 2 and 10 set this variable immediately after assignments to y. When node z has two children, then nodes y and z are

```
RB-DELETE(T, z)

1   y = z
2   y-original-color = y.color
3   if z.left == T.nil
4       x = z.right
5       RB-TRANSPLANT(T, z, z.right)        // replace z by its right child
6   elseif z.right == T.nil
7       x = z.left
8       RB-TRANSPLANT(T, z, z.left)         // replace z by its left child
9   else y = TREE-MINIMUM(z.right)          // y is z's successor
10       y-original-color = y.color
11       x = y.right
12       if y ≠ z.right                     // is y farther down the tree?
13           RB-TRANSPLANT(T, y, y.right)   // replace y by its right child
14           y.right = z.right              // z's right child becomes
15           y.right.p = y                  //     y's right child
16       else x.p = y                       // in case x is T.nil
17       RB-TRANSPLANT(T, z, y)             // replace z by its successor y
18       y.left = z.left                    // and give z's left child to y,
19       y.left.p = y                       //     which had no left child
20       y.color = z.color
21   if y-original-color == BLACK           // if any red-black violations occurred,
22       RB-DELETE-FIXUP(T, x)              //     correct them
```

distinct. In this case, line 17 moves y into z's original position in the tree (that is, z's location in the tree at the time RB-DELETE was called), and line 20 gives y the same color as z. When node y was originally black, removing or moving it could cause violations of the red-black properties, which are corrected by the call of RB-DELETE-FIXUP in line 22.

- As discussed, the procedure keeps track of the node x that moves into node y's original position at the time of call. The assignments in lines 4, 7, and 11 set x to point to either y's only child or, if y has no children, the sentinel $T.nil$.

- Since node x moves into node y's original position, the attribute $x.p$ must be set correctly. If node z has two children and y is z's right child, then y just moves into z's position, with x remaining a child of y. Line 12 checks for this case. Although you might think that setting $x.p$ to y in line 16 is unnecessary since x is a child of y, the call of RB-DELETE-FIXUP relies on $x.p$ being y even if x is $T.nil$. Thus, when z has two children and y is z's right child, executing line 16 is necessary if y's right child is $T.nil$, and otherwise it does not change anything.

Otherwise, node z is either the same as node y or it is a proper ancestor of y's original parent. In these cases, the calls of RB-TRANSPLANT in lines 5, 8, and 13 set $x.p$ correctly in line 6 of RB-TRANSPLANT. (In these calls of RB-TRANSPLANT, the third parameter passed is the same as x.)

- Finally, if node y was black, one or more violations of the red-black properties might arise. The call of RB-DELETE-FIXUP in line 22 restores the red-black properties. If y was red, the red-black properties still hold when y is removed or moved, for the following reasons:

  1. No black-heights in the tree have changed. (See Exercise 13.4-1.)
  2. No red nodes have been made adjacent. If z has at most one child, then y and z are the same node. That node is removed, with a child taking its place. If the removed node was red, then neither its parent nor its children can also be red, so moving a child to take its place cannot cause two red nodes to become adjacent. If, on the other hand, z has two children, then y takes z's place in the tree, along with z's color, so there cannot be two adjacent red nodes at y's new position in the tree. In addition, if y was not z's right child, then y's original right child x replaces y in the tree. Since y is red, x must be black, and so replacing y by x cannot cause two red nodes to become adjacent.
  3. Because y could not have been the root if it was red, the root remains black.

If node y was black, three problems may arise, which the call of RB-DELETE-FIXUP will remedy. First, if y was the root and a red child of y became the new root, property 2 is violated. Second, if both x and its new parent are red, then a violation of property 4 occurs. Third, moving y within the tree causes any simple path that previously contained y to have one less black node. Thus, property 5 is now violated by any ancestor of y in the tree. We can correct the violation of property 5 by saying that when the black node y is removed or moved, its blackness transfers to the node x that moves into y's original position, giving x an "extra" black. That is, if we add 1 to the count of black nodes on any simple path that contains x, then under this interpretation, property 5 holds. But now another problem emerges: node x is neither red nor black, thereby violating property 1. Instead, node x is either "doubly black" or "red-and-black," and it contributes either 2 or 1, respectively, to the count of black nodes on simple paths containing x. The *color* attribute of x will still be either RED (if x is red-and-black) or BLACK (if x is doubly black). In other words, the extra black on a node is reflected in x's pointing to the node rather than in the *color* attribute.

The procedure RB-DELETE-FIXUP on the next page restores properties 1, 2, and 4. Exercises 13.4-2 and 13.4-3 ask you to show that the procedure restores properties 2 and 4, and so in the remainder of this section, we focus on property 1. The goal of the **while** loop in lines 1–43 is to move the extra black up the tree until

1. x points to a red-and-black node, in which case line 44 colors x (singly) black;

2. x points to the root, in which case the extra black simply vanishes; or

3. having performed suitable rotations and recolorings, the loop exits.

Like RB-INSERT-FIXUP, the RB-DELETE-FIXUP procedure handles two symmetric situations: lines 3–22 for when node x is a left child, and lines 24–43 for when x is a right child. Our proof focuses on the four cases shown in lines 3–22.

Within the **while** loop, x always points to a nonroot doubly black node. Line 2 determines whether x is a left child or a right child of its parent $x.p$ so that either lines 3–22 or 24–43 will execute in a given iteration. The sibling of x is always denoted by a pointer w. Since node x is doubly black, node w cannot be $T.nil$, because otherwise, the number of blacks on the simple path from $x.p$ to the (singly black) leaf w would be smaller than the number on the simple path from $x.p$ to x.

Recall that the RB-DELETE procedure always assigns to $x.p$ before calling RB-DELETE-FIXUP (either within the call of RB-TRANSPLANT in line 13 or the assignment in line 16), even when node x is the sentinel $T.nil$. That is because RB-DELETE-FIXUP references x's parent $x.p$ in several places, and this attribute must point to the node that became x's parent in RB-DELETE—even if x is $T.nil$.

Figure 13.7 demonstrates the four cases in the code when node x is a left child. (As in RB-INSERT-FIXUP, the cases in RB-DELETE-FIXUP are not mutually exclusive.) Before examining each case in detail, let's look more generally at how we can verify that the transformation in each of the cases preserves property 5. The key idea is that in each case, the transformation applied preserves the number of black nodes (including x's extra black) from (and including) the root of the subtree shown to the roots of each of the subtrees $\alpha, \beta, \ldots, \zeta$. Thus, if property 5 holds prior to the transformation, it continues to hold afterward. For example, in Figure 13.7(a), which illustrates case 1, the number of black nodes from the root to the root of either subtree α or β is 3, both before and after the transformation. (Again, remember that node x adds an extra black.) Similarly, the number of black nodes from the root to the root of any of $\gamma, \delta, \varepsilon,$ and ζ is 2, both before and after the transformation.[2] In Figure 13.7(b), the counting must involve the value c of the *color* attribute of the root of the subtree shown, which can be either RED or BLACK.

---

[2] If property 5 holds, we can assume that paths from the roots of $\gamma, \delta, \varepsilon,$ and ζ down to leaves contain one more black than do paths from the roots of α and β down to leaves.

RB-DELETE-FIXUP(T, x)

```
 1  while x ≠ T.root and x.color == BLACK
 2      if x == x.p.left              // is x a left child?
 3          w = x.p.right             // w is x's sibling
 4          if w.color == RED
 5              w.color = BLACK
 6              x.p.color = RED                           ⎫
 7              LEFT-ROTATE(T, x.p)                        ⎬ case 1
 8              w = x.p.right                             ⎭
 9          if w.left.color == BLACK and w.right.color == BLACK
10              w.color = RED                             ⎫ case 2
11              x = x.p                                   ⎭
12          else
13              if w.right.color == BLACK
14                  w.left.color = BLACK                  ⎫
15                  w.color = RED                          ⎬ case 3
16                  RIGHT-ROTATE(T, w)                    ⎭
17                  w = x.p.right
18              w.color = x.p.color                       ⎫
19              x.p.color = BLACK                          ⎬ case 4
20              w.right.color = BLACK                     ⎭
21              LEFT-ROTATE(T, x.p)
22              x = T.root
23      else // same as lines 3–22, but with "right" and "left" exchanged
24          w = x.p.left
25          if w.color == RED
26              w.color = BLACK
27              x.p.color = RED
28              RIGHT-ROTATE(T, x.p)
29              w = x.p.left
30          if w.right.color == BLACK and w.left.color == BLACK
31              w.color = RED
32              x = x.p
33          else
34              if w.left.color == BLACK
35                  w.right.color = BLACK
36                  w.color = RED
37                  LEFT-ROTATE(T, w)
38                  w = x.p.left
39              w.color = x.p.color
40              x.p.color = BLACK
41              w.left.color = BLACK
42              RIGHT-ROTATE(T, x.p)
43              x = T.root
44  x.color = BLACK
```

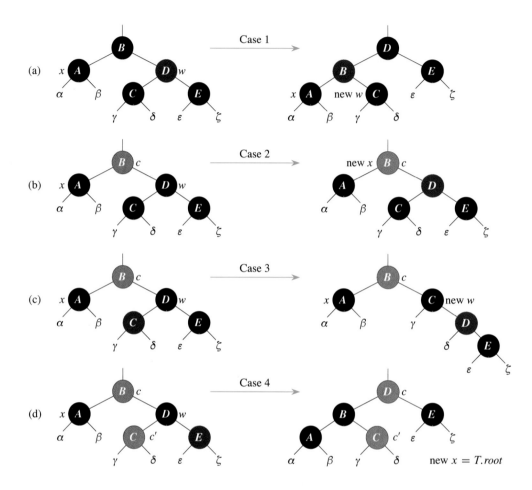

Figure 13.7   The cases in lines 3–22 of the procedure RB-DELETE-FIXUP. Brown nodes have *color* attributes represented by c and c', which may be either RED or BLACK. The letters $\alpha, \beta, \ldots, \zeta$ represent arbitrary subtrees. Each case transforms the configuration on the left into the configuration on the right by changing some colors and/or performing a rotation. Any node pointed to by x has an extra black and is either doubly black or red-and-black. Only case 2 causes the loop to repeat. **(a)** Case 1 is transformed into case 2, 3, or 4 by exchanging the colors of nodes B and D and performing a left rotation. **(b)** In case 2, the extra black represented by the pointer x moves up the tree by coloring node D red and setting x to point to node B. If case 2 is entered through case 1, the **while** loop terminates because the new node x is red-and-black, and therefore the value c of its *color* attribute is RED. **(c)** Case 3 is transformed to case 4 by exchanging the colors of nodes C and D and performing a right rotation. **(d)** Case 4 removes the extra black represented by x by changing some colors and performing a left rotation (without violating the red-black properties), and then the loop terminates.

If we define count(RED) $= 0$ and count(BLACK) $= 1$, then the number of black nodes from the root to α is $2 + \text{count}(c)$, both before and after the transformation. In this case, after the transformation, the new node x has *color* attribute c, but this node is really either red-and-black (if $c = \text{RED}$) or doubly black (if $c = \text{BLACK}$). You can verify the other cases similarly (see Exercise 13.4-6).

Case 1: x's sibling w is red

Case 1 (lines 5–8 and Figure 13.7(a)) occurs when node w, the sibling of node x, is red. Because w is red, it must have black children. This case switches the colors of w and $x.p$ and then performs a left-rotation on $x.p$ without violating any of the red-black properties. The new sibling of x, which is one of w's children prior to the rotation, is now black, and thus case 1 converts into one of cases 2, 3, or 4.

Cases 2, 3, and 4 occur when node w is black and are distinguished by the colors of w's children.

Case 2: x's sibling w is black, and both of w's children are black

In case 2 (lines 10–11 and Figure 13.7(b)), both of w's children are black. Since w is also black, this case removes one black from both x and w, leaving x with only one black and leaving w red. To compensate for x and w each losing one black, x's parent $x.p$ can take on an extra black. Line 11 does so by moving x up one level, so that the **while** loop repeats with $x.p$ as the new node x. If case 2 enters through case 1, the new node x is red-and-black, since the original $x.p$ was red. Hence, the value c of the *color* attribute of the new node x is RED, and the loop terminates when it tests the loop condition. Line 44 then colors the new node x (singly) black.

Case 3: x's sibling w is black, w's left child is red, and w's right child is black

Case 3 (lines 14–17 and Figure 13.7(c)) occurs when w is black, its left child is red, and its right child is black. This case switches the colors of w and its left child $w.left$ and then performs a right rotation on w without violating any of the red-black properties. The new sibling w of x is now a black node with a red right child, and thus case 3 falls through into case 4.

Case 4: x's sibling w is black, and w's right child is red

Case 4 (lines 18–22 and Figure 13.7(d)) occurs when node x's sibling w is black and w's right child is red. Some color changes and a left rotation on $x.p$ allow the extra black on x to vanish, making it singly black, without violating any of the red-black properties. Line 22 sets x to be the root, and the **while** loop terminates when it next tests the loop condition.

Analysis

What is the running time of RB-DELETE? Since the height of a red-black tree of n nodes is $O(\lg n)$, the total cost of the procedure without the call to RB-DELETE-FIXUP takes $O(\lg n)$ time. Within RB-DELETE-FIXUP, each of cases 1, 3, and 4 lead to termination after performing a constant number of color changes and at most three rotations. Case 2 is the only case in which the **while** loop can be repeated, and then the pointer x moves up the tree at most $O(\lg n)$ times, performing no rotations. Thus, the procedure RB-DELETE-FIXUP takes $O(\lg n)$ time and performs at most three rotations, and the overall time for RB-DELETE is therefore also $O(\lg n)$.

Exercises

13.4-1
Show that if node y in RB-DELETE is red, then no black-heights change.

13.4-2
Argue that after RB-DELETE-FIXUP executes, the root of the tree must be black.

13.4-3
Argue that if in RB-DELETE both x and $x.p$ are red, then property 4 is restored by the call to RB-DELETE-FIXUP(T, x).

13.4-4
In Exercise 13.3-2 on page 346, you found the red-black tree that results from successively inserting the keys $41, 38, 31, 12, 19, 8$ into an initially empty tree. Now show the red-black trees that result from the successive deletion of the keys in the order $8, 12, 19, 31, 38, 41$.

13.4-5
Which lines of the code for RB-DELETE-FIXUP might examine or modify the sentinel $T.nil$?

13.4-6
In each of the cases of Figure 13.7, give the count of black nodes from the root of the subtree shown to the roots of each of the subtrees $\alpha, \beta, \ldots, \zeta$, and verify that each count remains the same after the transformation. When a node has a *color* attribute c or c', use the notation count(c) or count(c') symbolically in your count.

13.4-7
Professors Skelton and Baron worry that at the start of case 1 of RB-DELETE-FIXUP, the node $x.p$ might not be black. If $x.p$ is not black, then lines 5–6 are

wrong. Show that $x.p$ must be black at the start of case 1, so that the professors need not be concerned.

13.4-8
A node x is inserted into a red-black tree with RB-INSERT and then is immediately deleted with RB-DELETE. Is the resulting red-black tree always the same as the initial red-black tree? Justify your answer.

★ 13.4-9
Consider the operation RB-ENUMERATE(T, r, a, b), which outputs all the keys k such that $a \leq k \leq b$ in a subtree rooted at node r in an n-node red-black tree T. Describe how to implement RB-ENUMERATE in $\Theta(m + \lg n)$ time, where m is the number of keys that are output. Assume that the keys in T are unique and that the values a and b appear as keys in T. How does your solution change if a and b might not appear in T?

Problems

13-1   *Persistent dynamic sets*
During the course of an algorithm, you sometimes find that you need to maintain past versions of a dynamic set as it is updated. We call such a set *persistent*. One way to implement a persistent set is to copy the entire set whenever it is modified, but this approach can slow down a program and also consume a lot of space. Sometimes, you can do much better.

Consider a persistent set S with the operations INSERT, DELETE, and SEARCH, which you implement using binary search trees as shown in Figure 13.8(a). Maintain a separate root for every version of the set. In order to insert the key 5 into the set, create a new node with key 5. This node becomes the left child of a new node with key 7, since you cannot modify the existing node with key 7. Similarly, the new node with key 7 becomes the left child of a new node with key 8 whose right child is the existing node with key 10. The new node with key 8 becomes, in turn, the right child of a new root r' with key 4 whose left child is the existing node with key 3. Thus, you copy only part of the tree and share some of the nodes with the original tree, as shown in Figure 13.8(b).

Assume that each tree node has the attributes *key*, *left*, and *right* but no parent. (See also Exercise 13.3-6 on page 346.)

a. For a persistent binary search tree (not a red-black tree, just a binary search tree), identify the nodes that need to change to insert or delete a node.

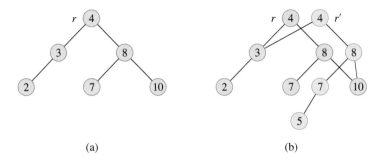

Figure 13.8 **(a)** A binary search tree with keys $2, 3, 4, 7, 8, 10$. **(b)** The persistent binary search tree that results from the insertion of key 5. The most recent version of the set consists of the nodes reachable from the root r', and the previous version consists of the nodes reachable from r. Blue nodes are added when key 5 is inserted.

b. Write a procedure PERSISTENT-TREE-INSERT(T, z) that, given a persistent binary search tree T and a node z to insert, returns a new persistent tree T' that is the result of inserting z into T. Assume that you have a procedure COPY-NODE(x) that makes a copy of node x, including all of its attributes.

c. If the height of the persistent binary search tree T is h, what are the time and space requirements of your implementation of PERSISTENT-TREE-INSERT? (The space requirement is proportional to the number of nodes that are copied.)

d. Suppose that you include the parent attribute in each node. In this case, the PERSISTENT-TREE-INSERT procedure needs to perform additional copying. Prove that PERSISTENT-TREE-INSERT then requires $\Omega(n)$ time and space, where n is the number of nodes in the tree.

e. Show how to use red-black trees to guarantee that the worst-case running time and space are $O(\lg n)$ per insertion or deletion. You may assume that all keys are distinct.

13-2   *Join operation on red-black trees*

The *join* operation takes two dynamic sets S_1 and S_2 and an element x such that for any $x_1 \in S_1$ and $x_2 \in S_2$, we have $x_1.key \leq x.key \leq x_2.key$. It returns a set $S = S_1 \cup \{x\} \cup S_2$. In this problem, we investigate how to implement the join operation on red-black trees.

a. Suppose that you store the black-height of a red-black tree T as the new attribute $T.bh$. Argue that RB-INSERT and RB-DELETE can maintain the *bh* attribute without requiring extra storage in the nodes of the tree and without increasing the asymptotic running times. Show how to determine the black-height of each node visited while descending through T, using $O(1)$ time per node visited.

Let T_1 and T_2 be red-black trees and x be a key value such that for any nodes x_1 in T_1 and x_2 in T_2, we have $x_1.key \leq x.key \leq x_2.key$. You will show how to implement the operation RB-JOIN(T_1, x, T_2), which destroys T_1 and T_2 and returns a red-black tree $T = T_1 \cup \{x\} \cup T_2$. Let n be the total number of nodes in T_1 and T_2.

b. Assume that $T_1.bh \geq T_2.bh$. Describe an $O(\lg n)$-time algorithm that finds a black node y in T_1 with the largest key from among those nodes whose black-height is $T_2.bh$.

c. Let T_y be the subtree rooted at y. Describe how $T_y \cup \{x\} \cup T_2$ can replace T_y in $O(1)$ time without destroying the binary-search-tree property.

d. What color should you make x so that red-black properties 1, 3, and 5 are maintained? Describe how to enforce properties 2 and 4 in $O(\lg n)$ time.

e. Argue that no generality is lost by making the assumption in part (b). Describe the symmetric situation that arises when $T_1.bh \leq T_2.bh$.

f. Argue that the running time of RB-JOIN is $O(\lg n)$.

13-3 AVL trees

An *AVL tree* is a binary search tree that is *height balanced*: for each node x, the heights of the left and right subtrees of x differ by at most 1. To implement an AVL tree, maintain an extra attribute h in each node such that $x.h$ is the height of node x. As for any other binary search tree T, assume that $T.root$ points to the root node.

a. Prove that an AVL tree with n nodes has height $O(\lg n)$. (*Hint:* Prove that an AVL tree of height h has at least F_h nodes, where F_h is the hth Fibonacci number.)

b. To insert into an AVL tree, first place a node into the appropriate place in binary search tree order. Afterward, the tree might no longer be height balanced. Specifically, the heights of the left and right children of some node might differ by 2. Describe a procedure BALANCE(x), which takes a subtree rooted at x whose left and right children are height balanced and have heights that differ by at most 2, so that $|x.right.h - x.left.h| \leq 2$, and alters the subtree rooted at x to be height balanced. The procedure should return a pointer to the node that is the root of the subtree after alterations occur. (*Hint:* Use rotations.)

c. Using part (b), describe a recursive procedure AVL-INSERT(T, z) that takes an AVL tree T and a newly created node z (whose key has already been filled in), and adds z into T, maintaining the property that T is an AVL tree. As in TREE-INSERT from Section 12.3, assume that $z.key$ has already been filled in and that $z.left = $ NIL and $z.right = $ NIL. Assume as well that $z.h = 0$.

d. Show that AVL-INSERT, run on an n-node AVL tree, takes $O(\lg n)$ time and performs $O(\lg n)$ rotations.

Chapter notes

The idea of balancing a search tree is due to Adel'son-Vel'skiĭ and Landis [2], who introduced a class of balanced search trees called "AVL trees" in 1962, described in Problem 13-3. Another class of search trees, called "2-3 trees," was introduced by J. E. Hopcroft (unpublished) in 1970. A 2-3 tree maintains balance by manipulating the degrees of nodes in the tree, where each node has either two or three children. Chapter 18 covers a generalization of 2-3 trees introduced by Bayer and McCreight [39], called "B-trees."

Red-black trees were invented by Bayer [38] under the name "symmetric binary B-trees." Guibas and Sedgewick [202] studied their properties at length and introduced the red/black color convention. Andersson [16] gives a simpler-to-code variant of red-black trees. Weiss [451] calls this variant AA-trees. An AA-tree is similar to a red-black tree except that left children can never be red.

Sedgewick and Wayne [402] present red-black trees as a modified version of 2-3 trees in which a node with three children is split into two nodes with two children each. One of these nodes becomes the left child of the other, and only left children can be red. They call this structure a "left-leaning red-black binary search tree." Although the code for left-leaning red-black binary search trees is more concise than the red-black tree pseudocode in this chapter, operations on left-leaning red-black binary search trees do not limit the number of rotations per operation to a constant. This distinction will matter in Chapter 17.

Treaps, a hybrid of binary search trees and heaps, were proposed by Seidel and Aragon [404]. They are the default implementation of a dictionary in LEDA [324], which is a well-implemented collection of data structures and algorithms.

There are many other variations on balanced binary trees, including weight-balanced trees [344], k-neighbor trees [318], and scapegoat trees [174]. Perhaps the most intriguing are the "splay trees" introduced by Sleator and Tarjan [418], which are "self-adjusting." (See Tarjan [429] for a good description of splay trees.) Splay trees maintain balance without any explicit balance condition such as color. Instead, "splay operations" (which involve rotations) are performed within the tree every time an access is made. The amortized cost (see Chapter 16) of each operation on an n-node tree is $O(\lg n)$. Splay trees have been conjectured to perform within a constant factor of the best offline rotation-based tree. The best known competitive ratio (see Chapter 27) for a rotation-based tree is the Tango Tree of Demaine et al. [109].

Skip lists [369] provide an alternative to balanced binary trees. A skip list is a linked list that is augmented with a number of additional pointers. Each dictionary operation runs in $O(\lg n)$ expected time on a skip list of n items.

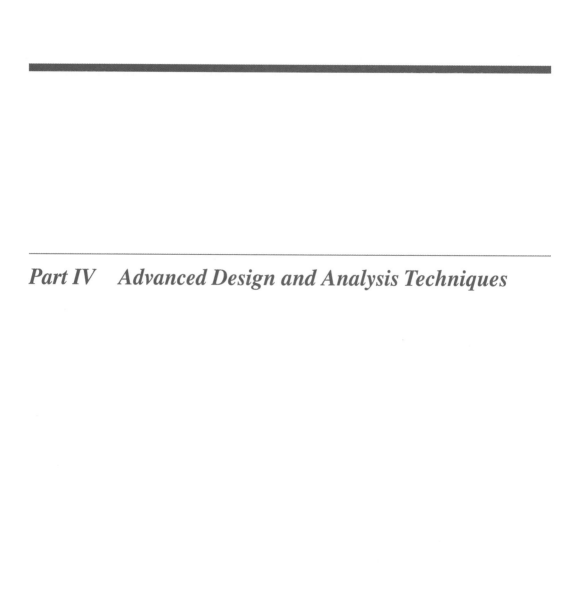

Part IV   Advanced Design and Analysis Techniques

Introduction

This part covers three important techniques used in designing and analyzing efficient algorithms: dynamic programming (Chapter 14), greedy algorithms (Chapter 15), and amortized analysis (Chapter 16). Earlier parts have presented other widely applicable techniques, such as divide-and-conquer, randomization, and how to solve recurrences. The techniques in this part are somewhat more sophisticated, but you will be able to use them solve many computational problems. The themes introduced in this part will recur later in this book.

Dynamic programming typically applies to optimization problems in which you make a set of choices in order to arrive at an optimal solution, each choice generates subproblems of the same form as the original problem, and the same subproblems arise repeatedly. The key strategy is to store the solution to each such subproblem rather than recompute it. Chapter 14 shows how this simple idea can sometimes transform exponential-time algorithms into polynomial-time algorithms.

Like dynamic-programming algorithms, greedy algorithms typically apply to optimization problems in which you make a set of choices in order to arrive at an optimal solution. The idea of a greedy algorithm is to make each choice in a locally optimal manner, resulting in a faster algorithm than you get with dynamic programming. Chapter 15 will help you determine when the greedy approach works.

The technique of amortized analysis applies to certain algorithms that perform a sequence of similar operations. Instead of bounding the cost of the sequence of operations by bounding the actual cost of each operation separately, an amortized analysis provides a worst-case bound on the actual cost of the entire sequence. One advantage of this approach is that although some operations might be expensive, many others might be cheap. You can use amortized analysis when designing algorithms, since the design of an algorithm and the analysis of its running time are often closely intertwined. Chapter 16 introduces three ways to perform an amortized analysis of an algorithm.

14 Dynamic Programming

Dynamic programming, like the divide-and-conquer method, solves problems by combining the solutions to subproblems. ("Programming" in this context refers to a tabular method, not to writing computer code.) As we saw in Chapters 2 and 4, divide-and-conquer algorithms partition the problem into disjoint subproblems, solve the subproblems recursively, and then combine their solutions to solve the original problem. In contrast, dynamic programming applies when the subproblems overlap—that is, when subproblems share subsubproblems. In this context, a divide-and-conquer algorithm does more work than necessary, repeatedly solving the common subsubproblems. A dynamic-programming algorithm solves each subsubproblem just once and then saves its answer in a table, thereby avoiding the work of recomputing the answer every time it solves each subsubproblem.

Dynamic programming typically applies to *optimization problems*. Such problems can have many possible solutions. Each solution has a value, and you want to find a solution with the optimal (minimum or maximum) value. We call such a solution *an* optimal solution to the problem, as opposed to *the* optimal solution, since there may be several solutions that achieve the optimal value.

To develop a dynamic-programming algorithm, follow a sequence of four steps:

1. Characterize the structure of an optimal solution.

2. Recursively define the value of an optimal solution.

3. Compute the value of an optimal solution, typically in a bottom-up fashion.

4. Construct an optimal solution from computed information.

Steps 1–3 form the basis of a dynamic-programming solution to a problem. If you need only the value of an optimal solution, and not the solution itself, then you can omit step 4. When you do perform step 4, it often pays to maintain additional information during step 3 so that you can easily construct an optimal solution.

The sections that follow use the dynamic-programming method to solve some optimization problems. Section 14.1 examines the problem of cutting a rod into

rods of smaller length in a way that maximizes their total value. Section 14.2
shows how to multiply a chain of matrices while performing the fewest total scalar
multiplications. Given these examples of dynamic programming, Section 14.3 discusses two key characteristics that a problem must have for dynamic programming
to be a viable solution technique. Section 14.4 then shows how to find the longest
common subsequence of two sequences via dynamic programming. Finally, Section 14.5 uses dynamic programming to construct binary search trees that are optimal, given a known distribution of keys to be looked up.

14.1   Rod cutting

Our first example uses dynamic programming to solve a simple problem in deciding where to cut steel rods. Serling Enterprises buys long steel rods and cuts them
into shorter rods, which it then sells. Each cut is free. The management of Serling
Enterprises wants to know the best way to cut up the rods.

Serling Enterprises has a table giving, for $i = 1, 2, \ldots,$ the price p_i in dollars
that they charge for a rod of length i inches. The length of each rod in inches is
always an integer. Figure 14.1 gives a sample price table.

The *rod-cutting problem* is the following. Given a rod of length n inches and
a table of prices p_i for $i = 1, 2, \ldots, n,$ determine the maximum revenue r_n ob-
tainable by cutting up the rod and selling the pieces. If the price p_n for a rod of
length n is large enough, an optimal solution might require no cutting at all.

Consider the case when $n = 4$. Figure 14.2 shows all the ways to cut up a rod
of 4 inches in length, including the way with no cuts at all. Cutting a 4-inch rod
into two 2-inch pieces produces revenue $p_2 + p_2 = 5 + 5 = 10$, which is optimal.

Serling Enterprises can cut up a rod of length n in 2^{n-1} different ways, since they
have an independent option of cutting, or not cutting, at distance i inches from the
left end, for $i = 1, 2, \ldots, n - 1$.[1] We denote a decomposition into pieces using
ordinary additive notation, so that $7 = 2 + 2 + 3$ indicates that a rod of length 7 is
cut into three pieces—two of length 2 and one of length 3. If an optimal solution
cuts the rod into k pieces, for some $1 \leq k \leq n$, then an optimal decomposition

$$n = i_1 + i_2 + \cdots + i_k$$

---

[1] If pieces are required to be cut in order of monotonically increasing size, there are fewer ways to
consider. For $n = 4$, only 5 such ways are possible: parts (a), (b), (c), (e), and (h) in Figure 14.2. The
number of ways is called the *partition function*, which is approximately equal to $e^{\pi\sqrt{2n/3}}/4n\sqrt{3}$.
This quantity is less than 2^{n-1}, but still much greater than any polynomial in n. We won't pursue
this line of inquiry further, however.

length i	1	2	3	4	5	6	7	8	9	10
price p_i	1	5	8	9	10	17	17	20	24	30

Figure 14.1   A sample price table for rods. Each rod of length i inches earns the company p_i dollars of revenue.

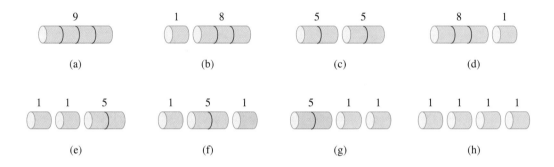

(a)   (b)   (c)   (d)

(e)   (f)   (g)   (h)

Figure 14.2   The 8 possible ways of cutting up a rod of length 4. Above each piece is the value of that piece, according to the sample price chart of Figure 14.1. The optimal strategy is part (c)— cutting the rod into two pieces of length 2—which has total value 10.

of the rod into pieces of lengths $i_1, i_2, \ldots, i_k$ provides maximum corresponding revenue

$$r_n = p_{i_1} + p_{i_2} + \cdots + p_{i_k} \, .$$

For the sample problem in Figure 14.1, you can determine the optimal revenue figures r_i, for $i = 1, 2, \ldots, 10$, by inspection, with the corresponding optimal decompositions

$$
\begin{aligned}
r_1 &= 1 && \text{from solution } 1 = 1 \quad \text{(no cuts)}, \\
r_2 &= 5 && \text{from solution } 2 = 2 \quad \text{(no cuts)}, \\
r_3 &= 8 && \text{from solution } 3 = 3 \quad \text{(no cuts)}, \\
r_4 &= 10 && \text{from solution } 4 = 2 + 2, \\
r_5 &= 13 && \text{from solution } 5 = 2 + 3, \\
r_6 &= 17 && \text{from solution } 6 = 6 \quad \text{(no cuts)}, \\
r_7 &= 18 && \text{from solution } 7 = 1 + 6 \text{ or } 7 = 2 + 2 + 3, \\
r_8 &= 22 && \text{from solution } 8 = 2 + 6, \\
r_9 &= 25 && \text{from solution } 9 = 3 + 6, \\
r_{10} &= 30 && \text{from solution } 10 = 10 \quad \text{(no cuts)}.
\end{aligned}
$$

More generally, we can express the values r_n for $n \geq 1$ in terms of optimal revenues from shorter rods:

$$r_n = \max \{p_n, r_1 + r_{n-1}, r_2 + r_{n-2}, \ldots, r_{n-1} + r_1\} \ . \tag{14.1}$$

The first argument, p_n, corresponds to making no cuts at all and selling the rod of length n as is. The other $n - 1$ arguments to max correspond to the maximum revenue obtained by making an initial cut of the rod into two pieces of size i and $n - i$, for each $i = 1, 2, \ldots, n - 1$, and then optimally cutting up those pieces further, obtaining revenues r_i and r_{n-i} from those two pieces. Since you don't know ahead of time which value of i optimizes revenue, you have to consider all possible values for i and pick the one that maximizes revenue. You also have the option of picking no i at all if the greatest revenue comes from selling the rod uncut.

To solve the original problem of size n, you solve smaller problems of the same type. Once you make the first cut, the two resulting pieces form independent instances of the rod-cutting problem. The overall optimal solution incorporates optimal solutions to the two resulting subproblems, maximizing revenue from each of those two pieces. We say that the rod-cutting problem exhibits *optimal substructure*: optimal solutions to a problem incorporate optimal solutions to related subproblems, which you may solve independently.

In a related, but slightly simpler, way to arrange a recursive structure for the rod-cutting problem, let's view a decomposition as consisting of a first piece of length i cut off the left-hand end, and then a right-hand remainder of length $n - i$. Only the remainder, and not the first piece, may be further divided. Think of every decomposition of a length-n rod in this way: as a first piece followed by some decomposition of the remainder. Then we can express the solution with no cuts at all by saying that the first piece has size $i = n$ and revenue p_n and that the remainder has size 0 with corresponding revenue $r_0 = 0$. We thus obtain the following simpler version of equation (14.1):

$$r_n = \max \{p_i + r_{n-i} : 1 \leq i \leq n\} \ . \tag{14.2}$$

In this formulation, an optimal solution embodies the solution to only *one* related subproblem—the remainder—rather than two.

Recursive top-down implementation

The CUT-ROD procedure on the following page implements the computation implicit in equation (14.2) in a straightforward, top-down, recursive manner. It takes as input an array $p[1:n]$ of prices and an integer n, and it returns the maximum revenue possible for a rod of length n. For length $n = 0$, no revenue is possible, and so CUT-ROD returns 0 in line 2. Line 3 initializes the maximum revenue q to $-\infty$, so that the **for** loop in lines 4–5 correctly computes

$q = \max\{p_i + \text{CUT-ROD}(p, n - i) : 1 \leq i \leq n\}$. Line 6 then returns this value. A simple induction on n proves that this answer is equal to the desired answer r_n, using equation (14.2).

CUT-ROD(p, n)

1 **if** $n == 0$
2   **return** 0
3 $q = -\infty$
4 **for** $i = 1$ **to** n
5      $q = \max\{q, p[i] + \text{CUT-ROD}(p, n - i)\}$
6 **return** q

If you code up CUT-ROD in your favorite programming language and run it on your computer, you'll find that once the input size becomes moderately large, your program takes a long time to run. For $n = 40$, your program may take several minutes and possibly more than an hour. For large values of n, you'll also discover that each time you increase n by 1, your program's running time approximately doubles.

Why is CUT-ROD so inefficient? The problem is that CUT-ROD calls itself recursively over and over again with the same parameter values, which means that it solves the same subproblems repeatedly. Figure 14.3 shows a recursion tree demonstrating what happens for $n = 4$: CUT-ROD(p, n) calls CUT-ROD$(p, n - i)$ for $i = 1, 2, \ldots, n$. Equivalently, CUT-ROD(p, n) calls CUT-ROD(p, j) for each $j = 0, 1, \ldots, n - 1$. When this process unfolds recursively, the amount of work done, as a function of n, grows explosively.

To analyze the running time of CUT-ROD, let $T(n)$ denote the total number of calls made to CUT-ROD(p, n) for a particular value of n. This expression equals the number of nodes in a subtree whose root is labeled n in the recursion tree. The count includes the initial call at its root. Thus, $T(0) = 1$ and

$$T(n) = 1 + \sum_{j=0}^{n-1} T(j) \, . \tag{14.3}$$

The initial 1 is for the call at the root, and the term $T(j)$ counts the number of calls (including recursive calls) due to the call CUT-ROD$(p, n - i)$, where $j = n - i$. As Exercise 14.1-1 asks you to show,

$$T(n) = 2^n \, , \tag{14.4}$$

and so the running time of CUT-ROD is exponential in n.

In retrospect, this exponential running time is not so surprising. CUT-ROD explicitly considers all possible ways of cutting up a rod of length n. How many ways

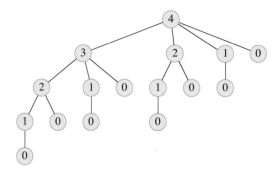

Figure 14.3 The recursion tree showing recursive calls resulting from a call CUT-ROD(p, n) for $n = 4$. Each node label gives the size n of the corresponding subproblem, so that an edge from a parent with label s to a child with label t corresponds to cutting off an initial piece of size $s - t$ and leaving a remaining subproblem of size t. A path from the root to a leaf corresponds to one of the 2^{n-1} ways of cutting up a rod of length n. In general, this recursion tree has 2^n nodes and 2^{n-1} leaves.

are there? A rod of length n has $n - 1$ potential locations to cut. Each possible way to cut up the rod makes a cut at some subset of these $n - 1$ locations, including the empty set, which makes for no cuts. Viewing each cut location as a distinct member of a set of $n - 1$ elements, you can see that there are 2^{n-1} subsets. Each leaf in the recursion tree of Figure 14.3 corresponds to one possible way to cut up the rod. Hence, the recursion tree has 2^{n-1} leaves. The labels on the simple path from the root to a leaf give the sizes of each remaining right-hand piece before making each cut. That is, the labels give the corresponding cut points, measured from the right-hand end of the rod.

Using dynamic programming for optimal rod cutting

Now, let's see how to use dynamic programming to convert CUT-ROD into an efficient algorithm.

The dynamic-programming method works as follows. Instead of solving the same subproblems repeatedly, as in the naive recursion solution, arrange for each subproblem to be solved *only once*. There's actually an obvious way to do so: the first time you solve a subproblem, *save its solution*. If you need to refer to this subproblem's solution again later, just look it up, rather than recomputing it.

Saving subproblem solutions comes with a cost: the additional memory needed to store solutions. Dynamic programming thus serves as an example of a *time-memory trade-off*. The savings may be dramatic. For example, we're about to use dynamic programming to go from the exponential-time algorithm for rod cutting down to a $\Theta(n^2)$-time algorithm. A dynamic-programming approach runs in polynomial time when the number of *distinct* subproblems involved is polynomial in the input size and you can solve each such subproblem in polynomial time.

There are usually two equivalent ways to implement a dynamic-programming approach. Solutions to the rod-cutting problem illustrate both of them.

The first approach is *top-down* with *memoization*.[2] In this approach, you write the procedure recursively in a natural manner, but modified to save the result of each subproblem (usually in an array or hash table). The procedure now first checks to see whether it has previously solved this subproblem. If so, it returns the saved value, saving further computation at this level. If not, the procedure computes the value in the usual manner but also saves it. We say that the recursive procedure has been *memoized*: it "remembers" what results it has computed previously.

The second approach is the *bottom-up method*. This approach typically depends on some natural notion of the "size" of a subproblem, such that solving any particular subproblem depends only on solving "smaller" subproblems. Solve the subproblems in size order, smallest first, storing the solution to each subproblem when it is first solved. In this way, when solving a particular subproblem, there are already saved solutions for all of the smaller subproblems its solution depends upon. You need to solve each subproblem only once, and when you first see it, you have already solved all of its prerequisite subproblems.

These two approaches yield algorithms with the same asymptotic running time, except in unusual circumstances where the top-down approach does not actually recurse to examine all possible subproblems. The bottom-up approach often has much better constant factors, since it has lower overhead for procedure calls.

The procedures MEMOIZED-CUT-ROD and MEMOIZED-CUT-ROD-AUX on the facing page demonstrate how to memoize the top-down CUT-ROD procedure. The main procedure MEMOIZED-CUT-ROD initializes a new auxiliary array $r[0:n]$ with the value $-\infty$ which, since known revenue values are always nonnegative, is a convenient choice for denoting "unknown." MEMOIZED-CUT-ROD then calls its helper procedure, MEMOIZED-CUT-ROD-AUX, which is just the memoized version of the exponential-time procedure, CUT-ROD. It first checks in line 1 to see whether the desired value is already known and, if it is, then line 2 returns it. Otherwise, lines 3–7 compute the desired value q in the usual manner, line 8 saves it in $r[n]$, and line 9 returns it.

The bottom-up version, BOTTOM-UP-CUT-ROD on the next page, is even simpler. Using the bottom-up dynamic-programming approach, BOTTOM-UP-CUT-ROD takes advantage of the natural ordering of the subproblems: a subproblem of

---

[2] The technical term "memoization" is not a misspelling of "memorization." The word "memoization" comes from "memo," since the technique consists of recording a value to be looked up later.

MEMOIZED-CUT-ROD(p, n)

```
1  let r[0:n] be a new array          // will remember solution values in r
2  for i = 0 to n
3      r[i] = -∞
4  return MEMOIZED-CUT-ROD-AUX(p, n, r)
```

MEMOIZED-CUT-ROD-AUX(p, n, r)

```
1  if r[n] ≥ 0                        // already have a solution for length n?
2      return r[n]
3  if n == 0
4      q = 0
5  else q = -∞
6      for i = 1 to n      // i is the position of the first cut
7          q = max {q, p[i] + MEMOIZED-CUT-ROD-AUX(p, n - i, r)}
8  r[n] = q                           // remember the solution value for length n
9  return q
```

BOTTOM-UP-CUT-ROD(p, n)

```
1  let r[0:n] be a new array          // will remember solution values in r
2  r[0] = 0
3  for j = 1 to n                     // for increasing rod length j
4      q = -∞
5      for i = 1 to j                 // i is the position of the first cut
6          q = max {q, p[i] + r[j - i]}
7      r[j] = q                       // remember the solution value for length j
8  return r[n]
```

size i is "smaller" than a subproblem of size j if $i < j$. Thus, the procedure solves subproblems of sizes $j = 0, 1, \ldots, n$, in that order.

Line 1 of BOTTOM-UP-CUT-ROD creates a new array $r[0:n]$ in which to save the results of the subproblems, and line 2 initializes $r[0]$ to 0, since a rod of length 0 earns no revenue. Lines 3–6 solve each subproblem of size j, for $j = 1, 2, \ldots, n$, in order of increasing size. The approach used to solve a problem of a particular size j is the same as that used by CUT-ROD, except that line 6 now directly references array entry $r[j - i]$ instead of making a recursive call to solve the subproblem of size $j - i$. Line 7 saves in $r[j]$ the solution to the subproblem of size j. Finally, line 8 returns $r[n]$, which equals the optimal value r_n.

The bottom-up and top-down versions have the same asymptotic running time. The running time of BOTTOM-UP-CUT-ROD is $\Theta(n^2)$, due to its doubly nested

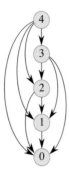

Figure 14.4   The subproblem graph for the rod-cutting problem with $n = 4$. The vertex labels give the sizes of the corresponding subproblems. A directed edge (x, y) indicates that solving subproblem x requires a solution to subproblem y. This graph is a reduced version of the recursion tree of Figure 14.3, in which all nodes with the same label are collapsed into a single vertex and all edges go from parent to child.

loop structure. The number of iterations of its inner **for** loop, in lines 5–6, forms an arithmetic series. The running time of its top-down counterpart, MEMOIZED-CUT-ROD, is also $\Theta(n^2)$, although this running time may be a little harder to see. Because a recursive call to solve a previously solved subproblem returns immediately, MEMOIZED-CUT-ROD solves each subproblem just once. It solves subproblems for sizes $0, 1, \ldots, n$. To solve a subproblem of size n, the **for** loop of lines 6–7 iterates n times. Thus, the total number of iterations of this **for** loop, over all recursive calls of MEMOIZED-CUT-ROD, forms an arithmetic series, giving a total of $\Theta(n^2)$ iterations, just like the inner **for** loop of BOTTOM-UP-CUT-ROD. (We actually are using a form of aggregate analysis here. We'll see aggregate analysis in detail in Section 16.1.)

Subproblem graphs

When you think about a dynamic-programming problem, you need to understand the set of subproblems involved and how subproblems depend on one another.

The *subproblem graph* for the problem embodies exactly this information. Figure 14.4 shows the subproblem graph for the rod-cutting problem with $n = 4$. It is a directed graph, containing one vertex for each distinct subproblem. The subproblem graph has a directed edge from the vertex for subproblem x to the vertex for subproblem y if determining an optimal solution for subproblem x involves directly considering an optimal solution for subproblem y. For example, the subproblem graph contains an edge from x to y if a top-down recursive procedure for solving x directly calls itself to solve y. You can think of the subproblem graph as a "reduced" or "collapsed" version of the recursion tree for the top-down recursive method, with all nodes for the same subproblem coalesced into a single vertex and all edges directed from parent to child.

The bottom-up method for dynamic programming considers the vertices of the subproblem graph in such an order that you solve the subproblems y adjacent to a given subproblem x before you solve subproblem x. (As Section B.4 notes, the adjacency relation in a directed graph is not necessarily symmetric.) Using terminology that we'll see in Section 20.4, in a bottom-up dynamic-programming algorithm, you consider the vertices of the subproblem graph in an order that is a "reverse topological sort," or a "topological sort of the transpose" of the subproblem graph. In other words, no subproblem is considered until all of the subproblems it depends upon have been solved. Similarly, using notions that we'll visit in Section 20.3, you can view the top-down method (with memoization) for dynamic programming as a "depth-first search" of the subproblem graph.

The size of the subproblem graph $G = (V, E)$ can help you determine the running time of the dynamic-programming algorithm. Since you solve each subproblem just once, the running time is the sum of the times needed to solve each subproblem. Typically, the time to compute the solution to a subproblem is proportional to the degree (number of outgoing edges) of the corresponding vertex in the subproblem graph, and the number of subproblems is equal to the number of vertices in the subproblem graph. In this common case, the running time of dynamic programming is linear in the number of vertices and edges.

Reconstructing a solution

The procedures MEMOIZED-CUT-ROD and BOTTOM-UP-CUT-ROD return the *value* of an optimal solution to the rod-cutting problem, but they do not return the solution *itself*: a list of piece sizes.

Let's see how to extend the dynamic-programming approach to record not only the optimal *value* computed for each subproblem, but also a *choice* that led to the optimal value. With this information, you can readily print an optimal solution. The procedure EXTENDED-BOTTOM-UP-CUT-ROD on the next page computes, for each rod size j, not only the maximum revenue r_j, but also s_j, the optimal size of the first piece to cut off. It's similar to BOTTOM-UP-CUT-ROD, except that it creates the array s in line 1, and it updates $s[j]$ in line 8 to hold the optimal size i of the first piece to cut off when solving a subproblem of size j.

The procedure PRINT-CUT-ROD-SOLUTION on the following page takes as input an array $p[1:n]$ of prices and a rod size n. It calls EXTENDED-BOTTOM-UP-CUT-ROD to compute the array $s[1:n]$ of optimal first-piece sizes. Then it prints out the complete list of piece sizes in an optimal decomposition of a rod of length n. For the sample price chart appearing in Figure 14.1, the call EXTENDED-BOTTOM-UP-CUT-ROD$(p, 10)$ returns the following arrays:

i	0	1	2	3	4	5	6	7	8	9	10
$r[i]$	0	1	5	8	10	13	17	18	22	25	30
$s[i]$		1	2	3	2	2	6	1	2	3	10

A call to PRINT-CUT-ROD-SOLUTION$(p, 10)$ prints just 10, but a call with $n = 7$ prints the cuts 1 and 6, which correspond to the first optimal decomposition for r_7 given earlier.

EXTENDED-BOTTOM-UP-CUT-ROD(p, n)

```
1   let r[0:n] and s[1:n] be new arrays
2   r[0] = 0
3   for j = 1 to n                  // for increasing rod length j
4       q = -∞
5       for i = 1 to j              // i is the position of the first cut
6           if q < p[i] + r[j - i]
7               q = p[i] + r[j - i]
8               s[j] = i            // best cut location so far for length j
9       r[j] = q                    // remember the solution value for length j
10  return r and s
```

PRINT-CUT-ROD-SOLUTION(p, n)

```
1   (r, s) = EXTENDED-BOTTOM-UP-CUT-ROD(p, n)
2   while n > 0
3       print s[n]          // cut location for length n
4       n = n - s[n]        // length of the remainder of the rod
```

Exercises

14.1-1
Show that equation (14.4) follows from equation (14.3) and the initial condition $T(0) = 1$.

14.1-2
Show, by means of a counterexample, that the following "greedy" strategy does not always determine an optimal way to cut rods. Define the *density* of a rod of length i to be p_i / i, that is, its value per inch. The greedy strategy for a rod of length n cuts off a first piece of length i, where $1 \leq i \leq n$, having maximum

density. It then continues by applying the greedy strategy to the remaining piece of length $n - i$.

14.1-3

Consider a modification of the rod-cutting problem in which, in addition to a price p_i for each rod, each cut incurs a fixed cost of c. The revenue associated with a solution is now the sum of the prices of the pieces minus the costs of making the cuts. Give a dynamic-programming algorithm to solve this modified problem.

14.1-4

Modify CUT-ROD and MEMOIZED-CUT-ROD-AUX so that their **for** loops go up to only $\lfloor n/2 \rfloor$, rather than up to n. What other changes to the procedures do you need to make? How are their running times affected?

14.1-5

Modify MEMOIZED-CUT-ROD to return not only the value but the actual solution.

14.1-6

The Fibonacci numbers are defined by recurrence (3.31) on page 69. Give an $O(n)$-time dynamic-programming algorithm to compute the nth Fibonacci number. Draw the subproblem graph. How many vertices and edges does the graph contain?

14.2 Matrix-chain multiplication

Our next example of dynamic programming is an algorithm that solves the problem of matrix-chain multiplication. Given a sequence (chain) $\langle A_1, A_2, \ldots, A_n \rangle$ of n matrices to be multiplied, where the matrices aren't necessarily square, the goal is to compute the product

$$A_1 A_2 \cdots A_n . \tag{14.5}$$

using the standard algorithm[3] for multiplying rectangular matrices, which we'll see in a moment, while minimizing the number of scalar multiplications.

You can evaluate the expression (14.5) using the algorithm for multiplying pairs of rectangular matrices as a subroutine once you have parenthesized it to resolve all ambiguities in how the matrices are multiplied together. Matrix multiplication is associative, and so all parenthesizations yield the same product. A product of

---

[3] None of the three methods from Sections 4.1 and Section 4.2 can be used directly, because they apply only to square matrices.

matrices is *fully parenthesized* if it is either a single matrix or the product of two fully parenthesized matrix products, surrounded by parentheses. For example, if the chain of matrices is $\langle A_1, A_2, A_3, A_4 \rangle$, then you can fully parenthesize the product $A_1 A_2 A_3 A_4$ in five distinct ways:

$(A_1(A_2(A_3 A_4)))$,
$(A_1((A_2 A_3) A_4))$,
$((A_1 A_2)(A_3 A_4))$,
$((A_1(A_2 A_3)) A_4)$,
$(((A_1 A_2) A_3) A_4)$.

How you parenthesize a chain of matrices can have a dramatic impact on the cost of evaluating the product. Consider first the cost of multiplying two rectangular matrices. The standard algorithm is given by the procedure RECTANGULAR-MATRIX-MULTIPLY, which generalizes the square-matrix multiplication procedure MATRIX-MULTIPLY on page 81. The RECTANGULAR-MATRIX-MULTIPLY procedure computes $C = C + A \cdot B$ for three matrices $A = (a_{ij})$, $B = (b_{ij})$, and $C = (c_{ij})$, where A is $p \times q$, B is $q \times r$, and C is $p \times r$.

RECTANGULAR-MATRIX-MULTIPLY(A, B, C, p, q, r)

1 **for** $i = 1$ **to** p
2   **for** $j = 1$ **to** r
3   **for** $k = 1$ **to** q
4              $c_{ij} = c_{ij} + a_{ik} \cdot b_{kj}$

The running time of RECTANGULAR-MATRIX-MULTIPLY is dominated by the number of scalar multiplications in line 4, which is pqr. Therefore, we'll consider the cost of multiplying matrices to be the number of scalar multiplications. (The number of scalar multiplications dominates even if we consider initializing $C = 0$ to perform just $C = A \cdot B$.)

To illustrate the different costs incurred by different parenthesizations of a matrix product, consider the problem of a chain $\langle A_1, A_2, A_3 \rangle$ of three matrices. Suppose that the dimensions of the matrices are 10×100, 100×5, and 5×50, respectively. Multiplying according to the parenthesization $((A_1 A_2) A_3)$ performs $10 \cdot 100 \cdot 5 = 5000$ scalar multiplications to compute the 10×5 matrix product $A_1 A_2$, plus another $10 \cdot 5 \cdot 50 = 2500$ scalar multiplications to multiply this matrix by A_3, for a total of 7500 scalar multiplications. Multiplying according to the alternative parenthesization $(A_1(A_2 A_3))$ performs $100 \cdot 5 \cdot 50 = 25{,}000$ scalar multiplications to compute the 100×50 matrix product $A_2 A_3$, plus another $10 \cdot 100 \cdot 50 = 50{,}000$ scalar multiplications to multiply A_1 by this matrix, for a total of 75,000 scalar multiplications. Thus, computing the product according to the first parenthesization is 10 times faster.

We state the *matrix-chain multiplication problem* as follows: given a chain $\langle A_1, A_2, \ldots, A_n \rangle$ of n matrices, where for $i = 1, 2, \ldots, n$, matrix A_i has dimension $p_{i-1} \times p_i$, fully parenthesize the product $A_1 A_2 \cdots A_n$ in a way that minimizes the number of scalar multiplications. The input is the sequence of dimensions $\langle p_0, p_1, p_2, \ldots, p_n \rangle$.

The matrix-chain multiplication problem does not entail actually multiplying matrices. The goal is only to determine an order for multiplying matrices that has the lowest cost. Typically, the time invested in determining this optimal order is more than paid for by the time saved later on when actually performing the matrix multiplications (such as performing only 7500 scalar multiplications instead of 75,000).

Counting the number of parenthesizations

Before solving the matrix-chain multiplication problem by dynamic programming, let us convince ourselves that exhaustively checking all possible parenthesizations is not an efficient algorithm. Denote the number of alternative parenthesizations of a sequence of n matrices by $P(n)$. When $n = 1$, the sequence consists of just one matrix, and therefore there is only one way to fully parenthesize the matrix product. When $n \geq 2$, a fully parenthesized matrix product is the product of two fully parenthesized matrix subproducts, and the split between the two subproducts may occur between the kth and $(k + 1)$st matrices for any $k = 1, 2, \ldots, n - 1$. Thus, we obtain the recurrence

$$P(n) = \begin{cases} 1 & \text{if } n = 1, \\ \sum_{k=1}^{n-1} P(k) P(n-k) & \text{if } n \geq 2. \end{cases} \tag{14.6}$$

Problem 12-4 on page 329 asked you to show that the solution to a similar recurrence is the sequence of *Catalan numbers*, which grows as $\Omega(4^n / n^{3/2})$. A simpler exercise (see Exercise 14.2-3) is to show that the solution to the recurrence (14.6) is $\Omega(2^n)$. The number of solutions is thus exponential in n, and the brute-force method of exhaustive search makes for a poor strategy when determining how to optimally parenthesize a matrix chain.

Applying dynamic programming

Let's use the dynamic-programming method to determine how to optimally parenthesize a matrix chain, by following the four-step sequence that we stated at the beginning of this chapter:

1. Characterize the structure of an optimal solution.

2. Recursively define the value of an optimal solution.

3. Compute the value of an optimal solution.

4. Construct an optimal solution from computed information.

We'll go through these steps in order, demonstrating how to apply each step to the problem.

Step 1: The structure of an optimal parenthesization

In the first step of the dynamic-programming method, you find the optimal sub-structure and then use it to construct an optimal solution to the problem from optimal solutions to subproblems. To perform this step for the matrix-chain multiplication problem, it's convenient to first introduce some notation. Let $A_{i:j}$, where $i \leq j$, denote the matrix that results from evaluating the product $A_i A_{i+1} \cdots A_j$. If the problem is nontrivial, that is, $i < j$, then to parenthesize the product $A_i A_{i+1} \cdots A_j$, the product must split between A_k and A_{k+1} for some integer k in the range $i \leq k < j$. That is, for some value of k, first compute the matrices $A_{i:k}$ and $A_{k+1:j}$, and then multiply them together to produce the final product $A_{i:j}$. The cost of parenthesizing this way is the cost of computing the matrix $A_{i:k}$, plus the cost of computing $A_{k+1:j}$, plus the cost of multiplying them together.

The optimal substructure of this problem is as follows. Suppose that to optimally parenthesize $A_i A_{i+1} \cdots A_j$, you split the product between A_k and A_{k+1}. Then the way you parenthesize the "prefix" subchain $A_i A_{i+1} \cdots A_k$ within this optimal parenthesization of $A_i A_{i+1} \cdots A_j$ must be an optimal parenthesization of $A_i A_{i+1} \cdots A_k$. Why? If there were a less costly way to parenthesize $A_i A_{i+1} \cdots A_k$, then you could substitute that parenthesization in the optimal parenthesization of $A_i A_{i+1} \cdots A_j$ to produce another way to parenthesize $A_i A_{i+1} \cdots A_j$ whose cost is lower than the optimum: a contradiction. A similar observation holds for how to parenthesize the subchain $A_{k+1} A_{k+2} \cdots A_j$ in the optimal parenthesization of $A_i A_{i+1} \cdots A_j$: it must be an optimal parenthesization of $A_{k+1} A_{k+2} \cdots A_j$.

Now let's use the optimal substructure to show how to construct an optimal solution to the problem from optimal solutions to subproblems. Any solution to a nontrivial instance of the matrix-chain multiplication problem requires splitting the product, and any optimal solution contains within it optimal solutions to subproblem instances. Thus, to build an optimal solution to an instance of the matrix-chain multiplication problem, split the problem into two subproblems (optimally parenthesizing $A_i A_{i+1} \cdots A_k$ and $A_{k+1} A_{k+2} \cdots A_j$), find optimal solutions to the two subproblem instances, and then combine these optimal subproblem solutions. To ensure that you've examined the optimal split, you must consider all possible splits.

Step 2: A recursive solution

The next step is to define the cost of an optimal solution recursively in terms of the optimal solutions to subproblems. For the matrix-chain multiplication problem, a subproblem is to determine the minimum cost of parenthesizing $A_i A_{i+1} \cdots A_j$ for $1 \leq i \leq j \leq n$. Given the input dimensions $\langle p_0, p_1, p_2, \ldots, p_n \rangle$, an index pair i, j specifies a subproblem. Let $m[i, j]$ be the minimum number of scalar multiplications needed to compute the matrix $A_{i:j}$. For the full problem, the lowest-cost way to compute $A_{1:n}$ is thus $m[1, n]$.

We can define $m[i, j]$ recursively as follows. If $i = j$, the problem is trivial: the chain consists of just one matrix $A_{i:i} = A_i$, so that no scalar multiplications are necessary to compute the product. Thus, $m[i, i] = 0$ for $i = 1, 2, \ldots, n$. To compute $m[i, j]$ when $i < j$, we take advantage of the structure of an optimal solution from step 1. Suppose that an optimal parenthesization splits the product $A_i A_{i+1} \cdots A_j$ between A_k and A_{k+1}, where $i \leq k < j$. Then, $m[i, j]$ equals the minimum cost $m[i, k]$ for computing the subproduct $A_{i:k}$, plus the minimum cost $m[k + 1, j]$ for computing the subproduct, $A_{k+1:j}$, plus the cost of multiplying these two matrices together. Because each matrix A_i is $p_{i-1} \times p_i$, computing the matrix product $A_{i:k} A_{k+1:j}$ takes $p_{i-1} p_k p_j$ scalar multiplications. Thus, we obtain

$$m[i, j] = m[i, k] + m[k + 1, j] + p_{i-1} p_k p_j .$$

This recursive equation assumes that you know the value of k. But you don't, at least not yet. You have to try all possible values of k. How many are there? Just $j - i$, namely $k = i, i + 1, \ldots, j - 1$. Since the optimal parenthesization must use one of these values for k, you need only check them all to find the best. Thus, the recursive definition for the minimum cost of parenthesizing the product $A_i A_{i+1} \cdots A_j$ becomes

$$m[i, j] = \begin{cases} 0 & \text{if } i = j , \\ \min \{ m[i, k] + m[k + 1, j] + p_{i-1} p_k p_j : i \leq k < j \} & \text{if } i < j . \end{cases}$$

$$(14.7)$$

The $m[i, j]$ values give the costs of optimal solutions to subproblems, but they do not provide all the information you need to construct an optimal solution. To help you do so, let's define $s[i, j]$ to be a value of k at which you split the product $A_i A_{i+1} \cdots A_j$ in an optimal parenthesization. That is, $s[i, j]$ equals a value k such that $m[i, j] = m[i, k] + m[k + 1, j] + p_{i-1} p_k p_j$.

Step 3: Computing the optimal costs

At this point, you could write a recursive algorithm based on recurrence (14.7) to compute the minimum cost $m[1, n]$ for multiplying $A_1 A_2 \cdots A_n$. But as we saw for the rod-cutting problem, and as we shall see in Section 14.3, this recursive algorithm takes exponential time. That's no better than the brute-force method of checking each way of parenthesizing the product.

Fortunately, there aren't all that many distinct subproblems: just one subproblem for each choice of i and j satisfying $1 \leq i \leq j \leq n$, or $\binom{n}{2} + n = \Theta(n^2)$ in all.[4] A recursive algorithm may encounter each subproblem many times in different branches of its recursion tree. This property of overlapping subproblems is the second hallmark of when dynamic programming applies (the first hallmark being optimal substructure).

Instead of computing the solution to recurrence (14.7) recursively, let's compute the optimal cost by using a tabular, bottom-up approach, as in the procedure MATRIX-CHAIN-ORDER. (The corresponding top-down approach using memoization appears in Section 14.3.) The input is a sequence $p = \langle p_0, p_1, \ldots, p_n \rangle$ of matrix dimensions, along with n, so that for $i = 1, 2, \ldots, n$, matrix A_i has dimensions $p_{i-1} \times p_i$. The procedure uses an auxiliary table $m[1:n, 1:n]$ to store the $m[i, j]$ costs and another auxiliary table $s[1:n-1, 2:n]$ that records which index k achieved the optimal cost in computing $m[i, j]$. The table s will help in constructing an optimal solution.

MATRIX-CHAIN-ORDER(p, n)

```
 1  let m[1:n, 1:n] and s[1:n − 1, 2:n] be new tables
 2  for i = 1 to n                    // chain length 1
 3      m[i, i] = 0
 4  for l = 2 to n                    // l is the chain length
 5      for i = 1 to n − l + 1        // chain begins at A_i
 6          j = i + l − 1             // chain ends at A_j
 7          m[i, j] = ∞
 8          for k = i to j − 1        // try A_{i:k} A_{k+1:j}
 9              q = m[i, k] + m[k + 1, j] + p_{i−1} p_k p_j
10              if q < m[i, j]
11                  m[i, j] = q       // remember this cost
12                  s[i, j] = k       // remember this index
13  return m and s
```

In what order should the algorithm fill in the table entries? To answer this question, let's see which entries of the table need to be accessed when computing the

---

[4] The $\binom{n}{2}$ term counts all pairs in which $i < j$. Because i and j may be equal, we need to add in the n term.

cost $m[i, j]$. Equation (14.7) tells us that to compute the cost of matrix product $A_{i:j}$, first the costs of the products $A_{i:k}$ and $A_{k+1:j}$ need to have been computed for all $k = i, i + 1, \dots, j - 1$. The chain $A_i A_{i+1} \cdots A_j$ consists of $j - i + 1$ matrices, and the chains $A_i A_{i+1} \dots A_k$ and $A_{k+1} A_{k+2} \dots A_j$ consist of $k - i + 1$ and $j - k$ matrices, respectively. Since $k < j$, a chain of $k - i + 1$ matrices consists of fewer than $j - i + 1$ matrices. Likewise, since $k \geq i$, a chain of $j - k$ matrices consists of fewer than $j - i + 1$ matrices. Thus, the algorithm should fill in the table m from shorter matrix chains to longer matrix chains. That is, for the subproblem of optimally parenthesizing the chain $A_i A_{i+1} \cdots A_j$, it makes sense to consider the subproblem size as the length $j - i + 1$ of the chain.

Now, let's see how the MATRIX-CHAIN-ORDER procedure fills in the $m[i, j]$ entries in order of increasing chain length. Lines 2–3 initialize $m[i, i] = 0$ for $i = 1, 2, \dots, n$, since any matrix chain with just one matrix requires no scalar multiplications. In the **for** loop of lines 4–12, the loop variable l denotes the length of matrix chains whose minimum costs are being computed. Each iteration of this loop uses recurrence (14.7) to compute $m[i, i + l - 1]$ for $i = 1, 2, \dots, n - l + 1$. In the first iteration, $l = 2$, and so the loop computes $m[i, i + 1]$ for $i = 1, 2, \dots, n - 1$: the minimum costs for chains of length $l = 2$. The second time through the loop, it computes $m[i, i + 2]$ for $i = 1, 2, \dots, n - 2$: the minimum costs for chains of length $l = 3$. And so on, ending with a single matrix chain of length $l = n$ and computing $m[1, n]$. When lines 7–12 compute an $m[i, j]$ cost, this cost depends only on table entries $m[i, k]$ and $m[k + 1, j]$, which have already been computed.

Figure 14.5 illustrates the m and s tables, as filled in by the MATRIX-CHAIN-ORDER procedure on a chain of $n = 6$ matrices. Since $m[i, j]$ is defined only for $i \leq j$, only the portion of the table m on or above the main diagonal is used. The figure shows the table rotated to make the main diagonal run horizontally. The matrix chain is listed along the bottom. Using this layout, the minimum cost $m[i, j]$ for multiplying a subchain $A_i A_{i+1} \cdots A_j$ of matrices appears at the intersection of lines running northeast from A_i and northwest from A_j. Reading across, each diagonal in the table contains the entries for matrix chains of the same length. MATRIX-CHAIN-ORDER computes the rows from bottom to top and from left to right within each row. It computes each entry $m[i, j]$ using the products $p_{i-1} p_k p_j$ for $k = i, i + 1, \dots, j - 1$ and all entries southwest and southeast from $m[i, j]$.

A simple inspection of the nested loop structure of MATRIX-CHAIN-ORDER yields a running time of $O(n^3)$ for the algorithm. The loops are nested three deep, and each loop index (l, i, and k) takes on at most $n - 1$ values. Exercise 14.2-5 asks you to show that the running time of this algorithm is in fact also $\Omega(n^3)$. The algorithm requires $\Theta(n^2)$ space to store the m and s tables. Thus, MATRIX-CHAIN-ORDER is much more efficient than the exponential-time method of enumerating all possible parenthesizations and checking each one.

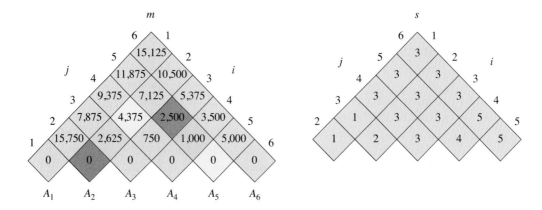

Figure 14.5   The m and s tables computed by MATRIX-CHAIN-ORDER for $n = 6$ and the following matrix dimensions:

matrix	A_1	A_2	A_3	A_4	A_5	A_6
dimension	30×35	35×15	15×5	5×10	10×20	20×25

The tables are rotated so that the main diagonal runs horizontally. The m table uses only the main diagonal and upper triangle, and the s table uses only the upper triangle. The minimum number of scalar multiplications to multiply the 6 matrices is $m[1, 6] = 15{,}125$. Of the entries that are not tan, the pairs that have the same color are taken together in line 9 when computing

$$
m[2, 5] = \min \begin{cases}
m[2, 2] + m[3, 5] + p_1 p_2 p_5 = 0 + 2500 + 35 \cdot 15 \cdot 20 & = 13{,}000 \,, \\
m[2, 3] + m[4, 5] + p_1 p_3 p_5 = 2625 + 1000 + 35 \cdot 5 \cdot 20 & = 7125 \,, \\
m[2, 4] + m[5, 5] + p_1 p_4 p_5 = 4375 + 0 + 35 \cdot 10 \cdot 20 & = 11{,}375
\end{cases}
$$
$$
= 7125 \,.
$$

Step 4: Constructing an optimal solution

Although MATRIX-CHAIN-ORDER determines the optimal number of scalar multiplications needed to compute a matrix-chain product, it does not directly show how to multiply the matrices. The table $s[1 : n - 1, 2 : n]$ provides the information needed to do so. Each entry $s[i, j]$ records a value of k such that an optimal parenthesization of $A_i A_{i+1} \cdots A_j$ splits the product between A_k and A_{k+1}. The final matrix multiplication in computing $A_{1:n}$ optimally is $A_{1:s[1,n]} A_{s[1,n]+1:n}$. The s table contains the information needed to determine the earlier matrix multiplications as well, using recursion: $s[1, s[1, n]]$ determines the last matrix multiplication when computing $A_{1:s[1,n]}$ and $s[s[1, n] + 1, n]$ determines the last matrix multiplication when computing $A_{s[1,n]+1:n}$. The recursive procedure PRINT-OPTIMAL-PARENS on the facing page prints an optimal parenthesization of the matrix chain product $A_i A_{i+1} \cdots A_j$, given the s table computed by MATRIX-CHAIN-ORDER and the indices i and j. The initial call PRINT-OPTIMAL-PARENS$(s, 1, n)$ prints an optimal parenthesization of the full matrix chain product $A_1 A_2 \cdots A_n$. In the example of Figure 14.5, the call PRINT-OPTIMAL-PARENS$(s, 1, 6)$ prints the optimal parenthesization $((A_1 (A_2 A_3))((A_4 A_5) A_6))$.

PRINT-OPTIMAL-PARENS(s, i, j)

```
1   if i == j
2       print "A"ᵢ
3   else print "("
4       PRINT-OPTIMAL-PARENS(s, i, s[i, j])
5       PRINT-OPTIMAL-PARENS(s, s[i, j] + 1, j)
6       print ")"
```

Exercises

14.2-1
Find an optimal parenthesization of a matrix-chain product whose sequence of dimensions is $\langle 5, 10, 3, 12, 5, 50, 6 \rangle$.

14.2-2
Give a recursive algorithm MATRIX-CHAIN-MULTIPLY(A, s, i, j) that actually performs the optimal matrix-chain multiplication, given the sequence of matrices $\langle A_1, A_2, \ldots, A_n \rangle$, the s table computed by MATRIX-CHAIN-ORDER, and the indices i and j. (The initial call is MATRIX-CHAIN-MULTIPLY$(A, s, 1, n)$.) Assume that the call RECTANGULAR-MATRIX-MULTIPLY(A, B) returns the product of matrices A and B.

14.2-3
Use the substitution method to show that the solution to the recurrence (14.6) is $\Omega(2^n)$.

14.2-4
Describe the subproblem graph for matrix-chain multiplication with an input chain of length n. How many vertices does it have? How many edges does it have, and which edges are they?

14.2-5
Let $R(i, j)$ be the number of times that table entry $m[i, j]$ is referenced while computing other table entries in a call of MATRIX-CHAIN-ORDER. Show that the total number of references for the entire table is

$$\sum_{i=1}^{n}\sum_{j=i}^{n} R(i,j) = \frac{n^3 - n}{3} .$$

(*Hint:* You may find equation (A.4) on page 1141 useful.)

14.2-6
Show that a full parenthesization of an n-element expression has exactly $n-1$ pairs of parentheses.

14.3   Elements of dynamic programming

Although you have just seen two complete examples of the dynamic-programming method, you might still be wondering just when the method applies. From an engineering perspective, when should you look for a dynamic-programming solution to a problem? In this section, we'll examine the two key ingredients that an optimization problem must have in order for dynamic programming to apply: optimal substructure and overlapping subproblems. We'll also revisit and discuss more fully how memoization might help you take advantage of the overlapping-subproblems property in a top-down recursive approach.

Optimal substructure

The first step in solving an optimization problem by dynamic programming is to characterize the structure of an optimal solution. Recall that a problem exhibits *optimal substructure* if an optimal solution to the problem contains within it optimal solutions to subproblems. When a problem exhibits optimal substructure, that gives you a good clue that dynamic programming might apply. (As Chapter 15 discusses, it also might mean that a greedy strategy applies, however.) Dynamic programming builds an optimal solution to the problem from optimal solutions to subproblems. Consequently, you must take care to ensure that the range of subproblems you consider includes those used in an optimal solution.

Optimal substructure was key to solving both of the previous problems in this chapter. In Section 14.1, we observed that the optimal way of cutting up a rod of length n (if Serling Enterprises makes any cuts at all) involves optimally cutting up the two pieces resulting from the first cut. In Section 14.2, we noted that an optimal parenthesization of the matrix chain product $A_i A_{i+1} \cdots A_j$ that splits the product between A_k and A_{k+1} contains within it optimal solutions to the problems of parenthesizing $A_i A_{i+1} \cdots A_k$ and $A_{k+1} A_{k+2} \cdots A_j$.

You will find yourself following a common pattern in discovering optimal substructure:

1. You show that a solution to the problem consists of making a choice, such as choosing an initial cut in a rod or choosing an index at which to split the matrix chain. Making this choice leaves one or more subproblems to be solved.

2. You suppose that for a given problem, you are given the choice that leads to an optimal solution. You do not concern yourself yet with how to determine this choice. You just assume that it has been given to you.

3. Given this choice, you determine which subproblems ensue and how to best characterize the resulting space of subproblems.

4. You show that the solutions to the subproblems used within an optimal solution to the problem must themselves be optimal by using a "cut-and-paste" technique. You do so by supposing that each of the subproblem solutions is not optimal and then deriving a contradiction. In particular, by "cutting out" the nonoptimal solution to each subproblem and "pasting in" the optimal one, you show that you can get a better solution to the original problem, thus contradicting your supposition that you already had an optimal solution. If an optimal solution gives rise to more than one subproblem, they are typically so similar that you can modify the cut-and-paste argument for one to apply to the others with little effort.

To characterize the space of subproblems, a good rule of thumb says to try to keep the space as simple as possible and then expand it as necessary. For example, the space of subproblems for the rod-cutting problem contained the problems of optimally cutting up a rod of length i for each size i. This subproblem space worked well, and it was not necessary to try a more general space of subproblems.

Conversely, suppose that you tried to constrain the subproblem space for matrix-chain multiplication to matrix products of the form $A_1 A_2 \cdots A_j$. As before, an optimal parenthesization must split this product between A_k and A_{k+1} for some $1 \le k < j$. Unless you can guarantee that k always equals $j - 1$, you will find that you have subproblems of the form $A_1 A_2 \cdots A_k$ and $A_{k+1} A_{k+2} \cdots A_j$. Moreover, the latter subproblem does not have the form $A_1 A_2 \cdots A_j$. To solve this problem by dynamic programming, you need to allow the subproblems to vary at "both ends." That is, both i and j need to vary in the subproblem of parenthesizing the product $A_i A_{i+1} \cdots A_j$.

Optimal substructure varies across problem domains in two ways:

1. how many subproblems an optimal solution to the original problem uses, and

2. how many choices you have in determining which subproblem(s) to use in an optimal solution.

In the rod-cutting problem, an optimal solution for cutting up a rod of size n uses just one subproblem (of size $n - i$), but we have to consider n choices for i in order to determine which one yields an optimal solution. Matrix-chain multiplication for the subchain $A_i A_{i+1} \cdots A_j$ serves an example with two subproblems and $j - i$ choices. For a given matrix A_k where the product splits, two subproblems arise—parenthesizing $A_i A_{i+1} \cdots A_k$ and parenthesizing $A_{k+1} A_{k+2} \cdots A_j$—and we have to solve *both* of them optimally. Once we determine the optimal solutions to subproblems, we choose from among $j - i$ candidates for the index k.

Informally, the running time of a dynamic-programming algorithm depends on the product of two factors: the number of subproblems overall and how many choices you look at for each subproblem. In rod cutting, we had $\Theta(n)$ subproblems overall, and at most n choices to examine for each, yielding an $O(n^2)$ running time. Matrix-chain multiplication had $\Theta(n^2)$ subproblems overall, and each had at most $n - 1$ choices, giving an $O(n^3)$ running time (actually, a $\Theta(n^3)$ running time, by Exercise 14.2-5).

Usually, the subproblem graph gives an alternative way to perform the same analysis. Each vertex corresponds to a subproblem, and the choices for a subproblem are the edges incident from that subproblem. Recall that in rod cutting, the subproblem graph has n vertices and at most n edges per vertex, yielding an $O(n^2)$ running time. For matrix-chain multiplication, if you were to draw the subproblem graph, it would have $\Theta(n^2)$ vertices and each vertex would have degree at most $n - 1$, giving a total of $O(n^3)$ vertices and edges.

Dynamic programming often uses optimal substructure in a bottom-up fashion. That is, you first find optimal solutions to subproblems and, having solved the subproblems, you find an optimal solution to the problem. Finding an optimal solution to the problem entails making a choice among subproblems as to which you will use in solving the problem. The cost of the problem solution is usually the subproblem costs plus a cost that is directly attributable to the choice itself. In rod cutting, for example, first we solved the subproblems of determining optimal ways to cut up rods of length i for $i = 0, 1, \ldots, n - 1$, and then we determined which of these subproblems yielded an optimal solution for a rod of length n, using equation (14.2). The cost attributable to the choice itself is the term p_i in equation (14.2). In matrix-chain multiplication, we determined optimal parenthesizations of subchains of $A_i A_{i+1} \cdots A_j$, and then we chose the matrix A_k at which to split the product. The cost attributable to the choice itself is the term $p_{i-1} p_k p_j$.

Chapter 15 explores "greedy algorithms," which have many similarities to dynamic programming. In particular, problems to which greedy algorithms apply have optimal substructure. One major difference between greedy algorithms and dynamic programming is that instead of first finding optimal solutions to subproblems and then making an informed choice, greedy algorithms first make a "greedy" choice—the choice that looks best at the time—and then solve a resulting subproblem, without bothering to solve all possible related smaller subproblems. Surprisingly, in some cases this strategy works!

Subtleties

You should be careful not to assume that optimal substructure applies when it does not. Consider the following two problems whose input consists of a directed graph $G = (V, E)$ and vertices $u, v \in V$.

Unweighted shortest path:[5] Find a path from u to v consisting of the fewest edges. Such a path must be simple, since removing a cycle from a path produces a path with fewer edges.

Unweighted longest simple path: Find a simple path from u to v consisting of the most edges. (Without the requirement that the path must be simple, the problem is undefined, since repeatedly traversing a cycle creates paths with an arbitrarily large number of edges.)

The unweighted shortest-path problem exhibits optimal substructure. Here's how. Suppose that $u \neq v$, so that the problem is nontrivial. Then, any path p from u to v must contain an intermediate vertex, say w. (Note that w may be u or v.) Then, we can decompose the path $u \overset{p}{\leadsto} v$ into subpaths $u \overset{p_1}{\leadsto} w \overset{p_2}{\leadsto} v$. The number of edges in p equals the number of edges in p_1 plus the number of edges in p_2. We claim that if p is an optimal (i.e., shortest) path from u to v, then p_1 must be a shortest path from u to w. Why? As suggested earlier, use a "cut-and-paste" argument: if there were another path, say p_1', from u to w with fewer edges than p_1, then we could cut out p_1 and paste in p_1' to produce a path $u \overset{p_1'}{\leadsto} w \overset{p_2}{\leadsto} v$ with fewer edges than p, thus contradicting p's optimality. Likewise, p_2 must be a shortest path from w to v. Thus, to find a shortest path from u to v, consider all intermediate vertices w, find a shortest path from u to w and a shortest path from w to v, and choose an intermediate vertex w that yields the overall shortest path. Section 23.2 uses a variant of this observation of optimal substructure to find a shortest path between every pair of vertices on a weighted, directed graph.

You might be tempted to assume that the problem of finding an unweighted longest simple path exhibits optimal substructure as well. After all, if we decompose a longest simple path $u \overset{p}{\leadsto} v$ into subpaths $u \overset{p_1}{\leadsto} w \overset{p_2}{\leadsto} v$, then mustn't p_1 be a longest simple path from u to w, and mustn't p_2 be a longest simple path from w to v? The answer is no! Figure 14.6 supplies an example. Consider the

---

[5] We use the term "unweighted" to distinguish this problem from that of finding shortest paths with weighted edges, which we shall see in Chapters 22 and 23. You can use the breadth-first search technique of Chapter 20 to solve the unweighted problem.

Figure 14.6 A directed graph showing that the problem of finding a longest simple path in an unweighted directed graph does not have optimal substructure. The path $q \rightarrow r \rightarrow t$ is a longest simple path from q to t, but the subpath $q \rightarrow r$ is not a longest simple path from q to r, nor is the subpath $r \rightarrow t$ a longest simple path from r to t.

path $q \rightarrow r \rightarrow t$, which is a longest simple path from q to t. Is $q \rightarrow r$ a longest simple path from q to r? No, for the path $q \rightarrow s \rightarrow t \rightarrow r$ is a simple path that is longer. Is $r \rightarrow t$ a longest simple path from r to t? No again, for the path $r \rightarrow q \rightarrow s \rightarrow t$ is a simple path that is longer.

This example shows that for longest simple paths, not only does the problem lack optimal substructure, but you cannot necessarily assemble a "legal" solution to the problem from solutions to subproblems. If you combine the longest simple paths $q \rightarrow s \rightarrow t \rightarrow r$ and $r \rightarrow q \rightarrow s \rightarrow t$, you get the path $q \rightarrow s \rightarrow t \rightarrow r \rightarrow q \rightarrow s \rightarrow t$, which is not simple. Indeed, the problem of finding an unweighted longest simple path does not appear to have any sort of optimal substructure. No efficient dynamic-programming algorithm for this problem has ever been found. In fact, this problem is NP-complete, which—as we shall see in Chapter 34—means that we are unlikely to find a way to solve it in polynomial time.

Why is the substructure of a longest simple path so different from that of a shortest path? Although a solution to a problem for both longest and shortest paths uses two subproblems, the subproblems in finding the longest simple path are not *independent*, whereas for shortest paths they are. What do we mean by subproblems being independent? We mean that the solution to one subproblem does not affect the solution to another subproblem of the same problem. For the example of Figure 14.6, we have the problem of finding a longest simple path from q to t with two subproblems: finding longest simple paths from q to r and from r to t. For the first of these subproblems, we chose the path $q \rightarrow s \rightarrow t \rightarrow r$, which used the vertices s and t. These vertices cannot appear in a solution to the second subproblem, since the combination of the two solutions to subproblems yields a path that is not simple. If vertex t cannot be in the solution to the second problem, then there is no way to solve it, since t is required to be on the path that forms the solution, and it is not the vertex where the subproblem solutions are "spliced" together (that vertex being r). Because vertices s and t appear in one subproblem solution, they cannot appear in the other subproblem solution. One of them must be in the solution to the other subproblem, however, and an optimal solution requires both.

Thus, we say that these subproblems are not independent. Looked at another way, using resources in solving one subproblem (those resources being vertices) renders them unavailable for the other subproblem.

Why, then, are the subproblems independent for finding a shortest path? The answer is that by nature, the subproblems do not share resources. We claim that if a vertex w is on a shortest path p from u to v, then we can splice together *any* shortest path $u \overset{p_1}{\rightsquigarrow} w$ and *any* shortest path $w \overset{p_2}{\rightsquigarrow} v$ to produce a shortest path from u to v. We are assured that, other than w, no vertex can appear in both paths p_1 and p_2. Why? Suppose that some vertex $x \neq w$ appears in both p_1 and p_2, so that we can decompose p_1 as $u \overset{p_{ux}}{\rightsquigarrow} x \rightsquigarrow w$ and p_2 as $w \rightsquigarrow x \overset{p_{xv}}{\rightsquigarrow} v$. By the optimal substructure of this problem, path p has as many edges as p_1 and p_2 together. Let's say that p has e edges. Now let us construct a path $p' = u \overset{p_{ux}}{\rightsquigarrow} x \overset{p_{xv}}{\rightsquigarrow} v$ from u to v. Because we have excised the paths from x to w and from w to x, each of which contains at least one edge, path p' contains at most $e - 2$ edges, which contradicts the assumption that p is a shortest path. Thus, we are assured that the subproblems for the shortest-path problem are independent.

The two problems examined in Sections 14.1 and 14.2 have independent sub-problems. In matrix-chain multiplication, the subproblems are multiplying sub-chains $A_i A_{i+1} \cdots A_k$ and $A_{k+1} A_{k+2} \cdots A_j$. These subchains are disjoint, so that no matrix could possibly be included in both of them. In rod cutting, to determine the best way to cut up a rod of length n, we looked at the best ways of cutting up rods of length i for $i = 0, 1, \ldots, n-1$. Because an optimal solution to the length-n problem includes just one of these subproblem solutions (after cutting off the first piece), independence of subproblems is not an issue.

Overlapping subproblems

The second ingredient that an optimization problem must have for dynamic pro-gramming to apply is that the space of subproblems must be "small" in the sense that a recursive algorithm for the problem solves the same subproblems over and over, rather than always generating new subproblems. Typically, the total number of distinct subproblems is a polynomial in the input size. When a recursive algo-rithm revisits the same problem repeatedly, we say that the optimization problem has *overlapping subproblems*.[6] In contrast, a problem for which a divide-and-

---

[6] It may seem strange that dynamic programming relies on subproblems being both independent and overlapping. Although these requirements may sound contradictory, they describe two different notions, rather than two points on the same axis. Two subproblems of the same problem are inde-pendent if they do not share resources. Two subproblems are overlapping if they are really the same subproblem that occurs as a subproblem of different problems.

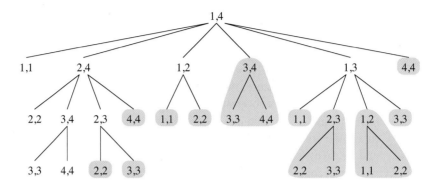

Figure 14.7 The recursion tree for the computation of RECURSIVE-MATRIX-CHAIN($p, 1, 4$). Each node contains the parameters i and j. The computations performed in a subtree shaded blue are replaced by a single table lookup in MEMOIZED-MATRIX-CHAIN.

conquer approach is suitable usually generates brand-new problems at each step of the recursion. Dynamic-programming algorithms typically take advantage of overlapping subproblems by solving each subproblem once and then storing the solution in a table where it can be looked up when needed, using constant time per lookup.

In Section 14.1, we briefly examined how a recursive solution to rod cutting makes exponentially many calls to find solutions of smaller subproblems. The dynamic-programming solution reduces the running time from the exponential time of the recursive algorithm down to quadratic time.

To illustrate the overlapping-subproblems property in greater detail, let's revisit the matrix-chain multiplication problem. Referring back to Figure 14.5, observe that MATRIX-CHAIN-ORDER repeatedly looks up the solution to subproblems in lower rows when solving subproblems in higher rows. For example, it references entry $m[3, 4]$ four times: during the computations of $m[2, 4]$, $m[1, 4]$, $m[3, 5]$, and $m[3, 6]$. If the algorithm were to recompute $m[3, 4]$ each time, rather than just looking it up, the running time would increase dramatically. To see how, consider the inefficient recursive procedure RECURSIVE-MATRIX-CHAIN on the facing page, which determines $m[i, j]$, the minimum number of scalar multiplications needed to compute the matrix-chain product $A_{i:j} = A_i A_{i+1} \cdots A_j$. The procedure is based directly on the recurrence (14.7). Figure 14.7 shows the recursion tree produced by the call RECURSIVE-MATRIX-CHAIN($p, 1, 4$). Each node is labeled by the values of the parameters i and j. Observe that some pairs of values occur many times.

In fact, the time to compute $m[1, n]$ by this recursive procedure is at least exponential in n. To see why, let $T(n)$ denote the time taken by RECURSIVE-MATRIX-

RECURSIVE-MATRIX-CHAIN(p, i, j)

```
1   if i == j
2       return 0
3   m[i, j] = ∞
4   for k = i to j − 1
5       q = RECURSIVE-MATRIX-CHAIN(p, i, k)
                + RECURSIVE-MATRIX-CHAIN(p, k + 1, j)
                + p_{i−1} p_k p_j
6       if q < m[i, j]
7           m[i, j] = q
8   return m[i, j]
```

CHAIN to compute an optimal parenthesization of a chain of n matrices. Because the execution of lines 1–2 and of lines 6–7 each take at least unit time, as does the multiplication in line 5, inspection of the procedure yields the recurrence

$$
T(n) \geq
\begin{cases}
1 & \text{if } n = 1, \\
1 + \displaystyle\sum_{k=1}^{n-1}(T(k) + T(n-k) + 1) & \text{if } n > 1.
\end{cases}
$$

Noting that for $i = 1, 2, \ldots, n-1$, each term $T(i)$ appears once as $T(k)$ and once as $T(n-k)$, and collecting the $n-1$ 1s in the summation together with the 1 out front, we can rewrite the recurrence as

$$
T(n) \geq 2 \sum_{i=1}^{n-1} T(i) + n .
\tag{14.8}
$$

Let's prove that $T(n) = \Omega(2^n)$ using the substitution method. Specifically, we'll show that $T(n) \geq 2^{n-1}$ for all $n \geq 1$. For the base case $n = 1$, the summation is empty, and we get $T(1) \geq 1 = 2^0$. Inductively, for $n \geq 2$ we have

$$
\begin{aligned}
T(n) &\geq 2 \sum_{i=1}^{n-1} 2^{i-1} + n \\
&= 2 \sum_{j=0}^{n-2} 2^j + n && \text{(letting } j = i - 1) \\
&= 2(2^{n-1} - 1) + n && \text{(by equation (A.6) on page 1142)} \\
&= 2^n - 2 + n \\
&\geq 2^{n-1},
\end{aligned}
$$

which completes the proof. Thus, the total amount of work performed by the call RECURSIVE-MATRIX-CHAIN$(p, 1, n)$ is at least exponential in n.

Compare this top-down, recursive algorithm (without memoization) with the bottom-up dynamic-programming algorithm. The latter is more efficient because it takes advantage of the overlapping-subproblems property. Matrix-chain multiplication has only $\Theta(n^2)$ distinct subproblems, and the dynamic-programming algorithm solves each exactly once. The recursive algorithm, on the other hand, must solve each subproblem every time it reappears in the recursion tree. Whenever a recursion tree for the natural recursive solution to a problem contains the same subproblem repeatedly, and the total number of distinct subproblems is small, dynamic programming can improve efficiency, sometimes dramatically.

Reconstructing an optimal solution

As a practical matter, you'll often want to store in a separate table which choice you made in each subproblem so that you do not have to reconstruct this information from the table of costs.

For matrix-chain multiplication, the table $s[i, j]$ saves a significant amount of work when we need to reconstruct an optimal solution. Suppose that the MATRIX-CHAIN-ORDER procedure on page 378 did not maintain the $s[i, j]$ table, so that it filled in only the table $m[i, j]$ containing optimal subproblem costs. The procedure chooses from among $j - i$ possibilities when determining which subproblems to use in an optimal solution to parenthesizing $A_i A_{i+1} \cdots A_j$, and $j - i$ is not a constant. Therefore, it would take $\Theta(j-i) = \omega(1)$ time to reconstruct which subproblems it chose for a solution to a given problem. Because MATRIX-CHAIN-ORDER stores in $s[i, j]$ the index of the matrix at which it split the product $A_i A_{i+1} \cdots A_j$, the PRINT-OPTIMAL-PARENS procedure on page 381 can look up each choice in $O(1)$ time.

Memoization

As we saw for the rod-cutting problem, there is an alternative approach to dynamic programming that often offers the efficiency of the bottom-up dynamic-programming approach while maintaining a top-down strategy. The idea is to *memoize* the natural, but inefficient, recursive algorithm. As in the bottom-up approach, you maintain a table with subproblem solutions, but the control structure for filling in the table is more like the recursive algorithm.

A memoized recursive algorithm maintains an entry in a table for the solution to each subproblem. Each table entry initially contains a special value to indicate that the entry has yet to be filled in. When the subproblem is first encountered as the recursive algorithm unfolds, its solution is computed and then stored in the table.

Each subsequent encounter of this subproblem simply looks up the value stored in the table and returns it.[7]

The procedure MEMOIZED-MATRIX-CHAIN is a memoized version of the procedure RECURSIVE-MATRIX-CHAIN on page 389. Note where it resembles the memoized top-down method on page 369 for the rod-cutting problem.

MEMOIZED-MATRIX-CHAIN(p, n)

1 let $m[1:n, 1:n]$ be a new table
2 **for** $i = 1$ **to** n
3   **for** $j = i$ **to** n
4          $m[i, j] = \infty$
5 **return** LOOKUP-CHAIN$(m, p, 1, n)$

LOOKUP-CHAIN(m, p, i, j)

1 **if** $m[i, j] < \infty$
2   **return** $m[i, j]$
3 **if** $i == j$
4      $m[i, j] = 0$
5 **else for** $k = i$ **to** $j - 1$
6          $q =$ LOOKUP-CHAIN(m, p, i, k)
                + LOOKUP-CHAIN$(m, p, k + 1, j) + p_{i-1} p_k p_j$
7   **if** $q < m[i, j]$
8          $m[i, j] = q$
9 **return** $m[i, j]$

The MEMOIZED-MATRIX-CHAIN procedure, like the bottom-up MATRIX-CHAIN-ORDER procedure on page 378, maintains a table $m[1:n, 1:n]$ of computed values of $m[i, j]$, the minimum number of scalar multiplications needed to compute the matrix $A_{i:j}$. Each table entry initially contains the value ∞ to indicate that the entry has yet to be filled in. Upon calling LOOKUP-CHAIN(m, p, i, j), if line 1 finds that $m[i, j] < \infty$, then the procedure simply returns the previously computed cost $m[i, j]$ in line 2. Otherwise, the cost is computed as in RECURSIVE-MATRIX-CHAIN, stored in $m[i, j]$, and returned. Thus, LOOKUP-CHAIN(m, p, i, j) always returns the value of $m[i, j]$, but it computes it only upon the first call of LOOKUP-CHAIN with these specific values of i and j.

---

[7] This approach presupposes that you know the set of all possible subproblem parameters and that you have established the relationship between table positions and subproblems. Another, more general, approach is to memoize by using hashing with the subproblem parameters as keys.

Figure 14.7 illustrates how MEMOIZED-MATRIX-CHAIN saves time compared with RECURSIVE-MATRIX-CHAIN. Subtrees shaded blue represent values that are looked up rather than recomputed.

Like the bottom-up procedure MATRIX-CHAIN-ORDER, the memoized procedure MEMOIZED-MATRIX-CHAIN runs in $O(n^3)$ time. To begin with, line 4 of MEMOIZED-MATRIX-CHAIN executes $\Theta(n^2)$ times, which dominates the running time outside of the call to LOOKUP-CHAIN in line 5. We can categorize the calls of LOOKUP-CHAIN into two types:

1. calls in which $m[i, j] = \infty$, so that lines 3–9 execute, and

2. calls in which $m[i, j] < \infty$, so that LOOKUP-CHAIN simply returns in line 2.

There are $\Theta(n^2)$ calls of the first type, one per table entry. All calls of the second type are made as recursive calls by calls of the first type. Whenever a given call of LOOKUP-CHAIN makes recursive calls, it makes $O(n)$ of them. Therefore, there are $O(n^3)$ calls of the second type in all. Each call of the second type takes $O(1)$ time, and each call of the first type takes $O(n)$ time plus the time spent in its recursive calls. The total time, therefore, is $O(n^3)$. Memoization thus turns an $\Omega(2^n)$-time algorithm into an $O(n^3)$-time algorithm.

We have seen how to solve the matrix-chain multiplication problem by either a top-down, memoized dynamic-programming algorithm or a bottom-up dynamic-programming algorithm in $O(n^3)$ time. Both the bottom-up and memoized methods take advantage of the overlapping-subproblems property. There are only $\Theta(n^2)$ distinct subproblems in total, and either of these methods computes the solution to each subproblem only once. Without memoization, the natural recursive algorithm runs in exponential time, since solved subproblems are repeatedly solved.

In general practice, if all subproblems must be solved at least once, a bottom-up dynamic-programming algorithm usually outperforms the corresponding top-down memoized algorithm by a constant factor, because the bottom-up algorithm has no overhead for recursion and less overhead for maintaining the table. Moreover, for some problems you can exploit the regular pattern of table accesses in the dynamic-programming algorithm to reduce time or space requirements even further. On the other hand, in certain situations, some of the subproblems in the subproblem space might not need to be solved at all. In that case, the memoized solution has the advantage of solving only those subproblems that are definitely required.

Exercises

14.3-1
Which is a more efficient way to determine the optimal number of multiplications in a matrix-chain multiplication problem: enumerating all the ways of parenthesiz-

ing the product and computing the number of multiplications for each, or running RECURSIVE-MATRIX-CHAIN? Justify your answer.

14.3-2

Draw the recursion tree for the MERGE-SORT procedure from Section 2.3.1 on an array of 16 elements. Explain why memoization fails to speed up a good divide-and-conquer algorithm such as MERGE-SORT.

14.3-3

Consider the antithetical variant of the matrix-chain multiplication problem where the goal is to parenthesize the sequence of matrices so as to maximize, rather than minimize, the number of scalar multiplications. Does this problem exhibit optimal substructure?

14.3-4

As stated, in dynamic programming, you first solve the subproblems and then choose which of them to use in an optimal solution to the problem. Professor Capulet claims that she does not always need to solve all the subproblems in order to find an optimal solution. She suggests that she can find an optimal solution to the matrix-chain multiplication problem by always choosing the matrix A_k at which to split the subproduct $A_i A_{i+1} \cdots A_j$ (by selecting k to minimize the quantity $p_{i-1} p_k p_j$) before solving the subproblems. Find an instance of the matrix-chain multiplication problem for which this greedy approach yields a suboptimal solution.

14.3-5

Suppose that the rod-cutting problem of Section 14.1 also had a limit l_i on the number of pieces of length i allowed to be produced, for $i = 1, 2, \ldots, n$. Show that the optimal-substructure property described in Section 14.1 no longer holds.

14.4 Longest common subsequence

Biological applications often need to compare the DNA of two (or more) different organisms. A strand of DNA consists of a string of molecules called *bases*, where the possible bases are adenine, cytosine, guanine, and thymine. Representing each of these bases by its initial letter, we can express a strand of DNA as a string over the 4-element set $\{A, C, G, T\}$. (See Section C.1 for the definition of a string.) For example, the DNA of one organism may be $S_1 = \text{ACCGGTCGAGTGCGCGGAAGCCGGCCGAA}$, and the DNA of another organism may be $S_2 = \text{GTCGTTCGGAATGCCGTTGCTCTGTAAA}$. One reason to compare two strands of DNA is to determine how "similar" the two strands are, as some measure of how closely related the two organisms are. We can, and do, define similarity in many different ways. For example, we can say that two DNA strands are similar if one is a substring of the other. (Chapter 32 explores algorithms to solve this problem.) In our example, neither S_1 nor S_2 is a substring of the other. Alternatively, we could say that two strands are similar if the number of changes needed to turn one into the other is small. (Problem 14-5 looks at this notion.) Yet another way to measure the similarity of strands S_1 and S_2 is by finding a third strand S_3 in which the bases in S_3 appear in each of S_1 and S_2. These bases must appear in the same order, but not necessarily consecutively. The longer the strand S_3 we can find, the more similar S_1 and S_2 are. In our example, the longest strand S_3 is GTCGTCGGAAGCCGGCCGAA.

We formalize this last notion of similarity as the longest-common-subsequence problem. A subsequence of a given sequence is just the given sequence with 0 or more elements left out. Formally, given a sequence $X = \langle x_1, x_2, \ldots, x_m \rangle$, another sequence $Z = \langle z_1, z_2, \ldots, z_k \rangle$ is a *subsequence* of X if there exists a strictly increasing sequence $\langle i_1, i_2, \ldots, i_k \rangle$ of indices of X such that for all $j = 1, 2, \ldots, k$, we have $x_{i_j} = z_j$. For example, $Z = \langle B, C, D, B \rangle$ is a subsequence of $X = \langle A, B, C, B, D, A, B \rangle$ with corresponding index sequence $\langle 2, 3, 5, 7 \rangle$.

Given two sequences X and Y, we say that a sequence Z is a *common subsequence* of X and Y if Z is a subsequence of both X and Y. For example, if $X = \langle A, B, C, B, D, A, B \rangle$ and $Y = \langle B, D, C, A, B, A \rangle$, the sequence $\langle B, C, A \rangle$ is a common subsequence of both X and Y. The sequence $\langle B, C, A \rangle$ is not a *longest common subsequence* (*LCS*) of X and Y, however, since it has length 3 and the sequence $\langle B, C, B, A \rangle$, which is also common to both sequences X and Y, has length 4. The sequence $\langle B, C, B, A \rangle$ is an LCS of X and Y, as is the sequence $\langle B, D, A, B \rangle$, since X and Y have no common subsequence of length 5 or greater.

In the *longest-common-subsequence problem*, the input is two sequences $X = \langle x_1, x_2, \ldots, x_m \rangle$ and $Y = \langle y_1, y_2, \ldots, y_n \rangle$, and the goal is to find a maximum-length common subsequence of X and Y. This section shows how to efficiently solve the LCS problem using dynamic programming.

Step 1: Characterizing a longest common subsequence

You can solve the LCS problem with a brute-force approach: enumerate all subsequences of X and check each subsequence to see whether it is also a subsequence of Y, keeping track of the longest subsequence you find. Each subsequence of X corresponds to a subset of the indices $\{1, 2, \ldots, m\}$ of X. Because X has 2^m subsequences, this approach requires exponential time, making it impractical for long sequences.

The LCS problem has an optimal-substructure property, however, as the following theorem shows. As we'll see, the natural classes of subproblems correspond to pairs of "prefixes" of the two input sequences. To be precise, given a sequence $X = \langle x_1, x_2, \ldots, x_m \rangle$, we define the ith *prefix* of X, for $i = 0, 1, \ldots, m$, as $X_i = \langle x_1, x_2, \ldots, x_i \rangle$. For example, if $X = \langle A, B, C, B, D, A, B \rangle$, then $X_4 = \langle A, B, C, B \rangle$ and X_0 is the empty sequence.

Theorem 14.1 (Optimal substructure of an LCS)
Let $X = \langle x_1, x_2, \ldots, x_m \rangle$ and $Y = \langle y_1, y_2, \ldots, y_n \rangle$ be sequences, and let $Z = \langle z_1, z_2, \ldots, z_k \rangle$ be any LCS of X and Y.

1. If $x_m = y_n$, then $z_k = x_m = y_n$ and Z_{k-1} is an LCS of X_{m-1} and Y_{n-1}.

2. If $x_m \neq y_n$ and $z_k \neq x_m$, then Z is an LCS of X_{m-1} and Y.

3. If $x_m \neq y_n$ and $z_k \neq y_n$, then Z is an LCS of X and Y_{n-1}.

Proof   (1) If $z_k \neq x_m$, then we could append $x_m = y_n$ to Z to obtain a common subsequence of X and Y of length $k + 1$, contradicting the supposition that Z is a *longest* common subsequence of X and Y. Thus, we must have $z_k = x_m = y_n$. Now, the prefix Z_{k-1} is a length-$(k - 1)$ common subsequence of X_{m-1} and Y_{n-1}. We wish to show that it is an LCS. Suppose for the purpose of contradiction that there exists a common subsequence W of X_{m-1} and Y_{n-1} with length greater than $k - 1$. Then, appending $x_m = y_n$ to W produces a common subsequence of X and Y whose length is greater than k, which is a contradiction.

(2) If $z_k \neq x_m$, then Z is a common subsequence of X_{m-1} and Y. If there were a common subsequence W of X_{m-1} and Y with length greater than k, then W would also be a common subsequence of X_m and Y, contradicting the assumption that Z is an LCS of X and Y.

(3) The proof is symmetric to (2).   ■

The way that Theorem 14.1 characterizes longest common subsequences says that an LCS of two sequences contains within it an LCS of prefixes of the two sequences. Thus, the LCS problem has an optimal-substructure property. A recursive solution also has the overlapping-subproblems property, as we'll see in a moment.

Step 2: A recursive solution

Theorem 14.1 implies that you should examine either one or two subproblems when finding an LCS of $X = \langle x_1, x_2, \ldots, x_m \rangle$ and $Y = \langle y_1, y_2, \ldots, y_n \rangle$. If $x_m = y_n$, you need to find an LCS of X_{m-1} and Y_{n-1}. Appending $x_m = y_n$ to this LCS yields an LCS of X and Y. If $x_m \neq y_n$, then you have to solve two subproblems: finding an LCS of X_{m-1} and Y and finding an LCS of X and Y_{n-1}.

Whichever of these two LCSs is longer is an LCS of X and Y. Because these cases exhaust all possibilities, one of the optimal subproblem solutions must appear within an LCS of X and Y.

The LCS problem has the overlapping-subproblems property. Here's how. To find an LCS of X and Y, you might need to find the LCSs of X and Y_{n-1} and of X_{m-1} and Y. But each of these subproblems has the subsubproblem of finding an LCS of X_{m-1} and Y_{n-1}. Many other subproblems share subsubproblems.

As in the matrix-chain multiplication problem, solving the LCS problem recursively involves establishing a recurrence for the value of an optimal solution. Let's define $c[i, j]$ to be the length of an LCS of the sequences X_i and Y_j. If either $i = 0$ or $j = 0$, one of the sequences has length 0, and so the LCS has length 0. The optimal substructure of the LCS problem gives the recursive formula

$$c[i, j] = \begin{cases} 0 & \text{if } i = 0 \text{ or } j = 0, \\ c[i-1, j-1] + 1 & \text{if } i, j > 0 \text{ and } x_i = y_j, \\ \max\{c[i, j-1], c[i-1, j]\} & \text{if } i, j > 0 \text{ and } x_i \neq y_j. \end{cases} \qquad (14.9)$$

In this recursive formulation, a condition in the problem restricts which subproblems to consider. When $x_i = y_j$, you can and should consider the subproblem of finding an LCS of X_{i-1} and Y_{j-1}. Otherwise, you instead consider the two subproblems of finding an LCS of X_i and Y_{j-1} and of X_{i-1} and Y_j. In the previous dynamic-programming algorithms we have examined—for rod cutting and matrix-chain multiplication—we didn't rule out any subproblems due to conditions in the problem. Finding an LCS is not the only dynamic-programming algorithm that rules out subproblems based on conditions in the problem. For example, the edit-distance problem (see Problem 14-5) has this characteristic.

Step 3: Computing the length of an LCS

Based on equation (14.9), you could write an exponential-time recursive algorithm to compute the length of an LCS of two sequences. Since the LCS problem has only $\Theta(mn)$ distinct subproblems (computing $c[i, j]$ for $0 \leq i \leq m$ and $0 \leq j \leq n$), dynamic programming can compute the solutions bottom up.

The procedure LCS-LENGTH on the next page takes two sequences $X = \langle x_1, x_2, \ldots, x_m \rangle$ and $Y = \langle y_1, y_2, \ldots, y_n \rangle$ as inputs, along with their lengths. It stores the $c[i, j]$ values in a table $c[0:m, 0:n]$, and it computes the entries in *row-major* order. That is, the procedure fills in the first row of c from left to right, then the second row, and so on. The procedure also maintains the table $b[1:m, 1:n]$ to help in constructing an optimal solution. Intuitively, $b[i, j]$ points to the table entry corresponding to the optimal subproblem solution chosen when computing $c[i, j]$. The procedure returns the b and c tables, where $c[m, n]$ contains the length of an LCS of X and Y. Figure 14.8 shows the tables produced by LCS-LENGTH on the sequences $X = \langle A, B, C, B, D, A, B \rangle$ and $Y = \langle B, D, C, A, B, A \rangle$. The running time of the procedure is $\Theta(mn)$, since each table entry takes $\Theta(1)$ time to compute.

LCS-LENGTH(X, Y, m, n)

```
 1  let b[1 : m, 1 : n] and c[0 : m, 0 : n] be new tables
 2  for i = 1 to m
 3      c[i, 0] = 0
 4  for j = 0 to n
 5      c[0, j] = 0
 6  for i = 1 to m              // compute table entries in row-major order
 7      for j = 1 to n
 8          if x_i == y_j
 9              c[i, j] = c[i − 1, j − 1] + 1
10              b[i, j] = "↖"
11          elseif c[i − 1, j] ≥ c[i, j − 1]
12              c[i, j] = c[i − 1, j]
13              b[i, j] = "↑"
14          else c[i, j] = c[i, j − 1]
15              b[i, j] = "←"
16  return c and b
```

PRINT-LCS(b, X, i, j)

```
 1  if i == 0 or j == 0
 2      return                 // the LCS has length 0
 3  if b[i, j] == "↖"
 4      PRINT-LCS(b, X, i − 1, j − 1)
 5      print x_i              // same as y_j
 6  elseif b[i, j] == "↑"
 7      PRINT-LCS(b, X, i − 1, j)
 8  else PRINT-LCS(b, X, i, j − 1)
```

Step 4: Constructing an LCS

With the b table returned by LCS-LENGTH, you can quickly construct an LCS of $X = \langle x_1, x_2, \ldots, x_m \rangle$ and $Y = \langle y_1, y_2, \ldots, y_n \rangle$. Begin at $b[m, n]$ and trace through the table by following the arrows. Each "↖" encountered in an entry $b[i, j]$ implies that $x_i = y_j$ is an element of the LCS that LCS-LENGTH found. This method gives you the elements of this LCS in reverse order. The recursive procedure PRINT-LCS prints out an LCS of X and Y in the proper, forward order.

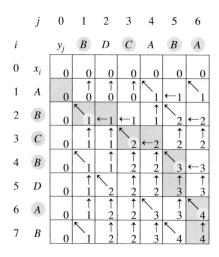

Figure 14.8 The c and b tables computed by LCS-LENGTH on the sequences $X = \langle A, B, C, B,$ $D, A, B \rangle$ and $Y = \langle B, D, C, A, B, A \rangle$. The square in row i and column j contains the value of $c[i, j]$ and the appropriate arrow for the value of $b[i, j]$. The entry 4 in $c[7, 6]$—the lower right-hand corner of the table—is the length of an LCS $\langle B, C, B, A \rangle$ of X and Y. For $i, j > 0$, entry $c[i, j]$ depends only on whether $x_i = y_j$ and the values in entries $c[i - 1, j], c[i, j - 1]$, and $c[i - 1, j - 1]$, which are computed before $c[i, j]$. To reconstruct the elements of an LCS, follow the $b[i, j]$ arrows from the lower right-hand corner, as shown by the sequence shaded blue. Each "↖" on the shaded-blue sequence corresponds to an entry (highlighted) for which $x_i = y_j$ is a member of an LCS.

The initial call is PRINT-LCS(b, X, m, n). For the b table in Figure 14.8, this procedure prints $BCBA$. The procedure takes $O(m + n)$ time, since it decrements at least one of i and j in each recursive call.

Improving the code

Once you have developed an algorithm, you will often find that you can improve on the time or space it uses. Some changes can simplify the code and improve constant factors but otherwise yield no asymptotic improvement in performance. Others can yield substantial asymptotic savings in time and space.

In the LCS algorithm, for example, you can eliminate the b table altogether. Each $c[i, j]$ entry depends on only three other c table entries: $c[i - 1, j - 1]$, $c[i - 1, j]$, and $c[i, j - 1]$. Given the value of $c[i, j]$, you can determine in $O(1)$ time which of these three values was used to compute $c[i, j]$, without inspecting table b. Thus, you can reconstruct an LCS in $O(m + n)$ time using a procedure similar to PRINT-LCS. (Exercise 14.4-2 asks you to give the pseudocode.) Although this method saves $\Theta(mn)$ space, the auxiliary space requirement for computing an LCS does not asymptotically decrease, since the c table takes $\Theta(mn)$ space anyway.

You can, however, reduce the asymptotic space requirements for LCS-LENGTH, since it needs only two rows of table c at a time: the row being computed and the previous row. (In fact, as Exercise 14.4-4 asks you to show, you can use only slightly more than the space for one row of c to compute the length of an LCS.) This improvement works if you need only the length of an LCS. If you need to reconstruct the elements of an LCS, the smaller table does not keep enough information to retrace the algorithm's steps in $O(m + n)$ time.

Exercises

14.4-1
Determine an LCS of $\langle 1, 0, 0, 1, 0, 1, 0, 1 \rangle$ and $\langle 0, 1, 0, 1, 1, 0, 1, 1, 0 \rangle$.

14.4-2
Give pseudocode to reconstruct an LCS from the completed c table and the original sequences $X = \langle x_1, x_2, \ldots, x_m \rangle$ and $Y = \langle y_1, y_2, \ldots, y_n \rangle$ in $O(m + n)$ time, without using the b table.

14.4-3
Give a memoized version of LCS-LENGTH that runs in $O(mn)$ time.

14.4-4
Show how to compute the length of an LCS using only $2 \cdot \min \{m, n\}$ entries in the c table plus $O(1)$ additional space. Then show how to do the same thing, but using $\min \{m, n\}$ entries plus $O(1)$ additional space.

14.4-5
Give an $O(n^2)$-time algorithm to find the longest monotonically increasing subsequence of a sequence of n numbers.

★ ***14.4-6***
Give an $O(n \lg n)$-time algorithm to find the longest monotonically increasing subsequence of a sequence of n numbers. (*Hint:* The last element of a candidate subsequence of length i is at least as large as the last element of a candidate subsequence of length $i - 1$. Maintain candidate subsequences by linking them through the input sequence.)

14.5   Optimal binary search trees

Suppose that you are designing a program to translate text from English to Latvian. For each occurrence of each English word in the text, you need to look up its Latvian equivalent. You can perform these lookup operations by building a binary search tree with n English words as keys and their Latvian equivalents as satellite data. Because you will search the tree for each individual word in the text, you want the total time spent searching to be as low as possible. You can ensure an $O(\lg n)$ search time per occurrence by using a red-black tree or any other balanced binary search tree. Words appear with different frequencies, however, and a frequently used word such as *the* can end up appearing far from the root while a rarely used word such as *naumachia* appears near the root. Such an organization would slow down the translation, since the number of nodes visited when searching for a key in a binary search tree equals 1 plus the depth of the node containing the key. You want words that occur frequently in the text to be placed nearer the root.[8] Moreover, some words in the text might have no Latvian translation,[9] and such words would not appear in the binary search tree at all. How can you organize a binary search tree so as to minimize the number of nodes visited in all searches, given that you know how often each word occurs?

What you need is an *optimal binary search tree*. Formally, given a sequence $K = \langle k_1, k_2, \ldots, k_n \rangle$ of n distinct keys such that $k_1 < k_2 < \cdots < k_n$, build a binary search tree containing them. For each key k_i, you are given the probability p_i that any given search is for key k_i. Since some searches may be for values not in K, you also have $n + 1$ "dummy" keys $d_0, d_1, d_2, \ldots, d_n$ representing those values. In particular, d_0 represents all values less than k_1, d_n represents all values greater than k_n, and for $i = 1, 2, \ldots, n - 1$, the dummy key d_i represents all values between k_i and k_{i+1}. For each dummy key d_i, you have the probability q_i that a search corresponds to d_i. Figure 14.9 shows two binary search trees for a set of $n = 5$ keys. Each key k_i is an internal node, and each dummy key d_i is a leaf. Since every search is either successful (finding some key k_i) or unsuccessful (finding some dummy key d_i), we have

$$\sum_{i=1}^{n} p_i + \sum_{i=0}^{n} q_i = 1 \, . \tag{14.10}$$

---

[8] If the subject of the text is ancient Rome, you might want *naumachia* to appear near the root.

[9] Yes, *naumachia* has a Latvian counterpart: *nomačija*.

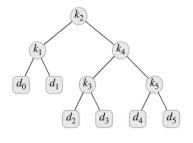 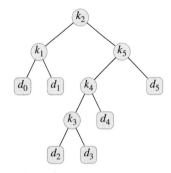

node	depth	probability	contribution		node	depth	probability	contribution
k_1	1	0.15	0.30		k_1	1	0.15	0.30
k_2	0	0.10	0.10		k_2	0	0.10	0.10
k_3	2	0.05	0.15		k_3	3	0.05	0.20
k_4	1	0.10	0.20		k_4	2	0.10	0.30
k_5	2	0.20	0.60		k_5	1	0.20	0.40
d_0	2	0.05	0.15		d_0	2	0.05	0.15
d_1	2	0.10	0.30		d_1	2	0.10	0.30
d_2	3	0.05	0.20		d_2	4	0.05	0.25
d_3	3	0.05	0.20		d_3	4	0.05	0.25
d_4	3	0.05	0.20		d_4	3	0.05	0.20
d_5	3	0.10	0.40		d_5	2	0.10	0.30
Total			2.80		Total			2.75

(a)   (b)

Figure 14.9   Two binary search trees for a set of $n = 5$ keys with the following probabilities:

i	0	1	2	3	4	5
p_i		0.15	0.10	0.05	0.10	0.20
q_i	0.05	0.10	0.05	0.05	0.05	0.10

(a) A binary search tree with expected search cost 2.80. **(b)** A binary search tree with expected search cost 2.75. This tree is optimal.

Knowing the probabilities of searches for each key and each dummy key allows us to determine the expected cost of a search in a given binary search tree T. Let us assume that the actual cost of a search equals the number of nodes examined, which is the depth of the node found by the search in T, plus 1. Then the expected cost of a search in T is

$$E[\text{search cost in } T] = \sum_{i=1}^{n}(\text{depth}_T(k_i) + 1) \cdot p_i + \sum_{i=0}^{n}(\text{depth}_T(d_i) + 1) \cdot q_i$$

$$= 1 + \sum_{i=1}^{n} \text{depth}_T(k_i) \cdot p_i + \sum_{i=0}^{n} \text{depth}_T(d_i) \cdot q_i , \quad (14.11)$$

where depth$_T$ denotes a node's depth in the tree T. The last equation follows from equation (14.10). Figure 14.9 shows how to calculate the expected search cost node by node.

For a given set of probabilities, your goal is to construct a binary search tree whose expected search cost is smallest. We call such a tree an *optimal binary search tree*. Figure 14.9(a) shows one binary search tree, with expected cost 2.80, for the probabilities given in the figure caption. Part (b) of the figure displays an optimal binary search tree, with expected cost 2.75. This example demonstrates that an optimal binary search tree is not necessarily a tree whose overall height is smallest. Nor does an optimal binary search tree always have the key with the greatest probability at the root. Here, key k_5 has the greatest search probability of any key, yet the root of the optimal binary search tree shown is k_2. (The lowest expected cost of any binary search tree with k_5 at the root is 2.85.)

As with matrix-chain multiplication, exhaustive checking of all possibilities fails to yield an efficient algorithm. You can label the nodes of any n-node binary tree with the keys $k_1, k_2, \ldots, k_n$ to construct a binary search tree, and then add in the dummy keys as leaves. In Problem 12-4 on page 329, we saw that the number of binary trees with n nodes is $\Omega(4^n / n^{3/2})$. Thus you would need to examine an exponential number of binary search trees to perform an exhaustive search. We'll see how to solve this problem more efficiently with dynamic programming.

Step 1: The structure of an optimal binary search tree

To characterize the optimal substructure of optimal binary search trees, we start with an observation about subtrees. Consider any subtree of a binary search tree. It must contain keys in a contiguous range $k_i, \ldots, k_j$, for some $1 \leq i \leq j \leq n$. In addition, a subtree that contains keys $k_i, \ldots, k_j$ must also have as its leaves the dummy keys $d_{i-1}, \ldots, d_j$.

Now we can state the optimal substructure: if an optimal binary search tree T has a subtree T' containing keys $k_i, \ldots, k_j$, then this subtree T' must be optimal as well for the subproblem with keys $k_i, \ldots, k_j$ and dummy keys $d_{i-1}, \ldots, d_j$. The usual cut-and-paste argument applies. If there were a subtree T'' whose expected cost is lower than that of T', then cutting T' out of T and pasting in T'' would result in a binary search tree of lower expected cost than T, thus contradicting the optimality of T.

With the optimal substructure in hand, here is how to construct an optimal solution to the problem from optimal solutions to subproblems. Given keys $k_i, \ldots, k_j$, one of these keys, say k_r ($i \leq r \leq j$), is the root of an optimal subtree containing these keys. The left subtree of the root k_r contains the keys $k_i, \ldots, k_{r-1}$ (and dummy keys $d_{i-1}, \ldots, d_{r-1}$), and the right subtree contains the keys $k_{r+1}, \ldots, k_j$ (and dummy keys $d_r, \ldots, d_j$). As long as you examine all candidate roots k_r, where $i \leq r \leq j$, and you determine all optimal binary search trees containing $k_i, \ldots, k_{r-1}$ and those containing $k_{r+1}, \ldots, k_j$, you are guaranteed to find an optimal binary search tree.

There is one technical detail worth understanding about "empty" subtrees. Suppose that in a subtree with keys $k_i, \ldots, k_j$, you select k_i as the root. By the above argument, k_i's left subtree contains the keys $k_i, \ldots, k_{i-1}$: no keys at all. Bear in mind, however, that subtrees also contain dummy keys. We adopt the convention that a subtree containing keys $k_i, \ldots, k_{i-1}$ has no actual keys but does contain the single dummy key d_{i-1}. Symmetrically, if you select k_j as the root, then k_j's right subtree contains the keys $k_{j+1}, \ldots, k_j$. This right subtree contains no actual keys, but it does contain the dummy key d_j.

Step 2: A recursive solution

To define the value of an optimal solution recursively, the subproblem domain is finding an optimal binary search tree containing the keys $k_i, \ldots, k_j$, where $i \geq 1$, $j \leq n$, and $j \geq i - 1$. (When $j = i - 1$, there is just the dummy key d_{i-1}, but no actual keys.) Let $e[i, j]$ denote the expected cost of searching an optimal binary search tree containing the keys $k_i, \ldots, k_j$. Your goal is to compute $e[1, n]$, the expected cost of searching an optimal binary search tree for all the actual and dummy keys.

The easy case occurs when $j = i - 1$. Then the subproblem consists of just the dummy key d_{i-1}. The expected search cost is $e[i, i - 1] = q_{i-1}$.

When $j \geq i$, you need to select a root k_r from among $k_i, \ldots, k_j$ and then make an optimal binary search tree with keys $k_i, \ldots, k_{r-1}$ as its left subtree and an optimal binary search tree with keys $k_{r+1}, \ldots, k_j$ as its right subtree. What happens to the expected search cost of a subtree when it becomes a subtree of a node? The depth of each node in the subtree increases by 1. By equation (14.11), the expected search cost of this subtree increases by the sum of all the probabilities in the subtree. For a subtree with keys $k_i, \ldots, k_j$, denote this sum of probabilities as

$$w(i, j) = \sum_{l=i}^{j} p_l + \sum_{l=i-1}^{j} q_l . \tag{14.12}$$

Thus, if k_r is the root of an optimal subtree containing keys $k_i, \ldots, k_j$, we have

$$e[i, j] = p_r + (e[i, r - 1] + w(i, r - 1)) + (e[r + 1, j] + w(r + 1, j)) .$$

Noting that

$$w(i, j) = w(i, r - 1) + p_r + w(r + 1, j) ,$$

we rewrite $e[i, j]$ as

$$e[i, j] = e[i, r - 1] + e[r + 1, j] + w(i, j) \,. \tag{14.13}$$

The recursive equation (14.13) assumes that you know which node k_r to use as the root. Of course, you choose the root that gives the lowest expected search cost, giving the final recursive formulation:

$$e[i, j] = \begin{cases} q_{i-1} & \text{if } j = i - 1 \,, \\ \min \{e[i, r - 1] + e[r + 1, j] + w(i, j) : i \leq r \leq j\} & \text{if } i \leq j \,. \end{cases} \tag{14.14}$$

The $e[i, j]$ values give the expected search costs in optimal binary search trees. To help keep track of the structure of optimal binary search trees, define $root[i, j]$, for $1 \leq i \leq j \leq n$, to be the index r for which k_r is the root of an optimal binary search tree containing keys $k_i, \ldots, k_j$. Although we'll see how to compute the values of $root[i, j]$, the construction of an optimal binary search tree from these values is left as Exercise 14.5-1.

Step 3: Computing the expected search cost of an optimal binary search tree

At this point, you may have noticed some similarities between our characterizations of optimal binary search trees and matrix-chain multiplication. For both problem domains, the subproblems consist of contiguous index subranges. A direct, recursive implementation of equation (14.14) would be just as inefficient as a direct, recursive matrix-chain multiplication algorithm. Instead, you can store the $e[i, j]$ values in a table $e[1 : n + 1, 0 : n]$. The first index needs to run to $n + 1$ rather than n because in order to have a subtree containing only the dummy key d_n, you need to compute and store $e[n + 1, n]$. The second index needs to start from 0 because in order to have a subtree containing only the dummy key d_0, you need to compute and store $e[1, 0]$. Only the entries $e[i, j]$ for which $j \geq i - 1$ are filled in. The table $root[i, j]$ records the root of the subtree containing keys $k_i, \ldots, k_j$ and uses only the entries for which $1 \leq i \leq j \leq n$.

One other table makes the dynamic-programming algorithm a little faster. Instead of computing the value of $w(i, j)$ from scratch every time you compute $e[i, j]$, which would take $\Theta(j - i)$ additions, store these values in a table $w[1 : n + 1, 0 : n]$. For the base case, compute $w[i, i - 1] = q_{i-1}$ for $1 \leq i \leq n + 1$. For $j \geq i$, compute

$$w[i, j] = w[i, j - 1] + p_j + q_j \,. \tag{14.15}$$

Thus, you can compute the $\Theta(n^2)$ values of $w[i, j]$ in $\Theta(1)$ time each.

The OPTIMAL-BST procedure on the next page takes as inputs the probabilities $p_1, \ldots, p_n$ and $q_0, \ldots, q_n$ and the size n, and it returns the tables e and $root$. From the description above and the similarity to the MATRIX-CHAIN-ORDER procedure in Section 14.2, you should find the operation of this procedure to be fairly straight-forward. The **for** loop of lines 2–4 initializes the values of $e[i, i-1]$ and $w[i, i-1]$. Then the **for** loop of lines 5–14 uses the recurrences (14.14) and (14.15) to compute $e[i, j]$ and $w[i, j]$ for all $1 \leq i \leq j \leq n$. In the first iteration, when $l = 1$, the loop computes $e[i, i]$ and $w[i, i]$ for $i = 1, 2, \ldots, n$. The second iteration, with $l = 2$, computes $e[i, i+1]$ and $w[i, i+1]$ for $i = 1, 2, \ldots, n-1$, and so on. The innermost **for** loop, in lines 10–14, tries each candidate index r to determine which key k_r to use as the root of an optimal binary search tree containing keys $k_i, \ldots, k_j$. This **for** loop saves the current value of the index r in $root[i, j]$ whenever it finds a better key to use as the root.

OPTIMAL-BST(p, q, n)

```
 1  let e[1 : n + 1, 0 : n], w[1 : n + 1, 0 : n],
                and root[1 : n, 1 : n] be new tables
 2  for i = 1 to n + 1          // base cases
 3      e[i, i − 1] = q_{i−1}       // equation (14.14)
 4      w[i, i − 1] = q_{i−1}
 5  for l = 1 to n
 6      for i = 1 to n − l + 1
 7          j = i + l − 1
 8          e[i, j] = ∞
 9          w[i, j] = w[i, j − 1] + p_j + q_j      // equation (14.15)
10          for r = i to j                 // try all possible roots r
11              t = e[i, r − 1] + e[r + 1, j] + w[i, j]  // equation (14.14)
12              if t < e[i, j]                        // new minimum?
13                  e[i, j] = t
14                  root[i, j] = r
15  return e and root
```

Figure 14.10 shows the tables $e[i, j]$, $w[i, j]$, and $root[i, j]$ computed by the procedure OPTIMAL-BST on the key distribution shown in Figure 14.9. As in the matrix-chain multiplication example of Figure 14.5, the tables are rotated to make the diagonals run horizontally. OPTIMAL-BST computes the rows from bottom to top and from left to right within each row.

The OPTIMAL-BST procedure takes $\Theta(n^3)$ time, just like MATRIX-CHAIN-ORDER. Its running time is $O(n^3)$, since its **for** loops are nested three deep and each loop index takes on at most n values. The loop indices in OPTIMAL-BST do not have exactly the same bounds as those in MATRIX-CHAIN-ORDER, but they are within at most 1 in all directions. Thus, like MATRIX-CHAIN-ORDER, the OPTIMAL-BST procedure takes $\Omega(n^3)$ time.

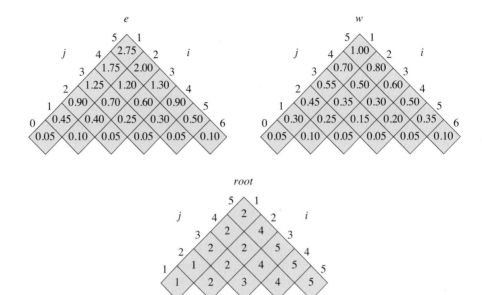

Figure 14.10 The tables $e[i, j]$, $w[i, j]$, and $root[i, j]$ computed by OPTIMAL-BST on the key distribution shown in Figure 14.9. The tables are rotated so that the diagonals run horizontally.

Exercises

14.5-1

Write pseudocode for the procedure CONSTRUCT-OPTIMAL-BST$(root, n)$ which, given the table $root[1:n, 1:n]$, outputs the structure of an optimal binary search tree. For the example in Figure 14.10, your procedure should print out the structure

k_2 is the root
k_1 is the left child of k_2
d_0 is the left child of k_1
d_1 is the right child of k_1
k_5 is the right child of k_2
k_4 is the left child of k_5
k_3 is the left child of k_4
d_2 is the left child of k_3
d_3 is the right child of k_3
d_4 is the right child of k_4
d_5 is the right child of k_5

corresponding to the optimal binary search tree shown in Figure 14.9(b).

14.5-2

Determine the cost and structure of an optimal binary search tree for a set of $n = 7$ keys with the following probabilities:

i	0	1	2	3	4	5	6	7
p_i		0.04	0.06	0.08	0.02	0.10	0.12	0.14
q_i	0.06	0.06	0.06	0.06	0.05	0.05	0.05	0.05

14.5-3

Suppose that instead of maintaining the table $w[i, j]$, you computed the value of $w(i, j)$ directly from equation (14.12) in line 9 of OPTIMAL-BST and used this computed value in line 11. How would this change affect the asymptotic running time of OPTIMAL-BST?

★ **14.5-4**

Knuth [264] has shown that there are always roots of optimal subtrees such that $root[i, j - 1] \leq root[i, j] \leq root[i + 1, j]$ for all $1 \leq i < j \leq n$. Use this fact to modify the OPTIMAL-BST procedure to run in $\Theta(n^2)$ time.

Problems

14-1 *Longest simple path in a directed acyclic graph*

You are given a directed acyclic graph $G = (V, E)$ with real-valued edge weights and two distinguished vertices s and t. The *weight* of a path is the sum of the weights of the edges in the path. Describe a dynamic-programming approach for finding a longest weighted simple path from s to t. What is the running time of your algorithm?

14-2 *Longest palindrome subsequence*

A *palindrome* is a nonempty string over some alphabet that reads the same forward and backward. Examples of palindromes are all strings of length 1, civic, racecar, and aibohphobia (fear of palindromes).

Give an efficient algorithm to find the longest palindrome that is a subsequence of a given input string. For example, given the input character, your algorithm should return carac. What is the running time of your algorithm?

14-3 *Bitonic euclidean traveling-salesperson problem*

In the *euclidean traveling-salesperson problem*, you are given a set of n points in the plane, and your goal is to find the shortest closed tour that connects all n points.

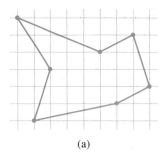 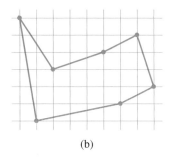

(a)   (b)

Figure 14.11   Seven points in the plane, shown on a unit grid. **(a)** The shortest closed tour, with length approximately 24.89. This tour is not bitonic. **(b)** The shortest bitonic tour for the same set of points. Its length is approximately 25.58.

Figure 14.11(a) shows the solution to a 7-point problem. The general problem is NP-hard, and its solution is therefore believed to require more than polynomial time (see Chapter 34).

J. L. Bentley has suggested simplifying the problem by considering only *bitonic tours*, that is, tours that start at the leftmost point, go strictly rightward to the rightmost point, and then go strictly leftward back to the starting point. Figure 14.11(b) shows the shortest bitonic tour of the same 7 points. In this case, a polynomial-time algorithm is possible.

Describe an $O(n^2)$-time algorithm for determining an optimal bitonic tour. You may assume that no two points have the same x-coordinate and that all operations on real numbers take unit time. (*Hint:* Scan left to right, maintaining optimal possibilities for the two parts of the tour.)

14-4   Printing neatly

Consider the problem of neatly printing a paragraph with a monospaced font (all characters having the same width). The input text is a sequence of n words of lengths $l_1, l_2, \ldots, l_n$, measured in characters, which are to be printed neatly on a number of lines that hold a maximum of M characters each. No word exceeds the line length, so that $l_i \leq M$ for $i = 1, 2, \ldots, n$. The criterion of "neatness" is as follows. If a given line contains words i through j, where $i \leq j$, and exactly one space appears between words, then the number of extra space characters at the end of the line is $M - j + i - \sum_{k=i}^{j} l_k$, which must be nonnegative so that the words fit on the line. The goal is to minimize the sum, over all lines except the last, of the cubes of the numbers of extra space characters at the ends of lines. Give a dynamic-programming algorithm to print a paragraph of n words neatly. Analyze the running time and space requirements of your algorithm.

14-5 Edit distance

In order to transform a source string of text $x[1:m]$ to a target string $y[1:n]$, you can perform various transformation operations. The goal is, given x and y, to produce a series of transformations that changes x to y. An array z—assumed to be large enough to hold all the characters it needs—holds the intermediate results. Initially, z is empty, and at termination, you should have $z[j] = y[j]$ for $j = 1, 2, \ldots, n$. The procedure for solving this problem maintains current indices i into x and j into z, and the operations are allowed to alter z and these indices. Initially, $i = j = 1$. Every character in x must be examined during the transformation, which means that at the end of the sequence of transformation operations, $i = m + 1$.

You may choose from among six transformation operations, each of which has a constant cost that depends on the operation:

Copy a character from x to z by setting $z[j] = x[i]$ and then incrementing both i and j. This operation examines $x[i]$ and has cost Q_C.

Replace a character from x by another character c, by setting $z[j] = c$, and then incrementing both i and j. This operation examines $x[i]$ and has cost Q_R.

Delete a character from x by incrementing i but leaving j alone. This operation examines $x[i]$ and has cost Q_D.

Insert the character c into z by setting $z[j] = c$ and then incrementing j, but leaving i alone. This operation examines no characters of x and has cost Q_I.

Twiddle (i.e., exchange) the next two characters by copying them from x to z but in the opposite order: setting $z[j] = x[i + 1]$ and $z[j + 1] = x[i]$, and then setting $i = i + 2$ and $j = j + 2$. This operation examines $x[i]$ and $x[i + 1]$ and has cost Q_T.

Kill the remainder of x by setting $i = m + 1$. This operation examines all characters in x that have not yet been examined. This operation, if performed, must be the final operation. It has cost Q_K.

Figure 14.12 gives one way to transform the source string `algorithm` to the target string `altruistic`. Several other sequences of transformation operations can transform `algorithm` to `altruistic`.

Assume that $Q_C < Q_D + Q_I$ and $Q_R < Q_D + Q_I$, since otherwise, the copy and replace operations would not be used. The cost of a given sequence of transformation operations is the sum of the costs of the individual operations in the sequence. For the sequence above, the cost of transforming `algorithm` to `altruistic` is $3Q_C + Q_R + Q_D + 4Q_I + Q_T + Q_K$.

a. Given two sequences $x[1:m]$ and $y[1:n]$ and the costs of the transformation operations, the *edit distance* from x to y is the cost of the least expensive op-

Operation	x	z
initial strings	a̲lgorithm	_
copy	al̲gorithm	a_
copy	al̲gorithm	al_
replace by t	alg̲orithm	alt_
delete	algo̲rithm	alt_
copy	algor̲ithm	altr_
insert u	algori̲thm	altru_
insert i	algori̲thm	altrui_
insert s	algori̲thm	altruis_
twiddle	algorit̲hm	altruisti_
insert c	algorith̲m	altruistic_
kill	algorithm̲_	altruistic_

Figure 14.12   A sequence of operations that transforms the source algorithm to the target string altruistic. The underlined characters are $x[i]$ and $z[j]$ after the operation.

eration sequence that transforms x to y. Describe a dynamic-programming algorithm that finds the edit distance from $x[1:m]$ to $y[1:n]$ and prints an optimal operation sequence. Analyze the running time and space requirements of your algorithm.

The edit-distance problem generalizes the problem of aligning two DNA sequences (see, for example, Setubal and Meidanis [405, Section 3.2]). There are several methods for measuring the similarity of two DNA sequences by aligning them. One such method to align two sequences x and y consists of inserting spaces at arbitrary locations in the two sequences (including at either end) so that the resulting sequences x' and y' have the same length but do not have a space in the same position (i.e., for no position j are both $x'[j]$ and $y'[j]$ a space). Then we assign a "score" to each position. Position j receives a score as follows:

- $+1$ if $x'[j] = y'[j]$ and neither is a space,

- -1 if $x'[j] \neq y'[j]$ and neither is a space,

- -2 if either $x'[j]$ or $y'[j]$ is a space.

The score for the alignment is the sum of the scores of the individual positions. For example, given the sequences x = GATCGGCAT and y = CAATGTGAATC, one alignment is

```
G ATCG GCAT
CAAT GTGAATC
-*++*+*+-++*
```

A + under a position indicates a score of +1 for that position, a − indicates a score of −1, and a ∗ indicates a score of −2, so that this alignment has a total score of $6 \cdot 1 - 2 \cdot 1 - 4 \cdot 2 = -4$.

b. Explain how to cast the problem of finding an optimal alignment as an edit-distance problem using a subset of the transformation operations copy, replace, delete, insert, twiddle, and kill.

14-6 Planning a company party

Professor Blutarsky is consulting for the president of a corporation that is planning a company party. The company has a hierarchical structure, that is, the supervisor relation forms a tree rooted at the president. The human resources department has ranked each employee with a conviviality rating, which is a real number. In order to make the party fun for all attendees, the president does not want both an employee and his or her immediate supervisor to attend.

Professor Blutarsky is given the tree that describes the structure of the corporation, using the left-child, right-sibling representation described in Section 10.3. Each node of the tree holds, in addition to the pointers, the name of an employee and that employee's conviviality ranking. Describe an algorithm to make up a guest list that maximizes the sum of the conviviality ratings of the guests. Analyze the running time of your algorithm.

14-7 Viterbi algorithm

Dynamic programming on a directed graph can play a part in speech recognition. A directed graph $G = (V, E)$ with labeled edges forms a formal model of a person speaking a restricted language. Each edge $(u, v) \in E$ is labeled with a sound $\sigma(u, v)$ from a finite set Σ of sounds. Each directed path in the graph starting from a distinguished vertex $v_0 \in V$ corresponds to a possible sequence of sounds produced by the model, with the label of a path being the concatenation of the labels of the edges on that path.

a. Describe an efficient algorithm that, given an edge-labeled directed graph G with distinguished vertex v_0 and a sequence $s = \langle \sigma_1, \sigma_2, \ldots, \sigma_k \rangle$ of sounds from Σ, returns a path in G that begins at v_0 and has s as its label, if any such path exists. Otherwise, the algorithm should return NO-SUCH-PATH. Analyze the running time of your algorithm. (*Hint:* You may find concepts from Chapter 20 useful.)

Now suppose that every edge $(u, v) \in E$ has an associated nonnegative probability $p(u, v)$ of being traversed, so that the corresponding sound is produced. The sum of the probabilities of the edges leaving any vertex equals 1. The probability of a path is defined to be the product of the probabilities of its edges. Think of the probability of a path beginning at vertex v_0 as the probability that a "random walk" beginning at v_0 follows the specified path, where the edge leaving a vertex u is taken randomly, according to the probabilities of the available edges leaving u.

b. Extend your answer to part (a) so that if a path is returned, it is a *most probable path* starting at vertex v_0 and having label s. Analyze the running time of your algorithm.

14-8   *Image compression by seam carving*

Suppose that you are given a color picture consisting of an $m \times n$ array $A[1:m, 1:n]$ of pixels, where each pixel specifies a triple of red, green, and blue (RGB) intensities. You want to compress this picture slightly, by removing one pixel from each of the m rows, so that the whole picture becomes one pixel narrower. To avoid incongruous visual effects, however, the pixels removed in two adjacent rows must lie in either the same column or adjacent columns. In this way, the pixels removed form a "seam" from the top row to the bottom row, where successive pixels in the seam are adjacent vertically or diagonally.

a. Show that the number of such possible seams grows at least exponentially in m, assuming that $n > 1$.

b. Suppose now that along with each pixel $A[i, j]$, you are given a real-valued disruption measure $d[i, j]$, indicating how disruptive it would be to remove pixel $A[i, j]$. Intuitively, the lower a pixel's disruption measure, the more similar the pixel is to its neighbors. Define the disruption measure of a seam as the sum of the disruption measures of its pixels.

Give an algorithm to find a seam with the lowest disruption measure. How efficient is your algorithm?

14-9   *Breaking a string*

A certain string-processing programming language allows you to break a string into two pieces. Because this operation copies the string, it costs n time units to break a string of n characters into two pieces. Suppose that you want to break a string into many pieces. The order in which the breaks occur can affect the total amount of time used. For example, suppose that you want to break a 20-character string after characters 2, 8, and 10 (numbering the characters in ascending order from the left-hand end, starting from 1). If you program the breaks to occur in left-to-right order, then the first break costs 20 time units, the second break costs 18 time units (breaking the string from characters 3 to 20 at character 8), and the third break costs 12 time units, totaling 50 time units. If you program the breaks to occur in right-to-left order, however, then the first break costs 20 time units, the second break costs 10 time units, and the third break costs 8 time units, totaling 38 time units. In yet another order, you could break first at 8 (costing 20), then break the left piece at 2 (costing another 8), and finally the right piece at 10 (costing 12), for a total cost of 40.

Design an algorithm that, given the numbers of characters after which to break, determines a least-cost way to sequence those breaks. More formally, given an array $L[1:m]$ containing the break points for a string of n characters, compute the lowest cost for a sequence of breaks, along with a sequence of breaks that achieves this cost.

14-10 *Planning an investment strategy*

Your knowledge of algorithms helps you obtain an exciting job with a hot startup, along with a $10,000 signing bonus. You decide to invest this money with the goal of maximizing your return at the end of 10 years. You decide to use your investment manager, G. I. Luvcache, to manage your signing bonus. The company that Luvcache works with requires you to observe the following rules. It offers n different investments, numbered 1 through n. In each year j, investment i provides a return rate of r_{ij}. In other words, if you invest d dollars in investment i in year j, then at the end of year j, you have dr_{ij} dollars. The return rates are guaranteed, that is, you are given all the return rates for the next 10 years for each investment. You make investment decisions only once per year. At the end of each year, you can leave the money made in the previous year in the same investments, or you can shift money to other investments, by either shifting money between existing investments or moving money to a new investment. If you do not move your money between two consecutive years, you pay a fee of f_1 dollars, whereas if you switch your money, you pay a fee of f_2 dollars, where $f_2 > f_1$. You pay the fee once per year at the end of the year, and it is the same amount, f_2, whether you move money in and out of only one investment, or in and out of many investments.

a. The problem, as stated, allows you to invest your money in multiple investments in each year. Prove that there exists an optimal investment strategy that, in each year, puts all the money into a single investment. (Recall that an optimal investment strategy maximizes the amount of money after 10 years and is not concerned with any other objectives, such as minimizing risk.)

b. Prove that the problem of planning your optimal investment strategy exhibits optimal substructure.

c. Design an algorithm that plans your optimal investment strategy. What is the running time of your algorithm?

d. Suppose that Luvcache's company imposes the additional restriction that, at any point, you can have no more than $15,000 in any one investment. Show that the problem of maximizing your income at the end of 10 years no longer exhibits optimal substructure.

14-11 *Inventory planning*

The Rinky Dink Company makes machines that resurface ice rinks. The demand for such products varies from month to month, and so the company needs to develop a strategy to plan its manufacturing given the fluctuating, but predictable, demand. The company wishes to design a plan for the next n months. For each month i, the company knows the demand d_i, that is, the number of machines that it will sell. Let $D = \sum_{i=1}^{n} d_i$ be the total demand over the next n months. The company keeps a full-time staff who provide labor to manufacture up to m machines per month. If the company needs to make more than m machines in a given month, it can hire additional, part-time labor, at a cost that works out to c dollars per machine. Furthermore, if the company is holding any unsold machines at the end of a month, it must pay inventory costs. The company can hold up to D machines, with the cost for holding j machines given as a function $h(j)$ for $j = 1, 2, \ldots, D$ that monotonically increases with j.

Give an algorithm that calculates a plan for the company that minimizes its costs while fulfilling all the demand. The running time should be polynomial in n and D.

14-12 *Signing free-agent baseball players*

Suppose that you are the general manager for a major-league baseball team. During the off-season, you need to sign some free-agent players for your team. The team owner has given you a budget of $\$X$ to spend on free agents. You are allowed to spend less than $\$X$, but the owner will fire you if you spend any more than $\$X$.

You are considering N different positions, and for each position, P free-agent players who play that position are available.[10] Because you do not want to overload your roster with too many players at any position, for each position you may sign at most one free agent who plays that position. (If you do not sign any players at a particular position, then you plan to stick with the players you already have at that position.)

---

[10] Although there are nine positions on a baseball team, N is not necessarily equal to 9 because some general managers have particular ways of thinking about positions. For example, a general manager might consider right-handed pitchers and left-handed pitchers to be separate "positions," as well as starting pitchers, long relief pitchers (relief pitchers who can pitch several innings), and short relief pitchers (relief pitchers who normally pitch at most only one inning).

To determine how valuable a player is going to be, you decide to use a saber-metric statistic[11] known as "WAR," or "wins above replacement." A player with a higher WAR is more valuable than a player with a lower WAR. It is not necessarily more expensive to sign a player with a higher WAR than a player with a lower WAR, because factors other than a player's value determine how much it costs to sign them.

For each available free-agent player p, you have three pieces of information:

- the player's position,

- $p.cost$, the amount of money it costs to sign the player, and

- $p.war$, the player's WAR.

Devise an algorithm that maximizes the total WAR of the players you sign while spending no more than $\$X$. You may assume that each player signs for a multiple of $\$100,000$. Your algorithm should output the total WAR of the players you sign, the total amount of money you spend, and a list of which players you sign. Analyze the running time and space requirement of your algorithm.

Chapter notes

Bellman [44] began the systematic study of dynamic programming in 1955, publishing a book about it in 1957. The word "programming," both here and in linear programming, refers to using a tabular solution method. Although optimization techniques incorporating elements of dynamic programming were known earlier, Bellman provided the area with a solid mathematical basis.

Galil and Park [172] classify dynamic-programming algorithms according to the size of the table and the number of other table entries each entry depends on. They call a dynamic-programming algorithm tD/eD if its table size is $O(n^t)$ and each entry depends on $O(n^e)$ other entries. For example, the matrix-chain multiplication algorithm in Section 14.2 is $2D/1D$, and the longest-common-subsequence algorithm in Section 14.4 is $2D/0D$.

The MATRIX-CHAIN-ORDER algorithm on page 378 is by Muraoka and Kuck [339]. Hu and Shing [230, 231] give an $O(n \lg n)$-time algorithm for the matrix-chain multiplication problem.

The $O(mn)$-time algorithm for the longest-common-subsequence problem appears to be a folk algorithm. Knuth [95] posed the question of whether subquadratic

---

[11] *Sabermetrics* is the application of statistical analysis to baseball records. It provides several ways to compare the relative values of individual players.

algorithms for the LCS problem exist. Masek and Paterson [316] answered this question in the affirmative by giving an algorithm that runs in $O(mn/\lg n)$ time, where $n \leq m$ and the sequences are drawn from a set of bounded size. For the special case in which no element appears more than once in an input sequence, Szymanski [425] shows how to solve the problem in $O((n + m)\lg(n + m))$ time. Many of these results extend to the problem of computing string edit distances (Problem 14-5).

An early paper on variable-length binary encodings by Gilbert and Moore [181], which had applications to constructing optimal binary search trees for the case in which all probabilities p_i are 0, contains an $O(n^3)$-time algorithm. Aho, Hopcroft, and Ullman [5] present the algorithm from Section 14.5. Splay trees [418], which modify the tree in response to the search queries, come within a constant factor of the optimal bounds without being initialized with the frequencies. Exercise 14.5-4 is due to Knuth [264]. Hu and Tucker [232] devised an algorithm for the case in which all probabilities p_i are 0 that uses $O(n^2)$ time and $O(n)$ space. Subsequently, Knuth [261] reduced the time to $O(n \lg n)$.

Problem 14-8 is due to Avidan and Shamir [30], who have posted on the web a wonderful video illustrating this image-compression technique.

15 Greedy Algorithms

Algorithms for optimization problems typically go through a sequence of steps, with a set of choices at each step. For many optimization problems, using dynamic programming to determine the best choices is overkill, and simpler, more efficient algorithms will do. A *greedy algorithm* always makes the choice that looks best at the moment. That is, it makes a locally optimal choice in the hope that this choice leads to a globally optimal solution. This chapter explores optimization problems for which greedy algorithms provide optimal solutions. Before reading this chapter, you should read about dynamic programming in Chapter 14, particularly Section 14.3.

Greedy algorithms do not always yield optimal solutions, but for many problems they do. We first examine, in Section 15.1, a simple but nontrivial problem, the activity-selection problem, for which a greedy algorithm efficiently computes an optimal solution. We'll arrive at the greedy algorithm by first considering a dynamic-programming approach and then showing that an optimal solution can result from always making greedy choices. Section 15.2 reviews the basic elements of the greedy approach, giving a direct approach for proving greedy algorithms correct. Section 15.3 presents an important application of greedy techniques: designing data-compression (Huffman) codes. Finally, Section 15.4 shows that in order to decide which blocks to replace when a miss occurs in a cache, the "furthest-in-future" strategy is optimal if the sequence of block accesses is known in advance.

The greedy method is quite powerful and works well for a wide range of problems. Later chapters will present many algorithms that you can view as applications of the greedy method, including minimum-spanning-tree algorithms (Chapter 21), Dijkstra's algorithm for shortest paths from a single source (Section 22.3), and a greedy set-covering heuristic (Section 35.3). Minimum-spanning-tree algorithms furnish a classic example of the greedy method. Although you can read this chapter and Chapter 21 independently of each other, you might find it useful to read them together.

15.1   An activity-selection problem

Our first example is the problem of scheduling several competing activities that re-quire exclusive use of a common resource, with a goal of selecting a maximum-size set of mutually compatible activities. Imagine that you are in charge of scheduling a conference room. You are presented with a set $S = \{a_1, a_2, \ldots, a_n\}$ of n pro-posed *activities* that wish to reserve the conference room, and the room can serve only one activity at a time. Each activity a_i has a *start time* s_i and a *finish time* f_i, where $0 \le s_i < f_i < \infty$. If selected, activity a_i takes place during the half-open time interval $[s_i, f_i)$. Activities a_i and a_j are *compatible* if the intervals $[s_i, f_i)$ and $[s_j, f_j)$ do not overlap. That is, a_i and a_j are compatible if $s_i \ge f_j$ or $s_j \ge f_i$. (Assume that if your staff needs time to change over the room from one activity to the next, the changeover time is built into the intervals.) In the *activity-selection problem*, your goal is to select a maximum-size subset of mutually compatible ac-tivities. Assume that the activities are sorted in monotonically increasing order of finish time:

$$f_1 \le f_2 \le f_3 \le \cdots \le f_{n-1} \le f_n . \tag{15.1}$$

(We'll see later the advantage that this assumption provides.) For example, con-sider the set of activities in Figure 15.1. The subset $\{a_3, a_9, a_{11}\}$ consists of mutu-ally compatible activities. It is not a maximum subset, however, since the subset $\{a_1, a_4, a_8, a_{11}\}$ is larger. In fact, $\{a_1, a_4, a_8, a_{11}\}$ is a largest subset of mutually compatible activities, and another largest subset is $\{a_2, a_4, a_9, a_{11}\}$.

We'll see how to solve this problem, proceeding in several steps. First we'll explore a dynamic-programming solution, in which you consider several choices when determining which subproblems to use in an optimal solution. We'll then observe that you need to consider only one choice—the greedy choice—and that when you make the greedy choice, only one subproblem remains. Based on these observations, we'll develop a recursive greedy algorithm to solve the activity-selection problem. Finally, we'll complete the process of developing a greedy solution by converting the recursive algorithm to an iterative one. Although the steps we go through in this section are slightly more involved than is typical when developing a greedy algorithm, they illustrate the relationship between greedy al-gorithms and dynamic programming.

i	1	2	3	4	5	6	7	8	9	10	11
s_i	1	3	0	5	3	5	6	7	8	2	12
f_i	4	5	6	7	9	9	10	11	12	14	16

Figure 15.1   A set $\{a_1, a_2, \ldots, a_{11}\}$ of activities. Activity a_i has start time s_i and finish time f_i.

The optimal substructure of the activity-selection problem

Let's verify that the activity-selection problem exhibits optimal substructure. Denote by S_{ij} the set of activities that start after activity a_i finishes and that finish before activity a_j starts. Suppose that you want to find a maximum set of mutually compatible activities in S_{ij}, and suppose further that such a maximum set is A_{ij}, which includes some activity a_k. By including a_k in an optimal solution, you are left with two subproblems: finding mutually compatible activities in the set S_{ik} (activities that start after activity a_i finishes and that finish before activity a_k starts) and finding mutually compatible activities in the set S_{kj} (activities that start after activity a_k finishes and that finish before activity a_j starts). Let $A_{ik} = A_{ij} \cap S_{ik}$ and $A_{kj} = A_{ij} \cap S_{kj}$, so that A_{ik} contains the activities in A_{ij} that finish before a_k starts and A_{kj} contains the activities in A_{ij} that start after a_k finishes. Thus, we have $A_{ij} = A_{ik} \cup \{a_k\} \cup A_{kj}$, and so the maximum-size set A_{ij} of mutually compatible activities in S_{ij} consists of $|A_{ij}| = |A_{ik}| + |A_{kj}| + 1$ activities.

The usual cut-and-paste argument shows that an optimal solution A_{ij} must also include optimal solutions to the two subproblems for S_{ik} and S_{kj}. If you could find a set A'_{kj} of mutually compatible activities in S_{kj} where $|A'_{kj}| > |A_{kj}|$, then you could use A'_{kj}, rather than A_{kj}, in a solution to the subproblem for S_{ij}. You would have constructed a set of $|A_{ik}| + |A'_{kj}| + 1 > |A_{ik}| + |A_{kj}| + 1 = |A_{ij}|$ mutually compatible activities, which contradicts the assumption that A_{ij} is an optimal solution. A symmetric argument applies to the activities in S_{ik}.

This way of characterizing optimal substructure suggests that you can solve the activity-selection problem by dynamic programming. Let's denote the size of an optimal solution for the set S_{ij} by $c[i, j]$. Then, the dynamic-programming approach gives the recurrence

$$c[i, j] = c[i, k] + c[k, j] + 1 .$$

Of course, if you do not know that an optimal solution for the set S_{ij} includes activity a_k, you must examine all activities in S_{ij} to find which one to choose, so that

$$c[i, j] = \begin{cases} 0 & \text{if } S_{ij} = \emptyset , \\ \max \{c[i, k] + c[k, j] + 1 : a_k \in S_{ij}\} & \text{if } S_{ij} \neq \emptyset . \end{cases} \tag{15.2}$$

You can then develop a recursive algorithm and memoize it, or you can work bottom-up and fill in table entries as you go along. But you would be overlooking another important characteristic of the activity-selection problem that you can use to great advantage.

Making the greedy choice

What if you could choose an activity to add to an optimal solution without having to first solve all the subproblems? That could save you from having to consider all the choices inherent in recurrence (15.2). In fact, for the activity-selection problem, you need to consider only one choice: the greedy choice.

What is the greedy choice for the activity-selection problem? Intuition suggests that you should choose an activity that leaves the resource available for as many other activities as possible. Of the activities you end up choosing, one of them must be the first one to finish. Intuition says, therefore, choose the activity in S with the earliest finish time, since that leaves the resource available for as many of the activities that follow it as possible. (If more than one activity in S has the earliest finish time, then choose any such activity.) In other words, since the activities are sorted in monotonically increasing order by finish time, the greedy choice is activity a_1. Choosing the first activity to finish is not the only way to think of making a greedy choice for this problem. Exercise 15.1-3 asks you to explore other possibilities.

Once you make the greedy choice, you have only one remaining subproblem to solve: finding activities that start after a_1 finishes. Why don't you have to consider activities that finish before a_1 starts? Because $s_1 < f_1$, and because f_1 is the earliest finish time of any activity, no activity can have a finish time less than or equal to s_1. Thus, all activities that are compatible with activity a_1 must start after a_1 finishes.

Furthermore, we have already established that the activity-selection problem exhibits optimal substructure. Let $S_k = \{a_i \in S : s_i \geq f_k\}$ be the set of activities that start after activity a_k finishes. If you make the greedy choice of activity a_1, then S_1 remains as the only subproblem to solve.[1] Optimal substructure says that if a_1 belongs to an optimal solution, then an optimal solution to the original problem consists of activity a_1 and all the activities in an optimal solution to the subproblem S_1.

One big question remains: Is this intuition correct? Is the greedy choice—in which you choose the first activity to finish—always part of some optimal solution? The following theorem shows that it is.

---

[1] We sometimes refer to the sets S_k as subproblems rather than as just sets of activities. The context will make it clear whether we are referring to S_k as a set of activities or as a subproblem whose input is that set.

Theorem 15.1

Consider any nonempty subproblem S_k, and let a_m be an activity in S_k with the earliest finish time. Then a_m is included in some maximum-size subset of mutually compatible activities of S_k.

Proof Let A_k be a maximum-size subset of mutually compatible activities in S_k, and let a_j be the activity in A_k with the earliest finish time. If $a_j = a_m$, we are done, since we have shown that a_m belongs to some maximum-size subset of mutually compatible activities of S_k. If $a_j \neq a_m$, let the set $A'_k = (A_k - \{a_j\}) \cup \{a_m\}$ be A_k but substituting a_m for a_j. The activities in A'_k are compatible, which follows because the activities in A_k are compatible, a_j is the first activity in A_k to finish, and $f_m \leq f_j$. Since $|A'_k| = |A_k|$, we conclude that A'_k is a maximum-size subset of mutually compatible activities of S_k, and it includes a_m. ∎

Although you might be able to solve the activity-selection problem with dynamic programming, Theorem 15.1 says that you don't need to. Instead, you can repeatedly choose the activity that finishes first, keep only the activities compatible with this activity, and repeat until no activities remain. Moreover, because you always choose the activity with the earliest finish time, the finish times of the activities that you choose must strictly increase. You can consider each activity just once overall, in monotonically increasing order of finish times.

An algorithm to solve the activity-selection problem does not need to work bottom-up, like a table-based dynamic-programming algorithm. Instead, it can work top-down, choosing an activity to put into the optimal solution that it constructs and then solving the subproblem of choosing activities from those that are compatible with those already chosen. Greedy algorithms typically have this top-down design: make a choice and then solve a subproblem, rather than the bottom-up technique of solving subproblems before making a choice.

A recursive greedy algorithm

Now that you know you can bypass the dynamic-programming approach and instead use a top-down, greedy algorithm, let's see a straightforward, recursive procedure to solve the activity-selection problem. The procedure RECURSIVE-ACTIVITY-SELECTOR on the following page takes the start and finish times of the activities, represented as arrays s and f,[2] the index k that defines the subproblem S_k it is to solve, and the size n of the original problem. It returns a maximum-

---

[2] Because the pseudocode takes s and f as arrays, it indexes into them with square brackets rather than with subscripts.

size set of mutually compatible activities in S_k. The procedure assumes that the n input activities are already ordered by monotonically increasing finish time, according to equation (15.1). If not, you can first sort them into this order in $O(n \lg n)$ time, breaking ties arbitrarily. In order to start, add the fictitious activity a_0 with $f_0 = 0$, so that subproblem S_0 is the entire set of activities S. The initial call, which solves the entire problem, is RECURSIVE-ACTIVITY-SELECTOR$(s, f, 0, n)$.

RECURSIVE-ACTIVITY-SELECTOR(s, f, k, n)

```
1   m = k + 1
2   while m ≤ n and s[m] < f[k]        // find the first activity in S_k to finish
3       m = m + 1
4   if m ≤ n
5       return {a_m} ∪ RECURSIVE-ACTIVITY-SELECTOR(s, f, m, n)
6   else return Ø
```

Figure 15.2 shows how the algorithm operates on the activities in Figure 15.1. In a given recursive call RECURSIVE-ACTIVITY-SELECTOR(s, f, k, n), the **while** loop of lines 2–3 looks for the first activity in S_k to finish. The loop examines $a_{k+1}, a_{k+2}, \ldots, a_n$, until it finds the first activity a_m that is compatible with a_k, which means that $s_m \geq f_k$. If the loop terminates because it finds such an activity, line 5 returns the union of $\{a_m\}$ and the maximum-size subset of S_m returned by the recursive call RECURSIVE-ACTIVITY-SELECTOR(s, f, m, n). Alternatively, the loop may terminate because $m > n$, in which case the procedure has examined all activities in S_k without finding one that is compatible with a_k. In this case, $S_k = \emptyset$, and so line 6 returns $\emptyset$.

Assuming that the activities have already been sorted by finish times, the running time of the call RECURSIVE-ACTIVITY-SELECTOR$(s, f, 0, n)$ is $\Theta(n)$. To see why, observe that over all recursive calls, each activity is examined exactly once in the **while** loop test of line 2. In particular, activity a_i is examined in the last call made in which $k < i$.

An iterative greedy algorithm

The recursive procedure can be converted to an iterative one because the procedure RECURSIVE-ACTIVITY-SELECTOR is almost "tail recursive" (see Problem 7-5): it ends with a recursive call to itself followed by a union operation. It is usually a straightforward task to transform a tail-recursive procedure to an iterative form. In fact, some compilers for certain programming languages perform this task automatically.

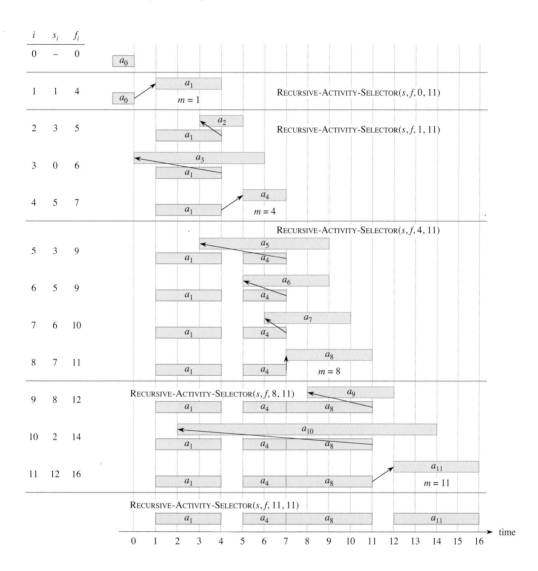

Figure 15.2   The operation of RECURSIVE-ACTIVITY-SELECTOR on the 11 activities from Figure 15.1. Activities considered in each recursive call appear between horizontal lines. The fictitious activity a_0 finishes at time 0, and the initial call RECURSIVE-ACTIVITY-SELECTOR$(s, f, 0, 11)$, selects activity a_1. In each recursive call, the activities that have already been selected are blue, and the activity shown in tan is being considered. If the starting time of an activity occurs before the finish time of the most recently added activity (the arrow between them points left), it is rejected. Otherwise (the arrow points directly up or to the right), it is selected. The last recursive call, RECURSIVE-ACTIVITY-SELECTOR$(s, f, 11, 11)$, returns $\emptyset$. The resulting set of selected activities is $\{a_1, a_4, a_8, a_{11}\}$.

The procedure GREEDY-ACTIVITY-SELECTOR is an iterative version of the procedure RECURSIVE-ACTIVITY-SELECTOR. It, too, assumes that the input activities are ordered by monotonically increasing finish time. It collects selected activities into a set A and returns this set when it is done.

GREEDY-ACTIVITY-SELECTOR(s, f, n)

```
1  A = {a₁}
2  k = 1
3  for m = 2 to n
4      if s[m] ≥ f[k]        // is aₘ in Sₖ?
5          A = A ∪ {aₘ}      // yes, so choose it
6          k = m             // and continue from there
7  return A
```

The procedure works as follows. The variable k indexes the most recent addition to A, corresponding to the activity a_k in the recursive version. Since the procedure considers the activities in order of monotonically increasing finish time, f_k is always the maximum finish time of any activity in A. That is,

$$f_k = \max \{ f_i : a_i \in A \} . \tag{15.3}$$

Lines 1–2 select activity a_1, initialize A to contain just this activity, and initialize k to index this activity. The **for** loop of lines 3–6 finds the earliest activity in S_k to finish. The loop considers each activity a_m in turn and adds a_m to A if it is compatible with all previously selected activities. Such an activity is the earliest in S_k to finish. To see whether activity a_m is compatible with every activity currently in A, it suffices by equation (15.3) to check (in line 4) that its start time s_m is not earlier than the finish time f_k of the activity most recently added to A. If activity a_m is compatible, then lines 5–6 add activity a_m to A and set k to m. The set A returned by the call GREEDY-ACTIVITY-SELECTOR(s, f) is precisely the set returned by the initial call RECURSIVE-ACTIVITY-SELECTOR$(s, f, 0, n)$.

Like the recursive version, GREEDY-ACTIVITY-SELECTOR schedules a set of n activities in $\Theta(n)$ time, assuming that the activities were already sorted initially by their finish times.

Exercises

15.1-1

Give a dynamic-programming algorithm for the activity-selection problem, based on recurrence (15.2). Have your algorithm compute the sizes $c[i, j]$ as defined above and also produce the maximum-size subset of mutually compatible activities.

Assume that the inputs have been sorted as in equation (15.1). Compare the running time of your solution to the running time of GREEDY-ACTIVITY-SELECTOR.

15.1-2

Suppose that instead of always selecting the first activity to finish, you instead select the last activity to start that is compatible with all previously selected activities. Describe how this approach is a greedy algorithm, and prove that it yields an optimal solution.

15.1-3

Not just any greedy approach to the activity-selection problem produces a maximum-size set of mutually compatible activities. Give an example to show that the approach of selecting the activity of least duration from among those that are compatible with previously selected activities does not work. Do the same for the approaches of always selecting the compatible activity that overlaps the fewest other remaining activities and always selecting the compatible remaining activity with the earliest start time.

15.1-4

You are given a set of activities to schedule among a large number of lecture halls, where any activity can take place in any lecture hall. You wish to schedule all the activities using as few lecture halls as possible. Give an efficient greedy algorithm to determine which activity should use which lecture hall.

(This problem is also known as the *interval-graph coloring problem*. It is modeled by an interval graph whose vertices are the given activities and whose edges connect incompatible activities. The smallest number of colors required to color every vertex so that no two adjacent vertices have the same color corresponds to finding the fewest lecture halls needed to schedule all of the given activities.)

15.1-5

Consider a modification to the activity-selection problem in which each activity a_i has, in addition to a start and finish time, a value v_i. The objective is no longer to maximize the number of activities scheduled, but instead to maximize the total value of the activities scheduled. That is, the goal is to choose a set A of compatible activities such that $\sum_{a_k \in A} v_k$ is maximized. Give a polynomial-time algorithm for this problem.

15.2   Elements of the greedy strategy

A greedy algorithm obtains an optimal solution to a problem by making a sequence of choices. At each decision point, the algorithm makes the choice that seems best at the moment. This heuristic strategy does not always produce an optimal solution, but as in the activity-selection problem, sometimes it does. This section discusses some of the general properties of greedy methods.

The process that we followed in Section 15.1 to develop a greedy algorithm was a bit more involved than is typical. It consisted of the following steps:

1. Determine the optimal substructure of the problem.

2. Develop a recursive solution. (For the activity-selection problem, we formulated recurrence (15.2), but bypassed developing a recursive algorithm based solely on this recurrence.)

3. Show that if you make the greedy choice, then only one subproblem remains.

4. Prove that it is always safe to make the greedy choice. (Steps 3 and 4 can occur in either order.)

5. Develop a recursive algorithm that implements the greedy strategy.

6. Convert the recursive algorithm to an iterative algorithm.

These steps highlighted in great detail the dynamic-programming underpinnings of a greedy algorithm. For example, the first cut at the activity-selection problem defined the subproblems S_{ij}, where both i and j varied. We then found that if you always make the greedy choice, you can restrict the subproblems to be of the form S_k.

An alternative approach is to fashion optimal substructure with a greedy choice in mind, so that the choice leaves just one subproblem to solve. In the activity-selection problem, start by dropping the second subscript and defining subproblems of the form S_k. Then prove that a greedy choice (the first activity a_m to finish in S_k), combined with an optimal solution to the remaining set S_m of compatible activities, yields an optimal solution to S_k. More generally, you can design greedy algorithms according to the following sequence of steps:

1. Cast the optimization problem as one in which you make a choice and are left with one subproblem to solve.

2. Prove that there is always an optimal solution to the original problem that makes the greedy choice, so that the greedy choice is always safe.

3. Demonstrate optimal substructure by showing that, having made the greedy choice, what remains is a subproblem with the property that if you combine an

optimal solution to the subproblem with the greedy choice you have made, you arrive at an optimal solution to the original problem.

Later sections of this chapter will use this more direct process. Nevertheless, beneath every greedy algorithm, there is almost always a more cumbersome dynamic-programming solution.

How can you tell whether a greedy algorithm will solve a particular optimization problem? No way works all the time, but the greedy-choice property and optimal substructure are the two key ingredients. If you can demonstrate that the problem has these properties, then you are well on the way to developing a greedy algorithm for it.

Greedy-choice property

The first key ingredient is the *greedy-choice property*: you can assemble a globally optimal solution by making locally optimal (greedy) choices. In other words, when you are considering which choice to make, you make the choice that looks best in the current problem, without considering results from subproblems.

Here is where greedy algorithms differ from dynamic programming. In dynamic programming, you make a choice at each step, but the choice usually depends on the solutions to subproblems. Consequently, you typically solve dynamic-programming problems in a bottom-up manner, progressing from smaller subproblems to larger subproblems. (Alternatively, you can solve them top down, but memoizing. Of course, even though the code works top down, you still must solve the subproblems before making a choice.) In a greedy algorithm, you make whatever choice seems best at the moment and then solve the subproblem that remains. The choice made by a greedy algorithm may depend on choices so far, but it cannot depend on any future choices or on the solutions to subproblems. Thus, unlike dynamic programming, which solves the subproblems before making the first choice, a greedy algorithm makes its first choice before solving any subproblems. A dynamic-programming algorithm proceeds bottom up, whereas a greedy strategy usually progresses top down, making one greedy choice after another, reducing each given problem instance to a smaller one.

Of course, you need to prove that a greedy choice at each step yields a globally optimal solution. Typically, as in the case of Theorem 15.1, the proof examines a globally optimal solution to some subproblem. It then shows how to modify the solution to substitute the greedy choice for some other choice, resulting in one similar, but smaller, subproblem.

You can usually make the greedy choice more efficiently than when you have to consider a wider set of choices. For example, in the activity-selection problem, assuming that the activities were already sorted in monotonically increasing order by finish times, each activity needed to be examined just once. By preprocessing the input or by using an appropriate data structure (often a priority queue), you often can make greedy choices quickly, thus yielding an efficient algorithm.

Optimal substructure

As we saw in Chapter 14, a problem exhibits *optimal substructure* if an optimal solution to the problem contains within it optimal solutions to subproblems. This property is a key ingredient of assessing whether dynamic programming applies, and it's also essential for greedy algorithms. As an example of optimal substructure, recall how Section 15.1 demonstrated that if an optimal solution to subproblem S_{ij} includes an activity a_k, then it must also contain optimal solutions to the subproblems S_{ik} and S_{kj}. Given this optimal substructure, we argued that if you know which activity to use as a_k, you can construct an optimal solution to S_{ij} by selecting a_k along with all activities in optimal solutions to the subproblems S_{ik} and S_{kj}. This observation of optimal substructure gave rise to the recurrence (15.2) that describes the value of an optimal solution.

You will usually use a more direct approach regarding optimal substructure when applying it to greedy algorithms. As mentioned above, you have the luxury of assuming that you arrived at a subproblem by having made the greedy choice in the original problem. All you really need to do is argue that an optimal solution to the subproblem, combined with the greedy choice already made, yields an optimal solution to the original problem. This scheme implicitly uses induction on the subproblems to prove that making the greedy choice at every step produces an optimal solution.

Greedy versus dynamic programming

Because both the greedy and dynamic-programming strategies exploit optimal substructure, you might be tempted to generate a dynamic-programming solution to a problem when a greedy solution suffices or, conversely, you might mistakenly think that a greedy solution works when in fact a dynamic-programming solution is required. To illustrate the subtle differences between the two techniques, let's investigate two variants of a classical optimization problem.

The *0-1 knapsack problem* is the following. A thief robbing a store wants to take the most valuable load that can be carried in a knapsack capable of carrying at most W pounds of loot. The thief can choose to take any subset of n items in the store. The ith item is worth v_i dollars and weighs w_i pounds, where v_i and w_i are integers. Which items should the thief take? (We call this the 0-1 knapsack problem because for each item, the thief must either take it or leave it behind. The thief cannot take a fractional amount of an item or take an item more than once.)

In the *fractional knapsack problem*, the setup is the same, but the thief can take fractions of items, rather than having to make a binary (0-1) choice for each item. You can think of an item in the 0-1 knapsack problem as being like a gold ingot and an item in the fractional knapsack problem as more like gold dust.

Both knapsack problems exhibit the optimal-substructure property. For the 0-1 problem, if the most valuable load weighing at most W pounds includes item j, then the remaining load must be the most valuable load weighing at most $W - w_j$ pounds that the thief can take from the $n - 1$ original items excluding item j. For the comparable fractional problem, if if the most valuable load weighing at most W pounds includes weight w of item j, then the remaining load must be the most valuable load weighing at most $W - w$ pounds that the thief can take from the $n - 1$ original items plus $w_j - w$ pounds of item j.

Although the problems are similar, a greedy strategy works to solve the fractional knapsack problem, but not the 0-1 problem. To solve the fractional problem, first compute the value per pound v_i / w_i for each item. Obeying a greedy strategy, the thief begins by taking as much as possible of the item with the greatest value per pound. If the supply of that item is exhausted and the thief can still carry more, then the thief takes as much as possible of the item with the next greatest value per pound, and so forth, until reaching the weight limit W. Thus, by sorting the items by value per pound, the greedy algorithm runs in $O(n \lg n)$ time. You are asked to prove that the fractional knapsack problem has the greedy-choice property in Exercise 15.2-1.

To see that this greedy strategy does not work for the 0-1 knapsack problem, consider the problem instance illustrated in Figure 15.3(a). This example has three items and a knapsack that can hold 50 pounds. Item 1 weighs 10 pounds and is worth \$60. Item 2 weighs 20 pounds and is worth \$100. Item 3 weighs 30 pounds and is worth \$120. Thus, the value per pound of item 1 is \$6 per pound, which is greater than the value per pound of either item 2 (\$5 per pound) or item 3 (\$4 per pound). The greedy strategy, therefore, would take item 1 first. As you can see from the case analysis in Figure 15.3(b), however, the optimal solution takes items 2 and 3, leaving item 1 behind. The two possible solutions that take item 1 are both suboptimal.

For the comparable fractional problem, however, the greedy strategy, which takes item 1 first, does yield an optimal solution, as shown in Figure 15.3(c). Taking item 1 doesn't work in the 0-1 problem, because the thief is unable to fill the knapsack to capacity, and the empty space lowers the effective value per pound of the load. In the 0-1 problem, when you consider whether to include an item in the knapsack, you must compare the solution to the subproblem that includes the item with the solution to the subproblem that excludes the item before you can make the choice. The problem formulated in this way gives rise to many overlapping sub-

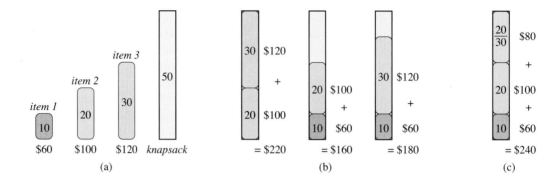

Figure 15.3 An example showing that the greedy strategy does not work for the 0-1 knapsack problem. **(a)** The thief must select a subset of the three items shown whose weight must not exceed 50 pounds. **(b)** The optimal subset includes items 2 and 3. Any solution with item 1 is suboptimal, even though item 1 has the greatest value per pound. **(c)** For the fractional knapsack problem, taking the items in order of greatest value per pound yields an optimal solution.

problems—a hallmark of dynamic programming, and indeed, as Exercise 15.2-2 asks you to show, you can use dynamic programming to solve the 0-1 problem.

Exercises

15.2-1
Prove that the fractional knapsack problem has the greedy-choice property.

15.2-2
Give a dynamic-programming solution to the 0-1 knapsack problem that runs in $O(n\,W)$ time, where n is the number of items and W is the maximum weight of items that the thief can put in the knapsack.

15.2-3
Suppose that in a 0-1 knapsack problem, the order of the items when sorted by increasing weight is the same as their order when sorted by decreasing value. Give an efficient algorithm to find an optimal solution to this variant of the knapsack problem, and argue that your algorithm is correct.

15.2-4
Professor Gekko has always dreamed of inline skating across North Dakota. The professor plans to cross the state on highway U.S. 2, which runs from Grand Forks, on the eastern border with Minnesota, to Williston, near the western border with Montana. The professor can carry two liters of water and can skate m miles before

running out of water. (Because North Dakota is relatively flat, the professor does not have to worry about drinking water at a greater rate on uphill sections than on flat or downhill sections.) The professor will start in Grand Forks with two full liters of water. The professor has an official North Dakota state map, which shows all the places along U.S. 2 to refill water and the distances between these locations.

The professor's goal is to minimize the number of water stops along the route across the state. Give an efficient method by which the professor can determine which water stops to make. Prove that your strategy yields an optimal solution, and give its running time.

15.2-5

Describe an efficient algorithm that, given a set $\{x_1, x_2, \ldots, x_n\}$ of points on the real line, determines the smallest set of unit-length closed intervals that contains all of the given points. Argue that your algorithm is correct.

★ *15.2-6*

Show how to solve the fractional knapsack problem in $O(n)$ time.

15.2-7

You are given two sets A and B, each containing n positive integers. You can choose to reorder each set however you like. After reordering, let a_i be the ith element of set A, and let b_i be the ith element of set B. You then receive a payoff of $\prod_{i=1}^{n} a_i{}^{b_i}$. Give an algorithm that maximizes your payoff. Prove that your algorithm maximizes the payoff, and state its running time, omitting the time for reordering the sets.

15.3 Huffman codes

Huffman codes compress data well: savings of 20% to 90% are typical, depending on the characteristics of the data being compressed. The data arrive as a sequence of characters. Huffman's greedy algorithm uses a table giving how often each character occurs (its frequency) to build up an optimal way of representing each character as a binary string.

Suppose that you have a 100,000-character data file that you wish to store compactly and you know that the 6 distinct characters in the file occur with the frequencies given by Figure 15.4. The character a occurs 45,000 times, the character b occurs 13,000 times, and so on.

You have many options for how to represent such a file of information. Here, we consider the problem of designing a *binary character code* (or *code* for short)

	a	b	c	d	e	f
Frequency (in thousands)	45	13	12	16	9	5
Fixed-length codeword	000	001	010	011	100	101
Variable-length codeword	0	101	100	111	1101	1100

Figure 15.4   A character-coding problem. A data file of 100,000 characters contains only the characters a–f, with the frequencies indicated. With each character represented by a 3-bit codeword, encoding the file requires 300,000 bits. With the variable-length code shown, the encoding requires only 224,000 bits.

in which each character is represented by a unique binary string, which we call a *codeword*. If you use a *fixed-length code*, you need $\lceil \lg n \rceil$ bits to represent $n \geq 2$ characters. For 6 characters, therefore, you need 3 bits: $a = 000$, $b = 001$, $c = 010$, $d = 011$, $e = 100$, and $f = 101$. This method requires 300,000 bits to encode the entire file. Can you do better?

A *variable-length code* can do considerably better than a fixed-length code. The idea is simple: give frequent characters short codewords and infrequent characters long codewords. Figure 15.4 shows such a code. Here, the 1-bit string 0 represents a, and the 4-bit string 1100 represents f. This code requires

$$(45 \cdot 1 + 13 \cdot 3 + 12 \cdot 3 + 16 \cdot 3 + 9 \cdot 4 + 5 \cdot 4) \cdot 1{,}000 = 224{,}000 \text{ bits}$$

to represent the file, a savings of approximately 25%. In fact, this is an optimal character code for this file, as we shall see.

Prefix-free codes

We consider here only codes in which no codeword is also a prefix of some other codeword. Such codes are called *prefix-free codes*. Although we won't prove it here, a prefix-free code can always achieve the optimal data compression among any character code, and so we suffer no loss of generality by restricting our attention to prefix-free codes.

Encoding is always simple for any binary character code: just concatenate the codewords representing each character of the file. For example, with the variable-length prefix-free code of Figure 15.4, the 4-character file face has the encoding $1100 \cdot 0 \cdot 100 \cdot 1101 = 110001001101$, where "·" denotes concatenation.

Prefix-free codes are desirable because they simplify decoding. Since no codeword is a prefix of any other, the codeword that begins an encoded file is unambiguous. You can simply identify the initial codeword, translate it back to the original character, and repeat the decoding process on the remainder of the encoded file. In our example, the string 100011001101 parses uniquely as $100 \cdot 0 \cdot 1100 \cdot 1101$, which decodes to cafe.

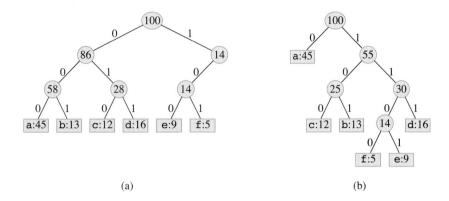

Figure 15.5   Trees corresponding to the coding schemes in Figure 15.4. Each leaf is labeled with a character and its frequency of occurrence. Each internal node is labeled with the sum of the frequencies of the leaves in its subtree. All frequencies are in thousands. **(a)** The tree corresponding to the fixed-length code $a = 000, b = 001, c = 010, d = 011, e = 100, f = 101$. **(b)** The tree corresponding to the optimal prefix-free code $a = 0, b = 101, c = 100, d = 111, e = 1101, f = 1100$.

The decoding process needs a convenient representation for the prefix-free code so that you can easily pick off the initial codeword. A binary tree whose leaves are the given characters provides one such representation. Interpret the binary codeword for a character as the simple path from the root to that character, where 0 means "go to the left child" and 1 means "go to the right child." Figure 15.5 shows the trees for the two codes of our example. Note that these are not binary search trees, since the leaves need not appear in sorted order and internal nodes do not contain character keys.

An optimal code for a file is always represented by a *full* binary tree, in which every nonleaf node has two children (see Exercise 15.3-2). The fixed-length code in our example is not optimal since its tree, shown in Figure 15.5(a), is not a full binary tree: it contains codewords beginning with 10, but none beginning with 11. Since we can now restrict our attention to full binary trees, we can say that if C is the alphabet from which the characters are drawn and all character frequencies are positive, then the tree for an optimal prefix-free code has exactly $|C|$ leaves, one for each letter of the alphabet, and exactly $|C| - 1$ internal nodes (see Exercise B.5-3 on page 1175).

Given a tree T corresponding to a prefix-free code, we can compute the number of bits required to encode a file. For each character c in the alphabet C, let the attribute $c.freq$ denote the frequency of c in the file and let $d_T(c)$ denote the depth of c's leaf in the tree. Note that $d_T(c)$ is also the length of the codeword for character c. The number of bits required to encode a file is thus

$$B(T) = \sum_{c \in C} c.freq \cdot d_T(c) \,, \qquad\qquad (15.4)$$

which we define as the *cost* of the tree T.

Constructing a Huffman code

Huffman invented a greedy algorithm that constructs an optimal prefix-free code, called a *Huffman code* in his honor. In line with our observations in Section 15.2, its proof of correctness relies on the greedy-choice property and optimal substructure. Rather than demonstrating that these properties hold and then developing pseudocode, we present the pseudocode first. Doing so will help clarify how the algorithm makes greedy choices.

The procedure HUFFMAN assumes that C is a set of n characters and that each character $c \in C$ is an object with an attribute $c.freq$ giving its frequency. The algorithm builds the tree T corresponding to an optimal code in a bottom-up manner. It begins with a set of $|C|$ leaves and performs a sequence of $|C| - 1$ "merging" operations to create the final tree. The algorithm uses a min-priority queue Q, keyed on the *freq* attribute, to identify the two least-frequent objects to merge together. The result of merging two objects is a new object whose frequency is the sum of the frequencies of the two objects that were merged.

HUFFMAN(C)

```
 1  n = |C|
 2  Q = C
 3  for i = 1 to n − 1
 4      allocate a new node z
 5      x = EXTRACT-MIN(Q)
 6      y = EXTRACT-MIN(Q)
 7      z.left = x
 8      z.right = y
 9      z.freq = x.freq + y.freq
10      INSERT(Q, z)
11  return EXTRACT-MIN(Q)      // the root of the tree is the only node left
```

For our example, Huffman's algorithm proceeds as shown in Figure 15.6. Since the alphabet contains 6 letters, the initial queue size is $n = 6$, and 5 merge steps build the tree. The final tree represents the optimal prefix-free code. The codeword for a letter is the sequence of edge labels on the simple path from the root to the letter.

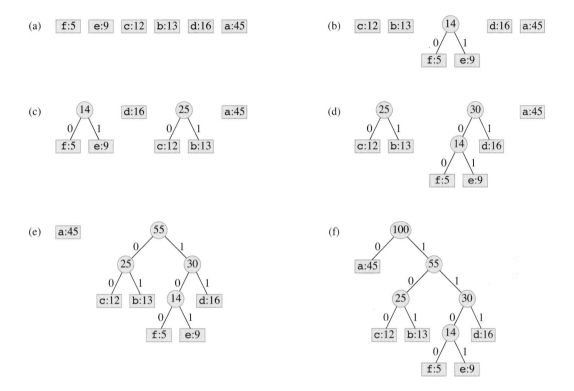

Figure 15.6 The steps of Huffman's algorithm for the frequencies given in Figure 15.4. Each part shows the contents of the queue sorted into increasing order by frequency. Each step merges the two trees with the lowest frequencies. Leaves are shown as rectangles containing a character and its frequency. Internal nodes are shown as circles containing the sum of the frequencies of their children. An edge connecting an internal node with its children is labeled 0 if it is an edge to a left child and 1 if it is an edge to a right child. The codeword for a letter is the sequence of labels on the edges connecting the root to the leaf for that letter. **(a)** The initial set of $n = 6$ nodes, one for each letter. **(b)–(e)** Intermediate stages. **(f)** The final tree.

The Huffman procedure works as follows. Line 2 initializes the min-priority queue Q with the characters in C. The **for** loop in lines 3–10 repeatedly extracts the two nodes x and y of lowest frequency from the queue and replaces them in the queue with a new node z representing their merger. The frequency of z is computed as the sum of the frequencies of x and y in line 9. The node z has x as its left child and y as its right child. (This order is arbitrary. Switching the left and right child of any node yields a different code of the same cost.) After $n - 1$ mergers, line 11 returns the one node left in the queue, which is the root of the code tree.

The algorithm produces the same result without the variables x and y, assigning the values returned by the EXTRACT-MIN calls directly to $z.left$ and $z.right$ in lines 7 and 8, and changing line 9 to $z.freq = z.left.freq + z.right.freq$. We'll use the node names x and y in the proof of correctness, however, so we leave them in.

The running time of Huffman's algorithm depends on how the min-priority queue Q is implemented. Let's assume that it's implemented as a binary min-heap (see Chapter 6). For a set C of n characters, the BUILD-MIN-HEAP procedure discussed in Section 6.3 can initialize Q in line 2 in $O(n)$ time. The **for** loop in lines 3–10 executes exactly $n - 1$ times, and since each heap operation runs in $O(\lg n)$ time, the loop contributes $O(n \lg n)$ to the running time. Thus, the total running time of HUFFMAN on a set of n characters is $O(n \lg n)$.

Correctness of Huffman's algorithm

To prove that the greedy algorithm HUFFMAN is correct, we'll show that the problem of determining an optimal prefix-free code exhibits the greedy-choice and optimal-substructure properties. The next lemma shows that the greedy-choice property holds.

Lemma 15.2 (Optimal prefix-free codes have the greedy-choice property)
Let C be an alphabet in which each character $c \in C$ has frequency $c.freq$. Let x and y be two characters in C having the lowest frequencies. Then there exists an optimal prefix-free code for C in which the codewords for x and y have the same length and differ only in the last bit.

Proof   The idea of the proof is to take the tree T representing an arbitrary optimal prefix-free code and modify it to make a tree representing another optimal prefix-free code such that the characters x and y appear as sibling leaves of maximum depth in the new tree. In such a tree, the codewords for x and y have the same length and differ only in the last bit.

Let a and b be any two characters that are sibling leaves of maximum depth in T. Without loss of generality, assume that $a.freq \leq b.freq$ and $x.freq \leq y.freq$. Since $x.freq$ and $y.freq$ are the two lowest leaf frequencies, in order, and $a.freq$ and $b.freq$ are two arbitrary frequencies, in order, we have $x.freq \leq a.freq$ and $y.freq \leq b.freq$.

In the remainder of the proof, it is possible that we could have $x.freq = a.freq$ or $y.freq = b.freq$, but $x.freq = b.freq$ implies that $a.freq = b.freq = x.freq = y.freq$ (see Exercise 15.3-1), and the lemma would be trivially true. Therefore, assume that $x.freq \neq b.freq$, which means that $x \neq b$.

As Figure 15.7 shows, imagine exchanging the positions in T of a and x to produce a tree T', and then exchanging the positions in T' of b and y to produce a

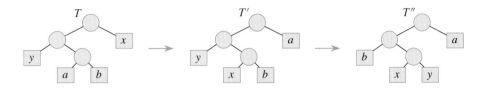

Figure 15.7 An illustration of the key step in the proof of Lemma 15.2. In the optimal tree T, leaves a and b are two siblings of maximum depth. Leaves x and y are the two characters with the lowest frequencies. They appear in arbitrary positions in T. Assuming that $x \neq b$, swapping leaves a and x produces tree T', and then swapping leaves b and y produces tree T''. Since each swap does not increase the cost, the resulting tree T'' is also an optimal tree.

tree T'' in which x and y are sibling leaves of maximum depth. (Note that if $x = b$ but $y \neq a$, then tree T'' does not have x and y as sibling leaves of maximum depth. Because we assume that $x \neq b$, this situation cannot occur.) By equation (15.4), the difference in cost between T and T' is

$$
\begin{aligned}
B(T) - B(T') \\
&= \sum_{c \in C} c.freq \cdot d_T(c) - \sum_{c \in C} c.freq \cdot d_{T'}(c) \\
&= x.freq \cdot d_T(x) + a.freq \cdot d_T(a) - x.freq \cdot d_{T'}(x) - a.freq \cdot d_{T'}(a) \\
&= x.freq \cdot d_T(x) + a.freq \cdot d_T(a) - x.freq \cdot d_T(a) - a.freq \cdot d_T(x) \\
&= (a.freq - x.freq)(d_T(a) - d_T(x)) \\
&\geq 0 ,
\end{aligned}
$$

because both $a.freq - x.freq$ and $d_T(a) - d_T(x)$ are nonnegative. More specifically, $a.freq - x.freq$ is nonnegative because x is a minimum-frequency leaf, and $d_T(a) - d_T(x)$ is nonnegative because a is a leaf of maximum depth in T. Similarly, exchanging y and b does not increase the cost, and so $B(T') - B(T'')$ is nonnegative. Therefore, $B(T'') \leq B(T') \leq B(T)$, and since T is optimal, we have $B(T) \leq B(T'')$, which implies $B(T'') = B(T)$. Thus, T'' is an optimal tree in which x and y appear as sibling leaves of maximum depth, from which the lemma follows.   ∎

Lemma 15.2 implies that the process of building up an optimal tree by mergers can, without loss of generality, begin with the greedy choice of merging together those two characters of lowest frequency. Why is this a greedy choice? We can view the cost of a single merger as being the sum of the frequencies of the two items being merged. Exercise 15.3-4 shows that the total cost of the tree constructed equals the sum of the costs of its mergers. Of all possible mergers at each step, HUFFMAN chooses the one that incurs the least cost.

The next lemma shows that the problem of constructing optimal prefix-free codes has the optimal-substructure property.

Lemma 15.3 (Optimal prefix-free codes have the optimal-substructure property)
Let C be a given alphabet with frequency $c.freq$ defined for each character $c \in C$. Let x and y be two characters in C with minimum frequency. Let C' be the alphabet C with the characters x and y removed and a new character z added, so that $C' = (C - \{x, y\}) \cup \{z\}$. Define *freq* for all characters in C' with the same values as in C, along with $z.freq = x.freq + y.freq$. Let T' be any tree representing an optimal prefix-free code for alphabet C'. Then the tree T, obtained from T' by replacing the leaf node for z with an internal node having x and y as children, represents an optimal prefix-free code for the alphabet C.

Proof We first show how to express the cost $B(T)$ of tree T in terms of the cost $B(T')$ of tree T', by considering the component costs in equation (15.4). For each character $c \in C - \{x, y\}$, we have that $d_T(c) = d_{T'}(c)$, and hence $c.freq \cdot d_T(c) = c.freq \cdot d_{T'}(c)$. Since $d_T(x) = d_T(y) = d_{T'}(z) + 1$, we have

$$
\begin{aligned}
x.freq \cdot d_T(x) + y.freq \cdot d_T(y) &= (x.freq + y.freq)(d_{T'}(z) + 1) \\
&= z.freq \cdot d_{T'}(z) + (x.freq + y.freq) \, ,
\end{aligned}
$$

from which we conclude that

$$B(T) = B(T') + x.freq + y.freq$$

or, equivalently,

$$B(T') = B(T) - x.freq - y.freq \, .$$

We now prove the lemma by contradiction. Suppose that T does not represent an optimal prefix-free code for C. Then there exists an optimal tree T'' such that $B(T'') < B(T)$. Without loss of generality (by Lemma 15.2), T'' has x and y as siblings. Let T''' be the tree T'' with the common parent of x and y replaced by a leaf z with frequency $z.freq = x.freq + y.freq$. Then

$$
\begin{aligned}
B(T''') &= B(T'') - x.freq - y.freq \\
&< B(T) - x.freq - y.freq \\
&= B(T') \, ,
\end{aligned}
$$

yielding a contradiction to the assumption that T' represents an optimal prefix-free code for C'. Thus, T must represent an optimal prefix-free code for the alphabet C.   ∎

Theorem 15.4
Procedure HUFFMAN produces an optimal prefix-free code.

Proof   Immediate from Lemmas 15.2 and 15.3.   ∎

Exercises

15.3-1
Explain why, in the proof of Lemma 15.2, if $x.freq = b.freq$, then we must have $a.freq = b.freq = x.freq = y.freq$.

15.3-2
Prove that a non-full binary tree cannot correspond to an optimal prefix-free code.

15.3-3
What is an optimal Huffman code for the following set of frequencies, based on the first 8 Fibonacci numbers?

a:1 b:1 c:2 d:3 e:5 f:8 g:13 h:21

Can you generalize your answer to find the optimal code when the frequencies are the first n Fibonacci numbers?

15.3-4
Prove that the total cost $B(T)$ of a full binary tree T for a code equals the sum, over all internal nodes, of the combined frequencies of the two children of the node.

15.3-5
Given an optimal prefix-free code on a set C of n characters, you wish to transmit the code itself using as few bits as possible. Show how to represent any optimal prefix-free code on C using only $2n - 1 + n \lceil \lg n \rceil$ bits. (*Hint:* Use $2n - 1$ bits to specify the structure of the tree, as discovered by a walk of the tree.)

15.3-6
Generalize Huffman's algorithm to ternary codewords (i.e., codewords using the symbols 0, 1, and 2), and prove that it yields optimal ternary codes.

15.3-7
A data file contains a sequence of 8-bit characters such that all 256 characters are about equally common: the maximum character frequency is less than twice the minimum character frequency. Prove that Huffman coding in this case is no more efficient than using an ordinary 8-bit fixed-length code.

15.3-8
Show that no lossless (invertible) compression scheme can guarantee that for every input file, the corresponding output file is shorter. (*Hint:* Compare the number of possible files with the number of possible encoded files.)

15.4   Offline caching

Computer systems can decrease the time to access data by storing a subset of the main memory in the *cache*: a small but faster memory. A cache organizes data into *cache blocks* typically comprising $32, 64$, or 128 bytes. You can also think of main memory as a cache for disk-resident data in a virtual-memory system. Here, the blocks are called *pages*, and 4096 bytes is a typical size.

As a computer program executes, it makes a sequence of memory requests. Say that there are n memory requests, to data in blocks $b_1, b_2, \ldots, b_n$, in that order. The blocks in the access sequence might not be distinct, and indeed, any given block is usually accessed multiple times. For example, a program that accesses four distinct blocks p, q, r, s might make a sequence of requests to blocks $s, q, s, q, q, s, p, p, r,$ s, s, q, p, r, q. The cache can hold up to some fixed number k of cache blocks. It starts out empty before the first request. Each request causes at most one block to enter the cache and at most one block to be evicted from the cache. Upon a request for block b_i, any one of three scenarios may occur:

1. Block b_i is already in the cache, due to a previous request for the same block. The cache remains unchanged. This situation is known as a *cache hit*.

2. Block b_i is not in the cache at that time, but the cache contains fewer than k blocks. In this case, block b_i is placed into the cache, so that the cache contains one more block than it did before the request.

3. Block b_i is not in the cache at that time and the cache is full: it contains k blocks. Block b_i is placed into the cache, but before that happens, some other block in the cache must be evicted from the cache in order to make room.

The latter two situations, in which the requested block is not already in the cache, are called *cache misses*. The goal is to minimize the number of cache misses or, equivalently, to maximize the number of cache hits, over the entire sequence of n requests. A cache miss that occurs while the cache holds fewer than k blocks—that is, as the cache is first being filled up—is known as a *compulsory miss*, since no prior decision could have kept the requested block in the cache. When a cache miss occurs and the cache is full, ideally the choice of which block to evict should allow for the smallest possible number of cache misses over the entire sequence of future requests.

Typically, caching is an online problem. That is, the computer has to decide which blocks to keep in the cache without knowing the future requests. Here, however, let's consider the offline version of this problem, in which the computer knows in advance the entire sequence of n requests and the cache size k, with a goal of minimizing the total number of cache misses.

To solve this offline problem, you can use a greedy strategy called *furthest-in-future*, which chooses to evict the block in the cache whose next access in the request sequence comes furthest in the future. Intuitively, this strategy makes sense: if you're not going to need something for a while, why keep it around? We'll show that the furthest-in-future strategy is indeed optimal by showing that the offline caching problem exhibits optimal substructure and that furthest-in-future has the greedy-choice property.

Now, you might be thinking that since the computer usually doesn't know the sequence of requests in advance, there is no point in studying the offline problem. Actually, there is. In some situations, you do know the sequence of requests in advance. For example, if you view the main memory as the cache and the full set of data as residing on disk (or a solid-state drive), there are algorithms that plan out the entire set of reads and writes in advance. Furthermore, we can use the number of cache misses produced by an optimal algorithm as a baseline for comparing how well online algorithms perform. We'll do just that in Section 27.3.

Offline caching can even model real-world problems. For example, consider a scenario where you know in advance a fixed schedule of n events at known locations. Events may occur at a location multiple times, not necessarily consecutively. You are managing a group of k agents, you need to ensure that you have one agent at each location when an event occurs, and you want to minimize the number of times that agents have to move. Here, the agents are like the blocks, the events are like the requests, and moving an agent is akin to a cache miss.

Optimal substructure of offline caching

To show that the offline problem exhibits optimal substructure, let's define the subproblem (C, i) as processing requests for blocks $b_i, b_{i+1}, \ldots, b_n$ with cache configuration C at the time that the request for block b_i occurs, that is, C is a subset of the set of blocks such that $|C| \leq k$. A solution to subproblem (C, i) is a sequence of decisions that specifies which block to evict (if any) upon each request for blocks $b_i, b_{i+1}, \ldots, b_n$. An optimal solution to subproblem (C, i) minimizes the number of cache misses.

Consider an optimal solution S to subproblem (C, i), and let C' be the contents of the cache after processing the request for block b_i in solution S. Let S' be the subsolution of S for the resulting subproblem $(C', i + 1)$. If the request for b_i results in a cache hit, then the cache remains unchanged, so that $C' = C$. If the request for block b_i results in a cache miss, then the contents of the cache change, so that $C' \neq C$. We claim that in either case, S' is an optimal solution to subproblem $(C', i + 1)$. Why? If S' is not an optimal solution to subproblem $(C', i + 1)$, then there exists another solution S'' to subproblem $(C', i + 1)$ that makes fewer cache misses than S'. Combining S'' with the decision of S at the request for block b_i yields another solution that makes fewer cache misses than S, which contradicts the assumption that S is an optimal solution to subproblem (C, i).

To quantify a recursive solution, we need a little more notation. Let $R_{C,i}$ be the set of all cache configurations that can immediately follow configuration C after processing a request for block b_i. If the request results in a cache hit, then the cache remains unchanged, so that $R_{C,i} = \{C\}$. If the request for b_i results in a cache miss, then there are two possibilities. If the cache is not full ($|C| < k$), then the cache is filling up and the only choice is to insert b_i into the cache, so that $R_{C,i} = \{C \cup \{b_i\}\}$. If the cache is full ($|C| = k$) upon a cache miss, then $R_{C,i}$ contains k potential configurations: one for each candidate block in C that could be evicted and replaced by block b_i. In this case, $R_{C,i} = \{(C - \{x\}) \cup \{b_i\} : x \in C\}$. For example, if $C = \{p, q, r\}$, $k = 3$, and block s is requested, then $R_{C,i} = \{\{p, q, s\}, \{p, r, s\}, \{q, r, s\}\}$.

Let $miss(C, i)$ denote the minimum number of cache misses in a solution for subproblem (C, i). Here is a recurrence for $miss(C, i)$:

$$
miss(C, i) = \begin{cases}
0 & \text{if } i = n \text{ and } b_n \in C , \\
1 & \text{if } i = n \text{ and } b_n \notin C , \\
miss(C, i + 1) & \text{if } i < n \text{ and } b_i \in C , \\
1 + \min\{miss(C', i + 1) : C' \in R_{C,i}\} & \text{if } i < n \text{ and } b_i \notin C .
\end{cases}
$$

Greedy-choice property

To prove that the furthest-in-future strategy yields an optimal solution, we need to show that optimal offline caching exhibits the greedy-choice property. Combined with the optimal-substructure property, the greedy-choice property will prove that furthest-in-future produces the minimum possible number of cache misses.

Theorem 15.5 (Optimal offline caching has the greedy-choice property)
Consider a subproblem (C, i) when the cache C contains k blocks, so that it is full, and a cache miss occurs. When block b_i is requested, let $z = b_m$ be the block in C whose next access is furthest in the future. (If some block in the cache will never again be referenced, then consider any such block to be block z, and add a dummy request for block $z = b_m = b_{n+1}$.) Then evicting block z upon a request for block b_i is included in some optimal solution for the subproblem (C, i).

Proof Let S be an optimal solution to subproblem (C, i). If S evicts block z upon the request for block b_i, then we are done, since we have shown that some optimal solution includes evicting z.

So now suppose that optimal solution S evicts some other block x when block b_i is requested. We'll construct another solution S' to subproblem (C, i) which, upon the request for b_i, evicts block z instead of x and induces no more cache misses than S does, so that S' is also optimal. Because different solutions may yield different cache configurations, denote by $C_{S,j}$ the configuration of the cache under solution S just before the request for some block b_j, and likewise for solution S' and $C_{S',j}$. We'll show how to construct S' with the following properties:

1. For $j = i + 1, \ldots, m$, let $D_j = C_{S,j} \cap C_{S',j}$. Then, $|D_j| \geq k - 1$, so that the cache configurations $C_{S,j}$ and $C_{S',j}$ differ by at most one block. If they differ, then $C_{S,j} = D_j \cup \{z\}$ and $C_{S',j} = D_j \cup \{y\}$ for some block $y \neq z$.

2. For each request of blocks $b_i, \ldots, b_{m-1}$, if solution S has a cache hit, then solution S' also has a cache hit.

3. For all $j > m$, the cache configurations $C_{S,j}$ and $C_{S',j}$ are identical.

4. Over the sequence of requests for blocks $b_i, \ldots, b_m$, the number of cache misses produced by solution S' is at most the number of cache misses produced by solution S.

We'll prove inductively that these properties hold for each request.

1. We proceed by induction on j, for $j = i + 1, \ldots, m$. For the base case, the initial caches $C_{S,i}$ and $C_{S',i}$ are identical. Upon the request for block b_i, solution S evicts x and solution S' evicts z. Thus, cache configurations $C_{S,i+1}$ and $C_{S',i+1}$ differ by just one block, $C_{S,i+1} = D_{i+1} \cup \{z\}$, $C_{S',i+1} = D_{i+1} \cup \{x\}$, and $x \neq z$.

    The inductive step defines how solution S' behaves upon a request for block b_j for $i + 1 \leq j \leq m - 1$. The inductive hypothesis is that property 1 holds when b_j is requested. Because $z = b_m$ is the block in $C_{S,i}$ whose next reference is furthest in the future, we know that $b_j \neq z$. We consider several scenarios:

    - If $C_{S,j} = C_{S',j}$ (so that $|D_j| = k$), then solution S' makes the same decision upon the request for b_j as S makes, so that $C_{S,j+1} = C_{S',j+1}$.
    - If $|D_j| = k - 1$ and $b_j \in D_j$, then both caches already contain block b_j, and both solutions S and S' have cache hits. Therefore, $C_{S,j+1} = C_{S,j}$ and $C_{S',j+1} = C_{S',j}$.
    - If $|D_j| = k - 1$ and $b_j \notin D_j$, then because $C_{S,j} = D_j \cup \{z\}$ and $b_j \neq z$, solution S has a cache miss. It evicts either block z or some block $w \in D_j$.
        - If solution S evicts block z, then $C_{S,j+1} = D_j \cup \{b_j\}$. There are two cases, depending on whether $b_j = y$:
            - If $b_j = y$, then solution S' has a cache hit, so that $C_{S',j+1} = C_{S',j} = D_j \cup \{b_j\}$. Thus, $C_{S,j+1} = C_{S',j+1}$.
            - If $b_j \neq y$, then solution S' has a cache miss. It evicts block y, so that $C_{S',j+1} = D_j \cup \{b_j\}$, and again $C_{S,j+1} = C_{S',j+1}$.

- ° If solution S evicts some block $w \in D_j$, then $C_{S,j+1} = (D_j - \{w\}) \cup \{b_j, z\}$. Once again, there are two cases, depending on whether $b_j = y$:
  - · If $b_j = y$, then solution S' has a cache hit, so that $C_{S',j+1} = C_{S',j} = D_j \cup \{b_j\}$. Since $w \in D_j$ and w was not evicted by solution S', we have $w \in C_{S',j+1}$. Therefore, $w \notin D_{j+1}$ and $b_j \in D_{j+1}$, so that $D_{j+1} = (D_j - \{w\}) \cup \{b_j\}$. Thus, $C_{S,j+1} = D_{j+1} \cup \{z\}$, $C_{S',j+1} = D_{j+1} \cup \{w\}$, and because $w \neq z$, property 1 holds when block b_{j+1} is requested. (In other words, block w replaces block y in property 1.)
  - · If $b_j \neq y$, then solution S' has a cache miss. It evicts block w, so that $C_{S',j+1} = (D_j - \{w\}) \cup \{b_j, y\}$. Therefore, we have that $D_{j+1} = (D_j - \{w\}) \cup \{b_j\}$ and so $C_{S,j+1} = D_{j+1} \cup \{z\}$ and $C_{S',j+1} = D_{j+1} \cup \{y\}$.

2. In the above discussion about maintaining property 1, solution S may have a cache hit in only the first two cases, and solution S' has a cache hit in these cases if and only if S does.

3. If $C_{S,m} = C_{S',m}$, then solution S' makes the same decision upon the request for block $z = b_m$ as S makes, so that $C_{S,m+1} = C_{S',m+1}$. If $C_{S,m} \neq C_{S',m}$, then by property 1, $C_{S,m} = D_m \cup \{z\}$ and $C_{S',m} = D_m \cup \{y\}$, where $y \neq z$. In this case, solution S has a cache hit, so that $C_{S,m+1} = C_{S,m} = D_m \cup \{z\}$. Solution S' evicts block y and brings in block z, so that $C_{S',m+1} = D_m \cup \{z\} = C_{S,m+1}$. Thus, regardless of whether or not $C_{S,m} = C_{S',m}$, we have $C_{S,m+1} = C_{S',m+1}$, and starting with the request for block b_{m+1}, solution S' simply makes the same decisions as S.

4. By property 2, upon the requests for blocks $b_i, \ldots, b_{m-1}$, whenever solution S has a cache hit, so does S'. Only the request for block $b_m = z$ remains to be considered. If S has a cache miss upon the request for b_m, then regardless of whether S' has a cache hit or a cache miss, we are done: S' has at most the same number of cache misses as S.

So now suppose that S has a cache hit and S' has a cache miss upon the request for b_m. We'll show that there exists a request for at least one of blocks $b_{i+1}, \ldots, b_{m-1}$ in which the request results in a cache miss for S and a cache hit for S', thereby compensating for what happens upon the request for block b_m. The proof is by contradiction. Assume that no request for blocks $b_{i+1}, \ldots, b_{m-1}$ results in a cache miss for S and a cache hit for S'.

We start by observing that once the caches $C_{S,j}$ and $C_{S'j}$ are equal for some $j > i$, they remain equal thereafter. Observe also that if $b_m \in C_{S,m}$ and $b_m \notin C_{S',m}$, then $C_{S,m} \neq C_{S',m}$. Therefore, solution S cannot have evicted block z upon the requests for blocks $b_i, \ldots, b_{m-1}$, for if it had, then these two cache configurations would be equal. The remaining possibility is that upon each of these requests, we had $C_{S,j} = D_j \cup \{z\}$, $C_{S',j} = D_j \cup \{y\}$ for some block $y \neq z$, and solution S evicted some block $w \in D_j$. Moreover, since none of these requests resulted in a cache miss for S and a cache hit for S', the case of $b_j = y$ never occurred. That is, for every request of blocks $b_{i+1}, \ldots, b_{m-1}$, the requested block b_j was never the block $y \in C_{S',j} - C_{S,j}$. In these cases, after processing the request, we had $C_{S',j+1} = D_{j+1} \cup \{y\}$: the difference between the two caches did not change. Now, let's go back to the request for block b_i, where afterward, we had $C_{S',i+1} = D_{i+1} \cup \{x\}$. Because every succeeding request until requesting block b_m did not change the difference between the caches, we had $C_{S',j} = D_j \cup \{x\}$ for $j = i + 1, \ldots, m$.

By definition, block $z = b_m$ is requested after block x. That means at least one of blocks $b_{i+1}, \ldots, b_{m-1}$ is block x. But for $j = i + 1, \ldots, m$, we have $x \in C_{S',j}$ and $x \notin C_{S,j}$, so that at least one of these requests had a cache hit for S' and a cache miss for S, a contradiction. We conclude that if solution S has a cache hit and solution S' has a cache miss upon the request for block b_m, then some earlier request had the opposite result, and so solution S' produces no more cache misses than solution S. Since S is assumed to be optimal, S' is optimal as well.   ∎

Along with the optimal-substructure property, Theorem 15.5 tells us that the furthest-in-future strategy yields the minimum number of cache misses.

Exercises

15.4-1
Write pseudocode for a cache manager that uses the furthest-in-future strategy. It should take as input a set C of blocks in the cache, the number of blocks k that the cache can hold, a sequence $b_1, b_2, \ldots, b_n$ of requested blocks, and the index i into the sequence for the block b_i being requested. For each request, it should print out whether a cache hit or cache miss occurs, and for each cache miss, it should also print out which block, if any, is evicted.

15.4-2
Real cache managers do not know the future requests, and so they often use the past to decide which block to evict. The *least-recently-used*, or *LRU*, strategy evicts the block that, of all blocks currently in the cache, was the least recently requested. (You can think of LRU as "furthest-in-past.") Give an example of a request sequence in which the LRU strategy is not optimal, by showing that it induces more cache misses than the furthest-in-future strategy does on the same request sequence.

15.4-3

Professor Croesus suggests that in the proof of Theorem 15.5, the last clause in property 1 can change to $C_{S',j} = D_j \cup \{x\}$ or, equivalently, require the block y given in property 1 to always be the block x evicted by solution S upon the request for block b_i. Show where the proof breaks down with this requirement.

15.4-4

This section has assumed that at most one block is placed into the cache whenever a block is requested. You can imagine, however, a strategy in which multiple blocks may enter the cache upon a single request. Show that for every solution that allows multiple blocks to enter the cache upon each request, there is another solution that brings in only one block upon each request and is at least as good.

Problems

15-1   *Coin changing*

Consider the problem of making change for n cents using the smallest number of coins. Assume that each coin's value is an integer.

a. Describe a greedy algorithm to make change consisting of quarters, dimes, nickels, and pennies. Prove that your algorithm yields an optimal solution.

b. Suppose that the available coins are in denominations that are powers of c: the denominations are $c^0, c^1, \ldots, c^k$ for some integers $c > 1$ and $k \geq 1$. Show that the greedy algorithm always yields an optimal solution.

c. Give a set of coin denominations for which the greedy algorithm does not yield an optimal solution. Your set should include a penny so that there is a solution for every value of n.

d. Give an $O(nk)$-time algorithm that makes change for any set of k different coin denominations using the smallest number of coins, assuming that one of the coins is a penny.

15-2   *Scheduling to minimize average completion time*

You are given a set $S = \{a_1, a_2, \ldots, a_n\}$ of tasks, where task a_i requires p_i units of processing time to complete. Let C_i be the *completion time* of task a_i, that is, the time at which task a_i completes processing. Your goal is to minimize the average completion time, that is, to minimize $(1/n) \sum_{i=1}^{n} C_i$. For example, suppose that there are two tasks a_1 and a_2 with $p_1 = 3$ and $p_2 = 5$, and consider the schedule in which a_2 runs first, followed by a_1. Then we have $C_2 = 5$, $C_1 = 8$, and the average completion time is $(5 + 8)/2 = 6.5$. If task a_1 runs first, however, then we have $C_1 = 3$, $C_2 = 8$, and the average completion time is $(3 + 8)/2 = 5.5$.

a. Give an algorithm that schedules the tasks so as to minimize the average completion time. Each task must run nonpreemptively, that is, once task a_i starts, it must run continuously for p_i units of time until it is done. Prove that your algorithm minimizes the average completion time, and analyze the running time of your algorithm.

b. Suppose now that the tasks are not all available at once. That is, each task cannot start until its *release time* b_i. Suppose also that tasks may be *preempted*, so that a task can be suspended and restarted at a later time. For example, a task a_i with processing time $p_i = 6$ and release time $b_i = 1$ might start running at time 1 and be preempted at time 4. It might then resume at time 10 but be preempted at time 11, and it might finally resume at time 13 and complete at time 15. Task a_i has run for a total of 6 time units, but its running time has been divided into three pieces. Give an algorithm that schedules the tasks so as to minimize the average completion time in this new scenario. Prove that your algorithm minimizes the average completion time, and analyze the running time of your algorithm.

Chapter notes

Much more material on greedy algorithms can be found in Lawler [276] and Papadimitriou and Steiglitz [353]. The greedy algorithm first appeared in the combinatorial optimization literature in a 1971 article by Edmonds [131].

The proof of correctness of the greedy algorithm for the activity-selection problem is based on that of Gavril [179].

Huffman codes were invented in 1952 [233]. Lelewer and Hirschberg [294] surveys data-compression techniques known as of 1987.

The furthest-in-future strategy was proposed by Belady [41], who suggested it for virtual-memory systems. Alternative proofs that furthest-in-future is optimal appear in articles by Lee et al. [284] and Van Roy [443].

16   Amortized Analysis

Imagine that you join Buff's Gym. Buff charges a membership fee of $60 per month, plus $3 for every time you use the gym. Because you are disciplined, you visit Buff's Gym every day during the month of November. On top of the $60 monthly charge for November, you pay another $3 \times 30 = \$90$ that month. Although you can think of your fees as a flat fee of $60 and another $90 in daily fees, you can think about it in another way. All together, you pay $150 over 30 days, or an average of $5 per day. When you look at your fees in this way, you are *amortizing* the monthly fee over the 30 days of the month, spreading it out at $2 per day.

You can do the same thing when you analyze running times. In an *amortized analysis*, you average the time required to perform a sequence of data-structure operations over all the operations performed. With amortized analysis, you show that if you average over a sequence of operations, then the average cost of an operation is small, even though a single operation within the sequence might be expensive. Amortized analysis differs from average-case analysis in that probability is not involved. An amortized analysis guarantees the *average performance of each operation in the worst case*.

The first three sections of this chapter cover the three most common techniques used in amortized analysis. Section 16.1 starts with aggregate analysis, in which you determine an upper bound $T(n)$ on the total cost of a sequence of n operations. The average cost per operation is then $T(n)/n$. You take the average cost as the amortized cost of each operation, so that all operations have the same amortized cost.

Section 16.2 covers the accounting method, in which you determine an amortized cost of each operation. When there is more than one type of operation, each type of operation may have a different amortized cost. The accounting method overcharges some operations early in the sequence, storing the overcharge as "prepaid credit" on specific objects in the data structure. Later in the sequence, the credit pays for operations that are charged less than they actually cost.

Section 16.3 discusses the potential method, which is like the accounting method in that you determine the amortized cost of each operation and may overcharge operations early on to compensate for undercharges later. The potential method maintains the credit as the "potential energy" of the data structure as a whole instead of associating the credit with individual objects within the data structure.

We'll use use two examples in this chapter to examine each of these three methods. One is a stack with the additional operation MULTIPOP, which pops several objects at once. The other is a binary counter that counts up from 0 by means of the single operation INCREMENT.

While reading this chapter, bear in mind that the charges assigned during an amortized analysis are for analysis purposes only. They need not—and should not—appear in the code. If, for example, you assign a credit to an object x when using the accounting method, you have no need to assign an appropriate amount to some attribute, such as $x.credit$, in the code.

When you perform an amortized analysis, you often gain insight into a particular data structure, and this insight can help you optimize the design. For example, Section 16.4 will use the potential method to analyze a dynamically expanding and contracting table.

16.1 Aggregate analysis

In *aggregate analysis*, you show that for all n, a sequence of n operations takes $T(n)$ *worst-case* time in total. In the worst case, the average cost, or *amortized cost*, per operation is therefore $T(n)/n$. This amortized cost applies to each operation, even when there are several types of operations in the sequence. The other two methods we shall study in this chapter, the accounting method and the potential method, may assign different amortized costs to different types of operations.

Stack operations

As the first example of aggregate analysis, let's analyze stacks that have been augmented with a new operation. Section 10.1.3 presented the two fundamental stack operations, each of which takes $O(1)$ time:

PUSH(S, x) pushes object x onto stack S.

POP(S) pops the top of stack S and returns the popped object. Calling POP on an empty stack generates an error.

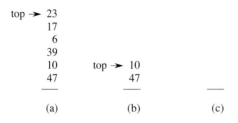

Figure 16.1 The action of Multipop on a stack S, shown initially in **(a)**. The top 4 objects are popped by Multipop$(S, 4)$, whose result is shown in **(b)**. The next operation is Multipop$(S, 7)$, which empties the stack—shown in **(c)**—since fewer than 7 objects remained.

Since each of these operations runs in $O(1)$ time, let us consider the cost of each to be 1. The total cost of a sequence of n Push and Pop operations is therefore n, and the actual running time for n operations is therefore $\Theta(n)$.

Now let's add the stack operation Multipop(S, k), which removes the k top objects of stack S, popping the entire stack if the stack contains fewer than k objects. Of course, the procedure assumes that k is positive, and otherwise, the Multipop operation leaves the stack unchanged. In the pseudocode for Multipop, the operation Stack-Empty returns TRUE if there are no objects currently on the stack, and FALSE otherwise. Figure 16.1 shows an example of Multipop.

```
Multipop(S, k)
1  while not Stack-Empty(S) and k > 0
2      Pop(S)
3      k = k − 1
```

What is the running time of Multipop(S, k) on a stack of s objects? The actual running time is linear in the number of Pop operations actually executed, and thus we can analyze Multipop in terms of the abstract costs of 1 each for Push and Pop. The number of iterations of the **while** loop is the number $\min\{s, k\}$ of objects popped off the stack. Each iteration of the loop makes one call to Pop in line 2. Thus, the total cost of Multipop is $\min\{s, k\}$, and the actual running time is a linear function of this cost.

Now let's analyze a sequence of n Push, Pop, and Multipop operations on an initially empty stack. The worst-case cost of a Multipop operation in the sequence is $O(n)$, since the stack size is at most n. The worst-case time of any stack operation is therefore $O(n)$, and hence a sequence of n operations costs $O(n^2)$, since the sequence contains at most n Multipop operations costing $O(n)$ each.

Although this analysis is correct, the $O(n^2)$ result, which came from considering the worst-case cost of each operation individually, is not tight.

Yes, a single MULTIPOP might be expensive, but an aggregate analysis shows that any sequence of n PUSH, POP, and MULTIPOP operations on an initially empty stack has an upper bound on its cost of $O(n)$. Why? An object cannot be popped from the stack unless it was first pushed. Therefore, the number of times that POP can be called on a nonempty stack, including calls within MULTIPOP, is at most the number of PUSH operations, which is at most n. For any value of n, any sequence of n PUSH, POP, and MULTIPOP operations takes a total of $O(n)$ time. Averaging over the n operations gives an average cost per operation of $O(n)/n = O(1)$. Aggregate analysis assigns the amortized cost of each operation to be the average cost. In this example, therefore, all three stack operations have an amortized cost of $O(1)$.

To recap: although the average cost, and hence the running time, of a stack operation is $O(1)$, the analysis did not rely on probabilistic reasoning. Instead, the analysis yielded a *worst-case* bound of $O(n)$ on a sequence of n operations. Dividing this total cost by n yielded that the average cost per operation—that is, the amortized cost—is $O(1)$.

Incrementing a binary counter

As another example of aggregate analysis, consider the problem of implementing a k-bit binary counter that counts upward from 0. An array $A[0:k-1]$ of bits represents the counter. A binary number x that is stored in the counter has its lowest-order bit in $A[0]$ and its highest-order bit in $A[k-1]$, so that $x = \sum_{i=0}^{k-1} A[i] \cdot 2^i$. Initially, $x = 0$, and thus $A[i] = 0$ for $i = 0, 1, \ldots, k-1$. To add 1 (modulo 2^k) to the value in the counter, call the INCREMENT procedure.

INCREMENT(A, k)

```
1   i = 0
2   while i < k and A[i] == 1
3       A[i] = 0
4       i = i + 1
5   if i < k
6       A[i] = 1
```

Figure 16.2 shows what happens to a binary counter when INCREMENT is called 16 times, starting with the initial value 0 and ending with the value 16. Each iteration of the **while** loop in lines 2–4 adds a 1 into position i. If $A[i] = 1$, then adding 1 flips the bit to 0 in position i and yields a carry of 1, to be added into

Counter value	$A[7]$	$A[6]$	$A[5]$	$A[4]$	$A[3]$	$A[2]$	$A[1]$	$A[0]$	Total cost
0	0	0	0	0	0	0	0	0	0
1	0	0	0	0	0	0	0	1	1
2	0	0	0	0	0	0	1	0	3
3	0	0	0	0	0	0	1	1	4
4	0	0	0	0	0	1	0	0	7
5	0	0	0	0	0	1	0	1	8
6	0	0	0	0	0	1	1	0	10
7	0	0	0	0	0	1	1	1	11
8	0	0	0	0	1	0	0	0	15
9	0	0	0	0	1	0	0	1	16
10	0	0	0	0	1	0	1	0	18
11	0	0	0	0	1	0	1	1	19
12	0	0	0	0	1	1	0	0	22
13	0	0	0	0	1	1	0	1	23
14	0	0	0	0	1	1	1	0	25
15	0	0	0	0	1	1	1	1	26
16	0	0	0	1	0	0	0	0	31

Figure 16.2   An 8-bit binary counter as its value goes from 0 to 16 by a sequence of 16 INCREMENT operations. Bits that flip to achieve the next value are shaded in blue. The running cost for flipping bits is shown at the right. The total cost is always less than twice the total number of INCREMENT operations.

position $i + 1$ during the next iteration of the loop. Otherwise, the loop ends, and then, if $i < k$, $A[i]$ must be 0, so that line 6 adds a 1 into position i, flipping the 0 to a 1. If the loop ends with $i = k$, then the call of INCREMENT flipped all k bits from 1 to 0. The cost of each INCREMENT operation is linear in the number of bits flipped.

As with the stack example, a cursory analysis yields a bound that is correct but not tight. A single execution of INCREMENT takes $\Theta(k)$ time in the worst case, in which all the bits in array A are 1. Thus, a sequence of n INCREMENT operations on an initially zero counter takes $O(nk)$ time in the worst case.

Although a single call of INCREMENT might flip all k bits, not all bits flip upon each call. (Note the similarity to MULTIPOP, where a single call might pop many objects, but not every call pops many objects.) As Figure 16.2 shows, $A[0]$ does flip each time INCREMENT is called. The next bit up, $A[1]$, flips only every other time: a sequence of n INCREMENT operations on an initially zero counter causes $A[1]$ to flip $\lfloor n/2 \rfloor$ times. Similarly, bit $A[2]$ flips only every fourth time, or $\lfloor n/4 \rfloor$ times in a sequence of n INCREMENT operations. In general, for $i = 0, 1, \ldots, k - 1$, bit $A[i]$ flips $\lfloor n/2^i \rfloor$ times in a sequence of n INCREMENT operations on an initially zero counter. For $i \geq k$, bit $A[i]$ does not exist, and so it cannot flip. The total number of flips in the sequence is thus

$$\sum_{i=0}^{k-1} \left\lfloor \frac{n}{2^i} \right\rfloor < n \sum_{i=0}^{\infty} \frac{1}{2^i}$$
$$= 2n \,,$$

by equation (A.7) on page 1142. Thus, a sequence of n INCREMENT operations on an initially zero counter takes $O(n)$ time in the worst case. The average cost of each operation, and therefore the amortized cost per operation, is $O(n)/n = O(1)$.

Exercises

16.1-1
If the set of stack operations includes a MULTIPUSH operation, which pushes k items onto the stack, does the $O(1)$ bound on the amortized cost of stack operations continue to hold?

16.1-2
Show that if a DECREMENT operation is included in the k-bit counter example, n operations can cost as much as $\Theta(nk)$ time.

16.1-3
Use aggregate analysis to determine the amortized cost per operation for a sequence of n operations on a data structure in which the ith operation costs i if i is an exact power of 2, and 1 otherwise.

16.2   The accounting method

In the *accounting method* of amortized analysis, you assign differing charges to different operations, with some operations charged more or less than they actually cost. The amount that you charge an operation is its *amortized cost*. When an operation's amortized cost exceeds its actual cost, you assign the difference to specific objects in the data structure as *credit*. Credit can help pay for later operations whose amortized cost is less than their actual cost. Thus, you can view the amortized cost of an operation as being split between its actual cost and credit that is either deposited or used up. Different operations may have different amortized costs. This method differs from aggregate analysis, in which all operations have the same amortized cost.

You must choose the amortized costs of operations carefully. If you want to use amortized costs to show that in the worst case the average cost per operation is small, you must ensure that the total amortized cost of a sequence of operations provides an upper bound on the total actual cost of the sequence. Moreover, as in aggregate analysis, the upper bound must apply to all sequences of operations. Let's denote the actual cost of the ith operation by c_i and the amortized cost of the ith operation by $\hat{c}_i$. Then you need to have

$$\sum_{i=1}^{n} \hat{c}_i \geq \sum_{i=1}^{n} c_i \tag{16.1}$$

for all sequences of n operations. The total credit stored in the data structure is the difference between the total amortized cost and the total actual cost, or $\sum_{i=1}^{n} \hat{c}_i - \sum_{i=1}^{n} c_i$. By inequality (16.1), the total credit associated with the data structure must be nonnegative at all times. If you ever allowed the total credit to become negative (the result of undercharging early operations with the promise of repaying the account later on), then the total amortized costs incurred at that time would be below the total actual costs incurred. In that case, for the sequence of operations up to that time, the total amortized cost would not be an upper bound on the total actual cost. Thus, you must take care that the total credit in the data structure never becomes negative.

Stack operations

To illustrate the accounting method of amortized analysis, we return to the stack example. Recall that the actual costs of the operations were

PUSH   1 ,
POP   1 ,
MULTIPOP $\min\{s, k\}$,

where k is the argument supplied to MULTIPOP and s is the stack size when it is called. Let us assign the following amortized costs:

PUSH   2 ,
POP   0 ,
MULTIPOP   0 .

The amortized cost of MULTIPOP is a constant (0), whereas the actual cost is variable, and thus all three amortized costs are constant. In general, the amortized costs of the operations under consideration may differ from each other, and they may even differ asymptotically.

Now let's see how to pay for any sequence of stack operations by charging the amortized costs. Let \$1 represent each unit of cost. At first, the stack is empty. Recall the analogy of Section 10.1.3 between the stack data structure and a stack of plates in a cafeteria. Upon pushing a plate onto the stack, use \$1 to pay the actual cost of the push, leaving a credit of $1 (out of the $2 charged). Place that $1 of credit on top of the plate. At any point in time, every plate on the stack has $1 of credit on it.

The $1 stored on the plate serves to prepay the cost of popping the plate from the stack. A POP operation incurs no charge: pay the actual cost of popping a plate by taking the $1 of credit off the plate. Thus, by charging the PUSH operation a little bit more, we can view the POP operation as free.

Moreover, the MULTIPOP operation also incurs no charge, since it's just repeated POP operations, each of which is free. If a MULTIPOP operation pops k plates, then the actual cost is paid by the k dollars stored on the k plates. Because each plate on the stack has $1 of credit on it, and the stack always has a nonnegative number of plates, the amount of credit is always nonnegative. Thus, for *any* sequence of n PUSH, POP, and MULTIPOP operations, the total amortized cost is an upper bound on the total actual cost. Since the total amortized cost is $O(n)$, so is the total actual cost.

Incrementing a binary counter

As another illustration of the accounting method, let's analyze the INCREMENT operation on a binary counter that starts at 0. Recall that the running time of this operation is proportional to the number of bits flipped, which serves as the cost for this example. Again, we'll use $1 to represent each unit of cost (the flipping of a bit in this example).

For the amortized analysis, the amortized cost to set a 0-bit to 1 is $2. When a bit is set to 1, $1 of the $2 pays to actually set the bit. The second $1 resides on the bit as credit to be used later if and when the bit is reset to 0. At any point in time, every 1-bit in the counter has $1 of credit on it, and thus resetting a bit to 0 can be viewed as costing nothing, and the $1 on the bit prepays for the reset.

Here is how to determine the amortized cost of INCREMENT. The cost of resetting the bits to 0 within the **while** loop is paid for by the dollars on the bits that are reset. The INCREMENT procedure sets at most one bit to 1, in line 6, and therefore the amortized cost of an INCREMENT operation is at most $2. The number of 1-bits in the counter never becomes negative, and thus the amount of credit stays nonnegative at all times. Thus, for n INCREMENT operations, the total amortized cost is $O(n)$, which bounds the total actual cost.

Exercises

16.2-1
You perform a sequence of PUSH and POP operations on a stack whose size never exceeds k. After every k operations, a copy of the entire stack is made automat-

ically, for backup purposes. Show that the cost of n stack operations, including copying the stack, is $O(n)$ by assigning suitable amortized costs to the various stack operations.

16.2-2
Redo Exercise 16.1-3 using an accounting method of analysis.

16.2-3
You wish not only to increment a counter but also to reset it to 0 (i.e., make all bits in it 0). Counting the time to examine or modify a bit as $\Theta(1)$, show how to implement a counter as an array of bits so that any sequence of n INCREMENT and RESET operations takes $O(n)$ time on an initially zero counter. (*Hint:* Keep a pointer to the high-order 1.)

16.3   The potential method

Instead of representing prepaid work as credit stored with specific objects in the data structure, the *potential method* of amortized analysis represents the prepaid work as "potential energy," or just "potential," which can be released to pay for future operations. The potential applies to the data structure as a whole rather than to specific objects within the data structure.

The potential method works as follows. Starting with an initial data structure D_0, a sequence of n operations occurs. For each $i = 1, 2, \ldots, n$, let c_i be the actual cost of the ith operation and D_i be the data structure that results after applying the ith operation to data structure D_{i-1}. A *potential function* Φ maps each data structure D_i to a real number $\Phi(D_i)$, which is the *potential* associated with D_i. The *amortized cost* $\hat{c}_i$ of the ith operation with respect to potential function Φ is defined by

$$\hat{c}_i = c_i + \Phi(D_i) - \Phi(D_{i-1}) . \tag{16.2}$$

The amortized cost of each operation is therefore its actual cost plus the change in potential due to the operation. By equation (16.2), the total amortized cost of the n operations is

$$\sum_{i=1}^{n} \hat{c}_i = \sum_{i=1}^{n} (c_i + \Phi(D_i) - \Phi(D_{i-1}))$$

$$= \sum_{i=1}^{n} c_i + \Phi(D_n) - \Phi(D_0) . \tag{16.3}$$

The second equation follows from equation (A.12) on page 1143 because the $\Phi(D_i)$ terms telescope.

If you can define a potential function Φ so that $\Phi(D_n) \geq \Phi(D_0)$, then the total amortized cost $\sum_{i=1}^{n} \hat{c}_i$ gives an upper bound on the total actual cost $\sum_{i=1}^{n} c_i$. In practice, you don't always know how many operations might be performed. Therefore, if you require that $\Phi(D_i) \geq \Phi(D_0)$ for all i, then you guarantee, as in the accounting method, that you've paid in advance. It's usually simplest to just define $\Phi(D_0)$ to be 0 and then show that $\Phi(D_i) \geq 0$ for all i. (See Exercise 16.3-1 for an easy way to handle cases in which $\Phi(D_0) \neq 0$.)

Intuitively, if the potential difference $\Phi(D_i) - \Phi(D_{i-1})$ of the ith operation is positive, then the amortized cost $\hat{c}_i$ represents an overcharge to the ith operation, and the potential of the data structure increases. If the potential difference is negative, then the amortized cost represents an undercharge to the ith operation, and the decrease in the potential pays for the actual cost of the operation.

The amortized costs defined by equations (16.2) and (16.3) depend on the choice of the potential function Φ. Different potential functions may yield different amortized costs, yet still be upper bounds on the actual costs. You will often find trade-offs that you can make in choosing a potential function. The best potential function to use depends on the desired time bounds.

Stack operations

To illustrate the potential method, we return once again to the example of the stack operations PUSH, POP, and MULTIPOP. We define the potential function Φ on a stack to be the number of objects in the stack. The potential of the empty initial stack D_0 is $\Phi(D_0) = 0$. Since the number of objects in the stack is never negative, the stack D_i that results after the ith operation has nonnegative potential, and thus

$$\Phi(D_i) \geq 0$$
$$= \Phi(D_0) .$$

The total amortized cost of n operations with respect to Φ therefore represents an upper bound on the actual cost.

Now let's compute the amortized costs of the various stack operations. If the ith operation on a stack containing s objects is a PUSH operation, then the potential difference is

$$\Phi(D_i) - \Phi(D_{i-1}) = (s + 1) - s$$
$$= 1 .$$

By equation (16.2), the amortized cost of this PUSH operation is

$$\begin{aligned}
\widehat{c}_i &= c_i + \Phi(D_i) - \Phi(D_{i-1}) \\
&= 1 + 1 \\
&= 2 \ .
\end{aligned}$$

Suppose that the ith operation on the stack of s objects is MULTIPOP(S, k), which causes $k' = \min\{s, k\}$ objects to be popped off the stack. The actual cost of the operation is k', and the potential difference is

$$\Phi(D_i) - \Phi(D_{i-1}) = -k' \ .$$

Thus, the amortized cost of the MULTIPOP operation is

$$\begin{aligned}
\widehat{c}_i &= c_i + \Phi(D_i) - \Phi(D_{i-1}) \\
&= k' - k' \\
&= 0 \ .
\end{aligned}$$

Similarly, the amortized cost of an ordinary POP operation is 0.

The amortized cost of each of the three operations is $O(1)$, and thus the total amortized cost of a sequence of n operations is $O(n)$. Since $\Phi(D_i) \geq \Phi(D_0)$, the total amortized cost of n operations is an upper bound on the total actual cost. The worst-case cost of n operations is therefore $O(n)$.

Incrementing a binary counter

As another example of the potential method, we revisit incrementing a k-bit binary counter. This time, the potential of the counter after the ith INCREMENT operation is defined to be the number of 1-bits in the counter after the ith operation, which we'll denote by b_i.

Here is how to compute the amortized cost of an INCREMENT operation. Suppose that the ith INCREMENT operation resets t_i bits to 0. The actual cost c_i of the operation is therefore at most $t_i + 1$, since in addition to resetting t_i bits, it sets at most one bit to 1. If $b_i = 0$, then the ith operation had reset all k bits to 0, and so $b_{i-1} = t_i = k$. If $b_i > 0$, then $b_i = b_{i-1} - t_i + 1$. In either case, $b_i \leq b_{i-1} - t_i + 1$, and the potential difference is

$$\begin{aligned}
\Phi(D_i) - \Phi(D_{i-1}) &\leq (b_{i-1} - t_i + 1) - b_{i-1} \\
&= 1 - t_i \ .
\end{aligned}$$

The amortized cost is therefore

$$\begin{aligned}
\widehat{c}_i &= c_i + \Phi(D_i) - \Phi(D_{i-1}) \\
&\leq (t_i + 1) + (1 - t_i) \\
&= 2 \ .
\end{aligned}$$

If the counter starts at 0, then $\Phi(D_0) = 0$. Since $\Phi(D_i) \geq 0$ for all i, the total amortized cost of a sequence of n INCREMENT operations is an upper bound on the total actual cost, and so the worst-case cost of n INCREMENT operations is $O(n)$.

The potential method provides a simple and clever way to analyze the counter even when it does not start at 0. The counter starts with b_0 1-bits, and after n INCREMENT operations it has b_n 1-bits, where $0 \leq b_0, b_n \leq k$. Rewrite equation (16.3) as

$$\sum_{i=1}^{n} c_i = \sum_{i=1}^{n} \hat{c}_i - \Phi(D_n) + \Phi(D_0) \,.$$

Since $\Phi(D_0) = b_0$, $\Phi(D_n) = b_n$, and $\hat{c}_i \leq 2$ for all $1 \leq i \leq n$, the total actual cost of n INCREMENT operations is

$$\sum_{i=1}^{n} c_i \leq \sum_{i=1}^{n} 2 - b_n + b_0$$
$$= 2n - b_n + b_0 \,.$$

In particular, $b_0 \leq k$ means that as long as $k = O(n)$, the total actual cost is $O(n)$. In other words, if at least $n = \Omega(k)$ INCREMENT operations occur, the total actual cost is $O(n)$, no matter what initial value the counter contains.

Exercises

16.3-1
Suppose you have a potential function Φ such that $\Phi(D_i) \geq \Phi(D_0)$ for all i, but $\Phi(D_0) \neq 0$. Show that there exists a potential function Φ' such that $\Phi'(D_0) = 0$, $\Phi'(D_i) \geq 0$ for all $i \geq 1$, and the amortized costs using Φ' are the same as the amortized costs using Φ.

16.3-2
Redo Exercise 16.1-3 using a potential method of analysis.

16.3-3
Consider an ordinary binary min-heap data structure supporting the instructions INSERT and EXTRACT-MIN that, when there are n items in the heap, implements each operation in $O(\lg n)$ worst-case time. Give a potential function Φ such that the amortized cost of INSERT is $O(\lg n)$ and the amortized cost of EXTRACT-MIN is $O(1)$, and show that your potential function yields these amortized time bounds. Note that in the analysis, n is the number of items currently in the heap, and you do not know a bound on the maximum number of items that can ever be stored in the heap.

16.3-4

What is the total cost of executing n of the stack operations PUSH, POP, and MULTIPOP, assuming that the stack begins with s_0 objects and finishes with s_n objects?

16.3-5

Show how to implement a queue with two ordinary stacks (Exercise 10.1-7) so that the amortized cost of each ENQUEUE and each DEQUEUE operation is $O(1)$.

16.3-6

Design a data structure to support the following two operations for a dynamic multiset S of integers, which allows duplicate values:

INSERT(S, x) inserts x into S.

DELETE-LARGER-HALF(S) deletes the largest $\lceil |S| / 2 \rceil$ elements from S.

Explain how to implement this data structure so that any sequence of m INSERT and DELETE-LARGER-HALF operations runs in $O(m)$ time. Your implementation should also include a way to output the elements of S in $O(|S|)$ time.

16.4   Dynamic tables

When you design an application that uses a table, you do not always know in advance how many items the table will hold. You might allocate space for the table, only to find out later that it is not enough. The program must then reallocate the table with a larger size and copy all items stored in the original table over into the new, larger table. Similarly, if many items have been deleted from the table, it might be worthwhile to reallocate the table with a smaller size. This section studies this problem of dynamically expanding and contracting a table. Amortized analyses will show that the amortized cost of insertion and deletion is only $O(1)$, even though the actual cost of an operation is large when it triggers an expansion or a contraction. Moreover, you'll see how to guarantee that the unused space in a dynamic table never exceeds a constant fraction of the total space.

Let's assume that the dynamic table supports the operations TABLE-INSERT and TABLE-DELETE. TABLE-INSERT inserts into the table an item that occupies a single *slot*, that is, a space for one item. Likewise, TABLE-DELETE removes an item from the table, thereby freeing a slot. The details of the data-structuring method used to organize the table are unimportant: it could be a stack (Section 10.1.3), a heap (Chapter 6), a hash table (Chapter 11), or something else.

It is convenient to use a concept introduced in Section 11.2, where we analyzed hashing. The *load factor* $\alpha(T)$ of a nonempty table T is defined as the number of items stored in the table divided by the size (number of slots) of the table. An empty table (one with no slots) has size 0, and its load factor is defined to be 1. If the load factor of a dynamic table is bounded below by a constant, the unused space in the table is never more than a constant fraction of the total amount of space.

We start by analyzing a dynamic table that allows only insertion and then move on to the more general case that supports both insertion and deletion.

16.4.1 Table expansion

Let's assume that storage for a table is allocated as an array of slots. A table fills up when all slots have been used or, equivalently, when its load factor is 1.[1] In some software environments, upon an attempt to insert an item into a full table, the only alternative is to abort with an error. The scenario in this section assumes, however, that the software environment, like many modern ones, provides a memory-management system that can allocate and free blocks of storage on request. Thus, upon inserting an item into a full table, the system can *expand* the table by allocating a new table with more slots than the old table had. Because the table must always reside in contiguous memory, the system must allocate a new array for the larger table and then copy items from the old table into the new table.

A common heuristic allocates a new table with twice as many slots as the old one. If the only table operations are insertions, then the load factor of the table is always at least $1/2$, and thus the amount of wasted space never exceeds half the total space in the table.

The TABLE-INSERT procedure on the following page assumes that T is an object representing the table. The attribute $T.table$ contains a pointer to the block of storage representing the table, $T.num$ contains the number of items in the table, and $T.size$ gives the total number of slots in the table. Initially, the table is empty: $T.num = T.size = 0$.

There are two types of insertion here: the TABLE-INSERT procedure itself and the *elementary insertion* into a table in lines 6 and 10. We can analyze the running time of TABLE-INSERT in terms of the number of elementary insertions by assigning a cost of 1 to each elementary insertion. In most computing environments, the overhead for allocating an initial table in line 2 is constant and the overhead for allocating and freeing storage in lines 5 and 7 is dominated by the cost of transfer-

---

[1] In some situations, such as an open-address hash table, it's better to consider a table to be full if its load factor equals some constant strictly less than 1. (See Exercise 16.4-2.)

TABLE-INSERT(T, x)

```
 1  if T.size == 0
 2      allocate T.table with 1 slot
 3          T.size = 1
 4  if T.num == T.size
 5      allocate new-table with 2 · T.size slots
 6      insert all items in T.table into new-table
 7      free T.table
 8          T.table = new-table
 9          T.size = 2 · T.size
10  insert x into T.table
11  T.num = T.num + 1
```

ring items in line 6. Thus, the actual running time of TABLE-INSERT is linear in the number of elementary insertions. An *expansion* occurs when lines 5–9 execute.

Now, we'll use all three amortized analysis techniques to analyze a sequence of n TABLE-INSERT operations on an initially empty table. First, we need to determine the actual cost c_i of the ith operation. If the current table has room for the new item (or if this is the first operation), then $c_i = 1$, since the only elementary insertion performed is the one in line 10. If the current table is full, however, and an expansion occurs, then $c_i = i$: the cost is 1 for the elementary insertion in line 10 plus $i - 1$ for the items copied from the old table to the new table in line 6. For n operations, the worst-case cost of an operation is $O(n)$, which leads to an upper bound of $O(n^2)$ on the total running time for n operations.

This bound is not tight, because the table rarely expands in the course of n TABLE-INSERT operations. Specifically, the ith operation causes an expansion only when $i - 1$ is an exact power of 2. The amortized cost of an operation is in fact $O(1)$, as an aggregate analysis shows. The cost of the ith operation is

$$
c_i = \begin{cases} i & \text{if } i - 1 \text{ is an exact power of 2 ,} \\ 1 & \text{otherwise .} \end{cases}
$$

The total cost of n TABLE-INSERT operations is therefore

$$
\sum_{i=1}^{n} c_i \leq n + \sum_{j=0}^{\lfloor \lg n \rfloor} 2^j
$$
$$
< n + 2n \qquad \text{(by equation (A.6) on page 1142)}
$$
$$
= 3n ,
$$

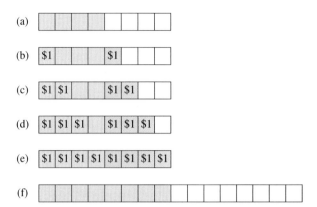

Figure 16.3   Analysis of table expansion by the accounting method. Each call of TABLE-INSERT charges $3 as follows: $1 to pay for the elementary insertion, $1 on the item inserted as prepayment for it to be reinserted later, and $1 on an item that was already in the table, also as prepayment for reinsertion. **(a)** The table immediately after an expansion, with 8 slots, 4 items (tan slots), and no stored credit. **(b)–(e)** After each of 4 calls to TABLE-INSERT, the table has one more item, with $1 stored on the new item and $1 stored on one of the 4 items that were present immediately after the expansion. Slots with these new items are blue. **(f)** Upon the next call to TABLE-INSERT, the table is full, and so it expands again. Each item had $1 to pay for it to be reinserted. Now the table looks as it did in part (a), with no stored credit but 16 slots and 8 items.

because at most n operations cost 1 each and the costs of the remaining operations form a geometric series. Since the total cost of n TABLE-INSERT operations is bounded by $3n$, the amortized cost of a single operation is at most 3.

The accounting method can provide some intuition for why the amortized cost of a TABLE-INSERT operation should be 3. You can think of each item paying for three elementary insertions: inserting itself into the current table, moving itself the next time that the table expands, and moving some other item that was already in the table the next time that the table expands. For example, suppose that the size of the table is m immediately after an expansion, as shown in Figure 16.3 for $m = 8$. Then the table holds $m/2$ items, and it contains no credit. Each call of TABLE-INSERT charges $3. The elementary insertion that occurs immediately costs $1. Another $1 resides on the item inserted as credit. The third $1 resides as credit on one of the $m/2$ items already in the table. The table will not fill again until another $m/2 - 1$ items have been inserted, and thus, by the time the table contains m items and is full, each item has $1 on it to pay for it to be reinserted it during the expansion.

Now, let's see how to use the potential method. We'll use it again in Section 16.4.2 to design a TABLE-DELETE operation that has an $O(1)$ amortized cost as well. Just as the accounting method had no stored credit immediately after an expansion—that is, when $T.num = T.size/2$—let's define the potential to be 0 when $T.num = T.size/2$. As elementary insertions occur, the potential needs to increase enough to pay for all the reinsertions that will happen when the table next expands. The table fills after another $T.size/2$ calls of TABLE-INSERT, when $T.num = T.size$. The next call of TABLE-INSERT after these $T.size/2$ calls triggers an expansion with a cost of $T.size$ to reinsert all the items. Therefore, over the course of $T.size/2$ calls of TABLE-INSERT, the potential must increase from 0 to $T.size$. To achieve this increase, let's design the potential so that each call of TABLE-INSERT increases it by

$$\frac{T.size}{T.size/2} = 2 \,,$$

until the table expands. You can see that the potential function

$$\Phi(T) = 2(T.num - T.size/2) \tag{16.4}$$

equals 0 immediately after the table expands, when $T.num = T.size/2$, and it increases by 2 upon each insertion until the table fills. Once the table fills, that is, when $T.num = T.size$, the potential $\Phi(T)$ equals $T.size$. The initial value of the potential is 0, and since the table is always at least half full, $T.num \geq T.size/2$, which implies that $\Phi(T)$ is always nonnegative. Thus, the sum of the amortized costs of n TABLE-INSERT operations gives an upper bound on the sum of the actual costs.

To analyze the amortized costs of table operations, it is convenient to think in terms of the change in potential due to each operation. Letting Φ_i denote the potential after the ith operation, we can rewrite equation (16.2) as

$$\widehat{c}_i = c_i + \Phi_i - \Phi_{i-1}$$
$$= c_i + \Delta\Phi_i \,,$$

where $\Delta\Phi_i$ is the change in potential due to the ith operation. First, consider the case when the ith insertion does not cause the table to expand. In this case, $\Delta\Phi_i$ is 2. Since the actual cost c_i is 1, the amortized cost is

$$\widehat{c}_i = c_i + \Delta\Phi_i$$
$$= 1 + 2$$
$$= 3 \,.$$

Now, consider the change in potential when the table does expand during the ith insertion because it was full immediately before the insertion. Let num_i denote the number of items stored in the table after the ith operation and $size_i$ denote the total size of the table after the ith operation, so that $size_{i-1} = num_{i-1} = i - 1$

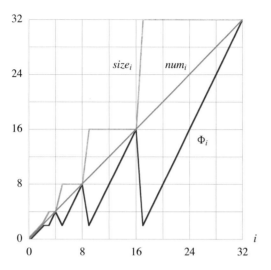

Figure 16.4 The effect of a sequence of n TABLE-INSERT operations on the number num_i of items in the table (the brown line), the number $size_i$ of slots in the table (the blue line), and the potential $\Phi_i = 2(num_i - size_i/2)$ (the red line), each being measured after the ith operation. Immediately before an expansion, the potential has built up to the number of items in the table, and therefore it can pay for moving all the items to the new table. Afterward, the potential drops to 0, but it immediately increases by 2 upon insertion of the item that caused the expansion.

and therefore $\Phi_{i-1} = 2(size_{i-1} - size_{i-1}/2) = size_{i-1} = i - 1$. Immediately after the expansion, the potential goes down to 0, and then the new item is inserted, causing the potential to increase to $\Phi_i = 2$. Thus, when the ith insertion triggers an expansion, $\Delta\Phi_i = 2 - (i - 1) = 3 - i$. When the table expands in the ith TABLE-INSERT operation, the actual cost c_i equals i (to reinsert $i - 1$ items and insert the ith item), giving an amortized cost of

$$\begin{aligned}
\widehat{c}_i &= c_i + \Delta\Phi_i \\
&= i + (3 - i) \\
&= 3 \,.
\end{aligned}$$

Figure 16.4 plots the values of num_i, $size_i$, and Φ_i against i. Notice how the potential builds to pay for expanding the table.

16.4.2 Table expansion and contraction

To implement a TABLE-DELETE operation, it is simple enough to remove the specified item from the table. In order to limit the amount of wasted space, however, you might want to *contract* the table when the load factor becomes too small. Table contraction is analogous to table expansion: when the number of items in the table drops too low, allocate a new, smaller table and then copy the items from the old table into the new one. You can then free the storage for the old table by returning it to the memory-management system. In order to not waste space, yet keep the amortized costs low, the insertion and deletion procedures should preserve two properties:

- the load factor of the dynamic table is bounded below by a positive constant, as well as above by 1, and

- the amortized cost of a table operation is bounded above by a constant.

The actual cost of each operation equals the number of elementary insertions or deletions.

You might think that if you double the table size upon inserting an item into a full table, then you should halve the size when deleting an item that would cause the table to become less than half full. This strategy does indeed guarantee that the load factor of the table never drops below $1/2$. Unfortunately, it can also cause the amortized cost of an operation to be quite large. Consider the following scenario. Perform n operations on a table T of size $n/2$, where n is an exact power of 2. The first $n/2$ operations are insertions, which by our previous analysis cost a total of $\Theta(n)$. At the end of this sequence of insertions, $T.num = T.size = n/2$. For the second $n/2$ operations, perform the following sequence:

insert, delete, delete, insert, insert, delete, delete, insert, insert, ...

The first insertion causes the table to expand to size n. The two deletions that follow cause the table to contract back to size $n/2$. Two further insertions cause another expansion, and so forth. The cost of each expansion and contraction is $\Theta(n)$, and there are $\Theta(n)$ of them. Thus, the total cost of the n operations is $\Theta(n^2)$, making the amortized cost of an operation $\Theta(n)$.

The problem with this strategy is that after the table expands, not enough deletions occur to pay for a contraction. Likewise, after the table contracts, not enough insertions take place to pay for an expansion.

How can we solve this problem? Allow the load factor of the table to drop below $1/2$. Specifically, continue to double the table size upon inserting an item into a full table, but halve the table size when deleting an item causes the table to become less than $1/4$ full, rather than $1/2$ full as before. The load factor of the table is therefore bounded below by the constant $1/4$, and the load factor is $1/2$ immediately after a contraction.

An expansion or contraction should exhaust all the built-up potential, so that immediately after expansion or contraction, when the load factor is $1/2$, the table's potential is 0. Figure 16.5 shows the idea. As the load factor deviates from $1/2$, the

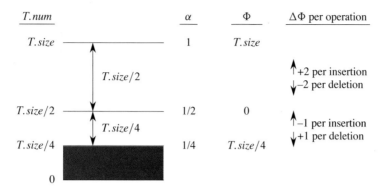

Figure 16.5 How to think about the potential function Φ for table insertion and deletion. When the load factor α is $1/2$, the potential is 0. In order to accumulate sufficient potential to pay for reinserting all $T.size$ items when the table fills, the potential needs to increase by 2 upon each insertion when $\alpha \geq 1/2$. Correspondingly, the potential decreases by 2 upon each deletion that leaves $\alpha \geq 1/2$. In order to accrue enough potential to cover the cost of reinserting all $T.size/4$ items when the table contracts, the potential needs to increase by 1 upon each deletion when $\alpha < 1/2$, and correspondingly the potential decreases by 1 upon each insertion that leaves $\alpha < 1/2$. The red area represents load factors less than $1/4$, which are not allowed.

potential increases so that by the time an expansion or contraction occurs, the table has garnered sufficient potential to pay for copying all the items into the newly allocated table. Thus, the potential function should grow to $T.num$ by the time that the load factor has either increased to 1 or decreased to $1/4$. Immediately after either expanding or contracting the table, the load factor goes back to $1/2$ and the table's potential reduces back to 0.

We omit the code for TABLE-DELETE, since it is analogous to TABLE-INSERT. We assume that if a contraction occurs during TABLE-DELETE, it occurs after the item is deleted from the table. The analysis assumes that whenever the number of items in the table drops to 0, the table occupies no storage. That is, if $T.num = 0$, then $T.size = 0$.

How do we design a potential function that gives constant amortized time for both insertion and deletion? When the load factor is at least $1/2$, the same potential function, $\Phi(T) = 2(T.num - T.size/2)$, that we used for insertion still works. When the table is at least half full, each insertion increases the potential by 2 if the table does not expand, and each deletion reduces the potential by 2 if it does not cause the load factor to drop below $1/2$.

What about when the load factor is less than $1/2$, that is, when $1/4 \leq \alpha(T) < 1/2$? As before, when $\alpha(T) = 1/2$, so that $T.num = T.size/2$, the potential $\Phi(T)$ should be 0. To get the load factor from $1/2$ down to $1/4$, $T.size/4$ deletions need to occur, at which time $T.num = T.size/4$. To pay for all the reinsertions, the potential must increase from 0 to $T.size/4$ over these $T.size/4$ deletions. Therefore, for each call of TABLE-DELETE until the table contracts, the potential should increase by

$$\frac{T.size/4}{T.size/4} = 1 \, .$$

Likewise, when $\alpha < 1/2$, each call of TABLE-INSERT should decrease the potential by 1. When $1/4 \le \alpha(T) < 1/2$, the potential function

$$\Phi(T) = T.size/2 - T.num$$

produces this desired behavior.

Putting the two cases together, we get the potential function

$$\Phi(T) = \begin{cases} 2(T.num - T.size/2) & \text{if } \alpha(T) \ge 1/2 \, , \\ T.size/2 - T.num & \text{if } \alpha(T) < 1/2 \, . \end{cases} \tag{16.5}$$

The potential of an empty table is 0 and the potential is never negative. Thus, the total amortized cost of a sequence of operations with respect to Φ provides an upper bound on the actual cost of the sequence. Figure 16.6 illustrates how the potential function behaves over a sequence of insertions and deletions.

Now, let's determine the amortized costs of each operation. As before, let num_i denote the number of items stored in the table after the ith operation, $size_i$ denote the total size of the table after the ith operation, $\alpha_i = num_i/size_i$ denote the load factor after the ith operation, Φ_i denote the potential after the ith operation, and $\Delta\Phi_i$ denote the change in potential due to the ith operation. Initially, $num_0 = 0$, $size_0 = 0$, and $\Phi_0 = 0$.

The cases in which the table does not expand or contract and the load factor does not cross $\alpha = 1/2$ are straightforward. As we have seen, if $\alpha_{i-1} \ge 1/2$ and the ith operation is an insertion that does not cause the table to expand, then $\Delta\Phi_i = 2$. Likewise, if the ith operation is a deletion and $\alpha_i \ge 1/2$, then $\Delta\Phi_i = -2$. Furthermore, if $\alpha_{i-1} < 1/2$ and the ith operation is a deletion that does not trigger a contraction, then $\Delta\Phi_i = 1$, and if the ith operation is an insertion and $\alpha_i < 1/2$, then $\Delta\Phi_i = -1$. In other words, if no expansion or contraction occurs and the load factor does not cross $\alpha = 1/2$, then

- if the load factor stays at or above $1/2$, then the potential increases by 2 for an insertion and decreases by 2 for a deletion, and

- if the load factor stays below $1/2$, then the potential increases by 1 for a deletion and decreases by 1 for an insertion.

In each of these cases, the actual cost c_i of the ith operation is just 1, and so

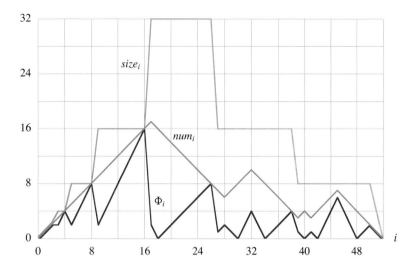

Figure 16.6 The effect of a sequence of n Table-Insert and Table-Delete operations on the number num_i of items in the table (the brown line), the number $size_i$ of slots in the table (the blue line), and the potential (the red line)

$$\Phi_i = \begin{cases} 2(num_i - size_i/2) & \text{if } \alpha_i \geq 1/2 \text{ ,} \\ size_i/2 - num_i & \text{if } \alpha_i < 1/2 \text{ ,} \end{cases}$$

where $\alpha_i = num_i / size_i$, each measured after the ith operation. Immediately before an expansion or contraction, the potential has built up to the number of items in the table, and therefore it can pay for moving all the items to the new table.

- if the ith operation is an insertion, its amortized cost $\hat{c}_i$ is $c_i + \Delta\Phi_i$, which is $1 + 2 = 3$ if the load factor stays at or above $1/2$, and $1 + (-1) = 0$ if the load factor stays below $1/2$, and

- if the ith operation is a deletion, its amortized cost $\hat{c}_i$ is $c_i + \Delta\Phi_i$, which is $1 + (-2) = -1$ if the load factor stays at or above $1/2$, and $1 + 1 = 2$ if the load factor stays below $1/2$.

Four cases remain: an insertion that takes the load factor from below $1/2$ to $1/2$, a deletion that takes the load factor from $1/2$ to below $1/2$, a deletion that causes the table to contract, and an insertion that causes the table to expand. We analyzed that last case at the end of Section 16.4.1 to show that its amortized cost is 3.

When the ith operation is a deletion that causes the table to contract, we have $num_{i-1} = size_{i-1}/4$ before the contraction, then the item is deleted, and finally $num_i = size_i/2 - 1$ after the contraction. Thus, by equation (16.5) we have

$$\Phi_{i-1} = size_{i-1}/2 - num_{i-1}$$
$$= size_{i-1}/2 - size_{i-1}/4$$
$$= size_{i-1}/4 \, ,$$

which also equals the actual cost c_i of deleting one item and copying $size_{i-1}/4 - 1$ items into the new, smaller table. Since $num_i = size_i/2 - 1$ after the operation has completed, $\alpha_i < 1/2$, and so

$$\Phi_i = size_i/2 - num_i$$
$$= 1 \, ,$$

giving $\Delta\Phi_i = 1 - size_{i-1}/4$. Therefore, when the ith operation is a deletion that triggers a contraction, its amortized cost is

$$\hat{c}_i = c_i + \Delta\Phi_i$$
$$= size_{i-1}/4 + (1 - size_{i-1}/4)$$
$$= 1 \, .$$

Finally, we handle the cases where the load factor fits one case of equation (16.5) before the operation and the other case afterward. We start with deletion, where we have $num_{i-1} = size_{i-1}/2$, so that $\alpha_{i-1} = 1/2$, beforehand, and $num_i = size_i/2-1$, so that $\alpha_i < 1/2$ afterward. Because $\alpha_{i-1} = 1/2$, we have $\Phi_{i-1} = 0$, and because $\alpha_i < 1/2$, we have $\Phi_i = size_i/2 - num_i = 1$. Thus we get that $\Delta\Phi_i = 1 - 0 = 1$. Since the ith operation is a deletion that does not cause a contraction, the actual cost c_i equals 1, and the amortized cost $\hat{c}_i$ is $c_i + \Delta\Phi_i = 1 + 1 = 2$.

Conversely, if the ith operation is an insertion that takes the load factor from below $1/2$ to equaling $1/2$, the change in potential $\Delta\Phi_i$ equals -1. Again, the actual cost c_i is 1, and now the amortized cost $\hat{c}_i$ is $c_i + \Delta\Phi_i = 1 + (-1) = 0$.

In summary, since the amortized cost of each operation is bounded above by a constant, the actual time for any sequence of n operations on a dynamic table is $O(n)$.

Exercises

16.4-1
Using the potential method, analyze the amortized cost of the first table insertion.

16.4-2
You wish to implement a dynamic, open-address hash table. Why might you consider the table to be full when its load factor reaches some value α that is strictly less than 1? Describe briefly how to make insertion into a dynamic, open-address hash table run in such a way that the expected value of the amortized cost per

insertion is $O(1)$. Why is the expected value of the actual cost per insertion not necessarily $O(1)$ for all insertions?

16.4-3
Discuss how to use the accounting method to analyze both the insertion and deletion operations, assuming that the table doubles in size when its load factor exceeds 1 and the table halves in size when its load factor goes below $1/4$.

16.4-4
Suppose that instead of contracting a table by halving its size when its load factor drops below $1/4$, you contract the table by multiplying its size by $2/3$ when its load factor drops below $1/3$. Using the potential function

$$\Phi(T) = |2(T.num - T.size/2)| \ ,$$

show that the amortized cost of a TABLE-DELETE that uses this strategy is bounded above by a constant.

Problems

16-1 *Binary reflected Gray code*
A *binary Gray code* represents a sequence of nonnegative integers in binary such that to go from one integer to the next, exactly one bit flips every time. The *binary reflected Gray code* represents a sequence of the integers 0 to $2^k - 1$ for some positive integer k according to the following recursive method:

- For $k = 1$, the binary reflected Gray code is $\langle 0, 1 \rangle$.

- For $k \geq 2$, first form the binary reflected Gray code for $k - 1$, giving the 2^{k-1} integers 0 to $2^{k-1} - 1$. Then form the reflection of this sequence, which is just the sequence in reverse. (That is, the jth integer in the sequence becomes the $(2^{k-1} - j - 1)$st integer in the reflection). Next, add 2^{k-1} to each of the 2^{k-1} integers in the reflected sequence. Finally, concatenate the two sequences.

For example, for $k = 2$, first form the binary reflected Gray code $\langle 0, 1 \rangle$ for $k = 1$. Its reflection is the sequence $\langle 1, 0 \rangle$. Adding $2^{k-1} = 2$ to each integer in the reflection gives the sequence $\langle 3, 2 \rangle$. Concatenating the two sequences gives $\langle 0, 1, 3, 2 \rangle$ or, in binary, $\langle 00, 01, 11, 10 \rangle$, so that each integer differs from its predecessor by exactly one bit. For $k = 3$, the reflection of the binary reflected Gray code for $k = 2$ is $\langle 2, 3, 1, 0 \rangle$ and adding $2^{k-1} = 4$ gives $\langle 6, 7, 5, 4 \rangle$. Concatenating produces the sequence $\langle 0, 1, 3, 2, 6, 7, 5, 4 \rangle$, which in binary is $\langle 000, 001, 011, 010, 110, 111, 101, 100 \rangle$. In the binary reflected Gray code, only one bit flips even when wrapping around from the last integer to the first.

a. Index the integers in a binary reflected Gray code from 0 to $2^k - 1$, and consider the ith integer in the binary reflected Gray code. To go from the $(i-1)$st integer to the ith integer in the binary reflected Gray code, exactly one bit flips. Show how to determine which bit flips, given the index i.

b. Assuming that given a bit number j, you can flip bit j of an integer in constant time, show how to compute the entire binary reflected Gray code sequence of 2^k numbers in $\Theta(2^k)$ time.

16-2 *Making binary search dynamic*

Binary search of a sorted array takes logarithmic search time, but the time to insert a new element is linear in the size of the array. You can improve the time for insertion by keeping several sorted arrays.

Specifically, suppose that you wish to support SEARCH and INSERT on a set of n elements. Let $k = \lceil \lg(n + 1) \rceil$, and let the binary representation of n be $\langle n_{k-1}, n_{k-2}, \ldots, n_0 \rangle$. Maintain k sorted arrays $A_0, A_1, \ldots, A_{k-1}$, where for $i = 0, 1, \ldots, k - 1$, the length of array A_i is 2^i. Each array is either full or empty, depending on whether $n_i = 1$ or $n_i = 0$, respectively. The total number of elements held in all k arrays is therefore $\sum_{i=0}^{k-1} n_i \, 2^i = n$. Although each individual array is sorted, elements in different arrays bear no particular relationship to each other.

a. Describe how to perform the SEARCH operation for this data structure. Analyze its worst-case running time.

b. Describe how to perform the INSERT operation. Analyze its worst-case and amortized running times, assuming that the only operations are INSERT and SEARCH.

c. Describe how to implement DELETE. Analyze its worst-case and amortized running times, assuming that there can be DELETE, INSERT, and SEARCH operations.

16-3 *Amortized weight-balanced trees*

Consider an ordinary binary search tree augmented by adding to each node x the attribute $x.size$, which gives the number of keys stored in the subtree rooted at x. Let α be a constant in the range $1/2 \le \alpha < 1$. We say that a given node x is *α-balanced* if $x.left.size \le \alpha \cdot x.size$ and $x.right.size \le \alpha \cdot x.size$. The tree as a whole is *α-balanced* if every node in the tree is α-balanced. The following amortized approach to maintaining weight-balanced trees was suggested by G. Varghese.

a. A $1/2$-balanced tree is, in a sense, as balanced as it can be. Given a node x in an arbitrary binary search tree, show how to rebuild the subtree rooted at x so that it becomes $1/2$-balanced. Your algorithm should run in $\Theta(x.size)$ time, and it can use $O(x.size)$ auxiliary storage.

b. Show that performing a search in an n-node α-balanced binary search tree takes $O(\lg n)$ worst-case time.

For the remainder of this problem, assume that the constant α is strictly greater than $1/2$. Suppose that you implement INSERT and DELETE as usual for an n-node binary search tree, except that after every such operation, if any node in the tree is no longer α-balanced, then you "rebuild" the subtree rooted at the highest such node in the tree so that it becomes $1/2$-balanced.

We'll analyze this rebuilding scheme using the potential method. For a node x in a binary search tree T, define

$$\Delta(x) = |x.left.size - x.right.size| \ .$$

Define the potential of T as

$$\Phi(T) = c \sum_{x \in T : \Delta(x) \geq 2} \Delta(x) \ ,$$

where c is a sufficiently large constant that depends on α.

c. Argue that any binary search tree has nonnegative potential and also that a $1/2$-balanced tree has potential 0.

d. Suppose that m units of potential can pay for rebuilding an m-node subtree. How large must c be in terms of α in order for it to take $O(1)$ amortized time to rebuild a subtree that is not α-balanced?

e. Show that inserting a node into or deleting a node from an n-node α-balanced tree costs $O(\lg n)$ amortized time.

16-4 *The cost of restructuring red-black trees*

There are four basic operations on red-black trees that perform *structural modifications*: node insertions, node deletions, rotations, and color changes. We have seen that RB-INSERT and RB-DELETE use only $O(1)$ rotations, node insertions, and node deletions to maintain the red-black properties, but they may make many more color changes.

a. Describe a legal red-black tree with n nodes such that calling RB-INSERT to add the $(n + 1)$st node causes $\Omega(\lg n)$ color changes. Then describe a legal red-black tree with n nodes for which calling RB-DELETE on a particular node causes $\Omega(\lg n)$ color changes.

Although the worst-case number of color changes per operation can be logarithmic, you will prove that any sequence of m RB-INSERT and RB-DELETE operations on an initially empty red-black tree causes $O(m)$ structural modifications in the worst case.

b. Some of the cases handled by the main loop of the code of both RB-INSERT-FIXUP and RB-DELETE-FIXUP are *terminating*: once encountered, they cause the loop to terminate after a constant number of additional operations. For each of the cases of RB-INSERT-FIXUP and RB-DELETE-FIXUP, specify which are terminating and which are not. (*Hint:* Look at Figures 13.5, 13.6, and 13.7 in Sections 13.3 and 13.4.)

You will first analyze the structural modifications when only insertions are performed. Let T be a red-black tree, and define $\Phi(T)$ to be the number of red nodes in T. Assume that one unit of potential can pay for the structural modifications performed by any of the three cases of RB-INSERT-FIXUP.

c. Let T' be the result of applying Case 1 of RB-INSERT-FIXUP to T. Argue that $\Phi(T') = \Phi(T) - 1$.

d. We can break the operation of the RB-INSERT procedure into three parts. List the structural modifications and potential changes resulting from lines 1–16 of RB-INSERT, from nonterminating cases of RB-INSERT-FIXUP, and from terminating cases of RB-INSERT-FIXUP.

e. Using part (d), argue that the amortized number of structural modifications performed by any call of RB-INSERT is $O(1)$.

Next you will prove that there are $O(m)$ structural modifications when both insertions and deletions occur. Define, for each node x,

$$w(x) = \begin{cases} 0 & \text{if } x \text{ is red}, \\ 1 & \text{if } x \text{ is black and has no red children}, \\ 0 & \text{if } x \text{ is black and has one red child}, \\ 2 & \text{if } x \text{ is black and has two red children}. \end{cases}$$

Now redefine the potential of a red-black tree T as

$$\Phi(T) = \sum_{x \in T} w(x),$$

and let T' be the tree that results from applying any nonterminating case of RB-INSERT-FIXUP or RB-DELETE-FIXUP to T.

f. Show that $\Phi(T') \leq \Phi(T) - 1$ for all nonterminating cases of RB-INSERT-FIXUP. Argue that the amortized number of structural modifications performed by any call of RB-INSERT-FIXUP is $O(1)$.

g. Show that $\Phi(T') \leq \Phi(T) - 1$ for all nonterminating cases of RB-DELETE-FIXUP. Argue that the amortized number of structural modifications performed by any call of RB-DELETE-FIXUP is $O(1)$.

h. Complete the proof that in the worst case, any sequence of m RB-INSERT and RB-DELETE operations performs $O(m)$ structural modifications.

Chapter notes

Aho, Hopcroft, and Ullman [5] used aggregate analysis to determine the running time of operations on a disjoint-set forest. We'll analyze this data structure using the potential method in Chapter 19. Tarjan [430] surveys the accounting and potential methods of amortized analysis and presents several applications. He attributes the accounting method to several authors, including M. R. Brown, R. E. Tarjan, S. Huddleston, and K. Mehlhorn. He attributes the potential method to D. D. Sleator. The term "amortized" is due to D. D. Sleator and R. E. Tarjan.

Potential functions are also useful for proving lower bounds for certain types of problems. For each configuration of the problem, define a potential function that maps the configuration to a real number. Then determine the potential Φ_{init} of the initial configuration, the potential Φ_{final} of the final configuration, and the maximum change in potential $\Delta\Phi_{\text{max}}$ due to any step. The number of steps must therefore be at least $|\Phi_{\text{final}} - \Phi_{\text{init}}| / |\Delta\Phi_{\text{max}}|$. Examples of potential functions to prove lower bounds in I/O complexity appear in works by Cormen, Sundquist, and Wisniewski [105], Floyd [146], and Aggarwal and Vitter [3]. Krumme, Cybenko, and Venkataraman [271] applied potential functions to prove lower bounds on *gossiping*: communicating a unique item from each vertex in a graph to every other vertex.

Part V   Advanced Data Structures

Introduction

This part returns to studying data structures that support operations on dynamic sets, but at a more advanced level than Part III. One of the chapters, for example, makes extensive use of the amortized analysis techniques from Chapter 16.

Chapter 17 shows how to augment red-black trees—adding additional information in each node—to support dynamic-set operations in addition to those covered in Chapters 12 and 13. The first example augments red-black trees to dynamically maintain order statistics for a set of keys. Another example augments them in a different way to maintain intervals of real numbers. Chapter 17 includes a theorem giving sufficient conditions for when a red-black tree can be augmented while maintaining the $O(\lg n)$ running times for insertion and deletion.

Chapter 18 presents B-trees, which are balanced search trees specifically designed to be stored on disks. Since disks operate much more slowly than random-access memory, B-tree performance depends not only on how much computing time the dynamic-set operations consume but also on how many disk accesses they perform. For each B-tree operation, the number of disk accesses increases with the height of the B-tree, but B-tree operations keep the height low.

Chapter 19 examines data structures for disjoint sets. Starting with a universe of n elements, each initially in its own singleton set, the operation UNION unites two sets. At all times, the n elements are partitioned into disjoint sets, even as calls to the UNION operation change the members of a set dynamically. The query FIND-SET identifies the unique set that contains a given element at the moment. Representing each set as a simple rooted tree yields surprisingly fast operations: a sequence of m operations runs in $O(m \, \alpha(n))$ time, where $\alpha(n)$ is an incredibly slowly growing function—$\alpha(n)$ is at most 4 in any conceivable application. The amortized analysis that proves this time bound is as complex as the data structure is simple.

The topics covered in this part are by no means the only examples of "advanced" data structures. Other advanced data structures include the following:

- *Fibonacci heaps* [156] implement mergeable heaps (see Problem 10-2 on page 268) with the operations INSERT, MINIMUM, and UNION taking only $O(1)$ actual and amortized time, and the operations EXTRACT-MIN and DELETE taking $O(\lg n)$ amortized time. The most significant advantage of these data structures, however, is that DECREASE-KEY takes only $O(1)$ amortized time. *Strict Fibonacci heaps* [73], developed later, made all of these time bounds actual. Because the DECREASE-KEY operation takes constant amortized time, (strict) Fibonacci heaps constitute key components of some of the asymptotically fastest algorithms to date for graph problems.

- *Dynamic trees* [415, 429] maintain a forest of disjoint rooted trees. Each edge in each tree has a real-valued cost. Dynamic trees support queries to find parents, roots, edge costs, and the minimum edge cost on a simple path from a node up to a root. Trees may be manipulated by cutting edges, updating all edge costs on a simple path from a node up to a root, linking a root into another tree, and making a node the root of the tree it appears in. One implementation of dynamic trees gives an $O(\lg n)$ amortized time bound for each operation, while a more complicated implementation yields $O(\lg n)$ worst-case time bounds. Dynamic trees are used in some of the asymptotically fastest network-flow algorithms.

- *Splay trees* [418, 429] are a form of binary search tree on which the standard search-tree operations run in $O(\lg n)$ amortized time. One application of splay trees simplifies dynamic trees.

- *Persistent* data structures allow queries, and sometimes updates as well, on past versions of a data structure. For example, linked data structures can be made persistent with only a small time and space cost [126]. Problem 13-1 gives a simple example of a persistent dynamic set.

- Several data structures allow a faster implementation of dictionary operations (INSERT, DELETE, and SEARCH) for a restricted universe of keys. By taking advantage of these restrictions, they are able to achieve better worst-case asymptotic running times than comparison-based data structures. If the keys are unique integers drawn from the set $\{0, 1, 2, \ldots, u - 1\}$, where u is an exact power of 2, then a recursive data structure known as a *van Emde Boas tree* [440, 441] supports each of the operations SEARCH, INSERT, DELETE, MINIMUM, MAXIMUM, SUCCESSOR, and PREDECESSOR in $O(\lg \lg u)$ time. *Fusion trees* [157] were the first data structure to allow faster dictionary operations when the universe is restricted to integers, implementing these operations in $O(\lg n / \lg \lg n)$ time. Several subsequent data structures, including *exponential search trees* [17], have also given improved bounds on some or all of the dictionary operations and are mentioned in the chapter notes throughout this book.

- *Dynamic graph data structures* support various queries while allowing the structure of a graph to change through operations that insert or delete vertices or edges. Examples of the queries that they support include vertex connectivity [214], edge connectivity, minimum spanning trees [213], biconnectivity, and transitive closure [212].

Chapter notes throughout this book mention additional data structures.

17 Augmenting Data Structures

Some solutions require no more than a "textbook" data structure—such as a doubly linked list, a hash table, or a binary search tree—but many others require a dash of creativity. Rarely will you need to create an entirely new type of data structure, though. More often, you can augment a textbook data structure by storing additional information in it. You can then program new operations for the data structure to support your application. Augmenting a data structure is not always straightforward, however, since the added information must be updated and maintained by the ordinary operations on the data structure.

This chapter discusses two data structures based on red-black trees that are augmented with additional information. Section 17.1 describes a data structure that supports general order-statistic operations on a dynamic set: quickly finding the ith smallest number or the rank of a given element. Section 17.2 abstracts the process of augmenting a data structure and provides a theorem that you can use when augmenting red-black trees. Section 17.3 uses this theorem to help design a data structure for maintaining a dynamic set of intervals, such as time intervals. You can use this data structure to quickly find an interval that overlaps a given query interval.

17.1 Dynamic order statistics

Chapter 9 introduced the notion of an order statistic. Specifically, the ith order statistic of a set of n elements, where $i \in \{1, 2, \ldots, n\}$, is simply the element in the set with the ith smallest key. In Chapter 9, you saw how to determine any order statistic in $O(n)$ time from an unordered set. This section shows how to modify red-black trees so that you can determine any order statistic for a dynamic set in $O(\lg n)$ time and also compute the *rank* of an element—its position in the linear order of the set—in $O(\lg n)$ time.

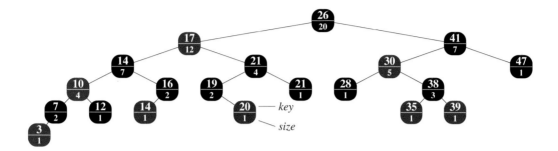

Figure 17.1 An order-statistic tree, which is an augmented red-black tree. In addition to its usual attributes, each node x has an attribute $x.size$, which is the number of nodes, other than the sentinel, in the subtree rooted at x.

Figure 17.1 shows a data structure that can support fast order-statistic operations. An *order-statistic tree* T is simply a red-black tree with additional information stored in each node. Each node x contains the usual red-black tree attributes $x.key$, $x.color$, $x.p$, $x.left$, and $x.right$, along with a new attribute, $x.size$. This attribute contains the number of internal nodes in the subtree rooted at x (including x itself, but not including any sentinels), that is, the size of the subtree. If we define the sentinel's size to be 0—that is, we set $T.nil.size$ to be 0—then we have the identity

$$x.size = x.left.size + x.right.size + 1 \ .$$

Keys need not be distinct in an order-statistic tree. For example, the tree in Figure 17.1 has two keys with value 14 and two keys with value 21. When equal keys are present, the above notion of rank is not well defined. We remove this ambiguity for an order-statistic tree by defining the rank of an element as the position at which it would be printed in an inorder walk of the tree. In Figure 17.1, for example, the key 14 stored in a black node has rank 5, and the key 14 stored in a red node has rank 6.

Retrieving the element with a given rank

Before we show how to maintain the size information during insertion and deletion, let's see how to implement two order-statistic queries that use this additional information. We begin with an operation that retrieves the element with a given rank. The procedure OS-SELECT(x, i) on the following page returns a pointer to the node containing the ith smallest key in the subtree rooted at x. To find the node with the ith smallest key in an order-statistic tree T, call OS-SELECT$(T.root, i)$.

Here is how OS-SELECT works. Line 1 computes r, the rank of node x within the subtree rooted at x. The value of $x.left.size$ is the number of nodes that come

OS-SELECT(x, i)

1    $r = x.left.size + 1$ // rank of x within the subtree rooted at x
2   **if** $i == r$
3   **return** x
4   **elseif** $i < r$
5   **return** OS-SELECT$(x.left, i)$
6   **else return** OS-SELECT$(x.right, i - r)$

before x in an inorder tree walk of the subtree rooted at x. Thus, $x.left.size + 1$ is the rank of x within the subtree rooted at x. If $i = r$, then node x is the ith smallest element, and so line 3 returns x. If $i < r$, then the ith smallest element resides in x's left subtree, and therefore, line 5 recurses on $x.left$. If $i > r$, then the ith smallest element resides in x's right subtree. Since the subtree rooted at x contains r elements that come before x's right subtree in an inorder tree walk, the ith smallest element in the subtree rooted at x is the $(i - r)$th smallest element in the subtree rooted at $x.right$. Line 6 determines this element recursively.

As an example of how OS-SELECT operates, consider a search for the 17th smallest element in the order-statistic tree of Figure 17.1. The search starts with x as the root, whose key is 26, and with $i = 17$. Since the size of 26's left subtree is 12, its rank is 13. Thus, the node with rank 17 is the $17 - 13 = 4$th smallest element in 26's right subtree. In the recursive call, x is the node with key 41, and $i = 4$. Since the size of 41's left subtree is 5, its rank within its subtree is 6. Therefore, the node with rank 4 is the 4th smallest element in 41's left subtree. In the recursive call, x is the node with key 30, and its rank within its subtree is 2. The procedure recurses once again to find the $4 - 2 = 2$nd smallest element in the subtree rooted at the node with key 38. Its left subtree has size 1, which means it is the second smallest element. Thus, the procedure returns a pointer to the node with key 38.

Because each recursive call goes down one level in the order-statistic tree, the total time for OS-SELECT is at worst proportional to the height of the tree. Since the tree is a red-black tree, its height is $O(\lg n)$, where n is the number of nodes. Thus, the running time of OS-SELECT is $O(\lg n)$ for a dynamic set of n elements.

Determining the rank of an element

Given a pointer to a node x in an order-statistic tree T, the procedure OS-RANK on the facing page returns the position of x in the linear order determined by an inorder tree walk of T.

OS-RANK(T, x)

```
1   r = x.left.size + 1          // rank of x within the subtree rooted at x
2   y = x                        // root of subtree being examined
3   while y ≠ T.root
4       if y == y.p.right                    // if root of a right subtree ...
5           r = r + y.p.left.size + 1        // ... add in parent and its left subtree
6       y = y.p                              // move y toward the root
7   return r
```

The OS-RANK procedure works as follows. You can think of node x's rank as the number of nodes preceding x in an inorder tree walk, plus 1 for x itself. OS-RANK maintains the following loop invariant:

> At the start of each iteration of the **while** loop of lines 3–6, r is the rank of $x.key$ in the subtree rooted at node y.

We use this loop invariant to show that OS-RANK works correctly as follows:

Initialization: Prior to the first iteration, line 1 sets r to be the rank of $x.key$ within the subtree rooted at x. Setting $y = x$ in line 2 makes the invariant true the first time the test in line 3 executes.

Maintenance: At the end of each iteration of the **while** loop, line 6 sets $y = y.p$. Thus, we must show that if r is the rank of $x.key$ in the subtree rooted at y at the start of the loop body, then r is the rank of $x.key$ in the subtree rooted at $y.p$ at the end of the loop body. In each iteration of the **while** loop, consider the subtree rooted at $y.p$. The value of r already includes the number of nodes in the subtree rooted at node y that precede x in an inorder walk, and so the procedure must add the nodes in the subtree rooted at y's sibling that precede x in an inorder walk, plus 1 for $y.p$ if it, too, precedes x. If y is a left child, then neither $y.p$ nor any node in $y.p$'s right subtree precedes x, and so OS-RANK leaves r alone. Otherwise, y is a right child and all the nodes in $y.p$'s left subtree precede x, as does $y.p$ itself. In this case, line 5 adds $y.p.left.size + 1$ to the current value of r.

Termination: Because each iteration of the loop moves y toward the root and the loop terminates when $y = T.root$, the loop eventually terminates. Moreover, the subtree rooted at y is the entire tree. Thus, the value of r is the rank of $x.key$ in the entire tree.

As an example, when OS-RANK runs on the order-statistic tree of Figure 17.1 to find the rank of the node with key 38, the following sequence of values of $y.key$ and r occurs at the top of the **while** loop:

iteration	$y.key$	r
1	38	2
2	30	4
3	41	4
4	26	17

The procedure returns the rank 17.

Since each iteration of the **while** loop takes $O(1)$ time, and y goes up one level in the tree with each iteration, the running time of OS-RANK is at worst proportional to the height of the tree: $O(\lg n)$ on an n-node order-statistic tree.

Maintaining subtree sizes

Given the *size* attribute in each node, OS-SELECT and OS-RANK can quickly compute order-statistic information. But if the basic modifying operations on red-black trees cannot efficiently maintain the *size* attribute, our work will have been for naught. Let's see how to maintain subtree sizes for both insertion and deletion without affecting the asymptotic running time of either operation.

Recall from Section 13.3 that insertion into a red-black tree consists of two phases. The first phase goes down the tree from the root, inserting the new node as a child of an existing node. The second phase goes up the tree, changing colors and performing rotations to maintain the red-black properties.

To maintain the subtree sizes in the first phase, simply increment $x.size$ for each node x on the simple path traversed from the root down toward the leaves. The new node added gets a *size* of 1. Since there are $O(\lg n)$ nodes on the traversed path, the additional cost of maintaining the *size* attributes is $O(\lg n)$.

In the second phase, the only structural changes to the underlying red-black tree are caused by rotations, of which there are at most two. Moreover, a rotation is a local operation: only two nodes have their *size* attributes invalidated. The link around which the rotation is performed is incident on these two nodes. Referring to the code for LEFT-ROTATE(T, x) on page 336, add the following lines:

```
13   y.size = x.size
14   x.size = x.left.size + x.right.size + 1
```

Figure 17.2 illustrates how the attributes are updated. The change to RIGHT-ROTATE is symmetric.

Since inserting into a red-black tree requires at most two rotations, updating the *size* attributes in the second phase costs only $O(1)$ additional time. Thus, the total time for insertion into an n-node order-statistic tree is $O(\lg n)$, which is asymptotically the same as for an ordinary red-black tree.

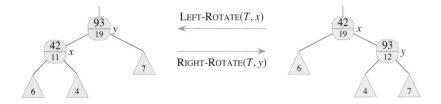

Figure 17.2 Updating subtree sizes during rotations. The updates are local, requiring only the *size* information stored in x, y, and the roots of the subtrees shown as triangles.

Deletion from a red-black tree also consists of two phases: the first operates on the underlying search tree, and the second causes at most three rotations and otherwise performs no structural changes. (See Section 13.4.) The first phase removes one node z from the tree and could move at most two other nodes within the tree (nodes y and x in Figure 12.4 on page 323). To update the subtree sizes, simply traverse a simple path from the lowest node that moves (starting from its original position within the tree) up to the root, decrementing the *size* attribute of each node on the path. Since this path has length $O(\lg n)$ in an n-node red-black tree, the additional time spent maintaining *size* attributes in the first phase is $O(\lg n)$. For the $O(1)$ rotations in the second phase of deletion, handle them in the same manner as for insertion. Thus, both insertion and deletion, including maintaining the *size* attributes, take $O(\lg n)$ time for an n-node order-statistic tree.

Exercises

17.1-1
Show how OS-SELECT$(T.root, 10)$ operates on the red-black tree T shown in Figure 17.1.

17.1-2
Show how OS-RANK(T, x) operates on the red-black tree T shown in Figure 17.1 and the node x with $x.key = 35$.

17.1-3
Write a nonrecursive version of OS-SELECT.

17.1-4
Write a procedure OS-KEY-RANK(T, k) that takes an order-statistic tree T and a key k and returns the rank of k in the dynamic set represented by T. Assume that the keys of T are distinct.

17.1-5

Given an element x in an n-node order-statistic tree and a natural number i, show how to determine the ith successor of x in the linear order of the tree in $O(\lg n)$ time.

17.1-6

The procedures OS-SELECT and OS-RANK use the *size* attribute of a node only to compute a rank. Suppose that you store in each node its rank in the subtree of which it is the root instead of the *size* attribute. Show how to maintain this information during insertion and deletion. (Remember that these two operations can cause rotations.)

17.1-7

Show how to use an order-statistic tree to count the number of inversions (see Problem 2-4 on page 47) in an array of n distinct elements in $O(n \lg n)$ time.

★ 17.1-8

Consider n chords on a circle, each defined by its endpoints. Describe an $O(n \lg n)$-time algorithm to determine the number of pairs of chords that intersect inside the circle. (For example, if the n chords are all diameters that meet at the center, then the answer is $\binom{n}{2}$.) Assume that no two chords share an endpoint.

17.2   How to augment a data structure

The process of augmenting a basic data structure to support additional functionality occurs quite frequently in algorithm design. We'll use it again in the next section to design a data structure that supports operations on intervals. This section examines the steps involved in such augmentation. It includes a useful theorem that allows you to augment red-black trees easily in many cases.

You can break the process of augmenting a data structure into four steps:

1. Choose an underlying data structure.

2. Determine additional information to maintain in the underlying data structure.

3. Verify that you can maintain the additional information for the basic modifying operations on the underlying data structure.

4. Develop new operations.

As with any prescriptive design method, you'll rarely be able to follow the steps precisely in the order given. Most design work contains an element of trial and error, and progress on all steps usually proceeds in parallel. There is no point, for example, in determining additional information and developing new operations (steps 2 and 4) if you cannot maintain the additional information efficiently. Nevertheless, this four-step method provides a good focus for your efforts in augmenting a data structure, and it is also a good framework for documenting an augmented data structure.

We followed these four steps in Section 17.1 to design order-statistic trees. For step 1, we chose red-black trees as the underlying data structure. Red-black trees seemed like a good starting point because they efficiently support other dynamic-set operations on a total order, such as MINIMUM, MAXIMUM, SUCCESSOR, and PREDECESSOR.

In Step 2, we added the *size* attribute, so that each node x stores the size of the subtree rooted at x. Generally, the additional information makes operations more efficient. For example, it is possible to implement OS-SELECT and OS-RANK using just the keys stored in the tree, but then they would not run in $O(\lg n)$ time. Sometimes, the additional information is pointer information rather than data, as in Exercise 17.2-1.

For step 3, we ensured that insertion and deletion can maintain the *size* attributes while still running in $O(\lg n)$ time. Ideally, you would like to update only a few elements of the data structure in order to maintain the additional information. For example, if each node simply stores its rank in the tree, the OS-SELECT and OS-RANK procedures run quickly, but inserting a new minimum element might cause a change to this information in every node of the tree. Because we chose to store subtree sizes instead, inserting a new element causes information to change in only $O(\lg n)$ nodes.

In Step 4, we developed the operations OS-SELECT and OS-RANK. After all, the need for new operations is why anyone bothers to augment a data structure in the first place. Occasionally, rather than developing new operations, you can use the additional information to expedite existing ones, as in Exercise 17.2-1.

Augmenting red-black trees

When red-black trees underlie an augmented data structure, we can prove that insertion and deletion can always efficiently maintain certain kinds of additional information, thereby simplifying step 3. The proof of the following theorem is similar to the argument from Section 17.1 that we can maintain the *size* attribute for order-statistic trees.

Theorem 17.1 (Augmenting a red-black tree)
Let f be an attribute that augments a red-black tree T of n nodes, and suppose that the value of f for each node x depends only the information in nodes $x, x.left$, and $x.right$ (possibly including $x.left.f$ and $x.right.f$), and that the value of $x.f$ can

be computed from this information in $O(1)$ time. Then, the insertion and deletion operations can maintain the values of f in all nodes of T without asymptotically affecting the $O(\lg n)$ running times of these operations.

Proof   The main idea of the proof is that a change to an f attribute in a node x propagates only to ancestors of x in the tree. That is, changing $x.f$ may require $x.p.f$ to be updated, but nothing else; updating $x.p.f$ may require $x.p.p.f$ to be updated, but nothing else; and so on up the tree. After updating $T.root.f$, no other node depends on the new value, and so the process terminates. Since the height of a red-black tree is $O(\lg n)$, changing an f attribute in a node costs $O(\lg n)$ time in updating all nodes that depend on the change.

As we saw in Section 13.3, insertion of a node x into red-black tree T consists of two phases. If the tree T is empty, then the first phase simply makes x be the root of T. If T is not empty, then the first phase inserts x as a child of an existing node. Because we assume that the value of $x.f$ depends only on information in the other attributes of x itself and the information in x's children, and because x's children are both the sentinel $T.nil$, it takes only $O(1)$ time to compute the value of $x.f$. Having computed $x.f$, the change propagates up the tree. Thus, the total time for the first phase of insertion is $O(\lg n)$. During the second phase, the only structural changes to the tree come from rotations. Since only two nodes change in a rotation, but a change to an attribute might need to propagate up to the root, the total time for updating the f attributes is $O(\lg n)$ per rotation. Since the number of rotations during insertion is at most two, the total time for insertion is $O(\lg n)$.

Like insertion, deletion has two phases, as Section 13.4 discusses. In the first phase, changes to the tree occur when a node is deleted, and at most two other nodes could move within the tree. Propagating the updates to f caused by these changes costs at most $O(\lg n)$, since the changes modify the tree locally along a simple path from the lowest changed node to the root. Fixing up the red-black tree during the second phase requires at most three rotations, and each rotation requires at most $O(\lg n)$ time to propagate the updates to f. Thus, like insertion, the total time for deletion is $O(\lg n)$.   ∎

In many cases, such as maintaining the *size* attributes in order-statistic trees, the cost of updating after a rotation is $O(1)$, rather than the $O(\lg n)$ derived in the proof of Theorem 17.1. Exercise 17.2-3 gives an example.

On the other hand, when an update after a rotation requires a traversal all the way up to the root, it is important that insertion into and deletion from a red-black tree require a constant number of rotations. The chapter notes for Chapter 13 list other schemes for balancing search trees that do not bound the number of rotations per insertion or deletion by a constant. If each operation might require $\Theta(\lg n)$ rotations and each rotation traverses a path up to the root, then a single operation could require $\Theta(\lg^2 n)$ time, rather than the $O(\lg n)$ time bound given by Theorem 17.1.

Exercises

17.2-1
Show, by adding pointers to the nodes, how to support each of the dynamic-set queries MINIMUM, MAXIMUM, SUCCESSOR, and PREDECESSOR in $O(1)$ worst-case time on an augmented order-statistic tree. The asymptotic performance of other operations on order-statistic trees should not be affected.

17.2-2
Can you maintain the black-heights of nodes in a red-black tree as attributes in the nodes of the tree without affecting the asymptotic performance of any of the red-black tree operations? Show how, or argue why not. How about maintaining the depths of nodes?

17.2-3
Let $\otimes$ be an associative binary operator, and let a be an attribute maintained in each node of a red-black tree. Suppose that you want to include in each node x an additional attribute f such that $x.f = x_1.a \otimes x_2.a \otimes \cdots \otimes x_m.a$, where $x_1, x_2, \ldots, x_m$ is the inorder listing of nodes in the subtree rooted at x. Show how to update the f attributes in $O(1)$ time after a rotation. Modify your argument slightly to apply it to the *size* attributes in order-statistic trees.

17.3   Interval trees

This section shows how to augment red-black trees to support operations on dynamic sets of intervals. In this section, we'll assume that intervals are closed. Extending the results to open and half-open intervals is conceptually straightforward. (See page 1157 for definitions of closed, open, and half-open intervals.)

Intervals are convenient for representing events that each occupy a continuous period of time. For example, you could query a database of time intervals to find out which events occurred during a given interval. The data structure in this section provides an efficient means for maintaining such an interval database.

A simple way to represent an interval $[t_1, t_2]$ is as an object i with attributes $i.low = t_1$ (the *low endpoint*) and $i.high = t_2$ (the *high endpoint*). We say that intervals i and i' *overlap* if $i \cap i' \neq \emptyset$, that is, if $i.low \leq i'.high$ and $i'.low \leq i.high$.

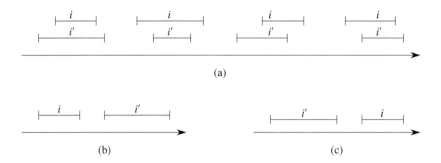

Figure 17.3 The interval trichotomy for two closed intervals i and i'. **(a)** If i and i' overlap, there are four situations, and in each, $i.low \leq i'.high$ and $i'.low \leq i.high$. **(b)** The intervals do not overlap, and $i.high < i'.low$. **(c)** The intervals do not overlap, and $i'.high < i.low$.

As Figure 17.3 shows, any two intervals i and i' satisfy the *interval trichotomy*, that is, exactly one of the following three properties holds:

a. i and i' overlap,

b. i is to the left of i' (i.e., $i.high < i'.low$),

c. i is to the right of i' (i.e., $i'.high < i.low$).

An *interval tree* is a red-black tree that maintains a dynamic set of elements, with each element x containing an interval $x.int$. Interval trees support the following operations:

INTERVAL-INSERT(T, x) adds the element x, whose *int* attribute is assumed to contain an interval, to the interval tree T.

INTERVAL-DELETE(T, x) removes the element x from the interval tree T.

INTERVAL-SEARCH(T, i) returns a pointer to an element x in the interval tree T such that $x.int$ overlaps interval i, or a pointer to the sentinel $T.nil$ if no such element belongs to the set.

Figure 17.4 shows how an interval tree represents a set of intervals. The four-step method from Section 17.2 will guide our design of an interval tree and the operations that run on it.

Step 1: Underlying data structure

A red-black tree serves as the underlying data structure. Each node x contains an interval $x.int$. The key of x is the low endpoint, $x.int.low$, of the interval. Thus, an inorder tree walk of the data structure lists the intervals in sorted order by low endpoint.

(a)

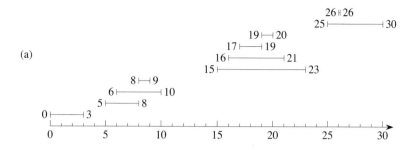

(b)

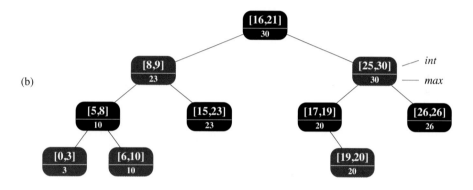

Figure 17.4   An interval tree. **(a)** A set of 10 intervals, shown sorted bottom to top by left endpoint. **(b)** The interval tree that represents them. Each node x contains an interval, shown above the dashed line, and the maximum value of any interval endpoint in the subtree rooted at x, shown below the dashed line. An inorder tree walk of the tree lists the nodes in sorted order by left endpoint.

Step 2: Additional information

In addition to the intervals themselves, each node x contains a value $x.max$, which is the maximum value of any interval endpoint stored in the subtree rooted at x.

Step 3: Maintaining the information

We must verify that insertion and deletion take $O(\lg n)$ time on an interval tree of n nodes. It is simple enough to determine $x.max$ in $O(1)$ time, given interval $x.int$ and the *max* values of node x's children:

$$x.max = \max \{x.int.high, x.left.max, x.right.max\} \ .$$

Thus, by Theorem 17.1, insertion and deletion run in $O(\lg n)$ time. In fact, you can use either Exercise 17.2-3 or 17.3-1 to show how to update all the *max* attributes that change after a rotation in just $O(1)$ time.

Step 4: Developing new operations

The only new operation is INTERVAL-SEARCH(T, i), which finds a node in tree T whose interval overlaps interval i. If there is no interval in the tree that overlaps i, the procedure returns a pointer to the sentinel $T.nil$.

INTERVAL-SEARCH(T, i)

```
1   x = T.root
2   while x ≠ T.nil and i does not overlap x.int
3       if x.left ≠ T.nil and x.left.max ≥ i.low
4           x = x.left   // overlap in left subtree or no overlap in right subtree
5       else x = x.right // no overlap in left subtree
6   return x
```

The search for an interval that overlaps i starts at the root of the tree and proceeds downward. It terminates when either it finds an overlapping interval or it reaches the sentinel $T.nil$. Since each iteration of the basic loop takes $O(1)$ time, and since the height of an n-node red-black tree is $O(\lg n)$, the INTERVAL-SEARCH procedure takes $O(\lg n)$ time.

Before we see why INTERVAL-SEARCH is correct, let's examine how it works on the interval tree in Figure 17.4. Let's look for an interval that overlaps the interval $i = [22, 25]$. Begin with x as the root, which contains $[16, 21]$ and does not overlap i. Since $x.left.max = 23$ is greater than $i.low = 22$, the loop continues with x as the left child of the root—the node containing $[8, 9]$, which also does not overlap i. This time, $x.left.max = 10$ is less than $i.low = 22$, and so the loop continues with the right child of x as the new x. Because the interval $[15, 23]$ stored in this node overlaps i, the procedure returns this node.

Now let's try an unsuccessful search, for an interval that overlaps $i = [11, 14]$ in the interval tree of Figure 17.4. Again, begin with x as the root. Since the root's interval $[16, 21]$ does not overlap i, and since $x.left.max = 23$ is greater than $i.low = 11$, go left to the node containing $[8, 9]$. Interval $[8, 9]$ does not overlap i, and $x.left.max = 10$ is less than $i.low = 11$, and so the search goes right. (No interval in the left subtree overlaps i.) Interval $[15, 23]$ does not overlap i, and its left child is $T.nil$, so again the search goes right, the loop terminates, and INTERVAL-SEARCH returns the sentinel $T.nil$.

To see why INTERVAL-SEARCH is correct, we must understand why it suffices to examine a single path from the root. The basic idea is that at any node x, if $x.int$ does not overlap i, the search always proceeds in a safe direction: the search will definitely find an overlapping interval if the tree contains one. The following theorem states this property more precisely.

Theorem 17.2
Any execution of INTERVAL-SEARCH(T, i) either returns a node whose interval overlaps i, or it returns $T.nil$ and the tree T contains no node whose interval overlaps i.

Proof The **while** loop of lines 2–5 terminates when either $x = T.nil$ or i overlaps $x.int$. In the latter case, it is certainly correct to return x. Therefore, we focus on the former case, in which the **while** loop terminates because $x = T.nil$, which is the node that INTERVAL-SEARCH returns.

We'll prove that if the procedure returns $T.nil$, then it did not miss any intervals in T that overlap i. The idea is to show that whether the search goes left in line 4 or right in line 5, it always heads toward a node containing an interval overlapping i, if any such interval exists. In particular, we'll prove that

1. If the search goes left in line 4, then the left subtree of node x contains an interval that overlaps i or the right subtree of x contains no interval that overlaps i. Therefore, even if x's left subtree contains no interval that overlaps i but the search goes left, it does not make a mistake, because x's right subtree does not contain an interval overlapping i, either.

2. If the search goes right in line 5, then the left subtree of x contains no interval that overlaps i. Thus, if the search goes right, it does not make a mistake.

For both cases, we rely on the interval trichotomy. Let's start with the case where the search goes right, whose proof is simpler. By the tests in line 3, we know that $x.left = T.nil$ or $x.left.max < i.low$. If $x.left = T.nil$, then x's left subtree contains no interval that overlaps i, since it contains no intervals at all. Now suppose that $x.left \neq T.nil$, so that we must have $x.left.max < i.low$. Consider any interval i' in x's left subtree. Because $x.left.max$ is the maximum endpoint in x's left subtree, we have $i'.high \leq x.left.max$. Thus, as Figure 17.5(a) shows,

$$i'.high \leq x.left.max$$
$$< i.low .$$

By the interval trichotomy, therefore, intervals i and i' do not overlap, and so x's left subtree contains no interval that overlaps i.

Now we examine the case in which the search goes left. If the left subtree of node x contains an interval that overlaps i, we're done, so let's assume that no node

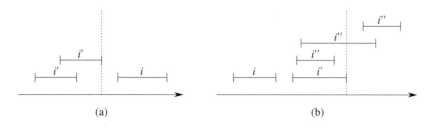

Figure 17.5 Intervals in the proof of Theorem 17.2. The value of $x.left.max$ is shown in each case as a dashed line. **(a)** The search goes right. No interval i' in x's left subtree can overlap i. **(b)** The search goes left. The left subtree of x contains an interval that overlaps i (situation not shown), or x's left subtree contains an interval i' such that $i'.high = x.left.max$. Since i does not overlap i', neither does it overlap any interval i'' in x's right subtree, since $i'.low \leq i''.low$.

in x's left subtree overlaps i. We need to show that in this case, no node in x's right subtree overlaps i, so that going left will not miss any overlaps in x's right subtree. By the tests in line 3, the left subtree of x is not empty and $x.left.max \geq i.low$. By the definition of the *max* attribute, x's left subtree contains some interval i' such that

$$
\begin{aligned}
i'.high \ &= \ x.left.max \\
&\geq \ i.low \, ,
\end{aligned}
$$

as illustrated in Figure 17.5(b). Since i' is in x's left subtree, it does not overlap i, and since $i'.high \geq i.low$, the interval trichotomy tells us that $i.high < i'.low$. Now we bring in the property that interval trees are keyed on the low endpoints of intervals. Because i' is in x's left subtree, we have $i'.low \leq x.int.low$. Now consider any interval i'' in x's right subtree, so that $x.int.low \leq i''.low$. Putting inequalities together, we get

$$
\begin{aligned}
i.high \ &< \ i'.low \\
&\leq \ x.int.low \\
&\leq \ i''.low \, .
\end{aligned}
$$

Because $i.high < i''.low$, the interval trichotomy tells us that i and i'' do not overlap. Since we chose i'' as any interval in x's right subtree, no node in x's right subtree overlaps i. ∎

Thus, the Interval-Search procedure works correctly.

Exercises

17.3-1
Write pseudocode for LEFT-ROTATE that operates on nodes in an interval tree and updates all the *max* attributes that change in $O(1)$ time.

17.3-2
Describe an efficient algorithm that, given an interval i, returns an interval overlapping i that has the minimum low endpoint, or $T.nil$ if no such interval exists.

17.3-3
Given an interval tree T and an interval i, describe how to list all intervals in T that overlap i in $O(\min\{n, k \lg n\})$ time, where k is the number of intervals in the output list. (*Hint:* One simple method makes several queries, modifying the tree between queries. A slightly more complicated method does not modify the tree.)

17.3-4
Suggest modifications to the interval-tree procedures to support the new operation INTERVAL-SEARCH-EXACTLY(T, i), where T is an interval tree and i is an interval. The operation should return a pointer to a node x in T such that $x.int.low = i.low$ and $x.int.high = i.high$, or $T.nil$ if T contains no such node. All operations, including INTERVAL-SEARCH-EXACTLY, should run in $O(\lg n)$ time on an n-node interval tree.

17.3-5
Show how to maintain a dynamic set Q of numbers that supports the operation MIN-GAP, which gives the absolute value of the difference of the two closest numbers in Q. For example, if we have $Q = \{1, 5, 9, 15, 18, 22\}$, then MIN-GAP$(Q)$ returns 3, since 15 and 18 are the two closest numbers in Q. Make the operations INSERT, DELETE, SEARCH, and MIN-GAP as efficient as possible, and analyze their running times.

★ ***17.3-6***
VLSI databases commonly represent an integrated circuit as a list of rectangles. Assume that each rectangle is rectilinearly oriented (sides parallel to the x- and y-axes), so that each rectangle is represented by four values: its minimum and maximum x- and y-coordinates. Give an $O(n \lg n)$-time algorithm to decide whether a set of n rectangles so represented contains two rectangles that overlap. Your algorithm need not report all intersecting pairs, but it must report that an overlap exists if one rectangle entirely covers another, even if the boundary lines do not intersect. (*Hint:* Move a "sweep" line across the set of rectangles.)

Problems

17-1   *Point of maximum overlap*

You wish to keep track of a *point of maximum overlap* in a set of intervals—a point with the largest number of intervals in the set that overlap it.

a. Show that there is always a point of maximum overlap that is an endpoint of one of the intervals.

b. Design a data structure that efficiently supports the operations INTERVAL-INSERT, INTERVAL-DELETE, and FIND-POM, which returns a point of maximum overlap. (*Hint:* Keep a red-black tree of all the endpoints. Associate a value of $+1$ with each left endpoint, and associate a value of -1 with each right endpoint. Augment each node of the tree with some extra information to maintain the point of maximum overlap.)

17-2   *Josephus permutation*

We define the *Josephus problem* as follows. A group of n people form a circle, and we are given a positive integer $m \leq n$. Beginning with a designated first person, proceed around the circle, removing every mth person. After each person is removed, counting continues around the circle that remains. This process continues until nobody remains in the circle. The order in which the people are removed from the circle defines the (n, m)-*Josephus permutation* of the integers $1, 2, \ldots, n$. For example, the $(7, 3)$-Josephus permutation is $\langle 3, 6, 2, 7, 5, 1, 4 \rangle$.

a. Suppose that m is a constant. Describe an $O(n)$-time algorithm that, given an integer n, outputs the (n, m)-Josephus permutation.

b. Suppose that m is not necessarily a constant. Describe an $O(n \lg n)$-time algorithm that, given integers n and m, outputs the (n, m)-Josephus permutation.

Chapter notes

In their book, Preparata and Shamos [364] describe several of the interval trees that appear in the literature, citing work by H. Edelsbrunner (1980) and E. M. McCreight (1981). The book details an interval tree that, given a static database of n intervals, allows us to enumerate all k intervals that overlap a given query interval in $O(k + \lg n)$ time.

18 B-Trees

B-trees are balanced search trees designed to work well on disk drives or other direct-access secondary storage devices. B-trees are similar to red-black trees (Chapter 13), but they are better at minimizing the number of operations that access disks. (We often say just "disk" instead of "disk drive.") Many database systems use B-trees, or variants of B-trees, to store information.

B-trees differ from red-black trees in that B-tree nodes may have many children, from a few to thousands. That is, the "branching factor" of a B-tree can be quite large, although it usually depends on characteristics of the disk drive used. B-trees are similar to red-black trees in that every n-node B-tree has height $O(\lg n)$, so that B-trees can implement many dynamic-set operations in $O(\lg n)$ time. But a B-tree has a larger branching factor than a red-black tree, so the base of the logarithm that expresses its height is larger, and hence its height can be considerably lower.

B-trees generalize binary search trees in a natural manner. Figure 18.1 shows a simple B-tree. If an internal B-tree node x contains $x.n$ keys, then x has $x.n + 1$ children. The keys in node x serve as dividing points separating the range of keys handled by x into $x.n + 1$ subranges, each handled by one child of x. A search for a key in a B-tree makes an $(x.n + 1)$-way decision based on comparisons with the $x.n$ keys stored at node x. An internal node contains pointers to its children, but a leaf node does not.

Section 18.1 gives a precise definition of B-trees and proves that the height of a B-tree grows only logarithmically with the number of nodes it contains. Section 18.2 describes how to search for a key and insert a key into a B-tree, and Section 18.3 discusses deletion. Before proceeding, however, we need to ask why we evaluate data structures designed to work on a disk drive differently from data structures designed to work in main random-access memory.

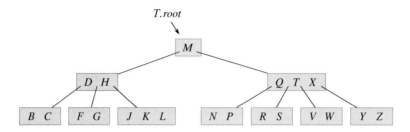

Figure 18.1   A B-tree whose keys are the consonants of English. An internal node x containing $x.n$ keys has $x.n + 1$ children. All leaves are at the same depth in the tree. The blue nodes are examined in a search for the letter R.

Data structures on secondary storage

Computer systems take advantage of various technologies that provide memory capacity. The *main memory* of a computer system normally consists of silicon memory chips. This technology is typically more than an order of magnitude more expensive per bit stored than magnetic storage technology, such as tapes or disk drives. Most computer systems also have *secondary storage* based on solid-state drives (SSDs) or magnetic disk drives. The amount of such secondary storage often exceeds the amount of primary memory by one to two orders of magnitude. SSDs have faster access times than magnetic disk drives, which are mechanical devices. In recent years, SSD capacities have increased while their prices have decreased. Magnetic disk drives typically have much higher capacities than SSDs, and they remain a more cost-effective means for storing massive amounts of information. Disk drives that store several terabytes[1] can be found for under $100.

Figure 18.2 shows a typical disk drive. The drive consists of one or more *platters*, which rotate at a constant speed around a common *spindle*. A magnetizable material covers the surface of each platter. The drive reads and writes each platter by a *head* at the end of an *arm*. The arms can move their heads toward or away from the spindle. The surface that passes underneath a given head when it is stationary is called a *track*.

Although disk drives are cheaper and have higher capacity than main memory, they are much, much slower because they have moving mechanical parts. The mechanical motion has two components: platter rotation and arm movement. As of this writing, commodity disk drives rotate at speeds of 5400–15,000 revolutions per minute (RPM). Typical speeds are 15,000 RPM in server-grade drives, 7200 RPM

---

[1] When specifying disk capacities, one terabyte is one trillion bytes, rather than 2^{40} bytes.

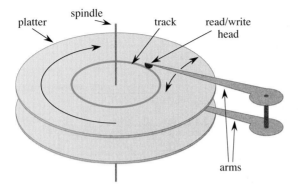

spindle

platter   track   read/write
                              head

arms

Figure 18.2   A typical magnetic disk drive. It consists of one or more platters covered with a magnetizable material (two platters are shown here) that rotate around a spindle. Each platter is read and written with a head, shown in red, at the end of an arm. Arms rotate around a common pivot axis. A track, drawn in blue, is the surface that passes beneath the read/write head when the head is stationary.

in drives for desktops, and 5400 RPM in drives for laptops. Although 7200 RPM may seem fast, one rotation takes 8.33 milliseconds, which is over 5 orders of magnitude longer than the 50 nanosecond access times (more or less) commonly found for main memory. In other words, if a computer waits a full rotation for a particular item to come under the read/write head, it could access main memory more than 100,000 times during that span. The average wait is only half a rotation, but still, the difference in access times for main memory compared with disk drives is enormous. Moving the arms also takes some time. As of this writing, average access times for commodity disk drives are around 4 milliseconds.

In order to amortize the time spent waiting for mechanical movements, also known as *latency*, disk drives access not just one item but several at a time. Information is divided into a number of equal-sized *blocks* of bits that appear consecutively within tracks, and each disk read or write is of one or more entire blocks.[2] Typical disk drives have block sizes running from 512 to 4096 bytes. Once the read/write head is positioned correctly and the platter has rotated to the beginning of the desired block, reading or writing a magnetic disk drive is entirely electronic (aside from the rotation of the platter), and the disk drive can quickly read or write large amounts of data.

---

[2] SSDs also exhibit greater latency than main memory and access data in blocks.

Often, accessing a block of information and reading it from a disk drive takes longer than processing all the information read. For this reason, in this chapter we'll look separately at the two principal components of the running time:

- the number of disk accesses, and
- the CPU (computing) time.

We measure the number of disk accesses in terms of the number of blocks of information that need to be read from or written to the disk drive. Although disk-access time is not constant—it depends on the distance between the current track and the desired track and also on the initial rotational position of the platters—the number of blocks read or written provides a good first-order approximation of the total time spent accessing the disk drive.

In a typical B-tree application, the amount of data handled is so large that all the data do not fit into main memory at once. The B-tree algorithms copy selected blocks from disk into main memory as needed and write back onto disk the blocks that have changed. B-tree algorithms keep only a constant number of blocks in main memory at any time, and thus the size of main memory does not limit the size of B-trees that can be handled.

B-tree procedures need to be able to read information from disk into main memory and write information from main memory to disk. Consider some object x. If x is currently in the computer's main memory, then the code can refer to the attributes of x as usual: $x.key$, for example. If x resides on disk, however, then the procedure must perform the operation DISK-READ(x) to read the block containing object x into main memory before it can refer to x's attributes. (Assume that if x is already in main memory, then DISK-READ(x) requires no disk accesses: it is a "no-op.") Similarly, procedures call DISK-WRITE(x) to save any changes that have been made to the attributes of object x by writing to disk the block containing x. Thus, the typical pattern for working with an object is as follows:

```
x = a pointer to some object
DISK-READ(x)
operations that access and/or modify the attributes of x
DISK-WRITE(x)          // omitted if no attributes of x were changed
other operations that access but do not modify attributes of x
```

The system can keep only a limited number of blocks in main memory at any one time. Our B-tree algorithms assume that the system automatically flushes from main memory blocks that are no longer in use.

Since in most systems the running time of a B-tree algorithm depends primarily on the number of DISK-READ and DISK-WRITE operations it performs, we

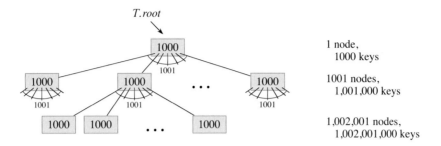

Figure 18.3 A B-tree of height 2 containing over one billion keys. Shown inside each node x is $x.n$, the number of keys in x. Each internal node and leaf contains 1000 keys. This B-tree has 1001 nodes at depth 1 and over one million leaves at depth 2.

typically want each of these operations to read or write as much information as possible. Thus, a B-tree node is usually as large as a whole disk block, and this size limits the number of children a B-tree node can have.

Large B-trees stored on disk drives often have branching factors between 50 and 2000, depending on the size of a key relative to the size of a block. A large branching factor dramatically reduces both the height of the tree and the number of disk accesses required to find any key. Figure 18.3 shows a B-tree with a branching factor of 1001 and height 2 that can store over one billion keys. Nevertheless, if the root node is kept permanently in main memory, at most two disk accesses suffice to find any key in this tree.

18.1   Definition of B-trees

To keep things simple, let's assume, as we have for binary search trees and red-black trees, that any satellite information associated with a key resides in the same node as the key. In practice, you might actually store with each key just a pointer to another disk block containing the satellite information for that key. The pseudocode in this chapter implicitly assumes that the satellite information associated with a key, or the pointer to such satellite information, travels with the key whenever the key is moved from node to node. A common variant on a B-tree, known as a ***B⁺-tree***, stores all the satellite information in the leaves and stores only keys and child pointers in the internal nodes, thus maximizing the branching factor of the internal nodes.

A ***B-tree*** T is a rooted tree with root $T.root$ having the following properties:

1. Every node x has the following attributes:

   a. $x.n$, the number of keys currently stored in node x,

   b. the $x.n$ keys themselves, $x.key_1, x.key_2, \ldots, x.key_{x.n}$, stored in monotonically increasing order, so that $x.key_1 \le x.key_2 \le \cdots \le x.key_{x.n}$,

   c. $x.leaf$, a boolean value that is TRUE if x is a leaf and FALSE if x is an internal node.

2. Each internal node x also contains $x.n + 1$ pointers $x.c_1, x.c_2, \ldots, x.c_{x.n+1}$ to its children. Leaf nodes have no children, and so their c_i attributes are undefined.

3. The keys $x.key_i$ separate the ranges of keys stored in each subtree: if k_i is any key stored in the subtree with root $x.c_i$, then

$$k_1 \le x.key_1 \le k_2 \le x.key_2 \le \cdots \le x.key_{x.n} \le k_{x.n+1} .$$

4. All leaves have the same depth, which is the tree's height h.

5. Nodes have lower and upper bounds on the number of keys they can contain, expressed in terms of a fixed integer $t \ge 2$ called the *minimum degree* of the B-tree:

   a. Every node other than the root must have at least $t - 1$ keys. Every internal node other than the root thus has at least t children. If the tree is nonempty, the root must have at least one key.

   b. Every node may contain at most $2t - 1$ keys. Therefore, an internal node may have at most $2t$ children. We say that a node is *full* if it contains exactly $2t - 1$ keys.[3]

The simplest B-tree occurs when $t = 2$. Every internal node then has either 2, 3, or 4 children, and it is a *2-3-4 tree*. In practice, however, much larger values of t yield B-trees with smaller height.

The height of a B-tree

The number of disk accesses required for most operations on a B-tree is proportional to the height of the B-tree. The following theorem bounds the worst-case height of a B-tree.

---

[3] Another common variant on a B-tree, known as a *B*-tree*, requires each internal node to be at least 2/3 full, rather than at least half full, as a B-tree requires.

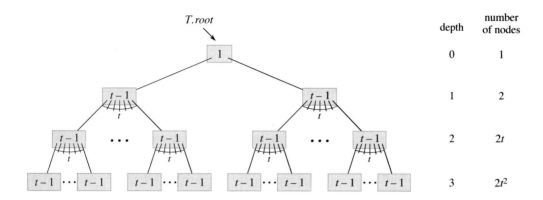

Figure 18.4 A B-tree of height 3 containing a minimum possible number of keys. Shown inside each node x is $x.n$.

Theorem 18.1

If $n \geq 1$, then for any n-key B-tree T of height h and minimum degree $t \geq 2$,

$$h \leq \log_t \frac{n+1}{2} .$$

Proof By definition, the root of a nonempty B-tree T contains at least one key, and all other nodes contain at least $t - 1$ keys. Let h be the height of T. Then T contains at least 2 nodes at depth 1, at least $2t$ nodes at depth 2, at least $2t^2$ nodes at depth 3, and so on, until at depth h, it has at least $2t^{h-1}$ nodes. Figure 18.4 illustrates such a tree for $h = 3$. The number n of keys therefore satisfies the inequality

$$
\begin{aligned}
n &\geq 1 + (t - 1) \sum_{i=1}^{h} 2t^{i-1} \\
&= 1 + 2(t - 1) \left(\frac{t^h - 1}{t - 1} \right) \quad \text{(by equation (A.6) on page 1142)} \\
&= 2t^h - 1 ,
\end{aligned}
$$

so that $t^h \leq (n + 1)/2$. Taking base-t logarithms of both sides proves the theorem. ∎

You can see the power of B-trees as compared with red-black trees. Although the height of the tree grows as $O(\log n)$ in both cases (recall that t is a constant), for B-trees the base of the logarithm can be many times larger. Thus, B-trees save a factor of about $\lg t$ over red-black trees in the number of nodes examined for most tree operations. Because examining an arbitrary node in a tree usually entails accessing the disk, B-trees avoid a substantial number of disk accesses.

Exercises

18.1-1
Why isn't a minimum degree of $t = 1$ allowed?

18.1-2
For what values of t is the tree of Figure 18.1 a legal B-tree?

18.1-3
Show all legal B-trees of minimum degree 2 that store the keys $1, 2, 3, 4, 5$.

18.1-4
As a function of the minimum degree t, what is the maximum number of keys that can be stored in a B-tree of height h?

18.1-5
Describe the data structure that results if each black node in a red-black tree absorbs its red children, incorporating their children with its own.

18.2   Basic operations on B-trees

This section presents the details of the operations B-TREE-SEARCH, B-TREE-CREATE, and B-TREE-INSERT. These procedures observe two conventions:

- The root of the B-tree is always in main memory, so that no procedure ever needs to perform a DISK-READ on the root. If any changes to the root node occur, however, then DISK-WRITE must be called on the root.

- Any nodes that are passed as parameters must already have had a DISK-READ operation performed on them.

The procedures are all "one-pass" algorithms that proceed downward from the root of the tree, without having to back up.

Searching a B-tree

Searching a B-tree is much like searching a binary search tree, except that instead of making a binary, or "two-way," branching decision at each node, the search makes a multiway branching decision according to the number of the node's children. More precisely, at each internal node x, the search makes an $(x.n + 1)$-way branching decision.

The procedure B-TREE-SEARCH generalizes the TREE-SEARCH procedure defined for binary search trees on page 316. It takes as input a pointer to the root node x of a subtree and a key k to be searched for in that subtree. The top-level call is thus of the form B-TREE-SEARCH($T.root, k$). If k is in the B-tree, then B-TREE-SEARCH returns the ordered pair (y, i) consisting of a node y and an index i such that $y.key_i = k$. Otherwise, the procedure returns NIL.

B-TREE-SEARCH(x, k)

```
1   i = 1
2   while i ≤ x.n and k > x.key_i
3       i = i + 1
4   if i ≤ x.n and k == x.key_i
5       return (x, i)
6   elseif x.leaf
7       return NIL
8   else DISK-READ(x.c_i)
9       return B-TREE-SEARCH(x.c_i, k)
```

Using a linear-search procedure, lines 1–3 of B-TREE-SEARCH find the smallest index i such that $k \leq x.key_i$, or else they set i to $x.n + 1$. Lines 4–5 check to see whether the search has discovered the key, returning if it has. Otherwise, if x is a leaf, then line 7 terminates the search unsuccessfully, and if x is an internal node, lines 8–9 recurse to search the appropriate subtree of x, after performing the necessary DISK-READ on that child. Figure 18.1 illustrates the operation of B-TREE-SEARCH. The blue nodes are those examined during a search for the key R.

As in the TREE-SEARCH procedure for binary search trees, the nodes encountered during the recursion form a simple path downward from the root of the tree. The B-TREE-SEARCH procedure therefore accesses $O(h) = O(\log_t n)$ disk blocks, where h is the height of the B-tree and n is the number of keys in the B-tree. Since $x.n < 2t$, the **while** loop of lines 2–3 takes $O(t)$ time within each node, and the total CPU time is $O(th) = O(t \log_t n)$.

Creating an empty B-tree

To build a B-tree T, first use the B-TREE-CREATE procedure on the next page to create an empty root node and then call the B-TREE-INSERT procedure on

page 508 to add new keys. Both of these procedures use an auxiliary procedure
ALLOCATE-NODE, whose pseudocode we omit and which allocates one disk block
to be used as a new node in $O(1)$ time. A node created by ALLOCATE-NODE
requires no DISK-READ, since there is as yet no useful information stored on the
disk for that node. B-TREE-CREATE requires $O(1)$ disk operations and $O(1)$ CPU
time.

B-TREE-CREATE(T)

```
1   x = ALLOCATE-NODE()
2   x.leaf = TRUE
3   x.n = 0
4   DISK-WRITE(x)
5   T.root = x
```

Inserting a key into a B-tree

Inserting a key into a B-tree is significantly more complicated than inserting a
key into a binary search tree. As with binary search trees, you search for the leaf
position at which to insert the new key. With a B-tree, however, you cannot simply
create a new leaf node and insert it, as the resulting tree would fail to be a valid
B-tree. Instead, you insert the new key into an existing leaf node. Since you cannot
insert a key into a leaf node that is full, you need an operation that *splits* a full
node y (having $2t - 1$ keys) around its *median key* $y.key_t$ into two nodes having
only $t - 1$ keys each. The median key moves up into y's parent to identify the
dividing point between the two new trees. But if y's parent is also full, you must
split it before you can insert the new key, and thus you could end up splitting full
nodes all the way up the tree.

To avoid having to go back up the tree, just split every full node you encounter
as you go down the tree. In this way, whenever you need to split a full node, you
are assured that its parent is not full. Inserting a key into a B-tree then requires
only a single pass down the tree from the root to a leaf.

Splitting a node in a B-tree

The procedure B-TREE-SPLIT-CHILD on the facing page takes as input a *nonfull*
internal node x (assumed to reside in main memory) and an index i such that $x.c_i$
(also assumed to reside in main memory) is a *full* child of x. The procedure splits
this child in two and adjusts x so that it has an additional child. To split a full root,
you first need to make the root a child of a new empty root node, so that you can

use B-TREE-SPLIT-CHILD. The tree thus grows in height by 1: splitting is the only means by which the tree grows taller.

B-TREE-SPLIT-CHILD(x, i)

```
 1   y = x.c_i                        // full node to split
 2   z = ALLOCATE-NODE()              // z will take half of y
 3   z.leaf = y.leaf
 4   z.n = t − 1
 5   for j = 1 to t − 1               // z gets y's greatest keys ...
 6       z.key_j = y.key_{j+t}
 7   if not y.leaf
 8       for j = 1 to t               // ... and its corresponding children
 9           z.c_j = y.c_{j+t}
10   y.n = t − 1                      // y keeps t − 1 keys
11   for j = x.n + 1 downto i + 1     // shift x's children to the right ...
12       x.c_{j+1} = x.c_j
13   x.c_{i+1} = z                    // ... to make room for z as a child
14   for j = x.n downto i            // shift the corresponding keys in x
15       x.key_{j+1} = x.key_j
16   x.key_i = y.key_t               // insert y's median key
17   x.n = x.n + 1                    // x has gained a child
18   DISK-WRITE(y)
19   DISK-WRITE(z)
20   DISK-WRITE(x)
```

Figure 18.5 illustrates how a node splits. B-TREE-SPLIT-CHILD splits the full node $y = x.c_i$ about its median key (S in the figure), which moves up into y's parent node x. Those keys in y that are greater than the median key move into a new node z, which becomes a new child of x.

B-TREE-SPLIT-CHILD works by straightforward cutting and pasting. Node x is the parent of the node y being split, which is x's ith child (set in line 1). Node y originally has $2t$ children and $2t − 1$ keys, but splitting reduces y to t children and $t − 1$ keys. The t largest children and $t − 1$ keys of node y move over to node z, which becomes a new child of x, positioned just after y in x's table of children. The median key of y moves up to become the key in node x that separates the pointers to nodes y and z.

Lines 2–9 create node z and give it the largest $t − 1$ keys and, if y and z are internal nodes, the corresponding t children of y. Line 10 adjusts the key count for y. Then, lines 11–17 shift keys and child pointers in x to the right in order to make room for x's new child, insert z as a new child of x, move the median key

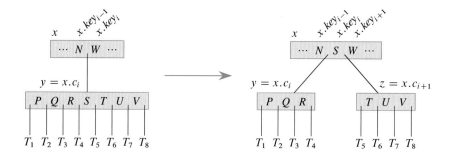

Figure 18.5 Splitting a node with $t = 4$. Node $y = x.c_i$ splits into two nodes, y and z, and the median key S of y moves up into y's parent.

from y up to x in order to separate y from z, and adjust x's key count. Lines 18–20 write out all modified disk blocks. The CPU time used by B-TREE-SPLIT-CHILD is $\Theta(t)$, due to the **for** loops in lines 5–6 and 8–9. (The **for** loops in lines 11–12 and 14–15 also run for $O(t)$ iterations.) The procedure performs $O(1)$ disk operations.

Inserting a key into a B-tree in a single pass down the tree

Inserting a key k into a B-tree T of height h requires just a single pass down the tree and $O(h)$ disk accesses. The CPU time required is $O(th) = O(t \log_t n)$. The B-TREE-INSERT procedure uses B-TREE-SPLIT-CHILD to guarantee that the recursion never descends to a full node. If the root is full, B-TREE-INSERT splits it by calling the procedure B-TREE-SPLIT-ROOT on the facing page.

B-TREE-INSERT(T, k)

1   $r = T.root$
2   **if** $r.n == 2t - 1$
3       $s =$ B-TREE-SPLIT-ROOT(T)
4   B-TREE-INSERT-NONFULL(s, k)
5   **else** B-TREE-INSERT-NONFULL(r, k)

B-TREE-INSERT works as follows. If the root is full, then line 3 calls B-TREE-SPLIT-ROOT in line 3 to split it. A new node s (with two children) becomes the root and is returned by B-TREE-SPLIT-ROOT. Splitting the root, illustrated in Figure 18.6, is the only way to increase the height of a B-tree. Unlike a binary search tree, a B-tree increases in height at the top instead of at the bottom. Regardless of whether the root split, B-TREE-INSERT finishes by calling B-TREE-INSERT-NONFULL to insert key k into the tree rooted at the nonfull root node,

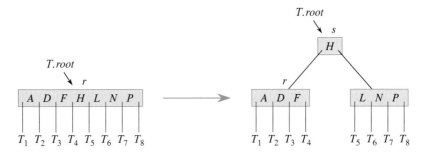

Figure 18.6   Splitting the root with $t = 4$. Root node r splits in two, and a new root node s is created. The new root contains the median key of r and has the two halves of r as children. The B-tree grows in height by one when the root is split. A B-tree's height increases only when the root splits.

which is either the new root (the call in line 4) or the original root (the call in line 5).

```
B-TREE-SPLIT-ROOT(T)
1   s = ALLOCATE-NODE()
2   s.leaf = FALSE
3   s.n = 0
4   s.c₁ = T.root
5   T.root = s
6   B-TREE-SPLIT-CHILD(s, 1)
7   return s
```

The auxiliary procedure B-TREE-INSERT-NONFULL on page 511 inserts key k into node x, which is assumed to be nonfull when the procedure is called. B-TREE-INSERT-NONFULL recurses as necessary down the tree, at all times guaranteeing that the node to which it recurses is not full by calling B-TREE-SPLIT-CHILD as necessary. The operation of B-TREE-INSERT and the recursive operation of B-TREE-INSERT-NONFULL guarantee that this assumption is true.

Figure 18.7 illustrates the various cases of how B-TREE-INSERT-NONFULL inserts a key into a B-tree. Lines 3–8 handle the case in which x is a leaf node by inserting key k into x, shifting to the right all keys in x that are greater than k. If x is not a leaf node, then k should go into the appropriate leaf node in the subtree rooted at internal node x. Lines 9–11 determine the child $x.c_i$ to which the recursion descends. Line 13 detects whether the recursion would descend to a full child, in which case line 14 calls B-TREE-SPLIT-CHILD to split that child into two non-

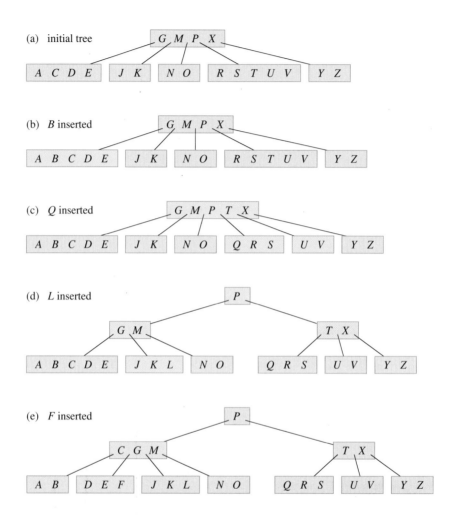

Figure 18.7   Inserting keys into a B-tree. The minimum degree t for this B-tree is 3, so that a node can hold at most 5 keys. Blue nodes are modified by the insertion process. **(a)** The initial tree for this example. **(b)** The result of inserting B into the initial tree. This case is a simple insertion into a leaf node. **(c)** The result of inserting Q into the previous tree. The node $RSTUV$ splits into two nodes containing RS and UV, the key T moves up to the root, and Q is inserted in the leftmost of the two halves (the RS node). **(d)** The result of inserting L into the previous tree. The root splits right away, since it is full, and the B-tree grows in height by one. Then L is inserted into the leaf containing JK. **(e)** The result of inserting F into the previous tree. The node $ABCDE$ splits before F is inserted into the rightmost of the two halves (the DE node).

B-TREE-INSERT-NONFULL(x, k)

```
1   i = x.n
2   if x.leaf                            // inserting into a leaf?
3       while i ≥ 1 and k < x.keyᵢ       // shift keys in x to make room for k
4           x.keyᵢ₊₁ = x.keyᵢ
5           i = i − 1
6       x.keyᵢ₊₁ = k                      // insert key k in x
7       x.n = x.n + 1                     // now x has 1 more key
8       DISK-WRITE(x)
9   else while i ≥ 1 and k < x.keyᵢ      // find the child where k belongs
10          i = i − 1
11      i = i + 1
12      DISK-READ(x.cᵢ)
13      if x.cᵢ.n == 2t − 1              // split the child if it's full
14          B-TREE-SPLIT-CHILD(x, i)
15          if k > x.keyᵢ                // does k go into x.cᵢ or x.cᵢ₊₁?
16              i = i + 1
17      B-TREE-INSERT-NONFULL(x.cᵢ, k)
```

full children, and lines 15–16 determine which of the two children is the correct one to descend to. (Note that DISK-READ$(x.c_i)$ is not needed after line 16 increments i, since the recursion descends in this case to a child that was just created by B-TREE-SPLIT-CHILD.) The net effect of lines 13–16 is thus to guarantee that the procedure never recurses to a full node. Line 17 then recurses to insert k into the appropriate subtree.

For a B-tree of height h, B-TREE-INSERT performs $O(h)$ disk accesses, since only $O(1)$ DISK-READ and DISK-WRITE operations occur at each level of the tree. The total CPU time used is $O(t)$ in each level of the tree, or $O(th) = O(t \log_t n)$ overall. Since B-TREE-INSERT-NONFULL is tail-recursive, you can instead implement it with a **while** loop, thereby demonstrating that the number of blocks that need to be in main memory at any time is $O(1)$.

Exercises

18.2-1
Show the results of inserting the keys

$$F, S, Q, K, C, L, H, T, V, W, M, R, N, P, A, B, X, Y, D, Z, E$$

in order into an empty B-tree with minimum degree 2. Draw only the configurations of the tree just before some node must split, and also draw the final configuration.

18.2-2

Explain under what circumstances, if any, redundant DISK-READ or DISK-WRITE operations occur during the course of executing a call to B-TREE-INSERT. (A redundant DISK-READ is a DISK-READ for a block that is already in memory. A redundant DISK-WRITE writes to disk a block of information that is identical to what is already stored there.)

18.2-3

Professor Bunyan asserts that the B-TREE-INSERT procedure always results in a B-tree with the minimum possible height. Show that the professor is mistaken by proving that with $t = 2$ and the set of keys $\{1, 2, \ldots, 15\}$, there is no insertion sequence that results in a B-tree with the minimum possible height.

★ 18.2-4

If you insert the keys $\{1, 2, \ldots, n\}$ into an empty B-tree with minimum degree 2, how many nodes does the final B-tree have?

18.2-5

Since leaf nodes require no pointers to children, they could conceivably use a different (larger) t value than internal nodes for the same disk block size. Show how to modify the procedures for creating and inserting into a B-tree to handle this variation.

18.2-6

Suppose that you implement B-TREE-SEARCH to use binary search rather than linear search within each node. Show that this change makes the required CPU time $O(\lg n)$, independent of how t might be chosen as a function of n.

18.2-7

Suppose that disk hardware allows you to choose the size of a disk block arbitrarily, but that the time it takes to read the disk block is $a + bt$, where a and b are specified constants and t is the minimum degree for a B-tree using blocks of the selected size. Describe how to choose t so as to minimize (approximately) the B-tree search time. Suggest an optimal value of t for the case in which $a = 5$ milliseconds and $b = 10$ microseconds.

18.3 Deleting a key from a B-tree

Deletion from a B-tree is analogous to insertion but a little more complicated, because you can delete a key from any node—not just a leaf—and when you delete a key from an internal node, you must rearrange the node's children. As in insertion, you must guard against deletion producing a tree whose structure violates the B-tree properties. Just as a node should not get too big due to insertion, a node must not get too small during deletion (except that the root is allowed to have fewer than the minimum number $t - 1$ of keys). And just as a simple insertion algorithm might have to back up if a node on the path to where the key is to be inserted is full, a simple approach to deletion might have to back up if a node (other than the root) along the path to where the key is to be deleted has the minimum number of keys.

The procedure B-TREE-DELETE deletes the key k from the subtree rooted at x. Unlike the procedures TREE-DELETE on page 325 and RB-DELETE on page 348, which are given the node to delete—presumably as the result of a prior search—B-TREE-DELETE combines the search for key k with the deletion process. Why do we combine search and deletion in B-TREE-DELETE? Just as B-TREE-INSERT prevents any node from becoming overfull (having more than $2t - 1$ keys) while making a single pass down the tree, B-TREE-DELETE prevents any node from becoming underfull (having fewer than $t - 1$ keys) while also making a single pass down the tree, searching for and ultimately deleting the key.

To prevent any node from becoming underfull, the design of B-TREE-DELETE guarantees that whenever it calls itself recursively on a node x, the number of keys in x is at least the minimum degree t at the time of the call. (Although the root may have fewer than t keys and a recursive call may be made *from* the root, no recursive call is made *on* the root.) This condition requires one more key than the minimum required by the usual B-tree conditions, and so a key might have to be moved from x into one of its child nodes (still leaving x with at least the minimum $t - 1$ keys) before a recursive call is made on that child, thus allowing deletion to occur in one downward pass without having to traverse back up the tree.

We describe how the procedure B-TREE-DELETE(T, k) deletes a key k from a B-tree T instead of presenting detailed pseudocode. We examine three cases, illustrated in Figure 18.8. The cases are for when the search arrives at a leaf, at an internal node containing key k, and at an internal node not containing key k. As mentioned above, in all three cases node x has at least t keys (with the possible exception of when x is the root). Cases 2 and 3—when x is an internal node—guarantee this property as the recursion descends through the B-tree.

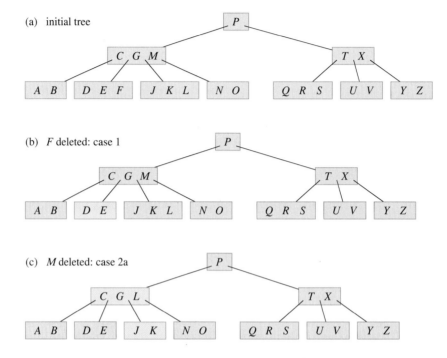

Figure 18.8 Deleting keys from a B-tree. The minimum degree for this B-tree is $t = 3$, so that, other than the root, every node must have at least 2 keys. Blue nodes are those that are modified by the deletion process. **(a)** The B-tree of Figure 18.7(e). **(b)** Deletion of F, which is case 1: simple deletion from a leaf when all nodes visited during the search (other than the root) have at least $t = 3$ keys. **(c)** Deletion of M, which is case 2a: the predecessor L of M moves up to take M's position.

Case 1: *The search arrives at a leaf node* x. If x contains key k, then delete k from x. If x does not contain key k, then k was not in the B-tree and nothing else needs to be done.

Case 2: *The search arrives at an internal node* x *that contains key* k. Let $k = x.key_i$. One of the following three cases applies, depending on the number of keys in $x.c_i$ (the child of x that precedes k) and $x.c_{i+1}$ (the child of x that follows k).

Case 2a: $x.c_i$ *has at least* t *keys.* Find the predecessor k' of k in the subtree rooted at $x.c_i$. Recursively delete k' from $x.c_i$, and replace k by k' in x. (Key k' can be found and deleted in a single downward pass.)

Case 2b: $x.c_i$ *has* $t - 1$ *keys and* $x.c_{i+1}$ *has at least* t *keys.* This case is symmetric to case 2a. Find the successor k' of k in the subtree rooted at $x.c_{i+1}$.

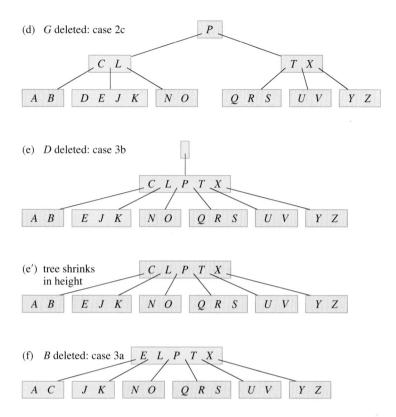

(d)   *G* deleted: case 2c

(e)   *D* deleted: case 3b

(e′)   tree shrinks
       in height

(f)   *B* deleted: case 3a

Figure 18.8, continued   **(d)** Deletion of G, which is case 2c: push G down to make node $DEGJK$ and then delete G from this leaf (case 1). **(e)** Deletion of D, which is case 3b: since the recursion cannot descend to node CL because it has only 2 keys, push P down and merge it with CL and TX to form $CLPTX$. Then delete D from a leaf (case 1). **(e′)** After (e), delete the empty root. The tree shrinks in height by 1. **(f)** Deletion of B, which is case 3a: C moves to fill B's position and E moves to fill C's position.

Recursively delete k' from $x.c_{i+1}$, and replace k by k' in x. (Again, finding and deleting k' can be done in a single downward pass.)

Case 2c: *Both $x.c_i$ and $x.c_{i+1}$ have $t-1$ keys.* Merge k and all of $x.c_{i+1}$ into $x.c_i$, so that x loses both k and the pointer to $x.c_{i+1}$, and $x.c_i$ now contains $2t-1$ keys. Then free $x.c_{i+1}$ and recursively delete k from $x.c_i$.

Case 3: *The search arrives at an internal node x that does not contain key k.* Continue searching down the tree while ensuring that each node visited has at least t keys. To do so, determine the root $x.c_i$ of the appropriate subtree that must contain k, if k is in the tree at all. If $x.c_i$ has only $t-1$ keys, execute case 3a or 3b as necessary to guarantee descending to a node containing at least t keys. Then finish by recursing on the appropriate child of x.

Case 3a: *$x.c_i$ has only $t - 1$ keys but has an immediate sibling with at least t keys.* Give $x.c_i$ an extra key by moving a key from x down into $x.c_i$, moving a key from $x.c_i$'s immediate left or right sibling up into x, and moving the appropriate child pointer from the sibling into $x.c_i$.

Case 3b: *$x.c_i$ and each of $x.c_i$'s immediate siblings have $t - 1$ keys.* (It is possible for $x.c_i$ to have either one or two siblings.) Merge $x.c_i$ with one sibling, which involves moving a key from x down into the new merged node to become the median key for that node.

In cases 2c and 3b, if node x is the root, it could end up having no keys. When this situation occurs, then x is deleted, and x's only child $x.c_1$ becomes the new root of the tree. This action decreases the height of the tree by one and preserves the property that the root of the tree contains at least one key (unless the tree is empty).

Since most of the keys in a B-tree are in the leaves, deletion operations often end up deleting keys from leaves. The B-TREE-DELETE procedure then acts in one downward pass through the tree, without having to back up. When deleting a key in an internal node x, however, the procedure might make a downward pass through the tree to find the key's predecessor or successor and then return to node x to replace the key with its predecessor or successor (cases 2a and 2b). Returning to node x does not require a traversal through all the levels between x and the node containing the predecessor or successor, however, since the procedure can just keep a pointer to x and the key position within x and put the predecessor or successor key directly there.

Although this procedure seems complicated, it involves only $O(h)$ disk operations for a B-tree of height h, since only $O(1)$ calls to DISK-READ and DISK-WRITE are made between recursive invocations of the procedure. The CPU time required is $O(th) = O(t \log_t n)$.

Exercises

18.3-1
Show the results of deleting C, P, and V, in order, from the tree of Figure 18.8(f).

18.3-2
Write pseudocode for B-TREE-DELETE.

Problems

18-1   *Stacks on secondary storage*

Consider implementing a stack in a computer that has a relatively small amount of fast primary memory and a relatively large amount of slower disk storage. The operations PUSH and POP work on single-word values. The stack can grow to be much larger than can fit in memory, and thus most of it must be stored on disk.

A simple, but inefficient, stack implementation keeps the entire stack on disk. Maintain in memory a stack pointer, which is the disk address of the top element on the stack. Indexing block numbers and word offsets within blocks from 0, if the pointer has value p, the top element is the $(p \bmod m)$th word on block $\lfloor p/m \rfloor$ of the disk, where m is the number of words per block.

To implement the PUSH operation, increment the stack pointer, read the appropriate block into memory from disk, copy the element to be pushed to the appropriate word on the block, and write the block back to disk. A POP operation is similar. Read in the appropriate block from disk, save the top of the stack, decrement the stack pointer, and return the saved value. You need not write back the block, since it was not modified, and the word in the block that contained the popped value is ignored.

As in the analyses of B-tree operations, two costs matter: the total number of disk accesses and the total CPU time. A disk access also incurs a cost in CPU time. In particular, any disk access to a block of m words incurs charges of one disk access and $\Theta(m)$ CPU time.

a. Asymptotically, what is the worst-case number of disk accesses for n stack operations using this simple implementation? What is the CPU time for n stack operations? Express your answer in terms of m and n for this and subsequent parts.

Now consider a stack implementation in which you keep one block of the stack in memory. (You also maintain a small amount of memory to record which block is currently in memory.) You can perform a stack operation only if the relevant disk block resides in memory. If necessary, you can write the block currently in memory to the disk and read the new block from the disk into memory. If the relevant disk block is already in memory, then no disk accesses are required.

b. What is the worst-case number of disk accesses required for n PUSH operations? What is the CPU time?

c. What is the worst-case number of disk accesses required for n stack operations? What is the CPU time?

Suppose that you now implement the stack by keeping two blocks in memory (in addition to a small number of words for bookkeeping).

d. Describe how to manage the stack blocks so that the amortized number of disk accesses for any stack operation is $O(1/m)$ and the amortized CPU time for any stack operation is $O(1)$.

18-2   *Joining and splitting 2-3-4 trees*

The *join* operation takes two dynamic sets S' and S'' and an element x such that $x'.key < x.key < x''.key$ for any $x' \in S'$ and $x'' \in S''$. It returns a set $S = S' \cup \{x\} \cup S''$. The *split* operation is like an "inverse" join: given a dynamic set S and an element $x \in S$, it creates a set S' that consists of all elements in $S - \{x\}$ whose keys are less than $x.key$ and another set S'' that consists of all elements in $S - \{x\}$ whose keys are greater than $x.key$. This problem investigates how to implement these operations on 2-3-4 trees (B-trees with $t = 2$). Assume for convenience that elements consist only of keys and that all key values are distinct.

a. Show how to maintain, for every node x of a 2-3-4 tree, the height of the subtree rooted at x as an attribute $x.height$. Make sure that your implementation does not affect the asymptotic running times of searching, insertion, and deletion.

b. Show how to implement the join operation. Given two 2-3-4 trees T' and T'' and a key k, the join operation should run in $O(1 + |h' - h''|)$ time, where h' and h'' are the heights of T' and T'', respectively.

c. Consider the simple path p from the root of a 2-3-4 tree T to a given key k, the set S' of keys in T that are less than k, and the set S'' of keys in T that are greater than k. Show that p breaks S' into a set of trees $\{T'_0, T'_1, \ldots, T'_m\}$ and a set of keys $\{k'_1, k'_2, \ldots, k'_m\}$ such that $y < k'_i < z$ for $i = 1, 2, \ldots, m$ and any keys $y \in T'_{i-1}$ and $z \in T'_i$. What is the relationship between the heights of T'_{i-1} and T'_i? Describe how p breaks S'' into sets of trees and keys.

d. Show how to implement the split operation on T. Use the join operation to assemble the keys in S' into a single 2-3-4 tree T' and the keys in S'' into a single 2-3-4 tree T''. The running time of the split operation should be $O(\lg n)$, where n is the number of keys in T. (*Hint:* The costs for joining should telescope.)

Chapter notes

Knuth [261], Aho, Hopcroft, and Ullman [5], and Sedgewick and Wayne [402] give further discussions of balanced-tree schemes and B-trees. Comer [99] provides a comprehensive survey of B-trees. Guibas and Sedgewick [202] discuss the relationships among various kinds of balanced-tree schemes, including red-black trees and 2-3-4 trees.

In 1970, J. E. Hopcroft invented 2-3 trees, a precursor to B-trees and 2-3-4 trees, in which every internal node has either two or three children. Bayer and McCreight [39] introduced B-trees in 1972 with no explanation of their choice of name.

Bender, Demaine, and Farach-Colton [47] studied how to make B-trees perform well in the presence of memory-hierarchy effects. Their *cache-oblivious* algorithms work efficiently without explicitly knowing the data transfer sizes within the memory hierarchy.

19　Data Structures for Disjoint Sets

Some applications involve grouping n distinct elements into a collection of disjoint sets—sets with no elements in common. These applications often need to perform two operations in particular: finding the unique set that contains a given element and uniting two sets. This chapter explores methods for maintaining a data structure that supports these operations.

Section 19.1 describes the operations supported by a disjoint-set data structure and presents a simple application. Section 19.2 looks at a simple linked-list implementation for disjoint sets. Section 19.3 presents a more efficient representation using rooted trees. The running time using the tree representation is theoretically superlinear, but for all practical purposes it is linear. Section 19.4 defines and discusses a very quickly growing function and its very slowly growing inverse, which appears in the running time of operations on the tree-based implementation, and then, by a complex amortized analysis, proves an upper bound on the running time that is just barely superlinear.

19.1　Disjoint-set operations

A *disjoint-set data structure* maintains a collection $\mathcal{S} = \{S_1, S_2, \ldots, S_k\}$ of disjoint dynamic sets. To identify each set, choose a *representative*, which is some member of the set. In some applications, it doesn't matter which member is used as the representative; it matters only that if you ask for the representative of a dynamic set twice without modifying the set between the requests, you get the same answer both times. Other applications may require a prespecified rule for choosing the representative, such as choosing the smallest member in the set (for a set whose elements can be ordered).

As in the other dynamic-set implementations we have studied, each element of a set is represented by an object. Letting x denote an object, we'll see how to support the following operations:

MAKE-SET(x), where x does not already belong to some other set, creates a new set whose only member (and thus representative) is x.

UNION(x, y) unites two disjoint, dynamic sets that contain x and y, say S_x and S_y, into a new set that is the union of these two sets. The representative of the resulting set is any member of $S_x \cup S_y$, although many implementations of UNION specifically choose the representative of either S_x or S_y as the new representative. Since the sets in the collection must at all times be disjoint, the UNION operation destroys sets S_x and S_y, removing them from the collection $\mathcal{S}$. In practice, implementations often absorb the elements of one of the sets into the other set.

FIND-SET(x) returns a pointer to the representative of the unique set containing x.

Throughout this chapter, we'll analyze the running times of disjoint-set data structures in terms of two parameters: n, the number of MAKE-SET operations, and m, the total number of MAKE-SET, UNION, and FIND-SET operations. Because the total number of operations m includes the n MAKE-SET operations, $m \geq n$. The first n operations are always MAKE-SET operations, so that after the first n operations, the collection consists of n singleton sets. Since the sets are disjoint at all times, each UNION operation reduces the number of sets by 1. After $n - 1$ UNION operations, therefore, only one set remains, and so at most $n - 1$ UNION operations can occur.

An application of disjoint-set data structures

One of the many applications of disjoint-set data structures arises in determining the connected components of an undirected graph (see Section B.4). Figure 19.1(a), for example, shows a graph with four connected components.

The procedure CONNECTED-COMPONENTS on the following page uses the disjoint-set operations to compute the connected components of a graph. Once the CONNECTED-COMPONENTS procedure has preprocessed the graph, the procedure SAME-COMPONENT answers queries about whether two vertices belong to the same connected component. In pseudocode, we denote the set of vertices of a graph G by $G.V$ and the set of edges by $G.E$.

The procedure CONNECTED-COMPONENTS initially places each vertex v in its own set. Then, for each edge (u, v), it unites the sets containing u and v. By Exercise 19.1-2, after all the edges are processed, two vertices belong to the same connected component if and only if the objects corresponding to the vertices belong

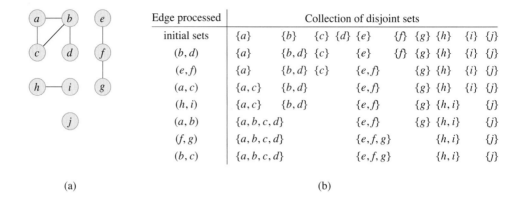

<table>
<tr><td colspan="2">Edge processed</td><td colspan="10">Collection of disjoint sets</td></tr>
</table>

Edge processed	Collection of disjoint sets									
initial sets	$\{a\}$	$\{b\}$	$\{c\}$	$\{d\}$	$\{e\}$		$\{f\}$	$\{g\}$ $\{h\}$	$\{i\}$	$\{j\}$
(b, d)	$\{a\}$	$\{b, d\}$	$\{c\}$		$\{e\}$		$\{f\}$	$\{g\}$ $\{h\}$	$\{i\}$	$\{j\}$
(e, f)	$\{a\}$	$\{b, d\}$	$\{c\}$		$\{e, f\}$			$\{g\}$ $\{h\}$	$\{i\}$	$\{j\}$
(a, c)	$\{a, c\}$	$\{b, d\}$			$\{e, f\}$			$\{g\}$ $\{h\}$	$\{i\}$	$\{j\}$
(h, i)	$\{a, c\}$	$\{b, d\}$			$\{e, f\}$			$\{g\}$ $\{h, i\}$		$\{j\}$
(a, b)	$\{a, b, c, d\}$				$\{e, f\}$			$\{g\}$ $\{h, i\}$		$\{j\}$
(f, g)	$\{a, b, c, d\}$				$\{e, f, g\}$			$\{h, i\}$		$\{j\}$
(b, c)	$\{a, b, c, d\}$				$\{e, f, g\}$			$\{h, i\}$		$\{j\}$

(a)   (b)

Figure 19.1 **(a)** A graph with four connected components: $\{a, b, c, d\}$, $\{e, f, g\}$, $\{h, i\}$, and $\{j\}$. **(b)** The collection of disjoint sets after processing each edge.

CONNECTED-COMPONENTS(G)

```
1   for each vertex v ∈ G.V
2       MAKE-SET(v)
3   for each edge (u, v) ∈ G.E
4       if FIND-SET(u) ≠ FIND-SET(v)
5           UNION(u, v)
```

SAME-COMPONENT(u, v)

```
1   if FIND-SET(u) == FIND-SET(v)
2       return TRUE
3   else return FALSE
```

to the same set. Thus CONNECTED-COMPONENTS computes sets in such a way that the procedure SAME-COMPONENT can determine whether two vertices are in the same connected component. Figure 19.1(b) illustrates how CONNECTED-COMPONENTS computes the disjoint sets.

In an actual implementation of this connected-components algorithm, the representations of the graph and the disjoint-set data structure would need to reference each other. That is, an object representing a vertex would contain a pointer to the corresponding disjoint-set object, and vice versa. Since these programming details depend on the implementation language, we do not address them further here.

When the edges of the graph are static—not changing over time—depth-first search can compute the connected components faster (see Exercise 20.3-12 on page 572). Sometimes, however, the edges are added dynamically, with the connected components updated as each edge is added. In this case, the implementation given here can be more efficient than running a new depth-first search for each new edge.

Exercises

19.1-1

The CONNECTED-COMPONENTS procedure is run on the undirected graph $G = (V, E)$, where $V = \{a, b, c, d, e, f, g, h, i, j, k\}$, and the edges of E are processed in the order $(d, i), (f, k), (g, i), (b, g), (a, h), (i, j), (d, k), (b, j), (d, f), (g, j), (a, e)$. List the vertices in each connected component after each iteration of lines 3–5.

19.1-2

Show that after all edges are processed by CONNECTED-COMPONENTS, two vertices belong to the same connected component if and only if they belong to the same set.

19.1-3

During the execution of CONNECTED-COMPONENTS on an undirected graph $G = (V, E)$ with k connected components, how many times is FIND-SET called? How many times is UNION called? Express your answers in terms of $|V|$, $|E|$, and k.

19.2   Linked-list representation of disjoint sets

Figure 19.2(a) shows a simple way to implement a disjoint-set data structure: each set is represented by its own linked list. The object for each set has attributes *head*, pointing to the first object in the list, and *tail*, pointing to the last object. Each object in the list contains a set member, a pointer to the next object in the list, and a pointer back to the set object. Within each linked list, the objects may appear in any order. The representative is the set member in the first object in the list.

With this linked-list representation, both MAKE-SET and FIND-SET require only $O(1)$ time. To carry out MAKE-SET(x), create a new linked list whose only object is x. For FIND-SET(x), just follow the pointer from x back to its set object and then return the member in the object that *head* points to. For example, in Figure 19.2(a), the call FIND-SET(g) returns f.

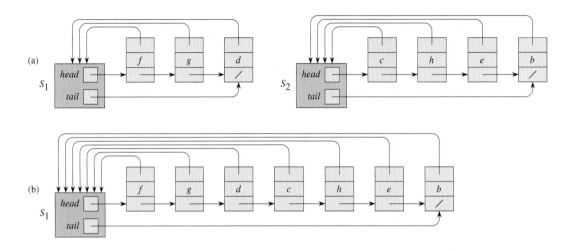

Figure 19.2 **(a)** Linked-list representations of two sets. Set S_1 contains members d, f, and g, with representative f, and set S_2 contains members b, c, e, and h, with representative c. Each object in the list contains a set member, a pointer to the next object in the list, and a pointer back to the set object. Each set object has pointers *head* and *tail* to the first and last objects, respectively. **(b)** The result of UNION(g, e), which appends the linked list containing e to the linked list containing g. The representative of the resulting set is f. The set object for e's list, S_2, is destroyed.

A simple implementation of union

The simplest implementation of the UNION operation using the linked-list set representation takes significantly more time than MAKE-SET or FIND-SET. As Figure 19.2(b) shows, the operation UNION(x, y) appends y's list onto the end of x's list. The representative of x's list becomes the representative of the resulting set. To quickly find where to append y's list, use the *tail* pointer for x's list. Because all members of y's list join x's list, the UNION operation destroys the set object for y's list. The UNION operation is where this implementation pays the price for FIND-SET taking constant time: UNION must also update the pointer to the set object for each object originally on y's list, which takes time linear in the length of y's list. In Figure 19.2, for example, the operation UNION(g, e) causes pointers to be updated in the objects for b, c, e, and h.

In fact, we can construct a sequence of m operations on n objects that requires $\Theta(n^2)$ time. Starting with objects $x_1, x_2, \ldots, x_n$, execute the sequence of n MAKE-SET operations followed by $n - 1$ UNION operations shown in Figure 19.3, so that $m = 2n - 1$. The n MAKE-SET operations take $\Theta(n)$ time. Because the ith UNION operation updates i objects, the total number of objects updated by all $n - 1$ UNION operations forms an arithmetic series:

Operation	Number of objects updated
MAKE-SET(x_1)	1
MAKE-SET(x_2)	1
$\vdots$	$\vdots$
MAKE-SET(x_n)	1
UNION(x_2, x_1)	1
UNION(x_3, x_2)	2
UNION(x_4, x_3)	3
$\vdots$	$\vdots$
UNION(x_n, x_{n-1})	$n-1$

Figure 19.3 A sequence of $2n - 1$ operations on n objects that takes $\Theta(n^2)$ time, or $\Theta(n)$ time per operation on average, using the linked-list set representation and the simple implementation of UNION.

$$\sum_{i=1}^{n-1} i = \Theta(n^2) \ .$$

The total number of operations is $2n - 1$, and so each operation on average requires $\Theta(n)$ time. That is, the amortized time of an operation is $\Theta(n)$.

A weighted-union heuristic

In the worst case, the above implementation of UNION requires an average of $\Theta(n)$ time per call, because it might be appending a longer list onto a shorter list, and the procedure must update the pointer to the set object for each member of the longer list. Suppose instead that each list also includes the length of the list (which can be maintained straightforwardly with constant overhead) and that the UNION procedure always appends the shorter list onto the longer, breaking ties arbitrarily. With this simple *weighted-union heuristic*, a single UNION operation can still take $\Omega(n)$ time if both sets have $\Omega(n)$ members. As the following theorem shows, however, a sequence of m MAKE-SET, UNION, and FIND-SET operations, n of which are MAKE-SET operations, takes $O(m + n \lg n)$ time.

Theorem 19.1
Using the linked-list representation of disjoint sets and the weighted-union heuristic, a sequence of m MAKE-SET, UNION, and FIND-SET operations, n of which are MAKE-SET operations, takes $O(m + n \lg n)$ time.

Proof Because each UNION operation unites two disjoint sets, at most $n - 1$ UNION operations occur over all. We now bound the total time taken by these

UNION operations. We start by determining, for each object, an upper bound on the number of times the object's pointer back to its set object is updated. Consider a particular object x. Each time x's pointer is updated, x must have started in the smaller set. The first time x's pointer is updated, therefore, the resulting set must have at least 2 members. Similarly, the next time x's pointer is updated, the resulting set must have had at least 4 members. Continuing on, for any $k \le n$, after x's pointer has been updated $\lceil \lg k \rceil$ times, the resulting set must have at least k members. Since the largest set has at most n members, each object's pointer is updated at most $\lceil \lg n \rceil$ times over all the UNION operations. Thus the total time spent updating object pointers over all UNION operations is $O(n \lg n)$. We must also account for updating the *tail* pointers and the list lengths, which take only $\Theta(1)$ time per UNION operation. The total time spent in all UNION operations is thus $O(n \lg n)$.

The time for the entire sequence of m operations follows. Each MAKE-SET and FIND-SET operation takes $O(1)$ time, and there are $O(m)$ of them. The total time for the entire sequence is thus $O(m + n \lg n)$. ∎

Exercises

19.2-1
Write pseudocode for MAKE-SET, FIND-SET, and UNION using the linked-list representation and the weighted-union heuristic. Make sure to specify the attributes that you assume for set objects and list objects.

19.2-2
Show the data structure that results and the answers returned by the FIND-SET operations in the following program. Use the linked-list representation with the weighted-union heuristic. Assume that if the sets containing x_i and x_j have the same size, then the operation UNION(x_i, x_j) appends x_j's list onto x_i's list.

```
 1  for i = 1 to 16
 2      MAKE-SET(x_i)
 3  for i = 1 to 15 by 2
 4      UNION(x_i, x_{i+1})
 5  for i = 1 to 13 by 4
 6      UNION(x_i, x_{i+2})
 7  UNION(x_1, x_5)
 8  UNION(x_11, x_13)
 9  UNION(x_1, x_10)
10  FIND-SET(x_2)
11  FIND-SET(x_9)
```

19.2-3

Adapt the aggregate proof of Theorem 19.1 to obtain amortized time bounds of $O(1)$ for MAKE-SET and FIND-SET and $O(\lg n)$ for UNION using the linked-list representation and the weighted-union heuristic.

19.2-4

Give a tight asymptotic bound on the running time of the sequence of operations in Figure 19.3 assuming the linked-list representation and the weighted-union heuristic.

19.2-5

Professor Gompers suspects that it might be possible to keep just one pointer in each set object, rather than two (*head* and *tail*), while keeping the number of pointers in each list element at two. Show that the professor's suspicion is well founded by describing how to represent each set by a linked list such that each operation has the same running time as the operations described in this section. Describe also how the operations work. Your scheme should allow for the weighted-union heuristic, with the same effect as described in this section. (*Hint:* Use the tail of a linked list as its set's representative.)

19.2-6

Suggest a simple change to the UNION procedure for the linked-list representation that removes the need to keep the *tail* pointer to the last object in each list. Regardless of whether the weighted-union heuristic is used, your change should not change the asymptotic running time of the UNION procedure. (*Hint:* Rather than appending one list to another, splice them together.)

19.3 Disjoint-set forests

A faster implementation of disjoint sets represents sets by rooted trees, with each node containing one member and each tree representing one set. In a *disjoint-set forest*, illustrated in Figure 19.4(a), each member points only to its parent. The root of each tree contains the representative and is its own parent. As we'll see, although the straightforward algorithms that use this representation are no faster than ones that use the linked-list representation, two heuristics—"union by rank" and "path compression"—yield an asymptotically optimal disjoint-set data structure.

The three disjoint-set operations have simple implementations. A MAKE-SET operation simply creates a tree with just one node. A FIND-SET operation follows parent pointers until it reaches the root of the tree. The nodes visited on this sim-

Figure 19.4 A disjoint-set forest. **(a)** Trees representing the two sets of Figure 19.2. The tree on the left represents the set $\{b, c, e, h\}$, with c as the representative, and the tree on the right represents the set $\{d, f, g\}$, with f as the representative. **(b)** The result of UNION(e, g).

ple path toward the root constitute the *find path*. A UNION operation, shown in Figure 19.4(b), simply causes the root of one tree to point to the root of the other.

Heuristics to improve the running time

So far, disjoint-set forests have not improved on the linked-list implementation. A sequence of $n - 1$ UNION operations could create a tree that is just a linear chain of n nodes. By using two heuristics, however, we can achieve a running time that is almost linear in the total number m of operations.

The first heuristic, *union by rank*, is similar to the weighted-union heuristic we used with the linked-list representation. The common-sense approach is to make the root of the tree with fewer nodes point to the root of the tree with more nodes. Rather than explicitly keeping track of the size of the subtree rooted at each node, however, we'll adopt an approach that eases the analysis. For each node, maintain a *rank*, which is an upper bound on the height of the node. Union by rank makes the root with smaller rank point to the root with larger rank during a UNION operation.

The second heuristic, *path compression*, is also quite simple and highly effective. As shown in Figure 19.5, FIND-SET operations use it to make each node on the find path point directly to the root. Path compression does not change any ranks.

Pseudocode for disjoint-set forests

The union-by-rank heuristic requires its implementation to keep track of ranks. With each node x, maintain the integer value $x.rank$, which is an upper bound on the height of x (the number of edges in the longest simple path from a descendant leaf to x). When MAKE-SET creates a singleton set, the single node in the

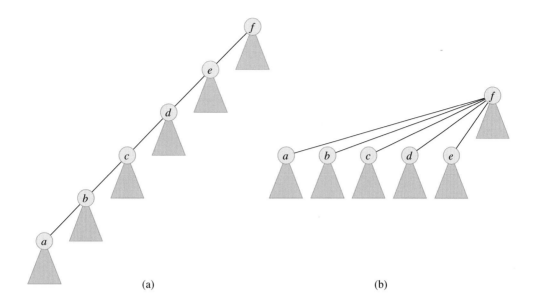

Figure 19.5 Path compression during the operation FIND-SET. Arrows and self-loops at roots are omitted. **(a)** A tree representing a set prior to executing FIND-SET(a). Triangles represent subtrees whose roots are the nodes shown. Each node has a pointer to its parent. **(b)** The same set after executing FIND-SET(a). Each node on the find path now points directly to the root.

corresponding tree has an initial rank of 0. Each FIND-SET operation leaves all ranks unchanged. The UNION operation has two cases, depending on whether the roots of the trees have equal rank. If the roots have unequal ranks, make the root with higher rank the parent of the root with lower rank, but don't change the ranks themselves. If the roots have equal ranks, arbitrarily choose one of the roots as the parent and increment its rank.

Let's put this method into pseudocode, appearing on the next page. The parent of node x is denoted by $x.p$. The LINK procedure, a subroutine called by UNION, takes pointers to two roots as inputs. The FIND-SET procedure with path compression, implemented recursively, turns out to be quite simple.

The FIND-SET procedure is a *two-pass method*: as it recurses, it makes one pass up the find path to find the root, and as the recursion unwinds, it makes a second pass back down the find path to update each node to point directly to the root. Each call of FIND-SET(x) returns $x.p$ in line 3. If x is the root, then FIND-SET skips line 2 and just returns $x.p$, which is x. In this case the recursion bottoms out. Otherwise, line 2 executes, and the recursive call with parameter $x.p$ returns

```
MAKE-SET(x)
1   x.p = x
2   x.rank = 0

UNION(x, y)
1   LINK(FIND-SET(x), FIND-SET(y))

LINK(x, y)
1   if x.rank > y.rank
2       y.p = x
3   else x.p = y
4       if x.rank == y.rank
5           y.rank = y.rank + 1

FIND-SET(x)
1   if x ≠ x.p                  // not the root?
2       x.p = FIND-SET(x.p)     // the root becomes the parent
3   return x.p                  // return the root
```

a pointer to the root. Line 2 updates node x to point directly to the root, and line 3 returns this pointer.

Effect of the heuristics on the running time

Separately, either union by rank or path compression improves the running time of the operations on disjoint-set forests, and combining the two heuristics yields an even greater improvement. Alone, union by rank yields a running time of $O(m \lg n)$ for a sequence of m operations, n of which are MAKE-SET (see Exercise 19.4-4), and this bound is tight (see Exercise 19.3-3). Although we won't prove it here, for a sequence of n MAKE-SET operations (and hence at most $n - 1$ UNION operations) and f FIND-SET operations, the worst-case running time using only the path-compression heuristic is $\Theta(n + f \cdot (1 + \log_{2+f/n} n))$.

Combining union by rank and path compression gives a worst-case running time of $O(m \, \alpha(n))$, where $\alpha(n)$ is a *very* slowly growing function, defined in Section 19.4. In any conceivable application of a disjoint-set data structure, $\alpha(n) \leq 4$, and thus, its running time is as good as linear in m for all practical purposes. Mathematically speaking, however, it is superlinear. Section 19.4 proves this $O(m \, \alpha(n))$ upper bound.

Exercises

19.3-1
Redo Exercise 19.2-2 using a disjoint-set forest with union by rank and path compression. Show the resulting forest with each node including its x_i and rank.

19.3-2
Write a nonrecursive version of FIND-SET with path compression.

19.3-3
Give a sequence of m MAKE-SET, UNION, and FIND-SET operations, n of which are MAKE-SET operations, that takes $\Omega(m \lg n)$ time when using only union by rank and not path compression.

19.3-4
Consider the operation PRINT-SET(x), which is given a node x and prints all the members of x's set, in any order. Show how to add just a single attribute to each node in a disjoint-set forest so that PRINT-SET(x) takes time linear in the number of members of x's set and the asymptotic running times of the other operations are unchanged. Assume that you can print each member of the set in $O(1)$ time.

★ ***19.3-5***
Show that any sequence of m MAKE-SET, FIND-SET, and LINK operations, where all the LINK operations appear before any of the FIND-SET operations, takes only $O(m)$ time when using both path compression and union by rank. You may assume that the arguments to LINK are roots within the disjoint-set forest. What happens in the same situation when using only path compression and not union by rank?

★ **19.4 Analysis of union by rank with path compression**

As noted in Section 19.3, the combined union-by-rank and path-compression heuristic runs in $O(m\, \alpha(n))$ time for m disjoint-set operations on n elements. In this section, we'll explore the function α to see just how slowly it grows. Then we'll analyze the running time using the potential method of amortized analysis.

A very quickly growing function and its very slowly growing inverse

For integers $j, k \geq 0$, we define the function $A_k(j)$ as

$$A_k(j) = \begin{cases} j+1 & \text{if } k = 0\,, \\ A_{k-1}^{(j+1)}(j) & \text{if } k \geq 1\,, \end{cases} \qquad (19.1)$$

where the expression $A_{k-1}^{(j+1)}(j)$ uses the functional-iteration notation defined in equation (3.30) on page 68. Specifically, equation (3.30) gives $A_{k-1}^{(0)}(j) = j$ and $A_{k-1}^{(i)}(j) = A_{k-1}(A_{k-1}^{(i-1)}(j))$ for $i \geq 1$. We call the parameter k the *level* of the function A.

The function $A_k(j)$ strictly increases with both j and k. To see just how quickly this function grows, we first obtain closed-form expressions for $A_1(j)$ and $A_2(j)$.

Lemma 19.2
For any integer $j \geq 1$, we have $A_1(j) = 2j + 1$.

Proof   We first use induction on i to show that $A_0^{(i)}(j) = j + i$. For the base case, $A_0^{(0)}(j) = j = j + 0$. For the inductive step, assume that $A_0^{(i-1)}(j) = j + (i-1)$. Then $A_0^{(i)}(j) = A_0(A_0^{(i-1)}(j)) = (j + (i-1)) + 1 = j + i$. Finally, we note that $A_1(j) = A_0^{(j+1)}(j) = j + (j+1) = 2j + 1$.   ∎

Lemma 19.3
For any integer $j \geq 1$, we have $A_2(j) = 2^{j+1}(j+1) - 1$.

Proof   We first use induction on i to show that $A_1^{(i)}(j) = 2^i(j+1) - 1$. For the base case, we have $A_1^{(0)}(j) = j = 2^0(j+1) - 1$. For the inductive step, assume that $A_1^{(i-1)}(j) = 2^{i-1}(j+1) - 1$. Then $A_1^{(i)}(j) = A_1(A_1^{(i-1)}(j)) = A_1(2^{i-1}(j+1) - 1) = 2 \cdot (2^{i-1}(j+1) - 1) + 1 = 2^i(j+1) - 2 + 1 = 2^i(j+1) - 1$. Finally, we note that $A_2(j) = A_1^{(j+1)}(j) = 2^{j+1}(j+1) - 1$.   ∎

Now we can see how quickly $A_k(j)$ grows by simply examining $A_k(1)$ for levels $k = 0, 1, 2, 3, 4$. From the definition of $A_0(j)$ and the above lemmas, we have $A_0(1) = 1 + 1 = 2$, $A_1(1) = 2 \cdot 1 + 1 = 3$, and $A_2(1) = 2^{1+1} \cdot (1+1) - 1 = 7$. We also have

$$
\begin{aligned}
A_3(1) &= A_2^{(2)}(1) \\
&= A_2(A_2(1)) \\
&= A_2(7) \\
&= 2^8 \cdot 8 - 1 \\
&= 2^{11} - 1 \\
&= 2047
\end{aligned}
$$

and

$$
\begin{aligned}
A_4(1) &= A_3^{(2)}(1) \\
&= A_3(A_3(1)) \\
&= A_3(2047) \\
&= A_2^{(2048)}(2047) \\
&\gg A_2(2047) \\
&= 2^{2048} \cdot 2048 - 1 \\
&= 2^{2059} - 1 \\
&> 2^{2056} \\
&= (2^4)^{514} \\
&= 16^{514} \\
&\gg 10^{80} \ ,
\end{aligned}
$$

which is the estimated number of atoms in the observable universe. (The symbol "$\gg$" denotes the "much-greater-than" relation.)

We define the inverse of the function $A_k(n)$, for integer $n \geq 0$, by

$$
\alpha(n) = \min\{k : A_k(1) \geq n\} \ . \tag{19.2}
$$

In words, $\alpha(n)$ is the lowest level k for which $A_k(1)$ is at least n. From the above values of $A_k(1)$, we see that

$$
\alpha(n) = \begin{cases}
0 & \text{for } 0 \leq n \leq 2 \ , \\
1 & \text{for } n = 3 \ , \\
2 & \text{for } 4 \leq n \leq 7 \ , \\
3 & \text{for } 8 \leq n \leq 2047 \ , \\
4 & \text{for } 2048 \leq n \leq A_4(1) \ .
\end{cases}
$$

It is only for values of n so large that the term "astronomical" understates them (greater than $A_4(1)$, a huge number) that $\alpha(n) > 4$, and so $\alpha(n) \leq 4$ for all practical purposes.

Properties of ranks

In the remainder of this section, we prove an $O(m\,\alpha(n))$ bound on the running time of the disjoint-set operations with union by rank and path compression. In order to prove this bound, we first prove some simple properties of ranks.

Lemma 19.4
For all nodes x, we have $x.rank \leq x.p.rank$, with strict inequality if $x \neq x.p$ (x is not a root). The value of $x.rank$ is initially 0, increases through time until $x \neq x.p$,

and from then on, $x.rank$ does not change. The value of $x.p.rank$ monotonically increases over time.

Proof The proof is a straightforward induction on the number of operations, using the implementations of MAKE-SET, UNION, and FIND-SET that appear on page 530, and is left as Exercise 19.4-1. ∎

Corollary 19.5
On the simple path from any node going up toward a root, node ranks strictly increase. ∎

Lemma 19.6
Every node has rank at most $n - 1$.

Proof Each node's rank starts at 0, and it increases only upon LINK operations. Because there are at most $n - 1$ UNION operations, there are also at most $n - 1$ LINK operations. Because each LINK operation either leaves all ranks alone or increases some node's rank by 1, all ranks are at most $n - 1$. ∎

Lemma 19.6 provides a weak bound on ranks. In fact, every node has rank at most $\lfloor \lg n \rfloor$ (see Exercise 19.4-2). The looser bound of Lemma 19.6 suffices for our purposes, however.

Proving the time bound

In order to prove the $O(m \, \alpha(n))$ time bound, we'll use the potential method of amortized analysis from Section 16.3. In performing the amortized analysis, it will be convenient to assume that we invoke the LINK operation rather than the UNION operation. That is, since the parameters of the LINK procedure are pointers to two roots, we act as though we perform the appropriate FIND-SET operations separately. The following lemma shows that even if we count the extra FIND-SET operations induced by UNION calls, the asymptotic running time remains unchanged.

Lemma 19.7
Suppose that we convert a sequence S' of m' MAKE-SET, UNION, and FIND-SET operations into a sequence S of m MAKE-SET, LINK, and FIND-SET operations by turning each UNION into two FIND-SET operations followed by one LINK. Then, if sequence S runs in $O(m \alpha(n))$ time, sequence S' runs in $O(m' \alpha(n))$ time.

Proof Since each UNION operation in sequence S' is converted into three operations in S, we have $m' \leq m \leq 3m'$, so that $m = \Theta(m')$, Thus, an $O(m \, \alpha(n))$

time bound for the converted sequence S implies an $O(m' \alpha(n))$ time bound for the original sequence S'. ∎

From now on, we assume that the initial sequence of m' MAKE-SET, UNION, and FIND-SET operations has been converted to a sequence of m MAKE-SET, LINK, and FIND-SET operations. We now prove an $O(m \alpha(n))$ time bound for the converted sequence and appeal to Lemma 19.7 to prove the $O(m' \alpha(n))$ running time of the original sequence of m' operations.

Potential function

The potential function we use assigns a potential $\phi_q(x)$ to each node x in the disjoint-set forest after q operations. For the potential Φ_q of the entire forest after q operations, sum the individual node potentials: $\Phi_q = \sum_x \phi_q(x)$. Because the forest is empty before the first operation, the sum is taken over an empty set, and so $\Phi_0 = 0$. No potential Φ_q is ever negative.

The value of $\phi_q(x)$ depends on whether x is a tree root after the qth operation. If it is, or if $x.rank = 0$, then $\phi_q(x) = \alpha(n) \cdot x.rank$.

Now suppose that after the qth operation, x is not a root and that $x.rank \geq 1$. We need to define two auxiliary functions on x before we can define $\phi_q(x)$. First we define

$$\text{level}(x) = \max \{k : x.p.rank \geq A_k(x.rank)\} \ . \tag{19.3}$$

That is, level(x) is the greatest level k for which A_k, applied to x's rank, is no greater than x's parent's rank.

We claim that

$$0 \leq \text{level}(x) < \alpha(n) \ , \tag{19.4}$$

which we see as follows. We have

$$\begin{aligned} x.p.rank \ &\geq \ x.rank + 1 \quad \text{(by Lemma 19.4 because x is not a root)} \\ &= \ A_0(x.rank) \quad \text{(by the definition (19.1) of $A_0(j)$)} \ , \end{aligned}$$

which implies that level$(x) \geq 0$, and

$$\begin{aligned} A_{\alpha(n)}(x.rank) \ &\geq \ A_{\alpha(n)}(1) \quad \text{(because $A_k(j)$ is strictly increasing)} \\ &\geq \ n \quad\quad\quad \text{(by the definition (19.2) of $\alpha(n)$)} \\ &> \ x.p.rank \quad \text{(by Lemma 19.6)} \ , \end{aligned}$$

which implies that level$(x) < \alpha(n)$.

For a given nonroot node x, the value of level(x) monotonically increases over time. Why? Because x is not a root, its rank does not change. The rank of $x.p$

monotonically increases over time, since if $x.p$ is not a root then its rank does not change, and if $x.p$ is a root then its rank can never decrease. Thus, the difference between $x.rank$ and $x.p.rank$ monotonically increases over time. Therefore, the value of k needed for $A_k(x.rank)$ to overtake $x.p.rank$ monotonically increases over time as well.

The second auxiliary function applies when $x.rank \geq 1$:

$$\text{iter}(x) = \max\left\{i : x.p.rank \geq A_{\text{level}(x)}^{(i)}(x.rank)\right\} . \tag{19.5}$$

That is, $\text{iter}(x)$ is the largest number of times we can iteratively apply $A_{\text{level}(x)}$, applied initially to x's rank, before exceeding x's parent's rank.

We claim that when $x.rank \geq 1$, we have

$$1 \leq \text{iter}(x) \leq x.rank , \tag{19.6}$$

which we see as follows. We have

$$
\begin{aligned}
x.p.rank &\geq A_{\text{level}(x)}(x.rank) &&\text{(by the definition (19.3) of level}(x)) \\
&= A_{\text{level}(x)}^{(1)}(x.rank) &&\text{(by the definition (3.30) of functional iteration) ,}
\end{aligned}
$$

which implies that $\text{iter}(x) \geq 1$. We also have

$$
\begin{aligned}
A_{\text{level}(x)}^{(x.rank+1)}(x.rank) &= A_{\text{level}(x)+1}(x.rank) &&\text{(by the definition (19.1) of } A_k(j)) \\
&> x.p.rank &&\text{(by the definition (19.3) of level}(x)) ,
\end{aligned}
$$

which implies that $\text{iter}(x) \leq x.rank$. Note that because $x.p.rank$ monotonically increases over time, in order for $\text{iter}(x)$ to decrease, $\text{level}(x)$ must increase. As long as $\text{level}(x)$ remains unchanged, $\text{iter}(x)$ must either increase or remain unchanged.

With these auxiliary functions in place, we are ready to define the potential of node x after q operations:

$$
\phi_q(x) =
\begin{cases}
\alpha(n) \cdot x.rank & \text{if } x \text{ is a root or } x.rank = 0 , \\
(\alpha(n) - \text{level}(x)) \cdot x.rank - \text{iter}(x) & \\
& \text{if } x \text{ is not a root and } x.rank \geq 1 .
\end{cases}
\tag{19.7}
$$

We next investigate some useful properties of node potentials.

Lemma 19.8
For every node x, and for all operation counts q, we have

$$0 \leq \phi_q(x) \leq \alpha(n) \cdot x.rank .$$

Proof If x is a root or $x.rank = 0$, then $\phi_q(x) = \alpha(n) \cdot x.rank$ by definition. Now suppose that x is not a root and that $x.rank \geq 1$. We can obtain a lower bound on $\phi_q(x)$ by maximizing $\text{level}(x)$ and $\text{iter}(x)$. The bounds (19.4) and (19.6) give $\alpha(n) - \text{level}(x) \geq 1$ and $\text{iter}(x) \leq x.rank$. Thus, we have

$$\phi_q(x) = (\alpha(n) - \text{level}(x)) \cdot x.rank - \text{iter}(x)$$
$$\geq x.rank - x.rank$$
$$= 0.$$

Similarly, minimizing level(x) and iter(x) provides an upper bound on $\phi_q(x)$. By the bound (19.4), level(x) ≥ 0, and by the bound (19.6), iter(x) ≥ 1. Thus, we have

$$\phi_q(x) \leq (\alpha(n) - 0) \cdot x.rank - 1$$
$$= \alpha(n) \cdot x.rank - 1$$
$$< \alpha(n) \cdot x.rank.$$ ∎

Corollary 19.9
If node x is not a root and $x.rank > 0$, then $\phi_q(x) < \alpha(n) \cdot x.rank$. ∎

Potential changes and amortized costs of operations

We are now ready to examine how the disjoint-set operations affect node potentials. Once we understand how each operation can change the potential, we can determine the amortized costs.

Lemma 19.10
Let x be a node that is not a root, and suppose that the qth operation is either a LINK or a FIND-SET. Then after the qth operation, $\phi_q(x) \leq \phi_{q-1}(x)$. Moreover, if $x.rank \geq 1$ and either level(x) or iter(x) changes due to the qth operation, then $\phi_q(x) \leq \phi_{q-1}(x) - 1$. That is, x's potential cannot increase, and if it has positive rank and either level(x) or iter(x) changes, then x's potential drops by at least 1.

Proof Because x is not a root, the qth operation does not change $x.rank$, and because n does not change after the initial n MAKE-SET operations, $\alpha(n)$ remains unchanged as well. Hence, these components of the formula for x's potential remain the same after the qth operation. If $x.rank = 0$, then $\phi_q(x) = \phi_{q-1}(x) = 0$.

Now assume that $x.rank \geq 1$. Recall that level(x) monotonically increases over time. If the qth operation leaves level(x) unchanged, then iter(x) either increases or remains unchanged. If both level(x) and iter(x) are unchanged, then $\phi_q(x) = \phi_{q-1}(x)$. If level($x$) is unchanged and iter($x$) increases, then it increases by at least 1, and so $\phi_q(x) \leq \phi_{q-1}(x) - 1$.

Finally, if the qth operation increases level(x), it increases by at least 1, so that the value of the term $(\alpha(n) - \text{level}(x)) \cdot x.rank$ drops by at least $x.rank$. Because level(x) increased, the value of iter(x) might drop, but according to the bound (19.6), the drop is by at most $x.rank - 1$. Thus, the increase in potential due to the change in iter(x) is less than the decrease in potential due to the change in level(x), yielding $\phi_q(x) \leq \phi_{q-1}(x) - 1$.   ∎

Our final three lemmas show that the amortized cost of each MAKE-SET, LINK, and FIND-SET operation is $O(\alpha(n))$. Recall from equation (16.2) on page 456 that the amortized cost of each operation is its actual cost plus the change in potential due to the operation.

Lemma 19.11
The amortized cost of each MAKE-SET operation is $O(1)$.

Proof   Suppose that the qth operation is MAKE-SET(x). This operation creates node x with rank 0, so that $\phi_q(x) = 0$. No other ranks or potentials change, and so $\Phi_q = \Phi_{q-1}$. Noting that the actual cost of the MAKE-SET operation is $O(1)$ completes the proof.   ∎

Lemma 19.12
The amortized cost of each LINK operation is $O(\alpha(n))$.

Proof   Suppose that the qth operation is LINK(x, y). The actual cost of the LINK operation is $O(1)$. Without loss of generality, suppose that the LINK makes y the parent of x.

To determine the change in potential due to the LINK, note that the only nodes whose potentials may change are x, y, and the children of y just prior to the operation. We'll show that the only node whose potential can increase due to the LINK is y, and that its increase is at most $\alpha(n)$:

- By Lemma 19.10, any node that is y's child just before the LINK cannot have its potential increase due to the LINK.

- From the definition (19.7) of $\phi_q(x)$, note that, since x was a root just before the qth operation, $\phi_{q-1}(x) = \alpha(n) \cdot x.rank$ at that time. If $x.rank = 0$, then $\phi_q(x) = \phi_{q-1}(x) = 0$. Otherwise,

$$\phi_q(x) < \alpha(n) \cdot x.rank \quad \text{(by Corollary 19.9)}$$
$$= \phi_{q-1}(x) \,,$$

  and so x's potential decreases.

- Because y is a root prior to the LINK, $\phi_{q-1}(y) = \alpha(n) \cdot y.rank$. After the LINK operation, y remains a root, so that y's potential still equals $\alpha(n)$ times its rank after the operation. The LINK operation either leaves y's rank alone or increases y's rank by 1. Therefore, either $\phi_q(y) = \phi_{q-1}(y)$ or $\phi_q(y) = \phi_{q-1}(y) + \alpha(n)$.

The increase in potential due to the LINK operation, therefore, is at most $\alpha(n)$. The amortized cost of the LINK operation is $O(1) + \alpha(n) = O(\alpha(n))$. ∎

Lemma 19.13
The amortized cost of each FIND-SET operation is $O(\alpha(n))$.

Proof Suppose that the qth operation is a FIND-SET and that the find path contains s nodes. The actual cost of the FIND-SET operation is $O(s)$. We will show that no node's potential increases due to the FIND-SET and that at least $\max\{0, s - (\alpha(n) + 2)\}$ nodes on the find path have their potential decrease by at least 1.

We first show that no node's potential increases. Lemma 19.10 takes care of all nodes other than the root. If x is the root, then its potential is $\alpha(n) \cdot x.rank$, which does not change due to the FIND-SET operation.

Now we show that at least $\max\{0, s - (\alpha(n) + 2)\}$ nodes have their potential decrease by at least 1. Let x be a node on the find path such that $x.rank > 0$ and x is followed somewhere on the find path by another node y that is not a root, where $\text{level}(y) = \text{level}(x)$ just before the FIND-SET operation. (Node y need not *immediately* follow x on the find path.) All but at most $\alpha(n) + 2$ nodes on the find path satisfy these constraints on x. Those that do not satisfy them are the first node on the find path (if it has rank 0), the last node on the path (i.e., the root), and the last node w on the path for which $\text{level}(w) = k$, for each $k = 0, 1, 2, \ldots, \alpha(n) - 1$.

Consider such a node x. It has positive rank and is followed somewhere on the find path by nonroot node y such that $\text{level}(y) = \text{level}(x)$ before the path compression occurs. We claim that the path compression decreases x's potential by at least 1. To prove this claim, let $k = \text{level}(x) = \text{level}(y)$ and $i = \text{iter}(x)$ before the path compression occurs. Just prior to the path compression caused by the FIND-SET, we have

$x.p.rank \geq A_k^{(i)}(x.rank)$ (by the definition (19.5) of $\text{iter}(x)$) ,

$y.p.rank \geq A_k(y.rank)$ (by the definition (19.3) of $\text{level}(y)$) ,

$y.rank \geq x.p.rank$ (by Corollary 19.5 and because
$\qquad\qquad\qquad\qquad$ y follows x on the find path) .

Putting these inequalities together gives

$$
\begin{aligned}
y.p.rank &\geq A_k(y.rank) \\
&\geq A_k(x.p.rank) \quad \text{(because } A_k(j) \text{ is strictly increasing)} \\
&\geq A_k(A_k^{(i)}(x.rank)) \\
&= A_k^{(i+1)}(x.rank) \quad \text{(by the definition (3.30) of functional iteration) .}
\end{aligned}
$$

Because path compression makes x and y have the same parent, after path compression we have $x.p.rank = y.p.rank$. The parent of y might change due to the path compression, but if it does, the rank of y's new parent compared with the rank of y's parent before path compression is either the same or greater. Since $x.rank$ does not change, $x.p.rank = y.p.rank \geq A_k^{(i+1)}(x.rank)$ after path compression. By the definition (19.5) of the iter function, the value of $\text{iter}(x)$ increases from i to at least $i + 1$. By Lemma 19.10, $\phi_q(x) \leq \phi_{q-1}(x) - 1$, so that x's potential decreases by at least 1.

The amortized cost of the FIND-SET operation is the actual cost plus the change in potential. The actual cost is $O(s)$, and we have shown that the total potential decreases by at least $\max\{0, s - (\alpha(n) + 2)\}$. The amortized cost, therefore, is at most $O(s) - (s - (\alpha(n) + 2)) = O(s) - s + O(\alpha(n)) = O(\alpha(n))$, since we can scale up the units of potential to dominate the constant hidden in $O(s)$. (See Exercise 19.4-6.)   ∎

Putting the preceding lemmas together yields the following theorem.

Theorem 19.14
A sequence of m MAKE-SET, UNION, and FIND-SET operations, n of which are MAKE-SET operations, can be performed on a disjoint-set forest with union by rank and path compression in $O(m \, \alpha(n))$ time.

Proof   Immediate from Lemmas 19.7, 19.11, 19.12, and 19.13.   ∎

Exercises

19.4-1
Prove Lemma 19.4.

19.4-2
Prove that every node has rank at most $\lfloor \lg n \rfloor$.

19.4-3
In light of Exercise 19.4-2, how many bits are necessary to store $x.rank$ for each node x?

19.4-4
Using Exercise 19.4-2, give a simple proof that operations on a disjoint-set forest with union by rank but without path compression run in $O(m \lg n)$ time.

19.4-5

Professor Dante reasons that because node ranks increase strictly along a simple path to the root, node levels must monotonically increase along the path. In other words, if $x.rank > 0$ and $x.p$ is not a root, then $\text{level}(x) \leq \text{level}(x.p)$. Is the professor correct?

19.4-6

The proof of Lemma 19.13 ends with scaling the units of potential to dominate the constant hidden in the $O(s)$ term. To be more precise in the proof, you need to change the definition (19.7) of the potential function to multiply each of the two cases by a constant, say c, that dominates the constant in the $O(s)$ term. How must the rest of the analysis change to accommodate this updated potential function?

★ 19.4-7

Consider the function $\alpha'(n) = \min\{k : A_k(1) \geq \lg(n + 1)\}$. Show that $\alpha'(n) \leq 3$ for all practical values of n and, using Exercise 19.4-2, show how to modify the potential-function argument to prove that performing a sequence of m MAKE-SET, UNION, and FIND-SET operations, n of which are MAKE-SET operations, on a disjoint-set forest with union by rank and path compression takes $O(m\alpha'(n))$ time.

Problems

19-1   *Offline minimum*

In the *offline minimum problem*, you maintain a dynamic set T of elements from the domain $\{1, 2, \ldots, n\}$ under the operations INSERT and EXTRACT-MIN. The input is a sequence S of n INSERT and m EXTRACT-MIN calls, where each key in $\{1, 2, \ldots, n\}$ is inserted exactly once. Your goal is to determine which key is returned by each EXTRACT-MIN call. Specifically, you must fill in an array *extracted*$[1 : m]$, where for $i = 1, 2, \ldots, m$, *extracted*$[i]$ is the key returned by the ith EXTRACT-MIN call. The problem is "offline" in the sense that you are allowed to process the entire sequence S before determining any of the returned keys.

a. Consider the following instance of the offline minimum problem, in which each operation INSERT(i) is represented by the value of i and each EXTRACT-MIN is represented by the letter E:

4, 8, E, 3, E, 9, 2, 6, E, E, E, 1, 7, E, 5 .

Fill in the correct values in the *extracted* array.

To develop an algorithm for this problem, break the sequence S into homogeneous subsequences. That is, represent S by

$$I_1, E, I_2, E, I_3, \ldots, I_m, E, I_{m+1} ,$$

where each E represents a single EXTRACT-MIN call and each I_j represents a (possibly empty) sequence of INSERT calls. For each subsequence I_j, initially place the keys inserted by these operations into a set K_j, which is empty if I_j is empty. Then execute the OFFLINE-MINIMUM procedure.

OFFLINE-MINIMUM(m, n)

```
1  for i = 1 to n
2      determine j such that i ∈ K_j
3      if j ≠ m + 1
4          extracted[j] = i
5          let l be the smallest value greater than j for which set K_l exists
6          K_l = K_j ∪ K_l, destroying K_j
7  return extracted
```

b. Argue that the array *extracted* returned by OFFLINE-MINIMUM is correct.

c. Describe how to implement OFFLINE-MINIMUM efficiently with a disjoint-set data structure. Give as tight a bound as you can on the worst-case running time of your implementation.

19-2   Depth determination

In the ***depth-determination problem***, you maintain a forest $\mathcal{F} = \{T_i\}$ of rooted trees under three operations:

MAKE-TREE(v) creates a tree whose only node is v.

FIND-DEPTH(v) returns the depth of node v within its tree.

GRAFT(r, v) makes node r, which is assumed to be the root of a tree, become the child of node v, which is assumed to be in a different tree from r but may or may not itself be a root.

a. Suppose that you use a tree representation similar to a disjoint-set forest: $v.p$ is the parent of node v, except that $v.p = v$ if v is a root. Suppose further that you implement GRAFT(r, v) by setting $r.p = v$ and FIND-DEPTH(v) by following the find path from v up to the root, returning a count of all nodes other than v encountered. Show that the worst-case running time of a sequence of m MAKE-TREE, FIND-DEPTH, and GRAFT operations is $\Theta(m^2)$.

By using the union-by-rank and path-compression heuristics, you can reduce the worst-case running time. Use the disjoint-set forest $\mathcal{S} = \{S_i\}$, where each set S_i (which is itself a tree) corresponds to a tree T_i in the forest $\mathcal{F}$. The tree structure within a set S_i, however, does not necessarily correspond to that of T_i. In fact, the implementation of S_i does not record the exact parent-child relationships but nevertheless allows you to determine any node's depth in T_i.

The key idea is to maintain in each node v a "pseudodistance" $v.d$, which is defined so that the sum of the pseudodistances along the simple path from v to the root of its set S_i equals the depth of v in T_i. That is, if the simple path from v to its root in S_i is $v_0, v_1, \ldots, v_k$, where $v_0 = v$ and v_k is S_i's root, then the depth of v in T_i is $\sum_{j=0}^{k} v_j.d$.

b. Give an implementation of MAKE-TREE.

c. Show how to modify FIND-SET to implement FIND-DEPTH. Your implementation should perform path compression, and its running time should be linear in the length of the find path. Make sure that your implementation updates pseudodistances correctly.

d. Show how to implement GRAFT(r, v), which combines the sets containing r and v, by modifying the UNION and LINK procedures. Make sure that your implementation updates pseudodistances correctly. Note that the root of a set S_i is not necessarily the root of the corresponding tree T_i.

e. Give a tight bound on the worst-case running time of a sequence of m MAKE-TREE, FIND-DEPTH, and GRAFT operations, n of which are MAKE-TREE operations.

19-3 *Tarjan's offline lowest-common-ancestors algorithm*

The *lowest common ancestor* of two nodes u and v in a rooted tree T is the node w that is an ancestor of both u and v and that has the greatest depth in T. In the *offline lowest-common-ancestors problem*, you are given a rooted tree T and an arbitrary set $P = \{\{u, v\}\}$ of unordered pairs of nodes in T, and you wish to determine the lowest common ancestor of each pair in P.

To solve the offline lowest-common-ancestors problem, the LCA procedure on the following page performs a tree walk of T with the initial call LCA($T.root$). Assume that each node is colored WHITE prior to the walk.

a. Argue that line 10 executes exactly once for each pair $\{u, v\} \in P$.

b. Argue that at the time of the call LCA(u), the number of sets in the disjoint-set data structure equals the depth of u in T.

LCA(u)

1 MAKE-SET(u)
2 FIND-SET(u).$ancestor = u$
3 **for** each child v of u in T
4   LCA(v)
5   UNION(u, v)
6   FIND-SET(u).$ancestor = u$
7 $u.color = $ BLACK
8 **for** each node v such that $\{u, v\} \in P$
9   **if** $v.color == $ BLACK
10   print "The lowest common ancestor of"
              u "and" v "is" FIND-SET(v).$ancestor$

c. Prove that LCA correctly prints the lowest common ancestor of u and v for each pair $\{u, v\} \in P$.

d. Analyze the running time of LCA, assuming that you use the implementation of the disjoint-set data structure in Section 19.3.

Chapter notes

Many of the important results for disjoint-set data structures are due at least in part to R. E. Tarjan. Using aggregate analysis, Tarjan [427, 429] gave the first tight upper bound in terms of the very slowly growing inverse $\hat{\alpha}(m, n)$ of Ackermann's function. (The function $A_k(j)$ given in Section 19.4 is similar to Ackermann's function, and the function $\alpha(n)$ is similar to $\hat{\alpha}(m, n)$. Both $\alpha(n)$ and $\hat{\alpha}(m, n)$ are at most 4 for all conceivable values of m and n.) An upper bound of $O(m \lg^* n)$ was proven earlier by Hopcroft and Ullman [5, 227]. The treatment in Section 19.4 is adapted from a later analysis by Tarjan [431], which is based on an analysis by Kozen [270]. Harfst and Reingold [209] give a potential-based version of Tarjan's earlier bound.

Tarjan and van Leeuwen [432] discuss variants on the path-compression heuristic, including "one-pass methods," which sometimes offer better constant factors in their performance than do two-pass methods. As with Tarjan's earlier analyses of the basic path-compression heuristic, the analyses by Tarjan and van Leeuwen are aggregate. Harfst and Reingold [209] later showed how to make a small change to the potential function to adapt their path-compression analysis to these one-pass variants. Goel et al. [182] prove that linking disjoint-set trees randomly yields the same asymptotic running time as union by rank. Gabow and Tarjan [166] show that in certain applications, the disjoint-set operations can be made to run in $O(m)$ time.

Tarjan [428] showed that a lower bound of $\Omega(m\,\hat{\alpha}(m,n))$ time is required for operations on any disjoint-set data structure satisfying certain technical conditions. This lower bound was later generalized by Fredman and Saks [155], who showed that in the worst case, $\Omega(m\,\hat{\alpha}(m,n))$ $(\lg n)$-bit words of memory must be accessed.

Part VI   Graph Algorithms

Introduction

Graph problems pervade computer science, and algorithms for working with them are fundamental to the field. Hundreds of interesting computational problems are couched in terms of graphs. This part touches on a few of the more significant ones.

Chapter 20 shows how to represent a graph in a computer and then discusses algorithms based on searching a graph using either breadth-first search or depth-first search. The chapter gives two applications of depth-first search: topologically sorting a directed acyclic graph and decomposing a directed graph into its strongly connected components.

Chapter 21 describes how to compute a minimum-weight spanning tree of a graph: the least-weight way of connecting all of the vertices together when each edge has an associated weight. The algorithms for computing minimum spanning trees serve as good examples of greedy algorithms (see Chapter 15).

Chapters 22 and 23 consider how to compute shortest paths between vertices when each edge has an associated length or "weight." Chapter 22 shows how to find shortest paths from a given source vertex to all other vertices, and Chapter 23 examines methods to compute shortest paths between every pair of vertices.

Chapter 24 shows how to compute a maximum flow of material in a flow network, which is a directed graph having a specified source vertex of material, a specified sink vertex, and specified capacities for the amount of material that can traverse each directed edge. This general problem arises in many forms, and a good algorithm for computing maximum flows can help solve a variety of related problems efficiently.

Finally, Chapter 25 explores matchings in bipartite graphs: methods for pairing up vertices that are partitioned into two sets by selecting edges that go between the sets. Bipartite-matching problems model several situations that arise in the real world. The chapter examines how to find a matching of maximum cardinality; the "stable-marriage problem," which has the highly practical application of matching medical residents to hospitals; and assignment problems, which maximize the total weight of a bipartite matching.

When we characterize the running time of a graph algorithm on a given graph $G = (V, E)$, we usually measure the size of the input in terms of the number of vertices $|V|$ and the number of edges $|E|$ of the graph. That is, we denote the size of the input with two parameters, not just one. We adopt a common notational convention for these parameters. Inside asymptotic notation (such as O-notation or Θ-notation), and *only* inside such notation, the symbol V denotes $|V|$ and the symbol E denotes $|E|$. For example, we might say, "the algorithm runs in $O(VE)$ time," meaning that the algorithm runs in $O(|V| \, |E|)$ time. This convention makes the running-time formulas easier to read, without risk of ambiguity.

Another convention we adopt appears in pseudocode. We denote the vertex set of a graph G by $G.V$ and its edge set by $G.E$. That is, the pseudocode views vertex and edge sets as attributes of a graph.

20 Elementary Graph Algorithms

This chapter presents methods for representing a graph and for searching a graph. Searching a graph means systematically following the edges of the graph so as to visit the vertices of the graph. A graph-searching algorithm can discover much about the structure of a graph. Many algorithms begin by searching their input graph to obtain this structural information. Several other graph algorithms elaborate on basic graph searching. Techniques for searching a graph lie at the heart of the field of graph algorithms.

Section 20.1 discusses the two most common computational representations of graphs: as adjacency lists and as adjacency matrices. Section 20.2 presents a simple graph-searching algorithm called breadth-first search and shows how to create a breadth-first tree. Section 20.3 presents depth-first search and proves some standard results about the order in which depth-first search visits vertices. Section 20.4 provides our first real application of depth-first search: topologically sorting a directed acyclic graph. A second application of depth-first search, finding the strongly connected components of a directed graph, is the topic of Section 20.5.

20.1 Representations of graphs

You can choose between two standard ways to represent a graph $G = (V, E)$: as a collection of adjacency lists or as an adjacency matrix. Either way applies to both directed and undirected graphs. Because the adjacency-list representation provides a compact way to represent *sparse* graphs—those for which $|E|$ is much less than $|V|^2$—it is usually the method of choice. Most of the graph algorithms presented in this book assume that an input graph is represented in adjacency-list form. You might prefer an adjacency-matrix representation, however, when the graph is *dense*—$|E|$ is close to $|V|^2$—or when you need to be able to tell quickly whether there is an edge connecting two given vertices. For example, two of the

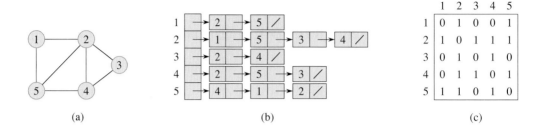

Figure 20.1   Two representations of an undirected graph. **(a)** An undirected graph G with 5 vertices and 7 edges. **(b)** An adjacency-list representation of G. **(c)** The adjacency-matrix representation of G.

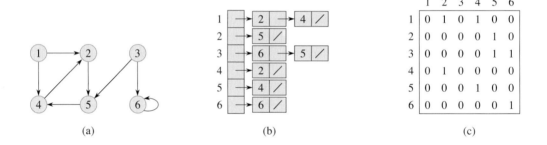

Figure 20.2   Two representations of a directed graph. **(a)** A directed graph G with 6 vertices and 8 edges. **(b)** An adjacency-list representation of G. **(c)** The adjacency-matrix representation of G.

all-pairs shortest-paths algorithms presented in Chapter 23 assume that their input graphs are represented by adjacency matrices.

The *adjacency-list representation* of a graph $G = (V, E)$ consists of an array *Adj* of $|V|$ lists, one for each vertex in V. For each $u \in V$, the adjacency list *Adj*[*u*] contains all the vertices v such that there is an edge $(u, v) \in E$. That is, *Adj*[*u*] consists of all the vertices adjacent to u in G. (Alternatively, it can contain pointers to these vertices.) Since the adjacency lists represent the edges of a graph, our pseudocode treats the array *Adj* as an attribute of the graph, just like the edge set E. In pseudocode, therefore, you will see notation such as $G.Adj[u]$. Figure 20.1(b) is an adjacency-list representation of the undirected graph in Figure 20.1(a). Similarly, Figure 20.2(b) is an adjacency-list representation of the directed graph in Figure 20.2(a).

If G is a directed graph, the sum of the lengths of all the adjacency lists is $|E|$, since an edge of the form (u, v) is represented by having v appear in *Adj*[*u*]. If G is an undirected graph, the sum of the lengths of all the adjacency lists is $2|E|$, since if (u, v) is an undirected edge, then u appears in v's adjacency list and vice versa. For both directed and undirected graphs, the adjacency-list representation has the desirable property that the amount of memory it requires is $\Theta(V + E)$. Finding each edge in the graph also takes $\Theta(V + E)$ time, rather than just $\Theta(E)$, since each of the $|V|$ adjacency lists must be examined. Of course, if $|E| = \Omega(V)$—such as in a connected, undirected graph or a strongly connected, directed graph—we can say that finding each edge takes $\Theta(E)$ time.

Adjacency lists can also represent *weighted graphs*, that is, graphs for which each edge has an associated *weight* given by a *weight function* $w : E \rightarrow \mathbb{R}$. For example, let $G = (V, E)$ be a weighted graph with weight function w. Then you can simply store the weight $w(u, v)$ of the edge $(u, v) \in E$ with vertex v in u's adjacency list. The adjacency-list representation is quite robust in that you can modify it to support many other graph variants.

A potential disadvantage of the adjacency-list representation is that it provides no quicker way to determine whether a given edge (u, v) is present in the graph than to search for v in the adjacency list $Adj[u]$. An adjacency-matrix representation of the graph remedies this disadvantage, but at the cost of using asymptotically more memory. (See Exercise 20.1-8 for suggestions of variations on adjacency lists that permit faster edge lookup.)

The *adjacency-matrix representation* of a graph $G = (V, E)$ assumes that the vertices are numbered $1, 2, \ldots, |V|$ in some arbitrary manner. Then the adjacency-matrix representation of a graph G consists of a $|V| \times |V|$ matrix $A = (a_{ij})$ such that

$$a_{ij} = \begin{cases} 1 & \text{if } (i, j) \in E, \\ 0 & \text{otherwise}. \end{cases}$$

Figures 20.1(c) and 20.2(c) are the adjacency matrices of the undirected and directed graphs in Figures 20.1(a) and 20.2(a), respectively. The adjacency matrix of a graph requires $\Theta(V^2)$ memory, independent of the number of edges in the graph. Because finding each edge in the graph requires examining the entire adjacency matrix, doing so takes $\Theta(V^2)$ time.

Observe the symmetry along the main diagonal of the adjacency matrix in Figure 20.1(c). Since in an undirected graph, (u, v) and (v, u) represent the same edge, the adjacency matrix A of an undirected graph is its own transpose: $A = A^{\mathrm{T}}$. In some applications, it pays to store only the entries on and above the diagonal of the adjacency matrix, thereby cutting the memory needed to store the graph almost in half.

Like the adjacency-list representation of a graph, an adjacency matrix can represent a weighted graph. For example, if $G = (V, E)$ is a weighted graph with edge-weight function w, you can store the weight $w(u, v)$ of the edge $(u, v) \in E$

as the entry in row u and column v of the adjacency matrix. If an edge does not exist, you can store a NIL value as its corresponding matrix entry, though for many problems it is convenient to use a value such as 0 or ∞.

Although the adjacency-list representation is asymptotically at least as space-efficient as the adjacency-matrix representation, adjacency matrices are simpler, and so you might prefer them when graphs are reasonably small. Moreover, adjacency matrices carry a further advantage for unweighted graphs: they require only one bit per entry.

Representing attributes

Most algorithms that operate on graphs need to maintain attributes for vertices and/or edges. We indicate these attributes using our usual notation, such as $v.d$ for an attribute d of a vertex v. When we indicate edges as pairs of vertices, we use the same style of notation. For example, if edges have an attribute f, then we denote this attribute for edge (u, v) by $(u, v).f$. For the purpose of presenting and understanding algorithms, our attribute notation suffices.

Implementing vertex and edge attributes in real programs can be another story entirely. There is no one best way to store and access vertex and edge attributes. For a given situation, your decision will likely depend on the programming language you are using, the algorithm you are implementing, and how the rest of your program uses the graph. If you represent a graph using adjacency lists, one design choice is to represent vertex attributes in additional arrays, such as an array $d[1 : |V|]$ that parallels the *Adj* array. If the vertices adjacent to u belong to *Adj*$[u]$, then the attribute $u.d$ can actually be stored in the array entry $d[u]$. Many other ways of implementing attributes are possible. For example, in an object-oriented programming language, vertex attributes might be represented as instance variables within a subclass of a `Vertex` class.

Exercises

20.1-1
Given an adjacency-list representation of a directed graph, how long does it take to compute the out-degree of every vertex? How long does it take to compute the in-degrees?

20.1-2
Give an adjacency-list representation for a complete binary tree on 7 vertices. Give an equivalent adjacency-matrix representation. Assume that the edges are undirected and that the vertices are numbered from 1 to 7 as in a binary heap.

20.1-3
The *transpose* of a directed graph $G = (V, E)$ is the graph $G^T = (V, E^T)$, where $E^T = \{(v, u) \in V \times V : (u, v) \in E\}$. That is, G^T is G with all its edges reversed. Describe efficient algorithms for computing G^T from G, for both the adjacency-list and adjacency-matrix representations of G. Analyze the running times of your algorithms.

20.1-4
Given an adjacency-list representation of a multigraph $G = (V, E)$, describe an $O(V + E)$-time algorithm to compute the adjacency-list representation of the "equivalent" undirected graph $G' = (V, E')$, where E' consists of the edges in E with all multiple edges between two vertices replaced by a single edge and with all self-loops removed.

20.1-5
The *square* of a directed graph $G = (V, E)$ is the graph $G^2 = (V, E^2)$ such that $(u, v) \in E^2$ if and only if G contains a path with at most two edges between u and v. Describe efficient algorithms for computing G^2 from G for both the adjacency-list and adjacency-matrix representations of G. Analyze the running times of your algorithms.

20.1-6
Most graph algorithms that take an adjacency-matrix representation as input require $\Omega(V^2)$ time, but there are some exceptions. Show how to determine whether a directed graph G contains a *universal sink*—a vertex with in-degree $|V| - 1$ and out-degree 0—in $O(V)$ time, given an adjacency matrix for G.

20.1-7
The *incidence matrix* of a directed graph $G = (V, E)$ with no self-loops is a $|V| \times |E|$ matrix $B = (b_{ij})$ such that

$$
b_{ij} = \begin{cases} -1 & \text{if edge } j \text{ leaves vertex } i \text{ ,} \\ 1 & \text{if edge } j \text{ enters vertex } i \text{ ,} \\ 0 & \text{otherwise .} \end{cases}
$$

Describe what the entries of the matrix product BB^T represent, where B^T is the transpose of B.

20.1-8
Suppose that instead of a linked list, each array entry $Adj[u]$ is a hash table containing the vertices v for which $(u, v) \in E$, with collisions resolved by chaining. Under the assumption of uniform independent hashing, if all edge lookups are equally likely, what is the expected time to determine whether an edge is in the graph?

What disadvantages does this scheme have? Suggest an alternate data structure for each edge list that solves these problems. Does your alternative have disadvantages compared with the hash table?

20.2   Breadth-first search

Breadth-first search is one of the simplest algorithms for searching a graph and the archetype for many important graph algorithms. Prim's minimum-spanning-tree algorithm (Section 21.2) and Dijkstra's single-source shortest-paths algorithm (Section 22.3) use ideas similar to those in breadth-first search.

Given a graph $G = (V, E)$ and a distinguished *source* vertex s, breadth-first search systematically explores the edges of G to "discover" every vertex that is reachable from s. It computes the distance from s to each reachable vertex, where the distance to a vertex v equals the smallest number of edges needed to go from s to v. Breadth-first search also produces a "breadth-first tree" with root s that contains all reachable vertices. For any vertex v reachable from s, the simple path in the breadth-first tree from s to v corresponds to a shortest path from s to v in G, that is, a path containing the smallest number of edges. The algorithm works on both directed and undirected graphs.

Breadth-first search is so named because it expands the frontier between discovered and undiscovered vertices uniformly across the breadth of the frontier. You can think of it as discovering vertices in waves emanating from the source vertex. That is, starting from s, the algorithm first discovers all neighbors of s, which have distance 1. Then it discovers all vertices with distance 2, then all vertices with distance 3, and so on, until it has discovered every vertex reachable from s.

In order to keep track of the waves of vertices, breadth-first search could maintain separate arrays or lists of the vertices at each distance from the source vertex. Instead, it uses a single first-in, first-out queue (see Section 10.1.3) containing some vertices at a distance k, possibly followed by some vertices at distance $k + 1$. The queue, therefore, contains portions of two consecutive waves at any time.

To keep track of progress, breadth-first search colors each vertex white, gray, or black. All vertices start out white, and vertices not reachable from the source vertex s stay white the entire time. A vertex that is reachable from s is *discovered* the first time it is encountered during the search, at which time it becomes gray, indicating that is now on the frontier of the search: the boundary between discovered and undiscovered vertices. The queue contains all the gray vertices. Eventually, all the edges of a gray vertex will be explored, so that all of its neighbors will be discovered. Once all of a vertex's edges have been explored, the vertex is behind the frontier of the search, and it goes from gray to black.[1]

Breadth-first search constructs a breadth-first tree, initially containing only its root, which is the source vertex s. Whenever the search discovers a white vertex v in the course of scanning the adjacency list of a gray vertex u, the vertex v and the edge (u, v) are added to the tree. We say that u is the *predecessor* or *parent* of v in the breadth-first tree. Since every vertex reachable from s is discovered at most once, each vertex reachable from s has exactly one parent. (There is one exception: because s is the root of the breadth-first tree, it has no parent.) Ancestor and descendant relationships in the breadth-first tree are defined relative to the root s as usual: if u is on the simple path in the tree from the root s to vertex v, then u is an ancestor of v and v is a descendant of u.

The breadth-first-search procedure BFS on the following page assumes that the graph $G = (V, E)$ is represented using adjacency lists. It denotes the queue by Q, and it attaches three additional attributes to each vertex v in the graph:

- $v.color$ is the color of v: WHITE, GRAY, or BLACK.

- $v.d$ holds the distance from the source vertex s to v, as computed by the algorithm.

- $v.\pi$ is v's predecessor in the breadth-first tree. If v has no predecessor because it is the source vertex or is undiscovered, then $v.\pi = $ NIL.

Figure 20.3 illustrates the progress of BFS on an undirected graph.

The procedure BFS works as follows. With the exception of the source vertex s, lines 1–4 paint every vertex white, set $u.d = \infty$ for each vertex u, and set the parent of every vertex to be NIL. Because the source vertex s is always the first vertex discovered, lines 5–7 paint s gray, set $s.d$ to 0, and set the predecessor of s to NIL. Lines 8–9 create the queue Q, initially containing just the source vertex.

The **while** loop of lines 10–18 iterates as long as there remain gray vertices, which are on the frontier: discovered vertices that have not yet had their adjacency lists fully examined. This **while** loop maintains the following invariant:

> At the test in line 10, the queue Q consists of the set of gray vertices.

Although we won't use this loop invariant to prove correctness, it is easy to see that it holds prior to the first iteration and that each iteration of the loop maintains the invariant. Prior to the first iteration, the only gray vertex, and the only vertex

---

[1] We distinguish between gray and black vertices to help us understand how breadth-first search operates. In fact, as Exercise 20.2-3 shows, we get the same result even if we do not distinguish between gray and black vertices.

BFS(G, s)

```
 1  for each vertex u ∈ G.V − {s}
 2      u.color = WHITE
 3      u.d = ∞
 4      u.π = NIL
 5  s.color = GRAY
 6  s.d = 0
 7  s.π = NIL
 8  Q = ∅
 9  ENQUEUE(Q, s)
10  while Q ≠ ∅
11      u = DEQUEUE(Q)
12      for each vertex v in G.Adj[u]      // search the neighbors of u
13          if v.color == WHITE            // is v being discovered now?
14              v.color = GRAY
15              v.d = u.d + 1
16              v.π = u
17              ENQUEUE(Q, v)              // v is now on the frontier
18      u.color = BLACK                    // u is now behind the frontier
```

in Q, is the source vertex s. Line 11 determines the gray vertex u at the head of the queue Q and removes it from Q. The **for** loop of lines 12–17 considers each vertex v in the adjacency list of u. If v is white, then it has not yet been discovered, and the procedure discovers it by executing lines 14–17. These lines paint vertex v gray, set v's distance $v.d$ to $u.d + 1$, record u as v's parent $v.\pi$, and place v at the tail of the queue Q. Once the procedure has examined all the vertices on u's adjacency list, it blackens u in line 18, indicating that u is now behind the frontier. The loop invariant is maintained because whenever a vertex is painted gray (in line 14) it is also enqueued (in line 17), and whenever a vertex is dequeued (in line 11) it is also painted black (in line 18).

The results of breadth-first search may depend upon the order in which the neighbors of a given vertex are visited in line 12: the breadth-first tree may vary, but the distances d computed by the algorithm do not. (See Exercise 20.2-5.)

A simple change allows the BFS procedure to terminate in many cases before the queue Q becomes empty. Because each vertex is discovered at most once and receives a finite d value only when it is discovered, the algorithm can terminate once every vertex has a finite d value. If BFS keeps count of how many vertices have been discovered, it can terminate once either the queue Q is empty or all $|V|$ vertices are discovered.

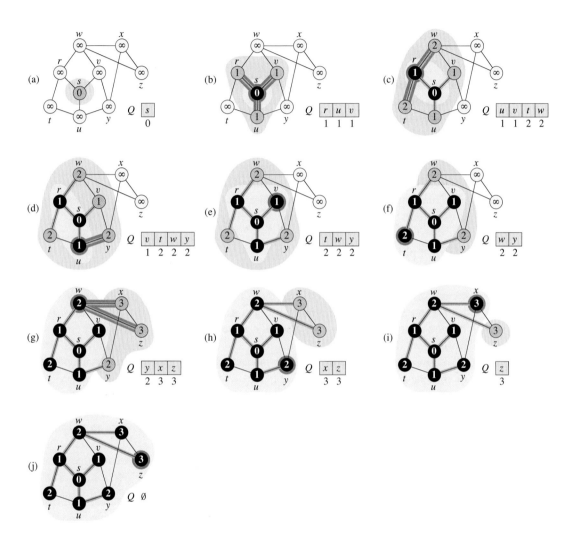

Figure 20.3 The operation of BFS on an undirected graph. Each part shows the graph and the queue Q at the beginning of each iteration of the **while** loop of lines 10–18. Vertex distances appear within each vertex and below vertices in the queue. The tan region surrounds the frontier of the search, consisting of the vertices in the queue. The light blue region surrounds the vertices behind the frontier, which have been dequeued. Each part highlights in orange the vertex dequeued and the breadth-first tree edges added, if any, in the previous iteration. Blue edges belong to the breadth-first tree constructed so far.

Analysis

Before proving the various properties of breadth-first search, let's take on the easier job of analyzing its running time on an input graph $G = (V, E)$. We use aggregate analysis, as we saw in Section 16.1. After initialization, breadth-first search never whitens a vertex, and thus the test in line 13 ensures that each vertex is enqueued at most once, and hence dequeued at most once. The operations of enqueuing and dequeuing take $O(1)$ time, and so the total time devoted to queue operations is $O(V)$. Because the procedure scans the adjacency list of each vertex only when the vertex is dequeued, it scans each adjacency list at most once. Since the sum of the lengths of all $|V|$ adjacency lists is $\Theta(E)$, the total time spent in scanning adjacency lists is $O(V + E)$. The overhead for initialization is $O(V)$, and thus the total running time of the BFS procedure is $O(V + E)$. Thus, breadth-first search runs in time linear in the size of the adjacency-list representation of G.

Shortest paths

Now, let's see why breadth-first search finds the shortest distance from a given source vertex s to each vertex in a graph. Define the *shortest-path distance* $\delta(s, v)$ from s to v as the minimum number of edges in any path from vertex s to vertex v. If there is no path from s to v, then $\delta(s, v) = \infty$. We call a path of length $\delta(s, v)$ from s to v a *shortest path*[2] from s to v. Before showing that breadth-first search correctly computes shortest-path distances, we investigate an important property of shortest-path distances.

Lemma 20.1
Let $G = (V, E)$ be a directed or undirected graph, and let $s \in V$ be an arbitrary vertex. Then, for any edge $(u, v) \in E$,

$$\delta(s, v) \leq \delta(s, u) + 1 .$$

Proof If u is reachable from s, then so is v. In this case, the shortest path from s to v cannot be longer than the shortest path from s to u followed by the edge (u, v), and thus the inequality holds. If u is not reachable from s, then $\delta(s, u) = \infty$, and again, the inequality holds.   ∎

Our goal is to show that the BFS procedure properly computes $v.d = \delta(s, v)$ for each vertex $v \in V$. We first show that $v.d$ bounds $\delta(s, v)$ from above.

---

[2] Chapters 22 and 23 generalize shortest paths to weighted graphs, in which every edge has a real-valued weight and the weight of a path is the sum of the weights of its constituent edges. The graphs considered in the present chapter are unweighted or, equivalently, all edges have unit weight.

Lemma 20.2
Let $G = (V, E)$ be a directed or undirected graph, and suppose that BFS is run on G from a given source vertex $s \in V$. Then, for each vertex $v \in V$, the value $v.d$ computed by BFS satisfies $v.d \geq \delta(s, v)$ at all times, including at termination.

Proof The lemma is true intuitively, because any finite value assigned to $v.d$ equals the number of edges on some path from s to v. The formal proof is by induction on the number of ENQUEUE operations. The inductive hypothesis is that $v.d \geq \delta(s, v)$ for all $v \in V$.

The base case of the induction is the situation immediately after enqueuing s in line 9 of BFS. The inductive hypothesis holds here, because $s.d = 0 = \delta(s, s)$ and $v.d = \infty \geq \delta(s, v)$ for all $v \in V - \{s\}$.

For the inductive step, consider a white vertex v that is discovered during the search from a vertex u. The inductive hypothesis implies that $u.d \geq \delta(s, u)$. The assignment performed by line 15 and Lemma 20.1 give

$$
\begin{aligned}
v.d &= u.d + 1 \\
&\geq \delta(s, u) + 1 \\
&\geq \delta(s, v) \ .
\end{aligned}
$$

Vertex v is then enqueued, and it is never enqueued again because it is also grayed and lines 14–17 execute only for white vertices. Thus, the value of $v.d$ never changes again, and the inductive hypothesis is maintained.   ∎

To prove that $v.d = \delta(s, v)$, we first show more precisely how the queue Q operates during the course of BFS. The next lemma shows that at all times, the d values of vertices in the queue either are all the same or form a sequence $\langle k, k, \ldots, k, k+1, k+1, \ldots, k+1 \rangle$ for some integer $k \geq 0$.

Lemma 20.3
Suppose that during the execution of BFS on a graph $G = (V, E)$, the queue Q contains the vertices $\langle v_1, v_2, \ldots, v_r \rangle$, where v_1 is the head of Q and v_r is the tail. Then, $v_r.d \leq v_1.d + 1$ and $v_i.d \leq v_{i+1}.d$ for $i = 1, 2, \ldots, r - 1$.

Proof The proof is by induction on the number of queue operations. Initially, when the queue contains only s, the lemma trivially holds.

For the inductive step, we must prove that the lemma holds after both dequeuing and enqueuing a vertex. First, we examine dequeuing. When the head v_1 of the queue is dequeued, v_2 becomes the new head. (If the queue becomes empty, then the lemma holds vacuously.) By the inductive hypothesis, $v_1.d \leq v_2.d$. But then we have $v_r.d \leq v_1.d + 1 \leq v_2.d + 1$, and the remaining inequalities are unaffected. Thus, the lemma follows with v_2 as the new head.

Now, we examine enqueuing. When line 17 of BFS enqueues a vertex v onto a queue containing vertices $\langle v_1, v_2, \ldots, v_r \rangle$, the enqueued vertex becomes v_{r+1}. If the queue was empty before v was enqueued, then after enqueuing v, we have $r = 1$ and the lemma trivially holds. Now suppose that the queue was nonempty when v was enqueued. At that time, the procedure has most recently removed vertex u, whose adjacency list is currently being scanned, from the queue Q. Just before u was removed, we had $u = v_1$ and the inductive hypothesis held, so that $u.d \leq v_2.d$ and $v_r.d \leq u.d + 1$. After u is removed from the queue, the vertex that had been v_2 becomes the new head v_1 of the queue, so that now $u.d \leq v_1.d$. Thus, $v_{r+1}.d = v.d = u.d + 1 \leq v_1.d + 1$. Since $v_r.d \leq u.d + 1$, we have $v_r.d \leq u.d + 1 = v.d = v_{r+1}.d$, and the remaining inequalities are unaffected. Thus, the lemma follows when v is enqueued.   ∎

The following corollary shows that the d values at the time that vertices are enqueued monotonically increase over time.

Corollary 20.4
Suppose that vertices v_i and v_j are enqueued during the execution of BFS, and that v_i is enqueued before v_j. Then $v_i.d \leq v_j.d$ at the time that v_j is enqueued.

Proof Immediate from Lemma 20.3 and the property that each vertex receives a finite d value at most once during the course of BFS.   ∎

We can now prove that breadth-first search correctly finds shortest-path distances.

Theorem 20.5 (Correctness of breadth-first search)
Let $G = (V, E)$ be a directed or undirected graph, and suppose that BFS is run on G from a given source vertex $s \in V$. Then, during its execution, BFS discovers every vertex $v \in V$ that is reachable from the source s, and upon termination, $v.d = \delta(s, v)$ for all $v \in V$. Moreover, for any vertex $v \neq s$ that is reachable from s, one of the shortest paths from s to v is a shortest path from s to $v.\pi$ followed by the edge $(v.\pi, v)$.

Proof Assume for the purpose of contradiction that some vertex receives a d value not equal to its shortest-path distance. Of all such vertices, let v be a vertex that has the minimum $\delta(s, v)$. By Lemma 20.2, we have $v.d \geq \delta(s, v)$, and thus $v.d > \delta(s, v)$. We cannot have $v = s$, because $s.d = 0$ and $\delta(s, s) = 0$. Vertex v must be reachable from s, for otherwise we would have $\delta(s, v) = \infty \geq v.d$. Let u be the vertex immediately preceding v on some shortest path from s to v (since $v \neq s$, vertex u must exist), so that $\delta(s, v) = \delta(s, u) + 1$. Because $\delta(s, u) < \delta(s, v)$, and because of how we chose v, we have $u.d = \delta(s, u)$. Putting these properties together gives

$$v.d > \delta(s, v) = \delta(s, u) + 1 = u.d + 1 \,. \tag{20.1}$$

Now consider the time when BFS chooses to dequeue vertex u from Q in line 11. At this time, vertex v is either white, gray, or black. We shall show that each of these cases leads to a contradiction of inequality (20.1). If v is white, then line 15 sets $v.d = u.d + 1$, contradicting inequality (20.1). If v is black, then it was already removed from the queue and, by Corollary 20.4, we have $v.d \le u.d$, again contradicting inequality (20.1). If v is gray, then it was painted gray upon dequeuing some vertex w, which was removed from Q earlier than u and for which $v.d = w.d + 1$. By Corollary 20.4, however, $w.d \le u.d$, and so $v.d = w.d + 1 \le u.d + 1$, once again contradicting inequality (20.1).

Thus we conclude that $v.d = \delta(s, v)$ for all $v \in V$. All vertices v reachable from s must be discovered, for otherwise they would have $\infty = v.d > \delta(s, v)$. To conclude the proof of the theorem, observe from lines 15–16 that if $v.\pi = u$, then $v.d = u.d + 1$. Thus, to form a shortest path from s to v, take a shortest path from s to $v.\pi$ and then traverse the edge $(v.\pi, v)$. ∎

Breadth-first trees

The blue edges in Figure 20.3 show the breadth-first tree built by the BFS procedure as it searches the graph. The tree corresponds to the π attributes. More formally, for a graph $G = (V, E)$ with source s, we define the *predecessor subgraph* of G as $G_\pi = (V_\pi, E_\pi)$, where

$$V_\pi = \{v \in V : v.\pi \ne \text{NIL}\} \cup \{s\} \tag{20.2}$$

and

$$E_\pi = \{(v.\pi, v) : v \in V_\pi - \{s\}\} \,. \tag{20.3}$$

The predecessor subgraph G_π is a *breadth-first tree* if V_π consists of the vertices reachable from s and, for all $v \in V_\pi$, the subgraph G_π contains a unique simple path from s to v that is also a shortest path from s to v in G. A breadth-first tree is in fact a tree, since it is connected and $|E_\pi| = |V_\pi| - 1$ (see Theorem B.2 on page 1169). We call the edges in E_π *tree edges*.

The following lemma shows that the predecessor subgraph produced by the BFS procedure is a breadth-first tree.

Lemma 20.6
When applied to a directed or undirected graph $G = (V, E)$, procedure BFS constructs π so that the predecessor subgraph $G_\pi = (V_\pi, E_\pi)$ is a breadth-first tree.

Proof   Line 16 of BFS sets $v.\pi = u$ if and only if $(u, v) \in E$ and $\delta(s, v) < \infty$—that is, if v is reachable from s—and thus V_π consists of the vertices in V reachable from s. Since the predecessor subgraph G_π forms a tree, by Theorem B.2, it contains a unique simple path from s to each vertex in V_π. Applying Theorem 20.5 inductively yields that every such path is a shortest path in G.   ∎

The PRINT-PATH procedure prints out the vertices on a shortest path from s to v, assuming that BFS has already computed a breadth-first tree. This procedure runs in time linear in the number of vertices in the path printed, since each recursive call is for a path one vertex shorter.

PRINT-PATH(G, s, v)

1   **if** $v == s$
2   print s
3   **elseif** $v.\pi ==$ NIL
4   print "no path from" s "to" v "exists"
5   **else** PRINT-PATH$(G, s, v.\pi)$
6   print v

Exercises

20.2-1
Show the d and π values that result from running breadth-first search on the directed graph of Figure 20.2(a), using vertex 3 as the source.

20.2-2
Show the d and π values that result from running breadth-first search on the undirected graph of Figure 20.3, using vertex u as the source. Assume that neighbors of a vertex are visited in alphabetical order.

20.2-3
Show that using a single bit to store each vertex color suffices by arguing that the BFS procedure produces the same result if line 18 is removed. Then show how to obviate the need for vertex colors altogether.

20.2-4
What is the running time of BFS if we represent its input graph by an adjacency matrix and modify the algorithm to handle this form of input?

20.2-5

Argue that in a breadth-first search, the value $u.d$ assigned to a vertex u is independent of the order in which the vertices appear in each adjacency list. Using Figure 20.3 as an example, show that the breadth-first tree computed by BFS can depend on the ordering within adjacency lists.

20.2-6

Give an example of a directed graph $G = (V, E)$, a source vertex $s \in V$, and a set of tree edges $E_\pi \subseteq E$ such that for each vertex $v \in V$, the unique simple path in the graph (V, E_π) from s to v is a shortest path in G, yet the set of edges E_π cannot be produced by running BFS on G, no matter how the vertices are ordered in each adjacency list.

20.2-7

There are two types of professional wrestlers: "faces" (short for "babyfaces," i.e., "good guys") and "heels" ("bad guys"). Between any pair of professional wrestlers, there may or may not be a rivalry. You are given the names of n professional wrestlers and a list of r pairs of wrestlers for which there are rivalries. Give an $O(n + r)$-time algorithm that determines whether it is possible to designate some of the wrestlers as faces and the remainder as heels such that each rivalry is between a face and a heel. If it is possible to perform such a designation, your algorithm should produce it.

★ ***20.2-8***

The *diameter* of a tree $T = (V, E)$ is defined as $\max \{\delta(u, v) : u, v \in V\}$, that is, the largest of all shortest-path distances in the tree. Give an efficient algorithm to compute the diameter of a tree, and analyze the running time of your algorithm.

20.3 Depth-first search

As its name implies, depth-first search searches "deeper" in the graph whenever possible. Depth-first search explores edges out of the most recently discovered vertex v that still has unexplored edges leaving it. Once all of v's edges have been explored, the search "backtracks" to explore edges leaving the vertex from which v was discovered. This process continues until all vertices that are reachable from the original source vertex have been discovered. If any undiscovered vertices remain, then depth-first search selects one of them as a new source, repeating the search from that source. The algorithm repeats this entire process until it has discovered every vertex.[3]

As in breadth-first search, whenever depth-first search discovers a vertex v during a scan of the adjacency list of an already discovered vertex u, it records this event by setting v's predecessor attribute $v.\pi$ to u. Unlike breadth-first search, whose predecessor subgraph forms a tree, depth-first search produces a predecessor subgraph that might contain several trees, because the search may repeat from multiple sources. Therefore, we define the *predecessor subgraph* of a depth-first search slightly differently from that of a breadth-first search: it always includes all vertices, and it accounts for multiple sources. Specifically, for a depth-first search the predecessor subgraph is $G_\pi = (V, E_\pi)$, where

$$E_\pi = \{(v.\pi, v) : v \in V \text{ and } v.\pi \neq \text{NIL}\} \ .$$

The predecessor subgraph of a depth-first search forms a *depth-first forest* comprising several *depth-first trees*. The edges in E_π are *tree edges*.

Like breadth-first search, depth-first search colors vertices during the search to indicate their state. Each vertex is initially white, is grayed when it is *discovered* in the search, and is blackened when it is *finished*, that is, when its adjacency list has been examined completely. This technique guarantees that each vertex ends up in exactly one depth-first tree, so that these trees are disjoint.

Besides creating a depth-first forest, depth-first search also *timestamps* each vertex. Each vertex v has two timestamps: the first timestamp $v.d$ records when v is first discovered (and grayed), and the second timestamp $v.f$ records when the search finishes examining v's adjacency list (and blackens v). These timestamps provide important information about the structure of the graph and are generally helpful in reasoning about the behavior of depth-first search.

The procedure DFS on the facing page records when it discovers vertex u in the attribute $u.d$ and when it finishes vertex u in the attribute $u.f$. These timestamps are integers between 1 and $2|V|$, since there is one discovery event and one finishing event for each of the $|V|$ vertices. For every vertex u,

$$u.d < u.f \ . \tag{20.4}$$

Vertex u is WHITE before time $u.d$, GRAY between time $u.d$ and time $u.f$, and BLACK thereafter. In the DFS procedure, the input graph G may be undirected or

---

[3] It may seem arbitrary that breadth-first search is limited to only one source whereas depth-first search may search from multiple sources. Although conceptually, breadth-first search could proceed from multiple sources and depth-first search could be limited to one source, our approach reflects how the results of these searches are typically used. Breadth-first search usually serves to find shortest-path distances and the associated predecessor subgraph from a given source. Depth-first search is often a subroutine in another algorithm, as we'll see later in this chapter.

directed. The variable *time* is a global variable used for timestamping. Figure 20.4 illustrates the progress of DFS on the graph shown in Figure 20.2 (but with vertices labeled by letters rather than numbers).

DFS(*G*)

```
1   for each vertex u ∈ G.V
2       u.color = WHITE
3       u.π = NIL
4   time = 0
5   for each vertex u ∈ G.V
6       if u.color == WHITE
7           DFS-VISIT(G, u)
```

DFS-VISIT(*G*, *u*)

```
1    time = time + 1              // white vertex u has just been discovered
2    u.d = time
3    u.color = GRAY
4    for each vertex v in G.Adj[u]   // explore each edge (u, v)
5        if v.color == WHITE
6            v.π = u
7            DFS-VISIT(G, v)
8    time = time + 1
9    u.f = time
10   u.color = BLACK              // blacken u; it is finished
```

The DFS procedure works as follows. Lines 1–3 paint all vertices white and initialize their π attributes to NIL. Line 4 resets the global time counter. Lines 5–7 check each vertex in V in turn and, when a white vertex is found, visit it by calling DFS-VISIT. Upon every call of DFS-VISIT(*G*, *u*) in line 7, vertex *u* becomes the root of a new tree in the depth-first forest. When DFS returns, every vertex *u* has been assigned a *discovery time u.d* and a *finish time u.f*.

In each call DFS-VISIT(*G*, *u*), vertex *u* is initially white. Lines 1–3 increment the global variable *time*, record the new value of *time* as the discovery time *u.d*, and paint *u* gray. Lines 4–7 examine each vertex *v* adjacent to *u* and recursively visit *v* if it is white. As line 4 considers each vertex $v \in Adj[u]$, the depth-first search *explores* edge (*u*, *v*). Finally, after every edge leaving *u* has been explored, lines 8–10 increment *time*, record the finish time in *u.f*, and paint *u* black.

The results of depth-first search may depend upon the order in which line 5 of DFS examines the vertices and upon the order in which line 4 of DFS-VISIT visits the neighbors of a vertex. These different visitation orders tend not to cause

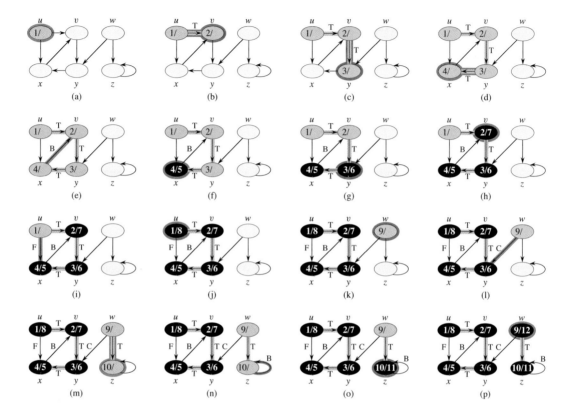

Figure 20.4 The progress of the depth-first-search algorithm DFS on a directed graph. Edges are classified as they are explored: tree edges are labeled T, back edges B, forward edges F, and cross edges C. Timestamps within vertices indicate discovery time/finish times. Tree edges are highlighted in blue. Orange highlights indicate vertices whose discovery or finish times change and edges that are explored in each step.

problems in practice, because many applications of depth-first search can use the result from any depth-first search.

What is the running time of DFS? The loops on lines 1–3 and lines 5–7 of DFS take $\Theta(V)$ time, exclusive of the time to execute the calls to DFS-VISIT. As we did for breadth-first search, we use aggregate analysis. The procedure DFS-VISIT is called exactly once for each vertex $v \in V$, since the vertex u on which DFS-VISIT is invoked must be white and the first thing DFS-VISIT does is paint vertex u gray. During an execution of DFS-VISIT(G, v), the loop in lines 4–7 executes $|Adj[v]|$ times. Since $\sum_{v \in V} |Adj[v]| = \Theta(E)$ and DFS-VISIT is called once per vertex, the total cost of executing lines 4–7 of DFS-VISIT is $\Theta(V + E)$. The running time of DFS is therefore $\Theta(V + E)$.

Properties of depth-first search

Depth-first search yields valuable information about the structure of a graph. Perhaps the most basic property of depth-first search is that the predecessor subgraph G_π does indeed form a forest of trees, since the structure of the depth-first trees exactly mirrors the structure of recursive calls of DFS-VISIT. That is, $u = v.\pi$ if and only if DFS-VISIT(G, v) was called during a search of u's adjacency list. Additionally, vertex v is a descendant of vertex u in the depth-first forest if and only if v is discovered during the time in which u is gray.

Another important property of depth-first search is that discovery and finish times have *parenthesis structure*. If the DFS-VISIT procedure were to print a left parenthesis "$(u$" when it discovers vertex u and to print a right parenthesis "$u)$" when it finishes u, then the printed expression would be well formed in the sense that the parentheses are properly nested. For example, the depth-first search of Figure 20.5(a) corresponds to the parenthesization shown in Figure 20.5(b). The following theorem provides another way to characterize the parenthesis structure.

Theorem 20.7 (Parenthesis theorem)
In any depth-first search of a (directed or undirected) graph $G = (V, E)$, for any two vertices u and v, exactly one of the following three conditions holds:

- the intervals $[u.d, u.f]$ and $[v.d, v.f]$ are entirely disjoint, and neither u nor v is a descendant of the other in the depth-first forest,

- the interval $[u.d, u.f]$ is contained entirely within the interval $[v.d, v.f]$, and u is a descendant of v in a depth-first tree, or

- the interval $[v.d, v.f]$ is contained entirely within the interval $[u.d, u.f]$, and v is a descendant of u in a depth-first tree.

Proof We begin with the case in which $u.d < v.d$. We consider two subcases, according to whether $v.d < u.f$. The first subcase occurs when $v.d < u.f$, so that v was discovered while u was still gray, which implies that v is a descendant of u. Moreover, since v was discovered after u, all of its outgoing edges are explored, and v is finished, before the search returns to and finishes u. In this case, therefore, the interval $[v.d, v.f]$ is entirely contained within the interval $[u.d, u.f]$. In the other subcase, $u.f < v.d$, and by inequality (20.4), $u.d < u.f < v.d < v.f$, and thus the intervals $[u.d, u.f]$ and $[v.d, v.f]$ are disjoint. Because the intervals are disjoint, neither vertex was discovered while the other was gray, and so neither vertex is a descendant of the other.

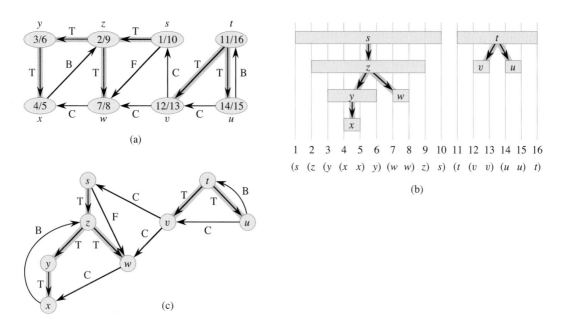

Figure 20.5 Properties of depth-first search. **(a)** The result of a depth-first search of a directed graph. Vertices are timestamped and edge types are indicated as in Figure 20.4. **(b)** Intervals for the discovery time and finish time of each vertex correspond to the parenthesization shown. Each rectangle spans the interval given by the discovery and finish times of the corresponding vertex. Only tree edges are shown. If two intervals overlap, then one is nested within the other, and the vertex corresponding to the smaller interval is a descendant of the vertex corresponding to the larger. **(c)** The graph of part (a) redrawn with all tree and forward edges going down within a depth-first tree and all back edges going up from a descendant to an ancestor.

The case in which $v.d < u.d$ is similar, with the roles of u and v reversed in the above argument. ∎

Corollary 20.8 (*Nesting of descendants' intervals*)
Vertex v is a proper descendant of vertex u in the depth-first forest for a (directed or undirected) graph G if and only if $u.d < v.d < v.f < u.f$.

Proof   Immediate from Theorem 20.7. ∎

The next theorem gives another important characterization of when one vertex is a descendant of another in the depth-first forest.

Theorem 20.9 (White-path theorem)
In a depth-first forest of a (directed or undirected) graph $G = (V, E)$, vertex v is a descendant of vertex u if and only if at the time $u.d$ that the search discovers u, there is a path from u to v consisting entirely of white vertices.

Proof   ⟹: If $v = u$, then the path from u to v contains just vertex u, which is still white when $u.d$ receives a value. Now, suppose that v is a proper descendant of u in the depth-first forest. By Corollary 20.8, $u.d < v.d$, and so v is white at time $u.d$. Since v can be any descendant of u, all vertices on the unique simple path from u to v in the depth-first forest are white at time $u.d$.

⟸: Suppose that there is a path of white vertices from u to v at time $u.d$, but v does not become a descendant of u in the depth-first tree. Without loss of generality, assume that every vertex other than v along the path becomes a descendant of u. (Otherwise, let v be the closest vertex to u along the path that doesn't become a descendant of u.) Let w be the predecessor of v in the path, so that w is a descendant of u (w and u may in fact be the same vertex). By Corollary 20.8, $w.f \leq u.f$. Because v must be discovered after u is discovered, but before w is finished, $u.d < v.d < w.f \leq u.f$. Theorem 20.7 then implies that the interval $[v.d, v.f]$ is contained entirely within the interval $[u.d, u.f]$. By Corollary 20.8, v must after all be a descendant of u.   ∎

Classification of edges

You can obtain important information about a graph by classifying its edges during a depth-first search. For example, Section 20.4 will show that a directed graph is acyclic if and only if a depth-first search yields no "back" edges (Lemma 20.11).

The depth-first forest G_π produced by a depth-first search on graph G can contain four types of edges:

1. *Tree edges* are edges in the depth-first forest G_π. Edge (u, v) is a tree edge if v was first discovered by exploring edge (u, v).

2. *Back edges* are those edges (u, v) connecting a vertex u to an ancestor v in a depth-first tree. We consider self-loops, which may occur in directed graphs, to be back edges.

3. *Forward edges* are those nontree edges (u, v) connecting a vertex u to a proper descendant v in a depth-first tree.

4. *Cross edges* are all other edges. They can go between vertices in the same depth-first tree, as long as one vertex is not an ancestor of the other, or they can go between vertices in different depth-first trees.

In Figures 20.4 and 20.5, edge labels indicate edge types. Figure 20.5(c) also shows how to redraw the graph of Figure 20.5(a) so that all tree and forward edges head downward in a depth-first tree and all back edges go up. You can redraw any graph in this fashion.

The DFS algorithm has enough information to classify some edges as it encounters them. The key idea is that when an edge (u, v) is first explored, the color of vertex v says something about the edge:

1. WHITE indicates a tree edge,

2. GRAY indicates a back edge, and

3. BLACK indicates a forward or cross edge.

The first case is immediate from the specification of the algorithm. For the second case, observe that the gray vertices always form a linear chain of descendants corresponding to the stack of active DFS-VISIT invocations. The number of gray vertices is 1 more than the depth in the depth-first forest of the vertex most recently discovered. Depth-first search always explores from the deepest gray vertex, so that an edge that reaches another gray vertex has reached an ancestor. The third case handles the remaining possibility. Exercise 20.3-5 asks you to show that such an edge (u, v) is a forward edge if $u.d < v.d$ and a cross edge if $u.d > v.d$.

According to the following theorem, forward and cross edges never occur in a depth-first search of an undirected graph.

Theorem 20.10
In a depth-first search of an undirected graph G, every edge of G is either a tree edge or a back edge.

Proof   Let (u, v) be an arbitrary edge of G, and suppose without loss of generality that $u.d < v.d$. Then, while u is gray, the search must discover and finish v before it finishes u, since v is on u's adjacency list. If the first time that the search explores edge (u, v), it is in the direction from u to v, then v is undiscovered (white) until that time, for otherwise the search would have explored this edge already in the direction from v to u. Thus, (u, v) becomes a tree edge. If the search explores (u, v) first in the direction from v to u, then (u, v) is a back edge, since there must be a path of tree edges from u to v.   ∎

Since (u, v) and (v, u) are really the same edge in an undirected graph, the proof of Theorem 20.10 says how to classify the edge. When searching from a vertex, which must be gray, if the adjacent vertex is white, then the edge is a tree edge. Otherwise, the edge is a back edge.

The next two sections apply the above theorems about depth-first search.

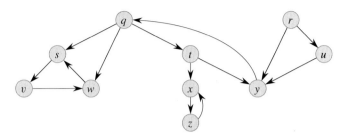

Figure 20.6 A directed graph for use in Exercises 20.3-2 and 20.5-2.

Exercises

20.3-1
Make a 3-by-3 chart with row and column labels WHITE, GRAY, and BLACK. In each cell (i, j), indicate whether, at any point during a depth-first search of a directed graph, there can be an edge from a vertex of color i to a vertex of color j. For each possible edge, indicate what edge types it can be. Make a second such chart for depth-first search of an undirected graph.

20.3-2
Show how depth-first search works on the graph of Figure 20.6. Assume that the **for** loop of lines 5–7 of the DFS procedure considers the vertices in alphabetical order, and assume that each adjacency list is ordered alphabetically. Show the discovery and finish times for each vertex, and show the classification of each edge.

20.3-3
Show the parenthesis structure of the depth-first search of Figure 20.4.

20.3-4
Show that using a single bit to store each vertex color suffices by arguing that the DFS procedure produces the same result if line 10 of DFS-VISIT is removed.

20.3-5
Show that in a directed graph, edge (u, v) is

a. a tree edge or forward edge if and only if $u.d < v.d < v.f < u.f$,

b. a back edge if and only if $v.d \le u.d < u.f \le v.f$, and

c. a cross edge if and only if $v.d < v.f < u.d < u.f$.

20.3-6
Rewrite the procedure DFS, using a stack to eliminate recursion.

20.3-7
Give a counterexample to the conjecture that if a directed graph G contains a path from u to v, and if $u.d < v.d$ in a depth-first search of G, then v is a descendant of u in the depth-first forest produced.

20.3-8
Give a counterexample to the conjecture that if a directed graph G contains a path from u to v, then any depth-first search must result in $v.d \leq u.f$.

20.3-9
Modify the pseudocode for depth-first search so that it prints out every edge in the directed graph G, together with its type. Show what modifications, if any, you need to make if G is undirected.

20.3-10
Explain how a vertex u of a directed graph can end up in a depth-first tree containing only u, even though u has both incoming and outgoing edges in G.

20.3-11
Let $G = (V, E)$ be a connected, undirected graph. Give an $O(V + E)$-time algorithm to compute a path in G that traverses each edge in E exactly once in each direction. Describe how you can find your way out of a maze if you are given a large supply of pennies.

20.3-12
Show how to use a depth-first search of an undirected graph G to identify the connected components of G, so that the depth-first forest contains as many trees as G has connected components. More precisely, show how to modify depth-first search so that it assigns to each vertex v an integer label $v.cc$ between 1 and k, where k is the number of connected components of G, such that $u.cc = v.cc$ if and only if u and v belong to the same connected component.

★ ***20.3-13***
A directed graph $G = (V, E)$ is *singly connected* if $u \rightsquigarrow v$ implies that G contains at most one simple path from u to v for all vertices $u, v \in V$. Give an efficient algorithm to determine whether a directed graph is singly connected.

20.4   Topological sort

This section shows how to use depth-first search to perform a topological sort of a directed acyclic graph, or a "dag" as it is sometimes called. A *topological sort* of a dag $G = (V, E)$ is a linear ordering of all its vertices such that if G contains an edge (u, v), then u appears before v in the ordering. Topological sorting is defined only on directed graphs that are acyclic; no linear ordering is possible when a directed graph contains a cycle. Think of a topological sort of a graph as an ordering of its vertices along a horizontal line so that all directed edges go from left to right. Topological sorting is thus different from the usual kind of "sorting" studied in Part II.

Many applications use directed acyclic graphs to indicate precedences among events. Figure 20.7 gives an example that arises when Professor Bumstead gets dressed in the morning. The professor must don certain garments before others (e.g., socks before shoes). Other items may be put on in any order (e.g., socks and pants). A directed edge (u, v) in the dag of Figure 20.7(a) indicates that garment u must be donned before garment v. A topological sort of this dag therefore gives a possible order for getting dressed. Figure 20.7(b) shows the topologically sorted dag as an ordering of vertices along a horizontal line such that all directed edges go from left to right.

The procedure TOPOLOGICAL-SORT topologically sorts a dag. Figure 20.7(b) shows how the topologically sorted vertices appear in reverse order of their finish times.

TOPOLOGICAL-SORT(G)

1   call DFS(G) to compute finish times $v.f$ for each vertex v
2   as each vertex is finished, insert it onto the front of a linked list
3   **return** the linked list of vertices

The TOPOLOGICAL-SORT procedure runs in $\Theta(V + E)$ time, since depth-first search takes $\Theta(V + E)$ time and it takes $O(1)$ time to insert each of the $|V|$ vertices onto the front of the linked list.

To prove the correctness of this remarkably simple and efficient algorithm, we start with the following key lemma characterizing directed acyclic graphs.

Lemma 20.11
A directed graph G is acyclic if and only if a depth-first search of G yields no back edges.

(a)

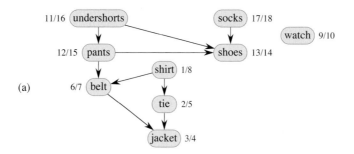

(b)

Figure 20.7   **(a)** Professor Bumstead topologically sorts his clothing when getting dressed. Each directed edge (u, v) means that garment u must be put on before garment v. The discovery and finish times from a depth-first search are shown next to each vertex. **(b)** The same graph shown topologically sorted, with its vertices arranged from left to right in order of decreasing finish time. All directed edges go from left to right.

Proof   ⇒: Suppose that a depth-first search produces a back edge (u, v). Then vertex v is an ancestor of vertex u in the depth-first forest. Thus, G contains a path from v to u, and the back edge (u, v) completes a cycle.

⇐: Suppose that G contains a cycle c. We show that a depth-first search of G yields a back edge. Let v be the first vertex to be discovered in c, and let (u, v) be the preceding edge in c. At time $v.d$, the vertices of c form a path of white vertices from v to u. By the white-path theorem, vertex u becomes a descendant of v in the depth-first forest. Therefore, (u, v) is a back edge.   ■

Theorem 20.12

Topological-Sort produces a topological sort of the directed acyclic graph provided as its input.

Proof   Suppose that DFS is run on a given dag $G = (V, E)$ to determine finish times for its vertices. It suffices to show that for any pair of distinct vertices $u, v \in V$, if G contains an edge from u to v, then $v.f < u.f$. Consider any edge (u, v) explored by DFS(G). When this edge is explored, v cannot be gray, since then v would be an ancestor of u and (u, v) would be a back edge, contradicting Lemma 20.11. Therefore, v must be either white or black. If v is

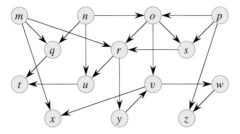

Figure 20.8   A dag for topological sorting.

white, it becomes a descendant of u, and so $v.f < u.f$. If v is black, it has already been finished, so that $v.f$ has already been set. Because the search is still exploring from u, it has yet to assign a timestamp to $u.f$, so that the timestamp eventually assigned to $u.f$ is greater than $v.f$. Thus, $v.f < u.f$ for any edge (u, v) in the dag, proving the theorem.   ∎

Exercises

20.4-1
Show the ordering of vertices produced by TOPOLOGICAL-SORT when it is run on the dag of Figure 20.8. Assume that the **for** loop of lines 5–7 of the DFS procedure considers the vertices in alphabetical order, and assume that each adjacency list is ordered alphabetically.

20.4-2
Give a linear-time algorithm that, given a directed acyclic graph $G = (V, E)$ and two vertices $a, b \in V$, returns the number of simple paths from a to b in G. For example, the directed acyclic graph of Figure 20.8 contains exactly four simple paths from vertex p to vertex v: $\langle p, o, v \rangle$, $\langle p, o, r, y, v \rangle$, $\langle p, o, s, r, y, v \rangle$, and $\langle p, s, r, y, v \rangle$. Your algorithm needs only to count the simple paths, not list them.

20.4-3
Give an algorithm that determines whether an undirected graph $G = (V, E)$ contains a simple cycle. Your algorithm should run in $O(V)$ time, independent of $|E|$.

20.4-4
Prove or disprove: If a directed graph G contains cycles, then the vertex ordering produced by TOPOLOGICAL-SORT(G) minimizes the number of "bad" edges that are inconsistent with the ordering produced.

20.4-5
Another way to topologically sort a directed acyclic graph $G = (V, E)$ is to repeatedly find a vertex of in-degree 0, output it, and remove it and all of its outgoing edges from the graph. Explain how to implement this idea so that it runs in
time $O(V + E)$. What happens to this algorithm if G has cycles?

20.5   Strongly connected components

We now consider a classic application of depth-first search: decomposing a directed graph into its strongly connected components. This section shows how to do
so using two depth-first searches. Many algorithms that work with directed graphs
begin with such a decomposition. After decomposing the graph into strongly connected components, such algorithms run separately on each one and then combine
the solutions according to the structure of connections among components.

Recall from Appendix B that a strongly connected component of a directed
graph $G = (V, E)$ is a maximal set of vertices $C \subseteq V$ such that for every pair
of vertices $u, v \in C$, both $u \rightsquigarrow v$ and $v \rightsquigarrow u$, that is, vertices u and v are reachable
from each other. Figure 20.9 shows an example.

The algorithm for finding the strongly connected components of a directed graph
$G = (V, E)$ uses the transpose of G, which we defined in Exercise 20.1-3 to be
the graph $G^{\mathrm{T}} = (V, E^{\mathrm{T}})$, where $E^{\mathrm{T}} = \{(u, v) : (v, u) \in E\}$. That is, E^{T} consists
of the edges of G with their directions reversed. Given an adjacency-list repre-
sentation of G, the time to create G^{T} is $\Theta(V + E)$. The graphs G and G^{T} have
exactly the same strongly connected components: u and v are reachable from each
other in G if and only if they are reachable from each other in G^{T}. Figure 20.9(b)
shows the transpose of the graph in Figure 20.9(a), with the strongly connected
components shaded blue in both parts.

The linear-time (i.e., $\Theta(V + E)$-time) procedure STRONGLY-CONNECTED-
COMPONENTS on the next page computes the strongly connected components of
a directed graph $G = (V, E)$ using two depth-first searches, one on G and one
on G^{T}.

The idea behind this algorithm comes from a key property of the *component
graph* $G^{\mathrm{SCC}} = (V^{\mathrm{SCC}}, E^{\mathrm{SCC}})$, defined as follows. Suppose that G has strongly
connected components $C_1, C_2, \ldots, C_k$. The vertex set V^{SCC} is $\{v_1, v_2, \ldots, v_k\}$,
and it contains one vertex v_i for each strongly connected component C_i of G.
There is an edge $(v_i, v_j) \in E^{\mathrm{SCC}}$ if G contains a directed edge (x, y) for some
$x \in C_i$ and some $y \in C_j$. Looked at another way, if we contract all edges whose
incident vertices are within the same strongly connected component of G so that

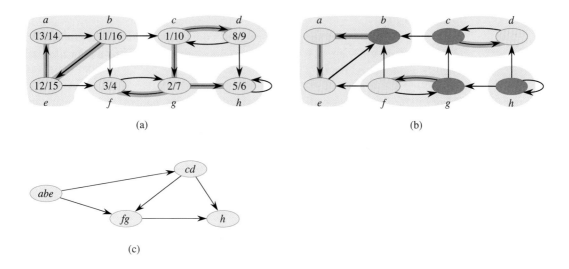

(a)   (b)

(c)

Figure 20.9 **(a)** A directed graph G. Each region shaded light blue is a strongly connected component of G. Each vertex is labeled with its discovery and finish times in a depth-first search, and tree edges are dark blue. **(b)** The graph G^{T}, the transpose of G, with the depth-first forest computed in line 3 of STRONGLY-CONNECTED-COMPONENTS shown and tree edges shaded dark blue. Each strongly connected component corresponds to one depth-first tree. Orange vertices b, c, g, and h are the roots of the depth-first trees produced by the depth-first search of G^{T}. **(c)** The acyclic component graph G^{SCC} obtained by contracting all edges within each strongly connected component of G so that only a single vertex remains in each component.

STRONGLY-CONNECTED-COMPONENTS(G)

1   call DFS(G) to compute finish times $u.f$ for each vertex u
2   create G^{T}
3   call DFS(G^{T}), but in the main loop of DFS, consider the vertices
     in order of decreasing $u.f$ (as computed in line 1)
4   output the vertices of each tree in the depth-first forest formed in line 3 as a
     separate strongly connected component

---

only a single vertex remains, the resulting graph is G^{SCC}. Figure 20.9(c) shows the component graph of the graph in Figure 20.9(a).

The following lemma gives the key property that the component graph is acyclic. We'll see that the algorithm uses this property to visit the vertices of the component graph in topologically sorted order, by considering vertices in the second depth-first search in decreasing order of the finish times that were computed in the first depth-first search.

Lemma 20.13

Let C and C' be distinct strongly connected components in directed graph $G = (V, E)$, let $u, v \in C$, let $u', v' \in C'$, and suppose that G contains a path $u \rightsquigarrow u'$. Then G cannot also contain a path $v' \rightsquigarrow v$.

Proof If G contains a path $v' \rightsquigarrow v$, then it contains paths $u \rightsquigarrow u' \rightsquigarrow v'$ and $v' \rightsquigarrow v \rightsquigarrow u$. Thus, u and v' are reachable from each other, thereby contradicting the assumption that C and C' are distinct strongly connected components.   ∎

Because the STRONGLY-CONNECTED-COMPONENTS procedure performs two depth-first searches, there are two distinct sets of discovery and finish times. In this section, discovery and finish times always refer to those computed by the *first* call of DFS, in line 1.

The notation for discovery and finish times extends to sets of vertices. For a subset U of vertices, $d(U)$ and $f(U)$ are the earliest discovery time and latest finish time, respectively, of any vertex in U: $d(U) = \min\{u.d : u \in U\}$ and $f(U) = \max\{u.f : u \in U\}$.

The following lemma and its corollary give a key property relating strongly connected components and finish times in the first depth-first search.

Lemma 20.14

Let C and C' be distinct strongly connected components in directed graph $G = (V, E)$. Suppose that there is an edge $(u, v) \in E$, where $u \in C'$ and $v \in C$. Then $f(C') > f(C)$.

Proof We consider two cases, depending on which strongly connected component, C or C', had the first discovered vertex during the first depth-first search.

If $d(C') < d(C)$, let x be the first vertex discovered in C'. At time $x.d$, all vertices in C and C' are white. At that time, G contains a path from x to each vertex in C' consisting only of white vertices. Because $(u, v) \in E$, for any vertex $w \in C$, there is also a path in G at time $x.d$ from x to w consisting only of white vertices: $x \rightsquigarrow u \rightarrow v \rightsquigarrow w$. By the white-path theorem, all vertices in C and C' become descendants of x in the depth-first tree. By Corollary 20.8, x has the latest finish time of any of its descendants, and so $x.f = f(C') > f(C)$.

Otherwise, $d(C') > d(C)$. Let y be the first vertex discovered in C, so that $y.d = d(C)$. At time $y.d$, all vertices in C are white and G contains a path from y to each vertex in C consisting only of white vertices. By the white-path theorem, all vertices in C become descendants of y in the depth-first tree, and by Corollary 20.8, $y.f = f(C)$. Because $d(C') > d(C) = y.d$, all vertices in C' are white at time $y.d$. Since there is an edge (u, v) from C' to C, Lemma 20.13 implies that there cannot be a path from C to C'. Hence, no vertex in C' is reachable from y. At time $y.f$, therefore, all vertices in C' are still white. Thus, for any vertex $w \in C'$, we have $w.f > y.f$, which implies that $f(C') > f(C)$. ∎

Corollary 20.15

Let C and C' be distinct strongly connected components in directed graph $G = (V, E)$, and suppose that $f(C) > f(C')$. Then E^{T} contains no edge (v, u) such that $u \in C'$ and $v \in C$.

Proof   The contrapositive of Lemma 20.14 says that if $f(C') < f(C)$, then there is no edge $(u, v) \in E$ such that $u \in C'$ and $v \in C$. Because the strongly connected components of G and G^{T} are the same, if there is no such edge $(u, v) \in E$, then there is no edge $(v, u) \in E^{\mathrm{T}}$ such that $u \in C'$ and $v \in C$. ∎

Corollary 20.15 provides the key to understanding why the strongly connected components algorithm works. Let's examine what happens during the second depth-first search, which is on G^{T}. The search starts from the vertex x whose finish time from the first depth-first search is maximum. This vertex belongs to some strongly connected component C, and since $x.f$ is maximum, $f(C)$ is maximum over all strongly connected components. When the search starts from x, it visits all vertices in C. By Corollary 20.15, G^{T} contains no edges from C to any other strongly connected component, and so the search from x never visits vertices in any other component. Thus, the tree rooted at x contains exactly the vertices of C. Having completed visiting all vertices in C, the second depth-first search selects as a new root a vertex from some other strongly connected component C' whose finish time $f(C')$ is maximum over all components other than C. Again, the search visits all vertices in C'. But by Corollary 20.15, if any edges in G^{T} go from C' to any other component, they must go to C, which the second depth-first search has already visited. In general, when the depth-first search of G^{T} in line 3 visits any strongly connected component, any edges out of that component must be to components that the search has already visited. Each depth-first tree, therefore, corresponds to exactly one strongly connected component. The following theorem formalizes this argument.

Theorem 20.16

The STRONGLY-CONNECTED-COMPONENTS procedure correctly computes the strongly connected components of the directed graph G provided as its input.

Proof   We argue by induction on the number of depth-first trees found in the depth-first search of G^{T} in line 3 that the vertices of each tree form a strongly connected component. The inductive hypothesis is that the first k trees produced in line 3 are strongly connected components. The basis for the induction, when $k = 0$, is trivial.

In the inductive step, we assume that each of the first k depth-first trees produced in line 3 is a strongly connected component, and we consider the $(k + 1)$st tree produced. Let the root of this tree be vertex u, and let u be in strongly connected component C. Because of how the depth-first search chooses roots in line 3, $u.f = f(C) > f(C')$ for any strongly connected component C' other than C that has yet to be visited. By the inductive hypothesis, at the time that the search visits u, all other vertices of C are white. By the white-path theorem, therefore, all other vertices of C are descendants of u in its depth-first tree. Moreover, by the inductive hypothesis and by Corollary 20.15, any edges in G^T that leave C must be to strongly connected components that have already been visited. Thus, no vertex in any strongly connected component other than C is a descendant of u during the depth-first search of G^T. The vertices of the depth-first tree in G^T that is rooted at u form exactly one strongly connected component, which completes the inductive step and the proof.   ■

Here is another way to look at how the second depth-first search operates. Consider the component graph $(G^\mathrm{T})^\mathrm{SCC}$ of G^T. If you map each strongly connected component visited in the second depth-first search to a vertex of $(G^\mathrm{T})^\mathrm{SCC}$, the second depth-first search visits vertices of $(G^\mathrm{T})^\mathrm{SCC}$ in the reverse of a topologically sorted order. If you reverse the edges of $(G^\mathrm{T})^\mathrm{SCC}$, you get the graph $((G^\mathrm{T})^\mathrm{SCC})^\mathrm{T}$. Because $((G^\mathrm{T})^\mathrm{SCC})^\mathrm{T} = G^\mathrm{SCC}$ (see Exercise 20.5-4), the second depth-first search visits the vertices of G^SCC in topologically sorted order.

Exercises

20.5-1
How can the number of strongly connected components of a graph change if a new edge is added?

20.5-2
Show how the procedure Strongly-Connected-Components works on the graph of Figure 20.6. Specifically, show the finish times computed in line 1 and the forest produced in line 3. Assume that the loop of lines 5–7 of DFS considers vertices in alphabetical order and that the adjacency lists are in alphabetical order.

20.5-3
Professor Bacon rewrites the algorithm for strongly connected components to use the original (instead of the transpose) graph in the second depth-first search and

scan the vertices in order of *increasing* finish times. Does this modified algorithm always produce correct results?

20.5-4
Prove that for any directed graph G, the transpose of the component graph of G^{T} is the same as the component graph of G. That is, $((G^{\mathrm{T}})^{\mathrm{SCC}})^{\mathrm{T}} = G^{\mathrm{SCC}}$.

20.5-5
Give an $O(V + E)$-time algorithm to compute the component graph of a directed graph $G = (V, E)$. Make sure that there is at most one edge between two vertices in the component graph your algorithm produces.

20.5-6
Give an $O(V + E)$-time algorithm that, given a directed graph $G = (V, E)$, constructs another graph $G' = (V, E')$ such that G and G' have the same strongly connected components, G' has the same component graph as G, and $|E'|$ is as small as possible.

20.5-7
A directed graph $G = (V, E)$ is *semiconnected* if, for all pairs of vertices $u, v \in V$, we have $u \rightsquigarrow v$ or $v \rightsquigarrow u$. Give an efficient algorithm to determine whether G is semiconnected. Prove that your algorithm is correct, and analyze its running time.

20.5-8
Let $G = (V, E)$ be a directed graph, and let $l : V \to \mathbb{R}$ be a function that assigns a real-valued label l to each vertex. For vertices $s, t \in V$, define

$$\Delta l(s, t) = \begin{cases} l(t) - l(s) & \text{if there is a path from } s \text{ to } t \text{ in } G, \\ -\infty & \text{otherwise .} \end{cases}$$

Give an $O(V + E)$-time algorithm to find vertices s and t such that $\Delta l(s, t)$ is maximum over all pairs of vertices. (*Hint:* Use Exercise 20.5-5.)

Problems

20-1 *Classifying edges by breadth-first search*
A depth-first forest classifies the edges of a graph into tree, back, forward, and cross edges. A breadth-first tree can also be used to classify the edges reachable from the source of the search into the same four categories.

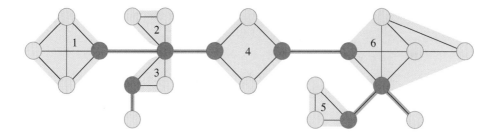

Figure 20.10 The articulation points, bridges, and biconnected components of a connected, undirected graph for use in Problem 20-2. The articulation points are the orange vertices, the bridges are the dark blue edges, and the biconnected components are the edges in the light blue regions, with a *bcc* numbering shown.

a. Prove that in a breadth-first search of an undirected graph, the following properties hold:

1. There are no back edges and no forward edges.
2. If (u, v) is a tree edge, then $v.d = u.d + 1$.
3. If (u, v) is a cross edge, then $v.d = u.d$ or $v.d = u.d + 1$.

b. Prove that in a breadth-first search of a directed graph, the following properties hold:

1. There are no forward edges.
2. If (u, v) is a tree edge, then $v.d = u.d + 1$.
3. If (u, v) is a cross edge, then $v.d \leq u.d + 1$.
4. If (u, v) is a back edge, then $0 \leq v.d \leq u.d$.

20-2   *Articulation points, bridges, and biconnected components*

Let $G = (V, E)$ be a connected, undirected graph. An *articulation point* of G is a vertex whose removal disconnects G. A *bridge* of G is an edge whose removal disconnects G. A *biconnected component* of G is a maximal set of edges such that any two edges in the set lie on a common simple cycle. Figure 20.10 illustrates these definitions. You can determine articulation points, bridges, and biconnected components using depth-first search. Let $G_\pi = (V, E_\pi)$ be a depth-first tree of G.

a. Prove that the root of G_π is an articulation point of G if and only if it has at least two children in G_π.

b. Let v be a nonroot vertex of G_π. Prove that v is an articulation point of G if and only if v has a child s such that there is no back edge from s or any descendant of s to a proper ancestor of v.

c. Let

$$v.low = \min \begin{cases} v.d\,, \\ w.d : (u, w) \text{ is a back edge for some descendant } u \text{ of } v\,. \end{cases}$$

Show how to compute $v.low$ for all vertices $v \in V$ in $O(E)$ time.

d. Show how to compute all articulation points in $O(E)$ time.

e. Prove that an edge of G is a bridge if and only if it does not lie on any simple cycle of G.

f. Show how to compute all the bridges of G in $O(E)$ time.

g. Prove that the biconnected components of G partition the nonbridge edges of G.

h. Give an $O(E)$-time algorithm to label each edge e of G with a positive integer $e.bcc$ such that $e.bcc = e'.bcc$ if and only if e and e' belong to the same biconnected component.

20-3 Euler tour

An *Euler tour* of a strongly connected, directed graph $G = (V, E)$ is a cycle that traverses each edge of G exactly once, although it may visit a vertex more than once.

a. Show that G has an Euler tour if and only if in-degree$(v) =$ out-degree(v) for each vertex $v \in V$.

b. Describe an $O(E)$-time algorithm to find an Euler tour of G if one exists. (*Hint:* Merge edge-disjoint cycles.)

20-4 Reachability

Let $G = (V, E)$ be a directed graph in which each vertex $u \in V$ is labeled with a unique integer $L(u)$ from the set $\{1, 2, \ldots, |V|\}$. For each vertex $u \in V$, let $R(u) = \{v \in V : u \rightsquigarrow v\}$ be the set of vertices that are reachable from u. Define $\min(u)$ to be the vertex in $R(u)$ whose label is minimum, that is, $\min(u)$ is the vertex v such that $L(v) = \min\{L(w) : w \in R(u)\}$. Give an $O(V + E)$-time algorithm that computes $\min(u)$ for all vertices $u \in V$.

20-5   Inserting and querying vertices in planar graphs

A *planar* graph is an undirected graph that can be drawn in the plane with no edges crossing. Euler proved that every planar graph has $|E| < 3|V|$.

Consider the following two operations on a planar graph G:

- INSERT$(G, v, \textit{neighbors})$ inserts a new vertex v into G, where *neighbors* is an array (possibly empty) of vertices that have already been inserted into G and will become all the neighbors of v in G when v is inserted.

- NEWEST-NEIGHBOR(G, v) returns the neighbor of vertex v that was most recently inserted into G, or NIL if v has no neighbors.

Design a data structure that supports these two operations such that NEWEST-NEIGHBOR takes $O(1)$ worst-case time and INSERT takes $O(1)$ amortized time. Note that the length of the array *neighbors* given to INSERT may vary. (*Hint:* Use a potential function for the amortized analysis.)

Chapter notes

Even [137] and Tarjan [429] are excellent references for graph algorithms.

Breadth-first search was discovered by Moore [334] in the context of finding paths through mazes. Lee [280] independently discovered the same algorithm in the context of routing wires on circuit boards.

Hopcroft and Tarjan [226] advocated the use of the adjacency-list representation over the adjacency-matrix representation for sparse graphs and were the first to recognize the algorithmic importance of depth-first search. Depth-first search has been widely used since the late 1950s, especially in artificial intelligence programs.

Tarjan [426] gave a linear-time algorithm for finding strongly connected components. The algorithm for strongly connected components in Section 20.5 is adapted from Aho, Hopcroft, and Ullman [6], who credit it to S. R. Kosaraju (unpublished) and Sharir [408]. Dijkstra [117, Chapter 25] also developed an algorithm for strongly connected components that is based on contracting cycles. Subsequently, Gabow [163] rediscovered this algorithm. Knuth [259] was the first to give a linear-time algorithm for topological sorting.

21   Minimum Spanning Trees

Electronic circuit designs often need to make the pins of several components electrically equivalent by wiring them together. To interconnect a set of n pins, the designer can use an arrangement of $n - 1$ wires, each connecting two pins. Of all such arrangements, the one that uses the least amount of wire is usually the most desirable.

To model this wiring problem, use a connected, undirected graph $G = (V, E)$, where V is the set of pins, E is the set of possible interconnections between pairs of pins, and for each edge $(u, v) \in E$, a weight $w(u, v)$ specifies the cost (amount of wire needed) to connect u and v. The goal is to find an acyclic subset $T \subseteq E$ that connects all of the vertices and whose total weight

$$w(T) = \sum_{(u,v) \in T} w(u, v)$$

is minimized. Since T is acyclic and connects all of the vertices, it must form a tree, which we call a *spanning tree* since it "spans" the graph G. We call the problem of determining the tree T the *minimum-spanning-tree problem*.[1] Figure 21.1 shows an example of a connected graph and a minimum spanning tree.

This chapter studies two ways to solve the minimum-spanning-tree problem. Kruskal's algorithm and Prim's algorithm both run in $O(E \lg V)$ time. Prim's algorithm achieves this bound by using a binary heap as a priority queue. By using Fibonacci heaps instead (see page 478), Prim's algorithm runs in $O(E + V \lg V)$ time. This bound is better than $O(E \lg V)$ whenever $|E|$ grows asymptotically faster than $|V|$.

---

[1] The phrase "minimum spanning tree" is a shortened form of the phrase "minimum-weight spanning tree." There is no point in minimizing the number of edges in T, since all spanning trees have exactly $|V| - 1$ edges by Theorem B.2 on page 1169.

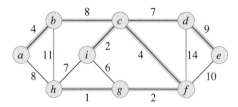

Figure 21.1   A minimum spanning tree for a connected graph. The weights on edges are shown, and the blue edges form a minimum spanning tree. The total weight of the tree shown is 37. This minimum spanning tree is not unique: removing the edge (b, c) and replacing it with the edge (a, h) yields another spanning tree with weight 37.

The two algorithms are greedy algorithms, as described in Chapter 15. Each step of a greedy algorithm must make one of several possible choices. The greedy strategy advocates making the choice that is the best at the moment. Such a strategy does not generally guarantee that it always finds globally optimal solutions to problems. For the minimum-spanning-tree problem, however, we can prove that certain greedy strategies do yield a spanning tree with minimum weight. Although you can read this chapter independently of Chapter 15, the greedy methods presented here are a classic application of the theoretical notions introduced there.

Section 21.1 introduces a "generic" minimum-spanning-tree method that grows a spanning tree by adding one edge at a time. Section 21.2 gives two algorithms that implement the generic method. The first algorithm, due to Kruskal, is similar to the connected-components algorithm from Section 19.1. The second, due to Prim, resembles Dijkstra's shortest-paths algorithm (Section 22.3).

Because a tree is a type of graph, in order to be precise we must define a tree in terms of not just its edges, but its vertices as well. Because this chapter focuses on trees in terms of their edges, we'll implicitly understand that the vertices of a tree T are those that some edge of T is incident on.

21.1   Growing a minimum spanning tree

The input to the minumum-spanning-tree problem is a connected, undirected graph $G = (V, E)$ with a weight function $w : E \rightarrow \mathbb{R}$. The goal is to find a minimum spanning tree for G. The two algorithms considered in this chapter use a greedy approach to the problem, although they differ in how they apply this approach.

This greedy strategy is captured by the procedure GENERIC-MST on the facing page, which grows the minimum spanning tree one edge at a time. The generic method manages a set A of edges, maintaining the following loop invariant:

Prior to each iteration, A is a subset of some minimum spanning tree.

GENERIC-MST(G, w)

1   $A = \emptyset$
2   **while** A does not form a spanning tree
3   find an edge (u, v) that is safe for A
4           $A = A \cup \{(u, v)\}$
5   **return** A

Each step determines an edge (u, v) that the procedure can add to A without violating this invariant, in the sense that $A \cup \{(u, v)\}$ is also a subset of a minimum spanning tree. We call such an edge a *safe edge* for A, since it can be added safely to A while maintaining the invariant.

This generic algorithm uses the loop invariant as follows:

Initialization: After line 1, the set A trivially satisfies the loop invariant.

Maintenance: The loop in lines 2–4 maintains the invariant by adding only safe edges.

Termination: All edges added to A belong to a minimum spanning tree, and the loop must terminate by the time it has considered all edges. Therefore, the set A returned in line 5 must be a minimum spanning tree.

The tricky part is, of course, finding a safe edge in line 3. One must exist, since when line 3 is executed, the invariant dictates that there is a spanning tree T such that $A \subseteq T$. Within the **while** loop body, A must be a proper subset of T, and therefore there must be an edge $(u, v) \in T$ such that $(u, v) \notin A$ and (u, v) is safe for A.

The remainder of this section provides a rule (Theorem 21.1) for recognizing safe edges. The next section describes two algorithms that use this rule to find safe edges efficiently.

We first need some definitions. A *cut* $(S, V - S)$ of an undirected graph $G = (V, E)$ is a partition of V. Figure 21.2 illustrates this notion. We say that an edge $(u, v) \in E$ *crosses* the cut $(S, V - S)$ if one of its endpoints belongs to S and the other belongs to $V - S$. A cut *respects* a set A of edges if no edge in A crosses the cut. An edge is a *light edge* crossing a cut if its weight is the minimum of any edge crossing the cut. There can be more than one light edge crossing a cut in the case of ties. More generally, we say that an edge is a *light edge* satisfying a given property if its weight is the minimum of any edge satisfying the property.

The following theorem gives the rule for recognizing safe edges.

Theorem 21.1

Let $G = (V, E)$ be a connected, undirected graph with a real-valued weight function w defined on E. Let A be a subset of E that is included in some minimum

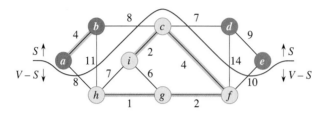

Figure 21.2   A cut $(S, V - S)$ of the graph from Figure 21.1. Orange vertices belong to the set S, and tan vertices belong to $V - S$. The edges crossing the cut are those connecting tan vertices with orange vertices. The edge (d, c) is the unique light edge crossing the cut. Blue edges form a subset A of the edges. The cut $(S, V - S)$ respects A, since no edge of A crosses the cut.

spanning tree for G, let $(S, V - S)$ be any cut of G that respects A, and let (u, v) be a light edge crossing $(S, V - S)$. Then, edge (u, v) is safe for A.

Proof   Let T be a minimum spanning tree that includes A, and assume that T does not contain the light edge (u, v), since if it does, we are done. We'll construct another minimum spanning tree T' that includes $A \cup \{(u, v)\}$ by using a cut-and-paste technique, thereby showing that (u, v) is a safe edge for A.

The edge (u, v) forms a cycle with the edges on the simple path p from u to v in T, as Figure 21.3 illustrates. Since u and v are on opposite sides of the cut $(S, V - S)$, at least one edge in T lies on the simple path p and also crosses the cut. Let (x, y) be any such edge. The edge (x, y) is not in A, because the cut respects A. Since (x, y) is on the unique simple path from u to v in T, removing (x, y) breaks T into two components. Adding (u, v) reconnects them to form a new spanning tree $T' = (T - \{(x, y)\}) \cup \{(u, v)\}$.

We next show that T' is a minimum spanning tree. Since (u, v) is a light edge crossing $(S, V - S)$ and (x, y) also crosses this cut, $w(u, v) \le w(x, y)$. Therefore,

$$w(T') = w(T) - w(x, y) + w(u, v)$$
$$\le w(T) .$$

But T is a minimum spanning tree, so that $w(T) \le w(T')$, and thus, T' must be a minimum spanning tree as well.

It remains to show that (u, v) is actually a safe edge for A. We have $A \subseteq T'$, since $A \subseteq T$ and $(x, y) \notin A$, and thus, $A \cup \{(u, v)\} \subseteq T'$. Consequently, since T' is a minimum spanning tree, (u, v) is safe for A.   ■

Theorem 21.1 provides insight into how the GENERIC-MST method works on a connected graph $G = (V, E)$. As the method proceeds, the set A is always acyclic, since it is a subset of a minimum spanning tree and a tree may not contain a cycle.

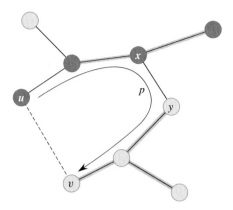

Figure 21.3   The proof of Theorem 21.1. Orange vertices belong to S, and tan vertices belong to $V - S$. Only edges in the minimum spanning tree T are shown, along with edge (u, v), which does not lie in T. The edges in A are blue, and (u, v) is a light edge crossing the cut $(S, V - S)$. The edge (x, y) is an edge on the unique simple path p from u to v in T. To form a minimum spanning tree T' that contains (u, v), remove the edge (x, y) from T and add the edge (u, v).

At any point in the execution, the graph $G_A = (V, A)$ is a forest, and each of the connected components of G_A is a tree. (Some of the trees may contain just one vertex, as is the case, for example, when the method begins: A is empty and the forest contains $|V|$ trees, one for each vertex.) Moreover, any safe edge (u, v) for A connects distinct components of G_A, since $A \cup \{(u, v)\}$ must be acyclic.

The **while** loop in lines 2–4 of GENERIC-MST executes $|V| - 1$ times because it finds one of the $|V| - 1$ edges of a minimum spanning tree in each iteration. Initially, when $A = \emptyset$, there are $|V|$ trees in G_A, and each iteration reduces that number by 1. When the forest contains only a single tree, the method terminates.

The two algorithms in Section 21.2 use the following corollary to Theorem 21.1.

Corollary 21.2
Let $G = (V, E)$ be a connected, undirected graph with a real-valued weight function w defined on E. Let A be a subset of E that is included in some minimum spanning tree for G, and let $C = (V_C, E_C)$ be a connected component (tree) in the forest $G_A = (V, A)$. If (u, v) is a light edge connecting C to some other component in G_A, then (u, v) is safe for A.

Proof   The cut $(V_C, V - V_C)$ respects A, and (u, v) is a light edge for this cut. Therefore, (u, v) is safe for A.   ■

Exercises

21.1-1
Let (u, v) be a minimum-weight edge in a connected graph G. Show that (u, v) belongs to some minimum spanning tree of G.

21.1-2
Professor Sabatier conjectures the following converse of Theorem 21.1. Let $G = (V, E)$ be a connected, undirected graph with a real-valued weight function w defined on E. Let A be a subset of E that is included in some minimum spanning tree for G, let $(S, V - S)$ be any cut of G that respects A, and let (u, v) be a safe edge for A crossing $(S, V - S)$. Then, (u, v) is a light edge for the cut. Show that the professor's conjecture is incorrect by giving a counterexample.

21.1-3
Show that if an edge (u, v) is contained in some minimum spanning tree, then it is a light edge crossing some cut of the graph.

21.1-4
Give a simple example of a connected graph such that the set of edges $\{(u, v) :$ there exists a cut $(S, V - S)$ such that (u, v) is a light edge crossing $(S, V - S)\}$ does not form a minimum spanning tree.

21.1-5
Let e be a maximum-weight edge on some cycle of connected graph $G = (V, E)$. Prove that there is a minimum spanning tree of $G' = (V, E - \{e\})$ that is also a minimum spanning tree of G. That is, there is a minimum spanning tree of G that does not include e.

21.1-6
Show that a graph has a unique minimum spanning tree if, for every cut of the graph, there is a unique light edge crossing the cut. Show that the converse is not true by giving a counterexample.

21.1-7
Argue that if all edge weights of a graph are positive, then any subset of edges that connects all vertices and has minimum total weight must be a tree. Give an example to show that the same conclusion does not follow if we allow some weights to be nonpositive.

21.1-8

Let T be a minimum spanning tree of a graph G, and let L be the sorted list of the edge weights of T. Show that for any other minimum spanning tree T' of G, the list L is also the sorted list of edge weights of T'.

21.1-9

Let T be a minimum spanning tree of a graph $G = (V, E)$, and let V' be a subset of V. Let T' be the subgraph of T induced by V', and let G' be the subgraph of G induced by V'. Show that if T' is connected, then T' is a minimum spanning tree of G'.

21.1-10

Given a graph G and a minimum spanning tree T, suppose that the weight of one of the edges in T decreases. Show that T is still a minimum spanning tree for G. More formally, let T be a minimum spanning tree for G with edge weights given by weight function w. Choose one edge $(x, y) \in T$ and a positive number k, and define the weight function w' by

$$w'(u, v) = \begin{cases} w(u, v) & \text{if } (u, v) \neq (x, y), \\ w(x, y) - k & \text{if } (u, v) = (x, y). \end{cases}$$

Show that T is a minimum spanning tree for G with edge weights given by w'.

★ 21.1-11

Given a graph G and a minimum spanning tree T, suppose that the weight of one of the edges *not* in T decreases. Give an algorithm for finding the minimum spanning tree in the modified graph.

21.2 The algorithms of Kruskal and Prim

The two minimum-spanning-tree algorithms described in this section elaborate on the generic method. They each use a specific rule to determine a safe edge in line 3 of GENERIC-MST. In Kruskal's algorithm, the set A is a forest whose vertices are all those of the given graph. The safe edge added to A is always a lowest-weight edge in the graph that connects two distinct components. In Prim's algorithm, the set A forms a single tree. The safe edge added to A is always a lowest-weight edge connecting the tree to a vertex not in the tree. Both algorithms assume that the input graph is connected and represented by adjacency lists.

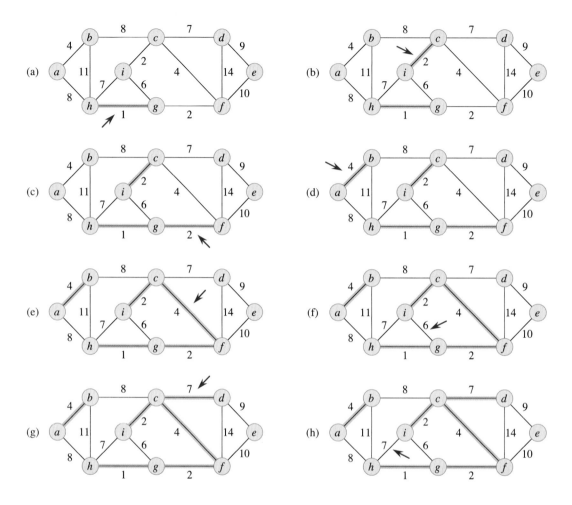

Figure 21.4 The execution of Kruskal's algorithm on the graph from Figure 21.1. Blue edges belong to the forest A being grown. The algorithm considers each edge in sorted order by weight. A red arrow points to the edge under consideration at each step of the algorithm. If the edge joins two distinct trees in the forest, it is added to the forest, thereby merging the two trees.

Kruskal's algorithm

Kruskal's algorithm finds a safe edge to add to the growing forest by finding, of all the edges that connect any two trees in the forest, an edge (u, v) with the lowest weight. Let C_1 and C_2 denote the two trees that are connected by (u, v). Since (u, v) must be a light edge connecting C_1 to some other tree, Corollary 21.2 implies

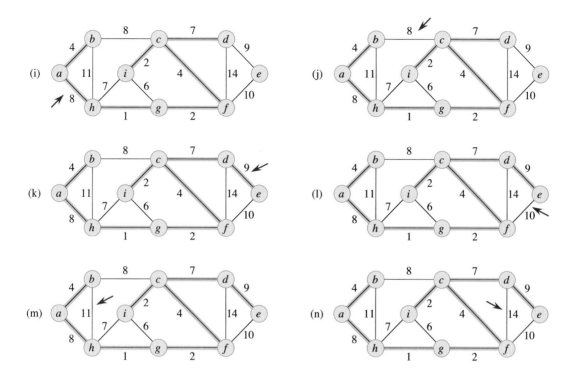

Figure 21.4, continued   Further steps in the execution of Kruskal's algorithm.

that (u, v) is a safe edge for C_1. Kruskal's algorithm qualifies as a greedy algorithm because at each step it adds to the forest an edge with the lowest possible weight.

Like the algorithm to compute connected components from Section 19.1, the procedure MST-KRUSKAL on the following page uses a disjoint-set data structure to maintain several disjoint sets of elements. Each set contains the vertices in one tree of the current forest. The operation FIND-SET(u) returns a representative element from the set that contains u. Thus, to determine whether two vertices u and v belong to the same tree, just test whether FIND-SET(u) equals FIND-SET(v). To combine trees, Kruskal's algorithm calls the UNION procedure.

Figure 21.4 shows how Kruskal's algorithm works. Lines 1–3 initialize the set A to the empty set and create $|V|$ trees, one containing each vertex. The **for** loop in lines 6–9 examines edges in order of weight, from lowest to highest. The loop checks, for each edge (u, v), whether the endpoints u and v belong to the same tree. If they do, then the edge (u, v) cannot be added to the forest without creating a cycle, and the edge is ignored. Otherwise, the two vertices belong to different

MST-KRUSKAL(G, w)

```
 1  A = ∅
 2  for each vertex v ∈ G.V
 3      MAKE-SET(v)
 4  create a single list of the edges in G.E
 5  sort the list of edges into monotonically increasing order by weight w
 6  for each edge (u, v) taken from the sorted list in order
 7      if FIND-SET(u) ≠ FIND-SET(v)
 8          A = A ∪ {(u, v)}
 9          UNION(u, v)
10  return A
```

trees. In this case, line 8 adds the edge (u, v) to A, and line 9 merges the vertices in the two trees.

The running time of Kruskal's algorithm for a graph $G = (V, E)$ depends on the specific implementation of the disjoint-set data structure. Let's assume that it uses the disjoint-set-forest implementation of Section 19.3 with the union-by-rank and path-compression heuristics, since that is the asymptotically fastest implementation known. Initializing the set A in line 1 takes $O(1)$ time, creating a single list of edges in line 4 takes $O(V + E)$ time (which is $O(E)$ because G is connected), and the time to sort the edges in line 5 is $O(E \lg E)$. (We'll account for the cost of the $|V|$ MAKE-SET operations in the **for** loop of lines 2–3 in a moment.) The **for** loop of lines 6–9 performs $O(E)$ FIND-SET and UNION operations on the disjoint-set forest. Along with the $|V|$ MAKE-SET operations, these disjoint-set operations take a total of $O((V + E) \, \alpha(V))$ time, where α is the very slowly growing function defined in Section 19.4. Because we assume that G is connected, we have $|E| \geq |V| - 1$, and so the disjoint-set operations take $O(E \, \alpha(V))$ time. Moreover, since $\alpha(|V|) = O(\lg V) = O(\lg E)$, the total running time of Kruskal's algorithm is $O(E \lg E)$. Observing that $|E| < |V|^2$, we have $\lg |E| = O(\lg V)$, and so we can restate the running time of Kruskal's algorithm as $O(E \lg V)$.

Prim's algorithm

Like Kruskal's algorithm, Prim's algorithm is a special case of the generic minimum-spanning-tree method from Section 21.1. Prim's algorithm operates much like Dijkstra's algorithm for finding shortest paths in a graph, which we'll see in Section 22.3. Prim's algorithm has the property that the edges in the set A always form a single tree. As Figure 21.5 shows, the tree starts from an arbitrary root vertex r and grows until it spans all the vertices in V. Each step adds to the tree A

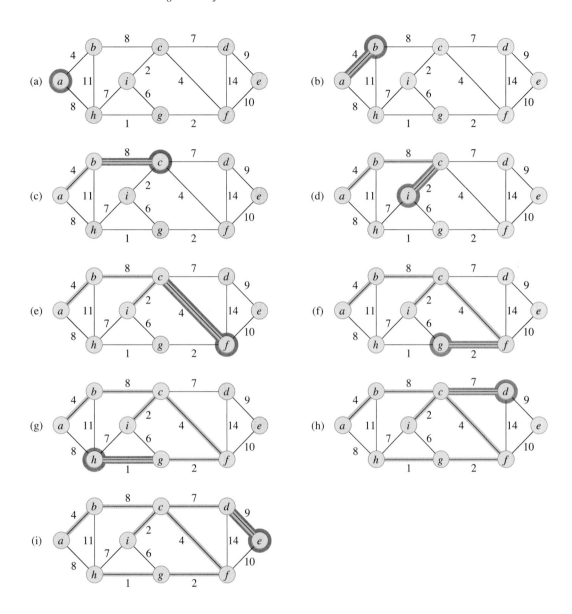

Figure 21.5 The execution of Prim's algorithm on the graph from Figure 21.1. The root vertex
is a. Blue vertices and edges belong to the tree being grown, and tan vertices have yet to be added
to the tree. At each step of the algorithm, the vertices in the tree determine a cut of the graph, and a
light edge crossing the cut is added to the tree. The edge and vertex added to the tree are highlighted
in orange. In the second step (part (c)), for example, the algorithm has a choice of adding either
edge (b, c) or edge (a, h) to the tree since both are light edges crossing the cut.

a light edge that connects A to an isolated vertex—one on which no edge of A is incident. By Corollary 21.2, this rule adds only edges that are safe for A. Therefore, when the algorithm terminates, the edges in A form a minimum spanning tree. This strategy qualifies as greedy since at each step it adds to the tree an edge that contributes the minimum amount possible to the tree's weight.

In the procedure MST-PRIM below, the connected graph G and the root r of the minimum spanning tree to be grown are inputs to the algorithm. In order to efficiently select a new edge to add into tree A, the algorithm maintains a min-priority queue Q of all vertices that are *not* in the tree, based on a *key* attribute. For each vertex v, the attribute $v.key$ is the minimum weight of any edge connecting v to a vertex in the tree, where by convention, $v.key = \infty$ if there is no such edge. The attribute $v.\pi$ names the parent of v in the tree. The algorithm implicitly maintains the set A from GENERIC-MST as

$$A = \{(v, v.\pi) : v \in V - \{r\} - Q\} \ ,$$

where we interpret the vertices in Q as forming a set. When the algorithm terminates, the min-priority queue Q is empty, and thus the minimum spanning tree A for G is

$$A = \{(v, v.\pi) : v \in V - \{r\}\} \ .$$

MST-PRIM(G, w, r)

```
 1  for each vertex u ∈ G.V
 2      u.key = ∞
 3      u.π = NIL
 4  r.key = 0
 5  Q = ∅
 6  for each vertex u ∈ G.V
 7      INSERT(Q, u)
 8  while Q ≠ ∅
 9      u = EXTRACT-MIN(Q)          // add u to the tree
10      for each vertex v in G.Adj[u]   // update keys of u's non-tree neighbors
11          if v ∈ Q and w(u, v) < v.key
12              v.π = u
13              v.key = w(u, v)
14              DECREASE-KEY(Q, v, w(u, v))
```

Figure 21.5 shows how Prim's algorithm works. Lines 1–7 set the key of each vertex to ∞ (except for the root r, whose key is set to 0 to make it the first vertex processed), set the parent of each vertex to NIL, and insert each vertex into the min-priority queue Q. The algorithm maintains the following three-part loop invariant:

Prior to each iteration of the **while** loop of lines 8–14,

1. $A = \{(v, v.\pi) : v \in V - \{r\} - Q\}$.
2. The vertices already placed into the minimum spanning tree are those in $V - Q$.
3. For all vertices $v \in Q$, if $v.\pi \neq$ NIL, then $v.key < \infty$ and $v.key$ is the weight of a light edge $(v, v.\pi)$ connecting v to some vertex already placed into the minimum spanning tree.

Line 9 identifies a vertex $u \in Q$ incident on a light edge that crosses the cut $(V - Q, Q)$ (with the exception of the first iteration, in which $u = r$ due to lines 4–7). Removing u from the set Q adds it to the set $V - Q$ of vertices in the tree, thus adding the edge $(u, u.\pi)$ to A. The **for** loop of lines 10–14 updates the *key* and π attributes of every vertex v adjacent to u but not in the tree, thereby maintaining the third part of the loop invariant. Whenever line 13 updates $v.key$, line 14 calls DECREASE-KEY to inform the min-priority queue that v's key has changed.

The running time of Prim's algorithm depends on the specific implementation of the min-priority queue Q. You can implement Q with a binary min-heap (see Chapter 6), including a way to map between vertices and their corresponding heap elements. The BUILD-MIN-HEAP procedure can perform lines 5–7 in $O(V)$ time. In fact, there is no need to call BUILD-MIN-HEAP. You can just put the key of r at the root of the min-heap, and because all other keys are ∞, they can go anywhere else in the min-heap. The body of the **while** loop executes $|V|$ times, and since each EXTRACT-MIN operation takes $O(\lg V)$ time, the total time for all calls to EXTRACT-MIN is $O(V \lg V)$. The **for** loop in lines 10–14 executes $O(E)$ times altogether, since the sum of the lengths of all adjacency lists is $2|E|$. Within the **for** loop, the test for membership in Q in line 11 can take constant time if you keep a bit for each vertex that indicates whether it belongs to Q and update the bit when the vertex is removed from Q. Each call to DECREASE-KEY in line 14 takes $O(\lg V)$ time. Thus, the total time for Prim's algorithm is $O(V \lg V + E \lg V) = O(E \lg V)$, which is asymptotically the same as for our implementation of Kruskal's algorithm.

You can further improve the asymptotic running time of Prim's algorithm by implementing the min-priority queue with a Fibonacci heap (see page 478). If a Fibonacci heap holds $|V|$ elements, an EXTRACT-MIN operation takes $O(\lg V)$ amortized time and each INSERT and DECREASE-KEY operation takes only $O(1)$ amortized time. Therefore, by using a Fibonacci heap to implement the min-priority queue Q, the running time of Prim's algorithm improves to $O(E + V \lg V)$.

Exercises

21.2-1
Kruskal's algorithm can return different spanning trees for the same input graph G, depending on how it breaks ties when the edges are sorted. Show that for each minimum spanning tree T of G, there is a way to sort the edges of G in Kruskal's algorithm so that the algorithm returns T.

21.2-2
Give a simple implementation of Prim's algorithm that runs in $O(V^2)$ time when the graph $G = (V, E)$ is represented as an adjacency matrix.

21.2-3
For a sparse graph $G = (V, E)$, where $|E| = \Theta(V)$, is the implementation of Prim's algorithm with a Fibonacci heap asymptotically faster than the binary-heap implementation? What about for a dense graph, where $|E| = \Theta(V^2)$? How must the sizes $|E|$ and $|V|$ be related for the Fibonacci-heap implementation to be asymptotically faster than the binary-heap implementation?

21.2-4
Suppose that all edge weights in a graph are integers in the range from 1 to $|V|$. How fast can you make Kruskal's algorithm run? What if the edge weights are integers in the range from 1 to W for some constant W?

21.2-5
Suppose that all edge weights in a graph are integers in the range from 1 to $|V|$. How fast can you make Prim's algorithm run? What if the edge weights are integers in the range from 1 to W for some constant W?

21.2-6
Professor Borden proposes a new divide-and-conquer algorithm for computing minimum spanning trees, which goes as follows. Given a graph $G = (V, E)$, partition the set V of vertices into two sets V_1 and V_2 such that $|V_1|$ and $|V_2|$ differ by at most 1. Let E_1 be the set of edges that are incident only on vertices in V_1, and let E_2 be the set of edges that are incident only on vertices in V_2. Recursively solve a minimum-spanning-tree problem on each of the two subgraphs $G_1 = (V_1, E_1)$ and $G_2 = (V_2, E_2)$. Finally, select the minimum-weight edge in E that crosses the cut (V_1, V_2), and use this edge to unite the resulting two minimum spanning trees into a single spanning tree.

Either argue that the algorithm correctly computes a minimum spanning tree of G, or provide an example for which the algorithm fails.

★ *21.2-7*

Suppose that the edge weights in a graph are uniformly distributed over the half-open interval $[0, 1)$. Which algorithm, Kruskal's or Prim's, can you make run faster?

★ *21.2-8*

Suppose that a graph G has a minimum spanning tree already computed. How quickly can you update the minimum spanning tree upon adding a new vertex and incident edges to G?

Problems

21-1 Second-best minimum spanning tree

Let $G = (V, E)$ be an undirected, connected graph whose weight function is $w : E \to \mathbb{R}$, and suppose that $|E| \geq |V|$ and all edge weights are distinct.

We define a second-best minimum spanning tree as follows. Let $\mathcal{T}$ be the set of all spanning trees of G, and let T be a minimum spanning tree of G. Then a *second-best minimum spanning tree* is a spanning tree T' such that $w(T') = \min \{w(T'') : T'' \in \mathcal{T} - \{T\}\}$.

a. Show that the minimum spanning tree is unique, but that the second-best minimum spanning tree need not be unique.

b. Let T be the minimum spanning tree of G. Prove that G contains some edge $(u, v) \in T$ and some edge $(x, y) \notin T$ such that $(T - \{(u, v)\}) \cup \{(x, y)\}$ is a second-best minimum spanning tree of G.

c. Now let T be any spanning tree of G and, for any two vertices $u, v \in V$, let *max[u, v]* denote an edge of maximum weight on the unique simple path between u and v in T. Describe an $O(V^2)$-time algorithm that, given T, computes *max[u, v]* for all $u, v \in V$.

d. Give an efficient algorithm to compute the second-best minimum spanning tree of G.

21-2 Minimum spanning tree in sparse graphs

For a very sparse connected graph $G = (V, E)$, it is possible to further improve upon the $O(E + V \lg V)$ running time of Prim's algorithm with a Fibonacci heap by preprocessing G to decrease the number of vertices before running Prim's algorithm. In particular, for each vertex u, choose the minimum-weight edge (u, v)

incident on u, and put (u, v) into the minimum spanning tree under construction. Then, contract all chosen edges (see Section B.4). Rather than contracting these edges one at a time, first identify sets of vertices that are united into the same new vertex. Then create the graph that would have resulted from contracting these edges one at a time, but do so by "renaming" edges according to the sets into which their endpoints were placed. Several edges from the original graph might be renamed the same as each other. In such a case, only one edge results, and its weight is the minimum of the weights of the corresponding original edges.

Initially, set the minimum spanning tree T being constructed to be empty, and for each edge $(u, v) \in E$, initialize the two attributes $(u, v).orig = (u, v)$ and $(u, v).c = w(u, v)$. Use the $orig$ attribute to reference the edge from the initial graph that is associated with an edge in the contracted graph. The c attribute holds the weight of an edge, and as edges are contracted, it is updated according to the above scheme for choosing edge weights. The procedure MST-REDUCE on the facing page takes inputs G and T, and it returns a contracted graph G' with updated attributes $orig'$ and c'. The procedure also accumulates edges of G into the minimum spanning tree T.

a. Let T be the set of edges returned by MST-REDUCE, and let A be the minimum spanning tree of the graph G' formed by the call MST-PRIM(G', c', r), where c' is the weight attribute on the edges of $G'.E$ and r is any vertex in $G'.V$. Prove that $T \cup \{(x, y).orig' : (x, y) \in A\}$ is a minimum spanning tree of G.

b. Argue that $|G'.V| \le |V|/2$.

c. Show how to implement MST-REDUCE so that it runs in $O(E)$ time. (*Hint:* Use simple data structures.)

d. Suppose that you run k phases of MST-REDUCE, using the output G' produced by one phase as the input G to the next phase and accumulating edges in T. Argue that the overall running time of the k phases is $O(kE)$.

e. Suppose that after running k phases of MST-REDUCE, as in part (d), you run Prim's algorithm by calling MST-PRIM(G', c', r), where G', with weight attribute c', is returned by the last phase and r is any vertex in $G'.V$. Show how to pick k so that the overall running time is $O(E \lg \lg V)$. Argue that your choice of k minimizes the overall asymptotic running time.

f. For what values of $|E|$ (in terms of $|V|$) does Prim's algorithm with preprocessing asymptotically beat Prim's algorithm without preprocessing?

```
MST-REDUCE(G, T)
 1  for each vertex v ∈ G.V
 2      v.mark = FALSE
 3      MAKE-SET(v)
 4  for each vertex u ∈ G.V
 5      if u.mark == FALSE
 6          choose v ∈ G.Adj[u] such that (u, v).c is minimized
 7          UNION(u, v)
 8          T = T ∪ {(u, v).orig}
 9          u.mark = TRUE
10          v.mark = TRUE
11  G'.V = {FIND-SET(v) : v ∈ G.V}
12  G'.E = ∅
13  for each edge (x, y) ∈ G.E
14      u = FIND-SET(x)
15      v = FIND-SET(y)
16      if u ≠ v
17          if (u, v) ∉ G'.E
18              G'.E = G'.E ∪ {(u, v)}
19              (u, v).orig' = (x, y).orig
20              (u, v).c' = (x, y).c
21          elseif (x, y).c < (u, v).c'
22              (u, v).orig' = (x, y).orig
23              (u, v).c' = (x, y).c
24  construct adjacency lists G'.Adj for G'
25  return G' and T
```

21-3 *Alternative minimum-spanning-tree algorithms*

Consider the three algorithms MAYBE-MST-A, MAYBE-MST-B, and MAYBE-MST-C on the next page. Each one takes a connected graph and a weight function as input and returns a set of edges T. For each algorithm, either prove that T is a minimum spanning tree or prove that T is not necessarily a minimum spanning tree. Also describe the most efficient implementation of each algorithm, regardless of whether it computes a minimum spanning tree.

21-4 *Bottleneck spanning tree*

A *bottleneck spanning tree* T of an undirected graph G is a spanning tree of G whose largest edge weight is minimum over all spanning trees of G. The value of the bottleneck spanning tree is the weight of the maximum-weight edge in T.

MAYBE-MST-A(G, w)

1 sort the edges into monotonically decreasing order of edge weights w
2 $T = E$
3 **for** each edge e, taken in monotonically decreasing order by weight
4   **if** $T - \{e\}$ is a connected graph
5          $T = T - \{e\}$
6 **return** T

MAYBE-MST-B(G, w)

1 $T = \emptyset$
2 **for** each edge e, taken in arbitrary order
3   **if** $T \cup \{e\}$ has no cycles
4          $T = T \cup \{e\}$
5 **return** T

MAYBE-MST-C(G, w)

1 $T = \emptyset$
2 **for** each edge e, taken in arbitrary order
3      $T = T \cup \{e\}$
4   **if** T has a cycle c
5   let e' be a maximum-weight edge on c
6          $T = T - \{e'\}$
7 **return** T

a. Argue that a minimum spanning tree is a bottleneck spanning tree.

Part (a) shows that finding a bottleneck spanning tree is no harder than finding a minimum spanning tree. In the remaining parts, you will show how to find a bottleneck spanning tree in linear time.

b. Give a linear-time algorithm that, given a graph G and an integer b, determines whether the value of the bottleneck spanning tree is at most b.

c. Use your algorithm for part (b) as a subroutine in a linear-time algorithm for the bottleneck-spanning-tree problem. (*Hint:* You might want to use a subroutine that contracts sets of edges, as in the MST-REDUCE procedure described in Problem 21-2.)

Chapter notes

Tarjan [429] surveys the minimum-spanning-tree problem and provides excellent advanced material. Graham and Hell [198] compiled a history of the minimum-spanning-tree problem.

Tarjan attributes the first minimum-spanning-tree algorithm to a 1926 paper by O. Borůvka. Borůvka's algorithm consists of running $O(\lg V)$ iterations of the procedure MST-REDUCE described in Problem 21-2. Kruskal's algorithm was reported by Kruskal [272] in 1956. The algorithm commonly known as Prim's algorithm was indeed invented by Prim [367], but it was also invented earlier by V. Jarník in 1930.

When $|E| = \Omega(V \lg V)$, Prim's algorithm, implemented with a Fibonacci heap, runs in $O(E)$ time. For sparser graphs, using a combination of the ideas from Prim's algorithm, Kruskal's algorithm, and Borůvka's algorithm, together with advanced data structures, Fredman and Tarjan [156] give an algorithm that runs in $O(E \lg^* V)$ time. Gabow, Galil, Spencer, and Tarjan [165] improved this algorithm to run in $O(E \lg \lg^* V)$ time. Chazelle [83] gives an algorithm that runs in $O(E \, \hat{\alpha}(E, V))$ time, where $\hat{\alpha}(E, V)$ is the functional inverse of Ackermann's function. (See the chapter notes for Chapter 19 for a brief discussion of Ackermann's function and its inverse.) Unlike previous minimum-spanning-tree algorithms, Chazelle's algorithm does not follow the greedy method. Pettie and Ramachandran [356] give an algorithm based on precomputed "MST decision trees" that also runs in $O(E \, \hat{\alpha}(E, V))$ time.

A related problem is *spanning-tree verification*: given a graph $G = (V, E)$ and a tree $T \subseteq E$, determine whether T is a minimum spanning tree of G. King [254] gives a linear-time algorithm to verify a spanning tree, building on earlier work of Komlós [269] and Dixon, Rauch, and Tarjan [120].

The above algorithms are all deterministic and fall into the comparison-based model described in Chapter 8. Karger, Klein, and Tarjan [243] give a randomized minimum-spanning-tree algorithm that runs in $O(V + E)$ expected time. This algorithm uses recursion in a manner similar to the linear-time selection algorithm in Section 9.3: a recursive call on an auxiliary problem identifies a subset of the edges E' that cannot be in any minimum spanning tree. Another recursive call on $E - E'$ then finds the minimum spanning tree. The algorithm also uses ideas from Borůvka's algorithm and King's algorithm for spanning-tree verification.

Fredman and Willard [158] showed how to find a minimum spanning tree in $O(V + E)$ time using a deterministic algorithm that is not comparison based. Their algorithm assumes that the data are b-bit integers and that the computer memory consists of addressable b-bit words.

22   Single-Source Shortest Paths

Suppose that you need to drive from Oceanside, New York, to Oceanside, California, by the shortest possible route. Your GPS contains information about the entire road network of the United States, including the road distance between each pair of adjacent intersections. How can your GPS determine this shortest route?

One possible way is to enumerate all the routes from Oceanside, New York, to Oceanside, California, add up the distances on each route, and select the shortest. But even disallowing routes that contain cycles, your GPS would need to examine an enormous number of possibilities, most of which are simply not worth considering. For example, a route that passes through Miami, Florida, is a poor choice, because Miami is several hundred miles out of the way.

This chapter and Chapter 23 show how to solve such problems efficiently. The input to a *shortest-paths problem* is a weighted, directed graph $G = (V, E)$, with a weight function $w : E \to \mathbb{R}$ mapping edges to real-valued weights. The *weight $w(p)$* of path $p = \langle v_0, v_1, \ldots, v_k \rangle$ is the sum of the weights of its constituent edges:

$$w(p) = \sum_{i=1}^{k} w(v_{i-1}, v_i) .$$

We define the *shortest-path weight $\delta(u, v)$* from u to v by

$$\delta(u, v) = \begin{cases} \min\{w(p) : u \overset{p}{\rightsquigarrow} v\} & \text{if there is a path from } u \text{ to } v , \\ \infty & \text{otherwise} . \end{cases}$$

A *shortest path* from vertex u to vertex v is then defined as any path p with weight $w(p) = \delta(u, v)$.

In the example of going from Oceanside, New York, to Oceanside, California, your GPS models the road network as a graph: vertices represent intersections, edges represent road segments between intersections, and edge weights represent road distances. The goal is to find a shortest path from a given intersection in

Oceanside, New York (say, Brower Avenue and Skillman Avenue) to a given intersection in Oceanside, California (say, Topeka Street and South Horne Street).

Edge weights can represent metrics other than distances, such as time, cost, penalties, loss, or any other quantity that accumulates linearly along a path and that you want to minimize.

The breadth-first-search algorithm from Section 20.2 is a shortest-paths algorithm that works on unweighted graphs, that is, graphs in which each edge has unit weight. Because many of the concepts from breadth-first search arise in the study of shortest paths in weighted graphs, you might want to review Section 20.2 before proceeding.

Variants

This chapter focuses on the *single-source shortest-paths problem*: given a graph $G = (V, E)$, find a shortest path from a given *source vertex* $s \in V$ to every vertex $v \in V$. The algorithm for the single-source problem can solve many other problems, including the following variants.

Single-destination shortest-paths problem: Find a shortest path to a given *destination vertex* t from each vertex v. By reversing the direction of each edge in the graph, you can reduce this problem to a single-source problem.

Single-pair shortest-path problem: Find a shortest path from u to v for given vertices u and v. If you solve the single-source problem with source vertex u, you solve this problem also. Moreover, all known algorithms for this problem have the same worst-case asymptotic running time as the best single-source algorithms.

All-pairs shortest-paths problem: Find a shortest path from u to v for every pair of vertices u and v. Although you can solve this problem by running a single-source algorithm once from each vertex, you often can solve it faster. Additionally, its structure is interesting in its own right. Chapter 23 addresses the all-pairs problem in detail.

Optimal substructure of a shortest path

Shortest-paths algorithms typically rely on the property that a shortest path between two vertices contains other shortest paths within it. (The Edmonds-Karp maximum-flow algorithm in Chapter 24 also relies on this property.) Recall that optimal substructure is one of the key indicators that dynamic programming (Chapter 14) and the greedy method (Chapter 15) might apply. Dijkstra's algorithm, which we shall see in Section 22.3, is a greedy algorithm, and the Floyd-Warshall algorithm, which finds a shortest path between every pair of vertices (see Section 23.2), is a dynamic-programming algorithm. The following lemma states the optimal-substructure property of shortest paths more precisely.

Lemma 22.1 (Subpaths of shortest paths are shortest paths)

Given a weighted, directed graph $G = (V, E)$ with weight function $w : E \to \mathbb{R}$, let $p = \langle v_0, v_1, \ldots, v_k \rangle$ be a shortest path from vertex v_0 to vertex v_k and, for any i and j such that $0 \le i \le j \le k$, let $p_{ij} = \langle v_i, v_{i+1}, \ldots, v_j \rangle$ be the subpath of p from vertex v_i to vertex v_j. Then, p_{ij} is a shortest path from v_i to v_j.

Proof   Decompose path p into $v_0 \overset{p_{0i}}{\rightsquigarrow} v_i \overset{p_{ij}}{\rightsquigarrow} v_j \overset{p_{jk}}{\rightsquigarrow} v_k$, so that $w(p) = w(p_{0i}) + w(p_{ij}) + w(p_{jk})$. Now, assume that there is a path p'_{ij} from v_i to v_j with weight $w(p'_{ij}) < w(p_{ij})$. Then, $v_0 \overset{p_{0i}}{\rightsquigarrow} v_i \overset{p'_{ij}}{\rightsquigarrow} v_j \overset{p_{jk}}{\rightsquigarrow} v_k$ is a path from v_0 to v_k whose weight $w(p_{0i}) + w(p'_{ij}) + w(p_{jk})$ is less than $w(p)$, which contradicts the assumption that p is a shortest path from v_0 to v_k.   ∎

Negative-weight edges

Some instances of the single-source shortest-paths problem may include edges whose weights are negative. If the graph $G = (V, E)$ contains no negative-weight cycles reachable from the source s, then for all $v \in V$, the shortest-path weight $\delta(s, v)$ remains well defined, even if it has a negative value. If the graph contains a negative-weight cycle reachable from s, however, shortest-path weights are not well defined. No path from s to a vertex on the cycle can be a shortest path—you can always find a path with lower weight by following the proposed "shortest" path and then traversing the negative-weight cycle. If there is a negative-weight cycle on some path from s to v, we define $\delta(s, v) = -\infty$.

Figure 22.1 illustrates the effect of negative weights and negative-weight cycles on shortest-path weights. Because there is only one path from s to a (the path $\langle s, a \rangle$), we have $\delta(s, a) = w(s, a) = 3$. Similarly, there is only one path from s to b, and so $\delta(s, b) = w(s, a) + w(a, b) = 3 + (-4) = -1$. There are infinitely many paths from s to c: $\langle s, c \rangle$, $\langle s, c, d, c \rangle$, $\langle s, c, d, c, d, c \rangle$, and so on. Because the cycle $\langle c, d, c \rangle$ has weight $6 + (-3) = 3 > 0$, the shortest path from s to c is $\langle s, c \rangle$, with weight $\delta(s, c) = w(s, c) = 5$, and the shortest path from s to d is $\langle s, c, d \rangle$, with weight $\delta(s, d) = w(s, c) + w(c, d) = 11$. Analogously, there are infinitely many paths from s to e: $\langle s, e \rangle$, $\langle s, e, f, e \rangle$, $\langle s, e, f, e, f, e \rangle$, and so on. Because the cycle $\langle e, f, e \rangle$ has weight $3 + (-6) = -3 < 0$, however, there is no shortest path from s to e. By traversing the negative-weight cycle $\langle e, f, e \rangle$ arbitrarily many times, you can find paths from s to e with arbitrarily large negative weights, and so $\delta(s, e) = -\infty$. Similarly, $\delta(s, f) = -\infty$. Because g is reachable from f, you can also find paths with arbitrarily large negative weights from s to g,

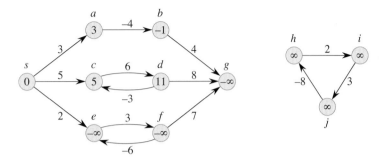

Figure 22.1 Negative edge weights in a directed graph. The shortest-path weight from source s appears within each vertex. Because vertices e and f form a negative-weight cycle reachable from s, they have shortest-path weights of $-\infty$. Because vertex g is reachable from a vertex whose shortest-path weight is $-\infty$, it, too, has a shortest-path weight of $-\infty$. Vertices such as h, i, and j are not reachable from s, and so their shortest-path weights are ∞, even though they lie on a negative-weight cycle.

and so $\delta(s, g) = -\infty$. Vertices h, i, and j also form a negative-weight cycle. They are not reachable from s, however, and so $\delta(s, h) = \delta(s, i) = \delta(s, j) = \infty$.

Some shortest-paths algorithms, such as Dijkstra's algorithm, assume that all edge weights in the input graph are nonnegative, as in a road network. Others, such as the Bellman-Ford algorithm, allow negative-weight edges in the input graph and produce a correct answer as long as no negative-weight cycles are reachable from the source. Typically, if there is such a negative-weight cycle, the algorithm can detect and report its existence.

Cycles

Can a shortest path contain a cycle? As we have just seen, it cannot contain a negative-weight cycle. Nor can it contain a positive-weight cycle, since removing the cycle from the path produces a path with the same source and destination vertices and a lower path weight. That is, if $p = \langle v_0, v_1, \ldots, v_k \rangle$ is a path and $c = \langle v_i, v_{i+1}, \ldots, v_j \rangle$ is a positive-weight cycle on this path (so that $v_i = v_j$ and $w(c) > 0$), then the path $p' = \langle v_0, v_1, \ldots, v_i, v_{j+1}, v_{j+2}, \ldots, v_k \rangle$ has weight $w(p') = w(p) - w(c) < w(p)$, and so p cannot be a shortest path from v_0 to v_k.

That leaves only 0-weight cycles. You can remove a 0-weight cycle from any path to produce another path whose weight is the same. Thus, if there is a shortest path from a source vertex s to a destination vertex v that contains a 0-weight cycle, then there is another shortest path from s to v without this cycle. As long as a shortest path has 0-weight cycles, you can repeatedly remove these cycles from the path until you have a shortest path that is cycle-free. Therefore, without loss of generality, assume that shortest paths have no cycles, that is, they are simple paths. Since any acyclic path in a graph $G = (V, E)$ contains at most $|V|$ distinct vertices, it also contains at most $|V| - 1$ edges. Assume, therefore, that any shortest path contains at most $|V| - 1$ edges.

Representing shortest paths

It is usually not enough to compute only shortest-path weights. Most applications of shortest paths need to know the vertices on shortest paths as well. For example, if your GPS told you the distance to your destination but not how to get there, it would not be terribly useful. We represent shortest paths similarly to how we represented breadth-first trees in Section 20.2. Given a graph $G = (V, E)$, maintain for each vertex $v \in V$ a *predecessor* $v.\pi$ that is either another vertex or NIL. The shortest-paths algorithms in this chapter set the π attributes so that the chain of predecessors originating at a vertex v runs backward along a shortest path from s to v. Thus, given a vertex v for which $v.\pi \neq$ NIL, the procedure PRINT-PATH(G, s, v) from Section 20.2 prints a shortest path from s to v.

In the midst of executing a shortest-paths algorithm, however, the π values might not indicate shortest paths. The *predecessor subgraph* $G_\pi = (V_\pi, E_\pi)$ induced by the π values is defined the same for single-source shortest paths as for breadth-first search in equations (20.2) and (20.3) on page 561:

$$V_\pi = \{v \in V : v.\pi \neq \text{NIL}\} \cup \{s\} \ ,$$
$$E_\pi = \{(v.\pi, v) \in E : v \in V_\pi - \{s\}\} \ .$$

We'll prove that the π values produced by the algorithms in this chapter have the property that at termination G_π is a "shortest-paths tree"—informally, a rooted tree containing a shortest path from the source s to every vertex that is reachable from s. A shortest-paths tree is like the breadth-first tree from Section 20.2, but it contains shortest paths from the source defined in terms of edge weights instead of numbers of edges. To be precise, let $G = (V, E)$ be a weighted, directed graph with weight function $w : E \rightarrow \mathbb{R}$, and assume that G contains no negative-weight cycles reachable from the source vertex $s \in V$, so that shortest paths are well defined. A *shortest-paths tree* rooted at s is a directed subgraph $G' = (V', E')$, where $V' \subseteq V$ and $E' \subseteq E$, such that

1. V' is the set of vertices reachable from s in G,

2. G' forms a rooted tree with root s, and

3. for all $v \in V'$, the unique simple path from s to v in G' is a shortest path from s to v in G.

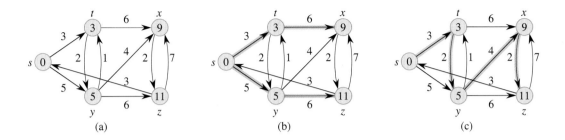

Figure 22.2 **(a)** A weighted, directed graph with shortest-path weights from source s. **(b)** The blue edges form a shortest-paths tree rooted at the source s. **(c)** Another shortest-paths tree with the same root.

Shortest paths are not necessarily unique, and neither are shortest-paths trees. For example, Figure 22.2 shows a weighted, directed graph and two shortest-paths trees with the same root.

Relaxation

The algorithms in this chapter use the technique of *relaxation*. For each vertex $v \in V$, the single-source shortest paths algorithms maintain an attribute $v.d$, which is an upper bound on the weight of a shortest path from source s to v. We call $v.d$ a *shortest-path estimate*. To initialize the shortest-path estimates and predecessors, call the $\Theta(V)$-time procedure INITIALIZE-SINGLE-SOURCE. After initialization, we have $v.\pi = \text{NIL}$ for all $v \in V$, $s.d = 0$ and $v.d = \infty$ for $v \in V - \{s\}$.

INITIALIZE-SINGLE-SOURCE(G, s)

1 **for** each vertex $v \in G.V$
2      $v.d = \infty$
3      $v.\pi = \text{NIL}$
4 $s.d = 0$

The process of *relaxing* an edge (u, v) consists of testing whether going through vertex u improves the shortest path to vertex v found so far and, if so, updating $v.d$ and $v.\pi$. A relaxation step might decrease the value of the shortest-path estimate $v.d$ and update v's predecessor attribute $v.\pi$. The RELAX procedure on the following page performs a relaxation step on edge (u, v) in $O(1)$ time. Figure 22.3 shows two examples of relaxing an edge, one in which a shortest-path estimate decreases and one in which no estimate changes.

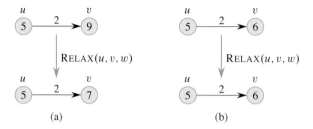

Figure 22.3   Relaxing an edge (u, v) with weight $w(u, v) = 2$. The shortest-path estimate of each vertex appears within the vertex. **(a)** Because $v.d > u.d + w(u, v)$ prior to relaxation, the value of $v.d$ decreases. **(b)** Since we have $v.d \leq u.d + w(u, v)$ before relaxing the edge, the relaxation step leaves $v.d$ unchanged.

$\text{RELAX}(u, v, w)$

1   **if** $v.d > u.d + w(u, v)$
2       $v.d = u.d + w(u, v)$
3       $v.\pi = u$

Each algorithm in this chapter calls INITIALIZE-SINGLE-SOURCE and then repeatedly relaxes edges.[1] Moreover, relaxation is the only means by which shortest-path estimates and predecessors change. The algorithms in this chapter differ in how many times they relax each edge and the order in which they relax edges. Dijkstra's algorithm and the shortest-paths algorithm for directed acyclic graphs relax each edge exactly once. The Bellman-Ford algorithm relaxes each edge $|V| - 1$ times.

Properties of shortest paths and relaxation

To prove the algorithms in this chapter correct, we'll appeal to several properties of shortest paths and relaxation. We state these properties here, and Section 22.5 proves them formally. For your reference, each property stated here includes the appropriate lemma or corollary number from Section 22.5. The latter five of these properties, which refer to shortest-path estimates or the predecessor subgraph, im-

---

[1] It may seem strange that the term "relaxation" is used for an operation that tightens an upper bound. The use of the term is historical. The outcome of a relaxation step can be viewed as a relaxation of the constraint $v.d \leq u.d + w(u, v)$, which, by the triangle inequality (Lemma 22.10 on page 633), must be satisfied if $u.d = \delta(s, u)$ and $v.d = \delta(s, v)$. That is, if $v.d \leq u.d + w(u, v)$, there is no "pressure" to satisfy this constraint, so the constraint is "relaxed."

plicitly assume that the graph is initialized with a call to INITIALIZE-SINGLE-SOURCE(G, s) and that the only way that shortest-path estimates and the predecessor subgraph change are by some sequence of relaxation steps.

Triangle inequality (Lemma 22.10)

For any edge $(u, v) \in E$, we have $\delta(s, v) \leq \delta(s, u) + w(u, v)$.

Upper-bound property (Lemma 22.11)

We always have $v.d \geq \delta(s, v)$ for all vertices $v \in V$, and once $v.d$ achieves the value $\delta(s, v)$, it never changes.

No-path property (Corollary 22.12)

If there is no path from s to v, then we always have $v.d = \delta(s, v) = \infty$.

Convergence property (Lemma 22.14)

If $s \rightsquigarrow u \rightarrow v$ is a shortest path in G for some $u, v \in V$, and if $u.d = \delta(s, u)$ at any time prior to relaxing edge (u, v), then $v.d = \delta(s, v)$ at all times afterward.

Path-relaxation property (Lemma 22.15)

If $p = \langle v_0, v_1, \ldots, v_k \rangle$ is a shortest path from $s = v_0$ to v_k, and the edges of p are relaxed in the order $(v_0, v_1), (v_1, v_2), \ldots, (v_{k-1}, v_k)$, then $v_k.d = \delta(s, v_k)$. This property holds regardless of any other relaxation steps that occur, even if they are intermixed with relaxations of the edges of p.

Predecessor-subgraph property (Lemma 22.17)

Once $v.d = \delta(s, v)$ for all $v \in V$, the predecessor subgraph is a shortest-paths tree rooted at s.

Chapter outline

Section 22.1 presents the Bellman-Ford algorithm, which solves the single-source shortest-paths problem in the general case in which edges can have negative weight. The Bellman-Ford algorithm is remarkably simple, and it has the further benefit of detecting whether a negative-weight cycle is reachable from the source. Section 22.2 gives a linear-time algorithm for computing shortest paths from a single source in a directed acyclic graph. Section 22.3 covers Dijkstra's algorithm, which has a lower running time than the Bellman-Ford algorithm but requires the edge weights to be nonnegative. Section 22.4 shows how to use the Bellman-Ford algorithm to solve a special case of linear programming. Finally, Section 22.5 proves the properties of shortest paths and relaxation stated above.

This chapter does arithmetic with infinities, and so we need some conventions for when ∞ or $-\infty$ appears in an arithmetic expression. We assume that for any real number $a \neq -\infty$, we have $a + \infty = \infty + a = \infty$. Also, to make our proofs hold in the presence of negative-weight cycles, we assume that for any real number $a \neq \infty$, we have $a + (-\infty) = (-\infty) + a = -\infty$.

All algorithms in this chapter assume that the directed graph G is stored in the adjacency-list representation. Additionally, stored with each edge is its weight, so that as each algorithm traverses an adjacency list, it can find edge weights in $O(1)$ time per edge.

22.1   The Bellman-Ford algorithm

The *Bellman-Ford algorithm* solves the single-source shortest-paths problem in the general case in which edge weights may be negative. Given a weighted, directed graph $G = (V, E)$ with source vertex s and weight function $w : E \rightarrow \mathbb{R}$, the Bellman-Ford algorithm returns a boolean value indicating whether there is a negative-weight cycle that is reachable from the source. If there is such a cycle, the algorithm indicates that no solution exists. If there is no such cycle, the algorithm produces the shortest paths and their weights.

The procedure BELLMAN-FORD relaxes edges, progressively decreasing an estimate $v.d$ on the weight of a shortest path from the source s to each vertex $v \in V$ until it achieves the actual shortest-path weight $\delta(s, v)$. The algorithm returns TRUE if and only if the graph contains no negative-weight cycles that are reachable from the source.

BELLMAN-FORD(G, w, s)

1 INITIALIZE-SINGLE-SOURCE(G, s)
2 **for** $i = 1$ **to** $|G.V| - 1$
3   **for** each edge $(u, v) \in G.E$
4   RELAX(u, v, w)
5 **for** each edge $(u, v) \in G.E$
6   **if** $v.d > u.d + w(u, v)$
7   **return** FALSE
8 **return** TRUE

Figure 22.4 shows the execution of the Bellman-Ford algorithm on a graph with 5 vertices. After initializing the d and π values of all vertices in line 1, the algorithm makes $|V| - 1$ passes over the edges of the graph. Each pass is one iteration of the **for** loop of lines 2–4 and consists of relaxing each edge of the graph once. Figures 22.4(b)–(e) show the state of the algorithm after each of the four passes over the edges. After making $|V| - 1$ passes, lines 5–8 check for a negative-weight cycle and return the appropriate boolean value. (We'll see a little later why this check works.)

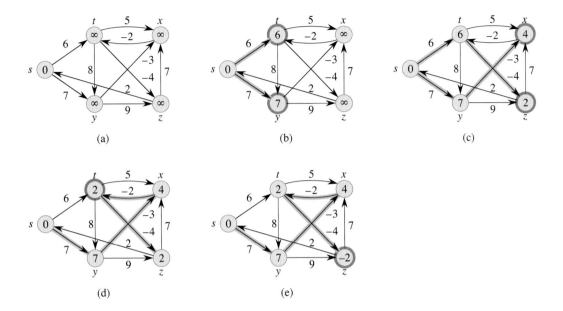

Figure 22.4 The execution of the Bellman-Ford algorithm. The source is vertex s. The d values appear within the vertices, and blue edges indicate predecessor values: if edge (u, v) is blue, then $v.\pi = u$. In this particular example, each pass relaxes the edges in the order $(t, x), (t, y), (t, z), (x, t), (y, x), (y, z), (z, x), (z, s), (s, t), (s, y)$. **(a)** The situation just before the first pass over the edges. **(b)–(e)** The situation after each successive pass over the edges. Vertices whose shortest-path estimates and predecessors have changed due to a pass are highlighted in orange. The d and π values in part (e) are the final values. The Bellman-Ford algorithm returns TRUE in this example.

The Bellman-Ford algorithm runs in $O(V^2 + VE)$ time when the graph is represented by adjacency lists, since the initialization in line 1 takes $\Theta(V)$ time, each of the $|V| - 1$ passes over the edges in lines 2–4 takes $\Theta(V + E)$ time (examining $|V|$ adjacency lists to find the $|E|$ edges), and the **for** loop of lines 5–7 takes $O(V + E)$ time. Fewer than $|V| - 1$ passes over the edges sometimes suffice (see Exercise 22.1-3), which is why we say $O(V^2 + VE)$ time, rather than $\Theta(V^2 + VE)$ time. In the frequent case where $|E| = \Omega(V)$, we can express this running time as $O(VE)$. Exercise 22.1-5 asks you to make the Bellman-Ford algorithm run in $O(VE)$ time even when $|E| = o(V)$.

To prove the correctness of the Bellman-Ford algorithm, we start by showing that if there are no negative-weight cycles, the algorithm computes correct shortest-path weights for all vertices reachable from the source.

Lemma 22.2

Let $G = (V, E)$ be a weighted, directed graph with source vertex s and weight function $w : E \rightarrow \mathbb{R}$, and assume that G contains no negative-weight cycles that are reachable from s. Then, after the $|V| - 1$ iterations of the **for** loop of lines 2–4 of BELLMAN-FORD, $v.d = \delta(s, v)$ for all vertices v that are reachable from s.

Proof   We prove the lemma by appealing to the path-relaxation property. Consider any vertex v that is reachable from s, and let $p = \langle v_0, v_1, \ldots, v_k \rangle$, where $v_0 = s$ and $v_k = v$, be any shortest path from s to v. Because shortest paths are simple, p has at most $|V| - 1$ edges, and so $k \leq |V| - 1$. Each of the $|V| - 1$ iterations of the **for** loop of lines 2–4 relaxes all $|E|$ edges. Among the edges relaxed in the ith iteration, for $i = 1, 2, \ldots, k$, is (v_{i-1}, v_i). By the path-relaxation property, therefore, $v.d = v_k.d = \delta(s, v_k) = \delta(s, v)$.   ∎

Corollary 22.3

Let $G = (V, E)$ be a weighted, directed graph with source vertex s and weight function $w : E \rightarrow \mathbb{R}$. Then, for each vertex $v \in V$, there is a path from s to v if and only if BELLMAN-FORD terminates with $v.d < \infty$ when it is run on G.

Proof   The proof is left as Exercise 22.1-2.   ∎

Theorem 22.4 (Correctness of the Bellman-Ford algorithm)

Let BELLMAN-FORD be run on a weighted, directed graph $G = (V, E)$ with source vertex s and weight function $w : E \rightarrow \mathbb{R}$. If G contains no negative-weight cycles that are reachable from s, then the algorithm returns TRUE, $v.d = \delta(s, v)$ for all vertices $v \in V$, and the predecessor subgraph G_π is a shortest-paths tree rooted at s. If G does contain a negative-weight cycle reachable from s, then the algorithm returns FALSE.

Proof   Suppose that graph G contains no negative-weight cycles that are reachable from the source s. We first prove the claim that at termination, $v.d = \delta(s, v)$ for all vertices $v \in V$. If vertex v is reachable from s, then Lemma 22.2 proves this claim. If v is not reachable from s, then the claim follows from the no-path property. Thus, the claim is proven. The predecessor-subgraph property, along with the claim, implies that G_π is a shortest-paths tree. Now we use the claim to show that BELLMAN-FORD returns TRUE. At termination, for all edges $(u, v) \in E$ we have

$$
\begin{aligned}
v.d &= \delta(s, v) \\
&\leq \delta(s, u) + w(u, v) \quad \text{(by the triangle inequality)} \\
&= u.d + w(u, v) \,,
\end{aligned}
$$

and so none of the tests in line 6 causes BELLMAN-FORD to return FALSE. Therefore, it returns TRUE.

Now, suppose that graph G contains a negative-weight cycle reachable from the source s. Let this cycle be $c = \langle v_0, v_1, \ldots, v_k \rangle$, where $v_0 = v_k$, in which case we have

$$\sum_{i=1}^{k} w(v_{i-1}, v_i) < 0 . \tag{22.1}$$

Assume for the purpose of contradiction that the Bellman-Ford algorithm returns TRUE. Thus, $v_i.d \leq v_{i-1}.d + w(v_{i-1}, v_i)$ for $i = 1, 2, \ldots, k$. Summing the inequalities around cycle c gives

$$\sum_{i=1}^{k} v_i.d \leq \sum_{i=1}^{k} (v_{i-1}.d + w(v_{i-1}, v_i))$$
$$= \sum_{i=1}^{k} v_{i-1}.d + \sum_{i=1}^{k} w(v_{i-1}, v_i) .$$

Since $v_0 = v_k$, each vertex in c appears exactly once in each of the summations $\sum_{i=1}^{k} v_i.d$ and $\sum_{i=1}^{k} v_{i-1}.d$, and so

$$\sum_{i=1}^{k} v_i.d = \sum_{i=1}^{k} v_{i-1}.d .$$

Moreover, by Corollary 22.3, $v_i.d$ is finite for $i = 1, 2, \ldots, k$. Thus,

$$0 \leq \sum_{i=1}^{k} w(v_{i-1}, v_i) ,$$

which contradicts inequality (22.1). We conclude that the Bellman-Ford algorithm returns TRUE if graph G contains no negative-weight cycles reachable from the source, and FALSE otherwise. ∎

Exercises

22.1-1
Run the Bellman-Ford algorithm on the directed graph of Figure 22.4, using vertex z as the source. In each pass, relax edges in the same order as in the figure, and show the d and π values after each pass. Now, change the weight of edge (z, x) to 4 and run the algorithm again, using s as the source.

22.1-2
Prove Corollary 22.3.

22.1-3

Given a weighted, directed graph $G = (V, E)$ with no negative-weight cycles, let m be the maximum over all vertices $v \in V$ of the minimum number of edges in a shortest path from the source s to v. (Here, the shortest path is by weight, not the number of edges.) Suggest a simple change to the Bellman-Ford algorithm that allows it to terminate in $m + 1$ passes, even if m is not known in advance.

22.1-4

Modify the Bellman-Ford algorithm so that it sets $v.d$ to $-\infty$ for all vertices v for which there is a negative-weight cycle on some path from the source to v.

22.1-5

Suppose that the graph given as input to the Bellman-Ford algorithm is represented with a list of $|E|$ edges, where each edge indicates the vertices it leaves and enters, along with its weight. Argue that the Bellman-Ford algorithm runs in $O(VE)$ time without the constraint that $|E| = \Omega(V)$. Modify the Bellman-Ford algorithm so that it runs in $O(VE)$ time in all cases when the input graph is represented with adjacency lists.

22.1-6

Let $G = (V, E)$ be a weighted, directed graph with weight function $w : E \to \mathbb{R}$. Give an $O(VE)$-time algorithm to find, for all vertices $v \in V$, the value $\delta^*(v) = \min \{\delta(u, v) : u \in V\}$.

22.1-7

Suppose that a weighted, directed graph $G = (V, E)$ contains a negative-weight cycle. Give an efficient algorithm to list the vertices of one such cycle. Prove that your algorithm is correct.

22.2   Single-source shortest paths in directed acyclic graphs

In this section, we introduce one further restriction on weighted, directed graphs: they are acyclic. That is, we are concerned with weighted dags. Shortest paths are always well defined in a dag, since even if there are negative-weight edges, no negative-weight cycles can exist. We'll see that if the edges of a weighted dag $G = (V, E)$ are relaxed according to a topological sort of its vertices, it takes only $\Theta(V + E)$ time to compute shortest paths from a single source.

The algorithm starts by topologically sorting the dag (see Section 20.4) to impose a linear ordering on the vertices. If the dag contains a path from vertex u to vertex v, then u precedes v in the topological sort. The DAG-SHORTEST-PATHS procedure makes just one pass over the vertices in the topologically sorted order. As it processes each vertex, it relaxes each edge that leaves the vertex. Figure 22.5 shows the execution of this algorithm.

DAG-SHORTEST-PATHS(G, w, s)

1   topologically sort the vertices of G
2   INITIALIZE-SINGLE-SOURCE(G, s)
3   **for** each vertex $u \in G.V$, taken in topologically sorted order
4   **for** each vertex v in $G.Adj[u]$
5   RELAX(u, v, w)

Let's analyze the running time of this algorithm. As shown in Section 20.4, the topological sort of line 1 takes $\Theta(V + E)$ time. The call of INITIALIZE-SINGLE-SOURCE in line 2 takes $\Theta(V)$ time. The **for** loop of lines 3–5 makes one iteration per vertex. Altogether, the **for** loop of lines 4–5 relaxes each edge exactly once. (We have used an aggregate analysis here.) Because each iteration of the inner **for** loop takes $\Theta(1)$ time, the total running time is $\Theta(V + E)$, which is linear in the size of an adjacency-list representation of the graph.

The following theorem shows that the DAG-SHORTEST-PATHS procedure correctly computes the shortest paths.

Theorem 22.5
If a weighted, directed graph $G = (V, E)$ has source vertex s and no cycles, then at the termination of the DAG-SHORTEST-PATHS procedure, $v.d = \delta(s, v)$ for all vertices $v \in V$, and the predecessor subgraph G_π is a shortest-paths tree.

Proof   We first show that $v.d = \delta(s, v)$ for all vertices $v \in V$ at termination. If v is not reachable from s, then $v.d = \delta(s, v) = \infty$ by the no-path property. Now, suppose that v is reachable from s, so that there is a shortest path $p = \langle v_0, v_1, \ldots, v_k \rangle$, where $v_0 = s$ and $v_k = v$. Because DAG-SHORTEST-PATHS processes the vertices in topologically sorted order, it relaxes the edges on p in the order $(v_0, v_1), (v_1, v_2), \ldots, (v_{k-1}, v_k)$. The path-relaxation property implies that $v_i.d = \delta(s, v_i)$ at termination for $i = 0, 1, \ldots, k$. Finally, by the predecessor-subgraph property, G_π is a shortest-paths tree.   ∎

A useful application of this algorithm arises in determining critical paths in *PERT chart*[2] analysis. A job consists of several tasks. Each task takes a certain

---

[2] "PERT" is an acronym for "program evaluation and review technique."

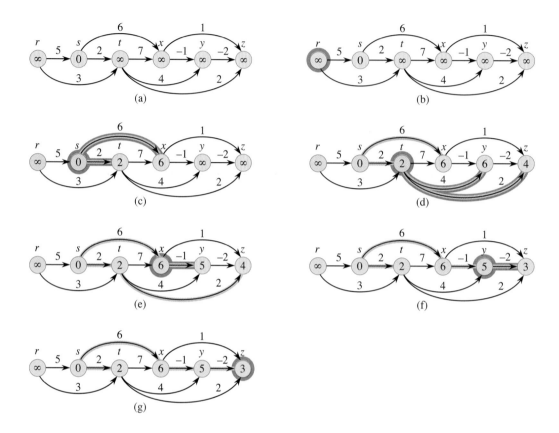

Figure 22.5 The execution of the algorithm for shortest paths in a directed acyclic graph. The vertices are topologically sorted from left to right. The source vertex is s. The d values appear within the vertices, and blue edges indicate the π values. **(a)** The situation before the first iteration of the **for** loop of lines 3–5. **(b)–(g)** The situation after each iteration of the **for** loop of lines 3–5. Blue vertices have had their outgoing edges relaxed. The vertex highlighted in orange was used as u in that iteration. Each edge highlighted in orange caused a d value to change when it was relaxed in that iteration. The values shown in part (g) are the final values.

amount of time, and some tasks must be completed before others can be started. For example, if the job is to build a house, then the foundation must be completed before starting to frame the exterior walls, which must be completed before starting on the roof. Some tasks require more than one other task to be completed before they can be started: before the drywall can be installed over the wall framing, both the electrical system and plumbing must be installed. A dag models the tasks and dependencies. Edges represent tasks, with the weight of an edge indicating the time required to perform the task. Vertices represent "milestones," which are achieved when all the tasks represented by the edges entering the vertex have been completed. If edge (u, v) enters vertex v and edge (v, x) leaves v, then task (u, v) must be completed before task (v, x) is started. A path through this dag represents a sequence of tasks that must be performed in a particular order. A *critical path* is a *longest* path through the dag, corresponding to the longest time to perform any sequence of tasks. Thus, the weight of a critical path provides a lower bound on the total time to perform all the tasks, even if as many tasks as possible are performed simultaneously. You can find a critical path by either

- negating the edge weights and running DAG-SHORTEST-PATHS, or

- running DAG-SHORTEST-PATHS, but replacing "∞" by "−∞" in line 2 of INITIALIZE-SINGLE-SOURCE and ">" by "<" in the RELAX procedure.

Exercises

22.2-1
Show the result of running DAG-SHORTEST-PATHS on the directed acyclic graph of Figure 22.5, using vertex r as the source.

22.2-2
Suppose that you change line 3 of DAG-SHORTEST-PATHS to read

3   **for** the first $|V| - 1$ vertices, taken in topologically sorted order

Show that the procedure remains correct.

22.2-3
An alternative way to represent a PERT chart looks more like the dag of Figure 20.7 on page 574. Vertices represent tasks and edges represent sequencing constraints, that is, edge (u, v) indicates that task u must be performed before task v. Vertices, not edges, have weights. Modify the DAG-SHORTEST-PATHS procedure so that it finds a longest path in a directed acyclic graph with weighted vertices in linear time.

★ ***22.2-4***
Give an efficient algorithm to count the total number of paths in a directed acyclic graph. The count should include all paths between all pairs of vertices and all paths with 0 edges. Analyze your algorithm.

22.3   Dijkstra's algorithm

Dijkstra's algorithm solves the single-source shortest-paths problem on a weighted, directed graph $G = (V, E)$, but it requires nonnegative weights on all edges: $w(u, v) \geq 0$ for each edge $(u, v) \in E$. As we shall see, with a good implementation, the running time of Dijkstra's algorithm is lower than that of the Bellman-Ford algorithm.

You can think of Dijkstra's algorithm as generalizing breadth-first search to weighted graphs. A wave emanates from the source, and the first time that a wave arrives at a vertex, a new wave emanates from that vertex. Whereas breadth-first search operates as if each wave takes unit time to traverse an edge, in a weighted graph, the time for a wave to traverse an edge is given by the edge's weight. Because a shortest path in a weighted graph might not have the fewest edges, a simple, first-in, first-out queue won't suffice for choosing the next vertex from which to send out a wave.

Instead, Dijkstra's algorithm maintains a set S of vertices whose final shortest-path weights from the source s have already been determined. The algorithm repeatedly selects the vertex $u \in V - S$ with the minimum shortest-path estimate, adds u into S, and relaxes all edges leaving u. The procedure DIJKSTRA replaces the first-in, first-out queue of breadth-first search by a min-priority queue Q of vertices, keyed by their d values.

DIJKSTRA(G, w, s)

1   INITIALIZE-SINGLE-SOURCE(G, s)
2   $S = \emptyset$
3   $Q = \emptyset$
4   **for** each vertex $u \in G.V$
5   INSERT(Q, u)
6   **while** $Q \neq \emptyset$
7       $u =$ EXTRACT-MIN(Q)
8       $S = S \cup \{u\}$
9   **for** each vertex v in $G.Adj[u]$
10   RELAX(u, v, w)
11   **if** the call of RELAX decreased $v.d$
12   DECREASE-KEY$(Q, v, v.d)$

Dijkstra's algorithm relaxes edges as shown in Figure 22.6. Line 1 initializes the d and π values in the usual way, and line 2 initializes the set S to the empty set. The algorithm maintains the invariant that $Q = V - S$ at the start of each iteration

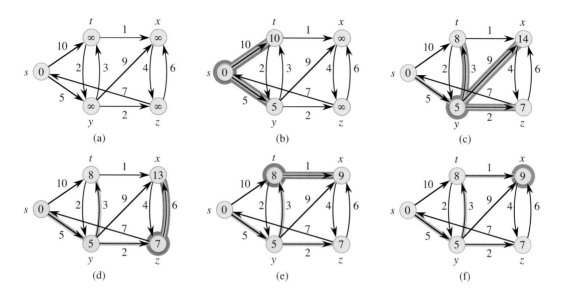

Figure 22.6 The execution of Dijkstra's algorithm. The source s is the leftmost vertex. The shortest-path estimates appear within the vertices, and blue edges indicate predecessor values. Blue vertices belong to the set S, and tan vertices are in the min-priority queue $Q = V - S$. **(a)** The situation just before the first iteration of the **while** loop of lines 6–12. **(b)–(f)** The situation after each successive iteration of the **while** loop. In each part, the vertex highlighted in orange was chosen as vertex u in line 7, and each edge highlighted in orange caused a d value and a predecessor to change when the edge was relaxed. The d values and predecessors shown in part (f) are the final values.

of the **while** loop of lines 6–12. Lines 3–5 initialize the min-priority queue Q to contain all the vertices in V. Since $S = \emptyset$ at that time, the invariant is true upon first reaching line 6. Each time through the **while** loop of lines 6–12, line 7 extracts a vertex u from $Q = V - S$ and line 8 adds it to set S, thereby maintaining the invariant. (The first time through this loop, $u = s$.) Vertex u, therefore, has the smallest shortest-path estimate of any vertex in $V - S$. Then, lines 9–12 relax each edge (u, v) leaving u, thus updating the estimate $v.d$ and the predecessor $v.\pi$ if the shortest path to v found so far improves by going through u. Whenever a relaxation step changes the d and π values, the call to DECREASE-KEY in line 12 updates the min-priority queue. The algorithm never inserts vertices into Q after the **for** loop of lines 4–5, and each vertex is extracted from Q and added to S exactly once, so that the **while** loop of lines 6–12 iterates exactly $|V|$ times.

Because Dijkstra's algorithm always chooses the "lightest" or "closest" vertex in $V - S$ to add to set S, you can think of it as using a greedy strategy. Chapter 15 explains greedy strategies in detail, but you need not have read that chapter to understand Dijkstra's algorithm. Greedy strategies do not always yield optimal

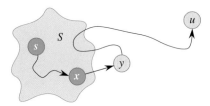

Figure 22.7 The proof of Theorem 22.6. Vertex u is selected to be added into set S in line 7 of DIJKSTRA. Vertex y is the first vertex on a shortest path from the source s to vertex u that is not in set S, and $x \in S$ is y's predecessor on that shortest path. The subpath from y to u may or may not re-enter set S.

results in general, but as the following theorem and its corollary show, Dijkstra's algorithm does indeed compute shortest paths. The key is to show that $u.d = \delta(s, u)$ each time it adds a vertex u to set S.

Theorem 22.6 (Correctness of Dijkstra's algorithm)
Dijkstra's algorithm, run on a weighted, directed graph $G = (V, E)$ with nonnegative weight function w and source vertex s, terminates with $u.d = \delta(s, u)$ for all vertices $u \in V$.

Proof We will show that at the start of each iteration of the **while** loop of lines 6–12, we have $v.d = \delta(s, v)$ for all $v \in S$. The algorithm terminates when $S = V$, so that $v.d = \delta(s, v)$ for all $v \in V$.

The proof is by induction on the number of iterations of the **while** loop, which equals $|S|$ at the start of each iteration. There are two bases: for $|S| = 0$, so that $S = \emptyset$ and the claim is trivially true, and for $|S| = 1$, so that $S = \{s\}$ and $s.d = \delta(s, s) = 0$.

For the inductive step, the inductive hypothesis is that $v.d = \delta(s, v)$ for all $v \in S$. The algorithm extracts vertex u from $V - S$. Because the algorithm adds u into S, we need to show that $u.d = \delta(s, u)$ at that time. If there is no path from s to u, then we are done, by the no-path property. If there is a path from s to u, then, as Figure 22.7 shows, let y be the first vertex on a shortest path from s to u that is not in S, and let $x \in S$ be the predecessor of y on that shortest path. (We could have $y = u$ or $x = s$.) Because y appears no later than u on the shortest path and all edge weights are nonnegative, we have $\delta(s, y) \leq \delta(s, u)$. Because the call of EXTRACT-MIN in line 7 returned u as having the minimum d value in $V - S$, we also have $u.d \leq y.d$, and the upper-bound property gives $\delta(s, u) \leq u.d$.

Since $x \in S$, the inductive hypothesis implies that $x.d = \delta(s, x)$. During the iteration of the **while** loop that added x into S, edge (x, y) was relaxed. By the convergence property, $y.d$ received the value of $\delta(s, y)$ at that time. Thus, we have

$\delta(s, y) \leq \delta(s, u) \leq u.d \leq y.d$ and $y.d = \delta(s, y)$,

so that

$\delta(s, y) = \delta(s, u) = u.d = y.d$.

Hence, $u.d = \delta(s, u)$, and by the upper-bound property, this value never changes again. $\blacksquare$

Corollary 22.7
After Dijkstra's algorithm is run on a weighted, directed graph $G = (V, E)$ with nonnegative weight function w and source vertex s, the predecessor subgraph G_π is a shortest-paths tree rooted at s.

Proof   Immediate from Theorem 22.6 and the predecessor-subgraph property. $\blacksquare$

Analysis

How fast is Dijkstra's algorithm? It maintains the min-priority queue Q by calling three priority-queue operations: INSERT (in line 5), EXTRACT-MIN (in line 7), and DECREASE-KEY (in line 12). The algorithm calls both INSERT and EXTRACT-MIN once per vertex. Because each vertex $u \in V$ is added to set S exactly once, each edge in the adjacency list $Adj[u]$ is examined in the **for** loop of lines 9–12 exactly once during the course of the algorithm. Since the total number of edges in all the adjacency lists is $|E|$, this **for** loop iterates a total of $|E|$ times, and thus the algorithm calls DECREASE-KEY at most $|E|$ times overall. (Observe once again that we are using aggregate analysis.)

Just as in Prim's algorithm, the running time of Dijkstra's algorithm depends on the specific implementation of the min-priority queue Q. A simple implementation takes advantage of the vertices being numbered 1 to $|V|$: simply store $v.d$ in the vth entry of an array. Each INSERT and DECREASE-KEY operation takes $O(1)$ time, and each EXTRACT-MIN operation takes $O(V)$ time (since it has to search through the entire array), for a total time of $O(V^2 + E) = O(V^2)$.

If the graph is sufficiently sparse—in particular, $E = o(V^2/\lg V)$—you can improve the running time by implementing the min-priority queue with a binary min-heap that includes a way to map between vertices and their corresponding heap elements. Each EXTRACT-MIN operation then takes $O(\lg V)$ time. As before, there are $|V|$ such operations. The time to build the binary min-heap is $O(V)$. (As noted in Section 21.2, you don't even need to call BUILD-MIN-HEAP.) Each DECREASE-KEY operation takes $O(\lg V)$ time, and there are still at most $|E|$ such operations. The total running time is therefore $O((V + E) \lg V)$, which is $O(E \lg V)$ in the typical case that $|E| = \Omega(V)$. This running time improves upon the straightforward $O(V^2)$-time implementation if $E = o(V^2/\lg V)$.

By implementing the min-priority queue with a Fibonacci heap (see page 478), you can improve the running time to $O(V \lg V + E)$. The amortized cost of each of the $|V|$ EXTRACT-MIN operations is $O(\lg V)$, and each DECREASE-KEY call, of which there are at most $|E|$, takes only $O(1)$ amortized time. Historically, the development of Fibonacci heaps was motivated by the observation that Dijkstra's algorithm typically makes many more DECREASE-KEY calls than EXTRACT-MIN calls, so that any method of reducing the amortized time of each DECREASE-KEY operation to $o(\lg V)$ without increasing the amortized time of EXTRACT-MIN would yield an asymptotically faster implementation than with binary heaps.

Dijkstra's algorithm resembles both breadth-first search (see Section 20.2) and Prim's algorithm for computing minimum spanning trees (see Section 21.2). It is like breadth-first search in that set S corresponds to the set of black vertices in a breadth-first search. Just as vertices in S have their final shortest-path weights, so do black vertices in a breadth-first search have their correct breadth-first distances. Dijkstra's algorithm is like Prim's algorithm in that both algorithms use a min-priority queue to find the "lightest" vertex outside a given set (the set S in Dijkstra's algorithm and the tree being grown in Prim's algorithm), add this vertex into the set, and adjust the weights of the remaining vertices outside the set accordingly.

Exercises

22.3-1
Run Dijkstra's algorithm on the directed graph of Figure 22.2, first using vertex s as the source and then using vertex z as the source. In the style of Figure 22.6, show the d and π values and the vertices in set S after each iteration of the **while** loop.

22.3-2
Give a simple example of a directed graph with negative-weight edges for which Dijkstra's algorithm produces an incorrect answer. Why doesn't the proof of Theorem 22.6 go through when negative-weight edges are allowed?

22.3-3
Suppose that you change line 6 of Dijkstra's algorithm to read

6   **while** $|Q| > 1$

This change causes the **while** loop to execute $|V| - 1$ times instead of $|V|$ times. Is this proposed algorithm correct?

22.3-4

Modify the DIJKSTRA procedure so that the priority queue Q is more like the queue in the BFS procedure in that it contains only vertices that have been reached from source s so far: $Q \subseteq V - S$ and $v \in Q$ implies $v.d \neq \infty$.

22.3-5

Professor Gaedel has written a program that he claims implements Dijkstra's algorithm. The program produces $v.d$ and $v.\pi$ for each vertex $v \in V$. Give an $O(V + E)$-time algorithm to check the output of the professor's program. It should determine whether the d and π attributes match those of some shortest-paths tree. You may assume that all edge weights are nonnegative.

22.3-6

Professor Newman thinks that he has worked out a simpler proof of correctness for Dijkstra's algorithm. He claims that Dijkstra's algorithm relaxes the edges of every shortest path in the graph in the order in which they appear on the path, and therefore the path-relaxation property applies to every vertex reachable from the source. Show that the professor is mistaken by constructing a directed graph for which Dijkstra's algorithm relaxes the edges of a shortest path out of order.

22.3-7

Consider a directed graph $G = (V, E)$ on which each edge $(u, v) \in E$ has an associated value $r(u, v)$, which is a real number in the range $0 \leq r(u, v) \leq 1$ that represents the reliability of a communication channel from vertex u to vertex v. Interpret $r(u, v)$ as the probability that the channel from u to v will not fail, and assume that these probabilities are independent. Give an efficient algorithm to find the most reliable path between two given vertices.

22.3-8

Let $G = (V, E)$ be a weighted, directed graph with positive weight function $w : E \rightarrow \{1, 2, \ldots, W\}$ for some positive integer W, and assume that no two vertices have the same shortest-path weights from source vertex s. Now define an unweighted, directed graph $G' = (V \cup V', E')$ by replacing each edge $(u, v) \in E$ with $w(u, v)$ unit-weight edges in series. How many vertices does G' have? Now suppose that you run a breadth-first search on G'. Show that the order in which the breadth-first search of G' colors vertices in V black is the same as the order in which Dijkstra's algorithm extracts the vertices of V from the priority queue when it runs on G.

22.3-9

Let $G = (V, E)$ be a weighted, directed graph with nonnegative weight function $w : E \rightarrow \{0, 1, \ldots, W\}$ for some nonnegative integer W. Modify Dijkstra's algorithm to compute the shortest paths from a given source vertex s in $O(WV + E)$ time.

22.3-10

Modify your algorithm from Exercise 22.3-9 to run in $O((V + E)\lg W)$ time. (*Hint:* How many distinct shortest-path estimates can $V - S$ contain at any point in time?)

22.3-11

Suppose that you are given a weighted, directed graph $G = (V, E)$ in which edges that leave the source vertex s may have negative weights, all other edge weights are nonnegative, and there are no negative-weight cycles. Argue that Dijkstra's algorithm correctly finds shortest paths from s in this graph.

22.3-12

Suppose that you have a weighted directed graph $G = (V, E)$ in which all edge weights are positive real values in the range $[C, 2C]$ for some positive constant C. Modify Dijkstra's algorithm so that it runs in $O(V + E)$ time.

22.4   Difference constraints and shortest paths

Chapter 29 studies the general linear-programming problem, showing how to optimize a linear function subject to a set of linear inequalities. This section investigates a special case of linear programming that reduces to finding shortest paths from a single source. The Bellman-Ford algorithm then solves the resulting single-source shortest-paths problem, thereby also solving the linear-programming problem.

Linear programming

In the general *linear-programming problem*, the input is an $m \times n$ matrix A, an m-vector b, and an n-vector c. The goal is to find a vector x of n elements that maximizes the *objective function* $\sum_{i=1}^{n} c_i x_i$ subject to the m constraints given by $Ax \le b$.

The most popular method for solving linear programs is the *simplex algorithm*, which Section 29.1 discusses. Although the simplex algorithm does not always run in time polynomial in the size of its input, there are other linear-programming algorithms that do run in polynomial time. We offer here two reasons to understand the setup of linear-programming problems. First, if you know that you can cast a given problem as a polynomial-sized linear-programming problem, then you immediately have a polynomial-time algorithm to solve the problem. Second, faster algorithms exist for many special cases of linear programming. For example, the single-pair shortest-path problem (Exercise 22.4-4) and the maximum-flow problem (Exercise 24.1-5) are special cases of linear programming.

Sometimes the objective function does not matter: it's enough just to find any *feasible solution*, that is, any vector x that satisfies $Ax \leq b$, or to determine that no feasible solution exists. This section focuses on one such *feasibility problem*.

Systems of difference constraints

In a *system of difference constraints*, each row of the linear-programming matrix A contains one 1 and one -1, and all other entries of A are 0. Thus, the constraints given by $Ax \leq b$ are a set of m *difference constraints* involving n unknowns, in which each constraint is a simple linear inequality of the form

$$x_j - x_i \leq b_k ,$$

where $1 \leq i, j \leq n, i \neq j$, and $1 \leq k \leq m$.

For example, consider the problem of finding a 5-vector $x = (x_i)$ that satisfies

$$\begin{pmatrix} 1 & -1 & 0 & 0 & 0 \\ 1 & 0 & 0 & 0 & -1 \\ 0 & 1 & 0 & 0 & -1 \\ -1 & 0 & 1 & 0 & 0 \\ -1 & 0 & 0 & 1 & 0 \\ 0 & 0 & -1 & 1 & 0 \\ 0 & 0 & -1 & 0 & 1 \\ 0 & 0 & 0 & -1 & 1 \end{pmatrix} \begin{pmatrix} x_1 \\ x_2 \\ x_3 \\ x_4 \\ x_5 \end{pmatrix} \leq \begin{pmatrix} 0 \\ -1 \\ 1 \\ 5 \\ 4 \\ -1 \\ -3 \\ -3 \end{pmatrix} .$$

This problem is equivalent to finding values for the unknowns x_1, x_2, x_3, x_4, x_5, satisfying the following 8 difference constraints:

$$x_1 - x_2 \leq 0 , \qquad (22.2)$$
$$x_1 - x_5 \leq -1 , \qquad (22.3)$$
$$x_2 - x_5 \leq 1 , \qquad (22.4)$$
$$x_3 - x_1 \leq 5 , \qquad (22.5)$$
$$x_4 - x_1 \leq 4 , \qquad (22.6)$$
$$x_4 - x_3 \leq -1 , \qquad (22.7)$$
$$x_5 - x_3 \leq -3 , \qquad (22.8)$$
$$x_5 - x_4 \leq -3 . \qquad (22.9)$$

One solution to this problem is $x = (-5, -3, 0, -1, -4)$, which you can verify directly by checking each inequality. In fact, this problem has more than one solution.

Another is $x' = (0, 2, 5, 4, 1)$. These two solutions are related: each component of x' is 5 larger than the corresponding component of x. This fact is not mere coincidence.

Lemma 22.8
Let $x = (x_1, x_2, \ldots, x_n)$ be a solution to a system $Ax \leq b$ of difference constraints, and let d be any constant. Then $x + d = (x_1 + d, x_2 + d, \ldots, x_n + d)$ is a solution to $Ax \leq b$ as well.

Proof   For each x_i and x_j, we have $(x_j + d) - (x_i + d) = x_j - x_i$. Thus, if x satisfies $Ax \leq b$, so does $x + d$.   ∎

Systems of difference constraints occur in various applications. For example, the unknowns x_i might be times at which events are to occur. Each constraint states that at least a certain amount of time, or at most a certain amount of time, must elapse between two events. Perhaps the events are jobs to be performed during the assembly of a product. If the manufacturer applies an adhesive that takes 2 hours to set at time x_1 and has to wait until it sets to install a part at time x_2, then there is a constraint that $x_2 \geq x_1 + 2$ or, equivalently, that $x_1 - x_2 \leq -2$. Alternatively, the manufacturer might require the part to be installed after the adhesive has been applied but no later than the time that the adhesive has set halfway. In this case, there is a pair of constraints $x_2 \geq x_1$ and $x_2 \leq x_1 + 1$ or, equivalently, $x_1 - x_2 \leq 0$ and $x_2 - x_1 \leq 1$.

If all the constraints have nonnegative numbers on the right-hand side—that is, if $b_i \geq 0$ for $i = 1, 2, \ldots, m$—then finding a feasible solution is trivial: just set all the unknowns x_i equal to each other. Then all the differences are 0, and every constraint is satisfied. The problem of finding a feasible solution to a system of difference constraints is interesting only if at least one constraint has $b_i < 0$.

Constraint graphs

We can interpret systems of difference constraints from a graph-theoretic point of view. For a system $Ax \leq b$ of difference constraints, let's view the $m \times n$ linear-programming matrix A as the transpose of an incidence matrix (see Exercise 20.1-7) for a graph with n vertices and m edges. Each vertex v_i in the graph, for $i = 1, 2, \ldots, n$, corresponds to one of the n unknown variables x_i. Each directed edge in the graph corresponds to one of the m inequalities involving two unknowns.

More formally, given a system $Ax \leq b$ of difference constraints, the corresponding *constraint graph* is a weighted, directed graph $G = (V, E)$, where

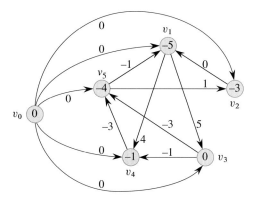

Figure 22.8   The constraint graph corresponding to the system (22.2)–(22.9) of difference constraints. The value of $\delta(v_0, v_i)$ appears in each vertex v_i. One feasible solution to the system is $x = (-5, -3, 0, -1, -4)$.

$$V = \{v_0, v_1, \ldots, v_n\}$$

and

$$E = \{(v_i, v_j) : x_j - x_i \leq b_k \text{ is a constraint}\}$$
$$\cup \{(v_0, v_1), (v_0, v_2), (v_0, v_3), \ldots, (v_0, v_n)\} \ .$$

The constraint graph includes the additional vertex v_0, as we shall see shortly, to guarantee that the graph has some vertex that can reach all other vertices. Thus, the vertex set V consists of a vertex v_i for each unknown x_i, plus an additional vertex v_0. The edge set E contains an edge for each difference constraint, plus an edge (v_0, v_i) for each unknown x_i. If $x_j - x_i \leq b_k$ is a difference constraint, then the weight of edge (v_i, v_j) is $w(v_i, v_j) = b_k$. The weight of each edge leaving v_0 is 0. Figure 22.8 shows the constraint graph for the system (22.2)–(22.9) of difference constraints.

The following theorem shows how to solve a system of difference constraints by finding shortest-path weights in the corresponding constraint graph.

Theorem 22.9
Given a system $Ax \leq b$ of difference constraints, let $G = (V, E)$ be the corresponding constraint graph. If G contains no negative-weight cycles, then

$$x = (\delta(v_0, v_1), \delta(v_0, v_2), \delta(v_0, v_3), \ldots, \delta(v_0, v_n)) \tag{22.10}$$

is a feasible solution for the system. If G contains a negative-weight cycle, then there is no feasible solution for the system.

Proof We first show that if the constraint graph contains no negative-weight cycles, then equation (22.10) gives a feasible solution. Consider any edge $(v_i, v_j) \in E$. The triangle inequality implies that $\delta(v_0, v_j) \leq \delta(v_0, v_i) + w(v_i, v_j)$, which is equivalent to $\delta(v_0, v_j) - \delta(v_0, v_i) \leq w(v_i, v_j)$. Thus, letting $x_i = \delta(v_0, v_i)$ and $x_j = \delta(v_0, v_j)$ satisfies the difference constraint $x_j - x_i \leq w(v_i, v_j)$ that corresponds to edge (v_i, v_j).

Now we show that if the constraint graph contains a negative-weight cycle, then the system of difference constraints has no feasible solution. Without loss of generality, let the negative-weight cycle be $c = \langle v_1, v_2, \ldots, v_k \rangle$, where $v_1 = v_k$. (The vertex v_0 cannot be on cycle c, because it has no entering edges.) Cycle c corresponds to the following difference constraints:

$$
\begin{aligned}
x_2 - x_1 &\leq w(v_1, v_2)\,, \\
x_3 - x_2 &\leq w(v_2, v_3)\,, \\
&\;\;\vdots \\
x_{k-1} - x_{k-2} &\leq w(v_{k-2}, v_{k-1})\,, \\
x_k - x_{k-1} &\leq w(v_{k-1}, v_k)\,.
\end{aligned}
$$

We'll assume that x has a solution satisfying each of these k inequalities and then derive a contradiction. The solution must also satisfy the inequality that results from summing the k inequalities together. In summing the left-hand sides, each unknown x_i is added in once and subtracted out once (remember that $v_1 = v_k$ implies $x_1 = x_k$), so that the left-hand side sums to 0. The right-hand side sums to the weight $w(c)$ of the cycle, giving $0 \leq w(c)$. But since c is a negative-weight cycle, $w(c) < 0$, and we obtain the contradiction that $0 \leq w(c) < 0$. ∎

Solving systems of difference constraints

Theorem 22.9 suggests how to use the Bellman-Ford algorithm to solve a system of difference constraints. Because the constraint graph contains edges from the source vertex v_0 to all other vertices, any negative-weight cycle in the constraint graph is reachable from v_0. If the Bellman-Ford algorithm returns TRUE, then the shortest-path weights give a feasible solution to the system. In Figure 22.8, for example, the shortest-path weights provide the feasible solution $x = (-5, -3, 0, -1, -4)$, and by Lemma 22.8, $x = (d - 5, d - 3, d, d - 1, d - 4)$ is also a feasible solution for any constant d. If the Bellman-Ford algorithm returns FALSE, there is no feasible solution to the system of difference constraints.

A system of difference constraints with m constraints on n unknowns produces a graph with $n + 1$ vertices and $n + m$ edges. Thus, the Bellman-Ford algorithm provides a way to solve the system in $O((n + 1)(n + m)) = O(n^2 + nm)$ time.

Exercise 22.4-5 asks you to modify the algorithm to run in $O(nm)$ time, even if m is much less than n.

Exercises

22.4-1
Find a feasible solution or determine that no feasible solution exists for the following system of difference constraints:

$$
\begin{aligned}
x_1 - x_2 &\leq 1, \\
x_1 - x_4 &\leq -4, \\
x_2 - x_3 &\leq 2, \\
x_2 - x_5 &\leq 7, \\
x_2 - x_6 &\leq 5, \\
x_3 - x_6 &\leq 10, \\
x_4 - x_2 &\leq 2, \\
x_5 - x_1 &\leq -1, \\
x_5 - x_4 &\leq 3, \\
x_6 - x_3 &\leq -8.
\end{aligned}
$$

22.4-2
Find a feasible solution or determine that no feasible solution exists for the following system of difference constraints:

$$
\begin{aligned}
x_1 - x_2 &\leq 4, \\
x_1 - x_5 &\leq 5, \\
x_2 - x_4 &\leq -6, \\
x_3 - x_2 &\leq 1, \\
x_4 - x_1 &\leq 3, \\
x_4 - x_3 &\leq 5, \\
x_4 - x_5 &\leq 10, \\
x_5 - x_3 &\leq -4, \\
x_5 - x_4 &\leq -8.
\end{aligned}
$$

22.4-3
Can any shortest-path weight from the new vertex v_0 in a constraint graph be positive? Explain.

22.4-4
Express the single-pair shortest-path problem as a linear program.

22.4-5
Show how to modify the Bellman-Ford algorithm slightly so that when using it to solve a system of difference constraints with m inequalities on n unknowns, the running time is $O(nm)$.

22.4-6
Consider adding *equality constraints* of the form $x_i = x_j + b_k$ to a system of difference constraints. Show how to solve this variety of constraint system.

22.4-7
Show how to solve a system of difference constraints by a Bellman-Ford-like algorithm that runs on a constraint graph without the extra vertex v_0.

★ **22.4-8**
Let $Ax \leq b$ be a system of m difference constraints in n unknowns. Show that the Bellman-Ford algorithm, when run on the corresponding constraint graph, maximizes $\sum_{i=1}^{n} x_i$ subject to $Ax \leq b$ and $x_i \leq 0$ for all x_i.

★ **22.4-9**
Show that the Bellman-Ford algorithm, when run on the constraint graph for a system $Ax \leq b$ of difference constraints, minimizes the quantity $(\max\{x_i\} - \min\{x_i\})$ subject to $Ax \leq b$. Explain how this fact might come in handy if the algorithm is used to schedule construction jobs.

22.4-10
Suppose that every row in the matrix A of a linear program $Ax \leq b$ corresponds to a difference constraint, a single-variable constraint of the form $x_i \leq b_k$, or a single-variable constraint of the form $-x_i \leq b_k$. Show how to adapt the Bellman-Ford algorithm to solve this variety of constraint system.

22.4-11
Give an efficient algorithm to solve a system $Ax \leq b$ of difference constraints when all of the elements of b are real-valued and all of the unknowns x_i must be integers.

★ **22.4-12**
Give an efficient algorithm to solve a system $Ax \leq b$ of difference constraints when all of the elements of b are real-valued and a specified subset of some, but not necessarily all, of the unknowns x_i must be integers.

22.5   Proofs of shortest-paths properties

Throughout this chapter, our correctness arguments have relied on the triangle inequality, upper-bound property, no-path property, convergence property, path-relaxation property, and predecessor-subgraph property. We stated these properties without proof on page 611. In this section, we prove them.

The triangle inequality

In studying breadth-first search (Section 20.2), we proved as Lemma 20.1 a simple property of shortest distances in unweighted graphs. The triangle inequality generalizes the property to weighted graphs.

Lemma 22.10 (Triangle inequality)
Let $G = (V, E)$ be a weighted, directed graph with weight function $w : E \to \mathbb{R}$ and source vertex s. Then, for all edges $(u, v) \in E$,

$$\delta(s, v) \leq \delta(s, u) + w(u, v) \ .$$

Proof   Suppose that p is a shortest path from source s to vertex v. Then p has no more weight than any other path from s to v. Specifically, path p has no more weight than the particular path that takes a shortest path from source s to vertex u and then takes edge (u, v).

Exercise 22.5-3 asks you to handle the case in which there is no shortest path from s to v.   ∎

Effects of relaxation on shortest-path estimates

The next group of lemmas describes how shortest-path estimates are affected by executing a sequence of relaxation steps on the edges of a weighted, directed graph that has been initialized by INITIALIZE-SINGLE-SOURCE.

Lemma 22.11 (Upper-bound property)
Let $G = (V, E)$ be a weighted, directed graph with weight function $w : E \to \mathbb{R}$. Let $s \in V$ be the source vertex, and let the graph be initialized by INITIALIZE-SINGLE-SOURCE(G, s). Then, $v.d \geq \delta(s, v)$ for all $v \in V$, and this invariant is maintained over any sequence of relaxation steps on the edges of G. Moreover, once $v.d$ achieves its lower bound $\delta(s, v)$, it never changes.

Proof   We prove the invariant $v.d \geq \delta(s, v)$ for all vertices $v \in V$ by induction over the number of relaxation steps.

For the base case, $v.d \geq \delta(s, v)$ holds after initialization, since if $v.d = \infty$, then $v.d \geq \delta(s, v)$ for all $v \in V - \{s\}$, and since $s.d = 0 \geq \delta(s, s)$. (Note that $\delta(s, s) = -\infty$ if s is on a negative-weight cycle and that $\delta(s, s) = 0$ otherwise.)

For the inductive step, consider the relaxation of an edge (u, v). By the inductive hypothesis, $x.d \geq \delta(s, x)$ for all $x \in V$ prior to the relaxation. The only d value that may change is $v.d$. If it changes, we have

$$
\begin{aligned}
v.d &= u.d + w(u, v) \\
&\geq \delta(s, u) + w(u, v) \quad \text{(by the inductive hypothesis)} \\
&\geq \delta(s, v) \quad\quad\quad\quad\;\; \text{(by the triangle inequality)} ,
\end{aligned}
$$

and so the invariant is maintained.

The value of $v.d$ never changes once $v.d = \delta(s, v)$ because, having achieved its lower bound, $v.d$ cannot decrease since we have just shown that $v.d \geq \delta(s, v)$, and it cannot increase because relaxation steps do not increase d values. ∎

Corollary 22.12 (No-path property)

Suppose that in a weighted, directed graph $G = (V, E)$ with weight function $w : E \rightarrow \mathbb{R}$, no path connects a source vertex $s \in V$ to a given vertex $v \in V$. Then, after the graph is initialized by INITIALIZE-SINGLE-SOURCE(G, s), we have $v.d = \delta(s, v) = \infty$, and this equation is maintained as an invariant over any sequence of relaxation steps on the edges of G.

Proof By the upper-bound property, we always have $\infty = \delta(s, v) \leq v.d$, and thus $v.d = \infty = \delta(s, v)$. ∎

Lemma 22.13

Let $G = (V, E)$ be a weighted, directed graph with weight function $w : E \rightarrow \mathbb{R}$, and let $(u, v) \in E$. Then, immediately after edge (u, v) is relaxed by a call of RELAX(u, v, w), we have $v.d \leq u.d + w(u, v)$.

Proof If, just prior to relaxing edge (u, v), we have $v.d > u.d + w(u, v)$, then $v.d = u.d + w(u, v)$ afterward. If, instead, $v.d \leq u.d + w(u, v)$ just before the relaxation, then neither $u.d$ nor $v.d$ changes, and so $v.d \leq u.d + w(u, v)$ afterward. ∎

Lemma 22.14 (Convergence property)

Let $G = (V, E)$ be a weighted, directed graph with weight function $w : E \rightarrow \mathbb{R}$, let $s \in V$ be a source vertex, and let $s \rightsquigarrow u \rightarrow v$ be a shortest path in G for some vertices $u, v \in V$. Suppose that G is initialized by INITIALIZE-SINGLE-SOURCE(G, s) and then a sequence of relaxation steps that includes the call

RELAX(u, v, w) is executed on the edges of G. If $u.d = \delta(s, u)$ at any time prior to the call, then $v.d = \delta(s, v)$ at all times after the call.

Proof   By the upper-bound property, if $u.d = \delta(s, u)$ at some point prior to relaxing edge (u, v), then this equation holds thereafter. In particular, after edge (u, v) is relaxed, we have

$$
\begin{aligned}
v.d &\leq u.d + w(u, v) &&\text{(by Lemma 22.13)} \\
    &= \delta(s, u) + w(u, v) \\
    &= \delta(s, v) &&\text{(by Lemma 22.1 on page 606)} .
\end{aligned}
$$

The upper-bound property gives $v.d \geq \delta(s, v)$, from which we conclude that $v.d = \delta(s, v)$, and this equation is maintained thereafter.   ∎

Lemma 22.15 (Path-relaxation property)

Let $G = (V, E)$ be a weighted, directed graph with weight function $w : E \to \mathbb{R}$, and let $s \in V$ be a source vertex. Consider any shortest path $p = \langle v_0, v_1, \ldots, v_k \rangle$ from $s = v_0$ to v_k. If G is initialized by INITIALIZE-SINGLE-SOURCE(G, s) and then a sequence of relaxation steps occurs that includes, in order, relaxing the edges $(v_0, v_1), (v_1, v_2), \ldots, (v_{k-1}, v_k)$, then $v_k.d = \delta(s, v_k)$ after these relaxations and at all times afterward. This property holds no matter what other edge relaxations occur, including relaxations that are intermixed with relaxations of the edges of p.

Proof   We show by induction that after the ith edge of path p is relaxed, we have $v_i.d = \delta(s, v_i)$. For the base case, $i = 0$, and before any edges of p have been relaxed, we have from the initialization that $v_0.d = s.d = 0 = \delta(s, s)$. By the upper-bound property, the value of $s.d$ never changes after initialization.

For the inductive step, assume that $v_{i-1}.d = \delta(s, v_{i-1})$. What happens when edge (v_{i-1}, v_i) is relaxed? By the convergence property, after this relaxation, we have $v_i.d = \delta(s, v_i)$, and this equation is maintained at all times thereafter.   ∎

Relaxation and shortest-paths trees

We now show that once a sequence of relaxations has caused the shortest-path estimates to converge to shortest-path weights, the predecessor subgraph G_π induced by the resulting π values is a shortest-paths tree for G. We start with the following lemma, which shows that the predecessor subgraph always forms a rooted tree whose root is the source.

Lemma 22.16

Let $G = (V, E)$ be a weighted, directed graph with weight function $w : E \to \mathbb{R}$, let $s \in V$ be a source vertex, and assume that G contains no negative-weight cycles that are reachable from s. Then, after the graph is initialized by INITIALIZE-SINGLE-SOURCE(G, s), the predecessor subgraph G_π forms a rooted tree with root s, and any sequence of relaxation steps on edges of G maintains this property as an invariant.

Proof   Initially, the only vertex in G_π is the source vertex, and the lemma is trivially true. Consider a predecessor subgraph G_π that arises after a sequence of relaxation steps. We first prove that G_π is acyclic. Suppose for the sake of contradiction that some relaxation step creates a cycle in the graph G_π. Let the cycle be $c = \langle v_0, v_1, \ldots, v_k \rangle$, where $v_k = v_0$. Then, $v_i.\pi = v_{i-1}$ for $i = 1, 2, \ldots, k$ and, without loss of generality, assume that relaxing edge (v_{k-1}, v_k) created the cycle in G_π.

We claim that all vertices on cycle c are reachable from the source vertex s. Why? Each vertex on c has a non-NIL predecessor, and so each vertex on c was assigned a finite shortest-path estimate when it was assigned its non-NIL π value. By the upper-bound property, each vertex on cycle c has a finite shortest-path weight, which means that it is reachable from s.

We'll examine the shortest-path estimates on cycle c immediately before the call RELAX(v_{k-1}, v_k, w) and show that c is a negative-weight cycle, thereby contradicting the assumption that G contains no negative-weight cycles that are reachable from the source. Just before the call, we have $v_i.\pi = v_{i-1}$ for $i = 1, 2, \ldots, k-1$. Thus, for $i = 1, 2, \ldots, k - 1$, the last update to $v_i.d$ was by the assignment $v_i.d = v_{i-1}.d + w(v_{i-1}, v_i)$. If $v_{i-1}.d$ changed since then, it decreased. Therefore, just before the call RELAX(v_{k-1}, v_k, w), we have

$$v_i.d \geq v_{i-1}.d + w(v_{i-1}, v_i) \qquad \text{for all } i = 1, 2, \ldots, k - 1 . \tag{22.11}$$

Because $v_k.\pi$ is changed by the call RELAX(v_{k-1}, v_k, w), immediately beforehand we also have the strict inequality

$$v_k.d > v_{k-1}.d + w(v_{k-1}, v_k) .$$

Summing this strict inequality with the $k - 1$ inequalities (22.11), we obtain the sum of the shortest-path estimates around cycle c:

$$\sum_{i=1}^{k} v_i.d > \sum_{i=1}^{k} (v_{i-1}.d + w(v_{i-1}, v_i))$$

$$= \sum_{i=1}^{k} v_{i-1}.d + \sum_{i=1}^{k} w(v_{i-1}, v_i) .$$

But

$$\sum_{i=1}^{k} v_i.d = \sum_{i=1}^{k} v_{i-1}.d ,$$

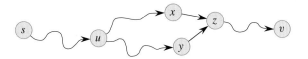

Figure 22.9 Showing that a simple path in G_π from source vertex s to vertex v is unique. If G_π contains two paths p_1 ($s \rightsquigarrow u \rightsquigarrow x \rightarrow z \rightsquigarrow v$) and p_2 ($s \rightsquigarrow u \rightsquigarrow y \rightarrow z \rightsquigarrow v$), where $x \neq y$, then $z.\pi = x$ and $z.\pi = y$, a contradiction.

since each vertex in the cycle c appears exactly once in each summation. This equation implies

$$0 > \sum_{i=1}^{k} w(v_{i-1}, v_i) \,.$$

Thus, the sum of weights around the cycle c is negative, which provides the desired contradiction.

We have now proven that G_π is a directed, acyclic graph. To show that it forms a rooted tree with root s, it suffices (see Exercise B.5-2 on page 1175) to prove that for each vertex $v \in V_\pi$, there is a unique simple path from s to v in G_π.

The vertices in V_π are those with non-NIL π values, plus s. Exercise 22.5-6 asks you to prove that a path from s exists to each vertex in V_π.

To complete the proof of the lemma, we now show that for any vertex $v \in V_\pi$, the graph G_π contains at most one simple path from s to v. Suppose otherwise. That is, suppose that, as Figure 22.9 illustrates, G_π contains two simple paths from s to some vertex v: p_1, which we decompose into $s \rightsquigarrow u \rightsquigarrow x \rightarrow z \rightsquigarrow v$, and p_2, which we decompose into $s \rightsquigarrow u \rightsquigarrow y \rightarrow z \rightsquigarrow v$, where $x \neq y$ (though u could be s and z could be v). But then, $z.\pi = x$ and $z.\pi = y$, which implies the contradiction that $x = y$. We conclude that G_π contains a unique simple path from s to v, and thus G_π forms a rooted tree with root s. ∎

We can now show that if all vertices have been assigned their true shortest-path weights after a sequence of relaxation steps, then the predecessor subgraph G_π is a shortest-paths tree.

Lemma 22.17 (Predecessor-subgraph property)
Let $G = (V, E)$ be a weighted, directed graph with weight function $w : E \rightarrow \mathbb{R}$, let $s \in V$ be a source vertex, and assume that G contains no negative-weight cycles that are reachable from s. Then, after a call to INITIALIZE-SINGLE-SOURCE(G, s) followed by any sequence of relaxation steps on edges of G that produces $v.d = \delta(s, v)$ for all $v \in V$, the predecessor subgraph G_π is a shortest-paths tree rooted at s.

Proof   We must prove that the three properties of shortest-paths trees given on page 608 hold for G_π. To show the first property, we must show that V_π is the set of vertices reachable from s. By definition, a shortest-path weight $\delta(s, v)$ is finite if and only if v is reachable from s, and thus the vertices that are reachable from s are exactly those with finite d values. But a vertex $v \in V - \{s\}$ has been assigned a finite value for $v.d$ if and only if $v.\pi \neq \text{NIL}$, since both assignments occur in RELAX. Thus, the vertices in V_π are exactly those reachable from s.

The second property, that G_π forms a rooted tree with root s, follows directly from Lemma 22.16.

It remains, therefore, to prove the last property of shortest-paths trees: for each vertex $v \in V_\pi$, the unique simple path $s \overset{p}{\leadsto} v$ in G_π is a shortest path from s to v in G. Let $p = \langle v_0, v_1, \ldots, v_k \rangle$, where $v_0 = s$ and $v_k = v$. Consider an edge (v_{i-1}, v_i) in path p. Because this edge belongs to G_π, the last relaxation that changed $v_i.d$ must have been of this edge. After that relaxation, we had $v_i.d = v_{i-1}.d + w(v_{i-1}, v_i)$. Subsequently, an edge entering v_{i-1} could have been relaxed, causing $v_{i-1}.d$ to decrease further, but without changing $v_i.d$. Therefore, we have $v_i.d \geq v_{i-1}.d + w(v_{i-1}, v_i)$. Thus, for $i = 1, 2, \ldots, k$, we have both $v_i.d = \delta(s, v_i)$ and $v_i.d \geq v_{i-1}.d + w(v_{i-1}, v_i)$, which together imply $w(v_{i-1}, v_i) \leq \delta(s, v_i) - \delta(s, v_{i-1})$. Summing the weights along path p yields

$$
\begin{aligned}
w(p) &= \sum_{i=1}^{k} w(v_{i-1}, v_i) \\
&\leq \sum_{i=1}^{k} (\delta(s, v_i) - \delta(s, v_{i-1})) \\
&= \delta(s, v_k) - \delta(s, v_0) \quad \text{(because the sum telescopes)} \\
&= \delta(s, v_k) \quad \text{(because } \delta(s, v_0) = \delta(s, s) = 0 \text{)} .
\end{aligned}
$$

Thus, we have $w(p) \leq \delta(s, v_k)$. Since $\delta(s, v_k)$ is a lower bound on the weight of any path from s to v_k, we conclude that $w(p) = \delta(s, v_k)$, and p is a shortest path from s to $v = v_k$.   ∎

Exercises

22.5-1
Give two shortest-paths trees for the directed graph of Figure 22.2 on page 609 other than the two shown.

22.5-2
Give an example of a weighted, directed graph $G = (V, E)$ with weight function $w : E \to \mathbb{R}$ and source vertex s such that G satisfies the following property: For

every edge $(u, v) \in E$, there is a shortest-paths tree rooted at s that contains (u, v) and another shortest-paths tree rooted at s that does not contain (u, v).

22.5-3

Modify the proof of Lemma 22.10 to handle cases in which shortest-path weights are ∞ or $-\infty$.

22.5-4

Let $G = (V, E)$ be a weighted, directed graph with source vertex s, and let G be initialized by INITIALIZE-SINGLE-SOURCE(G, s). Prove that if a sequence of relaxation steps sets $s.\pi$ to a non-NIL value, then G contains a negative-weight cycle.

22.5-5

Let $G = (V, E)$ be a weighted, directed graph with no negative-weight edges. Let $s \in V$ be the source vertex, and suppose that $v.\pi$ is allowed to be the predecessor of v on *any* shortest path to v from source s if $v \in V - \{s\}$ is reachable from s, and NIL otherwise. Give an example of such a graph G and an assignment of π values that produces a cycle in G_π. (By Lemma 22.16, such an assignment cannot be produced by a sequence of relaxation steps.)

22.5-6

Let $G = (V, E)$ be a weighted, directed graph with weight function $w : E \to \mathbb{R}$ and no negative-weight cycles. Let $s \in V$ be the source vertex, and let G be initialized by INITIALIZE-SINGLE-SOURCE(G, s). Use induction to prove that for every vertex $v \in V_\pi$, there exists a path from s to v in G_π and that this property is maintained as an invariant over any sequence of relaxations.

22.5-7

Let $G = (V, E)$ be a weighted, directed graph that contains no negative-weight cycles. Let $s \in V$ be the source vertex, and let G be initialized by INITIALIZE-SINGLE-SOURCE(G, s). Prove that there exists a sequence of $|V| - 1$ relaxation steps that produces $v.d = \delta(s, v)$ for all $v \in V$.

22.5-8

Let G be an arbitrary weighted, directed graph with a negative-weight cycle reachable from the source vertex s. Show how to construct an infinite sequence of relaxations of the edges of G such that every relaxation causes a shortest-path estimate to change.

Problems

22-1 *Yen's improvement to Bellman-Ford*

The Bellman-Ford algorithm does not specify the order in which to relax edges in each pass. Consider the following method for deciding upon the order. Before the first pass, assign an arbitrary linear order $v_1, v_2, \ldots, v_{|V|}$ to the vertices of the input graph $G = (V, E)$. Then partition the edge set E into $E_f \cup E_b$, where $E_f = \{(v_i, v_j) \in E : i < j\}$ and $E_b = \{(v_i, v_j) \in E : i > j\}$. (Assume that G contains no self-loops, so that every edge belongs to either E_f or E_b.) Define $G_f = (V, E_f)$ and $G_b = (V, E_b)$.

a. Prove that G_f is acyclic with topological sort $\langle v_1, v_2, \ldots, v_{|V|} \rangle$ and that G_b is acyclic with topological sort $\langle v_{|V|}, v_{|V|-1}, \ldots, v_1 \rangle$.

Suppose that each pass of the Bellman-Ford algorithm relaxes edges in the following way. First, visit each vertex in the order $v_1, v_2, \ldots, v_{|V|}$, relaxing edges of E_f that leave the vertex. Then visit each vertex in the order $v_{|V|}, v_{|V|-1}, \ldots, v_1$, relaxing edges of E_b that leave the vertex.

b. Prove that with this scheme, if G contains no negative-weight cycles that are reachable from the source vertex s, then after only $\lceil |V|/2 \rceil$ passes over the edges, $v.d = \delta(s, v)$ for all vertices $v \in V$.

c. Does this scheme improve the asymptotic running time of the Bellman-Ford algorithm?

22-2 *Nesting boxes*

A d-dimensional box with dimensions $(x_1, x_2, \ldots, x_d)$ *nests* within another box with dimensions $(y_1, y_2, \ldots, y_d)$ if there exists a permutation π on $\{1, 2, \ldots, d\}$ such that $x_{\pi(1)} < y_1, x_{\pi(2)} < y_2, \ldots, x_{\pi(d)} < y_d$.

a. Argue that the nesting relation is transitive.

b. Describe an efficient method to determine whether one d-dimensional box nests inside another.

c. You are given a set of n d-dimensional boxes $\{B_1, B_2, \ldots, B_n\}$. Give an efficient algorithm to find the longest sequence $\langle B_{i_1}, B_{i_2}, \ldots, B_{i_k} \rangle$ of boxes such that B_{i_j} nests within $B_{i_{j+1}}$ for $j = 1, 2, \ldots, k - 1$. Express the running time of your algorithm in terms of n and d.

22-3 Arbitrage

Arbitrage is the use of discrepancies in currency exchange rates to transform one unit of a currency into more than one unit of the same currency. For example, suppose that one U.S. dollar buys 64 Indian rupees, one Indian rupee buys 1.8 Japanese yen, and one Japanese yen buys 0.009 U.S. dollars. Then, by converting currencies, a trader can start with 1 U.S. dollar and buy $64 \times 1.8 \times 0.009 = 1.0368$ U.S. dollars, thus turning a profit of 3.68%.

Suppose that you are given n currencies $c_1, c_2, \ldots, c_n$ and an $n \times n$ table R of exchange rates, such that 1 unit of currency c_i buys $R[i, j]$ units of currency c_j.

a. Give an efficient algorithm to determine whether there exists a sequence of currencies $\langle c_{i_1}, c_{i_2}, \ldots, c_{i_k} \rangle$ such that

$$R[i_1, i_2] \cdot R[i_2, i_3] \cdots R[i_{k-1}, i_k] \cdot R[i_k, i_1] > 1 .$$

Analyze the running time of your algorithm.

b. Give an efficient algorithm to print out such a sequence if one exists. Analyze the running time of your algorithm.

22-4 Gabow's scaling algorithm for single-source shortest paths

A *scaling* algorithm solves a problem by initially considering only the highest-order bit of each relevant input value, such as an edge weight, assuming that these values are nonnegative integers. The algorithm then refines the initial solution by looking at the two highest-order bits. It progressively looks at more and more high-order bits, refining the solution each time, until it has examined all bits and computed the correct solution.

This problem examines an algorithm for computing the shortest paths from a single source by scaling edge weights. The input is a directed graph $G = (V, E)$ with nonnegative integer edge weights w. Let $W = \max \{w(u, v) : (u, v) \in E\}$ be the maximum weight of any edge. In this problem, you will develop an algorithm that runs in $O(E \lg W)$ time. Assume that all vertices are reachable from the source.

The scaling algorithm uncovers the bits in the binary representation of the edge weights one at a time, from the most significant bit to the least significant bit. Specifically, let $k = \lceil \lg(W + 1) \rceil$ be the number of bits in the binary representation of W, and for $i = 1, 2, \ldots, k$, let $w_i(u, v) = \lfloor w(u, v)/2^{k-i} \rfloor$. That is, $w_i(u, v)$ is the "scaled-down" version of $w(u, v)$ given by the i most significant bits of $w(u, v)$. (Thus, $w_k(u, v) = w(u, v)$ for all $(u, v) \in E$.) For example, if $k = 5$ and $w(u, v) = 25$, which has the binary representation $\langle 11001 \rangle$, then $w_3(u, v) = \langle 110 \rangle = 6$. Also with $k = 5$, if $w(u, v) = \langle 00100 \rangle = 4$, then $w_4(u, v) = \langle 0010 \rangle = 2$. Define $\delta_i(u, v)$ as the shortest-path weight from vertex u

to vertex v using weight function w_i, so that $\delta_k(u, v) = \delta(u, v)$ for all $u, v \in V$. For a given source vertex s, the scaling algorithm first computes the shortest-path weights $\delta_1(s, v)$ for all $v \in V$, then computes $\delta_2(s, v)$ for all $v \in V$, and so on, until it computes $\delta_k(s, v)$ for all $v \in V$. Assume throughout that $|E| \geq |V| - 1$. You will show how to compute δ_i from δ_{i-1} in $O(E)$ time, so that the entire algorithm takes $O(kE) = O(E \lg W)$ time.

a. Suppose that for all vertices $v \in V$, we have $\delta(s, v) \leq |E|$. Show how to compute $\delta(s, v)$ for all $v \in V$ in $O(E)$ time.

b. Show how to compute $\delta_1(s, v)$ for all $v \in V$ in $O(E)$ time.

Now focus on computing δ_i from δ_{i-1}.

c. Prove that for $i = 2, 3, \ldots, k$, either $w_i(u, v) = 2w_{i-1}(u, v)$ or $w_i(u, v) = 2w_{i-1}(u, v) + 1$. Then prove that

$$2\delta_{i-1}(s, v) \leq \delta_i(s, v) \leq 2\delta_{i-1}(s, v) + |V| - 1$$

for all $v \in V$.

d. Define, for $i = 2, 3, \ldots, k$ and all $(u, v) \in E$,

$$\widehat{w}_i(u, v) = w_i(u, v) + 2\delta_{i-1}(s, u) - 2\delta_{i-1}(s, v) \,.$$

Prove that for $i = 2, 3, \ldots, k$ and all $u, v \in V$, the "reweighted" value $\widehat{w}_i(u, v)$ of edge (u, v) is a nonnegative integer.

e. Now define $\widehat{\delta}_i(s, v)$ as the shortest-path weight from s to v using the weight function $\widehat{w}_i$. Prove that for $i = 2, 3, \ldots, k$ and all $v \in V$,

$$\delta_i(s, v) = \widehat{\delta}_i(s, v) + 2\delta_{i-1}(s, v)$$

and that $\widehat{\delta}_i(s, v) \leq |E|$.

f. Show how to compute $\delta_i(s, v)$ from $\delta_{i-1}(s, v)$ for all $v \in V$ in $O(E)$ time. Conclude that you can compute $\delta(s, v)$ for all $v \in V$ in $O(E \lg W)$ time.

22-5   *Karp's minimum mean-weight cycle algorithm*

Let $G = (V, E)$ be a directed graph with weight function $w : E \to \mathbb{R}$, and let $n = |V|$. We define the *mean weight* of a cycle $c = \langle e_1, e_2, \ldots, e_k \rangle$ of edges in E to be

$$\mu(c) = \frac{1}{k} \sum_{i=1}^{k} w(e_i) .$$

Let $\mu^* = \min \{\mu(c) : c \text{ is a directed cycle in } G\}$. We call a cycle c for which $\mu(c) = \mu^*$ a *minimum mean-weight cycle*. This problem investigates an efficient algorithm for computing μ^*.

Assume without loss of generality that every vertex $v \in V$ is reachable from a source vertex $s \in V$. Let $\delta(s, v)$ be the weight of a shortest path from s to v, and let $\delta_k(s, v)$ be the weight of a shortest path from s to v consisting of *exactly* k edges. If there is no path from s to v with exactly k edges, then $\delta_k(s, v) = \infty$.

a. Show that if $\mu^* = 0$, then G contains no negative-weight cycles and $\delta(s, v) = \min \{\delta_k(s, v) : 0 \le k \le n - 1\}$ for all vertices $v \in V$.

b. Show that if $\mu^* = 0$, then

$$\max \left\{ \frac{\delta_n(s, v) - \delta_k(s, v)}{n - k} : 0 \le k \le n - 1 \right\} \ge 0$$

for all vertices $v \in V$. (*Hint:* Use both properties from part (a).)

c. Let c be a 0-weight cycle, and let u and v be any two vertices on c. Suppose that $\mu^* = 0$ and that the weight of the simple path from u to v along the cycle is x. Prove that $\delta(s, v) = \delta(s, u) + x$. (*Hint:* The weight of the simple path from v to u along the cycle is $-x$.)

d. Show that if $\mu^* = 0$, then on each minimum mean-weight cycle there exists a vertex v such that

$$\max \left\{ \frac{\delta_n(s, v) - \delta_k(s, v)}{n - k} : 0 \le k \le n - 1 \right\} = 0 .$$

(*Hint:* Show how to extend a shortest path to any vertex on a minimum mean-weight cycle along the cycle to make a shortest path to the next vertex on the cycle.)

e. Show that if $\mu^* = 0$, then the minimum value of

$$\max \left\{ \frac{\delta_n(s, v) - \delta_k(s, v)}{n - k} : 0 \le k \le n - 1 \right\} ,$$

taken over all vertices $v \in V$, equals 0.

f. Show that if you add a constant t to the weight of each edge of G, then μ^* increases by t. Use this fact to show that μ^* equals the minimum value of

$$\max\left\{\frac{\delta_n(s,v) - \delta_k(s,v)}{n-k} : 0 \le k \le n-1\right\},$$

taken over all vertices $v \in V$.

g. Give an $O(VE)$-time algorithm to compute μ^*.

22-6   *Bitonic shortest paths*

A sequence is *bitonic* if it monotonically increases and then monotonically decreases, or if by a circular shift it monotonically increases and then monotonically decreases. For example the sequences $\langle 1, 4, 6, 8, 3, -2 \rangle$, $\langle 9, 2, -4, -10, -5 \rangle$, and $\langle 1, 2, 3, 4 \rangle$ are bitonic, but $\langle 1, 3, 12, 4, 2, 10 \rangle$ is not bitonic. (See Problem 14-3 on page 407 for the bitonic euclidean traveling-salesperson problem.)

Suppose that you are given a directed graph $G = (V, E)$ with weight function $w : E \to \mathbb{R}$, where all edge weights are unique, and you wish to find single-source shortest paths from a source vertex s. You are given one additional piece of information: for each vertex $v \in V$, the weights of the edges along any shortest path from s to v form a bitonic sequence.

Give the most efficient algorithm you can to solve this problem, and analyze its running time.

Chapter notes

The shortest-path problem has a long history that is nicely desribed in an article by Schrijver [400]. He credits the general idea of repeatedly executing edge relaxations to Ford [148]. Dijkstra's algorithm [116] appeared in 1959, but it contained no mention of a priority queue. The Bellman-Ford algorithm is based on separate algorithms by Bellman [45] and Ford [149]. The same algorithm is also attributed to Moore [334]. Bellman describes the relation of shortest paths to difference constraints. Lawler [276] describes the linear-time algorithm for shortest paths in a dag, which he considers part of the folklore.

When edge weights are relatively small nonnegative integers, more efficient algorithms result from using min-priority queues that require integer keys and rely on the sequence of values returned by the EXTRACT-MIN calls in Dijkstra's algorithm monotonically increasing over time. Ahuja, Mehlhorn, Orlin, and Tarjan [8] give an algorithm that runs in $O(E + V\sqrt{\lg W})$ time on graphs with nonnegative edge weights, where W is the largest weight of any edge in the graph. The best bounds are by Thorup [436], who gives an algorithm that runs in $O(E \lg \lg V)$ time, and by Raman [375], who gives an algorithm that runs in $O\left(E + V \min\left\{(\lg V)^{1/3+\epsilon}, (\lg W)^{1/4+\epsilon}\right\}\right)$ time. These two algorithms use an amount of space that depends on the word size of the underlying machine. Although the amount of space used can be unbounded in the size of the input, it can be reduced to be linear in the size of the input using randomized hashing.

For undirected graphs with integer weights, Thorup [435] gives an algorithm that runs in $O(V + E)$ time for single-source shortest paths. In contrast to the algorithms mentioned in the previous paragraph, the sequence of values returned by EXTRACT-MIN calls does not monotonically increase over time, and so this algorithm is not an implementation of Dijkstra's algorithm. Pettie and Ramachandran [357] remove the restriction of integer weights on undirected graphs. Their algorithm entails a preprocessing phase, followed by queries for specific source vertices. Preprocessing takes $O(MST(V, E) + \min\{V \lg V, V \lg \lg r\})$ time, where $MST(V, E)$ is the time to compute a minimum spanning tree and r is the ratio of the maximum edge weight to the minimum edge weight. After preprocessing, each query takes $O(E \lg \hat{\alpha}(E, V))$ time, where $\hat{\alpha}(E, V)$ is the inverse of Ackermann's function. (See the chapter notes for Chapter 19 for a brief discussion of Ackermann's function and its inverse.)

For graphs with negative edge weights, an algorithm due to Gabow and Tarjan [167] runs in $O(\sqrt{V}E \lg(VW))$ time, and one by Goldberg [186] runs in $O(\sqrt{V}E \lg W)$ time, where $W = \max\{|w(u, v)| : (u, v) \in E\}$. There has also been some progress based on methods that use continuous optimization and electrical flows. Cohen et al. [98] give such an algorithm, which is randomized and runs in $\widetilde{O}(E^{10/7} \lg W)$ expected time (see Problem 3-6 on page 73 for the definition of $\widetilde{O}$-notation). There is also a pseudopolyomial-time algorithm based on fast matrix multiplication. Sankowski [394] and Yuster and Zwick [465] designed an algorithm for shortest paths that runs in $\widetilde{O}(WV^{\omega})$ time, where two $n \times n$ matrices can be multiplied in $O(n^{\omega})$ time, giving a faster algorithm than the previously mentioned algorithms for small values of W on dense graphs.

Cherkassky, Goldberg, and Radzik [89] conducted extensive experiments comparing various shortest-path algorithms. Shortest-path algorithms are widely used in real-time navigation and route-planning applications. Typically based on Dijkstra's algorithm, these algorithms use many clever ideas to be able to compute shortest paths on networks with many millions of vertices and edges in fractions of a second. Bast et al. [36] survey many of these developments.

23 All-Pairs Shortest Paths

In this chapter, we turn to the problem of finding shortest paths between all pairs of vertices in a graph. A classic application of this problem occurs in computing a table of distances between all pairs of cities for a road atlas. Classic perhaps, but not a true application of finding shortest paths between *all* pairs of vertices. After all, a road map modeled as a graph has one vertex for *every* road intersection and one edge wherever a road connects intersections. A table of intercity distances in an atlas might include distances for 100 cities, but the United States has approximately 300,000 signal-controlled intersections[1] and many more uncontrolled intersections.

A legitimate application of all-pairs shortest paths is to determine the *diameter* of a network: the longest of all shortest paths. If a directed graph models a communication network, with the weight of an edge indicating the time required for a message to traverse a communication link, then the diameter gives the longest possible transit time for a message in the network.

As in Chapter 22, the input is a weighted, directed graph $G = (V, E)$ with a weight function $w : E \rightarrow \mathbb{R}$ that maps edges to real-valued weights. Now the goal is to find, for every pair of vertices $u, v \in V$, a shortest (least-weight) path from u to v, where the weight of a path is the sum of the weights of its constituent edges. For the all-pairs problem, the output typically takes a tabular form in which the entry in u's row and v's column is the weight of a shortest path from u to v.

You can solve an all-pairs shortest-paths problem by running a single-source shortest-paths algorithm $|V|$ times, once with each vertex as the source. If all edge weights are nonnegative, you can use Dijkstra's algorithm. If you implement the min-priority queue with a linear array, the running time is $O(V^3 + VE)$ which is $O(V^3)$. The binary min-heap implementation of the min-priority queue

---

[1] According to a report cited by U.S. Department of Transportation Federal Highway Administration, "a reasonable 'rule of thumb' is one signalized intersection per 1,000 population."

yields a running time of $O(V(V + E) \lg V)$. If $|E| = \Omega(V)$, the running time becomes $O(VE \lg V)$, which is faster than $O(V^3)$ if the graph is sparse. Alternatively, you can implement the min-priority queue with a Fibonacci heap, yielding a running time of $O(V^2 \lg V + VE)$.

If the graph contains negative-weight edges, Dijkstra's algorithm doesn't work, but you can run the slower Bellman-Ford algorithm once from each vertex. The resulting running time is $O(V^2 E)$, which on a dense graph is $O(V^4)$. This chapter shows how to guarantee a much better asymptotic running time. It also investigates the relation of the all-pairs shortest-paths problem to matrix multiplication.

Unlike the single-source algorithms, which assume an adjacency-list representation of the graph, most of the algorithms in this chapter represent the graph by an adjacency matrix. (Johnson's algorithm for sparse graphs, in Section 23.3, uses adjacency lists.) For convenience, we assume that the vertices are numbered $1, 2, \ldots, |V|$, so that the input is an $n \times n$ matrix $W = (w_{ij})$ representing the edge weights of an n-vertex directed graph $G = (V, E)$, where

$$
w_{ij} = \begin{cases} 0 & \text{if } i = j \text{ ,} \\ \text{the weight of directed edge } (i, j) & \text{if } i \neq j \text{ and } (i, j) \in E \text{ ,} \\ \infty & \text{if } i \neq j \text{ and } (i, j) \notin E \text{ .} \end{cases} \tag{23.1}
$$

The graph may contain negative-weight edges, but we assume for the time being that the input graph contains no negative-weight cycles.

The tabular output of each of the all-pairs shortest-paths algorithms presented in this chapter is an $n \times n$ matrix. The (i, j) entry of the output matrix contains $\delta(i, j)$, the shortest-path weight from vertex i to vertex j, as in Chapter 22.

A full solution to the all-pairs shortest-paths problem includes not only the shortest-path weights but also a *predecessor matrix* $\Pi = (\pi_{ij})$, where π_{ij} is NIL if either $i = j$ or there is no path from i to j, and otherwise π_{ij} is the predecessor of j on some shortest path from i. Just as the predecessor subgraph G_π from Chapter 22 is a shortest-paths tree for a given source vertex, the subgraph induced by the ith row of the Π matrix should be a shortest-paths tree with root i. For each vertex $i \in V$, the *predecessor subgraph* of G for i is $G_{\pi,i} = (V_{\pi,i}, E_{\pi,i})$, where

$$V_{\pi,i} = \{ j \in V : \pi_{ij} \neq \text{NIL} \} \cup \{i\} \text{ ,}$$
$$E_{\pi,i} = \{ (\pi_{ij}, j) : j \in V_{\pi,i} - \{i\} \} \text{ .}$$

If $G_{\pi,i}$ is a shortest-paths tree, then PRINT-ALL-PAIRS-SHORTEST-PATH on the following page, which is a modified version of the PRINT-PATH procedure from Chapter 20, prints a shortest path from vertex i to vertex j.

In order to highlight the essential features of the all-pairs algorithms in this chapter, we won't cover how to compute predecessor matrices and their properties as extensively as we dealt with predecessor subgraphs in Chapter 22. Some of the exercises cover the basics.

PRINT-ALL-PAIRS-SHORTEST-PATH(Π, i, j)

```
1   if i == j
2       print i
3   elseif π_ij == NIL
4       print "no path from" i "to" j "exists"
5   else PRINT-ALL-PAIRS-SHORTEST-PATH(Π, i, π_ij)
6       print j
```

Chapter outline

Section 23.1 presents a dynamic-programming algorithm based on matrix multiplication to solve the all-pairs shortest-paths problem. The technique of "repeated squaring" yields a running time of $\Theta(V^3 \lg V)$. Section 23.2 gives another dynamic-programming algorithm, the Floyd-Warshall algorithm, which runs in $\Theta(V^3)$ time. Section 23.2 also covers the problem of finding the transitive closure of a directed graph, which is related to the all-pairs shortest-paths problem. Finally, Section 23.3 presents Johnson's algorithm, which solves the all-pairs shortest-paths problem in $O(V^2 \lg V + VE)$ time and is a good choice for large, sparse graphs.

Before proceeding, we need to establish some conventions for adjacency-matrix representations. First, we generally assume that the input graph $G = (V, E)$ has n vertices, so that $n = |V|$. Second, we use the convention of denoting matrices by uppercase letters, such as W, L, or D, and their individual elements by subscripted lowercase letters, such as w_{ij}, l_{ij}, or d_{ij}. Finally, some matrices have parenthesized superscripts, as in $L^{(r)} = \left(l_{ij}^{(r)}\right)$ or $D^{(r)} = \left(d_{ij}^{(r)}\right)$, to indicate iterates.

23.1   Shortest paths and matrix multiplication

This section presents a dynamic-programming algorithm for the all-pairs shortest-paths problem on a directed graph $G = (V, E)$. Each major loop of the dynamic program invokes an operation similar to matrix multiplication, so that the algorithm looks like repeated matrix multiplication. We'll start by developing a $\Theta(V^4)$-time algorithm for the all-pairs shortest-paths problem, and then we'll improve its running time to $\Theta(V^3 \lg V)$.

Before proceeding, let's briefly recap the steps given in Chapter 14 for developing a dynamic-programming algorithm:

1. Characterize the structure of an optimal solution.

2. Recursively define the value of an optimal solution.

3. Compute the value of an optimal solution in a bottom-up fashion.

We reserve the fourth step—constructing an optimal solution from computed information—for the exercises.

The structure of a shortest path

Let's start by characterizing the structure of an optimal solution. Lemma 22.1 tells us that all subpaths of a shortest path are shortest paths. Consider a shortest path p from vertex i to vertex j, and suppose that p contains at most r edges. Assuming that there are no negative-weight cycles, r is finite. If $i = j$, then p has weight 0 and no edges. If vertices i and j are distinct, then decompose path p into $i \overset{p'}{\leadsto} k \to j$, where path p' now contains at most $r - 1$ edges. Lemma 22.1 says that p' is a shortest path from i to k, and so $\delta(i, j) = \delta(i, k) + w_{kj}$.

A recursive solution to the all-pairs shortest-paths problem

Now, let $l_{ij}^{(r)}$ be the minimum weight of any path from vertex i to vertex j that contains at most r edges. When $r = 0$, there is a shortest path from i to j with no edges if and only if $i = j$, yielding

$$l_{ij}^{(0)} = \begin{cases} 0 & \text{if } i = j , \\ \infty & \text{if } i \neq j . \end{cases} \tag{23.2}$$

For $r \geq 1$, one way to achieve a minimum-weight path from i to j with at most r edges is by taking a path containing at most $r - 1$ edges, so that $l_{ij}^{(r)} = l_{ij}^{(r-1)}$. Another way is by taking a path of at most $r - 1$ edges from i to some vertex k and then taking the edge (k, j), so that $l_{ij}^{(r)} = l_{ik}^{(r-1)} + w(k, j)$. Therefore, to examine paths from i to j consisting of at most r edges, try all possible predecessors k of j, giving the recursive definition

$$
\begin{aligned}
l_{ij}^{(r)} &= \min \left\{ l_{ij}^{(r-1)}, \min \left\{ l_{ik}^{(r-1)} + w_{kj} : 1 \leq k \leq n \right\} \right\} \\
&= \min \left\{ l_{ik}^{(r-1)} + w_{kj} : 1 \leq k \leq n \right\} .
\end{aligned}
\tag{23.3}
$$

The last equality follows from the observation that $w_{jj} = 0$ for all j.

What are the actual shortest-path weights $\delta(i, j)$? If the graph contains no negative-weight cycles, then whenever $\delta(i, j) < \infty$, there is a shortest path from vertex i to vertex j that is simple. (A path p from i to j that is not simple contains a cycle. Since each cycle's weight is nonnegative, removing all cycles from the path leaves a simple path with weight no greater than p's weight.) Because any simple path contains at most $n - 1$ edges, a path from vertex i to vertex j with more than $n - 1$ edges cannot have lower weight than a shortest path from i to j. The actual shortest-path weights are therefore given by

$$\delta(i,j) = l_{ij}^{(n-1)} = l_{ij}^{(n)} = l_{ij}^{(n+1)} = \cdots .$$ (23.4)

Computing the shortest-path weights bottom up

Taking as input the matrix $W = (w_{ij})$, let's see how to compute a series of matrices $L^{(0)}, L^{(1)}, \ldots, L^{(n-1)}$, where $L^{(r)} = \left(l_{ij}^{(r)}\right)$ for $r = 0, 1, \ldots, n-1$. The initial matrix is $L^{(0)}$ given by equation (23.2). The final matrix $L^{(n-1)}$ contains the actual shortest-path weights.

The heart of the algorithm is the procedure EXTEND-SHORTEST-PATHS, which implements equation (23.3) for all i and j. The four inputs are the matrix $L^{(r-1)}$ computed so far; the edge-weight matrix W; the output matrix $L^{(r)}$, which will hold the computed result and whose elements are all initialized to ∞ before invoking the procedure; and the number n of vertices. The superscripts r and $r-1$ help to make the correspondence of the pseudocode with equation (23.3) plain, but they play no actual role in the pseudocode. The procedure extends the shortest paths computed so far by one more edge, producing the matrix $L^{(r)}$ of shortest-path weights from the matrix $L^{(r-1)}$ computed so far. Its running time is $\Theta(n^3)$ due to the three nested **for** loops.

EXTEND-SHORTEST-PATHS$(L^{(r-1)}, W, L^{(r)}, n)$

1 **//** Assume that the elements of $L^{(r)}$ are initialized to ∞.
2 **for** $i = 1$ **to** n
3   **for** $j = 1$ **to** n
4   **for** $k = 1$ **to** n
5              $l_{ij}^{(r)} = \min \left\{ l_{ij}^{(r)}, l_{ik}^{(r-1)} + w_{kj} \right\}$

Let's now understand the relation of this computation to matrix multiplication. Consider how to compute the matrix product $C = A \cdot B$ of two $n \times n$ matrices A and B. The straightforward method used by MATRIX-MULTIPLY on page 81 uses a triply nested loop to implement equation (4.1), which we repeat here for convenience:

$$c_{ij} = \sum_{k=1}^{n} a_{ik} \cdot b_{kj} ,$$ (23.5)

for $i, j = 1, 2, \ldots, n$. Now make the substitutions

$$l^{(r-1)} \rightarrow a ,$$
$$w \rightarrow b ,$$
$$l^{(r)} \rightarrow c ,$$
$$\min \rightarrow + ,$$
$$+ \rightarrow \cdot$$

in equation (23.3). You get equation (23.5)! Making these changes to EXTEND-SHORTEST-PATHS, and also replacing ∞ (the identity for min) by 0 (the identity for $+$), yields the procedure MATRIX-MULTIPLY. We can see that the procedure EXTEND-SHORTEST-PATHS$(L^{(r-1)}, W, L^{(r)}, n)$ computes the matrix "product" $L^{(r)} = L^{(r-1)} \cdot W$ using this unusual definition of matrix multiplication.[2]

Thus, we can solve the all-pairs shortest-paths problem by repeatedly multiplying matrices. Each step extends the shortest-path weights computed so far by one more edge using EXTEND-SHORTEST-PATHS$(L^{(r-1)}, W, L^{(r)}, n)$ to perform the matrix multiplication. Starting with the matrix $L^{(0)}$, we produce the following sequence of $n - 1$ matrices corresponding to powers of W:

$$
\begin{aligned}
L^{(1)} &= L^{(0)} \cdot W &= W^1 , \\
L^{(2)} &= L^{(1)} \cdot W &= W^2 , \\
L^{(3)} &= L^{(2)} \cdot W &= W^3 , \\
&\vdots \\
L^{(n-1)} &= L^{(n-2)} \cdot W &= W^{n-1} .
\end{aligned}
$$

At the end, the matrix $L^{(n-1)} = W^{n-1}$ contains the shortest-path weights.

The procedure SLOW-APSP on the next page computes this sequence in $\Theta(n^4)$ time. The procedure takes the $n \times n$ matrices W and $L^{(0)}$ as inputs, along with n. Figure 23.1 illustrates its operation. The pseudocode uses two $n \times n$ matrices L and M to store powers of W, computing $M = L \cdot W$ on each iteration. Line 2 initializes $L = L^{(0)}$. For each iteration r, line 4 initializes $M = \infty$, where ∞ in this context is a matrix of scalar ∞ values. The rth iteration starts with the invariant $L = L^{(r-1)} = W^{r-1}$. Line 6 computes $M = L \cdot W = L^{(r-1)} \cdot W = W^{r-1} \cdot W = W^r = L^{(r)}$ so that the invariant can be restored for the next iteration by line 7, which sets $L = M$. At the end, the matrix $L = L^{(n-1)} = W^{n-1}$ of shortest-path weights is returned. The assignments to $n \times n$ matrices in lines 2, 4, and 7 implicitly run doubly nested loops that take $\Theta(n^2)$ time for each assignment.

---

[2] An algebraic *semiring* contains operations $\oplus$, which is commutative with identity $I_\oplus$, and $\otimes$, with identity $I_\otimes$, where $\otimes$ distributes over $\oplus$ on both the left and right, and where $I_\oplus \otimes x = x \otimes I_\oplus = I_\oplus$ for all x. Standard matrix multiplication, as in MATRIX-MULTIPLY, uses the semiring with $+$ for $\oplus$, $\cdot$ for $\otimes$, 0 for $I_\oplus$, and 1 for $I_\otimes$. The procedure EXTEND-SHORTEST-PATHS uses another semiring, known as the *tropical semiring*, with min for $\oplus$, $+$ for $\otimes$, ∞ for $I_\oplus$, and 0 for $I_\otimes$.

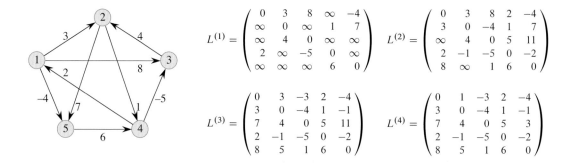

$$L^{(1)} = \begin{pmatrix} 0 & 3 & 8 & \infty & -4 \\ \infty & 0 & \infty & 1 & 7 \\ \infty & 4 & 0 & \infty & \infty \\ 2 & \infty & -5 & 0 & \infty \\ \infty & \infty & \infty & 6 & 0 \end{pmatrix} \quad L^{(2)} = \begin{pmatrix} 0 & 3 & 8 & 2 & -4 \\ 3 & 0 & -4 & 1 & 7 \\ \infty & 4 & 0 & 5 & 11 \\ 2 & -1 & -5 & 0 & -2 \\ 8 & \infty & 1 & 6 & 0 \end{pmatrix}$$

$$L^{(3)} = \begin{pmatrix} 0 & 3 & -3 & 2 & -4 \\ 3 & 0 & -4 & 1 & -1 \\ 7 & 4 & 0 & 5 & 11 \\ 2 & -1 & -5 & 0 & -2 \\ 8 & 5 & 1 & 6 & 0 \end{pmatrix} \quad L^{(4)} = \begin{pmatrix} 0 & 1 & -3 & 2 & -4 \\ 3 & 0 & -4 & 1 & -1 \\ 7 & 4 & 0 & 5 & 3 \\ 2 & -1 & -5 & 0 & -2 \\ 8 & 5 & 1 & 6 & 0 \end{pmatrix}$$

Figure 23.1 A directed graph and the sequence of matrices $L^{(r)}$ computed by SLOW-APSP. You might want to verify that $L^{(5)}$, defined as $L^{(4)} \cdot W$, equals $L^{(4)}$, and thus $L^{(r)} = L^{(4)}$ for all $r \geq 4$.

The $n-1$ invocations of EXTEND-SHORTEST-PATHS, each of which takes $\Theta(n^3)$ time, dominate the computation, yielding a total running time of $\Theta(n^4)$.

SLOW-APSP$(W, L^{(0)}, n)$

1   let $L = (l_{ij})$ and $M = (m_{ij})$ be new $n \times n$ matrices
2   $L = L^{(0)}$
3   **for** $r = 1$ **to** $n - 1$
4       $M = \infty$ // initialize M
5   // Compute the matrix "product" $M = L \cdot W$.
6   EXTEND-SHORTEST-PATHS(L, W, M, n)
7       $L = M$
8   **return** L

Improving the running time

Bear in mind that the goal is not to compute *all* the $L^{(r)}$ matrices: only the matrix $L^{(n-1)}$ matters. Recall that in the absence of negative-weight cycles, equation (23.4) implies $L^{(r)} = L^{(n-1)}$ for all integers $r \geq n - 1$. Just as traditional matrix multiplication is associative, so is matrix multiplication defined by the EXTEND-SHORTEST-PATHS procedure (see Exercise 23.1-4). In fact, we can compute $L^{(n-1)}$ with only $\lceil \lg(n - 1) \rceil$ matrix products by using the technique of *repeated squaring*:

$$
\begin{aligned}
L^{(1)} &= W\,, \\
L^{(2)} &= W^2 &= W \cdot W\,, \\
L^{(4)} &= W^4 &= W^2 \cdot W^2 \\
L^{(8)} &= W^8 &= W^4 \cdot W^4\,, \\
&\;\;\vdots \\
L^{(2^{\lceil \lg(n-1) \rceil})} &= W^{2^{\lceil \lg(n-1) \rceil}} &= W^{2^{\lceil \lg(n-1) \rceil - 1}} \cdot W^{2^{\lceil \lg(n-1) \rceil - 1}}\,.
\end{aligned}
$$

Since $2^{\lceil \lg(n-1) \rceil} \geq n-1$, the final product is $L^{(2^{\lceil \lg(n-1) \rceil})} = L^{(n-1)}$.

The procedure FASTER-APSP implements this idea. It takes just the $n \times n$ matrix W and the size n as inputs. Each iteration of the **while** loop of lines 4–8 starts with the invariant $L = W^r$, which it squares using EXTEND-SHORTEST-PATHS to obtain the matrix $M = L^2 = (W^r)^2 = W^{2r}$. At the end of each iteration, the value of r doubles, and L for the next iteration becomes M, restoring the invariant. Upon exiting the loop when $r \geq n-1$, the procedure returns $L = W^r = L^{(r)} = L^{(n-1)}$ by equation (23.4). As in SLOW-APSP, the assignments to $n \times n$ matrices in lines 2, 5, and 8 implicitly run doubly nested loops, taking $\Theta(n^2)$ time for each assignment.

FASTER-APSP(W, n)

1 let L and M be new $n \times n$ matrices
2 $L = W$
3 $r = 1$
4 **while** $r < n - 1$
5      $M = \infty$ **//** initialize M
6   EXTEND-SHORTEST-PATHS(L, L, M, n) **//** compute $M = L^2$
7      $r = 2r$
8      $L = M$ **//** ready for the next iteration
9 **return** L

Because each of the $\lceil \lg(n-1) \rceil$ matrix products takes $\Theta(n^3)$ time, FASTER-APSP runs in $\Theta(n^3 \lg n)$ time. The code is tight, containing no elaborate data structures, and the constant hidden in the Θ-notation is therefore small.

Exercises

23.1-1
Run SLOW-APSP on the weighted, directed graph of Figure 23.2, showing the matrices that result for each iteration of the loop. Then do the same for FASTER-APSP.

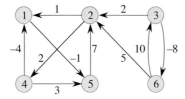

Figure 23.2   A weighted, directed graph for use in Exercises 23.1-1, 23.2-1, and 23.3-1.

23.1-2
Why is it convenient for both SLOW-APSP and FASTER-APSP that $w_{ii} = 0$ for $i = 1, 2, \ldots, n$?

23.1-3
What does the matrix

$$
L^{(0)} = \begin{pmatrix}
0 & \infty & \infty & \cdots & \infty \\
\infty & 0 & \infty & \cdots & \infty \\
\infty & \infty & 0 & \cdots & \infty \\
\vdots & \vdots & \vdots & \ddots & \vdots \\
\infty & \infty & \infty & \cdots & 0
\end{pmatrix}
$$

used in the shortest-paths algorithms correspond to in regular matrix multiplication?

23.1-4
Show that matrix multiplication defined by EXTEND-SHORTEST-PATHS is associative.

23.1-5
Show how to express the single-source shortest-paths problem as a product of matrices and a vector. Describe how evaluating this product corresponds to a Bellman-Ford-like algorithm (see Section 22.1).

23.1-6
Argue that we don't need the matrix M in SLOW-APSP because by substituting L for M and leaving out the initialization of M, the code still works correctly. (*Hint:* Relate line 5 of EXTEND-SHORTEST-PATHS to RELAX on page 610.) Do we need the matrix M in FASTER-APSP?

23.1-7

Suppose that you also want to compute the vertices on shortest paths in the algorithms of this section. Show how to compute the predecessor matrix Π from the completed matrix L of shortest-path weights in $O(n^3)$ time.

23.1-8

You can also compute the vertices on shortest paths along with computing the shortest-path weights. Define $\pi_{ij}^{(r)}$ as the predecessor of vertex j on any minimum-weight path from vertex i to vertex j that contains at most r edges. Modify the EXTEND-SHORTEST-PATHS and SLOW-APSP procedures to compute the matrices $\Pi^{(1)}, \Pi^{(2)}, \ldots, \Pi^{(n-1)}$ as they compute the matrices $L^{(1)}, L^{(2)}, \ldots, L^{(n-1)}$.

23.1-9

Modify FASTER-APSP so that it can determine whether the graph contains a negative-weight cycle.

23.1-10

Give an efficient algorithm to find the length (number of edges) of a minimum-length negative-weight cycle in a graph.

23.2   The Floyd-Warshall algorithm

Having already seen one dynamic-programming solution to the all-pairs shortest-paths problem, in this section we'll see another: the *Floyd-Warshall algorithm*, which runs in $\Theta(V^3)$ time. As before, negative-weight edges may be present, but not negative-weight cycles. As in Section 23.1, we develop the algorithm by following the dynamic-programming process. After studying the resulting algorithm, we present a similar method for finding the transitive closure of a directed graph.

The structure of a shortest path

In the Floyd-Warshall algorithm, we characterize the structure of a shortest path differently from how we characterized it in Section 23.1. The Floyd-Warshall algorithm considers the intermediate vertices of a shortest path, where an *intermediate* vertex of a simple path $p = \langle v_1, v_2, \ldots, v_l \rangle$ is any vertex of p other than v_1 or v_l, that is, any vertex in the set $\{v_2, v_3, \ldots, v_{l-1}\}$.

The Floyd-Warshall algorithm relies on the following observation. Numbering the vertices of G by $V = \{1, 2, \ldots, n\}$, take a subset $\{1, 2, \ldots, k\}$ of vertices for some $1 \leq k \leq n$. For any pair of vertices $i, j \in V$, consider all paths from i to j whose intermediate vertices are all drawn from $\{1, 2, \ldots, k\}$, and let p be a

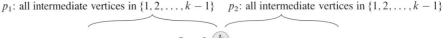

p_1: all intermediate vertices in $\{1, 2, \ldots, k-1\}$ p_2: all intermediate vertices in $\{1, 2, \ldots, k-1\}$

p: all intermediate vertices in $\{1, 2, \ldots, k\}$

Figure 23.3 Optimal substructure used by the Floyd-Warshall algorithm. Path p is a shortest path from vertex i to vertex j, and k is the highest-numbered intermediate vertex of p. Path p_1, the portion of path p from vertex i to vertex k, has all intermediate vertices in the set $\{1, 2, \ldots, k-1\}$. The same holds for path p_2 from vertex k to vertex j.

minimum-weight path from among them. (Path p is simple.) The Floyd-Warshall algorithm exploits a relationship between path p and shortest paths from i to j with all intermediate vertices in the set $\{1, 2, \ldots, k-1\}$. The details of the relationship depend on whether k is an intermediate vertex of path p or not.

- If k is not an intermediate vertex of path p, then all intermediate vertices of path p belong to the set $\{1, 2, \ldots, k-1\}$. Thus a shortest path from vertex i to vertex j with all intermediate vertices in the set $\{1, 2, \ldots, k-1\}$ is also a shortest path from i to j with all intermediate vertices in the set $\{1, 2, \ldots, k\}$.

- If k is an intermediate vertex of path p, then decompose p into $i \overset{p_1}{\rightsquigarrow} k \overset{p_2}{\rightsquigarrow} j$, as Figure 23.3 illustrates. By Lemma 22.1, p_1 is a shortest path from i to k with all intermediate vertices in the set $\{1, 2, \ldots, k\}$. In fact, we can make a slightly stronger statement. Because vertex k is not an *intermediate* vertex of path p_1, all intermediate vertices of p_1 belong to the set $\{1, 2, \ldots, k-1\}$. Therefore p_1 is a shortest path from i to k with all intermediate vertices in the set $\{1, 2, \ldots, k-1\}$. Likewise, p_2 is a shortest path from vertex k to vertex j with all intermediate vertices in the set $\{1, 2, \ldots, k-1\}$.

A recursive solution to the all-pairs shortest-paths problem

The above observations suggest a recursive formulation of shortest-path estimates that differs from the one in Section 23.1. Let $d_{ij}^{(k)}$ be the weight of a shortest path from vertex i to vertex j for which all intermediate vertices belong to the set $\{1, 2, \ldots, k\}$. When $k = 0$, a path from vertex i to vertex j with no intermediate vertex numbered higher than 0 has no intermediate vertices at all. Such a path has at most one edge, and hence $d_{ij}^{(0)} = w_{ij}$. Following the above discussion, define $d_{ij}^{(k)}$ recursively by

$$d_{ij}^{(k)} = \begin{cases} w_{ij} & \text{if } k = 0, \\ \min\left\{d_{ij}^{(k-1)}, d_{ik}^{(k-1)} + d_{kj}^{(k-1)}\right\} & \text{if } k \geq 1. \end{cases} \tag{23.6}$$

Because for any path, all intermediate vertices belong to the set $\{1, 2, \ldots, n\}$, the matrix $D^{(n)} = \left(d_{ij}^{(n)}\right)$ gives the final answer: $d_{ij}^{(n)} = \delta(i, j)$ for all $i, j \in V$.

Computing the shortest-path weights bottom up

Based on recurrence (23.6), the bottom-up procedure FLOYD-WARSHALL computes the values $d_{ij}^{(k)}$ in order of increasing values of k. Its input is an $n \times n$ matrix W defined as in equation (23.1). The procedure returns the matrix $D^{(n)}$ of shortest-path weights. Figure 23.4 shows the matrices $D^{(k)}$ computed by the Floyd-Warshall algorithm for the graph in Figure 23.1.

FLOYD-WARSHALL(W, n)

1   $D^{(0)} = W$
2   **for** $k = 1$ **to** n
3   let $D^{(k)} = \left(d_{ij}^{(k)}\right)$ be a new $n \times n$ matrix
4   **for** $i = 1$ **to** n
5   **for** $j = 1$ **to** n
6               $d_{ij}^{(k)} = \min\left\{d_{ij}^{(k-1)}, d_{ik}^{(k-1)} + d_{kj}^{(k-1)}\right\}$
7   **return** $D^{(n)}$

The running time of the Floyd-Warshall algorithm is determined by the triply nested **for** loops of lines 2–6. Because each execution of line 6 takes $O(1)$ time, the algorithm runs in $\Theta(n^3)$ time. As in the final algorithm in Section 23.1, the code is tight, with no elaborate data structures, and so the constant hidden in the Θ-notation is small. Thus, the Floyd-Warshall algorithm is quite practical for even moderate-sized input graphs.

Constructing a shortest path

There are a variety of different methods for constructing shortest paths in the Floyd-Warshall algorithm. One way is to compute the matrix D of shortest-path weights and then construct the predecessor matrix Π from the D matrix. Exercise 23.1-7 asks you to implement this method so that it runs in $O(n^3)$ time. Given the predecessor matrix Π, the PRINT-ALL-PAIRS-SHORTEST-PATH procedure prints the vertices on a given shortest path.

Alternatively, the predecessor matrix Π can be computed while the algorithm computes the matrices $D^{(0)}, D^{(1)}, \ldots, D^{(n)}$. Specifically, compute a sequence of

$$
D^{(0)} = \begin{pmatrix} 0 & 3 & 8 & \infty & -4 \\ \infty & 0 & \infty & 1 & 7 \\ \infty & 4 & 0 & \infty & \infty \\ 2 & \infty & -5 & 0 & \infty \\ \infty & \infty & \infty & 6 & 0 \end{pmatrix} \quad
\Pi^{(0)} = \begin{pmatrix} \text{NIL} & 1 & 1 & \text{NIL} & 1 \\ \text{NIL} & \text{NIL} & \text{NIL} & 2 & 2 \\ \text{NIL} & 3 & \text{NIL} & \text{NIL} & \text{NIL} \\ 4 & \text{NIL} & 4 & \text{NIL} & \text{NIL} \\ \text{NIL} & \text{NIL} & \text{NIL} & 5 & \text{NIL} \end{pmatrix}
$$

$$
D^{(1)} = \begin{pmatrix} 0 & 3 & 8 & \infty & -4 \\ \infty & 0 & \infty & 1 & 7 \\ \infty & 4 & 0 & \infty & \infty \\ 2 & 5 & -5 & 0 & -2 \\ \infty & \infty & \infty & 6 & 0 \end{pmatrix} \quad
\Pi^{(1)} = \begin{pmatrix} \text{NIL} & 1 & 1 & \text{NIL} & 1 \\ \text{NIL} & \text{NIL} & \text{NIL} & 2 & 2 \\ \text{NIL} & 3 & \text{NIL} & \text{NIL} & \text{NIL} \\ 4 & 1 & 4 & \text{NIL} & 1 \\ \text{NIL} & \text{NIL} & \text{NIL} & 5 & \text{NIL} \end{pmatrix}
$$

$$
D^{(2)} = \begin{pmatrix} 0 & 3 & 8 & 4 & -4 \\ \infty & 0 & \infty & 1 & 7 \\ \infty & 4 & 0 & 5 & 11 \\ 2 & 5 & -5 & 0 & -2 \\ \infty & \infty & \infty & 6 & 0 \end{pmatrix} \quad
\Pi^{(2)} = \begin{pmatrix} \text{NIL} & 1 & 1 & 2 & 1 \\ \text{NIL} & \text{NIL} & \text{NIL} & 2 & 2 \\ \text{NIL} & 3 & \text{NIL} & 2 & 2 \\ 4 & 1 & 4 & \text{NIL} & 1 \\ \text{NIL} & \text{NIL} & \text{NIL} & 5 & \text{NIL} \end{pmatrix}
$$

$$
D^{(3)} = \begin{pmatrix} 0 & 3 & 8 & 4 & -4 \\ \infty & 0 & \infty & 1 & 7 \\ \infty & 4 & 0 & 5 & 11 \\ 2 & -1 & -5 & 0 & -2 \\ \infty & \infty & \infty & 6 & 0 \end{pmatrix} \quad
\Pi^{(3)} = \begin{pmatrix} \text{NIL} & 1 & 1 & 2 & 1 \\ \text{NIL} & \text{NIL} & \text{NIL} & 2 & 2 \\ \text{NIL} & 3 & \text{NIL} & 2 & 2 \\ 4 & 3 & 4 & \text{NIL} & 1 \\ \text{NIL} & \text{NIL} & \text{NIL} & 5 & \text{NIL} \end{pmatrix}
$$

$$
D^{(4)} = \begin{pmatrix} 0 & 3 & -1 & 4 & -4 \\ 3 & 0 & -4 & 1 & -1 \\ 7 & 4 & 0 & 5 & 3 \\ 2 & -1 & -5 & 0 & -2 \\ 8 & 5 & 1 & 6 & 0 \end{pmatrix} \quad
\Pi^{(4)} = \begin{pmatrix} \text{NIL} & 1 & 4 & 2 & 1 \\ 4 & \text{NIL} & 4 & 2 & 1 \\ 4 & 3 & \text{NIL} & 2 & 1 \\ 4 & 3 & 4 & \text{NIL} & 1 \\ 4 & 3 & 4 & 5 & \text{NIL} \end{pmatrix}
$$

$$
D^{(5)} = \begin{pmatrix} 0 & 1 & -3 & 2 & -4 \\ 3 & 0 & -4 & 1 & -1 \\ 7 & 4 & 0 & 5 & 3 \\ 2 & -1 & -5 & 0 & -2 \\ 8 & 5 & 1 & 6 & 0 \end{pmatrix} \quad
\Pi^{(5)} = \begin{pmatrix} \text{NIL} & 3 & 4 & 5 & 1 \\ 4 & \text{NIL} & 4 & 2 & 1 \\ 4 & 3 & \text{NIL} & 2 & 1 \\ 4 & 3 & 4 & \text{NIL} & 1 \\ 4 & 3 & 4 & 5 & \text{NIL} \end{pmatrix}
$$

Figure 23.4 The sequence of matrices $D^{(k)}$ and $\Pi^{(k)}$ computed by the Floyd-Warshall algorithm for the graph in Figure 23.1.

matrices $\Pi^{(0)}, \Pi^{(1)}, \ldots, \Pi^{(n)}$, where $\Pi = \Pi^{(n)}$ and $\pi_{ij}^{(k)}$ is the predecessor of vertex j on a shortest path from vertex i with all intermediate vertices in the set $\{1, 2, \ldots, k\}$.

Here's a recursive formulation of $\pi_{ij}^{(k)}$. When $k = 0$, a shortest path from i to j has no intermediate vertices at all, and so

$$\pi_{ij}^{(0)} = \begin{cases} \text{NIL} & \text{if } i = j \text{ or } w_{ij} = \infty \,, \\ i & \text{if } i \neq j \text{ and } w_{ij} < \infty \,. \end{cases} \tag{23.7}$$

For $k \geq 1$, if the path has k as an intermediate vertex, so that it is $i \rightsquigarrow k \rightsquigarrow j$ where $k \neq j$, then choose as the predecessor of j on this path the same vertex as the predecessor of j chosen on a shortest path from k with all intermediate vertices in the set $\{1, 2, \dots, k - 1\}$. Otherwise, when the path from i to j does not have k as an intermediate vertex, choose the same predecessor of j as on a shortest path from i with all intermediate vertices in the set $\{1, 2, \dots, k - 1\}$. Formally, for $k \geq 1$,

$$\pi_{ij}^{(k)} = \begin{cases} \pi_{kj}^{(k-1)} & \text{if } d_{ij}^{(k-1)} > d_{ik}^{(k-1)} + d_{kj}^{(k-1)} \ (k \text{ is an intermediate vertex}) \,, \\ \pi_{ij}^{(k-1)} & \text{if } d_{ij}^{(k-1)} \leq d_{ik}^{(k-1)} + d_{kj}^{(k-1)} \ (k \text{ is not an intermediate vertex}) \,. \end{cases}$$
$$\tag{23.8}$$

Exercise 23.2-3 asks you to show how to incorporate the $\Pi^{(k)}$ matrix computations into the FLOYD-WARSHALL procedure. Figure 23.4 shows the sequence of $\Pi^{(k)}$ matrices that the resulting algorithm computes for the graph of Figure 23.1. The exercise also asks for the more difficult task of proving that the predecessor subgraph $G_{\pi,i}$ is a shortest-paths tree with root i. Exercise 23.2-7 asks for yet another way to reconstruct shortest paths.

Transitive closure of a directed graph

Given a directed graph $G = (V, E)$ with vertex set $V = \{1, 2, \dots, n\}$, you might wish to determine simply whether G contains a path from i to j for all vertex pairs $i, j \in V$, without regard to edge weights. We define the *transitive closure* of G as the graph $G^* = (V, E^*)$, where

$$E^* = \{(i, j) : \text{there is a path from vertex } i \text{ to vertex } j \text{ in } G\} \,.$$

One way to compute the transitive closure of a graph in $\Theta(n^3)$ time is to assign a weight of 1 to each edge of E and run the Floyd-Warshall algorithm. If there is a path from vertex i to vertex j, you get $d_{ij} < n$. Otherwise, you get $d_{ij} = \infty$.

There is another, similar way to compute the transitive closure of G in $\Theta(n^3)$ time, which can save time and space in practice. This method substitutes the logical operations $\lor$ (logical OR) and $\land$ (logical AND) for the arithmetic operations min and $+$ in the Floyd-Warshall algorithm. For $i, j, k = 1, 2, \dots, n$, define $t_{ij}^{(k)}$ to be 1 if there exists a path in graph G from vertex i to vertex j with all intermediate vertices in the set $\{1, 2, \dots, k\}$, and 0 otherwise. To construct the transitive closure $G^* = (V, E^*)$, put edge (i, j) into E^* if and only if $t_{ij}^{(n)} = 1$. A recursive definition of $t_{ij}^{(k)}$, analogous to recurrence (23.6), is

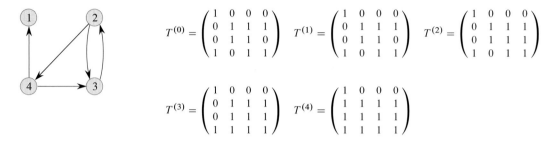

Figure 23.5   A directed graph and the matrices $T^{(k)}$ computed by the transitive-closure algorithm.

$$
t_{ij}^{(0)} = \begin{cases} 0 & \text{if } i \neq j \text{ and } (i,j) \notin E , \\ 1 & \text{if } i = j \text{ or } (i,j) \in E , \end{cases}
$$

and for $k \geq 1$,

$$
t_{ij}^{(k)} = t_{ij}^{(k-1)} \vee \left(t_{ik}^{(k-1)} \wedge t_{kj}^{(k-1)} \right) . \tag{23.9}
$$

As in the Floyd-Warshall algorithm, the TRANSITIVE-CLOSURE procedure computes the matrices $T^{(k)} = \left(t_{ij}^{(k)} \right)$ in order of increasing k.

TRANSITIVE-CLOSURE(G, n)

```
1   let T^(0) = (t_ij^(0)) be a new n × n matrix
2   for i = 1 to n
3       for j = 1 to n
4           if i == j or (i, j) ∈ G.E
5               t_ij^(0) = 1
6           else t_ij^(0) = 0
7   for k = 1 to n
8       let T^(k) = (t_ij^(k)) be a new n × n matrix
9       for i = 1 to n
10          for j = 1 to n
11              t_ij^(k) = t_ij^(k-1) ∨ (t_ik^(k-1) ∧ t_kj^(k-1))
12  return T^(n)
```

Figure 23.5 shows the matrices $T^{(k)}$ computed by the TRANSITIVE-CLOSURE procedure on a sample graph. The TRANSITIVE-CLOSURE procedure, like the Floyd-Warshall algorithm, runs in $\Theta(n^3)$ time. On some computers, though, logical operations on single-bit values execute faster than arithmetic operations on integer words of data. Moreover, because the direct transitive-closure algorithm uses only boolean values rather than integer values, its space requirement is less than the Floyd-Warshall algorithm's by a factor corresponding to the size of a word of computer storage.

Exercises

23.2-1
Run the Floyd-Warshall algorithm on the weighted, directed graph of Figure 23.2. Show the matrix $D^{(k)}$ that results for each iteration of the outer loop.

23.2-2
Show how to compute the transitive closure using the technique of Section 23.1.

23.2-3
Modify the FLOYD-WARSHALL procedure to compute the $\Pi^{(k)}$ matrices according to equations (23.7) and (23.8). Prove rigorously that for all $i \in V$, the predecessor subgraph $G_{\pi,i}$ is a shortest-paths tree with root i. (*Hint:* To show that $G_{\pi,i}$ is acyclic, first show that $\pi_{ij}^{(k)} = l$ implies $d_{ij}^{(k)} \geq d_{il}^{(k)} + w_{lj}$, according to the definition of $\pi_{ij}^{(k)}$. Then adapt the proof of Lemma 22.16.)

23.2-4
As it appears on page 657, the Floyd-Warshall algorithm requires $\Theta(n^3)$ space, since it creates $d_{ij}^{(k)}$ for $i, j, k = 1, 2, \ldots, n$. Show that the procedure FLOYD-WARSHALL', which simply drops all the superscripts, is correct, and thus only $\Theta(n^2)$ space is required.

```
FLOYD-WARSHALL'(W, n)
1   D = W
2   for k = 1 to n
3       for i = 1 to n
4           for j = 1 to n
5               d_ij = min {d_ij, d_ik + d_kj}
6   return D
```

23.2-5
Consider the following change to how equation (23.8) handles equality:

$$\pi_{ij}^{(k)} = \begin{cases} \pi_{kj}^{(k-1)} & \text{if } d_{ij}^{(k-1)} \geq d_{ik}^{(k-1)} + d_{kj}^{(k-1)} \ (k \text{ is an intermediate vertex}) , \\ \pi_{ij}^{(k-1)} & \text{if } d_{ij}^{(k-1)} < d_{ik}^{(k-1)} + d_{kj}^{(k-1)} \ (k \text{ is not an intermediate vertex}) . \end{cases}$$

Is this alternative definition of the predecessor matrix Π correct?

23.2-6
Show how to use the output of the Floyd-Warshall algorithm to detect the presence of a negative-weight cycle.

23.2-7
Another way to reconstruct shortest paths in the Floyd-Warshall algorithm uses values $\phi_{ij}^{(k)}$ for $i, j, k = 1, 2, \ldots, n$, where $\phi_{ij}^{(k)}$ is the highest-numbered intermediate vertex of a shortest path from i to j in which all intermediate vertices lie in the set $\{1, 2, \ldots, k\}$. Give a recursive formulation for $\phi_{ij}^{(k)}$, modify the FLOYD-WARSHALL procedure to compute the $\phi_{ij}^{(k)}$ values, and rewrite the PRINT-ALL-PAIRS-SHORTEST-PATH procedure to take the matrix $\Phi = \left(\phi_{ij}^{(n)}\right)$ as an input. How is the matrix Φ like the s table in the matrix-chain multiplication problem of Section 14.2?

23.2-8
Give an $O(VE)$-time algorithm for computing the transitive closure of a directed graph $G = (V, E)$. Assume that $|V| = O(E)$ and that the graph is represented with adjacency lists.

23.2-9
Suppose that it takes $f(|V|, |E|)$ time to compute the transitive closure of a directed acyclic graph, where f is a monotonically increasing function of both $|V|$ and $|E|$. Show that the time to compute the transitive closure $G^* = (V, E^*)$ of a general directed graph $G = (V, E)$ is then $f(|V|, |E|) + O(V + E^*)$.

23.3   Johnson's algorithm for sparse graphs

Johnson's algorithm finds shortest paths between all pairs in $O(V^2 \lg V + VE)$ time. For sparse graphs, it is asymptotically faster than either repeated squaring of matrices or the Floyd-Warshall algorithm. The algorithm either returns a matrix of shortest-path weights for all pairs of vertices or reports that the input graph contains a negative-weight cycle. Johnson's algorithm uses as subroutines both Dijkstra's algorithm and the Bellman-Ford algorithm, which Chapter 22 describes.

   Johnson's algorithm uses the technique of *reweighting*, which works as follows. If all edge weights w in a graph $G = (V, E)$ are nonnegative, Dijkstra's algorithm can find shortest paths between all pairs of vertices by running it once from each vertex. With the Fibonacci-heap min-priority queue, the running time of this all-pairs algorithm is $O(V^2 \lg V + VE)$. If G has negative-weight edges but no negative-weight cycles, first compute a new set of nonnegative edge weights so that Dijkstra's algorithm applies. The new set of edge weights $\widehat{w}$ must satisfy two important properties:

1. For all pairs of vertices $u, v \in V$, a path p is a shortest path from u to v using weight function w if and only if p is also a shortest path from u to v using weight function $\widehat{w}$.

2. For all edges (u, v), the new weight $\widehat{w}(u, v)$ is nonnegative.

As we'll see in a moment, preprocessing G to determine the new weight function $\widehat{w}$ takes $O(VE)$ time.

Preserving shortest paths by reweighting

The following lemma shows how to reweight the edges to satisfy the first property above. We use δ to denote shortest-path weights derived from weight function w and $\widehat{\delta}$ to denote shortest-path weights derived from weight function $\widehat{w}$.

Lemma 23.1 (Reweighting does not change shortest paths)
Given a weighted, directed graph $G = (V, E)$ with weight function $w : E \to \mathbb{R}$, let $h : V \to \mathbb{R}$ be any function mapping vertices to real numbers. For each edge $(u, v) \in E$, define

$$\widehat{w}(u, v) = w(u, v) + h(u) - h(v) . \tag{23.10}$$

Let $p = \langle v_0, v_1, \ldots, v_k \rangle$ be any path from vertex v_0 to vertex v_k. Then p is a shortest path from v_0 to v_k with weight function w if and only if it is a shortest path with weight function $\widehat{w}$. That is, $w(p) = \delta(v_0, v_k)$ if and only if $\widehat{w}(p) = \widehat{\delta}(v_0, v_k)$. Furthermore, G has a negative-weight cycle using weight function w if and only if G has a negative-weight cycle using weight function $\widehat{w}$.

Proof We start by showing that

$$\widehat{w}(p) = w(p) + h(v_0) - h(v_k) . \tag{23.11}$$

We have

$$\begin{aligned}
\widehat{w}(p) &= \sum_{i=1}^{k} \widehat{w}(v_{i-1}, v_i) \\
&= \sum_{i=1}^{k} (w(v_{i-1}, v_i) + h(v_{i-1}) - h(v_i)) \\
&= \sum_{i=1}^{k} w(v_{i-1}, v_i) + h(v_0) - h(v_k) \quad \text{(because the sum telescopes)} \\
&= w(p) + h(v_0) - h(v_k) .
\end{aligned}$$

Therefore, any path p from v_0 to v_k has $\widehat{w}(p) = w(p) + h(v_0) - h(v_k)$. Because $h(v_0)$ and $h(v_k)$ do not depend on the path, if one path from v_0 to v_k is shorter than another using weight function w, then it is also shorter using $\widehat{w}$. Thus, $w(p) = \delta(v_0, v_k)$ if and only if $\widehat{w}(p) = \widehat{\delta}(v_0, v_k)$.

Finally, we show that G has a negative-weight cycle using weight function w if and only if G has a negative-weight cycle using weight function $\widehat{w}$. Consider any cycle $c = \langle v_0, v_1, \ldots, v_k \rangle$, where $v_0 = v_k$. By equation (23.11),

$$
\begin{aligned}
\widehat{w}(c) &= w(c) + h(v_0) - h(v_k) \\
&= w(c) \,,
\end{aligned}
$$

and thus c has negative weight using w if and only if it has negative weight using $\widehat{w}$. ∎

Producing nonnegative weights by reweighting

Our next goal is to ensure that the second property holds: $\widehat{w}(u, v)$ must be nonnegative for all edges $(u, v) \in E$. Given a weighted, directed graph $G = (V, E)$ with weight function $w : E \to \mathbb{R}$, we'll see how to make a new graph $G' = (V', E')$, where $V' = V \cup \{s\}$ for some new vertex $s \notin V$ and $E' = E \cup \{(s, v) : v \in V\}$. To incorporate the new vertex s, extend the weight function w so that $w(s, v) = 0$ for all $v \in V$. Since no edges enter s, no shortest paths in G', other than those with source s, contain s. Moreover, G' has no negative-weight cycles if and only if G has no negative-weight cycles. Figure 23.6(a) shows the graph G' corresponding to the graph G of Figure 23.1.

Now suppose that G and G' have no negative-weight cycles. Define the function $h(v) = \delta(s, v)$ for all $v \in V'$. By the triangle inequality (Lemma 22.10 on page 633), we have $h(v) \le h(u) + w(u, v)$ for all edges $(u, v) \in E'$. Thus, by defining reweighted edge weights $\widehat{w}$ according to equation (23.10), we have $\widehat{w}(u, v) = w(u, v) + h(u) - h(v) \ge 0$, thereby satisfying the second property. Figure 23.6(b) shows the graph G' from Figure 23.6(a) with reweighted edges.

Computing all-pairs shortest paths

Johnson's algorithm to compute all-pairs shortest paths uses the Bellman-Ford algorithm (Section 22.1) and Dijkstra's algorithm (Section 22.3) as subroutines. The pseudocode appears in the procedure JOHNSON on page 666. It assumes implicitly that the edges are stored in adjacency lists. The algorithm returns the usual $|V| \times |V|$ matrix $D = (d_{ij})$, where $d_{ij} = \delta(i, j)$, or it reports that the input graph contains a negative-weight cycle. As is typical for an all-pairs shortest-paths algorithm, it assumes that the vertices are numbered from 1 to $|V|$.

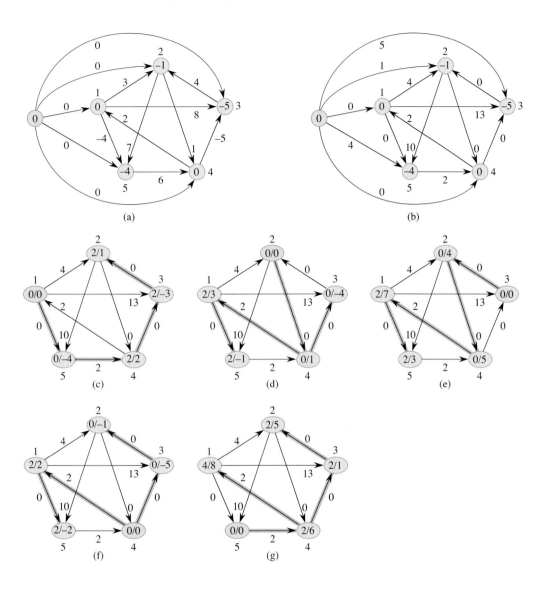

Figure 23.6 Johnson's all-pairs shortest-paths algorithm run on the graph of Figure 23.1. Vertex numbers appear outside the vertices. **(a)** The graph G' with the original weight function w. The new vertex s is blue. Within each vertex v is $h(v) = \delta(s, v)$. **(b)** After reweighting each edge (u, v) with weight function $\hat{w}(u, v) = w(u, v) + h(u) - h(v)$. **(c)**–**(g)** The result of running Dijkstra's algorithm on each vertex of G using weight function $\hat{w}$. In each part, the source vertex u is blue, and blue edges belong to the shortest-paths tree computed by the algorithm. Within each vertex v are the values $\hat{\delta}(u, v)$ and $\delta(u, v)$, separated by a slash. The value $d_{uv} = \delta(u, v)$ is equal to $\hat{\delta}(u, v) + h(v) - h(u)$.

JOHNSON(G, w)

1 compute G', where $G'.V = G.V \cup \{s\}$,
       $G'.E = G.E \cup \{(s, v) : v \in G.V\}$, and
       $w(s, v) = 0$ for all $v \in G.V$
2 **if** BELLMAN-FORD(G', w, s) == FALSE
3   print "the input graph contains a negative-weight cycle"
4 **else for** each vertex $v \in G'.V$
5   set $h(v)$ to the value of $\delta(s, v)$
               computed by the Bellman-Ford algorithm
6   **for** each edge $(u, v) \in G'.E$
7          $\widehat{w}(u, v) = w(u, v) + h(u) - h(v)$
8   let $D = (d_{uv})$ be a new $n \times n$ matrix
9   **for** each vertex $u \in G.V$
10   run DIJKSTRA$(G, \widehat{w}, u)$ to compute $\widehat{\delta}(u, v)$ for all $v \in G.V$
11   **for** each vertex $v \in G.V$
12             $d_{uv} = \widehat{\delta}(u, v) + h(v) - h(u)$
13   **return** D

The JOHNSON procedure simply performs the actions specified earlier. Line 1 produces G'. Line 2 runs the Bellman-Ford algorithm on G' with weight function w and source vertex s. If G', and hence G, contains a negative-weight cycle, line 3 reports the problem. Lines 4–12 assume that G' contains no negative-weight cycles. Lines 4–5 set $h(v)$ to the shortest-path weight $\delta(s, v)$ computed by the Bellman-Ford algorithm for all $v \in V'$. Lines 6–7 compute the new weights $\widehat{w}$. For each pair of vertices $u, v \in V$, the **for** loop of lines 9–12 computes the shortest-path weight $\widehat{\delta}(u, v)$ by calling Dijkstra's algorithm once from each vertex in V. Line 12 stores in matrix entry d_{uv} the correct shortest-path weight $\delta(u, v)$, calculated using equation (23.11). Finally, line 13 returns the completed D matrix. Figure 23.6 depicts the execution of Johnson's algorithm.

If the min-priority queue in Dijkstra's algorithm is implemented by a Fibonacci heap, Johnson's algorithm runs in $O(V^2 \lg V + VE)$ time. The simpler binary min-heap implementation yields a running time of $O(VE \lg V)$, which is still asymptotically faster than the Floyd-Warshall algorithm if the graph is sparse.

Exercises

23.3-1
Use Johnson's algorithm to find the shortest paths between all pairs of vertices in the graph of Figure 23.2. Show the values of h and $\widehat{w}$ computed by the algorithm.

23.3-2
What is the purpose of adding the new vertex s to V, yielding V'?

23.3-3
Suppose that $w(u, v) \geq 0$ for all edges $(u, v) \in E$. What is the relationship between the weight functions w and $\hat{w}$?

23.3-4
Professor Greenstreet claims that there is a simpler way to reweight edges than the method used in Johnson's algorithm. Letting $w^* = \min \{w(u, v) : (u, v) \in E\}$, just define $\hat{w}(u, v) = w(u, v) - w^*$ for all edges $(u, v) \in E$. What is wrong with the professor's method of reweighting?

23.3-5
Show that if G contains a 0-weight cycle c, then $\hat{w}(u, v) = 0$ for every edge (u, v) in c.

23.3-6
Professor Michener claims that there is no need to create a new source vertex in line 1 of JOHNSON. He suggests using $G' = G$ instead and letting s be any vertex. Give an example of a weighted, directed graph G for which incorporating the professor's idea into JOHNSON causes incorrect answers. Assume that $\infty - \infty$ is undefined, and in particular, it is not 0. Then show that if G is strongly connected (every vertex is reachable from every other vertex), the results returned by JOHNSON with the professor's modification are correct.

Problems

23-1   *Transitive closure of a dynamic graph*
You wish to maintain the transitive closure of a directed graph $G = (V, E)$ as you insert edges into E. That is, after inserting an edge, you update the transitive closure of the edges inserted so far. Start with G having no edges initially, and represent the transitive closure by a boolean matrix.

a. Show how to update the transitive closure $G^* = (V, E^*)$ of a graph $G = (V, E)$ in $O(V^2)$ time when a new edge is added to G.

b. Give an example of a graph G and an edge e such that $\Omega(V^2)$ time is required to update the transitive closure after inserting e into G, no matter what algorithm is used.

c. Give an algorithm for updating the transitive closure as edges are inserted into the graph. For any sequence of r insertions, your algorithm should run in time $\sum_{i=1}^{r} t_i = O(V^3)$, where t_i is the time to update the transitive closure upon inserting the ith edge. Prove that your algorithm attains this time bound.

23-2   *Shortest paths in ϵ-dense graphs*

A graph $G = (V, E)$ is ϵ-*dense* if $|E| = \Theta(V^{1+\epsilon})$ for some constant ϵ in the range $0 < \epsilon \leq 1$. d-ary min-heaps (see Problem 6-2 on page 179) provide a way to match the running times of Fibonacci-heap-based shortest-path algorithms on ϵ-dense graphs without using as complicated a data structure.

a. What are the asymptotic running times for the operations INSERT, EXTRACT-MIN, and DECREASE-KEY, as a function of d and the number n of elements in a d-ary min-heap? What are these running times if you choose $d = \Theta(n^\alpha)$ for some constant $0 < \alpha \leq 1$? Compare these running times to the amortized costs of these operations for a Fibonacci heap.

b. Show how to compute shortest paths from a single source on an ϵ-dense directed graph $G = (V, E)$ with no negative-weight edges in $O(E)$ time. (*Hint:* Pick d as a function of ϵ.)

c. Show how to solve the all-pairs shortest-paths problem on an ϵ-dense directed graph $G = (V, E)$ with no negative-weight edges in $O(VE)$ time.

d. Show how to solve the all-pairs shortest-paths problem in $O(VE)$ time on an ϵ-dense directed graph $G = (V, E)$ that may have negative-weight edges but has no negative-weight cycles.

Chapter notes

Lawler [276] has a good discussion of the all-pairs shortest-paths problem. He attributes the matrix-multiplication algorithm to the folklore. The Floyd-Warshall algorithm is due to Floyd [144], who based it on a theorem of Warshall [450] that describes how to compute the transitive closure of boolean matrices. Johnson's algorithm is taken from [238].

Several researchers have given improved algorithms for computing shortest paths via matrix multiplication. Fredman [153] shows how to solve the all-pairs shortest paths problem using $O(V^{5/2})$ comparisons between sums of edge weights and obtains an algorithm that runs in $O(V^3(\lg \lg V / \lg V)^{1/3})$ time, which is slightly better than the running time of the Floyd-Warshall algorithm. This bound has been improved several times, and the fastest algorithm is now by Williams [457], with a running time of $O(V^3/2^{\Omega(\lg^{1/2} V)})$.

Another line of research demonstrates how to apply algorithms for fast matrix multiplication (see the chapter notes for Chapter 4) to the all-pairs shortest paths problem. Let $O(n^\omega)$ be the running time of the fastest algorithm for multiplying two $n \times n$ matrices. Galil and Margalit [170, 171] and Seidel [403] designed algorithms that solve the all-pairs shortest paths problem in undirected, unweighted graphs in $(V^\omega p(V))$ time, where $p(n)$ denotes a particular function that is polylogarithmically bounded in n. In dense graphs, these algorithms are faster than the $O(VE)$ time needed to perform $|V|$ breadth-first searches. Several researchers have extended these results to give algorithms for solving the all-pairs shortest paths problem in undirected graphs in which the edge weights are integers in the range $\{1, 2, \ldots, W\}$. The asymptotically fastest such algorithm, by Shoshan and Zwick [410], runs in $O(WV^\omega p(VW))$ time. In directed graphs, the best algorithm to date is due to Zwick [467] and runs in $\widetilde{O}(W^{1/(4-\omega)}V^{2+1/(4-\omega)})$ time.

Karger, Koller, and Phillips [244] and independently McGeoch [320] have given a time bound that depends on E^*, the set of edges in E that participate in some shortest path. Given a graph with nonnegative edge weights, their algorithms run in $O(VE^* + V^2 \lg V)$ time and improve upon running Dijkstra's algorithm $|V|$ times when $|E^*| = o(E)$. Pettie [355] uses an approach based on component hierarchies to achieve a running time of $O(VE + V^2 \lg \lg V)$, and the same running time is also achieved by Hagerup [205].

Baswana, Hariharan, and Sen [37] examined decremental algorithms, which allow a sequence of intermixed edge deletions and queries, for maintaining all-pairs shortest paths and transitive-closure information. When a path exists, their randomized transitive-closure algorithm can fail to report it with probability $1/n^c$ for an arbitrary $c > 0$. The query times are $O(1)$ with high probability. For transitive closure, the amortized time for each update is $O(V^{4/3} \lg^{1/3} V)$. By comparison, Problem 23-1, in which edges are inserted, asks for an incremental algorithm. For all-pairs shortest paths, the update times depend on the queries. For queries just giving the shortest-path weights, the amortized time per update is $O(V^3/E \lg^2 V)$. To report the actual shortest path, the amortized update time is $\min\{O(V^{3/2}\sqrt{\lg V}), O(V^3/E \lg^2 V)\}$. Demetrescu and Italiano [111] showed how to handle update and query operations when edges are both inserted and deleted, as long as the range of edge weights is bounded.

Aho, Hopcroft, and Ullman [5] defined an algebraic structure known as a "closed semiring," which serves as a general framework for solving path problems in directed graphs. Both the Floyd-Warshall algorithm and the transitive-closure algorithm from Section 23.2 are instantiations of an all-pairs algorithm based on closed semirings. Maggs and Plotkin [309] showed how to find minimum spanning trees using a closed semiring.

Maximum Flow

Just as you can model a road map as a directed graph in order to find the shortest path from one point to another, you can also interpret a directed graph as a "flow network" and use it to answer questions about material flows. Imagine a material coursing through a system from a source, where the material is produced, to a sink, where it is consumed. The source produces the material at some steady rate, and the sink consumes the material at the same rate. The "flow" of the material at any point in the system is intuitively the rate at which the material moves. Flow networks can model many problems, including liquids flowing through pipes, parts through assembly lines, current through electrical networks, and information through communication networks.

You can think of each directed edge in a flow network as a conduit for the material. Each conduit has a stated capacity, given as a maximum rate at which the material can flow through the conduit, such as 200 gallons of liquid per hour through a pipe or 20 amperes of electrical current through a wire. Vertices are conduit junctions, and other than the source and sink, material flows through the vertices without collecting in them. In other words, the rate at which material enters a vertex must equal the rate at which it leaves the vertex. We call this property "flow conservation," and it is equivalent to Kirchhoff's current law when the material is electrical current.

The goal of the maximum-flow problem is to compute the greatest rate for shipping material from the source to the sink without violating any capacity constraints. It is one of the simplest problems concerning flow networks and, as we shall see in this chapter, this problem can be solved by efficient algorithms. Moreover, other network-flow problems are solvable by adapting the basic techniques used in maximum-flow algorithms.

This chapter presents two general methods for solving the maximum-flow problem. Section 24.1 formalizes the notions of flow networks and flows, formally defining the maximum-flow problem. Section 24.2 describes the classical method of Ford and Fulkerson for finding maximum flows. We finish up with a simple application of this method, finding a maximum matching in an undirected bipartite graph, in Section 24.3. (Section 25.1 will give a more efficient algorithm that is specifically designed to find a maximum matching in a bipartite graph.)

24.1   Flow networks

This section gives a graph-theoretic definition of flow networks, discusses their properties, and defines the maximum-flow problem precisely. It also introduces some helpful notation.

Flow networks and flows

A *flow network* $G = (V, E)$ is a directed graph in which each edge $(u, v) \in E$ has a nonnegative *capacity* $c(u, v) \geq 0$. We further require that if E contains an edge (u, v), then there is no edge (v, u) in the reverse direction. (We'll see shortly how to work around this restriction.) If $(u, v) \notin E$, then for convenience we define $c(u, v) = 0$, and we disallow self-loops. Each flow network contains two distinguished vertices: a *source* s and a *sink* t. For convenience, we assume that each vertex lies on some path from the source to the sink. That is, for each vertex $v \in V$, the flow network contains a path $s \rightsquigarrow v \rightsquigarrow t$. Because each vertex other than s has at least one entering edge, we have $|E| \geq |V| - 1$. Figure 24.1 shows an example of a flow network.

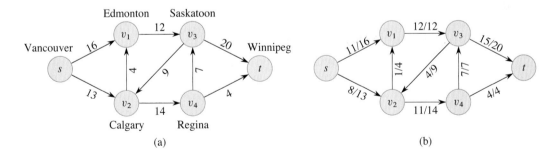

Figure 24.1 **(a)** A flow network $G = (V, E)$ for the Lucky Puck Company's trucking problem. The Vancouver factory is the source s, and the Winnipeg warehouse is the sink t. The company ships pucks through intermediate cities, but only $c(u, v)$ crates per day can go from city u to city v. Each edge is labeled with its capacity. **(b)** A flow f in G with value $|f| = 19$. Each edge (u, v) is labeled by $f(u, v)/c(u, v)$. The slash notation merely separates the flow and capacity and does not indicate division.

We are now ready to define flows more formally. Let $G = (V, E)$ be a flow network with a capacity function c. Let s be the source of the network, and let t be the sink. A *flow* in G is a real-valued function $f : V \times V \to \mathbb{R}$ that satisfies the following two properties:

Capacity constraint: For all $u, v \in V$, we require

$$0 \le f(u, v) \le c(u, v) \, .$$

The flow from one vertex to another must be nonnegative and must not exceed the given capacity.

Flow conservation: For all $u \in V - \{s, t\}$, we require

$$\sum_{v \in V} f(v, u) = \sum_{v \in V} f(u, v) \, .$$

The total flow into a vertex other than the source or sink must equal the total flow out of that vertex—informally, "flow in equals flow out."

When $(u, v) \notin E$, there can be no flow from u to v, and $f(u, v) = 0$.

We call the nonnegative quantity $f(u, v)$ the flow from vertex u to vertex v. The *value* $|f|$ of a flow f is defined as

$$|f| = \sum_{v \in V} f(s, v) - \sum_{v \in V} f(v, s) \, , \tag{24.1}$$

that is, the total flow out of the source minus the flow into the source. (Here, the $|\cdot|$ notation denotes flow value, not absolute value or cardinality.) Typically, a flow network does not have any edges into the source, and the flow into the source, given by the summation $\sum_{v \in V} f(v, s)$, is 0. We include it, however, because when we introduce residual networks later in this chapter, the flow into the source can be positive. In the *maximum-flow problem*, the input is a flow network G with source s and sink t, and the goal is to find a flow of maximum value.

An example of flow

A flow network can model the trucking problem shown in Figure 24.1(a). The Lucky Puck Company has a factory (source s) in Vancouver that manufactures hockey pucks, and it has a warehouse (sink t) in Winnipeg that stocks them. Lucky Puck leases space on trucks from another firm to ship the pucks from the factory to the warehouse. Because the trucks travel over specified routes (edges) between cities (vertices) and have a limited capacity, Lucky Puck can ship at most $c(u, v)$ crates per day between each pair of cities u and v in Figure 24.1(a). Lucky Puck

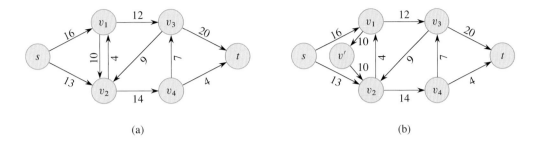

(a)   (b)

Figure 24.2   Converting a network with antiparallel edges to an equivalent one with no antiparallel edges. **(a)** A flow network containing both the edges (v_1, v_2) and (v_2, v_1). **(b)** An equivalent network with no antiparallel edges. A new vertex v' was added, and edge (v_1, v_2) was replaced by the pair of edges (v_1, v') and (v', v_2), both with the same capacity as (v_1, v_2).

has no control over these routes and capacities, and so the company cannot alter the flow network shown in Figure 24.1(a). They need to determine the largest number p of crates per day that they can ship and then to produce this amount, since there is no point in producing more pucks than they can ship to their warehouse. Lucky Puck is not concerned with how long it takes for a given puck to get from the factory to the warehouse. They care only that p crates per day leave the factory and p crates per day arrive at the warehouse.

A flow in this network models the "flow" of shipments because the number of crates shipped per day from one city to another is subject to a capacity constraint. Additionally, the model must obey flow conservation, for in a steady state, the rate at which pucks enter an intermediate city must equal the rate at which they leave. Otherwise, crates would accumulate at intermediate cities.

Modeling problems with antiparallel edges

Suppose that the trucking firm offers Lucky Puck the opportunity to lease space for 10 crates in trucks going from Edmonton to Calgary. It might seem natural to add this opportunity to our example and form the network shown in Figure 24.2(a). This network suffers from one problem, however: it violates the original assumption that if edge $(v_1, v_2) \in E$, then $(v_2, v_1) \notin E$. We call the two edges (v_1, v_2) and (v_2, v_1) *antiparallel*. Thus, to model a flow problem with antiparallel edges, the network must be transformed into an equivalent one containing no antiparallel edges. Figure 24.2(b) displays this equivalent network. To transform the network, choose one of the two antiparallel edges, in this case (v_1, v_2), and split it by adding a new vertex v' and replacing edge (v_1, v_2) with the pair of edges (v_1, v') and (v', v_2). Also set the capacity of both new edges to the capacity of the original edge. The resulting network satisfies the property that if an edge belongs to

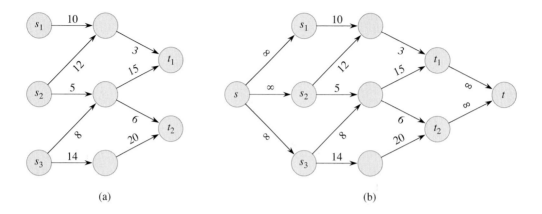

Figure 24.3 Converting a multiple-source, multiple-sink maximum-flow problem into a problem with a single source and a single sink. **(a)** A flow network with three sources $S = \{s_1, s_2, s_3\}$ and two sinks $T = \{t_1, t_2\}$. **(b)** An equivalent single-source, single-sink flow network. Add a supersource s and an edge with infinite capacity from s to each of the multiple sources. Also add a supersink t and an edge with infinite capacity from each of the multiple sinks to t.

the network, the reverse edge does not. As Exercise 24.1-1 asks you to prove, the resulting network is equivalent to the original one.

Networks with multiple sources and sinks

A maximum-flow problem may have several sources and sinks, rather than just one of each. The Lucky Puck Company, for example, might actually have a set of m factories $\{s_1, s_2, \ldots, s_m\}$ and a set of n warehouses $\{t_1, t_2, \ldots, t_n\}$, as shown in Figure 24.3(a). Fortunately, this problem is no harder than ordinary maximum flow.

The problem of determining a maximum flow in a network with multiple sources and multiple sinks reduces to an ordinary maximum-flow problem. Figure 24.3(b) shows how to convert the network from (a) to an ordinary flow network with only a single source and a single sink. Add a *supersource* s and add a directed edge (s, s_i) with capacity $c(s, s_i) = \infty$ for each $i = 1, 2, \ldots, m$. Similarly, create a new *supersink* t and add a directed edge (t_i, t) with capacity $c(t_i, t) = \infty$ for each $i = 1, 2, \ldots, n$. Intuitively, any flow in the network in (a) corresponds to a flow in the network in (b), and vice versa. The single supersource s provides as much flow as desired for the multiple sources s_i, and the single supersink t likewise consumes as much flow as desired for the multiple sinks t_i. Exercise 24.1-2 asks you to prove formally that the two problems are equivalent.

Exercises

24.1-1
Show that splitting an edge in a flow network yields an equivalent network. More formally, suppose that flow network G contains edge (u, v), and define a new flow network G' by creating a new vertex x and replacing (u, v) by new edges (u, x) and (x, v) with $c(u, x) = c(x, v) = c(u, v)$. Show that a maximum flow in G' has the same value as a maximum flow in G.

24.1-2
Extend the flow properties and definitions to the multiple-source, multiple-sink problem. Show that any flow in a multiple-source, multiple-sink flow network corresponds to a flow of identical value in the single-source, single-sink network obtained by adding a supersource and a supersink, and vice versa.

24.1-3
Suppose that a flow network $G = (V, E)$ violates the assumption that the network contains a path $s \rightsquigarrow v \rightsquigarrow t$ for all vertices $v \in V$. Let u be a vertex for which there is no path $s \rightsquigarrow u \rightsquigarrow t$. Show that there must exist a maximum flow f in G such that $f(u, v) = f(v, u) = 0$ for all vertices $v \in V$.

24.1-4
Let f be a flow in a network, and let α be a real number. The *scalar flow product*, denoted αf, is a function from $V \times V$ to $\mathbb{R}$ defined by

$$(\alpha f)(u, v) = \alpha \cdot f(u, v) \,.$$

Prove that the flows in a network form a *convex set*. That is, show that if f_1 and f_2 are flows, then so is $\alpha f_1 + (1 - \alpha) f_2$ for all α in the range $0 \le \alpha \le 1$.

24.1-5
State the maximum-flow problem as a linear-programming problem.

24.1-6
Professor Adam has two children who, unfortunately, dislike each other. The problem is so severe that not only do they refuse to walk to school together, but in fact each one refuses to walk on any block that the other child has stepped on that day. The children have no problem with their paths crossing at a corner. Fortunately both the professor's house and the school are on corners, but beyond that he is not sure if it is going to be possible to send both of his children to the same school. The professor has a map of his town. Show how to formulate the problem of determining whether both his children can go to the same school as a maximum-flow problem.

24.1-7

Suppose that, in addition to edge capacities, a flow network has *vertex capacities*. That is each vertex v has a limit $l(v)$ on how much flow can pass through v. Show how to transform a flow network $G = (V, E)$ with vertex capacities into an equivalent flow network $G' = (V', E')$ without vertex capacities, such that a maximum flow in G' has the same value as a maximum flow in G. How many vertices and edges does G' have?

24.2   The Ford-Fulkerson method

This section presents the Ford-Fulkerson method for solving the maximum-flow problem. We call it a "method" rather than an "algorithm" because it encompasses several implementations with differing running times. The Ford-Fulkerson method depends on three important ideas that transcend the method and are relevant to many flow algorithms and problems: residual networks, augmenting paths, and cuts. These ideas are essential to the important max-flow min-cut theorem (Theorem 24.6), which characterizes the value of a maximum flow in terms of cuts of the flow network. We end this section by presenting one specific implementation of the Ford-Fulkerson method and analyzing its running time.

The Ford-Fulkerson method iteratively increases the value of the flow. It starts with $f(u, v) = 0$ for all $u, v \in V$, giving an initial flow of value 0. Each iteration increases the flow value in G by finding an "augmenting path" in an associated "residual network" G_f. The edges of the augmenting path in G_f indicate on which edges in G to update the flow in order to increase the flow value. Although each iteration of the Ford-Fulkerson method increases the value of the flow, we'll see that the flow on any particular edge of G may increase or decrease. Although it might seem counterintuitive to decrease the flow on an edge, doing so may enable flow to increase on other edges, allowing more flow to travel from the source to the sink. The Ford-Fulkerson method, given in the procedure FORD-FULKERSON-METHOD, repeatedly augments the flow until the residual network has no more augmenting paths. The max-flow min-cut theorem shows that upon termination, this process yields a maximum flow.

FORD-FULKERSON-METHOD(G, s, t)

1   initialize flow f to 0
2   **while** there exists an augmenting path p in the residual network G_f
3   augment flow f along p
4   **return** f

In order to implement and analyze the Ford-Fulkerson method, we need to introduce several additional concepts.

Residual networks

Intuitively, given a flow network G and a flow f, the residual network G_f consists of edges whose capacities represent how the flow can change on edges of G. An edge of the flow network can admit an amount of additional flow equal to the edge's capacity minus the flow on that edge. If that value is positive, that edge goes into G_f with a "residual capacity" of $c_f(u, v) = c(u, v) - f(u, v)$. The only edges of G that belong to G_f are those that can admit more flow. Those edges (u, v) whose flow equals their capacity have $c_f(u, v) = 0$, and they do not belong to G_f.

You might be surprised that the residual network G_f can also contain edges that are not in G. As an algorithm manipulates the flow, with the goal of increasing the total flow, it might need to decrease the flow on a particular edge in order to increase the flow elsewhere. In order to represent a possible decrease in the positive flow $f(u, v)$ on an edge in G, the residual network G_f contains an edge (v, u) with residual capacity $c_f(v, u) = f(u, v)$—that is, an edge that can admit flow in the opposite direction to (u, v), at most canceling out the flow on (u, v). These reverse edges in the residual network allow an algorithm to send back flow it has already sent along an edge. Sending flow back along an edge is equivalent to *decreasing* the flow on the edge, which is a necessary operation in many algorithms.

More formally, for a flow network $G = (V, E)$ with source s, sink t, and a flow f, consider a pair of vertices $u, v \in V$. We define the *residual capacity* $c_f(u, v)$ by

$$
c_f(u, v) = \begin{cases} c(u, v) - f(u, v) & \text{if } (u, v) \in E, \\ f(v, u) & \text{if } (v, u) \in E, \\ 0 & \text{otherwise}. \end{cases} \tag{24.2}
$$

In a flow network, $(u, v) \in E$ implies $(v, u) \notin E$, and so exactly one case in equation (24.2) applies to each ordered pair of vertices.

As an example of equation (24.2), if $c(u, v) = 16$ and $f(u, v) = 11$, then $f(u, v)$ can increase by up to $c_f(u, v) = 5$ units before exceeding the capacity constraint on edge (u, v). Alternatively, up to 11 units of flow can return from v to u, so that $c_f(v, u) = 11$.

Given a flow network $G = (V, E)$ and a flow f, the *residual network* of G induced by f is $G_f = (V, E_f)$, where

$$
E_f = \{(u, v) \in V \times V : c_f(u, v) > 0\} . \tag{24.3}
$$

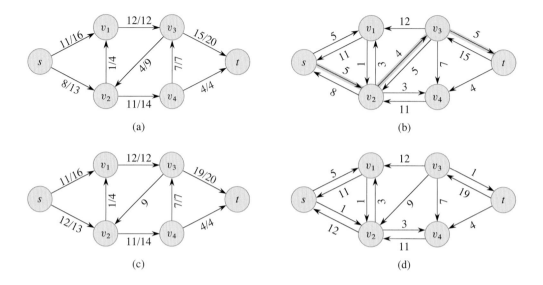

Figure 24.4 **(a)** The flow network G and flow f of Figure 24.1(b). **(b)** The residual network G_f with augmenting path p, having residual capacity $c_f(p) = c_f(v_2, v_3) = 4$, in blue. Edges with residual capacity equal to 0, such as (v_1, v_3), are not shown, a convention we follow in the remainder of this section. **(c)** The flow in G that results from augmenting along path p by its residual capacity 4. Edges carrying no flow, such as (v_3, v_2), are labeled only by their capacity, another convention we follow throughout. **(d)** The residual network induced by the flow in (c).

That is, as promised above, each edge of the residual network, or *residual edge*, can admit a flow that is greater than 0. Figure 24.4(a) repeats the flow network G and flow f of Figure 24.1(b), and Figure 24.4(b) shows the corresponding residual network G_f. The edges in E_f are either edges in E or their reversals, and thus

$$|E_f| \leq 2\,|E|\;.$$

Observe that the residual network G_f is similar to a flow network with capacities given by c_f. It does not satisfy the definition of a flow network, however, because it could contain antiparallel edges. Other than this difference, a residual network has the same properties as a flow network, and we can define a flow in the residual network as one that satisfies the definition of a flow, but with respect to capacities c_f in the residual network G_f.

A flow in a residual network provides a roadmap for adding flow to the original flow network. If f is a flow in G and f' is a flow in the corresponding residual network G_f, we define $f \uparrow f'$, the *augmentation* of flow f by f', to be a function from $V \times V$ to $\mathbb{R}$, defined by

$$(f \uparrow f')(u,v) = \begin{cases} f(u,v) + f'(u,v) - f'(v,u) & \text{if } (u,v) \in E , \\ 0 & \text{otherwise} . \end{cases} \qquad (24.4)$$

The intuition behind this definition follows the definition of the residual network. The flow on (u,v) increases by $f'(u,v)$, but decreases by $f'(v,u)$ because pushing flow on the reverse edge in the residual network signifies decreasing the flow in the original network. Pushing flow on the reverse edge in the residual network is also known as *cancellation*. For example, suppose that 5 crates of hockey pucks go from u to v and 2 crates go from v to u. That is equivalent (from the perspective of the final result) to sending 3 crates from u to v and none from v to u. Cancellation of this type is crucial for any maximum-flow algorithm.

The following lemma shows that augmenting a flow in G by a flow in G_f yields a new flow in G with a greater flow value.

Lemma 24.1
Let $G = (V, E)$ be a flow network with source s and sink t, and let f be a flow in G. Let G_f be the residual network of G induced by f, and let f' be a flow in G_f. Then the function $f \uparrow f'$ defined in equation (24.4) is a flow in G with value $|f \uparrow f'| = |f| + |f'|$.

Proof We first verify that $f \uparrow f'$ obeys the capacity constraint for each edge in E and flow conservation at each vertex in $V - \{s, t\}$.

For the capacity constraint, first observe that if $(u,v) \in E$, then $c_f(v,u) = f(u,v)$. Because f' is a flow in G_f, we have $f'(v,u) \leq c_f(v,u)$, which gives $f'(v,u) \leq f(u,v)$. Therefore,

$$\begin{aligned}
(f \uparrow f')(u,v) &= f(u,v) + f'(u,v) - f'(v,u) \quad \text{(by equation (24.4))} \\
&\geq f(u,v) + f'(u,v) - f(u,v) \quad \text{(because } f'(v,u) \leq f(u,v)) \\
&= f'(u,v) \\
&\geq 0 .
\end{aligned}$$

In addition,

$$\begin{aligned}
(f \uparrow f')(u,v) \\
&= f(u,v) + f'(u,v) - f'(v,u) \quad \text{(by equation (24.4))} \\
&\leq f(u,v) + f'(u,v) \quad \text{(because flows are nonnegative)} \\
&\leq f(u,v) + c_f(u,v) \quad \text{(capacity constraint)} \\
&= f(u,v) + c(u,v) - f(u,v) \quad \text{(definition of } c_f) \\
&= c(u,v) .
\end{aligned}$$

To show that flow conservation holds and that $|f \uparrow f'| = |f| + |f'|$, we first prove the claim that for all $u \in V$, we have

$$\sum_{v \in V} (f \uparrow f')(u, v) - \sum_{v \in V} (f \uparrow f')(v, u)$$

$$= \sum_{v \in V} f(u, v) - \sum_{v \in V} f(v, u) + \sum_{v \in V} f'(u, v) - \sum_{v \in V} f'(v, u) . \quad (24.5)$$

Because we disallow antiparallel edges in G (but not in G_f), we know that for each vertex u, there can be an edge (u, v) or (v, u) in G, but never both. For a fixed vertex u, define $V_l(u) = \{v : (u, v) \in E\}$ to be the set of vertices with edges in G leaving u, and define $V_e(u) = \{v : (v, u) \in E\}$ to be the set of vertices with edges in G entering u. We have $V_l(u) \cup V_e(u) \subseteq V$ and, because G contains no antiparallel edges, $V_l(u) \cap V_e(u) = \emptyset$. By the definition of flow augmentation in equation (24.4), only vertices v in $V_l(u)$ can have positive $(f \uparrow f')(u, v)$, and only vertices v in $V_e(u)$ can have positive $(f \uparrow f')(v, u)$. Starting from the left-hand side of equation (24.5), we use this fact and then reorder and group terms, giving

$$\sum_{v \in V} (f \uparrow f')(u, v) - \sum_{v \in V} (f \uparrow f')(v, u)$$

$$= \sum_{v \in V_l(u)} (f \uparrow f')(u, v) - \sum_{v \in V_e(u)} (f \uparrow f')(v, u)$$

$$= \sum_{v \in V_l(u)} (f(u, v) + f'(u, v) - f'(v, u)) - \sum_{v \in V_e(u)} (f(v, u) + f'(v, u) - f'(u, v))$$

$$= \sum_{v \in V_l(u)} f(u, v) + \sum_{v \in V_l(u)} f'(u, v) - \sum_{v \in V_l(u)} f'(v, u)$$

$$\quad - \sum_{v \in V_e(u)} f(v, u) - \sum_{v \in V_e(u)} f'(v, u) + \sum_{v \in V_e(u)} f'(u, v)$$

$$= \sum_{v \in V_l(u)} f(u, v) - \sum_{v \in V_e(u)} f(v, u)$$

$$\quad + \sum_{v \in V_l(u)} f'(u, v) + \sum_{v \in V_e(u)} f'(u, v) - \sum_{v \in V_l(u)} f'(v, u) - \sum_{v \in V_e(u)} f'(v, u)$$

$$= \sum_{v \in V_l(u)} f(u, v) - \sum_{v \in V_e(u)} f(v, u) + \sum_{v \in V_l(u) \cup V_e(u)} f'(u, v) - \sum_{v \in V_l(u) \cup V_e(u)} f'(v, u) . \quad (24.6)$$

In equation (24.6), all four summations can extend to sum over V, since each additional term has value 0. (Exercise 24.2-1 asks you to prove this formally.) Taking all four summations over V, instead of just subsets of V, proves the claim in equation (24.5).

Now we are ready to prove flow conservation for $f \uparrow f'$ and that $|f \uparrow f'| = |f| + |f'|$. For the latter property, let $u = s$ in equation (24.5). Then, we have

$$|f \uparrow f'| = \sum_{v \in V} (f \uparrow f')(s, v) - \sum_{v \in V} (f \uparrow f')(v, s)$$

$$= \sum_{v \in V} f(s, v) - \sum_{v \in V} f(v, s) + \sum_{v \in V} f'(s, v) - \sum_{v \in V} f'(v, s)$$

$$= |f| + |f'| .$$

For flow conservation, observe that for any vertex u that is neither s nor t, flow conservation for f and f' means that the right-hand side of equation (24.5) is 0, and thus $\sum_{v \in V} (f \uparrow f')(u, v) = \sum_{v \in V} (f \uparrow f')(v, u)$. ∎

Augmenting paths

Given a flow network $G = (V, E)$ and a flow f, an *augmenting path* p is a simple path from s to t in the residual network G_f. By the definition of the residual network, the flow on an edge (u, v) of an augmenting path may increase by up to $c_f(u, v)$ without violating the capacity constraint on whichever of (u, v) and (v, u) belongs to the original flow network G.

The blue path in Figure 24.4(b) is an augmenting path. Treating the residual network G_f in the figure as a flow network, the flow through each edge of this path can increase by up to 4 units without violating a capacity constraint, since the smallest residual capacity on this path is $c_f(v_2, v_3) = 4$. We call the maximum amount by which we can increase the flow on each edge in an augmenting path p the *residual capacity* of p, given by

$$c_f(p) = \min \{c_f(u, v) : (u, v) \text{ is in } p\} .$$

The following lemma, which Exercise 24.2-7 asks you to prove, makes the above argument more precise.

Lemma 24.2
Let $G = (V, E)$ be a flow network, let f be a flow in G, and let p be an augmenting path in G_f. Define a function $f_p : V \times V \to \mathbb{R}$ by

$$f_p(u, v) = \begin{cases} c_f(p) & \text{if } (u, v) \text{ is on } p , \\ 0 & \text{otherwise} . \end{cases} \tag{24.7}$$

Then, f_p is a flow in G_f with value $|f_p| = c_f(p) > 0$. ∎

The following corollary shows that augmenting f by f_p produces another flow in G whose value is closer to the maximum. Figure 24.4(c) shows the result of augmenting the flow f from Figure 24.4(a) by the flow f_p in Figure 24.4(b), and Figure 24.4(d) shows the ensuing residual network.

Corollary 24.3

Let $G = (V, E)$ be a flow network, let f be a flow in G, and let p be an augmenting path in G_f. Let f_p be defined as in equation (24.7), and suppose that f is augmented by f_p. Then the function $f \uparrow f_p$ is a flow in G with value $|f \uparrow f_p| = |f| + |f_p| > |f|$.

Proof   Immediate from Lemmas 24.1 and 24.2.   ∎

Cuts of flow networks

The Ford-Fulkerson method repeatedly augments the flow along augmenting paths until it has found a maximum flow. How do we know that when the algorithm terminates, it has actually found a maximum flow? The max-flow min-cut theorem, which we will prove shortly, tells us that a flow is maximum if and only if its residual network contains no augmenting path. To prove this theorem, though, we must first explore the notion of a cut of a flow network.

A *cut* (S, T) of flow network $G = (V, E)$ is a partition of V into S and $T = V - S$ such that $s \in S$ and $t \in T$. (This definition is similar to the definition of "cut" that we used for minimum spanning trees in Chapter 21, except that here we are cutting a directed graph rather than an undirected graph, and we insist that $s \in S$ and $t \in T$.) If f is a flow, then the *net flow* $f(S, T)$ across the cut (S, T) is defined to be

$$f(S, T) = \sum_{u \in S} \sum_{v \in T} f(u, v) - \sum_{u \in S} \sum_{v \in T} f(v, u) . \qquad (24.8)$$

The *capacity* of the cut (S, T) is

$$c(S, T) = \sum_{u \in S} \sum_{v \in T} c(u, v) . \qquad (24.9)$$

A *minimum cut* of a network is a cut whose capacity is minimum over all cuts of the network.

You probably noticed that the definitions of flow across a cut and capacity of a cut differ in that flow counts edges going in both directions across the cut, but capacity counts only edges going from the source side of the cut toward the sink side. This asymmetry is intentional and important. The reason for this difference will become apparent later in this section.

Figure 24.5 shows the cut $(\{s, v_1, v_2\}, \{v_3, v_4, t\})$ in the flow network of Figure 24.1(b). The net flow across this cut is

$$
\begin{aligned}
f(v_1, v_3) + f(v_2, v_4) - f(v_3, v_2) &= 12 + 11 - 4 \\
&= 19 ,
\end{aligned}
$$

and the capacity of this cut is

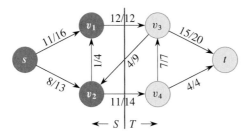

Figure 24.5   A cut (S, T) in the flow network of Figure 24.1(b), where $S = \{s, v_1, v_2\}$ and $T = \{v_3, v_4, t\}$. The vertices in S are orange, and the vertices in T are tan. The net flow across (S, T) is $f(S, T) = 19$, and the capacity is $c(S, T) = 26$.

$$
\begin{aligned}
c(v_1, v_3) + c(v_2, v_4) &= 12 + 14 \\
&= 26 \ .
\end{aligned}
$$

The following lemma shows that, for a given flow f, the net flow across any cut is the same, and it equals $|f|$, the value of the flow.

Lemma 24.4
Let f be a flow in a flow network G with source s and sink t, and let (S, T) be any cut of G. Then the net flow across (S, T) is $f(S, T) = |f|$.

Proof   For any vertex $u \in V - \{s, t\}$, rewrite the flow-conservation condition as

$$
\sum_{v \in V} f(u, v) - \sum_{v \in V} f(v, u) = 0 \ . \tag{24.10}
$$

Taking the definition of $|f|$ from equation (24.1) and adding the left-hand side of equation (24.10), which equals 0, summed over all vertices in $S - \{s\}$, gives

$$
|f| = \sum_{v \in V} f(s, v) - \sum_{v \in V} f(v, s) + \sum_{u \in S - \{s\}} \left(\sum_{v \in V} f(u, v) - \sum_{v \in V} f(v, u) \right) \ .
$$

Expanding the right-hand summation and regrouping terms yields

$$
\begin{aligned}
|f| &= \sum_{v \in V} f(s, v) - \sum_{v \in V} f(v, s) + \sum_{u \in S - \{s\}} \sum_{v \in V} f(u, v) - \sum_{u \in S - \{s\}} \sum_{v \in V} f(v, u) \\
&= \sum_{v \in V} \left(f(s, v) + \sum_{u \in S - \{s\}} f(u, v) \right) - \sum_{v \in V} \left(f(v, s) + \sum_{u \in S - \{s\}} f(v, u) \right) \\
&= \sum_{v \in V} \sum_{u \in S} f(u, v) - \sum_{v \in V} \sum_{u \in S} f(v, u) \ .
\end{aligned}
$$

Because $V = S \cup T$ and $S \cap T = \emptyset$, splitting each summation over V into summations over S and T gives

$$|f| = \sum_{v \in S} \sum_{u \in S} f(u, v) + \sum_{v \in T} \sum_{u \in S} f(u, v) - \sum_{v \in S} \sum_{u \in S} f(v, u) - \sum_{v \in T} \sum_{u \in S} f(v, u)$$

$$= \sum_{v \in T} \sum_{u \in S} f(u, v) - \sum_{v \in T} \sum_{u \in S} f(v, u)$$

$$+ \left(\sum_{v \in S} \sum_{u \in S} f(u, v) - \sum_{v \in S} \sum_{u \in S} f(v, u) \right) .$$

The two summations within the parentheses are actually the same, since for all vertices $x, y \in S$, the term $f(x, y)$ appears once in each summation. Hence, these summations cancel, yielding

$$|f| = \sum_{u \in S} \sum_{v \in T} f(u, v) - \sum_{u \in S} \sum_{v \in T} f(v, u)$$

$$= f(S, T) .$$ ■

A corollary to Lemma 24.4 shows how cut capacities bound the value of a flow.

Corollary 24.5

The value of any flow f in a flow network G is bounded from above by the capacity of any cut of G.

Proof   Let (S, T) be any cut of G and let f be any flow. By Lemma 24.4 and the capacity constraint,

$$|f| = f(S, T)$$

$$= \sum_{u \in S} \sum_{v \in T} f(u, v) - \sum_{u \in S} \sum_{v \in T} f(v, u)$$

$$\leq \sum_{u \in S} \sum_{v \in T} f(u, v)$$

$$\leq \sum_{u \in S} \sum_{v \in T} c(u, v)$$

$$= c(S, T) .$$ ■

Corollary 24.5 yields the immediate consequence that the value of a maximum flow in a network is bounded from above by the capacity of a minimum cut of the network. The important max-flow min-cut theorem, which we now state and prove, says that the value of a maximum flow is in fact equal to the capacity of a minimum cut.

Theorem 24.6 (Max-flow min-cut theorem)
If f is a flow in a flow network $G = (V, E)$ with source s and sink t, then the following conditions are equivalent:

1. f is a maximum flow in G.

2. The residual network G_f contains no augmenting paths.

3. $|f| = c(S, T)$ for some cut (S, T) of G.

Proof   (1) $\Rightarrow$ (2): Suppose for the sake of contradiction that f is a maximum flow in G but that G_f has an augmenting path p. Then, by Corollary 24.3, the flow found by augmenting f by f_p, where f_p is given by equation (24.7), is a flow in G with value strictly greater than $|f|$, contradicting the assumption that f is a maximum flow.

(2) $\Rightarrow$ (3): Suppose that G_f has no augmenting path, that is, that G_f contains no path from s to t. Define

$$S = \{v \in V : \text{there exists a path from } s \text{ to } v \text{ in } G_f\}$$

and $T = V - S$. The partition (S, T) is a cut: we have $s \in S$ trivially and $t \notin S$ because there is no path from s to t in G_f. Now consider a pair of vertices $u \in S$ and $v \in T$. If $(u, v) \in E$, we must have $f(u, v) = c(u, v)$, since otherwise $(u, v) \in E_f$, which would place v in set S. If $(v, u) \in E$, we must have $f(v, u) = 0$, because otherwise $c_f(u, v) = f(v, u)$ would be positive and we would have $(u, v) \in E_f$, which again would place v in S. Of course, if neither (u, v) nor (v, u) belongs to E, then $f(u, v) = f(v, u) = 0$. We thus have

$$
\begin{aligned}
f(S, T) &= \sum_{u \in S} \sum_{v \in T} f(u, v) - \sum_{v \in T} \sum_{u \in S} f(v, u) \\
&= \sum_{u \in S} \sum_{v \in T} c(u, v) - \sum_{v \in T} \sum_{u \in S} 0 \\
&= c(S, T) \, .
\end{aligned}
$$

By Lemma 24.4, therefore, $|f| = f(S, T) = c(S, T)$.

(3) $\Rightarrow$ (1): By Corollary 24.5, $|f| \leq c(S, T)$ for all cuts (S, T). The condition $|f| = c(S, T)$ thus implies that f is a maximum flow.   ∎

The basic Ford-Fulkerson algorithm

Each iteration of the Ford-Fulkerson method finds *some* augmenting path p and uses p to modify the flow f. As Lemma 24.2 and Corollary 24.3 suggest, replacing f by $f \uparrow f_p$ produces a new flow whose value is $|f| + |f_p|$. The procedure FORD-FULKERSON on the next page implements the method by updating the flow attribute $(u, v).f$ for each edge $(u, v) \in E$.[1] It assumes implicitly that $(u, v).f = 0$ if $(u, v) \notin E$. The procedure also assumes that the capacities $c(u, v)$ come with the flow network, and that $c(u, v) = 0$ if $(u, v) \notin E$. The procedure computes the residual capacity $c_f(u, v)$ in accordance with the formula (24.2). The expression $c_f(p)$ in the code is just a temporary variable that stores the residual capacity of the path p.

FORD-FULKERSON(G, s, t)

```
1   for each edge (u, v) ∈ G.E
2       (u, v).f = 0
3   while there exists a path p from s to t in the residual network G_f
4       c_f(p) = min {c_f(u, v) : (u, v) is in p}
5       for each edge (u, v) in p
6           if (u, v) ∈ G.E
7               (u, v).f = (u, v).f + c_f(p)
8           else (v, u).f = (v, u).f − c_f(p)
9   return f
```

The FORD-FULKERSON procedure simply expands on the FORD-FULKERSON-METHOD pseudocode given earlier. Figure 24.6 shows the result of each iteration in a sample run. Lines 1–2 initialize the flow f to 0. The **while** loop of lines 3–8 repeatedly finds an augmenting path p in G_f and augments flow f along p by the residual capacity $c_f(p)$. Each residual edge in path p is either an edge in the original network or the reversal of an edge in the original network. Lines 6–8 update the flow in each case appropriately, adding flow when the residual edge is an original edge and subtracting it otherwise. When no augmenting paths exist, the flow f is a maximum flow.

Analysis of Ford-Fulkerson

The running time of FORD-FULKERSON depends on the augmenting path p and how it's found in line 3. If the edge capacities are irrational numbers, it's possible to choose the augmenting path so that the algorithm never terminates: the value of the flow increases with successive augmentations, but never converges to the maximum flow value. The good news is that if the algorithm finds the augmenting path by using a breadth-first search (which we saw in Section 20.2), it runs in

---

[1] Recall from Section 20.1 that we represent an attribute f for edge (u, v) with the same style of notation—$(u, v).f$—that we use for an attribute of any other object.

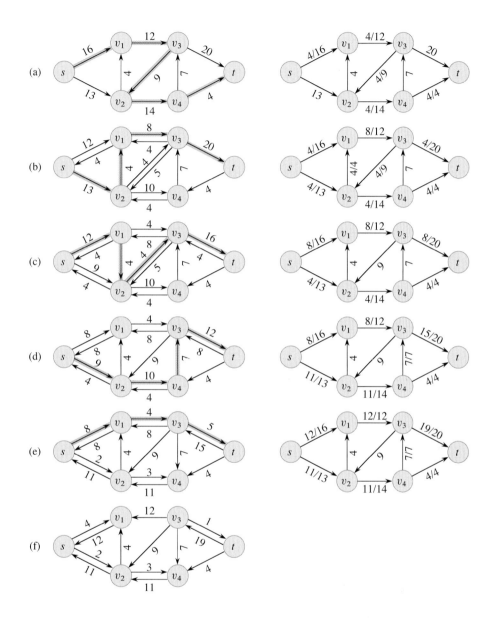

Figure 24.6   The execution of the basic Ford-Fulkerson algorithm. **(a)–(e)** Successive iterations of the **while** loop. The left side of each part shows the residual network G_f from line 3 with a blue augmenting path p. The right side of each part shows the new flow f that results from augmenting f by f_p. The residual network in (a) is the input flow network G. **(f)** The residual network at the last **while** loop test. It has no augmenting paths, and the flow f shown in (e) is therefore a maximum flow. The value of the maximum flow found is 23.

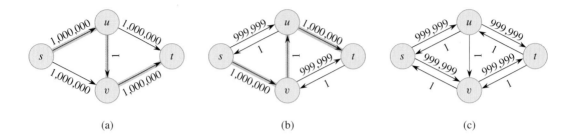

(a)   (b)   (c)

Figure 24.7 **(a)** A flow network for which FORD-FULKERSON can take $\Theta(E \,|f^*|)$ time, where f^* is a maximum flow, shown here with $|f^*| = 2{,}000{,}000$. The blue path is an augmenting path with residual capacity 1. **(b)** The resulting residual network, with another augmenting path whose residual capacity is 1. **(c)** The resulting residual network.

polynomial time. Before proving this result, we obtain a simple bound for the case in which all capacities are integers and the algorithm finds any augmenting path.

In practice, the maximum-flow problem often arises with integer capacities. If the capacities are rational numbers, an appropriate scaling transformation can make them all integers. If f^* denotes a maximum flow in the transformed network, then a straightforward implementation of FORD-FULKERSON executes the **while** loop of lines 3–8 at most $|f^*|$ times, since the flow value increases by at least 1 unit in each iteration.

A good implementation should perform the work done within the **while** loop efficiently. It should represent the flow network $G = (V, E)$ with the right data structure and find an augmenting path by a linear-time algorithm. Let's assume that the implementation keeps a data structure corresponding to a directed graph $G' = (V, E')$, where $E' = \{(u, v) : (u, v) \in E \text{ or } (v, u) \in E\}$. Edges in the network G are also edges in G', making it straightforward to maintain capacities and flows in this data structure. Given a flow f on G, the edges in the residual network G_f consist of all edges (u, v) of G' such that $c_f(u, v) > 0$, where c_f conforms to equation (24.2). The time to find a path in a residual network is therefore $O(V + E') = O(E)$ using either depth-first search or breadth-first search. Each iteration of the **while** loop thus takes $O(E)$ time, as does the initialization in lines 1–2, making the total running time of the FORD-FULKERSON algorithm $O(E \,|f^*|)$.

When the capacities are integers and the optimal flow value $|f^*|$ is small, the running time of the Ford-Fulkerson algorithm is good. Figure 24.7(a) shows an example of what can happen on a simple flow network for which $|f^*|$ is large. A maximum flow in this network has value 2,000,000: 1,000,000 units of flow traverse the path $s \rightarrow u \rightarrow t$, and another 1,000,000 units traverse the path $s \rightarrow v \rightarrow t$. If the first augmenting path found by FORD-FULKERSON is $s \rightarrow u \rightarrow v \rightarrow t$, shown in Figure 24.7(a), the flow has value 1 after the first iteration. The resulting residual network appears in Figure 24.7(b). If the second iteration finds the augmenting path $s \rightarrow v \rightarrow u \rightarrow t$, as shown in Figure 24.7(b), the flow then has value 2. Figure 24.7(c) shows the resulting residual network. If the algorithm continues alternately choosing the augmenting paths $s \rightarrow u \rightarrow v \rightarrow t$ and $s \rightarrow v \rightarrow u \rightarrow t$, it performs a total of 2,000,000 augmentations, increasing the flow value by only 1 unit in each.

The Edmonds-Karp algorithm

In the example of Figure 24.7, the algorithm never chooses the augmenting path with the fewest edges. It should have. By using breadth-first search to find an augmenting path in the residual network, the algorithm runs in polynomial time, independent of the maximum flow value. We call the Ford-Fulkerson method so implemented the *Edmonds-Karp algorithm*.

Let's now prove that the Edmonds-Karp algorithm runs in $O(VE^2)$ time. The analysis depends on the distances to vertices in the residual network G_f. The notation $\delta_f(u, v)$ denotes the shortest-path distance from u to v in G_f, where each edge has unit distance.

Lemma 24.7

If the Edmonds-Karp algorithm is run on a flow network $G = (V, E)$ with source s and sink t, then for all vertices $v \in V - \{s, t\}$, the shortest-path distance $\delta_f(s, v)$ in the residual network G_f increases monotonically with each flow augmentation.

Proof   We'll suppose that a flow augmentation occurs that causes the shortest-path distance from s to some vertex $v \in V - \{s, t\}$ to decrease and then derive a contradiction. Let f be the flow just before an augmentation that decreases some shortest-path distance, and let f' be the flow just afterward. Let v be a vertex with the minimum $\delta_{f'}(s, v)$ whose distance was decreased by the augmentation, so that $\delta_{f'}(s, v) < \delta_f(s, v)$. Let $p = s \rightsquigarrow u \rightarrow v$ be a shortest path from s to v in $G_{f'}$, so that $(u, v) \in E_{f'}$ and

$$\delta_{f'}(s, u) = \delta_{f'}(s, v) - 1 \,. \tag{24.11}$$

Because of how we chose v, we know that the distance of vertex u from the source s did not decrease, that is,

$$\delta_{f'}(s, u) \geq \delta_f(s, u) \,. \tag{24.12}$$

We claim that $(u, v) \notin E_f$. Why? If we have $(u, v) \in E_f$, then we also have

$$\delta_f(s, v) \le \delta_f(s, u) + 1 \quad \text{(by Lemma 22.10, the triangle inequality)}$$
$$\le \delta_{f'}(s, u) + 1 \quad \text{(by inequality (24.12))}$$
$$= \delta_{f'}(s, v) \quad \text{(by equation (24.11)) ,}$$

which contradicts our assumption that $\delta_{f'}(s, v) < \delta_f(s, v)$.

How can we have $(u, v) \notin E_f$ and $(u, v) \in E_{f'}$? The augmentation must have increased the flow from v to u, so that edge (v, u) was in the augmenting path. The augmenting path was a shortest path from s to t in G_f, and since any subpath of a shortest path is itself a shortest path, this augmenting path includes a shortest path from s to u in G_f that has (v, u) as its last edge. Therefore,

$$\delta_f(s, v) = \delta_f(s, u) - 1$$
$$\le \delta_{f'}(s, u) - 1 \quad \text{(by inequality (24.12))}$$
$$= \delta_{f'}(s, v) - 2 \quad \text{(by equation (24.11)) ,}$$

so that $\delta_{f'}(s, v) > \delta_f(s, v)$, contradicting our assumption that $\delta_{f'}(s, v) < \delta_f(s, v)$. We conclude that our assumption that such a vertex v exists is incorrect. ∎

The next theorem bounds the number of iterations of the Edmonds-Karp algorithm.

Theorem 24.8
If the Edmonds-Karp algorithm is run on a flow network $G = (V, E)$ with source s and sink t, then the total number of flow augmentations performed by the algorithm is $O(VE)$.

Proof We say that an edge (u, v) in a residual network G_f is ***critical*** on an augmenting path p if the residual capacity of p is the residual capacity of (u, v), that is, if $c_f(p) = c_f(u, v)$. After flow is augmented along an augmenting path, any critical edge on the path disappears from the residual network. Moreover, at least one edge on any augmenting path must be critical. We'll show that each of the $|E|$ edges can become critical at most $|V|/2$ times.

Let u and v be vertices in V that are connected by an edge in E. Since augmenting paths are shortest paths, when (u, v) is critical for the first time, we have

$$\delta_f(s, v) = \delta_f(s, u) + 1 .$$

Once the flow is augmented, the edge (u, v) disappears from the residual network. It cannot reappear later on another augmenting path until after the flow from u to v is decreased, which occurs only if (v, u) appears on an augmenting path. If f' is the flow in G when this event occurs, then we have

$$\delta_{f'}(s, u) = \delta_{f'}(s, v) + 1 .$$

Since $\delta_f(s, v) \le \delta_{f'}(s, v)$ by Lemma 24.7, we have

$$
\begin{aligned}
\delta_{f'}(s, u) &= \delta_{f'}(s, v) + 1 \\
&\ge \delta_f(s, v) + 1 \\
&= \delta_f(s, u) + 2 .
\end{aligned}
$$

Consequently, from the time (u, v) becomes critical to the time when it next becomes critical, the distance of u from the source increases by at least 2. The distance of u from the source is initially at least 0. Because edge (u, v) is on an augmenting path, and augmenting paths end at t, we know that u cannot be t, so that in any residual network that has a path from s to u, the shortest such path has at most $|V| - 2$ edges. Thus, after the first time that (u, v) becomes critical, it can become critical at most $(|V| - 2)/2 = |V|/2 - 1$ times more, for a total of at most $|V|/2$ times. Since there are $O(E)$ pairs of vertices that can have an edge between them in a residual network, the total number of critical edges during the entire execution of the Edmonds-Karp algorithm is $O(VE)$. Each augmenting path has at least one critical edge, and hence the theorem follows.   ■

Because each iteration of FORD-FULKERSON takes $O(E)$ time when it uses breadth-first search to find the augmenting path, the total running time of the Edmonds-Karp algorithm is $O(VE^2)$.

Exercises

24.2-1
Prove that the summations in equation (24.6) equal the summations on the right-hand side of equation (24.5).

24.2-2
In Figure 24.1(b), what is the net flow across the cut $(\{s, v_2, v_4\}, \{v_1, v_3, t\})$? What is the capacity of this cut?

24.2-3
Show the execution of the Edmonds-Karp algorithm on the flow network of Figure 24.1(a).

24.2-4
In the example of Figure 24.6, what is the minimum cut corresponding to the maximum flow shown? Of the augmenting paths appearing in the example, which one cancels flow?

24.2-5

The construction in Section 24.1 to convert a flow network with multiple sources and sinks into a single-source, single-sink network adds edges with infinite capacity. Prove that any flow in the resulting network has a finite value if the edges of the original network with multiple sources and sinks have finite capacity.

24.2-6

Suppose that each source s_i in a flow network with multiple sources and sinks produces exactly p_i units of flow, so that $\sum_{v \in V} f(s_i, v) = p_i$. Suppose also that each sink t_j consumes exactly q_j units, so that $\sum_{v \in V} f(v, t_j) = q_j$, where $\sum_i p_i = \sum_j q_j$. Show how to convert the problem of finding a flow f that obeys these additional constraints into the problem of finding a maximum flow in a single-source, single-sink flow network.

24.2-7

Prove Lemma 24.2.

24.2-8

Suppose that we redefine the residual network to disallow edges into s. Argue that the procedure FORD-FULKERSON still correctly computes a maximum flow.

24.2-9

Suppose that both f and f' are flows in a flow network. Does the augmented flow $f \uparrow f'$ satisfy the flow conservation property? Does it satisfy the capacity constraint?

24.2-10

Show how to find a maximum flow in a flow network $G = (V, E)$ by a sequence of at most $|E|$ augmenting paths. (*Hint:* Determine the paths *after* finding the maximum flow.)

24.2-11

The *edge connectivity* of an undirected graph is the minimum number k of edges that must be removed to disconnect the graph. For example, the edge connectivity of a tree is 1, and the edge connectivity of a cyclic chain of vertices is 2. Show how to determine the edge connectivity of an undirected graph $G = (V, E)$ by running a maximum-flow algorithm on at most $|V|$ flow networks, each having $O(V + E)$ vertices and $O(E)$ edges.

24.2-12

You are given a flow network G, where G contains edges entering the source s. Let f be a flow in G with $|f| \geq 0$ in which one of the edges (v, s) entering the source has $f(v, s) = 1$. Prove that there must exist another flow f' with $f'(v, s) = 0$ such that $|f| = |f'|$. Give an $O(E)$-time algorithm to compute f', given f and assuming that all edge capacities are integers.

24.2-13
Suppose that you wish to find, among all minimum cuts in a flow network G with integer capacities, one that contains the smallest number of edges. Show how to modify the capacities of G to create a new flow network G' in which any minimum cut in G' is a minimum cut with the smallest number of edges in G.

24.3   Maximum bipartite matching

Some combinatorial problems can be cast as maximum-flow problems, such as the multiple-source, multiple-sink maximum-flow problem from Section 24.1. Other combinatorial problems seem on the surface to have little to do with flow networks, but they can in fact be reduced to maximum-flow problems. This section presents one such problem: finding a maximum matching in a bipartite graph. In order to solve this problem, we'll take advantage of an integrality property provided by the Ford-Fulkerson method. We'll also see how to use the Ford-Fulkerson method to solve the maximum-bipartite-matching problem on a graph $G = (V, E)$ in $O(VE)$ time. Section 25.1 will present an algorithm specifically designed to solve this problem.

The maximum-bipartite-matching problem

Given an undirected graph $G = (V, E)$, a *matching* is a subset of edges $M \subseteq E$ such that for all vertices $v \in V$, at most one edge of M is incident on v. We say that a vertex $v \in V$ is *matched* by the matching M if some edge in M is incident on v, and otherwise, v is *unmatched*. A *maximum matching* is a matching of maximum cardinality, that is, a matching M such that for any matching M', we have $|M| \geq |M'|$. In this section, we restrict our attention to finding maximum matchings in bipartite graphs: graphs in which the vertex set can be partitioned into $V = L \cup R$, where L and R are disjoint and all edges in E go between L and R. We further assume that every vertex in V has at least one incident edge. Figure 24.8 illustrates the notion of a matching in a bipartite graph.

The problem of finding a maximum matching in a bipartite graph has many practical applications. As an example, consider matching a set L of machines with a set R of tasks to be performed simultaneously. An edge (u, v) in E signifies that

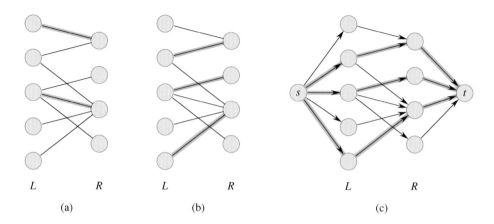

L   R   L   R   L   R

(a)   (b)   (c)

Figure 24.8 A bipartite graph $G = (V, E)$ with vertex partition $V = L \cup R$. **(a)** A matching with cardinality 2, indicated by blue edges. **(b)** A maximum matching with cardinality 3. **(c)** The corresponding flow network G' with a maximum flow shown. Each edge has unit capacity. Blue edges have a flow of 1, and all other edges carry no flow. The blue edges from L to R correspond to those in the maximum matching from (b).

a particular machine $u \in L$ is capable of performing a particular task $v \in R$. A maximum matching provides work for as many machines as possible.

Finding a maximum bipartite matching

The Ford-Fulkerson method provides a basis for finding a maximum matching in an undirected bipartite graph $G = (V, E)$ in time polynomial in $|V|$ and $|E|$. The trick is to construct a flow network in which flows correspond to matchings, as shown in Figure 24.8(c). We define the *corresponding flow network* $G' = (V', E')$ for the bipartite graph G as follows. Let the source s and sink t be new vertices not in V, and let $V' = V \cup \{s, t\}$. If the vertex partition of G is $V = L \cup R$, the directed edges of G' are the edges of E, directed from L to R, along with $|V|$ new directed edges:

$$
\begin{aligned}
E' = \ &\{(s, u) : u \in L\} \\
&\cup \{(u, v) : u \in L, v \in R, \text{ and } (u, v) \in E\} \\
&\cup \{(v, t) : v \in R\} \ .
\end{aligned}
$$

To complete the construction, assign unit capacity to each edge in E'. Since each vertex in V has at least one incident edge, $|E| \geq |V|/2$. Thus, $|E| \leq |E'| = |E| + |V| \leq 3|E|$, and so $|E'| = \Theta(E)$.

The following lemma shows that a matching in G corresponds directly to a flow in G's corresponding flow network G'. We say that a flow f on a flow network $G = (V, E)$ is ***integer-valued*** if $f(u, v)$ is an integer for all $(u, v) \in V \times V$.

Lemma 24.9
Let $G = (V, E)$ be a bipartite graph with vertex partition $V = L \cup R$, and let $G' = (V', E')$ be its corresponding flow network. If M is a matching in G, then there is an integer-valued flow f in G' with value $|f| = |M|$. Conversely, if f is an integer-valued flow in G', then there is a matching M in G with cardinality $|M| = |f|$ consisting of edges $(u, v) \in E$ such that $f(u, v) > 0$.

Proof   We first show that a matching M in G corresponds to an integer-valued flow f in G'. Define f as follows. If $(u, v) \in M$, then $f(s, u) = f(u, v) = f(v, t) = 1$. For all other edges $(u, v) \in E'$, define $f(u, v) = 0$. It is simple to verify that f satisfies the capacity constraint and flow conservation.

Intuitively, each edge $(u, v) \in M$ corresponds to 1 unit of flow in G' that traverses the path $s \to u \to v \to t$. Moreover, the paths induced by edges in M are vertex-disjoint, except for s and t. The net flow across cut $(L \cup \{s\}, R \cup \{t\})$ is equal to $|M|$, and thus, by Lemma 24.4, the value of the flow is $|f| = |M|$.

To prove the converse, let f be an integer-valued flow in G' and, as in the statement of the lemma, let

$$M = \{(u, v) : u \in L, \, v \in R, \text{ and } f(u, v) > 0\} \ .$$

Each vertex $u \in L$ has only one entering edge, namely (s, u), and its capacity is 1. Thus, each $u \in L$ has at most 1 unit of flow entering it, and if 1 unit of flow does enter, by flow conservation, 1 unit of flow must leave. Furthermore, since the flow f is integer-valued, for each $u \in L$, the 1 unit of flow can enter on at most one edge and can leave on at most one edge. Thus, 1 unit of flow enters u if and only if there is exactly one vertex $v \in R$ such that $f(u, v) = 1$, and at most one edge leaving each $u \in L$ carries positive flow. A symmetric argument applies to each $v \in R$. The set M is therefore a matching.

To see that $|M| = |f|$, observe that of the edges $(u, v) \in E'$ such that $u \in L$ and $v \in R$,

$$f(u, v) = \begin{cases} 1 & \text{if } (u, v) \in M \ , \\ 0 & \text{if } (u, v) \notin M \ . \end{cases}$$

Consequently, $f(L \cup \{s\}, R \cup \{t\})$, the net flow across cut $(L \cup \{s\}, R \cup \{t\})$, is equal to $|M|$. Lemma 24.4 gives that $|f| = f(L \cup \{s\}, R \cup \{t\}) = |M|$.   ∎

Based on Lemma 24.9, we would like to conclude that a maximum matching in a bipartite graph G corresponds to a maximum flow in its corresponding flow network G', and therefore running a maximum-flow algorithm on G' provides a maximum matching in G. The only hitch in this reasoning is that the maximum-flow algorithm might return a flow in G' for which some $f(u, v)$ is not an integer, even though the flow value $|f|$ must be an integer. The following theorem shows that the Ford-Fulkerson method cannot produce a solution with this problem.

Theorem 24.10 (Integrality theorem)
If the capacity function c takes on only integer values, then the maximum flow f produced by the Ford-Fulkerson method has the property that $|f|$ is an integer. Moreover, for all vertices u and v, the value of $f(u, v)$ is an integer.

Proof   Exercise 24.3-2 asks you to provide the proof by induction on the number of iterations.   ∎

We can now prove the following corollary to Lemma 24.9.

Corollary 24.11
The cardinality of a maximum matching M in a bipartite graph G equals the value of a maximum flow f in its corresponding flow network G'.

Proof   We use the nomenclature from Lemma 24.9. Suppose that M is a maximum matching in G and that the corresponding flow f in G' is not maximum. Then there is a maximum flow f' in G' such that $|f'| > |f|$. Since the capacities in G' are integer-valued, by Theorem 24.10, we can assume that f' is integer-valued. Thus, f' corresponds to a matching M' in G with cardinality $|M'| = |f'| > |f| = |M|$, contradicting our assumption that M is a maximum matching. In a similar manner, we can show that if f is a maximum flow in G', its corresponding matching is a maximum matching on G.   ∎

Thus, to find a maximum matching in a bipartite undirected graph G, create the flow network G', run the Ford-Fulkerson method on G', and convert the integer-valued maximum flow found into a maximum matching for G. Since any matching in a bipartite graph has cardinality at most $\min\{|L|, |R|\} = O(V)$, the value of the maximum flow in G' is $O(V)$. Therefore, finding a maximum matching in a bipartite graph takes $O(VE') = O(VE)$ time, since $|E'| = \Theta(E)$.

Exercises

24.3-1
Run the Ford-Fulkerson algorithm on the flow network in Figure 24.8(c) and show the residual network after each flow augmentation. Number the vertices in L top

to bottom from 1 to 5 and in R top to bottom from 6 to 9. For each iteration, pick the augmenting path that is lexicographically smallest.

24.3-2
Prove Theorem 24.10. Use induction on the number of iterations of the Ford-Fulkerson method.

24.3-3
Let $G = (V, E)$ be a bipartite graph with vertex partition $V = L \cup R$, and let G' be its corresponding flow network. Give a good upper bound on the length of any augmenting path found in G' during the execution of FORD-FULKERSON.

Problems

24-1 *Escape problem*
An $n \times n$ *grid* is an undirected graph consisting of n rows and n columns of vertices, as shown in Figure 24.9. We denote the vertex in the ith row and the jth column by (i, j). All vertices in a grid have exactly four neighbors, except for the boundary vertices, which are the points (i, j) for which $i = 1, i = n, j = 1,$ or $j = n$.

Given $m \le n^2$ starting points $(x_1, y_1), (x_2, y_2), \ldots, (x_m, y_m)$ in the grid, the *escape problem* is to determine whether there are m vertex-disjoint paths from the starting points to any m different points on the boundary. For example, the grid in Figure 24.9(a) has an escape, but the grid in Figure 24.9(b) does not.

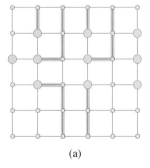
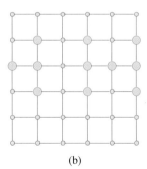

(a)   (b)

Figure 24.9 Grids for the escape problem. Starting points are blue, and other grid vertices are tan. **(a)** A grid with an escape, shown by blue paths. **(b)** A grid with no escape.

a. Consider a flow network in which vertices, as well as edges, have capacities. That is, the total positive flow entering any given vertex is subject to a capacity constraint. Show how to reduce the problem of determining the maximum flow in a network with edge and vertex capacities to an ordinary maximum-flow problem on a flow network of comparable size.

b. Describe an efficient algorithm to solve the escape problem, and analyze its running time.

24-2   Minimum path cover

A *path cover* of a directed graph $G = (V, E)$ is a set P of vertex-disjoint paths such that every vertex in V is included in exactly one path in P. Paths may start and end anywhere, and they may be of any length, including 0. A *minimum path cover* of G is a path cover containing the fewest possible paths.

a. Give an efficient algorithm to find a minimum path cover of a directed acyclic graph $G = (V, E)$. (*Hint:* Assuming that $V = \{1, 2, \ldots, n\}$, construct a flow network based on the graph $G' = (V', E')$, where

$$V' = \{x_0, x_1, \ldots, x_n\} \cup \{y_0, y_1, \ldots, y_n\} \ ,$$
$$E' = \{(x_0, x_i) : i \in V\} \cup \{(y_i, y_0) : i \in V\} \cup \{(x_i, y_j) : (i, j) \in E\} \ ,$$

and run a maximum-flow algorithm.)

b. Does your algorithm work for directed graphs that contain cycles? Explain.

24-3   Hiring consulting experts

Professor Fieri wants to open a consulting company for the food industry. He has identified n important food categories, which he represents by the set $C = \{C_1, C_2, \ldots, C_n\}$. In each category C_k, he can hire an expert in that category for $e_k > 0$ dollars. The consulting company has lined up a set $J = \{J_1, J_2, \ldots, J_m\}$ of potential jobs. In order to perform job J_i, the company needs to have hired experts in a subset $R_i \subseteq C$ of categories. Each expert can work on multiple jobs simultaneously. If the company chooses to accept job J_i, it must have hired experts in all categories in R_i, and it takes in revenue of $p_i > 0$ dollars.

Professor Fieri's job is to determine which categories to hire experts in and which jobs to accept in order to maximize the net revenue, which is the total income from jobs accepted minus the total cost of employing the experts.

Consider the following flow network G. It contains a source vertex s, vertices $C_1, C_2, \ldots, C_n$, vertices $J_1, J_2, \ldots, J_m$, and a sink vertex t. For $k = 1, 2 \ldots, n$, the flow network contains an edge (s, C_k) with capacity $c(s, C_k) = e_k$, and for $i = 1, 2, \ldots, m$, the flow network contains an edge (J_i, t) with capacity

$c(J_i, t) = p_i$. For $k = 1, 2, \ldots, n$ and $i = 1, 2, \ldots, m$, if $C_k \in R_i$, then G contains an edge (C_k, J_i) with capacity $c(C_k, J_i) = \infty$.

a. Show that if $J_i \in T$ for a finite-capacity cut (S, T) of G, then $C_k \in T$ for each $C_k \in R_i$.

b. Show how to determine the maximum net revenue from the capacity of a minimum cut of G and the given p_i values.

c. Give an efficient algorithm to determine which jobs to accept and which experts to hire. Analyze the running time of your algorithm in terms of m, n, and $r = \sum_{i=1}^{m} |R_i|$.

24-4 *Updating maximum flow*

Let $G = (V, E)$ be a flow network with source s, sink t, and integer capacities. Suppose that you are given a maximum flow in G.

a. Suppose that the capacity of a single edge $(u, v) \in E$ increases by 1. Give an $O(V + E)$-time algorithm to update the maximum flow.

b. Suppose that the capacity of a single edge $(u, v) \in E$ decreases by 1. Give an $O(V + E)$-time algorithm to update the maximum flow.

24-5 *Maximum flow by scaling*

Let $G = (V, E)$ be a flow network with source s, sink t, and an integer capacity $c(u, v)$ on each edge $(u, v) \in E$. Let $C = \max \{c(u, v) : (u, v) \in E\}$.

a. Argue that a minimum cut of G has capacity at most $C |E|$.

b. For a given number K, show how to find an augmenting path of capacity at least K in $O(E)$ time, if such a path exists.

The procedure MAX-FLOW-BY-SCALING appearing on the following page modifies the basic FORD-FULKERSON-METHOD procedure to compute a maximum flow in G.

c. Argue that MAX-FLOW-BY-SCALING returns a maximum flow.

d. Show that the capacity of a minimum cut of the residual network G_f is less than $2K |E|$ each time line 4 executes.

e. Argue that the inner **while** loop of lines 5–6 executes $O(E)$ times for each value of K.

MAX-FLOW-BY-SCALING(G, s, t)

```
1   C = max {c(u, v) : (u, v) ∈ E}
2   initialize flow f to 0
3   K = 2^⌊lg C⌋
4   while K ≥ 1
5       while there exists an augmenting path p of capacity at least K
6           augment flow f along p
7       K = K/2
8   return f
```

f. Conclude that MAX-FLOW-BY-SCALING can be implemented so that it runs in $O(E^2 \lg C)$ time.

24-6   *Widest augmenting path*

The Edmonds-Karp algorithm implements the Ford-Fulkerson algorithm by always choosing a shortest augmenting path in the residual network. Suppose instead that the Ford-Fulkerson algorithm chooses a *widest augmenting path*: an augmenting path with the greatest residual capacity. Assume that $G = (V, E)$ is a flow network with source s and sink t, that all capacities are integer, and that the largest capacity is C. In this problem, you will show that choosing a widest augmenting path results in at most $|E| \ln |f^*|$ augmentations to find a maximum flow f^*.

a. Show how to adjust Dijkstra's algorithm to find the widest augmenting path in the residual network.

b. Show that a maximum flow in G can be formed by successive flow augmentations along at most $|E|$ paths from s to t.

c. Given a flow f, argue that the residual network G_f has an augmenting path p with residual capacity $c_f(p) \geq (|f^*| - |f|)/|E|$.

d. Assuming that each augmenting path is a widest augmenting path, let f_i be the flow after augmenting the flow by the ith augmenting path, where f_0 has $f(u, v) = 0$ for all edges (u, v). Show that $|f^*| - |f_i| \leq |f^*|(1 - 1/|E|)^i$.

e. Show that $|f^*| - |f_i| < |f^*| e^{-i/|E|}$.

f. Conclude that after the flow is augmented at most $|E| \ln |f^*|$ times, the flow is a maximum flow.

24-7 Global minimum cut

A *global cut* in an undirected graph $G = (V, E)$ is a partition (see page 1156) of V into two nonempty sets V_1 and V_2. This definition is like the definition of cut that we have used in this chapter, except that we no longer have distinguished vertices s and t. Any edge (u, v) with $u \in V_1$ and $v \in V_2$ is said to *cross* the cut.

We can extend this definition of a cut to a multigraph $G = (V, E)$ (see page 1167), and we denote by $c(u, v)$ the number of edges in the multigraph with endpoints u and v. A global cut in a multigraph is still a partition of the vertices, and the value of a global cut (V_1, V_2) is $c(V_1, V_2) = \sum_{u \in V_1, v \in V_2} c(u, v)$. A solution to the *global-minimum-cut problem* is a cut (V_1, V_2) such that $c(V_1, V_2)$ is minimum. Let $\mu(G)$ denote the value of a global minimum cut in a graph or multigraph G.

a. Show how to find a global minimum cut of a graph $G = (V, E)$ by solving $\binom{|V|}{2}$ maximum-flow problems, each with a different pair of vertices as the source and sink, and taking the mininum value of the cuts found.

b. Give an algorithm to find a global minimum cut by solving only $\Theta(V)$ maximum-flow problems. What is the running time of your algorithm?

The remainder of this problem develops an algorithm for the global-minimum-cut problem that does not use any maximum-flow computations. It uses the notion of an edge contraction, defined on page 1168, with one crucial difference. The algorithm maintains a multigraph, so that upon contracting an edge (u, v), it creates a new vertex x, and for any other vertex $y \in V$, the number of edges between x and y is $c(u, y) + c(v, y)$. The algorithm does not maintain self-loops, and so it sets $c(x, x)$ to 0. Denote by $G/(u, v)$ the multigraph that results from contracting edge (u, v) in multigraph G.

Consider what can happen to the minimum cut when an edge is contracted. Assume that, at all points, the minimum cut in a multigraph G is unique. We'll remove this assumption later.

c. Show that for any edge (u, v), we have $\mu(G/(u, v)) \leq \mu(G)$. Under what conditions is $\mu(G/(u, v)) < \mu(G)$?

Next, you will show that if you pick an edge uniformly at random, the probability that it belongs to the minimum cut is small.

d. Show that for any multigraph $G = (V, E)$, the value of the global minimum cut is at most the average degree of a vertex: that $\mu(G) \leq 2|E|/|V|$, where $|E|$ denotes the total number of edges in the multigraph.

e. Using the results from parts (c) and (d), show that, if we pick an edge (u, v) uniformly at random, then the probability that (u, v) belongs to the minimum cut is at most $2/V$.

Consider the algorithm that repeatedly chooses an edge at random and contracts it until the multigraph has exactly two vertices, say u and v. At that point, the multigraph corresponds to a cut in the original graph, with vertex u representing all the nodes in one side of the original graph, and v representing all the vertices on the other side. The number of edges given by $c(u, v)$ corresponds exactly to the number of edges crossing the corresponding cut in the original graph. We call this algorithm the *contraction algorithm*.

f. Suppose that the contraction algorithm terminates with a multigraph whose only vertices are u and v. Show that $\Pr\{c(u, v) = \mu(G)\} = \Omega\left(1/\binom{|V|}{2}\right)$.

g. Prove that if the contraction algorithm repeats $\binom{|V|}{2} \ln |V|$ times, then the probability that at least one of the runs returns the minimum cut is at least $1 - 1/|V|$.

h. Give a detailed implementation of the contraction algorithm that runs in $O(V^2)$ time.

i. Combine the previous parts and remove the assumption that the minimum cut must be unique, to conclude that running the contraction algorithm $\binom{|V|}{2} \ln |V|$ times yields an algorithm that runs in $O(V^4 \lg V)$ time and returns a minimum cut with probability at least $1 - 1/V$.

Chapter notes

Ahuja, Magnanti, and Orlin [7], Even [137], Lawler [276], Papadimitriou and Steiglitz [353], Tarjan [429], and Williamson [458] are good references for network flows and related algorithms. Schrijver [399] has written an interesting review of historical developments in the field of network flows.

The Ford-Fulkerson method is due to Ford and Fulkerson [149], who originated the formal study of many of the problems in the area of network flow, including the maximum-flow and bipartite-matching problems. Many early implementations of the Ford-Fulkerson method found augmenting paths using breadth-first search. Edmonds and Karp [132], and independently Dinic [119], proved that this strategy yields a polynomial-time algorithm. A related idea, that of using "blocking flows," was also first developed by Dinic [119].

A class of algorithms known as *push-relabel algorithms*, due to Goldberg [185] and Goldberg and Tarjan [188], takes a different approach from the Ford-Fulkerson method. Push-relabel algorithms allow flow conservation to be violated at vertices other than the source and sink as they execute. Using an idea first developed by Karzonov [251], they allow a *preflow* in which the flow into a vertex may exceed the flow out of the vertex. Such a vertex is said to be *overflowing*. Initially, every edge leaving the source is filled to capacity, so that all neighbors of the source are overflowing. In a push-relabel algorithm, each vertex is assigned an integer height. An overflowing vertex may push flow to a neighboring vertex to which it has a residual edge provided that it is higher than the neighbor. If all residual edges from an overflowing vertex go to neighbors with equal or greater heights, then the vertex may increase its height. Once all vertices other than the sink are no longer overflowing, the preflow is not only a legal flow, but also a maximum flow.

Goldberg and Tarjan [188] gave an $O(V^3)$-time algorithm that uses a queue to maintain the set of overflowing vertices, as well as an algorithm that uses dynamic trees to achieve a running time of $O(VE \lg(V^2/E + 2))$. Several other researchers developed improved variants and implementations [9, 10, 15, 86, 87, 255, 358], the fastest of which, by King, Rao, and Tarjan [255], runs in $O(VE \log_{E/(V \lg V)} V)$ time.

Another efficient algorithm for maximum flow, by Goldberg and Rao [187], runs in $O\left(\min\left\{V^{2/3}, E^{1/2}\right\} E \lg(V^2/E + 2) \lg C\right)$ time, where C is the maximum capacity of any edge. Orlin [350] gave an algorithm in the same spirit as this algorithm that runs in $O(VE + E^{31/16} \lg^2 V)$ time. Combining it with the algorithm of King, Rao, and Tarjan results in an $O(VE)$-time algorithm.

A different approach to maximum flows and related problems is to use techniques from continuous optimization including electrical flows and interior-point methods. The first breakthrough in this line of work is due to Madry [308], who gave an $\widetilde{O}(E^{10/7})$-time algorithm for unit-capacity maximum flow and bipartite maximum matching. (See Problem 3-6 on page 73 for a definition of $\widetilde{O}$.) There has been a series of papers in this area for matchings, maximum flows, and minimum-cost flows. The fastest algorithm to date in this line of work for maximum flow is due to Lee and Sidford [285], taking $\widetilde{O}(\sqrt{V} E \lg^{O(1)} C)$ time. If the capacities are not too large, this algorithm is faster than the $O(VE)$-time algorithm mentioned above. Another algorithm, due to Liu and Sidford [303] runs in $\widetilde{O}(E^{11/8} C^{1/4})$ time, where C is the maximum capacity of any edge. This algorithm does not run in polynomial time, but for small enough capacities, it is faster than the previous ones.

In practice, push-relabel algorithms currently dominate algorithms based on augmenting paths, continuous-optimization, and linear programming for the maximum-flow problem [88] .

25   Matchings in Bipartite Graphs

Many real-world problems can be modeled as finding matchings in an undirected graph. For an undirected graph $G = (V, E)$, a *matching* is a subset of edges $M \subseteq E$ such that every vertex in V has at most one incident edge in M.

For example, consider the following scenario. You have one or more positions to fill and several candidates to interview. According to your schedule, you are able to interview candidates at certain time slots. You ask the candidates to indicate the subsets of time slots at which they are available. How can you schedule the interviews so that each time slot has at most one candidate scheduled, while maximizing the number of candidates that you can interview? You can model this scenario as a matching problem on a bipartite graph in which each vertex represents either a candidate or a time slot, with an edge between a candidate and a time slot if the candidate is available then. If an edge is included in the matching, that means you are scheduling a particular candidate for a particular time slot. Your goal is to find a *maximum matching*: a matching of maximum cardinality. One of the authors of this book was faced with exactly this situation when hiring teaching assistants for a large class. He used the Hopcroft-Karp algorithm in Section 25.1 to schedule the interviews.

Another application of matching is the U.S. National Resident Matching Program, in which medical students are matched to hospitals where they will be stationed as medical residents. Each student ranks the hospitals by preference, and each hospital ranks the students. The goal is to assign students to hospitals so that there is never a student and a hospital that both have regrets because the student was not assigned to the hospital, yet each ranked the other higher than who or where they were assigned. This scenario is perhaps the best-known real-world example of the "stable-marriage problem," which Section 25.2 examines.

Yet another instance where matching comes into play occurs when workers must be assigned to tasks in order to maximize the overall effectiveness of the assignment. For each worker and each task, the worker has some quantified effectiveness for that task. Assuming that there are equal numbers of workers and tasks, the goal is to find a matching with the maximum total effectiveness. Such a situation is an example of an assignment problem, which Section 25.3 shows how to solve.

The algorithms in this chapter find matchings in *bipartite* graphs. As in Section 24.3, the input is an undirected graph $G = (V, E)$, where $V = L \cup R$, the vertex sets L and R are disjoint, and every edge in E is incident on one vertex in L and one vertex in R. A matching, therefore, matches vertices in L with vertices in R. In some applications, the sets L and R have equal cardinality, and in other applications they need not be the same size.

An undirected graph need not be bipartite for the concept of matching to apply. Matching in general undirected graphs has applications in areas such as scheduling and computational chemistry. It models problems in which you want to pair up entities, represented by vertices. Two vertices are adjacent if they represent compatible entities, and you need to find a large set of compatible pairs. Maximum-matching and maximum-weight matching problems on general graphs can be solved by polynomial-time algorithms whose running times are similar to those for bipartite matching, but the algorithms are significantly more complicated. Exercise 25.2-5 discusses the general version of the stable-marriage problem, known as the "stable-roommates problem." Although matching applies to general undirected graphs, this chapter deals only with bipartite graphs.

25.1 Maximum bipartite matching (revisited)

Section 24.3 demonstrated one way to find a maximum matching in a bipartite graph, by finding a maximum flow. This section provides a more efficient method, the Hopcroft-Karp algorithm, which runs in $O(\sqrt{V}E)$ time. Figure 25.1(a) shows a matching in an undirected bipartite graph. A vertex that has an incident edge in matching M is *matched* under M, and otherwise, it is *unmatched*. A *maximal matching* is a matching M to which no other edges can be added, that is, for every edge $e \in E - M$, the edge set $M \cup \{e\}$ fails to be a matching. A maximum matching is always maximal, but the reverse does not always hold.

Many algorithms to find maximum matchings, the Hopcroft-Karp algorithm included, work by incrementally increasing the size of a matching. Given a matching M in an undirected graph $G = (V, E)$, an *M-alternating path* is a simple path whose edges alternate between being in M and being in $E - M$. Figure 25.1(b) depicts an *M-augmenting path* (sometimes called an augmenting path with respect to M): an M-alternating path whose first and last edges belong to $E - M$. Since an M-augmenting path contains one more edge in $E - M$ than in M, it must consist of an odd number of edges.

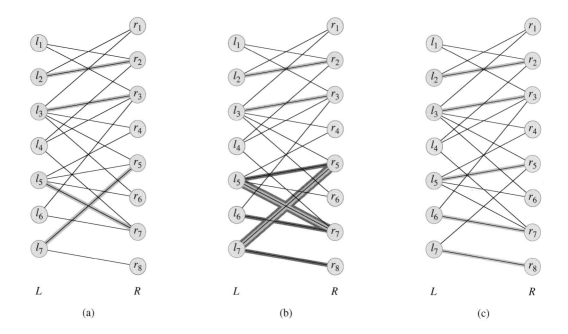

Figure 25.1   A bipartite graph, where $V = L \cup R$, $L = \{l_1, l_2, \ldots, l_7\}$, and $R = \{r_1, r_2, \ldots, r_8\}$. **(a)** A matching M with cardinality 4, highlighted in blue. Matched vertices are blue, and unmatched vertices are tan. **(b)** The five edges highlighted in orange form an M-augmenting path P going between vertices l_6 and r_8. **(c)** The set of edges $M' = M \oplus P$ highlighted in blue is a matching containing one more edge than M and adding l_6 and r_8 to the matched vertices. This matching is not a maximum matching (see Exercise 25.1-1).

Figure 25.1(c) demonstrates the following lemma, which shows that by removing from matching M the edges in an M-augmenting path that belong to M and adding to M the edges in the M-augmenting path that are not in M, the result is a new matching with one more edge than M. Since a matching is a set of edges, the lemma relies on the notion of the *symmetric difference* of two sets: $X \oplus Y = (X - Y) \cup (Y - X)$, that is, the elements that belong to X or Y, but not both. Alternatively, you can think of $X \oplus Y$ as $(X \cup Y) - (X \cap Y)$. The operator $\oplus$ is commutative and associative. Furthermore, $X \oplus X = \emptyset$ and $X \oplus \emptyset = \emptyset \oplus X = X$ for any set X, so that the empty set is the identity for $\oplus$.

Lemma 25.1

Let M be a matching in any undirected graph $G = (V, E)$, and let P be an M-augmenting path. Then the set of edges $M' = M \oplus P$ is also a matching in G with $|M'| = |M| + 1$.

Proof Let P contain q edges, so that $\lceil q/2 \rceil$ edges belong to $E - M$ and $\lfloor q/2 \rfloor$ edges belong to M, and let these q edges be $(v_1, v_2), (v_2, v_3), \ldots, (v_q, v_{q+1})$. Because P is an M-augmenting path, vertices v_1 and v_{q+1} are unmatched under M and all other vertices in P are matched. Edges $(v_1, v_2), (v_3, v_4), \ldots, (v_q, v_{q+1})$ belong to $E - M$, and edges $(v_2, v_3), (v_4, v_5), \ldots, (v_{q-1}, v_q)$ belong to M. The symmetric difference $M' = M \oplus P$ reverses these roles, so that edges $(v_1, v_2), (v_3, v_4), \ldots, (v_q, v_{q+1})$ belong to M' and $(v_2, v_3), (v_4, v_5), \ldots, (v_{q-1}, v_q)$ belong to $E - M'$. Each vertex $v_1, v_2, \ldots, v_q, v_{q+1}$ is matched under M', which gains one additional edge relative to M, and no other vertices or edges in G are affected by the change from M to M'. Hence, M' is a matching in G, and $|M'| = |M| + 1$. ∎

Since taking the symmetric difference of a matching M with an M-augmenting path increases the size of the matching by 1, the following corollary shows that taking the symmetric difference of M with k vertex-disjoint M-augmenting paths increases the size of the matching by k.

Corollary 25.2
Let M be a matching in any undirected graph $G = (V, E)$ and $P_1, P_2, \ldots, P_k$ be vertex-disjoint M-augmenting paths. Then the set of edges $M' = M \oplus (P_1 \cup P_2 \cup \cdots \cup P_k)$ is a matching in G with $|M'| = |M| + k$.

Proof Since the M-augmenting paths $P_1, P_2, \ldots, P_k$ are vertex-disjoint, we have that $P_1 \cup P_2 \cup \cdots \cup P_k = P_1 \oplus P_2 \oplus \cdots \oplus P_k$. Because the operator $\oplus$ is associative, we have

$$
\begin{aligned}
M \oplus (P_1 \cup P_2 \cup \cdots \cup P_k) &= M \oplus (P_1 \oplus P_2 \oplus \cdots \oplus P_k) \\
&= (\cdots((M \oplus P_1) \oplus P_2) \oplus \cdots \oplus P_{k-1}) \oplus P_k \, .
\end{aligned}
$$

A simple induction on i using Lemma 25.1 shows that $M \oplus (P_1 \cup P_2 \cup \cdots \cup P_{i-1})$ is a matching in G containing $|M| + i - 1$ edges and that path P_i is an augmenting path with respect to $M \oplus (P_1 \cup P_2 \cup \cdots \cup P_{i-1})$. Each of these augmenting paths increases the size of the matching by 1, and so $|M'| = |M| + k$. ∎

As the Hopcroft-Karp algorithm goes from matching to matching, it will be useful to consider the symmetric difference between two matchings.

Lemma 25.3
Let M and M^* be matchings in graph $G = (V, E)$, and consider the graph $G' = (V, E')$, where $E' = M \oplus M^*$. Then, G' is a disjoint union of simple paths, simple cycles, and/or isolated vertices. The edges in each such simple path or simple cycle

alternate between M and M^*. If $|M^*| > |M|$, then G' contains at least $|M^*| - |M|$ vertex-disjoint M-augmenting paths.

Proof   Each vertex in G' has degree 0, 1, or 2, since at most two edges of E' can be incident on a vertex: at most one edge from M and at most one edge from M^*. Therefore, each connected component of G' is either a singleton vertex, an even-length simple cycle with edges alternately in M and M^*, or a simple path with edges alternately in M and M^*. Since

$$E' = M \oplus M^*$$
$$= (M \cup M^*) - (M \cap M^*)$$

and $|M^*| > |M|$, the edge set E' must contain $|M^*| - |M|$ more edges from M^* than from M. Because each cycle in G' has an even number of edges drawn alternately from M and M^*, each cycle has an equal number of edges from M and M^*. Therefore, the simple paths in G' account for there being $|M^*| - |M|$ more edges from M^* than M. Each path containing a different number of edges from M and M^* either starts and ends with edges from M, containing one more edge from M than from M^*, or starts and ends with edges from M^*, containing one more edge from M^* than from M. Because E' contains $|M^*| - |M|$ more edges from M^* than from M, there are at least $|M^*| - |M|$ paths of the latter type, and each one is an M-augmenting path. Because each vertex has at most two incident edges from E', these paths must be vertex-disjoint.   ∎

If an algorithm finds a maximum matching by incrementally increasing the size of the matching, how does it determine when to stop? The following corollary gives the answer: when there are no augmenting paths.

Corollary 25.4
Matching M in graph $G = (V, E)$ is a maximum matching if and only if G contains no M-augmenting path.

Proof   We prove the contrapositive of both directions of the lemma statement. The contrapositive of the forward direction is straightforward. If there is an M-augmenting path P in G, then by Lemma 25.1, the matching $M \oplus P$ contains one more edge than M, meaning that M could not be a maximum matching.

To show the contrapositive of the backward direction—if M is not a maximum matching, then G contains an M-augmenting path—let M^* be a maximum matching in Lemma 25.3, so that $|M^*| > |M|$. Then G contains at least $|M^*| - |M| > 0$ vertex-disjoint M-augmenting paths.   ∎

We already have learned enough to create a maximum-matching algorithm that runs in $O(VE)$ time. Start with the matching M empty. Then repeatedly run a variant of either breadth-first search or depth-first search from an unmatched vertex that takes alternating paths until you find another unmatched vertex. Use the resulting M-augmenting path to increase the size of M by 1.

The Hopcroft-Karp algorithm

The Hopcroft-Karp algorithm improves the running time to $O(\sqrt{V}E)$. The procedure HOPCROFT-KARP is given an undirected bipartite graph, and it uses Corollary 25.2 to repeatedly increase the size of the matching M it finds. Corollary 25.4 proves that the algorithm is correct, since it terminates once there are no M-augmenting paths. It remains to show that the algorithm does run in $O(\sqrt{V}E)$ time. We'll see that the **repeat** loop of lines 2–5 iterates $O(\sqrt{V})$ times and how to implement line 3 so that it runs in $O(E)$ time in each iteration.

HOPCROFT-KARP(G)

1 $M = \emptyset$
2 **repeat**
3   let $\mathcal{P} = \{P_1, P_2, \ldots, P_k\}$ be a maximal set of vertex-disjoint
            shortest M-augmenting paths
4      $M = M \oplus (P_1 \cup P_2 \cup \cdots \cup P_k)$
5 **until** $\mathcal{P} == \emptyset$
6 **return** M

Let's first see how to find a maximal set of vertex-disjoint shortest M-augmenting paths in $O(E)$ time. There are three phases. The first phase forms a directed version G_M of the undirected bipartite graph G. The second phase creates a directed acyclic graph H from G_M via a variant of breadth-first search. The third phase finds a maximal set of vertex-disjoint shortest M-augmenting paths by running a variant of depth-first search on the transpose H^T of H. (Recall that the transpose of a directed graph reverses the direction of each edge. Since H is acyclic, so is H^T.)

Given a matching M, you can think of an M-augmenting path P as starting at an unmatched vertex in L, traversing an odd number of edges, and ending at an unmatched vertex in R. The edges in P traversed from L to R must belong to $E - M$, and the edges in P traversed from R to L must belong to M. The first phase, therefore, creates the directed graph G_M by directing the edges accordingly: $G_M = (V, E_M)$, where

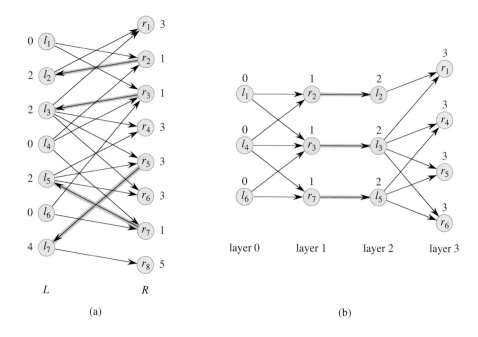

Figure 25.2 (a) The directed graph G_M created in the first phase for the undirected bipartite graph G and matching M in Figure 25.1(a). Breadth-first distances from any unmatched vertex in L appear next to each vertex. (b) The dag H created from G_M in the second phase. Because the smallest distance to an unmatched vertex in R is 3, vertices l_7 and r_8, with distances greater than 3, are not in H.

$$E_M = \{(l, r) : l \in L, r \in R, \text{ and } (l, r) \in E - M\} \quad \text{(edges from } L \text{ to } R)$$
$$\cup \{(r, l) : r \in R, l \in L, \text{ and } (l, r) \in M\} \quad \text{(edges from } R \text{ to } L) .$$

Figure 25.2(a) shows the graph G_M for the graph G and matching M in Figure 25.1(a).

The dag $H = (V_H, E_H)$ created by the second phase has layers of vertices. Figure 25.2(b) shows the dag H corresponding to the directed graph G_M in part (a) of the figure. Each layer contains only vertices from L or only vertices from R, alternating from layer to layer. The layer that a vertex resides in is given by that vertex's minimum breadth-first distance in G_M from any unmatched vertex in L. Vertices in L appear in even-numbered layers, and vertices in R appear in odd-numbered layers. Let q denote the smallest distance in G_M of any unmatched vertex in R. Then, the last layer in H contains the vertices in R with distance q. Vertices whose distance exceeds q do not appear in V_H. (The graph H in Figure 25.2(b) omits vertices l_7 and r_8 because their distances from any unmatched vertex in L exceed $q = 3$.) The edges in E_H form a subset of E_M:

$$E_H = \{(l, r) \in E_M : r.d \leq q \text{ and } r.d = l.d + 1\} \cup \{(r, l) \in E_M : l.d \leq q\} \ ,$$

where the attribute d of a vertex gives the vertex's breadth-first distance in G_M from any unmatched vertex in L. Edges that do not go between two consecutive layers are omitted from E_H.

To determine the breadth-first distances of vertices, run breadth-first search on the graph G_M, but starting from all the unmatched vertices in L. (In the BFS procedure on page 556, replace the root vertex s by the set of unmatched vertices in L.) The predecessor attributes π computed by the BFS procedure are not needed here, since H is a dag and not necessarily a tree.

Every path in H from a vertex in layer 0 to an unmatched vertex in layer q corresponds to a shortest M-augmenting path in the original bipartite graph G. Just use the undirected versions of the directed edges in H. Moreover, every shortest M-augmenting path in G is present in H.

The third phase identifies a maximal set of vertex-disjoint shortest M-augmenting paths. As Figure 25.3 shows, it starts by creating the transpose H^{T} of H. Then, for each unmatched vertex r in layer q, it performs a depth-first search starting from r until it either reaches a vertex in layer 0 or has exhausted all possible paths without reaching a vertex in layer 0. Instead of maintaining discovery and finish times, the depth-first search just needs to keep track of the predecessor attributes π in the depth-first tree of each search. Upon reaching a vertex in layer 0, tracing back along the predecessors identifies an M-augmenting path. Each vertex is searched from only when it is first discovered in any search. If the search from a vertex r in layer q cannot find a path of undiscovered vertices to an undiscovered vertex in layer 0, then no M-augmenting path including r goes into the maximal set.

Figure 25.3 shows the result of the third phase. The first depth-first search starts from vertex r_1. It identifies the M-augmenting path $\langle (r_1, l_3), (l_3, r_3), (r_3, l_1) \rangle$, which is highlighted in orange, and discovers vertices r_1, l_3, r_3, and l_1. The next depth-first search starts from vertex r_4. This search first examines the edge (r_4, l_3), but because l_3 was already discovered, it backtracks and examines edge (r_4, l_5). From there, it continues and identifies the M-augmenting path $\langle (r_4, l_5), (l_5, r_7), (r_7, l_6) \rangle$, which is highlighted in yellow, and discovers vertices r_4, l_5, r_7, and l_6. The depth-first search from vertex r_6 gets stuck at vertices l_3 and l_5, which have already been discovered, and so this search fails to find a path of undiscovered vertices to a vertex in layer 0. There is no depth-first search from vertex r_5 because it is matched, and depth-first searches start from unmatched vertices. Therefore, the maximal set of vertex-disjoint shortest M-augmenting paths found contains just the two M-augmenting paths $\langle (r_1, l_3), (l_3, r_3), (r_3, l_1) \rangle$ and $\langle (r_4, l_5), (l_5, r_7), (r_7, l_6) \rangle$.

You might have noticed that in this example, this maximal set of two vertex-disjoint shortest M-augmenting paths is not a maximum set. The graph contains three vertex-disjoint shortest M-augmenting paths: $\langle (r_1, l_2), (l_2, r_2), (r_2, l_1) \rangle$, $\langle (r_4, l_3), (l_3, r_3), (r_3, l_4) \rangle$, and $\langle (r_6, l_5), (l_5, r_7), (r_7, l_6) \rangle$. No matter: the algorithm

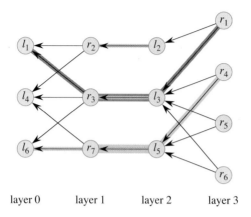

layer 0   layer 1   layer 2   layer 3

Figure 25.3   The transpose H^{T} of the dag H created in the third phase. The first depth-first search, starting from vertex r_1, identifies the M-augmenting path $\langle(r_1, l_3), (l_3, r_3), (r_3, l_1)\rangle$ highlighted in orange, and it discovers vertices r_1, l_3, r_3, l_1. The second depth-first search, starting from vertex r_4, identifies the M-augmenting path $\langle(r_4, l_5), (l_5, r_7), (r_7, l_6)\rangle$ highlighted in yellow, discovering vertices r_4, l_5, r_7, l_6.

requires the set of vertex-disjoint shortest M-augmenting paths found in line 3 of HOPCROFT-KARP to be only maximal, not necessarily maximum.

It remains to show that all three phases of line 3 take $O(E)$ time. We assume that in the original bipartite graph G, each vertex has at least one incident edge so that $|V| = O(E)$, which in turn implies that $|V| + |E| = O(E)$. The first phase creates the directed graph G_M by simply directing each edge of G, so that $|V_M| = |V|$ and $|E_M| = |E|$. The second phase performs a breadth-first search on G_M, taking $O(V_M + E_M) = O(E_M) = O(E)$ time. In fact, it can stop once the first distance in the queue within the breadth-first search exceeds the shortest distance q to an unmatched vertex in R. The dag H has $|V_H| \le |V_M|$ and $|E_H| \le |E_M|$, so that it takes $O(V_H + E_H) = O(E)$ time to construct. Finally, the third phase performs depth-first searches from the unmatched vertices in layer q. Once a vertex is discovered, it is not searched from again, and so the analysis of depth-first search from Section 20.3 applies here: $O(V_H + E_H) = O(E)$. Hence, all three phases take just $O(E)$ time.

Once the maximal set of vertex-disjoint shortest M-augmenting paths have been found in line 3, updating the matching in line 4 takes $O(E)$ time, as it is just a matter of going through the edges of the M-augmenting paths and adding edges to and removing edges from the matching M. Thus, each iteration of the **repeat** loop of lines 2–5 can run in $O(E)$ time.

It remains to show that the **repeat** loop iterates $O(\sqrt{V})$ times. We start with the following lemma, which shows that after each iteration of the **repeat** loop, the length of an augmenting path increases.

Lemma 25.5
Let $G = (V, E)$ be an undirected bipartite graph with matching M, and let q be the length of a shortest M-augmenting path. Let $\mathcal{P} = \{P_1, P_2, \ldots, P_k\}$ be a maximal set of vertex-disjoint M-augmenting paths of length q. Let $M' = M \oplus (P_1 \cup P_2 \cup \cdots \cup P_k)$, and suppose that P is a shortest M'-augmenting path. Then P has more than q edges.

Proof   We consider separately the cases in which P is vertex-disjoint from the augmenting paths in $\mathcal{P}$ and in which it is not vertex-disjoint.

First, assume that P is vertex-disjoint from the augmenting paths in $\mathcal{P}$. Then, P contains edges that are in M but are not in any of $P_1, P_2, \ldots, P_k$, so that P is also an M-augmenting path. Since P is disjoint from $P_1, P_2, \ldots, P_k$ but is also an M-augmenting path, and since $\mathcal{P}$ is a maximal set of shortest M-augmenting paths, P must be longer than any of the augmenting paths in $\mathcal{P}$, each of which has length q. Therefore, P has more than q edges.

Now, assume that P visits at least one vertex from the M-augmenting paths in $\mathcal{P}$. By Corollary 25.2, M' is a matching in G with $|M'| = |M| + k$. Since P is an M'-augmenting path, by Lemma 25.1, $M' \oplus P$ is a matching with $|M' \oplus P| = |M'| + 1 = |M| + k + 1$. Now let $A = M \oplus M' \oplus P$. We claim that $A = (P_1 \cup P_2 \cup \cdots \cup P_k) \oplus P$:

$$
\begin{aligned}
A &= M \oplus M' \oplus P \\
  &= M \oplus (M \oplus (P_1 \cup P_2 \cup \cdots \cup P_k)) \oplus P \\
  &= (M \oplus M) \oplus (P_1 \cup P_2 \cup \cdots \cup P_k) \oplus P && \text{(associativity of } \oplus) \\
  &= \emptyset \oplus (P_1 \cup P_2 \cup \cdots \cup P_k) \oplus P && (X \oplus X = \emptyset \text{ for all } X) \\
  &= (P_1 \cup P_2 \cup \cdots \cup P_k) \oplus P && (\emptyset \oplus X = X \text{ for all } X).
\end{aligned}
$$

Lemma 25.3 with $M^* = M' \oplus P$ gives that A contains at least $|M' \oplus P| - |M| = k + 1$ vertex-disjoint M-augmenting paths. Since each such M-augmenting path has at least q edges, we have $|A| \geq (k + 1)q = kq + q$.

Now we claim that P shares at least one edge with some M-augmenting path in $\mathcal{P}$. Under the matching M', every vertex in each M-augmenting path in $\mathcal{P}$ is matched. (Only the first and last vertex in each M-augmenting path P_i is unmatched under M, and under $M \oplus P_i$, all vertices in P_i are matched. Because the M-augmenting paths in $\mathcal{P}$ are vertex-disjoint, no other path in $\mathcal{P}$ can affect whether the vertices in P_i are matched. That is, the vertices in P_i are matched under $(M \oplus P_i) \oplus P_j$ if and only if they are matched under $M \oplus P_i$, for any other path $P_j \in \mathscr{P}$.) Suppose that P shares a vertex v with some path $P_i \in \mathscr{P}$. Vertex v cannot be an endpoint of P, because the endpoints of P are unmatched under M'. Therefore, v has an incident edge in P that belongs to M'. Since any vertex has at most one incident edge in a matching, this edge must also belong to P_i, thus proving the claim.

Because $A = (P_1 \cup P_2 \cup \cdots \cup P_k) \oplus P$ and P shares at least one edge with some $P_i \in \mathscr{P}$, we have that $|A| < |P_1 \cup P_2 \cup \cdots \cup P_k| + |P|$. Thus, we have

$$
\begin{aligned}
kq + q \;&\leq\; |A| \\
&<\; |P_1 \cup P_2 \cup \cdots \cup P_k| + |P| \\
&=\; kq + |P| \,,
\end{aligned}
$$

so that $q < |P|$. We conclude that P contains more than q edges. ∎

The next lemma bounds the size of a maximum matching, based on the length of a shortest augmenting path.

Lemma 25.6
Let M be a matching in graph $G = (V, E)$, and let a shortest M-augmenting path in G contain q edges. Then the size of a maximum matching in G is at most $|M| + |V|/(q + 1)$.

Proof Let M^* be a maximum matching in G. By Lemma 25.3, G contains at least $|M^*| - |M|$ vertex-disjoint M-augmenting paths. Each of these paths contains at least q edges, and hence at least $q + 1$ vertices. Because these paths are vertex-disjoint, we have $(|M^*| - |M|)(q + 1) \leq |V|$, so that $|M^*| \leq |M| + |V|/(q+1)$. ∎

The final lemma bounds the number of iterations of the **repeat** loop of lines 2–5.

Lemma 25.7
When the HOPCROFT-KARP procedure runs on an undirected bipartite graph $G = (V, E)$, the **repeat** loop of lines 2–5 iterates $O(\sqrt{V})$ times.

Proof By Lemma 25.5, the length q of the shortest M-augmenting paths found in line 3 increases from iteration to iteration. After $\lceil \sqrt{|V|} \rceil$ iterations, therefore, we must have $q \geq \lceil \sqrt{|V|} \rceil$. Consider the situation after the first time line 4 executes with M-augmenting paths whose length is at least $\lceil \sqrt{|V|} \rceil$. Since the size of a matching increases by at least one edge per iteration, Lemma 25.6 implies that the number of additional iterations before achieving a maximum matching is at most

$$
\frac{|V|}{\lceil \sqrt{|V|} \rceil + 1} \;<\; \frac{|V|}{\sqrt{|V|}} \;=\; \sqrt{|V|} \,.
$$

Hence, the total number of loop iterations is less than $2\sqrt{|V|}$. ∎

Thus, we have the following bound on the running time of the HOPCROFT-KARP procedure.

Theorem 25.8
The procedure HOPCROFT-KARP runs in $O(\sqrt{V}E)$ time on an undirected bipartite graph $G = (V, E)$.

Proof By Lemma 25.7 the **repeat** loop iterates $O(\sqrt{V})$ times, and we have seen how to implement each iteration in $O(E)$ time. ∎

Exercises

25.1-1
Use the Hopcroft-Karp algorithm to find a maximum matching for the graph in Figure 25.1.

25.1-2
How are M-augmenting paths and augmenting paths in flow networks similar? How do they differ?

25.1-3
What is the advantage of searching in the transpose H^{T} from unmatched vertices in layer q (the first layer that contains an unmatched vertex in R) to layer 0 versus searching in the dag H from layer 0 to layer q?

25.1-4
Show how to bound the number of iterations of the the **repeat** loop of lines 2–5 of HOPCROFT-KARP by $\lceil 3\sqrt{|V|}/2 \rceil$.

★ 25.1-5
A *perfect matching* is a matching under which every vertex is matched. Let $G = (V, E)$ be an undirected bipartite graph with vertex partition $V = L \cup R$, where $|L| = |R|$. For any $X \subseteq V$, define the *neighborhood* of X as

$$N(X) = \{y \in V : (x, y) \in E \text{ for some } x \in X\} ,$$

that is, the set of vertices adjacent to some member of X. Prove *Hall's theorem*: there exists a perfect matching in G if and only if $|A| \leq |N(A)|$ for every subset $A \subseteq L$.

25.1-6

In a ***d-regular*** graph, every vertex has degree d. If $G = (V, E)$ is bipartite with vertex partition $V = L \cup R$ and also d-regular, then $|L| = |R|$. Use Hall's theorem (see Exercise 25.1-5) to prove that every d-regular bipartite graph contains a perfect matching. Then use that result to prove that every d-regular bipartite graph contains d disjoint perfect matchings.

25.2   The stable-marriage problem

In Section 25.1, the goal was to find a maximum matching in an undirected bipartite graph. If you know that the graph $G = (V, E)$ with vertex partition $V = L \cup R$ is a ***complete bipartite graph***[1]—containing an edge from every vertex in L to every vertex in R—then you can find a maximum matching by a simple greedy algorithm.

When a graph can have several matchings, you might want to decide which matchings are most desirable. In Section 25.3, we'll add weights to the edges and find a matching of maximum weight. In this section, we will instead add some information to each vertex in a complete bipartite graph: a ranking of the vertices in the other side. That is, each vertex in L has an ordered list of all the vertices in R, and vice-versa. To keep things simple, let's assume that L and R each contain n vertices. The goal here is to match each vertex in L with a vertex in R in a "stable" way.

This problem derives its name, the ***stable-marriage problem***, from the notion of heterosexual marriage, viewing L as a set of women and R as a set of men.[2] Each woman ranks all the men in terms of desirability, and each man does the same with all the women. The goal is to pair up women and men (a matching) so that if a woman and a man are not matched to each other, then at least one of them prefers their assigned partner.

If a woman and a man are not matched to each other but each prefers the other over their assigned partner, they form a ***blocking pair***. A blocking pair has incentive to opt out of the assigned pairing and get together on their own. If that were to occur, then this pair would block the matching from being "stable." A ***stable***

---

[1] The definition of a complete bipartite graph differs from the definition of complete graph given on page 1167 because in a bipartite graph, there are no edges between vertices in L and no edges between vertices in R.

[2] Although marriage norms are changing, it's traditional to view the stable-marriage problem through the lens of heterosexual marriage.

matching, therefore, is a matching that has no blocking pair. If there is a blocking pair, then the matching is *unstable*.

Let's look at an example with four women—Wanda, Emma, Lacey, and Karen—and four men—Oscar, Davis, Brent, and Hank—having the following preferences:

Wanda: Brent, Hank, Oscar, Davis
Emma: Davis, Hank, Oscar, Brent
Lacey: Brent, Davis, Hank, Oscar
Karen: Brent, Hank, Davis, Oscar

Oscar: Wanda, Karen, Lacey, Emma
Davis: Wanda, Lacey, Karen, Emma
Brent: Lacey, Karen, Wanda, Emma
Hank: Lacey, Wanda, Emma, Karen

A stable matching comprises the following pairs:

Lacey and Brent
Wanda and Hank
Karen and Davis
Emma and Oscar

You can verify that this matching has no blocking pair. For example, even though Karen prefers Brent and Hank to her partner Davis, Brent prefers his partner Lacey to Karen, and Hank prefers his partner Wanda to Karen, so that neither Karen and Brent nor Karen and Hank form a blocking pair. In fact, this stable matching is unique. Suppose instead that the last two pairs were

Emma and Davis
Karen and Oscar

Then Karen and Davis would be a blocking pair, because they were not paired together, Karen prefers Davis to Oscar, and Davis prefers Karen to Emma. Therefore, this matching is not stable.

Stable matchings need not be unique. For example, suppose that there are three women—Monica, Phoebe, and Rachel—and three men—Chandler, Joey, and Ross—with these preferences:

Monica: Chandler, Joey, Ross
Phoebe: Joey, Ross, Chandler
Rachel: Ross, Chandler, Joey

Chandler: Phoebe, Rachel, Monica
Joey: Rachel, Monica, Phoebe
Ross: Monica, Phoebe, Rachel

In this case, there are three stable matchings:

Matching 1	Matching 2	Matching 3
Monica and Chandler	Phoebe and Chandler	Rachel and Chandler
Phoebe and Joey	Rachel and Joey	Monica and Joey
Rachel and Ross	Monica and Ross	Phoebe and Ross

In matching 1, all women get their first choice and all men get their last choice. Matching 2 is the opposite, with all men getting their first choice and all women getting their last choice. When all the women or all the men get their first choice, there plainly cannot be a blocking pair. In matching 3, everyone gets their second choice. You can verify that there are no blocking pairs.

You might wonder whether it is always possible to come up with a stable matching no matter what rankings each participant provides. The answer is yes. (Exercise 25.2-3 asks you to show that even in the scenario of the National Resident Matching Program, where each hospital takes on multiple students, it is always possible to devise a stable assignment.) A simple algorithm known as the Gale-Shapley algorithm always finds a stable matching. The algorithm has two variants, which mirror each other: "woman-oriented" and "man-oriented." Let's examine the woman-oriented version. Each participant is either "free" or "engaged." Everyone starts out free. Engagements occur when a free woman proposes to a man. When a man is first proposed to, he goes from free to engaged, and he always stays engaged, though not necessarily to the same woman. If an engaged man receives a proposal from a woman whom he prefers to the woman he's currently engaged to, that engagement is broken, the woman to whom he had been engaged becomes free, and the man and the woman whom he prefers become engaged. Each woman proposes to the men in her preference list, in order, until the last time she becomes engaged. When a woman is engaged, she temporarily stops proposing, but if she becomes free again, she continues down her list. Once everyone is engaged, the algorithm terminates. The procedure GALE-SHAPLEY on the next page makes this process more concrete. The procedure allows for some choice: any free woman may be selected in line 2. We'll see that the procedure produces a stable matching regardless of the order in which line 2 chooses free women. For the man-oriented version, just reverse the roles of men and women in the procedure.

Let's see how the GALE-SHAPLEY procedure executes on the example with Wanda, Emma, Lacey, Karen, Oscar, Davis, Brent, and Hank. After everyone is initialized to free, here is one possible version of what can occur in successive iterations of the **while** loop of lines 2–9:

1. Wanda proposes to Brent. Brent is free, so that Wanda and Brent become engaged and no longer free.

```
GALE-SHAPLEY (men, women, rankings)
 1   assign each woman and man as free
 2   while some woman w is free
 3       let m be the first man on w's ranked list to whom she has not proposed
 4       if m is free
 5           w and m become engaged to each other (and not free)
 6       elseif m ranks w higher than the woman w' he is currently engaged to
 7           m breaks the engagement to w', who becomes free
 8           w and m become engaged to each other (and not free)
 9       else m rejects w, with w remaining free
10   return the stable matching consisting of the engaged pairs
```

2. Emma proposes to Davis. Davis is free, so that Emma and Davis become engaged and no longer free.

3. Lacey proposes to Brent. Brent is engaged to Wanda, but he prefers Lacey. Brent breaks the engagement to Wanda, who becomes free. Lacey and Brent become engaged, with Lacey no longer free.

4. Karen proposes to Brent. Brent is engaged to Lacey, whom he prefers to Karen. Brent rejects Karen, who remains free.

5. Karen proposes to Hank. Hank is free, so that Karen and Hank become engaged and no longer free.

6. Wanda proposes to Hank. Hank is engaged to Karen, but he prefers Wanda. Hank breaks the engagement with Karen, who becomes free. Wanda and Hank become engaged, with Wanda no longer free.

7. Karen proposes to Davis. Davis is engaged to Emma, but he prefers Karen. Davis breaks the engagement to Emma, who becomes free. Karen and Davis become engaged, with Karen no longer free.

8. Emma proposes to Hank. Hank is engaged to Wanda, whom he prefers to Emma. Hank rejects Emma, who remains free.

9. Emma proposes to Oscar. Oscar is free, so that Emma and Oscar become engaged and no longer free.

At this point, everyone is engaged and nobody is free, so the **while** loop terminates. The procedure returns the stable matching we saw earlier.

The following theorem shows that not only does GALE-SHAPLEY terminate, but that it always returns a stable matching, thereby proving that a stable matching always exists.

Theorem 25.9
The procedure GALE-SHAPLEY always terminates and returns a stable matching.

Proof   Let's first show that the **while** loop of lines 2–9 always terminates, so that the procedure terminates. The proof is by contradiction. If the loop fails to terminate, it is because some woman remains free. In order for a woman to remain free, she must have proposed to all the men and been rejected by each one. In order for a man to reject a woman, he must be already engaged. Therefore, all the men are engaged. Once engaged, a man stays engaged (though not necessarily to the same woman). There are an equal number n of women and men, however, which means that every woman is engaged, leading to the contradiction that no women are free. We must also show that the **while** loop makes a bounded number of iterations. Since each of the n women goes through her ranking of the n men in order, possibly not reaching the end of her list, the total number of iterations is at most n^2. Therefore, the **while** loop always terminates, and the procedure returns a matching.

We need to show that there are no blocking pairs. We first observe that once a man m is engaged to a woman w, all subsequent actions for m occur in lines 6–8. Therefore, once a man is engaged, he stays engaged, and any time he breaks an engagement to a woman w, it's for a woman whom he prefers to w. Suppose that a woman w is matched with a man m, but she prefers man m'. We'll show that w and m' is not a blocking pair, because m' does not prefer w to his partner. Because w ranks m' higher than m, she must have proposed to m' before proposing to m, and m' either rejected her proposal or accepted it and later broke the engagement. If m' rejected the proposal from w, it is because he was already engaged to some woman he prefers to w. If m' accepted and later broke the engagement, he was at some point engaged to w but later accepted a proposal from a woman he prefers to w. In either case, he ultimately ends up with a partner whom he prefers to w. We conclude that even though w might prefer m' to her partner m, it is not also the case that m' prefers w to his partner. Therefore, the procedure returns a matching containing no blocking pairs.   ∎

Exercise 25.2-1 asks you to provide the proof of the following corollary.

Corollary 25.10
Given preference rankings for n women and n men, the Gale-Shapley algorithm can be implemented to run in $O(n^2)$ time.   ∎

Because line 2 can choose any free woman, you might wonder whether different choices can produce different stable matchings. The answer is no: as the following theorem shows, every execution of the GALE-SHAPLEY produces exactly the same result. Moreover, the stable matching returned is optimal for the women.

Theorem 25.11
Regardless of how women are chosen in line 2 of GALE-SHAPLEY, the procedure always returns the same stable matching, and in this stable matching, each woman has the best partner possible in any stable matching.

Proof   The proof that each woman has the best partner possible in any stable matching is by contradiction. Suppose that the GALE-SHAPLEY procedure returns a stable matching M, but that there is a different stable matching M' in which some woman w prefers her partner m' to the partner m she has in M. Because w ranks m' higher than m, she must have proposed to m' before proposing to m. Then there is a woman w' whom m' prefers to w, and m' was already engaged to w' when w proposed or m' accepted the proposal from w and later broke the engagement in favor of w'. Either way, there is a moment when m' decided against w in favor of w'. Now suppose, without loss of generality, that this moment was the first time that any man rejected a partner who belongs to some stable matching.

We claim that w' cannot have a partner m'' in a stable matching whom she prefers to m'. If there were such a man m'', then in order for w' to propose to m', she would have proposed to m'' and been rejected at some point before proposing to m'. If m' accepted the proposal from w and later broke it to accept w', then since this was the first rejection in a stable matching, we get the contradiction that m'' could not have rejected w' beforehand. If m' was already engaged to w' when w proposed, then again, m'' could not have rejected w' beforehand, thus proving the claim.

Since w' does not prefer anyone to m' in a stable matching and w' is not matched with m' in M (because m' is matched with w in M'), w' prefers m' to her partner in M'. Since w' prefers m' over her partner in M' and m' prefers w' over his partner w in M', the pair w' and m' is a blocking pair in M'. Because M' has a blocking pair, it cannot be a stable matching, thereby contradicting the assumption that there exists some stable matching in which each woman has the best partner possible other than the matching M returned by GALE-SHAPLEY.

We put no condition on the execution of the procedure, which means that all possible orders in which line 2 selects women result in the same stable matching being returned.   ∎

Corollary 25.12
There can be stable matchings that the GALE-SHAPLEY procedure does not return.

Proof   Theorem 25.11 says that for a given set of rankings, GALE-SHAPLEY returns just one matching, no matter how it chooses women in line 2. The earlier example of three women and three men with three different stable matchings shows that there can be multiple stable matchings for a given set of rankings. A call of GALE-SHAPLEY is capable of returning only one of these stable matchings.   ∎

Although the GALE-SHAPLEY procedure gives the best possible outcome for the women, the following corollary shows that it also produces the worst possible outcome for the men.

Corollary 25.13
In the stable matching returned by the procedure GALE-SHAPLEY, each man has the worst partner possible in any stable matching.

Proof   Let M be the matching returned by a call to GALE-SHAPLEY. Suppose that there is another stable matching M' and a man m who prefers his partner w in M to his partner w' in M'. Let the partner of w in M' be m'. By Theorem 25.11, m is the best partner that w can have in any stable matching, which means that w prefers m to m'. Since m prefers w to w', the pair w and m is a blocking pair in M', contradicting the assumption that M' is a stable matching.   ∎

Exercises

25.2-1
Describe how to implement the Gale-Shapley algorithm so that it runs in $O(n^2)$ time.

25.2-2
Is it possible to have an unstable matching with just two women and two men? If so, provide and justify an example. If not, argue why not.

25.2-3
The National Resident Matching Program differs from the scenario for the stable-marriage problem set out in this section in two ways. First, a hospital may be matched with more than one student, so that hospital h takes $r_h \geq 1$ students. Second, the number of students might not equal the number of hospitals. Describe how to modify the Gale-Shapley algorithm to fit the requirements of the National Resident Matching Program.

25.2-4
Prove the following property, which is known as *weak Pareto optimality*:

> Let M be the stable matching produced by the GALE-SHAPLEY procedure, with women proposing to men. Then, for a given instance of the stable-marriage problem there is no matching—stable or unstable—such that every

woman has a partner whom she prefers to her partner in the stable match-ing M.

25.2-5

The *stable-roommates problem* is similar to the stable-marriage problem, except that the graph is a complete graph, not bipartite, with an even number of ver-tices. Each vertex represents a person, and each person ranks all the other peo-ple. The definitions of blocking pairs and stable matching extend in the natural way: a blocking pair comprises two people who both prefer each other to their current partner, and a matching is stable if there are no blocking pairs. For exam-ple, consider four people—Wendy, Xenia, Yolanda, and Zelda—with the following preference lists:

> Wendy: Xenia, Yolanda, Zelda
> Xenia: Wendy, Zelda, Yolanda
> Yolanda: Wendy, Zelda, Xenia
> Zelda: Xenia, Yolanda, Wendy

You can verify that the following matching is stable:

> Wendy and Xenia
> Yolanda and Zelda

Unlike the stable-marriage problem, the stable-roommates problem can have inputs for which no stable matching exists. Find such an input and explain why no stable matching exists.

25.3   The Hungarian algorithm for the assignment problem

Let us once again add some information to a complete bipartite graph $G = (V, E)$, where $V = L \cup R$. This time, instead of having the vertices of each side rank the vertices on the other side, we assign a weight to each edge. Again, let's assume that the vertex sets L and R each contain n vertices, so that the graph contains n^2 edges. For $l \in L$ and $r \in R$, denote the weight of edge (l, r) by $w(l, r)$, which represents the utility gained by matching vertex l with vertex r.

The goal is to find a perfect matching M^* (see Exercises 25.1-5 and 25.1-6) whose edges have the maximum total weight over all perfect matchings. That is, letting $w(M) = \sum_{(l,r)\in M} w(l, r)$ denote the total weight of the edges in match-ing M, we want to find a perfect matching M^* such that

$$w(M^*) = \max \{w(M) : M \text{ is a perfect matching}\} .$$

We call finding such a maximum-weight perfect matching the *assignment problem*. A solution to the assignment problem is a perfect matching that maximizes the total utility. Like the stable-marriage problem, the assignment problem finds a matching that is "good," but with a different definition of good: maximizing total value rather than achieving stability.

Although you could enumerate all $n!$ perfect matchings to solve the assignment problem, an algorithm known as the *Hungarian algorithm* solves it much faster. This section will prove an $O(n^4)$ time bound, and Problem 25-2 asks you to refine the algorithm to reduce the running time to $O(n^3)$. Instead of working with the complete bipartite graph G, the Hungarian algorithm works with a subgraph of G called the "equality subgraph." The equality subgraph, which is defined below, changes over time and has the beneficial property that any perfect matching in the equality subgraph is also an optimal solution to the assignment problem.

The equality subgraph depends on assigning an attribute h to each vertex. We call h the *label* of a vertex, and we say that h is a *feasible vertex labeling* of G if

$$l.h + r.h \geq w(l,r) \text{ for all } l \in L \text{ and } r \in R .$$

A feasible vertex labeling always exists, such as the *default vertex labeling* given by

$$l.h = \max\{w(l,r) : r \in R\} \quad \text{for all } l \in L , \tag{25.1}$$
$$r.h = 0 \quad\quad\quad\quad\quad\quad \text{for all } r \in R . \tag{25.2}$$

Given a feasible vertex labeling h, the *equality subgraph* $G_h = (V, E_h)$ of G consists of the same vertices as G and the subset of edges

$$E_h = \{(l,r) \in E : l.h + r.h = w(l,r)\} .$$

The following theorem ties together a perfect matching in an equality subgraph and an optimal solution to the assignment problem.

Theorem 25.14
Let $G = (V, E)$, where $V = L \cup R$, be a complete bipartite graph where each edge $(l,r) \in E$ has weight $w(l,r)$. Let h be a feasible vertex labeling of G and G_h be the equality subgraph of G. If G_h contains a perfect matching M^*, then M^* is an optimal solution to the assignment problem on G.

Proof If G_h contains a perfect matching M^*, then because G_h and G have the same sets of vertices, M^* is also a perfect matching in G. Because each edge of M^* belongs to G_h and each vertex has exactly one incident edge from any perfect matching, we have

$$w(M^*) = \sum_{(l,r)\in M^*} w(l,r)$$

$$= \sum_{(l,r)\in M^*} (l.h + r.h) \quad \text{(because all edges in } M^* \text{ belong to } G_h)$$

$$= \sum_{l\in L} l.h + \sum_{r\in R} r.h \quad \text{(because } M^* \text{ is a perfect matching) .}$$

Letting M be any perfect matching in G, we have

$$w(M) = \sum_{(l,r)\in M} w(l,r)$$

$$\leq \sum_{(l,r)\in M} (l.h + r.h) \quad \text{(because } h \text{ is a feasible vertex labeling)}$$

$$= \sum_{l\in L} l.h + \sum_{r\in R} r.h \quad \text{(because } M \text{ is a perfect matching) .}$$

Thus, we have

$$w(M) \leq \sum_{l\in L} l.h + \sum_{r\in R} r.h = w(M^*) , \tag{25.3}$$

so that M^* is a maximum-weight perfect matching in G. ∎

The goal now becomes finding a perfect matching in an equality subgraph. Which equality subgraph? It does not matter! We have free rein to not only choose an equality subgraph, but to change which equality subgraph we choose as we go along. We just need to find *some* perfect matching in *some* equality subgraph.

To understand the equality subgraph better, consider again the proof of Theorem 25.14 and, in the second half, let M be any matching. The proof is still valid, in particular, inequality (25.3): the weight of any matching is always at most the sum of the vertex labels. If we choose any set of vertex labels that define an equality subgraph, then a maximum-cardinality matching in this equality subgraph has total value at most the sum of the vertex labels. If the set of vertex labels is the "right" one, then it will have total value equal to $w(M^*)$, and a maximum-cardinality matching in the equality subgraph is also a maximum-weight perfect matching. The Hungarian algorithm repeatedly modifies the matching and the vertex labels in order to achieve this goal.

The Hungarian algorithm starts with any feasible vertex labeling h and any matching M in the equality subgraph G_h. It repeatedly finds an M-augmenting path P in G_h and, using Lemma 25.1, updates the matching to be $M \oplus P$, thereby incrementing the size of the matching. As long as there is some equality subgraph that contains an M-augmenting path, the size of the matching can increase, until a perfect matching is achieved.

Four questions arise:

1. What initial feasible vertex labeling should the algorithm start with? Answer: the default vertex labeling given by equations (25.1) and (25.2).

2. What initial matching in G_h should the algorithm start with? Short answer: any matching, even an empty matching, but a greedy maximal matching works well.

3. If an M-augmenting path exists in G_h, how to find it? Short answer: use a variant of breadth-first search similar to the second phase of the procedure used in the Hopcroft-Karp algorithm to find a maximal set of shortest M-augmenting paths.

4. What if the search for an M-augmenting path fails? Short answer: update the feasible vertex labeling to bring in at least one new edge.

We'll elaborate on the short answers using the example that starts in Figure 25.4. Here, $L = \{l_1, l_2, \ldots, l_7\}$ and $R = \{r_1, r_2, \ldots, r_7\}$. The edge weights appear in the matrix shown in part (a), where the weight $w(l_i, r_j)$ appears in row i and column j. The feasible vertex labels, given by the default vertex labeling, appear to the left of and above the matrix. Matrix entries in red indicate edges (l_i, r_j) for which $l_i.h + r_j.h = w(l_i, r_j)$, that is, edges in the equality subgraph G_h appearing in part (b) of the figure.

Greedy maximal bipartite matching

There are several ways to implement a greedy method to find a maximal bipartite matching. The procedure GREEDY-BIPARTITE-MATCHING shows one. Edges in Figure 25.4(b) highlighted in blue indicate the initial greedy maximal matching in G_h. Exercise 25.3-2 asks you to show that the GREEDY-BIPARTITE-MATCHING procedure returns a matching that is at least half the size of a maximum matching.

```
GREEDY-BIPARTITE-MATCHING(G)

1   M = ∅
2   for each vertex l ∈ L
3       if l has an unmatched neighbor in R
4           choose any such unmatched neighbor r ∈ R
5               M = M ∪ {(l, r)}
6   return M
```

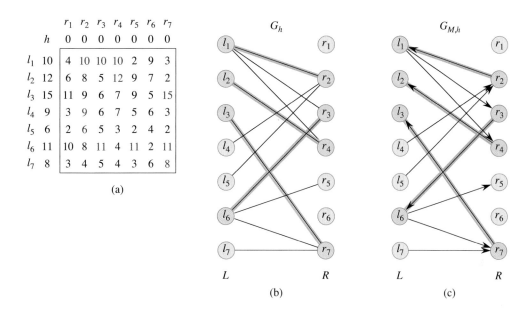

	h	r_1	r_2	r_3	r_4	r_5	r_6	r_7
		0	0	0	0	0	0	0
l_1	10	4	10	10	10	2	9	3
l_2	12	6	8	5	12	9	7	2
l_3	15	11	9	6	7	9	5	15
l_4	9	3	9	6	7	5	6	3
l_5	6	2	6	5	3	2	4	2
l_6	11	10	8	11	4	11	2	11
l_7	8	3	4	5	4	3	6	8

(a)

(b)

(c)

Figure 25.4 The start of the Hungarian algorithm. **(a)** The matrix of edge weights for a bipartite graph with $L = \{l_1, l_2, \ldots, l_7\}$ and $R = \{r_1, r_2, \ldots, r_7\}$. The value in row i and column j indicates $w(l_i, r_j)$. Feasible vertex labels appear above and next to the matrix. Red entries correspond to edges in the equality subgraph. **(b)** The equality subgraph G_h. Edges highlighted in blue belong to the initial greedy maximal matching M. Blue vertices are matched, and tan vertices are unmatched. **(c)** The directed equality subgraph $G_{M,h}$ created from G_h by directing edges in M from R to L and all other edges from L to R.

Finding an M-augmenting path in G_h

To find an M-augmenting path in the equality subgraph G_h with a matching M, the Hungarian algorithm first creates the ***directed equality subgraph*** $G_{M,h}$ from G_h, just as the Hopcroft-Karp algorithm creates G_M from G. As in the Hopcroft-Karp algorithm, you can think of an M-augmenting path as starting from an unmatched vertex in L, ending at an unmatched vertex in R, taking unmatched edges from L to R, and taking matched edges from R to L. Thus, $G_{M,h} = (V, E_{M,h})$, where

$$
\begin{aligned}
E_{M,h} = {} & \{(l, r) : l \in L, r \in R, \text{ and } (l, r) \in E_h - M\} \quad \text{(edges from } L \text{ to } R\text{)} \\
& \cup \{(r, l) : r \in R, l \in L, \text{ and } (l, r) \in M\} \quad \text{(edges from } R \text{ to } L\text{)} \, .
\end{aligned}
$$

Because an M-augmenting path in the directed equality subgraph $G_{M,h}$ is also an M-augmenting path in the equality subgraph G_h, it suffices to find M-augmenting paths in $G_{M,h}$. Figure 25.4(c) shows the directed equality subgraph $G_{M,h}$ corresponding to the equality subgraph G_h and matching M from part (b) of the figure.

With the directed equality subgraph $G_{M,h}$ in hand, the Hungarian algorithm searches for an M-augmenting path from any unmatched vertex in L to any unmatched vertex in R. Any exhaustive graph-search method suffices. Here, we'll use breadth-first search, starting from all the unmatched vertices in L (just as the Hopcroft-Karp algorithm does when creating the dag H), but stopping upon first discovering some unmatched vertex in R. Figure 25.5 shows the idea. To start from all the unmatched vertices in L, initialize the first-in, first-out queue with all the unmatched vertices in L, rather than just one source vertex. Unlike the dag H in the Hopcroft-Karp algorithm, here each vertex needs just one predecessor, so that the breadth-first search creates a ***breadth-first forest*** $F = (V_F, E_F)$. Each unmatched vertex in L is a root in F.

In Figure 25.5(g), the breadth-first search has found the M-augmenting path $\langle (l_4, r_2), (r_2, l_1), (l_1, r_3), (r_3, l_6), (l_6, r_5) \rangle$. Figure 25.6(a) shows the new matching created by taking the symmetric difference of the matching M in Figure 25.5(a) with this M-augmenting path.

When the search for an M-augmenting path fails

Having updated the matching M from an M-augmenting path, the Hungarian algorithm updates the directed equality subgraph $G_{M,h}$ according to the new matching and then starts a new breadth-first search from all the unmatched vertices in L. Figure 25.6 shows the start of this process, picking up from Figure 25.5.

In Figure 25.6(d), the queue contains vertices l_4 and l_3. Neither of these vertices has an edge that leaves it, however, so that once these vertices are removed from the queue, the queue becomes empty. The search terminates at this point, before discovering an unmatched vertex in R to yield an M-augmenting path. Whenever this situation occurs, the most recently discovered vertices must belong to L. Why? Whenever an unmatched vertex in R is discovered, the search has found an M-augmenting path, and when a matched vertex in R is discovered, it has an unvisited neighbor in L, which the search can then discover.

Recall that we have the freedom to work with any equality subgraph. We can change the directed equality subgraph "on the fly," as long we do not counteract the work already done. The Hungarian algorithm updates the feasible vertex labeling h to fulfill the following criteria:

1. No edge in the breadth-first forest F leaves the directed equality subgraph.

2. No edge in the matching M leaves the directed equality subgraph.

3. At least one edge (l, r), where $l \in L \cap V_F$ and $r \in R - V_F$ goes into E_h, and hence into $E_{M,h}$. Therefore, at least one vertex in R will be newly discovered.

Thus, at least one new edge enters the directed equality subgraph, and any edge that leaves the directed equality subgraph belongs to neither the matching M nor

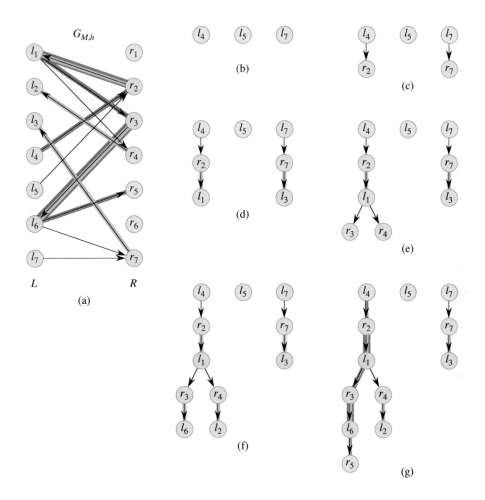

Figure 25.5   Finding an M-augmenting path in $G_{M,h}$ by breadth-first search. **(a)** The directed equality subgraph $G_{M,h}$ from Figure 25.4(c). **(b)–(g)** Successive versions of the breadth-first forest F, shown as the vertices at each distance from the roots—the unmatched vertices in L—are discovered. In parts (b)–(f), the layer of vertices closest to the bottom of the figure are those in the first-in, first-out queue. For example, in part (b), the queue contains the roots $\langle l_4, l_5, l_7 \rangle$, and in part (e), the queue contains $\langle r_3, r_4 \rangle$, at distance 3 from the roots. In part (g), the unmatched vertex r_5 is discovered, so the breadth-first search terminates. The path $\langle (l_4, r_2), (r_2, l_1), (l_1, r_3), (r_3, l_6), (l_6, r_5) \rangle$, highlighted in orange in parts (a) and (g), is an M-augmenting path. Taking its symmetric difference with the matching M yields a new matching with one more edge than M.

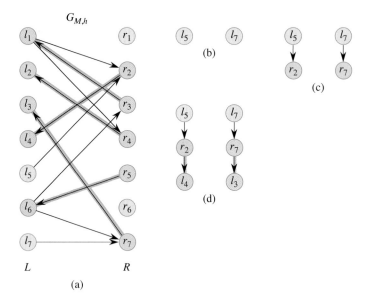

Figure 25.6 **(a)** The new matching M and the new directed equality subgraph $G_{M.h}$ after updating the matching in Figure 25.5(a) with the M-augmenting path in Figure 25.5(g). **(b)–(d)** Successive versions of the breadth-first forest F in a new breadth-first search with roots l_5 and l_7. After the vertices l_4 and l_3 in part (d) have been removed from the queue, the queue becomes empty before the search can discover an unmatched vertex in R.

the breadth-first forest F. Newly discovered vertices in R are enqueued, but their distances are not necessarily 1 greater than the distances of the most recently discovered vertices in L.

To update the feasible vertex labeling, the Hungarian algorithm first computes the value

$$\delta = \min \{l.h + r.h - w(l,r) : l \in F_L \text{ and } r \in R - F_R\} \, , \qquad (25.4)$$

where $F_L = L \cap V_F$ and $F_R = R \cap V_F$ denote the vertices in the breadth-first forest F that belong to L and R, respectively. That is, δ is the smallest difference by which an edge incident on a vertex in F_L missed being in the current equality subgraph G_h. The Hungarian algorithm then creates a new feasible vertex labeling, say h', by subtracting δ from $l.h$ for all vertices $l \in F_L$ and adding δ to $r.h$ for all vertices $r \in F_R$:

$$v.h' = \begin{cases} v.h - \delta & \text{if } v \in F_L \, , \\ v.h + \delta & \text{if } v \in F_R \, , \\ v.h & \text{otherwise } (v \in V - V_F) \, . \end{cases} \qquad (25.5)$$

The following lemma shows that these changes achieve the three criteria above.

Lemma 25.15

Let h be a feasible vertex labeling for the complete bipartite graph G with equality subgraph G_h, and let M be a matching for G_h and F be a breadth-first forest being constructed for the directed equality subgraph $G_{M,h}$. Then, the labeling h' in equation (25.5) is a feasible vertex labeling for G with the following properties:

1. If (u, v) is an edge in the breadth-first forest F for $G_{M,h}$, then $(u, v) \in E_{M,h'}$.

2. If (l, r) belongs to the matching M for G_h, then $(r, l) \in E_{M,h'}$.

3. There exist vertices $l \in F_L$ and $r \in R - F_R$ such that $(l, r) \notin E_{M,h}$ but $(l, r) \in E_{M,h'}$.

Proof We first show that h' is a feasible vertex labeling for G. Because h is a feasible vertex labeling, we have $l.h + r.h \geq w(l, r)$ for all $l \in L$ and $r \in R$. In order for h' to not be a feasible vertex labeling, we would need $l.h' + r.h' < l.h + r.h$ for some $l \in L$ and $r \in R$. The only way this could occur would be for some $l \in F_L$ and $r \in R - F_R$. In this instance, the amount of the decrease equals δ, so that $l.h' + r.h' = l.h - \delta + r.h$. By equation (25.4), we have that $l.h - \delta + r.h \geq w(l, r)$ for any $l \in F_L$ and $r \in R - F_R$, so that $l.h' + r.h' \geq w(l, r)$. For all other edges, we have $l.h' + r.h' \geq l.h + r.h \geq w(l, r)$. Thus, h' is a feasible vertex labeling.

Now we show that each of the three desired properties holds:

1. If $l \in F_L$ and $r \in F_R$, then we have $l.h' + r.h' = l.h + r.h$ because δ is added to the label of l and subtracted from the label of r. Therefore, if an edge belongs to F for the directed graph $G_{M,h}$, it also belongs to $G_{M,h'}$.

2. We claim that at the time the Hungarian algorithm computes the new feasible vertex labeling h', for every edge $(l, r) \in M$, we have $l \in F_L$ if and only if $r \in F_R$. To see why, consider a matched vertex r and let $(l, r) \in M$. First suppose that $r \in F_R$, so that the search discovered r and enqueued it. When r was removed from the queue, l was discovered, so $l \in F_L$. Now suppose that $r \notin F_R$, so r is undiscovered. We will show that $l \notin F_L$. The only edge in $G_{M,h}$ that enters l is (r, l), and since r is undiscovered, the search has not taken this edge; if $l \in F_L$, it is not because of the edge (r, l). The only other way that a vertex in L can be in F_L is if it is a root of the search, but only unmatched vertices in L are roots and l is matched. Thus, $l \notin F_L$, and the claim is proved.

   We already saw that $l \in F_L$ and $r \in F_R$ implies $l.h' + r.h' = l.h + r.h$. For the opposite case, when $l \in L - F_L$ and $R \in R - F_R$, we have that $l.h' = l.h$ and $r.h' = r.h$, so that again $l.h' + r.h' = l.h + r.h$. Thus, if edge (l, r) is in the matching M for the equality graph G_h, then $(r, l) \in E_{M,h'}$.

3. Let (l, r) be an edge not in E_h such that $l \in F_L$, $r \in R - F_R$, and $\delta = l.h + r.h - w(l, r)$. By the definition of δ, there is at least one such edge. Then, we have

$$
\begin{aligned}
l.h' + r.h' &= l.h - \delta + r.h \\
&= l.h - (l.h + r.h - w(l, r)) + r.h \\
&= w(l, r) \,,
\end{aligned}
$$

and thus $(l, r) \in E_{h'}$. Since (l, r) is not in E_h, it is not in the matching M, so that in $E_{M,h'}$ it must be directed from L to R. Thus, $(l, r) \in E_{M,h'}$.   ∎

It is possible for an edge to belong to $E_{M,h}$ but not to $E_{M,h'}$. By Lemma 25.15, any such edge belongs neither to the matching M nor to the breadth-first forest F at the time that the new feasible vertex labeling h' is computed. (See Exercise 25.3-3.)

Going back to Figure 25.6(d), the queue became empty before an M-augmenting path was found. Figure 25.7 shows the next steps taken by the algorithm. The value of $\delta = 1$ is achieved by the edge (l_5, r_3) because in Figure 25.4(a), $l_5.h + r_3.h - w(l_5, r_3) = 6 + 0 - 5 = 1$. In Figure 25.7(a), the values of $l_3.h$, $l_4.h$, $l_5.h$, and $l_7.h$ have decreased by 1 and the values of $r_2.h$ and $r_7.h$ have increased by 1 because these vertices are in F. As a result, the edges (l_1, r_2) and (l_6, r_7) leave $G_{M,h}$ and the edge (l_5, r_3) enters. Figure 25.7(b) shows the new directed equality subgraph $G_{M,h}$. With edge (l_5, r_3) now in $G_{M,h}$, Figure 25.7(c) shows that this edge is added to the breadth-first forest F, and r_3 is added to the queue. Parts (c)–(f) show the breadth-first forest continuing to be built until in part (f), the queue once again becomes empty after vertex l_2, which has no edges leaving, is removed. Again, the algorithm must update the feasible vertex labeling and the directed equality subgraph. Now the value of $\delta = 1$ is achieved by three edges: (l_1, r_6), (l_5, r_6), and (l_7, r_6).

As Figure 25.8 shows in parts (a) and (b), these edges enter $G_{M,h}$, and edge (l_6, r_3) leaves. Part (c) shows that edge (l_1, r_6) is added to the breadth-first forest. (Either of edges (l_5, r_6) or (l_7, r_6) could have been added instead.) Because r_6 is unmatched, the search has found the M-augmenting path $\langle (l_5, r_3), (r_3, l_1), (l_1, r_6) \rangle$, highlighted in orange.

Figure 25.9(a) shows $G_{M,h}$ after the matching M has been updated by taking its symmetric difference with the M-augmenting path. The Hungarian algorithm starts its last breadth-first search, with vertex l_7 as the only root. The search proceeds as shown in parts (b)–(h) of the figure, until the queue becomes empty after removing l_4. This time, we find that $\delta = 2$, achieved by the five edges (l_2, r_5), (l_3, r_1), (l_4, r_5), (l_5, r_1), and (l_5, r_5), each of which enters $G_{M,h}$. Figure 25.10(a) shows the results of decreasing the feasible vertex label of each vertex in F_L by 2 and increasing the feasible vertex label of each vertex in F_R

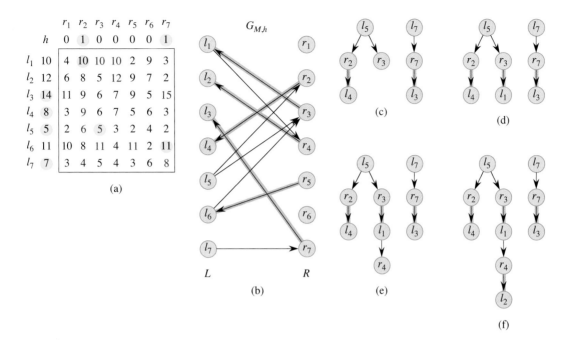

	h	r_1	r_2	r_3	r_4	r_5	r_6	r_7
		0	1	0	0	0	0	1
l_1	10	4	10	10	10	2	9	3
l_2	12	6	8	5	12	9	7	2
l_3	14	11	9	6	7	9	5	15
l_4	8	3	9	6	7	5	6	3
l_5	5	2	6	5	3	2	4	2
l_6	11	10	8	11	4	11	2	11
l_7	7	3	4	5	4	3	6	8

Figure 25.7   Updating the feasible vertex labeling and the directed equality subgraph $G_{M,h}$ when the queue becomes empty before finding an M-augmenting path. **(a)** With $\delta = 1$, the values of $l_3.h$, $l_4.h$, $l_5.h$, and $l_7.h$ decreased by 1 and $r_2.h$ and $r_7.h$ increased by 1. Edges (l_1, r_2) and (l_6, r_7) leave $G_{M,h}$, and edge (l_5, r_3) enters. These changes are highlighted in yellow. **(b)** The resulting directed equality subgraph $G_{M,h}$. **(c)–(f)** With edge (l_5, r_3) added to the breadth-first forest and r_3 added to the queue, the breadth-first search continues until the queue once again becomes empty in part (f).

by 2, and Figure 25.10(b) shows the resulting directed equality subgraph $G_{M,h}$. Part (c) shows that edge (l_3, r_1) is added to the breadth-first forest. Since r_1 is an unmatched vertex, the search terminates, having found the M-augmenting path $\langle (l_7, r_7), (r_7, l_3), (l_3, r_1) \rangle$, highlighted in orange. If r_1 had been matched, vertex r_5 would also have been added to the breadth-first forest, with any of l_2, l_4, or l_5 as its parent.

After updating the matching M, the algorithm arrives at the perfect matching shown for the equality subgraph G_h in Figure 25.11. By Theorem 25.14, the edges in M form an optimal solution to the original assignment problem given in the matrix. Here, the weights of edges $(l_1, r_6), (l_2, r_4), (l_3, r_1), (l_4, r_2), (l_5, r_3), (l_6, r_5)$, and (l_7, r_7) sum to 65, which is the maximum weight of any matching.

The weight of the maximum-weight matching equals the sum of all the feasible vertex labels. These problems—maximizing the weight of a matching and mini-

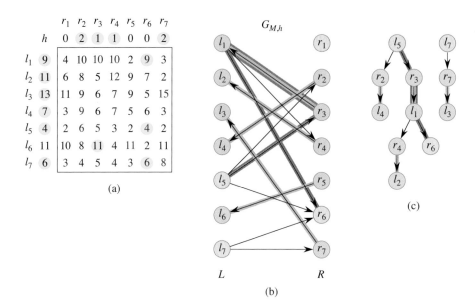

	h	r_1	r_2	r_3	r_4	r_5	r_6	r_7
		0	2	1	1	0	0	2
l_1	9	4	10	10	10	2	9	3
l_2	11	6	8	5	12	9	7	2
l_3	13	11	9	6	7	9	5	15
l_4	7	3	9	6	7	5	6	3
l_5	4	2	6	5	3	2	4	2
l_6	11	10	8	11	4	11	2	11
l_7	6	3	4	5	4	3	6	8

(a)

(b)

(c)

Figure 25.8 Another update to the feasible vertex labeling and directed equality subgraph $G_{M,h}$ because the queue became empty before finding an M-augmenting path. **(a)** With $\delta = 1$, the values of $l_1.h$, $l_2.h$, $l_3.h$, $l_4.h$, $l_5.h$, and $l_7.h$ decrease by 1, and $r_2.h$, $r_3.h$, $r_4.h$, and $r_7.h$ increase by 1. Edge (l_6, r_3) leaves $G_{M,h}$, and edges (l_1, r_6), (l_5, r_6) and (l_7, r_6) enter. **(b)** The resulting directed equality subgraph $G_{M,h}$. **(c)** With edge (l_1, r_6) added to the breadth-first forest and r_6 unmatched, the search terminates, having found the M-augmenting path $\langle (l_5, r_3), (r_3, l_1), (l_1, r_6) \rangle$, highlighted in orange in parts (b) and (c).

mizing the sum of the feasible vertex labels—are "duals" of each other, in a similar vein to how the value of a maximum flow equals the capacity of a minimum cut. Section 29.3 explores duality in more depth.

The Hungarian algorithm

The procedure HUNGARIAN on page 737 and its subroutine FIND-AUGMENTING-PATH on page 738 follow the steps we have just seen. The third property in Lemma 25.15 ensures that in line 23 of FIND-AUGMENTING-PATH the queue Q is nonempty. The pseudocode uses the attribute π to indicate predecessor vertices in the breadth-first forest. Instead of coloring vertices, as in the BFS procedure on page 556, the search puts the discovered vertices into the sets F_L and F_R. Because the Hungarian algorithm does not need breadth-first distances, the pseudocode omits the d attribute computed by the BFS procedure.

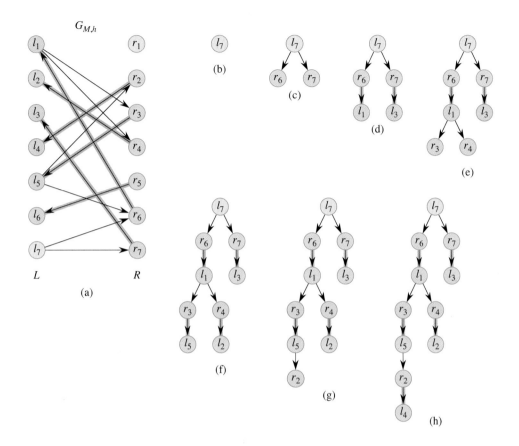

Figure 25.9 **(a)** The new matching M and the new directed equality subgraph $G_{M,h}$ after updating the matching in Figure 25.8 with the M-augmenting path in Figure 25.8 parts (b) and (c). **(b)–(h)** Successive versions of the breadth-first forest F in a new breadth-first search with root l_7. After the vertex l_4 in part (h) has been removed from the queue, the queue becomes empty before the search discovers an unmatched vertex in R.

Now, let's see why the Hungarian algorithm runs in $O(n^4)$ time, where $|V| = n/2$ and $|E| = n^2$ in the original graph G. (Below we outline how to reduce the running time to $O(n^3)$.) You can go through the pseudocode of HUNGARIAN to verify that lines 1–6 and 11 take $O(n^2)$ time. The **while** loop of lines 7–10 iterates at most n times, since each iteration increases the size of the matching M by 1. Each test in line 7 can take constant time by just checking whether $|M| < n$, each update of M in line 9 takes $O(n)$ time, and the updates in line 10 take $O(n^2)$ time.

To achieve the $O(n^4)$ time bound, it remains to show that each call of FIND-AUGMENTING-PATH runs in $O(n^3)$ time. Let's call each execution of lines 10–22

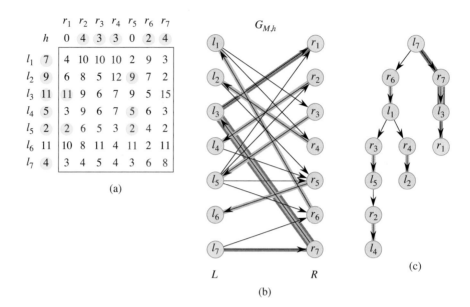

	h	r_1	r_2	r_3	r_4	r_5	r_6	r_7
		0	4	3	3	0	2	4
l_1	7	4	10	10	10	2	9	3
l_2	9	6	8	5	12	9	7	2
l_3	11	11	9	6	7	9	5	15
l_4	5	3	9	6	7	5	6	3
l_5	2	2	6	5	3	2	4	2
l_6	11	10	8	11	4	11	2	11
l_7	4	3	4	5	4	3	6	8

(a)

$G_{M,h}$

(b)

(c)

Figure 25.10 Updating the feasible vertex labeling and directed equality subgraph $G_{M,h}$. **(a)** Here, $\delta = 2$, so the values of $l_1.h$, $l_2.h$, $l_3.h$, $l_4.h$, $l_5.h$, and $l_7.h$ decreased by 2, and the values of $r_2.h$, $r_3.h$, $r_4.h$, $r_6.h$, and $r_7.h$ increased by 2. Edges (l_2, r_5), (l_3, r_1), (l_4, r_5), (l_5, r_1), and (l_5, r_5) enter $G_{M,h}$. **(b)** The resulting directed graph $G_{M,h}$. **(c)** With edge (l_3, r_1) added to the breadth-first forest and r_1 unmatched, the search terminates, having found the M-augmenting path $\langle (l_7, r_7), (r_7, l_3), (l_3, r_1) \rangle$, highlighted in orange in parts (b) and (c).

a *growth step*. Ignoring the growth steps, you can verify that FIND-AUGMENTING-PATH is a breadth-first search. With the sets F_L and F_R represented appropriately, the breadth-first search takes $O(V + E) = O(n^2)$ time. Within a call of FIND-AUGMENTING-PATH, at most n growth steps can occur, since each growth step is guaranteed to discover at least one vertex in R. Since there are at most n^2 edges in $G_{M,h}$, the **for** loop of lines 16–22 iterates at most n^2 times per call of FIND-AUGMENTING-PATH. The bottleneck is lines 10 and 15, which take $O(n^2)$ time, so that FIND-AUGMENTING-PATH takes $O(n^3)$ time.

Exercise 25.3-5 asks you to show that reconstructing the directed equality subgraph $G_{M,h}$ in line 15 is actually unnecessary, so that its cost can be eliminated. Reducing the cost of computing δ in line 10 to $O(n)$ takes a little more effort and is the subject of Problem 25-2. With these changes, each call of FIND-AUGMENTING-PATH takes $O(n^2)$ time, so that the Hungarian algorithm runs in $O(n^3)$ time.

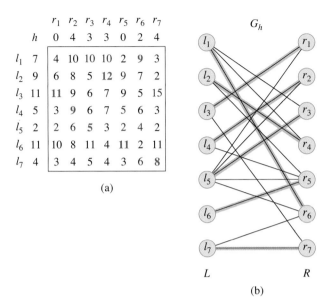

		r_1	r_2	r_3	r_4	r_5	r_6	r_7
h		0	4	3	3	0	2	4
l_1	7	4	10	10	10	2	9	3
l_2	9	6	8	5	12	9	7	2
l_3	11	11	9	6	7	9	5	15
l_4	5	3	9	6	7	5	6	3
l_5	2	2	6	5	3	2	4	2
l_6	11	10	8	11	4	11	2	11
l_7	4	3	4	5	4	3	6	8

(a)

(b)

Figure 25.11   The final matching, shown for the equality subgraph G_h with blue edges and blue entries in the matrix. The weights of the edges in the matching sum to 65, which is the maximum for any matching in the original complete bipartite graph G, as well as the sum of all the final feasible vertex labels.

HUNGARIAN(G)

```
 1  for each vertex l ∈ L
 2      l.h = max {w(l, r) : r ∈ R}   // from equation (25.1)
 3  for each vertex r ∈ R
 4      r.h = 0                        // from equation (25.2)
 5  let M be any matching in Gₕ (such as the matching returned by
        GREEDY-BIPARTITE-MATCHING)
 6  from G, M, and h, form the equality subgraph Gₕ
        and the directed equality subgraph G_{M,h}
 7  while M is not a perfect matching in Gₕ
 8      P = FIND-AUGMENTING-PATH(G_{M,h})
 9      M = M ⊕ P
10      update the equality subgraph Gₕ
            and the directed equality subgraph G_{M,h}
11  return M
```

FIND-AUGMENTING-PATH($G_{M,h}$)

```
 1  Q = ∅
 2  F_L = ∅
 3  F_R = ∅
 4  for each unmatched vertex l ∈ L
 5      l.π = NIL
 6      ENQUEUE(Q, l)
 7      F_L = F_L ∪ {l}        // forest F starts with unmatched vertices in L
 8  repeat
 9      if Q is empty          // ran out of vertices to search from?
10          δ = min {l.h + r.h − w(l, r) : l ∈ F_L and r ∈ R − F_R}
11          for each vertex l ∈ F_L
12              l.h = l.h − δ      // relabel according to equation (25.5)
13          for each vertex r ∈ F_R
14              r.h = r.h + δ      // relabel according to equation (25.5)
15          from G, M, and h, form a new directed equality graph G_{M,h}
16          for each new edge (l, r) in G_{M,h}      // continue search with new edges
17              if r ∉ F_R
18                  r.π = l                          // discover r, add it to F
19                  if r is unmatched
20                      an M-augmenting path has been found
                            (exit the repeat loop)
21                  else ENQUEUE(Q, r)      // can search from r later
22                      F_R = F_R ∪ {r}
23      u = DEQUEUE(Q)                        // search from u
24      for each neighbor v of u in G_{M,h}
25          if v ∈ L
26              v.π = u
27              F_L = F_L ∪ {v}              // discover v, add it to F
28              ENQUEUE(Q, v)                // can search from v later
29          elseif v ∉ F_R                   // v ∈ R, do same as lines 18–22
30              v.π = u
31              if v is unmatched
32                  an M-augmenting path has been found
                        (exit the repeat loop)
33              else ENQUEUE(Q, v)
34                  F_R = F_R ∪ {v}
35  until an M-augmenting path has been found
36  using the predecessor attributes π, construct an M-augmenting path P
        by tracing back from the unmatched vertex in R
37  return P
```

Exercises

25.3-1
The FIND-AUGMENTING-PATH procedure checks in two places (lines 19 and 31) whether a vertex it discovers in R is unmatched. Show how to rewrite the pseudocode so that it checks for an unmatched vertex in R in only one place. What is the downside of doing so?

25.3-2
Show that for any bipartite graph, the GREEDY-BIPARTITE-MATCHING procedure on page 726 returns a matching at least half the size of a maximum matching.

25.3-3
Show that if an edge (l, r) belongs to the directed equality subgraph $G_{M,h}$ but is not a member of $G_{M,h'}$, where h' is given by equation (25.5), then $l \in L - F_L$ and $r \in F_R$ at the time that h' is computed.

25.3-4
At line 29 in the FIND-AUGMENTING-PATH procedure, it has already been established that $v \in R$. This line checks to see whether v is already discovered by testing whether $v \in F_R$. Why doesn't the procedure need to check whether v is already discovered for the case when $v \in L$, in lines 26–28?

25.3-5
Professor Hrabosky asserts that the directed equality subgraph $G_{M,h}$ must be constructed and maintained by the Hungarian algorithm, so that line 6 of HUNGARIAN and line 15 of FIND-AUGMENTING-PATH are required. Argue that the professor is incorrect by showing how to determine whether an edge belongs to $E_{M,h}$ without explicitly constructing $G_{M,h}$.

25.3-6
How can you modify the Hungarian algorithm to find a matching of vertices in L to vertices in R that minimizes, rather than maximizes, the sum of the edge weights in the matching?

25.3-7
How can an assignment problem with $|L| \neq |R|$ be modified so that the Hungarian algorithm solves it?

Problems

25-1   *Perfect matchings in a regular bipartite graph*

a. Problem 20-3 asked about Euler tours in directed graphs. Prove that a connected, *undirected* graph $G = (V, E)$ has an Euler tour—a cycle traversing each edge exactly once, though it may visit a vertex multiple times—if and only if the degree of every vertex in V is even.

b. Assuming that G is connected, undirected, and every vertex in V has even degree, give an $O(E)$-time algorithm to find an Euler tour of G, as in Problem 20-3(b).

c. Exercise 25.1-6 states that if $G = (V, E)$ is a d-regular bipartite graph, then it contains d disjoint perfect matchings. Suppose that d is an exact power of 2. Give an algorithm to find all d disjoint perfect matchings in a d-regular bipartite graph in $\Theta(E \lg d)$ time.

25-2   *Reducing the running time of the Hungarian algorithm to $O(n^3)$*

In this problem, you will show how to reduce the running time of the Hungarian algorithm from $O(n^4)$ to $O(n^3)$ by showing how to reduce the running time of the FIND-AUGMENTING-PATH procedure from $O(n^3)$ to $O(n^2)$. Exercise 25.3-5 demonstrates that line 6 of HUNGARIAN and line 15 of FIND-AUGMENTING-PATH are unnecessary. Now you will show how to reduce the running time of each execution of line 10 in FIND-AUGMENTING-PATH to $O(n)$.

For each vertex $r \in R - F_R$, define a new attribute $r.\sigma$, where

$$r.\sigma = \min \{l.h + r.h - w(l, r) : l \in F_L\} \ .$$

That is, $r.\sigma$ indicates how close r is to being adjacent to some vertex $l \in F_L$ in the directed equality subgraph $G_{m,h}$. Initially, before placing any vertices into F_L, set $r.\sigma$ to ∞ for all $r \in R$.

a. Show how to compute δ in line 10 in $O(n)$ time, based on the σ attribute.

b. Show how to update all the σ attributes in $O(n)$ time after δ has been computed.

c. Show that updating all the σ attributes when F_L changes takes $O(n^2)$ time per call of FIND-AUGMENTING-PATH.

d. Conclude that the HUNGARIAN procedure can be implemented to run in $O(n^3)$ time.

25-3 *Other matching problems*

The Hungarian algorithm finds a maximum-weight perfect matching in a complete bipartite graph. It is possible to use the Hungarian algorithm to solve problems in other graphs by modifying the input graph, running the Hungarian algorithm, and then possibly modifying the output. Show how to solve the following matching problems in this manner.

a. Give an algorithm to find a maximum-weight matching in a weighted bipartite graph that is not necessarily complete and with all edge weights positive.

b. Redo part (a), but with edge weights allowed to also be 0 or negative.

c. A *cycle cover* in a directed graph, not necessarily bipartite, is a set of edge-disjoint directed cycles such that each vertex lies on at most one cycle. Given nonnegative edge weights $w(u, v)$, let C be the set of edges in a cycle cover, and define $w(C) = \sum_{(u,v) \in C} w(u, v)$ to be the weight of the cycle cover. Give an algorithm to find a maximum-weight cycle cover.

25-4 *Fractional matchings*

It is possible to define a *fractional matching*. Given a graph $G = (V, E)$, we define a fractional matching x as a function $x : E \rightarrow [0, 1]$ (real numbers between 0 and 1, inclusive) such that for every vertex $u \in V$, we have $\sum_{(u,v) \in E} x(u, v) \leq 1$. The value of a fractional matching is $\sum_{(u,v) \in E} x(u, v)$. The definition of a fractional matching is identical to that of a matching, except that a matching has the additional constraint that $x(u, v) \in \{0, 1\}$ for all edges $(u, v) \in E$. Given a graph, we let M^* denote a maximum matching and x^* denote a fractional matching with maximum value.

a. Argue that, for any bipartite graph, we must have $\sum_{(u,v) \in E} x^*(u, v) \geq |M^*|$.

b. Prove that, for any bipartite graph, we must have $\sum_{(u,v) \in E} x^*(e) \leq |M^*|$. (*Hint:* Give an algorithm that converts a fractional matching with an integer value to a matching.) Conclude that the maximum value of a fractional matching in a bipartite graph is the same as the size of the maximum cardinality matching.

c. We can define a fractional matching in a weighted graph in the same manner: the value of the matching is now $\sum_{(u,v) \in E} w(u, v)x(u, v)$. Extend the results of the previous parts to show that in a weighted bipartite graph, the maximum value of a weighted fractional matching is equal to the value of a maximum weighted matching.

d. In a general graph, the analogous results do not necessarily hold. Give an example of a small graph that is not bipartite for which the fractional matching with maximum value is not a maximum matching.

25-5 *Computing vertex labels*

You are given a complete bipartite graph $G = (V, E)$ with edge weights $w(l, r)$ for all $(l, r) \in E$. You are also given a maximum-weight perfect matching M^* for G. You wish to compute a feasible vertex labeling h such that M^* is a perfect matching in the equality subgraph G_h. That is, you want to compute a labeling h of vertices such that

$$l.h + r.h \geq w(l, r) \quad \text{for all } l \in L \text{ and } r \in R , \tag{25.6}$$

$$l.h + r.h = w(l, r) \quad \text{for all } (l, r) \in M^* . \tag{25.7}$$

(Requirement (25.6) holds for all edges, and the stronger requirement (25.7) holds for all edges in M^*.) Give an algorithm to compute the feasible vertex labeling h, and prove that it is correct. (*Hint:* Use the similarity between conditions (25.6) and (25.7) and some of the properties of shortest paths proved in Chapter 22, in particular the triangle inequality (Lemma 22.10) and the convergence property (Lemma 22.14).))

Chapter notes

Matching algorithms have a long history and have been central to many breakthroughs in algorithm design and analysis. The book by Lovász and Plummer [306] is an excellent reference on matching problems, and the chapter on matching in the book by Ahuja, Magnanti and Orlin [10] also has extensive references.

The Hopcroft-Karp algorithm is by Hopcroft and Karp [224]. Madry [308] gave an $\widetilde{O}(E^{10/7})$-time algorithm, which is asymptotically faster than Hopcroft-Karp for sparse graphs.

Corollary 25.4 is due to Berge [53], and it also holds in graphs that are not bipartite. Matching in general graphs requires more complicated algorithms. The first polynomial-time algorithm, running in $O(V^4)$ time, is due to Edmonds [130] (in a paper that also introduced the notion of a polynomial-time algorithm). Like the bipartite case, this algorithm also uses augmenting paths, although the algorithm for finding augmenting paths in general graphs is more involved than the one for bipartite graphs. Subsequently, several $O(\sqrt{V}E)$-time algorithms appeared, including ones by Gabow and Tarjan [168] as part of an algorithm for weighted matching and a simpler one by Gabow [164].

The Hungarian algorithm is described in the book by Bondy and Murty [67] and is based on work by Kuhn [273] and Munkres [337]. Kuhn adopted the name "Hungarian algorithm" because the algorithm derived from work by the Hungarian mathematicians D. Kőnig and J. Egervéry. The algorithm is an early example of a primal-dual algorithm. A faster algorithm that runs in $O(\sqrt{V} E \log(VW))$ time, where the edge weights are integers from 0 to W, was given by Gabow and Tarjan [167], and an algorithm with the same time bound for maximum-weight matching in general graphs was given by Duan, Pettie, and Su [127].

The stable-marriage problem was first defined and analyzed by Gale and Shapley [169]. The stable-marriage problem has numerous variants. The books by Gusfield and Irving [203], Knuth [266], and Manlove [313] serve as excellent sources for cataloging and solving them.

Part VII   Selected Topics

Introduction

This part contains a selection of algorithmic topics that extend and complement earlier material in this book. Some chapters introduce new models of computation such as circuits or parallel computers. Others cover specialized domains such as matrices or number theory. The last two chapters discuss some of the known limitations to the design of efficient algorithms and introduce techniques for coping with those limitations.

Chapter 26 presents an algorithmic model for parallel computing based on task-parallel computing, and more specifically, fork-join parallelism. The chapter introduces the basics of the model, showing how to quantify parallelism in terms of the measures of work and span. It then investigates several interesting fork-join algorithms, including algorithms for matrix multiplication and merge sorting.

An algorithm that receives its input over time, rather than having the entire input available at the start, is called an "online" algorithm. Chapter 27 examines techniques used in online algorithms, starting with the "toy" problem of how long to wait for an elevator before taking the stairs. It then studies the "move-to-front" heuristic for maintaining a linked list and finishes with the online version of the caching problem we saw back in Section 15.4. The analyses of these online algorithms are remarkable in that they prove that these algorithms, which do not know their future inputs, perform within a constant factor of optimal algorithms that know the future inputs.

Chapter 28 studies efficient algorithms for operating on matrices. It presents two general methods—LU decomposition and LUP decomposition—for solving linear equations by Gaussian elimination in $O(n^3)$ time. It also shows that matrix inversion and matrix multiplication can be performed equally fast. The chapter concludes by showing how to compute a least-squares approximate solution when a set of linear equations has no exact solution.

Chapter 29 studies how to model problems as linear programs, where the goal is to maximize or minimize an objective, given limited resources and competing constraints. Linear programming arises in a variety of practical application areas. The chapter also addresses the concept of "duality" which, by establishing that a maximization problem and minimization problem have the same objective value, helps to show that solutions to each are optimal.

Chapter 30 studies operations on polynomials and shows how to use a well-known signal-processing technique—the fast Fourier transform (FFT)—to multiply two degree-n polynomials in $O(n \lg n)$ time. It also derives a parallel circuit to compute the FFT.

Chapter 31 presents number-theoretic algorithms. After reviewing elementary number theory, it presents Euclid's algorithm for computing greatest common divisors. Next, it studies algorithms for solving modular linear equations and for raising one number to a power modulo another number. Then, it explores an important application of number-theoretic algorithms: the RSA public-key cryptosystem. This cryptosystem can be used not only to encrypt messages so that an adversary cannot read them, but also to provide digital signatures. The chapter finishes with the Miller-Rabin randomized primality test, which enables finding large primes efficiently—an essential requirement for the RSA system.

Chapter 32 studies the problem of finding all occurrences of a given pattern string in a given text string, a problem that arises frequently in text-editing programs. After examining the naive approach, the chapter presents an elegant approach due to Rabin and Karp. Then, after showing an efficient solution based on finite automata, the chapter presents the Knuth-Morris-Pratt algorithm, which modifies the automaton-based algorithm to save space by cleverly preprocessing the pattern. The chapter finishes by studying suffix arrays, which can not only find a pattern in a text string, but can do quite a bit more, such as finding the longest repeated substring in a text and finding the longest common substring appearing in two texts.

Chapter 33 examines three algorithms within the expansive field of machine learning. Machine-learning algorithms are designed to take in vast amounts of data, devise hypotheses about patterns in the data, and test these hypotheses. The chapter starts with k-means clustering, which groups data elements into k classes based on how similar they are to each other. It then shows how to use the technique of multiplicative weights to make predictions accurately based on a set of "experts" of varying quality. Perhaps surprisingly, even without knowing which experts are reliable and which are not, you can predict almost as accurately as the most reliable expert. The chapter finishes with gradient descent, an optimization technique that finds a local minimum value for a function. Gradient descent has many applications, including finding parameter settings for many machine-learning models.

Chapter 34 concerns NP-complete problems. Many interesting computational problems are NP-complete, but no polynomial-time algorithm is known for solving any of them. This chapter presents techniques for determining when a problem is NP-complete, using them to prove several classic problems NP-complete: determining whether a graph has a hamiltonian cycle (a cycle that includes every vertex), determining whether a boolean formula is satisfiable (whether there exists an assignment of boolean values to its variables that causes the formula to evaluate to TRUE), and determining whether a given set of numbers has a subset that adds up to a given target value. The chapter also proves that the famous traveling-salesperson problem (find a shortest route that starts and ends at the same location and visits each of a set of locations once) is NP-complete.

Chapter 35 shows how to find approximate solutions to NP-complete problems efficiently by using approximation algorithms. For some NP-complete problems, approximate solutions that are near optimal are quite easy to produce, but for others even the best approximation algorithms known work progressively more poorly as the problem size increases. Then, there are some problems for which investing increasing amounts of computation time yields increasingly better approximate solutions. This chapter illustrates these possibilities with the vertex-cover problem (unweighted and weighted versions), an optimization version of 3-CNF satisfiability, the traveling-salesperson problem, the set-covering problem, and the subset-sum problem.

26   Parallel Algorithms

The vast majority of algorithms in this book are *serial algorithms* suitable for running on a uniprocessor computer that executes only one instruction at a time. This chapter extends our algorithmic model to encompass *parallel algorithms*, where multiple instructions can execute simultaneously. Specifically, we'll explore the elegant model of task-parallel algorithms, which are amenable to algorithmic design and analysis. Our study focuses on fork-join parallel algorithms, the most basic and best understood kind of task-parallel algorithm. Fork-join parallel algorithms can be expressed cleanly using simple linguistic extensions to ordinary serial code. Moreover, they can be implemented efficiently in practice.

Parallel computers—computers with multiple processing units—are ubiquitous. Handheld, laptop, desktop, and cloud machines are all *multicore computers*, or simply, *multicores*, containing multiple processing "cores." Each processing core is a full-fledged processor that can directly access any location in a common *shared memory*. Multicores can be aggregated into larger systems, such as clusters, by using a network to interconnect them. These multicore clusters usually have a *distributed memory*, where one multicore's memory cannot be accessed directly by a processor in another multicore. Instead, the processor must explicitly send a message over the cluster network to a processor in the remote multicore to request any data it requires. The most powerful clusters are supercomputers, comprising many thousands of multicores. But since shared-memory programming tends to be conceptually easier than distributed-memory programming, and multicore machines are widely available, this chapter focuses on parallel algorithms for multicores.

One approach to programming multicores is *thread parallelism*. This processor-centric parallel-programming model employs a software abstraction of "virtual processors," or *threads* that share a common memory. Each thread maintains its own program counter and can execute code independently of the other threads. The operating system loads a thread onto a processing core for execution and switches it out when another thread needs to run.

Unfortunately, programming a shared-memory parallel computer using threads tends to be difficult and error-prone. One reason is that it can be complicated to dynamically partition the work among the threads so that each thread receives approximately the same load. For any but the simplest of applications, the programmer must use complex communication protocols to implement a scheduler that load-balances the work.

Task-parallel programming

The difficulty of thread programming has led to the creation of *task-parallel platforms*, which provide a layer of software on top of threads to coordinate, schedule, and manage the processors of a multicore. Some task-parallel platforms are built as runtime libraries, but others provide full-fledged parallel languages with compiler and runtime support.

Task-parallel programming allows parallelism to be specified in a "processor-oblivious" fashion, where the programmer identifies what computational tasks may run in parallel but does not indicate which thread or processor performs the task. Thus, the programmer is freed from worrying about communication protocols, load balancing, and other vagaries of thread programming. The task-parallel platform contains a scheduler, which automatically load-balances the tasks across the processors, thereby greatly simplifying the programmer's chore. *Task-parallel algorithms* provide a natural extension to ordinary serial algorithms, allowing performance to be reasoned about mathematically using "work/span analysis."

Fork-join parallelism

Although the functionality of task-parallel environments is still evolving and increasing, almost all support *fork-join parallelism*, which is typically embodied in two linguistic features: *spawning* and *parallel loops*. Spawning allows a subroutine to be "forked": executed like a subroutine call, except that the caller can continue to execute while the spawned subroutine computes its result. A parallel loop is like an ordinary **for** loop, except that multiple iterations of the loop can execute at the same time.

Fork-join parallel algorithms employ spawning and parallel loops to describe parallelism. A key aspect of this parallel model, inherited from the task-parallel model but different from the thread model, is that the programmer does not specify which tasks in a computation *must* run in parallel, only which tasks *may* run in parallel. The underlying runtime system uses threads to load-balance the tasks across the processors. This chapter investigates parallel algorithms described in the fork-join model, as well as how the underlying runtime system can schedule task-parallel computations (which include fork-join computations) efficiently.

Fork-join parallelism offers several important advantages:

- The fork-join programming model is a simple extension of the familiar serial programming model used in most of this book. To describe a fork-join parallel algorithm, the pseudocode in this book needs just three added keywords: **parallel**, **spawn**, and **sync**. Deleting these parallel keywords from the parallel pseudocode results in ordinary serial pseudocode for the same problem, which we call the "serial projection" of the parallel algorithm.

- The underlying task-parallel model provides a theoretically clean way to quantify parallelism based on the notions of "work" and "span."

- Spawning allows many divide-and-conquer algorithms to be parallelized naturally. Moreover, just as serial divide-and-conquer algorithms lend themselves to analysis using recurrences, so do parallel algorithms in the fork-join model.

- The fork-join programming model is faithful to how multicore programming has been evolving in practice. A growing number of multicore environments support one variant or another of fork-join parallel programming, including Cilk [290, 291, 383, 396], Habancro-Java [466], the Java Fork-Join Framework [279], OpenMP [81], Task Parallel Library [289], Threading Building Blocks [376], and X10 [82].

Section 26.1 introduces parallel pseudocode, shows how the execution of a task-parallel computation can be modeled as a directed acyclic graph, and presents the metrics of work, span, and parallelism, which you can use to analyze parallel algorithms. Section 26.2 investigates how to multiply matrices in parallel, and Section 26.3 tackles the tougher problem of designing an efficient parallel merge sort.

26.1   The basics of fork-join parallelism

Our exploration of parallel programming begins with the problem of computing Fibonacci numbers recursively in parallel. We'll look at a straightforward serial Fibonacci calculation, which, although inefficient, serves as a good illustration of how to express parallelism in pseudocode.

Recall that the Fibonacci numbers are defined by equation (3.31) on page 69:

$$F_i = \begin{cases} 0 & \text{if } i = 0\,, \\ 1 & \text{if } i = 1\,, \\ F_{i-1} + F_{i-2} & \text{if } i \geq 2\,. \end{cases}$$

To calculate the nth Fibonacci number recursively, you could use the ordinary serial algorithm in the procedure FIB on the facing page. You would not really want to compute large Fibonacci numbers this way, because this computation does needless repeated work, but parallelizing it can be instructive.

FIB(n)

1 **if** $n \leq 1$
2   **return** n
3 **else** $x = $ FIB($n - 1$)
4      $y = $ FIB($n - 2$)
5   **return** $x + y$

To analyze this algorithm, let $T(n)$ denote the running time of FIB(n). Since FIB(n) contains two recursive calls plus a constant amount of extra work, we obtain the recurrence

$$T(n) = T(n - 1) + T(n - 2) + \Theta(1) .$$

This recurrence has solution $T(n) = \Theta(F_n)$, which we can establish by using the substitution method (see Section 4.3). To show that $T(n) = O(F_n)$, we'll adopt the inductive hypothesis that $T(n) \leq a F_n - b$, where $a > 1$ and $b > 0$ are constants. Substituting, we obtain

$$
\begin{aligned}
T(n) &\leq (a F_{n-1} - b) + (a F_{n-2} - b) + \Theta(1) \\
&= a(F_{n-1} + F_{n-2}) - 2b + \Theta(1) \\
&\leq a F_n - b ,
\end{aligned}
$$

if we choose b large enough to dominate the upper-bound constant in the $\Theta(1)$ term. We can then choose a large enough to upper-bound the $\Theta(1)$ base case for small n. To show that $T(n) = \Omega(F_n)$, we use the inductive hypothesis $T(n) \geq a F_n - b$. Substituting and following reasoning similar to the asymptotic upper-bound argument, we establish this hypothesis by choosing b smaller than the lower-bound constant in the $\Theta(1)$ term and a small enough to lower-bound the $\Theta(1)$ base case for small n. Theorem 3.1 on page 56 then establishes that $T(n) = \Theta(F_n)$, as desired. Since $F_n = \Theta(\phi^n)$, where $\phi = (1 + \sqrt{5})/2$ is the golden ratio, by equation (3.34) on page 69, it follows that

$$T(n) = \Theta(\phi^n) . \tag{26.1}$$

Thus this procedure is a particularly slow way to compute Fibonacci numbers, since it runs in exponential time. (See Problem 31-3 on page 954 for faster ways.)

Let's see why the algorithm is inefficient. Figure 26.1 shows the tree of recursive procedure instances created when computing F_6 with the FIB procedure. The call to FIB(6) recursively calls FIB(5) and then FIB(4). But, the call to FIB(5) also

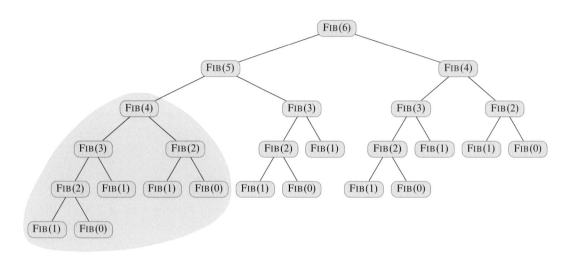

Figure 26.1   The invocation tree for FIB(6). Each node in the tree represents a procedure instance whose children are the procedure instances it calls during its execution. Since each instance of FIB with the same argument does the same work to produce the same result, the inefficiency of this algorithm for computing the Fibonacci numbers can be seen by the vast number of repeated calls to compute the same thing. The portion of the tree shaded blue appears in task-parallel form in Figure 26.2.

results in a call to FIB(4). Both instances of FIB(4) return the same result ($F_4 = 3$). Since the FIB procedure does not memoize (recall the definition of "memoize" from page 368), the second call to FIB(4) replicates the work that the first call performs, which is wasteful.

Although the FIB procedure is a poor way to compute Fibonacci numbers, it can help us warm up to parallelism concepts. Perhaps the most basic concept is to understand is that if two parallel tasks operate on entirely different data, then—absent other interference—they each produce the same outcomes when executed at the same time as when they run serially one after the other. Within FIB(n), for example, the two recursive calls in line 3 to FIB($n-1$) and in line 4 to FIB($n-2$) can safely execute in parallel because the computation performed by one in no way affects the other.

Parallel keywords

The P-FIB procedure on the next page computes Fibonacci numbers, but using the *parallel keywords* **spawn** and **sync** to indicate parallelism in the pseudocode.

If the keywords **spawn** and **sync** are deleted from P-FIB, the resulting pseudocode text is identical to FIB (other than renaming the procedure in the header

```
P-FIB(n)

1  if n ≤ 1
2      return n
3  else x = spawn P-FIB(n − 1)    // don't wait for subroutine to return
4      y = P-FIB(n − 2)            // in parallel with spawned subroutine
5      sync                       // wait for spawned subroutine to finish
6      return x + y
```

and in the two recursive calls). We define the *serial projection*[1] of a parallel algorithm to be the serial algorithm that results from ignoring the parallel directives, which in this case can be done by omitting the keywords **spawn** and **sync**. For **parallel for** loops, which we'll see later on, we omit the keyword **parallel**. Indeed, our parallel pseudocode possesses the elegant property that its serial projection is always ordinary serial pseudocode to solve the same problem.

Semantics of parallel keywords

Spawning occurs when the keyword **spawn** precedes a procedure call, as in line 3 of P-FIB. The semantics of a spawn differs from an ordinary procedure call in that the procedure instance that executes the spawn—the *parent*—may continue to execute in parallel with the spawned subroutine—its *child*—instead of waiting for the child to finish, as would happen in a serial execution. In this case, while the spawned child is computing P-FIB$(n − 1)$, the parent may go on to compute P-FIB$(n−2)$ in line 4 in parallel with the spawned child. Since the P-FIB procedure is recursive, these two subroutine calls themselves create nested parallelism, as do their children, thereby creating a potentially vast tree of subcomputations, all executing in parallel.

The keyword **spawn** does not say, however, that a procedure *must* execute in parallel with its spawned children, only that it *may*. The parallel keywords express the *logical parallelism* of the computation, indicating which parts of the computation may proceed in parallel. At runtime, it is up to a *scheduler* to determine which subcomputations actually run in parallel by assigning them to available pro-

---

[1] In mathematics, a projection is an idempotent function, that is, a function f such that $f \circ f = f$. In this case, the function f maps the set $\mathcal{P}$ of fork-join programs to the set $\mathcal{P}_S \subset \mathcal{P}$ of serial programs, which are themselves fork-join programs with no parallelism. For a fork-join program $x \in \mathcal{P}$, since we have $f(f(x)) = f(x)$, the serial projection, as we have defined it, is indeed a mathematical projection.

cessors as the computation unfolds. We'll discuss the theory behind task-parallel schedulers shortly (on page 759).

A procedure cannot safely use the values returned by its spawned children until after it executes a **sync** statement, as in line 5. The keyword **sync** indicates that the procedure must wait as necessary for all its spawned children to finish before proceeding to the statement after the **sync**—the "join" of a fork-join parallel computation. The P-FIB procedure requires a **sync** before the **return** statement in line 6 to avoid the anomaly that would occur if x and y were summed before P-FIB$(n-1)$ had finished and its return value had been assigned to x. In addition to explicit join synchronization provided by the **sync** statement, it is convenient to assume that every procedure executes a **sync** implicitly before it returns, thus ensuring that all children finish before their parent finishes.

A graph model for parallel execution

It helps to view the execution of a parallel computation—the dynamic stream of runtime instructions executed by processors under the direction of a parallel program—as a directed acyclic graph $G = (V, E)$, called a *(parallel) trace*.[2] Conceptually, the vertices in V are executed instructions, and the edges in E represent dependencies between instructions, where $(u, v) \in E$ means that the parallel program required instruction u to execute before instruction v.

It's sometimes inconvenient, especially if we want to focus on the parallel structure of a computation, for a vertex of a trace to represent only one executed instruction. Consequently, if a chain of instructions contains no parallel or procedural control (no **spawn**, **sync**, procedure call, or **return**—via either an explicit **return** statement or the return that happens implicitly upon reaching the end of a procedure), we group the entire chain into a single *strand*. As an example, Figure 26.2 shows the trace that results from computing P-FIB(4) in the portion of Figure 26.1 shaded blue. Strands do not include instructions that involve parallel or procedural control. These control dependencies must be represented as edges in the trace.

When a parent procedure calls a child, the trace contains an edge (u, v) from the strand u in the parent that executes the call to the first strand v of the spawned child, as illustrated in Figure 26.2 by the edge from the orange strand in P-FIB(4) to the blue strand in P-FIB(2). When the last strand v' in the child returns, the trace contains an edge (v', u') to the strand u', where u' is the successor strand of u in the parent, as with the edge from the white strand in P-FIB(2) to the white strand in P-FIB(4).

---

[2] Also called a *computation dag* in the literature.

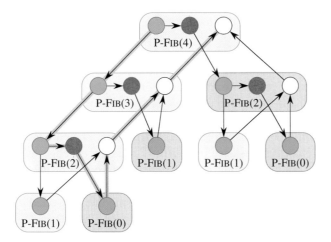

Figure 26.2   The trace of P-FIB(4) corresponding to the shaded portion of Figure 26.1. Each circle represents one strand, with blue circles representing any instructions executed in the part of the procedure (instance) up to the spawn of P-FIB($n - 1$) in line 3; orange circles representing the instructions executed in the part of the procedure that calls P-FIB($n - 2$) in line 4 up to the **sync** in line 5, where it suspends until the spawn of P-FIB($n - 1$) returns; and white circles representing the instructions executed in the part of the procedure after the **sync**, where it sums x and y, up to the point where it returns the result. Strands belonging to the same procedure are grouped into a rounded rectangle, blue for spawned procedures and tan for called procedures. Assuming that each strand takes unit time, the work is 17 time units, since there are 17 strands, and the span is 8 time units, since the critical path—shown with blue edges—contains 8 strands.

When the parent spawns a child, however, the trace is a little different. The edge (u, v) goes from parent to child as with a call, such as the edge from the blue strand in P-FIB(4) to the blue strand in P-FIB(3), but the trace contains another edge (u, u') as well, indicating that u's successor strand u' can continue to execute while v is executing. The edge from the blue strand in P-FIB(4) to the orange strand in P-FIB(4) illustrates one such edge. As with a call, there is an edge from the last strand v' in the child, but with a spawn, it no longer goes to u's successor. Instead, the edge is (v', x), where x is the strand immediately following the **sync** in the parent that ensures that the child has finished, as with the edge from the white strand in P-FIB(3) to the white strand in P-FIB(4).

You can figure out what parallel control created a particular trace. If a strand has two successors, one of them must have been spawned, and if a strand has multiple predecessors, the predecessors joined because of a **sync** statement. Thus, in the general case, the set V forms the set of strands, and the set E of directed edges represents dependencies between strands induced by parallel and procedural control. If G contains a directed path from strand u to strand v, we say that the two strands are *(logically) in series*. If there is no path in G either from u to v or from v to u, the strands are *(logically) in parallel*.

A fork-join parallel trace can be pictured as a dag of strands embedded in an *invocation tree* of procedure instances. For example, Figure 26.1 shows the invocation tree for FIB(6), which also serves as the invocation tree for P-FIB(6), the edges between procedure instances now representing either calls or spawns. Figure 26.2 zooms in on the subtree that is shaded blue, showing the strands that constitute each procedure instance in P-FIB(4). All directed edges connecting strands run either within a procedure or along undirected edges of the invocation tree in Figure 26.1. (More general task-parallel traces that are not fork-join traces may contain some directed edges that do not run along the undirected tree edges.)

Our analyses generally assume that parallel algorithms execute on an *ideal parallel computer*, which consists of a set of processors and a *sequentially consistent* shared memory. To understand sequential consistency, you first need to know that memory is accessed by *load instructions*, which copy data from a location in the memory to a register within a processor, and by *store instructions*, which copy data from a processor register to a location in the memory. A single line of pseudocode can entail several such instructions. For example, the line $x = y + z$ could result in load instructions to fetch each of y and z from memory into a processor, an instruction to add them together inside the processor, and a store instruction to place the result x back into memory. In a parallel computer, several processors might need to load or store at the same time. Sequential consistency means that even if multiple processors attempt to access the memory simultaneously, the shared memory behaves as if exactly one instruction from one of the processors is executed at a time, even though the actual transfer of data may happen at the same time. It is as if the instructions were executed one at a time sequentially according to some global linear order among all the processors that preserves the individual orders in which each processor executes its own instructions.

For task-parallel computations, which are scheduled onto processors automatically by a runtime system, the sequentially consistent shared memory behaves as if a parallel computation's executed instructions were executed one by one in the order of a topological sort (see Section 20.4) of its trace. That is, you can reason about the execution by imagining that the individual instructions (not generally the strands, which may aggregate many instructions) are interleaved in some linear order that preserves the partial order of the trace. Depending on scheduling, the linear order could vary from one run of the program to the next, but the behavior of any execution is always as if the instructions executed serially in a linear order consistent with the dependencies within the trace.

In addition to making assumptions about semantics, the ideal parallel-computer model makes some performance assumptions. Specifically, it assumes that each processor in the machine has equal computing power, and it ignores the cost of scheduling. Although this last assumption may sound optimistic, it turns out that for algorithms with sufficient "parallelism" (a term we'll define precisely a little later), the overhead of scheduling is generally minimal in practice.

Performance measures

We can gauge the theoretical efficiency of a task-parallel algorithm using *work/ span analysis*, which is based on two metrics: "work" and "span." The *work* of a task-parallel computation is the total time to execute the entire computation on one processor. In other words, the work is the sum of the times taken by each of the strands. If each strand takes unit time, the work is just the number of vertices in the trace. The *span* is the fastest possible time to execute the computation on an unlimited number of processors, which corresponds to the sum of the times taken by the strands along a longest path in the trace, where "longest" means that each strand is weighted by its execution time. Such a longest path is called the *critical path* of the trace, and thus the span is the weight of the longest (weighted) path in the trace. (Section 22.2, pages 617–619 shows how to find a critical path in a dag $G = (V, E)$ in $\Theta(V + E)$ time.) For a trace in which each strand takes unit time, the span equals the number of strands on the critical path. For example, the trace of Figure 26.2 has 17 vertices in all and 8 vertices on its critical path, so that if each strand takes unit time, its work is 17 time units and its span is 8 time units.

The actual running time of a task-parallel computation depends not only on its work and its span, but also on how many processors are available and how the scheduler allocates strands to processors. To denote the running time of a task-parallel computation on P processors, we subscript by P. For example, we might denote the running time of an algorithm on P processors by T_P. The work is the running time on a single processor, or T_1. The span is the running time if we could run each strand on its own processor—in other words, if we had an unlimited number of processors—and so we denote the span by T_∞.

The work and span provide lower bounds on the running time T_P of a task-parallel computation on P processors:

- In one step, an ideal parallel computer with P processors can do at most P units of work, and thus in T_P time, it can perform at most $P T_P$ work. Since the total work to do is T_1, we have $P T_P \geq T_1$. Dividing by P yields the *work law*:

$$T_P \geq T_1/P \ . \tag{26.2}$$

- A P-processor ideal parallel computer cannot run any faster than a machine with an unlimited number of processors. Looked at another way, a machine with an unlimited number of processors can emulate a P-processor machine by using just P of its processors. Thus, the *span law* follows:

$$T_P \geq T_\infty .\tag{26.3}$$

We define the *speedup* of a computation on P processors by the ratio T_1/T_P, which says how many times faster the computation runs on P processors than on one processor. By the work law, we have $T_P \geq T_1/P$, which implies that $T_1/T_P \leq P$. Thus, the speedup on a P-processor ideal parallel computer can be at most P. When the speedup is linear in the number of processors, that is, when $T_1/T_P = \Theta(P)$, the computation exhibits *linear speedup*. *Perfect linear speedup* occurs when $T_1/T_P = P$.

The ratio T_1/T_∞ of the work to the span gives the *parallelism* of the parallel computation. We can view the parallelism from three perspectives. As a ratio, the parallelism denotes the average amount of work that can be performed in parallel for each step along the critical path. As an upper bound, the parallelism gives the maximum possible speedup that can be achieved on any number of processors. Perhaps most important, the parallelism provides a limit on the possibility of attaining perfect linear speedup. Specifically, once the number of processors exceeds the parallelism, the computation cannot possibly achieve perfect linear speedup. To see this last point, suppose that $P > T_1/T_\infty$, in which case the span law implies that the speedup satisfies $T_1/T_P \leq T_1/T_\infty < P$. Moreover, if the number P of processors in the ideal parallel computer greatly exceeds the parallelism—that is, if $P \gg T_1/T_\infty$—then $T_1/T_P \ll P$, so that the speedup is much less than the number of processors. In other words, if the number of processors exceeds the parallelism, adding even more processors makes the speedup less perfect.

As an example, consider the computation P-FIB(4) in Figure 26.2, and assume that each strand takes unit time. Since the work is $T_1 = 17$ and the span is $T_\infty = 8$, the parallelism is $T_1/T_\infty = 17/8 = 2.125$. Consequently, achieving much more than double the performance is impossible, no matter how many processors execute the computation. For larger input sizes, however, we'll see that P-FIB(n) exhibits substantial parallelism.

We define the *(parallel) slackness* of a task-parallel computation executed on an ideal parallel computer with P processors to be the ratio $(T_1/T_\infty)/P = T_1/(PT_\infty)$, which is the factor by which the parallelism of the computation exceeds the number of processors in the machine. Restating the bounds on speedup, if the slackness is less than 1, perfect linear speedup is impossible, because $T_1/(PT_\infty) < 1$ and the span law imply that $T_1/T_P \leq T_1/T_\infty < P$. Indeed, as the slackness decreases from 1 and approaches 0, the speedup of the computation diverges further and further from perfect linear speedup. If the slackness is less than 1, additional parallelism in an algorithm can have a great impact on its execution efficiency. If the slackness is greater than 1, however, the work per processor is the limiting constraint. We'll see that as the slackness increases from 1, a good scheduler can achieve closer and closer to perfect linear speedup. But once the slackness is much greater than 1, the advantage of additional parallelism shows diminishing returns.

Scheduling

Good performance depends on more than just minimizing the work and span. The strands must also be scheduled efficiently onto the processors of the parallel machine. Our fork-join parallel-programming model provides no way for a programmer to specify which strands to execute on which processors. Instead, we rely on the runtime system's scheduler to map the dynamically unfolding computation to individual processors. In practice, the scheduler maps the strands to static threads, and the operating system schedules the threads on the processors themselves. But this extra level of indirection is unnecessary for our understanding of scheduling. We can just imagine that the scheduler maps strands to processors directly.

A task-parallel scheduler must schedule the computation without knowing in advance when procedures will be spawned or when they will finish—that is, it must operate *online*. Moreover, a good scheduler operates in a distributed fashion, where the threads implementing the scheduler cooperate to load-balance the computation. Provably good online, distributed schedulers exist, but analyzing them is complicated. Instead, to keep our analysis simple, we'll consider an online *centralized* scheduler that knows the global state of the computation at any moment.

In particular, we'll analyze *greedy schedulers*, which assign as many strands to processors as possible in each time step, never leaving a processor idle if there is work that can be done. We'll classify each step of a greedy scheduler as follows:

- *Complete step*: At least P strands are *ready* to execute, meaning that all strands on which they depend have finished execution. A greedy scheduler assigns any P of the ready strands to the processors, completely utilizing all the processor resources.

- *Incomplete step*: Fewer than P strands are ready to execute. A greedy scheduler assigns each ready strand to its own processor, leaving some processors idle for the step, but executing all the ready strands.

The work law tells us that the fastest running time T_P that we can hope for on P processors must be at least T_1/P. The span law tells us that the fastest possible running time must be at least T_∞. The following theorem shows that greedy scheduling is provably good in that it achieves the sum of these two lower bounds as an upper bound.

Theorem 26.1

On an ideal parallel computer with P processors, a greedy scheduler executes a task-parallel computation with work T_1 and span T_∞ in time

$$T_P \leq T_1/P + T_\infty \, . \tag{26.4}$$

Proof   Without loss of generality, assume that each strand takes unit time. (If necessary, replace each longer strand by a chain of unit-time strands.) We'll consider complete and incomplete steps separately.

In each complete step, the P processors together perform a total of P work. Thus, if the number of complete steps is k, the total work executing all the complete steps is kP. Since the greedy scheduler doesn't execute any strand more than once and only T_1 work needs to be performed, it follows that $kP \leq T_1$, from which we can conclude that the number k of complete steps is at most T_1/P.

Now, let's consider an incomplete step. Let G be the trace for the entire computation, let G' be the subtrace of G that has yet to be executed at the start of the incomplete step, and let G'' be the subtrace remaining to be executed after the incomplete step. Consider the set R of strands that are ready at the beginning of the incomplete step, where $|R| < P$. By definition, if a strand is ready, all its predecessors in trace G have executed. Thus the predecessors of strands in R do not belong to G'. A longest path in G' must necessarily start at a strand in R, since every other strand in G' has a predecessor and thus could not start a longest path. Because the greedy scheduler executes all ready strands during the incomplete step, the strands of G'' are exactly those in G' minus the strands in R. Consequently, the length of a longest path in G'' must be 1 less than the length of a longest path in G'. In other words, every incomplete step decreases the span of the trace remaining to be executed by 1. Hence, the number of incomplete steps can be at most T_∞.

Since each step is either complete or incomplete, the theorem follows.   ∎

The following corollary shows that a greedy scheduler always performs well.

Corollary 26.2

The running time T_P of any task-parallel computation scheduled by a greedy scheduler on a P-processor ideal parallel computer is within a factor of 2 of optimal.

Proof   Let T_P^* be the running time produced by an optimal scheduler on a machine with P processors, and let T_1 and T_∞ be the work and span of the computation, respectively. Since the work and span laws—inequalities (26.2) and (26.3)—give $T_P^* \geq \max\{T_1/P, T_\infty\}$, Theorem 26.1 implies that

$$\begin{aligned} T_P &\leq T_1/P + T_\infty \\ &\leq 2 \cdot \max\{T_1/P, T_\infty\} \\ &\leq 2T_P^* \, . \end{aligned}$$ ∎

The next corollary shows that, in fact, a greedy scheduler achieves near-perfect linear speedup on any task-parallel computation as the slackness grows.

Corollary 26.3

Let T_P be the running time of a task-parallel computation produced by a greedy scheduler on an ideal parallel computer with P processors, and let T_1 and T_∞ be the work and span of the computation, respectively. Then, if $P \ll T_1/T_\infty$, or equivalently, the parallel slackness is much greater than 1, we have $T_P \approx T_1/P$, a speedup of approximately P.

Proof   If we suppose that $P \ll T_1/T_\infty$, then it follows that $T_\infty \ll T_1/P$, and hence Theorem 26.1 gives $T_P \leq T_1/P + T_\infty \approx T_1/P$. Since the work law (26.2) dictates that $T_P \geq T_1/P$, we conclude that $T_P \approx T_1/P$, which is a speedup of $T_1/T_P \approx P$.   ■

The $\ll$ symbol denotes "much less," but how much is "much less"? As a rule of thumb, a slackness of at least 10—that is, 10 times more parallelism than processors—generally suffices to achieve good speedup. Then, the span term in the greedy bound, inequality (26.4), is less than 10% of the work-per-processor term, which is good enough for most engineering situations. For example, if a computation runs on only 10 or 100 processors, it doesn't make sense to value parallelism of, say 1,000,000, over parallelism of 10,000, even with the factor of 100 difference. As Problem 26-2 shows, sometimes reducing extreme parallelism yields algorithms that are better with respect to other concerns and which still scale up well on reasonable numbers of processors.

Analyzing parallel algorithms

We now have all the tools we need to analyze parallel algorithms using work/span analysis, allowing us to bound an algorithm's running time on any number of processors. Analyzing the work is relatively straightforward, since it amounts to nothing more than analyzing the running time of an ordinary serial algorithm, namely, the serial projection of the parallel algorithm. You should already be familiar with analyzing work, since that is what most of this textbook is about! Analyzing the span is the new thing that parallelism engenders, but it's generally no harder once you get the hang of it. Let's investigate the basic ideas using the P-FIB program.

Analyzing the work $T_1(n)$ of P-FIB(n) poses no hurdles, because we've already done it. The serial projection of P-FIB is effectively the original FIB procedure, and hence, we have $T_1(n) = T(n) = \Theta(\phi^n)$ from equation (26.1).

Figure 26.3 illustrates how to analyze the span. If two traces are joined in series, their spans add to form the span of their composition, whereas if they are joined

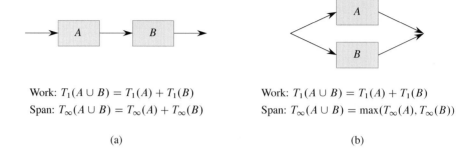

Work: $T_1(A \cup B) = T_1(A) + T_1(B)$

Span: $T_\infty(A \cup B) = T_\infty(A) + T_\infty(B)$

Work: $T_1(A \cup B) = T_1(A) + T_1(B)$

Span: $T_\infty(A \cup B) = \max(T_\infty(A), T_\infty(B))$

(a)   (b)

Figure 26.3 Series-parallel composition of parallel traces. **(a)** When two traces are joined in series, the work of the composition is the sum of their work, and the span of the composition is the sum of their spans. **(b)** When two traces are joined in parallel, the work of the composition remains the sum of their work, but the span of the composition is only the maximum of their spans.

in parallel, the span of their composition is the maximum of the spans of the two traces. As it turns out, the trace of any fork-join parallel computation can be built up from single strands by series-parallel composition.

Armed with an understanding of series-parallel composition, we can analyze the span of P-FIB(n). The spawned call to P-FIB$(n - 1)$ in line 3 runs in parallel with the call to P-FIB$(n - 2)$ in line 4. Hence, we can express the span of P-FIB(n) as the recurrence

$$
\begin{aligned}
T_\infty(n) &= \max\{T_\infty(n - 1), T_\infty(n - 2)\} + \Theta(1) \\
&= T_\infty(n - 1) + \Theta(1) \,,
\end{aligned}
$$

which has solution $T_\infty(n) = \Theta(n)$. (The second equality above follows from the first because P-FIB$(n - 1)$ uses P-FIB$(n - 2)$ in its computation, so that the span of P-FIB$(n - 1)$ must be at least as large as the span of P-FIB$(n - 2)$.)

The parallelism of P-FIB(n) is $T_1(n)/T_\infty(n) = \Theta(\phi^n/n)$, which grows dramatically as n gets large. Thus, Corollary 26.3 tells us that on even the largest parallel computers, a modest value for n suffices to achieve near perfect linear speedup for P-FIB(n), because this procedure exhibits considerable parallel slackness.

Parallel loops

Many algorithms contain loops for which all the iterations can operate in parallel. Although the **spawn** and **sync** keywords can be used to parallelize such loops, it is more convenient to specify directly that the iterations of such loops can run in parallel. Our pseudocode provides this functionality via the **parallel** keyword, which precedes the **for** keyword in a **for** loop statement.

As an example, consider the problem of multiplying a square $n \times n$ matrix $A = (a_{ij})$ by an n-vector $x = (x_j)$. The resulting n-vector $y = (y_i)$ is given by the equation

$$y_i = \sum_{j=1}^{n} a_{ij}x_j \, ,$$

for $i = 1, 2, \ldots, n$. The P-MAT-VEC procedure performs matrix-vector multiplication (actually, $y = y + Ax$) by computing all the entries of y in parallel. The **parallel for** keywords in line 1 of P-MAT-VEC indicate that the n iterations of the loop body, which includes a serial **for** loop, may be run in parallel. The initialization $y = 0$, if desired, should be performed before calling the procedure (and can be done with a **parallel for** loop).

P-MAT-VEC(A, x, y, n)

1   **parallel for** $i = 1$ to n // parallel loop
2   **for** $j = 1$ to n // serial loop
3           $y_i = y_i + a_{ij}x_j$

Compilers for fork-join parallel programs can implement **parallel for** loops in terms of **spawn** and **sync** by using recursive spawning. For example, for the **parallel for** loop in lines 1–3, a compiler can generate the auxiliary subroutine P-MAT-VEC-RECURSIVE and call P-MAT-VEC-RECURSIVE$(A, x, y, n, 1, n)$ in the place where the loop would be in the compiled code. As Figure 26.4 illustrates, this procedure recursively spawns the first half of the iterations of the loop to execute in parallel (line 5) with the second half of the iterations (line 6) and then executes a **sync** (line 7), thereby creating a binary tree of parallel execution. Each leaf represents a base case, which is the serial **for** loop of lines 2–3.

P-MAT-VEC-RECURSIVE(A, x, y, n, i, i')

1   **if** $i == i'$ // just one iteration to do?
2   **for** $j = 1$ to n // mimic P-MAT-VEC serial loop
3           $y_i = y_i + a_{ij}x_j$
4   **else** $mid = \lfloor (i + i')/2 \rfloor$ // parallel divide-and-conquer
5   **spawn** P-MAT-VEC-RECURSIVE(A, x, y, n, i, mid)
6   P-MAT-VEC-RECURSIVE$(A, x, y, n, mid + 1, i')$
7   **sync**

To calculate the work $T_1(n)$ of P-MAT-VEC on an $n \times n$ matrix, simply compute the running time of its serial projection, which comes from replacing the **parallel**

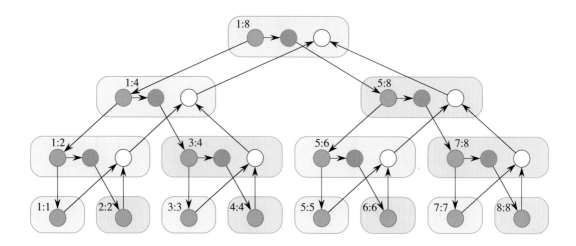

Figure 26.4 A trace for the computation of P-MAT-VEC-RECURSIVE($A, x, y, 8, 1, 8$). The two numbers within each rounded rectangle give the values of the last two parameters (i and i' in the procedure header) in the invocation (spawn, in blue, or call, in tan) of the procedure. The blue circles represent strands corresponding to the part of the procedure up to the spawn of P-MAT-VEC-RECURSIVE in line 5. The orange circles represent strands corresponding to the part of the procedure that calls P-MAT-VEC-RECURSIVE in line 6 up to the **sync** in line 7, where it suspends until the spawned subroutine in line 5 returns. The white circles represent strands corresponding to the (negligible) part of the procedure after the **sync** up to the point where it returns.

for loop in line 1 with an ordinary **for** loop. The running time of the resulting serial pseudocode is $\Theta(n^2)$, which means that $T_1(n) = \Theta(n^2)$. This analysis seems to ignore the overhead for recursive spawning in implementing the parallel loops, however. Indeed, the overhead of recursive spawning does increase the work of a parallel loop compared with that of its serial projection, but not asymptotically. To see why, observe that since the tree of recursive procedure instances is a full binary tree, the number of internal nodes is one less than the number of leaves (see Exercise B.5-3 on page 1175). Each internal node performs constant work to divide the iteration range, and each leaf corresponds to a base case, which takes at least constant time ($\Theta(n)$ time in this case). Thus, by amortizing the overhead of recursive spawning over the work of the iterations in the leaves, we see that the overall work increases by at most a constant factor.

To reduce the overhead of recursive spawning, task-parallel platforms sometimes *coarsen* the leaves of the recursion by executing several iterations in a single leaf, either automatically or under programmer control. This optimization comes at the expense of reducing the parallelism. If the computation has sufficient parallel slackness, however, near-perfect linear speedup won't be sacrificed.

Although recursive spawning doesn't affect the work of a parallel loop asymptotically, we must take it into account when analyzing the span. Consider a parallel loop with n iterations in which the ith iteration has span $iter_\infty(i)$. Since the depth of recursion is logarithmic in the number of iterations, the parallel loop's span is

$$T_\infty(n) = \Theta(\lg n) + \max \{iter_\infty(i) : 1 \le i \le n\} \ .$$

For example, let's compute the span of the doubly nested loops in lines 1–3 of P-Mat-Vec. The span for the **parallel for** loop control is $\Theta(\lg n)$. For each iteration of the outer parallel loop, the inner serial **for** loop contains n iterations of line 3. Since each iteration takes constant time, the total span for the inner serial **for** loop is $\Theta(n)$, no matter which iteration of the outer **parallel for** loop it's in. Thus, taking the maximum over all iterations of the outer loop and adding in the $\Theta(\lg n)$ for loop control yields an overall span of $T_\infty n = \Theta(n) + \Theta(\lg n) = \Theta(n)$ for the procedure. Since the work is $\Theta(n^2)$, the parallelism is $\Theta(n^2)/\Theta(n) = \Theta(n)$. (Exercise 26.1-7 asks you to provide an implementation with even more parallelism.)

Race conditions

A parallel algorithm is *deterministic* if it always does the same thing on the same input, no matter how the instructions are scheduled on the multicore computer. It is *nondeterministic* if its behavior might vary from run to run when the input is the same. A parallel algorithm that is intended to be deterministic may nevertheless act nondeterministically, however, if it contains a difficult-to-diagnose bug called a "determinacy race."

Famous race bugs include the Therac-25 radiation therapy machine, which killed three people and injured several others, and the Northeast Blackout of 2003, which left over 50 million people in the United States without power. These pernicious bugs are notoriously hard to find. You can run tests in the lab for days without a failure, only to discover that your software sporadically crashes in the field, sometimes with dire consequences.

A *determinacy race* occurs when two logically parallel instructions access the same memory location and at least one of the instructions modifies the value stored in the location. The toy procedure Race-Example on the following page illustrates a determinacy race. After initializing x to 0 in line 1, Race-Example creates two parallel strands, each of which increments x in line 3. Although it might seem that a call of Race-Example should always print the value 2 (its serial projection certainly does), it could instead print the value 1. Let's see how this anomaly might occur.

When a processor increments x, the operation is not indivisible, but is composed of a sequence of instructions:

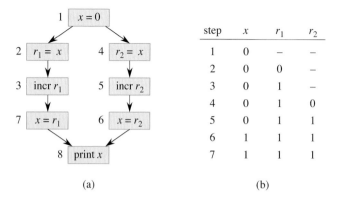

step	x	r_1	r_2
1	0	–	–
2	0	0	–
3	0	1	–
4	0	1	0
5	0	1	1
6	1	1	1
7	1	1	1

(a)   (b)

Figure 26.5 Illustration of the determinacy race in RACE-EXAMPLE. **(a)** A trace showing the dependencies among individual instructions. The processor registers are r_1 and r_2. Instructions unrelated to the race, such as the implementation of loop control, are omitted. **(b)** An execution sequence that elicits the bug, showing the values of x in memory and registers r_1 and r_2 for each step in the execution sequence.

RACE-EXAMPLE( )

1    $x = 0$
2   **parallel for** $i = 1$ **to** 2
3        $x = x + 1$ // determinacy race
4   print x

- Load x from memory into one of the processor's registers.

- Increment the value in the register.

- Store the value in the register back into x in memory.

Figure 26.5(a) illustrates a trace representing the execution of RACE-EXAMPLE, with the strands broken down to individual instructions. Recall that since an ideal parallel computer supports sequential consistency, you can view the parallel execution of a parallel algorithm as an interleaving of instructions that respects the dependencies in the trace. Part (b) of the figure shows the values in an execution of the computation that elicits the anomaly. The value x is kept in memory, and r_1 and r_2 are processor registers. In step 1, one of the processors sets x to 0. In steps 2 and 3, processor 1 loads x from memory into its register r_1 and increments it, producing the value 1 in r_1. At that point, processor 2 comes into the picture, executing instructions 4–6. Processor 2 loads x from memory into register r_2; increments it, producing the value 1 in r_2; and then stores this value into x, setting x to 1. Now, processor 1 resumes with step 7, storing the value 1 in r_1 into x, which leaves the value of x unchanged. Therefore, step 8 prints the value 1, rather than the value 2 that the serial projection would print.

Let's recap what happened. By sequential consistency, the effect of the parallel execution is as if the executed instructions of the two processors are interleaved. If processor 1 executes all its instructions before processor 2, a trivial interleaving, the value 2 is printed. Conversely, if processor 2 executes all its instructions before processor 1, the value 2 is still printed. When the instructions of the two processors interleave nontrivially, however, it is possible, as in this example execution, that one of the updates to x is lost, resulting in the value 1 being printed.

Of course, many executions do not elicit the bug. That's the problem with determinacy races. Generally, most instruction orderings produce correct results, such as any where the instructions on the left branch execute before the instructions on the right branch, or vice versa. But some orderings generate improper results when the instructions interleave. Consequently, races can be extremely hard to test for. Your program may fail, but you may be unable to reliably reproduce the failure in subsequent tests, confounding your attempts to locate the bug in your code and fix it. Task-parallel programming environments often provide race-detection productivity tools to help you isolate race bugs.

Many parallel programs in the real world are intentionally nondeterministic. They contain determinacy races, but they mitigate the dangers of nondeterminism through the use of mutual-exclusion locks and other methods of synchronization. For our purposes, however, we'll insist on an absence of determinacy races in the algorithms we develop. Nondeterministic programs are indeed interesting, but nondeterministic programming is a more advanced topic and unnecessary for a wide swath of interesting parallel algorithms.

To ensure that algorithms are deterministic, any two strands that operate in parallel should be *mutually noninterfering*: they only read, and do not modify, any memory locations accessed by both of them. Consequently, in a **parallel for** construct, such as the outer loop of P-MAT-VEC, we want all the iterations of the body, including any code an iteration executes in subroutines, to be mutually noninterfering. And between a **spawn** and its corresponding **sync**, we want the code executed by the spawned child and the code executed by the parent to be mutually noninterfering, once again including invoked subroutines.

As an example of how easy it is to write code with unintentional races, the P-MAT-VEC-WRONG procedure on the next page is a faulty parallel implementation of matrix-vector multiplication that achieves a span of $\Theta(\lg n)$ by parallelizing the inner **for** loop. This procedure is incorrect, unfortunately, due to determinacy races when updating y_i in line 3, which executes in parallel for all n values of j.

Index variables of **parallel for** loops, such as i in line 1 and j in line 2, do not cause races between iterations. Conceptually, each iteration of the loop creates an independent variable to hold the index of that iteration during that iteration's

P-MAT-VEC-WRONG(A, x, y, n)

1 **parallel for** $i = 1$ **to** n
2   **parallel for** $j = 1$ **to** n
3          $y_i = y_i + a_{ij} x_j$ // determinacy race

execution of the loop body. Even if two parallel iterations both access the same index variable, they really are accessing different variable instances—hence different memory locations—and no race occurs.

A parallel algorithm with races can sometimes be deterministic. As an example, two parallel threads might store the same value into a shared variable, and it wouldn't matter which stored the value first. For simplicity, however, we generally prefer code without determinacy races, even if the races are benign. And good parallel programmers frown on code with determinacy races that cause nondeterministic behavior, if deterministic code that performs comparably is an option.

But nondeterministic code does have its place. For example, you can't implement a parallel hash table, a highly practical data structure, without writing code containing determinacy races. Much research has centered around how to extend the fork-join model to incorporate limited "structured" nondeterminism while avoiding the full measure of complications that arise when nondeterminism is completely unrestricted.

A chess lesson

To illustrate the power of work/span analysis, this section closes with a true story that occurred during the development of one of the first world-class parallel chess-playing programs [106] many years ago. The timings below have been simplified for exposition.

The chess program was developed and tested on a 32-processor computer, but it was designed to run on a supercomputer with 512 processors. Since the supercomputer availability was limited and expensive, the developers ran benchmarks on the small computer and extrapolated performance to the large computer.

At one point, the developers incorporated an optimization into the program that reduced its running time on an important benchmark on the small machine from $T_{32} = 65$ seconds to $T'_{32} = 40$ seconds. Yet, the developers used the work and span performance measures to conclude that the optimized version, which was faster on 32 processors, would actually be slower than the original version on the 512 processors of the large machine. As a result, they abandoned the "optimization."

Here is their work/span analysis. The original version of the program had work $T_1 = 2048$ seconds and span $T_\infty = 1$ second. Let's treat inequality (26.4) on page 760 as the equation $T_P = T_1/P + T_\infty$, which we can use as an approximation to the running time on P processors. Then indeed we have $T_{32} = 2048/32 + 1 = 65$. With the optimization, the work becomes $T_1' = 1024$ seconds, and the span becomes $T_\infty' = 8$ seconds. Our approximation gives $T_{32}' = 1024/32 + 8 = 40$.

The relative speeds of the two versions switch when we estimate their running times on 512 processors, however. The first version has a running time of $T_{512} = 2048/512 + 1 = 5$ seconds, and the second version runs in $T_{512}' = 1024/512 + 8 = 10$ seconds. The optimization that speeds up the program on 32 processors makes the program run for twice as long on 512 processors! The optimized version's span of 8, which is not the dominant term in the running time on 32 processors, becomes the dominant term on 512 processors, nullifying the advantage from using more processors. The optimization does not scale up.

The moral of the story is that work/span analysis, and measurements of work and span, can be superior to measured running times alone in extrapolating an algorithm's scalability.

Exercises

26.1-1
What does a trace for the execution of a serial algorithm look like?

26.1-2
Suppose that line 4 of P-FIB spawns P-FIB$(n-2)$, rather than calling it as is done in the pseudocode. How would the trace of P-FIB(4) in Figure 26.2 change? What is the impact on the asymptotic work, span, and parallelism?

26.1-3
Draw the trace that results from executing P-FIB(5). Assuming that each strand in the computation takes unit time, what are the work, span, and parallelism of the computation? Show how to schedule the trace on 3 processors using greedy scheduling by labeling each strand with the time step in which it is executed.

26.1-4
Prove that a greedy scheduler achieves the following time bound, which is slightly stronger than the bound proved in Theorem 26.1:

$$T_P \leq \frac{T_1 - T_\infty}{P} + T_\infty . \tag{26.5}$$

26.1-5
Construct a trace for which one execution by a greedy scheduler can take nearly twice the time of another execution by a greedy scheduler on the same number of processors. Describe how the two executions would proceed.

26.1-6

Professor Karan measures her deterministic task-parallel algorithm on 4, 10, and 64 processors of an ideal parallel computer using a greedy scheduler. She claims that the three runs yielded $T_4 = 80$ seconds, $T_{10} = 42$ seconds, and $T_{64} = 10$ seconds. Argue that the professor is either lying or incompetent. (*Hint:* Use the work law (26.2), the span law (26.3), and inequality (26.5) from Exercise 26.1-4.)

26.1-7

Give a parallel algorithm to multiply an $n \times n$ matrix by an n-vector that achieves $\Theta(n^2 / \lg n)$ parallelism while maintaining $\Theta(n^2)$ work.

26.1-8

Analyze the work, span, and parallelism of the procedure P-TRANSPOSE, which transposes an $n \times n$ matrix A in place.

P-TRANSPOSE(A, n)

1   **parallel for** $j = 2$ **to** n
2   **parallel for** $i = 1$ **to** $j - 1$
3   exchange a_{ij} with a_{ji}

26.1-9

Suppose that instead of a **parallel for** loop in line 2, the P-TRANSPOSE procedure in Exercise 26.1-8 had an ordinary **for** loop. Analyze the work, span, and parallelism of the resulting algorithm.

26.1-10

For what number of processors do the two versions of the chess program run equally fast, assuming that $T_P = T_1/P + T_\infty$?

26.2   Parallel matrix multiplication

In this section, we'll explore how to parallelize the three matrix-multiplication algorithms from Sections 4.1 and 4.2. We'll see that each algorithm can be parallelized in a straightforward fashion using either parallel loops or recursive spawning. We'll analyze them using work/span analysis, and we'll see that each parallel algorithm attains the same performance on one processor as its corresponding serial algorithm, while scaling up to large numbers of processors.

A parallel algorithm for matrix multiplication using parallel loops

The first algorithm we'll study is P-MATRIX-MULTIPLY, which simply parallelizes the two outer loops in the procedure MATRIX-MULTIPLY on page 81.

P-MATRIX-MULTIPLY(A, B, C, n)

```
1   parallel for i = 1 to n          // compute entries in each of n rows
2       parallel for j = 1 to n      // compute n entries in row i
3           for k = 1 to n
4               c_ij = c_ij + a_ik · b_kj   // add in another term of equation (4.1)
```

Let's analyze P-MATRIX-MULTIPLY. Since the serial projection of the algorithm is just MATRIX-MULTIPLY, the work is the same as the running time of MATRIX-MULTIPLY: $T_1(n) = \Theta(n^3)$. The span is $T_\infty(n) = \Theta(n)$, because it follows a path down the tree of recursion for the **parallel for** loop starting in line 1, then down the tree of recursion for the **parallel for** loop starting in line 2, and then executes all n iterations of the ordinary **for** loop starting in line 3, resulting in a total span of $\Theta(\lg n) + \Theta(\lg n) + \Theta(n) = \Theta(n)$. Thus the parallelism is $\Theta(n^3)/\Theta(n) = \Theta(n^2)$. (Exercise 26.2-3 asks you to parallelize the inner loop to obtain a parallelism of $\Theta(n^3/\lg n)$, which you cannot do straightforwardly using **parallel for**, because you would create races.)

A parallel divide-and-conquer algorithm for matrix multiplication

Section 4.1 shows how to multiply $n \times n$ matrices serially in $\Theta(n^3)$ time using a divide-and-conquer strategy. Let's see how to parallelize that algorithm using recursive spawning instead of calls.

The serial MATRIX-MULTIPLY-RECURSIVE procedure on page 83 takes as input three $n \times n$ matrices A, B, and C and performs the matrix calculation $C = C + A \cdot B$ by recursively performing eight multiplications of $n/2 \times n/2$ submatrices of A and B. The P-MATRIX-MULTIPLY-RECURSIVE procedure on the following page implements the same divide-and-conquer strategy, but it uses spawning to perform the eight multiplications in parallel. To avoid determinacy races in updating the elements of C, it creates a temporary matrix D to store four of the submatrix products. At the end, it adds C and D together to produce the final result. (Problem 26-2 asks you to eliminate the temporary matrix D at the expense of some parallelism.)

Lines 2–3 of P-MATRIX-MULTIPLY-RECURSIVE handle the base case of multiplying 1×1 matrices. The remainder of the procedure deals with the recursive case. Line 4 allocates a temporary matrix D, and lines 5–7 zero it. Line 8 partitions each of the four matrices A, B, C, and D into $n/2 \times n/2$ submatrices. (As

P-MATRIX-MULTIPLY-RECURSIVE(A, B, C, n)

1 **if** $n == 1$ // just one element in each matrix?
2      $c_{11} = c_{11} + a_{11} \cdot b_{11}$
3   **return**
4 let D be a new $n \times n$ matrix   // temporary matrix
5 **parallel for** $i = 1$ **to** n // set $D = 0$
6   **parallel for** $j = 1$ **to** n
7          $d_{ij} = 0$
8 partition A, B, C, and D into $n/2 \times n/2$ submatrices
        $A_{11}, A_{12}, A_{21}, A_{22}; B_{11}, B_{12}, B_{21}, B_{22}; C_{11}, C_{12}, C_{21}, C_{22};$
        and $D_{11}, D_{12}, D_{21}, D_{22}$; respectively
9 **spawn** P-MATRIX-MULTIPLY-RECURSIVE$(A_{11}, B_{11}, C_{11}, n/2)$
10 **spawn** P-MATRIX-MULTIPLY-RECURSIVE$(A_{11}, B_{12}, C_{12}, n/2)$
11 **spawn** P-MATRIX-MULTIPLY-RECURSIVE$(A_{21}, B_{11}, C_{21}, n/2)$
12 **spawn** P-MATRIX-MULTIPLY-RECURSIVE$(A_{21}, B_{12}, C_{22}, n/2)$
13 **spawn** P-MATRIX-MULTIPLY-RECURSIVE$(A_{12}, B_{21}, D_{11}, n/2)$
14 **spawn** P-MATRIX-MULTIPLY-RECURSIVE$(A_{12}, B_{22}, D_{12}, n/2)$
15 **spawn** P-MATRIX-MULTIPLY-RECURSIVE$(A_{22}, B_{21}, D_{21}, n/2)$
16 **spawn** P-MATRIX-MULTIPLY-RECURSIVE$(A_{22}, B_{22}, D_{22}, n/2)$
17 **sync**   // wait for spawned submatrix products
18 **parallel for** $i = 1$ **to** n // update $C = C + D$
19   **parallel for** $j = 1$ **to** n
20          $c_{ij} = c_{ij} + d_{ij}$

with MATRIX-MULTIPLY-RECURSIVE on page 83, we're glossing over the subtle issue of how to use index calculations to represent submatrix sections of a matrix.) The spawned recursive call in line 9 sets $C_{11} = C_{11} + A_{11} \cdot B_{11}$, so that C_{11} accumulates the first of the two terms in equation (4.5) on page 82. Similarly, lines 10–12 cause each of C_{12}, C_{21}, and C_{22} in parallel to accumulate the first of the two terms in equations (4.6)–(4.8), respectively. Line 13 sets the submatrix D_{11} to the submatrix product $A_{12} \cdot B_{21}$, so that D_{11} equals the second of the two terms in equation (4.5). Lines 14–16 set each of D_{12}, D_{21}, and D_{22} in parallel to the second of the two terms in equations (4.6)–(4.8), respectively. The **sync** statement in line 17 ensures that all the spawned submatrix products in lines 9–16 have been computed, after which the doubly nested **parallel for** loops in lines 18–20 add the elements of D to the corresponding elements of C.

Let's analyze the P-MATRIX-MULTIPLY-RECURSIVE procedure. We start by analyzing the work $M_1(n)$, echoing the serial running-time analysis of its progenitor MATRIX-MULTIPLY-RECURSIVE. The recursive case allocates and zeros the temporary matrix D in $\Theta(n^2)$ time, partitions in $\Theta(1)$ time, performs eight recursive multiplications of $n/2 \times n/2$ matrices, and finishes up with the $\Theta(n^2)$ work from adding two $n \times n$ matrices. Thus the work outside the spawned recursive calls is $\Theta(n^2)$, and the recurrence for the work $M_1(n)$ becomes

$$
\begin{aligned}
M_1(n) &= 8M_1(n/2) + \Theta(n^2) \\
&= \Theta(n^3)
\end{aligned}
$$

by case 1 of the master theorem (Theorem 4.1). Not surprisingly, the work of this parallel algorithm is asymptotically the same as the running time of the procedure MATRIX-MULTIPLY on page 81, with its triply nested loops.

Let's determine the span $M_\infty(n)$ of P-MATRIX-MULTIPLY-RECURSIVE. Because the eight parallel recursive spawns all execute on matrices of the same size, the maximum span for any recursive spawn is just the span of a single one of them, or $M_\infty(n/2)$. The span for the doubly nested **parallel for** loops in lines 5–7 is $\Theta(\lg n)$ because each loop control adds $\Theta(\lg n)$ to the constant span of line 7. Similarly, the doubly nested **parallel for** loops in lines 18–20 add another $\Theta(\lg n)$. Matrix partitioning by index calculation has $\Theta(1)$ span, which is dominated by the $\Theta(\lg n)$ span of the nested loops. We obtain the recurrence

$$
M_\infty(n) = M_\infty(n/2) + \Theta(\lg n) \ . \tag{26.6}
$$

Since this recurrence falls under case 2 of the master theorem with $k = 1$, the solution is $M_\infty(n) = \Theta(\lg^2 n)$.

The parallelism of P-MATRIX-MULTIPLY-RECURSIVE is $M_1(n)/M_\infty(n) = \Theta(n^3/\lg^2 n)$, which is huge. (Problem 26-2 asks you to simplify this parallel algorithm at the expense of just a little less parallelism.)

Parallelizing Strassen's method

To parallelize Strassen's algorithm, we can follow the same general outline as on pages 86–87, but use spawning. You may find it helpful to compare each step below with the corresponding step there. We'll analyze costs as we go along to develop recurrences $T_1(n)$ and $T_\infty(n)$ for the overall work and span, respectively.

1. If $n = 1$, the matrices each contain a single element. Perform a single scalar multiplication and a single scalar addition, and return. Otherwise, partition the input matrices A and B and output matrix C into $n/2 \times n/2$ submatrices, as in equation (4.2) on page 82. This step takes $\Theta(1)$ work and $\Theta(1)$ span by index calculation.

2. Create $n/2 \times n/2$ matrices $S_1, S_2, \ldots, S_{10}$, each of which is the sum or difference of two submatrices from step 1. Create and zero the entries of seven $n/2 \times n/2$ matrices $P_1, P_2, \ldots, P_7$ to hold seven $n/2 \times n/2$ matrix products. All

17 matrices can be created, and the P_i initialized, with doubly nested **parallel for** loops using $\Theta(n^2)$ work and $\Theta(\lg n)$ span.

3. Using the submatrices from step 1 and the matrices $S_1, S_2, \ldots, S_{10}$ created in step 2, recursively spawn computations of each of the seven $n/2 \times n/2$ matrix products $P_1, P_2, \ldots, P_7$, taking $7T_1(n/2)$ work and $T_\infty(n/2)$ span.

4. Update the four submatrices $C_{11}, C_{12}, C_{21}, C_{22}$ of the result matrix C by adding or subtracting various P_i matrices. Using doubly nested **parallel for** loops, computing all four submatrices takes $\Theta(n^2)$ work and $\Theta(\lg n)$ span.

Let's analyze this algorithm. Since the serial projection is the same as the original serial algorithm, the work is just the running time of the serial projection, namely, $\Theta(n^{\lg 7})$. As we did with P-MATRIX-MULTIPLY-RECURSIVE, we can devise a recurrence for the span. In this case, seven recursive calls execute in parallel, but since they all operate on matrices of the same size, we obtain the same recurrence (26.6) as we did for P-MATRIX-MULTIPLY-RECURSIVE, with solution $\Theta(\lg^2 n)$. Thus the parallel version of Strassen's method has parallelism $\Theta(n^{\lg 7}/\lg^2 n)$, which is large. Although the parallelism is slightly less than that of P-MATRIX-MULTIPLY-RECURSIVE, that's just because the work is also less.

Exercises

26.2-1
Draw the trace for computing P-MATRIX-MULTIPLY on 2×2 matrices, labeling how the vertices in your diagram correspond to strands in the execution of the algorithm. Assuming that each strand executes in unit time, analyze the work, span, and parallelism of this computation.

26.2-2
Repeat Exercise 26.2-1 for P-MATRIX-MULTIPLY-RECURSIVE.

26.2-3
Give pseudocode for a parallel algorithm that multiplies two $n \times n$ matrices with work $\Theta(n^3)$ but span only $\Theta(\lg n)$. Analyze your algorithm.

26.2-4
Give pseudocode for an efficient parallel algorithm that multiplies a $p \times q$ matrix by a $q \times r$ matrix. Your algorithm should be highly parallel even if any of p, q, and r equal 1. Analyze your algorithm.

26.2-5
Give pseudocode for an efficient parallel version of the Floyd-Warshall algorithm (see Section 23.2), which computes shortest paths between all pairs of vertices in an edge-weighted graph. Analyze your algorithm.

26.3   Parallel merge sort

We first saw serial merge sort in Section 2.3.1, and in Section 2.3.2 we analyzed its running time and showed it to be $\Theta(n \lg n)$. Because merge sort already uses the divide-and-conquer method, it seems like a terrific candidate for implementing using fork-join parallelism.

The procedure P-MERGE-SORT modifies merge sort to spawn the first recursive call. Like its serial counterpart MERGE-SORT on page 39, the P-MERGE-SORT procedure sorts the subarray $A[p:r]$. After the **sync** statement in line 8 ensures that the two recursive spawns in lines 5 and 7 have finished, P-MERGE-SORT calls the P-MERGE procedure, a parallel merging algorithm, which is on page 779, but you don't need to bother looking at it right now.

P-MERGE-SORT(A, p, r)

```
 1  if p ≥ r                  // zero or one element?
 2      return
 3  q = ⌊(p + r)/2⌋           // midpoint of A[p : r]
 4  // Recursively sort A[p : q] in parallel.
 5  spawn P-MERGE-SORT(A, p, q)
 6  // Recursively sort A[q + 1 : r] in parallel.
 7  spawn P-MERGE-SORT(A, q + 1, r)
 8  sync                      // wait for spawns
 9  // Merge A[p : q] and A[q + 1 : r] into A[p : r].
10  P-MERGE(A, p, q, r)
```

First, let's use work/span analysis to get some intuition for why we need a parallel merge procedure. After all, it may seem as though there should be plenty of parallelism just by parallelizing MERGE-SORT without worrying about parallelizing the merge. But what would happen if the call to P-MERGE in line 10 of P-MERGE-SORT were replaced by a call to the serial MERGE procedure on page 36? Let's call the pseudocode so modified P-NAIVE-MERGE-SORT.

Let $T_1(n)$ be the (worst-case) work of P-NAIVE-MERGE-SORT on an n-element subarray, where $n = r - p + 1$ is the number of elements in $A[p:r]$, and let $T_\infty(n)$

be the span. Because MERGE is serial with running time $\Theta(n)$, both its work and span are $\Theta(n)$. Since the serial projection of P-NAIVE-MERGE-SORT is exactly MERGE-SORT, its work is $T_1(n) = \Theta(n \lg n)$. The two recursive calls in lines 5 and 7 run in parallel, and so its span is given by the recurrence

$$
\begin{aligned}
T_\infty(n) &= T_\infty(n/2) + \Theta(n) \\
&= \Theta(n) \, ,
\end{aligned}
$$

by case 1 of the master theorem. Thus the parallelism of P-NAIVE-MERGE-SORT is $T_1(n)/T_\infty(n) = \Theta(\lg n)$, which is an unimpressive amount of parallelism. To sort a million elements, for example, since $\lg 10^6 \approx 20$, it might achieve linear speedup on a few processors, but it would not scale up to dozens of processors.

The parallelism bottleneck in P-NAIVE-MERGE-SORT is plainly the MERGE procedure. If we asymptotically reduce the span of merging, the master theorem dictates that the span of parallel merge sort will also get smaller. When you look at the pseudocode for MERGE, it may seem that merging is inherently serial, but it's not. We can fashion a parallel merging algorithm. The goal is to reduce the span of parallel merging asymptotically, but if we want an efficient parallel algorithm, we must ensure that the $\Theta(n)$ bound on work doesn't increase.

Figure 26.6 depicts the divide-and-conquer strategy that we'll use in P-MERGE. The heart of the algorithm is a recursive auxiliary procedure P-MERGE-AUX that merges two sorted subarrays of an array A into a subarray of another array B in parallel. Specifically, P-MERGE-AUX merges $A[p_1 : r_1]$ and $A[p_2 : r_2]$ into subarray $B[p_3 : r_3]$, where $r_3 = p_3 + (r_1 - p_1 + 1) + (r_2 - p_2 + 1) - 1 = p_3 + (r_1 - p_1) + (r_2 - p_2) + 1$.

The key idea of the recursive merging algorithm in P-MERGE-AUX is to split each of the two sorted subarrays of A around a pivot x, such that all the elements in the lower part of each subarray are at most x and all the elements in the upper part of each subarray are at least x. The procedure can then recurse in parallel on two subtasks: merging the two lower parts, and merging the two upper parts. The trick is to find a pivot x so that the recursion is not too lopsided. We don't want a situation such as that in QUICKSORT on page 183, where bad partitioning elements lead to a dramatic loss of asymptotic efficiency. We could opt to partition around a random element, as RANDOMIZED-QUICKSORT on page 192 does, but because the input subarrays are sorted, P-MERGE-AUX can quickly determine a pivot that always works well.

Specifically, the recursive merging algorithm picks the pivot x as the middle element of the larger of the two input subarrays, which we can assume without loss of generality is $A[p_1 : r_1]$, since otherwise, the two subarrays can just switch roles. That is, $x = A[q_1]$, where $q_1 = \lfloor (p_1 + r_1)/2 \rfloor$. Because $A[p_1 : r_1]$ is sorted, x is a median of the subarray elements: every element in $A[p_1 : q_1 - 1]$ is no more than x, and every element in $A[q_1 + 1 : r_1]$ is no less than x. Then the

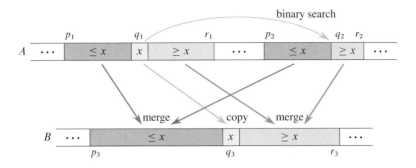

Figure 26.6   The idea behind P-MERGE-AUX, which merges two sorted subarrays $A[p_1:r_1]$ and $A[p_2:r_2]$ into the subarray $B[p_3:r_3]$ in parallel. Letting $x = A[q_1]$ (shown in yellow) be a median of $A[p_1:r_1]$ and q_2 be a place in $A[p_2:r_2]$ such that x would fall between $A[q_2 - 1]$ and $A[q_2]$, every element in the subarrays $A[p_1:q_1 - 1]$ and $A[p_2:q_2 - 1]$ (shown in orange) is at most x, and every element in the subarrays $A[q_1 + 1:r_1]$ and $A[q_2 + 1:r_2]$ (shown in blue) is at least x. To merge, compute the index q_3 where x belongs in $B[p_3:r_3]$, copy x into $B[q_3]$, and then recursively merge $A[p_1:q_1 - 1]$ with $A[p_2:q_2 - 1]$ into $B[p_3:q_3 - 1]$ and $A[q_1 + 1:r_1]$ with $A[q_2:r_2]$ into $B[q_3 + 1:r_3]$.

algorithm finds the "split point" q_2 in the smaller subarray $A[p_2:r_2]$ such that all the elements in $A[p_2:q_2 - 1]$ (if any) are at most x and all the elements in $A[q_2:r_2]$ (if any) are at least x. Intuitively, the subarray $A[p_2:r_2]$ would still be sorted if x were inserted between $A[q_2 - 1]$ and $A[q_2]$ (although the algorithm doesn't do that). Since $A[p_2:r_2]$ is sorted, a minor variant of binary search (see Exercise 2.3-6) with x as the search key can find the split point q_2 in $\Theta(\lg n)$ time in the worst case. As we'll see when we get to the analysis, even if x splits $A[p_2:r_2]$ badly—x is either smaller than all the subarray elements or larger—we'll still have at least $1/4$ of the elements in each of the two recursive merges. Thus the larger of the recursive merges operates on at most $3/4$ elements, and the recursion is guaranteed to bottom out after $\Theta(\lg n)$ recursive calls.

Now let's put these ideas into pseudocode. We start with the serial procedure FIND-SPLIT-POINT(A, p, r, x) on the next page, which takes as input a sorted subarray $A[p:r]$ and a key x. The procedure returns a split point of $A[p:r]$: an index q in the range $p \leq q \leq r + 1$ such that all the elements in $A[p:q - 1]$ (if any) are at most x and all the elements in $A[q:r]$ (if any) are at least x.

The FIND-SPLIT-POINT procedure uses binary search to find the split point. Lines 1 and 2 establish the range of indices for the search. Each time through the **while** loop, line 5 compares the middle element of the range with the search key x, and lines 6 and 7 narrow the search range to either the lower half or the upper half of the subarray, depending on the result of the test. In the end, after the range has been narrowed to a single index, line 8 returns that index as the split point.

FIND-SPLIT-POINT(A, p, r, x)

```
1   low = p                         // low end of search range
2   high = r + 1                    // high end of search range
3   while low < high                // more than one element?
4       mid = ⌊(low + high)/2⌋      // midpoint of range
5       if x ≤ A[mid]               // is answer q ≤ mid?
6           high = mid              // narrow search to A[low : mid]
7       else low = mid + 1          // narrow search to A[mid + 1 : high]
8   return low
```

Because FIND-SPLIT-POINT contains no parallelism, its span is just its serial running time, which is also its work. On a subarray $A[p:r]$ of size $n = r - p + 1$, each iteration of the **while** loop halves the search range, which means that the loop terminates after $\Theta(\lg n)$ iterations. Since each iteration takes constant time, the algorithm runs in $\Theta(\lg n)$ (worst-case) time. Thus the procedure has work and span $\Theta(\lg n)$.

Let's now look at the pseudocode for the parallel merging procedure P-MERGE on the next page. Most of the pseudocode is devoted to the recursive procedure P-MERGE-AUX. The procedure P-MERGE itself is just a "wrapper" that sets up for P-MERGE-AUX. It allocates a new array $B[p:r]$ to hold the output of P-MERGE-AUX in line 1. It then calls P-MERGE-AUX in line 2, passing the indices of the two subarrays to be merged and providing B as the output destination of the merged result, starting at index p. After P-MERGE-AUX returns, lines 3–4 perform a parallel copy of the output $B[p:r]$ into the subarray $A[p:r]$, which is where P-MERGE-SORT expects it.

The P-MERGE-AUX procedure is the interesting part of the algorithm. Let's start by understanding the parameters of this recursive parallel procedure. The input array A and the four indices p_1, r_1, p_2, r_2 specify the subarrays $A[p_1:r_1]$ and $A[p_2:r_2]$ to be merged. The array B and the index p_3 indicate that the merged result should be stored into $B[p_3:r_3]$, where $r_3 = p_3 + (r_1 - p_1) + (r_2 - p_2) + 1$, as we saw earlier. The end index r_3 of the output subarray is not needed by the pseudocode, but it helps conceptually to name the end index, as in the comment in line 13.

The procedure begins by checking the base case of the recursion and doing some bookkeeping to simplify the rest of the pseudocode. Lines 1 and 2 test whether the two subarrays are both empty, in which case the procedure returns. Line 3 checks whether the first subarray contains fewer elements than the second subarray. Since the number of elements in the first subarray is $r_1 - p_1 + 1$ and the number in the second subarray is $r_2 - p_2 + 1$, the test omits the two "+1's." If the first subarray

P-MERGE(A, p, q, r)

```
1   let B[p : r] be a new array          // allocate scratch array
2   P-MERGE-AUX(A, p, q, q + 1, r, B, p) // merge from A into B
3   parallel for i = p to r              // copy B back to A in parallel
4       A[i] = B[i]
```

P-MERGE-AUX($A, p_1, r_1, p_2, r_2, B, p_3$)

```
 1   if p_1 > r_1 and p_2 > r_2           // are both subarrays empty?
 2       return
 3   if r_1 − p_1 < r_2 − p_2             // second subarray bigger?
 4       exchange p_1 with p_2            // swap subarray roles
 5       exchange r_1 with r_2
 6   q_1 = ⌊(p_1 + r_1)/2⌋                // midpoint of A[p_1 : r_1]
 7   x = A[q_1]                           // median of A[p_1 : r_1] is pivot x
 8   q_2 = FIND-SPLIT-POINT(A, p_2, r_2, x) // split A[p_2 : r_2] around x
 9   q_3 = p_3 + (q_1 − p_1) + (q_2 − p_2) // where x belongs in B ...
10   B[q_3] = x                           // ... put it there
11   // Recursively merge A[p_1 : q_1 − 1] and A[p_2 : q_2 − 1] into B[p_3 : q_3 − 1].
12   spawn P-MERGE-AUX(A, p_1, q_1 − 1, p_2, q_2 − 1, B, p_3)
13   // Recursively merge A[q_1 + 1 : r_1] and A[q_2 : r_2] into B[q_3 + 1 : r_3].
14   spawn P-MERGE-AUX(A, q_1 + 1, r_1, q_2, r_2, B, q_3 + 1)
15   sync                                // wait for spawns
```

is the smaller of the two, lines 4 and 5 switch the roles of the subarrays so that $A[p_1, r_1]$ refers to the larger subarray for the balance of the procedure.

We're now at the crux of P-MERGE-AUX: implementing the parallel divide-and-conquer strategy. As we continue our pseudocode walk, you may find it helpful to refer again to Figure 26.6.

First the divide step. Line 6 computes the midpoint q_1 of $A[p_1 : r_1]$, which indexes a median $x = A[q_1]$ of this subarray to be used as the pivot, and line 7 determines x itself. Next, line 8 uses the FIND-SPLIT-POINT procedure to find the index q_2 in $A[p_2 : r_2]$ such that all elements in $A[p_2 : q_2 − 1]$ are at most x and all the elements in $A[q_2 : r_2]$ are at least x. Line 9 computes the index q_3 of the element that divides the output subarray $B[p_3 : r_3]$ into $B[p_3 : q_3 − 1]$ and $B[q_3 + 1 : r_3]$, and then line 10 puts x directly into $B[q_3]$, which is where it belongs in the output.

Next is the conquer step, which is where the parallel recursion occurs. Lines 12 and 14 each spawn P-MERGE-AUX to recursively merge from A into B, the first to merge the smaller elements and the second to merge the larger elements. The

sync statement in line 15 ensures that the subproblems finish before the procedure returns.

There is no combine step, as $B[p:r]$ already contains the correct sorted output.

Work/span analysis of parallel merging

Let's first analyze the worst-case span $T_\infty(n)$ of P-MERGE-AUX on input subarrays that together contain a total of n elements. The call to FIND-SPLIT-POINT in line 8 contributes $\Theta(\lg n)$ to the span in the worst case, and the procedure performs at most a constant amount of additional serial work outside of the two recursive spawns in lines 12 and 14.

Because the two recursive spawns operate logically in parallel, only one of them contributes to the overall worst-case span. We claimed earlier that neither recursive invocation ever operates on more than $3n/4$ elements. Let's see why. Let $n_1 = r_1 - p_1 + 1$ and $n_2 = r_2 - p_2 + 1$, where $n = n_1 + n_2$, be the sizes of the two subarrays when line 6 starts executing, that is, after we have established that $n_2 \le n_1$ by swapping the roles of the two subarrays, if necessary. Since the pivot x is a median of of $A[p_1:r_1]$, in the worst case, a recursive merge involves at most $n_1/2$ elements of $A[p_1:r_1]$, but it might involve all n_2 of the elements of $A[p_2:r_2]$. Thus we can bound the number of elements involved in a recursive invocation of P-MERGE-AUX by

$$
\begin{aligned}
n_1/2 + n_2 &= (2n_1 + 4n_2)/4 \\
&\le (3n_1 + 3n_2)/4 \quad \text{(since } n_2 \le n_1) \\
&= 3n/4 \,,
\end{aligned}
$$

proving the claim.

The worst-case span of P-MERGE-AUX can therefore be described by the following recurrence:

$$
T_\infty(n) = T_\infty(3n/4) + \Theta(\lg n) \,. \tag{26.7}
$$

Because this recurrence falls under case 2 of the master theorem with $k = 1$, its solution is $T_\infty(n) = \Theta(\lg^2 n)$.

Now let's verify that the work $T_1(n)$ of P-MERGE-AUX on n elements is linear. A lower bound of $\Omega(n)$ is straightforward, since each of the n elements is copied from array A to array B. We'll show that $T_1(n) = O(n)$ by deriving a recurrence for the worst-case work. The binary search in line 8 costs $\Theta(\lg n)$ in the worst case, which dominates the other work outside of the recursive spawns. For the recursive spawns, observe that although lines 12 and 14 might merge different numbers of elements, the two recursive spawns together merge at most $n - 1$ elements (since $x = A[q]$ is not merged). Moreover, as we saw when analyzing the span, a recursive spawn operates on at most $3n/4$ elements. We therefore obtain the recurrence

$$T_1(n) = T_1(\alpha n) + T_1((1 - \alpha)n) + \Theta(\lg n) , \qquad (26.8)$$

where α lies in the range $1/4 \leq \alpha \leq 3/4$. The value of α can vary from one recursive invocation to another.

We'll use the substitution method (see Section 4.3) to prove that the above recurrence (26.8) has solution $T_1(n) = O(n)$. (You could also use the Akra-Bazzi method from Section 4.7.) Assume that $T_1(n) \leq c_1 n - c_2 \lg n$ for some positive constants c_1 and c_2. Using the properties of logarithms on pages 66–67—in particular, to deduce that $\lg \alpha + \lg(1 - \alpha) = -\Theta(1)$—substitution yields

$$
\begin{aligned}
T_1(n) &\leq (c_1 \alpha n - c_2 \lg(\alpha n)) + (c_1(1 - \alpha)n - c_2 \lg((1 - \alpha)n)) + \Theta(\lg n) \\
&= c_1(\alpha + (1 - \alpha))n - c_2(\lg(\alpha n) + \lg((1 - \alpha)n)) + \Theta(\lg n) \\
&= c_1 n - c_2(\lg \alpha + \lg n + \lg(1 - \alpha) + \lg n) + \Theta(\lg n) \\
&= c_1 n - c_2 \lg n - c_2(\lg n + \lg \alpha + \lg(1 - \alpha)) + \Theta(\lg n) \\
&= c_1 n - c_2 \lg n - c_2(\lg n - \Theta(1)) + \Theta(\lg n) \\
&\leq c_1 n - c_2 \lg n ,
\end{aligned}
$$

if we choose c_2 large enough that the $c_2(\lg n - \Theta(1))$ term dominates the $\Theta(\lg n)$ term for sufficiently large n. Furthermore, we can choose c_1 large enough to satisfy the implied $\Theta(1)$ base cases of the recurrence, completing the induction. The lower and upper bounds of $\Omega(n)$ and $O(n)$ give $T_1(n) = \Theta(n)$, asymptotically the same work as for serial merging.

The execution of the pseudocode in the P-MERGE procedure itself does not add asymptotically to the work and span of P-MERGE-AUX. The **parallel for** loop in lines 3–4 has $\Theta(\lg n)$ span due to the loop control, and each iteration runs in constant time. Thus the $\Theta(\lg^2 n)$ span of P-MERGE-AUX dominates, yielding $\Theta(\lg^2 n)$ span overall for P-MERGE. The **parallel for** loop contains $\Theta(n)$ work, matching the asymptotic work of P-MERGE-AUX and yielding $\Theta(n)$ work overall for P-MERGE.

Analysis of parallel merge sort

The "heavy lifting" is done. Now that we have determined the work and span of P-MERGE, we can analyze P-MERGE-SORT. Let $T_1(n)$ and $T_\infty(n)$ be the work and span, respectively, of P-MERGE-SORT on an array of n elements. The call to P-MERGE in line 10 of P-MERGE-SORT dominates the costs of lines 1–3, for both work and span. Thus we obtain the recurrence

$$T_1(n) = 2T_1(n/2) + \Theta(n)$$

for the work of P-MERGE-SORT, and we obtain the recurrence

$$T_\infty(n) = T_\infty(n/2) + \Theta(\lg^2 n)$$

for its span. The work recurrence has solution $T_1(n) = \Theta(n \lg n)$ by case 2 of the master theorem with $k = 0$. The span recurrence has solution $T_\infty(n) = \Theta(\lg^3 n)$, also by case 2 of the master theorem, but with $k = 2$.

Parallel merging gives P-MERGE-SORT a parallelism advantage over P-NAIVE-MERGE-SORT. The parallelism of P-NAIVE-MERGE-SORT, which calls the serial MERGE procedure, is only $\Theta(\lg n)$. For P-MERGE-SORT, the parallelism is

$$
\begin{aligned}
T_1(n)/T_\infty(n) &= \Theta(n \lg n)/\Theta(\lg^3 n) \\
&= \Theta(n/\lg^2 n) \,,
\end{aligned}
$$

which is much better, both in theory and in practice. A good implementation in practice would sacrifice some parallelism by coarsening the base case in order to reduce the constants hidden by the asymptotic notation. For example, you could switch to an efficient serial sort, perhaps quicksort, when the number of elements to be sorted is sufficiently small.

Exercises

26.3-1
Explain how to coarsen the base case of P-MERGE.

26.3-2
Instead of finding a median element in the larger subarray, as P-MERGE does, suppose that the merge procedure finds a median of all the elements in the two sorted subarrays using the result of Exercise 9.3-10. Give pseudocode for an efficient parallel merging procedure that uses this median-finding procedure. Analyze your algorithm.

26.3-3
Give an efficient parallel algorithm for partitioning an array around a pivot, as is done by the PARTITION procedure on page 184. You need not partition the array in place. Make your algorithm as parallel as possible. Analyze your algorithm. (*Hint:* You might need an auxiliary array and might need to make more than one pass over the input elements.)

26.3-4
Give a parallel version of FFT on page 890. Make your implementation as parallel as possible. Analyze your algorithm.

★ ***26.3-5***
Show how to parallelize SELECT from Section 9.3. Make your implementation as parallel as possible. Analyze your algorithm.

Problems

26-1 Implementing parallel loops using recursive spawning
Consider the parallel procedure SUM-ARRAYS for performing pairwise addition on n-element arrays $A[1:n]$ and $B[1:n]$, storing the sums in $C[1:n]$.

SUM-ARRAYS(A, B, C, n)
1 **parallel for** $i = 1$ **to** n
2      $C[i] = A[i] + B[i]$

a. Rewrite the parallel loop in SUM-ARRAYS using recursive spawning in the manner of P-MAT-VEC-RECURSIVE. Analyze the parallelism.

Consider another implementation of the parallel loop in SUM-ARRAYS given by the procedure SUM-ARRAYS$'$, where the value *grain-size* must be specified.

SUM-ARRAYS$'(A, B, C, n)$
1 *grain-size* = ?   **//** to be determined
2 $r = \lceil n/\textit{grain-size} \rceil$
3 **for** $k = 0$ **to** $r - 1$
4   **spawn** ADD-SUBARRAY$(A, B, C, k \cdot \textit{grain-size} + 1,$
                     $\min\{(k + 1) \cdot \textit{grain-size}, n\})$
5 **sync**

ADD-SUBARRAY(A, B, C, i, j)
1 **for** $k = i$ **to** j
2      $C[k] = A[k] + B[k]$

b. Suppose that you set *grain-size* = 1. What is the resulting parallelism?

c. Give a formula for the span of SUM-ARRAYS$'$ in terms of n and *grain-size*. Derive the best value for *grain-size* to maximize parallelism.

26-2 Avoiding a temporary matrix in recursive matrix multiplication
The P-MATRIX-MULTIPLY-RECURSIVE procedure on page 772 must allocate a temporary matrix D of size $n \times n$, which can adversely affect the constants hidden by the Θ-notation. The procedure has high parallelism, however: $\Theta(n^3/\log^2 n)$.

For example, ignoring the constants in the Θ-notation, the parallelism for multiplying 1000×1000 matrices comes to approximately $1000^3 / 10^2 = 10^7$, since $\lg 1000 \approx 10$. Most parallel computers have far fewer than 10 million processors.

a. Parallelize MATRIX-MULTIPLY-RECURSIVE without using temporary matrices so that it retains its $\Theta(n^3)$ work. (*Hint:* Spawn the recursive calls, but insert a **sync** in a judicious location to avoid races.)

b. Give and solve recurrences for the work and span of your implementation.

c. Analyze the parallelism of your implementation. Ignoring the constants in the Θ-notation, estimate the parallelism on 1000×1000 matrices. Compare with the parallelism of P-MATRIX-MULTIPLY-RECURSIVE, and discuss whether the trade-off would be worthwhile.

26-3   Parallel matrix algorithms
Before attempting this problem, it may be helpful to read Chapter 28.

a. Parallelize the LU-DECOMPOSITION procedure on page 827 by giving pseudocode for a parallel version of this algorithm. Make your implementation as parallel as possible, and analyze its work, span, and parallelism.

b. Do the same for LUP-DECOMPOSITION on page 830.

c. Do the same for LUP-SOLVE on page 824.

d. Using equation (28.14) on page 835, write pseudocode for a parallel algorithm to invert a symmetric positive-definite matrix. Make your implementation as parallel as possible, and analyze its work, span, and parallelism.

26-4   Parallel reductions and scan (prefix) computations
A $\otimes$-*reduction* of an array $x[1 : n]$, where $\otimes$ is an associative operator, is the value $y = x[1] \otimes x[2] \otimes \cdots \otimes x[n]$. The REDUCE procedure computes the $\otimes$-reduction of a subarray $x[i : j]$ serially.

```
REDUCE(x, i, j)
1   y = x[i]
2   for k = i + 1 to j
3       y = y ⊗ x[k]
4   return y
```

a. Design and analyze a parallel algorithm P-REDUCE that uses recursive spawning to perform the same function with $\Theta(n)$ work and $\Theta(\lg n)$ span.

A related problem is that of computing a $\otimes$-*scan*, sometimes called a $\otimes$-*prefix
computation*, on an array $x[1:n]$, where $\otimes$ is once again an associative operator. The $\otimes$-scan, implemented by the serial procedure SCAN, produces the array $y[1:n]$ given by

$$y[1] = x[1] ,$$
$$y[2] = x[1] \otimes x[2] ,$$
$$y[3] = x[1] \otimes x[2] \otimes x[3] ,$$
$$\vdots$$
$$y[n] = x[1] \otimes x[2] \otimes x[3] \otimes \cdots \otimes x[n] ,$$

that is, all prefixes of the array x "summed" using the $\otimes$ operator.

SCAN(x, n)

1   let $y[1:n]$ be a new array
2   $y[1] = x[1]$
3   **for** $i = 2$ **to** n
4       $y[i] = y[i-1] \otimes x[i]$
5   **return** y

Parallelizing SCAN is not straightforward. For example, simply changing the **for**
loop to a **parallel for** loop would create races, since each iteration of the loop body
depends on the previous iteration. The procedures P-SCAN-1 and P-SCAN-1-AUX
perform the $\otimes$-scan in parallel, albeit inefficiently.

P-SCAN-1(x, n)

1   let $y[1:n]$ be a new array
2   P-SCAN-1-AUX$(x, y, 1, n)$
3   **return** y

P-SCAN-1-AUX(x, y, i, j)

1   **parallel for** $l = i$ **to** j
2       $y[l] = $ P-REDUCE$(x, 1, l)$

b. Analyze the work, span, and parallelism of P-SCAN-1.

The procedures P-SCAN-2 and P-SCAN-2-AUX use recursive spawning to perform a more efficient $\otimes$-scan.

P-SCAN-2(x, n)

1   let $y[1:n]$ be a new array
2   P-SCAN-2-AUX$(x, y, 1, n)$
3   **return** y

P-SCAN-2-AUX(x, y, i, j)

1   **if** $i == j$
2        $y[i] = x[i]$
3   **else** $k = \lfloor (i + j)/2 \rfloor$
4   **spawn** P-SCAN-2-AUX(x, y, i, k)
5   P-SCAN-2-AUX$(x, y, k + 1, j)$
6   **sync**
7   **parallel for** $l = k + 1$ **to** j
8            $y[l] = y[k] \otimes y[l]$

c. Argue that P-SCAN-2 is correct, and analyze its work, span, and parallelism.

To improve on both P-SCAN-1 and P-SCAN-2, perform the $\otimes$-scan in two distinct passes over the data. The first pass gathers the terms for various contiguous subarrays of x into a temporary array t, and the second pass uses the terms in t to compute the final result y. The pseudocode in the procedures P-SCAN-3, P-SCAN-UP, and P-SCAN-DOWN on the facing page implements this strategy, but certain expressions have been omitted.

d. Fill in the three missing expressions in line 8 of P-SCAN-UP and lines 5 and 6 of P-SCAN-DOWN. Argue that with the expressions you supplied, P-SCAN-3 is correct. (*Hint:* Prove that the value v passed to P-SCAN-DOWN(v, x, t, y, i, j) satisfies $v = x[1] \otimes x[2] \otimes \cdots \otimes x[i - 1]$.)

e. Analyze the work, span, and parallelism of P-SCAN-3.

f. Describe how to rewrite P-SCAN-3 so that it doesn't require the use of the temporary array t.

★ ***g.*** Give an algorithm P-SCAN-4(x, n) for a scan that operates in place. It should place its output in x and require only constant auxiliary storage.

h. Describe an efficient parallel algorithm that uses a $+$-scan to determine whether a string of parentheses is well formed. For example, the string (( ) ( )) ( )

is well formed, but the string (( ))) (( ) is not. (*Hint:* Interpret (as a 1 and) as a -1, and then perform a $+$-scan.)

P-SCAN-3(x, n)

1 let $y[1:n]$ and $t[1:n]$ be new arrays
2 $y[1] = x[1]$
3 **if** $n > 1$
4   P-SCAN-UP$(x, t, 2, n)$
5   P-SCAN-DOWN$(x[1], x, t, y, 2, n)$
6 **return** y

P-SCAN-UP(x, t, i, j)

1 **if** $i == j$
2   **return** $x[i]$
3 **else**
4      $k = \lfloor (i + j)/2 \rfloor$
5      $t[k] = $ **spawn** P-SCAN-UP(x, t, i, k)
6      $right = $ P-SCAN-UP$(x, t, k + 1, j)$
7   **sync**
8   **return** _____   // fill in the blank

P-SCAN-DOWN(v, x, t, y, i, j)

1 **if** $i == j$
2      $y[i] = v \otimes x[i]$
3 **else**
4      $k = \lfloor (i + j)/2 \rfloor$
5   **spawn** P-SCAN-DOWN$(\_\_\_\_\_, x, t, y, i, k)$ // fill in the blank
6   P-SCAN-DOWN$(\_\_\_\_\_, x, t, y, k + 1, j)$ // fill in the blank
7   **sync**

26-5 *Parallelizing a simple stencil calculation*

Computational science is replete with algorithms that require the entries of an array to be filled in with values that depend on the values of certain already computed neighboring entries, along with other information that does not change over the course of the computation. The pattern of neighboring entries does not change during the computation and is called a *stencil*. For example, Section 14.4 presents a stencil algorithm to compute a longest common subsequence, where the value in entry $c[i, j]$ depends only on the values in $c[i - 1, j]$, $c[i, j - 1]$, and $c[i - 1, j - 1]$, as well as the elements x_i and y_j within the two sequences given as inputs. The input sequences are fixed, but the algorithm fills in the two-dimensional array c so that it computes entry $c[i, j]$ after computing all three entries $c[i-1, j], c[i, j-1]$, and $c[i-1, j-1]$.

This problem examines how to use recursive spawning to parallelize a simple stencil calculation on an $n \times n$ array A in which the value placed into entry $A[i, j]$ depends only on values in $A[i', j']$, where $i' \leq i$ and $j' \leq j$ (and of course, $i' \neq i$ or $j' \neq j$). In other words, the value in an entry depends only on values in entries that are above it and/or to its left, along with static information outside of the array. Furthermore, we assume throughout this problem that once the entries upon which $A[i, j]$ depends have been filled in, the entry $A[i, j]$ can be computed in $\Theta(1)$ time (as in the LCS-LENGTH procedure of Section 14.4).

Partition the $n \times n$ array A into four $n/2 \times n/2$ subarrays as follows:

$$A = \begin{pmatrix} A_{11} & A_{12} \\ A_{21} & A_{22} \end{pmatrix}. \tag{26.9}$$

You can immediately fill in subarray A_{11} recursively, since it does not depend on the entries in the other three subarrays. Once the computation of A_{11} finishes, you can fill in A_{12} and A_{21} recursively in parallel, because although they both depend on A_{11}, they do not depend on each other. Finally, you can fill in A_{22} recursively.

a. Give parallel pseudocode that performs this simple stencil calculation using a divide-and-conquer algorithm SIMPLE-STENCIL based on the decomposition (26.9) and the discussion above. (Don't worry about the details of the base case, which depends on the specific stencil.) Give and solve recurrences for the work and span of this algorithm in terms of n. What is the parallelism?

b. Modify your solution to part (a) to divide an $n \times n$ array into nine $n/3 \times n/3$ subarrays, again recursing with as much parallelism as possible. Analyze this algorithm. How much more or less parallelism does this algorithm have compared with the algorithm from part (a)?

c. Generalize your solutions to parts (a) and (b) as follows. Choose an integer $b \geq 2$. Divide an $n \times n$ array into b^2 subarrays, each of size $n/b \times n/b$, recursing with as much parallelism as possible. In terms of n and b, what are the work, span, and parallelism of your algorithm? Argue that, using this approach, the parallelism must be $o(n)$ for any choice of $b \geq 2$. (*Hint:* For this argument, show that the exponent of n in the parallelism is strictly less than 1 for any choice of $b \geq 2$.)

d. Give pseudocode for a parallel algorithm for this simple stencil calculation that achieves $\Theta(n/\lg n)$ parallelism. Argue using notions of work and span that the problem has $\Theta(n)$ inherent parallelism. Unfortunately, simple fork-join parallelism does not let you achieve this maximal parallelism.

26-6 *Randomized parallel algorithms*

Like serial algorithms, parallel algorithms can employ random-number generators. This problem explores how to adapt the measures of work, span, and parallelism to handle the expected behavior of randomized task-parallel algorithms. It also asks you to design and analyze a parallel algorithm for randomized quicksort.

a. Explain how to modify the work law (26.2), span law (26.3), and greedy scheduler bound (26.4) to work with expectations when T_P, T_1, and T_∞ are all random variables.

b. Consider a randomized parallel algorithm for which 1% of the time, $T_1 = 10^4$ and $T_{10,000} = 1$, but for the remaining 99% of the time, $T_1 = T_{10,000} = 10^9$. Argue that the *speedup* of a randomized parallel algorithm should be defined as $\mathrm{E}\left[T_1\right]/\mathrm{E}\left[T_P\right]$, rather than $\mathrm{E}\left[T_1/T_P\right]$.

c. Argue that the *parallelism* of a randomized task-parallel algorithm should be defined as the ratio $\mathrm{E}\left[T_1\right]/\mathrm{E}\left[T_\infty\right]$.

d. Parallelize the RANDOMIZED-QUICKSORT algorithm on page 192 by using recursive spawning to produce P-RANDOMIZED-QUICKSORT. (Do not parallelize RANDOMIZED-PARTITION.)

e. Analyze your parallel algorithm for randomized quicksort. (*Hint:* Review the analysis of RANDOMIZED-SELECT on page 230.)

f. Parallelize RANDOMIZED-SELECT on page 230. Make your implementation as parallel as possible. Analyze your algorithm. (*Hint:* Use the partitioning algorithm from Exercise 26.3-3.)

Chapter notes

Parallel computers and algorithmic models for parallel programming have been around in various forms for years. Prior editions of this book included material on sorting networks and the PRAM (Parallel Random-Access Machine) model. The data-parallel model [58, 217] is another popular algorithmic programming model, which features operations on vectors and matrices as primitives. The notion of sequential consistency is due to Lamport [275].

Graham [197] and Brent [71] showed that there exist schedulers achieving the bound of Theorem 26.1. Eager, Zahorjan, and Lazowska [129] showed that any greedy scheduler achieves this bound and proposed the methodology of using work and span (although not by those names) to analyze parallel algorithms. Blelloch [57] developed an algorithmic programming model based on work and span (which he called "depth") for data-parallel programming. Blumofe and Leiserson [63] gave a distributed scheduling algorithm for task-parallel computations based on randomized "work-stealing" and showed that it achieves the bound $\mathrm{E}[T_P] \leq T_1/P + O(T_\infty)$. Arora, Blumofe, and Plaxton [20] and Blelloch, Gibbons, and Matias [61] also provided provably good algorithms for scheduling task-parallel computations. The recent literature contains many algorithms and strategies for scheduling parallel programs.

The parallel pseudocode and programming model were influenced by Cilk [290, 291, 383, 396]. The open-source project OpenCilk (www.opencilk.org) provides Cilk programming as an extension to the C and C++ programming languages. All of the parallel algorithms in this chapter can be coded straightforwardly in Cilk.

Concerns about nondeterministic parallel programs were expressed by Lee [281] and Bocchino, Adve, Adve, and Snir [64]. The algorithms literature contains many algorithmic strategies (see, for example, [60, 85, 118, 140, 160, 282, 283, 412, 461]) for detecting races and extending the fork-join model to avoid or safely embrace various kinds of nondeterminism. Blelloch, Fineman, Gibbons, and Shun [59] showed that deterministic parallel algorithms can often be as fast as, or even faster than, their nondeterministic counterparts.

Several of the parallel algorithms in this chapter appeared in unpublished lecture notes by C. E. Leiserson and H. Prokop and were originally implemented in Cilk. The parallel merge-sorting algorithm was inspired by an algorithm due to Akl [12].

27   Online Algorithms

Most problems described in this book have assumed that the entire input was available before the algorithm executes. In many situations, however, the input becomes available not in advance, but only as the algorithm executes. This idea was implicit in much of the discussion of data structures in Part III. The reason that you want to design, for example, a data structure that can handle n INSERT, DELETE, and SEARCH operations in $O(\lg n)$ time per operation is most likely because you are going to receive n such operation requests without knowing in advance what operations will be coming. This idea was also implicit in amortized analysis in Chapter 16, where we saw how to maintain a table that can grow or shrink in response to a sequence of insertion and deletion operations, yet with a constant amortized cost per operation.

An *online algorithm* receives its input progressively over time, rather than having the entire input available at the start, as in an *offline algorithm*. Online algorithms pertain to many situations in which information arrives gradually. A stock trader must make decisions today, without knowing what the prices will be tomorrow, yet wants to achieve good returns. A computer system must schedule arriving jobs without knowing what work will need to be done in the future. A store must decide when to order more inventory without knowing what the future demand will be. A driver for a ride-hailing service must decide whether to pick up a fare without knowing who will request rides in the future. In each of these situations, and many more, algorithmic decisions must be made without knowledge of the future.

There are several approaches for dealing with unknown future inputs. One approach is to form a probabilistic model of future inputs and design an algorithm that assumes future inputs conform to the model. This technique is common, for example, in the field of queuing theory, and it is also related to machine learning. Of course, you might not be able to develop a workable probabilistic model, or even if you can, some inputs might not conform to it. This chapter takes a different approach. Instead of assuming anything about the future input, we employ a conservative strategy of limiting how poor a solution any input can entail.

This chapter, therefore, adopts a worst-case approach, designing online algorithms that guarantee the quality of the solution for all possible future inputs. We'll analyze online algorithms by comparing the solution produced by the online algorithm with a solution produced by an optimal algorithm that knows the future inputs, and taking a worst-case ratio over all possible instances. We call this methodology *competitive analysis*. We'll use a similar approach when we study approximation algorithms in Chapter 35, where we'll compare the solution returned by an algorithm that might be suboptimal with the value of the optimal solution, and determine a worst-case ratio over all possible instances.

We start with a "toy" problem: deciding between whether to take the elevator or the stairs. This problem will introduce the basic methodology of thinking about online algorithms and how to analyze them via competitive analysis. We will then look at two problems that use competitive analysis. The first is how to maintain a search list so that the access time is not too large, and the second is about strategies for deciding which cache blocks to evict from a cache or other kind of fast computer memory.

27.1   Waiting for an elevator

Our first example of an online algorithm models a problem that you likely have encountered yourself: whether you should wait for an elevator to arrive or just take the stairs. Suppose that you enter a building and wish to visit an office that is k floors up. You have two choices: walk up the stairs or take the elevator. Let's assume, for convenience, that you can climb the stairs at the rate of one floor per minute. The elevator travels much faster than you can climb the stairs: it can ascend all k floors in just one minute. Your dilemma is that you do not know how long it will take for the elevator to arrive at the ground floor and pick you up. Should you take the elevator or the stairs? How do you decide?

Let's analyze the problem. Taking the stairs takes k minutes, no matter what. Suppose you know that the elevator takes at most $B - 1$ minutes to arrive for some value of B that is considerably higher than k. (The elevator could be going up when you call for it and then stop at several floors on its way down.) To keep things simple, let's also assume that the number of minutes for the elevator to arrive is an integer. Therefore, waiting for the elevator and taking it k floors up takes anywhere from one minute (if the elevator is already at the ground floor) to $(B-1)+1 = B$ minutes (the worst case). Although you know B and k, you don't know how long the elevator will take to arrive this time. You can use competitive analysis to inform your decision regarding whether to take the stairs or elevator. In the spirit of competitive analysis, you want to be sure that, no matter what the future brings (i.e., how long the elevator takes to arrive), you will not wait much longer than a seer who knows when the elevator will arrive.

Let us first consider what the seer would do. If the seer knows that the elevator is going to arrive in at most $k - 1$ minutes, the seer waits for the elevator, and otherwise, the seer takes the stairs. Letting m denote the number of minutes it takes for the elevator to arrive at the ground floor, we can express the time that the seer spends as the function

$$t(m) = \begin{cases} m + 1 & \text{if } m \leq k - 1, \\ k & \text{if } m \geq k. \end{cases} \tag{27.1}$$

We typically evaluate online algorithms by their *competitive ratio*. Let $\mathcal{U}$ denote the set (universe) of all possible inputs, and consider some input $I \in \mathcal{U}$. For a minimization problem, such as the stairs-versus-elevator problem, if an online algorithm A produces a solution with value $A(I)$ on input I and the solution from an algorithm F that knows the future has value $F(I)$ on the same input, then the competitive ratio of algorithm A is

$$\max \{A(I)/F(I) : I \in \mathcal{U}\} .$$

If an online algorithm has a competitive ratio of c, we say that it is *c-competitive*. The competitive ratio is always at least 1, so that we want an online algorithm with a competitive ratio as close to 1 as possible.

In the stairs-versus-elevator problem, the only input is the time for the elevator to arrive. Algorithm F knows this information, but an online algorithm has to make a decision without knowing when the elevator will arrive. Consider the algorithm "always take the stairs," which always takes exactly k minutes. Using equation (27.1), the competitive ratio is

$$\max \{k/t(m) : 0 \leq m \leq B - 1\} . \tag{27.2}$$

Enumerating the terms in equation (27.2) gives the competitive ratio as

$$\max \left\{ \frac{k}{1}, \frac{k}{2}, \frac{k}{3}, \ldots, \frac{k}{(k-1)}, \frac{k}{k}, \frac{k}{k}, \ldots, \frac{k}{k} \right\} = k ,$$

so that the competitive ratio is k. The maximum is achieved when the elevator arrives immediately. In this case, taking the stairs requires k minutes, but the optimal solution takes just 1 minute.

Now let's consider the opposite approach: "always take the elevator." If it takes m minutes for the elevator to arrive at the ground floor, then this algorithm will always take $m + 1$ minutes. Thus the competitive ratio becomes

$$\max \{(m + 1)/t(m) : 0 \leq m \leq B - 1\} ,$$

which we can again enumerate as

$$\max \left\{ \frac{1}{1}, \frac{2}{2}, \dots, \frac{k}{k}, \frac{k+1}{k}, \frac{k+2}{k}, \dots, \frac{B}{k} \right\} = \frac{B}{k}.$$

Now the maximum is achieved when the elevator takes $B - 1$ minutes to arrive, compared with the optimal approach of taking the stairs, which requires k minutes.

Hence, the algorithm "always take the stairs" has competitive ratio k, and the algorithm "always take the elevator" has competitive ratio B/k. Because we prefer the algorithm with smaller competitive ratio, if $k = 10$ and $B = 300$, we prefer "always take the stairs," with competitive ratio 10, over "always take the elevator," with competitive ratio 30. Taking the stairs is not always better, or necessarily more often better. It's just that taking the stairs guards better against the worst-case future.

These two approaches of always taking the stairs and always taking the elevator are extreme solutions, however. Instead, you can "hedge your bets" and guard even better against a worst-case future. In particular, you can wait for the elevator for a while, and then if it doesn't arrive, take the stairs. How long is "a while"? Let's say that "a while" is k minutes. Then the time $h(m)$ required by this hedging strategy, as a function of the number m of minutes before the elevator arrives, is

$$h(m) = \begin{cases} m + 1 & \text{if } m \le k, \\ 2k & \text{if } m > k. \end{cases}$$

In the second case, $h(m) = 2k$ because you wait for k minutes and then climb the stairs for k minutes. The competitive ratio is now

$$\max \{h(m)/t(m) : 0 \le m \le B - 1\}.$$

Enumerating this ratio yields

$$\max \left\{ \frac{1}{1}, \frac{2}{2}, \dots, \frac{k}{k}, \frac{k+1}{k}, \frac{2k}{k}, \frac{2k}{k}, \frac{2k}{k}, \dots, \frac{2k}{k} \right\} = 2.$$

The competitive ratio is now *independent* of k and B.

This example illustrates a common philosophy in online algorithms: we want an algorithm that guards against any possible worst case. Initially, waiting for the elevator guards against the case when the elevator arrives quickly, but eventually switching to the stairs guards against the case when the elevator takes a long time to arrive.

Exercises

27.1-1
Suppose that when hedging your bets, you wait for p minutes, instead of for k minutes, before taking the stairs. What is the competitive ratio as a function of p and k? How should you choose p to minimize the competitive ratio?

27.1-2
Imagine that you decide to take up downhill skiing. Suppose that a pair of skis costs r dollars to rent for a day and b dollars to buy, where $b > r$. If you knew in advance how many days you would ever ski, your decision whether to rent or buy would be easy. If you'll ski for at least $\lceil b/r \rceil$ days, then you should buy skis, and otherwise you should rent. This strategy minimizes the total that you ever spend. In reality, you don't know in advance how many days you'll eventually ski. Even after you have skied several times, you still don't know how many more times you'll ever ski. Yet you don't want to waste your money. Give and analyze an algorithm that has a competitive ratio of 2, that is, an algorithm guaranteeing that, no matter how many times you ski, you never spend more than twice what you would have spent if you knew from the outset how many times you'll ski.

27.1-3
In "concentration solitaire," a game for one person, you have n pairs of matching cards. The backs of the cards are all the same, but the fronts contain pictures of animals. One pair has pictures of aardvarks, one pair has pictures of bears, one pair has pictures of camels, and so on. At the start of the game, the cards are all placed face down. In each round, you can turn two cards face up to reveal their pictures. If the pictures match, then you remove that pair from the game. If they don't match, then you turn both of them over, hiding their pictures once again. The game ends when you have removed all n pairs, and your score is how many rounds you needed to do so. Suppose that you can remember the picture on every card that you have seen. Give an algorithm to play concentration solitaire that has a competitive ratio of 2.

27.2   Maintaining a search list

The next example of an online algorithm pertains to maintaining the order of elements in a linked list, as in Section 10.2. This problem often arises in practice for hash tables when collisions are resolved by chaining (see Section 11.2), since each slot contains a linked list. Reordering the linked list of elements in each slot of the hash table can boost the performance of searches measurably.

The list-maintenance problem can be set up as follows. You are given a list L of n elements $\{x_1, x_2, \ldots, x_n\}$. We'll assume that the list is doubly linked, although the algorithms and analysis work just as well for singly linked lists. Denote the position of element x_i in the list L by $r_L(x_i)$, where $1 \leq r_L(x_i) \leq n$. Calling LIST-SEARCH(L, x_i) on page 260 thus takes $\Theta(r_L(x_i))$ time.

If you know in advance something about the distribution of search requests, then it makes sense to arrange the list ahead of time to put the more frequently searched elements closer to the front, which minimizes the total cost (see Exercise 27.2-1). If instead you don't know anything about the search sequence, then no matter how you arrange the list, it is possible that every search is for whatever element appears at the tail of the list. The total searching time would then be $\Theta(nm)$, where m is the number of searches.

If you notice patterns in the access sequence or you observe differences in the frequencies in which elements are accessed, then you might want to rearrange the list as you perform searches. For example, if you discover that every search is for a particular element, you could move that element to the front of the list. In general, you could rearrange the list after each call to LIST-SEARCH. But how would you do so without knowing the future? After all, no matter how you move elements around, every search could be for the last element.

But it turns out that some search sequences are "easier" than others. Rather than just evaluate performance on the worst-case sequence, let's compare a reorganization scheme with whatever an optimal offline algorithm would do if it knew the search sequence in advance. That way, if the sequence is fundamentally hard, the optimal offline algorithm will also find it hard, but if the sequence is easy, we can hope to do reasonably well.

To ease analysis, we'll drop the asymptotic notation and say that the cost is just i to search for the ith element in the list. Let's also assume that the only way to reorder the elements in the list is by swapping two adjacent elements in the list. Because the list is doubly linked, each swap incurs a cost of 1. Thus, for example, a search for the sixth element followed by moving it forward two places (entailing two swaps) incurs a total cost 8. The goal is to minimize the total cost of calls to LIST-SEARCH plus the total number of swaps performed.

The online algorithm that we'll explore is MOVE-TO-FRONT(L, x). This procedure first searches for x in the doubly linked list L, and then it moves x to the front of the list.[1] If x is located at position $r = r_L(x)$ before the call, MOVE-TO-FRONT swaps x with the element in position $r - 1$, then with the element in position $r - 2$,

---

[1] The path-compression heuristic in Section 19.3 resembles MOVE-TO-FRONT, although it would be more accurately expressed as "move-to-next-to-front." Unlike MOVE-TO-FRONT in a doubly linked list, path compression can relocate multiple elements to become "next-to-front."

	FORESEE					MOVE-TO-FRONT				
element searched	L	search cost	swap cost	search + swap cost	cumulative cost	L	search cost	swap cost	search + swap cost	cumulative cost
5	$\langle 1,2,3,4,5 \rangle$	5	0	5	5	$\langle 1,2,3,4,5 \rangle$	5	4	9	9
3	$\langle 1,2,3,4,5 \rangle$	3	3	6	11	$\langle 5,1,2,3,4 \rangle$	4	3	7	16
4	$\langle 4,1,2,3,5 \rangle$	1	0	1	12	$\langle 3,5,1,2,4 \rangle$	5	4	9	25
4	$\langle 4,1,2,3,5 \rangle$	1	0	1	13	$\langle 4,3,5,1,2 \rangle$	1	0	1	26

Figure 27.1 The costs incurred by the procedures FORESEE and MOVE-TO-FRONT when searching for the elements 5, 3, 4, and 4, starting with the list $L = \langle 1, 2, 3, 4, 5 \rangle$. If FORESEE instead moved 3 to the front after the search for 5, the cumulative cost would not change, nor would the cumulative cost change if 4 moved to the second position after the search for 5.

and so on, until it finally swaps x with the element in position 1. Thus if the call MOVE-TO-FRONT$(L, 8)$ executes on the list $L = \langle 5, 3, 12, 4, 8, 9, 22 \rangle$, the list becomes $\langle 8, 5, 3, 12, 4, 9, 22 \rangle$. The call MOVE-TO-FRONT$(L, k)$ costs $2r_L(k) - 1$: it costs $r_L(k)$ to search for k, and it costs 1 for each of the $r_L(k) - 1$ swaps that move k to the front of the list.

We'll see that MOVE-TO-FRONT has a competitive ratio of 4. Let's think about what this means. MOVE-TO-FRONT performs a series of operations on a doubly linked list, accumulating cost. For comparison, suppose that there is an algorithm FORESEE that knows the future. Like MOVE-TO-FRONT, it also searches the list and moves elements around, but after each call it optimally rearranges the list for the future. (There may be more than one optimal order.) Thus FORESEE and MOVE-TO-FRONT maintain different lists of the same elements.

Consider the example shown in Figure 27.1. Starting with the list $\langle 1, 2, 3, 4, 5 \rangle$, four searches occur, for the elements 5, 3, 4, and 4. The hypothetical procedure FORESEE, after searching for 3, moves 4 to the front of the list, knowing that a search for 4 is imminent. It thus incurs a swap cost of 3 upon its second call, after which no further swap costs accrue. MOVE-TO-FRONT incurs swap costs in each step, moving the found element to the front. In this example, MOVE-TO-FRONT has a higher cost in each step, but that is not necessarily always the case.

The key to proving the competitive bound is to show that at any point, the total cost of MOVE-TO-FRONT is not much higher than that of FORESEE. Surprisingly, we can determine a bound on the costs incurred by MOVE-TO-FRONT relative to FORESEE even though MOVE-TO-FRONT cannot see the future.

If we compare any particular step, MOVE-TO-FRONT and FORESEE may be operating on very different lists and do very different things. If we focus on the search for 4 above, we observe that FORESEE actually moves it to the front of the list early, paying to move the element to the front before it is accessed. To capture this concept, we use the idea of an *inversion*: a pair of elements, say a and b, in which a appears before b in one list, but b appears before a in another list. For two lists L and L', let $I(L, L')$, called the *inversion count*, denote the number of inversions between the two lists, that is, the number of pairs of elements whose order differs in the two lists. For example, with lists $L = \langle 5, 3, 1, 4, 2 \rangle$ and $L' = \langle 3, 1, 2, 4, 5 \rangle$, then out of the $\binom{5}{2} = 10$ pairs, exactly five of them—$(1, 5), (2, 4), (2, 5), (3, 5), (4, 5)$—are inversions, since these pairs, and only these pairs, appear in different orders in the two lists. Thus the inversion count is $I(L, L') = 5$.

In order to analyze the algorithm, we define the following notation. Let L_i^M be the list maintained by MOVE-TO-FRONT immediately after the ith search, and similarly, let L_i^F be FORESEE's list immediately after the ith search. Let c_i^M and c_i^F be the costs incurred by MOVE-TO-FRONT and FORESEE on their ith calls, respectively. We don't know how many swaps FORESEE performs in its ith call, but we'll denote that number by t_i. Therefore, if the ith operation is a search for element x, then

$$c_i^M = 2r_{L_{i-1}^M}(x) - 1 , \tag{27.3}$$

$$c_i^F = r_{L_{i-1}^F}(x) + t_i . \tag{27.4}$$

In order to compare these costs more carefully, let's break down the elements into subsets, depending on their positions in the two lists before the ith search, relative to the element x being searched for in the ith search. We define three sets:

$BB = \{$elements before x in both L_{i-1}^M and $L_{i-1}^F\}$,

$BA = \{$elements before x in L_{i-1}^M but after x in $L_{i-1}^F\}$,

$AB = \{$elements after x in L_{i-1}^M but before x in $L_{i-1}^F\}$.

We can now relate the position of element x in L_{i-1}^F and L_{i-1}^M to the sizes of these sets:

$$r_{L_{i-1}^M}(x) = |BB| + |BA| + 1 , \tag{27.5}$$

$$r_{L_{i-1}^F}(x) = |BB| + |AB| + 1 . \tag{27.6}$$

When a swap occurs in one of the lists, it changes the relative positions of the two elements involved, which in turn changes the inversion count. Suppose that elements x and y are swapped in some list. Then the only possible difference in the inversion count between this list and *any* other list depends on whether (x, y) is an inversion. In fact, the inversion count of (x, y) with respect to any other list *must* change. If (x, y) is an inversion before the swap, it no longer is afterward, and vice versa. Therefore, if two consecutive elements x and y swap positions in a list L, then for any other list L', the value of the inversion count $I(L, L')$ either increases by 1 or decreases by 1.

As we compare MOVE-TO-FRONT and FORESEE searching and modifying their lists, we'll think about MOVE-TO-FRONT executing on its list for the ith time and then FORESEE executing on its list for the ith time. After MOVE-TO-FRONT has executed for the ith time and before FORESEE has executed for the ith time, we'll compare $I(L_{i-1}^M, L_{i-1}^F)$ (the inversion count immediately before the ith call of MOVE-TO-FRONT) with $I(L_i^M, L_{i-1}^F)$ (the inversion count after the ith call of MOVE-TO-FRONT but before the ith call of FORESEE). We'll concern ourselves later with what FORESEE does.

Let us analyze what happens to the inversion count after executing the ith call of MOVE-TO-FRONT, and suppose that it searches for element x. More precisely, we'll compute $I(L_i^M, L_{i-1}^F) - I(L_{i-1}^M, L_{i-1}^F)$, the change in the inversion count, which gives a rough idea of how much MOVE-TO-FRONT's list becomes more or less like FORESEE's list. After searching, MOVE-TO-FRONT performs a series of swaps with each of the elements on the list L_{i-1}^M that precedes x. Using the notation above, the number of such swaps is $|BB| + |BA|$. Bearing in mind that the list L_{i-1}^F has yet to be changed by the ith call of FORESEE, let's see how the inversion count changes.

Consider a swap with an element $y \in BB$. Before the swap, y precedes x in both L_{i-1}^M and L_{i-1}^F. After the swap, x precedes y in L_i^M, and L_{i-1}^F does not change. Therefore, the inversion count increases by 1 for each element in BB. Now consider a swap with an element $z \in BA$. Before the swap, z precedes x in L_{i-1}^M but x precedes z in L_{i-1}^F. After the swap, x precedes z in both lists. Therefore, the inversion count decreases by 1 for each element in BA. Thus altogether, the inversion count increases by

$$I(L_i^M, L_{i-1}^F) - I(L_{i-1}^M, L_{i-1}^F) = |BB| - |BA| \ . \tag{27.7}$$

We have laid the groundwork needed to analyze MOVE-TO-FRONT.

Theorem 27.1
Algorithm MOVE-TO-FRONT has a competitive ratio of 4.

Proof The proof uses a potential function, as described in Chapter 16 on amortized analysis. The value Φ_i of the potential function after the ith calls of MOVE-TO-FRONT and FORESEE depends on the inversion count:

$$\Phi_i = 2I(L_i^M, L_i^F) \ .$$

(Intuitively, the factor of 2 embodies the notion that each inversion represents a cost of 2 for MOVE-TO-FRONT relative to FORESEE: 1 for searching and 1 for swapping.) By equation (27.7), after the ith call of MOVE-TO-FRONT, but before the ith call of FORESEE, the potential increases by $2(|BB| - |BA|)$. Since the inversion count of the two lists is nonnegative, we have $\Phi_i \geq 0$ for all $i \geq 0$.

Assuming that MOVE-TO-FRONT and FORESEE start with the same list, the initial potential Φ_0 is 0, so that $\Phi_i \geq \Phi_0$ for all i.

Drawing from equation (16.2) on page 456, the amortized cost $\hat{c}_i^M$ of the ith MOVE-TO-FRONT operation is

$$\hat{c}_i^M = c_i^M + \Phi_i - \Phi_{i-1} \, ,$$

where c_i^M, the actual cost of the ith MOVE-TO-FRONT operation, is given by equation (27.3):

$$c_i^M = 2r_{L_{i-1}^M}(x) - 1 \, .$$

Now, let's consider the potential change $\Phi_i - \Phi_{i-1}$. Since both L^M and L^F change, let's consider the changes to one list at a time. Recall that when MOVE-TO-FRONT moves element x to the front, it increases the potential by exactly $2(|BB| - |BA|)$. We now consider how the optimal algorithm FORESEE changes its list L^F: it performs t_i swaps. Each swap performed by FORESEE either increases or decreases the potential by 2, and thus the increase in potential by FORESEE in the ith call can be at most $2t_i$. We therefore have

$$
\begin{aligned}
\hat{c}_i^M &= c_i^M + \Phi_i - \Phi_{i-1} \\
&\leq 2r_{L_{i-1}^M}(x) - 1 + 2(|BB| - |BA| + t_i) \\
&= 2r_{L_{i-1}^M}(x) - 1 + 2(|BB| - (r_{L_{i-1}^M}(x) - 1 - |BB|) + t_i) \\
&\qquad\qquad\qquad\qquad \text{(by equation (27.5))} \\
&= 4|BB| + 1 + 2t_i \\
&\leq 4|BB| + 4|AB| + 4 + 4t_i \qquad \text{(increasing some terms)} \\
&= 4(|BB| + |AB| + 1 + t_i) \\
&= 4(r_{L_{i-1}^F}(x) + t_i) \qquad\qquad \text{(by equation (27.6))} \\
&= 4c_i^F \qquad\qquad\qquad\qquad \text{(by equation (27.4))} \, . \qquad (27.8)
\end{aligned}
$$

We now finish the proof as in Chapter 16 by showing that the total amortized cost provides an upper bound on the total actual cost, because the initial potential function is 0 and the potential function is always nonnegative. By equation (16.3) on page 456, for any sequence of m MOVE-TO-FRONT operations, we have

$$
\begin{aligned}
\sum_{i=1}^{m} \hat{c}_i^M &= \sum_{i=1}^{m} c_i^M + \Phi_m - \Phi_0 \\
&\geq \sum_{i=1}^{m} c_i^M \qquad \text{(because } \Phi_m \geq \Phi_0\text{)} \, . \qquad (27.9)
\end{aligned}
$$

Therefore, we have

$$\sum_{i=1}^{m} c_i^M \leq \sum_{i=1}^{m} \hat{c}_i^M \qquad \text{(by equation (27.9))}$$

$$\leq \sum_{i=1}^{m} 4 c_i^F \qquad \text{(by equation (27.8))}$$

$$= 4 \sum_{i=1}^{m} c_i^F .$$

Thus the total cost of the m MOVE-TO-FRONT operations is at most 4 times the total cost of the m FORESEE operations, so MOVE-TO-FRONT is 4-competitive. ∎

Isn't it amazing that we can compare MOVE-TO-FRONT with the optimal algorithm FORESEE when we have no idea of the swaps that FORESEE makes? We were able to relate the performance of MOVE-TO-FRONT to the optimal algorithm by capturing how particular properties (swaps in this case) must evolve relative to the optimal algorithm, without actually knowing the optimal algorithm.

The online algorithm MOVE-TO-FRONT has a competitive ratio of 4: on any input sequence, it incurs a cost at most 4 times that of any other algorithm. On a particular input sequence, it could cost much less than 4 times the optimal algorithm, perhaps even matching the optimal algorithm.

Exercises

27.2-1
You are given a set $S = \{x_1, x_2, \ldots, x_n\}$ of n elements, and you wish to make a static list L (no rearranging once the list is created) containing the elements of S that is good for searching. Suppose that you have a probability distribution, where $p(x_i)$ is the probability that a given search searches for element x_i. Argue that the expected cost for m searches is

$$m \sum_{i=1}^{n} p(x_i) \cdot r_L(x_i) .$$

Prove that this sum is minimized when the elements of L are sorted in decreasing order with respect to $p(x_i)$.

27.2-2
Professor Carnac claims that since FORESEE is an optimal algorithm that knows the future, then at each step it must incur no more cost than MOVE-TO-FRONT. Either prove that Professor Carnac is correct or provide a counterexample.

27.2-3
Another way to maintain a linked list for efficient searching is for each element to maintain a *frequency count*: the number of times that the element has been searched for. The idea is to rearrange list elements after searches so that the list is always sorted by decreasing frequency count, from largest to smallest. Either show that this algorithm is $O(1)$-competitive, or prove that it is not.

27.2-4
The model in this section charged a cost of 1 for each swap. We can consider an alternative cost model in which, after accessing x, you can move x anywhere earlier in the list, and there is no cost for doing so. The only cost is the cost of the actual accesses. Show that MOVE-TO-FRONT is 2-competitive in this cost model, assuming that the number requests is sufficiently large. (*Hint:* Use the potential function $\Phi_i = I(L_i^M, L_i^F)$.)

27.3   Online caching

In Section 15.4, we studied the caching problem, in which *blocks* of data from the main memory of a computer are stored in the *cache*: a small but faster memory. In that section, we studied the offline version of the problem, in which we assumed that we knew the sequence of memory requests in advance, and we designed an algorithm to minimize the number of cache misses. In almost all computer systems, caching is, in fact, an online problem. We do not generally know the series of cache requests in advance; they are presented to the algorithm only as the requests for blocks are actually made. To gain a better understanding of this more realistic scenario, we analyze online algorithms for caching. We will first see that all deterministic online algorithms for caching have a lower bound of $\Omega(k)$ for the competitive ratio, where k is the size of the cache. We will then present an algorithm with a competitive ratio of $\Theta(n)$, where the input size is n, and one with a competitive ratio of $O(k)$, which matches the lower bound. We will end by showing how to use randomization to design an algorithm with a much better competitive ratio of $\Theta(\lg k)$. We will also discuss the assumptions that underlie randomized online algorithms, via the notion of an adversary, such as we saw in Chapter 11 and will see in Chapter 31.

You can find the terminology used to describe the caching problem in Section 15.4, which you might wish to review before proceeding.

27.3.1   Deterministic caching algorithms

In the caching problem, the input comprises a sequence of n memory requests, for data in blocks $b_1, b_2, \dots, b_n$, in that order. The blocks requested are not necessarily distinct: each block may appear multiple times within the request sequence. After block b_i is requested, it resides in a cache that can hold up to k blocks, where k is a fixed cache size. We assume that $n > k$, since otherwise we are assured that the cache can hold all the requested blocks at once. When a block b_i is requested, if it is already in the cache, then a *cache hit* occurs and the cache remains unchanged. If b_i is not in the cache, then a *cache miss* occurs. If the cache contains fewer than k blocks upon a cache miss, block b_i is placed into the cache, which now contains one block more than before. If a cache miss occurs with an already full cache, however, some block must be evicted from the cache before b_i can enter. Thus, a caching algorithm must decide which block to evict from the cache upon a cache miss when the cache is full. The goal is to minimize the number of cache misses over the entire request sequence. The caching algorithms considered in this chapter differ only in which block they decide to evict upon a cache miss. We do not consider abilities such as prefetching, in which a block is brought into the cache before an upcoming request in order to avert a future cache miss.

There are many online caching policies to determine which block to evict, including the following:

- First-in, first-out (FIFO): evict the block that has been in the cache the longest time.

- Last-in, first-out (LIFO): evict the block that has been in the cache the shortest time.

- Least Recently Used (LRU): evict the block whose last use is furthest in the past.

- Least Frequently Used (LFU): evict the block that has been accessed the fewest times, breaking ties by choosing the block that has been in the cache the longest.

To analyze these algorithms, we assume that the cache starts out empty, so that no evictions occur during the first k requests. We wish to compare the performance of an online algorithm to an optimal offline algorithm that knows the future requests. As we will soon see, all these deterministic online algorithms have a lower bound of $\Omega(k)$ for their competitive ratio. Some deterministic algorithms also have a competitive ratio with an $O(k)$ upper bound, but some other deterministic algorithms are considerably worse, having a competitive ratio of $\Theta(n/k)$.

We now proceed to analyze the LIFO and LRU policies. In addition to assuming that $n > k$, we will assume that at least k distinct blocks are requested. Otherwise, the cache never fills up and no blocks are evicted, so that all algorithms exhibit the same behavior. We begin by showing that LIFO has a large competitive ratio.

Theorem 27.2

LIFO has a competitive ratio of $\Theta(n/k)$ for the online caching problem with n requests and a cache of size k.

Proof We first show a lower bound of $\Omega(n/k)$. Suppose that the input consists of $k+1$ blocks, numbered $1, 2, \ldots, k+1$, and the request sequence is

$$1, \ 2, \ 3, \ 4, \ \ldots, \ k, \ k+1, \ k, \ k+1, \ k, \ k+1, \ \ldots,$$

where after the initial $1, 2, \ldots, k, k+1$, the remainder of the sequence alternates between k and $k+1$, with a total of n requests. The sequence ends on block k if n and k are either both even or both odd, and otherwise, the sequence ends on block $k+1$. That is, $b_i = i$ for $i = 1, 2, \ldots k-1, b_i = k+1$ for $i = k+1, k+3, \ldots$ and $b_i = k$ for $i = k, k+2, \ldots$. How many blocks does LIFO evict? After the first k requests (which are considered to be cache misses), the cache is filled with blocks $1, 2, \ldots, k$. The $(k+1)$st request, which is for block $k+1$, causes block k to be evicted. The $(k+2)$nd request, which is for block k, forces block $k+1$ to be evicted, since that block was just placed into the cache. This behavior continues, alternately evicting blocks k and $k+1$ for the remaining requests. LIFO, therefore, suffers a cache miss on every one of the n requests.

The optimal offline algorithm knows the entire sequence of requests in advance. Upon the first request of block $k+1$, it just evicts any block except block k, and then it never evicts another block. Thus, the optimal offline algorithm evicts only once. Since the first k requests are considered cache misses, the total number of cache misses is $k+1$. The competitive ratio, therefore, is $n/(k+1)$, or $\Omega(n/k)$.

For the upper bound, observe that on any input of size n, any caching algorithm incurs at most n cache misses. Because the input contains at least k distinct blocks, any caching algorithm, including the optimal offline algorithm, must incur at least k cache misses. Therefore, LIFO has a competitive ratio of $O(n/k)$. ∎

We call such a competitive ratio ***unbounded***, because it grows with the input size. Exercise 27.3-2 asks you to show that LFU also has an unbounded competitive ratio.

FIFO and LRU have a much better competitive ratio of $\Theta(k)$. There is a big difference between competitive ratios of $\Theta(n/k)$ and $\Theta(k)$. The cache size k is independent of the input sequence and does not grow as more requests arrive over time. A competitive ratio that depends on n, on the other hand, does grow with the size of the input sequence and thus can get quite large. It is preferable to use an algorithm with a competitive ratio that does not grow with the input sequence's size, when possible.

We now show that LRU has a competitive ratio of $\Theta(k)$, first showing the upper bound.

Theorem 27.3
LRU has a competitive ratio of $O(k)$ for the online caching problem with n requests and a cache of size k.

Proof To analyze LRU, we will divide the sequence of requests into *epochs*. Epoch 1 begins with the first request. Epoch i, for $i > 1$, begins upon encountering the $(k + 1)$st distinct request since the beginning of epoch $i - 1$. Consider the following example of requests with $k = 3$:

$$1, 2, 1, 5, 4, 4, 1, 2, 4, 2, 3, 4, 5, 2, 2, 1, 2, 2 . \qquad (27.10)$$

The first $k = 3$ distinct requests are for blocks $1, 2$ and 5, so epoch 2 begins with the first request for block 4. In epoch 2, the first 3 distinct requests are for blocks $4, 1$, and 2. Requests for these blocks recur until the request for block 3, and with this request epoch 3 begins. Thus, this example has four epochs:

$$1, 2, 1, 5 \qquad 4, 4, 1, 2, 4, 2 \qquad 3, 4, 5 \qquad 2, 2, 1, 2, 2 . \qquad (27.11)$$

Now we consider the behavior of LRU. In each epoch, the first time a request for a particular block appears, it may cause a cache miss, but subsequent requests for that block within the epoch cannot cause a cache miss, since the block is now one of the k most recently used. For example, in epoch 2, the first request for block 4 causes a cache miss, but the subsequent requests for block 4 do not. (Exercise 27.3-1 asks you to show the contents of the cache after each request.) In epoch 3, requests for blocks 3 and 5 cause cache misses, but the request for block 4 does not, because it was recently accessed in epoch 2. Since only the first request for a block within an epoch can cause a cache miss and the cache holds k blocks, each epoch incurs at most k cache misses.

Now consider the behavior of the optimal algorithm. The first request in each epoch must cause a cache miss, even for an optimal algorithm. The miss occurs because, by the definition of an epoch, there *must* have been k other blocks accessed since the last access to this block.

Since, for each epoch, the optimal algorithm incurs at least one miss and LRU incurs at most k, the competitive ratio is at most $k/1 = O(k)$. ∎

Exercise 27.3-3 asks you to show that FIFO also has a competitive ratio of $O(k)$.

We could show lower bounds of $\Omega(k)$ on LRU and FIFO, but in fact, we can make a much stronger statement: *any* deterministic online caching algorithm must have a competitive ratio of $\Omega(k)$. The proof relies on an adversary who knows the online algorithm being used and can tailor the future requests to cause the online algorithm to incur more cache misses than the optimal offline algorithm.

Consider a scenario in which the cache has size k and the set of possible blocks to request is $\{1, 2, \ldots, k + 1\}$. The first k requests are for blocks $1, 2, \ldots, k$, so that both the adversary and the deterministic online algorithm place these blocks into the cache. The next request is for block $k + 1$. In order to make room in the cache for block $k + 1$, the online algorithm evicts some block b_1 from the cache. The adversary, knowing that the online algorithm has just evicted block b_1, makes the next request be for b_1, so that the online algorithm must evict some other block b_2 to clear room in the cache for b_1. As you might have guessed, the adversary makes the next request be for block b_2, so that the online algorithm evicts some other block b_3 to make room for b_2. The online algorithm and the adversary continue in this manner. The online algorithm incurs a cache miss on every request and therefore incurs n cache misses over the n requests.

Now let's consider an optimal offline algorithm, which knows the future. As discussed in Section 15.4, this algorithm is known as furthest-in-future, and it always evicts the block whose next request is furthest in the future. Since there are only $k + 1$ unique blocks, when furthest-in-future evicts a block, we know that it will not be accessed during at least the next k requests. Thus, after the first k cache misses, the optimal algorithm incurs a cache miss at most once every k requests. Therefore, the number of cache misses over n requests is at most $k + n/k$.

Since the deterministic online algorithm incurs n cache misses and the optimal offline algorithm incurs at most $k + n/k$ cache misses, the competitive ratio is at least

$$\frac{n}{k + n/k} = \frac{nk}{n + k^2} \, .$$

For $n \geq k^2$, the above expression is at least

$$\frac{nk}{n + k^2} \geq \frac{nk}{2n} = \frac{k}{2} \, .$$

Thus, for sufficiently long request sequences, we have shown the following:

Theorem 27.4
Any deterministic online algorithm for caching with a cache size of k has competitive ratio $\Omega(k)$.   ∎

Although we can analyze the common caching strategies from the point of view of competitive analysis, the results are somewhat unsatisfying. Yes, we can distinguish between algorithms with a competitive ratio of $\Theta(k)$ and those with unbounded competitive ratios. In the end, however, all of these competitive ratios are rather high. The online algorithms we have seen so far are deterministic, and it is this property that the adversary is able to exploit.

27.3.2   Randomized caching algorithms

If we don't limit ourselves to deterministic online algorithms, we can use randomization to develop an online caching algorithm with a significantly smaller competitive ratio. Before describing the algorithm, let's discuss randomization in online algorithms in general. Recall that we analyze online algorithms with respect to an adversary who knows the online algorithm and can design requests knowing the decisions made by the online algorithm. With randomization, we must ask whether the adversary also knows the random choices made by the online algorithm. An adversary who does not know the random choices is *oblivious*, and an adversary who knows the random choices is *nonoblivious*. Ideally, we prefer to design algorithms against a nonoblivious adversary, as this adversary is stronger than an oblivious one. Unfortunately, a nonoblivious adversary mitigates much of the power of randomness, as an adversary who knows the outcome of random choices typically can act as if the online algorithm is deterministic. The oblivious adversary, on the other hand, does not know the random choices of the online algorithm, and that is the adversary we typically use.

As a simple illustration of the difference between an oblivious and nonoblivious adversary, imagine that you are flipping a fair coin n times, and the adversary wants to know how many heads you flipped. A nonoblivious adversary knows, after each flip, whether the coin came up heads or tails, and hence knows how many heads you flipped. An oblivious adversary, on the other hand, knows only that you are flipping a fair coin n times. The oblivious adversary, therefore, can reason that the number of heads follows a binomial distribution, so that the expected number of heads is $n/2$ (by equation (C.41) on page 1199) and the variance is $n/4$ (by equation (C.44) on page 1200). But the oblivious adversary has no way of knowing exactly how many heads you actually flipped.

Let's return to caching. We'll start with a deterministic algorithm and then randomize it. The algorithm we'll use is an approximation of LRU called MARKING. Rather than "least recently used," think of MARKING as simply "recently used." MARKING maintains a 1-bit attribute *mark* for each block in the cache. Initially, all blocks in the cache are unmarked. When a block is requested, if it is already in the cache, it is marked. If the request is a cache miss, MARKING checks to see whether there are any unmarked blocks in the cache. If all blocks are marked, then they are all changed to unmarked. Now, regardless of whether all blocks in the cache were marked when the request occurred, there is at least one unmarked block in the cache, and so an arbitrary unmarked block is evicted, and the requested block is placed into the cache and marked.

How should the block to evict from among the unmarked blocks in the cache be chosen? The procedure RANDOMIZED-MARKING on the next page shows the process when the block is chosen randomly. The procedure takes as input a block b being requested.

RANDOMIZED-MARKING(b)

1   **if** block b resides in the cache,
2       $b.mark = 1$
3   **else**
4   **if** all blocks b' in the cache have $b'.mark = 1$
5   unmark all blocks b' in the cache, setting $b'.mark = 0$
6   select an unmarked block u with $u.mark = 0$ uniformly at random
7   evict block u
8   place block b into the cache
9       $b.mark = 1$

For the purpose of analysis, we say that a new epoch begins immediately after each time line 5 executes. An epoch starts with no marked blocks in the cache. The first time a block is requested during an epoch, the number of marked blocks increases by 1, and any subsequent requests to that block do not change the number of marked blocks. Therefore, the number of marked blocks monotonically increases within an epoch. Under this view, epochs are the same as in the proof of Theorem 27.3: with a cache that holds k blocks, an epoch comprises requests for k distinct blocks (possibly fewer for the final epoch), and the next epoch begins upon a request for a block not in those k.

Because we are going to analyze a randomized algorithm, we will compute the expected competitive ratio. Recall that for an input I, we denote the solution value of an online algorithm A by $A(I)$ and the solution value of an optimal algorithm F by $F(I)$. Online algorithm A has an *expected competitive ratio* c if for all inputs I, we have

$$E[A(I)] \leq cF(I) , \tag{27.12}$$

where the expectation is taken over the random choices made by A.

Although the deterministic MARKING algorithm has a competitive ratio of $\Theta(k)$ (Theorem 27.4 provides the lower bound and see Exercise 27.3-4 for the upper bound), RANDOMIZED-MARKING has a much smaller expected competitive ratio, namely $O(\lg k)$. The key to the improved competitive ratio is that the adversary cannot always make a request for a block that is not in the cache, since an oblivious adversary does not know which blocks are in the cache.

Theorem 27.5
RANDOMIZED-MARKING has an expected competitive ratio of $O(\lg k)$ for the online caching problem with n requests and a cache of size k, against an oblivious adversary.

Before proving Theorem 27.5, we prove a basic probabilistic fact.

Lemma 27.6
Suppose that a bag contains $x + y$ balls: $x - 1$ blue balls, y white balls, and 1 red ball. You repeatedly choose a ball at random and remove it from the bag until you have chosen a total of m balls that are either blue or red, where $m \leq x$. You set aside each white ball you choose. Then, one of the balls chosen is the red ball with probability m/x.

Proof Choosing a white ball does not affect how many blue or red balls are chosen in any way. Therefore, we can continue the analysis as if there were no white balls and the bag contains just $x - 1$ blue balls and 1 red ball.

Let A be the event that the red ball is not chosen, and let A_i be the event that the ith draw does not choose the red ball. By equation (C.22) on page 1190, we have

$$\begin{aligned}
\Pr\{A\} &= \Pr\{A_1 \cap A_2 \cap \cdots \cap A_m\} \\
&= \Pr\{A_1\} \cdot \Pr\{A_2 \mid A_1\} \cdot \Pr\{A_3 \mid A_1 \cap A_2\} \cdots \\
&\quad \Pr\{A_m \mid A_1 \cap A_2 \cap \cdots \cap A_{m-1}\} \; .
\end{aligned} \tag{27.13}$$

The probability $\Pr\{A_1\}$ that the first ball is blue equals $(x - 1)/x$, since initially there are $x - 1$ blue balls and 1 red ball. More generally, we have

$$\Pr\{A_i \mid A_1 \cap \cdots \cap A_{i-1}\} = \frac{x - i}{x - i + 1} \; , \tag{27.14}$$

since the ith draw is from $x - i$ blue balls and 1 red ball. Equations (27.13) and (27.14) give

$$\Pr\{A\} = \left(\frac{x-1}{x}\right)\left(\frac{x-2}{x-1}\right)\left(\frac{x-3}{x-2}\right) \cdots \left(\frac{x-m+1}{x-m+2}\right)\left(\frac{x-m}{x-m+1}\right) \; . \tag{27.15}$$

The right-hand side of equation (27.15) is a telescoping product, similar to the telescoping series in equation (A.12) on page 1143. The numerator of one term equals the denominator of the next, so that everything except the first denominator and last numerator cancel, and we obtain $\Pr\{A\} = (x - m)/x$. Since we actually want to compute $\Pr\{\bar{A}\} = 1 - \Pr\{A\}$, that is, the probability that the red ball *is* chosen, we get $\Pr\{\bar{A}\} = 1 - (x - m)/x = m/x$. ∎

Now we can prove Theorem 27.5.

Proof   We'll analyze RANDOMIZED-MARKING one epoch at a time. Within epoch i, any request for a block b that is not the first request for block b in epoch i must result in a cache hit, since after the first request in epoch i, block b resides in the cache and is marked, so that it cannot be evicted during the epoch. Therefore, since we are counting cache misses, we'll consider only the first request for each block within each epoch, disregarding all other requests.

We can classify the requests in an epoch as either old or new. If block b resides in the cache at the start of epoch i, each request for block b during epoch i is an *old request*. Old requests in epoch i are for blocks requested in epoch $i - 1$. If a request in epoch i is not old, it is a *new request*, and it is for a block not requested in epoch $i - 1$. All requests in epoch 1 are new. For example, let's look again at the request sequence in example (27.11):

$$1,\ 2,\ 1,\ 5 \qquad 4,\ 4,\ 1,\ 2,\ 4,\ 2 \qquad 3,\ 4,\ 5 \qquad 2,\ 2,\ 1,\ 2,\ 2\ .$$

Since we can disregard all requests for a block within an epoch other than the first request, to analyze the cache behavior, we can view this request sequence as just

$$1,\ 2,\ 5 \qquad 4,\ 1,\ 2 \qquad 3,\ 4,\ 5 \qquad 2,\ 1\ .$$

All three requests in epoch 1 are new. In epoch 2, the requests for blocks 1 and 2 are old, but the request for block 4 is new. In epoch 3, the request for block 4 is old, and the requests for blocks 3 and 5 are new. Both requests in epoch 4 are new.

Within an epoch, each new request must cause a cache miss since, by definition, the block is not already in the cache. An old request, on the other hand, may or may not cause a cache miss. The old block is in the cache at the beginning of the epoch, but other requests might cause it to be evicted. Returning to our example, in epoch 2, the request for block 4 must cause a cache miss, as this request is new. The request for block 1, which is old, may or may not cause a cache miss. If block 1 was evicted when block 4 was requested, then a cache miss occurs and block 1 must be brought back into the cache. If instead block 1 was not evicted when block 4 was requested, then the request for block 1 results in a cache hit. The request for block 2 could incur a cache miss under two scenarios. One is if block 2 was evicted when block 4 was requested. The other is if block 1 was evicted when block 4 was requested, and then block 2 was evicted when block 1 was requested. We see that, within an epoch, each ensuing old request has an increasing chance of causing a cache miss.

Because we consider only the first request for each block within an epoch, we assume that each epoch contains exactly k requests, and each request within an epoch is for a unique block. (The last epoch might contain fewer than k requests. If it does, just add dummy requests to fill it out to k requests.) In epoch i, denote the number of new requests by $r_i \geq 1$ (an epoch must contain at least one new request), so that the number of old requests is $k - r_i$. As mentioned above, a new request always incurs a cache miss.

Let us now focus on an arbitrary epoch i to obtain a bound on the expected number of cache misses within that epoch. In particular, let's think about the jth old request within the epoch, where $1 \leq j < k$. Denote by b_{ij} the block requested in the jth old request of epoch i, and denote by n_{ij} and o_{ij} the number of new and old requests, respectively, that occur within epoch i but before the jth old request. Because $j - 1$ old requests occur before the jth old request, we have $o_{ij} = j - 1$. We will show that the probability of a cache miss upon the jth old request is $n_{ij}/(k - o_{ij})$, or $n_{ij}/(k - j + 1)$.

Start by considering the first old request, for block $b_{i,1}$. What is the probability that this request causes a cache miss? It causes a cache miss precisely when one of the $n_{i,1}$ previous requests resulted in $b_{i,1}$ being evicted. We can determine the probability that $b_{i,1}$ was chosen for eviction by using Lemma 27.6: consider the k blocks in the cache to be k balls, with block $b_{i,1}$ as the red ball, the other $k - 1$ blocks as the $k - 1$ blue balls, and no white balls. Each of the $n_{i,1}$ requests chooses a block to evict with equal probability, corresponding to drawing balls $n_{i,1}$ times. Thus, we can apply Lemma 27.6 with $x = k$, $y = 0$, and $m = n_{i,1}$, deriving the probability of a cache miss upon the first old request as $n_{i,1}/k$, which equals $n_{ij}/(k - j + 1)$ since $j = 1$.

In order to determine the probability of a cache miss for subsequent old requests, we'll need an additional observation. Let's consider the second old request, which is for block $b_{i,2}$. This request causes a cache miss precisely when one of the previous requests evicts $b_{i,2}$. Let's consider two cases, based on the request for $b_{i,1}$. In the first case, suppose that the request for $b_{i,1}$ did not cause an eviction, because $b_{i,1}$ was already in the cache. Then, the only way that $b_{i,2}$ could have been evicted is by one of the $n_{i,2}$ new requests that precedes it. What is the probability that this eviction happens? There are $n_{i,2}$ chances for $b_{i,2}$ to be evicted, but we also know that there is one block in the cache, namely $b_{i,1}$, that is not evicted. Thus, we can again apply Lemma 27.6, but with $b_{i,1}$ as the white ball, $b_{i,2}$ as the red ball, the remaining blocks as the blue balls, and drawing balls $n_{i,2}$ times. Applying Lemma 27.6, with $x = k - 1$, $y = 1$, and $m = n_{i,2}$, we find that the probability of a cache miss is $n_{i,2}/(k - 1)$. In the second case, the request for $b_{i,1}$ does cause an eviction, which can happen only if one of the new requests preceding the request for $b_{i,1}$ evicts $b_{i,1}$. Then, the request for $b_{i,1}$ brings $b_{i,1}$ back into the cache and evicts some other block. In this case, we know that of the new requests, one of them did not result in $b_{i,2}$ being evicted, since $b_{i,1}$ was evicted. Therefore, $n_{i,2} - 1$ new requests could evict $b_{i,2}$, as could the request for $b_{i,1}$, so that the number of requests that could evict $b_{i,2}$ is $n_{i,2}$. Each such request evicts a block chosen from among $k - 1$ blocks, since the request that resulted in evicting $b_{i,1}$ did not also cause $b_{i,2}$ to be evicted. Therefore, we can apply Lemma 27.6, with $x = k - 1$,

$y = 1$, and $m = n_{i,2}$, and get that the probability of a miss is $n_{i,2}/(k-1)$. In both cases the probability is the same, and it equals $n_{ij}/(k-j+1)$ since $j = 2$.

More generally, o_{ij} old requests occur before the jth old request. Each of these prior old requests either caused an eviction or did not. For those that caused an eviction, it is because they were evicted by a previous request, and for those that did not cause an eviction, it is because they were not evicted by any previous request. In either case, we can decrease the number of blocks that the random process is choosing from by 1 for each old request, and thus o_{ij} requests cannot cause b_{ij} to be evicted. Therefore, we can use Lemma 27.6 to determine the probability that b_{ij} was evicted by a previous request, with $x = k - o_{ij}$, $y = o_{ij}$ and $m = n_{ij}$. Thus, we have proven our claim that the probability of a cache miss on the jth request for an old block is $n_{ij}/(k-o_{ij})$, or $n_{ij}/(k-j+1)$. Since $n_{ij} \leq r_i$ (recall that r_i is the number of new requests during epoch i), we have an upper bound of $r_i/(k-j+1)$ on the probability that the jth old request incurs a cache miss.

We can now compute the expected number of misses during epoch i using indicator random variables, as introduced in Section 5.2. We define indicator random variables

$$Y_{ij} = I\{\text{the } j\text{th old request in epoch } i \text{ incurs a cache miss}\},$$

$$Z_{ij} = I\{\text{the } j\text{th new request in epoch } i \text{ incurs a cache miss}\}.$$

We have $Z_{ij} = 1$ for $j = 1, 2, \ldots, r_i$, since every new request results in a cache miss. Let X_i be the random variable denoting the number of cache misses during epoch i, so that

$$X_i = \sum_{j=1}^{k-r_i} Y_{ij} + \sum_{j=1}^{r_i} Z_{ij},$$

and so

$$\begin{aligned}
\mathrm{E}[X_i] &= \mathrm{E}\left[\sum_{j=1}^{k-r_i} Y_{ij} + \sum_{j=1}^{r_i} Z_{ij}\right] \\
&= \sum_{j=1}^{k-r_i} \mathrm{E}[Y_{ij}] + \sum_{j=1}^{r_i} \mathrm{E}[Z_{ij}] \quad \text{(by linearity of expectation)} \\
&\leq \sum_{j=1}^{k-r_i} \frac{r_i}{k-j+1} + \sum_{j=1}^{r_i} 1 \quad \text{(by Lemma 5.1 on page 130)} \\
&= r_i \left(\sum_{j=1}^{k-r_i} \frac{1}{k-j+1} + 1\right)
\end{aligned}$$

$$\leq r_i \left(\sum_{j=1}^{k-1} \frac{1}{k-j+1} + 1 \right)$$

$$= r_i H_k \qquad \text{(by equation (A.8) on page 1142)} , \qquad (27.16)$$

where H_k is the kth harmonic number.

To compute the expected total number of cache misses, we sum over all epochs. Let p denote the number of epochs and X be the random variable denoting the number of cache misses. Then, we have $X = \sum_{i=1}^{p} X_i$, so that

$$\mathrm{E}[X] = \mathrm{E}\left[\sum_{i=1}^{p} X_i \right]$$

$$= \sum_{i=1}^{p} \mathrm{E}[X_i] \qquad \text{(by linearity of expectation)}$$

$$\leq \sum_{i=1}^{p} r_i H_k \qquad \text{(by inequality (27.16))}$$

$$= H_k \sum_{i=1}^{p} r_i . \qquad (27.17)$$

To complete the analysis, we need to understand the behavior of the optimal offline algorithm. It could make a completely different set of decisions from those made by RANDOMIZED-MARKING, and at any point its cache may look nothing like the cache of the randomized algorithm. Yet, we want to relate the number of cache misses of the optimal offline algorithm to the value in inequality (27.17), in order to have a competitive ratio that does not depend on $\sum_{i=1}^{p} r_i$. Focusing on individual epochs won't suffice. At the beginning of any epoch, the offline algorithm might have loaded the cache with exactly the blocks that will be requested in that epoch. Therefore, we cannot take any one epoch in isolation and claim that an offline algorithm must suffer any cache misses during that epoch.

If we consider two consecutive epochs, however, we can better analyze the optimal offline algorithm. Consider two consecutive epochs, $i-1$ and i. Each contains k requests for k different blocks. (Recall our assumption that all requests are first requests in an epoch.) Epoch i contains r_i requests for new blocks, that is, blocks that were not requested during epoch $i-1$. Therefore, the number of distinct requests during epochs $i-1$ and i is exactly $k+r_i$. No matter what the cache contents were at the beginning of epoch $i-1$, after $k+r_i$ distinct requests, there must be at least r_i cache misses. There could be more, but there is no way to have fewer. Letting m_i denote the number of cache misses of the offline algorithm during epoch i, we have just argued that

$$m_{i-1} + m_i \geq r_i . \qquad (27.18)$$

The total number of cache misses of the offline algorithm is

$$
\begin{aligned}
\sum_{i=1}^{P} m_i &= \frac{1}{2} \sum_{i=1}^{P} 2m_i \\
&= \frac{1}{2} \left(m_1 + \sum_{i=2}^{P} (m_{i-1} + m_i) + m_p \right) \\
&\geq \frac{1}{2} \left(m_1 + \sum_{i=2}^{P} (m_{i-1} + m_i) \right) \\
&\geq \frac{1}{2} \left(m_1 + \sum_{i=2}^{P} r_i \right) \qquad \text{(by inequality (27.18))} \\
&= \frac{1}{2} \sum_{i=1}^{P} r_i \qquad \text{(because } m_1 = r_1 \text{)} .
\end{aligned}
$$

The justification $m_1 = r_1$ for the last equality follows because, by our assumptions, the cache starts out empty and every request incurs a cache miss in the first epoch, even for the optimal offline adversary.

To conclude the analysis, because we have an upper bound of $H_k \sum_{i=1}^{P} r_i$ on the expected number of cache misses for RANDOMIZED-MARKING and a lower bound of $\frac{1}{2} \sum_{i=1}^{P} r_i$ on the number of cache misses for the optimal offline algorithm, the expected competitive ratio is at most

$$
\begin{aligned}
\frac{H_k \sum_{i=1}^{P} r_i}{\frac{1}{2} \sum_{i=1}^{P} r_i} &= 2H_k \\
&= 2 \ln k + O(1) \quad \text{(by equation (A.9) on page 1142)} \\
&= O(\lg k) .
\end{aligned}
$$ ■

Exercises

27.3-1
For the cache sequence (27.10), show the contents of the cache after each request and count the number of cache misses. How many misses does each epoch incur?

27.3-2
Show that LFU has a competitive ratio of $\Theta(n/k)$ for the online caching problem with n requests and a cache of size k.

27.3-3
Show that FIFO has a competitive ratio of $O(k)$ for the online caching problem with n requests and a cache of size k.

27.3-4

Show that the deterministic MARKING algorithm has a competitive ratio of $O(k)$ for the online caching problem with n requests and a cache of size k.

27.3-5

Theorem 27.4 shows that any deterministic online algorithm for caching has a competitive ratio of $\Omega(k)$, where k is the cache size. One way in which an algorithm might be able to perform better is to have some ability to know what the next few requests will be. We say that an algorithm is *l-lookahead* if it has the ability to look ahead at the next l requests. Prove that for every constant $l \geq 0$ and every cache size $k \geq 1$, every deterministic l-lookahead algorithm has competitive ratio $\Omega(k)$.

Problems

27-1 *Cow-path problem*

The Appalachian Trail (AT) is a marked hiking trail in the eastern United States extending between Springer Mountain in Georgia and Mount Katahdin in Maine. The trail is about 2,190 miles long. You decide that you are going to hike the AT from Georgia to Maine and back. You plan to learn more about algorithms while on the trail, and so you bring along your copy of *Introduction to Algorithms* in your backpack.[2] You have already read through this chapter before starting out. Because the beauty of the trail distracts you, you forget about reading this book until you have reached Maine and hiked halfway back to Georgia. At that point, you decide that you have already seen the trail and want to continue reading the rest of the book, starting with Chapter 28. Unfortunately, you find that the book is no longer in your pack. You must have left it somewhere along the trail, but you don't know where. It could be anywhere between Georgia and Maine. You want to find the book, but now that you have learned something about online algorithms, you want your algorithm for finding it to have a good competitive ratio. That is, no matter where the book is, if its distance from you is x miles away, you would like to be sure that you do not walk more than cx miles to find it, for some constant c. You do not know x, though you may assume that $x \geq 1$.[3]

---

[2] This book is heavy. We do not recommend that you carry it on a long hike.

[3] In case you're wondering what this problem has to do with cows, some papers about it frame the problem as a cow looking for a field in which to graze.

What algorithm should you use, and what constant c can you prove bounds the total distance cx that you would have to walk? Your algorithm should work for a trail of any length, not just the 2,190-mile-long AT.

27-2   *Online scheduling to minimize average completion time*

Problem 15-2 discusses scheduling to minimize average completion time on one machine, without release times and preemption and with release times and preemption. Now you will develop an online algorithm for nonpreemptively scheduling a set of tasks with release times. Suppose you are given a set $S = \{a_1, a_2, \ldots, a_n\}$ of tasks, where task a_i has *release time* r_i, before which it cannot start, and requires p_i units of processing time to complete once it has started. You have one computer on which to run the tasks. Tasks cannot be *preempted*, which is to say that once started, a task must run to completion without interruption. (See Problem 15-2 on page 446 for a more detailed description of this problem.) Given a schedule, let C_i be the *completion time* of task a_i, that is, the time at which task a_i completes processing. Your goal is to find a schedule that minimizes the average completion time, that is, to minimize $(1/n) \sum_{i=1}^{n} C_i$.

In the online version of this problem, you learn about task i only when it arrives at its release time r_i, and at that point, you know its processing time p_i. The offline version of this problem is NP-hard (see Chapter 34), but you will develop a 2-competitive online algorithm.

a. Show that, if there are release times, scheduling by shortest processing time (when the machine becomes idle, start the already released task with the smallest processing time that has not yet run) is not d-competitive for any constant d.

In order to develop an online algorithm, consider the preemptive version of this problem, which is discussed in Problem 15-2(b). One way to schedule is to run the tasks according to the shortest remaining processing time (SRPT) order. That is, at any point, the machine is running the available task with the smallest amount of remaining processing time.

b. Explain how to run SRPT as an online algorithm.

c. Suppose that you run SRPT and obtain completion times $C_1^P, \ldots, C_n^P$. Show that

$$\sum_{i=1}^{n} C_i^P \leq \sum_{i=1}^{n} C_i^*,$$

where the C_i^* are the completion times in an optimal nonpreemptive schedule.

Consider the (offline) algorithm COMPLETION-TIME-SCHEDULE.

COMPLETION-TIME-SCHEDULE(S)

1   compute an optimal schedule for the preemptive version of the problem
2   renumber the tasks so that the completion times in the optimal
    preemptive schedule are ordered by their completion times
    $C_1^P < C_2^P < \cdots < C_n^P$ in SRPT order
3   greedily schedule the tasks nonpreemptively in the renumbered
    order $a_1, \ldots, a_n$
4   let $C_1, \ldots, C_n$ be the completion times of renumbered tasks $a_1, \ldots, a_n$
    in this nonpreemptive schedule
5   **return** $C_1, \ldots, C_n$

d. Prove that $C_i^P \geq \max \left\{ \sum_{j=1}^{i} p_j, \max \{ r_j : j \leq i \} \right\}$ for $i = 1, \ldots, n$.

e. Prove that $C_i \leq \max \{ r_j : j \leq i \} + \sum_{j=1}^{i} p_j$ for $i = 1, \ldots, n$.

f. Algorithm COMPLETION-TIME-SCHEDULE is an offline algorithm. Explain how to modify it to produce an online algorithm.

g. Combine parts (c)–(f) to show that the online version of COMPLETION-TIME-SCHEDULE is 2-competitive.

Chapter notes

Online algorithms are widely used in many domains. Some good overviews include the textbook by Borodin and El-Yaniv [68], the collection of surveys edited by Fiat and Woeginger [142], and the survey by Albers [14].

The move-to-front heuristic from Section 27.2 was analyzed by Sleator and Tarjan [416, 417] as part of their early work on amortized analysis. This rule works quite well in practice.

Competitive analysis of online caching also originated with Sleator and Tarjan [417]. The randomized marking algorithm was proposed and analyzed by Fiat et al. [141]. Young [464] surveys online caching and paging algorithms, and Buchbinder and Naor [76] survey primal-dual online algorithms.

Specific types of online algorithms are described using other names. *Dynamic graph algorithms* are online algorithms on graphs, where at each step a vertex or edge undergoes modification. Typically a vertex or edge is either inserted or deleted, or some associated property, such as edge weight, changes. Some graph problems need to be solved again after each change to the graph, and a good dynamic graph algorithm will not need to solve from scratch. For example, edges are inserted and deleted, and after each change to the graph, the minimum spanning tree is recomputed. Exercise 21.2-8 asks such a question. Similar questions can be asked for other graph algorithms, such as shortest paths, connectivity, or matching. The first paper in this field is credited to Even and Shiloach [138], who study how to maintain a shortest-path tree as edges are being deleted from a graph. Since then hundreds of papers have been published. Demetrescu et al. [110] survey early developments in dynamic graph algorithms.

For massive data sets, the input data might be too large to store. *Streaming algorithms* model this situation by requiring the memory used by an algorithm to be significantly smaller than the input size. For example, you may have a graph with n vertices and m edges with $m \gg n$, but the memory allowed may be only $O(n)$. Or you may have n numbers, but the memory allowed may only be $O(\lg n)$ or $O(\sqrt{n})$. A streaming algorithm is measured by the number of passes made over the data in addition to the running time of the algorithm. McGregor [322] surveys streaming algorithms for graphs and Muthukrishnan [341] surveys general streaming algorithms.

28 Matrix Operations

Because operations on matrices lie at the heart of scientific computing, efficient algorithms for working with matrices have many practical applications. This chapter focuses on how to multiply matrices and solve sets of simultaneous linear equations. Appendix D reviews the basics of matrices.

Section 28.1 shows how to solve a set of linear equations using LUP decompositions. Then, Section 28.2 explores the close relationship between multiplying and inverting matrices. Finally, Section 28.3 discusses the important class of symmetric positive-definite matrices and shows how to use them to find a least-squares solution to an overdetermined set of linear equations.

One important issue that arises in practice is *numerical stability*. Because actual computers have limits to how precisely they can represent floating-point numbers, round-off errors in numerical computations may become amplified over the course of a computation, leading to incorrect results. Such computations are called *numerically unstable*. Although we'll briefly consider numerical stability on occasion, we won't focus on it in this chapter. We refer you to the excellent book by Higham [216] for a thorough discussion of stability issues.

28.1 Solving systems of linear equations

Numerous applications need to solve sets of simultaneous linear equations. A linear system can be cast as a matrix equation in which each matrix or vector element belongs to a field, typically the real numbers $\mathbb{R}$. This section discusses how to solve a system of linear equations using a method called LUP decomposition.

The process starts with a set of linear equations in n unknowns $x_1, x_2, \ldots, x_n$:

$$
\begin{aligned}
a_{11}x_1 + a_{12}x_2 + \cdots + a_{1n}x_n &= b_1\,, \\
a_{21}x_1 + a_{22}x_2 + \cdots + a_{2n}x_n &= b_2\,, \\
&\;\;\vdots \\
a_{n1}x_1 + a_{n2}x_2 + \cdots + a_{nn}x_n &= b_n\,.
\end{aligned}
\tag{28.1}
$$

A *solution* to the equations (28.1) is a set of values for $x_1, x_2, \ldots, x_n$ that satisfy all of the equations simultaneously. In this section, we treat only the case in which there are exactly n equations in n unknowns.

Next, rewrite equations (28.1) as the matrix-vector equation

$$
\begin{pmatrix}
a_{11} & a_{12} & \cdots & a_{1n} \\
a_{21} & a_{22} & \cdots & a_{2n} \\
\vdots & \vdots & \ddots & \vdots \\
a_{n1} & a_{n2} & \cdots & a_{nn}
\end{pmatrix}
\begin{pmatrix}
x_1 \\ x_2 \\ \vdots \\ x_n
\end{pmatrix}
=
\begin{pmatrix}
b_1 \\ b_2 \\ \vdots \\ b_n
\end{pmatrix}
$$

or, equivalently, letting $A = (a_{ij})$, $x = (x_i)$, and $b = (b_i)$, as

$$
Ax = b\,.
\tag{28.2}
$$

If A is nonsingular, it possesses an inverse A^{-1}, and

$$
x = A^{-1}b
\tag{28.3}
$$

is the solution vector. We can prove that x is the unique solution to equation (28.2) as follows. If there are two solutions, x and x', then $Ax = Ax' = b$ and, letting I denote an identity matrix,

$$
\begin{aligned}
x &= Ix \\
&= (A^{-1}A)x \\
&= A^{-1}(Ax) \\
&= A^{-1}(Ax') \\
&= (A^{-1}A)x' \\
&= Ix' \\
&= x'\,.
\end{aligned}
$$

This section focuses on the case in which A is nonsingular or, equivalently (by Theorem D.1 on page 1220), the rank of A equals the number n of unknowns. There are other possibilities, however, which merit a brief discussion. If the number of equations is less than the number n of unknowns—or, more generally, if the rank of A is less than n—then the system is *underdetermined*. An underdetermined system typically has infinitely many solutions, although it may have no solutions at all if the equations are inconsistent. If the number of equations exceeds the number n of unknowns, the system is *overdetermined*, and there may not exist any solutions. Section 28.3 addresses the important problem of finding good approximate solutions to overdetermined systems of linear equations.

Let's return to the problem of solving the system $Ax = b$ of n equations in n unknowns. One option is to compute A^{-1} and then, using equation (28.3), multiply b by A^{-1}, yielding $x = A^{-1}b$. This approach suffers in practice from numerical instability. Fortunately, another approach—LUP decomposition—is numerically stable and has the further advantage of being faster in practice.

Overview of LUP decomposition

The idea behind LUP decomposition is to find three $n \times n$ matrices L, U, and P such that

$$PA = LU \,, \tag{28.4}$$

where

- L is a unit lower-triangular matrix,
- U is an upper-triangular matrix, and
- P is a permutation matrix.

We call matrices L, U, and P satisfying equation (28.4) an *LUP decomposition* of the matrix A. We'll show that every nonsingular matrix A possesses such a decomposition.

Computing an LUP decomposition for the matrix A has the advantage that linear systems can be efficiently solved when they are triangular, as is the case for both matrices L and U. If you have an LUP decomposition for A, you can solve equation (28.2), $Ax = b$, by solving only triangular linear systems, as follows. Multiply both sides of $Ax = b$ by P, yielding the equivalent equation $PAx = Pb$. By Exercise D.1-4 on page 1219, multiplying both sides by a permutation matrix amounts to permuting the equations (28.1). By the decomposition (28.4), substituting LU for PA gives

$$LUx = Pb \,.$$

You can now solve this equation by solving two triangular linear systems. Define $y = Ux$, where x is the desired solution vector. First, solve the lower-triangular system

$$Ly = Pb \tag{28.5}$$

for the unknown vector y by a method called "forward substitution." Having solved for y, solve the upper-triangular system

$$Ux = y \tag{28.6}$$

for the unknown x by a method called "back substitution." Why does this process solve $Ax = b$? Because the permutation matrix P is invertible (see Exercise D.2-3 on page 1223), multiplying both sides of equation (28.4) by P^{-1} gives $P^{-1}PA = P^{-1}LU$, so that

$$A = P^{-1}LU . \tag{28.7}$$

Hence, the vector x that satisfies $Ux = y$ is the solution to $Ax = b$:

$$
\begin{aligned}
Ax &= P^{-1}LUx & \text{(by equation (28.7))} \\
&= P^{-1}Ly & \text{(by equation (28.6))} \\
&= P^{-1}Pb & \text{(by equation (28.5))} \\
&= b .
\end{aligned}
$$

The next step is to show how forward and back substitution work and then attack the problem of computing the LUP decomposition itself.

Forward and back substitution

Forward substitution can solve the lower-triangular system (28.5) in $\Theta(n^2)$ time, given L, P, and b. An array $\pi[1:n]$ provides a more compact format to represent the permutation P than an $n \times n$ matrix that is mostly 0s. For $i = 1, 2, \ldots, n$, the entry $\pi[i]$ indicates that $P_{i,\pi[i]} = 1$ and $P_{ij} = 0$ for $j \neq \pi[i]$. Thus, PA has $a_{\pi[i],j}$ in row i and column j, and Pb has $b_{\pi[i]}$ as its ith element. Since L is unit lower-triangular, the matrix equation $Ly = Pb$ is equivalent to the n equations

$$
\begin{aligned}
y_1 &= b_{\pi[1]} , \\
l_{21}y_1 + y_2 &= b_{\pi[2]} , \\
l_{31}y_1 + l_{32}y_2 + y_3 &= b_{\pi[3]} , \\
&\vdots \\
l_{n1}y_1 + l_{n2}y_2 + l_{n3}y_3 + \cdots + y_n &= b_{\pi[n]} .
\end{aligned}
$$

The first equation gives $y_1 = b_{\pi[1]}$ directly. Knowing the value of y_1, you can substitute it into the second equation, yielding

$$y_2 = b_{\pi[2]} - l_{21}y_1 .$$

Next, you can substitute both y_1 and y_2 into the third equation, obtaining

$$y_3 = b_{\pi[3]} - (l_{31}y_1 + l_{32}y_2) .$$

In general, you substitute $y_1, y_2, \ldots, y_{i-1}$ "forward" into the ith equation to solve for y_i:

$$y_i = b_{\pi[i]} - \sum_{j=1}^{i-1} l_{ij} y_j \ .$$

Once you've solved for y, you can solve for x in equation (28.6) using **back substitution**, which is similar to forward substitution. This time, you solve the nth equation first and work backward to the first equation. Like forward substitution, this process runs in $\Theta(n^2)$ time. Since U is upper-triangular, the matrix equation $Ux = y$ is equivalent to the n equations

$$
\begin{aligned}
u_{11}x_1 + u_{12}x_2 + \cdots + \quad u_{1,n-2}x_{n-2} + \quad u_{1,n-1}x_{n-1} + \quad u_{1n}x_n &= y_1 \ , \\
u_{22}x_2 + \cdots + \quad u_{2,n-2}x_{n-2} + \quad u_{2,n-1}x_{n-1} + \quad u_{2n}x_n &= y_2 \ , \\
&\ \ \vdots \\
u_{n-2,n-2}x_{n-2} + u_{n-2,n-1}x_{n-1} + u_{n-2,n}x_n &= y_{n-2} \ , \\
u_{n-1,n-1}x_{n-1} + u_{n-1,n}x_n &= y_{n-1} \ , \\
u_{n,n}x_n &= y_n \ .
\end{aligned}
$$

Thus, you can solve for $x_n, x_{n-1}, \ldots, x_1$ successively as follows:

$$
\begin{aligned}
x_n &= y_n / u_{n,n} \ , \\
x_{n-1} &= (y_{n-1} - u_{n-1,n}x_n)/u_{n-1,n-1} \ , \\
x_{n-2} &= (y_{n-2} - (u_{n-2,n-1}x_{n-1} + u_{n-2,n}x_n))/u_{n-2,n-2} \ , \\
&\ \ \vdots
\end{aligned}
$$

or, in general,

$$x_i = \left(y_i - \sum_{j=i+1}^{n} u_{ij}x_j \right) \Big/ u_{ii} \ .$$

Given P, L, U, and b, the procedure LUP-SOLVE on the next page solves for x by combining forward and back substitution. The permutation matrix P is represented by the array π. The procedure first solves for y using forward substitution in lines 2–3, and then it solves for x using backward substitution in lines 4–5. Since the summation within each of the **for** loops includes an implicit loop, the running time is $\Theta(n^2)$.

As an example of these methods, consider the system of linear equations defined by $Ax = b$, where

$$A = \begin{pmatrix} 1 & 2 & 0 \\ 3 & 4 & 4 \\ 5 & 6 & 3 \end{pmatrix} \text{ and } b = \begin{pmatrix} 3 \\ 7 \\ 8 \end{pmatrix} \ ,$$

LUP-SOLVE(L, U, π, b, n)

1   let x and y be new vectors of length n
2   **for** $i = 1$ **to** n
3       $y_i = b_{\pi[i]} - \sum_{j=1}^{i-1} l_{ij} y_j$
4   **for** $i = n$ **downto** 1
5       $x_i = \left(y_i - \sum_{j=i+1}^{n} u_{ij} x_j \right) / u_{ii}$
6   **return** x

and we want to solve for the unknown x. The LUP decomposition is

$$L = \begin{pmatrix} 1 & 0 & 0 \\ 0.2 & 1 & 0 \\ 0.6 & 0.5 & 1 \end{pmatrix}, \quad U = \begin{pmatrix} 5 & 6 & 3 \\ 0 & 0.8 & -0.6 \\ 0 & 0 & 2.5 \end{pmatrix}, \quad \text{and } P = \begin{pmatrix} 0 & 0 & 1 \\ 1 & 0 & 0 \\ 0 & 1 & 0 \end{pmatrix}.$$

(You might want to verify that $PA = LU$.) Using forward substitution, solve $Ly = Pb$ for y:

$$\begin{pmatrix} 1 & 0 & 0 \\ 0.2 & 1 & 0 \\ 0.6 & 0.5 & 1 \end{pmatrix} \begin{pmatrix} y_1 \\ y_2 \\ y_3 \end{pmatrix} = \begin{pmatrix} 8 \\ 3 \\ 7 \end{pmatrix},$$

obtaining

$$y = \begin{pmatrix} 8 \\ 1.4 \\ 1.5 \end{pmatrix}$$

by computing first y_1, then y_2, and finally y_3. Then, using back substitution, solve $Ux = y$ for x:

$$\begin{pmatrix} 5 & 6 & 3 \\ 0 & 0.8 & -0.6 \\ 0 & 0 & 2.5 \end{pmatrix} \begin{pmatrix} x_1 \\ x_2 \\ x_3 \end{pmatrix} = \begin{pmatrix} 8 \\ 1.4 \\ 1.5 \end{pmatrix},$$

thereby obtaining the desired answer

$$x = \begin{pmatrix} -1.4 \\ 2.2 \\ 0.6 \end{pmatrix}$$

by computing first x_3, then x_2, and finally x_1.

Computing an LU decomposition

Given an LUP decomposition for a nonsingular matrix A, you can use forward and back substitution to solve the system $Ax = b$ of linear equations. Now let's see how to efficiently compute an LUP decomposition for A. We start with the simpler case in which A is an $n \times n$ nonsingular matrix and P is absent (or, equivalently, $P = I_n$, the $n \times n$ identity matrix), so that $A = LU$. We call the two matrices L and U an *LU decomposition* of A.

To create an LU decomposition, we'll use a process known as *Gaussian elimination*. Start by subtracting multiples of the first equation from the other equations in order to remove the first variable from those equations. Then subtract multiples of the second equation from the third and subsequent equations so that now the first and second variables are removed from them. Continue this process until the system that remains has an upper-triangular form—this is the matrix U. The matrix L comprises the row multipliers that cause variables to be eliminated.

To implement this strategy, let's start with a recursive formulation. The input is an $n \times n$ nonsingular matrix A. If $n = 1$, then nothing needs to be done: just choose $L = I_1$ and $U = A$. For $n > 1$, break A into four parts:

$$
A = \begin{pmatrix} a_{11} & a_{12} & \cdots & a_{1n} \\ a_{21} & a_{22} & \cdots & a_{2n} \\ \vdots & \vdots & \ddots & \vdots \\ a_{n1} & a_{n2} & \cdots & a_{nn} \end{pmatrix}
$$

$$
= \begin{pmatrix} a_{11} & w^{\mathrm{T}} \\ v & A' \end{pmatrix}, \tag{28.8}
$$

where $v = (a_{21}, a_{31}, \ldots, a_{n1})$ is a column $(n-1)$-vector, $w^{\mathrm{T}} = (a_{12}, a_{13}, \ldots, a_{1n})^{\mathrm{T}}$ is a row $(n - 1)$-vector, and A' is an $(n - 1) \times (n - 1)$ matrix. Then, using matrix algebra (verify the equations by simply multiplying through), factor A as

$$
A = \begin{pmatrix} a_{11} & w^{\mathrm{T}} \\ v & A' \end{pmatrix}
$$

$$
= \begin{pmatrix} 1 & 0 \\ v/a_{11} & I_{n-1} \end{pmatrix} \begin{pmatrix} a_{11} & w^{\mathrm{T}} \\ 0 & A' - vw^{\mathrm{T}}/a_{11} \end{pmatrix}. \tag{28.9}
$$

The 0s in the first and second matrices of equation (28.9) are row and column $(n - 1)$-vectors, respectively. The term vw^{T}/a_{11} is an $(n - 1) \times (n - 1)$ matrix formed by taking the outer product of v and w and dividing each element of the result by a_{11}. Thus it conforms in size to the matrix A' from which it is subtracted. The resulting $(n - 1) \times (n - 1)$ matrix

$$
A' - vw^{\mathrm{T}}/a_{11} \tag{28.10}
$$

is called the *Schur complement* of A with respect to a_{11}.

We claim that if A is nonsingular, then the Schur complement is nonsingular, too. Why? Suppose that the Schur complement, which is $(n - 1) \times (n - 1)$, is singular. Then by Theorem D.1, it has row rank strictly less than $n - 1$. Because the bottom $n - 1$ entries in the first column of the matrix

$$\begin{pmatrix} a_{11} & w^{\mathrm{T}} \\ 0 & A' - vw^{\mathrm{T}}/a_{11} \end{pmatrix}$$

are all 0, the bottom $n - 1$ rows of this matrix must have row rank strictly less than $n - 1$. The row rank of the entire matrix, therefore, is strictly less than n. Applying Exercise D.2-8 on page 1223 to equation (28.9), A has rank strictly less than n, and from Theorem D.1, we derive the contradiction that A is singular.

Because the Schur complement is nonsingular, it, too, has an LU decomposition, which we can find recursively. Let's say that

$$A' - vw^{\mathrm{T}}/a_{11} = L'U',$$

where L' is unit lower-triangular and U' is upper-triangular. The LU decomposition of A is then $A = LU$, with

$$L = \begin{pmatrix} 1 & 0 \\ v/a_{11} & L' \end{pmatrix} \text{ and } U = \begin{pmatrix} a_{11} & w^{\mathrm{T}} \\ 0 & U' \end{pmatrix},$$

as shown by

$$\begin{aligned} A &= \begin{pmatrix} 1 & 0 \\ v/a_{11} & I_{n-1} \end{pmatrix} \begin{pmatrix} a_{11} & w^{\mathrm{T}} \\ 0 & A' - vw^{\mathrm{T}}/a_{11} \end{pmatrix} \quad \text{(by equation (28.9))} \\ &= \begin{pmatrix} 1 & 0 \\ v/a_{11} & I_{n-1} \end{pmatrix} \begin{pmatrix} a_{11} & w^{\mathrm{T}} \\ 0 & L'U' \end{pmatrix} \\ &= \begin{pmatrix} a_{11} & w^{\mathrm{T}} \\ v & vw^{\mathrm{T}}/a_{11} + L'U' \end{pmatrix} \\ &= \begin{pmatrix} 1 & 0 \\ v/a_{11} & L' \end{pmatrix} \begin{pmatrix} a_{11} & w^{\mathrm{T}} \\ 0 & U' \end{pmatrix} \\ &= LU. \end{aligned}$$

Because L' is unit lower-triangular, so is L, and because U' is upper-triangular, so is U.

Of course, if $a_{11} = 0$, this method doesn't work, because it divides by 0. It also doesn't work if the upper leftmost entry of the Schur complement $A' - vw^{\mathrm{T}}/a_{11}$ is 0, since the next step of the recursion will divide by it. The denominators in each step of LU decomposition are called *pivots*, and they occupy the diagonal elements of the matrix U. The permutation matrix P included in LUP decomposition provides a way to avoid dividing by 0, as we'll see below. Using permutations to avoid division by 0 (or by small numbers, which can contribute to numerical instability), is called *pivoting*.

An important class of matrices for which LU decomposition always works correctly is the class of symmetric positive-definite matrices. Such matrices require no pivoting to avoid dividing by 0 in the recursive strategy outlined above. We will prove this result, as well as several others, in Section 28.3.

The pseudocode in the procedure LU-DECOMPOSITION follows the recursive strategy, except that an iteration loop replaces the recursion. (This transformation is a standard optimization for a "tail-recursive" procedure—one whose last operation is a recursive call to itself. See Problem 7-5 on page 202.) The procedure initializes the matrix U with 0s below the diagonal and matrix L with 1s on its diagonal and 0s above the diagonal. Each iteration works on a square submatrix, using its upper leftmost element as the pivot to compute the v and w vectors and the Schur complement, which becomes the square submatrix worked on by the next iteration.

LU-DECOMPOSITION(A, n)

```
 1   let L and U be new n × n matrices
 2   initialize U with 0s below the diagonal
 3   initialize L with 1s on the diagonal and 0s above the diagonal
 4   for k = 1 to n
 5       u_kk = a_kk
 6       for i = k + 1 to n
 7           l_ik = a_ik/a_kk          // a_ik holds v_i
 8           u_ki = a_ki               // a_ki holds w_i
 9       for i = k + 1 to n            // compute the Schur complement ...
10           for j = k + 1 to n
11               a_ij = a_ij − l_ik u_kj   // ... and store it back into A
12   return L and U
```

Each recursive step in the description above takes place in one iteration of the outer **for** loop of lines 4–11. Within this loop, line 5 determines the pivot to be $u_{kk} = a_{kk}$. The **for** loop in lines 6–8 (which does not execute when $k = n$) uses the v and w vectors to update L and U. Line 7 determines the below-diagonal elements of L, storing v_i / a_{kk} in l_{ik}, and line 8 computes the above-diagonal elements of U, storing w_i in u_{ki}. Finally, lines 9–11 compute the elements of the Schur complement and store them back into the matrix A. (There is no need to divide by a_{kk} in line 11 because that already happened when line 7 computed l_{ik}.) Because line 11 is triply nested, LU-DECOMPOSITION runs in $\Theta(n^3)$ time.

Figure 28.1 illustrates the operation of LU-DECOMPOSITION. It shows a standard optimization of the procedure that stores the significant elements of L and U in place in the matrix A. Each element a_{ij} corresponds to either l_{ij} (if $i > j$) or u_{ij} (if $i \leq j$), so that the matrix A holds both L and U when the procedure terminates. To obtain the pseudocode for this optimization from the pseudocode for the LU-DECOMPOSITION procedure, just replace each reference to l or u by a. You can verify that this transformation preserves correctness.

$$
\begin{array}{cccc}
2 & 3 & 1 & 5 \\
6 & 13 & 5 & 19 \\
2 & 19 & 10 & 23 \\
4 & 10 & 11 & 31
\end{array}
\qquad
\begin{array}{cccc}
2 & 3 & 1 & 5 \\
3 & 4 & 2 & 4 \\
1 & 16 & 9 & 18 \\
2 & 4 & 9 & 21
\end{array}
\qquad
\begin{array}{cccc}
2 & 3 & 1 & 5 \\
3 & 4 & 2 & 4 \\
1 & 4 & 1 & 2 \\
2 & 1 & 7 & 17
\end{array}
\qquad
\begin{array}{cccc}
2 & 3 & 1 & 5 \\
3 & 4 & 2 & 4 \\
1 & 4 & 1 & 2 \\
2 & 1 & 7 & 3
\end{array}
$$

(a) (b) (c) (d)

$$
\begin{pmatrix}
2 & 3 & 1 & 5 \\
6 & 13 & 5 & 19 \\
2 & 19 & 10 & 23 \\
4 & 10 & 11 & 31
\end{pmatrix}
=
\begin{pmatrix}
1 & 0 & 0 & 0 \\
3 & 1 & 0 & 0 \\
1 & 4 & 1 & 0 \\
2 & 1 & 7 & 1
\end{pmatrix}
\begin{pmatrix}
2 & 3 & 1 & 5 \\
0 & 4 & 2 & 4 \\
0 & 0 & 1 & 2 \\
0 & 0 & 0 & 3
\end{pmatrix}
$$

A L U

(e)

Figure 28.1 The operation of LU-DECOMPOSITION. **(a)** The matrix A. **(b)** The result of the first iteration of the outer **for** loop of lines 4–11. The element $a_{11} = 2$ highlighted in blue is the pivot, the tan column is v/a_{11}, and the tan row is w^T. The elements of U computed thus far are above the horizontal line, and the elements of L are to the left of the vertical line. The Schur complement matrix $A' - vw^T/a_{11}$ occupies the lower right. **(c)** The result of the next iteration of the outer **for** loop, on the Schur complement matrix from part (b). The element $a_{22} = 4$ highlighted in blue is the pivot, and the tan column and row are v/a_{22} and w^T (in the partitioning of the Schur complement), respectively. Lines divide the matrix into the elements of U computed so far (above), the elements of L computed so far (left), and the new Schur complement (lower right). **(d)** After the next iteration, the matrix A is factored. The element 3 in the new Schur complement becomes part of U when the recursion terminates.) **(e)** The factorization $A = LU$.

Computing an LUP decomposition

If the diagonal of the matrix given to LU-DECOMPOSITION contains any 0s, then the procedure will attempt to divide by 0, which would cause disaster. Even if the diagonal contains no 0s, but does have numbers with small absolute values, dividing by such numbers can cause numerical instabilities. Therefore, LUP decomposition pivots on entries with the largest absolute values that it can find.

In LUP decomposition, the input is an $n \times n$ nonsingular matrix A, with a goal of finding a permutation matrix P, a unit lower-triangular matrix L, and an upper-triangular matrix U such that $PA = LU$. Before partitioning the matrix A, as LU decomposition does, LUP decomposition moves a nonzero element, say a_{k1}, from somewhere in the first column to the $(1, 1)$ position of the matrix. For the greatest numerical stability, LUP decomposition chooses the element in the first column with the greatest absolute value as a_{k1}. (The first column cannot contain only 0s, for then A would be singular, because its determinant would be 0, by Theorems D.4 and D.5 on page 1221.) In order to preserve the set of equations, LUP decomposition exchanges row 1 with row k, which is equivalent to multiplying A by a permutation matrix Q on the left (Exercise D.1-4 on page 1219). Thus, the analog to equation (28.8) expresses QA as

$$QA = \begin{pmatrix} a_{k1} & w^{\mathrm{T}} \\ v & A' \end{pmatrix},$$

where $v = (a_{21}, a_{31}, \ldots, a_{n1})$, except that a_{11} replaces a_{k1}; $w^{\mathrm{T}} = (a_{k2}, a_{k3}, \ldots, a_{kn})^{\mathrm{T}}$; and A' is an $(n - 1) \times (n - 1)$ matrix. Since $a_{k1} \neq 0$, the analog to equation (28.9) guarantees no division by 0:

$$\begin{aligned}
QA &= \begin{pmatrix} a_{k1} & w^{\mathrm{T}} \\ v & A' \end{pmatrix} \\
&= \begin{pmatrix} 1 & 0 \\ v/a_{k1} & I_{n-1} \end{pmatrix} \begin{pmatrix} a_{k1} & w^{\mathrm{T}} \\ 0 & A' - vw^{\mathrm{T}}/a_{k1} \end{pmatrix}.
\end{aligned}$$

Just as in LU decomposition, if A is nonsingular, then the Schur complement $A' - vw^{\mathrm{T}}/a_{k1}$ is nonsingular, too. Therefore, you can recursively find an LUP decomposition for it, with unit lower-triangular matrix L', upper-triangular matrix U', and permutation matrix P', such that

$$P'(A' - vw^{\mathrm{T}}/a_{k1}) = L'U'.$$

Define

$$P = \begin{pmatrix} 1 & 0 \\ 0 & P' \end{pmatrix} Q,$$

which is a permutation matrix, since it is the product of two permutation matrices (Exercise D.1-4 on page 1219). This definition of P gives

$$\begin{aligned}
PA &= \begin{pmatrix} 1 & 0 \\ 0 & P' \end{pmatrix} QA \\
&= \begin{pmatrix} 1 & 0 \\ 0 & P' \end{pmatrix} \begin{pmatrix} 1 & 0 \\ v/a_{k1} & I_{n-1} \end{pmatrix} \begin{pmatrix} a_{k1} & w^{\mathrm{T}} \\ 0 & A' - vw^{\mathrm{T}}/a_{k1} \end{pmatrix} \\
&= \begin{pmatrix} 1 & 0 \\ P'v/a_{k1} & P' \end{pmatrix} \begin{pmatrix} a_{k1} & w^{\mathrm{T}} \\ 0 & A' - vw^{\mathrm{T}}/a_{k1} \end{pmatrix} \\
&= \begin{pmatrix} 1 & 0 \\ P'v/a_{k1} & I_{n-1} \end{pmatrix} \begin{pmatrix} a_{k1} & w^{\mathrm{T}} \\ 0 & P'(A' - vw^{\mathrm{T}}/a_{k1}) \end{pmatrix} \\
&= \begin{pmatrix} 1 & 0 \\ P'v/a_{k1} & I_{n-1} \end{pmatrix} \begin{pmatrix} a_{k1} & w^{\mathrm{T}} \\ 0 & L'U' \end{pmatrix} \\
&= \begin{pmatrix} 1 & 0 \\ P'v/a_{k1} & L' \end{pmatrix} \begin{pmatrix} a_{k1} & w^{\mathrm{T}} \\ 0 & U' \end{pmatrix} \\
&= LU,
\end{aligned}$$

which yields the LUP decomposition. Because L' is unit lower-triangular, so is L, and because U' is upper-triangular, so is U.

Notice that in this derivation, unlike the one for LU decomposition, both the column vector v/a_{k1} and the Schur complement $A' - vw^{\mathrm{T}}/a_{k1}$ are multiplied by the permutation matrix P'. The procedure LUP-DECOMPOSITION gives the pseudocode for LUP decomposition.

LUP-DECOMPOSITION(A, n)

```
 1   let π[1 : n] be a new array
 2   for i = 1 to n
 3       π[i] = i                          // initialize π to the identity permutation
 4   for k = 1 to n
 5       p = 0
 6       for i = k to n                    // find largest absolute value in column k
 7           if |a_{ik}| > p
 8               p = |a_{ik}|
 9               k' = i                     // row number of the largest found so far
10       if p == 0
11           error "singular matrix"
12       exchange π[k] with π[k']
13       for i = 1 to n
14           exchange a_{ki} with a_{k'i}   // exchange rows k and k'
15       for i = k + 1 to n
16           a_{ik} = a_{ik}/a_{kk}
17           for j = k + 1 to n
18               a_{ij} = a_{ij} - a_{ik}a_{kj}   // compute L and U in place in A
```

Like LU-DECOMPOSITION, the LUP-DECOMPOSITION procedure replaces the recursion with an iteration loop. As an improvement over a direct implementation of the recursion, the procedure dynamically maintains the permutation matrix P as an array π, where $\pi[i] = j$ means that the ith row of P contains a 1 in column j. The LUP-DECOMPOSITION procedure also implements the improvement mentioned earlier, computing L and U in place in the matrix A. Thus, when the procedure terminates,

$$a_{ij} = \begin{cases} l_{ij} & \text{if } i > j\,, \\ u_{ij} & \text{if } i \leq j\,. \end{cases}$$

Figure 28.2 illustrates how LUP-DECOMPOSITION factors a matrix. Lines 2–3 initialize the array π to represent the identity permutation. The outer **for** loop of lines 4–18 implements the recursion, finding an LUP decomposition of

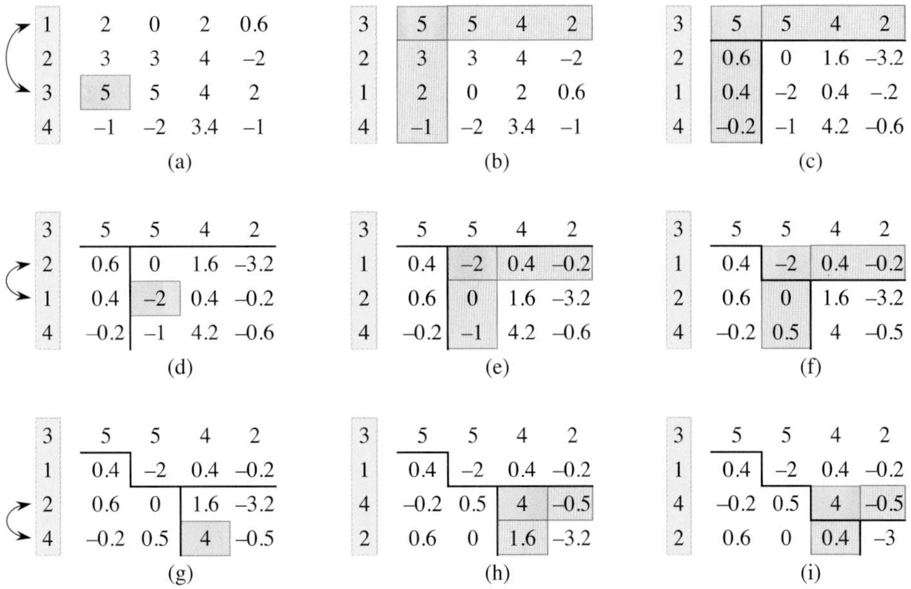

$$\underbrace{\begin{pmatrix} 0 & 0 & 1 & 0 \\ 1 & 0 & 0 & 0 \\ 0 & 0 & 0 & 1 \\ 0 & 1 & 0 & 0 \end{pmatrix}}_{P} \underbrace{\begin{pmatrix} 2 & 0 & 2 & 0.6 \\ 3 & 3 & 4 & -2 \\ 5 & 5 & 4 & 2 \\ -1 & -2 & 3.4 & -1 \end{pmatrix}}_{A} = \underbrace{\begin{pmatrix} 1 & 0 & 0 & 0 \\ 0.4 & 1 & 0 & 0 \\ -0.2 & 0.5 & 1 & 0 \\ 0.6 & 0 & 0.4 & 1 \end{pmatrix}}_{L} \underbrace{\begin{pmatrix} 5 & 5 & 4 & 2 \\ 0 & -2 & 0.4 & -0.2 \\ 0 & 0 & 4 & -0.5 \\ 0 & 0 & 0 & -3 \end{pmatrix}}_{U}$$

(j)

Figure 28.2 The operation of LUP-DECOMPOSITION. **(a)** The input matrix A with the identity permutation of the rows in yellow on the left. The first step of the algorithm determines that the element 5 highlighted in blue in the third row is the pivot for the first column. **(b)** Rows 1 and 3 are swapped and the permutation is updated. The tan column and row represent v and w^{T}. **(c)** The vector v is replaced by $v/5$, and the lower right of the matrix is updated with the Schur complement. Lines divide the matrix into three regions: elements of U (above), elements of L (left), and elements of the Schur complement (lower right). **(d)–(f)** The second step. **(g)–(i)** The third step. No further changes occur on the fourth (final) step. **(j)** The LUP decomposition $PA = LU$.

the $(n - k + 1) \times (n - k + 1)$ submatrix whose upper left is in row k and column k. Each time through the outer loop, lines 5–9 determine the element $a_{k'k}$ with the largest absolute value of those in the current first column (column k) of the $(n - k + 1) \times (n - k + 1)$ submatrix that the procedure is currently working on. If all elements in the current first column are 0, lines 10–11 report that the matrix is singular. To pivot, line 12 exchanges $\pi[k']$ with $\pi[k]$, and lines 13–14 exchange the kth and k'th rows of A, thereby making the pivot element a_{kk}. (The entire rows are swapped because in the derivation of the method above, not only is $A' - vw^T/a_{k1}$ multiplied by P', but so is v/a_{k1}.) Finally, the Schur complement is computed by lines 15–18 in much the same way as it is computed by lines 6–11 of LU-DECOMPOSITION, except that here the operation is written to work in place.

Because of its triply nested loop structure, LUP-DECOMPOSITION has a running time of $\Theta(n^3)$, which is the same as that of LU-DECOMPOSITION. Thus, pivoting costs at most a constant factor in time.

Exercises

28.1-1
Solve the equation

$$
\begin{pmatrix} 1 & 0 & 0 \\ 4 & 1 & 0 \\ -6 & 5 & 1 \end{pmatrix} \begin{pmatrix} x_1 \\ x_2 \\ x_3 \end{pmatrix} = \begin{pmatrix} 3 \\ 14 \\ -7 \end{pmatrix}
$$

by using forward substitution.

28.1-2
Find an LU decomposition of the matrix

$$
\begin{pmatrix} 4 & -5 & 6 \\ 8 & -6 & 7 \\ 12 & -7 & 12 \end{pmatrix}.
$$

28.1-3
Solve the equation

$$
\begin{pmatrix} 1 & 5 & 4 \\ 2 & 0 & 3 \\ 5 & 8 & 2 \end{pmatrix} \begin{pmatrix} x_1 \\ x_2 \\ x_3 \end{pmatrix} = \begin{pmatrix} 12 \\ 9 \\ 5 \end{pmatrix}
$$

by using an LUP decomposition.

28.1-4
Describe the LUP decomposition of a diagonal matrix.

28.1-5
Describe the LUP decomposition of a permutation matrix, and prove that it is unique.

28.1-6
Show that for all $n \geq 1$, there exists a singular $n \times n$ matrix that has an LU decomposition.

28.1-7
In LU-DECOMPOSITION, is it necessary to perform the outermost **for** loop iteration when $k = n$? How about in LUP-DECOMPOSITION?

28.2 Inverting matrices

Although you can use equation (28.3) to solve a system of linear equations by computing a matrix inverse, in practice you are better off using more numerically stable techniques, such as LUP decomposition. Sometimes, however, you really do need to compute a matrix inverse. This section shows how to use LUP decomposition to compute a matrix inverse. It also proves that matrix multiplication and computing the inverse of a matrix are equivalently hard problems, in that (subject to technical conditions) an algorithm for one can solve the other in the same asymptotic running time. Thus, you can use Strassen's algorithm (see Section 4.2) for matrix multiplication to invert a matrix. Indeed, Strassen's original paper was motivated by the idea that a set of a linear equations could be solved more quickly than by the usual method.

Computing a matrix inverse from an LUP decomposition

Suppose that you have an LUP decomposition of a matrix A in the form of three matrices L, U, and P such that $PA = LU$. Using LUP-SOLVE, you can solve an equation of the form $Ax = b$ in $\Theta(n^2)$ time. Since the LUP decomposition depends on A but not b, you can run LUP-SOLVE on a second set of equations of the form $Ax = b'$ in $\Theta(n^2)$ additional time. In general, once you have the LUP decomposition of A, you can solve, in $\Theta(kn^2)$ time, k versions of the equation $Ax = b$ that differ only in the vector b.

Let's think of the equation

$$AX = I_n , \tag{28.11}$$

which defines the matrix X, the inverse of A, as a set of n distinct equations of the form $Ax = b$. To be precise, let X_i denote the ith column of X, and recall that the unit vector e_i is the ith column of I_n. You can then solve equation (28.11) for X by using the LUP decomposition for A to solve each equation

$$AX_i = e_i$$

separately for X_i. Once you have the LUP decomposition, you can compute each of the n columns X_i in $\Theta(n^2)$ time, and so you can compute X from the LUP decomposition of A in $\Theta(n^3)$ time. Since you find the LUP decomposition of A in $\Theta(n^3)$ time, you can compute the inverse A^{-1} of a matrix A in $\Theta(n^3)$ time.

Matrix multiplication and matrix inversion

Now let's see how the theoretical speedups obtained for matrix multiplication translate to speedups for matrix inversion. In fact, we'll prove something stronger: matrix inversion is equivalent to matrix multiplication, in the following sense. If $M(n)$ denotes the time to multiply two $n \times n$ matrices, then a nonsingular $n \times n$ matrix can be inverted in $O(M(n))$ time. Moreover, if $I(n)$ denotes the time to invert a nonsingular $n \times n$ matrix, then two $n \times n$ matrices can be multiplied in $O(I(n))$ time. We prove these results as two separate theorems.

Theorem 28.1 (Multiplication is no harder than inversion)
If an $n \times n$ matrix can be inverted in $I(n)$ time, where $I(n) = \Omega(n^2)$ and $I(n)$ satisfies the regularity condition $I(3n) = O(I(n))$, then two $n \times n$ matrices can be multiplied in $O(I(n))$ time.

Proof   Let A and B be $n \times n$ matrices. To compute their product $C = AB$, define the $3n \times 3n$ matrix D by

$$D = \begin{pmatrix} I_n & A & 0 \\ 0 & I_n & B \\ 0 & 0 & I_n \end{pmatrix}.$$

The inverse of D is

$$D^{-1} = \begin{pmatrix} I_n & -A & AB \\ 0 & I_n & -B \\ 0 & 0 & I_n \end{pmatrix},$$

and thus to compute the product AB, just take the upper right $n \times n$ submatrix of D^{-1}.

Constructing matrix D takes $\Theta(n^2)$ time, which is $O(I(n))$ from the assumption that $I(n) = \Omega(n^2)$, and inverting D takes $O(I(3n)) = O(I(n))$ time, by the regularity condition on $I(n)$. We thus have $M(n) = O(I(n))$.   ■

Note that $I(n)$ satisfies the regularity condition whenever $I(n) = \Theta(n^c \lg^d n)$ for any constants $c > 0$ and $d \geq 0$.

The proof that matrix inversion is no harder than matrix multiplication relies on some properties of symmetric positive-definite matrices proved in Section 28.3.

Theorem 28.2 (Inversion is no harder than multiplication)
Suppose that two $n \times n$ real matrices can be multiplied in $M(n)$ time, where $M(n) = \Omega(n^2)$ and $M(n)$ satisfies the following two regularity conditions:

1. $M(n + k) = O(M(n))$ for any k in the range $0 \leq k < n$, and

2. $M(n/2) \leq cM(n)$ for some constant $c < 1/2$.

Then the inverse of any real nonsingular $n \times n$ matrix can be computed in $O(M(n))$ time.

Proof Let A be an $n \times n$ matrix with real-valued entries that is nonsingular. Assume that n is an exact power of 2 (i.e., $n = 2^l$ for some integer l); we'll see at the end of the proof what to do if n is not an exact power of 2.

For the moment, assume that the $n \times n$ matrix A is symmetric and positive-definite. Partition each of A and its inverse A^{-1} into four $n/2 \times n/2$ submatrices:

$$A = \begin{pmatrix} B & C^{\mathrm{T}} \\ C & D \end{pmatrix} \text{ and } A^{-1} = \begin{pmatrix} R & T \\ U & V \end{pmatrix} . \tag{28.12}$$

Then, if we let

$$S = D - CB^{-1}C^{\mathrm{T}} \tag{28.13}$$

be the Schur complement of A with respect to B (we'll see more about this form of Schur complement in Section 28.3), we have

$$A^{-1} = \begin{pmatrix} R & T \\ U & V \end{pmatrix} = \begin{pmatrix} B^{-1} + B^{-1}C^{\mathrm{T}}S^{-1}CB^{-1} & -B^{-1}C^{\mathrm{T}}S^{-1} \\ -S^{-1}CB^{-1} & S^{-1} \end{pmatrix} , \tag{28.14}$$

since $AA^{-1} = I_n$, as you can verify by performing the matrix multiplication. Because A is symmetric and positive-definite, Lemmas 28.4 and 28.5 in Section 28.3 imply that B and S are both symmetric and positive-definite. By Lemma 28.3 in Section 28.3, therefore, the inverses B^{-1} and S^{-1} exist, and by Exercise D.2-6 on page 1223, B^{-1} and S^{-1} are symmetric, so that $(B^{-1})^{\mathrm{T}} = B^{-1}$ and $(S^{-1})^{\mathrm{T}} = S^{-1}$. Therefore, to compute the submatrices

$$R = B^{-1} + B^{-1}C^{\mathrm{T}}S^{-1}CB^{-1} ,$$
$$T = -B^{-1}C^{\mathrm{T}}S^{-1} ,$$
$$U = -S^{-1}CB^{-1} , \text{ and}$$
$$V = S^{-1}$$

of A^{-1}, do the following, where all matrices mentioned are $n/2 \times n/2$:

1. Form the submatrices B, C, C^T, and D of A.

2. Recursively compute the inverse B^{-1} of B.

3. Compute the matrix product $W = CB^{-1}$, and then compute its transpose W^T, which equals $B^{-1}C^T$ (by Exercise D.1-2 on page 1219 and $(B^{-1})^T = B^{-1}$).

4. Compute the matrix product $X = WC^T$, which equals $CB^{-1}C^T$, and then compute the matrix $S = D - X = D - CB^{-1}C^T$.

5. Recursively compute the inverse S^{-1} of S.

6. Compute the matrix product $Y = S^{-1}W$, which equals $S^{-1}CB^{-1}$, and then compute its transpose Y^T, which equals $B^{-1}C^TS^{-1}$ (by Exercise D.1-2, $(B^{-1})^T = B^{-1}$, and $(S^{-1})^T = S^{-1}$).

7. Compute the matrix product $Z = W^TY$, which equals $B^{-1}C^TS^{-1}CB^{-1}$.

8. Set $R = B^{-1} + Z$.

9. Set $T = -Y^T$.

10. Set $U = -Y$.

11. Set $V = S^{-1}$.

Thus, to invert an $n \times n$ symmetric positive-definite matrix, invert two $n/2 \times n/2$ matrices in steps 2 and 5; perform four multiplications of $n/2 \times n/2$ matrices in steps 3, 4, 6, and 7; plus incur an additional cost of $O(n^2)$ for extracting submatrices from A, inserting submatrices into A^{-1}, and performing a constant number of additions, subtractions, and transposes on $n/2 \times n/2$ matrices. The running time is given by the recurrence

$$
\begin{aligned}
I(n) &\le 2I(n/2) + 4M(n/2) + O(n^2) \\
&= 2I(n/2) + \Theta(M(n)) \\
&= O(M(n)) \,.
\end{aligned}
\tag{28.15}
$$

The second line follows from the assumption that $M(n) = \Omega(n^2)$ and from the second regularity condition in the statement of the theorem, which implies that $4M(n/2) < 2M(n)$. Because $M(n) = \Omega(n^2)$, case 3 of the master theorem (Theorem 4.1) applies to the recurrence (28.15), giving the $O(M(n))$ result.

It remains to prove how to obtain the same asymptotic running time for matrix multiplication as for matrix inversion when A is invertible but not symmetric and positive-definite. The basic idea is that for any nonsingular matrix A, the matrix A^TA is symmetric (by Exercise D.1-2) and positive-definite (by Theorem D.6 on page 1222). The trick, then, is to reduce the problem of inverting A to the problem of inverting A^TA.

The reduction is based on the observation that when A is an $n \times n$ nonsingular matrix, we have

$$A^{-1} = (A^{\mathrm{T}} A)^{-1} A^{\mathrm{T}} ,$$

since $((A^{\mathrm{T}} A)^{-1} A^{\mathrm{T}}) A = (A^{\mathrm{T}} A)^{-1} (A^{\mathrm{T}} A) = I_n$ and a matrix inverse is unique. Therefore, to compute A^{-1}, first multiply A^{T} by A to obtain $A^{\mathrm{T}} A$, then invert the symmetric positive-definite matrix $A^{\mathrm{T}} A$ using the above divide-and-conquer algorithm, and finally multiply the result by A^{T}. Each of these three steps takes $O(M(n))$ time, and thus any nonsingular matrix with real entries can be inverted in $O(M(n))$ time.

The above proof assumed that A is an $n \times n$ matrix, where n is an exact power of 2. If n is not an exact power of 2, then let $k < n$ be such that $n + k$ is an exact power of 2, and define the $(n + k) \times (n + k)$ matrix A' as

$$A' = \begin{pmatrix} A & 0 \\ 0 & I_k \end{pmatrix} .$$

Then the inverse of A' is

$$\begin{pmatrix} A & 0 \\ 0 & I_k \end{pmatrix}^{-1} = \begin{pmatrix} A^{-1} & 0 \\ 0 & I_k \end{pmatrix} ,$$

Apply the method of the proof to A' to compute the inverse of A', and take the first n rows and n columns of the result as the desired answer A^{-1}. The first regularity condition on $M(n)$ ensures that enlarging the matrix in this way increases the running time by at most a constant factor.   ∎

The proof of Theorem 28.2 suggests how to solve the equation $Ax = b$ by using LU decomposition without pivoting, so long as A is nonsingular. Let $y = A^{\mathrm{T}} b$. Multiply both sides of the equation $Ax = b$ by A^{T}, yielding $(A^{\mathrm{T}} A) x = A^{\mathrm{T}} b = y$. This transformation doesn't affect the solution x, since A^{T} is invertible. Because $A^{\mathrm{T}} A$ is symmetric positive-definite, it can be factored by computing an LU decomposition. Then, use forward and back substitution to solve for x in the equation $(A^{\mathrm{T}} A) x = y$. Although this method is theoretically correct, in practice the procedure LUP-DECOMPOSITION works much better. LUP decomposition requires fewer arithmetic operations by a constant factor, and it has somewhat better numerical properties.

Exercises

28.2-1
Let $M(n)$ be the time to multiply two $n \times n$ matrices, and let $S(n)$ denote the time required to square an $n \times n$ matrix. Show that multiplying and squaring matrices have essentially the same difficulty: an $M(n)$-time matrix-multiplication algorithm implies an $O(M(n))$-time squaring algorithm, and an $S(n)$-time squaring algorithm implies an $O(S(n))$-time matrix-multiplication algorithm.

28.2-2

Let $M(n)$ be the time to multiply two $n \times n$ matrices. Show that an $M(n)$-time matrix-multiplication algorithm implies an $O(M(n))$-time LUP-decomposition algorithm. (The LUP decomposition your method produces need not be the same as the result produced by the LUP-DECOMPOSITION procedure.)

28.2-3

Let $M(n)$ be the time to multiply two $n \times n$ boolean matrices, and let $T(n)$ be the time to find the transitive closure of an $n \times n$ boolean matrix. (See Section 23.2.) Show that an $M(n)$-time boolean matrix-multiplication algorithm implies an $O(M(n) \lg n)$-time transitive-closure algorithm, and a $T(n)$-time transitive-closure algorithm implies an $O(T(n))$-time boolean matrix-multiplication algorithm.

28.2-4

Does the matrix-inversion algorithm based on Theorem 28.2 work when matrix elements are drawn from the field of integers modulo 2? Explain.

★ 28.2-5

Generalize the matrix-inversion algorithm of Theorem 28.2 to handle matrices of complex numbers, and prove that your generalization works correctly. (*Hint:* Instead of the transpose of A, use the *conjugate transpose* A^*, which you obtain from the transpose of A by replacing every entry with its complex conjugate. Instead of symmetric matrices, consider *Hermitian* matrices, which are matrices A such that $A = A^*$.)

28.3   Symmetric positive-definite matrices and least-squares approximation

Symmetric positive-definite matrices have many interesting and desirable properties. An $n \times n$ matrix A is *symmetric positive-definite* if $A = A^T$ (A is symmetric) and $x^T A x > 0$ for all n-vectors $x \neq 0$ (A is positive-definite). Symmetric positive-definite matrices are nonsingular, and an LU decomposition on them will not divide by 0. This section proves these and several other important properties of symmetric positive-definite matrices. We'll also see an interesting application to curve fitting by a least-squares approximation.

The first property we prove is perhaps the most basic.

Lemma 28.3

Any positive-definite matrix is nonsingular.

Proof Suppose that a matrix A is singular. Then by Corollary D.3 on page 1221, there exists a nonzero vector x such that $Ax = 0$. Hence, $x^{\mathrm{T}}Ax = 0$, and A cannot be positive-definite. $\blacksquare$

The proof that an LU decomposition on a symmetric positive-definite matrix A won't divide by 0 is more involved. We begin by proving properties about certain submatrices of A. Define the kth *leading submatrix* of A to be the matrix A_k consisting of the intersection of the first k rows and first k columns of A.

Lemma 28.4
If A is a symmetric positive-definite matrix, then every leading submatrix of A is symmetric and positive-definite.

Proof Since A is symmetric, each leading submatrix A_k is also symmetric. We'll prove that A_k is positive-definite by contradiction. If A_k is not positive-definite, then there exists a k-vector $x_k \neq 0$ such that $x_k^{\mathrm{T}} A_k x_k \leq 0$. Let A be $n \times n$, and

$$A = \begin{pmatrix} A_k & B^{\mathrm{T}} \\ B & C \end{pmatrix} \tag{28.16}$$

for submatrices B (which is $(n-k) \times k$) and C (which is $(n-k) \times (n-k)$). Define the n-vector $x = (\ x_k^{\mathrm{T}} \ \ 0\ )^{\mathrm{T}}$, where $n - k$ 0s follow x_k. Then we have

$$\begin{aligned} x^{\mathrm{T}}Ax &= (\ x_k^{\mathrm{T}} \ \ 0\ ) \begin{pmatrix} A_k & B^{\mathrm{T}} \\ B & C \end{pmatrix} \begin{pmatrix} x_k \\ 0 \end{pmatrix} \\ &= (\ x_k^{\mathrm{T}} \ \ 0\ ) \begin{pmatrix} A_k x_k \\ B x_k \end{pmatrix} \\ &= x_k^{\mathrm{T}} A_k x_k \\ &\leq 0\ , \end{aligned}$$

which contradicts A being positive-definite. $\blacksquare$

We now turn to some essential properties of the Schur complement. Let A be a symmetric positive-definite matrix, and let A_k be a leading $k \times k$ submatrix of A. Partition A once again according to equation (28.16). Equation (28.10) generalizes to define the *Schur complement* S of A with respect to A_k as

$$S = C - BA_k^{-1}B^{\mathrm{T}}\ . \tag{28.17}$$

(By Lemma 28.4, A_k is symmetric and positive-definite, and therefore, A_k^{-1} exists by Lemma 28.3, and S is well defined.) The earlier definition (28.10) of the Schur complement is consistent with equation (28.17) by letting $k = 1$.

The next lemma shows that the Schur-complement matrices of symmetric positive-definite matrices are themselves symmetric and positive-definite. We used this result in Theorem 28.2, and its corollary will help prove that LU decomposition works for symmetric positive-definite matrices.

Lemma 28.5 (Schur complement lemma)

If A is a symmetric positive-definite matrix and A_k is a leading $k \times k$ submatrix of A, then the Schur complement S of A with respect to A_k is symmetric and positive-definite.

Proof   Because A is symmetric, so is the submatrix C. By Exercise D.2-6 on page 1223, the product $BA_k^{-1}B^{\mathrm{T}}$ is symmetric. Since C and $BA_k^{-1}B^{\mathrm{T}}$ are symmetric, then by Exercise D.1-1 on page 1219, so is S.

It remains to show that S is positive-definite. Consider the partition of A given in equation (28.16). For any nonzero vector x, we have $x^{\mathrm{T}}Ax > 0$ by the assumption that A is positive-definite. Let the subvectors y and z consist of the first k and last $n - k$ elements in x, respectively, and thus they are compatible with A_k and C, respectively. Because A_k^{-1} exists, we have

$$
\begin{aligned}
x^{\mathrm{T}}Ax &= (\; y^{\mathrm{T}} \quad z^{\mathrm{T}} \;)\begin{pmatrix} A_k & B^{\mathrm{T}} \\ B & C \end{pmatrix}\begin{pmatrix} y \\ z \end{pmatrix} \\
&= (\; y^{\mathrm{T}} \quad z^{\mathrm{T}} \;)\begin{pmatrix} A_k y + B^{\mathrm{T}}z \\ By + Cz \end{pmatrix} \\
&= y^{\mathrm{T}}A_k y + y^{\mathrm{T}}B^{\mathrm{T}}z + z^{\mathrm{T}}By + z^{\mathrm{T}}Cz \\
&= (y + A_k^{-1}B^{\mathrm{T}}z)^{\mathrm{T}}A_k(y + A_k^{-1}B^{\mathrm{T}}z) + z^{\mathrm{T}}(C - BA_k^{-1}B^{\mathrm{T}})z \, , \qquad (28.18)
\end{aligned}
$$

This last equation, which you can verify by multiplying through, amounts to "completing the square" of the quadratic form. (See Exercise 28.3-2.)

Since $x^{\mathrm{T}}Ax > 0$ holds for any nonzero x, pick any nonzero z and then choose $y = -A_k^{-1}B^{\mathrm{T}}z$, which causes the first term in equation (28.18) to vanish, leaving

$$
z^{\mathrm{T}}(C - BA_k^{-1}B^{\mathrm{T}})z = z^{\mathrm{T}}Sz
$$

as the value of the expression. For any $z \neq 0$, we therefore have $z^{\mathrm{T}}Sz = x^{\mathrm{T}}Ax > 0$, and thus S is positive-definite.   ∎

Corollary 28.6

LU decomposition of a symmetric positive-definite matrix never causes a division by 0.

Proof   Let A be an $n \times n$ symmetric positive-definite matrix. In fact, we'll prove a stronger result than the statement of the corollary: every pivot is strictly positive. The first pivot is a_{11}. Let e_1 be the length-n unit vector $(\; 1 \quad 0 \quad 0 \quad \cdots \quad 0\;)^{\mathrm{T}}$, so that $a_{11} = e_1^{\mathrm{T}}Ae_1$, which is positive because e_1 is nonzero and A is positive definite. Since the first step of LU decomposition produces the Schur complement of A with respect to $A_1 = (a_{11})$, Lemma 28.5 implies by induction that all pivots are positive. ∎

Least-squares approximation

One important application of symmetric positive-definite matrices arises in fitting curves to given sets of data points. You are given a set of m data points

$$(x_1, y_1), (x_2, y_2), \ldots, (x_m, y_m) \, ,$$

where you know that the y_i are subject to measurement errors. You wish to determine a function $F(x)$ such that the approximation errors

$$\eta_i = F(x_i) - y_i \tag{28.19}$$

are small for $i = 1, 2, \ldots, m$. The form of the function F depends on the problem at hand. Let's assume that it has the form of a linearly weighted sum

$$F(x) = \sum_{j=1}^{n} c_j f_j(x) \, ,$$

where the number n of summands and the specific *basis functions* f_j are chosen based on knowledge of the problem at hand. A common choice is $f_j(x) = x^{j-1}$, which means that

$$F(x) = c_1 + c_2 x + c_3 x^2 + \cdots + c_n x^{n-1}$$

is a polynomial of degree $n - 1$ in x. Thus, if you are given m data points $(x_1, y_1), (x_2, y_2), \ldots, (x_m, y_m)$, you need to calculate n coefficients $c_1, c_2, \ldots, c_n$ that minimize the approximation errors $\eta_1, \eta_2, \ldots, \eta_m$.

By choosing $n = m$, you can calculate each y_i *exactly* in equation (28.19). Such a high-degree polynomial F "fits the noise" as well as the data, however, and generally gives poor results when used to predict y for previously unseen values of x. It is usually better to choose n significantly smaller than m and hope that by choosing the coefficients c_j well, you can obtain a function F that finds the significant patterns in the data points without paying undue attention to the noise. Some theoretical principles exist for choosing n, but they are beyond the scope of this text. In any case, once you choose a value of n that is less than m, you end up with an overdetermined set of equations whose solution you wish to approximate. Let's see how to do so.

Let

$$
A = \begin{pmatrix}
f_1(x_1) & f_2(x_1) & \cdots & f_n(x_1) \\
f_1(x_2) & f_2(x_2) & \cdots & f_n(x_2) \\
\vdots & \vdots & \ddots & \vdots \\
f_1(x_m) & f_2(x_m) & \cdots & f_n(x_m)
\end{pmatrix}
$$

denote the matrix of values of the basis functions at the given points, that is, $a_{ij} = f_j(x_i)$. Let $c = (c_k)$ denote the desired n-vector of coefficients. Then,

$$
\begin{aligned}
Ac &= \begin{pmatrix}
f_1(x_1) & f_2(x_1) & \cdots & f_n(x_1) \\
f_1(x_2) & f_2(x_2) & \cdots & f_n(x_2) \\
\vdots & \vdots & \ddots & \vdots \\
f_1(x_m) & f_2(x_m) & \cdots & f_n(x_m)
\end{pmatrix}
\begin{pmatrix}
c_1 \\
c_2 \\
\vdots \\
c_n
\end{pmatrix} \\
&= \begin{pmatrix}
F(x_1) \\
F(x_2) \\
\vdots \\
F(x_m)
\end{pmatrix}
\end{aligned}
$$

is the m-vector of "predicted values" for y. Thus,

$$
\eta = Ac - y
$$

is the m-vector of **approximation errors**.

To minimize approximation errors, let's minimize the norm of the error vector η, which gives a **least-squares solution**, since

$$
\|\eta\| = \left(\sum_{i=1}^{m} \eta_i^2 \right)^{1/2} .
$$

Because

$$
\|\eta\|^2 = \|Ac - y\|^2 = \sum_{i=1}^{m} \left(\sum_{j=1}^{n} a_{ij} c_j - y_i \right)^2 ,
$$

to minimize $\|\eta\|$, differentiate $\|\eta\|^2$ with respect to each c_k and then set the result to 0:

$$
\frac{d \|\eta\|^2}{d c_k} = \sum_{i=1}^{m} 2 \left(\sum_{j=1}^{n} a_{ij} c_j - y_i \right) a_{ik} = 0 . \tag{28.20}
$$

The n equations (28.20) for $k = 1, 2, \ldots, n$ are equivalent to the single matrix equation

$$(Ac - y)^{\mathrm{T}} A = 0$$

or, equivalently (using Exercise D.1-2 on page 1219), to

$$A^{\mathrm{T}}(Ac - y) = 0 \, ,$$

which implies

$$A^{\mathrm{T}} Ac = A^{\mathrm{T}} y \, . \tag{28.21}$$

In statistics, equation (28.21) is called the ***normal equation***. The matrix $A^{\mathrm{T}} A$ is symmetric by Exercise D.1-2, and if A has full column rank, then by Theorem D.6 on page 1222, $A^{\mathrm{T}} A$ is positive-definite as well. Hence, $(A^{\mathrm{T}} A)^{-1}$ exists, and the solution to equation (28.21) is

$$\begin{aligned} c &= \left((A^{\mathrm{T}} A)^{-1} A^{\mathrm{T}} \right) y \\ &= A^{+} y \, , \end{aligned} \tag{28.22}$$

where the matrix $A^{+} = \left((A^{\mathrm{T}} A)^{-1} A^{\mathrm{T}} \right)$ is the ***pseudoinverse*** of the matrix A. The pseudoinverse naturally generalizes the notion of a matrix inverse to the case in which A is not square. (Compare equation (28.22) as the approximate solution to $Ac = y$ with the solution $A^{-1} b$ as the exact solution to $Ax = b$.)

As an example of producing a least-squares fit, suppose that you have five data points

$$\begin{aligned} (x_1, y_1) &= (-1, 2) \, , \\ (x_2, y_2) &= (1, 1) \, , \\ (x_3, y_3) &= (2, 1) \, , \\ (x_4, y_4) &= (3, 0) \, , \\ (x_5, y_5) &= (5, 3) \, , \end{aligned}$$

shown as orange dots in Figure 28.3, and you want to fit these points with a quadratic polynomial

$$F(x) = c_1 + c_2 x + c_3 x^2 \, .$$

Start with the matrix of basis-function values

$$A = \begin{pmatrix} 1 & x_1 & x_1^2 \\ 1 & x_2 & x_2^2 \\ 1 & x_3 & x_3^2 \\ 1 & x_4 & x_4^2 \\ 1 & x_5 & x_5^2 \end{pmatrix} = \begin{pmatrix} 1 & -1 & 1 \\ 1 & 1 & 1 \\ 1 & 2 & 4 \\ 1 & 3 & 9 \\ 1 & 5 & 25 \end{pmatrix} \, ,$$

whose pseudoinverse is

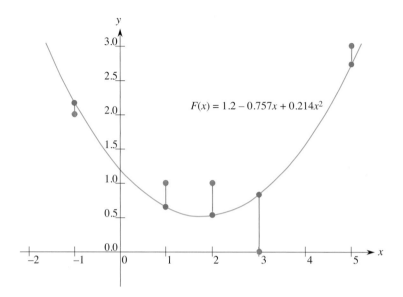

Figure 28.3 The least-squares fit of a quadratic polynomial to the set of five data points $\{(-1, 2), (1, 1), (2, 1), (3, 0), (5, 3)\}$. The orange dots are the data points, and the blue dots are their estimated values predicted by the polynomial $F(x) = 1.2 - 0.757x + 0.214x^2$, the quadratic polynomial that minimizes the sum of the squared errors, plotted in blue. Each orange line shows the error for one data point.

$$A^+ = \begin{pmatrix} 0.500 & 0.300 & 0.200 & 0.100 & -0.100 \\ -0.388 & 0.093 & 0.190 & 0.193 & -0.088 \\ 0.060 & -0.036 & -0.048 & -0.036 & 0.060 \end{pmatrix}.$$

Multiplying y by A^+ gives the coefficient vector

$$c = \begin{pmatrix} 1.200 \\ -0.757 \\ 0.214 \end{pmatrix},$$

which corresponds to the quadratic polynomial

$$F(x) = 1.200 - 0.757x + 0.214x^2$$

as the closest-fitting quadratic to the given data, in a least-squares sense.

As a practical matter, you would typically solve the normal equation (28.21) by multiplying y by A^{T} and then finding an LU decomposition of $A^{\mathrm{T}}A$. If A has full rank, the matrix $A^{\mathrm{T}}A$ is guaranteed to be nonsingular, because it is symmetric and positive-definite. (See Exercise D.1-2 and Theorem D.6.)

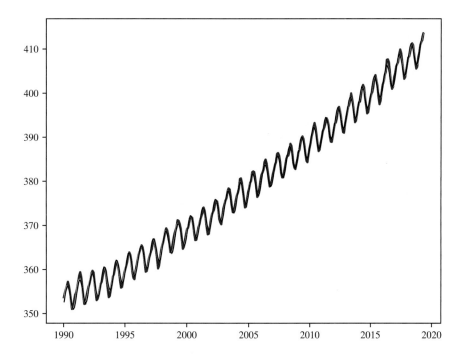

Figure 28.4 A least-squares fit of a curve of the form

$$c_1 + c_2 x + c_3 x^2 + c_4 \sin(2\pi x) + c_5 \cos(2\pi x)$$

for the carbon-dioxide concentrations measured in Mauna Loa, Hawaii from 1990[1] to 2019, where x is the number of years elapsed since 1990. This curve is the famous "Keeling curve," illustrating curve-fitting to nonpolynomial formulas. The sine and cosine terms allow modeling of seasonal variations in CO_2 concentrations. The red curve shows the measured CO_2 concentrations. The best fit, shown in black, has the form

$$352.83 + 1.39x + 0.02x^2 + 2.83 \sin(2\pi x) - 0.94 \cos(2\pi x) .$$

We close this section with an example in Figure 28.4, illustrating that a curve can also fit a nonpolynomial function. The curve confirms one aspect of climate change: that carbon dioxide (CO_2) concentrations have steadily increased over a period of 29 years. Linear and quadratic terms model the annual increase, and sine and cosine terms model seasonal variations.

---

[1] The year in which *Introduction to Algorithms* was first published.

Exercises

28.3-1
Prove that every diagonal element of a symmetric positive-definite matrix is positive.

28.3-2
Let $A = \begin{pmatrix} a & b \\ b & c \end{pmatrix}$ be a 2×2 symmetric positive-definite matrix. Prove that its determinant $ac - b^2$ is positive by "completing the square" in a manner similar to that used in the proof of Lemma 28.5.

28.3-3
Prove that the maximum element in a symmetric positive-definite matrix lies on the diagonal.

28.3-4
Prove that the determinant of each leading submatrix of a symmetric positive-definite matrix is positive.

28.3-5
Let A_k denote the kth leading submatrix of a symmetric positive-definite matrix A. Prove that $\det(A_k)/\det(A_{k-1})$ is the kth pivot during LU decomposition, where, by convention, $\det(A_0) = 1$.

28.3-6
Find the function of the form

$$F(x) = c_1 + c_2 x \lg x + c_3 e^x$$

that is the best least-squares fit to the data points

$$(1, 1), (2, 1), (3, 3), (4, 8) .$$

28.3-7
Show that the pseudoinverse A^+ satisfies the following four equations:

$$
\begin{aligned}
AA^+A &= A , \\
A^+AA^+ &= A^+ , \\
(AA^+)^{\mathrm{T}} &= AA^+ , \\
(A^+A)^{\mathrm{T}} &= A^+A .
\end{aligned}
$$

Problems

28-1 Tridiagonal systems of linear equations

Consider the tridiagonal matrix

$$A = \begin{pmatrix} 1 & -1 & 0 & 0 & 0 \\ -1 & 2 & -1 & 0 & 0 \\ 0 & -1 & 2 & -1 & 0 \\ 0 & 0 & -1 & 2 & -1 \\ 0 & 0 & 0 & -1 & 2 \end{pmatrix}.$$

a. Find an LU decomposition of A.

b. Solve the equation $Ax = (1 \quad 1 \quad 1 \quad 1 \quad 1)^{\mathrm{T}}$ by using forward and back substitution.

c. Find the inverse of A.

d. Show how to solve the equation $Ax = b$ for any $n \times n$ symmetric positive-definite, tridiagonal matrix A and any n-vector b in $O(n)$ time by performing an LU decomposition. Argue that any method based on forming A^{-1} is asymptotically more expensive in the worst case.

e. Show how to solve the equation $Ax = b$ for any $n \times n$ nonsingular, tridiagonal matrix A and any n-vector b in $O(n)$ time by performing an LUP decomposition.

28-2 Splines

A practical method for interpolating a set of points with a curve is to use *cubic splines*. You are given a set $\{(x_i, y_i) : i = 0, 1, \ldots, n\}$ of $n + 1$ point-value pairs, where $x_0 < x_1 < \cdots < x_n$. Your goal is to fit a piecewise-cubic curve (spline) $f(x)$ to the points. That is, the curve $f(x)$ is made up of n cubic polynomials $f_i(x) = a_i + b_i x + c_i x^2 + d_i x^3$ for $i = 0, 1, \ldots, n-1$, where if x falls in the range $x_i \leq x \leq x_{i+1}$, then the value of the curve is given by $f(x) = f_i(x - x_i)$. The points x_i at which the cubic polynomials are "pasted" together are called *knots*. For simplicity, assume that $x_i = i$ for $i = 0, 1, \ldots, n$.

To ensure continuity of $f(x)$, require that

$$f(x_i) \quad = \quad f_i(0) \; = \; y_i \, ,$$
$$f(x_{i+1}) \; = \; f_i(1) \; = \; y_{i+1}$$

for $i = 0, 1, \ldots, n - 1$. To ensure that $f(x)$ is sufficiently smooth, also require the first derivative to be continuous at each knot:

$$f'(x_{i+1}) = f_i'(1) = f_{i+1}'(0)$$

for $i = 0, 1, \ldots, n - 2$.

a. Suppose that for $i = 0, 1, \ldots, n$, in addition to the point-value pairs $\{(x_i, y_i)\}$, you are also given the first derivative $D_i = f'(x_i)$ at each knot. Express each coefficient a_i, b_i, c_i, and d_i in terms of the values y_i, y_{i+1}, D_i, and D_{i+1}. (Remember that $x_i = i$.) How quickly can you compute the $4n$ coefficients from the point-value pairs and first derivatives?

The question remains of how to choose the first derivatives of $f(x)$ at the knots. One method is to require the second derivatives to be continuous at the knots:

$$f''(x_{i+1}) = f_i''(1) = f_{i+1}''(0)$$

for $i = 0, 1, \ldots, n-2$. At the first and last knots, assume that $f''(x_0) = f_0''(0) = 0$ and $f''(x_n) = f_{n-1}''(1) = 0$. These assumptions make $f(x)$ a *natural* cubic spline.

b. Use the continuity constraints on the second derivative to show that for $i = 1, 2, \ldots, n - 1$,

$$D_{i-1} + 4D_i + D_{i+1} = 3(y_{i+1} - y_{i-1}) . \tag{28.23}$$

c. Show that

$$2D_0 + D_1 = 3(y_1 - y_0) , \tag{28.24}$$
$$D_{n-1} + 2D_n = 3(y_n - y_{n-1}) . \tag{28.25}$$

d. Rewrite equations (28.23)–(28.25) as a matrix equation involving the vector $D = (\, D_0 \quad D_1 \quad D_2 \quad \cdots \quad D_n \,)^{\mathrm{T}}$ of unknowns. What attributes does the matrix in your equation have?

e. Argue that a natural cubic spline can interpolate a set of $n + 1$ point-value pairs in $O(n)$ time (see Problem 28-1).

f. Show how to determine a natural cubic spline that interpolates a set of $n + 1$ points (x_i, y_i) satisfying $x_0 < x_1 < \cdots < x_n$, even when x_i is not necessarily equal to i. What matrix equation must your method solve, and how quickly does your algorithm run?

Chapter notes

Many excellent texts describe numerical and scientific computation in much greater detail than we have room for here. The following are especially readable: George and Liu [180], Golub and Van Loan [192], Press, Teukolsky, Vetterling, and Flannery [365, 366], and Strang [422, 423].

Golub and Van Loan [192] discuss numerical stability. They show why $\det(A)$ is not necessarily a good indicator of the stability of a matrix A, proposing instead to use $\|A\|_\infty \|A^{-1}\|_\infty$, where $\|A\|_\infty = \max\left\{ \sum_{j=1}^n |a_{ij}| : 1 \le i \le n \right\}$. They also address the question of how to compute this value without actually computing A^{-1}.

Gaussian elimination, upon which the LU and LUP decompositions are based, was the first systematic method for solving linear systems of equations. It was also one of the earliest numerical algorithms. Although it was known earlier, its discovery is commonly attributed to C. F. Gauss (1777–1855). In his famous paper [424], Strassen showed that an $n \times n$ matrix can be inverted in $O(n^{\lg 7})$ time. Winograd [460] originally proved that matrix multiplication is no harder than matrix inversion, and the converse is due to Aho, Hopcroft, and Ullman [5].

Another important matrix decomposition is the *singular value decomposition*, or *SVD*. The SVD factors an $m \times n$ matrix A into $A = Q_1 \Sigma Q_2^{\mathrm{T}}$, where Σ is an $m \times n$ matrix with nonzero values only on the diagonal, Q_1 is $m \times m$ with mutually orthonormal columns, and Q_2 is $n \times n$, also with mutually orthonormal columns. Two vectors are *orthonormal* if their inner product is 0 and each vector has a norm of 1. The books by Strang [422, 423] and Golub and Van Loan [192] contain good treatments of the SVD.

Strang [423] has an excellent presentation of symmetric positive-definite matrices and of linear algebra in general.

29   Linear Programming

Many problems take the form of maximizing or minimizing an objective, given limited resources and competing constraints. If you can specify the objective as a linear function of certain variables, and if you can specify the constraints on resources as equalities or inequalities on those variables, then you have a *linear-programming problem*. Linear programs arise in a variety of practical applications. We begin by studying an application in electoral politics.

A political problem

Suppose that you are a politician trying to win an election. Your district has three different types of areas—urban, suburban, and rural. These areas have, respectively, 100,000, 200,000, and 50,000 registered voters. Although not all the registered voters actually go to the polls, you decide that to govern effectively, you would like at least half the registered voters in each of the three regions to vote for you. You are honorable and would never consider supporting policies you don't believe in. You realize, however, that certain issues may be more effective in winning votes in certain places. Your primary issues are preparing for a zombie apocalypse, equipping sharks with lasers, building highways for flying cars, and allowing dolphins to vote.

According to your campaign staff's research, you can estimate how many votes you win or lose from each population segment by spending $1,000 on advertising on each issue. This information appears in the table of Figure 29.1. In this table, each entry indicates the number of thousands of either urban, suburban, or rural voters who would be won over by spending $1,000 on advertising in support of a particular issue. Negative entries denote votes that would be lost. Your task is to figure out the minimum amount of money that you need to spend in order to win 50,000 urban votes, 100,000 suburban votes, and 25,000 rural votes.

You could, by trial and error, devise a strategy that wins the required number of votes, but the strategy you come up with might not be the least expensive one. For example, you could devote $20,000 of advertising to preparing for a zombie

policy	urban	suburban	rural
zombie apocalypse	−2	5	3
sharks with lasers	8	2	−5
highways for flying cars	0	0	10
dolphins voting	10	0	−2

Figure 29.1   The effects of policies on voters. Each entry describes the number of thousands of urban, suburban, or rural voters who could be won over by spending $1,000 on advertising support of a policy on a particular issue. Negative entries denote votes that would be lost.

apocalypse, $0 to equipping sharks with lasers, $4,000 to building highways for flying cars, and $9,000 to allowing dolphins to vote. In this case, you would win $(20 \cdot -2) + (0 \cdot 8) + (4 \cdot 0) + (9 \cdot 10) = 50$ thousand urban votes, $(20 \cdot 5) + (0 \cdot 2) + (4 \cdot 0) + (9 \cdot 0) = 100$ thousand suburban votes, and $(20 \cdot 3) + (0 \cdot -5) + (4 \cdot 10) + (9 \cdot -2) = 82$ thousand rural votes. You would win the exact number of votes desired in the urban and suburban areas and more than enough votes in the rural area. (In fact, according to your model, in the rural area you would receive more votes than there are voters.) In order to garner these votes, you would have paid for $20 + 0 + 4 + 9 = 33$ thousand dollars of advertising.

It's natural to wonder whether this strategy is the best possible. That is, can you achieve your goals while spending less on advertising? Additional trial and error might help you to answer this question, but a better approach is to formulate (or *model*) this question mathematically.

The first step is to decide what decisions you have to make and to introduce variables that capture these decisions. Since you have four decisions, you introduce four *decision variables*:

- x_1 is the number of thousands of dollars spent on advertising on preparing for a zombie apocalypse,

- x_2 is the number of thousands of dollars spent on advertising on equipping sharks with lasers,

- x_3 is the number of thousands of dollars spent on advertising on building highways for flying cars, and

- x_4 is the number of thousands of dollars spent on advertising on allowing dolphins to vote.

You then think about *constraints*, which are limits, or restrictions, on the values that the decision variables can take. You can write the requirement that you win at least 50,000 urban votes as

$$-2x_1 + 8x_2 + 0x_3 + 10x_4 \geq 50 . \tag{29.1}$$

Similarly, you can write the requirements that you win at least 100,000 suburban votes and 25,000 rural votes as

$$5x_1 + 2x_2 + 0x_3 + 0x_4 \geq 100 \tag{29.2}$$

and

$$3x_1 - 5x_2 + 10x_3 - 2x_4 \geq 25 . \tag{29.3}$$

Any setting of the variables x_1, x_2, x_3, x_4 that satisfies inequalities (29.1)–(29.3) yields a strategy that wins a sufficient number of each type of vote.

Finally, you think about your *objective*, which is the quantity that you wish to either minimize or maximize. In order to keep costs as small as possible, you would like to minimize the amount spent on advertising. That is, you want to minimize the expression

$$x_1 + x_2 + x_3 + x_4 . \tag{29.4}$$

Although negative advertising often occurs in political campaigns, there is no such thing as negative-cost advertising. Consequently, you require that

$$x_1 \geq 0, \ x_2 \geq 0, \ x_3 \geq 0, \text{ and } x_4 \geq 0 . \tag{29.5}$$

Combining inequalities (29.1)–(29.3) and (29.5) with the objective of minimizing (29.4) produces what is known as a "linear program." We can format this problem tabularly as

$$\text{minimize} \quad x_1 + x_2 + x_3 + x_4 \tag{29.6}$$

subject to

$$
\begin{array}{rcrcrcrcr}
-2x_1 & + & 8x_2 & + & 0x_3 & + & 10x_4 & \geq & 50 \\
5x_1 & + & 2x_2 & + & 0x_3 & + & 0x_4 & \geq & 100 \\
3x_1 & - & 5x_2 & + & 10x_3 & - & 2x_4 & \geq & 25 \\
& & & & x_1, x_2, x_3, x_4 & \geq & 0 & &
\end{array}
$$

$$\tag{29.7}$$
$$\tag{29.8}$$
$$\tag{29.9}$$
$$\tag{29.10}$$

The solution to this linear program yields your optimal strategy.

The remainder of this chapter covers how to formulate linear programs and is an introduction to modeling in general. Modeling refers to the general process of converting a problem into a mathematical form amenable to solution by an algorithm. Section 29.1 discusses briefly the algorithmic aspects of linear programming, although it does not include the details of a linear-programming algorithm. Throughout this book, we have seen ways to model problems, such as by shortest paths and connectivity in a graph. When modeling a problem as a linear program, you go through the steps used in this political example—identifying the decision variables, specifying the constraints, and formulating the objective function. In order to model a problem as a linear program, the constraints and objectives must be linear. In Section 29.2, we will see several other examples of modeling via linear programs. Section 29.3 discusses duality, an important concept in linear programming and other optimization algorithms.

29.1   Linear programming formulations and algorithms

Linear programs take a particular form, which we will examine in this section. Multiple algorithms have been developed to solve linear programs. Some run in polynomial time, some do not, but they are all too complicated to show here. Instead, we will give an example that demonstrates some ideas behind the simplex algorithm, which is currently the most commonly deployed solution method.

General linear programs

In the general linear-programming problem, we wish to optimize a linear function subject to a set of linear inequalities. Given a set of real numbers $a_1, a_2, \ldots, a_n$ and a set of variables $x_1, x_2, \ldots, x_n$, we define a *linear function* f on those variables by

$$f(x_1, x_2, \ldots, x_n) = a_1 x_1 + a_2 x_2 + \cdots + a_n x_n = \sum_{j=1}^{n} a_j x_j \, .$$

If b is a real number and f is a linear function, then the equation

$$f(x_1, x_2, \ldots, x_n) = b$$

is a *linear equality* and the inequalities

$$f(x_1, x_2, \ldots, x_n) \le b \quad \text{and} \quad f(x_1, x_2, \ldots, x_n) \ge b$$

are *linear inequalities*. We use the general term *linear constraints* to denote either linear equalities or linear inequalities. Linear programming does not allow strict inequalities. Formally, a *linear-programming problem* is the problem of either minimizing or maximizing a linear function subject to a finite set of linear constraints. If minimizing, we call the linear program a *minimization linear program*, and if maximizing, we call the linear program a *maximization linear program*.

In order to discuss linear-programming algorithms and properties, it will be helpful to use a standard notation for the input. By convention, a maximization linear program takes as input n real numbers $c_1, c_2, \ldots, c_n$; m real numbers $b_1, b_2, \ldots, b_m$; and mn real numbers a_{ij} for $i = 1, 2, \ldots, m$ and $j = 1, 2, \ldots, n$.

The goal is to find n real numbers $x_1, x_2, \ldots, x_n$ that

maximize $\displaystyle\sum_{j=1}^{n} c_j x_j$ (29.11)

subject to

$$\sum_{j=1}^{n} a_{ij} x_j \le b_i \text{ for } i = 1, 2, \ldots, m \qquad (29.12)$$
$$x_j \ge 0 \text{ for } j = 1, 2, \ldots, n . \qquad (29.13)$$

We call expression (29.11) the *objective function* and the $n + m$ inequalities in lines (29.12) and (29.13) the *constraints*. The n constraints in line (29.13) are the *nonnegativity constraints*. It can sometimes be more convenient to express a linear program in a more compact form. If we create an $m \times n$ matrix $A = (a_{ij})$, an m-vector $b = (b_i)$, an n-vector $c = (c_j)$, and an n-vector $x = (x_j)$, then we can rewrite the linear program defined in (29.11)–(29.13) as

maximize $c^{\mathrm{T}} x$ (29.14)

subject to

$$Ax \le b \qquad (29.15)$$
$$x \ge 0 . \qquad (29.16)$$

In line (29.14), $c^{\mathrm{T}} x$ is the inner product of two n-vectors. In inequality (29.15), Ax is the m-vector that is the product of an $m \times n$ matrix and an n-vector, and in inequality (29.16), $x \ge 0$ means that each entry of the vector x must be nonnegative. We call this representation the *standard form* for a linear program, and we adopt the convention that A, b, and c always have the dimensions given above.

The standard form above may not naturally correspond to real-life situations you are trying to model. For example, you might have equality constraints or variables that can take on negative values. Exercises 29.1-6 and 29.1-7 ask you to show how to convert any linear program into this standard form.

We now introduce terminology to describe solutions to linear programs. We denote a particular setting of the values in a variable, say x, by putting a bar over the variable name: $\bar{x}$. If $\bar{x}$ satisfies all the constraints, then it is a *feasible solution*, but if it fails to satisfy at least one constraint, then it is an *infeasible solution*. We say that a solution $\bar{x}$ has *objective value* $c^{\mathrm{T}} \bar{x}$. A feasible solution $\bar{x}$ whose objective value is maximum over all feasible solutions is an *optimal solution*, and we call its objective value $c^{\mathrm{T}} \bar{x}$ the *optimal objective value*. If a linear program has no feasible solutions, we say that the linear program is *infeasible*, and otherwise, it is *feasible*. The set of points that satisfy all the constraints is the *feasible region*. If a linear program has some feasible solutions but does not have a finite optimal objective value, then the feasible region is *unbounded* and so is the linear program. Exercise 29.1-5 asks you to show that a linear program can have a finite optimal objective value even if the feasible region is unbounded.

One of the reasons for the power and popularity of linear programming is that
linear programs can, in general, be solved efficiently. There are two classes of
algorithms, known as ellipsoid algorithms and interior-point algorithms, that solve
linear programs in polynomial time. In addition, the simplex algorithm is widely
used. Although it does not run in polynomial time in the worst case, it tends to
perform well in practice.

We will not give a detailed algorithm for linear programming, but will discuss a
few important ideas. First, we will give an example of using a geometric procedure
to solve a two-variable linear program. Although this example does not immediately generalize to an efficient algorithm for larger problems, it introduces some
important concepts for linear programming and for optimization in general.

A two-variable linear program

Let us first consider the following linear program with two variables:

$$\text{maximize} \quad x_1 + x_2 \tag{29.17}$$

subject to

$$4x_1 - x_2 \le 8 \tag{29.18}$$

$$2x_1 + x_2 \le 10 \tag{29.19}$$

$$5x_1 - 2x_2 \ge -2 \tag{29.20}$$

$$x_1, x_2 \ge 0 \ . \tag{29.21}$$

Figure 29.2(a) graphs the constraints in the (x_1, x_2)-Cartesian coordinate system.
The feasible region in the two-dimensional space (highlighted in blue in the figure) is convex.[1] Conceptually, you could evaluate the objective function $x_1 + x_2$ at
each point in the feasible region, and then identify a point that has the maximum
objective value as an optimal solution. For this example (and for most linear programs), however, the feasible region contains an infinite number of points, and so
to solve this linear program, you need an efficient way to find a point that achieves
the maximum objective value without explicitly evaluating the objective function
at every point in the feasible region.

In two dimensions, you can optimize via a graphical procedure. The set of points
for which $x_1 + x_2 = z$, for any z, is a line with a slope of -1. Plotting $x_1 + x_2 = 0$
produces the line with slope -1 through the origin, as in Figure 29.2(b). The
intersection of this line and the feasible region is the set of feasible solutions that
have an objective value of 0. In this case, that intersection of the line with the
feasible region is the single point $(0, 0)$. More generally, for any value z, the

---

[1] An intuitive definition of a convex region is that it fulfills the requirement that for any two points
in the region, all points on a line segment between them are also in the region.

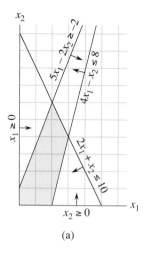
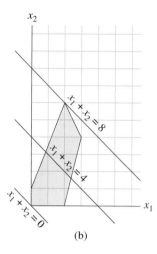

(a)   (b)

Figure 29.2   **(a)** The linear program given in (29.18)–(29.21). Each constraint is represented by a line and a direction. The intersection of the constraints, which is the feasible region, is highlighted in blue. **(b)** The red lines show, respectively, the points for which the objective value is 0, 4, and 8. The optimal solution to the linear program is $x_1 = 2$ and $x_2 = 6$ with objective value 8.

intersection of the line $x_1 + x_2 = z$ and the feasible region is the set of feasible solutions that have objective value z. Figure 29.2(b) shows the lines $x_1 + x_2 = 0$, $x_1 + x_2 = 4$, and $x_1 + x_2 = 8$. Because the feasible region in Figure 29.2 is bounded, there must be some maximum value z for which the intersection of the line $x_1 + x_2 = z$ and the feasible region is nonempty. Any point in the feasible region that maximizes $x_1 + x_2$ is an optimal solution to the linear program, which in this case is the vertex of the feasible region at $x_1 = 2$ and $x_2 = 6$, with objective value 8.

It is no accident that an optimal solution to the linear program occurs at a vertex of the feasible region. The maximum value of z for which the line $x_1 + x_2 = z$ intersects the feasible region must be on the boundary of the feasible region, and thus the intersection of this line with the boundary of the feasible region is either a single vertex or a line segment. If the intersection is a single vertex, then there is just one optimal solution, and it is that vertex. If the intersection is a line segment, every point on that line segment must have the same objective value. In particular, both endpoints of the line segment are optimal solutions. Since each endpoint of a line segment is a vertex, there is an optimal solution at a vertex in this case as well.

Although you cannot easily graph linear programs with more than two variables, the same intuition holds. If you have three variables, then each constraint corresponds to a half-space in three-dimensional space. The intersection of these half-spaces forms the feasible region. The set of points for which the objective function obtains a given value z is now a plane (assuming no degenerate conditions). If all coefficients of the objective function are nonnegative, and if the origin is a feasible solution to the linear program, then as you move this plane away from the origin, in a direction normal to the objective function, you find points of increasing objective value. (If the origin is not feasible or if some coefficients in the objective function are negative, the intuitive picture becomes slightly more complicated.) As in two dimensions, because the feasible region is convex, the set of points that achieve the optimal objective value must include a vertex of the feasible region. Similarly, if you have n variables, each constraint defines a half-space in n-dimensional space. We call the feasible region formed by the intersection of these half-spaces a *simplex*. The objective function is now a hyperplane and, because of convexity, an optimal solution still occurs at a vertex of the simplex. Any algorithm for linear programming must also identify linear programs that have no solutions, as well as linear programs that have no finite optimal solution.

The *simplex algorithm* takes as input a linear program and returns an optimal solution. It starts at some vertex of the simplex and performs a sequence of iterations. In each iteration, it moves along an edge of the simplex from a current vertex to a neighboring vertex whose objective value is no smaller than that of the current vertex (and usually is larger.) The simplex algorithm terminates when it reaches a local maximum, which is a vertex from which all neighboring vertices have a smaller objective value. Because the feasible region is convex and the objective function is linear, this local optimum is actually a global optimum. In Section 29.3, we'll see an important concept called "duality," which we'll use to prove that the solution returned by the simplex algorithm is indeed optimal.

The simplex algorithm, when implemented carefully, often solves general linear programs quickly in practice. With some carefully contrived inputs, however, the simplex algorithm can require exponential time. The first polynomial-time algorithm for linear programming was the *ellipsoid algorithm*, which runs slowly in practice. A second class of polynomial-time algorithms are known as *interior-point methods*. In contrast to the simplex algorithm, which moves along the exterior of the feasible region and maintains a feasible solution that is a vertex of the simplex at each iteration, these algorithms move through the interior of the feasible region. The intermediate solutions, while feasible, are not necessarily vertices of the simplex, but the final solution is a vertex. For large inputs, interior-point algorithms can run as fast as, and sometimes faster than, the simplex algorithm. The chapter notes point you to more information about these algorithms.

If you add to a linear program the additional requirement that all variables take on integer values, you have an *integer linear program*. Exercise 34.5-3 on page 1098 asks you to show that just finding a feasible solution to this problem is NP-hard. Since no polynomial-time algorithms are known for any NP-hard problems, there is no known polynomial-time algorithm for integer linear programming. In contrast, a general linear-programming problem can be solved in polynomial time.

Exercises

29.1-1
Consider the linear program

minimize $-2x_1 + 3x_2$

subject to

$$
\begin{aligned}
x_1 + x_2 &= 7 \\
x_1 - 2x_2 &\leq 4 \\
x_1 &\geq 0 \ .
\end{aligned}
$$

Give three feasible solutions to this linear program. What is the objective value of each one?

29.1-2
Consider the following linear program, which has a nonpositivity constraint:

minimize $2x_1 + 7x_2 + x_3$

subject to

$$
\begin{aligned}
x_1 \quad\quad - x_3 &= 7 \\
3x_1 + x_2 \quad\quad &\geq 24 \\
x_2 &\geq 0 \\
x_3 &\leq 0 \ .
\end{aligned}
$$

Give three feasible solutions to this linear program. What is the objective value of each one?

29.1-3
Show that the following linear program is infeasible:

maximize $3x_1 - 2x_2$

subject to

$$
\begin{aligned}
x_1 + x_2 &\leq 2 \\
-2x_1 - 2x_2 &\leq -10 \\
x_1, x_2 &\geq 0 \ .
\end{aligned}
$$

29.1-4

Show that the following linear program is unbounded:

$$\text{maximize} \quad x_1 - x_2$$

subject to

$$-2x_1 + x_2 \leq -1$$
$$-x_1 - 2x_2 \leq -2$$
$$x_1, x_2 \geq 0 \ .$$

29.1-5

Give an example of a linear program for which the feasible region is not bounded, but the optimal objective value is finite.

29.1-6

Sometimes, in a linear program, you need to convert constraints from one form to another.

a. Show how to convert an equality constraint into an equivalent set of inequalities. That is, given a constraint $\sum_{j=1}^{n} a_{ij}x_j = b_i$, give a set of inequalities that will be satisfied if and only if $\sum_{j=1}^{n} a_{ij}x_j = b_i$,

b. Show how to convert an inequality constraint $\sum_{j=1}^{n} a_{ij}x_j \leq b_i$ into an equality constraint and a nonnegativity constraint. You will need to introduce an additional variable s, and use the constraint that $s \geq 0$.

29.1-7

Explain how to convert a minimization linear program to an equivalent maximization linear program, and argue that your new linear program is equivalent to the original one.

29.1-8

In the political problem at the beginning of this chapter, there are feasible solutions that correspond to winning more voters than there actually are in the district. For example, you can set x_2 to 200, x_3 to 200, and $x_1 = x_4 = 0$. That solution is feasible, yet it seems to say that you will win 400,000 suburban voters, even though there are only 200,000 actual suburban voters. What constraints can you add to the linear program to ensure that you never seem to win more voters than there actually are? Even if you don't add these constraints, argue that the optimal solution to this linear program can never win more voters than there actually are in the district.

29.2   Formulating problems as linear programs

Linear programming has many applications. Any textbook on operations research is filled with examples of linear programming, and linear programming has become a standard tool taught to students in most business schools. The election scenario is one typical example. Here are two more examples:

- An airline wishes to schedule its flight crews. The Federal Aviation Administration imposes several constraints, such as limiting the number of consecutive hours that each crew member can work and insisting that a particular crew work only on one model of aircraft during each month. The airline wants to schedule crews on all of its flights using as few crew members as possible.

- An oil company wants to decide where to drill for oil. Siting a drill at a particular location has an associated cost and, based on geological surveys, an expected payoff of some number of barrels of oil. The company has a limited budget for locating new drills and wants to maximize the amount of oil it expects to find, given this budget.

Linear programs also model and solve graph and combinatorial problems, such as those appearing in this book. We have already seen a special case of linear programming used to solve systems of difference constraints in Section 22.4. In this section, we'll study how to formulate several graph and network-flow problems as linear programs. Section 35.4 uses linear programming as a tool to find an approximate solution to another graph problem.

Perhaps the most important aspect of linear programming is to be able to recognize when you can formulate a problem as a linear program. Once you cast a problem as a polynomial-sized linear program, you can solve it in polynomial time by the ellipsoid algorithm or interior-point methods. Several linear-programming software packages can solve problems efficiently, so that once the problem is in the form of a linear program, such a package can solve it.

We'll look at several concrete examples of linear-programming problems. We start with two problems that we have already studied: the single-source shortest-paths problem from Chapter 22 and the maximum-flow problem from Chapter 24. We then describe the minimum-cost-flow problem. (Although the minimum-cost-flow problem has a polynomial-time algorithm that is not based on linear programming, we won't describe the algorithm.) Finally, we describe the multicommodity-flow problem, for which the only known polynomial-time algorithm is based on linear programming.

When we solved graph problems in Part VI, we used attribute notation, such as $v.d$ and $(u, v).f$. Linear programs typically use subscripted variables rather than objects with attached attributes, however. Therefore, when we express variables in linear programs, we indicate vertices and edges through subscripts. For example, we denote the shortest-path weight for vertex v not by $v.d$ but by d_v, and we denote the flow from vertex u to vertex v not by $(u, v).f$ but by f_{uv}. For quantities that are given as inputs to problems, such as edge weights or capacities, we continue to use notations such as $w(u, v)$ and $c(u, v)$.

Shortest paths

We can formulate the single-source shortest-paths problem as a linear program. We'll focus on how to formulate the single-pair shortest-path problem, leaving the extension to the more general single-source shortest-paths problem as Exercise 29.2-2.

In the single-pair shortest-path problem, the input is a weighted, directed graph $G = (V, E)$, with weight function $w : E \to \mathbb{R}$ mapping edges to real-valued weights, a source vertex s, and destination vertex t. The goal is to compute the value d_t, which is the weight of a shortest path from s to t. To express this problem as a linear program, you need to determine a set of variables and constraints that define when you have a shortest path from s to t. The triangle inequality (Lemma 22.10 on page 633) gives $d_v \leq d_u + w(u, v)$ for each edge $(u, v) \in E$. The source vertex initially receives a value $d_s = 0$, which never changes. Thus the following linear program expresses the shortest-path weight from s to t:

maximize d_t (29.22)

subject to

$$d_v \leq d_u + w(u, v) \text{ for each edge } (u, v) \in E \tag{29.23}$$

$$d_s = 0 . \tag{29.24}$$

You might be surprised that this linear program maximizes an objective function when it is supposed to compute shortest paths. Minimizing the objective function would be a mistake, because when all the edge weights are nonnegative, setting $\bar{d}_v = 0$ for all $v \in V$ (recall that a bar over a variable name denotes a specific setting of the variable's value) would yield an optimal solution to the linear program without solving the shortest-paths problem. Maximizing is the right thing to do because an optimal solution to the shortest-paths problem sets each $\bar{d}_v$ to $\min \{\bar{d}_u + w(u, v) : u \in V \text{ and } (u, v) \in E\}$, so that $\bar{d}_v$ is the largest value that is less than or equal to all of the values in the set $\{\bar{d}_u + w(u, v)\}$. Therefore, it makes sense to maximize d_v for all vertices v on a shortest path from s to t subject to these constraints, and maximizing d_t achieves this goal.

This linear program has $|V|$ variables d_v, one for each vertex $v \in V$. It also has $|E| + 1$ constraints: one for each edge, plus the additional constraint that the source vertex's shortest-path weight always has the value 0.

Maximum flow

Next, let's express the maximum-flow problem as a linear program. Recall that the input is a directed graph $G = (V, E)$ in which each edge $(u, v) \in E$ has a nonnegative capacity $c(u, v) \geq 0$, and two distinguished vertices: a source s and a sink t. As defined in Section 24.1, a flow is a nonnegative real-valued function $f : V \times V \to \mathbb{R}$ that satisfies the capacity constraint and flow conservation. A maximum flow is a flow that satisfies these constraints and maximizes the flow value, which is the total flow coming out of the source minus the total flow into the source. A flow, therefore, satisfies linear constraints, and the value of a flow is a linear function. Recalling also that we assume that $c(u, v) = 0$ if $(u, v) \notin E$ and that there are no antiparallel edges, the maximum-flow problem can be expressed as a linear program:

$$\text{maximize} \quad \sum_{v \in V} f_{sv} - \sum_{v \in V} f_{vs} \tag{29.25}$$

subject to

$$f_{uv} \leq c(u, v) \quad \text{for each } u, v \in V \tag{29.26}$$

$$\sum_{v \in V} f_{vu} = \sum_{v \in V} f_{uv} \quad \text{for each } u \in V - \{s, t\} \tag{29.27}$$

$$f_{uv} \geq 0 \quad\quad \text{for each } u, v \in V \ . \tag{29.28}$$

This linear program has $|V|^2$ variables, corresponding to the flow between each pair of vertices, and it has $2|V|^2 + |V| - 2$ constraints.

It is usually more efficient to solve a smaller-sized linear program. The linear program in (29.25)–(29.28) has, for ease of notation, a flow and capacity of 0 for each pair of vertices u, v with $(u, v) \notin E$. It is more efficient to rewrite the linear program so that it has $O(V + E)$ constraints. Exercise 29.2-4 asks you to do so.

Minimum-cost flow

In this section, we have used linear programming to solve problems for which we already knew efficient algorithms. In fact, an efficient algorithm designed specifically for a problem, such as Dijkstra's algorithm for the single-source shortest-paths problem, will often be more efficient than linear programming, both in theory and in practice.

The real power of linear programming comes from the ability to solve new problems. Recall the problem faced by the politician in the beginning of this chapter. The problem of obtaining a sufficient number of votes, while not spending too much money, is not solved by any of the algorithms that we have studied in this book, yet it can be solved by linear programming. Books abound with such real-world problems that linear programming can solve. Linear programming is also

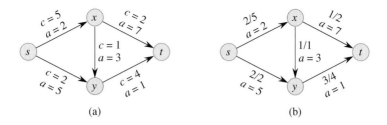

Figure 29.3 **(a)** An example of a minimum-cost-flow problem. Capacities are denoted by c and costs by a. Vertex s is the source, and vertex t is the sink. The goal is to send 4 units of flow from s to t. **(b)** A solution to the minimum-cost flow problem in which 4 units of flow are sent from s to t. For each edge, the flow and capacity are written as flow/capacity.

particularly useful for solving variants of problems for which we may not already know of an efficient algorithm.

Consider, for example, the following generalization of the maximum-flow problem. Suppose that, in addition to a capacity $c(u, v)$ for each edge (u, v), you are given a real-valued cost $a(u, v)$. As in the maximum-flow problem, assume that $c(u, v) = 0$ if $(u, v) \notin E$ and that there are no antiparallel edges. If you send f_{uv} units of flow over edge (u, v), you incur a cost of $a(u, v) \cdot f_{uv}$. You are also given a flow demand d. You wish to send d units of flow from s to t while minimizing the total cost $\sum_{(u,v) \in E} a(u, v) \cdot f_{uv}$ incurred by the flow. This problem is known as the ***minimum-cost-flow problem***.

Figure 29.3(a) shows an example of the minimum-cost-flow problem, with a goal of sending 4 units of flow from s to t while incurring the minimum total cost. Any particular legal flow, that is, a function f satisfying constraints (29.26)–(29.28), incurs a total cost of $\sum_{(u,v) \in E} a(u, v) \cdot f_{uv}$. What is the particular 4-unit flow that minimizes this cost? Figure 29.3(b) shows an optimal solution, with total cost $\sum_{(u,v) \in E} a(u, v) \cdot f_{uv} = (2 \cdot 2) + (5 \cdot 2) + (3 \cdot 1) + (7 \cdot 1) + (1 \cdot 3) = 27$.

There are polynomial-time algorithms specifically designed for the minimum-cost-flow problem, but they are beyond the scope of this book. The minimum-cost-flow problem can be expressed as a linear program, however. The linear program looks similar to the one for the maximum-flow problem with the additional constraint that the value of the flow must be exactly d units, and with the new objective function of minimizing the cost:

$$\text{minimize} \quad \sum_{(u,v) \in E} a(u,v) \cdot f_{uv} \tag{29.29}$$

subject to

$$f_{uv} \leq c(u,v) \quad \text{for each } u, v \in V$$

$$\sum_{v \in V} f_{vu} - \sum_{v \in V} f_{uv} = 0 \qquad \text{for each } u \in V - \{s,t\}$$

$$\sum_{v \in V} f_{sv} - \sum_{v \in V} f_{vs} = d$$

$$f_{uv} \geq 0 \qquad \text{for each } u, v \in V \ . \tag{29.30}$$

Multicommodity flow

As a final example, let's consider another flow problem. Suppose that the Lucky Puck company from Section 24.1 decides to diversify its product line and ship not only hockey pucks, but also hockey sticks and hockey helmets. Each piece of equipment is manufactured in its own factory, has its own warehouse, and must be shipped, each day, from factory to warehouse. The sticks are manufactured in Vancouver and are needed in Saskatoon, and the helmets are manufactured in Edmonton and must be shipped to Regina. The capacity of the shipping network does not change, however, and the different items, or *commodities*, must share the same network.

    This example is an instance of a *multicommodity-flow problem*. The input to this problem is once again a directed graph $G = (V, E)$ in which each edge $(u, v) \in E$ has a nonnegative capacity $c(u, v) \geq 0$. As in the maximum-flow problem, implicitly assume that $c(u, v) = 0$ for $(u, v) \notin E$ and that the graph has no antiparallel edges. In addition, there are k different commodities, $K_1, K_2, \ldots, K_k$, with commodity i specified by the triple $K_i = (s_i, t_i, d_i)$. Here, vertex s_i is the source of commodity i, vertex t_i is the sink of commodity i, and d_i is the demand for commodity i, which is the desired flow value for the commodity from s_i to t_i. We define a flow for commodity i, denoted by f_i, (so that f_{iuv} is the flow of commodity i from vertex u to vertex v) to be a real-valued function that satisfies the flow-conservation and capacity constraints. We define f_{uv}, the *aggregate flow*, to be the sum of the various commodity flows, so that $f_{uv} = \sum_{i=1}^{k} f_{iuv}$. The aggregate flow on edge (u, v) must be no more than the capacity of edge (u, v). This problem has no objective function: the question is to determine whether such a flow exists. Thus the linear program for this problem has a "null" objective function:

minimize   0

subject to

$$\sum_{i=1}^{k} f_{iuv} \le c(u, v) \text{ for each } u, v \in V$$

$$\sum_{v \in V} f_{iuv} - \sum_{v \in V} f_{ivu} = 0 \qquad \begin{array}{l} \text{for each } i = 1, 2, \ldots, k \text{ and} \\ \text{for each } u \in V - \{s_i, t_i\} \end{array}$$

$$\sum_{v \in V} f_{i, s_i, v} - \sum_{v \in V} f_{i, v, s_i} = d_i \qquad \text{for each } i = 1, 2, \ldots, k$$

$$f_{iuv} \ge 0 \qquad \begin{array}{l} \text{for each } u, v \in V \text{ and} \\ \text{for each } i = 1, 2, \ldots, k \end{array}.$$

The only known polynomial-time algorithm for this problem expresses it as a linear program and then solves it with a polynomial-time linear-programming algorithm.

Exercises

29.2-1
Write out explicitly the linear program corresponding to finding the shortest path from vertex s to vertex x in Figure 22.2(a) on page 609.

29.2-2
Given a graph G, write a linear program for the single-source shortest-paths problem. The solution should have the property that d_v is the shortest-path weight from the source vertex s to v for each vertex $v \in V$.

29.2-3
Write out explicitly the linear program corresponding to finding the maximum flow in Figure 24.1(a).

29.2-4
Rewrite the linear program for maximum flow (29.25)–(29.28) so that it uses only $O(V + E)$ constraints.

29.2-5
Write a linear program that, given a bipartite graph $G = (V, E)$, solves the maximum-bipartite-matching problem.

29.2-6
There can be more than one way to model a particular problem as a linear program. This exercise gives an alternative formulation for the maximum-flow problem. Let $\mathcal{P} = \{P_1, P_2, \ldots, P_p\}$ be the set of *all* possible directed simple paths from source s

to sink t. Using decision variables $x_1, \ldots, x_p$, where x_i is the amount of flow on path i, formulate a linear program for the maximum-flow problem. What is an upper bound on p, the number of directed simple paths from s to t?

29.2-7

In the ***minimum-cost multicommodity-flow problem***, the input is a directed graph $G = (V, E)$ in which each edge $(u, v) \in E$ has a nonnegative capacity $c(u, v) \geq 0$ and a cost $a(u, v)$. As in the multicommodity-flow problem, there are k different commodities, $K_1, K_2, \ldots, K_k$, with commodity i specified by the triple $K_i = (s_i, t_i, d_i)$. We define the flow f_i for commodity i and the aggregate flow f_{uv} on edge (u, v) as in the multicommodity-flow problem. A feasible flow is one in which the aggregate flow on each edge (u, v) is no more than the capacity of edge (u, v). The cost of a flow is $\sum_{u,v \in V} a(u, v) \cdot f_{uv}$, and the goal is to find the feasible flow of minimum cost. Express this problem as a linear program.

29.3   Duality

We will now introduce a powerful concept called ***linear-programming duality***. In general, given a maximization problem, duality allows you to formulate a related minimization problem that has the same objective value. The idea of duality is actually more general than linear programming, but we restrict our attention to linear programming in this section.

Duality enables us to prove that a solution is indeed optimal. We saw an example of duality in Chapter 24 with Theorem 24.6, the max-flow min-cut theorem. Suppose that, given an instance of a maximum-flow problem, you find a flow f with value $|f|$. How do you know whether f is a maximum flow? By the max-flow min-cut theorem, if you can find a cut whose value is also $|f|$, then you have verified that f is indeed a maximum flow. This relationship provides an example of duality: given a maximization problem, define a related minimization problem such that the two problems have the same optimal objective values.

Given a linear program in standard form in which the objective is to maximize, let's see how to formulate a *dual* linear program in which the objective is to minimize and whose optimal value is identical to that of the original linear program. When referring to dual linear programs, we call the original linear program the *primal*.

Given the primal linear program

$$\text{maximize} \quad \sum_{j=1}^{n} c_j x_j \tag{29.31}$$

subject to

$$\sum_{j=1}^{n} a_{ij} x_j \leq b_i \quad \text{for } i = 1, 2, \ldots, m \tag{29.32}$$

$$x_j \geq 0 \quad \text{for } j = 1, 2, \ldots, n \ , \tag{29.33}$$

its dual is

$$\text{minimize} \quad \sum_{i=1}^{m} b_i y_i \tag{29.34}$$

subject to

$$\sum_{i=1}^{m} a_{ij} y_i \geq c_j \quad \text{for } j = 1, 2, \ldots, n \tag{29.35}$$

$$y_i \geq 0 \quad \text{for } i = 1, 2, \ldots, m \ . \tag{29.36}$$

Mechanically, to form the dual, change the maximization to a minimization, exchange the roles of coefficients on the right-hand sides and in the objective function, and replace each $\leq$ by $\geq$. Each of the m constraints in the primal corresponds to a variable y_i in the dual. Likewise, each of the n constraints in the dual corresponds to a variable x_j in the primal. For example, consider the following primal linear program:

$$\text{maximize} \quad 3x_1 + x_2 + 4x_3 \tag{29.37}$$

subject to

$$x_1 + x_2 + 3x_3 \leq 30 \tag{29.38}$$

$$2x_1 + 2x_2 + 5x_3 \leq 24 \tag{29.39}$$

$$4x_1 + x_2 + 2x_3 \leq 36 \tag{29.40}$$

$$x_1, x_2, x_3 \geq 0 \ . \tag{29.41}$$

Its dual is

$$\text{minimize} \quad 30y_1 + 24y_2 + 36y_3 \tag{29.42}$$

subject to

$$y_1 + 2y_2 + 4y_3 \geq 3 \tag{29.43}$$

$$y_1 + 2y_2 + y_3 \geq 1 \tag{29.44}$$

$$3y_1 + 5y_2 + 2y_3 \geq 4 \tag{29.45}$$

$$y_1, y_2, y_3 \geq 0 \ . \tag{29.46}$$

Although forming the dual can be considered a mechanical operation, there is an intuitive explanation. Consider the primal maximization problem (29.37)–(29.41). Each constraint gives an upper bound on the objective function. In addition, if you take one or more constraints and add together nonnegative multiples of them, you get a valid constraint. For example, you can add constraints (29.38) and (29.39) to obtain the constraint $3x_1 + 3x_2 + 8x_3 \leq 54$. Any feasible solution to the primal must satisfy this new constraint, but there is something else interesting about it. Comparing this new constraint to the objective function (29.37), you can see that for each variable, the corresponding coefficient is at least as large as the coefficient in the objective function. Thus, since the variables x_1, x_2 and x_3 are nonnegative, we have that

$$3x_1 + x_2 + 4x_3 \ \leq \ 3x_1 + 3x_2 + 8x_3 \ \leq \ 54 \,,$$

and so the solution value to the primal is at most 54. In other words, adding these two constraints together has generated an upper bound on the objective value.

In general, for any nonnegative multipliers y_1, y_2, and y_3, you can generate a constraint

$$y_1(x_1+x_2+3x_3)+y_2(2x_1+2x_2+5x_3)+y_3(4x_1+x_2+2x_3) \leq 30y_1+24y_2+36y_3$$

from the primal constraints or, by distributing and regrouping,

$$(y_1+2y_2+4y_3)x_1+(y_1+2y_2+y_3)x_2+(3y_1+5y_2+2y_3)x_3 \leq 30y_1+24y_2+36y_3 \,.$$

Now, as long as this constraint has coefficients of x_1, x_2, and x_3 that are at least their objective-function coefficients, it is a valid upper bound. That is, as long as

$$y_1 + 2y_2 + 4y_3 \geq 3 \,,$$
$$y_1 + 2y_2 + \ y_3 \geq 1 \,,$$
$$3y_1 + 5y_2 + 2y_3 \geq 4 \,,$$

you have a valid upper bound of $30y_1+24y_2+36y_3$. The multipliers y_1, y_2, and y_3 must be nonnegative, because otherwise you cannot combine the inequalities. Of course, you would like the upper bound to be as small as possible, and so you want to choose y to minimize $30y_1 + 24y_2 + 36y_3$. Observe that we have just described the dual linear program as the problem of finding the smallest possible upper bound on the primal.

We'll formalize this idea and show in Theorem 29.4 that, if the linear program and its dual are feasible and bounded, then the optimal value of the dual linear program is always equal to the optimal value of the primal linear program. We begin by demonstrating *weak duality*, which states that any feasible solution to the primal linear program has a value no greater than that of any feasible solution to the dual linear program.

Lemma 29.1 (Weak linear-programming duality)
Let $\bar{x}$ be any feasible solution to the primal linear program in (29.31)–(29.33), and let $\bar{y}$ be any feasible solution to its dual linear program in (29.34)–(29.36). Then

$$\sum_{j=1}^{n} c_j \bar{x}_j \leq \sum_{i=1}^{m} b_i \bar{y}_i \; .$$

Proof   We have

$$
\begin{aligned}
\sum_{j=1}^{n} c_j \bar{x}_j &\leq \sum_{j=1}^{n} \left(\sum_{i=1}^{m} a_{ij} \bar{y}_i \right) \bar{x}_j && \text{(by inequalities (29.35))} \\
&= \sum_{i=1}^{m} \left(\sum_{j=1}^{n} a_{ij} \bar{x}_j \right) \bar{y}_i && \\
&\leq \sum_{i=1}^{m} b_i \bar{y}_i && \text{(by inequalities (29.32))} \; .
\end{aligned}
$$ ∎

Corollary 29.2

Let $\bar{x}$ be a feasible solution to the primal linear program in (29.31)–(29.33), and let $\bar{y}$ be a feasible solution to its dual linear program in (29.34)–(29.36). If

$$\sum_{j=1}^{n} c_j \bar{x}_j = \sum_{i=1}^{m} b_i \bar{y}_i \; ,$$

then $\bar{x}$ and $\bar{y}$ are optimal solutions to the primal and dual linear programs, respectively.

Proof   By Lemma 29.1, the objective value of a feasible solution to the primal cannot exceed that of a feasible solution to the dual. The primal linear program is a maximization problem and the dual is a minimization problem. Thus, if feasible solutions $\bar{x}$ and $\bar{y}$ have the same objective value, neither can be improved. ∎

We now show that, at optimality, the primal and dual objective values are indeed equal. To prove linear programming duality, we will require one lemma from linear algebra, known as Farkas's lemma, the proof of which Problem 29-4 asks you to provide. Farkas's lemma can take several forms, each of which is about when a set of linear equalities has a solution. In stating the lemma, we use $m + 1$ as a dimension because it matches our use below.

Lemma 29.3 (Farkas's lemma)

Given $M \in \mathbb{R}^{(m+1) \times n}$ and $g \in \mathbb{R}^{m+1}$, exactly one of the following statements is true:

1. There exists $v \in \mathbb{R}^n$ such that $Mv \leq g$,

2. There exists $w \in \mathbb{R}^{m+1}$ such that $w \geq 0$, $w^{\mathrm{T}} M = 0$ (an n-vector of all zeros), and $w^{\mathrm{T}} g < 0$. ∎

Theorem 29.4 (Linear-programming duality)

Given the primal linear program in (29.31)–(29.33) and its corresponding dual in (29.34)–(29.36), if both are feasible and bounded, then for optimal solutions x^* and y^*, we have $c^{\mathrm{T}} x^* = b^{\mathrm{T}} y^*$.

Proof   Let $\mu = b^{\mathrm{T}} y^*$ be the optimal value of the dual linear program given in (29.34)–(29.36). Consider an augmented set of primal constraints in which we add a constraint to (29.31)–(29.33) that the objective value is at least μ. We write out this *augmented primal* as

$$Ax \leq b, \tag{29.47}$$

$$c^{\mathrm{T}} x \geq \mu . \tag{29.48}$$

We can multiply (29.48) through by -1 and rewrite (29.47)–(29.48) as

$$\begin{pmatrix} A \\ -c^{\mathrm{T}} \end{pmatrix} x \leq \begin{pmatrix} b \\ -\mu \end{pmatrix} . \tag{29.49}$$

Here, $\begin{pmatrix} A \\ -c^{\mathrm{T}} \end{pmatrix}$ denotes an $(m+1) \times n$ matrix, x is an n-vector, and $\begin{pmatrix} b \\ -\mu \end{pmatrix}$ denotes an $(m+1)$-vector.

We claim that if there is a feasible solution $\bar{x}$ to the augmented primal, then the theorem is proved. To establish this claim, observe that $\bar{x}$ is also a feasible solution to the original primal and that it has objective value at least μ. We can then apply Lemma 29.1, which states that the objective value of the primal is at most μ, to complete the proof of the theorem.

It therefore remains to show that the augmented primal has a feasible solution. Suppose, for the purpose of contradiction, that the augmented primal is infeasible, which means that there is no $v \in \mathbb{R}^n$ such that $\begin{pmatrix} A \\ -c^{\mathrm{T}} \end{pmatrix} v \leq \begin{pmatrix} b \\ -\mu \end{pmatrix}$. We can apply Farkas's lemma, Lemma 29.3, to inequalty (29.49) with

$$M = \begin{pmatrix} A \\ -c^{\mathrm{T}} \end{pmatrix} \quad \text{and} \quad g = \begin{pmatrix} b \\ -\mu \end{pmatrix} .$$

Because the augmented primal is infeasible, condition 1 of Farkas's lemma does not hold. Therefore, condition 2 must apply, so that there must exist a $w \in \mathbb{R}^{m+1}$ such that $w \geq 0$, $w^{\mathrm{T}} M = 0$, and $w^{\mathrm{T}} g < 0$. Let's write w as $w = \begin{pmatrix} \bar{y} \\ \lambda \end{pmatrix}$ for some $\bar{y} \in \mathbb{R}^m$ and $\lambda \in \mathbb{R}$, where $\bar{y} \geq 0$ and $\lambda \geq 0$. Substituting for w, M, and g in condition 2 gives

$$\begin{pmatrix} \bar{y} \\ \lambda \end{pmatrix}^{\mathrm{T}} \begin{pmatrix} A \\ -c^{\mathrm{T}} \end{pmatrix} = 0 \quad \text{and} \quad \begin{pmatrix} \bar{y} \\ \lambda \end{pmatrix}^{\mathrm{T}} \begin{pmatrix} b \\ -\mu \end{pmatrix} < 0 .$$

Unpacking the matrix notation gives

$$\bar{y}^{\mathrm{T}}A - \lambda c^{\mathrm{T}} = 0 \text{ and } \bar{y}^{\mathrm{T}}b - \lambda\mu < 0. \tag{29.50}$$

We now show that the requirements in (29.50) contradict the assumption that μ is the optimal solution value for the dual linear program. We consider two cases.

The first case is when $\lambda = 0$. In this case, (29.50) simplifies to

$$\bar{y}^{\mathrm{T}}A = 0 \text{ and } \bar{y}^{\mathrm{T}}b < 0. \tag{29.51}$$

We'll now construct a dual feasible solution y' with an objective value smaller than $b^{\mathrm{T}}y^*$. Set $y' = y^* + \epsilon\bar{y}$, for any $\epsilon > 0$. Since

$$
\begin{aligned}
y'^{\mathrm{T}}A &= (y^* + \epsilon\bar{y})^{\mathrm{T}}A \\
&= y^{*\mathrm{T}}A + \epsilon\bar{y}^{\mathrm{T}}A \\
&= y^{*\mathrm{T}}A && \text{(by (29.51))} \\
&\geq c^{\mathrm{T}} && \text{(because } y^* \text{ is feasible)},
\end{aligned}
$$

y' is feasible. Now consider the objective value

$$
\begin{aligned}
b^{\mathrm{T}}y' &= b^{\mathrm{T}}(y^* + \epsilon\bar{y}) \\
&= b^{\mathrm{T}}y^* + \epsilon b^{\mathrm{T}}\bar{y} \\
&< b^{\mathrm{T}}y^*,
\end{aligned}
$$

where the last inequality follows because $\epsilon > 0$ and, by (29.51), $\bar{y}^{\mathrm{T}}b = b^{\mathrm{T}}\bar{y} < 0$ (since both $\bar{y}^{\mathrm{T}}b$ and $b^{\mathrm{T}}\bar{y}$ are the inner product of b and $\bar{y}$), and so their product is negative. Thus we have a feasible dual solution of value less than μ, which contradicts μ being the optimal objective value.

We now consider the second case, where $\lambda > 0$. In this case, we can take (29.50) and divide through by λ to obtain

$$(\bar{y}^{\mathrm{T}}/\lambda)A - (\lambda/\lambda)c^{\mathrm{T}} = 0 \text{ and } (\bar{y}^{\mathrm{T}}/\lambda)b - (\lambda/\lambda)\mu < 0. \tag{29.52}$$

Now set $y' = \bar{y}/\lambda$ in (29.52), giving

$$y'^{\mathrm{T}}A = c^{\mathrm{T}} \text{ and } y'^{\mathrm{T}}b < \mu.$$

Thus, y' is a feasible dual solution with objective value strictly less than μ, a contradiction. We conclude that the augmented primal has a feasible solution, and the theorem is proved.   ∎

Fundamental theorem of linear programming

We conclude this chapter by stating the fundamental theorem of linear programming, which extends Theorem 29.4 to the cases when the linear program may be either feasible or unbounded. Exercise 29.3-8 asks you to provide the proof.

Theorem 29.5 (Fundamental theorem of linear programming)
Any linear program, given in standard form, either

1. has an optimal solution with a finite objective value,

2. is infeasible, or

3. is unbounded.   ∎

Exercises

29.3-1
Formulate the dual of the linear program given in lines (29.6)–(29.10) on page 852.

29.3-2
You have a linear program that is not in standard form. You could produce the dual by first converting it to standard form, and then taking the dual. It would be more convenient, however, to produce the dual directly. Explain how to directly take the dual of an arbitrary linear program.

29.3-3
Write down the dual of the maximum-flow linear program, as given in lines (29.25)–(29.28) on page 862. Explain how to interpret this formulation as a minimum-cut problem.

29.3-4
Write down the dual of the minimum-cost-flow linear program, as given in lines (29.29)–(29.30) on page 864. Explain how to interpret this problem in terms of graphs and flows.

29.3-5
Show that the dual of the dual of a linear program is the primal linear program.

29.3-6
Which result from Chapter 24 can be interpreted as weak duality for the maximum-flow problem?

29.3-7
Consider the following 1-variable primal linear program:

maximize tx

subject to

$$rx \leq s$$
$$x \geq 0 \, ,$$

where r, s, and t are arbitrary real numbers. State for which values of r, s, and t you can assert that

1. Both the primal linear program and its dual have optimal solutions with finite objective values.

2. The primal is feasible, but the dual is infeasible.

3. The dual is feasible, but the primal is infeasible.

4. Neither the primal nor the dual is feasible.

29.3-8
Prove the fundamental theorem of linear programming, Theorem 29.5.

Problems

29-1 *Linear-inequality feasibility*
Given a set of m linear inequalities on n variables $x_1, x_2, \ldots, x_n$, the *linear-inequality feasibility problem* asks whether there is a setting of the variables that simultaneously satisfies each of the inequalities.

a. Given an algorithm for the linear-programming problem, show how to use it to solve a linear-inequality feasibility problem. The number of variables and constraints that you use in the linear-programming problem should be polynomial in n and m.

b. Given an algorithm for the linear-inequality feasibility problem, show how to use it to solve a linear-programming problem. The number of variables and linear inequalities that you use in the linear-inequality feasibility problem should be polynomial in n and m, the number of variables and constraints in the linear program.

29-2 *Complementary slackness*
Complementary slackness describes a relationship between the values of primal variables and dual constraints and between the values of dual variables and primal constraints. Let $\bar{x}$ be a feasible solution to the primal linear program given in (29.31)–(29.33), and let $\bar{y}$ be a feasible solution to the dual linear program given in (29.34)–(29.36). Complementary slackness states that the following conditions are necessary and sufficient for $\bar{x}$ and $\bar{y}$ to be optimal:

$$\sum_{i=1}^{m} a_{ij}\bar{y}_i = c_j \text{ or } \bar{x}_j = 0 \text{ for } j = 1, 2, \ldots, n$$

and

$$\sum_{j=1}^{n} a_{ij}\bar{x}_j = b_i \text{ or } \bar{y}_i = 0 \text{ for } i = 1, 2, \ldots, m .$$

a. Verify that complementary slackness holds for the linear program in lines (29.37)–(29.41).

b. Prove that complementary slackness holds for any primal linear program and its corresponding dual.

c. Prove that a feasible solution $\bar{x}$ to a primal linear program given in lines (29.31)–(29.33) is optimal if and only if there exist values $\bar{y} = (\bar{y}_1, \bar{y}_2, \ldots, \bar{y}_m)$ such that

1. $\bar{y}$ is a feasible solution to the dual linear program given in (29.34)–(29.36),
2. $\sum_{i=1}^{m} a_{ij}\bar{y}_i = c_j$ for all j such that $\bar{x}_j > 0$, and
3. $\bar{y}_i = 0$ for all i such that $\sum_{j=1}^{n} a_{ij}\bar{x}_j < b_i$.

29-3   Integer linear programming

An *integer linear-programming problem* is a linear-programming problem with the additional constraint that the variables x must take on integer values. Exercise 34.5-3 on page 1098 shows that just determining whether an integer linear program has a feasible solution is NP-hard, which means that there is no known polynomial-time algorithm for this problem.

a. Show that weak duality (Lemma 29.1) holds for an integer linear program.

b. Show that duality (Theorem 29.4) does not always hold for an integer linear program.

c. Given a primal linear program in standard form, let P be the optimal objective value for the primal linear program, D be the optimal objective value for its dual, IP be the optimal objective value for the integer version of the primal (that is, the primal with the added constraint that the variables take on integer values), and ID be the optimal objective value for the integer version of the dual. Assuming that both the primal integer program and the dual integer program are feasible and bounded, show that

$$IP \leq P = D \leq ID .$$

29-4　Farkas's lemma
Prove Farkas's lemma, Lemma 29.3.

29-5　Minimum-cost circulation
This problem considers a variant of the minimum-cost-flow problem from Section 29.2 in which there is no demand, source, or sink. Instead, the input, as before, contains a flow network, capacity constraints $c(u, v)$, and edge costs $a(u, v)$. A flow is feasible if it satisfies the capacity constraint on every edge and flow conservation at *every* vertex. The goal is to find, among all feasible flows, the one of minimum cost. We call this problem the ***minimum-cost-circulation problem.***

a. Formulate the minimum-cost-circulation problem as a linear program.

b. Suppose that for all edges $(u, v) \in E$, we have $a(u, v) > 0$. What does an optimal solution to the minimum-cost-circulation problem look like?

c. Formulate the maximum-flow problem as a minimum-cost-circulation problem linear program. That is, given a maximum-flow problem instance $G = (V, E)$ with source s, sink t and edge capacities c, create a minimum-cost-circulation problem by giving a (possibly different) network $G' = (V', E')$ with edge capacities c' and edge costs a' such that you can derive a solution to the maximum-flow problem from a solution to the minimum-cost-circulation problem.

d. Formulate the single-source shortest-path problem as a minimum-cost-circulation problem linear program.

Chapter notes

This chapter only begins to study the wide field of linear programming. A number of books are devoted exclusively to linear programming, including those by Chvátal [94], Gass [178], Karloff [246], Schrijver [398], and Vanderbei [444]. Many other books give a good coverage of linear programming, including those by Papadimitriou and Steiglitz [353] and Ahuja, Magnanti, and Orlin [7]. The coverage in this chapter draws on the approach taken by Chvátal.

The simplex algorithm for linear programming was invented by G. Dantzig in 1947. Shortly after, researchers discovered how to formulate a number of problems in a variety of fields as linear programs and solve them with the simplex algorithm. As a result, applications of linear programming flourished, along with several algorithms. Variants of the simplex algorithm remain the most popular methods for solving linear-programming problems. This history appears in a number of places, including the notes in [94] and [246].

The ellipsoid algorithm was the first polynomial-time algorithm for linear programming and is due to L. G. Khachian in 1979. It was based on earlier work by N. Z. Shor, D. B. Judin, and A. S. Nemirovskii. Grötschel, Lovász, and Schrijver [201] describe how to use the ellipsoid algorithm to solve a variety of problems in combinatorial optimization. To date, the ellipsoid algorithm does not appear to be competitive with the simplex algorithm in practice.

Karmarkar's paper [247] includes a description of the first interior-point algorithm. Many subsequent researchers designed interior-point algorithms. Good surveys appear in the article of Goldfarb and Todd [189] and the book by Ye [463].

Analysis of the simplex algorithm remains an active area of research. V. Klee and G. J. Minty constructed an example on which the simplex algorithm runs through $2^n - 1$ iterations. The simplex algorithm usually performs well in practice, and many researchers have tried to give theoretical justification for this empirical observation. A line of research begun by K. H. Borgwardt, and carried on by many others, shows that under certain probabilistic assumptions on the input, the simplex algorithm converges in expected polynomial time. Spielman and Teng [421] made progress in this area, introducing the "smoothed analysis of algorithms" and applying it to the simplex algorithm.

The simplex algorithm is known to run efficiently in certain special cases. Particularly noteworthy is the network-simplex algorithm, which is the simplex algorithm, specialized to network-flow problems. For certain network problems, including the shortest-paths, maximum-flow, and minimum-cost-flow problems, variants of the network-simplex algorithm run in polynomial time. See, for example, the article by Orlin [349] and the citations therein.

The straightforward method of adding two polynomials of degree n takes $\Theta(n)$ time, but the straightforward method of multiplying them takes $\Theta(n^2)$ time. This chapter will show how the fast Fourier transform, or FFT, can reduce the time to multiply polynomials to $\Theta(n \lg n)$.

The most common use for Fourier transforms, and hence the FFT, is in signal processing. A signal is given in the *time domain*: as a function mapping time to amplitude. Fourier analysis expresses the signal as a weighted sum of phase-shifted sinusoids of varying frequencies. The weights and phases associated with the frequencies characterize the signal in the *frequency domain*. Among the many everyday applications of FFT's are compression techniques used to encode digital video and audio information, including MP3 files. Many fine books delve into the rich area of signal processing, and the chapter notes reference a few of them.

Polynomials

A *polynomial* in the variable x over an algebraic field F represents a function $A(x)$ as a formal sum:

$$A(x) = \sum_{j=0}^{n-1} a_j x^j \ .$$

The values $a_0, a_1, \ldots, a_{n-1}$ are the *coefficients* of the polynomial. The coefficients and x are drawn from a field F, typically the set $\mathbb{C}$ of complex numbers. A polynomial $A(x)$ has *degree* k if its highest nonzero coefficient is a_k, in which case we say that $\text{degree}(A) = k$. Any integer strictly greater than the degree of a polynomial is a *degree-bound* of that polynomial. Therefore, the degree of a polynomial of degree-bound n may be any integer between 0 and $n - 1$, inclusive.

A variety of operations extend to polynomials. For *polynomial addition*, if $A(x)$ and $B(x)$ are polynomials of degree-bound n, their *sum* is a polynomial $C(x)$, also of degree-bound n, such that $C(x) = A(x) + B(x)$ for all x in the underlying field. That is, if

$$A(x) = \sum_{j=0}^{n-1} a_j x^j \quad \text{and} \quad B(x) = \sum_{j=0}^{n-1} b_j x^j ,$$

then

$$C(x) = \sum_{j=0}^{n-1} c_j x^j ,$$

where $c_j = a_j + b_j$ for $j = 0, 1, \ldots, n - 1$. For example, given the polynomials $A(x) = 6x^3 + 7x^2 - 10x + 9$ and $B(x) = -2x^3 + 4x - 5$, their sum is $C(x) = 4x^3 + 7x^2 - 6x + 4$.

For *polynomial multiplication*, if $A(x)$ and $B(x)$ are polynomials of degree-bound n, their *product* $C(x)$ is a polynomial of degree-bound $2n - 1$ such that $C(x) = A(x)B(x)$ for all x in the underlying field. You probably have multiplied polynomials before, by multiplying each term in $A(x)$ by each term in $B(x)$ and then combining terms with equal powers. For example, you can multiply $A(x) = 6x^3 + 7x^2 - 10x + 9$ and $B(x) = -2x^3 + 4x - 5$ as follows:

$$
\begin{array}{rl}
6x^3 + 7x^2 - 10x + 9 & \\
-2x^3 + 4x - 5 & \\
\hline
-30x^3 - 35x^2 + 50x - 45 & \text{(multiply } A(x) \text{ by } -5) \\
24x^4 + 28x^3 - 40x^2 + 36x & \text{(multiply } A(x) \text{ by } 4x) \\
-12x^6 - 14x^5 + 20x^4 - 18x^3 & \text{(multiply } A(x) \text{ by } -2x^3) \\
\hline
-12x^6 - 14x^5 + 44x^4 - 20x^3 - 75x^2 + 86x - 45 &
\end{array}
$$

Another way to express the product $C(x)$ is

$$C(x) = \sum_{j=0}^{2n-2} c_j x^j , \tag{30.1}$$

where

$$c_j = \sum_{k=0}^{j} a_k b_{j-k} , \tag{30.2}$$

(By the definition of degree, $a_k = 0$ for all $k > \text{degree}(A)$ and $b_k = 0$ for all $k > \text{degree}(B)$.) If A is a polynomial of degree-bound n_a and B is a polynomial of degree-bound n_b, then C must be a polynomial of degree-bound $n_a + n_b - 1$, because $\text{degree}(C) = \text{degree}(A) + \text{degree}(B)$. Since a polynomial of degree-bound k is also a polynomial of degree-bound $k + 1$, we normally make the somewhat simpler statement that the product polynomial C is a polynomial of degree-bound $n_a + n_b$.

Chapter outline

Section 30.1 presents two ways to represent polynomials: the coefficient representation and the point-value representation. The straightforward method for multiplying polynomials of degree n — equations (30.1) and (30.2) — takes $\Theta(n^2)$ time with polynomials represented in coefficient form, but only $\Theta(n)$ time with point-value form. Converting between the two representations, however, reduces the time to multiply polynomials to just $\Theta(n \lg n)$. To see why this approach works, you must first understand complex roots of unity, which Section 30.2 covers. Section 30.2 then uses the FFT and its inverse to perform the conversions. Because the FFT is used so often in signal processing, it is often implemented as a circuit in hardware, and Section 30.3 illustrates the structure of such circuits.

This chapter relies on complex numbers, and within this chapter the symbol i denotes $\sqrt{-1}$ exclusively.

30.1 Representing polynomials

The coefficient and point-value representations of polynomials are in a sense equivalent: a polynomial in point-value form has a unique counterpart in coefficient form. This section introduces the two representations and shows how to combine them in order to multiply two degree-bound n polynomials in $\Theta(n \lg n)$ time.

Coefficient representation

A *coefficient representation* of a polynomial $A(x) = \sum_{j=0}^{n-1} a_j x^j$ of degree-bound n is a vector of coefficients $a = (a_0, a_1, \ldots, a_{n-1})$. Matrix equations in this chapter generally treat vectors as column vectors.

The coefficient representation is convenient for certain operations on polynomials. For example, the operation of *evaluating* the polynomial $A(x)$ at a given point x_0 consists of computing the value of $A(x_0)$. To evaluate a polynomial in $\Theta(n)$ time, use *Horner's rule*:

$$A(x_0) = a_0 + x_0 \left(a_1 + x_0 \left(a_2 + \cdots + x_0 \left(a_{n-2} + x_0(a_{n-1}) \right) \cdots \right) \right) .$$

Similarly, adding two polynomials represented by the coefficient vectors $a = (a_0, a_1, \ldots, a_{n-1})$ and $b = (b_0, b_1, \ldots, b_{n-1})$ takes $\Theta(n)$ time: just produce the coefficient vector $c = (c_0, c_1, \ldots, c_{n-1})$, where $c_j = a_j + b_j$ for $j = 0, 1, \ldots, n-1$.

Now, consider multiplying two degree-bound n polynomials $A(x)$ and $B(x)$ represented in coefficient form. The method described by equations (30.1) and (30.2) takes $\Theta(n^2)$ time, since it multiplies each coefficient in the vector a by each coefficient in the vector b. The operation of multiplying polynomials in coefficient form seems to be considerably more difficult than that of evaluating a polynomial or adding two polynomials. The resulting coefficient vector c, given by equation (30.2), is also called the *convolution* of the input vectors a and b, denoted $c = a \otimes b$. Since multiplying polynomials and computing convolutions are fundamental computational problems of considerable practical importance, this chapter concentrates on efficient algorithms for them.

Point-value representation

A *point-value representation* of a polynomial $A(x)$ of degree-bound n is a set of n *point-value pairs*

$$\{(x_0, y_0), (x_1, y_1), \ldots, (x_{n-1}, y_{n-1})\}$$

such that all of the x_k are distinct and

$$y_k = A(x_k) \tag{30.3}$$

for $k = 0, 1, \ldots, n - 1$. A polynomial has many different point-value representations, since any set of n distinct points $x_0, x_1, \ldots, x_{n-1}$ can serve as a basis for the representation.

Computing a point-value representation for a polynomial given in coefficient form is in principle straightforward, since all you have to do is select n distinct points $x_0, x_1, \ldots, x_{n-1}$ and then evaluate $A(x_k)$ for $k = 0, 1, \ldots, n - 1$. With Horner's method, evaluating a polynomial at n points takes $\Theta(n^2)$ time. We'll see later that if you choose the points x_k cleverly, you can accelerate this computation to run in $\Theta(n \lg n)$ time.

The inverse of evaluation—determining the coefficient form of a polynomial from a point-value representation—is *interpolation*. The following theorem shows that interpolation is well defined when the desired interpolating polynomial must have a degree-bound equal to the given number of point-value pairs.

Theorem 30.1 (Uniqueness of an interpolating polynomial)
For any set $\{(x_0, y_0), (x_1, y_1), \ldots, (x_{n-1}, y_{n-1})\}$ of n point-value pairs such that all the x_k values are distinct, there is a unique polynomial $A(x)$ of degree-bound n such that $y_k = A(x_k)$ for $k = 0, 1, \ldots, n - 1$.

Proof   The proof relies on the existence of the inverse of a certain matrix. Equation (30.3) is equivalent to the matrix equation

$$\begin{pmatrix} 1 & x_0 & x_0^2 & \cdots & x_0^{n-1} \\ 1 & x_1 & x_1^2 & \cdots & x_1^{n-1} \\ \vdots & \vdots & \vdots & \ddots & \vdots \\ 1 & x_{n-1} & x_{n-1}^2 & \cdots & x_{n-1}^{n-1} \end{pmatrix} \begin{pmatrix} a_0 \\ a_1 \\ \vdots \\ a_{n-1} \end{pmatrix} = \begin{pmatrix} y_0 \\ y_1 \\ \vdots \\ y_{n-1} \end{pmatrix}. \qquad (30.4)$$

The matrix on the left is denoted $V(x_0, x_1, \ldots, x_{n-1})$ and is known as a *Vandermonde matrix*. By Problem D-1 on page 1223, this matrix has determinant

$$\prod_{0 \le j < k \le n-1} (x_k - x_j) \,,$$

and therefore, by Theorem D.5 on page 1221, it is invertible (that is, nonsingular) if the x_k are distinct. To solve for the coefficients a_j uniquely given the point-value representation, use the inverse of the Vandermonde matrix:

$$a = V(x_0, x_1, \ldots, x_{n-1})^{-1} y \,. \qquad \blacksquare$$

The proof of Theorem 30.1 describes an algorithm for interpolation based on solving the set (30.4) of linear equations. Section 28.1 shows how to solve these equations in $O(n^3)$ time.

A faster algorithm for n-point interpolation is based on *Lagrange's formula*:

$$A(x) = \sum_{k=0}^{n-1} y_k \frac{\prod_{j \ne k} (x - x_j)}{\prod_{j \ne k} (x_k - x_j)} \,. \qquad (30.5)$$

You might want to verify that the right-hand side of equation (30.5) is a polynomial of degree-bound n that satisfies $A(x_k) = y_k$ for all k. Exercise 30.1-5 asks you how to compute the coefficients of A using Lagrange's formula in $\Theta(n^2)$ time.

Thus, n-point evaluation and interpolation are well-defined inverse operations that transform between the coefficient representation of a polynomial and a point-value representation.[1] The algorithms described above for these problems take $\Theta(n^2)$ time.

The point-value representation is quite convenient for many operations on polynomials. For addition, if $C(x) = A(x) + B(x)$, then $C(x_k) = A(x_k) + B(x_k)$ for any point x_k. More precisely, given point-value representations for A,

$$\{(x_0, y_0), (x_1, y_1), \ldots, (x_{n-1}, y_{n-1})\} \,,$$

---

[1] Interpolation is a notoriously tricky problem from the point of view of numerical stability. Although the approaches described here are mathematically correct, small differences in the inputs or round-off errors during computation can cause large differences in the result.

and for B,

$$\{(x_0, y_0'), (x_1, y_1'), \ldots, (x_{n-1}, y_{n-1}')\} \ ,$$

where A and B are evaluated at the *same n* points, then a point-value representation for C is

$$\{(x_0, y_0 + y_0'), (x_1, y_1 + y_1'), \ldots, (x_{n-1}, y_{n-1} + y_{n-1}')\} \ .$$

Thus the time to add two polynomials of degree-bound n in point-value form is $\Theta(n)$.

Similarly, the point-value representation is convenient for multiplying polynomials. If $C(x) = A(x)B(x)$, then $C(x_k) = A(x_k)B(x_k)$ for any point x_k, and to obtain a point-value representation for C, just pointwise multiply a point-value representation for A by a point-value representation for B. Polynomial multiplication differs from polynomial addition in one key aspect, however: $\text{degree}(C) = \text{degree}(A) + \text{degree}(B)$, so that if A and B have degree-bound n, then C has degree-bound $2n$. A standard point-value representation for A and B consists of n point-value pairs for each polynomial. Multiplying these together gives n point-value pairs, but $2n$ pairs are necessary to interpolate a unique polynomial C of degree-bound $2n$. (See Exercise 30.1-4.) Instead, begin with "extended" point-value representations for A and for B consisting of $2n$ point-value pairs each. Given an extended point-value representation for A,

$$\{(x_0, y_0), (x_1, y_1), \ldots, (x_{2n-1}, y_{2n-1})\} \ ,$$

and a corresponding extended point-value representation for B,

$$\{(x_0, y_0'), (x_1, y_1'), \ldots, (x_{2n-1}, y_{2n-1}')\} \ ,$$

then a point-value representation for C is

$$\{(x_0, y_0 y_0'), (x_1, y_1 y_1'), \ldots, (x_{2n-1}, y_{2n-1} y_{2n-1}')\} \ .$$

Given two input polynomials in extended point-value form, multiplying them to obtain the point-value form of the result takes just $\Theta(n)$ time, much less than the $\Theta(n^2)$ time required to multiply polynomials in coefficient form.

Finally, let's consider how to evaluate a polynomial given in point-value form at a new point. For this problem, the simplest approach known is to first convert the polynomial to coefficient form and then evaluate it at the new point.

Fast multiplication of polynomials in coefficient form

Can the linear-time multiplication method for polynomials in point-value form expedite polynomial multiplication in coefficient form? The answer hinges on

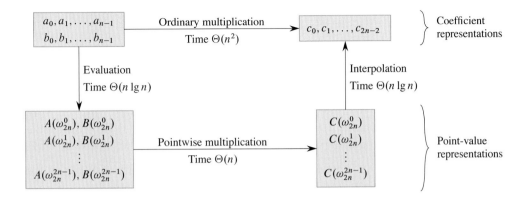

Figure 30.1 A graphical outline of an efficient polynomial-multiplication process. Representations on the top are in coefficient form, and those on the bottom are in point-value form. The arrows from left to right correspond to the multiplication operation. The ω_{2n} terms are complex $(2n)$th roots of unity.

whether it is possible convert a polynomial quickly from coefficient form to point-value form (evaluate) and vice versa (interpolate).

Any points can serve as evaluation points, but certain evaluation points allow conversion between representations in only $\Theta(n \lg n)$ time. As we'll see in Section 30.2, if "complex roots of unity" are the evaluation points, then the discrete Fourier transform (or DFT) evaluates and the inverse DFT interpolates. Section 30.2 shows how the FFT accomplishes the DFT and inverse DFT operations in $\Theta(n \lg n)$ time.

Figure 30.1 shows this strategy graphically. One minor detail concerns degree-bounds. The product of two polynomials of degree-bound n is a polynomial of degree-bound $2n$. Before evaluating the input polynomials A and B, therefore, first double their degree-bounds to $2n$ by adding n high-order coefficients of 0. Because the vectors have $2n$ elements, use "complex $(2n)$th roots of unity," which are denoted by the ω_{2n} terms in Figure 30.1.

The following procedure takes advantage of the FFT to multiply two polynomials $A(x)$ and $B(x)$ of degree-bound n in $\Theta(n \lg n)$-time, where the input and output representations are in coefficient form. The procedure assumes that n is an exact power of 2, so if it isn't, just add high-order zero coefficients.

1. **Double degree-bound:** Create coefficient representations of $A(x)$ and $B(x)$ as degree-bound $2n$ polynomials by adding n high-order zero coefficients to each.

2. **Evaluate:** Compute point-value representations of $A(x)$ and $B(x)$ of length $2n$ by applying the FFT of order $2n$ on each polynomial. These representations contain the values of the two polynomials at the $(2n)$th roots of unity.

3. **Pointwise multiply:** Compute a point-value representation for the polynomial $C(x) = A(x)B(x)$ by multiplying these values together pointwise. This representation contains the value of $C(x)$ at each $(2n)$th root of unity.

4. **Interpolate:** Create the coefficient representation of the polynomial $C(x)$ by applying the FFT on $2n$ point-value pairs to compute the inverse DFT.

Steps (1) and (3) take $\Theta(n)$ time, and steps (2) and (4) take $\Theta(n \lg n)$ time. Thus, once we show how to use the FFT, we will have proven the following.

Theorem 30.2
Two polynomials of degree-bound n with both the input and output representations in coefficient form can be multiplied in $\Theta(n \lg n)$ time.   ∎

Exercises

30.1-1
Multiply the polynomials $A(x) = 7x^3 - x^2 + x - 10$ and $B(x) = 8x^3 - 6x + 3$ using equations (30.1) and (30.2).

30.1-2
Another way to evaluate a polynomial $A(x)$ of degree-bound n at a given point x_0 is to divide $A(x)$ by the polynomial $(x - x_0)$, obtaining a quotient polynomial $q(x)$ of degree-bound $n - 1$ and a remainder r, such that

$$A(x) = q(x)(x - x_0) + r .$$

Then we have $A(x_0) = r$. Show how to compute the remainder r and the coefficients of $q(x)$ from x_0 and the coefficients of A in $\Theta(n)$ time.

30.1-3
Given a polynomial $A(x) = \sum_{j=0}^{n-1} a_j x^j$, define $A^{\text{rev}}(x) = \sum_{j=0}^{n-1} a_{n-1-j} x^j$. Show how to derive a point-value representation for $A^{\text{rev}}(x)$ from a point-value representation for $A(x)$, assuming that none of the points is 0.

30.1-4
Prove that n distinct point-value pairs are necessary to uniquely specify a polynomial of degree-bound n, that is, if fewer than n distinct point-value pairs are given, they fail to specify a unique polynomial of degree-bound n. (*Hint:* Using Theorem 30.1, what can you say about a set of $n - 1$ point-value pairs to which you add one more arbitrarily chosen point-value pair?)

30.1-5
Show how to use equation (30.5) to interpolate in $\Theta(n^2)$ time. (*Hint:* First compute the coefficient representation of the polynomial $\prod_j (x - x_j)$ and then divide by $(x - x_k)$ as necessary for the numerator of each term (see Exercise 30.1-2). You can compute each of the n denominators in $O(n)$ time.)

30.1-6
Explain what is wrong with the "obvious" approach to polynomial division using a point-value representation: dividing the corresponding y values. Discuss separately the case in which the division comes out exactly and the case in which it doesn't.

30.1-7
Consider two sets A and B, each having n integers in the range from 0 to $10n$. The *Cartesian sum* of A and B is defined by

$$C = \{x + y : x \in A \text{ and } y \in B\} \ .$$

The integers in C lie in the range from 0 to $20n$. Show how, in $O(n \lg n)$ time, to find the elements of C and the number of times each element of C is realized as a sum of elements in A and B. (*Hint:* Represent A and B as polynomials of degree at most $10n$.)

30.2   The DFT and FFT

In Section 30.1, we claimed that by computing the DFT and its inverse by using the FFT, it is possible to evaluate and interpolate a degree n polynomial at the complex roots of unity in $\Theta(n \lg n)$ time. This section defines complex roots of unity, studies their properties, defines the DFT, and then shows how the FFT computes the DFT and its inverse in $\Theta(n \lg n)$ time.

Complex roots of unity

A *complex nth root of unity* is a complex number ω such that

$$\omega^n = 1 \ .$$

There are exactly n complex nth roots of unity: $e^{2\pi i k/n}$ for $k = 0, 1, \ldots, n-1$. To interpret this formula, use the definition of the exponential of a complex number:

$$e^{iu} = \cos(u) + i \sin(u) \ .$$

Figure 30.2 shows that the n complex roots of unity are equally spaced around the circle of unit radius centered at the origin of the complex plane. The value

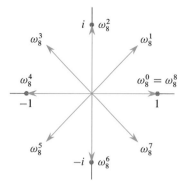

Figure 30.2   The values of $\omega_8^0, \omega_8^1, \ldots, \omega_8^7$ in the complex plane, where $\omega_8 = e^{2\pi i/8}$ is the principal 8th root of unity.

$$\omega_n = e^{2\pi i/n} \tag{30.6}$$

is the *principal nth root of unity*.[2] All other complex nth roots of unity are powers of ω_n.

The n complex nth roots of unity,

$$\omega_n^0, \omega_n^1, \ldots, \omega_n^{n-1} ,$$

form a group under multiplication (see Section 31.3). This group has the same structure as the additive group $(\mathbb{Z}_n, +)$ modulo n, since $\omega_n^n = \omega_n^0 = 1$ implies that $\omega_n^j \omega_n^k = \omega_n^{j+k} = \omega_n^{(j+k) \bmod n}$. Similarly, $\omega_n^{-1} = \omega_n^{n-1}$. The following lemmas furnish some essential properties of the complex nth roots of unity.

Lemma 30.3 (Cancellation lemma)
For any integers $n > 0, k \geq 0,$ and $d > 0,$

$$\omega_{dn}^{dk} = \omega_n^k . \tag{30.7}$$

Proof   The lemma follows directly from equation (30.6), since

$$
\begin{aligned}
\omega_{dn}^{dk} &= \left(e^{2\pi i/dn}\right)^{dk} \\
&= \left(e^{2\pi i/n}\right)^{k} \\
&= \omega_n^k .
\end{aligned}
$$

$\blacksquare$

---

[2] Many other authors define ω_n differently: $\omega_n = e^{-2\pi i/n}$. This alternative definition tends to be used for signal-processing applications. The underlying mathematics is substantially the same with either definition of ω_n.

Corollary 30.4
For any even integer $n > 0$,

$$\omega_n^{n/2} = \omega_2 = -1 \ .$$

Proof   The proof is left as Exercise 30.2-1.   ∎

Lemma 30.5 (Halving lemma)
If $n > 0$ is even, then the squares of the n complex nth roots of unity are the $n/2$ complex $(n/2)$th roots of unity.

Proof   By the cancellation lemma, $(\omega_n^k)^2 = \omega_{n/2}^k$ for any nonnegative integer k. Squaring all of the complex nth roots of unity produces each $(n/2)$th root of unity exactly twice, since

$$\begin{aligned}
(\omega_n^{k+n/2})^2 &= \omega_n^{2k+n} \\
&= \omega_n^{2k}\omega_n^{n} \\
&= \omega_n^{2k} \\
&= (\omega_n^k)^2 \ .
\end{aligned}$$

Thus ω_n^k and $\omega_n^{k+n/2}$ have the same square. We could also have used Corollary 30.4 to prove this property, since $\omega_n^{n/2} = -1$ implies $\omega_n^{k+n/2} = \omega_n^k \omega_n^{n/2} = -\omega_n^k$, and thus $(\omega_n^{k+n/2})^2 = (-\omega_n^k)^2 = (\omega_n^k)^2$.   ∎

As we'll see, the halving lemma is essential to the divide-and-conquer approach for converting between coefficient and point-value representations of polynomials, since it guarantees that the recursive subproblems are only half as large.

Lemma 30.6 (Summation lemma)
For any integer $n \geq 1$ and nonzero integer k not divisible by n,

$$\sum_{j=0}^{n-1} \left(\omega_n^k\right)^j = 0 \ .$$

Proof   Equation (A.6) on page 1142 applies to complex values as well as to reals, giving

$$\sum_{j=0}^{n-1} (\omega_n^k)^j = \frac{(\omega_n^k)^n - 1}{\omega_n^k - 1}$$

$$= \frac{(\omega_n^n)^k - 1}{\omega_n^k - 1}$$

$$= \frac{(1)^k - 1}{\omega_n^k - 1}$$

$$= 0 .$$

To see that the denominator is not 0, note that $\omega_n^k = 1$ only when k is divisible by n, which the lemma statement prohibits.   ∎

The DFT

Recall the goal of evaluating a polynomial

$$A(x) = \sum_{j=0}^{n-1} a_j x^j$$

of degree-bound n at $\omega_n^0, \omega_n^1, \omega_n^2, \ldots, \omega_n^{n-1}$ (that is, at the n complex nth roots of unity).[3] The polynomial A is given in coefficient form: $a = (a_0, a_1, \ldots, a_{n-1})$. Let us define the results y_k, for $k = 0, 1, \ldots, n-1$, by

$$y_k = A(\omega_n^k)$$

$$= \sum_{j=0}^{n-1} a_j \omega_n^{kj} . \tag{30.8}$$

The vector $y = (y_0, y_1, \ldots, y_{n-1})$ is the *discrete Fourier transform (DFT)* of the coefficient vector $a = (a_0, a_1, \ldots, a_{n-1})$. We also write $y = \mathrm{DFT}_n(a)$.

The FFT

The *fast Fourier transform (FFT)* takes advantage of the special properties of the complex roots of unity to compute $\mathrm{DFT}_n(a)$ in $\Theta(n \lg n)$ time, as opposed to the $\Theta(n^2)$ time of the straightforward method. Assume throughout that n is an exact power of 2. Although strategies for dealing with sizes that are not exact powers of 2 are known, they are beyond the scope of this book.

---

[3] The length n is actually what Section 30.1 referred to as $2n$, since the degree-bound of the given polynomials doubles prior to evaluation. In the context of polynomial multiplication, therefore, we are actually working with complex $(2n)$th roots of unity.

The FFT method employs a divide-and-conquer strategy, using the even-indexed and odd-indexed coefficients of $A(x)$ separately to define the two new polynomials $A^{\text{even}}(x)$ and $A^{\text{odd}}(x)$ of degree-bound $n/2$:

$$A^{\text{even}}(x) = a_0 + a_2 x + a_4 x^2 + \cdots + a_{n-2} x^{n/2-1} \, ,$$
$$A^{\text{odd}}(x) = a_1 + a_3 x + a_5 x^2 + \cdots + a_{n-1} x^{n/2-1} \, .$$

Note that A^{even} contains all the even-indexed coefficients of A (the binary representation of the index ends in 0) and A^{odd} contains all the odd-indexed coefficients (the binary representation of the index ends in 1). It follows that

$$A(x) = A^{\text{even}}(x^2) + x A^{\text{odd}}(x^2) \, , \tag{30.9}$$

so that the problem of evaluating $A(x)$ at $\omega_n^0, \omega_n^1, \ldots, \omega_n^{n-1}$ reduces to

1. evaluating the degree-bound $n/2$ polynomials $A^{\text{even}}(x)$ and $A^{\text{odd}}(x)$ at the points

    $$(\omega_n^0)^2, (\omega_n^1)^2, \ldots, (\omega_n^{n-1})^2 \, , \tag{30.10}$$

    and then

2. combining the results according to equation (30.9).

By the halving lemma, the list of values (30.10) consists not of n distinct values but only of the $n/2$ complex $(n/2)$th roots of unity, with each root occurring exactly twice. Therefore, the FFT recursively evaluates the polynomials A^{even} and A^{odd} of degree-bound $n/2$ at the $n/2$ complex $(n/2)$th roots of unity. These subproblems have exactly the same form as the original problem, but are half the size, dividing an n-element DFT_n computation into two $n/2$-element $\text{DFT}_{n/2}$ computations. This decomposition is the basis for the FFT procedure on the next page, which computes the DFT of an n-element vector $a = (a_0, a_1, \ldots, a_{n-1})$, where n is an exact power of 2.

The FFT procedure works as follows. Lines 1–2 represent the base case of the recursion. The DFT of 1 element is the element itself, since in this case

$$y_0 = a_0 \, \omega_1^0$$
$$= a_0 \cdot 1$$
$$= a_0 \, .$$

Lines 5–6 define the coefficient vectors for the polynomials A^{even} and A^{odd}. Lines 3, 4, and 12 guarantee that ω is updated properly so that whenever lines 10–11 are executed, $\omega = \omega_n^k$. (Keeping a running value of ω from iteration to iteration saves

FFT(a, n)

```
 1  if n == 1
 2      return a                          // DFT of 1 element is the element itself
 3  ωₙ = e^{2πi/n}
 4  ω = 1
 5  a^{even} = (a₀, a₂, …, a_{n-2})
 6  a^{odd} = (a₁, a₃, …, a_{n-1})
 7  y^{even} = FFT(a^{even}, n/2)
 8  y^{odd} = FFT(a^{odd}, n/2)
 9  for k = 0 to n/2 − 1                   // at this point, ω = ωₙᵏ
10      y_k = y_k^{even} + ω y_k^{odd}
11      y_{k+(n/2)} = y_k^{even} − ω y_k^{odd}
12      ω = ω ωₙ
13  return y
```

time over computing ω_n^k from scratch each time through the **for** loop.[4]) Lines 7–8 perform the recursive $\mathrm{DFT}_{n/2}$ computations, setting, for $k = 0, 1, \ldots, n/2 - 1$,

$$y_k^{\mathrm{even}} = A^{\mathrm{even}}(\omega_{n/2}^k) \,,$$
$$y_k^{\mathrm{odd}} = A^{\mathrm{odd}}(\omega_{n/2}^k) \,,$$

or, since $\omega_{n/2}^k = \omega_n^{2k}$ by the cancellation lemma,

$$y_k^{\mathrm{even}} = A^{\mathrm{even}}(\omega_n^{2k}) \,,$$
$$y_k^{\mathrm{odd}} = A^{\mathrm{odd}}(\omega_n^{2k}) \,.$$

Lines 10–11 combine the results of the recursive $\mathrm{DFT}_{n/2}$ calculations. For the first $n/2$ results $y_0, y_1, \ldots, y_{n/2-1}$, line 10 yields

$$
\begin{aligned}
y_k &= y_k^{\mathrm{even}} + \omega_n^k y_k^{\mathrm{odd}} \\
    &= A^{\mathrm{even}}(\omega_n^{2k}) + \omega_n^k A^{\mathrm{odd}}(\omega_n^{2k}) \\
    &= A(\omega_n^k) \qquad\qquad \text{(by equation (30.9))} \,.
\end{aligned}
$$

For $y_{n/2}, y_{n/2+1}, \ldots, y_{n-1}$, letting $k = 0, 1, \ldots, n/2 - 1$, line 11 yields

---

[4] The downside of iteratively updating ω is that round-off errors can accumulate, especially for larger input sizes. Several techniques to limit the magnitude of FFT round-off errors have been proposed, but are beyond the scope of this book. If several FFTs are going to be run on inputs of the same size, then it might be worthwhile to directly precompute a table of all $n/2$ values of ω_n^k.

$$
\begin{aligned}
y_{k+(n/2)} &= y_k^{\text{even}} - \omega_n^k y_k^{\text{odd}} \\
&= y_k^{\text{even}} + \omega_n^{k+(n/2)} y_k^{\text{odd}} && \text{(since } \omega_n^{k+(n/2)} = -\omega_n^k) \\
&= A^{\text{even}}(\omega_n^{2k}) + \omega_n^{k+(n/2)} A^{\text{odd}}(\omega_n^{2k}) \\
&= A^{\text{even}}(\omega_n^{2k+n}) + \omega_n^{k+(n/2)} A^{\text{odd}}(\omega_n^{2k+n}) && \text{(since } \omega_n^{2k+n} = \omega_n^{2k}) \\
&= A(\omega_n^{k+(n/2)}) && \text{(by equation (30.9))} .
\end{aligned}
$$

Thus the vector y returned by FFT is indeed the DFT of the input vector a.

Lines 10 and 11 multiply each value y_k^{odd} by ω_n^k, for $k = 0, 1, \ldots, n/2 - 1$. Line 10 adds this product to y_k^{even}, and line 11 subtracts it. Because each factor ω_n^k appears in both its positive and negative forms, we call the factors ω_n^k *twiddle factors*.

To determine the running time of the procedure FFT, note that exclusive of the recursive calls, each invocation takes $\Theta(n)$ time, where n is the length of the input vector. The recurrence for the running time is therefore

$$
\begin{aligned}
T(n) &= 2T(n/2) + \Theta(n) \\
&= \Theta(n \lg n) ,
\end{aligned}
$$

by case 2 of the master theorem (Theorem 4.1). Thus the FFT can evaluate a polynomial of degree-bound n at the complex nth roots of unity in $\Theta(n \lg n)$ time.

Interpolation at the complex roots of unity

The polynomial multiplication scheme entails converting from coefficient form to point-value form by evaluating the polynomial at the complex roots of unity, point-wise multiplying, and finally converting from point-value form back to coefficient form by interpolating. We've just seen how to evaluate, so now we'll see how to interpolate the complex roots of unity by a polynomial. To interpolate, we'll write the DFT as a matrix equation and then look at the form of the matrix inverse.

From equation (30.4), we can write the DFT as the matrix product $y = V_n a$, where V_n is a Vandermonde matrix containing the appropriate powers of ω_n:

$$
\begin{pmatrix}
y_0 \\
y_1 \\
y_2 \\
y_3 \\
\vdots \\
y_{n-1}
\end{pmatrix}
=
\begin{pmatrix}
1 & 1 & 1 & 1 & \cdots & 1 \\
1 & \omega_n & \omega_n^2 & \omega_n^3 & \cdots & \omega_n^{n-1} \\
1 & \omega_n^2 & \omega_n^4 & \omega_n^6 & \cdots & \omega_n^{2(n-1)} \\
1 & \omega_n^3 & \omega_n^6 & \omega_n^9 & \cdots & \omega_n^{3(n-1)} \\
\vdots & \vdots & \vdots & \vdots & \ddots & \vdots \\
1 & \omega_n^{n-1} & \omega_n^{2(n-1)} & \omega_n^{3(n-1)} & \cdots & \omega_n^{(n-1)(n-1)}
\end{pmatrix}
\begin{pmatrix}
a_0 \\
a_1 \\
a_2 \\
a_3 \\
\vdots \\
a_{n-1}
\end{pmatrix} .
$$

The (k, j) entry of V_n is ω_n^{kj}, for $j, k = 0, 1, \ldots, n - 1$. The exponents of the entries of V_n form a multiplication table for factors 0 to $n - 1$.

For the inverse operation, which we write as $a = \text{DFT}_n^{-1}(y)$, multiply y by the matrix V_n^{-1}, the inverse of V_n.

Theorem 30.7
For $j, k = 0, 1, \ldots, n - 1$, the (j, k) entry of V_n^{-1} is ω_n^{-jk}/n.

Proof We show that $V_n^{-1}V_n = I_n$, the $n \times n$ identity matrix. Consider the (k, k') entry of $V_n^{-1}V_n$:

$$[V_n^{-1}V_n]_{kk'} = \sum_{j=0}^{n-1} (\omega_n^{-jk}/n)(\omega_n^{jk'})$$

$$= \sum_{j=0}^{n-1} \omega_n^{j(k'-k)}/n .$$

This summation equals 1 if $k' = k$, and it is 0 otherwise by the summation lemma (Lemma 30.6). Note that in order for the summation lemma to apply, $k' - k$ must not be divisible by n. Indeed, it is not, since $-(n-1) \leq k' - k \leq n - 1$. ∎

With the inverse matrix V_n^{-1} defined, $\text{DFT}_n^{-1}(y)$ is given by

$$a_j = \sum_{k=0}^{n-1} y_k \frac{\omega^{-jk}}{n}$$

$$= \frac{1}{n} \sum_{k=0}^{n-1} y_k \omega_n^{-kj} \tag{30.11}$$

for $j = 0, 1, \ldots, n - 1$. By comparing equations (30.8) and (30.11), you can see that if you modify the FFT algorithm to switch the roles of a and y, replace ω_n by ω_n^{-1}, and divide each element of the result by n, you get the inverse DFT (see Exercise 30.2-4). Thus, DFT_n^{-1} is computable in $\Theta(n \lg n)$ time as well.

Thus, the FFT and the inverse FFT provide a way to transform a polynomial of degree-bound n back and forth between its coefficient representation and a point-value representation in only $\Theta(n \lg n)$ time. In the context of polynomial multiplication, we have shown the following about the convolution $a \otimes b$ of vectors a and b:

Theorem 30.8 (Convolution theorem)
For any two vectors a and b of length n, where n is an exact power of 2,

$$a \otimes b = \text{DFT}_{2n}^{-1}(\text{DFT}_{2n}(a) \cdot \text{DFT}_{2n}(b)) ,$$

where the vectors a and b are padded with 0s to length $2n$ and $\cdot$ denotes the componentwise product of two $2n$-element vectors. ∎

Exercises

30.2-1
Prove Corollary 30.4.

30.2-2
Compute the DFT of the vector $(0, 1, 2, 3)$.

30.2-3
Do Exercise 30.1-1 by using the $\Theta(n \lg n)$-time scheme.

30.2-4
Write pseudocode to compute DFT_n^{-1} in $\Theta(n \lg n)$ time.

30.2-5
Describe the generalization of the FFT procedure to the case in which n is an exact power of 3. Give a recurrence for the running time, and solve the recurrence.

★ **30.2-6**
Instead of performing an n-element FFT over the field of complex numbers (where n is an exact power of 2), let's use the ring $\mathbb{Z}_m$ of integers modulo m, where $m = 2^{tn/2} + 1$ and t is an arbitrary positive integer. We can use $\omega = 2^t$ instead of ω_n as a principal nth root of unity, modulo m. Prove that the DFT and the inverse DFT are well defined in this system.

30.2-7
Given a list of values $z_0, z_1, \ldots, z_{n-1}$ (possibly with repetitions), show how to find the coefficients of a polynomial $P(x)$ of degree-bound $n + 1$ that has zeros only at $z_0, z_1, \ldots, z_{n-1}$ (possibly with repetitions). Your procedure should run in $O(n \lg^2 n)$ time. (*Hint:* The polynomial $P(x)$ has a zero at z_j if and only if $P(x)$ is a multiple of $(x - z_j)$.)

★ **30.2-8**
The *chirp transform* of a vector $a = (a_0, a_1, \ldots, a_{n-1})$ is the vector $y = (y_0, y_1, \ldots, y_{n-1})$, where $y_k = \sum_{j=0}^{n-1} a_j z^{kj}$ and z is any complex number. The DFT is therefore a special case of the chirp transform, obtained by taking $z = \omega_n$. Show how to evaluate the chirp transform for any complex number z in $O(n \lg n)$ time. (*Hint:* Use the equation

$$y_k = z^{k^2/2} \sum_{j=0}^{n-1} \left(a_j z^{j^2/2} \right) \left(z^{-(k-j)^2/2} \right)$$

to view the chirp transform as a convolution.)

30.3   FFT circuits

Many of the FFT's applications in signal processing require the utmost speed, and so the FFT is often implemented as a circuit in hardware. The FFT's divide-and-conquer structure enables the circuit to have a parallel structure so that the *depth* of the circuit—the maximum number of computational elements between any output and any input that can reach it—is $\Theta(\lg n)$. Moreover, the structure of the FFT circuit has several interesting mathematical properties, which we won't go into here.

Butterfly operations

Notice that the **for** loop of lines 9–12 of the FFT procedure computes the value $\omega_n^k \, y_k^{\mathrm{odd}}$ twice per iteration: once in line 10 and once in line 11. A good optimizing compiler produces code that evaluates this *common subexpression* just once, storing its value into a temporary variable, so that lines 10–11 are treated like the three lines

$$
\begin{aligned}
t &= \omega \, y_k^{\mathrm{odd}} \\
y_k &= y_k^{\mathrm{even}} + t \\
y_{k+(n/2)} &= y_k^{\mathrm{even}} - t
\end{aligned}
$$

This operation, multiplying the twiddle factor $\omega = \omega_n^k$ by y_k^{odd}, storing the product into the temporary variable t, and adding and subtracting t from y_k^{even}, is known as a *butterfly operation*. Figure 30.3 shows it as a circuit, and you can see how it vaguely resembles the shape of a butterfly. (Although less colorfully, it could have been called a "bowtie" operation.)

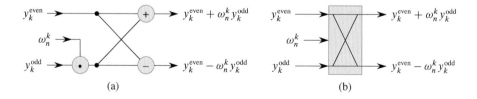

(a)   (b)

Figure 30.3   A circuit for a butterfly operation. **(a)** The two input values enter from the left, the twiddle factor ω_n^k is multiplied by y_k^{odd}, and the sum and difference are output on the right. **(b)** A simplified drawing of a butterfly operation, which we'll use when drawing the parallel FFT circuit.

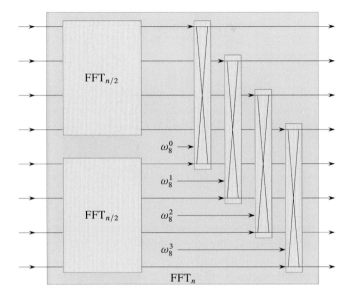

Figure 30.4   The schema for the conquer and combine steps of an n-input, n-output FFT circuit, FFT$_n$, shown for $n = 8$. Inputs enter from the left, and outputs exit from the right. The input values first go through two FFT$_{n/2}$ circuits, and then $n/2$ butterfly circuits combine the results. Only the top and bottom wires entering a butterfly interact with it: wires that pass through the middle of a butterfly do not affect that butterfly, nor are their values changed by that butterfly.

Recursive circuit structure

The FFT procedure follows the divide-and-conquer strategy that we first saw in Section 2.3.1:

Divide the n-element input vector into its $n/2$ even-indexed and $n/2$ odd-indexed elements.

Conquer by recursively computing the DFTs of the two subproblems, each of size $n/2$.

Combine by performing $n/2$ butterfly operations. These butterfly operations work with twiddle factors $\omega_n^0, \omega_n^1, \ldots, \omega_n^{n/2-1}$.

The circuit schema in Figure 30.4 follows the conquer and combine steps of this pattern for an FFT circuit with n inputs and n outputs, denoted by FFT$_n$. Each line is a wire that carries a value. Inputs enter from the left, one per wire, and outputs exit from the right. The conquer step runs the inputs through two FFT$_{n/2}$ circuits, which are also constructed recursively. The values produced by the two FFT$_{n/2}$ circuits feed into $n/2$ butterfly circuits, with twiddle factors $\omega_n^0, \omega_n^1, \ldots, \omega_n^{n/2} - 1$,

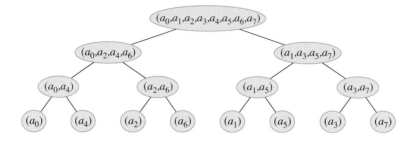

Figure 30.5 The tree of input vectors to the recursive calls of the FFT procedure. The initial invocation is for $n = 8$.

to combine the results. The base case of the recursion occurs when $n = 1$, where the sole output value equals the sole input value. An FFT_1 circuit, therefore, does nothing, and so the smallest nontrivial FFT circuit is FFT_2, a single butterfly operation whose twiddle factor is $\omega_2^0 = 1$.

Permuting the inputs

How does the divide step enter into the circuit design? Let's examine how input vectors to the various recursive calls of the FFT procedure relate to the original input vector, so that the circuit can emulate the divide step at the start for all levels of recursion. Figure 30.5 arranges the input vectors to the recursive calls in an invocation of FFT in a tree structure, where the initial call is for $n = 8$. The tree has one node for each call of the procedure, labeled by the elements of the initial call as they appear in the corresponding input vector. Each FFT invocation makes two recursive calls, unless it has received a 1-element vector. The first call appears in the left child, and the second call appears in the right child.

Looking at the tree, observe that if you arrange the elements of the initial vector a into the order in which they appear in the leaves, you can trace the execution of the FFT procedure, but bottom up instead of top down. First, take the elements in pairs, compute the DFT of each pair using one butterfly operation, and replace the pair with its DFT. The vector then holds $n/2$ two-element DFTs. Next, take these $n/2$ DFTs in pairs and compute the DFT of the four vector elements they come from by executing two butterfly operations, replacing two two-element DFTs with one four-element DFT. The vector then holds $n/4$ four-element DFTs. Continue in this manner until the vector holds two $(n/2)$-element DFTs, which $n/2$ butterfly operations combine into the final n-element DFT. In other words, you can start with the elements of the initial vector a, but rearranged as in the leaves of Figure 30.5, and then feed them directly into a circuit that follows the schema in Figure 30.4.

Let's think about the permutation that rearranges the input vector. The order in which the leaves appear in Figure 30.5 is a *bit-reversal permutation*. That is, letting rev(k) be the lg n-bit integer formed by reversing the bits of the binary representation of k, then vector element a_k moves to position rev(k). In Figure 30.5, for example, the leaves appear in the order $0, 4, 2, 6, 1, 5, 3, 7$. This sequence in binary is $000, 100, 010, 110, 001, 101, 011, 111$, and you can obtain it by reversing the bits of each number in the sequence $0, 1, 2, 3, 4, 6, 7$ or, in binary, $000, 001, 010, 011, 100, 101, 110, 111$. To see in general that the input vector should be rearranged by a bit-reversal permutation, note that at the top level of the tree, indices whose low-order bit is 0 go into the left subtree and indices whose low-order bit is 1 go into the right subtree. Stripping off the low-order bit at each level, continue this process down the tree, until you get the order given by the bit-reversal permutation at the leaves.

The full FFT circuit

Figure 30.6 depicts the entire circuit for $n = 8$. The circuit begins with a bit-reversal permutation of the inputs, followed by lg n stages, each stage consisting of $n/2$ butterflies executed in parallel. Assuming that each butterfly circuit has constant depth, the full circuit has depth $\Theta(\lg n)$. The butterfly operations at each level of recursion in the FFT procedure are independent, and so the circuit performs them in parallel. The figure shows wires running from left to right, carrying values through the lg n stages. For $s = 1, 2, \ldots, \lg n$, stage s consists of $n/2^s$ groups of butterflies, with 2^{s-1} butterflies per group. The twiddle factors in stage s are $\omega_m^0, \omega_m^1, \ldots, \omega_m^{m/2-1}$, where $m = 2^s$.

Exercises

30.3-1
Show the values on the wires for each butterfly input and output in the FFT circuit of Figure 30.6, given the input vector $(0, 2, 3, -1, 4, 5, 7, 9)$.

30.3-2
Consider an FFT_n circuit, such as in Figure 30.6, with wires $0, 1, \ldots, n-1$ (wire j has output y_j) and stages numbered as in the figure. Stage s, for $s = 1, 2 \ldots, \lg n$, consists of $n/2^s$ groups of butterflies. Which two wires are inputs and outputs for the jth butterfly circuit in the gth group in stage s?

30.3-3
Consider a b-bit integer k in the range $0 \le k < 2^b$. Treating k as a b-element vector over $\{0, 1\}$, describe a $b \times b$ matrix M such that the matrix-vector product Mk is the binary representation of rev(k).

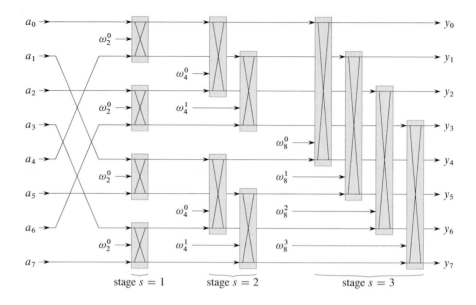

Figure 30.6 A full circuit that computes the FFT in parallel, here shown for $n = 8$ inputs. It has $\lg n$ stages, and each stage comprises $n/2$ butterflies that can operate in parallel. As in Figure 30.4, only the top and bottom wires entering a butterfly interact with it. For example, the top butterfly in stage 2 has inputs and outputs only on wires 0 and 2 (the wires with outputs y_0 and y_2, respectively). This circuit has depth $\Theta(\lg n)$ and performs $\Theta(n \lg n)$ butterfly operations altogether.

30.3-4
Write pseudocode for the procedure BIT-REVERSE-PERMUTATION(a, n), which performs the bit-reversal permutation on a vector a of length n in-place. Assume that you may call the procedure BIT-REVERSE-OF(k, b), which returns an integer that is the b-bit reversal of the nonnegative integer k, where $0 \le k < 2^b$.

★ *30.3-5*
Suppose that the adders within the butterfly operations of a given FFT circuit sometimes fail in such a manner that they always produce a 0 output, independent of their inputs. In addition, suppose that exactly one adder has failed, but you don't know which one. Describe how you can identify the failed adder by supplying inputs to the overall FFT circuit and observing the outputs. How efficient is your method?

Problems

30-1 *Divide-and-conquer multiplication*

a. Show how to multiply two linear polynomials $ax + b$ and $cx + d$ using only three multiplications. (*Hint:* One of the multiplications is $(a + b) \cdot (c + d)$.)

b. Give two divide-and-conquer algorithms for multiplying two polynomials of degree-bound n in $\Theta(n^{\lg 3})$ time. The first algorithm should divide the input polynomial coefficients into a high half and a low half, and the second algorithm should divide them according to whether their index is odd or even.

c. Show how to multiply two n-bit integers in $O(n^{\lg 3})$ steps, where each step operates on at most a constant number of 1-bit values.

30-2 *Multidimensional fast Fourier transform*

The 1-dimensional discrete Fourier transform defined by equation (30.8) generalizes to d dimensions. The input is a d-dimensional array $A = (a_{j_1, j_2, \ldots, j_d})$ whose dimensions are $n_1, n_2, \ldots, n_d$, where $n_1 n_2 \cdots n_d = n$. The d-dimensional discrete Fourier transform is defined by the equation

$$
y_{k_1, k_2, \ldots, k_d} = \sum_{j_1 = 0}^{n_1 - 1} \sum_{j_2 = 0}^{n_2 - 1} \cdots \sum_{j_d = 0}^{n_d - 1} a_{j_1, j_2, \ldots, j_d} \, \omega_{n_1}^{j_1 k_1} \omega_{n_2}^{j_2 k_2} \cdots \omega_{n_d}^{j_d k_d}
$$

for $0 \leq k_1 < n_1, 0 \leq k_2 < n_2, \ldots, 0 \leq k_d < n_d$.

a. Show how to produce a d-dimensional DFT by computing 1-dimensional DFTs on each dimension in turn. That is, first compute n/n_1 separate 1-dimensional DFTs along dimension 1. Then, using the result of the DFTs along dimension 1 as the input, compute n/n_2 separate 1-dimensional DFTs along dimension 2. Using this result as the input, compute n/n_3 separate 1-dimensional DFTs along dimension 3, and so on, through dimension d.

b. Show that the ordering of dimensions does not matter, so that if you compute the 1-dimensional DFTs in any order of the d dimensions, you compute the d-dimensional DFT.

c. Show that if you compute each 1-dimensional DFT by computing the fast Fourier transform, the total time to compute a d-dimensional DFT is $O(n \lg n)$, independent of d.

30-3   Evaluating all derivatives of a polynomial at a point

Given a polynomial $A(x)$ of degree-bound n, we define its tth derivative by

$$
A^{(t)}(x) = \begin{cases}
A(x) & \text{if } t = 0, \\
\frac{d}{dx} A^{(t-1)}(x) & \text{if } 1 \le t \le n - 1, \\
0 & \text{if } t \ge n.
\end{cases}
$$

In this problem, you will show how to determine $A^{(t)}(x_0)$ for $t = 0, 1, \ldots, n - 1$, given the coefficient representation $(a_0, a_1, \ldots, a_{n-1})$ of $A(x)$ and a point x_0.

a. Given coefficients $b_0, b_1, \ldots, b_{n-1}$ such that

$$
A(x) = \sum_{j=0}^{n-1} b_j (x - x_0)^j,
$$

show how to compute $A^{(t)}(x_0)$, for $t = 0, 1, \ldots, n - 1$, in $O(n)$ time.

b. Explain how to find $b_0, b_1, \ldots, b_{n-1}$ in $O(n \lg n)$ time, given $A(x_0 + \omega_n^k)$ for $k = 0, 1, \ldots, n - 1$.

c. Prove that

$$
A(x_0 + \omega_n^k) = \sum_{r=0}^{n-1} \left(\frac{\omega_n^{kr}}{r!} \sum_{j=0}^{n-1} f(j) g(r - j) \right),
$$

where $f(j) = a_j \cdot j!$ and

$$
g(l) = \begin{cases}
x_0^{-l}/(-l)! & \text{if } -(n - 1) \le l \le 0, \\
0 & \text{if } 1 \le l \le n - 1.
\end{cases}
$$

d. Explain how to evaluate $A(x_0 + \omega_n^k)$ for $k = 0, 1, \ldots, n - 1$ in $O(n \lg n)$ time. Conclude that you can evaluate all nontrivial derivatives of $A(x)$ at x_0 in $O(n \lg n)$ time.

30-4   Polynomial evaluation at multiple points

Problem 2-3 showed how to evaluate a polynomial of degree-bound n at a single point in $O(n)$ time using Horner's rule. This chapter described how to evaluate such a polynomial at all n complex roots of unity in $O(n \lg n)$ time using the FFT. Now, you will show how to evaluate a polynomial of degree-bound n at n arbitrary points in $O(n \lg^2 n)$ time.

To do so, assume that you can compute the polynomial remainder when one such polynomial is divided by another in $O(n \lg n)$ time. For example, the remainder of $3x^3 + x^2 - 3x + 1$ when divided by $x^2 + x + 2$ is

$$(3x^3 + x^2 - 3x + 1) \bmod (x^2 + x + 2) = -7x + 5 \, .$$

Given the coefficient representation of a polynomial $A(x) = \sum_{k=0}^{n-1} a_k x^k$ and n points $x_0, x_1, \ldots, x_{n-1}$, your goal is to compute the n values $A(x_0), A(x_1), \ldots, A(x_{n-1})$. For $0 \leq i \leq j \leq n - 1$, define the polynomials $P_{ij}(x) = \prod_{k=i}^{j}(x - x_k)$ and $Q_{ij}(x) = A(x) \bmod P_{ij}(x)$. Note that $Q_{ij}(x)$ has degree at most $j - i$.

a. Prove that $A(x) \bmod (x - z) = A(z)$ for any point z.

b. Prove that $Q_{kk}(x) = A(x_k)$ and that $Q_{0,n-1}(x) = A(x)$.

c. Prove that for $i \leq k \leq j$, we have both $Q_{ik}(x) = Q_{ij}(x) \bmod P_{ik}(x)$ and $Q_{kj}(x) = Q_{ij}(x) \bmod P_{kj}(x)$.

d. Give an $O(n \lg^2 n)$-time algorithm to evaluate $A(x_0), A(x_1), \ldots, A(x_{n-1})$.

30-5 FFT using modular arithmetic

As defined, the discrete Fourier transform requires computation with complex numbers, which can result in a loss of precision due to round-off errors. For some problems, the answer is known to contain only integers, and a variant of the FFT based on modular arithmetic can guarantee that the answer is calculated exactly. An example of such a problem is that of multiplying two polynomials with integer coefficients. Exercise 30.2-6 gives one approach, using a modulus of length $\Omega(n)$ bits to handle a DFT on n points. This problem explores another approach that uses a modulus of the more reasonable length $O(\lg n)$, but it requires that you understand the material of Chapter 31. Let n be an exact power of 2.

a. You wish to search for the smallest k such that $p = kn + 1$ is prime. Give a simple heuristic argument why you might expect k to be approximately $\ln n$. (The value of k might be much larger or smaller, but you can reasonably expect to examine $O(\lg n)$ candidate values of k on average.) How does the expected length of p compare to the length of n?

Let g be a generator of $\mathbb{Z}_p^*$, and let $w = g^k \bmod p$.

b. Argue that the DFT and the inverse DFT are well-defined inverse operations modulo p, where w is used as a principal nth root of unity.

c. Show how to make the FFT and its inverse work modulo p in $O(n \lg n)$ time, where operations on words of $O(\lg n)$ bits take unit time. Assume that the algorithm is given p and w.

d. Compute the DFT modulo $p = 17$ of the vector $(0, 5, 3, 7, 7, 2, 1, 6)$. (*Hint:* Verify and use the fact that $g = 3$ is a generator of $\mathbb{Z}_{17}^*$.)

Chapter notes

Van Loan's book [442] provides an outstanding treatment of the fast Fourier transform. Press, Teukolsky, Vetterling, and Flannery [365, 366] offer a good description of the fast Fourier transform and its applications. For an excellent introduction to signal processing, a popular FFT application area, see the texts by Oppenheim and Schafer [347] and Oppenheim and Willsky [348]. The Oppenheim and Schafer book also shows how to handle cases in which n is not an exact power of 2.

Fourier analysis is not limited to 1-dimensional data. It is widely used in image processing to analyze data in two or more dimensions. The books by Gonzalez and Woods [194] and Pratt [363] discuss multidimensional Fourier transforms and their use in image processing, and books by Tolimieri, An, and Lu [439] and Van Loan [442] discuss the mathematics of multidimensional fast Fourier transforms.

Cooley and Tukey [101] are widely credited with devising the FFT in the 1960s. The FFT had in fact been discovered many times previously, but its importance was not fully realized before the advent of modern digital computers. Although Press, Teukolsky, Vetterling, and Flannery attribute the origins of the method to Runge and König in 1924, an article by Heideman, Johnson, and Burrus [211] traces the history of the FFT as far back as C. F. Gauss in 1805.

Frigo and Johnson [161] developed a fast and flexible implementation of the FFT, called FFTW ("fastest Fourier transform in the West"). FFTW is designed for situations requiring multiple DFT computations on the same problem size. Before actually computing the DFTs, FFTW executes a "planner," which, by a series of trial runs, determines how best to decompose the FFT computation for the given problem size on the host machine. FFTW adapts to use the hardware cache efficiently, and once subproblems are small enough, FFTW solves them with optimized, straight-line code. Moreover, FFTW has the advantage of taking $\Theta(n \lg n)$ time for any problem size n, even when n is a large prime.

Although the standard Fourier transform assumes that the input represents points that are uniformly spaced in the time domain, other techniques can approximate the FFT on "nonequispaced" data. The article by Ware [449] provides an overview.

31 Number-Theoretic Algorithms

Number theory was once viewed as a beautiful but largely useless subject in pure mathematics. Today number-theoretic algorithms are used widely, due in large part to the invention of cryptographic schemes based on large prime numbers. These schemes are feasible because we can find large primes quickly, and they are secure because we do not know how to factor the product of large primes (or solve related problems, such as computing discrete logarithms) efficiently. This chapter presents some of the number theory and related algorithms that underlie such applications.

We start in Section 31.1 by introducing basic concepts of number theory, such as divisibility, modular equivalence, and unique prime factorization. Section 31.2 studies one of the world's oldest algorithms: Euclid's algorithm for computing the greatest common divisor of two integers, and Section 31.3 reviews concepts of modular arithmetic. Section 31.4 then explores the set of multiples of a given number a, modulo n, and shows how to find all solutions to the equation $ax = b$ (mod n) by using Euclid's algorithm. The Chinese remainder theorem is presented in Section 31.5. Section 31.6 considers powers of a given number a, modulo n, and presents a repeated-squaring algorithm for efficiently computing a^b mod n, given a, b, and n. This operation is at the heart of efficient primality testing and of much modern cryptography, such as the RSA public-key cryptosystem described in Section 31.7. We wrap up in Section 31.8, which examines a randomized primality test. This test finds large primes efficiently, an essential step in creating keys for the RSA cryptosystem.

Size of inputs and cost of arithmetic computations

Because we'll be working with large integers, we need to adjust how to think about the size of an input and about the cost of elementary arithmetic operations.

In this chapter, a "large input" typically means an input containing "large integers" rather than an input containing "many integers" (as for sorting). Thus, the size of an input depends on the *number of bits* required to represent that input, not just the number of integers in the input. An algorithm with integer inputs $a_1, a_2, \ldots, a_k$ is a *polynomial-time algorithm* if it runs in time polynomial in $\lg a_1, \lg a_2, \ldots, \lg a_k$, that is, polynomial in the lengths of its binary-encoded inputs.

Most of this book considers the elementary arithmetic operations (multiplications, divisions, or computing remainders) as primitive operations that take one unit of time. Counting the number of such arithmetic operations that an algorithm performs provides a basis for making a reasonable estimate of the algorithm's actual running time on a computer. Elementary operations can be time-consuming, however, when their inputs are large. It thus becomes appropriate to measure how many *bit operations* a number-theoretic algorithm requires. In this model, multiplying two β-bit integers by the ordinary method uses $\Theta(\beta^2)$ bit operations. Similarly, dividing a β-bit integer by a shorter integer or taking the remainder of a β-bit integer when divided by a shorter integer requires $\Theta(\beta^2)$ time by simple algorithms. (See Exercise 31.1-12.) Faster methods are known. For example, a simple divide-and-conquer method for multiplying two β-bit integers has a running time of $\Theta(\beta^{\lg 3})$, and $O(\beta \lg \beta \lg \lg \beta)$ time is possible. For practical purposes, however, the $\Theta(\beta^2)$ algorithm is often best, and we use this bound as a basis for our analyses. In this chapter, we'll usually analyze algorithms in terms of both the number of arithmetic operations and the number of bit operations they require.

31.1   Elementary number-theoretic notions

This section provides a brief review of notions from elementary number theory concerning the set $\mathbb{Z} = \{\ldots, -2, -1, 0, 1, 2, \ldots\}$ of integers and the set $\mathbb{N} = \{0, 1, 2, \ldots\}$ of natural numbers.

Divisibility and divisors

The notion of one integer being divisible by another is key to the theory of numbers. The notation $d \mid a$ (read "d *divides* a") means that $a = kd$ for some integer k. Every integer divides 0. If $a > 0$ and $d \mid a$, then $|d| \leq |a|$. If $d \mid a$, then we also say that a is a *multiple* of d. If d does not divide a, we write $d \nmid a$.

If $d \mid a$ and $d \geq 0$, then d is a *divisor* of a. Since $d \mid a$ if and only if $-d \mid a$, without loss of generality, we define the divisors of a to be nonnegative, with the understanding that the negative of any divisor of a also divides a. A divisor of a nonzero integer a is at least 1 but not greater than $|a|$. For example, the divisors of 24 are 1, 2, 3, 4, 6, 8, 12, and 24.

Every positive integer a is divisible by the *trivial divisors* 1 and a. The nontrivial divisors of a are the *factors* of a. For example, the factors of 20 are 2, 4, 5, and 10.

Prime and composite numbers

An integer $a > 1$ whose only divisors are the trivial divisors 1 and a is a *prime number* or, more simply, a *prime*. Primes have many special properties and play a critical role in number theory. The first 20 primes, in order, are

2, 3, 5, 7, 11, 13, 17, 19, 23, 29, 31, 37, 41, 43, 47, 53, 59, 61, 67, 71 .

Exercise 31.1-2 asks you to prove that there are infinitely many primes. An integer $a > 1$ that is not prime is a *composite number* or, more simply, a *composite*. For example, 39 is composite because $3 \mid 39$. We call the integer 1 a *unit*, and it is neither prime nor composite. Similarly, the integer 0 and all negative integers are neither prime nor composite.

The division theorem, remainders, and modular equivalence

Given an integer n, we can partition the integers into those that are multiples of n and those that are not multiples of n. Much number theory is based upon refining this partition by classifying the integers that are not multiples of n according to their remainders when divided by n. The following theorem provides the basis for this refinement. We omit the proof (but see, for example, Niven and Zuckerman [345]).

Theorem 31.1 (Division theorem)
For any integer a and any positive integer n, there exist unique integers q and r such that $0 \le r < n$ and $a = qn + r$.   ∎

The value $q = \lfloor a/n \rfloor$ is the *quotient* of the division. The value $r = a \bmod n$ is the *remainder* (or *residue*) of the division, so that $n \mid a$ if and only if $a \bmod n = 0$.

The integers partition into n equivalence classes according to their remainders modulo n. The *equivalence class modulo n* containing an integer a is

$$[a]_n = \{a + kn : k \in \mathbb{Z}\} .$$

For example, $[3]_7 = \{\ldots, -11, -4, 3, 10, 17, \ldots\}$, and $[-4]_7$ and $[10]_7$ also denote this set. With the notation defined on page 64, writing $a \in [b]_n$ is the same as writing $a = b \pmod{n}$. The set of all such equivalence classes is

$$\mathbb{Z}_n = \{[a]_n : 0 \le a \le n - 1\} . \tag{31.1}$$

When you see the definition

$$\mathbb{Z}_n = \{0, 1, \ldots, n - 1\} , \tag{31.2}$$

you should read it as equivalent to equation (31.1) with the understanding that 0 represents $[0]_n$, 1 represents $[1]_n$, and so on. Each class is represented by its smallest nonnegative element. You should keep the underlying equivalence classes in mind, however. For example, if we refer to -1 as a member of $\mathbb{Z}_n$, we are really referring to $[n-1]_n$, since $-1 = n-1 \pmod{n}$.

Common divisors and greatest common divisors

If d is a divisor of a and d is also a divisor of b, then d is a *common divisor* of a and b. For example, the divisors of 30 are 1, 2, 3, 5, 6, 10, 15, and 30, and so the common divisors of 24 and 30 are 1, 2, 3, and 6. Any pair of integers has a common divisor of 1.

An important property of common divisors is that

$$\text{if } d \mid a \text{ and } d \mid b, \text{ then } d \mid (a+b) \text{ and } d \mid (a-b) \,. \tag{31.3}$$

More generally, for any integers x and y,

$$\text{if } d \mid a \text{ and } d \mid b, \text{ then } d \mid (ax+by) \,. \tag{31.4}$$

Also, if $a \mid b$, then either $|a| \le |b|$ or $b = 0$, which implies that

$$\text{if } a \mid b \text{ and } b \mid a, \text{ then } a = \pm b \,. \tag{31.5}$$

The *greatest common divisor* of two integers a and b which are not both 0, denoted by $\gcd(a, b)$, is the largest of the common divisors of a and b. For example, $\gcd(24, 30) = 6$, $\gcd(5, 7) = 1$, and $\gcd(0, 9) = 9$. If a and b are both nonzero, then $\gcd(a, b)$ is an integer between 1 and $\min\{|a|, |b|\}$. We define $\gcd(0, 0)$ to be 0, so that standard properties of the gcd function (such as equation (31.9) below) hold universally.

Exercise 31.1-9 asks you to prove the following elementary properties of the gcd function:

$$\gcd(a, b) = \gcd(b, a) \,, \tag{31.6}$$

$$\gcd(a, b) = \gcd(-a, b) \,, \tag{31.7}$$

$$\gcd(a, b) = \gcd(|a|, |b|) \,, \tag{31.8}$$

$$\gcd(a, 0) = |a| \,, \tag{31.9}$$

$$\gcd(a, ka) = |a| \quad \text{for any } k \in \mathbb{Z} \,. \tag{31.10}$$

The following theorem provides an alternative and useful way to characterize $\gcd(a, b)$.

Theorem 31.2

If a and b are any integers, not both zero, then $\gcd(a, b)$ is the smallest positive element of the set $\{ax + by : x, y \in \mathbb{Z}\}$ of linear combinations of a and b.

Proof Let s be the smallest positive such linear combination of a and b, and let $s = ax + by$ for some $x, y \in \mathbb{Z}$. Let $q = \lfloor a/s \rfloor$. Equation (3.11) on page 64 then implies

$$
\begin{aligned}
a \bmod s &= a - qs \\
&= a - q(ax + by) \\
&= a(1 - qx) + b(-qy) ,
\end{aligned}
$$

so that $a \bmod s$ is a linear combination of a and b as well. Because s is the smallest *positive* such linear combination and $0 \le a \bmod s < s$ (inequality (3.12) on page 64), $a \bmod s$ cannot be positive. Hence, $a \bmod s = 0$. Therefore, we have that $s \mid a$ and, by analogous reasoning, $s \mid b$. Thus, s is a common divisor of a and b, so that $\gcd(a, b) \ge s$. By definition, $\gcd(a, b)$ divides both a and b, and s is defined as a linear combination of a and b. Equation (31.4) therefore implies that $\gcd(a, b) \mid s$. But $\gcd(a, b) \mid s$ and $s > 0$ imply that $\gcd(a, b) \le s$. Combining $\gcd(a, b) \ge s$ and $\gcd(a, b) \le s$ yields $\gcd(a, b) = s$. We conclude that s, the smallest positive linear combination of a and b, is also their greatest common divisor. ∎

Theorem 31.2 engenders three useful corollaries.

Corollary 31.3
For any integers a and b, if $d \mid a$ and $d \mid b$, then $d \mid \gcd(a, b)$.

Proof This corollary follows from equation (31.4) and Theorem 31.2, because $\gcd(a, b)$ is a linear combination of a and b, ∎

Corollary 31.4
For all integers a and b and any nonnegative integer n, we have

$$
\gcd(an, bn) = n \gcd(a, b) .
$$

Proof If $n = 0$, the corollary is trivial. If $n > 0$, then $\gcd(an, bn)$ is the smallest positive element of the set $\{anx + bny : x, y \in \mathbb{Z}\}$, which in turn is n times the smallest positive element of the set $\{ax + by : x, y \in \mathbb{Z}\}$. ∎

Corollary 31.5
For all positive integers n, a, and b, if $n \mid ab$ and $\gcd(a, n) = 1$, then $n \mid b$.

Proof Exercise 31.1-5 asks you to provide the proof. ∎

Relatively prime integers

Two integers a and b are *relatively prime* if their only common divisor is 1, that is, if $\gcd(a, b) = 1$. For example, 8 and 15 are relatively prime, since the divisors of 8 are 1, 2, 4, and 8, and the divisors of 15 are 1, 3, 5, and 15. The following theorem states that if two integers are each relatively prime to an integer p, then their product is relatively prime to p.

Theorem 31.6
For any integers a, b, and p, we have $\gcd(ab, p) = 1$ if and only if $\gcd(a, p) = 1$ and $\gcd(b, p) = 1$ both hold.

Proof If $\gcd(a, p) = 1$ and $\gcd(b, p) = 1$, then it follows from Theorem 31.2 that there exist integers x, y, x', and y' such that

$$ax + py = 1,$$
$$bx' + py' = 1.$$

Multiplying these equations and rearranging gives

$$ab(xx') + p(ybx' + y'ax + pyy') = 1.$$

Since 1 is thus a positive linear combination of ab and p, it is the smallest positive linear combination. Applying Theorem 31.2 implies $\gcd(ab, p) = 1$, completing the proof in this direction.

Conversely, if $\gcd(ab, p) = 1$, then Theorem 31.2 implies that there exist integers x and y such that

$$abx + py = 1.$$

Writing abx as $a(bx)$ and applying Theorem 31.2 again proves that $\gcd(a, p) = 1$. Proving that $\gcd(b, p) = 1$ is similar. ∎

Integers $n_1, n_2, \ldots, n_k$ are *pairwise relatively prime* if $\gcd(n_i, n_j) = 1$ for $1 \leq i < j \leq k$.

Unique prime factorization

An elementary but important fact about divisibility by primes is the following.

Theorem 31.7
For all primes p and all integers a and b, if $p \mid ab$, then $p \mid a$ or $p \mid b$ (or both).

Proof Assume for the purpose of contradiction that $p \mid ab$, but that $p \nmid a$ and $p \nmid b$. Because $p > 1$ and $ab = kp$ for some $k \in \mathbb{Z}$, equation (31.10) gives that $\gcd(ab, p) = p$. We also have that $\gcd(a, p) = 1$ and $\gcd(b, p) = 1$, since the only divisors of p are 1 and p, and we assumed that p divides neither a nor b. Theorem 31.6 then implies that $\gcd(ab, p) = 1$, contradicting $\gcd(ab, p) = p$. This contradiction completes the proof. ∎

A consequence of Theorem 31.7 is that any composite integer can be uniquely factored into a product of primes. Exercise 31.1-11 asks you to provide a proof.

Theorem 31.8 (Unique prime factorization)
There is exactly one way to write any composite integer a as a product of the form

$$a = p_1^{e_1} p_2^{e_2} \cdots p_r^{e_r} \, ,$$

where the p_i are prime, $p_1 < p_2 < \cdots < p_r$, and the e_i are positive integers. ∎

As an example, the unique prime factorization of the number 6000 is $2^4 \cdot 3^1 \cdot 5^3$.

Exercises

31.1-1
Prove that if $a > b > 0$ and $c = a + b$, then $c \bmod a = b$.

31.1-2
Prove that there are infinitely many primes. (*Hint:* Show that none of the primes $p_1, p_2, \ldots, p_k$ divide $(p_1 p_2 \cdots p_k) + 1$.)

31.1-3
Prove that if $a \mid b$ and $b \mid c$, then $a \mid c$.

31.1-4
Prove that if p is prime and $0 < k < p$, then $\gcd(k, p) = 1$.

31.1-5
Prove Corollary 31.5.

31.1-6
Prove that if p is prime and $0 < k < p$, then $p \mid \binom{p}{k}$. Conclude that for all integers a and b and all primes p,

$$(a + b)^p = a^p + b^p \pmod{p} \, .$$

31.1-7
Prove that if a and b are any positive integers such that $a \mid b$, then

$(x \bmod b) \bmod a = x \bmod a$

for any x. Prove, under the same assumptions, that

$x = y \pmod{b}$ implies $x = y \pmod{a}$

for any integers x and y.

31.1-8
For any integer $k > 0$, an integer n is a ***kth power*** if there exists an integer a such that $a^k = n$. Furthermore, $n > 1$ is a ***nontrivial power*** if it is a kth power for some integer $k > 1$. Show how to determine whether a given β-bit integer n is a nontrivial power in time polynomial in β.

31.1-9
Prove equations (31.6)–(31.10).

31.1-10
Show that the gcd operator is associative. That is, prove that for all integers a, b, and c, we have

$$\gcd(a, \gcd(b, c)) = \gcd(\gcd(a, b), c) \, .$$

★ 31.1-11
Prove Theorem 31.8.

31.1-12
Give efficient algorithms for the operations of dividing a β-bit integer by a shorter integer and of taking the remainder of a β-bit integer when divided by a shorter integer. Your algorithms should run in $\Theta(\beta^2)$ time.

31.1-13
Give an efficient algorithm to convert a given β-bit (binary) integer to a decimal representation. Argue that if multiplication or division of integers whose length is at most β takes $M(\beta)$ time, where $M(\beta) = \Omega(\beta)$, then you can convert binary to decimal in $O(M(\beta) \lg \beta)$ time. (*Hint:* Use a divide-and-conquer approach, obtaining the top and bottom halves of the result with separate recursions.)

31.1-14
Professor Marshall sets up n lightbulbs in a row. The lightbulbs all have switches, so that if he presses a bulb, it toggles on if it was off and off if it was on. The lightbulbs all start off. For $i = 1, 2, 3, \ldots, n$, the professor presses bulb $i, 2i, 3i, \ldots$. After the last press, which lightbulbs are on? Prove your answer.

31.2 Greatest common divisor

In this section, we describe Euclid's algorithm for efficiently computing the greatest common divisor of two integers. When we analyze the running time, we'll see a surprising connection with the Fibonacci numbers, which yield a worst-case input for Euclid's algorithm.

We restrict ourselves in this section to nonnegative integers. This restriction is justified by equation (31.8), which states that $\gcd(a, b) = \gcd(|a|, |b|)$.

In principle, for positive integers a and b, their prime factorizations suffice to compute $\gcd(a, b)$. Indeed, if

$$a = p_1^{e_1} p_2^{e_2} \cdots p_r^{e_r} , \tag{31.11}$$
$$b = p_1^{f_1} p_2^{f_2} \cdots p_r^{f_r} , \tag{31.12}$$

with 0 exponents being used to make the set of primes $p_1, p_2, \ldots, p_r$ the same for both a and b, then, as Exercise 31.2-1 asks you to show,

$$\gcd(a, b) = p_1^{\min\{e_1, f_1\}} p_2^{\min\{e_2, f_2\}} \cdots p_r^{\min\{e_r, f_r\}} . \tag{31.13}$$

The best algorithms to date for factoring do not run in polynomial time. Thus, this approach to computing greatest common divisors seems unlikely to yield an efficient algorithm.

Euclid's algorithm for computing greatest common divisors relies on the following theorem.

Theorem 31.9 (GCD recursion theorem)
For any nonnegative integer a and any positive integer b,

$$\gcd(a, b) = \gcd(b, a \bmod b) .$$

Proof We will show that $\gcd(a, b)$ and $\gcd(b, a \bmod b)$ divide each other. Since they are both nonnegative, equation (31.5) then implies that they must be equal.

We first show that $\gcd(a, b) \mid \gcd(b, a \bmod b)$. If we let $d = \gcd(a, b)$, then $d \mid a$ and $d \mid b$. By equation (3.11) on page 64, $a \bmod b = a - qb$, where $q = \lfloor a/b \rfloor$. Since $a \bmod b$ is thus a linear combination of a and b, equation (31.4) implies that $d \mid (a \bmod b)$. Therefore, since $d \mid b$ and $d \mid (a \bmod b)$, Corollary 31.3 implies that $d \mid \gcd(b, a \bmod b)$, that is,

$$\gcd(a, b) \mid \gcd(b, a \bmod b) . \tag{31.14}$$

Showing that $\gcd(b, a \bmod b) \mid \gcd(a, b)$ is almost the same. If we now let $d = \gcd(b, a \bmod b)$, then $d \mid b$ and $d \mid (a \bmod b)$. Since $a = qb + (a \bmod b)$, where $q = \lfloor a/b \rfloor$, we have that a is a linear combination of b and $(a \bmod b)$. By equation (31.4), we conclude that $d \mid a$. Since $d \mid b$ and $d \mid a$, we have that $d \mid \gcd(a, b)$ by Corollary 31.3, so that

$$\gcd(b, a \bmod b) \mid \gcd(a, b) . \tag{31.15}$$

Using equation (31.5) to combine equations (31.14) and (31.15) completes the proof.   ■

Euclid's algorithm

Euclid's *Elements* (circa 300 B.C.E.) describes the following gcd algorithm, although its origin might be even earlier. The recursive procedure EUCLID implements Euclid's algorithm, based directly on Theorem 31.9. The inputs a and b are arbitrary nonnegative integers.

EUCLID(a, b)

1   **if** $b == 0$
2   **return** a
3   **else return** EUCLID$(b, a \bmod b)$

For example, here is how the procedure computes $\gcd(30, 21)$:

$$\begin{aligned}
\text{EUCLID}(30, 21) &= \text{EUCLID}(21, 9) \\
&= \text{EUCLID}(9, 3) \\
&= \text{EUCLID}(3, 0) \\
&= 3 .
\end{aligned}$$

This computation calls EUCLID recursively three times.

The correctness of EUCLID follows from Theorem 31.9 and the property that if the algorithm returns a in line 2, then $b = 0$, so that by equation (31.9), $\gcd(a, b) = \gcd(a, 0) = a$. The algorithm cannot recurse indefinitely, since the second argument strictly decreases in each recursive call and is always nonnegative. Therefore, EUCLID always terminates with the correct answer.

The running time of Euclid's algorithm

Let's analyze the worst-case running time of EUCLID as a function of the size of a and b. The overall running time of EUCLID is proportional to the number of recursive calls it makes. The analysis assumes that $a > b \geq 0$, that is, the first argument is greater than the second argument. Why? If $b = a > 0$, then $a \bmod b = 0$ and the procedure terminates after one recursive call. If $b > a \geq 0$, then the procedure makes just one more recursive call than when $a > b$, because in this case EUCLID(a, b) immediately makes the recursive call EUCLID(b, a), and now the first argument is greater than the second.

Our analysis relies on the Fibonacci numbers F_k, defined by the recurrence equation (3.31) on page 69.

Lemma 31.10
If $a > b \geq 1$ and the call EUCLID(a, b) performs $k \geq 1$ recursive calls, then $a \geq F_{k+2}$ and $b \geq F_{k+1}$.

Proof   The proof proceeds by induction on k. For the base case of the induction, let $k = 1$. Then, $b \geq 1 = F_2$, and since $a > b$, we must have $a \geq 2 = F_3$. Since $b > (a \bmod b)$, in each recursive call the first argument is strictly larger than the second. The assumption that $a > b$ therefore holds for each recursive call.

Assuming inductively that the lemma holds if the procedure makes $k - 1$ recursive calls, we shall prove that the lemma holds for k recursive calls. Since $k > 0$, we have $b > 0$, and EUCLID(a, b) calls EUCLID$(b, a \bmod b)$ recursively, which in turn makes $k - 1$ recursive calls. The inductive hypothesis then implies that $b \geq F_{k+1}$ (thus proving part of the lemma), and $a \bmod b \geq F_k$. We have

$$b + (a \bmod b) = b + (a - b \lfloor a/b \rfloor) \qquad \text{(by equation (3.11))}$$
$$\leq a \,,$$

since $a > b > 0$ implies $\lfloor a/b \rfloor \geq 1$. Thus,

$$a \geq b + (a \bmod b)$$
$$\geq F_{k+1} + F_k$$
$$= F_{k+2} \,. \qquad \blacksquare$$

The following theorem is an immediate corollary of this lemma.

Theorem 31.11 (Lamé's theorem)
For any integer $k \geq 1$, if $a > b \geq 1$ and $b < F_{k+1}$, then the call EUCLID(a, b) makes fewer than k recursive calls. $\blacksquare$

To show that the upper bound of Theorem 31.11 is the best possible, we'll show that the call EUCLID(F_{k+1}, F_k) makes exactly $k - 1$ recursive calls when $k \geq 2$. We use induction on k. For the base case, $k = 2$, and the call EUCLID(F_3, F_2) makes exactly one recursive call, to EUCLID$(1, 0)$. (We have to start at $k = 2$, because when $k = 1$ we do not have $F_2 > F_1$.) For the inductive step, assume that EUCLID(F_k, F_{k-1}) makes exactly $k - 2$ recursive calls. For $k > 2$, we have $F_k > F_{k-1} > 0$ and $F_{k+1} = F_k + F_{k-1}$, and so by Exercise 31.1-1, we have $F_{k+1} \bmod F_k = F_{k-1}$. Because EUCLID$(a, b)$ calls EUCLID$(b, a \bmod b)$ when $b > 0$, the call EUCLID(F_{k+1}, F_k) recurses one time more than the call EUCLID(F_k, F_{k-1}), or exactly $k - 1$ times, which meets the upper bound given by Theorem 31.11.

Since F_k is approximately $\phi^k / \sqrt{5}$, where ϕ is the golden ratio $(1 + \sqrt{5})/2$ defined by equation (3.32) on page 69, the number of recursive calls in EUCLID is $O(\lg b)$. (See Exercise 31.2-5 for a tighter bound.) Therefore, a call of EUCLID on two β-bit numbers performs $O(\beta)$ arithmetic operations and $O(\beta^3)$ bit operations (assuming that multiplication and division of β-bit numbers take $O(\beta^2)$ bit operations). Problem 31-2 asks you to prove an $O(\beta^2)$ bound on the number of bit operations.

The extended form of Euclid's algorithm

By rewriting Euclid's algorithm, we can gain additional useful information. Specifically, let's extend the algorithm to compute the integer coefficients x and y such that

$$d = \gcd(a, b) = ax + by \,, \tag{31.16}$$

where either or both of x and y may be zero or negative. These coefficients will prove useful later for computing modular multiplicative inverses. The procedure EXTENDED-EUCLID takes as input a pair of nonnegative integers and returns a triple of the form (d, x, y) that satisfies equation (31.16). As an example, Figure 31.1 traces out the call EXTENDED-EUCLID$(99, 78)$.

EXTENDED-EUCLID(a, b)

1   **if** $b == 0$
2   **return** $(a, 1, 0)$
3   **else** $(d', x', y') =$ EXTENDED-EUCLID$(b, a \bmod b)$
4       $(d, x, y) = (d', y', x' - \lfloor a/b \rfloor y')$
5   **return** (d, x, y)

The EXTENDED-EUCLID procedure is a variation of the EUCLID procedure. Line 1 is equivalent to the test "$b == 0$" in line 1 of EUCLID. If $b = 0$, then EXTENDED-EUCLID returns not only $d = a$ in line 2, but also the coefficients $x = 1$ and $y = 0$, so that $a = ax + by$. If $b \neq 0$, EXTENDED-EUCLID first computes (d', x', y') such that $d' = \gcd(b, a \bmod b)$ and

$$d' = bx' + (a \bmod b)y' \,. \tag{31.17}$$

As in the EUCLID procedure, we have $d = \gcd(a, b) = d' = \gcd(b, a \bmod b)$. To obtain x and y such that $d = ax + by$, let's rewrite equation (31.17), setting

a	b	$\lfloor a/b \rfloor$	d	x	y
99	78	1	3	−11	14
78	21	3	3	3	−11
21	15	1	3	−2	3
15	6	2	3	1	−2
6	3	2	3	0	1
3	0	—	3	1	0

Figure 31.1 How EXTENDED-EUCLID computes gcd(99, 78). Each line shows one level of the recursion: the values of the inputs a and b, the computed value $\lfloor a/b \rfloor$, and the values d, x, and y returned. The triple (d, x, y) returned becomes the triple (d', x', y') used at the next higher level of recursion. The call EXTENDED-EUCLID(99, 78) returns $(3, -11, 14)$, so that gcd(99, 78) = 3 = $99 \cdot (-11) + 78 \cdot 14$.

$d = d'$ and using equation (3.11):

$$
\begin{aligned}
d &= bx' + (a - b \lfloor a/b \rfloor) y' \\
  &= ay' + b(x' - \lfloor a/b \rfloor y') \,.
\end{aligned}
$$

Thus, choosing $x = y'$ and $y = x' - \lfloor a/b \rfloor y'$ satisfies the equation $d = ax + by$, thereby proving the correctness of EXTENDED-EUCLID.

Since the number of recursive calls made in EUCLID is equal to the number of recursive calls made in EXTENDED-EUCLID, the running times of EUCLID and EXTENDED-EUCLID are the same, to within a constant factor. That is, for $a > b > 0$, the number of recursive calls is $O(\lg b)$.

Exercises

31.2-1
Prove that equations (31.11) and (31.12) imply equation (31.13).

31.2-2
Compute the values (d, x, y) that the call EXTENDED-EUCLID(899, 493) returns.

31.2-3
Prove that for all integers a, k, and n,

$$
\gcd(a, n) = \gcd(a + kn, n) \,. \tag{31.18}
$$

Use equation (31.18) to show that $a = 1 \pmod{n}$ implies $\gcd(a, n) = 1$.

31.2-4
Rewrite EUCLID in an iterative form that uses only a constant amount of memory (that is, stores only a constant number of integer values).

31.2-5
If $a > b \geq 0$, show that the call EUCLID(a, b) makes at most $1 + \log_\phi b$ recursive calls. Improve this bound to $1 + \log_\phi(b/\gcd(a, b))$.

31.2-6
What does EXTENDED-EUCLID(F_{k+1}, F_k) return? Prove your answer correct.

31.2-7
Define the gcd function for more than two arguments by the recursive equation $\gcd(a_0, a_1, \ldots, a_n) = \gcd(a_0, \gcd(a_1, a_2, \ldots, a_n))$. Show that the gcd function returns the same answer independent of the order in which its arguments are specified. Also show how to find integers $x_0, x_1, \ldots, x_n$ such that $\gcd(a_0, a_1, \ldots, a_n) = a_0 x_0 + a_1 x_1 + \cdots + a_n x_n$. Show that the number of divisions performed by your algorithm is $O(n + \lg(\max\{a_0, a_1, \ldots, a_n\}))$.

31.2-8
The *least common multiple* $\text{lcm}(a_1, a_2, \ldots, a_n)$ of integers $a_1, a_2, \ldots, a_n$ is the smallest nonnegative integer that is a multiple of each a_i. Show how to compute $\text{lcm}(a_1, a_2, \ldots, a_n)$ efficiently using the (two-argument) gcd operation as a subroutine.

31.2-9
Prove that n_1, n_2, n_3, and n_4 are pairwise relatively prime if and only if

$$\gcd(n_1 n_2, n_3 n_4) = \gcd(n_1 n_3, n_2 n_4) = 1 .$$

More generally, show that $n_1, n_2, \ldots, n_k$ are pairwise relatively prime if and only if a set of $\lceil \lg k \rceil$ pairs of numbers derived from the n_i are relatively prime.

31.3   Modular arithmetic

Informally, you can think of modular arithmetic as arithmetic as usual over the integers, except that when working modulo n, then every result x is replaced by the element of $\{0, 1, \ldots, n - 1\}$ that is equivalent to x, modulo n (so that x is replaced by $x \bmod n$). This informal model suffices if you stick to the operations of addition, subtraction, and multiplication. A more formal model for modular arithmetic, which follows, is best described within the framework of group theory.

Finite groups

A *group* $(S, \oplus)$ is a set S together with a binary operation $\oplus$ defined on S for which the following properties hold:

1. **Closure:** For all $a, b \in S$, we have $a \oplus b \in S$.

2. **Identity:** There exists an element $e \in S$, called the *identity* of the group, such that $e \oplus a = a \oplus e = a$ for all $a \in S$.

3. **Associativity:** For all $a, b, c \in S$, we have $(a \oplus b) \oplus c = a \oplus (b \oplus c)$.

4. **Inverses:** For each $a \in S$, there exists a unique element $b \in S$, called the *inverse* of a, such that $a \oplus b = b \oplus a = e$.

As an example, consider the familiar group $(\mathbb{Z}, +)$ of the integers $\mathbb{Z}$ under the operation of addition: 0 is the identity, and the inverse of a is $-a$. An *abelian group* $(S, \oplus)$ satisfies the *commutative law* $a \oplus b = b \oplus a$ for all $a, b \in S$. The *size* of group $(S, \oplus)$ is $|S|$, and if $|S| < \infty$, then $(S, \oplus)$ is a *finite group*.

The groups defined by modular addition and multiplication

We can form two finite abelian groups by using addition and multiplication modulo n, where n is a positive integer. These groups are based on the equivalence classes of the integers modulo n, defined in Section 31.1.

To define a group on $\mathbb{Z}_n$, we need suitable binary operations, which we obtain by redefining the ordinary operations of addition and multiplication. We can define addition and multiplication operations for $\mathbb{Z}_n$, because the equivalence class of two integers uniquely determines the equivalence class of their sum or product. That is, if $a = a' \pmod{n}$ and $b = b' \pmod{n}$, then

$$a + b = a' + b' \pmod{n},$$
$$ab = a'b' \pmod{n}.$$

Thus, we define addition and multiplication modulo n, denoted $+_n$ and $\cdot_n$, by

$$[a]_n +_n [b]_n = [a + b]_n, \tag{31.19}$$
$$[a]_n \cdot_n [b]_n = [ab]_n.$$

(We can define subtraction similarly on $\mathbb{Z}_n$ by $[a]_n -_n [b]_n = [a - b]_n$, but division is more complicated, as we'll see.) These facts justify the common and convenient practice of using the smallest nonnegative element of each equivalence class as its representative when performing computations in $\mathbb{Z}_n$. We add, subtract, and multiply as usual on the representatives, but we replace each result x by the representative of its class, that is, by $x \bmod n$.

$+_6$	0	1	2	3	4	5
0	0	1	2	3	4	5
1	1	2	3	4	5	0
2	2	3	4	5	0	1
3	3	4	5	0	1	2
4	4	5	0	1	2	3
5	5	0	1	2	3	4

$\cdot_{15}$	1	2	4	7	8	11	13	14
1	1	2	4	7	8	11	13	14
2	2	4	8	14	1	7	11	13
4	4	8	1	13	2	14	7	11
7	7	14	13	4	11	2	1	8
8	8	1	2	11	4	13	14	7
11	11	7	14	2	13	1	8	4
13	13	11	7	1	14	8	4	2
14	14	13	11	8	7	4	2	1

(a)   (b)

Figure 31.2   Two finite groups. Equivalence classes are denoted by their representative elements. **(a)** The group $(\mathbb{Z}_6, +_6)$. **(b)** The group $(\mathbb{Z}_{15}^*, \cdot_{15})$.

Using this definition of addition modulo n, we define the *additive group modulo n* as $(\mathbb{Z}_n, +_n)$. The size of the additive group modulo n is $|\mathbb{Z}_n| = n$. Figure 31.2(a) gives the operation table for the group $(\mathbb{Z}_6, +_6)$.

Theorem 31.12
The system $(\mathbb{Z}_n, +_n)$ is a finite abelian group.

Proof   Equation (31.19) shows that $(\mathbb{Z}_n, +_n)$ is closed. Associativity and commutativity of $+_n$ follow from the associativity and commutativity of $+$:

$$([a]_n +_n [b]_n) +_n [c]_n = [a+b]_n +_n [c]_n$$
$$= [(a+b)+c]_n$$
$$= [a+(b+c)]_n$$
$$= [a]_n +_n [b+c]_n$$
$$= [a]_n +_n ([b]_n +_n [c]_n) ,$$

$$[a]_n +_n [b]_n = [a+b]_n$$
$$= [b+a]_n$$
$$= [b]_n +_n [a]_n .$$

The identity element of $(\mathbb{Z}_n, +_n)$ is 0 (that is, $[0]_n$). The (additive) inverse of an element a (that is, of $[a]_n$) is the element $-a$ (that is, $[-a]_n$ or $[n-a]_n$), since $[a]_n +_n [-a]_n = [a-a]_n = [0]_n$.   ■

Using the definition of multiplication modulo n, we define the *multiplicative group modulo n* as $(\mathbb{Z}_n^*, \cdot_n)$. The elements of this group are the set $\mathbb{Z}_n^*$ of elements in $\mathbb{Z}_n$ that are relatively prime to n, so that each one has a unique inverse, modulo n:

$$\mathbb{Z}_n^* = \{[a]_n \in \mathbb{Z}_n : \gcd(a, n) = 1\} \ .$$

To see that $\mathbb{Z}_n^*$ is well defined, note that for $0 \le a < n$, we have $a = (a + kn)$ (mod n) for all integers k. By Exercise 31.2-3, therefore, $\gcd(a, n) = 1$ implies $\gcd(a + kn, n) = 1$ for all integers k. Since $[a]_n = \{a + kn : k \in \mathbb{Z}\}$, the set $\mathbb{Z}_n^*$ is well defined. An example of such a group is

$$\mathbb{Z}_{15}^* = \{1, 2, 4, 7, 8, 11, 13, 14\} \ ,$$

where the group operation is multiplication modulo 15. (We have denoted an element $[a]_{15}$ as a, and thus, for example, we denote $[7]_{15}$ as 7.) Figure 31.2(b) shows the group $(\mathbb{Z}_{15}^*, \cdot_{15})$. For example, $8 \cdot 11 = 13$ (mod 15), working in $\mathbb{Z}_{15}^*$. The identity for this group is 1.

Theorem 31.13
The system $(\mathbb{Z}_n^*, \cdot_n)$ is a finite abelian group.

Proof Theorem 31.6 implies that $(\mathbb{Z}_n^*, \cdot_n)$ is closed. Associativity and commutativity can be proved for $\cdot_n$ as they were for $+_n$ in the proof of Theorem 31.12. The identity element is $[1]_n$. To show the existence of inverses, let a be an element of $\mathbb{Z}_n^*$ and let (d, x, y) be returned by EXTENDED-EUCLID(a, n). Then we have $d = 1$, since $a \in \mathbb{Z}_n^*$, and

$$ax + ny = 1 \ , \tag{31.20}$$

or equivalently,

$$ax = 1 \pmod{n} \ .$$

Thus $[x]_n$ is a multiplicative inverse of $[a]_n$, modulo n. Furthermore, we claim that $[x]_n \in \mathbb{Z}_n^*$. To see why, equation (31.20) demonstrates that the smallest positive linear combination of x and n must be 1. Therefore, Theorem 31.2 implies that $\gcd(x, n) = 1$. We defer the proof that inverses are uniquely defined until Corollary 31.26 in Section 31.4. ∎

As an example of computing multiplicative inverses, suppose that $a = 5$ and $n = 11$. Then EXTENDED-EUCLID(a, n) returns $(d, x, y) = (1, -2, 1)$, so that $1 = 5 \cdot (-2) + 11 \cdot 1$. Thus, $[-2]_{11}$ (i.e., $[9]_{11}$) is the multiplicative inverse of $[5]_{11}$.

When working with the groups $(\mathbb{Z}_n, +_n)$ and $(\mathbb{Z}_n^*, \cdot_n)$ in the remainder of this chapter, we follow the convenient practice of denoting equivalence classes by their representative elements and denoting the operations $+_n$ and $\cdot_n$ by the usual arithmetic notations $+$ and $\cdot$ (or juxtaposition, so that $ab = a \cdot b$) respectively. Furthermore, equivalences modulo n may also be interpreted as equations in $\mathbb{Z}_n$. For example, the following two statements are equivalent:

$$ax = b \pmod{n}$$

and

$$[a]_n \cdot_n [x]_n = [b]_n .$$

As a further convenience, we sometimes refer to a group $(S, \oplus)$ merely as S when the operation $\oplus$ is understood from context. We may thus refer to the groups $(\mathbb{Z}_n, +_n)$ and $(\mathbb{Z}_n^*, \cdot_n)$ as just $\mathbb{Z}_n$ and $\mathbb{Z}_n^*$, respectively.

We denote the (multiplicative) inverse of an element a by $(a^{-1} \bmod n)$. Division in $\mathbb{Z}_n^*$ is defined by the equation $a/b = ab^{-1} \pmod{n}$. For example, in $\mathbb{Z}_{15}^*$ we have that $7^{-1} = 13 \pmod{15}$, since $7 \cdot 13 = 91 = 1 \pmod{15}$, so that $2/7 = 2 \cdot 13 = 11 \pmod{15}$.

The size of $\mathbb{Z}_n^*$ is denoted $\phi(n)$. This function, known as *Euler's phi function*, satisfies the equation

$$\phi(n) = n \prod_{p \text{ prime such that } p \mid n} \left(1 - \frac{1}{p}\right) , \tag{31.21}$$

so that p runs over all the primes dividing n (including n itself, if n is prime). We won't prove this formula here. Intuitively, begin with a list of the n remainders $\{0, 1, \ldots, n - 1\}$ and then, for each prime p that divides n, cross out every multiple of p in the list. For example, since the prime divisors of 45 are 3 and 5,

$$\begin{aligned}
\phi(45) &= 45 \left(1 - \frac{1}{3}\right)\left(1 - \frac{1}{5}\right) \\
&= 45 \left(\frac{2}{3}\right)\left(\frac{4}{5}\right) \\
&= 24 .
\end{aligned}$$

If p is prime, then $\mathbb{Z}_p^* = \{1, 2, \ldots, p - 1\}$, and

$$\begin{aligned}
\phi(p) &= p \left(1 - \frac{1}{p}\right) \\
&= p - 1 .
\end{aligned} \tag{31.22}$$

If n is composite, then $\phi(n) < n - 1$, although it can be shown that

$$\phi(n) > \frac{n}{e^\gamma \ln \ln n + 3/\ln \ln n} \tag{31.23}$$

for $n \geq 3$, where $\gamma = 0.5772156649\ldots$ is *Euler's constant*. A somewhat simpler (but looser) lower bound for $n > 5$ is

$$\phi(n) > \frac{n}{6 \ln \ln n} . \tag{31.24}$$

The lower bound (31.23) is essentially the best possible, since

$$\liminf_{n \to \infty} \frac{\phi(n)}{n / \ln \ln n} = e^{-\gamma} . \tag{31.25}$$

Subgroups

If $(S, \oplus)$ is a group, $S' \subseteq S$, and $(S', \oplus)$ is also a group, then $(S', \oplus)$ is a *subgroup* of $(S, \oplus)$. For example, the even integers form a subgroup of the integers under the operation of addition. The following theorem, whose proof we leave as Exercise 31.3-3, provides a useful tool for recognizing subgroups.

Theorem 31.14 (A nonempty closed subset of a finite group is a subgroup)
If $(S, \oplus)$ is a finite group and S' is any nonempty subset of S such that $a \oplus b \in S'$ for all $a, b \in S'$, then $(S', \oplus)$ is a subgroup of $(S, \oplus)$. ∎

For example, the set $\{0, 2, 4, 6\}$ forms a subgroup of $\mathbb{Z}_8$, since it is nonempty and closed under the operation $+$ (that is, it is closed under $+_8$).

The following theorem, whose proof is omitted, provides an extremely useful constraint on the size of a subgroup.

Theorem 31.15 (Lagrange's theorem)
If $(S, \oplus)$ is a finite group and $(S', \oplus)$ is a subgroup of $(S, \oplus)$, then $|S'|$ is a divisor of $|S|$. ∎

A subgroup S' of a group S is a *proper* subgroup if $S' \neq S$. We'll use the following corollary in the analysis in Section 31.8 of the Miller-Rabin primality test procedure.

Corollary 31.16
If S' is a proper subgroup of a finite group S, then $|S'| \leq |S|/2$. ∎

Subgroups generated by an element

Theorem 31.14 affords us a straightforward way to produce a subgroup of a finite group $(S, \oplus)$: choose an element a and take all elements that can be generated from a using the group operation. Specifically, define $a^{(k)}$ for $k \geq 1$ by

$$a^{(k)} = \bigoplus_{i=1}^{k} a = \underbrace{a \oplus a \oplus \cdots \oplus a}_{k} \ .$$

For example, taking $a = 2$ in the group $\mathbb{Z}_6$ yields the sequence

$$a^{(1)}, a^{(2)}, a^{(3)}, \ldots = 2, 4, 0, 2, 4, 0, 2, 4, 0, \ldots \ .$$

We have $a^{(k)} = ka \bmod n$ in the group $\mathbb{Z}_n$, and $a^{(k)} = a^k \bmod n$ in the group $\mathbb{Z}_n^*$. We define the *subgroup generated by a*, denoted $\langle a \rangle$ or $(\langle a \rangle, \oplus)$, by

$$\langle a \rangle = \{a^{(k)} : k \geq 1\} \ .$$

We say that a *generates* the subgroup $\langle a \rangle$ or that a is a *generator* of $\langle a \rangle$. Since S is finite, $\langle a \rangle$ is a finite subset of S, possibly including all of S. Since the associativity of $\oplus$ implies

$$a^{(i)} \oplus a^{(j)} = a^{(i+j)} \ ,$$

$\langle a \rangle$ is closed and therefore, by Theorem 31.14, $\langle a \rangle$ is a subgroup of S. For example, in $\mathbb{Z}_6$, we have

$$\langle 0 \rangle = \{0\} \ ,$$
$$\langle 1 \rangle = \{0, 1, 2, 3, 4, 5\} \ ,$$
$$\langle 2 \rangle = \{0, 2, 4\} \ .$$

Similarly, in $\mathbb{Z}_7^*$, we have

$$\langle 1 \rangle = \{1\} \ ,$$
$$\langle 2 \rangle = \{1, 2, 4\} \ ,$$
$$\langle 3 \rangle = \{1, 2, 3, 4, 5, 6\} \ .$$

The *order* of a (in the group S), denoted $\mathrm{ord}(a)$, is defined as the smallest positive integer t such that $a^{(t)} = e$. (Recall that $e \in S$ is the group identity.)

Theorem 31.17
For any finite group $(S, \oplus)$ and any $a \in S$, the order of a is equal to the size of the subgroup it generates, or $\mathrm{ord}(a) = |\langle a \rangle|$.

Proof Let $t = \mathrm{ord}(a)$. Since $a^{(t)} = e$ and $a^{(t+k)} = a^{(t)} \oplus a^{(k)} = a^{(k)}$ for $k \geq 1$, if $i > t$, then $a^{(i)} = a^{(j)}$ for some $j < i$. Therefore, as we generate elements by a, we see no new elements after $a^{(t)}$. Thus, $\langle a \rangle = \{a^{(1)}, a^{(2)}, \ldots, a^{(t)}\}$, and so $|\langle a \rangle| \leq t$. To show that $|\langle a \rangle| \geq t$, we show that each element of the sequence $a^{(1)}, a^{(2)}, \ldots, a^{(t)}$ is distinct. Suppose for the purpose of contradiction that $a^{(i)} = a^{(j)}$ for some i and j satisfying $1 \leq i < j \leq t$. Then, $a^{(i+k)} = a^{(j+k)}$ for

$k \geq 0$. But this equation implies that $a^{(i+(t-j))} = a^{(j+(t-j))} = e$, a contradiction, since $i + (t - j) < t$ but t is the least positive value such that $a^{(t)} = e$. Therefore, each element of the sequence $a^{(1)}, a^{(2)}, \ldots, a^{(t)}$ is distinct, and $|\langle a \rangle| \geq t$. We conclude that $\mathrm{ord}(a) = |\langle a \rangle|$. ∎

Corollary 31.18
The sequence $a^{(1)}, a^{(2)}, \ldots$ is periodic with period $t = \mathrm{ord}(a)$, that is, $a^{(i)} = a^{(j)}$ if and only if $i = j \pmod{t}$. ∎

Consistent with the above corollary, we define $a^{(0)}$ as e and $a^{(i)}$ as $a^{(i \bmod t)}$, where $t = \mathrm{ord}(a)$, for all integers i.

Corollary 31.19
If $(S, \oplus)$ is a finite group with identity e, then for all $a \in S$,

$$a^{(|S|)} = e \ .$$

Proof Lagrange's theorem (Theorem 31.15) implies that $\mathrm{ord}(a) \mid |S|$, and so $|S| = 0 \pmod{t}$, where $t = \mathrm{ord}(a)$. Therefore, $a^{(|S|)} = a^{(0)} = e$. ∎

Exercises

31.3-1
Draw the group operation tables for the groups $(\mathbb{Z}_4, +_4)$ and $(\mathbb{Z}_5^*, \cdot_5)$. Show that these groups are isomorphic by exhibiting a one-to-one correspondence f between $\mathbb{Z}_4$ and $\mathbb{Z}_5^*$ such that $a + b = c \pmod{4}$ if and only if $f(a) \cdot f(b) = f(c) \pmod{5}$.

31.3-2
List all subgroups of $\mathbb{Z}_9$ and of $\mathbb{Z}_{13}^*$.

31.3-3
Prove Theorem 31.14.

31.3-4
Show that if p is prime and e is a positive integer, then

$$\phi(p^e) = p^{e-1}(p - 1) \ .$$

31.3-5
Show that for any integer $n > 1$ and for any $a \in \mathbb{Z}_n^*$, the function $f_a : \mathbb{Z}_n^* \to \mathbb{Z}_n^*$ defined by $f_a(x) = ax \bmod n$ is a permutation of $\mathbb{Z}_n^*$.

31.4   Solving modular linear equations

We now consider the problem of finding solutions to the equation

$$ax = b \pmod{n},\tag{31.26}$$

where $a > 0$ and $n > 0$. This problem has several applications. For example, we'll use it in Section 31.7 as part of the procedure to find keys in the RSA public-key cryptosystem. We assume that a, b, and n are given, and we wish to find all values of x, modulo n, that satisfy equation (31.26). The equation may have zero, one, or more than one such solution.

Let $\langle a \rangle$ denote the subgroup of $\mathbb{Z}_n$ generated by a. Since $\langle a \rangle = \{a^{(x)} : x > 0\} = \{ax \bmod n : x > 0\}$, equation (31.26) has a solution if and only if $[b] \in \langle a \rangle$. Lagrange's theorem (Theorem 31.15) tells us that $|\langle a \rangle|$ must be a divisor of n. The following theorem gives us a precise characterization of $\langle a \rangle$.

Theorem 31.20
For any positive integers a and n, if $d = \gcd(a, n)$, then we have

$$\langle a \rangle = \langle d \rangle$$
$$= \{0, d, 2d, \ldots, ((n/d) - 1)d\}$$

in $\mathbb{Z}_n$, and thus

$$|\langle a \rangle| = n/d .$$

Proof   We begin by showing that $d \in \langle a \rangle$. Recall that EXTENDED-EUCLID(a, n) returns a triple (d, x, y) such that $ax + ny = d$. Thus, $ax = d \pmod{n}$, so that $d \in \langle a \rangle$. In other words, d is a multiple of a in $\mathbb{Z}_n$.

Since $d \in \langle a \rangle$, it follows that every multiple of d belongs to $\langle a \rangle$, because any multiple of a multiple of a is itself a multiple of a. Thus, $\langle a \rangle$ contains every element in $\{0, d, 2d, \ldots, ((n/d) - 1)d\}$. That is, $\langle d \rangle \subseteq \langle a \rangle$.

We now show that $\langle a \rangle \subseteq \langle d \rangle$. If $m \in \langle a \rangle$, then $m = ax \bmod n$ for some integer x, and so $m = ax + ny$ for some integer y. Because $d = \gcd(a, n)$, we know that $d \mid a$ and $d \mid n$, and so $d \mid m$ by equation (31.4). Therefore, $m \in \langle d \rangle$.

Combining these results, we have that $\langle a \rangle = \langle d \rangle$. To see that $|\langle a \rangle| = n/d$, observe that there are exactly n/d multiples of d between 0 and $n - 1$, inclusive. ∎

Corollary 31.21
The equation $ax = b \pmod{n}$ is solvable for the unknown x if and only if $d \mid b$, where $d = \gcd(a, n)$.

Proof The equation $ax = b \pmod{n}$ is solvable if and only if $[b] \in \langle a \rangle$, which is the same as saying

$$(b \bmod n) \in \{0, d, 2d, \ldots, ((n/d) - 1)d\} \ ,$$

by Theorem 31.20. If $0 \le b < n$, then $b \in \langle a \rangle$ if and only if $d \mid b$, since the members of $\langle a \rangle$ are precisely the multiples of d. If $b < 0$ or $b \ge n$, the corollary then follows from the observation that $d \mid b$ if and only if $d \mid (b \bmod n)$, since b and $b \bmod n$ differ by a multiple of n, which is itself a multiple of d. ∎

Corollary 31.22
The equation $ax = b \pmod{n}$ either has d distinct solutions modulo n, where $d = \gcd(a, n)$, or it has no solutions.

Proof If $ax = b \pmod{n}$ has a solution, then $b \in \langle a \rangle$. By Theorem 31.17, $\text{ord}(a) = |\langle a \rangle|$, and so Corollary 31.18 and Theorem 31.20 imply that the sequence $ai \bmod n$, for $i = 0, 1, \ldots$, is periodic with period $|\langle a \rangle| = n/d$. If $b \in \langle a \rangle$, then b appears exactly d times in the sequence $ai \bmod n$, for $i = 0, 1, \ldots, n - 1$, since the length-(n/d) block of values $\langle a \rangle$ repeats exactly d times as i increases from 0 to $n-1$. The indices x of the d positions for which $ax \bmod n = b$ are the solutions of the equation $ax = b \pmod{n}$. ∎

Theorem 31.23
Let $d = \gcd(a, n)$, and suppose that $d = ax' + ny'$ for some integers x' and y' (for example, as computed by EXTENDED-EUCLID). If $d \mid b$, then the equation $ax = b \pmod{n}$ has as one of its solutions the value x_0, where

$$x_0 = x'(b/d) \bmod n \ .$$

Proof We have

$$
\begin{aligned}
ax_0 &= ax'(b/d) &&\pmod{n} \\
&= d(b/d) &&\pmod{n} &&\text{(because } ax' = d \pmod{n}) \\
&= b &&\pmod{n} \ ,
\end{aligned}
$$

and thus x_0 is a solution to $ax = b \pmod{n}$. ∎

Theorem 31.24
Suppose that the equation $ax = b \pmod{n}$ is solvable (that is, $d \mid b$, where $d = \gcd(a, n)$) and that x_0 is any solution to this equation. Then, this equation has exactly d distinct solutions, modulo n, given by $x_i = x_0 + i(n/d)$ for $i = 0, 1, \ldots, d - 1$.

Proof Because $n/d > 0$ and $0 \le i(n/d) < n$ for $i = 0, 1, \ldots, d - 1$, the values $x_0, x_1, \ldots, x_{d-1}$ are all distinct, modulo n. Since x_0 is a solution of $ax = b$ (mod n), we have $ax_0 \bmod n = b$ (mod n). Thus, for $i = 0, 1, \ldots, d - 1$, we have

$$
\begin{aligned}
ax_i \bmod n &= a(x_0 + in/d) \bmod n \\
&= (ax_0 + ain/d) \bmod n \\
&= ax_0 \bmod n \quad \text{(because } d \mid a \text{ implies that } ain/d \text{ is a multiple of } n) \\
&= b \pmod{n} ,
\end{aligned}
$$

and hence $ax_i = b$ (mod n), making x_i a solution, too. By Corollary 31.22, the equation $ax = b$ (mod n) has exactly d solutions, so that $x_0, x_1, \ldots, x_{d-1}$ must be all of them. ∎

We have now developed the mathematics needed to solve the equation $ax = b$ (mod n). The procedure MODULAR-LINEAR-EQUATION-SOLVER prints all solutions to this equation. The inputs a and n are arbitrary positive integers, and b is an arbitrary integer.

MODULAR-LINEAR-EQUATION-SOLVER(a, b, n)

1 $(d, x', y') = $ EXTENDED-EUCLID(a, n)
2 **if** $d \mid b$
3      $x_0 = x'(b/d) \bmod n$
4   **for** $i = 0$ **to** $d - 1$
5   print $(x_0 + i(n/d)) \bmod n$
6 **else** print "no solutions"

As an example of the operation of MODULAR-LINEAR-EQUATION-SOLVER, consider the equation $14x = 30$ (mod 100) (and thus $a = 14$, $b = 30$, and $n = 100$). Calling EXTENDED-EUCLID in line 1 gives $(d, x', y') = (2, -7, 1)$. Since $2 \mid 30$, lines 3–5 execute. Line 3 computes $x_0 = (-7)(15) \bmod 100 = 95$. The **for** loop of lines 4–5 prints the two solutions, 95 and 45.

The procedure MODULAR-LINEAR-EQUATION-SOLVER works as follows. The call to EXTENDED-EUCLID in line 1 returns a triple (d, x', y') such that $d = \gcd(a, n)$ and $d = ax' + ny'$. Therefore, x' is a solution to the equation $ax' = d$ (mod n). If d does not divide b, then the equation $ax = b$ (mod n) has no solution, by Corollary 31.21. Line 2 checks to see whether $d \mid b$, and if not, line 6 reports that there are no solutions. Otherwise, line 3 computes a solution x_0 to $ax = b$ (mod n), as Theorem 31.23 suggests. Given one solution, Theorem 31.24 states that adding multiples of (n/d), modulo n, yields the other

$d - 1$ solutions. The **for** loop of lines 4–5 prints out all d solutions, beginning with x_0 and spaced n/d apart, modulo n.

MODULAR-LINEAR-EQUATION-SOLVER performs $O(\lg n + \gcd(a, n))$ arithmetic operations, since EXTENDED-EUCLID performs $O(\lg n)$ arithmetic operations, and each iteration of the **for** loop of lines 4–5 performs a constant number of arithmetic operations.

The following corollaries of Theorem 31.24 give specializations of particular interest.

Corollary 31.25
For any $n > 1$, if $\gcd(a, n) = 1$, then the equation $ax = b \pmod{n}$ has a unique solution, modulo n. ∎

If $b = 1$, a common case of considerable interest, the x that solves the equation is a *multiplicative inverse* of a, modulo n.

Corollary 31.26
For any $n > 1$, if $\gcd(a, n) = 1$, then the equation $ax = 1 \pmod{n}$ has a unique solution, modulo n. Otherwise, it has no solution. ∎

Thanks to Corollary 31.26, the notation $a^{-1} \bmod n$ refers to *the* multiplicative inverse of a, modulo n, when a and n are relatively prime. If $\gcd(a, n) = 1$, then the unique solution to the equation $ax = 1 \pmod{n}$ is the integer x returned by EXTENDED-EUCLID, since the equation

$$\gcd(a, n) = 1 = ax + ny$$

implies $ax = 1 \pmod{n}$. Thus, EXTENDED-EUCLID can compute $a^{-1} \bmod n$ efficiently.

Exercises

31.4-1
Find all solutions to the equation $35x = 10 \pmod{50}$.

31.4-2
Prove that the equation $ax = ay \pmod{n}$ implies $x = y \pmod{n}$ whenever $\gcd(a, n) = 1$. Show that the condition $\gcd(a, n) = 1$ is necessary by supplying a counterexample with $\gcd(a, n) > 1$.

31.4-3

Consider the following change to line 3 of the procedure MODULAR-LINEAR-EQUATION-SOLVER:

3        $x_0 = x'(b/d) \bmod (n/d)$

With this change, will the procedure still work? Explain why or why not.

★ ***31.4-4***

Let p be prime and $f(x) = (f_0 + f_1 x + \cdots + f_t x^t) \pmod{p}$ be a polynomial of degree t, with coefficients f_i drawn from $\mathbb{Z}_p$. We say that $a \in \mathbb{Z}_p$ is a ***zero*** of f if $f(a) = 0 \pmod{p}$. Prove that if a is a zero of f, then $f(x) = (x - a)g(x) \pmod{p}$ for some polynomial $g(x)$ of degree $t - 1$. Prove by induction on t that if p is prime, then a polynomial $f(x)$ of degree t can have at most t distinct zeros modulo p.

31.5   The Chinese remainder theorem

Around 100 C.E., the Chinese mathematician Sun-Tsŭ solved the problem of finding those integers x that leave remainders $2, 3$, and 2 when divided by $3, 5$, and 7 respectively. One such solution is $x = 23$, and all solutions are of the form $23 + 105k$ for arbitrary integers k. The "Chinese remainder theorem" provides a correspondence between a system of equations modulo a set of pairwise relatively prime moduli (for example, $3, 5$, and 7) and an equation modulo their product (for example, 105).

The Chinese remainder theorem has two major applications. Let the integer n be factored as $n = n_1 n_2 \cdots n_k$, where the factors n_i are pairwise relatively prime. First, the Chinese remainder theorem is a descriptive "structure theorem" that describes the structure of $\mathbb{Z}_n$ as identical to that of the Cartesian product $\mathbb{Z}_{n_1} \times \mathbb{Z}_{n_2} \times \cdots \times \mathbb{Z}_{n_k}$ with componentwise addition and multiplication modulo n_i in the ith component. Second, this description helps in designing efficient algorithms, since working in each of the systems $\mathbb{Z}_{n_i}$ can be more efficient (in terms of bit operations) than working modulo n.

Theorem 31.27 (Chinese remainder theorem)

Let $n = n_1 n_2 \cdots n_k$, where the n_i are pairwise relatively prime. Consider the correspondence

$$a \leftrightarrow (a_1, a_2, \ldots, a_k) \,, \qquad\qquad (31.27)$$

where $a \in \mathbb{Z}_n$, $a_i \in \mathbb{Z}_{n_i}$, and

$a_i = a \bmod n_i$

for $i = 1, 2, \ldots, k$. Then, mapping (31.27) is a one-to-one mapping (bijection) between $\mathbb{Z}_n$ and the Cartesian product $\mathbb{Z}_{n_1} \times \mathbb{Z}_{n_2} \times \cdots \times \mathbb{Z}_{n_k}$. Operations performed on the elements of $\mathbb{Z}_n$ can be equivalently performed on the corresponding k-tuples by performing the operations independently in each coordinate position in the appropriate system. That is, if

$$a \leftrightarrow (a_1, a_2, \ldots, a_k) \,,$$
$$b \leftrightarrow (b_1, b_2, \ldots, b_k) \,,$$

then

$$(a + b) \bmod n \; \leftrightarrow \; ((a_1 + b_1) \bmod n_1, \ldots, (a_k + b_k) \bmod n_k) \,, \qquad (31.28)$$

$$(a - b) \bmod n \; \leftrightarrow \; ((a_1 - b_1) \bmod n_1, \ldots, (a_k - b_k) \bmod n_k) \,, \qquad (31.29)$$

$$(ab) \bmod n \quad \leftrightarrow \; (a_1 b_1 \bmod n_1, \ldots, a_k b_k \bmod n_k) \,. \qquad (31.30)$$

Proof   Let's see how to translate between the two representations. Going from a to $(a_1, a_2, \ldots, a_k)$ requires only k "mod" operations. The reverse—computing a from inputs $(a_1, a_2, \ldots, a_k)$—is only slightly more complicated.

We begin by defining $m_i = n/n_i$ for $i = 1, 2, \ldots, k$. Thus, m_i is the product of all of the n_j's other than n_i: $m_i = n_1 n_2 \cdots n_{i-1} n_{i+1} \cdots n_k$. We next define

$$c_i = m_i (m_i^{-1} \bmod n_i) \qquad (31.31)$$

for $i = 1, 2, \ldots, k$. Equation (31.31) is well defined: since m_i and n_i are relatively prime (by Theorem 31.6), Corollary 31.26 guarantees that $m_i^{-1} \bmod n_i$ exists. Here is how to compute a as a function of the a_i and c_i:

$$a = (a_1 c_1 + a_2 c_2 + \cdots + a_k c_k) \pmod{n} \,. \qquad (31.32)$$

We now show that equation (31.32) ensures that $a = a_i \pmod{n_i}$ for $i = 1, 2, \ldots, k$. If $j \neq i$, then $m_j = 0 \pmod{n_i}$, which implies that $c_j = m_j = 0 \pmod{n_i}$. Note also that $c_i = 1 \pmod{n_i}$, from equation (31.31). We thus have the appealing and useful correspondence

$$c_i \leftrightarrow (0, 0, \ldots, 0, 1, 0, \ldots, 0) \,,$$

a vector that has 0s everywhere except in the ith coordinate, where it has a 1. The c_i thus form a "basis" for the representation, in a certain sense. For each i, therefore, we have

$$\begin{aligned}
a &= a_i c_i & \pmod{n_i} \\
&= a_i m_i (m_i^{-1} \bmod n_i) & \pmod{n_i} \\
&= a_i & \pmod{n_i} \,,
\end{aligned}$$

which is what we wished to show: our method of computing a from the a_i's produces a result a that satisfies the constraints $a = a_i \pmod{n_i}$ for $i = 1, 2, \ldots, k$. The correspondence is one-to-one, since we can transform in both directions. Finally, equations (31.28)–(31.30) follow directly from Exercise 31.1-7, since $x \bmod n_i = (x \bmod n) \bmod n_i$ for any x and $i = 1, 2, \ldots, k$. ■

We'll use the following corollaries later in this chapter.

Corollary 31.28

If $n_1, n_2, \ldots, n_k$ are pairwise relatively prime and $n = n_1 n_2 \cdots n_k$, then for any integers $a_1, a_2, \ldots, a_k$, the set of simultaneous equations

$$x = a_i \pmod{n_i},$$

for $i = 1, 2, \ldots, k$, has a unique solution modulo n for the unknown x. ■

Corollary 31.29

If $n_1, n_2, \ldots, n_k$ are pairwise relatively prime and $n = n_1 n_2 \cdots n_k$, then for all integers x and a,

$$x = a \pmod{n_i}$$

for $i = 1, 2, \ldots, k$ if and only if

$$x = a \pmod{n}.$$ ■

As an example of the application of the Chinese remainder theorem, suppose that you are given the two equations

$$a = 2 \pmod 5,$$
$$a = 3 \pmod{13},$$

so that $a_1 = 2$, $n_1 = m_2 = 5$, $a_2 = 3$, and $n_2 = m_1 = 13$, and you wish to compute $a \bmod 65$, since $n = n_1 n_2 = 65$. Because $13^{-1} = 2 \pmod 5$ and $5^{-1} = 8 \pmod{13}$, you compute

$$c_1 = 13 \cdot (2 \bmod 5) = 26,$$
$$c_2 = 5 \cdot (8 \bmod 13) = 40,$$

and

$$\begin{aligned}
a &= 2 \cdot 26 + 3 \cdot 40 &&\pmod{65} \\
&= 52 + 120 &&\pmod{65} \\
&= 42 &&\pmod{65}.
\end{aligned}$$

	0	1	2	3	4	5	6	7	8	9	10	11	12
0	0	40	15	55	30	5	45	20	60	35	10	50	25
1	26	1	41	16	56	31	6	46	21	61	36	11	51
2	52	27	2	42	17	57	32	7	47	22	62	37	12
3	13	53	28	3	43	18	58	33	8	48	23	63	38
4	39	14	54	29	4	44	19	59	34	9	49	24	64

Figure 31.3   An illustration of the Chinese remainder theorem for $n_1 = 5$ and $n_2 = 13$. For this example, $c_1 = 26$ and $c_2 = 40$. In row i, column j is shown the value of a, modulo 65, such that $a \bmod 5 = i$ and $a \bmod 13 = j$. Note that row 0, column 0 contains a 0. Similarly, row 4, column 12 contains a 64 (equivalent to -1). Since $c_1 = 26$, moving down a row increases a by 26. Similarly, $c_2 = 40$ means that moving right by a column increases a by 40. Increasing a by 1 corresponds to moving diagonally downward and to the right, wrapping around from the bottom to the top and from the right to the left.

See Figure 31.3 for an illustration of the Chinese remainder theorem, modulo 65.

Thus, you can work modulo n by working modulo n directly or by working in the transformed representation using separate modulo n_i computations, as convenient. The computations are entirely equivalent.

Exercises

31.5-1
Find all solutions to the equations $x = 4 \pmod 5$ and $x = 5 \pmod{11}$.

31.5-2
Find all integers x that leave remainders 1, 2, and 3 when divided by 9, 8, and 7, respectively.

31.5-3
Argue that, under the definitions of Theorem 31.27, if $\gcd(a, n) = 1$, then

$$(a^{-1} \bmod n) \leftrightarrow ((a_1^{-1} \bmod n_1), (a_2^{-1} \bmod n_2), \ldots, (a_k^{-1} \bmod n_k)) \, .$$

31.5-4
Under the definitions of Theorem 31.27, prove that for any polynomial f, the number of roots of the equation $f(x) = 0 \pmod n$ equals the product of the number of roots of each of the equations $f(x) = 0 \pmod{n_1}$, $f(x) = 0 \pmod{n_2}$, $\ldots$, $f(x) = 0 \pmod{n_k}$.

31.6   Powers of an element

Along with considering the multiples of a given element a, modulo n, we often consider the sequence of powers of a, modulo n, where $a \in \mathbb{Z}_n^*$:

$$a^0, a^1, a^2, a^3, \ldots,$$

modulo n. Indexing from 0, the 0th value in this sequence is $a^0 \bmod n = 1$, and the ith value is $a^i \bmod n$. For example, the powers of 3 modulo 7 are

i	0	1	2	3	4	5	6	7	8	9	10	11	$\cdots$
$3^i \bmod 7$	1	3	2	6	4	5	1	3	2	6	4	5	$\cdots$

and the powers of 2 modulo 7 are

i	0	1	2	3	4	5	6	7	8	9	10	11	$\cdots$
$2^i \bmod 7$	1	2	4	1	2	4	1	2	4	1	2	4	$\cdots$

In this section, let $\langle a \rangle$ denote the subgroup of $\mathbb{Z}_n^*$ generated by a through repeated multiplication, and let $\mathrm{ord}_n(a)$ (the "order of a, modulo n") denote the order of a in $\mathbb{Z}_n^*$. For example, $\langle 2 \rangle = \{1, 2, 4\}$ in $\mathbb{Z}_7^*$, and $\mathrm{ord}_7(2) = 3$. Using the definition of the Euler phi function $\phi(n)$ as the size of $\mathbb{Z}_n^*$ (see Section 31.3), we now translate Corollary 31.19 into the notation of $\mathbb{Z}_n^*$ to obtain Euler's theorem and specialize it to $\mathbb{Z}_p^*$, where p is prime, to obtain Fermat's theorem.

Theorem 31.30 (Euler's theorem)
For any integer $n > 1$,

$$a^{\phi(n)} = 1 \pmod{n} \text{ for all } a \in \mathbb{Z}_n^* \, . \qquad \blacksquare$$

Theorem 31.31 (Fermat's theorem)
If p is prime, then

$$a^{p-1} = 1 \pmod{p} \text{ for all } a \in \mathbb{Z}_p^* \, .$$

Proof   By equation (31.22), $\phi(p) = p - 1$ if p is prime. $\blacksquare$

Fermat's theorem applies to every element in $\mathbb{Z}_p$ except 0, since $0 \notin \mathbb{Z}_p^*$. For all $a \in \mathbb{Z}_p$, however, we have $a^p = a \pmod{p}$ if p is prime.

If $\mathrm{ord}_n(g) = |\mathbb{Z}_n^*|$, then every element in $\mathbb{Z}_n^*$ is a power of g, modulo n, and g is a ***primitive root*** or a ***generator*** of $\mathbb{Z}_n^*$. For example, 3 is a primitive root, modulo 7, but 2 is not a primitive root, modulo 7. If $\mathbb{Z}_n^*$ possesses a primitive root, the group $\mathbb{Z}_n^*$ is ***cyclic***. We omit the proof of the following theorem, which is proven by Niven and Zuckerman [345].

Theorem 31.32

The values of $n > 1$ for which $\mathbb{Z}_n^*$ is cyclic are 2, 4, p^e, and $2p^e$, for all primes $p > 2$ and all positive integers e.   ∎

If g is a primitive root of $\mathbb{Z}_n^*$ and a is any element of $\mathbb{Z}_n^*$, then there exists a z such that $g^z = a \pmod{n}$. This z is a *discrete logarithm* or an *index* of a, modulo n, to the base g. We denote this value as $\mathrm{ind}_{n,g}(a)$.

Theorem 31.33 (Discrete logarithm theorem)

If g is a primitive root of $\mathbb{Z}_n^*$, then the equation $g^x = g^y \pmod{n}$ holds if and only if the equation $x = y \pmod{\phi(n)}$ holds.

Proof   Suppose first that $x = y \pmod{\phi(n)}$. Then, we have $x = y + k\phi(n)$ for some integer k, and thus

$$
\begin{aligned}
g^x &= g^{y+k\phi(n)} &&\pmod{n} \\
    &= g^y \cdot (g^{\phi(n)})^k &&\pmod{n} \\
    &= g^y \cdot 1^k &&\pmod{n} \qquad \text{(by Euler's theorem)} \\
    &= g^y &&\pmod{n}.
\end{aligned}
$$

Conversely, suppose that $g^x = g^y \pmod{n}$. Because the sequence of powers of g generates every element of $\langle g \rangle$ and $|\langle g \rangle| = \phi(n)$, Corollary 31.18 implies that the sequence of powers of g is periodic with period $\phi(n)$. Therefore, if $g^x = g^y \pmod{n}$, we must have $x = y \pmod{\phi(n)}$.   ∎

Let's now turn our attention to the square roots of 1, modulo a prime power. The following properties will be useful to justify the primality-testing algorithm in Section 31.8.

Theorem 31.34

If p is an odd prime and $e \geq 1$, then the equation

$$x^2 = 1 \pmod{p^e} \tag{31.33}$$

has only two solutions, namely $x = 1$ and $x = -1$.

Proof   By Exercise 31.6-2, equation (31.33) is equivalent to

$$p^e \mid (x-1)(x+1).$$

Since $p > 2$, we can have $p \mid (x-1)$ or $p \mid (x+1)$, but not both. (Otherwise, by property (31.3), p would also divide their difference $(x+1) - (x-1) = 2$.) If $p \nmid (x-1)$, then $\gcd(p^e, x-1) = 1$, and by Corollary 31.5, we would have $p^e \mid (x+1)$. That is, $x = -1 \pmod{p^e}$. Symmetrically, if $p \nmid (x+1)$, then $\gcd(p^e, x + 1) = 1$, and Corollary 31.5 implies that $p^e \mid (x - 1)$, so that $x = 1 \pmod{p^e}$. Therefore, either $x = -1 \pmod{p^e}$ or $x = 1 \pmod{p^e}$. ∎

A number x is a ***nontrivial square root of 1, modulo n***, if it satisfies the equation $x^2 = 1 \pmod n$ but x is equivalent to neither of the two "trivial" square roots: 1 or -1, modulo n. For example, 6 is a nontrivial square root of 1, modulo 35. We'll use the following corollary to Theorem 31.34 in Section 31.8 to prove the Miller-Rabin primality-testing procedure correct.

Corollary 31.35
If there exists a nontrivial square root of 1, modulo n, then n is composite.

Proof   By the contrapositive of Theorem 31.34, if there exists a nontrivial square root of 1, modulo n, then n cannot be an odd prime or a power of an odd prime. Nor can n be 2, because if $x^2 = 1 \pmod 2$, then $x = 1 \pmod 2$, and therefore, all square roots of 1, modulo 2, are trivial. Thus, n cannot be prime. Finally, we must have $n > 1$ for a nontrivial square root of 1 to exist. Therefore, n must be composite. ∎

Raising to powers with repeated squaring

A frequently occurring operation in number-theoretic computations is raising one number to a power modulo another number, also known as ***modular exponentiation***. More precisely, we would like an efficient way to compute $a^b \bmod n$, where a and b are nonnegative integers and n is a positive integer. Modular exponentiation is an essential operation in many primality-testing routines and in the RSA public-key cryptosystem. The method of ***repeated squaring*** solves this problem efficiently.

Repeated squaring is based on the following formula to compute a^b for nonnegative integers a and b:

$$a^b = \begin{cases} 1 & \text{if } b = 0 \,, \\ (a^{b/2})^2 & \text{if } b > 0 \text{ and } b \text{ is even} \,, \\ a \cdot a^{b-1} & \text{if } b > 0 \text{ and } b \text{ is odd} \,. \end{cases} \tag{31.34}$$

The last case, where b is odd, reduces to the one of the first two cases, since if b is odd, then $b - 1$ is even. The recursive procedure MODULAR-EXPONENTIATION on the next page computes $a^b \bmod n$ using equation (31.34), but performing all computations modulo n. The term "repeated squaring" comes from squaring the intermediate result $d = a^{b/2}$ in line 5. Figure 31.4 shows the values of the parameter b, the local variable d, and the value returned at each level of the recursion for the call MODULAR-EXPONENTIATION$(7, 560, 561)$, which returns the result 1.

b	560	280	140	70	35	34	17	16	8	4	2	1	0
d	67	166	298	241	355	160	103	526	157	49	7	1	–
returned value	1	67	166	298	241	355	160	103	526	157	49	7	1

Figure 31.4 The values of the parameter b, the local variable d, and the value returned for recursive calls of MODULAR-EXPONENTIATION with parameter values $a = 7$, $b = 560$, and $n = 561$. The value returned by each recursive call is assigned directly to d. The result of the call with $a = 7$, $b = 560$, and $n = 561$ is 1.

MODULAR-EXPONENTIATION(a, b, n)

1   **if** $b == 0$
2   **return** 1
3   **elseif** $b \bmod 2 == 0$
4       $d = $ MODULAR-EXPONENTIATION$(a, b/2, n)$ **//** b is even
5   **return** $(d \cdot d) \bmod n$
6   **else** $d = $ MODULAR-EXPONENTIATION$(a, b - 1, n)$ **//** b is odd
7   **return** $(a \cdot d) \bmod n$

The total number of recursive calls depends on the number of bits of b and the values of these bits. Assume that $b > 0$ and that the most significant bit of b is a 1. Each 0 generates one recursive call (in line 4), and each 1 generates two recursive calls (one in line 6 followed by one in line 4 because if b is odd, then $b - 1$ is even). If the inputs a, b, and n are β-bit numbers, then there are between β and $2\beta - 1$ recursive calls altogether, the total number of arithmetic operations required is $O(\beta)$, and the total number of bit operations required is $O(\beta^3)$.

Exercises

31.6-1
Draw a table showing the order of every element in $\mathbb{Z}_{11}^*$. Pick the smallest primitive root g and compute a table giving $\mathrm{ind}_{11,g}(x)$ for all $x \in \mathbb{Z}_{11}^*$.

31.6-2
Show that $x^2 = 1 \pmod{p^e}$ is equivalent to $p^e \mid (x - 1)(x + 1)$.

31.6-3
Rewrite the third case of MODULAR-EXPONENTIATION, where b is odd, so that if b has β bits and the most significant bit is 1, then there are always exactly β recursive calls.

31.6-4

Give a nonrecursive (i.e., iterative) version of MODULAR-EXPONENTIATION.

31.6-5

Assuming that you know $\phi(n)$, explain how to compute $a^{-1} \bmod n$ for any $a \in \mathbb{Z}_n^*$ using the procedure MODULAR-EXPONENTIATION.

31.7   The RSA public-key cryptosystem

With a public-key cryptosystem, you can *encrypt* messages sent between two communicating parties so that an eavesdropper who overhears the encrypted messages will not be able to decode, or *decrypt*, them. A public-key cryptosystem also enables a party to append an unforgeable "digital signature" to the end of an electronic message. Such a signature is the electronic version of a handwritten signature on a paper document. It can be easily checked by anyone, forged by no one, yet loses its validity if any bit of the message is altered. It therefore provides authentication of both the identity of the signer and the contents of the signed message. It is the perfect tool for electronically signed business contracts, electronic checks, electronic purchase orders, and other electronic communications that parties wish to authenticate.

The RSA public-key cryptosystem relies on the dramatic difference between the ease of finding large prime numbers and the difficulty of factoring the product of two large prime numbers. Section 31.8 describes an efficient procedure for finding large prime numbers.

Public-key cryptosystems

In a public-key cryptosystem, each participant has both a *public key* and a *secret key*. Each key is a piece of information. For example, in the RSA cryptosystem, each key consists of a pair of integers. The participants "Alice" and "Bob" are traditionally used in cryptography examples. We denote the public keys for Alice and Bob as P_A and P_B, respectively, and likewise the secret keys are S_A for Alice and S_B for Bob.

Each participant creates his or her own public and secret keys. Secret keys are kept secret, but public keys can be revealed to anyone or even published. In fact, it is often convenient to assume that everyone's public key is available in a public directory, so that any participant can easily obtain the public key of any other participant.

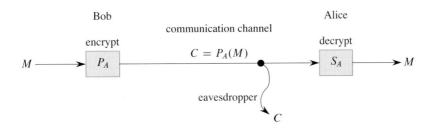

Figure 31.5   Encryption in a public key system. Bob encrypts the message M using Alice's public key P_A and transmits the resulting ciphertext $C = P_A(M)$ over a communication channel to Alice. An eavesdropper who captures the transmitted ciphertext gains no information about M. Alice receives C and decrypts it using her secret key to obtain the original message $M = S_A(C)$.

The public and secret keys specify functions that can be applied to any message. Let $\mathcal{D}$ denote the set of permissible messages. For example, $\mathcal{D}$ might be the set of all finite-length bit sequences. The simplest, and original, formulation of public-key cryptography requires one-to-one functions from $\mathcal{D}$ to itself, based on the public and secret keys. We denote the function based on Alice's public key P_A by $P_A()$ and the function based on her secret key S_A by $S_A()$. The functions $P_A()$ and $S_A()$ are thus permutations of $\mathcal{D}$. We assume that the functions $P_A()$ and $S_A()$ are efficiently computable given the corresponding keys P_A and S_A.

The public and secret keys for any participant are a "matched pair" in that they specify functions that are inverses of each other. That is,

$$M = S_A(P_A(M)) \,, \tag{31.35}$$
$$M = P_A(S_A(M)) \tag{31.36}$$

for any message $M \in \mathcal{D}$. Transforming M with the two keys P_A and S_A successively, in either order, yields back the original message M.

A public-key cryptosystem requires that Alice, and only Alice, be able to compute the function $S_A()$ in any practical amount of time. This assumption is crucial to keeping encrypted messages sent to Alice private and to knowing that Alice's digital signatures are authentic. Alice must keep her key S_A secret. If she does not, whoever else has access to S_A can decrypt messages intended only for Alice and can also forge her digital signature. The assumption that only Alice can reasonably compute $S_A()$ must hold even though everyone knows P_A and can compute $P_A()$, the inverse function to $S_A()$, efficiently. These requirements appear formidable, but we'll see how to satisfy them.

In a public-key cryptosystem, encryption works as shown in Figure 31.5. Suppose that Bob wishes to send Alice a message M encrypted so that it looks like

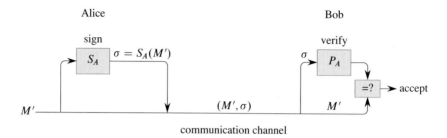

Figure 31.6 Digital signatures in a public-key system. Alice signs the message M' by appending her digital signature $\sigma = S_A(M')$ to it. She transmits the message/signature pair (M', σ) to Bob, who verifies it by checking the equation $M' = P_A(\sigma)$. If the equation holds, he accepts (M', σ) as a message that Alice has signed.

unintelligible gibberish to an eavesdropper. The scenario for sending the message goes as follows.

- Bob obtains Alice's public key P_A, perhaps from a public directory or perhaps directly from Alice.

- Bob computes the *ciphertext* $C = P_A(M)$ corresponding to the message M and sends C to Alice.

- When Alice receives the ciphertext C, she applies her secret key S_A to retrieve the original message: $S_A(C) = S_A(P_A(M)) = M$.

Because $S_A()$ and $P_A()$ are inverse functions, Alice can compute M from C. Because only Alice is able to compute $S_A()$, only Alice can compute M from C. Because Bob encrypts M using $P_A()$, only Alice can understand the transmitted message.

Digital signatures can be implemented within this formulation of a public-key cryptosystem. (There are other ways to construct digital signatures, but we won't go into them here.) Suppose now that Alice wishes to send Bob a digitally signed response M'. Figure 31.6 shows how the digital-signature scenario proceeds.

- Alice computes her *digital signature* σ for the message M' using her secret key S_A and the equation $\sigma = S_A(M')$.

- Alice sends the message/signature pair (M', σ) to Bob.

- When Bob receives (M', σ), he can verify that it originated from Alice by using Alice's public key to verify the equation $M' = P_A(\sigma)$. (Presumably, M' contains Alice's name, so that Bob knows whose public key to use.) If the equation holds, then Bob concludes that the message M' was actually signed by Alice. If the equation fails to hold, Bob concludes either that the information he received was corrupted by transmission errors or that the pair (M', σ) is an attempted forgery.

Because a digital signature provides both authentication of the signer's identity and authentication of the contents of the signed message, it is analogous to a handwritten signature at the end of a written document.

A digital signature must be verifiable by anyone who has access to the signer's public key. A signed message can be verified by one party and then passed on to other parties who can also verify the signature. For example, the message might be an electronic check from Alice to Bob. After Bob verifies Alice's signature on the check, he can give the check to his bank, who can then also verify the signature and effect the appropriate funds transfer.

A signed message may or may not be encrypted. The message can be "in the clear" and not protected from disclosure. By composing the above protocols for encryption and for signatures, Alice can create a message to Bob that is both signed and encrypted. Alice first appends her digital signature to the message and then encrypts the resulting message/signature pair with Bob's public key. Bob decrypts the received message with his secret key to obtain both the original message and its digital signature. Bob can then verify the signature using Alice's public key. The corresponding combined process using paper-based systems would be to sign the paper document and then seal the document inside a paper envelope that is opened only by the intended recipient.

The RSA cryptosystem

In the *RSA public-key cryptosystem*, a participant creates a public key and a secret key with the following procedure:

1. Select at random two large prime numbers p and q such that $p \neq q$. The primes p and q might be, say, 1024 bits each.

2. Compute $n = pq$.

3. Select a small odd integer e that is relatively prime to $\phi(n)$, which, by equation (31.21), equals $(p - 1)(q - 1)$.

4. Compute d as the multiplicative inverse of e, modulo $\phi(n)$. (Corollary 31.26 guarantees that d exists and is uniquely defined. You can use the technique of Section 31.4 to compute d, given e and $\phi(n)$.)

5. Publish the pair $P = (e, n)$ as the participant's *RSA public key*.

6. Keep secret the pair $S = (d, n)$ as the participant's *RSA secret key*.

For this scheme, the domain $\mathcal{D}$ is the set $\mathbb{Z}_n$. To transform a message M associated with a public key $P = (e, n)$, compute

$$P(M) = M^e \bmod n .$$
(31.37)

To transform a ciphertext C associated with a secret key $S = (d, n)$, compute

$$S(C) = C^d \bmod n .$$
(31.38)

These equations apply to both encryption and signatures. To create a signature, the signer's secret key is applied to the message to be signed, rather than to a ciphertext. To verify a signature, the public key of the signer is applied to the signature rather than to a message to be encrypted.

To implement the public-key and secret-key operations (31.37) and (31.38), you can use the procedure MODULAR-EXPONENTIATION described in Section 31.6. To analyze the running time of these operations, assume that the public key (e, n) and secret key (d, n) satisfy $\lg e = O(1)$, $\lg d \leq \beta$, and $\lg n \leq \beta$. Then, applying a public key requires $O(1)$ modular multiplications and uses $O(\beta^2)$ bit operations. Applying a secret key requires $O(\beta)$ modular multiplications, using $O(\beta^3)$ bit operations.

Theorem 31.36 (Correctness of RSA)
The RSA equations (31.37) and (31.38) define inverse transformations of $\mathbb{Z}_n$ satisfying equations (31.35) and (31.36).

Proof   From equations (31.37) and (31.38), we have that for any $M \in \mathbb{Z}_n$,

$$P(S(M)) = S(P(M)) = M^{ed} \pmod{n} .$$

Since e and d are multiplicative inverses modulo $\phi(n) = (p-1)(q-1)$,

$$ed = 1 + k(p-1)(q-1)$$

for some integer k. But then, if $M \not\equiv 0 \pmod{p}$, we have

$$
\begin{aligned}
M^{ed} &= M(M^{p-1})^{k(q-1)} && \pmod{p} \\
&= M((M \bmod p)^{p-1})^{k(q-1)} && \pmod{p} \\
&= M(1)^{k(q-1)} && \pmod{p} && \text{(by Theorem 31.31)} \\
&= M && \pmod{p} .
\end{aligned}
$$

Also, $M^{ed} = M \pmod{p}$ if $M = 0 \pmod{p}$. Thus,

$$M^{ed} = M \pmod{p}$$

for all M. Similarly,

$M^{ed} = M \pmod{q}$

for all M. Thus, by Corollary 31.29 to the Chinese remainder theorem,

$M^{ed} = M \pmod{n}$

for all M.   ∎

The security of the RSA cryptosystem rests in large part on the difficulty of factoring large integers. If an adversary can factor the modulus n in a public key, then the adversary can derive the secret key from the public key, using the knowledge of the factors p and q in the same way that the creator of the public key used them. Therefore, if factoring large integers is easy, then breaking the RSA cryptosystem is easy. The converse statement, that if factoring large integers is hard, then breaking RSA is hard, is unproven. After two decades of research, however, no easier method has been found to break the RSA public-key cryptosystem than to factor the modulus n. And factoring large integers is surprisingly difficult. By randomly selecting and multiplying together two 1024-bit primes, you can create a public key that cannot be "broken" in any feasible amount of time with current technology. In the absence of a fundamental breakthrough in the design of number-theoretic algorithms, and when implemented with care following recommended standards, the RSA cryptosystem is capable of providing a high degree of security in applications.

In order to achieve security with the RSA cryptosystem, however, you should use integers that are quite long—more than 1000 bits—to resist possible advances in the art of factoring. In 2021, RSA moduli are commonly in the range of 2048 to 4096 bits. To create moduli of such sizes, you must find large primes efficiently. Section 31.8 addresses this problem.

For efficiency, RSA is often used in a "hybrid" or "key-management" mode with fast cryptosystems that are not public-key cryptosystems. With such a *symmetric-key* system, the encryption and decryption keys are identical. If Alice wishes to send a long message M to Bob privately, she selects a random key K for the fast symmetric-key cryptosystem and encrypts M using K, obtaining ciphertext C, where C is as long as M, but K is quite short. Then she encrypts K using Bob's public RSA key. Since K is short, computing $P_B(K)$ is fast (much faster than computing $P_B(M)$). She then transmits $(C, P_B(K))$ to Bob, who decrypts $P_B(K)$ to obtain K and then uses K to decrypt C, obtaining M.

A similar hybrid approach creates digital signatures efficiently. This approach combines RSA with a public *collision-resistant hash function h*—a function that is easy to compute but for which it is computationally infeasible to find two messages M and M' such that $h(M) = h(M')$. The value $h(M)$ is a short (say, 256-bit) "fingerprint" of the message M. If Alice wishes to sign a message M, she first applies h to M to obtain the fingerprint $h(M)$, which she then encrypts with her secret key. She sends $(M, S_A(h(M)))$ to Bob as her signed version of M.

Bob can verify the signature by computing $h(M)$ and verifying that P_A applied to $S_A(h(M))$ as received equals $h(M)$. Because no one can create two messages with the same fingerprint, it is computationally infeasible to alter a signed message and preserve the validity of the signature.

One way to distribute public keys uses *certificates*. For example, assume that there is a "trusted authority" T whose public key is known by everyone. Alice can obtain from T a signed message (her certificate) stating that "Alice's public key is P_A." This certificate is "self-authenticating" since everyone knows P_T. Alice can include her certificate with her signed messages, so that the recipient has Alice's public key immediately available in order to verify her signature. Because her key was signed by T, the recipient knows that Alice's key is really Alice's.

Exercises

31.7-1
Consider an RSA key set with $p = 11$, $q = 29$, $n = 319$, and $e = 3$. What value of d should be used in the secret key? What is the encryption of the message $M = 100$?

31.7-2
Prove that if Alice's public exponent e is 3 and an adversary obtains Alice's secret exponent d, where $0 < d < \phi(n)$, then the adversary can factor Alice's modulus n in time polynomial in the number of bits in n. (Although you are not asked to prove it, you might be interested to know that this result remains true even if the condition $e = 3$ is removed. See Miller [327].)

★ *31.7-3*
Prove that RSA is multiplicative in the sense that

$$P_A(M_1)P_A(M_2) = P_A(M_1 M_2) \pmod{n} .$$

Use this fact to prove that if an adversary had a procedure that could efficiently decrypt 1% of messages from $\mathbb{Z}_n$ encrypted with P_A, then the adversary could employ a probabilistic algorithm to decrypt every message encrypted with P_A with high probability.

★ 31.8   Primality testing

This section shows how to find large primes. We begin with a discussion of the density of primes, proceed to examine a plausible, but incomplete, approach to primality testing, and then present an effective randomized primality test due to Miller and Rabin.

The density of prime numbers

Many applications, such as cryptography, call for finding large "random" primes. Fortunately, large primes are not too rare, so that it is feasible to test random integers of the appropriate size until you find one that is prime. The *prime distribution function* $\pi(n)$ specifies the number of primes that are less than or equal to n. For example, $\pi(10) = 4$, since there are 4 prime numbers less than or equal to 10, namely, 2, 3, 5, and 7. The prime number theorem gives a useful approximation to $\pi(n)$.

Theorem 31.37 (Prime number theorem)

$$\lim_{n \to \infty} \frac{\pi(n)}{n / \ln n} = 1 .$$ ∎

The approximation $n / \ln n$ gives reasonably accurate estimates of $\pi(n)$ even for small n. For example, it is off by less than 6% at $n = 10^9$, where $\pi(n) = 50{,}847{,}534$ and $n / \ln n \approx 48{,}254{,}942$. (To a number theorist, 10^9 is a small number.)

The process of randomly selecting an integer n and determining whether it is prime is really just a Bernoulli trial (see Section C.4). By the prime number theorem, the probability of a success—that is, the probability that n is prime—is approximately $1 / \ln n$. The geometric distribution says how many trials must occur to obtain a success, and by equation (C.36) on page 1197, the expected number of trials is approximately $\ln n$. Thus, in order to find a prime that has the same length as n by testing integers chosen randomly near n, the expected number examined would be approximately $\ln n$. For example, the expectation is that finding a 1024-bit prime would require testing approximately $\ln 2^{1024} \approx 710$ randomly chosen 1024-bit numbers for primality. (Of course, to cut this figure in half, choose only odd integers.)

The remainder of this section shows how to determine whether a large odd integer n is prime. For notational convenience, we assume that n has the prime factorization

$$n = p_1^{e_1} p_2^{e_2} \cdots p_r^{e_r} ,$$

where $r \geq 1$, $p_1, p_2, \ldots, p_r$ are the prime factors of n, and $e_1, e_2, \ldots, e_r$ are positive integers. The integer n is prime if and only if $r = 1$ and $e_1 = 1$.

One simple approach to the problem of testing for primality is *trial division*: try dividing n by each integer $2, 3, 5, 7, 9, \ldots, \lfloor \sqrt{n} \rfloor$, skipping even integers greater than 2. We can conclude that n is prime if and only if none of the trial divisors divides n. Assuming that each trial division takes constant time, the worst-case running time is $\Theta(\sqrt{n})$, which is exponential in the length of n. (Recall that if n is encoded in binary using β bits, then $\beta = \lceil \lg(n+1) \rceil$, and so $\sqrt{n} = \Theta(2^{\beta/2})$.) Thus, trial division works well only if n is very small or happens to have a small prime factor. When it works, trial division has the advantage that it not only determines whether n is prime or composite, it also determines one of n's prime factors if n is composite.

This section focuses on finding out whether a given number n is prime. If n is composite, we won't worry about finding its prime factorization. Computing the prime factorization of a number is computationally expensive. You might be surprised that it turns out to be much easier to ascertain whether a given number is prime than it is to determine the prime factorization of the number if it is not prime.

Pseudoprimality testing

We'll start with a method for primality testing that "almost works" and, in fact, is good enough for many practical applications. Later on, we'll refine this method to remove the small defect. Let $\mathbb{Z}_n^+$ denote the nonzero elements of $\mathbb{Z}_n$:

$$\mathbb{Z}_n^+ = \{1, 2, \ldots, n-1\} \ .$$

If n is prime, then $\mathbb{Z}_n^+ = \mathbb{Z}_n^*$.

We say that n is a *base-a pseudoprime* if n is composite and

$$a^{n-1} \equiv 1 \pmod{n} \ . \tag{31.39}$$

Fermat's theorem (Theorem 31.31 on page 932) implies that if n is prime, then n satisfies equation (31.39) for every a in $\mathbb{Z}_n^+$. Thus, if there is any $a \in \mathbb{Z}_n^+$ such that n does *not* satisfy equation (31.39), then n is certainly composite. Surprisingly, the converse *almost* holds, so that this criterion forms an almost perfect test for primality. Instead of trying every value of $a \in \mathbb{Z}_n^+$, test to see whether n satisfies equation (31.39) for just $a = 2$. If not, then declare n to be composite by returning COMPOSITE. Otherwise, return PRIME, guessing that n is prime (when, in fact, all we know is that n is either prime or a base-2 pseudoprime).

The procedure PSEUDOPRIME on the next page pretends in this manner to check whether n is prime. It uses the procedure MODULAR-EXPONENTIATION from Section 31.6. It assumes that the input n is an odd integer greater than 2. This procedure can make errors, but only of one type. That is, if it says that n is composite, then it is always correct. If it says that n is prime, however, then it makes an error only if n is a base-2 pseudoprime.

How often does PSEUDOPRIME err? Surprisingly rarely. There are only 22 values of n less than 10,000 for which it errs, the first four of which are 341, 561, 645,

PSEUDOPRIME(*n*)

```
1   if MODULAR-EXPONENTIATION(2, n − 1, n) ≠ 1  (mod n)
2        return COMPOSITE        // definitely
3   else return PRIME           // we hope!
```

and 1105. We won't prove it, but the probability that this program makes an error on a randomly chosen β-bit number goes to 0 as β approaches ∞. Using more precise estimates due to Pomerance [361] of the number of base-2 pseudoprimes of a given size, a randomly chosen 512-bit number that is called prime by PSEUDOPRIME has less than one chance in 10^{20} of being a base-2 pseudoprime, and a randomly chosen 1024-bit number that is called prime has less than one chance in 10^{41} of being a base-2 pseudoprime. Thus, if you are merely trying to find a large prime for some application, for all practical purposes you almost never go wrong by choosing large numbers at random until one of them causes PSEUDOPRIME to return PRIME. But when the numbers being tested for primality are not randomly chosen, you might need a better approach for testing primality. As we'll see, a little more cleverness, and some randomization, will yield a primality-testing method that works well on all inputs.

Since PSEUDOPRIME checks equation (31.39) for only $a = 2$, you might think that you could eliminate all the errors by simply checking equation (31.39) for a second base number, say $a = 3$. Better yet, you could check equation (31.39) for even more values of a. Unfortunately, even checking for several values of a does not eliminate all errors, because there exist composite integers n, known as *Carmichael numbers*, that satisfy equation (31.39) for *all* $a \in \mathbb{Z}_n^*$. (The equation does fail when $\gcd(a, n) > 1$—that is, when $a \notin \mathbb{Z}_n^*$—but demonstrating that n is composite by finding such an a can be difficult if n has only large prime factors.) The first three Carmichael numbers are 561, 1105, and 1729. Carmichael numbers are extremely rare. For example, only 255 of them are less than 100,000,000. Exercise 31.8-2 helps explain why they are so rare.

Let's see how to improve the primality test so that Carmichael numbers won't fool it.

The Miller-Rabin randomized primality test

The Miller-Rabin primality test overcomes the problems of the simple procedure PSEUDOPRIME with two modifications:

- It tries several randomly chosen base values a instead of just one base value.

- While computing each modular exponentiation, it looks for a nontrivial square root of 1, modulo n, during the final set of squarings. If it finds one, it stops and returns COMPOSITE. Corollary 31.35 from Section 31.6 justifies detecting composites in this manner.

The pseudocode for the Miller-Rabin primality test appears in the procedures MILLER-RABIN and WITNESS. The input $n > 2$ to MILLER-RABIN is the odd number to be tested for primality, and s is the number of randomly chosen base values from $\mathbb{Z}_n^+$ to be tried. The code uses the random-number generator RANDOM described on page 129: RANDOM$(2, n - 2)$ returns a randomly chosen integer a satisfying $2 \le a \le n - 2$. (This range of values avoids having $a = \pm 1 \pmod{n}$.) The call of the auxiliary procedure WITNESS(a, n) returns TRUE if and only if a is a "witness" to the compositeness of n—that is, if it is possible using a to prove (in a manner that we will see) that n is composite. The test WITNESS(a, n) is an extension of, but more effective than, the test in equation (31.39) that formed the basis for PSEUDOPRIME, using $a = 2$.

Let's first understand how WITNESS works, and then we'll see how the Miller-Rabin primality test uses it. Let $n - 1 = 2^t u$ where $t \ge 1$ and u is odd. That is, the binary representation of $n - 1$ is the binary representation of the odd integer u followed by exactly t zeros. Therefore, $a^{n-1} = (a^u)^{2^t} \pmod{n}$, so that one way to compute $a^{n-1} \bmod n$ is to first compute $a^u \bmod n$ and then square the result t times successively.

MILLER-RABIN(n, s) // $n > 2$ is odd

```
1   for j = 1 to s
2       a = RANDOM(2, n − 2)
3       if WITNESS(a, n)
4           return COMPOSITE      // definitely
5   return PRIME                  // almost surely
```

WITNESS(a, n)

```
1   let t and u be such that t ≥ 1, u is odd, and n − 1 = 2ᵗu
2   x₀ = MODULAR-EXPONENTIATION(a, u, n)
3   for i = 1 to t
4       xᵢ = xᵢ₋₁² mod n
5       if xᵢ == 1 and xᵢ₋₁ ≠ 1 and xᵢ₋₁ ≠ n − 1
6           return TRUE           // found a nontrivial square root of 1
7   if xₜ ≠ 1
8       return TRUE               // composite, as in PSEUDOPRIME
9   return FALSE
```

This pseudocode for WITNESS computes a^{n-1} mod n by first computing the value $x_0 = a^u$ mod n in line 2 and then repeatedly squaring the result t times in the **for** loop of lines 3–6. By induction on i, the sequence $x_0, x_1, \ldots, x_t$ of values computed satisfies the equation $x_i = a^{2^i u} \pmod{n}$ for $i = 0, 1, \ldots, t$, so that in particular $x_t = a^{n-1} \pmod{n}$. After line 4 performs a squaring step, however, the loop will terminate early if lines 5–6 detect that a nontrivial square root of 1 has just been discovered. (We'll explain these tests shortly.) If so, the procedure stops and returns TRUE. Lines 7–8 return TRUE if the value computed for $x_t = a^{n-1} \pmod{n}$ is not equal to 1, just as the PSEUDOPRIME procedure returns COMPOSITE in this case. Line 9 returns FALSE if lines 6 or 8 have not returned TRUE.

The following lemma proves the correctness of WITNESS.

Lemma 31.38

If WITNESS(a, n) returns TRUE, then a proof that n is composite can be constructed using a as a witness.

Proof If WITNESS returns TRUE from line 8, it's because line 7 determined that $x_t = a^{n-1}$ mod $n \neq 1$. If n is prime, however, Fermat's theorem (Theorem 31.31) says that $a^{n-1} = 1 \pmod{n}$ for all $a \in \mathbb{Z}_n^*$. Since $\mathbb{Z}_n^+ = \mathbb{Z}_n^*$ if n is prime, Fermat's theorem also says that $a^{n-1} = 1 \pmod{n}$ for all $a \in \mathbb{Z}_n^+$. Therefore, n cannot be prime, and the equation a^{n-1} mod $n \neq 1$ proves this fact.

If WITNESS returns TRUE from line 6, then it has discovered that x_{i-1} is a nontrivial square root of 1, modulo n, since we have that $x_{i-1} \neq \pm 1 \pmod{n}$ yet $x_i = x_{i-1}^2 = 1 \pmod{n}$. Corollary 31.35 on page 934 states that only if n is composite can there exist a nontrivial square root of 1, modulo n, so that demonstrating that x_{i-1} is a nontrivial square root of 1, modulo n proves that n is composite. ∎

Thus, if the call WITNESS(a, n) returns TRUE, then n is surely composite, and the witness a, along with the reason that the procedure returns TRUE (did it return from line 6 or from line 8?), provides a proof that n is composite.

Let's explore an alternative view of the behavior of WITNESS as a function of the sequence $X = \langle x_0, x_1, \ldots, x_t \rangle$. We'll find this view useful later on, when we analyze the error rate of the Miller-Rabin primality test. Note that if $x_i = 1$ for some $0 \leq i < t$, WITNESS might not compute the rest of the sequence. If it were to do so, however, each value $x_{i+1}, x_{i+2}, \ldots, x_t$ would be 1, so we can consider these positions in the sequence X as being all 1s. There are four cases:

1. $X = \langle \ldots, d \rangle$, where $d \neq 1$: the sequence X does not end in 1. Return TRUE in line 8, since a is a witness to the compositeness of n (by Fermat's Theorem).

2. $X = \langle 1, 1, \ldots, 1 \rangle$: the sequence X is all 1s. Return FALSE, since a is not a witness to the compositeness of n.

3. $X = \langle \ldots, -1, 1, \ldots, 1 \rangle$: the sequence X ends in 1, and the last non-1 is equal to -1. Return FALSE, since a is not a witness to the compositeness of n.

4. $X = \langle \ldots, d, 1, \ldots, 1 \rangle$, where $d \neq \pm 1$: the sequence X ends in 1, but the last non-1 is not -1. Return TRUE in line 6: a is a witness to the compositeness of n, since d is a nontrivial square root of 1.

Now, let's examine the Miller-Rabin primality test based on how it uses the WITNESS procedure. As before, assume that n is an odd integer greater than 2.

The procedure MILLER-RABIN is a probabilistic search for a proof that n is composite. The main loop (beginning on line 1) picks up to s random values of a from $\mathbb{Z}_n^+$, except for 1 and $n-1$ (line 2). If it picks a value of a that is a witness to the compositeness of n, then MILLER-RABIN returns COMPOSITE on line 4. Such a result is always correct, by the correctness of WITNESS. If MILLER-RABIN finds no witness in s trials, then the procedure assumes that it found no witness because no witnesses exist, and therefore it assumes that n is prime. We'll see that this result is likely to be correct if s is large enough, but there is still a tiny chance that the procedure could be unlucky in its choice of s random values of a, so that even though the procedure failed to find a witness, at least one witness exists.

To illustrate the operation of MILLER-RABIN, let n be the Carmichael number 561, so that $n - 1 = 560 = 2^4 \cdot 35$, $t = 4$, and $u = 35$. If the procedure chooses $a = 7$ as a base, the column for $b = 35$ in Figure 31.4 (Section 31.6) shows that WITNESS computes $x_0 = a^{35} = 241 \pmod{561}$. Because of how the MODULAR-EXPONENTIATION procedure operates recursively on its parameter b, the first four columns in Figure 31.4 represent the factor 2^4 of 560—the rightmost four zeros in the binary representation of 560—reading these four zeros from right to left in the binary representation. Thus WITNESS computes the sequence $X = \langle 241, 298, 166, 67, 1 \rangle$. Then, in the last squaring step, WITNESS discovers that a^{280} is a nontrivial square root of 1 since $a^{280} = 67 \pmod{n}$ and $(a^{280})^2 = a^{560} = 1 \pmod{n}$. Therefore, $a = 7$ is a witness to the compositeness of n, WITNESS$(7, n)$ returns TRUE, and MILLER-RABIN returns COMPOSITE.

If n is a β-bit number, MILLER-RABIN requires $O(s\beta)$ arithmetic operations and $O(s\beta^3)$ bit operations, since it requires asymptotically no more work than s modular exponentiations.

Error rate of the Miller-Rabin primality test

If MILLER-RABIN returns PRIME, then there is a very slim chance that it has made an error. Unlike PSEUDOPRIME, however, the chance of error does not depend on n: there are no bad inputs for this procedure. Rather, it depends on the size of s

and the "luck of the draw" in choosing base values a. Moreover, since each test is more stringent than a simple check of equation (31.39), we can expect on general principles that the error rate should be small for randomly chosen integers n. The following theorem presents a more precise argument.

Theorem 31.39

If n is an odd composite number, then the number of witnesses to the compositeness of n is at least $(n - 1)/2$.

Proof The proof shows that the number of nonwitnesses is at most $(n - 1)/2$, which implies the theorem.

We start by claiming that any nonwitness must be a member of $\mathbb{Z}_n^*$. Why? Consider any nonwitness a. It must satisfy $a^{n-1} = 1 \pmod{n}$ or, equivalently, $a \cdot a^{n-2} = 1 \pmod{n}$. Thus the equation $ax = 1 \pmod{n}$ has a solution, namely a^{n-2}. By Corollary 31.21 on page 924, $\gcd(a, n) \mid 1$, which in turn implies that $\gcd(a, n) = 1$. Therefore, a is a member of $\mathbb{Z}_n^*$, and all nonwitnesses belong to $\mathbb{Z}_n^*$.

To complete the proof, we show that not only are all nonwitnesses contained in $\mathbb{Z}_n^*$, they are all contained in a proper subgroup B of $\mathbb{Z}_n^*$ (recall that B is a *proper* subgroup of $\mathbb{Z}_n^*$ when B is subgroup of $\mathbb{Z}_n^*$ but B is not equal to $\mathbb{Z}_n^*$). By Corollary 31.16 on page 921, we then have $|B| \leq |\mathbb{Z}_n^*|/2$. Since $|\mathbb{Z}_n^*| \leq n - 1$, we obtain $|B| \leq (n - 1)/2$. Therefore, if all nonwitnesses are contained in a proper subgroup of $\mathbb{Z}_n^*$, then the number of nonwitnesses is at most $(n - 1)/2$, so that the number of witnesses must be at least $(n - 1)/2$.

To find a proper subgroup B of $\mathbb{Z}_n^*$ containing all of the nonwitnesses, we consider two cases.

Case 1: There exists an $x \in \mathbb{Z}_n^*$ such that

$$x^{n-1} \neq 1 \pmod{n} .$$

In other words, n is not a Carmichael number. Since, as noted earlier, Carmichael numbers are extremely rare, case 1 is the more typical case (e.g., when n has been chosen randomly and is being tested for primality).

Let $B = \{b \in \mathbb{Z}_n^* : b^{n-1} = 1 \pmod{n}\}$. The set B must be nonempty, since $1 \in B$. The set B is closed under multiplication modulo n, and so B is a subgroup of $\mathbb{Z}_n^*$ by Theorem 31.14. Every nonwitness belongs to B, since a nonwitness a satisfies $a^{n-1} = 1 \pmod{n}$. Since $x \in \mathbb{Z}_n^* - B$, we have that B is a proper subgroup of $\mathbb{Z}_n^*$.

Case 2: For all $x \in \mathbb{Z}_n^*$,

$$x^{n-1} = 1 \pmod{n} . \tag{31.40}$$

In other words, n is a Carmichael number. This case is extremely rare in practice. Unlike a pseudoprimality test, however, the Miller-Rabin test can efficiently determine that Carmichael numbers are composite, as we're about to see.

In this case, n cannot be a prime power. To see why, suppose to the contrary that $n = p^e$, where p is a prime and $e > 1$. We derive a contradiction as follows. Since we assume that n is odd, p must also be odd. Theorem 31.32 on page 933 implies that $\mathbb{Z}_n^*$ is a cyclic group: it contains a generator g such that $\mathrm{ord}_n(g) = |\mathbb{Z}_n^*| = \phi(n) = p^e(1 - 1/p) = (p - 1)p^{e-1}$. (The formula for $\phi(n)$ comes from equation (31.21) on page 920.) By equation (31.40), we have $g^{n-1} = 1 \pmod{n}$. Then the discrete logarithm theorem (Theorem 31.33 on page 933, taking $y = 0$) implies that $n - 1 = 0 \pmod{\phi(n)}$, or

$$(p - 1)p^{e-1} \mid p^e - 1 .$$

This statement is a contradiction for $e > 1$, since $(p - 1)p^{e-1}$ is divisible by the prime p, but $p^e - 1$ is not. Thus n is not a prime power.

Since the odd composite number n is not a prime power, we decompose it into a product $n_1 n_2$, where n_1 and n_2 are odd numbers greater than 1 that are relatively prime to each other. (There may be several ways to decompose n, and it does not matter which one we choose. For example, if $n = p_1^{e_1} p_2^{e_2} \cdots p_r^{e_r}$, then we can choose $n_1 = p_1^{e_1}$ and $n_2 = p_2^{e_2} p_3^{e_3} \cdots p_r^{e_r}$.)

Recall that t and u are such that $n - 1 = 2^t u$, where $t \geq 1$ and u is odd, and that for an input a, the procedure WITNESS computes the sequence

$$X = \langle a^u, a^{2u}, a^{2^2 u}, \ldots, a^{2^t u} \rangle$$

where all computations are performed modulo n.

Let us call a pair (v, j) of integers *acceptable* if $v \in \mathbb{Z}_n^*$, $j \in \{0, 1, \ldots, t\}$, and

$$v^{2^j u} = -1 \pmod{n} .$$

Acceptable pairs certainly exist, since u is odd. Choose $v = n - 1$ and $j = 0$, and let $u = 2k + 1$, so that $v^{2^j u} = (n - 1)^u = (n - 1)^{2k+1}$. Taking this number modulo n gives $(n - 1)^{2k+1} = (n - 1)^{2k} \cdot (n - 1) = (-1)^{2k} \cdot -1 = -1 \pmod{n}$. Thus, $(n - 1, 0)$ is an acceptable pair. Now pick the largest possible j such that there exists an acceptable pair (v, j), and fix v so that (v, j) is an acceptable pair. Let

$$B = \{x \in \mathbb{Z}_n^* : x^{2^j u} = \pm 1 \pmod{n}\} .$$

Since B is closed under multiplication modulo n, it is a subgroup of $\mathbb{Z}_n^*$. By Theorem 31.15 on page 921, therefore, $|B|$ divides $|\mathbb{Z}_n^*|$. Every nonwitness must be a member of B, since the sequence X produced by a nonwitness must either be all 1s or else contain a -1 no later than the jth position, by the maximality of j.

(If (a, j') is acceptable, where a is a nonwitness, we must have $j' \leq j$ by how we chose j.)

We now use the existence of v to demonstrate that there exists a $w \in \mathbb{Z}_n^* - B$, and hence that B is a proper subgroup of $\mathbb{Z}_n^*$. Since $v^{2^j u} \equiv -1 \pmod{n}$, we also have $v^{2^j u} \equiv -1 \pmod{n_1}$ by Corollary 31.29 to the Chinese remainder theorem. By Corollary 31.28, there exists a w simultaneously satisfying the equations

$$w \equiv v \pmod{n_1},$$
$$w \equiv 1 \pmod{n_2}.$$

Therefore,

$$w^{2^j u} \equiv -1 \pmod{n_1},$$
$$w^{2^j u} \equiv 1 \pmod{n_2}.$$

Corollary 31.29 gives that $w^{2^j u} \not\equiv 1 \pmod{n_1}$ implies $w^{2^j u} \not\equiv 1 \pmod{n}$ and also that $w^{2^j u} \not\equiv -1 \pmod{n_2}$ implies $w^{2^j u} \not\equiv -1 \pmod{n}$. Hence, we conclude that $w^{2^j u} \not\equiv \pm 1 \pmod{n}$, and so $w \notin B$.

It remains to show that $w \in \mathbb{Z}_n^*$. We start by working separately modulo n_1 and modulo n_2. Working modulo n_1, since $v \in \mathbb{Z}_n^*$, we have that $\gcd(v, n) = 1$. Also, we have $\gcd(v, n_1) = 1$, since if v does not have any common divisors with n, then it certainly does not have any common divisors with n_1. Since $w \equiv v \pmod{n_1}$, we see that $\gcd(w, n_1) = 1$. Working modulo n_2, we have $w \equiv 1 \pmod{n_2}$ implies $\gcd(w, n_2) = 1$ by Exercise 31.2-3. Since $\gcd(w, n_1) = 1$ and $\gcd(w, n_2) = 1$, Theorem 31.6 on page 908 yields $\gcd(w, n_1 n_2) = \gcd(w, n) = 1$. That is, $w \in \mathbb{Z}_n^*$.

Therefore, we have $w \in \mathbb{Z}_n^* - B$, and we can conclude in case 2 that B, which includes all nonwitnesses, is a proper subgroup of $\mathbb{Z}_n^*$ and therefore has size at most $(n-1)/2$.

In either case, the number of witnesses to the compositeness of n is at least $(n-1)/2$. ∎

Theorem 31.40
For any odd integer $n > 2$ and positive integer s, the probability that MILLER-RABIN(n, s) errs is at most 2^{-s}.

Proof By Theorem 31.39, if n is composite, then each execution of the **for** loop of lines 1–4 of MILLER-RABIN has a probability of at least $1/2$ of discovering a witness to the compositeness of n. MILLER-RABIN makes an error only if it is so unlucky as to miss discovering a witness to the compositeness of n on each of the s iterations of the main loop. The probability of such a sequence of misses is at most 2^{-s}. ∎

If n is prime, MILLER-RABIN always reports PRIME, and if n is composite, the chance that MILLER-RABIN reports PRIME is at most 2^{-s}.

When applying MILLER-RABIN to a large randomly chosen integer n, however, we need to consider as well the prior probability that n is prime, in order to correctly interpret MILLER-RABIN's result. Suppose that we fix a bit length β and choose at random an integer n of length β bits to be tested for primality, so that $\beta \approx \lg n \approx 1.443 \ln n$. Let A denote the event that n is prime. By the prime number theorem (Theorem 31.37), the probability that n is prime is approximately

$$\Pr\{A\} \approx 1/\ln n$$
$$\approx 1.443/\beta \ .$$

Now let B denote the event that MILLER-RABIN returns PRIME. We have that $\Pr\{\overline{B} \mid A\} = 0$ (or equivalently, that $\Pr\{B \mid A\} = 1$) and $\Pr\{B \mid \overline{A}\} \leq 2^{-s}$ (or equivalently, that $\Pr\{\overline{B} \mid \overline{A}\} > 1 - 2^{-s}$).

But what is $\Pr\{A \mid B\}$, the probability that n is prime, given that MILLER-RABIN has returned PRIME? By the alternate form of Bayes's theorem (equation (C.20) on page 1189) and approximating $\Pr\{B \mid \overline{A}\}$ by 2^{-s}, we have

$$\Pr\{A \mid B\} = \frac{\Pr\{A\}\Pr\{B \mid A\}}{\Pr\{A\}\Pr\{B \mid A\} + \Pr\{\overline{A}\}\Pr\{B \mid \overline{A}\}}$$
$$\approx \frac{(1/\ln n) \cdot 1}{(1/\ln n) \cdot 1 + (1 - 1/\ln n) \cdot 2^{-s}}$$
$$\approx \frac{1}{1 + 2^{-s}(\ln n - 1)} \ .$$

This probability does not exceed $1/2$ until s exceeds $\lg(\ln n - 1)$. Intuitively, that many initial trials are needed just for the confidence derived from failing to find a witness to the compositeness of n to overcome the prior bias in favor of n being composite. For a number with $\beta = 1024$ bits, this initial testing requires about

$$\lg(\ln n - 1) \approx \lg(\beta/1.443)$$
$$\approx 9$$

trials. In any case, choosing $s = 50$ should suffice for almost any imaginable application.

In fact, the situation is much better. If you are trying to find large primes by applying MILLER-RABIN to large randomly chosen odd integers, then choosing a small value of s (say 3) is unlikely to lead to erroneous results, though we won't prove it here. The reason is that for a randomly chosen odd composite integer n, the expected number of nonwitnesses to the compositeness of n is likely to be considerably smaller than $(n-1)/2$.

If the integer n is not chosen randomly, however, the best that can be proven is that the number of nonwitnesses is at most $(n - 1)/4$, using an improved version of Theorem 31.39. Furthermore, there do exist integers n for which the number of nonwitnesses is $(n - 1)/4$.

Exercises

31.8-1
Prove that if an odd integer $n > 1$ is not a prime or a prime power, then there exists a nontrivial square root of 1, modulo n.

★ *31.8-2*
It is possible to strengthen Euler's theorem (Theorem 31.30) slightly to the form

$$a^{\lambda(n)} = 1 \pmod{n} \text{ for all } a \in \mathbb{Z}_n^* ,$$

where $n = p_1^{e_1} \cdots p_r^{e_r}$ and $\lambda(n)$ is defined by

$$\lambda(n) = \text{lcm}(\phi(p_1^{e_1}), \ldots, \phi(p_r^{e_r})) .$$

Prove that $\lambda(n) \mid \phi(n)$. A composite number n is a Carmichael number if $\lambda(n) \mid n - 1$. The smallest Carmichael number is $561 = 3 \cdot 11 \cdot 17$, for which $\lambda(n) = \text{lcm}(2, 10, 16) = 80$, which divides 560. Prove that Carmichael numbers must be both "square-free" (not divisible by the square of any prime) and the product of at least three primes. (For this reason, they are not common.)

31.8-3
Prove that if x is a nontrivial square root of 1, modulo n, then $\gcd(x - 1, n)$ and $\gcd(x + 1, n)$ are both nontrivial divisors of n.

Problems

31-1 Binary gcd algorithm
Most computers can perform the operations of subtraction, testing the parity (odd or even) of a binary integer, and halving more quickly than computing remainders. This problem investigates the *binary gcd algorithm*, which avoids the remainder computations used in Euclid's algorithm.

a. Prove that if a and b are both even, then $\gcd(a, b) = 2 \cdot \gcd(a/2, b/2)$.

b. Prove that if a is odd and b is even, then $\gcd(a, b) = \gcd(a, b/2)$.

c. Prove that if a and b are both odd, then $\gcd(a, b) = \gcd((a - b)/2, b)$.

d. Design an efficient binary gcd algorithm for input integers a and b, where $a \geq b$, that runs in $O(\lg a)$ time. Assume that each subtraction, parity test, and halving takes unit time.

31-2   *Analysis of bit operations in Euclid's algorithm*

a. Consider the ordinary "paper and pencil" algorithm for long division: dividing a by b, which yields a quotient q and remainder r. Show that this method requires $O((1 + \lg q) \lg b)$ bit operations.

b. Define $\mu(a, b) = (1 + \lg a)(1 + \lg b)$. Show that the number of bit operations performed by EUCLID in reducing the problem of computing $\gcd(a, b)$ to that of computing $\gcd(b, a \bmod b)$ is at most $c(\mu(a, b) - \mu(b, a \bmod b))$ for some sufficiently large constant $c > 0$.

c. Show that EUCLID(a, b) requires $O(\mu(a, b))$ bit operations in general and $O(\beta^2)$ bit operations when applied to two β-bit inputs.

31-3   *Three algorithms for Fibonacci numbers*

This problem compares the efficiency of three methods for computing the nth Fibonacci number F_n, given n. Assume that the cost of adding, subtracting, or multiplying two numbers is $O(1)$, independent of the size of the numbers.

a. Show that the running time of the straightforward recursive method for computing F_n based on recurrence (3.31) on page 69 is exponential in n. (See, for example, the FIB procedure on page 751.)

b. Show how to compute F_n in $O(n)$ time using memoization.

c. Show how to compute F_n in $O(\lg n)$ time using only integer addition and multiplication. (*Hint:* Consider the matrix $\begin{pmatrix} 0 & 1 \\ 1 & 1 \end{pmatrix}$ and its powers.)

d. Assume now that adding two β-bit numbers takes $\Theta(\beta)$ time and that multiplying two β-bit numbers takes $\Theta(\beta^2)$ time. What is the running time of these three methods under this more reasonable cost measure for the elementary arithmetic operations?

31-4   *Quadratic residues*

Let p be an odd prime. A number $a \in Z_p^*$ is a *quadratic residue* modulo p, if the equation $x^2 = a \pmod{p}$ has a solution for the unknown x.

a. Show that there are exactly $(p - 1)/2$ quadratic residues, modulo p.

b. If p is prime, we define the *Legendre symbol* $\left(\frac{a}{p}\right)$, for $a \in \mathbb{Z}_p^*$, to be 1 if a is a quadratic residue, modulo p, and -1 otherwise. Prove that if $a \in \mathbb{Z}_p^*$, then

$$\left(\frac{a}{p}\right) = a^{(p-1)/2} \pmod{p} \,.$$

Give an efficient algorithm that determines whether a given number a is a quadratic residue, modulo p. Analyze the efficiency of your algorithm.

c. Prove that if p is a prime of the form $4k + 3$ and a is a quadratic residue in $\mathbb{Z}_p^*$, then $a^{k+1} \bmod p$ is a square root of a, modulo p. How much time is required to find the square root of a quadratic residue a, modulo p?

d. Describe an efficient randomized algorithm for finding a nonquadratic residue, modulo an arbitrary prime p, that is, a member of $\mathbb{Z}_p^*$ that is not a quadratic residue. How many arithmetic operations does your algorithm require on average?

Chapter notes

Knuth [260] contains a good discussion of algorithms for finding the greatest common divisor, as well as other basic number-theoretic algorithms. Dixon [121] gives an overview of factorization and primality testing. Bach [33], Riesel [378], and Bach and Shallit [34] provide overviews of the basics of computational number theory; Shoup [411] provides a more recent survey. The conference proceedings edited by Pomerance [362] contains several excellent survey articles.

Knuth [260] discusses the origin of Euclid's algorithm. It appears in Book 7, Propositions 1 and 2, of the Greek mathematician Euclid's *Elements*, which was written around 300 B.C.E. Euclid's description may have been derived from an algorithm due to Eudoxus around 375 B.C.E. Euclid's algorithm may hold the honor of being the oldest nontrivial algorithm, rivaled only by an algorithm for multiplication known to the ancient Egyptians. Shallit [407] chronicles the history of the analysis of Euclid's algorithm.

Knuth attributes a special case of the Chinese remainder theorem (Theorem 31.27) to the Chinese mathematician Sun-Tsŭ, who lived sometime between 200 B.C.E. and 200 C.E.—the date is quite uncertain. The same special case was given by the Greek mathematician Nichomachus around 100 C.E. It was generalized by Qin Jiushao in 1247. The Chinese remainder theorem was finally stated and proved in its full generality by L. Euler in 1734.

The randomized primality-testing algorithm presented here is due to Miller [327] and Rabin [373] and is the fastest randomized primality-testing algorithm known, to within constant factors. The proof of Theorem 31.40 is a slight adaptation of one suggested by Bach [32]. A proof of a stronger result for MILLER-RABIN was given by Monier [332, 333]. For many years primality-testing was the classic example of a problem where randomization appeared to be necessary to obtain an efficient (polynomial-time) algorithm. In 2002, however, Agrawal, Kayal, and Saxena [4] surprised everyone with their deterministic polynomial-time primality-testing algorithm. Until then, the fastest deterministic primality testing algorithm known, due to Cohen and Lenstra [97], ran in $(\lg n)^{O(\lg \lg \lg n)}$ time on input n, which is just slightly superpolynomial. Nonetheless, for practical purposes, randomized primality-testing algorithms remain more efficient and are generally preferred.

Beauchemin, Brassard, Crépeau, Goutier, and Pomerance [40] nicely discuss the problem of finding large "random" primes.

The concept of a public-key cryptosystem is due to Diffie and Hellman [115]. The RSA cryptosystem was proposed in 1977 by Rivest, Shamir, and Adleman [380]. Since then, the field of cryptography has blossomed. Our understanding of the RSA cryptosystem has deepened, and modern implementations use significant refinements of the basic techniques presented here. In addition, many new techniques have been developed for proving cryptosystems to be secure. For example, Goldwasser and Micali [190] show that randomization can be an effective tool in the design of secure public-key encryption schemes. For signature schemes, Goldwasser, Micali, and Rivest [191] present a digital-signature scheme for which every conceivable type of forgery is provably as difficult as factoring. Katz and Lindell [253] provide an overview of modern cryptography.

The best algorithms for factoring large numbers have a running time that grows roughly exponentially with the cube root of the length of the number n to be factored. The general number-field sieve factoring algorithm (as developed by Buhler, Lenstra, and Pomerance [77] as an extension of the ideas in the number-field sieve factoring algorithm by Pollard [360] and Lenstra et al. [295] and refined by Coppersmith [102] and others) is perhaps the most efficient such algorithm in general for large inputs. Although it is difficult to give a rigorous analysis of this algorithm, under reasonable assumptions we can derive a running-time estimate of $L(1/3, n)^{1.902+o(1)}$, where $L(\alpha, n) = e^{(\ln n)^{\alpha}(\ln \ln n)^{1-\alpha}}$.

The elliptic-curve method due to Lenstra [296] may be more effective for some inputs than the number-field sieve method, since it can find a small prime factor p quite quickly. With this method, the time to find p is estimated to be $L(1/2, p)^{\sqrt{2}+o(1)}$.

32 String Matching

Text-editing programs frequently need to find all occurrences of a pattern in the text. Typically, the text is a document being edited, and the pattern searched for is a particular word supplied by the user. Efficient algorithms for this problem —called "string matching"—can greatly aid the responsiveness of the text-editing program. Among their many other applications, string-matching algorithms search for particular patterns in DNA sequences. Internet search engines also use them to find web pages relevant to queries.

The string-matching problem can be stated formally as follows. The text is given as an array $T[1:n]$ of length n, and the pattern is an array $P[1:m]$ of length $m \leq n$. The elements of P and T are characters drawn from an alphabet Σ, which is a finite set of characters. For example, Σ could be the set $\{0, 1\}$, or it could be the set $\{a, b, \ldots, z\}$. The character arrays P and T are often called *strings* of characters.

As Figure 32.1 shows, pattern P *occurs with shift s* in text T (or, equivalently, that pattern P *occurs beginning at position $s + 1$* in text T) if $0 \leq s \leq n - m$ and $T[s + 1 : s + m] = P[1 : m]$, that is, if $T[s + j] = P[j]$, for $1 \leq j \leq m$. If P occurs with shift s in T, then s is a *valid shift*, and otherwise, s is an *invalid shift*. The *string-matching problem* is the problem of finding all valid shifts with which a given pattern P occurs in a given text T.

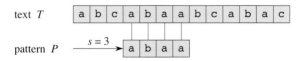

Figure 32.1 An example of the string-matching problem to find all occurrences of the pattern $P = \text{abaa}$ in the text $T = \text{abcabaabcabac}$. The pattern occurs only once in the text, at shift $s = 3$, which is a valid shift. A vertical line connects each character of the pattern to its matching character in the text, and all matched characters are shaded blue.

Except for the naive brute-force algorithm in Section 32.1, each string-matching algorithm in this chapter performs some preprocessing based on the pattern and then finds all valid shifts. We call this latter phase "matching." Here are the pre-processing and matching times for each of the string-matching algorithms in this chapter. The total running time of each algorithm is the sum of the preprocessing and matching times:

Algorithm	Preprocessing time	Matching time
Naive	0	$O((n - m + 1)m)$
Rabin-Karp	$\Theta(m)$	$O((n - m + 1)m)$
Finite automaton	$O(m\,\lvert\Sigma\rvert)$	$\Theta(n)$
Knuth-Morris-Pratt	$\Theta(m)$	$\Theta(n)$
Suffix array[1]	$O(n \lg n)$	$O(m \lg n + km)$

Section 32.2 presents an interesting string-matching algorithm, due to Rabin and Karp. Although the $\Theta((n - m + 1)m)$ worst-case running time of this algorithm is no better than that of the naive method, it works much better on average and in practice. It also generalizes nicely to other pattern-matching problems. Section 32.3 then describes a string-matching algorithm that begins by constructing a finite automaton specifically designed to search for occurrences of the given pattern P in a text. This algorithm takes $O(m\,\lvert\Sigma\rvert)$ preprocessing time, but only $\Theta(n)$ matching time. Section 32.4 presents the similar, but much cleverer, Knuth-Morris-Pratt (or KMP) algorithm, which has the same $\Theta(n)$ matching time, but it reduces the preprocessing time to only $\Theta(m)$.

A completely different approach appears in Section 32.5, which examines suffix arrays and the longest common prefix array. You can use these arrays not only to find a pattern in a text, but also to answer other questions, such as what is the longest repeated substring in the text and what is the longest common substring between two texts. The algorithm to form the suffix array in Section 32.5 takes $O(n \lg n)$ time and, given the suffix array, the section shows how to compute the longest common prefix array in $O(n)$ time.

Notation and terminology

We denote by Σ^* (read "sigma-star") the set of all finite-length strings formed using characters from the alphabet Σ. This chapter considers only finite-length

---

[1] For suffix arrays, the preprocessing time of $O(n \lg n)$ comes from the algorithm presented in Section 32.5. It can be reduced to $\Theta(n)$ by using the algorithm in Problem 32-2. The factor k in the matching time denotes the number of occurrences of the pattern in the text.

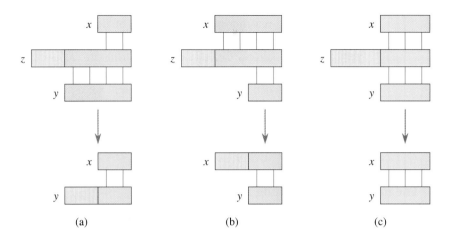

Figure 32.2   A graphical proof of Lemma 32.1. Suppose that $x \sqsupset z$ and $y \sqsupset z$. The three parts of the figure illustrate the three cases of the lemma. Vertical lines connect matching regions (shown in blue) of the strings. **(a)** If $|x| \leq |y|$, then $x \sqsupset y$. **(b)** If $|x| \geq |y|$, then $y \sqsupset x$. **(c)** If $|x| = |y|$, then $x = y$.

strings. The 0-length *empty string*, denoted ε, also belongs to Σ^*. The length of a string x is denoted $|x|$. The *concatenation* of two strings x and y, denoted xy, has length $|x| + |y|$ and consists of the characters from x followed by the characters from y.

A string w is a *prefix* of a string x, denoted $w \sqsubset x$, if $x = wy$ for some string $y \in \Sigma^*$. Note that if $w \sqsubset x$, then $|w| \leq |x|$. Similarly, a string w is a *suffix* of a string x, denoted $w \sqsupset x$, if $x = yw$ for some $y \in \Sigma^*$. As with a prefix, $w \sqsupset x$ implies $|w| \leq |x|$. For example, $ab \sqsubset abcca$ and $cca \sqsupset abcca$. A string w is a *proper prefix* of x if $w \sqsubset x$ and $|w| < |x|$, and likewise for a *proper suffix*. The empty string ε is both a suffix and a prefix of every string. For any strings x and y and any character a, we have $x \sqsupset y$ if and only if $xa \sqsupset ya$. The $\sqsubset$ and $\sqsupset$ relations are transitive. The following lemma will be useful later.

Lemma 32.1 (*Overlapping-suffix lemma*)
Suppose that x, y, and z are strings such that $x \sqsupset z$ and $y \sqsupset z$. If $|x| \leq |y|$, then $x \sqsupset y$. If $|x| \geq |y|$, then $y \sqsupset x$. If $|x| = |y|$, then $x = y$.

Proof   See Figure 32.2 for a graphical proof.   ∎

For convenience, denote the k-character prefix $P[1:k]$ of the pattern $P[1:m]$ by $P[:k]$. Thus, we can write $P[:0] = \varepsilon$ and $P[:m] = P = P[1:m]$. Similarly, denote the k-character prefix of the text T by $T[:k]$. Using this notation, we can state the string-matching problem as that of finding all shifts s in the range $0 \leq s \leq n - m$ such that $P \sqsupset T[:s+m]$.

Our pseudocode allows two equal-length strings to be compared for equality as a primitive operation. If the strings are compared from left to right and the comparison stops when a mismatch is discovered, we assume that the time taken by such a test is a linear function of the number of matching characters discovered. To be precise, the test "$x == y$" is assumed to take $\Theta(t)$ time, where t is the length of the longest string z such that $z \sqsubset x$ and $z \sqsubset y$.

32.1   The naive string-matching algorithm

The NAIVE-STRING-MATCHER procedure finds all valid shifts using a loop that checks the condition $P[1:m] = T[s+1:s+m]$ for each of the $n - m + 1$ possible values of s.

NAIVE-STRING-MATCHER(T, P, n, m)

1 **for** $s = 0$ **to** $n - m$
2   **if** $P[1:m] == T[s+1:s+m]$
3   print "Pattern occurs with shift" s

Figure 32.3 portrays the naive string-matching procedure as sliding a "template" containing the pattern over the text, noting for which shifts all of the characters on the template equal the corresponding characters in the text. The **for** loop of lines 1–3 considers each possible shift explicitly. The test in line 2 determines whether the current shift is valid. This test implicitly loops to check corresponding character positions until all positions match successfully or a mismatch is found. Line 3 prints out each valid shift s.

Procedure NAIVE-STRING-MATCHER takes $O((n - m + 1)m)$ time, and this bound is tight in the worst case. For example, consider the text string a^n (a string of n a's) and the pattern a^m. For each of the $n - m + 1$ possible values of the shift s, the implicit loop on line 2 to compare corresponding characters must execute m times to validate the shift. The worst-case running time is thus $\Theta((n - m + 1)m)$, which is $\Theta(n^2)$ if $m = \lfloor n/2 \rfloor$. Because it requires no preprocessing, NAIVE-STRING-MATCHER's running time equals its matching time.

NAIVE-STRING-MATCHER is far from an optimal procedure for this problem. Indeed, this chapter will show that the Knuth-Morris-Pratt algorithm is much better in the worst case. The naive string-matcher is inefficient because it entirely ignores information gained about the text for one value of s when it considers other values of s. Such information can be quite valuable, however. For example, if $P = \mathsf{aaab}$

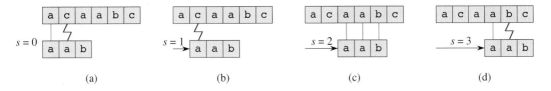

Figure 32.3   The operation of the NAIVE-STRING-MATCHER procedure for the pattern $P = $ aab and the text $T = $ acaabc. Imagine the pattern P as a template that slides next to the text. **(a)–(d)** The four successive alignments tried by the naive string matcher. In each part, vertical lines connect corresponding regions found to match (shown in blue), and a red jagged line connects the first mismatched character found, if any. The algorithm finds one occurrence of the pattern, at shift $s = 2$, shown in part (c).

and $s = 0$ is valid, then none of the shifts 1, 2, or 3 are valid, since $T[4] = $ b. The following sections examine several ways to make effective use of this sort of information.

Exercises

32.1-1
Show the comparisons the naive string matcher makes for the pattern $P = $ 0001 in the text $T = $ 000010001010001.

32.1-2
Suppose that all characters in the pattern P are different. Show how to accelerate NAIVE-STRING-MATCHER to run in $O(n)$ time on an n-character text T.

32.1-3
Suppose that pattern P and text T are *randomly* chosen strings of length m and n, respectively, from the d-ary alphabet $\Sigma_d = \{0, 1, \dots, d-1\}$, where $d \geq 2$. Show that the *expected* number of character-to-character comparisons made by the implicit loop in line 2 of the naive algorithm is

$$(n - m + 1)\frac{1 - d^{-m}}{1 - d^{-1}} \leq 2(n - m + 1)$$

over all executions of this loop. (Assume that the naive algorithm stops comparing characters for a given shift once it finds a mismatch or matches the entire pattern.) Thus, for randomly chosen strings, the naive algorithm is quite efficient.

32.1-4
Suppose that the pattern P may contain occurrences of a *gap character* $\diamond$ that can match an *arbitrary* string of characters (even one of 0 length). For example, the pattern ab$\diamond$ba$\diamond$c occurs in the text cabccbacbacab as

```
c ab cc ba cba c ab
  ab  ◇  ba  ◇  c
```

and as

```
c ab ccbac ba     c ab .
  ab   ◇  ba ◇  c
```

The gap character may occur an arbitrary number of times in the pattern but not at all in the text. Give a polynomial-time algorithm to determine whether such a pattern P occurs in a given text T, and analyze the running time of your algorithm.

32.2   The Rabin-Karp algorithm

Rabin and Karp proposed a string-matching algorithm that performs well in practice and that also generalizes to other algorithms for related problems, such as two-dimensional pattern matching. The Rabin-Karp algorithm uses $\Theta(m)$ preprocessing time, and its worst-case running time is $\Theta((n-m+1)m)$. Based on certain assumptions, however, its average-case running time is better.

This algorithm makes use of elementary number-theoretic notions such as the equivalence of two numbers modulo a third number. You might want to refer to Section 31.1 for the relevant definitions.

For expository purposes, let's assume that $\Sigma = \{0, 1, 2, \ldots, 9\}$, so that each character is a decimal digit. (In the general case, you can assume that each character is a digit in radix-d notation, so that it has a numerical value in the range 0 to $d-1$, where $d = |\Sigma|$.) You can then view a string of k consecutive characters as representing a length-k decimal number. For example, the character string 31415 corresponds to the decimal number 31,415. Because we interpret the input characters as both graphical symbols and digits, it will be convenient in this section to denote them as digits in standard text font.

Given a pattern $P[1:m]$, let p denote its corresponding decimal value. In a similar manner, given a text $T[1:n]$, let t_s denote the decimal value of the length-m substring $T[s+1:s+m]$, for $s = 0, 1, \ldots, n-m$. Certainly, $t_s = p$ if and only if $T[s+1:s+m] = P[1:m]$, and thus, s is a valid shift if and only if $t_s = p$. If you could compute p in $\Theta(m)$ time and all the t_s values in a total of $\Theta(n-m+1)$ time,[2] then you could determine all valid shifts s in $\Theta(m) + \Theta(n-m+1) = \Theta(n)$

---

[2] We write $\Theta(n-m+1)$ instead of $\Theta(n-m)$ because s takes on $n-m+1$ different values. The "+1" is significant in an asymptotic sense because when $m = n$, computing the lone t_s value takes $\Theta(1)$ time, not $\Theta(0)$ time.

time by comparing p with each of the t_s values. (For the moment, let's not worry about the possibility that p and the t_s values might be very large numbers.)

Indeed, you can compute p in $\Theta(m)$ time using Horner's rule (see Problem 2-3):

$$p = P[m] + 10 \left(P[m-1] + 10 \left(P[m-2] + \cdots + 10(P[2] + 10P[1]) \cdots \right) \right).$$

Similarly, you can compute t_0 from $T[1:m]$ in $\Theta(m)$ time.

To compute the remaining values $t_1, t_2, \ldots, t_{n-m}$ in $\Theta(n-m)$ time, observe that you can compute t_{s+1} from t_s in constant time, since

$$t_{s+1} = 10 \left(t_s - 10^{m-1} T[s+1] \right) + T[s+m+1]. \tag{32.1}$$

Subtracting $10^{m-1} T[s+1]$ removes the high-order digit from t_s, multiplying the result by 10 shifts the number left by one digit position, and adding $T[s+m+1]$ brings in the appropriate low-order digit. For example, suppose that $m = 5$, $t_s = 31415$, and the new low-order digit is $T[s+5+1] = 2$. The high-order digit to remove is $T[s+1] = 3$, and so

$$\begin{aligned} t_{s+1} &= 10\,(31415 - 10000 \cdot 3) + 2 \\ &= 14152. \end{aligned}$$

If you precompute the constant 10^{m-1} (which you can do in $O(\lg m)$ time using the techniques of Section 31.6, although for this application a straightforward $O(m)$-time method suffices), then each execution of equation (32.1) takes a constant number of arithmetic operations. Thus, you can compute p in $\Theta(m)$ time, and you can compute all of $t_0, t_1, \ldots, t_{n-m}$ in $\Theta(n-m+1)$ time. Therefore, you can find all occurrences of the pattern $P[1:m]$ in the text $T[1:n]$ with $\Theta(m)$ preprocessing time and $\Theta(n-m+1)$ matching time.

This scheme works well if P is short enough and the alphabet Σ is small enough that arithmetic operations on p and t_s take constant time. But what if P is long, or if the size of Σ means that instead of powers of 10 in equation (32.1) you have to use powers of a larger number (such as powers of 256 for the extended ASCII character set)? Then the values of p and t_s might be too large to work with in constant time. Fortunately, this problem can be solved, as Figure 32.4 shows: compute p and the t_s values modulo a suitable modulus q. You can compute p modulo q in $\Theta(m)$ time and all the t_s values modulo q in $\Theta(n-m+1)$ time. With $|\Sigma| = 10$, if you choose the modulus q as a prime such that $10q$ just fits within one computer word, then you can perform all the necessary computations with single-precision arithmetic. In general, with a d-ary alphabet $\{0, 1, \ldots, d-1\}$, choose q so that dq fits within a computer word and adjust the recurrence equation (32.1) to work modulo q, so that it becomes

$$t_{s+1} = \left(d(t_s - T[s+1]h) + T[s+m+1] \right) \bmod q, \tag{32.2}$$

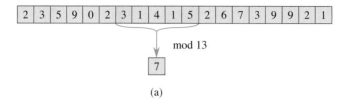

(a)

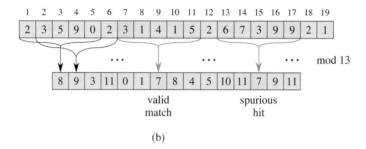

(b)

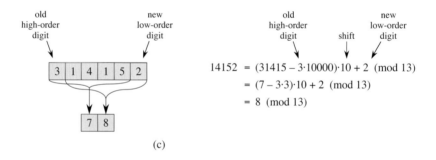

(c)

Figure 32.4 The Rabin-Karp algorithm. Each character is a decimal digit. Values are computed modulo 13. **(a)** A text string. A window of length 5 is shaded blue. The numerical value of the blue number, computed modulo 13, yields the value 7. **(b)** The same text string with values computed modulo 13 for each possible position of a length-5 window. Assuming the pattern $P = 31415$, look for windows whose value modulo 13 is 7, since $31415 = 7 \pmod{13}$. The algorithm finds two such windows, shaded blue in the figure. The first, beginning at text position 7, is indeed an occurrence of the pattern. The second window, beginning at text position 13, is a spurious hit. **(c)** How to compute the value for a window in constant time, given the value for the previous window. The first window has value 31415. Dropping the high-order digit 3, shifting left (multiplying by 10), and then adding in the low-order digit 2 gives the new value 14152. Because all computations are performed modulo 13, the value for the first window is 7, and the value for the new window is 8.

where $h = d^{m-1} \bmod q$ is the value of the digit "1" in the high-order position of an m-digit text window.

The solution of working modulo q is not perfect, however: $t_s = p \pmod{q}$ does not automatically mean that $t_s = p$. On the other hand, if $t_s \neq p \pmod{q}$, then you definitely know that $t_s \neq p$, so that shift s is invalid. Thus you can use the test $t_s = p \pmod{q}$ as a fast heuristic test to rule out invalid shifts. If $t_s = p \pmod{q}$—a *hit*—then you need to test further to see whether s is really valid or you just have a *spurious hit*. This additional test explicitly checks the condition $P[1:m] = T[s+1:s+m]$. If q is large enough, then you would hope that spurious hits occur infrequently enough that the cost of the extra checking is low.

The procedure RABIN-KARP-MATCHER on the next page makes these ideas precise. The inputs to the procedure are the text T, the pattern P, their lengths n and m, the radix d to use (which is typically taken to be $|\Sigma|$), and the prime q to use. The procedure works as follows. All characters are interpreted as radix-d digits. The subscripts on t are provided only for clarity: the procedure works correctly if all the subscripts are dropped. Line 1 initializes h to the value of the high-order digit position of an m-digit window. Lines 2–6 compute p as the value of $P[1:m] \bmod q$ and t_0 as the value of $T[1:m] \bmod q$. The **for** loop of lines 7–12 iterates through all possible shifts s, maintaining the following invariant:

Whenever line 8 is executed, $t_s = T[s+1:s+m] \bmod q$.

If a hit occurs because $p = t_s$ in line 8, then line 9 determines whether s is a valid shift or the hit was spurious via the test $P[1:m] == T[s+1:s+m]$. Line 10 prints out any valid shifts that are found. If $s < n-m$ (checked in line 11), then the **for** loop will iterate at least one more time, and so line 12 first executes to ensure that the loop invariant holds upon the next iteration. Line 12 computes the value of $t_{s+1} \bmod q$ from the value of $t_s \bmod q$ in constant time using equation (32.2) directly.

RABIN-KARP-MATCHER takes $\Theta(m)$ preprocessing time, and its matching time is $\Theta((n-m+1)m)$ in the worst case, since (like the naive string-matching algorithm) the Rabin-Karp algorithm explicitly verifies every valid shift. If $P = \mathtt{a}^m$ and $T = \mathtt{a}^n$, then verifying takes $\Theta((n-m+1)m)$ time, since each of the $n-m+1$ possible shifts is valid.

In many applications, you expect few valid shifts—perhaps some constant c of them. In such applications, the expected matching time of the algorithm is only $O((n-m+1)+cm) = O(n+m)$, plus the time required to process spurious hits. We can base a heuristic analysis on the assumption that reducing values modulo q acts like a random mapping from Σ^* to $\mathbb{Z}_q$. The expected number of spurious hits is then $O(n/q)$, because we can estimate the chance that an arbitrary t_s will be equivalent to p, modulo q, as $1/q$. Since there are $O(n)$ positions at which the

RABIN-KARP-MATCHER(T, P, n, m, d, q)

```
1   h = d^(m-1) mod q
2   p = 0
3   t_0 = 0
4   for i = 1 to m                              // preprocessing
5       p = (dp + P[i]) mod q
6       t_0 = (dt_0 + T[i]) mod q
7   for s = 0 to n - m                          // matching—try all possible shifts
8       if p == t_s                             // a hit?
9           if P[1 : m] == T[s + 1 : s + m]     // valid shift?
10              print "Pattern occurs with shift" s
11      if s < n - m
12          t_(s+1) = (d(t_s - T[s + 1]h) + T[s + m + 1]) mod q
```

test of line 8 fails (actually, at most $n - m + 1$ positions) and checking each hit takes $O(m)$ time in line 9, the expected matching time taken by the Rabin-Karp algorithm is

$$O(n) + O(m(v + n/q)),$$

where v is the number of valid shifts. This running time is $O(n)$ if $v = O(1)$ and you choose $q \geq m$. That is, if the expected number of valid shifts is small ($O(1)$) and you choose the prime q to be larger than the length of the pattern, then you can expect the Rabin-Karp procedure to use only $O(n + m)$ matching time. Since $m \leq n$, this expected matching time is $O(n)$.

Exercises

32.2-1
Working modulo $q = 11$, how many spurious hits does the Rabin-Karp matcher encounter in the text $T = 3141592653589793$ when looking for the pattern $P = 26$?

32.2-2
Describe how to extend the Rabin-Karp method to the problem of searching a text string for an occurrence of any one of a given set of k patterns. Start by assuming that all k patterns have the same length. Then generalize your solution to allow the patterns to have different lengths.

32.2-3
Show how to extend the Rabin-Karp method to handle the problem of looking for a given $m \times m$ pattern in an $n \times n$ array of characters. (The pattern may be shifted vertically and horizontally, but it may not be rotated.)

32.2-4

Alice has a copy of a long n-bit file $A = \langle a_{n-1}, a_{n-2}, \ldots, a_0 \rangle$, and Bob similarly has an n-bit file $B = \langle b_{n-1}, b_{n-2}, \ldots, b_0 \rangle$. Alice and Bob wish to know if their files are identical. To avoid transmitting all of A or B, they use the following fast probabilistic check. Together, they select a prime $q > 1000n$ and randomly select an integer x from $\{0, 1, \ldots, q-1\}$. Letting

$$A(x) = \left(\sum_{i=0}^{n-1} a_i x^i \right) \bmod q \quad \text{and} \quad B(x) = \left(\sum_{i=0}^{n-1} b_i x^i \right) \bmod q \, ,$$

Alice evaluates $A(x)$ and Bob evaluates $B(x)$. Prove that if $A \neq B$, there is at most one chance in 1000 that $A(x) = B(x)$, whereas if the two files are the same, $A(x)$ is necessarily the same as $B(x)$. (*Hint:* See Exercise 31.4-4.)

32.3 String matching with finite automata

Many string-matching algorithms build a finite automaton—a simple machine for processing information—that scans the text string T for all occurrences of the pattern P. This section presents a method for building such an automaton. These string-matching automata are efficient: they examine each text character *exactly once*, taking constant time per text character. The matching time used—after preprocessing the pattern to build the automaton—is therefore $\Theta(n)$. The time to build the automaton, however, can be large if Σ is large. Section 32.4 describes a clever way around this problem.

We begin this section with the definition of a finite automaton. We then examine a special string-matching automaton and show how to use it to find occurrences of a pattern in a text. Finally, we'll see how to construct the string-matching automaton for a given input pattern.

Finite automata

A *finite automaton* M, illustrated in Figure 32.5, is a 5-tuple $(Q, q_0, A, \Sigma, \delta)$, where

- Q is a finite set of *states*,
- $q_0 \in Q$ is the *start state*,
- $A \subseteq Q$ is a distinguished set of *accepting states*,
- Σ is a finite *input alphabet*,
- δ is a function from $Q \times \Sigma$ into Q, called the *transition function* of M.

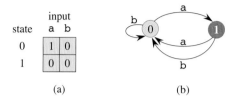

	input	
state	a	b
0	1	0
1	0	0

(a)   (b)

Figure 32.5 A simple two-state finite automaton with state set $Q = \{0, 1\}$, start state $q_0 = 0$, and input alphabet $\Sigma = \{a, b\}$. **(a)** A tabular representation of the transition function δ. **(b)** An equivalent state-transition diagram. State 1, in orange, is the only accepting state. Directed edges represent transitions. For example, the edge from state 1 to state 0 labeled b indicates that $\delta(1, b) = 0$. This automaton accepts those strings that end in an odd number of a's. More precisely, it accepts a string x if and only if $x = yz$, where $y = \varepsilon$ or y ends with a b, and $z = a^k$, where k is odd. For example, on input abaaa, including the start state, this automaton enters the sequence of states $\langle 0, 1, 0, 1, 0, 1 \rangle$, and so it accepts this input. For input abbaa, it enters the sequence of states $\langle 0, 1, 0, 0, 1, 0 \rangle$, and so it rejects this input.

The finite automaton begins in state q_0 and reads the characters of its input string one at a time. If the automaton is in state q and reads input character a, it moves ("makes a transition") from state q to state $\delta(q, a)$. Whenever its current state q is a member of A, the machine M has **accepted** the string read so far. An input that is not accepted is **rejected**.

A finite automaton M induces a function ϕ, called the **final-state function**, from Σ^* to Q such that $\phi(w)$ is the state M ends up in after reading the string w. Thus, M accepts a string w if and only if $\phi(w) \in A$. We define the function ϕ recursively, using the transition function:

$$\phi(\varepsilon) = q_0 \, ,$$
$$\phi(wa) = \delta(\phi(w), a) \quad \text{for } w \in \Sigma^*, a \in \Sigma \, .$$

String-matching automata

For a given pattern P, a preprocessing step constructs a string-matching automaton specific to P. The automaton then searches the text string for occurrences of P. Figure 32.6 illustrates the automaton for the pattern $P = \text{ababaca}$. From now on, let's assume that P is fixed, and for brevity, we won't bother to indicate the dependence upon P in our notation.

In order to specify the string-matching automaton corresponding to a given pattern $P[1:m]$, we first define an auxiliary function σ, called the **suffix function** corresponding to the pattern P. The function σ maps Σ^* to $\{0, 1, \ldots, m\}$ such that $\sigma(x)$ is the length of the longest prefix of P that is also a suffix of x:

$$\sigma(x) = \max \{k : P[:k] \sqsupseteq x\} \, . \tag{32.3}$$

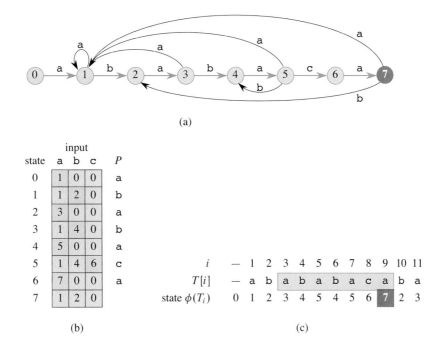

(a)

(b)

state	input a	b	c	P
0	1	0	0	a
1	1	2	0	b
2	3	0	0	a
3	1	4	0	b
4	5	0	0	a
5	1	4	6	c
6	7	0	0	a
7	1	2	0	

(c)

i	—	1	2	3	4	5	6	7	8	9	10	11
$T[i]$	—	a	b	a	b	a	b	a	c	a	b	a
state $\phi(T_i)$	0	1	2	3	4	5	4	5	6	7	2	3

Figure 32.6 (a) A state-transition diagram for the string-matching automaton that accepts all strings ending in the string `ababaca`. State 0 is the start state, and state 7 (in orange) is the only accepting state. The transition function δ is defined by equation (32.4), and a directed edge from state i to state j labeled a represents $\delta(i, a) = j$. The right-going edges forming the "spine" of the automaton, shown in blue, correspond to successful matches between pattern and input characters. Except for the edges from state 7 to states 1 and 2, the left-going edges correspond to mismatches. Some edges corresponding to mismatches are omitted: by convention, if a state i has no outgoing edge labeled a for some $a \in \Sigma$, then $\delta(i, a) = 0$. (b) The corresponding transition function δ, and the pattern string $P = $ `ababaca`. The entries corresponding to successful matches between pattern and input characters are shown in blue. (c) The operation of the automaton on the text $T = $ `ababababacaba`. Under each text character $T[i]$ appears the state $\phi(T[:i])$ that the automaton is in after processing the prefix $T[:i]$. The substring of the pattern that occurs in the text is highlighted in blue. The automaton finds this one occurrence of the pattern, ending in position 9.

The suffix function σ is well defined since the empty string $P[:0] = \varepsilon$ is a suffix of every string. As examples, for the pattern $P = $ `ab`, we have $\sigma(\varepsilon) = 0$, $\sigma(\text{ccaca}) = 1$, and $\sigma(\text{ccab}) = 2$. For a pattern P of length m, we have $\sigma(x) = m$ if and only if $P \sqsupset x$. From the definition of the suffix function, $x \sqsupset y$ implies $\sigma(x) \le \sigma(y)$ (see Exercise 32.3-4).

We are now ready to define the string-matching automaton that corresponds to a given pattern $P[1:m]$:

- The state set Q is $\{0, 1, \dots, m\}$. The start state q_0 is state 0, and state m is the only accepting state.

- The transition function δ is defined, for any state q and character a, by

$$\delta(q, a) = \sigma(P[:q]a) . \tag{32.4}$$

As the automaton consumes characters of the text T, it is trying to build a match of the pattern P against the most recently seen characters of T. At any time, the state number q gives the length of the longest prefix of P that matches the most recently seen text characters. Whenever the automaton reaches state m, the m most recently seen text characters match the first m characters of P. Since P has length m, reaching state m means that the m most recently seen text characters match the entire pattern, so that the automaton has found a match.

With this intuition behind the design of the automaton, here is the reasoning behind defining $\delta(q, a) = \sigma(P[:q]a)$. Suppose that the automaton is in state q after reading the first i characters of the text, that is, $q = \phi(T[:i])$. The intuitive idea then says that q also equals the length of the longest prefix of P that matches a suffix of $T[:i]$ or, equivalently, that $q = \sigma(T[:i])$. Thus, since $\phi(T[:i])$ and $\sigma(T[:i])$ both equal q, we will see (in Theorem 32.4 on page 973) that the automaton maintains the following invariant:

$$\phi(T[:i]) = \sigma(T[:i]) . \tag{32.5}$$

If the automaton is in state q and reads the next character $T[i + 1] = a$, then the transition should lead to the state corresponding to the longest prefix of P that is a suffix of $T[:i]a$. That state is $\sigma(T[:i]a)$, and equation (32.5) gives $\phi(T[:i]a) = \sigma(T[:i]a)$. Because $P[:q]$ is the longest prefix of P that is a suffix of $T[:i]$, the longest prefix of P that is a suffix of $T[:i]a$ has length not only $\sigma(T[:i]a)$, but also $\sigma(P[:q]a)$, and so $\phi(T[:i]a) = \sigma(P[:q]a)$. (Lemma 32.3 on page 972 will prove that $\sigma(T[:i]a) = \sigma(P[:q]a)$.) Thus, when the automaton is in state q, the transition function δ on character a should take the automaton to state $\delta(q, a) = \delta(\phi(T[:i]), a) = \phi(T[:i]a) = \sigma(P[:q]a)$ (with the last equality following from equation (32.5)).

There are two cases to consider, depending on whether the next character continues to match the pattern. In the first case, $a = P[q + 1]$, so that the character a continues to match the pattern. In this case, because $\delta(q, a) = q + 1$, the transition continues to go along the "spine" of the automaton (the blue edges in Figure 32.6(a)). In the second case, $a \neq P[q + 1]$, so that a does not extend the match being built. In this case, we need to find the longest prefix of P that is also a suffix of $T[:i]a$, which will have length at most q. The preprocessing step matches the pattern against itself when creating the string-matching automaton, so that the transition function can quickly identify the longest such smaller prefix of P.

Let's look at an example. Consider state 5 in the string-matching automaton of Figure 32.6. In state 5, the five most recently read characters of T are ababa, the characters along the spine of the automaton that reach state 5. If the next character of T is c, then the most recently read characters of T are ababac, which is the prefix of P with length 6. The automaton should continue along the spine to state 6. This is the first case, in which the match continues, and $\delta(5, c) = 6$. To illustrate the second case, suppose that in state 5, the next character of T is b, so the most recently read characters of T are ababab. Here, the longest prefix of P that matches the most recently read characters of T—that is, a suffix of the portion of T read so far—is abab, with length 4, so $\delta(5, b) = 4$.

To clarify the operation of a string-matching automaton, the simple and efficient procedure FINITE-AUTOMATON-MATCHER simulates the behavior of such an automaton (represented by its transition function δ) in finding occurrences of a pattern P of length m in an input text $T[1:n]$. As for any string-matching automaton for a pattern of length m, the state set Q is $\{0, 1, \ldots, m\}$, the start state is 0, and the only accepting state is state m. From the simple loop structure of FINITE-AUTOMATON-MATCHER, you can see that its matching time on a text string of length n is $\Theta(n)$, assuming that each lookup of the transition function δ takes constant time. This matching time, however, does not include the preprocessing time required to compute the transition function. We address this problem later, after first proving that the procedure FINITE-AUTOMATON-MATCHER operates correctly.

FINITE-AUTOMATON-MATCHER(T, δ, n, m)

```
1  q = 0
2  for i = 1 to n
3      q = δ(q, T[i])
4      if q == m
5          print "Pattern occurs with shift" i − m
```

Let's examine how the automaton operates on an input text $T[1:n]$. We will prove that the automaton is in state $\sigma(T[:i])$ after reading character $T[i]$. Since $\sigma(T[:i]) = m$ if and only if $P \sqsupset T[:i]$, the machine is in the accepting state m if and only if it has just read the pattern P. We start with two lemmas about the suffix function σ.

Lemma 32.2 (Suffix-function inequality)
For any string x and character a, we have $\sigma(xa) \leq \sigma(x) + 1$.

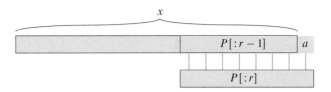

Figure 32.7 An illustration for the proof of Lemma 32.2. The figure shows that $r \leq \sigma(x) + 1$, where $r = \sigma(xa)$.

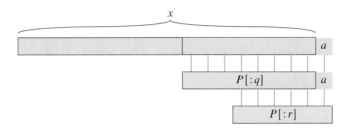

Figure 32.8 An illustration for the proof of Lemma 32.3. The figure shows that $r = \sigma(P[:q]a)$, where $q = \sigma(x)$ and $r = \sigma(xa)$.

Proof Referring to Figure 32.7, let $r = \sigma(xa)$. If $r = 0$, then the conclusion $\sigma(xa) = r \leq \sigma(x) + 1$ is trivially satisfied since $\sigma(x)$ is nonnegative. Now assume that $r > 0$. Then, $P[:r] \sqsupset xa$, by the definition of σ. Thus, $P[:r-1] \sqsupset x$, by dropping the a from both the end of $P[:r]$ and the end of xa. Therefore, $r - 1 \leq \sigma(x)$, since $\sigma(x)$ is the largest k such that $P[:k] \sqsupset x$, and thus $\sigma(xa) = r \leq \sigma(x) + 1$. ∎

Lemma 32.3 (Suffix-function recursion lemma)
For any string x and character a, if $q = \sigma(x)$, then $\sigma(xa) = \sigma(P[:q]a)$.

Proof The definition of σ gives that $P[:q] \sqsupset x$. As Figure 32.8 shows, we also have $P[:q]a \sqsupset xa$. Let $r = \sigma(xa)$. Then $P[:r] \sqsupset xa$ and, by Lemma 32.2, $r \leq q + 1$. Thus, we have $|P[:r]| = r \leq q + 1 = |P[:q]a|$. Since $P[:q]a \sqsupset xa$, $P[:r] \sqsupset xa$, and $|P[:r]| \leq |P[:q]a|$, Lemma 32.1 on page 959 implies that $P[:r] \sqsupset P[:q]a$. Therefore, $r \leq \sigma(P[:q]a)$, that is, $\sigma(xa) \leq \sigma(P[:q]a)$. But we also have $\sigma(P[:q]a) \leq \sigma(xa)$, since $P[:q]a \sqsupset xa$. Thus, $\sigma(xa) = \sigma(P[:q]a)$. ∎

We are now ready to prove the main theorem characterizing the behavior of a string-matching automaton on a given input text. As noted above, this theorem shows that the automaton is merely keeping track, at each step, of the longest prefix of the pattern that is a suffix of what has been read so far. In other words, the automaton maintains the invariant (32.5).

Theorem 32.4

If ϕ is the final-state function of a string-matching automaton for a given pattern P and $T[1:n]$ is an input text for the automaton, then

$$\phi(T[:i]) = \sigma(T[:i])$$

for $i = 0, 1, \ldots, n$.

Proof   The proof is by induction on i. For $i = 0$, the theorem is trivially true, since $T[:0] = \varepsilon$. Thus, $\phi(T[:0]) = 0 = \sigma(T[:0])$.

Now assume that $\phi(T[:i]) = \sigma(T[:i])$. We will prove that $\phi(T[:i+1]) = \sigma(T[:i+1])$. Let q denote $\phi(T[:i])$, so that $q = \sigma(T[:i])$, and let a denote $T[i+1]$. Then,

$$
\begin{aligned}
\phi(T[:i+1]) &= \phi(T[:i]a) && \text{(by the definitions of } T[:i+1] \text{ and } a) \\
&= \delta(\phi(T[:i]), a) && \text{(by the definition of } \phi) \\
&= \delta(q, a) && \text{(by the definition of } q) \\
&= \sigma(P[:q]a) && \text{(by the definition (32.4) of } \delta) \\
&= \sigma(T[:i]a) && \text{(by Lemma 32.3)} \\
&= \sigma(T[:i+1]) && \text{(by the definition of } T[:i+1]) \, . \quad \blacksquare
\end{aligned}
$$

By Theorem 32.4, if the machine enters state q on line 3, then q is the largest value such that $P[:q] \sqsupset T[:i]$. Thus, in line 4, $q = m$ if and only if the machine has just read an occurrence of the pattern P. Therefore, FINITE-AUTOMATON-MATCHER operates correctly.

Computing the transition function

The procedure COMPUTE-TRANSITION-FUNCTION on the following page computes the transition function δ from a given pattern $P[1:m]$. It computes $\delta(q, a)$ in a straightforward manner according to its definition in equation (32.4). The nested loops beginning on lines 1 and 2 consider all states q and all characters a, and lines 3–6 set $\delta(q, a)$ to be the largest k such that $P[:k] \sqsupset P[:q]a$. The code starts with the largest conceivable value of k, which is $q + 1$, unless $q = m$, in which case k cannot be larger than m. It then decreases k until $P[:k]$ is a suffix of $P[:q]a$, which must eventually occur, since $P[:0] = \varepsilon$ is a suffix of every string.

COMPUTE-TRANSITION-FUNCTION(P, Σ, m)

```
1   for q = 0 to m
2       for each character a ∈ Σ
3           k = min {m, q + 1}
4           while P[:k] is not a suffix of P[:q]a
5               k = k - 1
6           δ(q, a) = k
7   return δ
```

The running time of COMPUTE-TRANSITION-FUNCTION is $O(m^3 |\Sigma|)$, because the outer loops contribute a factor of $m |\Sigma|$, the inner **while** loop can run at most $m + 1$ times, and the test for whether $P[:k]$ is a suffix of $P[:q]a$ on line 4 can require comparing up to m characters. Much faster procedures exist. By utilizing some cleverly computed information about the pattern P (see Exercise 32.4-8), the time required to compute δ from P improves to $O(m |\Sigma|)$. This improved procedure for computing δ provides a way to find all occurrences of a length-m pattern in a length-n text over an alphabet Σ with $O(m |\Sigma|)$ preprocessing time and $\Theta(n)$ matching time.

Exercises

32.3-1
Draw a state-transition diagram for the string-matching automaton for the pattern $P =$ aabab over the alphabet $\Sigma = \{a, b\}$ and illustrate its operation on the text string $T =$ aaababaabaababaab.

32.3-2
Draw a state-transition diagram for the string-matching automaton for the pattern $P =$ ababbabbababbababbabb over the alphabet $\Sigma = \{a, b\}$.

32.3-3
A pattern P is *nonoverlappable* if $P[:k] \sqsupset P[:q]$ implies $k = 0$ or $k = q$. Describe the state-transition diagram of the string-matching automaton for a nonoverlappable pattern.

32.3-4
Let x and y be prefixes of the pattern P. Prove that $x \sqsupset y$ implies $\sigma(x) \leq \sigma(y)$.

★ *32.3-5*

Given two patterns P and P', describe how to construct a finite automaton that determines all occurrences of *either* pattern. Try to minimize the number of states in your automaton.

32.3-6

Given a pattern P containing gap characters (see Exercise 32.1-4), show how to build a finite automaton that can find an occurrence of P in a text T in $O(n)$ matching time, where $n = |T|$.

★   **32.4   The Knuth-Morris-Pratt algorithm**

Knuth, Morris, and Pratt developed a linear-time string matching algorithm that avoids computing the transition function δ altogether. Instead, the KMP algorithm uses an auxiliary function π, which it precomputes from the pattern in $\Theta(m)$ time and stores in an array $\pi[1:m]$. The array π allows the algorithm to compute the transition function δ efficiently (in an amortized sense) "on the fly" as needed. Loosely speaking, for any state $q = 0, 1, \dots, m$ and any character $a \in \Sigma$, the value $\pi[q]$ contains the information needed to compute $\delta(q, a)$ but that does not depend on a. Since the array π has only m entries, whereas δ has $\Theta(m\,|\Sigma|)$ entries, the KMP algorithm saves a factor of $|\Sigma|$ in the preprocessing time by computing π rather than δ. Like the procedure FINITE-AUTOMATON-MATCHER, once preprocessing has completed, the KMP algorithm uses $\Theta(n)$ matching time.

The prefix function for a pattern

The prefix function π for a pattern encapsulates knowledge about how the pattern matches against shifts of itself. The KMP algorithm takes advantage of this information to avoid testing useless shifts in the naive pattern-matching algorithm and to avoid precomputing the full transition function δ for a string-matching automaton.

Consider the operation of the naive string matcher. Figure 32.9(a) shows a particular shift s of a template containing the pattern $P = \text{ababaca}$ against a text T. For this example, $q = 5$ of the characters have matched successfully, but the 6th pattern character fails to match the corresponding text character. The information that q characters have matched successfully determines the corresponding text characters. Because these q text characters match, certain shifts must be invalid. In the example of the figure, the shift $s + 1$ is necessarily invalid, since the first pattern character (a) would be aligned with a text character that does not match the first pattern character, but does match the second pattern character (b). The shift

$s' = s + 2$ shown in part (b) of the figure, however, aligns the first three pattern characters with three text characters that necessarily match.

More generally, suppose that you know that $P[:q] \sqsupset T[:s + q]$ or, equivalently, that $P[1:q] = T[s + 1:s + q]$. You want to shift P so that some shorter prefix $P[:k]$ of P matches a suffix of $T[:s+q]$, if possible. You might have more than one choice for how much to shift, however. In Figure 32.9(b), shifting P by 2 positions works, so that $P[:3] \sqsupset T[:s+q]$, but so does shifting P by 4 positions, so that $P[:1] \sqsupset T[:s+q]$ in Figure 32.9(c). If more than one shift amount works, you should choose the smallest shift amount so that you do not miss any potential matches. Put more precisely, you want to answer this question:

Given that pattern characters $P[1:q]$ match text characters $T[s + 1:s + q]$ (that is, $P[:q] \sqsupset T[:s + q]$), what is the least shift $s' > s$ such that for some $k < q$,

$$P[1:k] = T[s' + 1:s' + k],\qquad (32.6)$$

(that is, $P[:k] \sqsupset T[:s' + k]$), where $s' + k = s + q$?

Here's another way to look at this question. If you know $P[:q] \sqsupset T[:s + q]$, then how do you find the longest proper prefix $P[:k]$ of $P[:q]$ that is also a suffix of $T[:s + q]$? These questions are equivalent because given s and q, requiring $s' + k = s + q$ means that finding the smallest shift s' (2 in Figure 32.9(b)) is tantamount to finding the longest prefix length k (3 in Figure 32.9(b)). If you add the difference $q - k$ in the lengths of these prefixes of P to the shift s, you get the new shift s', so that $s' = s + (q - k)$. In the best case, $k = 0$, so that $s' = s + q$, immediately ruling out shifts $s + 1, s + 2, \ldots, s + q - 1$. In any case, at the new shift s', it is redundant to compare the first k characters of P with the corresponding characters of T, since equation (32.6) guarantees that they match.

As Figure 32.9(d) demonstrates, you can precompute the necessary information by comparing the pattern against itself. Since $T[s' + 1:s' + k]$ is part of the matched portion of the text, it is a suffix of the string $P[:q]$. Therefore, think of equation (32.6) as asking for the greatest $k < q$ such that $P[:k] \sqsupset P[:q]$. Then, the new shift $s' = s + (q - k)$ is the next potentially valid shift. It will be convenient to store, for each value of q, the number k of matching characters at the new shift s', rather than storing, say, the amount $s' - s$ to shift by.

Let's look at the precomputed information a little more formally. For a given pattern $P[1:m]$, the *prefix function* for P is the function $\pi : \{1, 2, \ldots, m\} \to \{0, 1, \ldots, m - 1\}$ such that

$$\pi[q] = \max \{k : k < q \text{ and } P[:k] \sqsupset P[:q]\} \,.$$

That is, $\pi[q]$ is the length of the longest prefix of P that is a proper suffix of $P[:q]$. Here is the complete prefix function π for the pattern ababaca:

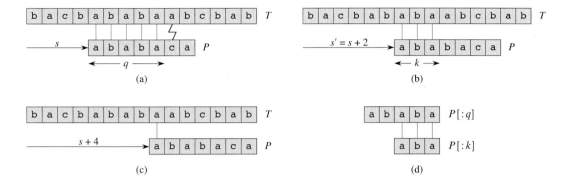

(a)

(b)

(c)

(d)

Figure 32.9   The prefix function π. **(a)** The pattern $P = \texttt{ababaca}$ aligns with a text T so that the first $q = 5$ characters match. Matching characters, in blue, are connected by blue lines. **(b)** Knowing these particular 5 matched characters ($P[:5]$) suffices to deduce that a shift of $s + 1$ is invalid, but that a shift of $s' = s + 2$ is consistent with everything known about the text and therefore is potentially valid. The prefix $P[:k]$, where $k = 3$, aligns with the text seen so far. **(c)** A shift of $s + 4$ is also potentially valid, but it leaves only the prefix $P[:1]$ aligned with the text seen so far. **(d)** To precompute useful information for such deductions, compare the pattern with itself. Here, the longest prefix of P that is also a proper suffix of $P[:5]$ is $P[:3]$. The array π represents this precomputed information, so that $\pi[5] = 3$. Given that q characters have matched successfully at shift s, the next potentially valid shift is at $s' = s + (q - \pi[q])$ as shown in part (b).

i	1	2	3	4	5	6	7
$P[i]$	a	b	a	b	a	c	a
$\pi[i]$	0	0	1	2	3	0	1

The procedure KMP-MATCHER on the following page gives the Knuth-Morris-Pratt matching algorithm. The procedure follows from FINITE-AUTOMATON-MATCHER for the most part. To compute π, KMP-MATCHER calls the auxiliary procedure COMPUTE-PREFIX-FUNCTION. These two procedures have much in common, because both match a string against the pattern P: KMP-MATCHER matches the text T against P, and COMPUTE-PREFIX-FUNCTION matches P against itself.

Next, let's analyze the running times of these procedures. Then we'll prove them correct, which will be more complicated.

Running-time analysis

The running time of COMPUTE-PREFIX-FUNCTION is $\Theta(m)$, which we show by using the aggregate method of amortized analysis (see Section 16.1). The only tricky part is showing that the **while** loop of lines 5–6 executes $O(m)$ times alto-

KMP-MATCHER(T, P, n, m)

```
1   π = COMPUTE-PREFIX-FUNCTION(P, m)
2   q = 0                        // number of characters matched
3   for i = 1 to n               // scan the text from left to right
4       while q > 0 and P[q + 1] ≠ T[i]
5           q = π[q]             // next character does not match
6       if P[q + 1] == T[i]
7           q = q + 1            // next character matches
8       if q == m               // is all of P matched?
9           print "Pattern occurs with shift" i − m
10          q = π[q]            // look for the next match
```

COMPUTE-PREFIX-FUNCTION(P, m)

```
1   let π[1 : m] be a new array
2   π[1] = 0
3   k = 0
4   for q = 2 to m
5       while k > 0 and P[k + 1] ≠ P[q]
6           k = π[k]
7       if P[k + 1] == P[q]
8           k = k + 1
9       π[q] = k
10  return π
```

gether. Starting with some observations about k, we'll show that it makes at most $m-1$ iterations. First, line 3 starts k at 0, and the only way that k increases is by the increment operation in line 8, which executes at most once per iteration of the **for** loop of lines 4–9. Thus, the total increase in k is at most $m-1$. Second, since $k < q$ upon entering the **for** loop and each iteration of the loop increments q, we always have $k < q$. Therefore, the assignments in lines 2 and 9 ensure that $\pi[q] < q$ for all $q = 1, 2, \ldots, m$, which means that each iteration of the **while** loop decreases k. Third, k never becomes negative. Putting these facts together, we see that the total decrease in k from the **while** loop is bounded from above by the total increase in k over all iterations of the **for** loop, which is $m - 1$. Thus, the **while** loop iterates at most $m - 1$ times in all, and COMPUTE-PREFIX-FUNCTION runs in $\Theta(m)$ time.

Exercise 32.4-4 asks you to show, by a similar aggregate analysis, that the matching time of KMP-MATCHER is $\Theta(n)$.

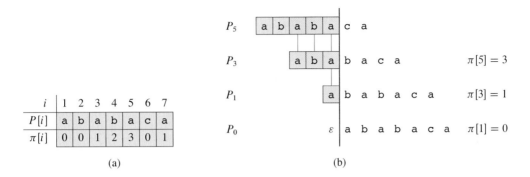

i	1	2	3	4	5	6	7
$P[i]$	a	b	a	b	a	c	a
$\pi[i]$	0	0	1	2	3	0	1

(a)

(b)

Figure 32.10   An illustration of Lemma 32.5 for the pattern $P = \mathtt{ababaca}$ and $q = 5$. **(a)** The π function for the given pattern. Since $\pi[5] = 3$, $\pi[3] = 1$, and $\pi[1] = 0$, iterating π gives $\pi^*[5] = \{3, 1, 0\}$. **(b)** Sliding the template containing the pattern P to the right and noting when some prefix $P[:k]$ of P matches up with some proper suffix of $P[:5]$. Matches occur when $k = 3$, 1, and 0. In the figure, the first row gives P, and the vertical red line is drawn just after $P[:5]$. Successive rows show all the shifts of P that cause some prefix $P[:k]$ of P to match some suffix of $P[:5]$. Successfully matched characters are shown in blue. Blue lines connect aligned matching characters. Thus, $\{k : k < 5$ and $P[:k] \sqsupset P[:5]\} = \{3, 1, 0\}$. Lemma 32.5 claims that $\pi^*[q] = \{k : k < q$ and $P[:k] \sqsupset P[:q]\}$ for all q.

Compared with FINITE-AUTOMATON-MATCHER, by using π rather than δ, the KMP algorithm reduces the time for preprocessing the pattern from $O(m\,|\Sigma|)$ to $\Theta(m)$, while keeping the actual matching time bounded by $\Theta(n)$.

Correctness of the prefix-function computation

We'll see a little later that the prefix function π helps to simulate the transition function δ in a string-matching automaton. But first, we need to prove that the procedure COMPUTE-PREFIX-FUNCTION does indeed compute the prefix function correctly. Doing so requires finding all prefixes $P[:k]$ that are proper suffixes of a given prefix $P[:q]$. The value of $\pi[q]$ gives us the length of the longest such prefix, but the following lemma, illustrated in Figure 32.10, shows that iterating the prefix function π generates all the prefixes $P[:k]$ that are proper suffixes of $P[:q]$. Let

$$\pi^*[q] = \{\pi[q], \pi^{(2)}[q], \pi^{(3)}[q], \ldots, \pi^{(t)}[q]\}\ ,$$

where $\pi^{(i)}[q]$ is defined in terms of functional iteration, so that $\pi^{(0)}[q] = q$ and $\pi^{(i)}[q] = \pi[\pi^{(i-1)}[q]]$ for $i \geq 1$ (so that $\pi[q] = \pi^{(1)}[q]$), and where the sequence in $\pi^*[q]$ stops upon reaching $\pi^{(t)}[q] = 0$ for some $t \geq 1$.

Lemma 32.5 (Prefix-function iteration lemma)

Let P be a pattern of length m with prefix function π. Then, for $q = 1, 2, \ldots, m$, we have $\pi^*[q] = \{k : k < q \text{ and } P[:k] \sqsupset P[:q]\}$.

Proof We first prove that $\pi^*[q] \subseteq \{k : k < q \text{ and } P[:k] \sqsupset P[:q]\}$ or, equivalently,

$$i \in \pi^*[q] \text{ implies } P[:i] \sqsupset P[:q] \,. \tag{32.7}$$

If $i \in \pi^*[q]$, then $i = \pi^{(u)}[q]$ for some $u > 0$. We prove equation (32.7) by induction on u. For $u = 1$, we have $i = \pi[q]$, and the claim follows since $i < q$ and $P[:\pi[q]] \sqsupset P[:q]$ by the definition of π. Now consider some $u \geq 1$ such that both $\pi^{(u)}[q]$ and $\pi^{(u+1)}[q]$ belong to $\pi^*[q]$. Let $i = \pi^{(u)}[q]$, so that $\pi[i] = \pi^{(u+1)}[q]$. The inductive hypothesis is that $P[:i] \sqsupset P[:q]$. Because the relations $<$ and $\sqsupset$ are transitive, we have $\pi[i] < i < q$ and $P[:\pi[i]] \sqsupset P[:i] \sqsupset P[:q]$, which establishes equation (32.7) for all i in $\pi^*[q]$. Therefore, $\pi^*[q] \subseteq \{k : k < q \text{ and } P[:k] \sqsupset P[:q]\}$.

We now prove that $\{k : k < q \text{ and } P[:k] \sqsupset P[:q]\} \subseteq \pi^*[q]$ by contradiction. Suppose to the contrary that the set $\{k : k < q \text{ and } P[:k] \sqsupset P[:q]\} - \pi^*[q]$ is nonempty, and let j be the largest number in the set. Because $\pi[q]$ is the largest value in $\{k : k < q \text{ and } P[:k] \sqsupset P[:q]\}$ and $\pi[q] \in \pi^*[q]$, it must be the case that $j < \pi[q]$. Having established that $\pi^*[q]$ contains at least one integer greater than j, let j' denote the smallest such integer. (We can choose $j' = \pi[q]$ if no other number in $\pi^*[q]$ is greater than j.) We have $P[:j] \sqsupset P[:q]$ because $j \in \{k : k < q \text{ and } P[:k] \sqsupset P[:q]\}$, and from $j' \in \pi^*[q]$ and equation (32.7), we have $P[:j'] \sqsupset P[:q]$. Thus, $P[:j] \sqsupset P[:j']$ by Lemma 32.1, and j is the largest value less than j' with this property. Therefore, we must have $\pi[j'] = j$ and, since $j' \in \pi^*[q]$, we must have $j \in \pi^*[q]$ as well. This contradiction proves the lemma. ∎

The algorithm COMPUTE-PREFIX-FUNCTION computes $\pi[q]$, in order, for $q = 1, 2, \ldots, m$. Setting $\pi[1]$ to 0 in line 2 of COMPUTE-PREFIX-FUNCTION is certainly correct, since $\pi[q] < q$ for all q. We'll use the following lemma and its corollary to prove that COMPUTE-PREFIX-FUNCTION computes $\pi[q]$ correctly for $q > 1$.

Lemma 32.6

Let P be a pattern of length m, and let π be the prefix function for P. For $q = 1, 2, \ldots, m$, if $\pi[q] > 0$, then $\pi[q] - 1 \in \pi^*[q - 1]$.

Proof Let $r = \pi[q] > 0$, so that $r < q$ and $P[:r] \sqsupset P[:q]$, and thus, $r - 1 < q - 1$ and $P[:r - 1] \sqsupset P[:q - 1]$ (by dropping the last character from

$P[:r]$ and $P[:q]$, which we can do because $r > 0$). By Lemma 32.5, therefore, $r - 1 \in \pi^*[q - 1]$. Thus, we have $\pi[q] - 1 = r - 1 \in \pi^*[q - 1]$. ∎

For $q = 2, 3, \ldots, m$, define the subset $E_{q-1} \subseteq \pi^*[q - 1]$ by

$$E_{q-1} = \{k \in \pi^*[q - 1] : P[k + 1] = P[q]\}$$
$$= \{k : k < q - 1 \text{ and } P[:k] \sqsupset P[:q - 1] \text{ and } P[k + 1] = P[q]\}$$
$$\text{(by Lemma 32.5)}$$
$$= \{k : k < q - 1 \text{ and } P[:k + 1] \sqsupset P[:q]\} .$$

The set E_{q-1} consists of the values $k < q - 1$ for which $P[:k] \sqsupset P[:q - 1]$ and for which, because $P[k + 1] = P[q]$, we have $P[:k + 1] \sqsupset P[:q]$. Thus, E_{q-1} consists of those values $k \in \pi^*[q - 1]$ such that extending $P[:k]$ to $P[:k + 1]$ produces a proper suffix of $P[:q]$.

Corollary 32.7
Let P be a pattern of length m, and let π be the prefix function for P. Then, for $q = 2, 3, \ldots, m$,

$$\pi[q] = \begin{cases} 0 & \text{if } E_{q-1} = \emptyset , \\ 1 + \max E_{q-1} & \text{if } E_{q-1} \neq \emptyset . \end{cases}$$

Proof If E_{q-1} is empty, there is no $k \in \pi^*[q - 1]$ (including $k = 0$) such that extending $P[:k]$ to $P[:k + 1]$ produces a proper suffix of $P[:q]$. Therefore, $\pi[q] = 0$.

If, instead, E_{q-1} is nonempty, then for each $k \in E_{q-1}$, we have $k + 1 < q$ and $P[:k + 1] \sqsupset P[:q]$. Therefore, the definition of $\pi[q]$ gives

$$\pi[q] \geq 1 + \max E_{q-1} . \tag{32.8}$$

Note that $\pi[q] > 0$. Let $r = \pi[q] - 1$, so that $r + 1 = \pi[q] > 0$, and therefore $P[:r + 1] \sqsupset P[:q]$. If a nonempty string is a suffix of another, then the two strings must have the same last character. Since $r + 1 > 0$, the prefix $P[:r + 1]$ is nonempty, and so $P[r + 1] = P[q]$. Furthermore, $r \in \pi^*[q - 1]$ by Lemma 32.6. Therefore, $r \in E_{q-1}$, and so $\pi[q] - 1 = r \leq \max E_{q-1}$ or, equivalently,

$$\pi[q] \leq 1 + \max E_{q-1} . \tag{32.9}$$

Combining equations (32.8) and (32.9) completes the proof. ∎

We now finish the proof that COMPUTE-PREFIX-FUNCTION computes π correctly. The key is to combine the definition of E_{q-1} with the statement of Corollary 32.7, so that $\pi[q]$ equals 1 plus the greatest value of k in $\pi^*[q - 1]$ such that

$P[k + 1] = P[q]$. First, in COMPUTE-PREFIX-FUNCTION, $k = \pi[q - 1]$ at the start of each iteration of the **for** loop of lines 4–9. This condition is enforced by lines 2 and 3 when the loop is first entered, and it remains true in each successive iteration because of line 9. Lines 5–8 adjust k so that it becomes the correct value of $\pi[q]$. The **while** loop of lines 5–6 searches through all values $k \in \pi^*[q - 1]$ in decreasing order to find the value of $\pi[q]$. The loop terminates either because k reaches 0 or $P[k + 1] = P[q]$. Because the "and" operator short-circuits, if the loop terminates because $P[k + 1] = P[q]$, then k must have also been positive, and so k is the greatest value in E_{q-1}. In this case, lines 7–9 set $\pi[q]$ to $k + 1$, according to Corollary 32.7. If, instead, the **while** loop terminates because $k = 0$, then there are two possibilities. If $P[1] = P[q]$, then $E_{q-1} = \{0\}$, and lines 7–9 set both k and $\pi[q]$ to 1. If $k = 0$ and $P[1] \neq P[q]$, however, then $E_{q-1} = \emptyset$. In this case, line 9 sets $\pi[q]$ to 0, again according to Corollary 32.7, which completes the proof of the correctness of COMPUTE-PREFIX-FUNCTION.

Correctness of the Knuth-Morris-Pratt algorithm

You can think of the procedure KMP-MATCHER as a reimplemented version of the procedure FINITE-AUTOMATON-MATCHER, but using the prefix function π to compute state transitions. Specifically, we'll prove that in the ith iteration of the **for** loops of both KMP-MATCHER and FINITE-AUTOMATON-MATCHER, the state q has the same value upon testing for equality with m (at line 8 in KMP-MATCHER and at line 4 in FINITE-AUTOMATON-MATCHER). Once we have argued that KMP-MATCHER simulates the behavior of FINITE-AUTOMATON-MATCHER, the correctness of KMP-MATCHER follows from the correctness of FINITE-AUTOMATON-MATCHER (though we'll see a little later why line 10 in KMP-MATCHER is necessary).

Before formally proving that KMP-MATCHER correctly simulates FINITE-AUTOMATON-MATCHER, let's take a moment to understand how the prefix function π replaces the δ transition function. Recall that when a string-matching automaton is in state q and it scans a character $a = T[i]$, it moves to a new state $\delta(q, a)$. If $a = P[q + 1]$, so that a continues to match the pattern, then the state number is incremented: $\delta(q, a) = q + 1$. Otherwise, $a \neq P[q + 1]$, so that a does not continue to match the pattern, and the state number does not increase: $0 \leq \delta(q, a) \leq q$. In the first case, when a continues to match, KMP-MATCHER moves to state $q + 1$ without referring to the π function: the **while** loop test in line 4 immediately comes up false, the test in line 6 comes up true, and line 7 increments q.

The π function comes into play when the character a does not continue to match the pattern, so that the new state $\delta(q, a)$ is either q or to the left of q along the spine of the automaton. The **while** loop of lines 4–5 in KMP-MATCHER iterates through the states in $\pi^*[q]$, stopping either when it arrives in a state, say q', such that a matches $P[q' + 1]$ or q' has gone all the way down to 0. If a matches $P[q' + 1]$, then line 7 sets the new state to $q'+1$, which should equal $\delta(q, a)$ for the simulation to work correctly. In other words, the new state $\delta(q, a)$ should be either state 0 or a state numbered 1 more than some state in $\pi^*[q]$.

Let's look at the example in Figures 32.6 and 32.10, which are for the pattern $P = \mathtt{ababaca}$. Suppose that the automaton is in state $q = 5$, having matched $\mathtt{ababa}$. The states in $\pi^*[5]$ are, in descending order, 3, 1, and 0. If the next character scanned is $\mathtt{c}$, then you can see that the automaton moves to state $\delta(5, \mathtt{c}) = 6$ in both FINITE-AUTOMATON-MATCHER (line 3) and KMP-MATCHER (line 7). Now suppose that the next character scanned is instead $\mathtt{b}$, so that the automaton should move to state $\delta(5, \mathtt{b}) = 4$. The **while** loop in KMP-MATCHER exits after executing line 5 once, and the automaton arrives in state $q' = \pi[5] = 3$. Since $P[q' + 1] = P[4] = \mathtt{b}$, the test in line 6 comes up true, and the automaton moves to the new state $q' + 1 = 4 = \delta(5, \mathtt{b})$. Finally, suppose that the next character scanned is instead $\mathtt{a}$, so that the automaton should move to state $\delta(5, \mathtt{a}) = 1$. The first three times that the test in line 4 executes, the test comes up true. The first time finds that $P[6] = \mathtt{c} \neq \mathtt{a}$, and the automaton moves to state $\pi[5] = 3$ (the first state in $\pi^*[5]$). The second time finds that $P[4] = \mathtt{b} \neq \mathtt{a}$, and the automaton moves to state $\pi[3] = 1$ (the second state in $\pi^*[5]$). The third time finds that $P[2] = \mathtt{b} \neq \mathtt{a}$, and the automaton moves to state $\pi[1] = 0$ (the last state in $\pi^*[5]$). The **while** loop exits once it arrives in state $q' = 0$. Now line 6 finds that $P[q' + 1] = P[1] = \mathtt{a}$, and line 7 moves the automaton to the new state $q' + 1 = 1 = \delta(5, \mathtt{a})$.

Thus, the intuition is that KMP-MATCHER iterates through the states in $\pi^*[q]$ in decreasing order, stopping at some state q' and then possibly moving to state $q'+1$. Although that might seem like a lot of work just to simulate computing $\delta(q, a)$, bear in mind that asymptotically, KMP-MATCHER is no slower than FINITE-AUTOMATON-MATCHER.

We are now ready to formally prove the correctness of the Knuth-Morris-Pratt algorithm. By Theorem 32.4, we have that $q = \sigma(T[:i])$ after each time line 3 of FINITE-AUTOMATON-MATCHER executes. Therefore, it suffices to show that the same property holds with regard to the **for** loop in KMP-MATCHER. The proof proceeds by induction on the number of loop iterations. Initially, both procedures set q to 0 as they enter their respective **for** loops for the first time. Consider iteration i of the **for** loop in KMP-MATCHER. By the inductive hypothesis, the state number q equals $\sigma(T[:i - 1])$ at the start of the loop iteration. We need to show that when line 8 is reached, the new value of q is $\sigma(T[:i])$. (Again, we'll handle line 10 separately.)

Considering q to be the state number at the start of the **for** loop iteration, when KMP-MATCHER considers the character $T[i]$, the longest prefix of P that is a suffix of $T[:i]$ is either $P[:q + 1]$ (if $P[q + 1] = T[i]$) or some prefix (not necessarily proper, and possibly empty) of $P[:q]$. We consider separately the three cases in which $\sigma(T[:i]) = 0$, $\sigma(T[:i]) = q + 1$, and $0 < \sigma(T[:i]) \le q$.

- If $\sigma(T[:i]) = 0$, then $P[:0] = \varepsilon$ is the only prefix of P that is a suffix of $T[:i]$. The **while** loop of lines 4–5 iterates through each value q' in $\pi^*[q]$, but although $P[:q'] \sqsupset P[:q] \sqsupset T[:i-1]$ for every $q' \in \pi^*[q]$ (because $<$ are $\sqsupset$ are transitive relations), the loop never finds a q' such that $P[q'+1] = T[i]$. The loop terminates when q reaches 0, and of course line 7 does not execute. Therefore, $q = 0$ at line 8, so that now $q = \sigma(T[:i])$.

- If $\sigma(T[:i]) = q+1$, then $P[q+1] = T[i]$, and the **while** loop test in line 4 fails the first time through. Line 7 executes, incrementing the state number to $q + 1$, which equals $\sigma(T[:i])$.

- If $0 < \sigma(T[:i]) \le q'$, then the **while** loop of lines 4–5 iterates at least once, checking in decreasing order each value in $\pi^*[q]$ until it stops at some $q' < q$. Thus, $P[:q']$ is the longest prefix of $P[:q]$ for which $P[q'+1] = T[i]$, so that when the **while** loop terminates, $q' + 1 = \sigma(P[:q]T[i])$. Since $q = \sigma(T[:i-1])$, Lemma 32.3 implies that $\sigma(T[:i-1]T[i]) = \sigma(P[:q]T[i])$. Thus we have

$$
\begin{aligned}
q' + 1 &= \sigma(P[:q]T[i]) \\
&= \sigma(T[:i-1]T[i]) \\
&= \sigma(T[:i])
\end{aligned}
$$

when the **while** loop terminates. After line 7 increments q, the new state number q equals $\sigma(T[:i])$.

Line 10 is necessary in KMP-MATCHER, because otherwise, line 4 might try to reference $P[m + 1]$ after finding an occurrence of P. (The argument that $q = \sigma(T[:i - 1])$ upon the next execution of line 4 remains valid by the hint given in Exercise 32.4-8: that $\delta(m, a) = \delta(\pi[m], a)$ or, equivalently, $\sigma(Pa) = \sigma(P[:\pi[m]]a)$ for any $a \in \Sigma$.) The remaining argument for the correctness of the Knuth-Morris-Pratt algorithm follows from the correctness of FINITE-AUTOMATON-MATCHER, since we have shown that KMP-MATCHER simulates the behavior of FINITE-AUTOMATON-MATCHER.

Exercises

32.4-1
Compute the prefix function π for the pattern `ababbabbabbababbabb`.

32.4-2
Give an upper bound on the size of $\pi^*[q]$ as a function of q. Give an example to show that your bound is tight.

32.4-3
Explain how to determine the occurrences of pattern P in the text T by examining the π function for the string PT (the string of length $m+n$ that is the concatenation of P and T).

32.4-4
Use an aggregate analysis to show that the running time of KMP-MATCHER is $\Theta(n)$.

32.4-5
Use a potential function to show that the running time of KMP-MATCHER is $\Theta(n)$.

32.4-6
Show how to improve KMP-MATCHER by replacing the occurrence of π in line 5 (but not line 10) by π', where π' is defined recursively for $q = 1, 2, \dots, m - 1$ by the equation

$$
\pi'[q] = \begin{cases}
0 & \text{if } \pi[q] = 0 , \\
\pi'[\pi[q]] & \text{if } \pi[q] \neq 0 \text{ and } P[\pi[q] + 1] = P[q + 1] , \\
\pi[q] & \text{if } \pi[q] \neq 0 \text{ and } P[\pi[q] + 1] \neq P[q + 1] .
\end{cases}
$$

Explain why the modified algorithm is correct, and explain in what sense this change constitutes an improvement.

32.4-7
Give a linear-time algorithm to determine whether a text T is a cyclic rotation of another string T'. For example, `braze` and `zebra` are cyclic rotations of each other.

★ 32.4-8
Give an $O(m\,|\Sigma|)$-time algorithm for computing the transition function δ for the string-matching automaton corresponding to a given pattern P. (*Hint:* Prove that $\delta(q, a) = \delta(\pi[q], a)$ if $q = m$ or $P[q + 1] \neq a$.)

32.5   Suffix arrays

The algorithms we have seen thus far in this chapter can efficiently find all occurrences of a pattern in a text. That is, however, all they can do. This section presents a different approach—suffix arrays—with which you can find all occurrences of a pattern in a text, but also quite a bit more. A suffix array won't find all occurrences

i	1	2	3	4	5	6	7
$T[i]$	r	a	t	a	t	a	t

i	$SA[i]$	$rank[i]$	$LCP[i]$	suffix $T[SA[i]:]$
1	6	4	0	at
2	4	3	2	atat
3	2	7	4	atatat
4	1	2	0	ratatat
5	7	6	0	t
6	5	1	1	tat
7	3	5	3	tatat

Figure 32.11 The suffix array SA, rank array $rank$, longest common prefix array LCP, and lexicographically sorted suffixes of the text $T =$ `ratatat` with length $n = 7$. The value of $rank[i]$ indicates the position of the suffix $T[i:]$ in the lexicographically sorted order: $rank[SA[i]] = i$ for $i = 1, 2, \ldots, n$. The $rank$ array is used to compute the LCP array.

of a pattern as quickly as, say, the Knuth-Morris-Pratt algorithm, but its additional flexibility makes it well worth studying.

A suffix array is simply a compact way to represent the lexicographically sorted order of all n suffixes of a length-n text. Given a text $T[1:n]$, let $T[i:]$ denote the suffix $T[i:n]$. The *suffix array $SA[1:n]$* of T is defined such that if $SA[i] = j$, then $T[j:]$ is the ith suffix of T in lexicographic order.[3] That is, the ith suffix of T in lexicographic order is $T[SA[i]:]$. Along with the suffix array, another useful array is the *longest common prefix array $LCP[1:n]$*. The entry $LCP[i]$ gives the length of the longest common prefix between the ith and $(i-1)$st suffixes in the sorted order (with $LCP[SA[1]]$ defined to be 0, since there is no prefix lexicographically smaller than $T[SA[1]:]$). Figure 32.11 shows the suffix array and longest common prefix array for the 7-character text `ratatat`.

Given the suffix array for a text, you can search for a pattern via binary search on the suffix array. Each occurrence of a pattern in the text starts some suffix of the text, and because the suffix array is in lexicographically sorted order, all occurrences of a pattern will appear at the start of consecutive entries of the suffix array. For example, in Figure 32.11, the three occurrences of `at` in `ratatat` appear in entries 1 through 3 of the suffix array. If you find the length-m pattern in the length-n suffix array via binary search (taking $O(m \lg n)$ time because each comparison takes $O(m)$ time), then you can find all occurrences of the pattern in the text by searching backward and forward from that spot until you find a suffix that does not start with the pattern (or you go beyond the bounds of the suffix array). If the pattern occurs k times, then the time to find all k occurrences is $O(m \lg n + km)$.

---

[3] Informally, lexicographic order is "alphabetical order" in the underlying character set. A more precise definition of lexicographic order appears in Problem 12-2 on page 327.

With the longest common prefix array, you can find a longest repeated substring, that is, the longest substring that occurs more than once in the text. If $LCP[i]$ contains a maximum value in the LCP array, then a longest repeated substring appears in $T[SA[i]:SA[i] + LCP[i] - 1]$. In the example of Figure 32.11, the LCP array has one maximum value: $LCP[3] = 4$. Therefore, since $SA[3] = 2$, the longest repeated substring is $T[2:5] = \mathtt{atat}$. Exercise 32.5-3 asks you to use the suffix array and longest common prefix array to find the longest common substrings between two texts. Next, we'll see how to compute the suffix array for an n-character text in $O(n \lg n)$ time and, given the suffix array and the text, how to compute the longest common prefix array in $\Theta(n)$ time.

Computing the suffix array

There are several algorithms to compute the suffix array of a length-n text. Some run in linear time, but are rather complicated. One such algorithm is given in Problem 32-2. Here we'll explore a simpler algorithm that runs in $\Theta(n \lg n)$ time.

The idea behind the $O(n \lg n)$-time procedure COMPUTE-SUFFIX-ARRAY on the following page is to lexicographically sort substrings of the text with increasing lengths. The procedure makes several passes over the text, with the substring length doubling each time. By the $\lceil \lg n \rceil$th pass, the procedure is sorting all the suffixes, thereby gaining the information needed to construct the suffix array. The key to attaining an $O(n \lg n)$-time algorithm will be to have each pass after the first sort in linear time, which will indeed be possible by using radix sort.

Let's start with a simple observation. Consider any two strings, s_1 and s_2. Decompose s_1 into s_1' and s_1'', so that s_1 is s_1' concatenated with s_1''. Likewise, let s_2 be s_2' concatenated with s_2''. Now, suppose that s_1' is lexicographically smaller than s_2'. Then, regardless of s_1'' and s_2'', it must be the case that s_1 is lexicographically smaller than s_2. For example, let $s_1 = \mathtt{aaz}$ and $s_2 = \mathtt{aba}$, and decompose s_1 into $s_1' = \mathtt{aa}$ and $s_1'' = \mathtt{z}$ and s_2 into $s_2' = \mathtt{ab}$ and $s_2'' = \mathtt{a}$. Because s_1' is lexicographically smaller than s_2', it follows that s_1 is lexicographically smaller than s_2, even though s_2'' is lexicographically smaller than s_1''.

Instead of comparing substrings directly, COMPUTE-SUFFIX-ARRAY represents substrings of the text with integer *ranks*. Ranks have the simple property that one substring is lexicographically smaller than another if and only if it has a smaller rank. Identical substrings have equal ranks.

Where do these ranks come from? Initially, the substrings being considered are just single characters from the text. Assume that, as in many programming languages, there is a function, ord, that maps a character to its underlying encoding, which is a positive integer. The ord function could be the ASCII or Unicode encodings or any other function that produces a relative ordering of the characters. For example if all the characters are known to be lowercase letters, then ord($\mathtt{a}$) = 1,

COMPUTE-SUFFIX-ARRAY(T, n)

 1 allocate arrays *substr-rank*$[1:n]$, *rank*$[1:n]$, and *SA*$[1:n]$
 2 **for** $i = 1$ **to** n
 3   *substr-rank*$[i]$.*left-rank* $= \text{ord}(T[i])$
 4   **if** $i < n$
 5   *substr-rank*$[i]$.*right-rank* $= \text{ord}(T[i + 1])$
 6   **else** *substr-rank*$[i]$.*right-rank* $= 0$
 7   *substr-rank*$[i]$.*index* $= i$
 8 sort the array *substr-rank* into monotonically increasing order based
        on the *left-rank* attributes, using the *right-rank* attributes to break ties;
        if still a tie, the order does not matter
 9 $l = 2$
10 **while** $l < n$
11   MAKE-RANKS$(substr\text{-}rank, rank, n)$
12   **for** $i = 1$ **to** n
13   *substr-rank*$[i]$.*left-rank* $= rank[i]$
14   **if** $i + l \le n$
15   *substr-rank*$[i]$.*right-rank* $= rank[i + l]$
16   **else** *substr-rank*$[i]$.*right-rank* $= 0$
17   *substr-rank*$[i]$.*index* $= i$
18   sort the array *substr-rank* into monotonically increasing order based
            on the *left-rank* attributes, using the *right-rank* attributes
            to break ties; if still a tie, the order does not matter
19      $l = 2l$
20 **for** $i = 1$ **to** n
21      $SA[i] = substr\text{-}rank[i].index$
22 **return** *SA*

MAKE-RANKS$(substr\text{-}rank, rank, n)$

 1 $r = 1$
 2 $rank[substr\text{-}rank[1].index] = r$
 3 **for** $i = 2$ **to** n
 4   **if** *substr-rank*$[i]$.*left-rank* $\neq$ *substr-rank*$[i-1]$.*left-rank*
                or *substr-rank*$[i]$.*right-rank* $\neq$ *substr-rank*$[i-1]$.*right-rank*
 5          $r = r + 1$
 6      $rank[substr\text{-}rank[i].index] = r$

i	left-rank	right-rank	index	substring	i	left-rank	right-rank	index	substring
	After lines 2–7					*After line 8*			
1	114	97	1	ra	1	97	116	2	at
2	97	116	2	at	2	97	116	4	at
3	116	97	3	ta	3	97	116	6	at
4	97	116	4	at	4	114	97	1	ra
5	116	97	5	ta	5	116	0	7	t
6	97	116	6	at	6	116	97	3	ta
7	116	0	7	t	7	116	97	5	ta

Figure 32.12   The *substr-rank* array for indices $i = 1, 2, \ldots, 7$ after the **for** loop of lines 2–7 and after the sorting step in line 8 for input string $T = \texttt{ratatat}$.

$\mathrm{ord}(\texttt{b}) = 2, \ldots, \mathrm{ord}(\texttt{z}) = 26$ would work. Once the substrings being considered contain multiple characters, their ranks will be positive integers less than or equal to n, coming from their relative order after being sorted. An empty substring always has rank 0, since it is lexicographically less than any nonempty substring.

The COMPUTE-SUFFIX-ARRAY procedure uses objects internally to keep track of the relative ordering of the substrings according to their ranks. When considering substrings of a given length, the procedure creates and sorts an array *substr-rank*[1 : n] of n objects, each with the following attributes:

- *left-rank* contains the rank of the left part of the substring.

- *right-rank* contains the rank of the right part of the substring.

- *index* contains the index into the text T of where the substring starts.

Before delving into the details of how the procedure works, let's look at how it operates on the input text $\texttt{ratatat}$, with $n = 7$. Assuming that the ord function returns the ASCII code for a character, Figure 32.12 shows the *substr-rank* array after the **for** loop of lines 2–7 and then after the sorting step in line 8. The *left-rank* and *right-rank* values after lines 2–7 are the ranks of length-1 substrings in positions i and $i + 1$, for $i = 1, 2, \ldots, n$. These initial ranks are the ASCII values of the characters. At this point, the *left-rank* and *right-rank* values give the ranks of the left and right part of each substring of length 2. Because the substring starting at index 7 consists of only one character, its right part is empty and so its *right-rank* is 0. After the sorting step in line 8, the *substr-rank* array gives the relative lexicographic order of all the substrings of length 2, with starting points of these substrings in the *index* attribute. For example, the lexicographically smallest length-2 substring is $\texttt{at}$, which starts at position *substr-rank*[1].*index*, which equals 2. This substring also occurs at positions *substr-rank*[2].*index* $= 4$ and *substr-rank*[3].*index* $= 6$.

The procedure then enters the **while** loop of lines 10–19. The loop variable l gives an upper bound on the length of substrings that have been sorted thus far.

| After line 11 | | | | | After lines 12–17 | | | | | | After line 18 | | | |
i	rank		i	left-rank	right-rank	index	substring		i	left-rank	right-rank	index	substring
1	2		1	2	4	1	rata		1	1	0	6	at
2	1		2	1	1	2	atat		2	1	1	2	atat
3	4		3	4	4	3	tata		3	1	1	4	atat
4	1		4	1	1	4	atat		4	2	4	1	rata
5	4		5	4	3	5	tat		5	3	0	7	t
6	1		6	1	0	6	at		6	4	3	5	tat
7	3		7	3	0	7	t		7	4	4	3	tata

Figure 32.13 The *rank* array after line 11 and the *substr-rank* array after lines 12–17 and after line 18 in the first iteration of the **while** loop of lines 10–19, where $l = 2$.

Entering the **while** loop, therefore, the substrings of length at most $l = 2$ are sorted. The call of MAKE-RANKS in line 11 gives each of these substrings its rank in the sorted order, from 1 up to the number of unique length-2 substrings, based on the values it finds in the *substr-rank* array. With $l = 2$, MAKE-RANKS sets *rank*[i] to be the rank of the length-2 substring $T[i : i + 1]$. Figure 32.13 shows these new ranks, which are not necessarily unique. For example, since the length-2 substring `at` occurs at positions 2, 4, and 6, MAKE-RANKS finds that *substr-rank*[1], *substr-rank*[2], and *substr-rank*[3] have equal values in *left-rank* and in *right-rank*. Since *substr-rank*[1].*index* = 2, *substr-rank*[2].*index* = 4, and *substr-rank*[3].*index* = 6, and since `at` is the smallest substring in lexicographic order, MAKE-RANKS sets *rank*[2] = *rank*[4] = *rank*[6] = 1.

This iteration of the **while** loop will sort the substrings of length at most 4 based on the ranks from sorting the substrings of length at most 2. The **for** loop of lines 12–17 reconstitutes the *substr-rank* array, with *substr-rank*[i].*left-rank* based on *rank*[i] (the rank of the length-2 substring $T[i : i+1]$) and *substr-rank*[i].*right-rank* based on *rank*[$i + 2$] (the rank of the length-2 substring $T[i + 2 : i + 3]$, which is 0 if this substring starts beyond the end of the length-n text). Together, these two ranks give the relative rank of the length-4 substring $T[i : i + 3]$. Figure 32.13 shows the effect of lines 12–17. The figure also shows the result of sorting the *substr-rank* array in line 18, based on the *left-rank* attribute, and using the *right-rank* attribute to break ties. Now *substr-rank* gives the lexicographically sorted order of all substrings with length at most 4.

The next iteration of the **while** loop, with $l = 4$, sorts the substrings of length at most 8 based on the ranks from sorting the substrings of length at most[4] 4. Figure 32.14 shows the ranks of the length-4 substrings and the *substr-rank* array

---

[4] Why keep saying "length at most"? Because for a given value of l, a substring of length l starting at position i is $T[i : i + l - 1]$. If $i + l - 1 > n$, then the substring cuts off at the end of the text.

After line 11		After lines 12–17					After line 18				
i	rank		i	left-rank	right-rank	index	substring		i	left-rank	right-rank	index	substring

After line 11		After lines 12–17					After line 18				
i	rank	i	left-rank	right-rank	index	substring	i	left-rank	right-rank	index	substring
1	3	1	3	5	1	ratatat	1	1	0	6	at
2	2	2	2	1	2	atatat	2	2	0	4	atat
3	6	3	6	4	3	tatat	3	2	1	2	atatat
4	2	4	2	0	4	atat	4	3	5	1	ratatat
5	5	5	5	0	5	tat	5	4	0	7	t
6	1	6	1	0	6	at	6	5	0	5	tat
7	4	7	4	0	7	t	7	6	4	3	tatat

Figure 32.14 The *rank* array after line 11 and the *substr-rank* array after lines 12–17 and after line 18 in the second—and final—iteration of the **while** loop of lines 10–19, where $l = 4$.

before and after sorting. This iteration is the final one, since with the length n of the text equaling 7, the procedure has sorted all substrings.

In general, as the loop variable l increases, more and more of the right parts of the substrings are empty. Therefore, more of the *right-rank* values are 0. Because i is at most n within the loop of lines 12–17, the left part of each substring is always nonempty, and so all *left-rank* values are always positive.

This example illuminates why the Compute-Suffix-Array procedure works. The initial ranks established in lines 2–7 are simply the ord values of the characters in the text, and so when line 8 sorts the *substr-rank* array, its ordering corresponds to the lexicographic ordering of the length-2 substrings. Each iteration of the **while** loop of lines 10–19 takes sorted substrings of length l and produces sorted substrings of length $2l$. Once l reaches or exceeds n, all substrings have been sorted.

Within an iteration of the **while** loop, the Make-Ranks procedure "re-ranks" the substrings that were sorted, either by line 8 before the first iteration or by line 18 in the previous iteration. Make-Ranks takes a *substr-rank* array, which has been sorted, and fills in an array $rank[1:n]$ so that $rank[i]$ is the rank of the ith substring represented in the *substr-rank* array. Each rank is a positive integer, starting from 1, and going up to the number of unique substrings of length $2l$. Substrings with equal values of *left-rank* and *right-rank* receive the same rank. Otherwise, a substring that is lexicographically smaller than another appears earlier in the *substr-rank* array, and it receives a smaller rank. Once the substrings of length $2l$ are re-ranked, line 18 sorts them by rank, preparing for the next iteration of the **while** loop.

Once l reaches or exceeds n and all substrings are sorted, the values in the *index* attributes give the starting positions of the sorted substrings. These indices are precisely the values that constitute the suffix array.

Let's analyze the running time of Compute-Suffix-Array. Lines 1–7 take $\Theta(n)$ time. Line 8 takes $O(n \lg n)$ time, using either merge sort (see Section 2.3.1) or heapsort (see Chapter 6). Because the value of l doubles in each iteration of the **while** loop of lines 10–19, this loop makes $\lceil \lg n \rceil - 1$ iterations. Within each iteration, the call of MAKE-RANKS takes $\Theta(n)$ time, as does the **for** loop of lines 12–17. Line 18, like line 8, takes $O(n \lg n)$ time, using either merge sort or heapsort. Finally, the **for** loop of lines 20–21 takes $\Theta(n)$ time. The total time works out to $O(n \lg^2 n)$.

A simple observation allows us to reduce the running time to $\Theta(n \lg n)$. The values of *left-rank* and *right-rank* being sorted in line 18 are always integers in the range 0 to n. Therefore, radix sort can sort the *substr-rank* array in $\Theta(n)$ time by first running counting sort (see Chapter 8) based on *right-rank* and then running counting sort based on *left-rank*. Now each iteration of the **while** loop of lines 10–19 takes only $\Theta(n)$ time, giving a total time of $\Theta(n \lg n)$.

Exercise 32.5-2 asks you to make a simple modification to COMPUTE-SUFFIX-ARRAY that allows the **while** loop of lines 10–19 to iterate fewer than $\lceil \lg n \rceil - 1$ times for certain inputs.

Computing the *LCP* array

Recall that *LCP*[i] is defined as the length of the longest common prefix of the $(i - 1)$st and ith lexicographically smallest suffixes $T[SA[i-1]:]$ and $T[SA[i]:]$. Because $T[SA[1]:]$ is the lexicographically smallest suffix, we define *LCP*[1] to be 0.

In order to compute the *LCP* array, we need an array *rank* that is the inverse of the *SA* array, just like the final *rank* array in COMPUTE-SUFFIX-ARRAY: if $SA[i] = j$, then $rank[j] = i$. That is, we have $rank[SA[i]] = i$ for $i = 1, 2, \ldots, n$. For a suffix $T[i:]$, the value of $rank[i]$ gives the position of this suffix in the lexicographically sorted order. Figure 32.11 includes the *rank* array for the `ratatat` example. For example, the suffix `tat` is $T[5:]$. To find this suffix's position in the sorted order, look up $rank[5] = 6$.

To compute the *LCP* array, we will need to determine where in the lexicographically sorted order a suffix appears, but with its first character removed. The *rank* array helps. Consider the ith smallest suffix, which is $T[SA[i]:]$. Dropping its first character gives the suffix $T[SA[i] + 1:]$, that is, the suffix starting at position $SA[i] + 1$ in the text. The location of this suffix in the sorted order is given by $rank[SA[i] + 1]$. For example, for the suffix `atat`, let's see where to find `tat` (`atat` with its first character removed) in the lexicographically sorted order. The suffix `atat` appears in position 2 of the suffix array, and $SA[2] = 4$. Thus, $rank[SA[2] + 1] = rank[5] = 6$, and sure enough the suffix `tat` appears in location 6 in the sorted order.

The procedure COMPUTE-LCP on the next page produces the *LCP* array. The following lemma helps show that the procedure is correct.

COMPUTE-LCP(T, SA, n)

```
 1  allocate arrays rank[1 : n] and LCP[1 : n]
 2  for i = 1 to n
 3      rank[SA[i]] = i              // by definition
 4  LCP[1] = 0                       // also by definition
 5  l = 0                           // initialize length of LCP
 6  for i = 1 to n
 7      if rank[i] > 1
 8          j = SA[rank[i] − 1]     // T[j :] precedes T[i :] lexicographically
 9          m = max {i, j}
10          while m + l ≤ n and T[i + l] == T[j + l]
11              l = l + 1           // next character is in common prefix
12          LCP[rank[i]] = l        // length of LCP of T[j :] and T[i :]
13          if l > 0
14              l = l − 1           // peel off first character of common prefix
15  return LCP
```

Lemma 32.8

Consider suffixes $T[i − 1 :]$ and $T[i :]$, which appear at positions $rank[i − 1]$ and $rank[i]$, respectively, in the lexicographically sorted order of suffixes. If $LCP[rank[i − 1]] = l > 1$, then the suffix $T[i :]$, which is $T[i − 1 :]$ with its first character removed, has $LCP[rank[i]] \geq l − 1$.

Proof The suffix $T[i − 1 :]$ appears at position $rank[i − 1]$ in the lexicographically sorted order. The suffix immediately preceding it in the sorted order appears at position $rank[i − 1] − 1$ and is $T[SA[rank[i − 1] − 1] :]$. By assumption and the definition of the LCP array, these two suffixes, $T[SA[rank[i−1]−1] :]$ and $T[i−1 :]$, have a longest common prefix of length $l > 1$. Removing the first character from each of these suffixes gives the suffixes $T[SA[rank[i − 1] − 1] + 1 :]$ and $T[i :]$, respectively. These suffixes have a longest common prefix of length $l − 1$. If $T[SA[rank[i − 1] − 1] + 1 :]$ immediately precedes $T[i :]$ in the lexicographically sorted order (that is, if $rank[SA[rank[i − 1]−1]+1] = rank[i]−1$), then the lemma is proven.

So now assume that $T[SA[rank[i − 1] − 1] + 1 :]$ does not immediately precede $T[i :]$ in the sorted order. Since $T[SA[rank[i − 1] − 1] :]$ immediately precedes $T[i − 1 :]$ and they have the same first $l > 1$ characters, $T[SA[rank[i−1]−1]+1 :]$ must appear in the sorted order somewhere before $T[i :]$, with one or more other suffixes intervening. Each of these suffixes must start with the same $l − 1$ characters as $T[SA[rank[i−1]−1]+1 :]$ and $T[i :]$, for otherwise it would appear either before

$T[SA[rank[i-1]-1]+1:]$ or after $T[i:]$. Therefore, whichever suffix appears in position $rank[i]-1$, immediately before $T[i:]$, has at least its first $l-1$ characters in common with $T[i:]$. Thus, $LCP[rank[i]] \geq l-1$.   ∎

The COMPUTE-LCP procedure works as follows. After allocating the *rank* and *LCP* arrays in line 1, lines 2–3 fill in the *rank* array and line 4 pegs $LCP[1]$ to 0, per the definition of the *LCP* array.

The **for** loop of lines 6–14 fills in the rest of the *LCP* array going by decreasing-length suffixes. That is, it fills the position of the *LCP* array in the order $rank[1]$, $rank[2], rank[3], \ldots, rank[n]$, with the assignment occurring in line 12. Upon considering a suffix $T[i:]$, line 8 determines the suffix $T[j:]$ that immediately precedes $T[i:]$ in the lexicographically sorted order. At this point, the longest common prefix of $T[j:]$ and $T[i:]$ has length at least l. This property certainly holds upon the first iteration of the **for** loop, when $l = 0$. Assuming that line 12 sets $LCP[rank[i]]$ correctly, line 14 (which decrements l if it is positive) and Lemma 32.8 maintain this property for the next iteration. The longest common prefix of $T[j:]$ and $T[i:]$ might be even longer than the value of l at the start of the iteration, however. Lines 9–11 increment l for each additional character the prefixes have in common so that it achieves the length of the longest common prefix. The index m is set in line 9 and used in the test in line 10 to make sure that the test $T[i+l] == T[j+l]$ for extending the longest common prefix does not run off the end of the text T. When the **while** loop of lines 10–11 terminates, l is the length of the longest common prefix of $T[j:]$ and $T[i:]$.

As a simple aggregate analysis shows, the COMPUTE-LCP procedure runs in $\Theta(n)$ time. Each of the two **for** loops iterates n times, and so it remains only to bound the total number of iterations by the **while** loop of lines 10–11. Each iteration increases l by 1, and the test $m + l \leq n$ ensures that l is always less than n. Because l has an initial value of 0 and decreases at most $n-1$ times in line 14, line 11 increments l fewer than $2n$ times. Thus, COMPUTE-LCP takes $\Theta(n)$ time.

Exercises

32.5-1
Show the *substr-rank* and *rank* arrays before each iteration of the **while** loop of lines 10–19 and after the last iteration of the **while** loop, the suffix array *SA* returned, and the sorted suffixes when COMPUTE-SUFFIX-ARRAY is run on the text `hippityhoppity`. Use the position of each letter in the alphabet as its ord value, so that ord(b) = 2. Then show the *LCP* array after each iteration of the **for** loop of lines 6–14 of COMPUTE-LCP given the text `hippityhoppity` and its suffix array.

32.5-2
For some inputs, the COMPUTE-SUFFIX-ARRAY procedure can produce the correct result with fewer than $\lceil \lg n \rceil - 1$ iterations of the **while** loop of lines 10–19. Modify COMPUTE-SUFFIX-ARRAY (and, if necessary, MAKE-RANKS) so that the procedure can stop before making all $\lceil \lg n \rceil - 1$ iterations in some cases. Describe an input that allows the procedure to make $O(1)$ iterations. Describe an input that forces the procedure to make the maximum number of iterations.

32.5-3
Given two texts, T_1 of length n_1 and T_2 of length n_2, show how to use the suffix array and longest common prefix array to find all of the *longest common substrings*, that is, the longest substrings that appear in both T_1 and T_2. Your algorithm should run in $O(n \lg n + kl)$ time, where $n = n_1 + n_2$ and there are k such longest substrings, each with length l.

32.5-4
Professor Markram proposes the following method to find the longest palindromes in a string $T[1:n]$ by using its suffix array and LCP array. (Recall from Problem 14-2 that a palindrome is a nonempty string that reads the same forward and backward.)

> Let @ be a character that does not appear in T. Construct the text T' as the concatenation of T, @, and the reverse of T. Denote the length of T' by $n' = 2n + 1$. Create the suffix array SA and LCP array LCP for T'. Since the indices for a palindrome and its reverse appear in consecutive positions in the suffix array, find the entries with the maximum LCP value $LCP[i]$ such that $SA[i-1] = n' - SA[i] - LCP[i] + 2$. (This constraint prevents a substring—and its reverse—from being construed as a palindrome unless it really is one.) For each such index i, one of the longest palindromes is $T'[SA[i] : SA[i] + LCP[i] - 1]$.

For example, if the text T is $\mathtt{unreferenced}$, with $n = 12$, then the text T' is $\mathtt{unreferenced@decnerefernu}$, with $n' = 25$ and the following suffix array and LCP array:

i	1	2	3	4	5	6	7	8	9	10	11	12	13	14	15	16	17	18	19	20	21	22	23	24	25
$T'[i]$	u	n	r	e	f	e	r	e	n	c	e	d	@	d	e	c	n	e	r	e	f	e	r	n	u
$SA[i]$	13	10	16	12	14	15	11	4	20	8	18	6	22	5	21	9	17	2	24	3	19	7	23	25	1
$LCP[i]$	0	0	1	0	1	0	1	1	4	1	1	3	2	0	3	0	1	1	1	0	5	2	1	0	1

The maximum LCP value is achieved at $LCP[21] = 5$, and $SA[20] = 3 = n' - SA[21] - LCP[21] + 2$. The suffixes of T' starting at indices $SA[20]$ and $SA[21]$ are $\mathtt{referenced@decnerefernu}$ and $\mathtt{refernu}$, both of which start with the length-5 palindrome $\mathtt{refer}$.

Alas, this method is not foolproof. Give an input string T that causes this method to give results that are shorter than the longest palindrome contained within T, and explain why your input causes the method to fail.

Problems

32-1 *String matching based on repetition factors*

Let y^i denote the concatenation of string y with itself i times. For example, $(ab)^3 = $ ababab. We say that a string $x \in \Sigma^*$ has *repetition factor r* if $x = y^r$ for some string $y \in \Sigma^*$ and some $r > 0$. Let $\rho(x)$ denote the largest r such that x has repetition factor r.

a. Give an efficient algorithm that takes as input a pattern $P[1:m]$ and computes the value $\rho(P[:i])$ for $i = 1, 2, \ldots, m$. What is the running time of your algorithm?

b. For any pattern $P[1:m]$, let $\rho^*(P)$ be defined as max $\{\rho(P[:i]) : 1 \le i \le m\}$. Prove that if the pattern P is chosen randomly from the set of all binary strings of length m, then the expected value of $\rho^*(P)$ is $O(1)$.

c. Argue that the procedure REPETITION-MATCHER correctly finds all occurrences of pattern $P[1:m]$ in text $T[1:n]$ in $O(\rho^*(P)n + m)$ time. (This algorithm is due to Galil and Seiferas. By extending these ideas greatly, they obtained a linear-time string-matching algorithm that uses only $O(1)$ storage beyond what is required for P and T.)

```
REPETITION-MATCHER(T, P, n, m)
1   k = 1 + ρ*(P)
2   q = 0
3   s = 0
4   while s ≤ n − m
5       if T[s + q + 1] == P[q + 1]
6           q = q + 1
7           if q == m
8               print "Pattern occurs with shift" s
9       if q == m or T[s + q + 1] ≠ P[q + 1]
10          s = s + max {1, ⌈q/k⌉}
11          q = 0
```

32-2 *A linear-time suffix-array algorithm*

In this problem, you will develop and analyze a linear-time divide-and-conquer algorithm to compute the suffix array of a text $T[1:n]$. As in Section 32.5, assume that each character in the text is represented by an underlying encoding, which is a positive integer.

The idea behind the linear-time algorithm is to compute the suffix array for the suffixes starting at $2/3$ of the positions in the text, recursing as needed, use the resulting information to sort the suffixes starting at the remaining $1/3$ of the positions, and then merge the sorted information in linear time to produce the full suffix array.

For $i = 1, 2, \ldots, n$, if $i \bmod 3$ equals 1 or 2, then i is a *sample position*, and the suffixes starting at such positions are *sample suffixes*. Positions $3, 6, 9, \ldots$ are *nonsample positions*, and the suffixes starting at nonsample positions are *nonsample suffixes*.

The algorithm sorts the sample suffixes, sorts the nonsample suffixes (aided by the result of sorting the sample suffixes), and merges the sorted sample and nonsample suffixes. Using the example text $T = \texttt{bippityboppityboo}$, here is the algorithm in detail, listing substeps of each of the above steps:

1. The sample suffixes comprise about $2/3$ of the suffixes. Sort them by the following substeps, which work with a heavily modified version of T and may require recursion. In part (a) of this problem on page 999, you will show that the orders of the suffixes of T and the suffixes of the modified version of T are the same.

   A. Construct two texts P_1 and P_2 made up of "metacharacters" that are actually substrings of three consecutive characters from T. We delimit each such metacharacter with parentheses. Construct

   $$P_1 = (T[1:3]) (T[4:6]) (T[7:9]) \cdots (T[n' : n' + 2]),$$

   where n' is the largest integer congruent to 1, modulo 3, that is less than or equal to n and T is extended beyond position n with the special character $\varnothing$, with encoding 0. With the example text $T = \texttt{bippityboppityboo}$, we get that

   $$P_1 = (\texttt{bip}) (\texttt{pit}) (\texttt{ybo}) (\texttt{ppi}) (\texttt{tyb}) (\texttt{oo}\varnothing).$$

   Similarly, construct

   $$P_2 = (T[2:4]) (T[5:7]) (T[8:10]) \cdots (T[n'' : n'' + 2]),$$

   where n'' is the largest integer congruent to 2, modulo 3, that is less than or equal to n. For our example, we have

   $$P_2 = (\texttt{ipp}) (\texttt{ity}) (\texttt{bop}) (\texttt{pit}) (\texttt{ybo}) (\texttt{o}\varnothing\varnothing).$$

position in T	1	4	7	10	13	16	2	5	8	11	14	17
metacharacter in P	(bip)	(pit)	(ybo)	(ppi)	(tyb)	(oo∅)	(ipp)	(ity)	(bop)	(pit)	(ybo)	(o∅∅)
character in P'	1	7	10	8	9	6	3	4	2	7	10	5
position in P'	1	2	3	4	5	6	7	8	9	10	11	12
$SA_{P'}$	1	9	7	8	12	6	10	2	4	5	11	3
positions in T of sorted sample suffixes of T	1	8	2	5	17	16	11	4	10	13	14	7

Figure 32.15 Computed values when sorting the sample suffixes of the linear-time suffix-array algorithm for the text $T = $ bippityboppityboo.

If n is a multiple of 3, append the metacharacter $(∅∅∅)$ to the end of P_1. In this way, P_1 is guaranteed to end with a metacharacter containing $∅$. (This property helps in part (a) of this problem.) The text P_2 may or may not end with a metacharacter containing $∅$.

B. Concatenate P_1 and P_2 to form a new text P. Figure 32.15 shows P for our example, along with the corresponding positions of T.

C. Sort and rank the unique metacharacters of P, with ranks starting from 1. In the example, P has 10 unique metacharacters: in sorted order, they are (bip), (bop), (ipp), (ity), (o∅∅), (oo∅), (pit), (ppi), (tyb), (ybo). The metacharacters (pit) and (ybo) each appear twice.

D. As Figure 32.15 shows, construct a new "text" P' by renaming each metacharacter in P by its rank. If P contains k unique metacharacters, then each "character" in P' is an integer from 1 to k. The suffix arrays for P and P' are identical.

E. Compute the suffix array $SA_{P'}$ of P'. If the characters of P' (i.e., the ranks of metacharacters in P) are unique, then you can compute its suffix array directly, since the ordering of the individual characters gives the suffix array. Otherwise, recurse to compute the suffix array of P', treating the ranks in P' as the input characters in the recursive call. Figure 32.15 shows the suffix array $SA_{P'}$ for our example. Since the number of metacharacters in P, and hence the length of P', is approximately $2n/3$, this recursive subproblem is smaller than the current problem.

F. From $SA_{P'}$ and the positions in T corresponding to the sample positions, compute the list of positions of the sorted sample suffixes of the original text T. Figure 32.15 shows the list of positions in T of the sorted sample suffixes in our example.

2. The nonsample suffixes comprise about $1/3$ of the suffixes. Using the sorted sample suffixes, sort the nonsample suffixes by the following substeps.

i	1	2	3	4	5	6	7	8	9	10	11	12	13	14	15	16	17	18	19
$T[i]$	b	i	p	p	i	t	y	b	o	p	p	i	t	y	b	o	o	∅	∅
r_i	1	3	□	8	4	□	12	2	□	9	7	□	10	11	□	6	5	0	0

Figure 32.16 The ranks r_1 through r_{n+3} for the text $T = $ bippityboppityboo with $n = 17$.

G. Extending the text T by the two special characters ∅∅, so that T now has $n + 2$ characters, consider each suffix $T[i :]$ for $i = 1, 2, \ldots, n + 2$. Assign a rank r_i to each suffix $T[i :]$. For the two special characters ∅∅, set $r_{n+1} = r_{n+2} = 0$. For the sample positions of T, base the rank on the list of sorted sample positions of T. The rank is currently undefined for the nonsample positions of T. For these positions, set $r_i = □$. Figure 32.16 shows the ranks for $T = $ bippityboppityboo with $n = 17$.

H. Sort the nonsample suffixes by comparing tuples $(T[i], r_{i+1})$. In our example, we get $T[15:] < T[12:] < T[9:] < T[3:] < T[6:]$ because $(\text{b}, 6) < (\text{i}, 10) < (\text{o}, 9) < (\text{p}, 8) < (\text{t}, 12)$.

3. Merge the sorted sets of suffixes. From the sorted set of suffixes, determine the suffix array of T.

This completes the description of a linear-time algorithm for computing suffix arrays. The following parts of this problem ask you to show that certain steps of this algorithm are correct and to analyze the algorithm's running time.

a. Define a *nonempty suffix* at position i of the text P created in substep B as all metacharacters from position i of P up to and including the first metacharacter of P in which ∅ appears or the end of P. In the example shown in Figure 32.15, the nonempty suffixes of P starting at positions 1, 4, and 11 of P are (bip)(pit)(ybo)(ppi)(tyb)(oo∅), (ppi)(tyb)(oo∅), and (ybo)(o∅∅), respectively. Prove that the order of suffixes of P is the same as the order of its nonempty suffixes. Conclude that the order of suffixes of P gives the order of the sample suffixes of T. (*Hint:* If P contains duplicate metacharacters, consider separately the cases in which two suffixes both start in P_1, both start in P_2, and one starts in P_1 and the other starts in P_2. Use the property that ∅ appears in the last metacharacter of P_1.)

b. Show how to perform substep C in $\Theta(n)$ time, bearing in mind that in a recursive call, the characters in T are actually ranks in P' in the caller.

c. Argue that the tuples in substep H are unique. Then show how to perform this substep in $\Theta(n)$ time.

d. Consider two suffixes $T[i:]$ and $T[j:]$, where $T[i:]$ is a sample suffix and $T[j:]$ is a nonsample suffix. Show how to determine in $\Theta(1)$ time whether $T[i:]$ is lexicographically smaller than $T[j:]$. (*Hint:* Consider separately the cases in which $i \bmod 3 = 1$ and $i \bmod 3 = 2$. Compare tuples whose elements are characters in T and ranks as shown in Figure 32.16. The number of elements per tuple may depend on whether $i \bmod 3$ equals 1 or 2.) Conclude that step 3 can be performed in $\Theta(n)$ time.

e. Justify the recurrence $T(n) \le T(2n/3 + 2) + \Theta(n)$ for the running time of the full algorithm, and show that its solution is $O(n)$. Conclude that the algorithm runs in $\Theta(n)$ time.

32-3   *Burrows-Wheeler transform*

The ***Burrows-Wheeler transform***, or BWT, for a text T is defined as follows. First, append a new character that compares as lexicographically less than every character of T, and denote this character by $ and the resulting string by T'. Letting n be the length of T', create n rows of characters, where each row is one of the n cyclic rotations of T'. Next, sort the rows lexicographically. The BWT is then the string of n characters in the rightmost column, read top to bottom.

For example, let $T = \texttt{rutabaga}$, so that $T' = \texttt{rutabaga\$}$. The cyclic rotations are

```
rutabaga$
utabaga$r
tabaga$ru
abaga$rut
baga$ruta
aga$rutab
ga$rutaba
a$rutabag
$rutabaga
```

Sorting the rows and numbering the sorted rows gives

```
1  $rutabaga
2  a$rutabag
3  abaga$rut
4  aga$rutab
5  baga$ruta
6  ga$rutaba
7  rutabaga$
8  tabaga$ru
9  utabaga$r
```

The BWT is the rightmost column, `agtbaa$ur`. (The row numbering will be helpful in understanding how to compute the inverse BWT.)

The BWT has applications in bioinformatics, and it can also be a step in text compression. That is because it tends to place identical characters together, as in the BWT of `rutabaga`, which places two of the instances of `a` together. When identical characters are placed together, or even nearby, additional means of compressing become available. Following the BWT, combinations of move-to-front encoding, run-length encoding, and Huffman coding (see Section 15.3) can provide significant text compression. Compression ratios with the BWT tend improve as the text length increases.

a. Given the suffix array for T', show how to compute the BWT in $\Theta(n)$ time.

In order to decompress, the BWT must be invertible. Assuming that the alphabet size is constant, the inverse BWT can be computed in $\Theta(n)$ time from the BWT. Let's look at the BWT of `rutabaga`, denoting it by $BWT[1:n]$. Each character in the BWT has a unique lexicographic rank from 1 to n. Denote the rank of $BWT[i]$ by $rank[i]$. If a character appears multiple times in the BWT, each instance of the character has a rank 1 greater than the previous instance of the character. Here are BWT and $rank$ for `rutabaga`:

i	1	2	3	4	5	6	7	8	9
$BWT[i]$	a	g	t	b	a	a	$	u	r
$rank[i]$	2	6	8	5	3	4	1	9	7

For example, $rank[1] = 2$ because $BWT[1] = $ a and the only character that precedes the first a lexicographically is $ (which we defined to precede all other characters, so that $ has rank 1). Next, we have $rank[2] = 6$ because $BWT[2] = $ g and five characters in the BWT precede g lexicographically: $, the three instances of a, and b. Jumping ahead to $rank[5] = 3$, that is because $BWT[5] = $ a, and because this a is the second instance of a in the BWT, its $rank$ value is 1 greater than the $rank$ value for the previous instance of a, in position 1.

There is enough information in BWT and $rank$ to reconstruct T' from back to front. Suppose that you know the rank r of a character c in T'. Then c is the first character in row r of the sorted cyclic rotations. The last character in row r must be the character that precedes c in T'. But you know which character is the last character in row r, because it is $BWT[r]$. To reconstruct T' from back to front, start with $, which you can find in BWT. Then work backward using BWT and $rank$ to reconstruct T'.

Let's see how this strategy works for `rutabaga`. The last character of T', $, appears in position 7 of BWT. Since $rank[7] = 1$, row 1 of the sorted cyclic rotations of T' begins with $. The character that precedes $ in T' is the last character in row 1, which is $BWT[1]$: a. Now we know that the last two characters of T'

are a\$. Looking up *rank*[1], it equals 2, so that row 2 of the sorted cyclic rotations of T' begins with a. The last character in row 2 precedes a in T', and that character is *BWT*[2] = g. Now we know that the last three characters of T' are ga\$. Continuing on, we have *rank*[2] = 6, so that row 6 of the sorted cyclic rotations begins with g. The character preceding g in T' is *BWT*[6] = a, and so the last four characters of T' are aga\$. Because *rank*[6] = 4, a begins row 4 of the sorted cyclic rotations of T'. The character preceding a in T' is the last character in row 4, *BWT*[4] = b, and the last five characters of T' are baga\$. And so on, until all n characters of T' have been identified, from back to front.

b. Given the array *BWT*[1 : n], write pseudcode to compute the array *rank*[1 : n] in $\Theta(n)$ time, assuming that the alphabet size is constant.

c. Given the arrays *BWT*[1 : n] and *rank*[1 : n], write pseudocode to compute T' in $\Theta(n)$ time.

Chapter notes

The relation of string matching to the theory of finite automata is discussed by Aho, Hopcroft, and Ullman [5]. The Knuth-Morris-Pratt algorithm [267] was invented independently by Knuth and Pratt and by Morris, but they published their work jointly. Matiyasevich [317] earlier discovered a similar algorithm, which applied only to an alphabet with two characters and was specified for a Turing machine with a two-dimensional tape. Reingold, Urban, and Gries [377] give an alternative treatment of the Knuth-Morris-Pratt algorithm. The Rabin-Karp algorithm was proposed by Karp and Rabin [250]. Galil and Seiferas [173] give an interesting deterministic linear-time string-matching algorithm that uses only $O(1)$ space beyond that required to store the pattern and text.

The suffix-array algorithm in Section 32.5 is by Manber and Myers [312], who first proposed the notion of suffix arrays. The linear-time algorithm to compute the longest common prefix array presented here is by Kasai et al. [252]. Problem 32-2 is based on the DC3 algorithm by Kärkkäinen, Sanders, and Burkhardt [245]. For a survey of suffix-array algorithms, see the article by Puglisi, Smyth, and Turpin [370]. To learn more about the Burrows-Wheeler transform from Problem 32-3, see the articles by Burrows and Wheeler [78] and Manzini [314].

33   Machine-Learning Algorithms

Machine learning may be viewed as a subfield of artificial intelligence. Broadly speaking, artificial intelligence aims to enable computers to carry out complex perception and information-processing tasks with human-like performance. The field of AI is vast and uses many different algorithmic methods.

Machine learning is rich and fascinating, with strong ties to statistics and optimization. Technology today produces enormous amounts of data, providing myriad opportunities for machine-learning algorithms to formulate and test hypotheses about patterns within the data. These hypotheses can then be used to make predictions about the characteristics or classifications in new data. Because machine learning is particularly good with challenging tasks involving uncertainty, where observed data follows unknown rules, it has markedly transformed fields such as medicine, advertising, and speech recognition.

This chapter presents three important machine-learning algorithms: k-means clustering, multiplicative weights, and gradient descent. You can view each of these tasks as a learning problem, whereby an algorithm uses the data collected so far to produce a hypothesis that describes the regularities learned and/or makes predictions about new data. The boundaries of machine learning are imprecise and evolving—some might say that the k-means clustering algorithm should be called "data science" and not "machine learning," and gradient descent, though an immensely important algorithm for machine learning, also has a multitude of applications outside of machine learning (most notably for optimization problems).

Machine learning typically starts with a *training phase* followed by a *prediction phase* in which predictions are made about new data. For *online learning*, the training and prediction phases are intermingled. The training phase takes as input *training data*, where each input data point has an associated output or *label*; the label might be a category name or some real-valued attribute. It then produces as an output one or more *hypotheses* about how the labels depend on the attributes of the input data points. Hypotheses can take many forms, typically some type of formula or algorithm. The learning algorithm used is often a form of gradient descent. The prediction phase then uses the hypothesis on new data in order to make *predictions* regarding the labels of new data points.

The type of learning just described is known as ***supervised learning***, since it starts with a set of inputs that are each labeled. As an example, consider a machine-learning algorithm to recognize spam emails. The training data comprises a collection of emails, each of which is labeled either "spam" or "not spam." The machine-learning algorithm frames a hypothesis, possibly a rule of the form "if an email has one of a set of words, then it is likely to be spam." Or it might learn rules that assign a spam score to each word and then evaluates a document by the sum of the spam scores of its constituent words, so that a document with a total score above a certain threshold value is classified as spam. The machine-learning algorithm can then predict whether a new email is spam or not.

A second form of machine learning is ***unsupervised learning***, where the training data is unlabeled, as in the clustering problem of Section 33.1. Here the machine-learning algorithm produces hypotheses regarding the centers of groups of input data points.

A third form of machine learning (not covered further here) is ***reinforcement learning***, where the machine-learning algorithm takes actions in an environment, receives feedback for those actions from the environment, and then updates its model of the environment based on the feedback. The learner is in an environment that has some state, and the actions of the learner have an effect on that state. Reinforcement learning is a natural choice for situations such as game playing or operating a self-driving car.

Sometimes the goal in a supervised machine-learning application is not making accurate predictions of labels for new examples, but rather performing causal ***inference***: finding an explanatory model that describes how the various features of an input data point affect its associated label. Finding a model that fits a given set of training data well can be tricky. It may involve sophisticated optimization methods that need to balance between producing a hypothesis that fits the data well and producing a hypothesis that is simple.

This chapter focuses on three problem domains: finding hypotheses that group the input data points well (using a clustering algorithm), learning which predictors (experts) to rely upon for making predictions in an online learning problem (using the multiplicative-weights algorithm), and fitting a model to data (using gradient descent).

Section 33.1 considers the clustering problem: how to divide a given set of n training data points into a given number k of groups, or "clusters," based on a measure of how similar (or more accurately, how dissimilar) points are to each other. The approach is iterative, beginning with an arbitrary initial clustering and incorporating successive improvements until no further improvements occur. Clustering is often used as an initial step when working on a machine-learning problem to discover what structure exists in the data.

Section 33.2 shows how to make online predictions quite accurately when you have a set of predictors, often called "experts," to rely on, many of which might be poor predictors, but some of which are good predictors. At first, you do not know which predictors are poor and which are good. The goal is to make predictions on new examples that are nearly as good as the predictions made by the best predictor. We study an effective multiplicative-weights prediction method that associates a positive real weight with each predictor and multiplicatively decreases the weights associated with predictors when they make poor predictions. The model in this section is online (see Chapter 27): at each step, we do not know anything about the future examples. In addition, we are able to make predictions even in the presence of adversarial experts, who are collaborating against us, a situation that actually happens in game-playing settings.

Finally, Section 33.3 introduces gradient descent, a powerful optimization technique used to find parameter settings in machine-learning models. Gradient descent also has many applications outside of machine learning. Intuitively, gradient descent finds the value that produces a local minimum for a function by "walking downhill." In a learning application, a "downhill step" is a step that adjusts hypothesis parameters so that the hypothesis does better on the given set of labeled examples.

This chapter makes extensive use of vectors. In contrast to the rest of the book, vector names in this chapter appear in boldface, such as $\mathbf{x}$, to more clearly delineate which quantities are vectors. Components of vectors do not appear in boldface, so if vector $\mathbf{x}$ has d dimensions, we might write $\mathbf{x} = (x_1, x_2, \ldots, x_d)$.

33.1 Clustering

Suppose that you have a large number of data points (examples), and you wish to group them into classes based on how similar they are to each other. For example, each data point might represent a celestial star, giving its temperature, size, and spectral characteristics. Or, each data point might represent a fragment of recorded speech. Grouping these speech fragments appropriately might reveal the set of accents of the fragments. Once a grouping of the training data points is found, new data can be placed into an appropriate group, facilitating star-type recognition or speech recognition.

These situations, along with many others, fall under the umbrella of clustering. The input to a *clustering* problem is a set of n examples (objects) and an integer k, with the goal of dividing the examples into at most k disjoint clusters such that the examples in each cluster are similar to each other. The clustering problem has several variations. For example, the integer k might not be given, but instead arises out of the clustering procedure. In this section we presume that k is given.

Feature vectors and similarity

Let's formally define the clustering problem. The input is a set of n *examples*. Each example has a set of *attributes* in common with all other examples, though the attribute values may vary among examples. For example, the clustering problem shown in Figure 33.1 clusters $n = 49$ examples—48 state capitals plus the District of Columbia—into $k = 4$ clusters. Each example has two attributes: the latitude and longitude of the capital. In a given clustering problem, each example has d attributes, with an example $\mathbf{x}$ specified by a d-dimensional *feature vector*

$$\mathbf{x} = (x_1, x_2, \ldots, x_d) \, .$$

Here, x_a for $a = 1, 2, \ldots, d$ is a real number giving the value of attribute a for example $\mathbf{x}$. We call $\mathbf{x}$ the *point* in $\mathbb{R}^d$ representing the example. For the example in Figure 33.1, each capital $\mathbf{x}$ has its latitude in x_1 and its longitude in x_2.

In order to cluster similar points together, we need to define similarity. Instead, let's define the opposite: the *dissimilarity* $\Delta(\mathbf{x}, \mathbf{y})$ of points $\mathbf{x}$ and $\mathbf{y}$ is the squared Euclidean distance between them:

$$\begin{aligned}
\Delta(\mathbf{x}, \mathbf{y}) &= \|\mathbf{x} - \mathbf{y}\|^2 \\
&= \sum_{a=1}^{d} (x_a - y_a)^2 \, .
\end{aligned} \tag{33.1}$$

Of course, for $\Delta(\mathbf{x}, \mathbf{y})$ to be well defined, all attribute values must be present. If any are missing, then you might just ignore that example, or you could fill in a missing attribute value with the median value for that attribute.

The attribute values are often "messy" in other ways, so that some "data cleaning" is necessary before the clustering algorithm is run. For example, the scale of attribute values can vary widely across attributes. In the example of Figure 33.1, the scales of the two attributes vary by a factor of 2, since latitude ranges from -90 to $+90$ degrees but longitude ranges from -180 to $+180$ degrees. You can imagine other scenarios where the differences in scales are even greater. If the examples contain information about students, one attribute might be grade-point average but another might be family income. Therefore, the attribute values are usually scaled or normalized, so that no single attribute can dominate the others when computing dissimilarities. One way to do so is by scaling attribute values with a linear transform so that the minimum value becomes 0 and the maximum value becomes 1. If the attribute values are binary values, then no scaling may be needed. Another

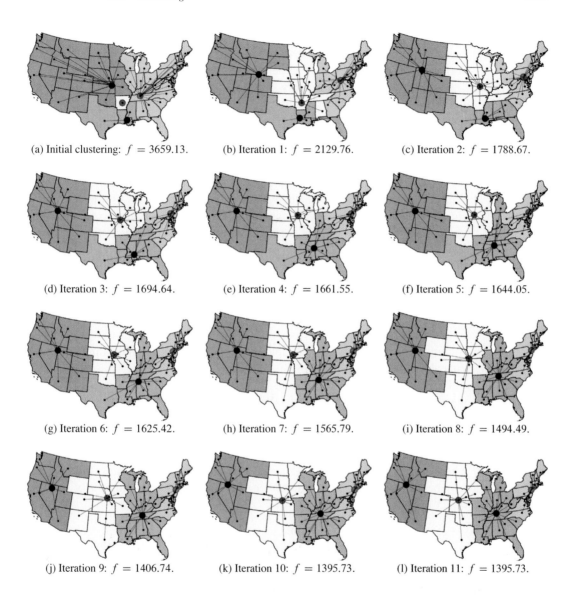

(a) Initial clustering: $f = 3659.13$.   (b) Iteration 1: $f = 2129.76$.   (c) Iteration 2: $f = 1788.67$.

(d) Iteration 3: $f = 1694.64$.   (e) Iteration 4: $f = 1661.55$.   (f) Iteration 5: $f = 1644.05$.

(g) Iteration 6: $f = 1625.42$.   (h) Iteration 7: $f = 1565.79$.   (i) Iteration 8: $f = 1494.49$.

(j) Iteration 9: $f = 1406.74$.   (k) Iteration 10: $f = 1395.73$.   (l) Iteration 11: $f = 1395.73$.

Figure 33.1   The iterations of Lloyd's procedure when clustering the capitals of the lower 48 states and the District of Columbia into $k = 4$ clusters. Each capital has two attributes: latitude and longitude. Each iteration reduces the value f, measuring the sum of squares of distances of all capitals to their cluster centers, until the value of f does not change. **(a)** The initial four clusters, with the capitals of Arkansas, Kansas, Louisiana, and Tennessee chosen as centers. **(b)–(k)** Iterations of Lloyd's procedure. **(l)** The 11th iteration results in the same value of f as the 10th iteration in part (k), and so the procedure terminates.

option is scaling so that the values for each attribute have mean 0 and unit variance. Sometimes it makes sense to choose the same scaling rule for several related attributes (for example, if they are lengths measured to the same scale).

Also, the choice of dissimilarity measure is somewhat arbitrary. The use of the sum of squared differences as in equation (33.1) is not required, but it is a conventional choice and mathematically convenient. For the example of Figure 33.1, you might use the actual distance between capitals rather than equation (33.1).

Clusterings

With the notion of similarity (actually, *dis*similarity) defined, let's see how to define clusters of similar points. Let S denote the given set of n points in $\mathbb{R}^d$. In some applications the points are not necessarily distinct, so that S is a multiset rather than a set.

Because the goal is to create k clusters, we define a *k-clustering* of S as a decomposition of S into a sequence $\langle S^{(1)}, S^{(2)}, \ldots, S^{(k)} \rangle$ of k disjoint subsets, or *clusters*, so that

$$S = S^{(1)} \cup S^{(2)} \cup \cdots \cup S^{(k)} \ .$$

A cluster may be empty, for example if $k > 1$ but all of the points in S have the same attribute values.

There are many ways to define a k-clustering of S and many ways to evaluate the quality of a given k-clustering. We consider here only k-clusterings of S that are defined by a sequence C of k *centers*

$$C = \langle \mathbf{c}^{(1)}, \mathbf{c}^{(2)}, \ldots, \mathbf{c}^{(k)} \rangle \ ,$$

where each center is a point in $\mathbb{R}^d$, and the *nearest-center rule* says that a point $\mathbf{x}$ may belong to cluster $S^{(\ell)}$ if the center of no other cluster is closer to $\mathbf{x}$ than the center $\mathbf{c}^{(\ell)}$ of $S^{(\ell)}$:

$$\mathbf{x} \in S^{(\ell)} \text{ only if } \Delta(\mathbf{x}, \mathbf{c}^{(\ell)}) = \min \{ \Delta(\mathbf{x}, \mathbf{c}^{(j)}) : 1 \leq j \leq k \} \ .$$

A center can be anywhere, and not necessarily a point in S.

Ties are possible and must be broken so that each point lies in exactly one cluster. In general, ties may be broken arbitrarily, although we'll need the property that we never change which cluster a point $\mathbf{x}$ is assigned to unless the distance from $\mathbf{x}$ to its new cluster center is *strictly smaller* than the distance from $\mathbf{x}$ to its old cluster center. That is, if the current cluster has a center that is one of the closest cluster centers to $\mathbf{x}$, then don't change which cluster $\mathbf{x}$ is assigned to.

The *k-means problem* is then the following: given a set S of n points and a positive integer k, find a sequence $C = \langle \mathbf{c}^{(1)}, \mathbf{c}^{(2)}, \ldots, \mathbf{c}^{(k)} \rangle$ of k center points minimizing the sum $f(S, C)$ of the squared distance from each point to its nearest center, where

$$f(S, C) = \sum_{\mathbf{x} \in S} \min \{\Delta(\mathbf{x}, \mathbf{c}^{(j)}) : 1 \leq j \leq k\}$$

$$= \sum_{\ell=1}^{k} \sum_{\mathbf{x} \in S^{(\ell)}} \Delta(\mathbf{x}, \mathbf{c}^{(\ell)}) \,. \tag{33.2}$$

In the second line, the k-clustering $\langle S^{(1)}, S^{(2)}, \ldots, S^{(k)} \rangle$ is defined by the centers C and the nearest-center rule. See Exercise 33.1-1 for an alternative formulation based on pairwise interpoint distances.

Is there a polynomial-time algorithm for the k-means problem? Probably not, because it is NP-hard [310]. As we'll see in Chapter 34, NP-hard problems have no known polynomial-time algorithm, but nobody has ever proven that polynomial-time algorithms for NP-hard problems cannot exist. Although we know of no polynomial-time algorithm that finds the global minimum over all clusterings (according to equation (33.2)), we *can* find a local minimum.

Lloyd [304] proposed a simple procedure that finds a sequence C of k centers that yields a local minimum of $f(S, C)$. A local minimum in the k-means problem satisfies two simple properties: each cluster has an optimal center (defined below), and each point is assigned to the cluster (or one of the clusters) with the closest center. Lloyd's procedure finds a good clustering—possibly optimal—that satisfies these two properties. These properties are necessary, but not sufficient, for optimality.

Optimal center for a given cluster

In an optimal solution to the k-means problem, each center point must be the *centroid*, or *mean*, of the points in its cluster. The centroid is a d-dimensional point, where the value in each dimension is the mean of the values of all the points in the cluster in that dimension (that is, the mean of the corresponding attribute values in the cluster). That is, if $\mathbf{c}^{(\ell)}$ is the centroid for cluster $S^{(\ell)}$, then for attributes $a = 1, 2, \ldots, d$, we have

$$c_a^{(\ell)} = \frac{1}{|S^{(\ell)}|} \sum_{\mathbf{x} \in S^{(\ell)}} x_a \,.$$

Over all attributes, we write

$$\mathbf{c}^{(\ell)} = \frac{1}{|S^{(\ell)}|} \sum_{\mathbf{x} \in S^{(\ell)}} \mathbf{x} \,. \tag{33.3}$$

Theorem 33.1
Given a nonempty cluster $S^{(\ell)}$, its centroid (or mean) is the unique choice for the cluster center $\mathbf{c}^{(\ell)} \in \mathbb{R}^d$ that minimizes

$$\sum_{\mathbf{x} \in S^{(\ell)}} \Delta(\mathbf{x}, \mathbf{c}^{(\ell)}) \, .$$

Proof   We wish to minimize, by choosing $\mathbf{c}^{(\ell)} \in \mathbb{R}^d$, the sum

$$\sum_{\mathbf{x} \in S^{(\ell)}} \Delta(\mathbf{x}, \mathbf{c}^{(\ell)}) = \sum_{\mathbf{x} \in S^{(\ell)}} \sum_{a=1}^{d} (x_a - c_a^{(\ell)})^2$$

$$= \sum_{a=1}^{d} \left(\sum_{\mathbf{x} \in S^{(\ell)}} x_a^2 - 2 \left(\sum_{\mathbf{x} \in S^{(\ell)}} x_a \right) c_a^{(\ell)} + \left| S^{(\ell)} \right| (c_a^{(\ell)})^2 \right) \, .$$

For each attribute a, the term summed is a convex quadratic function in $c_a^{(\ell)}$. To minimize this function, take its derivative with respect to $c_a^{(\ell)}$ and set it to 0:

$$-2 \sum_{\mathbf{x} \in S^{(\ell)}} x_a + 2 \left| S^{(\ell)} \right| c_a^{(\ell)} = 0$$

or, equivalently,

$$c_a^{(\ell)} = \frac{1}{|S^{(\ell)}|} \sum_{\mathbf{x} \in S^{(\ell)}} x_a \, .$$

Since the minimum is obtained uniquely when each coordinate of $c_a^{(\ell)}$ is the average of the corresponding coordinate for $\mathbf{x} \in S^{(\ell)}$, the overall minimum is obtained when $\mathbf{c}^{(\ell)}$ is the centroid of the points $\mathbf{x}$, as in equation (33.3).   ■

Optimal clusters for given centers

The following theorem shows that the nearest-center rule—assigning each point $\mathbf{x}$ to one of the clusters whose center is nearest to $\mathbf{x}$—yields an optimal solution to the k-means problem.

Theorem 33.2
Given a set S of n points and a sequence $\langle \mathbf{c}^{(1)}, \mathbf{c}^{(2)}, \ldots, \mathbf{c}^{(k)} \rangle$ of k centers, a clustering $\langle S^{(1)}, S^{(2)}, \ldots, S^{(k)} \rangle$ minimizes

$$\sum_{\ell=1}^{k} \sum_{\mathbf{x} \in S^{(\ell)}} \Delta(\mathbf{x}, \mathbf{c}^{(\ell)}) \tag{33.4}$$

if and only if it assigns each point $\mathbf{x} \in S$ to a cluster $S^{(\ell)}$ that minimizes $\Delta(\mathbf{x}, \mathbf{c}^{(\ell)})$.

Proof   The proof is straightforward: each point $\mathbf{x} \in S$ contributes exactly once to the sum (33.4), and choosing to put $\mathbf{x}$ in a cluster whose center is nearest minimizes the contribution from $\mathbf{x}$.   ∎

Lloyd's procedure

Lloyd's procedure just iterates two operations—assigning points to clusters based on the nearest-center rule, followed by recomputing the centers of clusters to be their centroids—until the results converge. Here is Lloyd's procedure:

Input: A set S of points in $\mathbb{R}^d$, and a positive integer k.

Output: A k-clustering $\langle S^{(1)}, S^{(2)}, \ldots, S^{(k)} \rangle$ of S with a sequence of centers $\langle \mathbf{c}^{(1)}, \mathbf{c}^{(2)}, \ldots, \mathbf{c}^{(k)} \rangle$.

1. **Initialize centers:** Generate an initial sequence $\langle \mathbf{c}^{(1)}, \mathbf{c}^{(2)}, \ldots, \mathbf{c}^{(k)} \rangle$ of k centers by picking k points independently from S at random. (If the points are not necessarily distinct, see Exercise 33.1-3.) Assign all points to cluster $S^{(1)}$ to begin.

2. **Assign points to clusters:** Use the nearest-center rule to define the clustering $\langle S^{(1)}, S^{(2)}, \ldots, S^{(k)} \rangle$. That is, assign each point $\mathbf{x} \in S$ to a cluster $S^{(\ell)}$ having a nearest center (breaking ties arbitrarily, but not changing the assignment for a point $\mathbf{x}$ unless the new cluster center is strictly closer to $\mathbf{x}$ than the old one).

3. **Stop if no change:** If step 2 did not change the assignments of any points to clusters, then stop and return the clustering $\langle S^{(1)}, S^{(2)}, \ldots, S^{(k)} \rangle$ and the associated centers $\langle \mathbf{c}^{(1)}, \mathbf{c}^{(2)}, \ldots, \mathbf{c}^{(k)} \rangle$. Otherwise, go to step 4.

4. **Recompute centers as centroids:** For $\ell = 1, 2, \ldots, k$, compute the center $\mathbf{c}^{(\ell)}$ of cluster $S^{(\ell)}$ as the centroid of the points in $S^{(\ell)}$. (If $S^{(\ell)}$ is empty, let $\mathbf{c}^{(\ell)}$ be the zero vector.) Then go to step 2.

It is possible for some of the clusters returned to be empty, particularly if many of the input points are identical.

   Lloyd's procedure always terminates. By Theorem 33.1, recomputing the centers of each cluster as the cluster centroid cannot increase $f(S, C)$. Lloyd's procedure ensures that a point is reassigned to a different cluster only when such an operation strictly decreases $f(S, C)$. Thus each iteration of Lloyd's procedure, except the last iteration, must strictly decrease $f(S, C)$. Since there are only a finite number of possible k-clusterings of S (at most k^n), the procedure must terminate. Furthermore, once one iteration of Lloyd's procedure yields no decrease in f, further iterations would not change anything, and the procedure can stop at this locally optimum assignment of points to clusters.

If Lloyd's procedure really required k^n iterations, it would be impractical. In practice, it sometimes suffices to terminate the procedure when the percentage decrease in $f(S, C)$ in the latest iteration falls below a predetermined threshold. Because Lloyd's procedure is guaranteed to find only a locally optimal clustering, one approach to finding a good clustering is to run Lloyd's procedure many times with different randomly chosen initial centers, taking the best result.

The running time of Lloyd's procedure is proportional to the number T of iterations. In one iteration, assigning points to clusters based on the nearest-center rule requires $O(dkn)$ time, and recomputing new centers for each cluster requires $O(dn)$ time (because each point is in one cluster). The overall running time of the k-means procedure is thus $O(Tdkn)$.

Lloyd's algorithm illustrates an approach common to many machine-learning algorithms:

- First, define a hypothesis space in terms an appropriate sequence θ of parameters, so that each θ is associated with a specific hypothesis h_θ. (For the k-means problem, θ is a dk-dimensional vector, equivalent to C, containing the d-dimensional center of each of the k clusters, and h_θ is the hypothesis that each data point $\mathbf{x}$ should be grouped with a cluster having a center closest to $\mathbf{x}$.)

- Second, define a measure $f(E, \theta)$ describing how poorly hypothesis h_θ fits the given training data E. Smaller values of $f(E, \theta)$ are better, and a (locally) optimal solution (locally) minimizes $f(E, \theta)$. (For the k-means problem, $f(E, \theta)$ is just $f(S, C)$.)

- Third, given a set of training data E, use a suitable optimization procedure to find a value of θ^* that minimizes $f(E, \theta^*)$, at least locally. (For the k-means problem, this value of θ^* is the sequence C of k center points returned by Lloyd's algorithm.)

- Return θ^* as the answer.

In this framework, we see that optimization becomes a powerful tool for machine learning. Using optimization in this way is flexible. For example, *regularization* terms can be incorporated in the function to be minimized, in order to penalize hypotheses that are "too complicated" and that "overfit" the training data. (Regularization is a complex topic that isn't pursued further here.)

Examples

Figure 33.1 demonstrates Lloyd's procedure on a set of $n = 49$ cities: 48 U.S. state capitals and the District of Columbia. Each city has $d = 2$ dimensions: latitude and longitude. The initial clustering in part (a) of the figure has the initial cluster centers arbitrarily chosen as the capitals of Arkansas, Kansas, Louisiana, and Tennessee. As the procedure iterates, the value of the function f decreases, until the 11th iteration in part (l), where it remains the same as in the 10th iteration in part (k). Lloyd's procedure then terminates with the clusters shown in part (l).

As Figure 33.2 shows, Lloyd's procedure can also apply to "vector quantization." Here, the goal is to reduce the number of distinct colors required to represent a photograph, thereby allowing the photograph to be greatly compressed (albeit in a lossy manner). In part (a) of the figure, an original photograph 700 pixels wide and 500 pixels high uses 24 bits (three bytes) per pixel to encode a triple of red, green, and blue (RGB) primary color intensities. Parts (b)–(e) of the figure show the results of using Lloyd's procedure to compress the picture from a initial space of 2^{24} possible values per pixel to a space of only $k = 4, k = 16, k = 64$, or $k = 256$ possible values per pixel; these k values are the cluster centers. The photograph can then be represented with only 2, 4, 6, or 8 bits per pixel, respectively, instead of the 24-bits per pixel needed by the initial photograph. An auxiliary table, the "palette," accompanies the compressed image; it holds the k 24-bit cluster centers and is used to map each pixel value to its 24-bit cluster center when the photo is decompressed.

Exercises

33.1-1
Show that the objective function $f(S, C)$ of equation (33.2) may be alternatively written as

$$f(S, C) = \sum_{\ell=1}^{k} \frac{1}{2 \, |S^{(\ell)}|} \sum_{\mathbf{x} \in S^{(\ell)}} \sum_{\mathbf{y} \in S^{(\ell)} : \mathbf{x} \neq \mathbf{y}} \Delta(\mathbf{x}, \mathbf{y}) \, .$$

33.1-2
Give an example in the plane with $n = 4$ points and $k = 2$ clusters where an iteration of Lloyd's procedure does not improve $f(S, C)$, yet the k-clustering is not optimal.

33.1-3
When the input to Lloyd's procedure contains many repeated points, a different initialization procedure might be used. Describe a way to pick a number of centers at random that maximizes the number of distinct centers picked. (*Hint:* See Exercise 5.3-5.)

33.1-4
Show how to find an optimal k-clustering in polynomial time when there is just one attribute ($d = 1$).

(a) Original

(b) $k = 4$ ($f = 1.29 \times 10^9$; 31 iterations)

(c) $k = 16$ ($f = 3.31 \times 10^8$; 36 iterations)

(d) $k = 64$ ($f = 5.50 \times 10^7$; 59 iterations)

(e) $k = 256$ ($f = 1.52 \times 10^7$; 104 iterations)

Figure 33.2 Using Lloyd's procedure for vector quantization to compress a photo by using fewer colors. **(a)** The original photo has 350,000 pixels (700 $\times$ 500), each a 24-bit RGB (red/blue/green) triple of 8-bit values; these pixels (colors) are the "points" to be clustered. Points repeat, so there are only 79,083 distinct colors (less than 2^{24}). After compression, only k distinct colors are used, so each pixel is represented by only $\lceil \lg k \rceil$ bits instead of 24. A "palette" maps these values back to 24-bit RGB values (the cluster centers). **(b)–(e)** The same photo with $k = 4, 16, 64,$ and 256 colors. (Photo from standuppaddle, pixabay.com.)

33.2 Multiplicative-weights algorithms

This section considers problems that require you to make a series of decisions. After each decision you receive feedback as to whether your decision was correct. We will study a class of algorithms that are called *multiplicative-weights algorithms*. This class of algorithms has a wide variety of applications, including game playing in economics, approximately solving linear-programming and multicommodity-flow problems, and various applications in online machine learning. We emphasize the online nature of the problem here: you have to make a sequence of decisions, but some of the information needed to make the ith decision appears only after you have already made the $(i-1)$st decision. In this section, we look at one particular problem, known as "learning from experts," and develop an example of a multiplicative-weights algorithm, called the weighted-majority algorithm.

Suppose that a series of events will occur, and you want to make predictions about these events. For example, over a series of days, you want to predict whether it is going to rain. Or perhaps you want to predict whether the price of a stock will increase or decrease. One way to approach this problem is to assemble a group of "experts" and use their collective wisdom in order to make good predictions. Let's denote the experts, n of them, by $E_1, E_2, \ldots, E_n$, and let's say that T events are going to take place. Each event has an outcome of either 0 or 1, with $o^{(t)}$ denoting the outcome of the tth event. Before event t, each expert $E^{(i)}$ makes a prediction $q_i^{(t)} \in \{0, 1\}$. You, as the "learner," then take the set of n expert predictions for event t and produce a single prediction $p^{(t)} \in \{0, 1\}$ of your own. You base your prediction only on the predictions of the experts and anything you have learned about the experts from their previous predictions. You do not use any additional information about the event. Only after making your prediction do you ascertain the outcome $o^{(t)}$ of event t. If your prediction $p^{(t)}$ matches $o^{(t)}$, then you were correct; otherwise, you made a mistake. The goal is to minimize the total number m of mistakes, where $m = \sum_{t=1}^{T} |p^{(t)} - o^{(t)}|$. You can also keep track of the number of mistakes each expert makes: expert E_i makes m_i mistakes, where $m_i = \sum_{t=1}^{T} |q_i^{(t)} - o^{(t)}|$.

For example, suppose that you are following the price of a stock, and each day you decide whether to invest in it for just that day by buying it at the beginning of the day and selling it at the end of the day. If, on some day, you buy the stock and it goes up, then you made the correct decision, but if the stock goes down, then you made a mistake. Similarly, if on some day, you do not buy the stock and it goes down, then you made the correct decision, but if the stock goes up, then you made a mistake. Since you would like to make as few mistakes as possible, you use the advice of the experts to make your decisions.

We'll assume nothing about the movement of the stock. We'll also assume nothing about the experts: the experts' predictions could be correlated, they could be chosen to deceive you, or perhaps some are not really experts after all. What algorithm would you use?

Before designing an algorithm for this problem, we need to consider what is a fair way to evaluate our algorithm. It is reasonable to expect that our algorithm performs better when the expert predictions are better, and that it performs worse when the expert predictions are worse. The goal of the algorithm is to limit the number of mistakes you make to be close to the number of mistakes that the best of the experts makes. At first, this goal might seem impossible, because you do not know until the end which expert is best. We'll see, however, that by taking the advice provided by all the experts into account, you can achieve this goal. More formally, we use the notion of "regret," which compares our algorithm to the performance of the best expert (in hindsight) over all. Letting $m^* = \min\{m_i : 1 \leq i \leq n\}$ denote the number of mistakes made by the best expert, the *regret* is $m - m^*$. The goal is to design an algorithm with low regret. (Regret can be negative, although it typically isn't, since it is rare that you do better than the best expert.)

As a warm-up, let's consider the case in which one of the experts makes a correct prediction each time. Even without knowing who that expert is, you can still achieve good results.

Lemma 33.3

Suppose that out of n experts, there is one who always makes the correct prediction for all T events. Then there is an algorithm that makes at most $\lceil \lg n \rceil$ mistakes.

Proof   The algorithm maintains a set S consisting of experts who have not yet made a mistake. Initially, S contains all n experts. The algorithm's prediction is always the majority vote of the predictions of the experts remaining in set S. In case of a tie, the algorithm makes any prediction. After each outcome is learned, set S is updated to remove all the experts who made an incorrect prediction about that outcome.

We now analyze the algorithm. The expert who always makes the correct prediction will always be in set S. Every time the algorithm makes a mistake, at least half of the experts who were still in S also make a mistake, and these experts are removed from S. If S' is the set of experts remaining after removing those who made a mistake, we have that $|S'| \leq |S|/2$. The size of S can be halved at most $\lceil \lg n \rceil$ times until $|S| = 1$. From this point on, we know that the algorithm never makes a mistake, since the set S consists only of the one expert who never makes a mistake. Therefore, overall the algorithm makes at most $\lceil \lg n \rceil$ mistakes.   ■

Exercise 33.2-1 asks you to generalize this result to the case when there is no expert who makes perfect predictions and show that, for any set of experts, there is an algorithm that makes at most $m^* \lceil \lg n \rceil$ mistakes. The generalized algorithm begins in the same way. The set S might become empty at some point, however. If that ever happens, reset S to contain all the experts and continue the algorithm.

You can substantially improve your prediction ability by not just tracking which experts have not made any mistakes, or have not made any mistakes recently, to a more nuanced evaluation of the quality of each expert. The key idea is to use the feedback you receive to update your evaluation of how much trust to put in each expert. As the experts make predictions, you observe whether they were correct and decrease your confidence in the experts who make more mistakes. In this way, you can learn over time which experts are more reliable and which are less reliable, and weight their predictions accordlingly. The change in weights is accomplished via multiplication, hence the term "multiplicative weights."

The algorithm appears in the procedure WEIGHTED-MAJORITY on the following page, which takes a set $E = \{E_1, E_2, \ldots, E_n\}$ of experts, a number T of events, the number n of experts, and a parameter $0 < \gamma \leq 1/2$ that controls how the weights change. The algorithm maintains weights $w_i^{(t)}$ for $i = 1, 2, \ldots, n$ and $t = 1, 2, \ldots, T$, where $0 < w_i^{(t)} \leq 1$. The **for** loop of lines 1–2 sets the initial weights $w_i^{(1)}$ to 1, capturing the idea that with no knowledge, you trust each expert equally. Each iteration of the main **for** loop of lines 3–18 does the following for an event $t = 1, 2, \ldots, T$. Each expert E_i makes a prediction for event t in line 4. Lines 5–8 compute *upweight*$^{(t)}$, the sum of the weights of the experts who predict 1 for event t, and *downweight*$^{(t)}$, the sum of the weights of the experts who predict 0 for the event. Lines 9–11 decide the algorithm's prediction $p^{(t)}$ for event t based on whichever weighted sum is larger (breaking ties in favor of deciding 1). The outcome of event t is revealed in line 12. Finally, lines 14–17 decrease the weights of the experts who made an incorrect prediction for event t by multiplying their weights by $1 - \gamma$, leaving alone the weights of the experts who correctly predicted the event's outcome. Thus, the fewer mistakes each expert makes, the higher that expert's weight.

The WEIGHTED-MAJORITY procedure doesn't do much worse than any expert. In particular, it doesn't do much worse than the best expert. To quantify this claim, let $m^{(t)}$ be the number of mistakes made by the procedure through event t, and let $m_i^{(t)}$ be the number of mistakes made by expert E_i through event t. The following theorem is the key.

WEIGHTED-MAJORITY(E, T, n, γ)

```
 1  for i = 1 to n
 2      w_i^{(1)} = 1                           // trust each expert equally
 3  for t = 1 to T
 4      each expert E_i ∈ E makes a prediction q_i^{(t)}
 5      U = {E_i : q_i^{(t)} = 1}               // experts who predicted 1
 6      upweight^{(t)} = ∑_{i:E_i∈U} w_i^{(t)}  // sum of weights of who predicted 1
 7      D = {E_i : q_i^{(t)} = 0}               // experts who predicted 0
 8      downweight^{(t)} = ∑_{i:E_i∈D} w_i^{(t)} // sum of weights of who predicted 0
 9      if upweight^{(t)} ≥ downweight^{(t)}
10          p^{(t)} = 1                         // algorithm predicts 1
11      else p^{(t)} = 0                        // algorithm predicts 0
12      outcome o^{(t)} is revealed
13      // If p^{(t)} ≠ o^{(t)}, the algorithm made a mistake.
14      for i = 1 to n
15          if q_i^{(t)} ≠ o^{(t)}              // if expert E^{(i)} made a mistake …
16              w_i^{(t+1)} = (1 − γ)w_i^{(t)}  // … then decrease that expert's weight
17          else w_i^{(t+1)} = w_i^{(t)}
18      return p^{(t)}
```

Theorem 33.4

When running WEIGHTED-MAJORITY, we have, for every expert E_i and every event $T' \leq T$,

$$m^{(T')} \leq 2(1 + \gamma)m_i^{(T')} + \frac{2\ln n}{\gamma} . \tag{33.5}$$

Proof Every time an expert E_i makes a mistake, its weight, which is initially 1, is multiplied by $1 - \gamma$, and so we have

$$w_i^{(t)} = (1 - \gamma)^{m_i^{(t)}} \tag{33.6}$$

for $t = 1, 2, \ldots, T$.

We use a potential function $W(t) = \sum_{i=1}^{n} w_i^{(t)}$, summing the weights for all n experts after iteration t of the **for** loop of lines 3–18. Initially, we have $W(0) = n$ since all n weights start out with the value 1. Because each expert belongs to either the set U or the set D (defined in lines 5 and 7 of WEIGHTED-MAJORITY), we always have $W(t) = upweight^{(t)} + downweight^{(t)}$ after each execution of line 8.

Consider an iteration t in which the algorithm makes a mistake in its prediction, which means that either the algorithm predicts 1 and the outcome is 0 or the algorithm predicts 0 and the outcome is 1. Without loss of generality, assume that the algorithm predicts 1 and the outcome is 0. The algorithm predicted 1 because $upweight^{(t)} \geq downweight^{(t)}$ in line 9, which implies that

$$upweight^{(t)} \geq W(t)/2 \ . \tag{33.7}$$

Each expert in U then has its weight multiplied by $1 - \gamma$, and each expert in D has its weight unchanged. Thus, we have

$$
\begin{aligned}
W(t + 1) &= upweight^{(t)}(1 - \gamma) + downweight^{(t)} \\
&= upweight^{(t)} + downweight^{(t)} - \gamma \cdot upweight^{(t)} \\
&= W(t) - \gamma \cdot upweight^{(t)} \\
&\leq W(t) - \gamma \frac{W(t)}{2} \qquad \text{(by inequality (33.7))} \\
&= W(t)(1 - \gamma/2) \ .
\end{aligned}
$$

Therefore, for every iteration t in which the algorithm makes a mistake, we have

$$W(t + 1) \leq (1 - \gamma/2)W(t) \ . \tag{33.8}$$

In an iteration where the algorithm does not make a mistake, some of the weights decrease and some remain unchanged, so that we have

$$W(t + 1) \leq W(t) \ . \tag{33.9}$$

Since there are $m^{(T')}$ mistakes made through iteration T', and $W(1) = n$, we can repeatedly apply inequality (33.8) to iterations where the algorithm makes a mistake and inequality (33.9) to iterations where the algorithm does not make a mistake, obtaining

$$W(T') \leq n(1 - \gamma/2)^{m^{(T')}} \ . \tag{33.10}$$

Because the function W is the sum of the weights and all weights are positive, its value exceeds any single weight. Therefore, using equation (33.6) we have, for any expert E_i and for any iteration $T' \leq T$,

$$W(T') \geq w_i^{(T')} = (1 - \gamma)^{m_i^{(T')}} \ . \tag{33.11}$$

Combining inequalities (33.10) and (33.11) gives

$$(1 - \gamma)^{m_i^{(T')}} \leq n(1 - \gamma/2)^{m^{(T')}} \ .$$

Taking the natural logarithm of both sides yields

$$m_i^{(T')} \ln(1 - \gamma) \leq m^{(T')} \ln(1 - \gamma/2) + \ln n \ . \tag{33.12}$$

We now use the Taylor series expansion to derive upper and lower bounds on the logarithmic factors in inequality (33.12). The Taylor series for $\ln(1+x)$ is given in equation (3.22) on page 67. Substituting $-x$ for x, we have that for $0 < x \leq 1/2$,

$$\ln(1-x) = -x - \frac{x^2}{2} - \frac{x^3}{3} - \frac{x^4}{4} - \cdots . \tag{33.13}$$

Since each term on the right-hand side is negative, we can drop all terms except the first and obtain an upper bound of $\ln(1-x) \leq -x$. Since $0 < \gamma \leq 1/2$, we have

$$\ln(1 - \gamma/2) \leq -\gamma/2 . \tag{33.14}$$

For the lower bound, Exercise 33.2-2 asks you to show that $\ln(1-x) \geq -x - x^2$ when $0 < x \leq 1/2$, so that

$$-\gamma - \gamma^2 \leq \ln(1 - \gamma) . \tag{33.15}$$

Thus, we have

$$
\begin{aligned}
m_i^{(T')}(-\gamma - \gamma^2) &\leq m_i^{(T')} \ln(1-\gamma) && \text{(by inequality (33.15))} \\
&\leq m^{(T')} \ln(1 - \gamma/2) + \ln n && \text{(by inequality (33.12)} \\
&\leq m^{(T')}(-\gamma/2) + \ln n && \text{(by inequality (33.14)) ,}
\end{aligned}
$$

so that

$$m_i^{(T')}(-\gamma - \gamma^2) \leq m^{(T')}(-\gamma/2) + \ln n . \tag{33.16}$$

Subtracting $\ln n$ from both sides of inequality (33.16) and then multiplying both sides by $-2/\gamma$ yields $m^{(T')} \leq 2(1+\gamma)m_i^{(T')} + (2 \ln n)/\gamma$, thus proving the theorem. ∎

Theorem 33.4 applies to any expert and any event $T' \leq T$. In particular, we can compare against the best expert after all events have occurred, producing the following corollary.

Corollary 33.5
At the end of procedure WEIGHTED-MAJORITY, we have

$$m^{(T)} \leq 2(1+\gamma)m^* + \frac{2 \ln n}{\gamma} . \tag{33.17}$$

∎

Let's explore this bound. Assuming that $\sqrt{\ln n / m^*} \leq 1/2$, we can choose $\gamma = \sqrt{\ln n / m^*}$ and plug into inequality (33.17) to obtain

$$m^{(T)} \leq 2\left(1 + \sqrt{\frac{\ln n}{m^*}}\right)m^* + \frac{2\ln n}{\sqrt{\ln n / m^*}}$$
$$= 2m^* + 2\sqrt{m^* \ln n} + 2\sqrt{m^* \ln n}$$
$$= 2m^* + 4\sqrt{m^* \ln n} \ ,$$

and so the number of errors is at most twice the number of errors made by the best expert plus a term that is often slower growing than m^*. Exercise 33.2-4 shows that you can decrease the bound on the number of errors by a factor of 2 by using randomization, which leads to much stronger bounds. In particular, the upper bound on regret $(m - m^*)$ is reduced from $(1 + 2\gamma)m^* + (2\ln n)/\gamma$ to an expected value of $\epsilon m^* + (\ln n)/\epsilon$, where both γ and ϵ are at most $1/2$. Numerically, we can see that if $\gamma = 1/2$, WEIGHTED-MAJORITY makes at most 3 times the number of errors as the best expert, plus $4\ln n$ errors. As another example, suppose that $T = 1000$ predictions are being made by $n = 20$ experts, and the best expert is correct 95% of the time, making 50 errors. Then WEIGHTED-MAJORITY makes at most $100(1+\gamma)+2\ln 20/\gamma$ errors. By choosing $\gamma = 1/4$, WEIGHTED-MAJORITY makes at most 149 errors, or a success rate of at least 85%.

Multiplicative weights methods typically refer to a broader class of algorithms that includes WEIGHTED-MAJORITY. The outcomes and predictions need not be only 0 or 1, but can be real numbers, and there can be a loss associated with a particular outcome and prediction. The weights can be updated by a multiplicative factor that depends on the loss, and the algorithm can, given a set of weights, treat them as a distribution on experts and use them to choose an expert to follow in each event. Even in these more general settings, bounds similar to Theorem 33.4 hold.

Exercises

33.2-1
The proof of Lemma 33.3 assumes that some expert never makes a mistake. It is possible to generalize the algorithm and analysis to remove this assumption. The new algorithm begins in the same way. The set S might become empty at some point, however. If that ever happens, reset S to contain all the experts and continue the algorithm. Show that the number of mistakes that this algorithm makes is at most $m^* \lceil \lg n \rceil$.

33.2-2
Show that $\ln(1 - x) \geq -x - x^2$ when $0 < x \leq 1/2$. (*Hint:* Start with equation (33.13), group all the terms after the first three, and use equation (A.7) on page 1142.)

33.2-3

Consider a randomized variant of the algorithm given in the proof of Lemma 33.3, in which some expert never makes a mistake. At each step, choose an expert E_i uniformly at random from the set S and then make the same predication as E_i. Show that the expected number of mistakes made by this algorithm is $\lceil \lg n \rceil$.

33.2-4

Consider a randomized version of WEIGHTED-MAJORITY. The algorithm is the same, except for the prediction step, which interprets the weights as a probability distribution over the experts and chooses an expert E_i according to that distribution. It then chooses its prediction to be the same as the prediction made by expert E_i. Show that, for any $0 < \epsilon < 1/2$, the expected number of mistakes made by this algorithm is at most $(1 + \epsilon)m^* + (\ln n)/\epsilon$.

33.3   Gradient descent

Suppose that you have a set $\{p_1, p_2, \ldots, p_n\}$ of points and you want to find the line that best fits these points. For any line ℓ, there is a distance d_i between each point p_i and the line. You want to find the line that minimizes some function $f(d_1, \ldots, d_n)$. There are many possible choices for the definition of distance and for the function f. For example, the distance can be the projection distance to the line and the function can be the sum of the squares of the distances. This type of problem is common in data science and machine learning—the line is the hypothesis that best describes the data—where the particular definition of best is determined by the definition of distance and the objective f. If the definition of distance and the function f are linear, then we have a linear-programming problem, as discussed in Chapter 29. Although the linear-programming framework captures several important problems, many other problems, including various machine-learning problems, have objectives and constraints that are not necessarily linear. We need frameworks and algorithms to solve such problems.

In this section, we consider the problem of optimizing a continuous function and discuss one of the most popular methods to do so: gradient descent. Gradient descent is a general method for finding a local minimum of a function $f : \mathbb{R}^n \to \mathbb{R}$, where informally, a local minimum of a function f is a point $\mathbf{x}$ for which $f(\mathbf{x}) \leq f(\mathbf{x}')$ for all $\mathbf{x}'$ that are "near" $\mathbf{x}$. When the function is convex, it can find a point near the *global minimizer* of f: an n-vector argument $\mathbf{x} = (x_1, x_2, \ldots, x_n)$ such that $f(\mathbf{x})$ is minimum. For the intuitive idea behind gradient descent, imagine being in a landscape of hills and valleys, and wanting to get to a low point as quickly as possible. You survey the terrain and choose to move in the direction that takes you downhill the fastest from your current position. You move in that direction, but only for a short while, because as you proceed, the terrain changes and you might need to choose a different direction. So you stop, reevaluate the possible directions and move another short distance in the steepest downhill direction, which might differ from the direction of your previous movement. You continue this process until you reach a point from which all directions lead up. Such a point is a local minimum.

In order to make this informal procedure more formal, we need to define the gradient of a function, which in the analogy above is a measure of the steepness of the various directions. Given a function $f : \mathbb{R}^n \to \mathbb{R}$, its *gradient* ∇f is a function $\nabla f : \mathbb{R}^n \to \mathbb{R}^n$ comprising n partial derivatives: $(\nabla f)(\mathbf{x}) = \left(\frac{\partial f}{\partial x_1}, \frac{\partial f}{\partial x_2}, \ldots, \frac{\partial f}{\partial x_n} \right)$. Analogous to the derivative of a function of a single variable, the gradient can be viewed as a direction in which the function value locally increases the fastest, and the rate of that increase. This view is informal; in order to make it formal we would have to define what local means and place certain conditions, such as continuity or existence of derivatives, on the function. Nevertheless, this view motivates the key step of gradient descent—move in the direction opposite to the gradient, by a distance influenced by the magnitude of the gradient.

The general procedure of gradient descent proceeds in steps. You start at some initial point $\mathbf{x}^{(0)}$, which is an n-vector. At each step t, you compute the value of the gradient of f at point $\mathbf{x}^{(t)}$, that is, $(\nabla f)(\mathbf{x}^{(t)})$, which is also an n-vector. You then move in the direction opposite to the gradient in each dimension at $\mathbf{x}^{(t)}$ to arrive at the next point $\mathbf{x}^{(t+1)}$, which again is an n-vector. Because you moved in a monotonically decreasing direction in each dimension, you should have that $f(\mathbf{x}^{(t+1)}) \leq f(\mathbf{x}^{(t)})$. Several details are needed to turn this idea into an actual algorithm. The two main details are that you need an initial point and that you need to decide how far to move in the direction of the negative gradient. You also need to understand when to stop and what you can conclude about the quality of the solution found. We will explore these issues further in this section, for both constrained minimization, where there are additional constraints on the points, and unconstrained minimization, where there are none.

Unconstrained gradient descent

In order to gain intuition, let's consider unconstrained gradient descent in just one dimension, that is, when f is a function of a scalar x, so that $f : \mathbb{R} \to \mathbb{R}$. In this case, the gradient ∇f of f is just $f'(x)$, the derivative of f with respect to x. Consider the function f shown in blue in Figure 33.3, with minimizer x^* and starting point $x^{(0)}$. The gradient (derivative) $f'(x^{(0)})$, shown in orange, has a negative slope, so that a small step from $x^{(0)}$ in the direction of increasing x results in a point x' for which $f(x') < f(x^{(0)})$. Too large a step, however, results in a

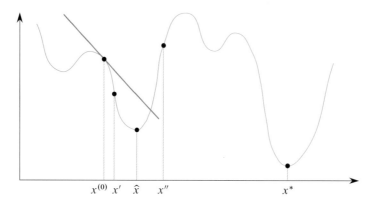

$x^{(0)}$ x' $\hat{x}$ x'' x^*

Figure 33.3 A function $f : \mathbb{R} \rightarrow \mathbb{R}$, shown in blue. Its gradient at point $x^{(0)}$, in orange, has a negative slope, and so a small increase in x from $x^{(0)}$ to x' results in $f(x') < f(x^{(0)})$. Small increases in x from $x^{(0)}$ head toward $\hat{x}$, which gives a local minimum. Too large an increase in x can end up at x'', where $f(x'') > f(x^{(0)})$. Small steps starting from $x^{(0)}$ and going only in the direction of decreasing values of f cannot end up at the global minimizer x^*.

point x'' for which $f(x'') > f(x^{(0)})$, so this is a bad idea. Restricting ourselves to small steps, where each one has $f(x') < f(x)$, eventually results in getting close to point $\hat{x}$, which gives a local minimum. By taking only small downhill steps, however, gradient descent has no chance to get to the global minimizer x^*, given the starting point $x^{(0)}$.

We draw two observations from this simple example. First, gradient descent converges toward a local minimum, and not necessarily a global minimum. Second, the speed at which it converges and how it behaves are related to properties of the function, to the initial point, and to the step size of the algorithm.

The procedure GRADIENT-DESCENT on the facing page takes as input a function f, an initial point $\mathbf{x}^{(0)} \in \mathbb{R}^n$, a fixed step-size multiplier $\gamma > 0$, and a number $T > 0$ of steps to take. Each iteration of the **for** loop of lines 2–4 performs a step by computing the n-dimensional gradient at point $\mathbf{x}^{(t)}$ and then moving distance γ in the opposite direction in the n-dimensional space. The complexity of computing the gradient depends on the function f and can sometimes be expensive. Line 3 sums the points visited. After the loop terminates, line 6 returns **x-avg**, the average of all the points visited except for the last one, $\mathbf{x}^{(T)}$. It might seem more natural to return $\mathbf{x}^{(T)}$, and in fact, in many circumstances, you might prefer to have the function return $\mathbf{x}^{(T)}$. For the version we will analyze, however, we use **x-avg**.

GRADIENT-DESCENT$(f, \mathbf{x}^{(0)}, \gamma, T)$

```
1  sum = 0                              // n-dimensional vector, initially all 0
2  for t = 0 to T − 1
3      sum = sum + x⁽ᵗ⁾                 // add each of n dimensions into sum
4      x⁽ᵗ⁺¹⁾ = x⁽ᵗ⁾ − γ · (∇f)(x⁽ᵗ⁾)   // (∇f)(x⁽ᵗ⁾), x⁽ᵗ⁺¹⁾ are n-dimensional
5  x-avg = sum/T                        // divide each of n dimensions by T
6  return x-avg
```

Figure 33.4 depicts how gradient descent ideally runs on a convex 1-dimensional function.[1] We'll define convexity more formally below, but the figure shows that each iteration moves in the direction opposite to the gradient, with the distance moved being proportional to the magnitude of the gradient. As the iterations proceed, the magnitude of the gradient decreases, and thus the distance moved along the horizontal axis decreases. After each iteration, the distance to the optimal point $\mathbf{x}^*$ decreases. This ideal behavior is not guaranteed to occur in general, but the analysis in the remainder of this section formalizes when this behavior occurs and quantifies the number of iterations needed. Gradient descent does not always work, however. We have already seen that if the function is not convex, gradient descent can converge to a local, rather than global, minimum. We have also seen that if the step size is too large, GRADIENT-DESCENT can overshoot the minimum and wind up farther away. (It is also possible to overshoot the minimum and wind up closer to the optimum.)

Analysis of unconstrained gradient descent for convex functions

Our analysis of gradient descent focuses on convex functions. Inequality (C.29) on page 1194 defines a convex function of one variable, as shown in Figure 33.5. We can extend that definition to a function $f : \mathbb{R}^n \to \mathbb{R}$ and say that f is *convex* if for all $\mathbf{x}, \mathbf{y} \in \mathbb{R}^n$ and for all $0 \leq \lambda \leq 1$, we have

$$f(\lambda \mathbf{x} + (1 - \lambda)\mathbf{y}) \leq \lambda f(\mathbf{x}) + (1 - \lambda) f(\mathbf{y}) . \tag{33.18}$$

(Inequalities (33.18) and (C.29) are the same, except for the dimensions of $\mathbf{x}$ and $\mathbf{y}$.) We also assume that our convex functions are closed[2] and differentiable.

---

[1] Although the curve in Figure 33.4 looks concave, according to the definition of convexity that we'll see below, the function f in the figure is convex.

[2] A function $f : \mathbb{R}^n \to \mathbb{R}$ is closed if, for each $\alpha \in \mathbb{R}$, the set $\{\mathbf{x} \in \mathrm{dom}(f) : f(\mathbf{x}) \leq \alpha\}$ is closed, where $\mathrm{dom}(f)$ is the domain of f.

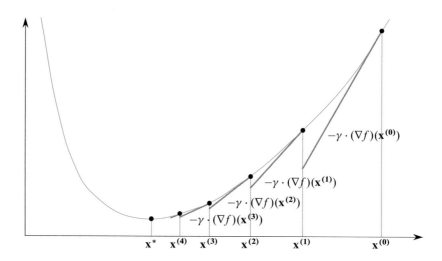

Figure 33.4   An example of running gradient descent on a convex function $f : \mathbb{R} \to \mathbb{R}$, shown in blue. Beginning at point $\mathbf{x}^{(0)}$, each iteration moves in the direction opposite to the gradient, and the distance moved is proportional to the magnitude of the gradient. Orange lines represent the negative of the gradient at each point, scaled by the step size γ. As the iterations proceed, the magnitude of the gradient decreases, and the distance moved decreases correspondingly. After each iteration, the distance to the optimal point $\mathbf{x}^*$ decreases.

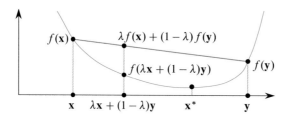

Figure 33.5   A convex function $f : \mathbb{R} \to \mathbb{R}$, shown in blue, with local and global minimizer $\mathbf{x}^*$. Because f is convex, $f(\lambda \mathbf{x} + (1 - \lambda)\mathbf{y}) \leq \lambda f(\mathbf{x}) + (1 - \lambda)f(\mathbf{y})$ for any two values $\mathbf{x}$ and $\mathbf{y}$ and all $0 \leq \lambda \leq 1$, shown for a particular value of λ. Here, the orange line segment represents all values $\lambda f(\mathbf{x}) + (1 - \lambda)f(\mathbf{y})$ for $0 \leq \lambda \leq 1$, and it is above the blue line.

A convex function has the property that any local minimum is also a global minimum. To verify this property, consider inequality (33.18), and suppose for the purpose of contradiction that $\mathbf{x}$ is a local minimum but not a global minimum and $\mathbf{y} \neq \mathbf{x}$ is a global minimum, so $f(\mathbf{y}) < f(\mathbf{x})$. Then we have

$$
\begin{aligned}
f(\lambda \mathbf{x} + (1 - \lambda)\mathbf{y}) &\leq \lambda f(\mathbf{x}) + (1 - \lambda)f(\mathbf{y}) \quad \text{(by inequality (33.18))} \\
&< \lambda f(\mathbf{x}) + (1 - \lambda)f(\mathbf{x}) \\
&= f(\mathbf{x}) \, .
\end{aligned}
$$

Thus, letting λ approach 1, we see that there is another point near $\mathbf{x}$, say $\mathbf{x}'$, such that $f(\mathbf{x}') < f(\mathbf{x})$, so $\mathbf{x}$ is not a local minimum.

Convex functions have several useful properties. The first property, whose proof we leave as Exercise 33.3-1, says that a convex function always lies above its tangent hyperplane. In the context of gradient descent, angle brackets denote the notation for inner product defined on page 1219 rather than denoting a sequence.

Lemma 33.6
For any convex differentiable function $f : \mathbb{R}^n \to \mathbb{R}$ and for all $x, y \in \mathbb{R}^n$, we have $f(\mathbf{x}) \leq f(\mathbf{y}) + \langle (\nabla f)(\mathbf{x}), \mathbf{x} - \mathbf{y} \rangle.$ ∎

The second property, which Exercise 33.3-2 asks you to prove, is a repeated application of the definition of convexity in inequality (33.18).

Lemma 33.7
For any convex function $f : \mathbb{R}^n \to \mathbb{R}$, for any integer $T \geq 1$, and for all $\mathbf{x}^{(0)}, \ldots, \mathbf{x}^{(T-1)} \in \mathbb{R}^n$, we have

$$f\left(\frac{\mathbf{x}^{(0)} + \cdots + \mathbf{x}^{(T-1)}}{T}\right) \leq \frac{f(\mathbf{x}^{(0)}) + \cdots + f(\mathbf{x}^{(T-1)})}{T}. \tag{33.19}$$

∎

The left-hand side of inequality (33.19) is the value of f at the vector **x-avg** that GRADIENT-DESCENT returns.

We now proceed to analyze GRADIENT-DESCENT. It might not return the exact global minimizer $\mathbf{x}^*$. We use an error bound ϵ, and we want to choose T so that $f(\mathbf{x\text{-}avg}) - f(\mathbf{x}^*) \leq \epsilon$ at termination. The value of ϵ depends on the number T of iterations and two additional values. First, since you expect it to be better to start close to the global minimizer, ϵ is a function of

$$R = \|\mathbf{x}^{(0)} - \mathbf{x}^*\|, \tag{33.20}$$

the euclidean norm (or distance, defined on page 1219) of the difference between $\mathbf{x}^{(0)}$ and $\mathbf{x}^*$. The error bound ϵ is also a function of a quantity we call L, which is an upper bound on the magnitude $\|(\nabla f)(\mathbf{x})\|$ of the gradient, so that

$$\|(\nabla f)(\mathbf{x})\| \leq L, \tag{33.21}$$

where $\mathbf{x}$ ranges over all the points $\mathbf{x}^{(0)}, \ldots, \mathbf{x}^{(T-1)}$ whose gradients are computed by GRADIENT-DESCENT. Of course, we don't know the values of L and R, but for now let's assume that we do. We'll discuss later how to remove these assumptions. The analysis of GRADIENT-DESCENT is summarized in the following theorem.

Theorem 33.8

Let $\mathbf{x}^* \in \mathbb{R}^n$ be the minimizer of a convex function f, and suppose that an execution of GRADIENT-DESCENT$(f, \mathbf{x}^{(0)}, \gamma, T)$ returns **x-avg**, where $\gamma = R/(L\sqrt{T})$ and R and L are defined in equations (33.20) and (33.21). Let $\epsilon = RL/\sqrt{T}$. Then we have $f(\mathbf{x\text{-avg}}) - f(\mathbf{x}^*) \leq \epsilon$. ∎

We now prove this theorem. We do not give an absolute bound on how much progress each iteration makes. Instead, we use a potential function, as in Section 16.3. Here, we define a potential $\Phi(t)$ after computing $\mathbf{x}^{(t)}$, such that $\Phi(t) \geq 0$ for $t = 0, \ldots, T$. We define the *amortized progress* in the iteration that computes $\mathbf{x}^{(t)}$ as

$$p(t) = f(\mathbf{x}^{(t)}) - f(\mathbf{x}^*) + \Phi(t+1) - \Phi(t) . \tag{33.22}$$

Along with including the change in potential $(\Phi(t+1) - \Phi(t))$, equation (33.22) also subtracts the minimum value $f(\mathbf{x}^*)$ because ultimately, you care not about the values $f(\mathbf{x}^{(t)})$ but about how close they are to $f(\mathbf{x}^*)$. Suppose that we can show that $p(t) \leq B$ for some value B and $t = 0, \ldots, T-1$. Then we can substitute for $p(t)$ using equation (33.22), giving

$$f(\mathbf{x}^{(t)}) - f(\mathbf{x}^*) \leq B - \Phi(t+1) + \Phi(t) . \tag{33.23}$$

Summing inequality (33.23) over $t = 0, \ldots, T-1$ yields

$$\sum_{t=0}^{T-1}(f(\mathbf{x}^{(t)}) - f(\mathbf{x}^*)) \leq \sum_{t=0}^{T-1}(B - \Phi(t+1) + \Phi(t)) .$$

Observing that we have a telescoping series on the right and regrouping terms, we have that

$$\left(\sum_{t=0}^{T-1} f(\mathbf{x}^{(t)})\right) - T \cdot f(\mathbf{x}^*) \leq TB - \Phi(T) + \Phi(0) .$$

Dividing by T and dropping the positive term $\Phi(T)$ gives

$$\frac{\sum_{t=0}^{T-1} f(\mathbf{x}^{(t)})}{T} - f(\mathbf{x}^*) \leq B + \frac{\Phi(0)}{T} , \tag{33.24}$$

and thus we have

$$\begin{aligned}
f(\mathbf{x\text{-avg}}) - f(\mathbf{x}^*) &= f\left(\frac{\sum_{t=0}^{T-1} \mathbf{x}^{(t)}}{T}\right) - f(\mathbf{x}^*) \quad \text{(by the definition of \textbf{x-avg})} \\
&\leq \frac{\sum_{t=0}^{T-1} f(\mathbf{x}^{(t)})}{T} - f(\mathbf{x}^*) \quad \text{(by Lemma 33.7)} \\
&\leq B + \frac{\Phi(0)}{T} \quad \text{(by inequality (33.24)) .} \tag{33.25}
\end{aligned}$$

In other words, if we can show that $p(t) \leq B$ for some value B and choose a potential function where $\Phi(0)$ is not too large, then inequality (33.25) tells us how close the function value $f(\mathbf{x\text{-}avg})$ is to the function value $f(\mathbf{x}^*)$ after T iterations. That is, we can set the error bound ϵ to $B + \Phi(0)/T$.

In order to bound the amortized progress, we need to come up with a concrete potential function. Define the potential function $\Phi(t)$ by

$$\Phi(t) = \frac{\left\| \mathbf{x}^{(t)} - \mathbf{x}^* \right\|^2}{2\gamma} , \tag{33.26}$$

that is, the potential function is proportional to the square of the distance between the current point and the minimizer $\mathbf{x}^*$. With this potential function in hand, the next lemma provides a bound on the amortized progress made in any iteration of GRADIENT-DESCENT.

Lemma 33.9
Let $\mathbf{x}^* \in \mathbb{R}^n$ be the minimizer of a convex function f, and consider an execution of GRADIENT-DESCENT$(f, \mathbf{x}^{(0)}, \gamma, T)$. Then for each point $\mathbf{x}^{(t)}$ computed by the procedure, we have that

$$p(t) = f(\mathbf{x}^{(t)}) - f(\mathbf{x}^*) + \Phi(t+1) - \Phi(t) \leq \frac{\gamma L^2}{2} .$$

Proof   We first bound the potential change $\Phi(t+1) - \Phi(t)$. Using the definition of $\Phi(t)$ from equation (33.26), we have

$$\Phi(t+1) - \Phi(t) = \frac{1}{2\gamma} \left\| \mathbf{x}^{(t+1)} - \mathbf{x}^* \right\|^2 - \frac{1}{2\gamma} \left\| \mathbf{x}^{(t)} - \mathbf{x}^* \right\|^2 . \tag{33.27}$$

From line 4 in GRADIENT-DESCENT, we know that

$$\mathbf{x}^{(t+1)} - \mathbf{x}^{(t)} = -\gamma \cdot (\nabla f)(\mathbf{x}^{(t)}) , \tag{33.28}$$

and so we would like to rewrite equation (33.27) to have $\mathbf{x}^{(t+1)} - \mathbf{x}^{(t)}$ terms. As Exercise 33.3-3 asks you to prove, for any two vectors $\mathbf{a}, \mathbf{b} \in \mathbb{R}^n$, we have

$$\|\mathbf{a} + \mathbf{b}\|^2 - \|\mathbf{a}\|^2 = 2\langle \mathbf{b}, \mathbf{a} \rangle + \|\mathbf{b}\|^2 . \tag{33.29}$$

Letting $\mathbf{a} = \mathbf{x}^{(t)} - \mathbf{x}^*$ and $\mathbf{b} = \mathbf{x}^{(t+1)} - \mathbf{x}^{(t)}$, we can write the right-hand side of equation (33.27) as $\frac{1}{2\gamma} \left(\|\mathbf{a} + \mathbf{b}\|^2 - \|\mathbf{a}\|^2 \right)$. Then we can express the potential change as

$$\Phi(t+1) - \Phi(t)$$

$$= \frac{1}{2\gamma} \left\| \mathbf{x}^{(t+1)} - \mathbf{x}^* \right\|^2 - \frac{1}{2\gamma} \left\| \mathbf{x}^{(t)} - \mathbf{x}^* \right\|^2 \qquad \text{(by equation (33.27))}$$

$$= \frac{1}{2\gamma} \left(2 \langle \mathbf{x}^{(t+1)} - \mathbf{x}^{(t)}, \mathbf{x}^{(t)} - \mathbf{x}^* \rangle + \left\| \mathbf{x}^{(t+1)} - \mathbf{x}^{(t)} \right\|^2 \right) \quad \text{(by equation (33.29))}$$

$$= \frac{1}{2\gamma} \left(2 \langle -\gamma \cdot (\nabla f)(\mathbf{x}^{(t)}), \mathbf{x}^{(t)} - \mathbf{x}^* \rangle + \left\| -\gamma \cdot (\nabla f)(\mathbf{x}^{(t)}) \right\|^2 \right)$$

$$\text{(by equation (33.28))}$$

$$= -\langle (\nabla f)(\mathbf{x}^{(t)}), \mathbf{x}^{(t)} - \mathbf{x}^* \rangle + \frac{\gamma}{2} \left\| (\nabla f)(\mathbf{x}^{(t)}) \right\|^2 \qquad (33.30)$$

$$\text{(by equation (D.3) on page 1219)}$$

$$\leq -(f(\mathbf{x}^{(t)}) - f(\mathbf{x}^*)) + \frac{\gamma}{2} \left\| (\nabla f)(\mathbf{x}^{(t)}) \right\|^2 \qquad \text{(by Lemma 33.6)} ,$$

and thus we have

$$\Phi(t+1) - \Phi(t) \leq -(f(\mathbf{x}^{(t)}) - f(\mathbf{x}^*)) + \frac{\gamma}{2} \left\| (\nabla f)(\mathbf{x}^{(t)}) \right\|^2 \qquad (33.31)$$

We can now proceed to bound $p(t)$. By the bound on the potential change from inequality (33.31), and using the definition of L (inequality (33.21)), we have

$$p(t) = f(\mathbf{x}^{(t)}) - f(\mathbf{x}^*) + \Phi(t+1) - \Phi(t) \qquad \text{(by equation (33.22))}$$

$$\leq f(\mathbf{x}^{(t)}) - f(\mathbf{x}^*) - (f(\mathbf{x}^{(t)}) - f(\mathbf{x}^*)) + \frac{\gamma}{2} \left\| (\nabla f)(\mathbf{x}^{(t)}) \right\|^2$$

$$\text{(by inequality (33.31))}$$

$$= \frac{\gamma}{2} \left\| (\nabla f)(\mathbf{x}^{(t)}) \right\|^2$$

$$\leq \frac{\gamma L^2}{2} \qquad \text{(by inequality (33.21))} . \quad \blacksquare$$

Having bounded the amortized progress in one step, we now analyze the entire GRADIENT-DESCENT procedure, completing the proof of Theorem 33.8.

Proof of Theorem 33.8   Inequality (33.25) tells us that if we have an upper bound of B for $p(t)$, then we also have the bound $f(\mathbf{x}\text{-}\mathbf{avg}) - f(\mathbf{x}^*) \leq B + \Phi(0)/T$. By equations (33.20) and (33.26), we have that $\Phi(0) = R^2/(2\gamma)$. Lemma 33.9 gives us the upper bound of $B = \gamma L^2/2$, and so we have

$$f(\mathbf{x}\text{-}\mathbf{avg}) - f(\mathbf{x}^*) \leq B + \frac{\Phi(0)}{T} \qquad \text{(by inequality (33.25))}$$

$$= \frac{\gamma L^2}{2} + \frac{R^2}{2\gamma T} .$$

Our choice of $\gamma = R/(L\sqrt{T})$ in the statement of Theorem 33.8 balances the two terms, and we obtain

$$
\begin{aligned}
\frac{\gamma L^2}{2} + \frac{R^2}{2\gamma T} &= \frac{R}{L\sqrt{T}} \cdot \frac{L^2}{2} + \frac{R^2}{2T} \cdot \frac{L\sqrt{T}}{R} \\
&= \frac{RL}{2\sqrt{T}} + \frac{RL}{2\sqrt{T}} \\
&= \frac{RL}{\sqrt{T}}.
\end{aligned}
$$

Since we chose $\epsilon = RL/\sqrt{T}$ in the theorem statement, the proof is complete. ∎

Continuing under the assumption that we know R (from equation (33.20)) and L (from inequality (33.21)), we can think of the analysis in a slightly different way. We can presume that we have a target accuracy ϵ and then compute the number of iterations needed. That is, we can solve $\epsilon = RL/\sqrt{T}$ for T, obtaining $T = R^2 L^2 / \epsilon^2$. The number of iterations thus depends on the square of R and L and, most importantly, on $1/\epsilon^2$. (The definition of L from inequality (33.21) depends on T, but we may know an upper bound on L that doesn't depend on the particular value of T.) Thus, if you want to halve your error bound, you need to run four times as many iterations.

It is quite possible that we don't really know R and L, since you'd need to know $\mathbf{x}^*$ in order to know R (since $R = \|\mathbf{x}^{(0)} - \mathbf{x}^*\|$), and you might not have an explicit upper bound on the gradient, which would provide L. You can, however, interpret the analysis of gradient descent as a proof that there is some step size for which the procedure makes progress toward the minimum. You can then compute a step size γ for which $f(\mathbf{x}^{(t)}) - f(\mathbf{x}^{(t+1)})$ is large enough. In fact, not having a fixed step size multiplier can actually help in practice, as you are free to use any step size s that achieves sufficient decrease in the value of f. You can search for a step size that achieves a large decrease via a binary-search-like routine, which is often called *line search*. For a given function f and step size s, define the function $g(\mathbf{x}^{(t)}, s) = f(\mathbf{x}^{(t)}) - s(\nabla f)(\mathbf{x}^{(t)})$. Start with a small step size s for which $g(\mathbf{x}^{(t)}, s) \leq f(\mathbf{x}^{(t)})$. Then repeatedly double s until $g(\mathbf{x}^{(t)}, 2s) \geq g(\mathbf{x}^{(t)}, s)$, and then perform a binary search in the interval $[s, 2s]$. This procedure can produce a step size that achieves a significant decrease in the objective function. In other circumstances, however, you may know good upper bounds on R and L, typically from problem-specific information, which can suffice.

The dominant computational step in each iteration of the **for** loop of lines 2–4 is computing the gradient. The complexity of computing and evaluating a gradient varies widely, depending on the application at hand. We'll discuss several applications later.

Constrained gradient descent

We can adapt gradient descent for constrained minimization to minimize a closed convex function $f(\mathbf{x})$, subject to the additional requirement that $\mathbf{x} \in K$, where K is a closed convex body. A *body* $K \subseteq \mathbb{R}^n$ is *convex* if for all $\mathbf{x}, \mathbf{y} \in K$, the convex combination $\lambda \mathbf{x} + (1-\lambda)\mathbf{y} \in K$ for all $0 \le \lambda \le 1$. A *closed* convex body contains its limit points. Somewhat surprisingly, restricting to the constrained problem does not significantly increase the number of iterations of gradient descent. The idea is that you run the same algorithm, but in each iteration, check whether the current point $\mathbf{x}^{(t)}$ is still within the convex body K. If it is not, just move to the closest point in K. Moving to the closest point is known as *projection*. We formally define the projection $\Pi_K(\mathbf{x})$ of a point $\mathbf{x}$ in n dimensions onto a convex body K as the point $\mathbf{y} \in K$ such that $\|\mathbf{x} - \mathbf{y}\| = \min\{\|\mathbf{x} - \mathbf{z}\| : \mathbf{z} \in K\}$. If we have $\mathbf{x} \in K$, then $\Pi_K(\mathbf{x}) = \mathbf{x}$.

This one change yields the procedure GRADIENT-DESCENT-CONSTRAINED, in which line 4 of GRADIENT-DESCENT is replaced by two lines. It assumes that $\mathbf{x}^{(0)} \in K$. Line 4 of GRADIENT-DESCENT-CONSTRAINED moves in the direction of the negative gradient, and line 5 projects back onto K. The lemma that follows helps to show that when $\mathbf{x}^* \in K$, if the projection step in line 5 moves from a point outside of K to a point in K, it cannot be moving away from $\mathbf{x}^*$.

GRADIENT-DESCENT-CONSTRAINED$(f, \mathbf{x}^{(0)}, \gamma, T, K)$

1 **sum** $= 0$ // n-dimensional vector, initially all 0
2 **for** $t = 0$ **to** $T - 1$
3   **sum** $=$ **sum** $+ \mathbf{x}^{(t)}$ // add each of n dimensions into **sum**
4    $\mathbf{x}'^{(t+1)} = \mathbf{x}^{(t)} - \gamma \cdot (\nabla f)(\mathbf{x}^{(t)})$ // $(\nabla f)(\mathbf{x}^{(t)}), \mathbf{x}'^{(t+1)}$ are n-dimensional
5    $\mathbf{x}^{(t+1)} = \Pi_K(\mathbf{x}'^{(t+1)})$ // project onto K
6 **x-avg** $=$ **sum**$/T$ // divide each of n dimensions by T
7 **return x-avg**

Lemma 33.10
Consider a convex body $K \subseteq \mathbb{R}^n$ and points $\mathbf{a} \in K$ and $\mathbf{b}' \in \mathbb{R}^n$. Let $\mathbf{b} = \Pi_K(\mathbf{b}')$. Then $\|\mathbf{b} - \mathbf{a}\|^2 \le \|\mathbf{b}' - \mathbf{a}\|^2$.

Proof   If $\mathbf{b}' \in K$, then $\mathbf{b} = \mathbf{b}'$ and the claim is true. Otherwise, $\mathbf{b}' \ne \mathbf{b}$, and as Figure 33.6 shows, we can extend the line segment between $\mathbf{b}$ and $\mathbf{b}'$ to a line ℓ. Let $\mathbf{c}$ be the projection of $\mathbf{a}$ onto ℓ. Point $\mathbf{c}$ may or may not be in K, and if $\mathbf{a}$ is on the boundary of K, then $\mathbf{c}$ could coincide with $\mathbf{b}$. If $\mathbf{c}$ coincides with $\mathbf{b}$ (part (c) of the figure), then $\mathbf{a}\mathbf{b}\mathbf{b}'$ is a right triangle, and so $\|\mathbf{b} - \mathbf{a}\|^2 \le \|\mathbf{b}' - \mathbf{a}\|^2$.

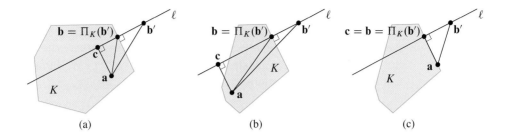

Figure 33.6   Projecting a point $\mathbf{b}'$ outside the convex body K to the closest point $\mathbf{b} = \Pi_K(\mathbf{b}')$ in K. Line ℓ is the line containing $\mathbf{b}$ and $\mathbf{b}'$, and point $\mathbf{c}$ is the projection of $\mathbf{a}$ onto ℓ. **(a)** When $\mathbf{c}$ is in K. **(b)** When $\mathbf{c}$ is not in K. **(c)** When $\mathbf{a}$ is on the boundary of K and $\mathbf{c}$ coincides with $\mathbf{b}$.

If $\mathbf{c}$ does not coincide with $\mathbf{b}$ (parts (a) and (b) of the figure), then because of convexity, the angle $\angle\mathbf{abb}'$ must be obtuse. Because angle $\angle\mathbf{abb}'$ is obtuse, $\mathbf{b}$ lies between $\mathbf{c}$ and $\mathbf{b}'$ on ℓ. Furthermore, because $\mathbf{c}$ is the projection of $\mathbf{a}$ onto line ℓ, $\mathbf{acb}$ and $\mathbf{acb}'$ must be right triangles. By the Pythagorean theorem, we have that $\|\mathbf{b}' - \mathbf{a}\|^2 = \|\mathbf{a} - \mathbf{c}\|^2 + \|\mathbf{c} - \mathbf{b}'\|^2$ and $\|\mathbf{b} - \mathbf{a}\|^2 = \|\mathbf{a} - \mathbf{c}\|^2 + \|\mathbf{c} - \mathbf{b}\|^2$. Subtracting these two equations gives $\|\mathbf{b}' - \mathbf{a}\|^2 - \|\mathbf{b} - \mathbf{a}\|^2 = \|\mathbf{c} - \mathbf{b}'\|^2 - \|\mathbf{c} - \mathbf{b}\|^2$. Because $\mathbf{b}$ is between $\mathbf{c}$ and $\mathbf{b}'$, we must have $\|\mathbf{c} - \mathbf{b}'\|^2 \geq \|\mathbf{c} - \mathbf{b}\|^2$, and thus $\|\mathbf{b}' - \mathbf{a}\|^2 - \|\mathbf{b} - \mathbf{a}\|^2 \geq 0$. The lemma follows. ∎

We can now repeat the entire proof for the unconstrained case and obtain the same bounds. Lemma 33.10 with $\mathbf{a} = \mathbf{x}^*$, $\mathbf{b} = \mathbf{x}^{(t+1)}$, and $\mathbf{b}' = \mathbf{x}'^{(t+1)}$ tells us that $\|\mathbf{x}^{(t+1)} - \mathbf{x}^*\|^2 \leq \|\mathbf{x}'^{(t+1)} - \mathbf{x}^*\|^2$. We can therefore derive an upper bound that matches inequality (33.31). We continue to define $\Phi(t)$ as in equation (33.26), but noting that $\mathbf{x}^{(t+1)}$, computed in line 5 of Gradient-Descent-Constrained, has a different meaning here from in inequality (33.31):

$$\Phi(t + 1) - \Phi(t)$$

$$= \frac{1}{2\gamma} \left\| \mathbf{x}^{(t+1)} - \mathbf{x}^* \right\|^2 - \frac{1}{2\gamma} \left\| \mathbf{x}^{(t)} - \mathbf{x}^* \right\|^2 \qquad \text{(by equation (33.27))}$$

$$\leq \frac{1}{2\gamma} \left\| \mathbf{x}'^{(t+1)} - \mathbf{x}^* \right\|^2 - \frac{1}{2\gamma} \left\| \mathbf{x}^{(t)} - \mathbf{x}^* \right\|^2 \qquad \text{(by Lemma 33.10)}$$

$$= \frac{1}{2\gamma} \left(2\langle \mathbf{x}'^{(t+1)} - \mathbf{x}^{(t)}, \mathbf{x}^{(t)} - \mathbf{x}^* \rangle + \left\| \mathbf{x}'^{(t+1)} - \mathbf{x}^* \right\|^2 \right)$$
$$\qquad\qquad\qquad\qquad\qquad\qquad \text{(by equation (33.29))}$$

$$= \frac{1}{2\gamma} \left(2\langle -\gamma \cdot (\nabla f)(\mathbf{x}^{(t)}), \mathbf{x}^{(t)} - \mathbf{x}^* \rangle + \left\| -\gamma \cdot (\nabla f)(\mathbf{x}^{(t)}) \right\|^2 \right)$$
$$\qquad\qquad\qquad \text{(by line 4 of Gradient-Descent-Constrained)}$$

$$= -\langle (\nabla f)(\mathbf{x}^{(t)}), \mathbf{x}^{(t)} - \mathbf{x}^* \rangle + \frac{\gamma}{2} \left\| (\nabla f)(\mathbf{x}^{(t)}) \right\|^2 .$$

With the same upper bound on the change in the potential function as in equation (33.30), the entire proof of Lemma 33.9 can proceed as before. We can therefore conclude that the procedure GRADIENT-DESCENT-CONSTRAINED has the same asymptotic complexity as GRADIENT-DESCENT. We summarize this result in the following theorem.

Theorem 33.11
Let $K \subseteq \mathbb{R}^n$ be a convex body, $\mathbf{x}^* \in \mathbb{R}^n$ be the minimizer of a convex function f over K, and $\gamma = R/(L\sqrt{T})$, where R and L are defined in equations (33.20) and (33.21). Suppose that the vector **x-avg** is returned by an execution of GRADIENT-DESCENT-CONSTRAINED$(f, \mathbf{x}^{(0)}, \gamma, T, K)$. Let $\epsilon = RL/\sqrt{T}$. Then we have $f(\mathbf{x}\text{-}\mathbf{avg}) - f(\mathbf{x}^*) \le \epsilon$. ∎

Applications of gradient descent

Gradient descent has many applications to minimizing functions and is widely used in optimization and machine learning. Here we sketch how it can be used to solve linear systems. Then we discuss an application to machine learning: prediction using linear regression.

In Chapter 28, we saw how to use Gaussian elimination to solve a system of linear equations $A\mathbf{x} = \mathbf{b}$, thereby computing $\mathbf{x} = A^{-1}\mathbf{b}$. If A is an $n \times n$ matrix and $\mathbf{b}$ is a length-n vector, then the running time of Gaussian elimination is $\Theta(n^3)$, which for large matrices might be prohibitively expensive. If an approximate solution is acceptable, however, you can use gradient descent.

First, let's see how to use gradient descent as a roundabout—and admittedly inefficient—way to solve for x in the scalar equation $ax = b$, where $a, x, b \in \mathbb{R}$. This equation is equivalent to $ax - b = 0$. If $ax - b$ is the derivative of a convex function $f(x)$, then $ax - b = 0$ for the value of x that minimizes $f(x)$. Given $f(x)$, gradient descent can then determine this minimizer. Of course, $f(x)$ is just the integral of $ax - b$, that is, $f(x) = \frac{1}{2}ax^2 - bx$, which is convex if $a \ge 0$. Therefore, one way to solve $ax = b$ for $a \ge 0$ is to find the minimizer for $\frac{1}{2}ax^2 - bx$ via gradient descent.

We now generalize this idea to higher dimensions, where using gradient descent may actually lead to a faster algorithm. One n-dimensional analog is the function $f(\mathbf{x}) = \frac{1}{2}\mathbf{x}^{\mathrm{T}}A\mathbf{x} - \mathbf{b}^{\mathrm{T}}\mathbf{x}$, where A is an $n \times n$ matrix. The gradient of f with respect to $\mathbf{x}$ is the function $A\mathbf{x} - \mathbf{b}$. To find the value of $\mathbf{x}$ that minimizes f, we set the gradient of f to 0 and solve for $\mathbf{x}$. Solving $A\mathbf{x} - \mathbf{b} = 0$ for $\mathbf{x}$, we obtain $\mathbf{x} = A^{-1}\mathbf{b}$, Thus, minimizing $f(\mathbf{x})$ is equivalent to solving $A\mathbf{x} = \mathbf{b}$. If $f(\mathbf{x})$ is convex, then gradient descent can approximately compute this minimum.

A 1-dimensional function is convex when its second derivative is positive. The equivalent definition for a multidimensional function is that it is convex when its

Hessian matrix is positive-semidefinite (see page 1222 for a definition), where the
Hessian matrix $(\nabla^2 f)(\mathbf{x})$ of a function $f(\mathbf{x})$ is the matrix in which entry (i, j) is
the partial derivative of f with respect to i and j:

$$(\nabla^2 f)(\mathbf{x}) = \begin{pmatrix} \frac{\partial^2 f}{\partial x_1 \partial x_1} & \frac{\partial^2 f}{\partial x_1 \partial x_2} & \cdots & \frac{\partial^2 f}{\partial x_1 \partial x_n} \\ \frac{\partial^2 f}{\partial x_2 \partial x_1} & \frac{\partial^2 f}{\partial x_2 \partial x_2} & \cdots & \frac{\partial^2 f}{\partial x_2 \partial x_n} \\ \vdots & \vdots & \ddots & \vdots \\ \frac{\partial^2 f}{\partial x_n \partial x_1} & \frac{\partial^2 f}{\partial x_n \partial x_2} & \cdots & \frac{\partial^2 f}{\partial x_n \partial x_n} \end{pmatrix}.$$

Analogous to the 1-dimensional case, the Hessian of f is just A, and so if A is
a positive-semidefinite matrix, then we can use gradient descent to find a point $\mathbf{x}$
where $A\mathbf{x} \approx \mathbf{b}$. If R and L are not too large, then this method is faster than using
Gaussian elimination.

Gradient descent in machine learning

As a concrete example of supervised learning for prediction, suppose that you want
to predict whether a patient will develop heart disease. For each of m patients, you
have n different attributes. For example, you might have $n = 4$ and the four pieces
of data are age, height, blood pressure, and number of close family members with
heart disease. Denote the data for patient i as a vector $\mathbf{x}^{(i)} \in \mathbb{R}^n$, with $x_j^{(i)}$ giving
the jth entry in vector $\mathbf{x}^{(i)}$. The *label* of patient i is denoted by a scalar $y^{(i)} \in \mathbb{R}$,
signifying the severity of the patient's heart disease. The hypothesis should capture
a relationship between the $\mathbf{x}^{(i)}$ values and $y^{(i)}$. For this example, we make the
modeling assumption that the relationship is linear, and therefore the goal is to
compute the "best" linear relationship between the $\mathbf{x}^{(i)}$ values and $y^{(i)}$: a linear
function $f : \mathbb{R}^n \to \mathbb{R}$ such that $f(\mathbf{x}^{(i)}) \approx y^{(i)}$ for each patient i. Of course, no
such function may exist, but you would like one that comes as close as possible.
A linear function f can be defined by a vector of weights $\mathbf{w} = (w_0, w_1, \ldots, w_n)$,
with

$$f(\mathbf{x}) = w_0 + \sum_{j=1}^{n} w_j x_j . \tag{33.32}$$

When evaluating a machine-learning model, you need to measure how close
each value $f(\mathbf{x}^{(i)})$ is to its corresponding label $y^{(i)}$. In this example, we define
the error $e^{(i)} \in \mathbb{R}$ associated with patient i as $e^{(i)} = f(\mathbf{x}^{(i)}) - y^{(i)}$. The objective
function we choose is to minimize the sum of squares of the errors, which is

$$\sum_{i=1}^{m} \left(e^{(i)}\right)^2 = \sum_{i=1}^{m} \left(f(\mathbf{x}^{(i)}) - y^{(i)}\right)^2$$

$$= \sum_{i=1}^{m} \left(w_0 + \sum_{j=1}^{n} w_j x_j^{(i)} - y^{(i)}\right)^2 . \qquad (33.33)$$

The objective function is typically called the *loss function*, and the *least-squares error* given by equation (33.33) is just one example of many possible loss functions. The goal is then, given the $\mathbf{x}^{(i)}$ and $y^{(i)}$ values, to compute the weights $w_0, w_1, \ldots, w_n$ so as to minimize the loss function in equation (33.33). The variables here are the weights $w_0, w_1, \ldots, w_n$ and not the $\mathbf{x}^{(i)}$ or $y^{(i)}$ values.

This particular objective is sometimes known as a *least-squares fit*, and the problem of finding a linear function to fit data and minimize the least-squares error is called *linear regression*. Finding a least-squares fit is also addressed in Section 28.3.

When the function f is linear, the loss function defined in equation (33.33) is convex, because it is the sum of squares of linear functions, which are themselves convex. Therefore, we can apply gradient descent to compute a set of weights to approximately minimize the least-squares error. The concrete goal of learning is to be able to make predictions on new data. Informally, if the features are all reported in the same units and are from the same range (perhaps from being normalized), then the weights tend to have a natural interpretation because the features of the data that are better predictors of the label have a larger associated weight. For example, you would expect that, after normalization, the weight associated with the number of family members with heart disease would be larger than the weight associated with height.

The computed weights form a model of the data. Once you have a model, you can make predictions, so that given new data, you can predict its label. In our example, given a new patient $\mathbf{x}'$ who is not part of the original training data set, you would still hope to predict the chance that the new patient develops heart disease. You can do so by computing the label $f(\mathbf{x}')$, incorporating the weights computed by gradient descent.

For this linear-regression problem, the objective is to minimize the expression in equation (33.33), which is a quadratic in each of the $n+1$ weights w_j. Thus, entry j in the gradient is linear in w_j. Exercise 33.3-5 asks you to explicitly compute the gradient and see that it can be computed in $O(nm)$ time, which is linear in the input size. Compared with the exact method of solving equation (33.33) in Chapter 28, which needs to invert a matrix, gradient descent is typically much faster.

Section 33.1 briefly discussed regularization—the idea that a complicated hypothesis should be penalized in order to avoid overfitting the training data. Regularization often involves adding a term to the objective function, but it can also be achieved by adding a constraint. One way to regularize this example would be to explicitly limit the norm of the weights, adding a constraint that $\|\mathbf{w}\| \leq B$ for some bound $B > 0$. (Recall again that the components of the vector $\mathbf{w}$ are the variables in the present application.) Adding this constraint controls the complexity of the model, as the number of values w_j that can have large absolute value is now limited.

In order to run GRADIENT-DESCENT-CONSTRAINED for any problem, you need to implement the projection step, as well as to compute bounds on R and L. We conclude this section by describing these calculations for gradient descent with the constraint $\|\mathbf{w}\| \leq B$. First, consider the projection step in line 5. Suppose that the update in line 4 results in a vector $\mathbf{w}'$. The projection is implemented by computing $\Pi_k(\mathbf{w}')$ where K is defined by $\|\mathbf{w}\| \leq B$. This particular projection can be accomplished by simply scaling $\mathbf{w}'$, since we know that closest point in K to $\mathbf{w}'$ must be the point along the vector whose norm is exactly B. The amount z by which we need to scale $\mathbf{w}'$ to hit the boundary of K is the solution to the equation $z \|\mathbf{w}'\| = B$, which is solved by $z = B/\|\mathbf{w}'\|$. Hence line 5 is implemented by computing $\mathbf{w} = \mathbf{w}'B/\|\mathbf{w}'\|$. Because we always have $\|\mathbf{w}\| \leq B$, Exercise 33.3-6 asks you to show that the upper bound on the magnitude L of the gradient is $O(B)$. We also get a bound on R, as follows. By the constraint $\|\mathbf{w}\| \leq B$, we know that both $\|\mathbf{w}^{(0)}\| \leq B$ and $\|\mathbf{w}^*\| \leq B$, and thus $\|\mathbf{w}^{(0)} - \mathbf{w}^*\| \leq 2B$. Using the definition of R in equation (33.20), we have $R = O(B)$. The bound $RL/\sqrt{T}$ on the accuracy of the solution after T iterations in Theorem 33.11 becomes $O(B)L/\sqrt{T} = O(B^2/\sqrt{T})$.

Exercises

33.3-1
Prove Lemma 33.6. Start from the definition of a convex function given in equation (33.18). (*Hint:* You can prove the statement when $n = 1$ first. The proof for general values of n is similar.)

33.3-2
Prove Lemma 33.7.

33.3-3
Prove equation (33.29). (*Hint:* The proof for $n = 1$ dimension is straightforward. The proof for general values of n dimensions follows along similar lines.)

33.3-4
Show that the function f in equation (33.32) is a convex function of the variables $w_0, w_1, \ldots, w_n$.

33.3-5
Compute the gradient of expression (33.33) and explain how to evaluate the gradient in $O(nm)$ time.

33.3-6
Consider the function f defined in equation (33.32), and suppose that you have a bound $\|\mathbf{w}\| \leq B$, as is considered in the discussion on regularization. Show that $L = O(B)$ in this case.

33.3-7
Equation (33.2) on page 1009 gives a function that, when minimized, gives an optimal solution to the k-means problem. Explain how to use gradient descent to solve the k-means problem.

Problems

33-1 Newton's method
Gradient descent iteratively moves closer to a desired value (the minimum) of a function. Another algorithm in this spirit is known as *Newton's method*, which is an iterative algorithm that finds the root of a function. Here, we consider Newton's method which, given a function $f : \mathbb{R} \to \mathbb{R}$, finds a value x^* such that $f(x^*) = 0$. The algorithm moves through a series of points $x^{(0)}, x^{(1)}, \ldots$. If the algorithm is currently at a point $x^{(t)}$, then to find point $x^{(t+1)}$, it first takes the equation of the line tangent to the curve at $x = x^{(t)}$,

$$y = f'(x^{(t)})(x - x^{(t)}) + f(x^{(t)}) .$$

It then uses the x-intercept of this line as the next point $x^{(t+1)}$.

a. Show that the algorithm described above can be summarized by the update rule

$$x^{(t+1)} = x^{(t)} - \frac{f(x^{(t)})}{f'(x^{(t)})} .$$

We restrict our attention to some domain I and assume that $f'(x) \neq 0$ for all $x \in I$ and that $f''(x)$ is continuous. We also assume that the starting point $x^{(0)}$ is sufficiently close to x^*, where "sufficiently close" means that we can use only the first two terms of the Taylor expansion of $f(x^*)$ about $x^{(0)}$, namely

$$f(x^*) = f(x^{(0)}) + f'(x^{(0)})(x^* - x^{(0)}) + \frac{1}{2}f''(\gamma^{(0)})(x^* - x^{(0)})^2 , \tag{33.34}$$

where $\gamma^{(0)}$ is some value between $x^{(0)}$ and x^*. If the approximation in equation (33.34) holds for $x^{(0)}$, it also holds for any point closer to x^*.

b. Assume that the function f has exactly one point x^* for which $f(x^*) = 0$. Let $\epsilon^{(t)} = |x^{(t)} - x^*|$. Using the Taylor expansion in equation (33.34), show that

$$\epsilon^{(t+1)} = \frac{|f''(\gamma^{(t)})|}{2|f'(\gamma^{(t)})|}\epsilon^{(t)} ,$$

where $\gamma^{(t)}$ is some value between $x^{(t)}$ and x^*.

c. If

$$\frac{|f''(\gamma^{(t)})|}{2|f'(\gamma^{(t)})|} \leq c$$

for some constant c and $\epsilon^{(0)} < 1$, then we say that the function f has *quadratic convergence*, since the error decreases quadratically. Assuming that f has quadratic convergence, how many iterations are needed to find a root of $f(x)$ to an accuracy of δ? Your answer should include δ.

d. Suppose you wish to find a root of the function $f(x) = (x - 3)^2$, which is also the minimizer, and you start at $x^{(0)} = 3.5$. Compare the number of iterations needed by gradient descent to find the minimizer and Newton's method to find the root.

33-2 Hedge

Another variant in the multiplicative-weights framework is known as HEDGE. It differs from WEIGHTED MAJORITY in two ways. First, HEDGE makes the prediction randomly—in iteration t, it assigns a probability $p_i^{(t)} = w_i^{(t)}/Z^{(t)}$ to expert E_i, where $Z^{(t)} = \sum_{i=1}^{n} w_i^{(t)}$. It then chooses an expert $E_{i'}$ according to this probability distribution and predicts according to $E_{i'}$. Second, the update rule is different. If an expert makes a mistake, line 16 updates that expert's weight by the rule $w_i^{(t+1)} = w_i^{(t)}e^{-\epsilon}$, for some $0 < \epsilon < 1$. Show that the expected number of mistakes made by HEDGE, running for T rounds, is at most $m^* + (\ln n)/\epsilon + \epsilon T$.

33-3 Nonoptimality of Lloyd's procedure in one dimension

Give an example to show that even in one dimension, Lloyd's procedure for finding clusters does not always return an optimum result. That is, Lloyd's procedure may terminate and return as a result a set C of clusters that does not minimize $f(S, C)$, even when S is a set of points on a line.

33-4   Stochastic gradient descent

Consider the problem described in Section 33.3 of fitting a line $f(x) = ax + b$ to a given set of point/value pairs $S = \{(x_1, y_1), ..., (x_T, y_T)\}$ by optimizing the choice of the parameters a and b using gradient descent to find a best least-squares fit. Here we consider the case where x is a real-valued variable, rather than a vector.

Suppose that you are not given the point/value pairs in S all at once, but only one at a time in an online manner. Furthermore, the points are given in random order. That is, you know that there are n points, but in iteration t you are given only (x_i, y_i) where i is independently and randomly chosen from $\{1, \ldots, T\}$.

You can use gradient descent to compute an estimate to the function. As each point (x_i, y_i) is considered, you can update the current values of a and b by taking the derivative with respect to a and b of the term of the objective function depending on (x_i, y_i). Doing so gives you a stochastic estimate of the gradient, and you can then take a small step in the opposite direction.

Give pseudocode to implement this variant of gradient descent. What would the expected value of the error be as a function of T, L, and R? (*Hint:* Replicate the analysis of GRADIENT-DESCENT in Section 33.3 for this variant.)

This procedure and its variants are known as *stochastic gradient descent*.

Chapter notes

For a general introduction to artificial intelligence, we recommend Russell and Norvig [391]. For a general introduction to machine learning, we recommend Murphy [340].

Lloyd's procedure for the k-means problem was first proposed by Lloyd [304] and also later by Forgy [151]. It is sometimes called "Lloyd's algorithm" or the "Lloyd-Forgy algorithm." Although Mahajan et al. [310] showed that finding an optimal clustering is NP-hard, even in the plane, Kanungo et al. [241] have shown that there is an approximation algorithm for the k-means problem with approximation ratio $9 + \epsilon$, for any $\epsilon > 0$.

The multiplicative-weights method is surveyed by Arora, Hazan, and Kale [25]. The main idea of updating weights based on feedback has been rediscovered many times. One early use is in game theory, where Brown defined "Fictitious Play" [74] and conjectured its convergence to the value of a zero-sum game. The convergence properties were established by Robinson [382].

In machine learning, the first use of multiplicative weights was by Littlestone in the Winnow algorithm [300], which was later extended by Littlestone and Warmuth to the weighted-majority algorithm described in Section 33.2 [301]. This work is closely connected to the boosting algorithm, originally due to Freund and Shapire

[159]. The multiplicative-weights idea is also closely related to several more general optimization algorithms, including the perceptron algorithm [328] and algorithms for optimization problems such as packing linear programs [177, 359].

The treatment of gradient descent in this chapter draws heavily on the unpublished manuscript of Bansal and Gupta [35]. They emphasize the idea of using a potential function and using ideas from amortized analysis to explain gradient descent. Other presentations and analyses of gradient descent include works by Bubeck [75], Boyd and Vanderberghe [69], and Nesterov [343].

Gradient descent is known to converge faster when functions obey stronger properties than general convexity. For example, a function f is *α-strongly convex* if $f(\mathbf{y}) \geq f(\mathbf{x}) + \langle (\nabla f)(\mathbf{x}), (\mathbf{y} - \mathbf{x}) \rangle + \alpha \|\mathbf{y} - \mathbf{x}\|$ for all $\mathbf{x}, \mathbf{y} \in \mathbb{R}^n$. In this case, GRADIENT-DESCENT can use a variable step size and return $\mathbf{x}^{(T)}$. The step size at step t becomes $\gamma_t = 1/(\alpha(t + 1))$, and the procedure returns a point such that $f(\mathbf{x}\text{-avg}) - f(\mathbf{x}^*) \leq L^2/(\alpha(T + 1))$. This convergence is better than that of Theorem 33.8 because the number of iterations needed is linear, rather than quadratic, in the desired error parameter ϵ, and because the performance is independent of the initial point.

Another case in which gradient descent can be shown to perform better than the analysis in Section 33.3 suggests is for smooth convex functions. We say that a function is *β-smooth* if $f(\mathbf{y}) \leq f(\mathbf{x}) + \langle (\nabla f)(\mathbf{x}), (\mathbf{y} - \mathbf{x}) \rangle + \frac{\beta}{2} \|\mathbf{y} - \mathbf{x}\|^2$. This inequality goes in the opposite direction from the one for α-strong convexity. Better bounds on gradient descent are possible here as well.

34 NP-Completeness

Almost all the algorithms we have studied thus far have been *polynomial-time algorithms*: on inputs of size n, their worst-case running time is $O(n^k)$ for some constant k. You might wonder whether *all* problems can be solved in polynomial time. The answer is no. For example, there are problems, such as Turing's famous "Halting Problem," that cannot be solved by any computer, no matter how long you're willing to wait for an answer.[1] There are also problems that can be solved, but not in $O(n^k)$ time for any constant k. Generally, we think of problems that are solvable by polynomial-time algorithms as being tractable, or "easy," and problems that require superpolynomial time as being intractable, or "hard."

The subject of this chapter, however, is an interesting class of problems, called the "NP-complete" problems, whose status is unknown. No polynomial-time algorithm has yet been discovered for an NP-complete problem, nor has anyone yet been able to prove that no polynomial-time algorithm can exist for any one of them. This so-called P $\neq$ NP question has been one of the deepest, most perplexing open research problems in theoretical computer science since it was first posed in 1971.

Several NP-complete problems are particularly tantalizing because they seem on the surface to be similar to problems that we know how to solve in polynomial time. In each of the following pairs of problems, one is solvable in polynomial time and the other is NP-complete, but the difference between the problems appears to be slight:

Shortest versus longest simple paths: In Chapter 22, we saw that even with negative edge weights, we can find *shortest* paths from a single source in a directed

---

[1] For the Halting Problem and other unsolvable problems, there are proofs that no algorithm can exist that, for every input, eventually produces the correct answer. A procedure attempting to solve an unsolvable problem might always produce an answer but is sometimes incorrect, or all the answers it produces might be correct but for some inputs it never produces an answer.

graph $G = (V, E)$ in $O(VE)$ time. Finding a *longest* simple path between two vertices is difficult, however. Merely determining whether a graph contains a simple path with at least a given number of edges is NP-complete.

Euler tour versus hamiltonian cycle: An *Euler tour* of a strongly connected, directed graph $G = (V, E)$ is a cycle that traverses each *edge* of G exactly once, although it is allowed to visit each vertex more than once. Problem 20-3 on page 583 asks you to show how to determine whether a strongly connected, directed graph has an Euler tour and, if it does, the order of the edges in the Euler tour, all in $O(E)$ time. A *hamiltonian cycle* of a directed graph $G = (V, E)$ is a simple cycle that contains each *vertex* in V. Determining whether a directed graph has a hamiltonian cycle is NP-complete. (Later in this chapter, we'll prove that determining whether an *undirected* graph has a hamiltonian cycle is NP-complete.)

2-CNF satisfiability versus 3-CNF satisfiability: Boolean formulas contain binary variables whose values are 0 or 1; boolean connectives such as $\wedge$ (AND), $\vee$ (OR), and $\neg$ (NOT); and parentheses. A boolean formula is *satisfiable* if there exists some assignment of the values 0 and 1 to its variables that causes it to evaluate to 1. We'll define terms more formally later in this chapter, but informally, a boolean formula is in *k-conjunctive normal form*, or *k*-CNF if it is the AND of clauses of ORs of exactly *k* variables or their negations. For example, the boolean formula $(x_1 \vee x_2) \wedge (\neg x_1 \vee x_3) \wedge (\neg x_2 \vee \neg x_3)$ is in 2-CNF (with satisfying assignment $x_1 = 1$, $x_2 = 0$, and $x_3 = 1$). Although there is a polynomial-time algorithm to determine whether a 2-CNF formula is satisfiable, we'll see later in this chapter that determining whether a 3-CNF formula is satisfiable is NP-complete.

NP-completeness and the classes P and NP

Throughout this chapter, we refer to three classes of problems: P, NP, and NPC, the latter class being the NP-complete problems. We describe them informally here, with formal definitions to appear later on.

The class P consists of those problems that are solvable in polynomial time. More specifically, they are problems that can be solved in $O(n^k)$ time for some constant k, where n is the size of the input to the problem. Most of the problems examined in previous chapters belong to P.

The class NP consists of those problems that are "verifiable" in polynomial time. What do we mean by a problem being verifiable? If you were somehow given a "certificate" of a solution, then you could verify that the certificate is correct in time polynomial in the size of the input to the problem. For example, in the hamiltonian-cycle problem, given a directed graph $G = (V, E)$, a certificate would be a sequence $\langle v_1, v_2, v_3, \ldots, v_{|V|} \rangle$ of $|V|$ vertices. You could check in polynomial time that the sequence contains each of the $|V|$ vertices exactly once, that $(v_i, v_{i+1}) \in E$ for $i = 1, 2, 3, \ldots, |V| - 1$, and that $(v_{|V|}, v_1) \in E$. As another example, for 3-CNF satisfiability, a certificate could be an assignment of values to variables. You could check in polynomial time that this assignment satisfies the boolean formula.

Any problem in P also belongs to NP, since if a problem belongs to P then it is solvable in polynomial time without even being supplied a certificate. We'll formalize this notion later in this chapter, but for now you can believe that P $\subseteq$ NP. The famous open question is whether P is a proper subset of NP.

Informally, a problem belongs to the class NPC—and we call it *NP-complete* —if it belongs to NP and is as "hard" as any problem in NP. We'll formally define what it means to be as hard as any problem in NP later in this chapter. In the meantime, we state without proof that if *any* NP-complete problem can be solved in polynomial time, then *every* problem in NP has a polynomial-time algorithm. Most theoretical computer scientists believe that the NP-complete problems are intractable, since given the wide range of NP-complete problems that have been studied to date—without anyone having discovered a polynomial-time solution to any of them—it would be truly astounding if all of them could be solved in polynomial time. Yet, given the effort devoted thus far to proving that NP-complete problems are intractable—without a conclusive outcome—we cannot rule out the possibility that the NP-complete problems could turn out to be solvable in polynomial time.

To become a good algorithm designer, you must understand the rudiments of the theory of NP-completeness. If you can establish a problem as NP-complete, you provide good evidence for its intractability. As an engineer, you would then do better to spend your time developing an approximation algorithm (see Chapter 35) or solving a tractable special case, rather than searching for a fast algorithm that solves the problem exactly. Moreover, many natural and interesting problems that on the surface seem no harder than sorting, graph searching, or network flow are in fact NP-complete. Therefore, you should become familiar with this remarkable class of problems.

Overview of showing problems to be NP-complete

The techniques used to show that a particular problem is NP-complete differ fundamentally from the techniques used throughout most of this book to design and analyze algorithms. If you can demonstrate that a problem is NP-complete, you are making a statement about how hard it is (or at least how hard we think it is), rather than about how easy it is. If you prove a problem NP-complete, you are saying that searching for efficient algorithm is likely to be a fruitless endeavor. In this way, NP-completeness proofs bear some similarity to the proof in Section 8.1 of an $\Omega(n \lg n)$-time lower bound for any comparison sort algorithm, although the specific techniques used for showing NP-completeness differ from the decision-tree method used in Section 8.1.

We rely on three key concepts in showing a problem to be NP-complete:

Decision problems versus optimization problems

Many problems of interest are *optimization problems*, in which each feasible (i.e., "legal") solution has an associated value, and the goal is to find a feasible solution with the best value. For example, in a problem that we call SHORTEST-PATH, the input is an undirected graph G and vertices u and v, and the goal is to find a path from u to v that uses the fewest edges. In other words, SHORTEST-PATH is the single-pair shortest-path problem in an unweighted, undirected graph. NP-completeness applies directly not to optimization problems, however, but to *decision problems*, in which the answer is simply "yes" or "no" (or, more formally, "1" or "0").

Although NP-complete problems are confined to the realm of decision problems, there is usually a way to cast a given optimization problem as a related decision problem by imposing a bound on the value to be optimized. For example, a decision problem related to SHORTEST-PATH is PATH: given an undirected graph G, vertices u and v, and an integer k, does a path exist from u to v consisting of at most k edges?

The relationship between an optimization problem and its related decision problem works in your favor when you try to show that the optimization problem is "hard." That is because the decision problem is in a sense "easier," or at least "no harder." As a specific example, you can solve PATH by solving SHORTEST-PATH and then comparing the number of edges in the shortest path found to the value of the decision-problem parameter k. In other words, if an optimization problem is easy, its related decision problem is easy as well. Stated in a way that has more relevance to NP-completeness, if you can provide evidence that a decision problem is hard, you also provide evidence that its related optimization problem is hard. Thus, even though it restricts attention to decision problems, the theory of NP-completeness often has implications for optimization problems as well.

Reductions

The above notion of showing that one problem is no harder or no easier than another applies even when both problems are decision problems. Almost every NP-completeness proof takes advantage of this idea, as follows. Consider a decision problem A, which you would like to solve in polynomial time. We call the input to a particular problem an *instance* of that problem. For example, in PATH, an

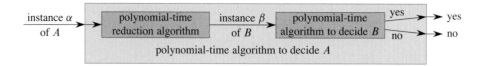

Figure 34.1 How to use a polynomial-time reduction algorithm to solve a decision problem A in polynomial time, given a polynomial-time decision algorithm for another problem B. In polynomial time, transform an instance α of A into an instance β of B, solve B in polynomial time, and use the answer for β as the answer for α.

instance is a particular graph G, particular vertices u and v of G, and a particular integer k. Now suppose that you already know how to solve a different decision problem B in polynomial time. Finally, suppose that you have a procedure that transforms any instance α of A into some instance β of B with the following characteristics:

- The transformation takes polynomial time.

- The answers are the same. That is, the answer for α is "yes" if and only if the answer for β is also "yes."

We call such a procedure a polynomial-time *reduction algorithm* and, as Figure 34.1 shows, it provides us a way to solve problem A in polynomial time:

1. Given an instance α of problem A, use a polynomial-time reduction algorithm to transform it to an instance β of problem B.

2. Run the polynomial-time decision algorithm for B on the instance β.

3. Use the answer for β as the answer for α.

As long as each of these steps takes polynomial time, all three together do also, and so you have a way to decide on α in polynomial time. In other words, by "reducing" solving problem A to solving problem B, you use the "easiness" of B to prove the "easiness" of A.

Recalling that NP-completeness is about showing how hard a problem is rather than how easy it is, you use polynomial-time reductions in the opposite way to show that a problem is NP-complete. Let's take the idea a step further and show how you can use polynomial-time reductions to show that no polynomial-time algorithm can exist for a particular problem B. Suppose that you have a decision problem A for which you already know that no polynomial-time algorithm can exist. (Ignore for the moment how to find such a problem A.) Suppose further that you have a polynomial-time reduction transforming instances of A to instances of B. Now you can use a simple proof by contradiction to show that no polynomial-time algorithm can exist for B. Suppose otherwise, that is, suppose that B has a polynomial-time algorithm. Then, using the method shown in Figure 34.1, you would have a way to solve problem A in polynomial time, which contradicts the assumption that there is no polynomial-time algorithm for A.

To prove that a problem B is NP-complete, the methodology is similar. Although you cannot assume that there is absolutely no polynomial-time algorithm for problem A, you prove that problem B is NP-complete on the assumption that problem A is also NP-complete.

A first NP-complete problem

Because the technique of reduction relies on having a problem already known to be NP-complete in order to prove a different problem NP-complete, there must be some "first" NP-complete problem. We'll use the circuit-satisfiability problem, in which the input is a boolean combinational circuit composed of AND, OR, and NOT gates, and the question is whether there exists some set of boolean inputs to this circuit that causes its output to be 1. Section 34.3 will prove that this first problem is NP-complete.

Chapter outline

This chapter studies the aspects of NP-completeness that bear most directly on the analysis of algorithms. Section 34.1 formalizes the notion of "problem" and defines the complexity class P of polynomial-time solvable decision problems. We'll also see how these notions fit into the framework of formal-language theory. Section 34.2 defines the class NP of decision problems whose solutions are verifiable in polynomial time. It also formally poses the $P \neq NP$ question.

Section 34.3 shows how to relate problems via polynomial-time "reductions." It defines NP-completeness and sketches a proof that the circuit-satisfiability problem is NP-complete. With one problem proven NP-complete, Section 34.4 demonstrates how to prove other problems to be NP-complete much more simply by the methodology of reductions. To illustrate this methodology, the section shows that two formula-satisfiability problems are NP-complete. Section 34.5 proves a variety of other problems to be NP-complete by using reductions. You will probably find several of these reductions to be quite creative, because they convert a problem in one domain to a problem in a completely different domain.

34.1   Polynomial time

Since NP-completeness relies on notions of solving a problem and verifying a certificate in polynomial time, let's first examine what it means for a problem to be solvable in polynomial time.

Recall that we generally regard problems that have polynomial-time solutions as tractable. Here are three reasons why:

1. Although no reasonable person considers a problem that requires $\Theta(n^{100})$ time to be tractable, few practical problems require time on the order of such a high-degree polynomial. The polynomial-time computable problems encountered in practice typically require much less time. Experience has shown that once the first polynomial-time algorithm for a problem has been discovered, more efficient algorithms often follow. Even if the current best algorithm for a problem has a running time of $\Theta(n^{100})$, an algorithm with a much better running time will likely soon be discovered.

2. For many reasonable models of computation, a problem that can be solved in polynomial time in one model can be solved in polynomial time in another. For example, the class of problems solvable in polynomial time by the serial random-access machine used throughout most of this book is the same as the class of problems solvable in polynomial time on abstract Turing machines.[2] It is also the same as the class of problems solvable in polynomial time on a parallel computer when the number of processors grows polynomially with the input size.

3. The class of polynomial-time solvable problems has nice closure properties, since polynomials are closed under addition, multiplication, and composition. For example, if the output of one polynomial-time algorithm is fed into the input of another, the composite algorithm is polynomial. Exercise 34.1-5 asks you to show that if an algorithm makes a constant number of calls to polynomial-time subroutines and performs an additional amount of work that also takes polynomial time, then the running time of the composite algorithm is polynomial.

Abstract problems

To understand the class of polynomial-time solvable problems, you must first have a formal notion of what a "problem" is. We define an *abstract problem Q* to be a

---

[2] See the books by Hopcroft and Ullman [228], Lewis and Papadimitriou [299], or Sipser [413] for a thorough treatment of the Turing-machine model.

binary relation on a set I of problem *instances* and a set S of problem *solutions*. For example, an instance for SHORTEST-PATH is a triple consisting of a graph and two vertices. A solution is a sequence of vertices in the graph, with perhaps the empty sequence denoting that no path exists. The problem SHORTEST-PATH itself is the relation that associates each instance of a graph and two vertices with a shortest path in the graph that connects the two vertices. Since shortest paths are not necessarily unique, a given problem instance may have more than one solution.

This formulation of an abstract problem is more general than necessary for our purposes. As we saw above, the theory of NP-completeness restricts attention to *decision problems*: those having a yes/no solution. In this case, we can view an abstract decision problem as a function that maps the instance set I to the solution set $\{0, 1\}$. For example, a decision problem related to SHORTEST-PATH is the problem PATH that we saw earlier. If $i = \langle G, u, v, k \rangle$ is an instance of PATH, then PATH$(i) = 1$ (yes) if G contains a path from u to v with at most k edges, and PATH$(i) = 0$ (no) otherwise. Many abstract problems are not decision problems, but rather *optimization problems*, which require some value to be minimized or maximized. As we saw above, however, you can usually recast an optimization problem as a decision problem that is no harder.

Encodings

In order for a computer program to solve an abstract problem, its problem instances must appear in a way that the program understands. An *encoding* of a set S of abstract objects is a mapping e from S to the set of binary strings.[3] For example, we are all familiar with encoding the natural numbers $\mathbb{N} = \{0, 1, 2, 3, 4, \ldots\}$ as the strings $\{0, 1, 10, 11, 100, \ldots\}$. Using this encoding, $e(17) = 10001$. If you have looked at computer representations of keyboard characters, you probably have seen the ASCII code, where, for example, the encoding of A is 01000001. You can encode a compound object as a binary string by combining the representations of its constituent parts. Polygons, graphs, functions, ordered pairs, programs—all can be encoded as binary strings.

Thus, a computer algorithm that "solves" some abstract decision problem actually takes an encoding of a problem instance as input. The *size* of an instance i is just the length of its string, which we denote by $|i|$. We call a problem whose instance set is the set of binary strings a *concrete problem*. We say that an algorithm *solves* a concrete problem in $O(T(n))$ time if, when it is provided a problem instance i of length $n = |i|$, the algorithm can produce the solution in $O(T(n))$

---

[3] The codomain of e need not be *binary* strings: any set of strings over a finite alphabet having at least two symbols will do.

time.[4] A concrete problem is *polynomial-time solvable*, therefore, if there exists an algorithm to solve it in $O(n^k)$ time for some constant k.

We can now formally define the *complexity class* **P** as the set of concrete decision problems that are polynomial-time solvable.

Encodings map abstract problems to concrete problems. Given an abstract decision problem Q mapping an instance set I to $\{0, 1\}$, an encoding $e : I \rightarrow \{0, 1\}^*$ can induce a related concrete decision problem, which we denote by $e(Q)$.[5] If the solution to an abstract-problem instance $i \in I$ is $Q(i) \in \{0, 1\}$, then the solution to the concrete-problem instance $e(i) \in \{0, 1\}^*$ is also $Q(i)$. As a technicality, some binary strings might represent no meaningful abstract-problem instance. For convenience, assume that any such string maps arbitrarily to 0. Thus, the concrete problem produces the same solutions as the abstract problem on binary-string instances that represent the encodings of abstract-problem instances.

We would like to extend the definition of polynomial-time solvability from concrete problems to abstract problems by using encodings as the bridge, ideally with the definition independent of any particular encoding. That is, the efficiency of solving a problem should not depend on how the problem is encoded. Unfortunately, it depends quite heavily on the encoding. For example, suppose that the sole input to an algorithm is an integer k, and suppose that the running time of the algorithm is $\Theta(k)$. If the integer k is provided in *unary*—a string of k 1s—then the running time of the algorithm is $O(n)$ on length-n inputs, which is polynomial time. If the input k is provided using the more natural binary representation, however, then the input length is $n = \lfloor \lg k \rfloor + 1$, so the size of the unary encoding is exponential in the size of the binary encoding. With the binary representation, the running time of the algorithm is $\Theta(k) = \Theta(2^n)$, which is exponential in the size of the input. Thus, depending on the encoding, the algorithm runs in either polynomial or superpolynomial time.

The encoding of an abstract problem matters quite a bit to how we understand polynomial time. We cannot really talk about solving an abstract problem without first specifying an encoding. Nevertheless, in practice, if we rule out "expensive" encodings such as unary ones, the actual encoding of a problem makes little difference to whether the problem can be solved in polynomial time. For example, representing integers in base 3 instead of binary has no effect on whether a problem is solvable in polynomial time, since we can convert an integer represented in base 3 to an integer represented in base 2 in polynomial time.

---

[4] We assume that the algorithm's output is separate from its input. Because it takes at least one time step to produce each bit of the output and the algorithm takes $O(T(n))$ time steps, the size of the output is $O(T(n))$.

[5] The notation $\{0, 1\}^*$ denotes the set of all strings composed of symbols from the set $\{0, 1\}$.

We say that a function $f : \{0, 1\}^* \to \{0, 1\}^*$ is *polynomial-time computable* if there exists a polynomial-time algorithm A that, given any input $x \in \{0, 1\}^*$, produces as output $f(x)$. For some set I of problem instances, we say that two encodings e_1 and e_2 are *polynomially related* if there exist two polynomial-time computable functions f_{12} and f_{21} such that for any $i \in I$, we have $f_{12}(e_1(i)) = e_2(i)$ and $f_{21}(e_2(i)) = e_1(i)$.[6] That is, a polynomial-time algorithm can compute the encoding $e_2(i)$ from the encoding $e_1(i)$, and vice versa. If two encodings e_1 and e_2 of an abstract problem are polynomially related, whether the problem is polynomial-time solvable or not is independent of which encoding we use, as the following lemma shows.

Lemma 34.1
Let Q be an abstract decision problem on an instance set I, and let e_1 and e_2 be polynomially related encodings on I. Then, $e_1(Q) \in \text{P}$ if and only if $e_2(Q) \in \text{P}$.

Proof We need only prove the forward direction, since the backward direction is symmetric. Suppose, therefore, that $e_1(Q)$ can be solved in $O(n^k)$ time for some constant k. Furthermore, suppose that for any problem instance i, the encoding $e_1(i)$ can be computed from the encoding $e_2(i)$ in $O(n^c)$ time for some constant c, where $n = |e_2(i)|$. To solve problem $e_2(Q)$ on input $e_2(i)$, first compute $e_1(i)$ and then run the algorithm for $e_1(Q)$ on $e_1(i)$. How long does this procedure take? Converting encodings takes $O(n^c)$ time, and therefore $|e_1(i)| = O(n^c)$, since the output of a serial computer cannot be longer than its running time. Solving the problem on $e_1(i)$ takes $O(|e_1(i)|^k) = O(n^{ck})$ time, which is polynomial since both c and k are constants. ∎

Thus, whether an abstract problem has its instances encoded in binary or base 3 does not affect its "complexity," that is, whether it is polynomial-time solvable or not. If instances are encoded in unary, however, its complexity may change. In order to be able to converse in an encoding-independent fashion, we generally assume that problem instances are encoded in any reasonable, concise fashion, unless we specifically say otherwise. To be precise, we assume that the encoding of an integer is polynomially related to its binary representation, and that the encoding of a finite set is polynomially related to its encoding as a list of its elements, enclosed in braces and separated by commas. (ASCII is one such encoding scheme.) With

---

[6] Technically, we also require the functions f_{12} and f_{21} to "map noninstances to noninstances." A *noninstance* of an encoding e is a string $x \in \{0, 1\}^*$ such that there is no instance i for which $e(i) = x$. We require that $f_{12}(x) = y$ for every noninstance x of encoding e_1, where y is some noninstance of e_2, and that $f_{21}(x') = y'$ for every noninstance x' of e_2, where y' is some noninstance of e_1.

such a "standard" encoding in hand, we can derive reasonable encodings of other mathematical objects, such as tuples, graphs, and formulas. To denote the standard encoding of an object, we enclose the object in angle brackets. Thus, $\langle G \rangle$ denotes the standard encoding of a graph G.

As long as the encoding implicitly used is polynomially related to this standard encoding, we can talk directly about abstract problems without reference to any particular encoding, knowing that the choice of encoding has no effect on whether the abstract problem is polynomial-time solvable. From now on, we will generally assume that all problem instances are binary strings encoded using the standard encoding, unless we explicitly specify the contrary. We'll also typically neglect the distinction between abstract and concrete problems. You should watch out for problems that arise in practice, however, in which a standard encoding is not obvious and the encoding does make a difference.

A formal-language framework

By focusing on decision problems, we can take advantage of the machinery of formal-language theory. Let's review some definitions from that theory. An *alphabet* Σ is a finite set of symbols. A *language* L over Σ is any set of strings made up of symbols from Σ. For example, if $\Sigma = \{0, 1\}$, the set $L = \{10, 11, 101, 111, 1011, 1101, 10001, \ldots\}$ is the language of binary representations of prime numbers. We denote the *empty string* by ε, the *empty language* by $\emptyset$, and the language of all strings over Σ by Σ^*. For example, if $\Sigma = \{0, 1\}$, then $\Sigma^* = \{\varepsilon, 0, 1, 00, 01, 10, 11, 000, \ldots\}$ is the set of all binary strings. Every language L over Σ is a subset of Σ^*.

Languages support a variety of operations. Set-theoretic operations, such as *union* and *intersection*, follow directly from the set-theoretic definitions. We define the *complement* of a language L by $\overline{L} = \Sigma^* - L$. The *concatenation* $L_1 L_2$ of two languages L_1 and L_2 is the language

$$L = \{x_1 x_2 : x_1 \in L_1 \text{ and } x_2 \in L_2\} \ .$$

The *closure* or *Kleene star* of a language L is the language

$$L^* = \{\varepsilon\} \cup L \cup L^2 \cup L^3 \cup \cdots ,$$

where L^k is the language obtained by concatenating L to itself k times.

From the point of view of language theory, the set of instances for any decision problem Q is simply the set Σ^*, where $\Sigma = \{0, 1\}$. Since Q is entirely characterized by those problem instances that produce a 1 (yes) answer, we can view Q as a language L over $\Sigma = \{0, 1\}$, where

$$L = \{x \in \Sigma^* : Q(x) = 1\} \ .$$

For example, the decision problem PATH has the corresponding language

PATH $= \{\langle G, u, v, k \rangle :$ $G = (V, E)$ is an undirected graph,

$\qquad\qquad\qquad\quad u, v \in V,$

$\qquad\qquad\qquad\quad k \geq 0$ is an integer, and

$\qquad\qquad\qquad\quad G$ contains a path from u to v with at most k edges$\}$.

(Where convenient, we'll sometimes use the same name—PATH in this case—to refer to both a decision problem and its corresponding language.)

The formal-language framework allows us to express concisely the relation between decision problems and algorithms that solve them. We say that an algorithm A *accepts* a string $x \in \{0, 1\}^*$ if, given input x, the algorithm's output $A(x)$ is 1. The language *accepted* by an algorithm A is the set of strings $L = \{x \in \{0, 1\}^* : A(x) = 1\}$, that is, the set of strings that the algorithm accepts. An algorithm A *rejects* a string x if $A(x) = 0$.

Even if language L is accepted by an algorithm A, the algorithm does not necessarily reject a string $x \notin L$ provided as input to it. For example, the algorithm might loop forever. A language L is *decided* by an algorithm A if every binary string in L is accepted by A and every binary string not in L is rejected by A. A language L is *accepted in polynomial time* by an algorithm A if it is accepted by A and if in addition there exists a constant k such that for any length-n string $x \in L$, algorithm A accepts x in $O(n^k)$ time. A language L is *decided in polynomial time* by an algorithm A if there exists a constant k such that for any length-n string $x \in \{0, 1\}^*$, the algorithm correctly decides whether $x \in L$ in $O(n^k)$ time. Thus, to accept a language, an algorithm need only produce an answer when provided a string in L, but to decide a language, it must correctly accept or reject every string in $\{0, 1\}^*$.

As an example, the language PATH can be accepted in polynomial time. One polynomial-time accepting algorithm verifies that G encodes an undirected graph, verifies that u and v are vertices in G, uses breadth-first search to compute a path from u to v in G with the fewest edges, and then compares the number of edges on the path obtained with k. If G encodes an undirected graph and the path found from u to v has at most k edges, the algorithm outputs 1 and halts. Otherwise, the algorithm runs forever. This algorithm does not decide PATH, however, since it does not explicitly output 0 for instances in which a shortest path has more than k edges. A decision algorithm for PATH must explicitly reject binary strings that do not belong to PATH. For a decision problem such as PATH, such a decision algorithm is straightforward to design: instead of running forever when there is not a path from u to v with at most k edges, it outputs 0 and halts. (It must also output 0 and halt if the input encoding is faulty.) For other problems, such as Turing's Halting Problem, there exists an accepting algorithm, but no decision algorithm exists.

We can informally define a *complexity class* as a set of languages, membership in which is determined by a *complexity measure*, such as running time, of an algorithm that determines whether a given string x belongs to language L. The actual definition of a complexity class is somewhat more technical.[7]

Using this language-theoretic framework, we can provide an alternative definition of the complexity class P:

$$P = \{L \subseteq \{0, 1\}^* : \text{there exists an algorithm } A \text{ that decides } L \\ \text{in polynomial time}\} \ .$$

In fact, as the following theorem shows, P is also the class of languages that can be accepted in polynomial time.

Theorem 34.2
$P = \{L : L \text{ is accepted by a polynomial-time algorithm}\} \ .$

Proof   Because the class of languages decided by polynomial-time algorithms is a subset of the class of languages accepted by polynomial-time algorithms, we need only show that if L is accepted by a polynomial-time algorithm, it is decided by a polynomial-time algorithm. Let L be the language accepted by some polynomial-time algorithm A. We use a classic "simulation" argument to construct another polynomial-time algorithm A' that decides L. Because A accepts L in $O(n^k)$ time for some constant k, there also exists a constant c such that A accepts L in at most cn^k steps. For any input string x, the algorithm A' simulates cn^k steps of A. After simulating cn^k steps, algorithm A' inspects the behavior of A. If A has accepted x, then A' accepts x by outputting a 1. If A has not accepted x, then A' rejects x by outputting a 0. The overhead of A' simulating A does not increase the running time by more than a polynomial factor, and thus A' is a polynomial-time algorithm that decides L.   ∎

The proof of Theorem 34.2 is nonconstructive. For a given language $L \in P$, we may not actually know a bound on the running time for the algorithm A that accepts L. Nevertheless, we know that such a bound exists, and therefore, that an algorithm A' exists that can check the bound, even though we may not be able to find the algorithm A' easily.

---

[7] For more on complexity classes, see the seminal paper by Hartmanis and Stearns [210].

Exercises

34.1-1

Define the optimization problem LONGEST-PATH-LENGTH as the relation that associates each instance of an undirected graph and two vertices with the number of edges in a longest simple path between the two vertices. Define the decision problem LONGEST-PATH $= \{\langle G, u, v, k \rangle : G = (V, E)$ is an undirected graph, $u, v \in V$, $k \geq 0$ is an integer, and there exists a simple path from u to v in G consisting of at least k edges$\}$. Show that the optimization problem LONGEST-PATH-LENGTH can be solved in polynomial time if and only if LONGEST-PATH $\in$ P.

34.1-2

Give a formal definition for the problem of finding the longest simple cycle in an undirected graph. Give a related decision problem. Give the language corresponding to the decision problem.

34.1-3

Give a formal encoding of directed graphs as binary strings using an adjacency-matrix representation. Do the same using an adjacency-list representation. Argue that the two representations are polynomially related.

34.1-4

Is the dynamic-programming algorithm for the 0-1 knapsack problem that is asked for in Exercise 15.2-2 a polynomial-time algorithm? Explain your answer.

34.1-5

Show that if an algorithm makes at most a constant number of calls to polynomial-time subroutines and performs an additional amount of work that also takes polynomial time, then it runs in polynomial time. Also show that a polynomial number of calls to polynomial-time subroutines may result in an exponential-time algorithm.

34.1-6

Show that the class P, viewed as a set of languages, is closed under union, intersection, concatenation, complement, and Kleene star. That is, if $L_1, L_2 \in$ P, then $L_1 \cup L_2 \in$ P, $L_1 \cap L_2 \in$ P, $L_1 L_2 \in$ P, $\overline{L}_1 \in$ P, and $L_1^* \in$ P.

34.2   Polynomial-time verification

Now, let's look at algorithms that verify membership in languages. For example, suppose that for a given instance $\langle G, u, v, k \rangle$ of the decision problem PATH, you are also given a path p from u to v. You can check whether p is a path in G and whether the length of p is at most k, and if so, you can view p as a "certificate" that the instance indeed belongs to PATH. For the decision problem PATH, this certificate doesn't seem to buy much. After all, PATH belongs to P—in fact, you can solve PATH in linear time—and so verifying membership from a given certificate takes as long as solving the problem from scratch. Instead, let's examine a problem for which we know of no polynomial-time decision algorithm and yet, given a certificate, verification is easy.

Hamiltonian cycles

The problem of finding a hamiltonian cycle in an undirected graph has been studied for over a hundred years. Formally, a *hamiltonian cycle* of an undirected graph $G = (V, E)$ is a simple cycle that contains each vertex in V. A graph that contains a hamiltonian cycle is said to be *hamiltonian*, and otherwise, it is *nonhamiltonian*. The name honors W. R. Hamilton, who described a mathematical game on the dodecahedron (Figure 34.2(a)) in which one player sticks five pins in any five consecutive vertices and the other player must complete the path to form a cycle containing all the vertices.[8] The dodecahedron is hamiltonian, and Figure 34.2(a) shows one hamiltonian cycle. Not all graphs are hamiltonian, however. For example, Figure 34.2(b) shows a bipartite graph with an odd number of vertices. Exercise 34.2-2 asks you to show that all such graphs are nonhamiltonian.

Here is how to define the *hamiltonian-cycle problem*, "Does a graph G have a hamiltonian cycle?" as a formal language:

HAM-CYCLE $= \{\langle G \rangle : G$ is a hamiltonian graph$\}$.

How might an algorithm decide the language HAM-CYCLE? Given a problem instance $\langle G \rangle$, one possible decision algorithm lists all permutations of the vertices of G and then checks each permutation to see whether it is a hamiltonian cycle.

---

[8] In a letter dated 17 October 1856 to his friend John T. Graves, Hamilton [206, p. 624] wrote, "I have found that some young persons have been much amused by trying a new mathematical game which the Icosion furnishes, one person sticking five pins in any five consecutive points ... and the other player then aiming to insert, which by the theory in this letter can always be done, fifteen other pins, in cyclical succession, so as to cover all the other points, and to end in immediate proximity to the pin wherewith his antagonist had begun."

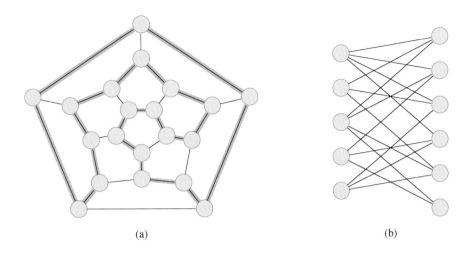

(a)   (b)

Figure 34.2 **(a)** A graph representing the vertices, edges, and faces of a dodecahedron, with a hamiltonian cycle shown by edges highlighted in blue. **(b)** A bipartite graph with an odd number of vertices. Any such graph is nonhamiltonian.

What is the running time of this algorithm? It depends on the encoding of the graph G. Let's say that G is encoded as its adjacency matrix. If the adjacency matrix contains n entries, so that the length of the encoding of G equals n, then the number m of vertices in the graph is $\Omega(\sqrt{n})$. There are $m!$ possible permutations of the vertices, and therefore the running time is $\Omega(m!) = \Omega(\sqrt{n}!) = \Omega(2^{\sqrt{n}})$, which is not $O(n^k)$ for any constant k. Thus, this naive algorithm does not run in polynomial time. In fact, the hamiltonian-cycle problem is NP-complete, as we'll prove in Section 34.5.

Verification algorithms

Consider a slightly easier problem. Suppose that a friend tells you that a given graph G is hamiltonian, and then the friend offers to prove it by giving you the vertices in order along the hamiltonian cycle. It would certainly be easy enough to verify the proof: simply verify that the provided cycle is hamiltonian by checking whether it is a permutation of the vertices of V and whether each of the consecutive edges along the cycle actually exists in the graph. You could certainly implement this verification algorithm to run in $O(n^2)$ time, where n is the length of the encoding of G. Thus, a proof that a hamiltonian cycle exists in a graph can be verified in polynomial time.

We define a *verification algorithm* as being a two-argument algorithm A, where one argument is an ordinary input string x and the other is a binary string y called a *certificate*. A two-argument algorithm A *verifies* an input string x if there exists a certificate y such that $A(x, y) = 1$. The *language verified* by a verification algorithm A is

$$L = \{x \in \{0, 1\}^* : \text{there exists } y \in \{0, 1\}^* \text{ such that } A(x, y) = 1\} \ .$$

Think of an algorithm A as verifying a language L if, for any string $x \in L$, there exists a certificate y that A can use to prove that $x \in L$. Moreover, for any string $x \notin L$, there must be no certificate proving that $x \in L$. For example, in the hamiltonian-cycle problem, the certificate is the list of vertices in some hamiltonian cycle. If a graph is hamiltonian, the hamiltonian cycle itself offers enough information to verify that the graph is indeed hamiltonian. Conversely, if a graph is not hamiltonian, there can be no list of vertices that fools the verification algorithm into believing that the graph is hamiltonian, since the verification algorithm carefully checks the so-called cycle to be sure.

The complexity class NP

The *complexity class* **NP** is the class of languages that can be verified by a polynomial-time algorithm.[9] More precisely, a language L belongs to NP if and only if there exist a two-input polynomial-time algorithm A and a constant c such that

$$L = \{x \in \{0, 1\}^* : \text{there exists a certificate } y \text{ with } |y| = O(|x|^c)$$
$$\text{such that } A(x, y) = 1\} \ .$$

We say that algorithm A *verifies* language L *in polynomial time*.

From our earlier discussion about the hamiltonian-cycle problem, you can see that HAM-CYCLE $\in$ NP. (It is always nice to know that an important set is nonempty.) Moreover, if $L \in$ P, then $L \in$ NP, since if there is a polynomial-time algorithm to decide L, the algorithm can be converted to a two-argument verification algorithm that simply ignores any certificate and accepts exactly those input strings it determines to belong to L. Thus, P $\subseteq$ NP.

That leaves the question of whether P $=$ NP. A definitive answer is unknown, but most researchers believe that P and NP are not the same class. Think of the class P as consisting of problems that can be solved quickly and the class NP as

---

[9] The name "NP" stands for "nondeterministic polynomial time." The class NP was originally studied in the context of nondeterminism, but this book uses the somewhat simpler yet equivalent notion of verification. Hopcroft and Ullman [228] give a good presentation of NP-completeness in terms of nondeterministic models of computation.

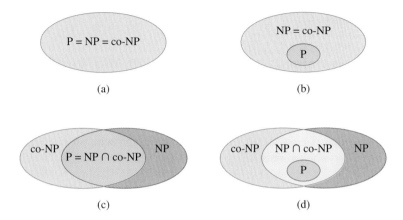

Figure 34.3 Four possibilities for relationships among complexity classes. In each diagram, one region enclosing another indicates a proper-subset relation. **(a)** P = NP = co-NP. Most researchers regard this possibility as the most unlikely. **(b)** If NP is closed under complement, then NP = co-NP, but it need not be the case that P = NP. **(c)** P = NP ∩ co-NP, but NP is not closed under complement. **(d)** NP ≠ co-NP and P ≠ NP ∩ co-NP. Most researchers regard this possibility as the most likely.

consisting of problems for which a solution can be verified quickly. You may have learned from experience that it is often more difficult to solve a problem from scratch than to verify a clearly presented solution, especially when working under time constraints. Theoretical computer scientists generally believe that this analogy extends to the classes P and NP, and thus that NP includes languages that do not belong to P.

There is more compelling, though not conclusive, evidence that P ≠ NP—the existence of languages that are "NP-complete." Section 34.3 will study this class.

Many other fundamental questions beyond the P ≠ NP question remain unresolved. Figure 34.3 shows some possible scenarios. Despite much work by many researchers, no one even knows whether the class NP is closed under complement. That is, does $L \in$ NP imply $\overline{L} \in$ NP? We define the *complexity class* co-NP as the set of languages L such that $\overline{L} \in$ NP, so that the question of whether NP is closed under complement is also whether NP = co-NP. Since P is closed under complement (Exercise 34.1-6), it follows from Exercise 34.2-9 (P ⊆ co-NP) that P ⊆ NP ∩ co-NP. Once again, however, no one knows whether P = NP ∩ co-NP or whether there is some language in (NP ∩ co-NP) − P.

Thus our understanding of the precise relationship between P and NP is woefully incomplete. Nevertheless, even though we might not be able to prove that a particular problem is intractable, if we can prove that it is NP-complete, then we have gained valuable information about it.

Exercises

34.2-1
Consider the language GRAPH-ISOMORPHISM = $\{\langle G_1, G_2 \rangle : G_1$ and G_2 are isomorphic graphs$\}$. Prove that GRAPH-ISOMORPHISM $\in$ NP by describing a polynomial-time algorithm to verify the language.

34.2-2
Prove that if G is an undirected bipartite graph with an odd number of vertices, then G is nonhamiltonian.

34.2-3
Show that if HAM-CYCLE $\in$ P, then the problem of listing the vertices of a hamiltonian cycle, in order, is polynomial-time solvable.

34.2-4
Prove that the class NP of languages is closed under union, intersection, concatenation, and Kleene star. Discuss the closure of NP under complement.

34.2-5
Show that any language in NP can be decided by an algorithm with a running time of $2^{O(n^k)}$ for some constant k.

34.2-6
A *hamiltonian path* in a graph is a simple path that visits every vertex exactly once. Show that the language HAM-PATH = $\{\langle G, u, v \rangle :$ there is a hamiltonian path from u to v in graph $G\}$ belongs to NP.

34.2-7
Show that the hamiltonian-path problem from Exercise 34.2-6 can be solved in polynomial time on directed acyclic graphs. Give an efficient algorithm for the problem.

34.2-8
Let ϕ be a boolean formula constructed from the boolean input variables $x_1, x_2, \ldots, x_k$, negations ($\neg$), ANDs ($\wedge$), ORs ($\vee$), and parentheses. The formula ϕ is a *tautology* if it evaluates to 1 for every assignment of 1 and 0 to the input variables. Define TAUTOLOGY as the language of boolean formulas that are tautologies. Show that TAUTOLOGY $\in$ co-NP.

34.2-9
Prove that P $\subseteq$ co-NP.

34.2-10
Prove that if NP $\neq$ co-NP, then P $\neq$ NP.

34.2-11
Let G be a connected, undirected graph with at least three vertices, and let G^3 be the graph obtained by connecting all pairs of vertices that are connected by a path in G of length at most 3. Prove that G^3 is hamiltonian. (*Hint:* Construct a spanning tree for G, and use an inductive argument.)

34.3 NP-completeness and reducibility

Perhaps the most compelling reason why theoretical computer scientists believe that P $\neq$ NP comes from the existence of the class of NP-complete problems. This class has the intriguing property that if *any* NP-complete problem can be solved in polynomial time, then *every* problem in NP has a polynomial-time solution, that is, P $=$ NP. Despite decades of study, though, no polynomial-time algorithm has ever been discovered for any NP-complete problem.

The language HAM-CYCLE is one NP-complete problem. If there were an algorithm to decide HAM-CYCLE in polynomial time, then every problem in NP could be solved in polynomial time. The NP-complete languages are, in a sense, the "hardest" languages in NP. In fact, if NP $-$ P turns out to be nonempty, we will be able to say with certainty that HAM-CYCLE $\in$ NP $-$ P.

This section starts by showing how to compare the relative "hardness" of languages using a precise notion called "polynomial-time reducibility." It then formally defines the NP-complete languages, finishing by sketching a proof that one such language, called CIRCUIT-SAT, is NP-complete. Sections 34.4 and 34.5 will use the notion of reducibility to show that many other problems are NP-complete.

Reducibility

One way that sometimes works for solving a problem is to recast it as a different problem. We call that strategy "reducing" one problem to another. Think of a problem Q as being reducible to another problem Q' if any instance of Q can be recast as an instance of Q', and the solution to the instance of Q' provides a solution to the instance of Q. For example, the problem of solving linear equations in an indeterminate x reduces to the problem of solving quadratic equations. Given a linear-equation instance $ax + b = 0$ (with solution $x = -b/a$), you can transform it to the quadratic equation $ax^2 + bx + 0 = 0$. This quadratic equation has the solutions $x = (-b \pm \sqrt{b^2 - 4ac})/2a$, where $c = 0$, so that $\sqrt{b^2 - 4ac} = b$. The

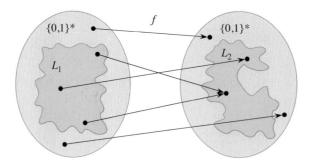

Figure 34.4 A function f that reduces language L_1 to language L_2. For any input $x \in \{0, 1\}^*$, the question of whether $x \in L_1$ has the same answer as the question of whether $f(x) \in L_2$.

solutions are then $x = (-b + b)/2a = 0$ and $x = (-b - b)/2a = -b/a$, thereby providing a solution to $ax + b = 0$. Thus, if a problem Q reduces to another problem Q', then Q is, in a sense, "no harder to solve" than Q'.

Returning to our formal-language framework for decision problems, we say that a language L_1 is *polynomial-time reducible* to a language L_2, written $L_1 \leq_P L_2$, if there exists a polynomial-time computable function $f : \{0, 1\}^* \rightarrow \{0, 1\}^*$ such that for all $x \in \{0, 1\}^*$,

$$x \in L_1 \text{ if and only if } f(x) \in L_2 . \tag{34.1}$$

We call the function f the *reduction function*, and a polynomial-time algorithm F that computes f is a *reduction algorithm*.

Figure 34.4 illustrates the idea of a reduction from a language L_1 to another language L_2. Each language is a subset of $\{0, 1\}^*$. The reduction function f provides a mapping such that if $x \in L_1$, then $f(x) \in L_2$. Moreover, if $x \notin L_1$, then $f(x) \notin L_2$. Thus, the reduction function maps any instance x of the decision problem represented by the language L_1 to an instance $f(x)$ of the problem represented by L_2. Providing an answer to whether $f(x) \in L_2$ directly provides the answer to whether $x \in L_1$. If, in addition, f can be computed in polynomial time, it is a polynomial-time reduction function.

Polynomial-time reductions give us a powerful tool for proving that various languages belong to P.

Lemma 34.3
If $L_1, L_2 \subseteq \{0, 1\}^*$ are languages such that $L_1 \leq_P L_2$, then $L_2 \in P$ implies $L_1 \in P$.

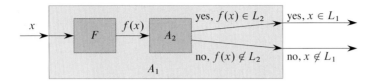

Figure 34.5   The proof of Lemma 34.3. The algorithm F is a reduction algorithm that computes the reduction function f from L_1 to L_2 in polynomial time, and A_2 is a polynomial-time algorithm that decides L_2. Algorithm A_1 decides whether $x \in L_1$ by using F to transform any input x into $f(x)$ and then using A_2 to decide whether $f(x) \in L_2$.

Proof   Let A_2 be a polynomial-time algorithm that decides L_2, and let F be a polynomial-time reduction algorithm that computes the reduction function f. We show how to construct a polynomial-time algorithm A_1 that decides L_1.

Figure 34.5 illustrates how we construct A_1. For a given input $x \in \{0, 1\}^*$, algorithm A_1 uses F to transform x into $f(x)$, and then it uses A_2 to test whether $f(x) \in L_2$. Algorithm A_1 takes the output from algorithm A_2 and produces that answer as its own output.

The correctness of A_1 follows from condition (34.1). The algorithm runs in polynomial time, since both F and A_2 run in polynomial time (see Exercise 34.1-5). ∎

NP-completeness

Polynomial-time reductions allow us to formally show that one problem is at least as hard as another, to within a polynomial-time factor. That is, if $L_1 \leq_P L_2$, then L_1 is not more than a polynomial factor harder than L_2, which is why the "less than or equal to" notation for reduction is mnemonic. We can now define the set of NP-complete languages, which are the hardest problems in NP.

A language $L \subseteq \{0, 1\}^*$ is *NP-complete* if

1. $L \in$ NP, and

2. $L' \leq_P L$ for every $L' \in$ NP.

If a language L satisfies property 2, but not necessarily property 1, we say that L is *NP-hard*. We also define NPC to be the class of NP-complete languages.

As the following theorem shows, NP-completeness is at the crux of deciding whether P is in fact equal to NP.

Theorem 34.4
If any NP-complete problem is polynomial-time solvable, then P $=$ NP. Equivalently, if any problem in NP is not polynomial-time solvable, then no NP-complete problem is polynomial-time solvable.

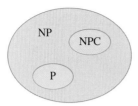

Figure 34.6 How most theoretical computer scientists view the relationships among P, NP, and NPC. Both P and NPC are wholly contained within NP, and $P \cap NPC = \emptyset$.

Proof Suppose that $L \in$ P and also that $L \in$ NPC. For any $L' \in$ NP, we have $L' \leq_P L$ by property 2 of the definition of NP-completeness. Thus, by Lemma 34.3, we also have that $L' \in$ P, which proves the first statement of the theorem.

To prove the second statement, consider the contrapositive of the first statement: if P $\neq$ NP, then there does not exist an NP-complete problem that is polynomial-time solvable. But P $\neq$ NP means that there is some problem in NP that is not polynomial-time solvable, and hence the second statement is the contrapositive of the first statement. ∎

It is for this reason that research into the P $\neq$ NP question centers around the NP-complete problems. Most theoretical computer scientists believe that P $\neq$ NP, which leads to the relationships among P, NP, and NPC shown in Figure 34.6. For all we know, however, someone may yet come up with a polynomial-time algorithm for an NP-complete problem, thus proving that P $=$ NP. Nevertheless, since no polynomial-time algorithm for any NP-complete problem has yet been discovered, a proof that a problem is NP-complete provides excellent evidence that it is intractable.

Circuit satisfiability

We have defined the notion of an NP-complete problem, but up to this point, we have not actually proved that any problem is NP-complete. Once we prove that at least one problem is NP-complete, polynomial-time reducibility becomes a tool to prove other problems to be NP-complete. Thus, we now focus on demonstrating the existence of an NP-complete problem: the circuit-satisfiability problem.

Unfortunately, the formal proof that the circuit-satisfiability problem is NP-complete requires technical detail beyond the scope of this text. Instead, we'll informally describe a proof that relies on a basic understanding of boolean combinational circuits.

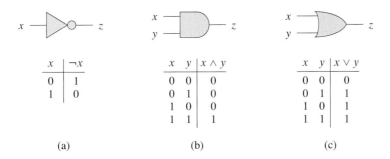

x	$\neg x$
0	1
1	0

x	y	$x \wedge y$
0	0	0
0	1	0
1	0	0
1	1	1

x	y	$x \vee y$
0	0	0
0	1	1
1	0	1
1	1	1

(a)   (b)   (c)

Figure 34.7 Three basic logic gates, with binary inputs and outputs. Under each gate is the truth table that describes the gate's operation. (a) The NOT gate. (b) The AND gate. (c) The OR gate.

Boolean combinational circuits are built from boolean combinational elements that are interconnected by wires. A *boolean combinational element* is any circuit element that has a constant number of boolean inputs and outputs and that performs a well-defined function. Boolean values are drawn from the set $\{0, 1\}$, where 0 represents FALSE and 1 represents TRUE.

The boolean combinational elements appearing in the circuit-satisfiability problem compute simple boolean functions, and they are known as *logic gates*. Figure 34.7 shows the three basic logic gates used in the circuit-satisfiability problem: the *NOT gate* (or *inverter*), the *AND gate*, and the *OR gate*. The NOT gate takes a single binary *input x*, whose value is either 0 or 1, and produces a binary *output z* whose value is opposite that of the input value. Each of the other two gates takes two binary inputs x and y and produces a single binary output z.

The operation of each gate, or of any boolean combinational element, is defined by a *truth table*, shown under each gate in Figure 34.7. A truth table gives the outputs of the combinational element for each possible setting of the inputs. For example, the truth table for the OR gate says that when the inputs are $x = 0$ and $y = 1$, the output value is $z = 1$. The symbol $\neg$ denotes the NOT function, $\wedge$ denotes the AND function, and $\vee$ denotes the OR function. Thus, for example, $0 \vee 1 = 1$.

AND and OR gates are not limited to just two inputs. An AND gate's output is 1 if all of its inputs are 1, and its output is 0 otherwise. An OR gate's output is 1 if any of its inputs are 1, and its output is 0 otherwise.

A *boolean combinational circuit* consists of one or more boolean combinational elements interconnected by *wires*. A wire can connect the output of one element to the input of another, so that the output value of the first element becomes an input value of the second. Figure 34.8 shows two similar boolean combinational circuits, differing in only one gate. Part (a) of the figure also shows the values on

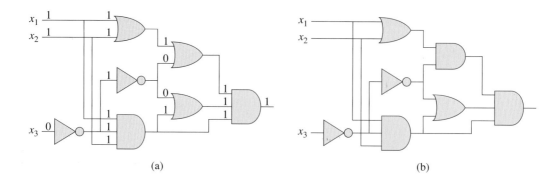

(a)   (b)

Figure 34.8 Two instances of the circuit-satisfiability problem. **(a)** The assignment $\langle x_1 = 1,$ $x_2 = 1, x_3 = 0 \rangle$ to the inputs of this circuit causes the output of the circuit to be 1. The circuit is therefore satisfiable. **(b)** No assignment to the inputs of this circuit can cause the output of the circuit to be 1. The circuit is therefore unsatisfiable.

the individual wires, given the input $\langle x_1 = 1, x_2 = 1, x_3 = 0 \rangle$. Although a single wire may have no more than one combinational-element output connected to it, it can feed several element inputs. The number of element inputs fed by a wire is called the *fan-out* of the wire. If no element output is connected to a wire, the wire is a *circuit input*, accepting input values from an external source. If no element input is connected to a wire, the wire is a *circuit output*, providing the results of the circuit's computation to the outside world. (An internal wire can also fan out to a circuit output.) For the purpose of defining the circuit-satisfiability problem, we limit the number of circuit outputs to 1, though in actual hardware design, a boolean combinational circuit may have multiple outputs.

Boolean combinational circuits contain no cycles. In other words, for a given combinational circuit, imagine a directed graph $G = (V, E)$ with one vertex for each combinational element and with k directed edges for each wire whose fan-out is k, where the graph contains a directed edge (u, v) if a wire connects the output of element u to an input of element v. Then G must be acyclic.

A *truth assignment* for a boolean combinational circuit is a set of boolean input values. We say that a 1-output boolean combinational circuit is *satisfiable* if it has a *satisfying assignment*: a truth assignment that causes the output of the circuit to be 1. For example, the circuit in Figure 34.8(a) has the satisfying assignment $\langle x_1 = 1, x_2 = 1, x_3 = 0 \rangle$, and so it is satisfiable. As Exercise 34.3-1 asks you to show, no assignment of values to x_1, x_2, and x_3 causes the circuit in Figure 34.8(b) to produce a 1 output. Since it always produces 0, it is unsatisfiable.

The *circuit-satisfiability problem* is, "Given a boolean combinational circuit composed of AND, OR, and NOT gates, is it satisfiable?" In order to pose this question formally, however, we must agree on a standard encoding for circuits. The *size* of a boolean combinational circuit is the number of boolean combinational elements plus the number of wires in the circuit. We could devise a graph-like encoding that maps any given circuit C into a binary string $\langle C \rangle$ whose length is polynomial in the size of the circuit itself. As a formal language, we can therefore define

CIRCUIT-SAT $= \{\langle C \rangle : C$ is a satisfiable boolean combinational circuit$\}$.

The circuit-satisfiability problem arises in the area of computer-aided hardware optimization. If a subcircuit always produces 0, that subcircuit is unnecessary: the designer can replace it by a simpler subcircuit that omits all logic gates and provides the constant 0 value as its output. You can see the value in having a polynomial-time algorithm for this problem.

Given a circuit C, you can determine whether it is satisfiable by simply checking all possible assignments to the inputs. Unfortunately, if the circuit has k inputs, then you would have to check up to 2^k possible assignments. When the size of C is polynomial in k, checking all possible assignments to the inputs takes $\Omega(2^k)$ time, which is superpolynomial in the size of the circuit.[10] In fact, as we have claimed, there is strong evidence that no polynomial-time algorithm exists that solves the circuit-satisfiability problem because circuit satisfiability is NP-complete. We break the proof of this fact into two parts, based on the two parts of the definition of NP-completeness.

Lemma 34.5
The circuit-satisfiability problem belongs to the class NP.

Proof We provide a two-input, polynomial-time algorithm A that can verify CIRCUIT-SAT. One of the inputs to A is (a standard encoding of) a boolean combinational circuit C. The other input is a certificate corresponding to an assignment of a boolean value to each of the wires in C. (See Exercise 34.3-4 for a smaller certificate.)

The algorithm A works as follows. For each logic gate in the circuit, it checks that the value provided by the certificate on the output wire is correctly computed as a function of the values on the input wires. Then, if the output of the entire circuit is 1, algorithm A outputs 1, since the values assigned to the inputs of C provide a satisfying assignment. Otherwise, A outputs 0.

---

[10] On the other hand, if the size of the circuit C is $\Theta(2^k)$, then an algorithm whose running time is $O(2^k)$ has a running time that is polynomial in the circuit size. Even if P $\neq$ NP, this situation would not contradict the NP-completeness of the problem. The existence of a polynomial-time algorithm for a special case does not imply that there is a polynomial-time algorithm for all cases.

Whenever a satisfiable circuit C is input to algorithm A, there exists a certificate whose length is polynomial in the size of C and that causes A to output a 1. Whenever an unsatisfiable circuit is input, no certificate can fool A into believing that the circuit is satisfiable. Algorithm A runs in polynomial time, and with a good implementation, linear time suffices. Thus, CIRCUIT-SAT is verifiable in polynomial time, and CIRCUIT-SAT $\in$ NP. ∎

The second part of proving that CIRCUIT-SAT is NP-complete is to show that the language is NP-hard: that *every* language in NP is polynomial-time reducible to CIRCUIT-SAT. The actual proof of this fact is full of technical intricacies, and so instead we'll sketch the proof based on some understanding of the workings of computer hardware.

A computer program is stored in the computer's memory as a sequence of instructions. A typical instruction encodes an operation to be performed, addresses of operands in memory, and an address where the result is to be stored. A special memory location, called the *program counter*, keeps track of which instruction is to be executed next. The program counter automatically increments when each instruction is fetched, thereby causing the computer to execute instructions sequentially. Certain instructions can cause a value to be written to the program counter, however, which alters the normal sequential execution and allows the computer to loop and perform conditional branches.

At any point while a program executes, the computer's memory holds the entire state of the computation. (Consider the memory to include the program itself, the program counter, working storage, and any of the various bits of state that a computer maintains for bookkeeping.) We call any particular state of computer memory a *configuration*. When an instruction executes, it transforms the configuration. Think of an instruction as mapping one configuration to another. The computer hardware that accomplishes this mapping can be implemented as a boolean combinational circuit, which we denote by M in the proof of the following lemma.

Lemma 34.6
The circuit-satisfiability problem is NP-hard.

Proof   Let L be any language in NP. We'll describe a polynomial-time algorithm F computing a reduction function f that maps every binary string x to a circuit $C = f(x)$ such that $x \in L$ if and only if $C \in$ CIRCUIT-SAT.

Since $L \in$ NP, there must exist an algorithm A that verifies L in polynomial time. The algorithm F that we construct uses the two-input algorithm A to compute the reduction function f.

Let $T(n)$ denote the worst-case running time of algorithm A on length-n input strings, and let $k \geq 1$ be a constant such that $T(n) = O(n^k)$ and the length of the

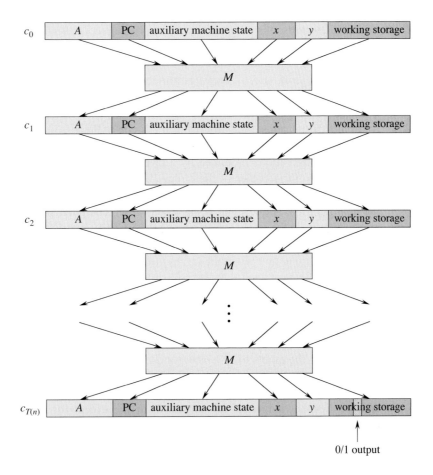

Figure 34.9 The sequence of configurations produced by an algorithm A running on an input x and certificate y. Each configuration represents the state of the computer for one step of the computation and, besides A, x, and y, includes the program counter (PC), auxiliary machine state, and working storage. Except for the certificate y, the initial configuration c_0 is constant. A boolean combinational circuit M maps each configuration to the next configuration. The output is a distinguished bit in the working storage.

certificate is $O(n^k)$. (The running time of A is actually a polynomial in the total input size, which includes both an input string and a certificate, but since the length of the certificate is polynomial in the length n of the input string, the running time is polynomial in n.)

The basic idea of the proof is to represent the computation of A as a sequence of configurations. As Figure 34.9 illustrates, consider each configuration as comprising a few parts: the program for A, the program counter and auxiliary machine state, the input x, the certificate y, and working storage. The combinational circuit M, which implements the computer hardware, maps each configuration c_i to the next configuration c_{i+1}, starting from the initial configuration c_0. Algorithm A writes its output—0 or 1—to some designated location by the time it finishes executing. After A halts, the output value never changes. Thus, if the algorithm runs for at most $T(n)$ steps, the output appears as one of the bits in $c_{T(n)}$.

The reduction algorithm F constructs a single combinational circuit that computes all configurations produced by a given initial configuration. The idea is to paste together $T(n)$ copies of the circuit M. The output of the ith circuit, which produces configuration c_i, feeds directly into the input of the $(i+1)$st circuit. Thus, the configurations, rather than being stored in the computer's memory, simply reside as values on the wires connecting copies of M.

Recall what the polynomial-time reduction algorithm F must do. Given an input x, it must compute a circuit $C = f(x)$ that is satisfiable if and only if there exists a certificate y such that $A(x, y) = 1$. When F obtains an input x, it first computes $n = |x|$ and constructs a combinational circuit C' consisting of $T(n)$ copies of M. The input to C' is an initial configuration corresponding to a computation on $A(x, y)$, and the output is the configuration $c_{T(n)}$.

Algorithm F modifies circuit C' slightly to construct the circuit $C = f(x)$. First, it wires the inputs to C' corresponding to the program for A, the initial program counter, the input x, and the initial state of memory directly to these known values. Thus, the only remaining inputs to the circuit correspond to the certificate y. Second, it ignores all outputs from C', except for the one bit of $c_{T(n)}$ corresponding to the output of A. This circuit C, so constructed, computes $C(y) = A(x, y)$ for any input y of length $O(n^k)$. The reduction algorithm F, when provided an input string x, computes such a circuit C and outputs it.

We need to prove two properties. First, we must show that F correctly computes a reduction function f. That is, we must show that C is satisfiable if and only if there exists a certificate y such that $A(x, y) = 1$. Second, we must show that F runs in polynomial time.

To show that F correctly computes a reduction function, suppose that there exists a certificate y of length $O(n^k)$ such that $A(x, y) = 1$. Then, upon applying the bits of y to the inputs of C, the output of C is $C(y) = A(x, y) = 1$. Thus, if a certificate exists, then C is satisfiable. For the other direction, suppose that C is satisfiable. Hence, there exists an input y to C such that $C(y) = 1$, from which we conclude that $A(x, y) = 1$. Thus, F correctly computes a reduction function.

To complete the proof sketch, we need to show that F runs in time polynomial in $n = |x|$. First, the number of bits required to represent a configuration is polynomial in n. Why? The program for A itself has constant size, independent of the length of its input x. The length of the input x is n, and the length of the certificate y is $O(n^k)$. Since the algorithm runs for at most $O(n^k)$ steps, the amount of working storage required by A is polynomial in n as well. (We implicitly assume that this memory is contiguous. Exercise 34.3-5 asks you to extend the argument to the situation in which the locations accessed by A are scattered across a much larger region of memory and the particular pattern of scattering can differ for each input x.)

The combinational circuit M implementing the computer hardware has size polynomial in the length of a configuration, which is $O(n^k)$, and hence, the size of M is polynomial in n. (Most of this circuitry implements the logic of the memory system.) The circuit C consists of $O(n^k)$ copies of M, and hence it has size polynomial in n. The reduction algorithm F can construct C from x in polynomial time, since each step of the construction takes polynomial time. ∎

The language CIRCUIT-SAT is therefore at least as hard as any language in NP, and since it belongs to NP, it is NP-complete.

Theorem 34.7
The circuit-satisfiability problem is NP-complete.

Proof Immediate from Lemmas 34.5 and 34.6 and from the definition of NP-completeness. ∎

Exercises

34.3-1
Verify that the circuit in Figure 34.8(b) is unsatisfiable.

34.3-2
Show that the $\leq_P$ relation is a transitive relation on languages. That is, show that if $L_1 \leq_P L_2$ and $L_2 \leq_P L_3$, then $L_1 \leq_P L_3$.

34.3-3
Prove that $L \leq_P \overline{L}$ if and only if $\overline{L} \leq_P L$.

34.3-4
Show that an alternative proof of Lemma 34.5 can use a satisfying assignment as a certificate. Which certificate makes for an easier proof?

34.3-5
The proof of Lemma 34.6 assumes that the working storage for algorithm A occupies a contiguous region of polynomial size. Where does the proof exploit this assumption? Argue that this assumption does not involve any loss of generality.

34.3-6

A language L is *complete* for a language class C with respect to polynomial-time reductions if $L \in C$ and $L' \leq_P L$ for all $L' \in C$. Show that $\emptyset$ and $\{0, 1\}^*$ are the only languages in P that are not complete for P with respect to polynomial-time reductions.

34.3-7

Show that, with respect to polynomial-time reductions (see Exercise 34.3-6), L is complete for NP if and only if $\overline{L}$ is complete for co-NP.

34.3-8

The reduction algorithm F in the proof of Lemma 34.6 constructs the circuit $C = f(x)$ based on knowledge of x, A, and k. Professor Sartre observes that the string x is input to F, but only the existence of A, k, and the constant factor implicit in the $O(n^k)$ running time is known to F (since the language L belongs to NP), not their actual values. Thus, the professor concludes that F cannot possibly construct the circuit C and that the language CIRCUIT-SAT is not necessarily NP-hard. Explain the flaw in the professor's reasoning.

34.4   NP-completeness proofs

The proof that the circuit-satisfiability problem is NP-complete showed directly that $L \leq_P$ CIRCUIT-SAT for every language $L \in$ NP. This section shows how to prove that languages are NP-complete without directly reducing *every* language in NP to the given language. We'll explore examples of this methodology by proving that various formula-satisfiability problems are NP-complete. Section 34.5 provides many more examples.

The following lemma provides a foundation for showing that a given language is NP-complete.

Lemma 34.8

If L is a language such that $L' \leq_P L$ for some $L' \in$ NPC, then L is NP-hard. If, in addition, we have $L \in$ NP, then $L \in$ NPC.

Proof   Since L' is NP-complete, for all $L'' \in$ NP, we have $L'' \leq_P L'$. By supposition, we have $L' \leq_P L$, and thus by transitivity (Exercise 34.3-2), we have $L'' \leq_P L$, which shows that L is NP-hard. If $L \in$ NP, we also have $L \in$ NPC.   ∎

In other words, by reducing a known NP-complete language L' to L, we implicitly reduce every language in NP to L. Thus, Lemma 34.8 provides a method for proving that a language L is NP-complete:

1. Prove $L \in$ NP.

2. Prove that L is NP-hard:

   a. Select a known NP-complete language L'.

   b. Describe an algorithm that computes a function f mapping every instance $x \in \{0, 1\}^*$ of L' to an instance $f(x)$ of L.

   c. Prove that the function f satisfies $x \in L'$ if and only if $f(x) \in L$ for all $x \in \{0, 1\}^*$.

   d. Prove that the algorithm computing f runs in polynomial time.

This methodology of reducing from a single known NP-complete language is far simpler than the more complicated process of showing directly how to reduce from every language in NP. Proving CIRCUIT-SAT $\in$ NPC furnishes a starting point. Knowing that the circuit-satisfiability problem is NP-complete makes it much easier to prove that other problems are NP-complete. Moreover, as the catalog of known NP-complete problems grows, so will the choices for languages from which to reduce.

Formula satisfiability

To illustrate the reduction methodology, let's see an NP-completeness proof for the problem of determining whether a boolean *formula*, not a *circuit*, is satisfiable. This problem has the historical honor of being the first problem ever shown to be NP-complete.

We formulate the *(formula) satisfiability* problem in terms of the language SAT as follows. An instance of SAT is a boolean formula ϕ composed of

1. n boolean variables: $x_1, x_2, \ldots, x_n$;

2. m boolean connectives: any boolean function with one or two inputs and one output, such as $\wedge$ (AND), $\vee$ (OR), $\neg$ (NOT), $\rightarrow$ (implication), $\leftrightarrow$ (if and only if); and

3. parentheses. (Without loss of generality, assume that there are no redundant parentheses, i.e., a formula contains at most one pair of parentheses per boolean connective.)

We can encode a boolean formula ϕ in a length that is polynomial in $n + m$. As in boolean combinational circuits, a *truth assignment* for a boolean formula ϕ

is a set of values for the variables of ϕ, and a *satisfying assignment* is a truth assignment that causes it to evaluate to 1. A formula with a satisfying assignment is a *satisfiable* formula. The satisfiability problem asks whether a given boolean formula is satisfiable, which we can express in formal-language terms as

$$\text{SAT} = \{\langle \phi \rangle : \phi \text{ is a satisfiable boolean formula}\}\ .$$

As an example, the formula

$$\phi = ((x_1 \to x_2) \vee \neg((\neg x_1 \leftrightarrow x_3) \vee x_4)) \wedge \neg x_2$$

has the satisfying assignment $\langle x_1 = 0, x_2 = 0, x_3 = 1, x_4 = 1 \rangle$, since

$$
\begin{aligned}
\phi &= ((0 \to 0) \vee \neg((\neg 0 \leftrightarrow 1) \vee 1)) \wedge \neg 0 &\text{(34.2)}\\
&= (1 \vee \neg(1 \vee 1)) \wedge 1 \\
&= (1 \vee 0) \wedge 1 \\
&= 1\ ,
\end{aligned}
$$

and thus this formula ϕ belongs to SAT.

The naive algorithm to determine whether an arbitrary boolean formula is satisfiable does not run in polynomial time. A formula with n variables has 2^n possible assignments. If the length of $\langle \phi \rangle$ is polynomial in n, then checking every assignment requires $\Omega(2^n)$ time, which is superpolynomial in the length of $\langle \phi \rangle$. As the following theorem shows, a polynomial-time algorithm is unlikely to exist.

Theorem 34.9
Satisfiability of boolean formulas is NP-complete.

Proof   We start by arguing that $\text{SAT} \in \text{NP}$. Then we prove that SAT is NP-hard by showing that $\text{CIRCUIT-SAT} \leq_P \text{SAT}$, which by Lemma 34.8 will prove the theorem.

To show that SAT belongs to NP, we show that a certificate consisting of a satisfying assignment for an input formula ϕ can be verified in polynomial time. The verifying algorithm simply replaces each variable in the formula with its corresponding value and then evaluates the expression, much as we did in equation (34.2) above. This task can be done in polynomial time. If the expression evaluates to 1, then the algorithm has verified that the formula is satisfiable. Thus, SAT belongs to NP.

To prove that SAT is NP-hard, we show that $\text{CIRCUIT-SAT} \leq_P \text{SAT}$. In other words, we need to show how to reduce any instance of circuit satisfiability to an instance of formula satisfiability in polynomial time. We can use induction to express any boolean combinational circuit as a boolean formula. We simply look at the gate that produces the circuit output and inductively express each of the

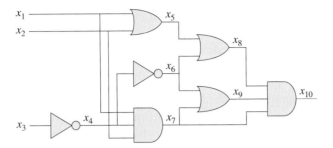

Figure 34.10   Reducing circuit satisfiability to formula satisfiability. The formula produced by the reduction algorithm has a variable for each wire in the circuit and a clause for each logic gate.

gate's inputs as formulas. We then obtain the formula for the circuit by writing an expression that applies the gate's function to its inputs' formulas.

Unfortunately, this straightforward method does not amount to a polynomial-time reduction. As Exercise 34.4-1 asks you to show, shared subformulas — which arise from gates whose output wires have fan-out of 2 or more — can cause the size of the generated formula to grow exponentially. Thus, the reduction algorithm must be somewhat more clever.

Figure 34.10 illustrates how to overcome this problem, using as an example the circuit from Figure 34.8(a). For each wire x_i in the circuit C, the formula ϕ has a variable x_i. To express how each gate operates, construct a small formula involving the variables of its incident wires. The formula has the form of an "if and only if" ($\leftrightarrow$), with the variable for the gate's output on the left and on the right a logical expression encapsulating the gate's function on its inputs. For example, the operation of the output AND gate (the rightmost gate in the figure) is $x_{10} \leftrightarrow (x_7 \wedge x_8 \wedge x_9)$. We call each of these small formulas a *clause*.

The formula ϕ produced by the reduction algorithm is the AND of the circuit-output variable with the conjunction of clauses describing the operation of each gate. For the circuit in the figure, the formula is

$$
\begin{aligned}
\phi \;=\; & x_{10} \wedge (x_4 \leftrightarrow \neg x_3) \\
& \wedge (x_5 \leftrightarrow (x_1 \vee x_2)) \\
& \wedge (x_6 \leftrightarrow \neg x_4) \\
& \wedge (x_7 \leftrightarrow (x_1 \wedge x_2 \wedge x_4)) \\
& \wedge (x_8 \leftrightarrow (x_5 \vee x_6)) \\
& \wedge (x_9 \leftrightarrow (x_6 \vee x_7)) \\
& \wedge (x_{10} \leftrightarrow (x_7 \wedge x_8 \wedge x_9)) \, .
\end{aligned}
$$

Given a circuit C, it is straightforward to produce such a formula ϕ in polynomial time.

Why is the circuit C satisfiable exactly when the formula ϕ is satisfiable? If C has a satisfying assignment, then each wire of the circuit has a well-defined value, and the output of the circuit is 1. Therefore, when wire values are assigned to variables in ϕ, each clause of ϕ evaluates to 1, and thus the conjunction of all evaluates to 1. Conversely, if some assignment causes ϕ to evaluate to 1, the circuit C is satisfiable by an analogous argument. Thus, we have shown that CIRCUIT-SAT $\leq_P$ SAT, which completes the proof.   ∎

3-CNF satisfiability

Reducing from formula satisfiability gives us an avenue to prove many problems NP-complete. The reduction algorithm must handle any input formula, though, and this requirement can lead to a huge number of cases to consider. Instead, it is usually simpler to reduce from a restricted language of boolean formulas. Of course, the restricted language must not be polynomial-time solvable. One convenient language is 3-CNF satisfiability, or 3-CNF-SAT.

In order to define 3-CNF satisfiability, we first need to define a few terms. A *literal* in a boolean formula is an occurrence of a variable (such as x_1) or its negation ($\neg x_1$). A *clause* is the OR of one or more literals, such as $x_1 \vee \neg x_2 \vee \neg x_3$. A boolean formula is in *conjunctive normal form*, or *CNF*, if it is expressed as an AND of clauses, and it's in *3-conjunctive normal form*, or *3-CNF*, if each clause contains exactly three distinct literals.

For example, the boolean formula

$$(x_1 \vee \neg x_1 \vee \neg x_2) \wedge (x_3 \vee x_2 \vee x_4) \wedge (\neg x_1 \vee \neg x_3 \vee \neg x_4)$$

is in 3-CNF. The first of its three clauses is $(x_1 \vee \neg x_1 \vee \neg x_2)$, which contains the three literals $x_1, \neg x_1$, and $\neg x_2$.

The language 3-CNF-SAT consists of encodings of boolean formulas in 3-CNF that are satisfiable. The following theorem shows that a polynomial-time algorithm that can determine the satisfiability of boolean formulas is unlikely to exist, even when they are expressed in this simple normal form.

Theorem 34.10
Satisfiability of boolean formulas in 3-conjunctive normal form is NP-complete.

Proof   The argument from the proof of Theorem 34.9 to show that SAT ∈ NP applies equally well here to show that 3-CNF-SAT ∈ NP. By Lemma 34.8, therefore, we need only show that SAT $\leq_P$ 3-CNF-SAT.

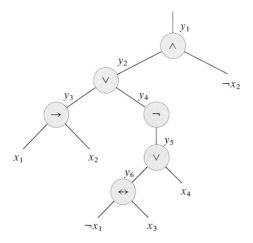

Figure 34.11 The tree corresponding to the formula $\phi = ((x_1 \rightarrow x_2) \vee \neg((\neg x_1 \leftrightarrow x_3) \vee x_4)) \wedge \neg x_2$.

We break the reduction algorithm into three basic steps. Each step progressively transforms the input formula ϕ closer to the desired 3-conjunctive normal form.

The first step is similar to the one used to prove CIRCUIT-SAT $\leq_P$ SAT in Theorem 34.9. First, construct a binary "parse" tree for the input formula ϕ, with literals as leaves and connectives as internal nodes. Figure 34.11 shows such a parse tree for the formula

$$\phi = ((x_1 \rightarrow x_2) \vee \neg((\neg x_1 \leftrightarrow x_3) \vee x_4)) \wedge \neg x_2 \ . \tag{34.3}$$

If the input formula contains a clause such as the OR of several literals, use associativity to parenthesize the expression fully so that every internal node in the resulting tree has just one or two children. The binary parse tree is like a circuit for computing the function.

Mimicking the reduction in the proof of Theorem 34.9, introduce a variable y_i for the output of each internal node. Then rewrite the original formula ϕ as the AND of the variable at the root of the parse tree and a conjunction of clauses describing the operation of each node. For the formula (34.3), the resulting expression is

$$
\begin{aligned}
\phi' = \ & y_1 \wedge (y_1 \leftrightarrow (y_2 \wedge \neg x_2)) \\
& \wedge (y_2 \leftrightarrow (y_3 \vee y_4)) \\
& \wedge (y_3 \leftrightarrow (x_1 \rightarrow x_2)) \\
& \wedge (y_4 \leftrightarrow \neg y_5) \\
& \wedge (y_5 \leftrightarrow (y_6 \vee x_4)) \\
& \wedge (y_6 \leftrightarrow (\neg x_1 \leftrightarrow x_3)) \ .
\end{aligned}
$$

y_1	y_2	x_2	$(y_1 \leftrightarrow (y_2 \wedge \neg x_2))$
1	1	1	0
1	1	0	1
1	0	1	0
1	0	0	0
0	1	1	1
0	1	0	0
0	0	1	1
0	0	0	1

Figure 34.12   The truth table for the clause $(y_1 \leftrightarrow (y_2 \wedge \neg x_2))$.

The formula ϕ' thus obtained is a conjunction of clauses ϕ'_i, each of which has at most three literals. These clauses are not yet ORs of three literals.

The second step of the reduction converts each clause ϕ'_i into conjunctive normal form. Construct a truth table for ϕ'_i by evaluating all possible assignments to its variables. Each row of the truth table consists of a possible assignment of the variables of the clause, together with the value of the clause under that assignment. Using the truth-table entries that evaluate to 0, build a formula in *disjunctive normal form* (or *DNF*)—an OR of ANDs—that is equivalent to $\neg\phi'_i$. Then negate this formula and convert it into a CNF formula ϕ''_i by using *DeMorgan's laws* for propositional logic,

$$\neg(a \wedge b) = \neg a \vee \neg b \,,$$
$$\neg(a \vee b) = \neg a \wedge \neg b \,,$$

to complement all literals, change ORs into ANDs, and change ANDs into ORs.

In our example, the clause $\phi'_1 = (y_1 \leftrightarrow (y_2 \wedge \neg x_2))$ converts into CNF as follows. The truth table for ϕ'_1 appears in Figure 34.12. The DNF formula equivalent to $\neg\phi'_1$ is

$$(y_1 \wedge y_2 \wedge x_2) \vee (y_1 \wedge \neg y_2 \wedge x_2) \vee (y_1 \wedge \neg y_2 \wedge \neg x_2) \vee (\neg y_1 \wedge y_2 \wedge \neg x_2) \,.$$

Negating and applying DeMorgan's laws yields the CNF formula

$$\phi''_1 = (\neg y_1 \vee \neg y_2 \vee \neg x_2) \wedge (\neg y_1 \vee y_2 \vee \neg x_2)$$
$$\wedge (\neg y_1 \vee y_2 \vee x_2) \wedge (y_1 \vee \neg y_2 \vee x_2) \,,$$

which is equivalent to the original clause ϕ'_1.

At this point, each clause ϕ'_i of the formula ϕ' has been converted into a CNF formula ϕ''_i, and thus ϕ' is equivalent to the CNF formula ϕ'' consisting of the conjunction of the ϕ''_i. Moreover, each clause of ϕ'' has at most three literals.

The third and final step of the reduction further transforms the formula so that each clause has *exactly* three distinct literals. From the clauses of the CNF formula ϕ'', construct the final 3-CNF formula ϕ'''. This formula also uses two auxiliary variables, p and q. For each clause C_i of ϕ'', include the following clauses in ϕ''':

- If C_i contains three distinct literals, then simply include C_i as a clause of ϕ'''.

- If C_i contains exactly two distinct literals, that is, if $C_i = (l_1 \vee l_2)$, where l_1 and l_2 are literals, then include $(l_1 \vee l_2 \vee p) \wedge (l_1 \vee l_2 \vee \neg p)$ as clauses of ϕ'''. The literals p and $\neg p$ merely fulfill the syntactic requirement that each clause of ϕ''' contain exactly three distinct literals. Whether $p = 0$ or $p = 1$, one of the clauses is equivalent to $l_1 \vee l_2$, and the other evaluates to 1, which is the identity for AND.

- If C_i contains just one distinct literal l, then include $(l \vee p \vee q) \wedge (l \vee p \vee \neg q) \wedge (l \vee \neg p \vee q) \wedge (l \vee \neg p \vee \neg q)$ as clauses of ϕ'''. Regardless of the values of p and q, one of the four clauses is equivalent to l, and the other three evaluate to 1.

We can see that the 3-CNF formula ϕ''' is satisfiable if and only if ϕ is satisfiable by inspecting each of the three steps. Like the reduction from CIRCUIT-SAT to SAT, the construction of ϕ' from ϕ in the first step preserves satisfiability. The second step produces a CNF formula ϕ'' that is algebraically equivalent to ϕ'. Then the third step produces a 3-CNF formula ϕ''' that is effectively equivalent to ϕ'', since any assignment to the variables p and q produces a formula that is algebraically equivalent to ϕ''.

We must also show that the reduction can be computed in polynomial time. Constructing ϕ' from ϕ introduces at most one variable and one clause per connective in ϕ. Constructing ϕ'' from ϕ' can introduce at most eight clauses into ϕ'' for each clause from ϕ', since each clause of ϕ' contains at most three variables, and the truth table for each clause has at most $2^3 = 8$ rows. The construction of ϕ''' from ϕ'' introduces at most four clauses into ϕ''' for each clause of ϕ''. Thus the size of the resulting formula ϕ''' is polynomial in the length of the original formula. Each of the constructions can be accomplished in polynomial time. ∎

Exercises

34.4-1
Consider the straightforward (nonpolynomial-time) reduction in the proof of Theorem 34.9. Describe a circuit of size n that, when converted to a formula by this method, yields a formula whose size is exponential in n.

34.4-2

Show the 3-CNF formula that results upon using the method of Theorem 34.10 on the formula (34.3).

34.4-3

Professor Jagger proposes to show that SAT $\leq_P$ 3-CNF-SAT by using only the truth-table technique in the proof of Theorem 34.10, and not the other steps. That is, the professor proposes to take the boolean formula ϕ, form a truth table for its variables, derive from the truth table a formula in 3-DNF that is equivalent to $\neg\phi$, and then negate and apply DeMorgan's laws to produce a 3-CNF formula equivalent to ϕ. Show that this strategy does not yield a polynomial-time reduction.

34.4-4

Show that the problem of determining whether a boolean formula is a tautology is complete for co-NP. (*Hint:* See Exercise 34.3-7.)

34.4-5

Show that the problem of determining the satisfiability of boolean formulas in disjunctive normal form is polynomial-time solvable.

34.4-6

Someone gives you a polynomial-time algorithm to decide formula satisfiability. Describe how to use this algorithm to find satisfying assignments in polynomial time.

34.4-7

Let 2-CNF-SAT be the set of satisfiable boolean formulas in CNF with exactly two literals per clause. Show that 2-CNF-SAT $\in$ P. Make your algorithm as efficient as possible. (*Hint:* Observe that $x \vee y$ is equivalent to $\neg x \rightarrow y$. Reduce 2-CNF-SAT to an efficiently solvable problem on a directed graph.)

34.5   NP-complete problems

NP-complete problems arise in diverse domains: boolean logic, graphs, arithmetic, network design, sets and partitions, storage and retrieval, sequencing and scheduling, mathematical programming, algebra and number theory, games and puzzles, automata and language theory, program optimization, biology, chemistry, physics, and more. This section uses the reduction methodology to provide NP-completeness proofs for a variety of problems drawn from graph theory and set partitioning.

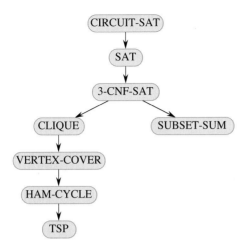

Figure 34.13   The structure of NP-completeness proofs in Sections 34.4 and 34.5. All proofs ultimately follow by reduction from the NP-completeness of CIRCUIT-SAT.

Figure 34.13 outlines the structure of the NP-completeness proofs in this section and Section 34.4. We prove each language in the figure to be NP-complete by reduction from the language that points to it. At the root is CIRCUIT-SAT, which we proved NP-complete in Theorem 34.7. This section concludes with a recap of reduction strategies.

34.5.1   The clique problem

A *clique* in an undirected graph $G = (V, E)$ is a subset $V' \subseteq V$ of vertices, each pair of which is connected by an edge in E. In other words, a clique is a complete subgraph of G. The *size* of a clique is the number of vertices it contains. The *clique problem* is the optimization problem of finding a clique of maximum size in a graph. The corresponding decision problem asks simply whether a clique of a given size k exists in the graph. The formal definition is

CLIQUE $= \{\langle G, k \rangle : G$ is a graph containing a clique of size $k\}$.

A naive algorithm for determining whether a graph $G = (V, E)$ with $|V|$ vertices contains a clique of size k lists all k-subsets of V and checks each one to see whether it forms a clique. The running time of this algorithm is $\Omega(k^2 \binom{|V|}{k})$, which is polynomial if k is a constant. In general, however, k could be near $|V|/2$, in which case the algorithm runs in superpolynomial time. Indeed, an efficient algorithm for the clique problem is unlikely to exist.

Theorem 34.11
The clique problem is NP-complete.

Proof   First, we show that CLIQUE $\in$ NP. For a given graph $G = (V, E)$, use the set $V' \subseteq V$ of vertices in the clique as a certificate for G. To check whether V' is a clique in polynomial time, check whether, for each pair $u, v \in V'$, the edge (u, v) belongs to E.

We next prove that 3-CNF-SAT $\leq_P$ CLIQUE, which shows that the clique problem is NP-hard. You might be surprised that the proof reduces an instance of 3-CNF-SAT to an instance of CLIQUE, since on the surface logical formulas seem to have little to do with graphs.

The reduction algorithm begins with an instance of 3-CNF-SAT. Let $\phi = C_1 \wedge C_2 \wedge \cdots \wedge C_k$ be a boolean formula in 3-CNF with k clauses. For $r = 1, 2, \ldots, k$, each clause C_r contains exactly three distinct literals: l_1^r, l_2^r, and l_3^r. We will construct a graph G such that ϕ is satisfiable if and only if G contains a clique of size k.

We construct the undirected graph $G = (V, E)$ as follows. For each clause $C_r = (l_1^r \vee l_2^r \vee l_3^r)$ in ϕ, place a triple of vertices v_1^r, v_2^r, and v_3^r into V. Add edge (v_i^r, v_j^s) into E if both of the following hold:

- v_i^r and v_j^s are in different triples, that is, $r \neq s$, and

- their corresponding literals are ***consistent***, that is, l_i^r is not the negation of l_j^s.

We can build this graph from ϕ in polynomial time. As an example of this construction, if

$$\phi = (x_1 \vee \neg x_2 \vee \neg x_3) \wedge (\neg x_1 \vee x_2 \vee x_3) \wedge (x_1 \vee x_2 \vee x_3) \,,$$

then G is the graph shown in Figure 34.14.

We must show that this transformation of ϕ into G is a reduction. First, suppose that ϕ has a satisfying assignment. Then each clause C_r contains at least one literal l_i^r that is assigned 1, and each such literal corresponds to a vertex v_i^r. Picking one such "true" literal from each clause yields a set V' of k vertices. We claim that V' is a clique. For any two vertices $v_i^r, v_j^s \in V'$, where $r \neq s$, both corresponding literals l_i^r and l_j^s map to 1 by the given satisfying assignment, and thus the literals cannot be complements. Thus, by the construction of G, the edge (v_i^r, v_j^s) belongs to E.

Conversely, suppose that G contains a clique V' of size k. No edges in G connect vertices in the same triple, and so V' contains exactly one vertex per triple. If $v_i^r \in V'$, then assign 1 to the corresponding literal l_i^r. Since G contains no edges between inconsistent literals, no literal and its complement are both assigned 1. Each clause is satisfied, and so ϕ is satisfied. (Any variables that do not correspond to a vertex in the clique may be set arbitrarily.)   ∎

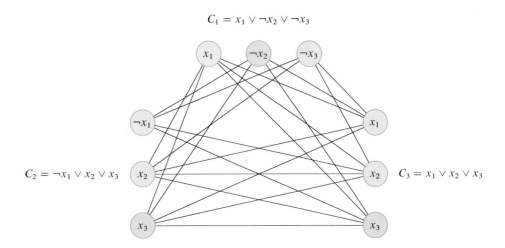

Figure 34.14 The graph G derived from the 3-CNF formula $\phi = C_1 \wedge C_2 \wedge C_3$, where $C_1 = (x_1 \vee \neg x_2 \vee \neg x_3)$, $C_2 = (\neg x_1 \vee x_2 \vee x_3)$, and $C_3 = (x_1 \vee x_2 \vee x_3)$, in reducing 3-CNF-SAT to CLIQUE. A satisfying assignment of the formula has $x_2 = 0$, $x_3 = 1$, and x_1 set to either 0 or 1. This assignment satisfies C_1 with $\neg x_2$, and it satisfies C_2 and C_3 with x_3, corresponding to the clique with blue vertices.

In the example of Figure 34.14, a satisfying assignment of ϕ has $x_2 = 0$ and $x_3 = 1$. A corresponding clique of size $k = 3$ consists of the vertices corresponding to $\neg x_2$ from the first clause, x_3 from the second clause, and x_3 from the third clause. Because the clique contains no vertices corresponding to either x_1 or $\neg x_1$, this satisfying assignment can set x_1 to either 0 or 1.

The proof of Theorem 34.11 reduced an arbitrary instance of 3-CNF-SAT to an instance of CLIQUE with a particular structure. You might think that we have shown only that CLIQUE is NP-hard in graphs in which the vertices are restricted to occur in triples and in which there are no edges between vertices in the same triple. Indeed, we have shown that CLIQUE is NP-hard only in this restricted case, but this proof suffices to show that CLIQUE is NP-hard in general graphs. Why? If there were a polynomial-time algorithm that solves CLIQUE on general graphs, it would also solve CLIQUE on restricted graphs.

The opposite approach—reducing instances of 3-CNF-SAT with a special structure to general instances of CLIQUE—does not suffice, however. Why not? Perhaps the instances of 3-CNF-SAT that we choose to reduce from are "easy," and so we would not have reduced an NP-hard problem to CLIQUE.

Moreover, the reduction uses the instance of 3-CNF-SAT, but not the solution. We would have erred if the polynomial-time reduction had relied on knowing

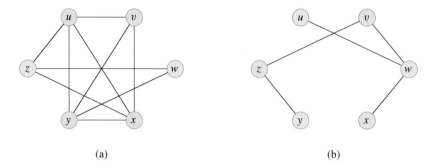

(a)   (b)

Figure 34.15   Reducing CLIQUE to VERTEX-COVER. **(a)** An undirected graph $G = (V, E)$ with clique $V' = \{u, v, x, y\}$, shown in blue. **(b)** The graph $\overline{G}$ produced by the reduction algorithm that has vertex cover $V - V' = \{w, z\}$, in blue.

whether the formula ϕ is satisfiable, since we do not know how to decide whether ϕ is satisfiable in polynomial time.

34.5.2   The vertex-cover problem

A *vertex cover* of an undirected graph $G = (V, E)$ is a subset $V' \subseteq V$ such that if $(u, v) \in E$, then $u \in V'$ or $v \in V'$ (or both). That is, each vertex "covers" its incident edges, and a vertex cover for G is a set of vertices that covers all the edges in E. The *size* of a vertex cover is the number of vertices in it. For example, the graph in Figure 34.15(b) has a vertex cover $\{w, z\}$ of size 2.

The *vertex-cover problem* is to find a vertex cover of minimum size in a given graph. For this optimization problem, the corresponding decision problem asks whether a graph has a vertex cover of a given size k. As a language, we define

VERTEX-COVER $= \{\langle G, k \rangle :$ graph G has a vertex cover of size $k\}$.

The following theorem shows that this problem is NP-complete.

Theorem 34.12
The vertex-cover problem is NP-complete.

Proof   We first show that VERTEX-COVER $\in$ NP. Given a graph $G = (V, E)$ and an integer k, the certificate is the vertex cover $V' \subseteq V$ itself. The verification algorithm affirms that $|V'| = k$, and then it checks, for each edge $(u, v) \in E$, that $u \in V'$ or $v \in V'$. It is easy to verify the certificate in polynomial time.

To prove that the vertex-cover problem is NP-hard, we reduce from the clique problem, showing that CLIQUE $\leq_P$ VERTEX-COVER. This reduction relies on the notion of the complement of a graph. Given an undirected graph $G = (V, E)$, we define the *complement* of G as a graph $\overline{G} = (V, \overline{E})$, where $\overline{E} = \{(u, v) : u, v \in V, u \neq v, \text{ and } (u, v) \notin E\}$. In other words, $\overline{G}$ is the graph containing exactly those edges that are not in G. Figure 34.15 shows a graph and its complement and illustrates the reduction from CLIQUE to VERTEX-COVER.

The reduction algorithm takes as input an instance $\langle G, k \rangle$ of the clique problem and computes the complement $\overline{G}$ in polynomial time. The output of the reduction algorithm is the instance $\langle \overline{G}, |V| - k \rangle$ of the vertex-cover problem. To complete the proof, we show that this transformation is indeed a reduction: the graph G contains a clique of size k if and only if the graph $\overline{G}$ has a vertex cover of size $|V| - k$.

Suppose that G contains a clique $V' \subseteq V$ with $|V'| = k$. We claim that $V - V'$ is a vertex cover in $\overline{G}$. Let (u, v) be any edge in $\overline{E}$. Then, $(u, v) \notin E$, which implies that at least one of u or v does not belong to V', since every pair of vertices in V' is connected by an edge of E. Equivalently, at least one of u or v belongs to $V - V'$, which means that edge (u, v) is covered by $V - V'$. Since (u, v) was chosen arbitrarily from $\overline{E}$, every edge of $\overline{E}$ is covered by a vertex in $V - V'$. Hence the set $V - V'$, which has size $|V| - k$, forms a vertex cover for $\overline{G}$.

Conversely, suppose that $\overline{G}$ has a vertex cover $V' \subseteq V$, where $|V'| = |V| - k$. Then for all $u, v \in V$, if $(u, v) \in \overline{E}$, then $u \in V'$ or $v \in V'$ or both. The contrapositive of this implication is that for all $u, v \in V$, if $u \notin V'$ and $v \notin V'$, then $(u, v) \in E$. In other words, $V - V'$ is a clique, and it has size $|V| - |V'| = k$. ∎

Since VERTEX-COVER is NP-complete, we don't expect to find a polynomial-time algorithm for finding a minimum-size vertex cover. Section 35.1 presents a polynomial-time "approximation algorithm," however, which produces "approximate" solutions for the vertex-cover problem. The size of a vertex cover produced by the algorithm is at most twice the minimum size of a vertex cover.

Thus, you shouldn't give up hope just because a problem is NP-complete. You might be able to design a polynomial-time approximation algorithm that obtains near-optimal solutions, even though finding an optimal solution is NP-complete. Chapter 35 gives several approximation algorithms for NP-complete problems.

34.5.3 The hamiltonian-cycle problem

We now return to the hamiltonian-cycle problem defined in Section 34.2.

Theorem 34.13
The hamiltonian cycle problem is NP-complete.

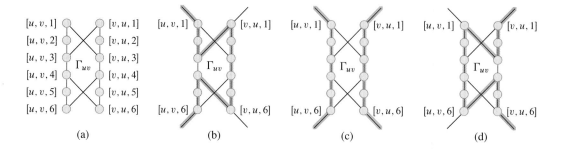

Figure 34.16 The gadget used in reducing the vertex-cover problem to the hamiltonian-cycle problem. An edge (u, v) of graph G corresponds to gadget Γ_{uv} in the graph G' created in the reduction. **(a)** The gadget, with individual vertices labeled. **(b)–(d)** The paths highlighted in blue are the only possible ones through the gadget that include all vertices, assuming that the only connections from the gadget to the remainder of G' are through vertices $[u, v, 1]$, $[u, v, 6]$, $[v, u, 1]$, and $[v, u, 6]$.

Proof We first show that HAM-CYCLE $\in$ NP. Given an undirected graph $G = (V, E)$, the certificate is the sequence of $|V|$ vertices that makes up the hamiltonian cycle. The verification algorithm checks that this sequence contains each vertex in V exactly once and that with the first vertex repeated at the end, it forms a cycle in G. That is, it checks that there is an edge between each pair of consecutive vertices and between the first and last vertices. This certificate can be verified in polynomial time.

We now prove that VERTEX-COVER $\leq_P$ HAM-CYCLE, which shows that HAM-CYCLE is NP-complete. Given an undirected graph $G = (V, E)$ and an integer k, we construct an undirected graph $G' = (V', E')$ that has a hamiltonian cycle if and only if G has a vertex cover of size k. We assume without loss of generality that G contains no isolated vertices (that is, every vertex in V has at least one incident edge) and that $k \leq |V|$. (If an isolated vertex belongs to a vertex cover of size k, then there also exists a vertex cover of size $k - 1$, and for any graph, the entire set V is always a vertex cover.)

Our construction uses a *gadget*, which is a piece of a graph that enforces certain properties. Figure 34.16(a) shows the gadget we use. For each edge $(u, v) \in E$, the constructed graph G' contains one copy of this gadget, which we denote by Γ_{uv}. We denote each vertex in Γ_{uv} by $[u, v, i]$ or $[v, u, i]$, where $1 \leq i \leq 6$, so that each gadget Γ_{uv} contains 12 vertices. Gadget Γ_{uv} also contains the 14 edges shown in Figure 34.16(a).

Along with the internal structure of the gadget, we enforce the properties we want by limiting the connections between the gadget and the remainder of the graph G' that we construct. In particular, only vertices $[u, v, 1]$, $[u, v, 6]$, $[v, u, 1]$, and $[v, u, 6]$ will have edges incident from outside Γ_{uv}. Any hamiltonian cycle of G' must traverse the edges of Γ_{uv} in one of the three ways shown in Figures 34.16(b)–(d). If the cycle enters through vertex $[u, v, 1]$, it must exit through vertex $[u, v, 6]$, and it either visits all 12 of the gadget's vertices (Figure 34.16(b)) or the six vertices $[u, v, 1]$ through $[u, v, 6]$ (Figure 34.16(c)). In the latter case, the cycle will have to reenter the gadget to visit vertices $[v, u, 1]$ through $[v, u, 6]$. Similarly, if the cycle enters through vertex $[v, u, 1]$, it must exit through vertex $[v, u, 6]$, and either it visits all 12 of the gadget's vertices (Figure 34.16(d)) or it visits the six vertices $[v, u, 1]$ through $[v, u, 6]$ and reenters to visit $[u, v, 1]$ through $[u, v, 6]$ (Figure 34.16(c)). No other paths through the gadget that visit all 12 vertices are possible. In particular, it is impossible to construct two vertex-disjoint paths, one of which connects $[u, v, 1]$ to $[v, u, 6]$ and the other of which connects $[v, u, 1]$ to $[u, v, 6]$, such that the union of the two paths contains all of the gadget's vertices.

The only other vertices in V' other than those of gadgets are **selector vertices** $s_1, s_2, \ldots, s_k$. We'll use edges incident on selector vertices in G' to select the k vertices of the cover in G.

In addition to the edges in gadgets, E' contains two other types of edges, which Figure 34.17 shows. First, for each vertex $u \in V$, edges join pairs of gadgets in order to form a path containing all gadgets corresponding to edges incident on u in G. We arbitrarily order the vertices adjacent to each vertex $u \in V$ as $u^{(1)}, u^{(2)}, \ldots, u^{(\text{degree}(u))}$, where degree$(u)$ is the number of vertices adjacent to u. To create a path in G' through all the gadgets corresponding to edges incident on u, E' contains the edges $\{([u, u^{(i)}, 6], [u, u^{(i+1)}, 1]) : 1 \leq i \leq \text{degree}(u) - 1\}$. In Figure 34.17, for example, we order the vertices adjacent to w as $\langle x, y, z \rangle$, and so graph G' in part (b) of the figure includes the edges $([w, x, 6], [w, y, 1])$ and $([w, y, 6], [w, z, 1])$. The vertices adjacent to x are ordered as $\langle w, y \rangle$, so that G' includes the edge $([x, w, 6], [x, y, 1])$. For each vertex $u \in V$, these edges in G' fill in a path containing all gadgets corresponding to edges incident on u in G.

The intuition behind these edges is that if vertex $u \in V$ belongs to the vertex cover of G, then G' contains a path from $[u, u^{(1)}, 1]$ to $[u, u^{(\text{degree}(u))}, 6]$ that "covers" all gadgets corresponding to edges incident on u. That is, for each of these gadgets, say $\Gamma_{u,u^{(i)}}$, the path either includes all 12 vertices (if u belongs to the vertex cover but $u^{(i)}$ does not) or just the six vertices $[u, u^{(i)}, 1]$ through $[u, u^{(i)}, 6]$ (if both u and $u^{(i)}$ belong to the vertex cover).

The final type of edge in E' joins the first vertex $[u, u^{(1)}, 1]$ and the last vertex $[u, u^{(\text{degree}(u))}, 6]$ of each of these paths to each of the selector vertices. That is, E' includes the edges

$$\{(s_j, [u, u^{(1)}, 1]) : u \in V \text{ and } 1 \leq j \leq k\}$$
$$\cup \{(s_j, [u, u^{(\text{degree}(u))}, 6]) : u \in V \text{ and } 1 \leq j \leq k\} .$$

(a)

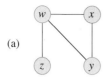

(b)

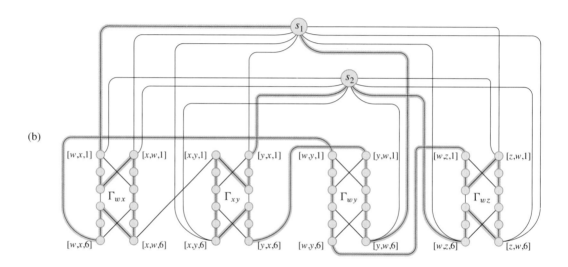

Figure 34.17 Reducing an instance of the vertex-cover problem to an instance of the hamiltonian-cycle problem. **(a)** An undirected graph G with a vertex cover of size 2, consisting of the blue vertices w and y. **(b)** The undirected graph G' produced by the reduction, with the hamiltonian cycle corresponding to the vertex cover highlighted in blue. The vertex cover $\{w, y\}$ corresponds to edges $(s_1, [w, x, 1])$ and $(s_2, [y, x, 1])$ appearing in the hamiltonian cycle.

Next we show that the size of G' is polynomial in the size of G, and hence it takes time polynomial in the size of G to construct G'. The vertices of G' are those in the gadgets, plus the selector vertices. With 12 vertices per gadget, plus $k \le |V|$ selector vertices, G' contains a total of

$$|V'| = 12\,|E| + k$$
$$\le 12\,|E| + |V|$$

vertices. The edges of G' are those in the gadgets, those that go between gadgets, and those connecting selector vertices to gadgets. Each gadget contains 14 edges, totaling $14\,|E|$ in all gadgets. For each vertex $u \in V$, graph G' has degree$(u) - 1$ edges going between gadgets, so that summed over all vertices in V,

$$\sum_{u \in V} (\mathrm{degree}(u) - 1) = 2\,|E| - |V|$$

edges go between gadgets. Finally, G' has two edges for each pair consisting of a selector vertex and a vertex of V, totaling $2k\,|V|$ such edges. The total number of edges of G' is therefore

$$
\begin{aligned}
|E'| &= (14\,|E|) + (2\,|E| - |V|) + (2k\,|V|) \\
&= 16\,|E| + (2k - 1)\,|V| \\
&\leq 16\,|E| + (2\,|V| - 1)\,|V| \ .
\end{aligned}
$$

Now we show that the transformation from graph G to G' is a reduction. That is, we must show that G has a vertex cover of size k if and only if G' has a hamiltonian cycle.

Suppose that $G = (V, E)$ has a vertex cover $V^* \subseteq V$, where $|V^*| = k$. Let $V^* = \{u_1, u_2, \ldots, u_k\}$. As Figure 34.17 shows, we can construct a hamiltonian cycle in G' by including the following edges[11] for each vertex $u_j \in V^*$. Start by including edges $\{([u_j, u_j^{(i)}, 6], [u_j, u_j^{(i+1)}, 1]) : 1 \leq i \leq \mathrm{degree}(u_j) - 1\}$, which connect all gadgets corresponding to edges incident on u_j. Also include the edges within these gadgets as Figures 34.16(b)–(d) show, depending on whether the edge is covered by one or two vertices in V^*. The hamiltonian cycle also includes the edges

$$
\begin{aligned}
\{(s_j, [u_j, u_j^{(1)}, 1]) &: 1 \leq j \leq k\} \\
\cup \{(s_{j+1}, [u_j, u_j^{(\mathrm{degree}(u_j))}, 6]) &: 1 \leq j \leq k - 1\} \\
\cup \{(s_1, [u_k, u_k^{(\mathrm{degree}(u_k))}, 6])\} \ .
\end{aligned}
$$

By inspecting Figure 34.17, you can verify that these edges form a cycle, where $u_1 = w$ and $u_2 = y$. The cycle starts at s_1, visits all gadgets corresponding to edges incident on u_1, then visits s_2, visits all gadgets corresponding to edges incident on u_2, and so on, until it returns to s_1. The cycle visits each gadget either once or twice, depending on whether one or two vertices of V^* cover its corresponding edge. Because V^* is a vertex cover for G, each edge in E is incident on some vertex in V^*, and so the cycle visits each vertex in each gadget of G'. Because the cycle also visits every selector vertex, it is hamiltonian.

Conversely, suppose that $G' = (V', E')$ contains a hamiltonian cycle $C \subseteq E'$. We claim that the set

$$V^* = \{u \in V : (s_j, [u, u^{(1)}, 1]) \in C \text{ for some } 1 \leq j \leq k\} \tag{34.4}$$

---

[11] Technically, a cycle is defined as a sequence of vertices rather than edges (see Section B.4). In the interest of clarity, we abuse notation here and define the hamiltonian cycle by its edges.

is a vertex cover for G.

We first argue that the set V^* is well defined, that is, for each selector vertex s_j, exactly one of the incident edges in the hamiltonian cycle C is of the form $(s_j, [u, u^{(1)}, 1])$ for some vertex $u \in V$. To see why, partition the hamiltonian cycle C into maximal paths that start at some selector vertex s_i, visit one or more gadgets, and end at some selector vertex s_j without passing through any other selector vertex. Let's call each of these maximal paths a "cover path." Let P be one such cover path, and orient it going from s_i to s_j. If P contains the edge $(s_i, [u, u^{(1)}, 1])$ for some vertex $u \in V$, then we have shown that one edge incident on s_i has the required form. Assume, then, that P contains the edge $(s_i, [v, v^{(\text{degree}(v))}, 6])$ for some vertex $v \in V$. This path enters a gadget from the bottom, as drawn in Figures 34.16 and 34.17, and it leaves from the top. It might go through several gadgets, but it always enters from the bottom of a gadget and leaves from the top. The only edges incident on vertices at the top of a gadget either go to the bottoms of other gadgets or to selector vertices. Therefore, after the last gadget in the series of gadgets visited by P, the edge taken must go to a selector vertex s_j, so that P contains an edge of the form $(s_j, [u, u^{(1)}, 1])$, where $[u, u^{(1)}, 1]$ is a vertex at the top of some gadget. To see that not both edges incident on s_j have this form, simply reverse the direction of traversing P in the above argument.

Having established that the set V^* is well defined, let's see why it is a vertex cover for G. We have already established that each cover path starts at some s_i, takes the edge $(s_i, [u, u^{(1)}, 1])$ for some vertex $u \in V$, passes through all the gadgets corresponding to edges in E incident on u, and then ends at some selector vertex s_j. (This orientation is the reverse of the orientation in the paragraph above.) Let's call this cover path P_u, and by equation (34.4), the vertex cover V^* includes u. Each gadget visited by P_u must be Γ_{uv} or Γ_{vu} for some $v \in V$. For each gadget visited by P_u, its vertices are visited by either one or two cover paths. If they are visited by one cover path, then edge $(u, v) \in E$ is covered in G by vertex u. If two cover paths visit the gadget, then the other cover path must be P_v, which implies that $v \in V^*$, and edge $(u, v) \in E$ is covered by both u and v. Because each vertex in each gadget is visited by some cover path, we see that each edge in E is covered by some vertex in V^*.   ∎

34.5.4   The traveling-salesperson problem

In the *traveling-salesperson problem*, which is closely related to the hamiltonian-cycle problem, a salesperson must visit n cities. Let's model the problem as a complete graph with n vertices, so that the salesperson wishes to make a *tour*, or hamiltonian cycle, visiting each city exactly once and finishing at the starting city. The salesperson incurs a nonnegative integer cost $c(i, j)$ to travel from city i

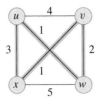

Figure 34.18 An instance of the traveling-salesperson problem. Edges highlighted in blue represent a minimum-cost tour, with cost 7.

to city j. In the optimization version of the problem, the salesperson wishes to make the tour whose total cost is minimum, where the total cost is the sum of the individual costs along the edges of the tour. For example, in Figure 34.18, a minimum-cost tour is $\langle u, w, v, x, u \rangle$, with cost 7. The formal language for the corresponding decision problem is

$$
\begin{aligned}
\text{TSP} = \{ \langle G, c, k \rangle : \ &G = (V, E) \text{ is a complete graph,} \\
&c \text{ is a function from } V \times V \to \mathbb{N}, \\
&k \in \mathbb{N}, \text{ and} \\
&G \text{ has a traveling-salesperson tour with cost at most } k \}.
\end{aligned}
$$

The following theorem shows that a fast algorithm for the traveling-salesperson problem is unlikely to exist.

Theorem 34.14
The traveling-salesperson problem is NP-complete.

Proof We first show that TSP $\in$ NP. Given an instance of the problem, the certificate is the sequence of n vertices in the tour. The verification algorithm checks that this sequence contains each vertex exactly once, sums up the edge costs, and checks that the sum is at most k. This process can certainly be done in polynomial time.

To prove that TSP is NP-hard, we show that HAM-CYCLE $\leq_P$ TSP. Given an instance $G = (V, E)$ of HAM-CYCLE, construct an instance of TSP by forming the complete graph $G' = (V, E')$, where $E' = \{(i, j) : i, j \in V \text{ and } i \neq j\}$, with the cost function c defined as

$$
c(i, j) = \begin{cases} 0 & \text{if } (i, j) \in E, \\ 1 & \text{if } (i, j) \notin E. \end{cases}
$$

(Because G is undirected, it contains no self-loops, and so $c(v, v) = 1$ for all vertices $v \in V$.) The instance of TSP is then $\langle G', c, 0 \rangle$, which can be created in polynomial time.

We now show that graph G has a hamiltonian cycle if and only if graph G' has a tour of cost at most 0. Suppose that graph G has a hamiltonian cycle H. Each edge in H belongs to E and thus has cost 0 in G'. Thus, H is a tour in G' with cost 0. Conversely, suppose that graph G' has a tour H' of cost at most 0. Since the costs of the edges in E' are 0 and 1, the cost of tour H' is exactly 0 and each edge on the tour must have cost 0. Therefore, H' contains only edges in E. We conclude that H' is a hamiltonian cycle in graph G.   ∎

34.5.5 The subset-sum problem

We next consider an arithmetic NP-complete problem. The *subset-sum problem* takes as inputs a finite set S of positive integers and an integer *target* $t > 0$. It asks whether there exists a subset $S' \subseteq S$ whose elements sum to exactly t. For example, if $S = \{1, 2, 7, 14, 49, 98, 343, 686, 2409, 2793, 16808, 17206, 117705, 117993\}$ and $t = 138457$, then the subset $S' = \{1, 2, 7, 98, 343, 686, 2409, 17206, 117705\}$ is a solution.

As usual, we express the problem as a language:

$$\text{SUBSET-SUM} = \left\{ \langle S, t \rangle : \text{there exists a subset } S' \subseteq S \text{ such that } t = \sum_{s \in S'} s \right\} .$$

As with any arithmetic problem, it is important to recall that our standard encoding assumes that the input integers are coded in binary. With this assumption in mind, we can show that the subset-sum problem is unlikely to have a fast algorithm.

Theorem 34.15
The subset-sum problem is NP-complete.

Proof To show that SUBSET-SUM $\in$ NP, for an instance $\langle S, t \rangle$ of the problem, let the subset S' be the certificate. A verification algorithm can check whether $t = \sum_{s \in S'} s$ in polynomial time.

We now show that 3-CNF-SAT $\leq_P$ SUBSET-SUM. Given a 3-CNF formula ϕ over variables $x_1, x_2, \ldots, x_n$ with clauses $C_1, C_2, \ldots, C_k$, each containing exactly three distinct literals, the reduction algorithm constructs an instance $\langle S, t \rangle$ of the subset-sum problem such that ϕ is satisfiable if and only if there exists a subset of S whose sum is exactly t. Without loss of generality, we make two simplifying assumptions about the formula ϕ. First, no clause contains both a variable and its negation, for such a clause is automatically satisfied by any assignment of values to the variables. Second, each variable appears in at least one clause, because it does not matter what value is assigned to a variable that appears in no clauses.

The reduction creates two numbers in set S for each variable x_i and two numbers in S for each clause C_j. The numbers will be represented in base 10, with each number containing $n + k$ digits and each digit corresponding to either one variable

		x_1	x_2	x_3	C_1	C_2	C_3	C_4
v_1	=	1	0	0	1	0	0	1
v_1'	=	1	0	0	0	1	1	0
v_2	=	0	1	0	0	0	0	1
v_2'	=	0	1	0	1	1	1	0
v_3	=	0	0	1	0	0	1	1
v_3'	=	0	0	1	1	1	0	0
s_1	=	0	0	0	1	0	0	0
s_1'	=	0	0	0	2	0	0	0
s_2	=	0	0	0	0	1	0	0
s_2'	=	0	0	0	0	2	0	0
s_3	=	0	0	0	0	0	1	0
s_3'	=	0	0	0	0	0	2	0
s_4	=	0	0	0	0	0	0	1
s_4'	=	0	0	0	0	0	0	2
t	=	1	1	1	4	4	4	4

Figure 34.19   The reduction of 3-CNF-SAT to SUBSET-SUM. The formula in 3-CNF is $\phi = C_1 \wedge C_2 \wedge C_3 \wedge C_4$, where $C_1 = (x_1 \vee \neg x_2 \vee \neg x_3)$, $C_2 = (\neg x_1 \vee \neg x_2 \vee \neg x_3)$, $C_3 = (\neg x_1 \vee \neg x_2 \vee x_3)$, and $C_4 = (x_1 \vee x_2 \vee x_3)$. A satisfying assignment of ϕ is $\langle x_1 = 0, x_2 = 0, x_3 = 1 \rangle$. The set S produced by the reduction consists of the base-10 numbers shown: reading from top to bottom, $S = \{1001001, 1000110, 100001, 101110, 10011, 11100, 1000, 2000, 100, 200, 10, 20, 1, 2\}$. The target t is 1114444. The subset $S' \subseteq S$ is shaded blue, and it contains v_1', v_2', and v_3, corresponding to the satisfying assignment. Subset S' also contains slack variables $s_1, s_1', s_2', s_3, s_4$, and s_4' to achieve the target value of 4 in the digits labeled by C_1 through C_4.

or one clause. Base 10 (and other bases, as we shall see) has the property we need of preventing carries from lower digits to higher digits.

As Figure 34.19 shows, we construct set S and target t as follows. Label each digit position by either a variable or a clause. The least significant k digits are labeled by the clauses, and the most significant n digits are labeled by variables.

- The target t has a 1 in each digit labeled by a variable and a 4 in each digit labeled by a clause.

- For each variable x_i, set S contains two integers v_i and v_i'. Each of v_i and v_i' has a 1 in the digit labeled by x_i and 0s in the other variable digits. If literal x_i appears in clause C_j, then the digit labeled by C_j in v_i contains a 1. If literal $\neg x_i$ appears in clause C_j, then the digit labeled by C_j in v_i' contains a 1. All other digits labeled by clauses in v_i and v_i' are 0.

All v_i and v_i' values in set S are unique. Why? For $\ell \neq i$, no v_ℓ or v_ℓ' values can equal v_i and v_i' in the most significant n digits. Furthermore, by our simplifying assumptions above, no v_i and v_i' can be equal in all k least significant digits. If v_i and v_i' were equal, then x_i and $\neg x_i$ would have to appear in exactly the same set of clauses. But we assume that no clause contains both x_i and $\neg x_i$ and that either x_i or $\neg x_i$ appears in some clause, and so there must be some clause C_j for which v_i and v_i' differ.

- For each clause C_j, set S contains two integers s_j and s_j'. Each of s_j and s_j' has 0s in all digits other than the one labeled by C_j. For s_j, there is a 1 in the C_j digit, and s_j' has a 2 in this digit. These integers are "slack variables," which we use to get each clause-labeled digit position to add to the target value of 4.

  Simple inspection of Figure 34.19 demonstrates that all s_j and s_j' values in S are unique in set S.

The greatest sum of digits in any one digit position is 6, which occurs in the digits labeled by clauses (three 1s from the v_i and v_i' values, plus 1 and 2 from the s_j and s_j' values). Interpreting these numbers in base 10, therefore, no carries can occur from lower digits to higher digits.[12]

The reduction can be performed in polynomial time. The set S consists of $2n + 2k$ values, each of which has $n + k$ digits, and the time to produce each digit is polynomial in $n + k$. The target t has $n + k$ digits, and the reduction produces each in constant time.

Let's now show that the 3-CNF formula ϕ is satisfiable if and only if there exists a subset $S' \subseteq S$ whose sum is t. First, suppose that ϕ has a satisfying assignment. For $i = 1, 2, \ldots, n$, if $x_i = 1$ in this assignment, then include v_i in S'. Otherwise, include v_i'. In other words, S' includes exactly the v_i and v_i' values that correspond to literals with the value 1 in the satisfying assignment. Having included either v_i or v_i', but not both, for all i, and having put 0 in the digits labeled by variables in all s_j and s_j', we see that for each variable-labeled digit, the sum of the values of S' must be 1, which matches those digits of the target t. Because each clause is satisfied, the clause contains some literal with the value 1. Therefore, each digit labeled by a clause has at least one 1 contributed to its sum by a v_i or v_i' value in S'. In fact, one, two, or three literals may be 1 in each clause, and so each clause-labeled digit has a sum of 1, 2, or 3 from the v_i and v_i' values in S'. In Figure 34.19 for example, literals $\neg x_1, \neg x_2$, and x_3 have the value 1 in a satisfying assignment. Each of clauses C_1 and C_4 contains exactly one of these literals, and so together v_1', v_2', and v_3 contribute 1 to the sum in the digits for C_1 and C_4.

---

[12] In fact, any base $b \geq 7$ works. The instance at the beginning of this subsection is the set S and target t in Figure 34.19 interpreted in base 7, with S listed in sorted order.

Clause C_2 contains two of these literals, and v_1', v_2', and v_3 contribute 2 to the sum in the digit for C_2. Clause C_3 contains all three of these literals, and v_1', v_2', and v_3 contribute 3 to the sum in the digit for C_3. To achieve the target of 4 in each digit labeled by clause C_j, include in S' the appropriate nonempty subset of slack variables $\{s_j, s_j'\}$. In Figure 34.19, S' includes s_1, s_1', s_2', s_3, s_4, and s_4'. Since S' matches the target in all digits of the sum, and no carries can occur, the values of S' sum to t.

Now suppose that some subset $S' \subseteq S$ sums to t. The subset S' must include exactly one of v_i and v_i' for each $i = 1, 2, \ldots, n$, for otherwise the digits labeled by variables would not sum to 1. If $v_i \in S'$, then set $x_i = 1$. Otherwise, $v_i' \in S'$, and set $x_i = 0$. We claim that every clause C_j, for $j = 1, 2, \ldots, k$, is satisfied by this assignment. To prove this claim, note that to achieve a sum of 4 in the digit labeled by C_j, the subset S' must include at least one v_i or v_i' value that has a 1 in the digit labeled by C_j, since the contributions of the slack variables s_j and s_j' together sum to at most 3. If S' includes a v_i that has a 1 in C_j's position, then the literal x_i appears in clause C_j. Since $x_i = 1$ when $v_i \in S'$, clause C_j is satisfied. If S' includes a v_i' that has a 1 in that position, then the literal $\neg x_i$ appears in C_j. Since $x_i = 0$ when $v_i' \in S'$, clause C_j is again satisfied. Thus, all clauses of ϕ are satisfied, which completes the proof. ■

34.5.6 Reduction strategies

From the reductions in this section, you can see that no single strategy applies to all NP-complete problems. Some reductions are straightforward, such as reducing the hamiltonian-cycle problem to the traveling-salesperson problem. Others are considerably more complicated. Here are a few things to keep in mind and some strategies that you can often bring to bear.

Pitfalls

Make sure that you don't get the reduction backward. That is, in trying to show that problem Y is NP-complete, you might take a known NP-complete problem X and give a polynomial-time reduction from Y to X. That is the wrong direction. The reduction should be from X to Y, so that a solution to Y gives a solution to X.

Remember also that reducing a known NP-complete problem X to a problem Y does not in itself prove that Y is NP-complete. It proves that Y is NP-hard. In order to show that Y is NP-complete, you additionally need to prove that it's in NP by showing how to verify a certificate for Y in polynomial time.

Go from general to specific

When reducing problem X to problem Y, you always have to start with an arbitrary input to problem X. But you are allowed to restrict the input to problem Y as much as you like. For example, when reducing 3-CNF satisfiability to the subset-sum problem, the reduction had to be able to handle *any* 3-CNF formula as its input, but the input to the subset-sum problem that it produced had a particular structure: $2n + 2k$ integers in the set, and each integer was formed in a particular way. The reduction did not need to produce *every* possible input to the subset-sum problem. The point is that one way to solve the 3-CNF satisfiability problem transforms the input into an input to the subset-sum problem and then uses the answer to the subset-sum problem as the answer to the 3-CNF satisfiability problem.

Take advantage of structure in the problem you are reducing from

When you are choosing a problem to reduce from, you might consider two problems in the same domain, but one problem has more structure than the other. For example, it's almost always much easier to reduce from 3-CNF satisfiability than to reduce from formula satisfiability. Boolean formulas can be arbitrarily complicated, but you can exploit the structure of 3-CNF formulas when reducing.

Likewise, it is usually more straightforward to reduce from the hamiltonian-cycle problem than from the traveling-salesperson problem, even though they are so similar. That's because you can view the hamiltonian-cycle problem as taking a complete graph but with edge weights of just 0 or 1, as they would appear in the adjacency matrix. In that sense, the hamiltonian-cycle problem has more structure than the traveling-salesperson problem, in which edge weights are unrestricted.

Look for special cases

Several NP-complete problems are just special cases of other NP-complete problems. For example, consider the decision version of the 0-1 knapsack problem: given a set of n items, each with a weight and a value, does there exist a subset of items whose total weight is at most a given weight W and whose total value is at least a given value V? You can view the set-partition problem in Exercise 34.5-5 as a special case of the 0-1 knapsack problem: let the value of each item equal its weight, and set both W and V to half the total weight. If problem X is NP-hard and it is a special case of problem Y, then problem Y must be NP-hard as well. That is because a polynomial-time solution for problem Y automatically gives a polynomial-time solution for problem X. More intuitively, problem Y, being more general than problem X, is at least as hard.

Select an appropriate problem to reduce from

It's often a good strategy to reduce from a problem in a domain that is the same as, or at least related to, the domain of the problem that you're trying to prove NP-complete. For example, we saw that the vertex-cover problem—a graph problem—was NP-hard by reducing from the clique problem—also a graph problem. From the vertex-cover problem, we reduced to the hamiltonian-cycle problem, and from the hamiltonian-cycle problem, we reduced to the traveling-salesperson problem. All of these problems take undirected graphs as inputs.

Sometimes, however, you will find that is it better to cross over from one domain to another, such as when we reduced from 3-CNF satisfiability to the clique problem or to the subset-sum problem. 3-CNF satisfiability often turns out to be a good choice as a problem to reduce from when crossing domains.

Within graph problems, if you need to select a portion of the graph, without regard to ordering, then the vertex-cover problem is often a good place to start. If ordering matters, then consider starting from the hamiltonian-cycle or hamiltonian-path problem (see Exercise 34.5-6).

Make big rewards and big penalties

The strategy for reducing the hamiltonian-cycle problem with a graph G to the traveling-salesperson problem encouraged using edges present in G when choosing edges for the traveling-salesperson tour. The reduction did so by giving these edges a low weight: 0. In other words, we gave a big reward for using these edges.

Alternatively, the reduction could have given the edges in G a finite weight and given edges not in G infinite weight, thereby exacting a hefty penalty for using edges not in G. With this approach, if each edge in G has weight W, then the target weight of the traveling-salesperson tour becomes $W \cdot |V|$. You can sometimes think of the penalties as a way to enforce requirements. For example, if the traveling-salesperson tour includes an edge with infinite weight, then it violates the requirement that the tour should include only edges belonging to G.

Design gadgets

The reduction from the vertex-cover problem to the hamiltonian-cycle problem uses the gadget shown in Figure 34.16. This gadget is a subgraph that is connected to other parts of the constructed graph in order to restrict the ways that a cycle can visit each vertex in the gadget once. More generally, a gadget is a component that enforces certain properties. Gadgets can be complicated, as in the reduction to the hamiltonian-cycle problem. Or they can be simple: in the reduction of 3-CNF satisfiability to the subset-sum problem, you can view the slack variables s_j and s'_j

as gadgets enabling each clause-labeled digit position to achieve the target value of 4.

Exercises

34.5-1
The *subgraph-isomorphism problem* takes two undirected graphs G_1 and G_2, and asks whether G_1 is isomorphic to a subgraph of G_2. Show that the subgraph-isomorphism problem is NP-complete.

34.5-2
Given an integer $m \times n$ matrix A and an integer m-vector b, the *0-1 integer-programming problem* asks whether there exists an integer n-vector x with elements in the set $\{0, 1\}$ such that $Ax \leq b$. Prove that 0-1 integer programming is NP-complete. (*Hint:* Reduce from 3-CNF-SAT.)

34.5-3
The *integer linear-programming problem* is like the 0-1 integer-programming problem given in Exercise 34.5-2, except that the values of the vector x may be any integers rather than just 0 or 1. Assuming that the 0-1 integer-programming problem is NP-hard, show that the integer linear-programming problem is NP-complete.

34.5-4
Show how to solve the subset-sum problem in polynomial time if the target value t is expressed in unary.

34.5-5
The *set-partition problem* takes as input a set S of numbers. The question is whether the numbers can be partitioned into two sets A and $\overline{A} = S - A$ such that $\sum_{x \in A} x = \sum_{x \in \overline{A}} x$. Show that the set-partition problem is NP-complete.

34.5-6
Show that the hamiltonian-path problem is NP-complete.

34.5-7
The *longest-simple-cycle problem* is the problem of determining a simple cycle (no repeated vertices) of maximum length in a graph. Formulate a related decision problem, and show that the decision problem is NP-complete.

34.5-8

In the *half 3-CNF satisfiability* problem, the input is a 3-CNF formula ϕ with n variables and m clauses, where m is even. The question is whether there exists a truth assignment to the variables of ϕ such that exactly half the clauses evaluate to 0 and exactly half the clauses evaluate to 1. Prove that the half 3-CNF satisfiability problem is NP-complete.

34.5-9

The proof that VERTEX-COVER $\leq_P$ HAM-CYCLE assumes that the graph G given as input to the vertex-cover problem has no isolated vertices. Show how the reduction in the proof can break down if G has an isolated vertex.

Problems

34-1 *Independent set*

An *independent set* of a graph $G = (V, E)$ is a subset $V' \subseteq V$ of vertices such that each edge in E is incident on at most one vertex in V'. The *independent-set problem* is to find a maximum-size independent set in G.

a. Formulate a related decision problem for the independent-set problem, and prove that it is NP-complete. (*Hint:* Reduce from the clique problem.)

b. You are given a "black-box" subroutine to solve the decision problem you defined in part (a). Give an algorithm to find an independent set of maximum size. The running time of your algorithm should be polynomial in $|V|$ and $|E|$, counting queries to the black box as a single step.

Although the independent-set decision problem is NP-complete, certain special cases are polynomial-time solvable.

c. Give an efficient algorithm to solve the independent-set problem when each vertex in G has degree 2. Analyze the running time, and prove that your algorithm works correctly.

d. Give an efficient algorithm to solve the independent-set problem when G is bipartite. Analyze the running time, and prove that your algorithm works correctly. (*Hint:* First prove that in a bipartite graph, the size of the maximimum independent set plus the size of the maximum matching is equal to $|V|$. Then use a maximum-matching algorithm (see Section 25.1) as a first step in an algorithm to find an independent set.)

34-2 *Bonnie and Clyde*

Bonnie and Clyde have just robbed a bank. They have a bag of money and want to divide it up. For each of the following scenarios, either give a polynomial-time algorithm to divide the money or prove that the problem of dividing the money in the manner described is NP-complete. The input in each case is a list of the n items in the bag, along with the value of each.

a. The bag contains n coins, but only two different denominations: some coins are worth x dollars, and some are worth y dollars. Bonnie and Clyde wish to divide the money exactly evenly.

b. The bag contains n coins, with an arbitrary number of different denominations, but each denomination is a nonnegative exact power of 2, so that the possible denominations are 1 dollar, 2 dollars, 4 dollars, etc. Bonnie and Clyde wish to divide the money exactly evenly.

c. The bag contains n checks, which are, in an amazing coincidence, made out to "Bonnie or Clyde." They wish to divide the checks so that they each get the exact same amount of money.

d. The bag contains n checks as in part (c), but this time Bonnie and Clyde are willing to accept a split in which the difference is no larger than 100 dollars.

34-3 *Graph coloring*

Mapmakers try to use as few colors as possible when coloring countries on a map, subject to the restriction that if two countries share a border, they must have different colors. You can model this problem with an undirected graph $G = (V, E)$ in which each vertex represents a country and vertices whose respective countries share a border are adjacent. Then, a *k-coloring* is a function $c : V \rightarrow \{1, 2, \ldots, k\}$ such that $c(u) \neq c(v)$ for every edge $(u, v) \in E$. In other words, the numbers $1, 2, \ldots, k$ represent the k colors, and adjacent vertices must have different colors. The *graph-coloring problem* is to determine the minimum number of colors needed to color a given graph.

a. Give an efficient algorithm to determine a 2-coloring of a graph, if one exists.

b. Cast the graph-coloring problem as a decision problem. Show that your decision problem is solvable in polynomial time if and only if the graph-coloring problem is solvable in polynomial time.

c. Let the language 3-COLOR be the set of graphs that can be 3-colored. Show that if 3-COLOR is NP-complete, then your decision problem from part (b) is NP-complete.

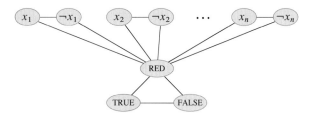

Figure 34.20 The subgraph of G in Problem 34-3 formed by the literal edges. The special vertices TRUE, FALSE, and RED form a triangle, and for each variable x_i, the vertices x_i, $\neg x_i$, and RED form a triangle.

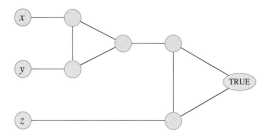

Figure 34.21 The gadget corresponding to a clause $(x \vee y \vee z)$, used in Problem 34-3.

To prove that 3-COLOR is NP-complete, you can reduce from 3-CNF-SAT. Given a formula ϕ of m clauses on n variables $x_1, x_2, \ldots, x_n$, construct a graph $G = (V, E)$ as follows. The set V consists of a vertex for each variable, a vertex for the negation of each variable, five vertices for each clause, and three special vertices: TRUE, FALSE, and RED. The edges of the graph are of two types: "literal" edges that are independent of the clauses and "clause" edges that depend on the clauses. As Figure 34.20 shows, the literal edges form a triangle on the three special vertices TRUE, FALSE, and RED, and they also form a triangle on x_i, $\neg x_i$, and RED for $i = 1, 2, \ldots, n$.

d. Consider a graph containing the literal edges. Argue that in any 3-coloring c of such a graph, exactly one of a variable and its negation is colored $c(\text{TRUE})$ and the other is colored $c(\text{FALSE})$. Then argue that for any truth assignment for ϕ, there exists a 3-coloring of the graph containing just the literal edges.

The gadget shown in Figure 34.21 helps to enforce the condition corresponding to a clause $(x \vee y \vee z)$, where x, y, and z are literals. Each clause requires a unique copy of the five blue vertices in the figure. They connect as shown to the literals of the clause and the special vertex TRUE.

e. Argue that if each of x, y, and z is colored $c(\text{TRUE})$ or $c(\text{FALSE})$, then the gadget is 3-colorable if and only if at least one of x, y, or z is colored $c(\text{TRUE})$.

f. Complete the proof that 3-COLOR is NP-complete.

34-4   Scheduling with profits and deadlines

You have one computer and a set of n tasks $\{a_1, a_2, \ldots, a_n\}$ requiring time on the computer. Each task a_j requires t_j time units on the computer (its processing time), yields a profit of p_j, and has a deadline d_j. The computer can process only one task at a time, and task a_j must run without interruption for t_j consecutive time units. If task a_j completes by its deadline d_j, you receive a profit p_j. If instead task a_j completes after its deadline, you receive no profit. As an optimization problem, given the processing times, profits, and deadlines for a set of n tasks, you wish to find a schedule that completes all the tasks and returns the greatest amount of profit. The processing times, profits, and deadlines are all nonnegative numbers.

a. State this problem as a decision problem.

b. Show that the decision problem is NP-complete.

c. Give a polynomial-time algorithm for the decision problem, assuming that all processing times are integers from 1 to n. (*Hint:* Use dynamic programming.)

d. Give a polynomial-time algorithm for the optimization problem, assuming that all processing times are integers from 1 to n.

Chapter notes

The book by Garey and Johnson [176] provides a wonderful guide to NP-completeness, discussing the theory at length and providing a catalogue of many problems that were known to be NP-complete in 1979. The proof of Theorem 34.13 is adapted from their book, and the list of NP-complete problem domains at the beginning of Section 34.5 is drawn from their table of contents. Johnson wrote a series of 23 columns in the *Journal of Algorithms* between 1981 and 1992 reporting new developments in NP-completeness. Fortnow's book [152] gives a history of NP-completeness, along with societal implications. Hopcroft, Motwani, and Ullman [225], Lewis and Papadimitriou [299], Papadimitriou [352], and Sipser [413] have good treatments of NP-completeness in the context of complexity theory. NP-completeness and several reductions also appear in books by Aho, Hopcroft, and Ullman [5], Dasgupta, Papadimitriou, and Vazirani [107], Johnsonbaugh and

Schaefer [239], and Kleinberg and Tardos [257]. The book by Hromkovič [229] studies various methods for solving hard problems.

The class P was introduced in 1964 by Cobham [96] and, independently, in 1965 by Edmonds [130], who also introduced the class NP and conjectured that $P \neq NP$. The notion of NP-completeness was proposed in 1971 by Cook [100], who gave the first NP-completeness proofs for formula satisfiability and 3-CNF satisfiability. Levin [297] independently discovered the notion, giving an NP-completeness proof for a tiling problem. Karp [248] introduced the methodology of reductions in 1972 and demonstrated the rich variety of NP-complete problems. Karp's paper included the original NP-completeness proofs of the clique, vertex-cover, and hamiltonian-cycle problems. Since then, thousands of problems have been proven to be NP-complete by many researchers.

Work in complexity theory has shed light on the complexity of computing approximate solutions. This work gives a new definition of NP using "probabilistically checkable proofs." This new definition implies that for problems such as clique, vertex cover, the traveling-salesperson problem with the triangle inequality, and many others, computing good approximate solutions (see Chapter 35) is NP-hard and hence no easier than computing optimal solutions. An introduction to this area can be found in Arora's thesis [21], a chapter by Arora and Lund in Hochbaum [221], a survey article by Arora [22], a book edited by Mayr, Prömel, and Steger [319], a survey article by Johnson [237], and a chapter in the textbook by Arora and Barak [24].

35 Approximation Algorithms

Many problems of practical significance are NP-complete, yet they are too important to abandon merely because nobody knows how to find an optimal solution in polynomial time. Even if a problem is NP-complete, there may be hope. You have at least three options to get around NP-completeness. First, if the actual inputs are small, an algorithm with exponential running time might be fast enough. Second, you might be able to isolate important special cases that you can solve in polynomial time. Third, you can try to devise an approach to find a *near-optimal* solution in polynomial time (either in the worst case or the expected case). In practice, near-optimality is often good enough. We call an algorithm that returns near-optimal solutions an *approximation algorithm*. This chapter presents polynomial-time approximation algorithms for several NP-complete problems.

Performance ratios for approximation algorithms

Suppose that you are working on an optimization problem in which each potential solution has a positive cost, and you want to find a near-optimal solution. Depending on the problem, you could define an optimal solution as one with maximum possible cost or as one with minimum possible cost, which is to say that the problem might be either a maximization or a minimization problem.

We say that an algorithm for a problem has an *approximation ratio* of $\rho(n)$ if, for any input of size n, the cost C of the solution produced by the algorithm is within a factor of $\rho(n)$ of the cost C^* of an optimal solution:

$$\max \left\{ \frac{C}{C^*}, \frac{C^*}{C} \right\} \le \rho(n) . \tag{35.1}$$

If an algorithm achieves an approximation ratio of $\rho(n)$, we call it a $\rho(n)$-*approximation algorithm*. The definitions of approximation ratio and $\rho(n)$-approximation algorithm apply to both minimization and maximization problems. For a maximization problem, $0 < C \le C^*$, and the ratio C^*/C gives the factor by which the cost of an optimal solution is larger than the cost of the approximate solution. Similarly, for a minimization problem, $0 < C^* \leq C$, and the ratio C/C^* gives the factor by which the cost of the approximate solution is larger than the cost of an optimal solution. Because we assume that all solutions have positive cost, these ratios are always well defined. The approximation ratio of an approximation algorithm is never less than 1, since $C/C^* \leq 1$ implies $C^*/C \geq 1$. Therefore, a 1-approximation algorithm[1] produces an optimal solution, and an approximation algorithm with a large approximation ratio may return a solution that is much worse than optimal.

For many problems, we know of polynomial-time approximation algorithms with small constant approximation ratios, although for other problems, the best known polynomial-time approximation algorithms have approximation ratios that grow as functions of the input size n. An example of such a problem is the set-cover problem presented in Section 35.3.

Some polynomial-time approximation algorithms can achieve increasingly better approximation ratios by using more and more computation time. For such problems, you can trade computation time for the quality of the approximation. An example is the subset-sum problem studied in Section 35.5. This situation is important enough to deserve a name of its own.

An *approximation scheme* for an optimization problem is an approximation algorithm that takes as input not only an instance of the problem, but also a value $\epsilon > 0$ such that for any fixed ϵ, the scheme is a $(1 + \epsilon)$-approximation algorithm. We say that an approximation scheme is a *polynomial-time approximation scheme* if for any fixed $\epsilon > 0$, the scheme runs in time polynomial in the size n of its input instance.

The running time of a polynomial-time approximation scheme can increase very rapidly as ϵ decreases. For example, the running time of a polynomial-time approximation scheme might be $O(n^{2/\epsilon})$. Ideally, if ϵ decreases by a constant factor, the running time to achieve the desired approximation should not increase by more than a constant factor (though not necessarily the same constant factor by which ϵ decreased).

We say that an approximation scheme is a *fully polynomial-time approximation scheme* if it is an approximation scheme and its running time is polynomial in both $1/\epsilon$ and the size n of the input instance. For example, the scheme might have a running time of $O((1/\epsilon)^2 n^3)$. With such a scheme, any constant-factor decrease in ϵ comes with a corresponding constant-factor increase in the running time.

---

[1] When the approximation ratio is independent of n, we use the terms "approximation ratio of ρ" and "ρ-approximation algorithm," indicating no dependence on n.

Chapter outline

The first four sections of this chapter present some examples of polynomial-time approximation algorithms for NP-complete problems, and the fifth section gives a fully polynomial-time approximation scheme. We begin in Section 35.1 with a study of the vertex-cover problem, an NP-complete minimization problem that has an approximation algorithm with an approximation ratio of 2. Section 35.2 looks at a version of the traveling-salesperson problem in which the cost function satisfies the triangle inequality and presents an approximation algorithm with an approximation ratio of 2. The section also shows that without the triangle inequality, for any constant $\rho \geq 1$, a ρ-approximation algorithm cannot exist unless P = NP. Section 35.3 applies a greedy method as an effective approximation algorithm for the set-covering problem, obtaining a covering whose cost is at worst a logarithmic factor larger than the optimal cost. Section 35.4 uses randomization and linear programming to develop two more approximation algorithms. The section first defines the optimization version of 3-CNF satisfiability and gives a simple randomized algorithm that produces a solution with an expected approximation ratio of 8/7. Then Section 35.4 examines a weighted variant of the vertex-cover problem and exhibits how to use linear programming to develop a 2-approximation algorithm. Finally, Section 35.5 presents a fully polynomial-time approximation scheme for the subset-sum problem.

35.1   The vertex-cover problem

Section 34.5.2 defined the vertex-cover problem and proved it NP-complete. Recall that a *vertex cover* of an undirected graph $G = (V, E)$ is a subset $V' \subseteq V$ such that if (u, v) is an edge of G, then either $u \in V'$ or $v \in V'$ (or both). The size of a vertex cover is the number of vertices in it.

The *vertex-cover problem* is to find a vertex cover of minimum size in a given undirected graph. We call such a vertex cover an *optimal vertex cover*. This problem is the optimization version of an NP-complete decision problem.

Even though nobody knows how to find an optimal vertex cover in a graph G in polynomial time, there is an efficient algorithm to find a vertex cover that is near-optimal. The approximation algorithm APPROX-VERTEX-COVER on the facing page takes as input an undirected graph G and returns a vertex cover whose size is guaranteed to be no more than twice the size of an optimal vertex cover.

Figure 35.1 illustrates how APPROX-VERTEX-COVER operates on an example graph. The variable C contains the vertex cover being constructed. Line 1 initializes C to the empty set. Line 2 sets E' to be a copy of the edge set $G.E$ of the graph. The **while** loop of lines 3–6 repeatedly picks an edge (u, v) from E', adds

```
APPROX-VERTEX-COVER(G)
1  C = ∅
2  E' = G.E
3  while E' ≠ ∅
4      let (u, v) be an arbitrary edge of E'
5      C = C ∪ {u, v}
6      remove from E' edge (u, v) and every edge incident on either u or v
7  return C
```

its endpoints u and v into C, and deletes all edges in E' that u or v covers. Finally, line 7 returns the vertex cover C. The running time of this algorithm is $O(V + E)$, using adjacency lists to represent E'.

Theorem 35.1
APPROX-VERTEX-COVER is a polynomial-time 2-approximation algorithm.

Proof We have already shown that APPROX-VERTEX-COVER runs in polynomial time.

The set C of vertices that is returned by APPROX-VERTEX-COVER is a vertex cover, since the algorithm loops until every edge in $G.E$ has been covered by some vertex in C.

To see that APPROX-VERTEX-COVER returns a vertex cover that is at most twice the size of an optimal cover, let A denote the set of edges that line 4 of APPROX-VERTEX-COVER picked. In order to cover the edges in A, any vertex cover—in particular, an optimal cover C^*—must include at least one endpoint of each edge in A. No two edges in A share an endpoint, since once an edge is picked in line 4, all other edges that are incident on its endpoints are deleted from E' in line 6. Thus, no two edges in A are covered by the same vertex from C^*, meaning that for every vertex in C^*, there is at most one edge in A, giving the lower bound

$$|C^*| \geq |A| \tag{35.2}$$

on the size of an optimal vertex cover. Each execution of line 4 picks an edge for which neither of its endpoints is already in C, yielding an upper bound (an exact upper bound, in fact) on the size of the vertex cover returned:

$$|C| = 2|A| . \tag{35.3}$$

Combining equations (35.2) and (35.3) yields

$$\begin{aligned} |C| &= 2|A| \\ &\leq 2|C^*| , \end{aligned}$$

thereby proving the theorem. ∎

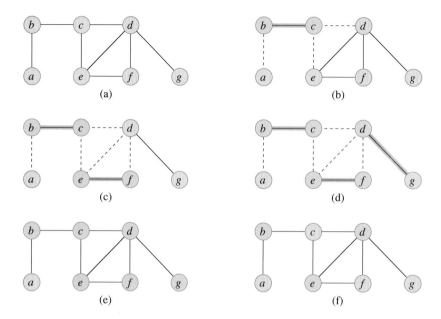

Figure 35.1 The operation of APPROX-VERTEX-COVER. **(a)** The input graph G, which has 7 vertices and 8 edges. **(b)** The highlighted edge (b, c) is the first edge chosen by APPROX-VERTEX-COVER. Vertices b and c, in blue, are added to the set C containing the vertex cover being created. Dashed edges (a, b), (c, e), and (c, d) are removed since they are now covered by some vertex in C. **(c)** Edge (e, f) is chosen, and vertices e and f are added to C. **(d)** Edge (d, g) is chosen, and vertices d and g are added to C. **(e)** The set C, which is the vertex cover produced by APPROX-VERTEX-COVER, contains the six vertices b, c, d, e, f, g. **(f)** The optimal vertex cover for this problem contains only three vertices: b, d, and e.

Let us reflect on this proof. At first, you might wonder how you can possibly prove that the size of the vertex cover returned by APPROX-VERTEX-COVER is at most twice the size of an optimal vertex cover, when you don't even know the size of an optimal vertex cover. Instead of requiring that you know the exact size of an optimal vertex cover, you find a lower bound on the size. As Exercise 35.1-2 asks you to show, the set A of edges that line 4 of APPROX-VERTEX-COVER selects is actually a maximal matching in the graph G. (A *maximal matching* is a matching to which no edges can be added and still have a matching.) The size of a maximal matching is, as we argued in the proof of Theorem 35.1, a lower bound on the size of an optimal vertex cover. The algorithm returns a vertex cover whose size is at most twice the size of the maximal matching A. The approximation ratio comes from relating the size of the solution returned to the lower bound. We will use this methodology in later sections as well.

Exercises

35.1-1
Give an example of a graph for which APPROX-VERTEX-COVER always yields a suboptimal solution.

35.1-2
Prove that the set of edges picked in line 4 of APPROX-VERTEX-COVER forms a maximal matching in the graph G.

★ *35.1-3*
Consider the following heuristic to solve the vertex-cover problem. Repeatedly select a vertex of highest degree, and remove all of its incident edges. Give an example to show that this heuristic does not provide an approximation ratio of 2. (*Hint:* Try a bipartite graph with vertices of uniform degree on the left and vertices of varying degree on the right.)

35.1-4
Give an efficient greedy algorithm that finds an optimal vertex cover for a tree in linear time.

35.1-5
The proof of Theorem 34.12 on page 1084 illustrates that the vertex-cover problem and the NP-complete clique problem are complementary in the sense that an optimal vertex cover is the complement of a maximum-size clique in the complement graph. Does this relationship imply that there is a polynomial-time approximation algorithm with a constant approximation ratio for the clique problem? Justify your answer.

35.2   The traveling-salesperson problem

The input to the traveling-salesperson problem, introduced in Section 34.5.4, is a complete undirected graph $G = (V, E)$ that has a nonnegative integer cost $c(u, v)$ associated with each edge $(u, v) \in E$. The goal is to find a hamiltonian cycle (a tour) of G with minimum cost. As an extension of our notation, let $c(A)$ denote the total cost of the edges in the subset $A \subseteq E$:

$$c(A) = \sum_{(u,v) \in A} c(u, v) .$$

In many practical situations, the least costly way to go from a place u to a place w is to go directly, with no intermediate steps. Put another way, cutting out an intermediate stop never increases the cost. Such a cost function c satisfies the *triangle inequality*: for all vertices $u, v, w \in V$,

$$c(u, w) \le c(u, v) + c(v, w) .$$

The triangle inequality seems as though it should naturally hold, and it is automatically satisfied in several applications. For example, if the vertices of the graph are points in the plane and the cost of traveling between two vertices is the ordinary euclidean distance between them, then the triangle inequality is satisfied. Furthermore, many cost functions other than euclidean distance satisfy the triangle inequality.

As Exercise 35.2-2 shows, the traveling-salesperson problem is NP-complete even if you require the cost function to satisfy the triangle inequality. Thus, you should not expect to find a polynomial-time algorithm for solving this problem exactly. Your time would be better spent looking for good approximation algorithms.

In Section 35.2.1, we examine a 2-approximation algorithm for the traveling-salesperson problem with the triangle inequality. In Section 35.2.2, we show that without the triangle inequality, a polynomial-time approximation algorithm with a constant approximation ratio does not exist unless P = NP.

35.2.1   The traveling-salesperson problem with the triangle inequality

Applying the methodology of the previous section, start by computing a structure —a minimum spanning tree—whose weight gives a lower bound on the length of an optimal traveling-salesperson tour. Then use the minimum spanning tree to create a tour whose cost is no more than twice that of the minimum spanning tree's weight, as long as the cost function satisfies the triangle inequality. The procedure APPROX-TSP-TOUR on the next page implements this approach, calling the minimum-spanning-tree algorithm MST-PRIM on page 596 as a subroutine. The parameter G is a complete undirected graph, and the cost function c satisfies the triangle inequality.

Recall from Section 12.1 that a preorder tree walk recursively visits every vertex in the tree, listing a vertex when it is first encountered, before visiting any of its children.

Figure 35.2 illustrates the operation of APPROX-TSP-TOUR. Part (a) of the figure shows a complete undirected graph, and part (b) shows the minimum spanning tree T grown from root vertex a by MST-PRIM. Part (c) shows how a preorder walk of T visits the vertices, and part (d) displays the corresponding tour, which is the tour returned by APPROX-TSP-TOUR. Part (e) displays an optimal tour, which is about 23% shorter.

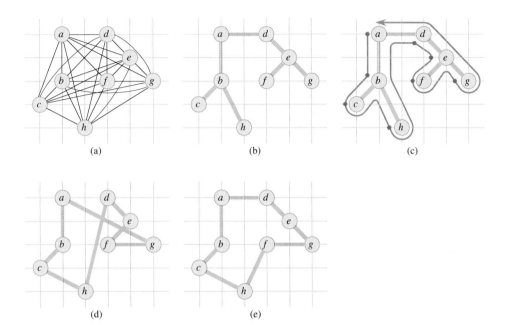

(a)   (b)   (c)

(d)   (e)

Figure 35.2 The operation of APPROX-TSP-TOUR. **(a)** A complete undirected graph. Vertices lie on intersections of integer grid lines. For example, f is one unit to the right and two units up from h. The cost function between two points is the ordinary euclidean distance. **(b)** A minimum spanning tree T of the complete graph, as computed by MST-PRIM. Vertex a is the root vertex. Only edges in the minimum spanning tree are shown. The vertices happen to be labeled in such a way that they are added to the main tree by MST-PRIM in alphabetical order. **(c)** A walk of T, starting at a. A full walk of the tree visits the vertices in the order $a, b, c, b, h, b, a, d, e, f, e, g, e, d, a$. A preorder walk of T lists a vertex just when it is first encountered, as indicated by the dot next to each vertex, yielding the ordering a, b, c, h, d, e, f, g. **(d)** A tour obtained by visiting the vertices in the order given by the preorder walk, which is the tour H returned by APPROX-TSP-TOUR. Its total cost is approximately 19.074. **(e)** An optimal tour H^* for the original complete graph. Its total cost is approximately 14.715.

APPROX-TSP-TOUR(G, c)

1 select a vertex $r \in G.V$ to be a "root" vertex
2 compute a minimum spanning tree T for G from root r
       using MST-PRIM(G, c, r)
3 let H be a list of vertices, ordered according to when they are first visited
       in a preorder tree walk of T
4 **return** the hamiltonian cycle H

By Exercise 21.2-2, even with a simple implementation of MST-PRIM, the running time of APPROX-TSP-TOUR is $\Theta(V^2)$. We now show that if the cost function for an instance of the traveling-salesperson problem satisfies the triangle inequality, then APPROX-TSP-TOUR returns a tour whose cost is at most twice the cost of an optimal tour.

Theorem 35.2
When the triangle inequality holds, APPROX-TSP-TOUR is a polynomial-time 2-approximation algorithm for the traveling-salesperson problem.

Proof   We have already seen that APPROX-TSP-TOUR runs in polynomial time.

Let H^* denote an optimal tour for the given set of vertices. Deleting any edge from a tour yields a spanning tree, and each edge cost is nonnegative. Therefore, the weight of the minimum spanning tree T computed in line 2 of APPROX-TSP-TOUR provides a lower bound on the cost of an optimal tour:

$$c(T) \leq c(H^*) . \tag{35.4}$$

A *full walk* of T lists the vertices when they are first visited and also whenever they are returned to after a visit to a subtree. Let's call this full walk W. The full walk of our example gives the order

$$a, b, c, b, h, b, a, d, e, f, e, g, e, d, a .$$

Since the full walk traverses every edge of T exactly twice, by extending the definition of the cost c in the natural manner to handle multisets of edges, we have

$$c(W) = 2c(T) . \tag{35.5}$$

Inequality (35.4) and equation (35.5) imply that

$$c(W) \leq 2c(H^*) , \tag{35.6}$$

and so the cost of W is within a factor of 2 of the cost of an optimal tour.

Of course, the full walk W is not a tour, since it visits some vertices more than once. By the triangle inequality, however, deleting a visit to any vertex from W does not increase the cost. (When a vertex v is deleted from W between visits to u and w, the resulting ordering specifies going directly from u to w.) Repeatedly apply this operation on each visit to a vertex after the first time it's visited in W, so that W is left with only the first visit to each vertex. In our example, this process leaves the ordering

$$a, b, c, h, d, e, f, g .$$

This ordering is the same as that obtained by a preorder walk of the tree T. Let H be the cycle corresponding to this preorder walk. It is a hamiltonian cycle, since every vertex is visited exactly once, and in fact it is the cycle computed by APPROX-TSP-TOUR. Since H is obtained by deleting vertices from the full walk W, we have

$$c(H) \leq c(W) . \tag{35.7}$$

Combining inequalities (35.6) and (35.7) gives $c(H) \leq 2c(H^*)$, which completes the proof.   ∎

Despite the small approximation ratio provided by Theorem 35.2, APPROX-TSP-TOUR is usually not the best practical choice for this problem. There are other approximation algorithms that typically perform much better in practice. (See the references at the end of this chapter.)

35.2.2   The general traveling-salesperson problem

When the cost function c does not satisfy the triangle inequality, there is no way to find good approximate tours in polynomial time unless P = NP.

Theorem 35.3
If P $\neq$ NP, then for any constant $\rho \geq 1$, there is no polynomial-time approximation algorithm with approximation ratio ρ for the general traveling-salesperson problem.

Proof   The proof is by contradiction. Suppose to the contrary that for some number $\rho \geq 1$, there is a polynomial-time approximation algorithm A with approximation ratio ρ. Without loss of generality, assume that ρ is an integer, by rounding it up if necessary. We will show how to use A to solve instances of the hamiltonian-cycle problem (defined in Section 34.2) in polynomial time. Since Theorem 34.13 on page 1085 says that the hamiltonian-cycle problem is NP-complete, Theorem 34.4 on page 1063 implies that if it has a polynomial-time algorithm, then P = NP.

Let $G = (V, E)$ be an instance of the hamiltonian-cycle problem. We will show how to determine efficiently whether G contains a hamiltonian cycle by making use of the hypothesized approximation algorithm A. Convert G into an instance of the traveling-salesperson problem as follows. Let $G' = (V, E')$ be the complete graph on V, that is,

$$E' = \{(u, v) : u, v \in V \text{ and } u \neq v\} .$$

Assign an integer cost to each edge in E' as follows:

$$c(u, v) = \begin{cases} 1 & \text{if } (u, v) \in E , \\ \rho|V| + 1 & \text{otherwise} . \end{cases}$$

Given a representation of G, it takes time polynomial in $|V|$ and $|E|$ to create representations of G' and c.

Now consider the traveling-salesperson problem (G', c). If the original graph G has a hamiltonian cycle H, then the cost function c assigns to each edge of H a cost of 1, and so (G', c) contains a tour of cost $|V|$. On the other hand, if G does not contain a hamiltonian cycle, then any tour of G' must use some edge not in E. But any tour that uses an edge not in E has a cost of at least

$$(\rho |V| + 1) + (|V| - 1) = \rho |V| + |V|$$
$$> \rho |V| \ .$$

Because edges not in G are so costly, there is a gap of at least $\rho |V|$ between the cost of a tour that is a hamiltonian cycle in G (cost $|V|$) and the cost of any other tour (cost at least $\rho |V| + |V|$). Therefore, the cost of a tour that is not a hamiltonian cycle in G is at least a factor of $\rho + 1$ greater than the cost of a tour that is a hamiltonian cycle in G.

What happens upon applying the approximation algorithm A to the traveling-salesperson problem (G', c)? Because A is guaranteed to return a tour of cost no more than ρ times the cost of an optimal tour, if G contains a hamiltonian cycle, then A must return it. If G has no hamiltonian cycle, then A returns a tour of cost more than $\rho |V|$. Therefore, using A solves the hamiltonian-cycle problem in polynomial time. ∎

The proof of Theorem 35.3 serves as an example of a general technique to prove that no good approximation algorithm exists for a particular problem. Given an NP-hard decision problem X, produce in polynomial time a minimization problem Y such that "yes" instances of X correspond to instances of Y with value at most k (for some k), but that "no" instances of X correspond to instances of Y with value greater than ρk. This technique shows that, unless P = NP, there is no polynomial-time ρ-approximation algorithm for problem Y.

Exercises

35.2-1
Let $G = (V, E)$ be a complete undirected graph containing at least 3 vertices, and let c be a cost function that satisfies the triangle inequality. Prove that $c(u, v) \geq 0$ for all $u, v \in V$.

35.2-2
Show how in polynomial time to transform one instance of the traveling-salesperson problem into another instance whose cost function satisfies the triangle inequality. The two instances must have the same set of optimal tours. Explain why

such a polynomial-time transformation does not contradict Theorem 35.3, assuming that $P \neq NP$.

35.2-3

Consider the following *closest-point heuristic* for building an approximate traveling-salesperson tour whose cost function satisfies the triangle inequality. Begin with a trivial cycle consisting of a single arbitrarily chosen vertex. At each step, identify the vertex u that is not on the cycle but whose distance to any vertex on the cycle is minimum. Suppose that the vertex on the cycle that is nearest u is vertex v. Extend the cycle to include u by inserting u just after v. Repeat until all vertices are on the cycle. Prove that this heuristic returns a tour whose total cost is not more than twice the cost of an optimal tour.

35.2-4

A solution to the *bottleneck traveling-salesperson problem* is the hamiltonian cycle that minimizes the cost of the most costly edge in the cycle. Assuming that the cost function satisfies the triangle inequality, show that there exists a polynomial-time approximation algorithm with approximation ratio 3 for this problem. (*Hint:* Show recursively how to visit all the nodes in a bottleneck spanning tree, as discussed in Problem 21-4 on page 601, exactly once by taking a full walk of the tree and skipping nodes, but without skipping more than two consecutive intermediate nodes. Show that the costliest edge in a bottleneck spanning tree has a cost bounded from above by the cost of the costliest edge in a bottleneck hamiltonian cycle.)

35.2-5

Suppose that the vertices for an instance of the traveling-salesperson problem are points in the plane and that the cost $c(u, v)$ is the euclidean distance between points u and v. Show that an optimal tour never crosses itself.

35.2-6

Adapt the proof of Theorem 35.3 to show that for any constant $c \geq 0$, there is no polynomial-time approximation algorithm with approximation ratio $|V|^c$ for the general traveling-salesperson problem.

35.3   The set-covering problem

The set-covering problem is an optimization problem that models many problems that require resources to be allocated. Its corresponding decision problem generalizes the NP-complete vertex-cover problem and is therefore also NP-hard. The approximation algorithm developed to handle the vertex-cover problem doesn't apply here, however. Instead, this section investigates a simple greedy heuristic with a logarithmic approximation ratio. That is, as the size of the instance gets larger, the size of the approximate solution may grow, relative to the size of an optimal solution. Because the logarithm function grows rather slowly, however, this approximation algorithm may nonetheless give useful results.

An instance $(X, \mathcal{F})$ of the **set-covering problem** consists of a finite set X and a family $\mathcal{F}$ of subsets of X, such that every element of X belongs to at least one subset in $\mathcal{F}$:

$$X = \bigcup_{S \in \mathcal{F}} S \,.$$

We say that a subfamily $\mathcal{C} \subseteq \mathcal{F}$ *covers* a set of elements U if

$$U \subseteq \bigcup_{S \in \mathcal{C}} S \,.$$

The problem is to find a minimum-size subfamily $\mathcal{C} \subseteq \mathcal{F}$ whose members cover all of X:

$$X = \bigcup_{S \in \mathcal{C}} S \,.$$

Figure 35.3 illustrates the set-covering problem. The size of $\mathcal{C}$ is the number of sets it contains, rather than the number of individual elements in these sets, since every subfamily $\mathcal{C}$ that covers X must contain all $|X|$ individual elements. In Figure 35.3, the minimum set cover has size 3.

The set-covering problem abstracts many commonly arising combinatorial problems. As a simple example, suppose that X represents a set of skills that are needed to solve a problem and that you have a given set of people available to work on the problem. You wish to form a committee, containing as few people as possible, such that for every requisite skill in X, at least one member of the committee has that skill. The decision version of the set-covering problem asks whether a covering exists with size at most k, where k is an additional parameter specified in the problem instance. The decision version of the problem is NP-complete, as Exercise 35.3-2 asks you to show.

A greedy approximation algorithm

The greedy method in the procedure GREEDY-SET-COVER on the facing page works by picking, at each stage, the set S that covers the greatest number of remaining elements that are uncovered. In the example of Figure 35.3, GREEDY-SET-COVER adds to $\mathcal{C}$, in order, the sets S_1, S_4, and S_5, followed by either S_3 or S_6.

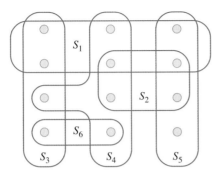

Figure 35.3   An instance $(X, \mathcal{F})$ of the set-covering problem, where X consists of the 12 tan points and $\mathcal{F} = \{S_1, S_2, S_3, S_4, S_5, S_6\}$. Each set $S_i \in \mathcal{F}$ is outlined in blue. A minimum-size set cover is $\mathcal{C} = \{S_3, S_4, S_5\}$, with size 3. The greedy algorithm produces a cover of size 4 by selecting either the sets S_1, S_4, S_5, and S_3 or the sets S_1, S_4, S_5, and S_6, in order.

$\text{GREEDY-SET-COVER}(X, \mathcal{F})$

1   $U_0 = X$
2   $\mathcal{C} = \emptyset$
3   $i = 0$
4   **while** $U_i \neq \emptyset$
5   $\qquad$ select $S \in \mathcal{F}$ that maximizes $|S \cap U_i|$
6   $\qquad U_{i+1} = U_i - S$
7   $\qquad \mathcal{C} = \mathcal{C} \cup \{S\}$
8   $\qquad i = i + 1$
9   **return** $\mathcal{C}$

The greedy algorithm works as follows. At the start of each iteration, U_i is a subset of X containing the remaining uncovered elements, with the initial subset U_0 containing all the elements in X. The set $\mathcal{C}$ contains the subfamily being constructed. Line 5 is the greedy decision-making step, choosing a subset S that covers as many uncovered elements as possible (breaking ties arbitrarily). After S is selected, line 6 updates the set of remaining uncovered elements, denoting it by U_{i+1}, and line 7 places S into $\mathcal{C}$. When the algorithm terminates, $\mathcal{C}$ is a subfamily of $\mathcal{F}$ that covers X.

Analysis

We now show that the greedy algorithm returns a set cover that is not too much larger than an optimal set cover.

Theorem 35.4
The procedure GREEDY-SET-COVER run on a set X and family of subsets $\mathcal{F}$ is a polynomial-time $O(\lg |X|)$-approximation algorithm.

Proof   Let's first show that the algorithm runs in time that is polynomial in $|X|$ and $|\mathcal{F}|$. The number of iterations of the loop in lines 4–7 is bounded above by $\min\{|X|, |\mathcal{F}|\} = O(|X| + |\mathcal{F}|)$. The loop body can be implemented to run in $O(|X| \cdot |\mathcal{F}|)$ time. Thus the algorithm runs in $O(|X| \cdot |\mathcal{F}| \cdot (|X| + |\mathcal{F}|))$ time, which is polynomial in the input size. (Exercise 35.3-3 asks for a linear-time algorithm.)

To prove the approximation bound, let $\mathcal{C}^*$ be an optimal set cover for the original instance $(X, \mathcal{F})$, and let $k = |\mathcal{C}^*|$. Since $\mathcal{C}^*$ is also a set cover of each subset U_i of X constructed by the algorithm, we know that any subset U_i constructed by the algorithm can be covered by k sets. Therefore, if $(U_i, \mathcal{F})$ is an instance of the set-covering problem, its optimal set cover has size at most k.

If an optimal set cover for an instance $(U_i, \mathcal{F})$ has size at most k, at least one of the sets in $\mathcal{C}$ covers at least $|U_i|/k$ new elements. Thus, line 5 of GREEDY-SET-COVER, which chooses a set with the maximum number of uncovered elements, must choose a set in which the number of newly covered elements is at least $|U_i|/k$. These elements are removed when constructing U_{i+1}, giving

$$
\begin{aligned}
|U_{i+1}| &\le |U_i| - |U_i|/k \\
&= |U_i|(1 - 1/k) .
\end{aligned}
\tag{35.8}
$$

Iterating inequality (35.8) gives

$$
\begin{aligned}
|U_0| &= |X| , \\
|U_1| &\le |U_0|(1 - 1/k) , \\
|U_2| &\le |U_1|(1 - 1/k) \le |U_0|(1 - 1/k)^2 ,
\end{aligned}
$$

and in general

$$
|U_i| \le |U_0|(1 - 1/k)^i = |X|(1 - 1/k)^i .
\tag{35.9}
$$

The algorithm stops when $U_i = \emptyset$, which means that $|U_i| < 1$. Thus an upper bound on the number of iterations of the algorithm is the smallest value of i for which $|U_i| < 1$.

Since $1 + x \le e^x$ for all real x (see inequality (3.14) on page 66), by letting $x = -1/k$, we have $1 - 1/k \le e^{-1/k}$, so that $(1 - 1/k)^k \le (e^{-1/k})^k = 1/e$. Denoting the number i of iterations by ck for some nonnegative integer c, we want c such that

$$
|X|(1 - 1/k)^{ck} \le |X|e^{-c} < 1 .
\tag{35.10}
$$

Multiplying both sides by e^c and then taking the natural logarithm of both sides gives $c > \ln |X|$, so we can choose for c any integer that is greater than $\ln |X|$.

We choose $c = \lceil \ln |X| \rceil + 1$. Since $i = ck$ is an upper bound on the number of iterations, which equals the size of $\mathcal{C}$, and $k = |\mathcal{C}^*|$, we have $|\mathcal{C}| \le i = ck = c|\mathcal{C}^*| = |\mathcal{C}^*|(\lceil \ln |X| \rceil + 1)$, and the theorem follows. ∎

Exercises

35.3-1
Consider each of the following words as a set of letters: {arid, dash, drain, heard, lost, nose, shun, slate, snare, thread}. Show which set cover GREEDY-SET-COVER produces when you break ties in favor of the word that appears first in the dictionary.

35.3-2
Show that the decision version of the set-covering problem is NP-complete by reducing the vertex-cover problem to it.

35.3-3
Show how to implement GREEDY-SET-COVER to run in $O\left(\sum_{S \in \mathcal{F}} |S|\right)$ time.

35.3-4
The proof of Theorem 35.4 says that when GREEDY-SET-COVER, run on the instance $(X, \mathcal{F})$, returns the subfamily $\mathcal{C}$, then $|\mathcal{C}| \le |\mathcal{C}^*| \lceil \ln X \rceil$. Show that the following weaker bound is trivially true:

$$|\mathcal{C}| \le |\mathcal{C}^*| \max\{|S| : S \in \mathcal{F}\} .$$

35.3-5
GREEDY-SET-COVER can return a number of different solutions, depending on how it breaks ties in line 5. Give a procedure BAD-SET-COVER-INSTANCE(n) that returns an n-element instance of the set-covering problem for which, depending on how line 5 breaks ties, GREEDY-SET-COVER can return a number of different solutions that is exponential in n.

35.4   Randomization and linear programming

This section studies two useful techniques for designing approximation algorithms: randomization and linear programming. It starts with a simple randomized algorithm for an optimization version of 3-CNF satisfiability, and then it shows how to design an approximation algorithm for a weighted version of the vertex-cover problem based on linear programming. This section only scratches the surface of these two powerful techniques. The chapter notes give references for further study of these areas.

A randomized approximation algorithm for MAX-3-CNF satisfiability

Just as some randomized algorithms compute exact solutions, some randomized algorithms compute approximate solutions. We say that a randomized algorithm for a problem has an *approximation ratio* of $\rho(n)$ if, for any input of size n, the *expected* cost C of the solution produced by the randomized algorithm is within a factor of $\rho(n)$ of the cost C^* of an optimal solution:

$$\max \left\{ \frac{C}{C^*}, \frac{C^*}{C} \right\} \leq \rho(n) \,. \tag{35.11}$$

We call a randomized algorithm that achieves an approximation ratio of $\rho(n)$ a *randomized $\rho(n)$-approximation algorithm.* In other words, a randomized approximation algorithm is like a deterministic approximation algorithm, except that the approximation ratio is for an expected cost.

A particular instance of 3-CNF satisfiability, as defined in Section 34.4, may or may not be satisfiable. In order to be satisfiable, there must exist an assignment of the variables so that every clause evaluates to 1. If an instance is not satisfiable, you might instead want to know how "close" to satisfiable it is, that is, find an assignment of the variables that satisfies as many clauses as possible. We call the resulting maximization problem *MAX-3-CNF satisfiability.* The input to MAX-3-CNF satisfiability is the same as for 3-CNF satisfiability, and the goal is to return an assignment of the variables that maximizes the number of clauses evaluating to 1. You might be surprised that randomly setting each variable to 1 with probability $1/2$ and to 0 with probability $1/2$ yields a randomized 8/7-approximation algorithm, but we're about to see why. Recall that the definition of 3-CNF satisfiability from Section 34.4 requires each clause to consist of exactly three distinct literals. We now further assume that no clause contains both a variable and its negation. Exercise 35.4-1 asks you to remove this last assumption.

Theorem 35.5
Given an instance of MAX-3-CNF satisfiability with n variables $x_1, x_2, \ldots, x_n$ and m clauses, the randomized algorithm that independently sets each variable to 1 with probability $1/2$ and to 0 with probability $1/2$ is a randomized 8/7-approximation algorithm.

Proof Suppose that each variable is independently set to 1 with probability $1/2$ and to 0 with probability $1/2$. Define, for $i = 1, 2, \ldots, m$, the indicator random variable

$$Y_i = \mathrm{I} \{\text{clause } i \text{ is satisfied}\} \;,$$

so that $Y_i = 1$ as long as at least one of the literals in the ith clause is set to 1. Since no literal appears more than once in the same clause, and since we assume that no variable and its negation appear in the same clause, the settings of the three literals in each clause are independent. A clause is not satisfied only if all three of its literals are set to 0, and so $\Pr \{\text{clause } i \text{ is not satisfied}\} = (1/2)^3 = 1/8$. Thus, we have $\Pr \{\text{clause } i \text{ is satisfied}\} = 1 - 1/8 = 7/8$, and Lemma 5.1 on page 130 gives $\mathrm{E}[Y_i] = 7/8$. Let Y be the number of satisfied clauses overall, so that $Y = Y_1 + Y_2 + \cdots + Y_m$. Then, we have

$$
\begin{aligned}
\mathrm{E}[Y] &= \mathrm{E}\left[\sum_{i=1}^{m} Y_i\right] \\
&= \sum_{i=1}^{m} \mathrm{E}[Y_i] \qquad \text{(by linearity of expectation)} \\
&= \sum_{i=1}^{m} 7/8 \\
&= 7m/8 \;.
\end{aligned}
$$

Since m is an upper bound on the number of satisfied clauses, the approximation ratio is at most $m/(7m/8) = 8/7$. ∎

Approximating weighted vertex cover using linear programming

The *minimum-weight vertex-cover problem* takes as input an undirected graph $G = (V, E)$ in which each vertex $v \in V$ has an associated positive weight $w(v)$. The weight $w(V')$ of a vertex cover $V' \subseteq V$ is the sum of the weights of its vertices: $w(V') = \sum_{v \in V'} w(v)$. The goal is to find a vertex cover of minimum weight.

The approximation algorithm for unweighted vertex cover from Section 35.1 won't work here, because the solution it returns could be far from optimal for the weighted problem. Instead, we'll first compute a lower bound on the weight of the minimum-weight vertex cover, by using a linear program. Then we'll "round" this solution and use it to obtain a vertex cover.

Start by associating a variable $x(v)$ with each vertex $v \in V$, and require that $x(v)$ equals either 0 or 1 for each $v \in V$. The vertex cover includes v if and only if $x(v) = 1$. Then the constraint that for any edge (u, v), at least one of u and v must belong to the vertex cover can be expressed as $x(u) + x(v) \geq 1$. This view gives rise to the following *0-1 integer program* for finding a minimum-weight vertex cover:

$$\text{minimize} \quad \sum_{v \in V} w(v)\, x(v) \tag{35.12}$$

subject to

$$x(u) + x(v) \ge 1 \qquad \text{for each } (u, v) \in E \tag{35.13}$$

$$x(v) \in \{0, 1\} \quad \text{for each } v \in V . \tag{35.14}$$

In the special case in which all the weights $w(v)$ equal 1, this formulation is the optimization version of the NP-hard vertex-cover problem. Let's remove the constraint that $x(v) \in \{0, 1\}$ and replace it by $0 \le x(v) \le 1$, resulting in the following linear program:

$$\text{minimize} \quad \sum_{v \in V} w(v)\, x(v) \tag{35.15}$$

subject to

$$x(u) + x(v) \ge 1 \quad \text{for each } (u, v) \in E \tag{35.16}$$

$$x(v) \le 1 \quad \text{for each } v \in V \tag{35.17}$$

$$x(v) \ge 0 \quad \text{for each } v \in V . \tag{35.18}$$

We refer to this linear program as the ***linear-programming relaxation***. Any feasible solution to the 0-1 integer program in lines (35.12)–(35.14) is also a feasible solution to its linear-programming relaxation in lines (35.15)–(35.18). Therefore, the value of an optimal solution to the linear-programming relaxation provides a lower bound on the value of an optimal solution to the 0-1 integer program, and hence a lower bound on the optimal weight in the minimum-weight vertex-cover problem.

The procedure APPROX-MIN-WEIGHT-VC on the facing page starts with a solution to the linear-programming relaxation and uses it to construct an approximate solution to the minimum-weight vertex-cover problem. The procedure works as follows. Line 1 initializes the vertex cover to be empty. Line 2 formulates the linear-programming relaxation in lines (35.15)–(35.18) and then solves this linear program. An optimal solution gives each vertex v an associated value $\bar{x}(v)$, where $0 \le \bar{x}(v) \le 1$. The procedure uses this value to guide the choice of which vertices to add to the vertex cover C in lines 3–5: the vertex cover C includes vertex v if and only if $\bar{x}(v) \ge 1/2$. In effect, the procedure "rounds" each fractional variable in the solution to the linear-programming relaxation to either 0 or 1 in order to obtain a solution to the 0-1 integer program in lines (35.12)–(35.14). Finally, line 6 returns the vertex cover C.

Theorem 35.6
Algorithm APPROX-MIN-WEIGHT-VC is a polynomial-time 2-approximation algorithm for the minimum-weight vertex-cover problem.

APPROX-MIN-WEIGHT-VC(G, w)

1   $C = \emptyset$
2   compute $\bar{x}$, an optimal solution to the linear-programming relaxation
       in lines (35.15)–(35.18)
3   **for** each vertex $v \in V$
4   **if** $\bar{x}(v) \geq 1/2$
5         $C = C \cup \{v\}$
6   **return** C

Proof   Because there is a polynomial-time algorithm to solve the linear program in line 2, and because the **for** loop of lines 3–5 runs in polynomial time, APPROX-MIN-WEIGHT-VC is a polynomial-time algorithm.

It remains to show that APPROX-MIN-WEIGHT-VC is a 2-approximation algorithm. Let C^* be an optimal solution to the minimum-weight vertex-cover problem, and let z^* be the value of an optimal solution to the linear-programming relaxation in lines (35.15)–(35.18). Since an optimal vertex cover is a feasible solution to the linear-programming relaxation, z^* must be a lower bound on $w(C^*)$, that is,

$$z^* \leq w(C^*) . \tag{35.19}$$

Next, we claim that rounding the fractional values of the variables $\bar{x}(v)$ in lines 3–5 produces a set C that is a vertex cover and satisfies $w(C) \leq 2z^*$. To see that C is a vertex cover, consider any edge $(u, v) \in E$. By constraint (35.16), we know that $x(u) + x(v) \geq 1$, which implies that at least one of $\bar{x}(u)$ and $\bar{x}(v)$ is at least $1/2$. Therefore, at least one of u and v is included in the vertex cover, and so every edge is covered.

Now we consider the weight of the cover. We have

$$
\begin{aligned}
z^* &= \sum_{v \in V} w(v)\,\bar{x}(v) \\
&\geq \sum_{v \in V : \bar{x}(v) \geq 1/2} w(v)\,\bar{x}(v) \\
&\geq \sum_{v \in V : \bar{x}(v) \geq 1/2} w(v) \cdot \frac{1}{2} \\
&= \sum_{v \in C} w(v) \cdot \frac{1}{2} \\
&= \frac{1}{2} \sum_{v \in C} w(v) \\
&= \frac{1}{2} w(C) .
\end{aligned}
\tag{35.20}
$$

Combining inequalities (35.19) and (35.20) gives

$$w(C) \le 2z^* \le 2w(C^*) \, ,$$

and hence APPROX-MIN-WEIGHT-VC is a 2-approximation algorithm.   ■

Exercises

35.4-1
Show that even if a clause is allowed to contain both a variable and its negation, randomly setting each variable to 1 with probability $1/2$ and to 0 with probability $1/2$ still yields a randomized 8/7-approximation algorithm.

35.4-2
The ***MAX-CNF satisfiability problem*** is like the MAX-3-CNF satisfiability problem, except that it does not restrict each clause to have exactly three literals. Give a randomized 2-approximation algorithm for the MAX-CNF satisfiability problem.

35.4-3
In the MAX-CUT problem, the input is an unweighted undirected graph $G = (V, E)$. We define a cut $(S, V - S)$ as in Chapter 21 and the ***weight*** of a cut as the number of edges crossing the cut. The goal is to find a cut of maximum weight. Suppose that each vertex v is randomly and independently placed into S with probability $1/2$ and into $V - S$ with probability $1/2$. Show that this algorithm is a randomized 2-approximation algorithm.

35.4-4
Show that the constraints in line (35.17) are redundant in the sense that removing them from the linear-programming relaxation in lines (35.15)–(35.18) yields a linear program for which any optimal solution x must satisfy $x(v) \le 1$ for each $v \in V$.

35.5   The subset-sum problem

Recall from Section 34.5.5 that an instance of the subset-sum problem is given by a pair (S, t), where S is a set $\{x_1, x_2, \ldots, x_n\}$ of positive integers and t is a positive integer. This decision problem asks whether there exists a subset of S that adds up exactly to the target value t. As we saw in Section 34.5.5, this problem is NP-complete.

The optimization problem associated with this decision problem arises in practical applications. The optimization problem seeks a subset of $\{x_1, x_2, \ldots, x_n\}$

whose sum is as large as possible but not larger than t. For example, consider a truck that can carry no more than t pounds, which is to be loaded with up to n different boxes, the ith of which weighs x_i pounds. How heavy a load can the truck take without exceeding the t-pound weight limit?

We start this section with an exponential-time algorithm to compute the optimal value for this optimization problem. Then we show how to modify the algorithm so that it becomes a fully polynomial-time approximation scheme. (Recall that a fully polynomial-time approximation scheme has a running time that is polynomial in $1/\epsilon$ as well as in the size of the input.)

An exponential-time exact algorithm

Suppose that you compute, for each subset S' of S, the sum of the elements in S', and then you select, among the subsets whose sum does not exceed t, the one whose sum is closest to t. This algorithm returns the optimal solution, but it might take exponential time. To implement this algorithm, you can use an iterative procedure that, in iteration i, computes the sums of all subsets of $\{x_1, x_2, \ldots, x_i\}$, using as a starting point the sums of all subsets of $\{x_1, x_2, \ldots, x_{i-1}\}$. In doing so, you would realize that once a particular subset S' has a sum exceeding t, there is no reason to maintain it, since no superset of S' can be an optimal solution. Let's see how to implement this strategy.

The procedure EXACT-SUBSET-SUM takes an input set $S = \{x_1, x_2, \ldots, x_n\}$, the size $n = |S|$, and a target value t. This procedure iteratively computes L_i, the list of sums of all subsets of $\{x_1, \ldots, x_i\}$ that do not exceed t, and then it returns the maximum value in L_n.

If L is a list of positive integers and x is another positive integer, then let $L + x$ denote the list of integers derived from L by increasing each element of L by x. For example, if $L = \langle 1, 2, 3, 5, 9 \rangle$, then $L + 2 = \langle 3, 4, 5, 7, 11 \rangle$. This notation extends to sets, so that

$$S + x = \{s + x : s \in S\} .$$

EXACT-SUBSET-SUM(S, n, t)

```
1   L₀ = ⟨0⟩
2   for i = 1 to n
3       Lᵢ = MERGE-LISTS(Lᵢ₋₁, Lᵢ₋₁ + xᵢ)
4           remove from Lᵢ every element that is greater than t
5   return the largest element in Lₙ
```

EXACT-SUBSET-SUM invokes an auxiliary procedure MERGE-LISTS(L, L'), which returns the sorted list that is the merge of its two sorted input lists L and L', with duplicate values removed. Like the MERGE procedure we used in merge sort on page 36, MERGE-LISTS runs in $O(|L| + |L'|)$ time. We omit the pseudocode for MERGE-LISTS.

To see how EXACT-SUBSET-SUM works, let P_i denote the set of values obtained by selecting each (possibly empty) subset of $\{x_1, x_2, \ldots, x_i\}$ and summing its members. For example, if $S = \{1, 4, 5\}$, then

$$P_1 = \{0, 1\} \,,$$
$$P_2 = \{0, 1, 4, 5\} \,,$$
$$P_3 = \{0, 1, 4, 5, 6, 9, 10\} \,.$$

Given the identity

$$P_i = P_{i-1} \cup (P_{i-1} + x_i) \,, \tag{35.21}$$

you can prove by induction on i (see Exercise 35.5-1) that the list L_i is a sorted list containing every element of P_i whose value is not more than t. Since the length of L_i can be as much as 2^i, EXACT-SUBSET-SUM is an exponential-time algorithm in general, although it is a polynomial-time algorithm in the special cases in which t is polynomial in $|S|$ or all the numbers in S are bounded by a polynomial in $|S|$.

A fully polynomial-time approximation scheme

The key to devising a fully polynomial-time approximation scheme for the subset-sum problem is to "trim" each list L_i after it is created. Here's the idea behind trimming: if two values in L are close to each other, then since the goal is just an approximate solution, there is no need to maintain both of them explicitly. More precisely, use a trimming parameter δ such that $0 < \delta < 1$. When *trimming* a list L by δ, remove as many elements from L as possible, in such a way that if L' is the result of trimming L, then for every element y that was removed from L, some element z still in L' approximates y. For z to approximate y, it must be no greater than y and also within a factor of $1 + \delta$ of y, so that

$$\frac{y}{1 + \delta} \leq z \leq y \,. \tag{35.22}$$

You can think of such a z as "representing" y in the new list L'. Each removed element y is represented by a remaining element z satisfying inequality (35.22). For example, suppose that $\delta = 0.1$ and

$$L = \langle 10, 11, 12, 15, 20, 21, 22, 23, 24, 29 \rangle \,.$$

Then trimming L results in

$$L' = \langle 10, 12, 15, 20, 23, 29 \rangle \,,$$

where the deleted value 11 is represented by 10, the deleted values 21 and 22 are represented by 20, and the deleted value 24 is represented by 23. Because every element of the trimmed version of the list is also an element of the original version of the list, trimming can dramatically decrease the number of elements kept while keeping a close (and slightly smaller) representative value in the list for each deleted element.

The procedure TRIM trims list $L = \langle y_1, y_2, \ldots, y_m \rangle$ in $\Theta(m)$ time, given L and the trimming parameter δ. It assumes that L is sorted into monotonically increasing order. The output of the procedure is a trimmed, sorted list. The procedure scans the elements of L in monotonically increasing order. A number is appended onto the returned list L' only if it is the first element of L or if it cannot be represented by the most recent number placed into L'.

TRIM(L, δ)

1 let m be the length of L
2 $L' = \langle y_1 \rangle$
3 $last = y_1$
4 **for** $i = 2$ **to** m
5   **if** $y_i > last \cdot (1 + \delta)$ // $y_i \geq last$ because L is sorted
6   append y_i onto the end of L'
7          $last = y_i$
8 **return** L'

Given the procedure TRIM, the procedure APPROX-SUBSET-SUM on the following page implements the approximation scheme. This procedure takes as input a set $S = \{x_1, x_2, \ldots, x_n\}$ of n integers (in arbitrary order), the size $n = |S|$, the target integer t, and an approximation parameter ϵ, where

$$0 < \epsilon < 1 . \tag{35.23}$$

It returns a value z^* whose value is within a factor of $1 + \epsilon$ of the optimal solution.

The APPROX-SUBSET-SUM procedure works as follows. Line 1 initializes the list L_0 to be the list containing just the element 0. The **for** loop in lines 2–5 computes L_i as a sorted list containing a suitably trimmed version of the set P_i, with all elements larger than t removed. Since the procedure creates L_i from L_{i-1}, it must ensure that the repeated trimming doesn't introduce too much compounded inaccuracy. That's why instead of the trimming parameter being ϵ in the call to TRIM, it has the smaller value $\epsilon/2n$. We'll soon see that APPROX-SUBSET-SUM returns a correct approximation if one exists.

APPROX-SUBSET-SUM(S, n, t, ϵ)

1 $L_0 = \langle 0 \rangle$
2 **for** $i = 1$ **to** n
3      $L_i = \text{MERGE-LISTS}(L_{i-1}, L_{i-1} + x_i)$
4      $L_i = \text{TRIM}(L_i, \epsilon/2n)$
5   remove from L_i every element that is greater than t
6 let z^* be the largest value in L_n
7 **return** z^*

As an example, suppose that APPROX-SUBSET-SUM is given

$$S = \langle 104, 102, 201, 101 \rangle$$

with $t = 308$ and $\epsilon = 0.40$. The trimming parameter δ is $\epsilon/2n = 0.40/8 = 0.05$. The procedure computes the following values on the indicated lines:

line 1: $L_0 = \langle 0 \rangle$,

line 3: $L_1 = \langle 0, 104 \rangle$,
line 4: $L_1 = \langle 0, 104 \rangle$,
line 5: $L_1 = \langle 0, 104 \rangle$,

line 3: $L_2 = \langle 0, 102, 104, 206 \rangle$,
line 4: $L_2 = \langle 0, 102, 206 \rangle$,
line 5: $L_2 = \langle 0, 102, 206 \rangle$,

line 3: $L_3 = \langle 0, 102, 201, 206, 303, 407 \rangle$,
line 4: $L_3 = \langle 0, 102, 201, 303, 407 \rangle$,
line 5: $L_3 = \langle 0, 102, 201, 303 \rangle$,

line 3: $L_4 = \langle 0, 101, 102, 201, 203, 302, 303, 404 \rangle$,
line 4: $L_4 = \langle 0, 101, 201, 302, 404 \rangle$,
line 5: $L_4 = \langle 0, 101, 201, 302 \rangle$.

The procedure returns $z^* = 302$ as its answer, which is well within $\epsilon = 40\%$ of the optimal answer $307 = 104 + 102 + 101$. In fact, it is within 2%.

Theorem 35.7
APPROX-SUBSET-SUM is a fully polynomial-time approximation scheme for the subset-sum problem.

Proof The operations of trimming L_i in line 4 and removing from L_i every element that is greater than t maintain the property that every element of L_i is also a member of P_i. Therefore, the value z^* returned in line 7 is indeed the sum of some subset of S, that is, $z^* \in P_n$. Let $y^* \in P_n$ denote an optimal solution to the subset-sum problem, so that it is the greatest value in P_n that is less than or equal to t. Because line 5 ensures that $z^* \leq t$, we know that $z^* \leq y^*$. By inequality (35.1), we need to show that $y^*/z^* \leq 1 + \epsilon$. We must also show that the running time of this algorithm is polynomial in both $1/\epsilon$ and the size of the input.

As Exercise 35.5-2 asks you to show, for every element y in P_i that is at most t, there exists an element $z \in L_i$ such that

$$\frac{y}{(1 + \epsilon/2n)^i} \leq z \leq y. \qquad (35.24)$$

Inequality (35.24) must hold for $y^* \in P_n$, and therefore there exists an element $z \in L_n$ such that

$$\frac{y^*}{(1 + \epsilon/2n)^n} \leq z \leq y^*,$$

and thus

$$\frac{y^*}{z} \leq \left(1 + \frac{\epsilon}{2n}\right)^n. \qquad (35.25)$$

Since there exists an element $z \in L_n$ fulfilling inequality (35.25), the inequality must hold for z^*, which is the largest value in L_n, which is to say

$$\frac{y^*}{z^*} \leq \left(1 + \frac{\epsilon}{2n}\right)^n. \qquad (35.26)$$

Now we show that $y^*/z^* \leq 1+\epsilon$. We do so by showing that $(1+\epsilon/2n)^n \leq 1+\epsilon$. First, inequality (35.23), $0 < \epsilon < 1$, implies that

$$(\epsilon/2)^2 \leq \epsilon/2. \qquad (35.27)$$

Next, from equation (3.16) on page 66, we have $\lim_{n \to \infty}(1 + \epsilon/2n)^n = e^{\epsilon/2}$. Exercise 35.5-3 asks you to show that

$$\frac{d}{dn}\left(1 + \frac{\epsilon}{2n}\right)^n > 0. \qquad (35.28)$$

Therefore, the function $(1 + \epsilon/2n)^n$ increases with n as it approaches its limit of $e^{\epsilon/2}$, and we have

$$\begin{aligned}
\left(1 + \frac{\epsilon}{2n}\right)^n &\leq e^{\epsilon/2} \\
&\leq 1 + \epsilon/2 + (\epsilon/2)^2 \quad \text{(by inequality (3.15) on page 66)} \\
&\leq 1 + \epsilon \quad\quad\quad\quad\quad\quad \text{(by inequality (35.27))} . \qquad (35.29)
\end{aligned}$$

Combining inequalities (35.26) and (35.29) completes the analysis of the approximation ratio.

To show that APPROX-SUBSET-SUM is a fully polynomial-time approximation scheme, we derive a bound on the length of L_i. After trimming, successive elements z and z' of L_i must have the relationship $z'/z > 1+\epsilon/2n$. That is, they must differ by a factor of at least $1 + \epsilon/2n$. Each list, therefore, contains the value 0, possibly the value 1, and up to $\lfloor \log_{1+\epsilon/2n} t \rfloor$ additional values. The number of elements in each list L_i is at most

$$
\begin{aligned}
\log_{1+\epsilon/2n} t + 2 &= \frac{\ln t}{\ln(1 + \epsilon/2n)} + 2 \\
&\leq \frac{2n(1 + \epsilon/2n)\ln t}{\epsilon} + 2 \quad \text{(by inequality (3.23) on page 67)} \\
&< \frac{3n \ln t}{\epsilon} + 2 \quad\quad\quad \text{(by inequality (35.23), } 0 < \epsilon < 1 \text{) .}
\end{aligned}
$$

This bound is polynomial in the size of the input—which is the number of bits $\lg t$ needed to represent t plus the number of bits needed to represent the set S, which in turn is polynomial in n—and in $1/\epsilon$. Since the running time of APPROX-SUBSET-SUM is polynomial in the lengths of the lists L_i, we conclude that APPROX-SUBSET-SUM is a fully polynomial-time approximation scheme. ∎

Exercises

35.5-1
Prove equation (35.21). Then show that after executing line 4 of EXACT-SUBSET-SUM, L_i is a sorted list containing every element of P_i whose value is not more than t.

35.5-2
Using induction on i, prove inequality (35.24).

35.5-3
Prove inequality (35.28).

35.5-4
How can you modify the approximation scheme presented in this section to find a good approximation to the smallest value not less than t that is a sum of some subset of the given input list?

35.5-5
Modify the APPROX-SUBSET-SUM procedure to also return the subset of S that sums to the value z^*.

Problems

35-1 *Bin packing*

You are given a set of n objects, where the size s_i of the ith object satisfies $0 < s_i < 1$. Your goal is to pack all the objects into the minimum number of unit-size bins. Each bin can hold any subset of the objects whose total size does not exceed 1.

a. Prove that the problem of determining the minimum number of bins required is NP-hard. (*Hint:* Reduce from the subset-sum problem.)

The *first-fit* heuristic takes each object in turn and places it into the first bin that can accommodate it, as follows. It maintains an ordered list of bins. Let b denote the number of bins in the list, where b increases over the course of the algorithm, and let $\langle B_1, \ldots, B_b \rangle$ be the list of bins. Initially $b = 0$ and the list is empty. The algorithm takes each object i in turn and places it in the lowest-numbered bin that can still accommodate it. If no bin can accommodate object i, then b is incremented and a new bin B_b is opened, containing object i. Let $S = \sum_{i=1}^{n} s_i$.

b. Argue that the optimal number of bins required is at least $\lceil S \rceil$.

c. Argue that the first-fit heuristic leaves at most one bin at most half full.

d. Prove that the number of bins used by the first-fit heuristic never exceeds $\lceil 2S \rceil$.

e. Prove an approximation ratio of 2 for the first-fit heuristic.

f. Give an efficient implementation of the first-fit heuristic, and analyze its running time.

35-2 *Approximating the size of a maximum clique*

Let $G = (V, E)$ be an undirected graph. For any $k \geq 1$, define $G^{(k)}$ to be the undirected graph $(V^{(k)}, E^{(k)})$, where $V^{(k)}$ is the set of all ordered k-tuples of vertices from V and $E^{(k)}$ is defined so that $(v_1, v_2, \ldots, v_k)$ is adjacent to $(w_1, w_2, \ldots, w_k)$ if and only if for $i = 1, 2, \ldots, k$, either vertex v_i is adjacent to w_i in G, or else $v_i = w_i$.

a. Prove that the size of the maximum clique in $G^{(k)}$ is equal to the kth power of the size of the maximum clique in G.

b. Argue that if there is an approximation algorithm that has a constant approximation ratio for finding a maximum-size clique, then there is a polynomial-time approximation scheme for the problem.

35-3   Weighted set-covering problem

Suppose that sets have weights in the set-covering problem, so that each set S_i in the family $\mathcal{F}$ has an associated weight w_i. The weight of a cover $\mathcal{C}$ is $\sum_{S_i \in \mathcal{C}} w_i$. The goal is wish to determine a minimum-weight cover. (Section 35.3 handles the case in which $w_i = 1$ for all i.)

Show how to generalize the greedy set-covering heuristic in a natural manner to provide an approximate solution for any instance of the weighted set-covering problem. Letting d be the maximum size of any set S_i, show that your heuristic has an approximation ratio of $H(d) = \sum_{i=1}^{d} 1/i$.

35-4   Maximum matching

Recall that for an undirected graph G, a matching is a set of edges such that no two edges in the set are incident on the same vertex. Section 25.1 showed how to find a maximum matching in a bipartite graph, that is, a matching such that no other matching in G contains more edges. This problem examines matchings in undirected graphs that are not required to be bipartite.

a. Show that a maximal matching need not be a maximum matching by exhibiting an undirected graph G and a maximal matching M in G that is not a maximum matching. (*Hint:* You can find such a graph with only four vertices.)

b. Consider a connected, undirected graph $G = (V, E)$. Give an $O(E)$-time greedy algorithm to find a maximal matching in G.

This problem concentrates on a polynomial-time approximation algorithm for maximum matching. Whereas the fastest known algorithm for maximum matching takes superlinear (but polynomial) time, the approximation algorithm here will run in linear time. You will show that the linear-time greedy algorithm for maximal matching in part (b) is a 2-approximation algorithm for maximum matching.

c. Show that the size of a maximum matching in G is a lower bound on the size of any vertex cover for G.

d. Consider a maximal matching M in $G = (V, E)$. Let $T = \{v \in V : \text{some edge in } M \text{ is incident on } v\}$. What can you say about the subgraph of G induced by the vertices of G that are not in T?

e. Conclude from part (d) that $2\,|M|$ is the size of a vertex cover for G.

f. Using parts (c) and (e), prove that the greedy algorithm in part (b) is a 2-approximation algorithm for maximum matching.

35-5 *Parallel machine scheduling*

In the *parallel-machine-scheduling problem*, the input has two parts: n jobs, $J_1, J_2, \ldots, J_n$, where each job J_k has an associated nonnegative processing time of p_k, and m identical machines, $M_1, M_2, \ldots, M_m$. Any job can run on any machine. A *schedule* specifies, for each job J_k, the machine on which it runs and the time period during which it runs. Each job J_k must run on some machine M_i for p_k consecutive time units, and during that time period no other job may run on M_i. Let C_k denote the *completion time* of job J_k, that is, the time at which job J_k completes processing. Given a schedule, define $C_{max} = \max \{C_j : 1 \le j \le n\}$ to be the *makespan* of the schedule. The goal is to find a schedule whose makespan is minimum.

For example, consider an input with two machines M_1 and M_2, and four jobs J_1, J_2, J_3, and J_4 with $p_1 = 2$, $p_2 = 12$, $p_3 = 4$, and $p_4 = 5$. Then one possible schedule runs, on machine M_1, job J_1 followed by job J_2, and on machine M_2, job J_4 followed by job J_3. For this schedule, $C_1 = 2, C_2 = 14, C_3 = 9, C_4 = 5$, and $C_{max} = 14$. An optimal schedule runs job J_2 on machine M_1 and jobs J_1, J_3, and J_4 on machine M_2. For this schedule, we have $C_1 = 2, C_2 = 12, C_3 = 6$, and $C_4 = 11$, and so $C_{max} = 12$.

Given the input to a parallel-machine-scheduling problem, let C_{max}^* denote the makespan of an optimal schedule.

a. Show that the optimal makespan is at least as large as the greatest processing time, that is,

$$C_{max}^* \ge \max \{p_k : 1 \le k \le n\} .$$

b. Show that the optimal makespan is at least as large as the average machine load, that is,

$$C_{max}^* \ge \frac{1}{m} \sum_{k=1}^{n} p_k .$$

Consider the following greedy algorithm for parallel machine scheduling: whenever a machine is idle, schedule any job that has not yet been scheduled.

c. Write pseudocode to implement this greedy algorithm. What is the running time of your algorithm?

d. For the schedule returned by the greedy algorithm, show that

$$C_{max} \le \frac{1}{m} \sum_{k=1}^{n} p_k + \max \{p_k : 1 \le k \le n\} .$$

Conclude that this algorithm is a polynomial-time 2-approximation algorithm.

35-6   Approximating a maximum spanning tree

Let $G = (V, E)$ be an undirected graph with distinct edge weights $w(u, v)$ on each edge $(u, v) \in E$. For each vertex $v \in V$, denote by $\max(v)$ the maximum-weight edge incident on that vertex. Let $S_G = \{\max(v) : v \in V\}$ be the set of maximum-weight edges incident on each vertex, and let T_G be the maximum-weight spanning tree of G, that is, the spanning tree of maximum total weight. For any subset of edges $E' \subseteq E$, define $w(E') = \sum_{(u,v) \in E'} w(u, v)$.

a. Give an example of a graph with at least 4 vertices for which $S_G = T_G$.

b. Give an example of a graph with at least 4 vertices for which $S_G \neq T_G$.

c. Prove that $S_G \subseteq T_G$ for any graph G.

d. Prove that $w(S_G) \geq w(T_G)/2$ for any graph G.

e. Give an $O(V + E)$-time algorithm to compute a 2-approximation to the maximum spanning tree.

35-7   An approximation algorithm for the 0-1 knapsack problem

Recall the knapsack problem from Section 15.2. The input includes n items, where the ith item is worth v_i dollars and weighs w_i pounds. The input also includes the capacity of a knapsack, which is W pounds. Here, we add the further assumptions that each weight w_i is at most W and that the items are indexed in monotonically decreasing order of their values: $v_1 \geq v_2 \geq \cdots \geq v_n$.

In the 0-1 knapsack problem, the goal is to find a subset of the items whose total weight is at most W and whose total value is maximum. The fractional knapsack problem is like the 0-1 knapsack problem, except that a fraction of each item may be put into the knapsack, rather than either all or none of each item. If a fraction x_i of item i goes into the knapsack, where $0 \leq x_i \leq 1$, it contributes $x_i w_i$ to the weight of the knapsack and adds value $x_i v_i$. The goal of this problem is to develop a polynomial-time 2-approximation algorithm for the 0-1 knapsack problem.

In order to design a polynomial-time algorithm, let's consider restricted instances of the 0-1 knapsack problem. Given an instance I of the knapsack problem, form restricted instances I_j, for $j = 1, 2, \ldots, n$, by removing items $1, 2, \ldots, j-1$ and requiring the solution to include item j (all of item j in both the fractional and 0-1 knapsack problems). No items are removed in instance I_1. For instance I_j, let P_j denote an optimal solution to the 0-1 problem and Q_j denote an optimal solution to the fractional problem.

a. Argue that an optimal solution to instance I of the 0-1 knapsack problem is one of $\{P_1, P_2, \ldots, P_n\}$.

b. Prove that to find an optimal solution Q_j to the fractional problem for instance I_j, you can include item j and then use the greedy algorithm in which each step takes as much as possible of the unchosen item with the maximum value per pound v_i/w_i in the set $\{j + 1, j + 2, \ldots, n\}$.

c. Prove that there is always an optimal solution Q_j to the fractional problem for instance I_j that includes at most one item fractionally. That is, for all items except possibly one, either all of the item or none of the item goes into the knapsack.

d. Given an optimal solution Q_j to the fractional problem for instance I_j, form solution R_j from Q_j by deleting any fractional items from Q_j. Let $v(S)$ denote the total value of items taken in a solution S. Prove that $v(R_j) \geq v(Q_j)/2 \geq v(P_j)/2$.

e. Give a polynomial-time algorithm that returns a maximum-value solution from the set $\{R_1, R_2, \ldots, R_n\}$, and prove that your algorithm is a polynomial-time 2-approximation algorithm for the 0-1 knapsack problem.

Chapter notes

Although methods that do not necessarily compute exact solutions have been known for thousands of years (for example, methods to approximate the value of π), the notion of an approximation algorithm is much more recent. Hochbaum [221] credits Garey, Graham, and Ullman [175] and Johnson [236] with formalizing the concept of a polynomial-time approximation algorithm. The first such algorithm is often credited to Graham [197].

Since this early work, thousands of approximation algorithms have been designed for a wide range of problems, and there is a wealth of literature on this field. Texts by Ausiello et al. [29], Hochbaum [221], Vazirani [446], and Williamson and Shmoys [459] deal exclusively with approximation algorithms, as do surveys by Shmoys [409] and Klein and Young [256]. Several other texts, such as Garey and Johnson [176] and Papadimitriou and Steiglitz [353], have significant coverage of approximation algorithms as well. Books edited by Lawler, Lenstra, Rinnooy Kan, and Shmoys [277] and by Gutin and Punnen [204] provide extensive treatments of approximation algorithms and heuristics for the traveling-salesperson problem.

Papadimitriou and Steiglitz attribute the algorithm APPROX-VERTEX-COVER to F. Gavril and M. Yannakakis. The vertex-cover problem has been studied extensively (Hochbaum [221] lists 16 different approximation algorithms for this problem), but all the approximation ratios are at least $2 - o(1)$.

The algorithm APPROX-TSP-TOUR appears in a paper by Rosenkrantz, Stearns, and Lewis [384]. Christofides improved on this algorithm and gave a $3/2$-approximation algorithm for the traveling-salesperson problem with the triangle inequality. Arora [23] and Mitchell [330] have shown that if the points lie in the euclidean plane, there is a polynomial-time approximation scheme. Theorem 35.3 is due to Sahni and Gonzalez [392].

The algorithm APPROX-SUBSET-SUM and its analysis are loosely modeled after related approximation algorithms for the knapsack and subset-sum problems by Ibarra and Kim [234].

Problem 35-7 is a combinatorial version of a more general result on approximating knapsack-type integer programs by Bienstock and McClosky [55].

The randomized algorithm for MAX-3-CNF satisfiability is implicit in the work of Johnson [236]. The weighted vertex-cover algorithm is by Hochbaum [220]. Section 35.4 only touches on the power of randomization and linear programming in the design of approximation algorithms. A combination of these two ideas yields a technique called "randomized rounding," which formulates a problem as an integer linear program, solves the linear-programming relaxation, and interprets the variables in the solution as probabilities. These probabilities then help guide the solution of the original problem. This technique was first used by Raghavan and Thompson [374], and it has had many subsequent uses. (See Motwani, Naor, and Raghavan [335] for a survey.) Several other notable ideas in the field of approximation algorithms include the primal-dual method (see Goemans and Williamson [184] for a survey), finding sparse cuts for use in divide-and-conquer algorithms [288], and the use of semidefinite programming [183].

As mentioned in the chapter notes for Chapter 34, results in probabilistically checkable proofs have led to lower bounds on the approximability of many problems, including several in this chapter. In addition to the references there, the chapter by Arora and Lund [26] contains a good description of the relationship between probabilistically checkable proofs and the hardness of approximating various problems.

Part VIII   Appendix: Mathematical Background

Introduction

When you analyze algorithms, you often need to draw upon a body of mathematical tools. Some of these tools are as simple as high-school algebra, but others may be new to you. In Part I, we saw how to manipulate asymptotic notations and solve recurrences. This appendix comprises a compendium of several other concepts and methods used in analyzing algorithms. As noted in the introduction to Part I, you may have seen much of the material in this appendix before having read this book, although some of the specific notational conventions appearing here might differ from those you have seen elsewhere. Hence, you should treat this appendix as reference material. As in the rest of this book, however, we have included exercises and problems, in order for you to improve your skills in these areas.

Appendix A offers methods for evaluating and bounding summations, which occur frequently in the analysis of algorithms. Many of the formulas here appear in any calculus text, but you will find it convenient to have these methods compiled in one place.

Appendix B contains basic definitions and notations for sets, relations, functions, graphs, and trees. It also gives some basic properties of these mathematical objects.

Appendix C begins with elementary principles of counting: permutations, combinations, and the like. The remainder contains definitions and properties of basic probability. Most of the algorithms in this book require no probability for their analysis, and thus you can easily omit the latter sections of the chapter on a first reading, even without skimming them. Later, when you encounter a probabilistic analysis that you want to understand better, you will find Appendix C well organized for reference purposes.

Appendix D defines matrices, their operations, and some of their basic properties. You have probably seen most of this material already if you have taken a course in linear algebra. But you might find it helpful to have one place to look for notations and definitions.

A   Summations

When an algorithm contains an iterative control construct such as a **while** or **for** loop, you can express its running time as the sum of the times spent on each execution of the body of the loop. For example, Section 2.2 argued that the ith iteration of insertion sort took time proportional to i in the worst case. Adding up the time spent on each iteration produced the summation (or series) $\sum_{i=2}^{n} i$. Evaluating this summation resulted in a bound of $\Theta(n^2)$ on the worst-case running time of the algorithm. This example illustrates why you should know how to manipulate and bound summations.

Section A.1 lists several basic formulas involving summations. Section A.2 offers useful techniques for bounding summations. The formulas in Section A.1 appear without proof, though proofs for some of them appear in Section A.2 to illustrate the methods of that section. You can find most of the other proofs in any calculus text.

A.1   Summation formulas and properties

Given a sequence $a_1, a_2, \ldots, a_n$ of numbers, where n is a nonnegative integer, the finite sum $a_1 + a_2 + \cdots + a_n$ can be expressed as $\sum_{k=1}^{n} a_k$. If $n = 0$, the value of the summation is defined to be 0. The value of a finite series is always well defined, and the order in which its terms are added does not matter.

Given an infinite sequence $a_1, a_2, \ldots$ of numbers, we can write their infinite sum $a_1 + a_2 + \cdots$ as $\sum_{k=1}^{\infty} a_k$, which means $\lim_{n \to \infty} \sum_{k=1}^{n} a_k$. If the limit does not exist, the series *diverges*, and otherwise, it *converges*. The terms of a convergent series cannot always be added in any order. You can, however, rearrange the terms of an *absolutely convergent series*, that is, a series $\sum_{k=1}^{\infty} a_k$ for which the series $\sum_{k=1}^{\infty} |a_k|$ also converges.

Linearity

For any real number c and any finite sequences $a_1, a_2, \ldots, a_n$ and $b_1, b_2, \ldots, b_n$,

$$\sum_{k=1}^{n}(ca_k + b_k) = c\sum_{k=1}^{n}a_k + \sum_{k=1}^{n}b_k \ .$$

The linearity property also applies to infinite convergent series.

The linearity property applies to summations incorporating asymptotic notation. For example,

$$\sum_{k=1}^{n}\Theta(f(k)) = \Theta\left(\sum_{k=1}^{n}f(k)\right) \ .$$

In this equation, the Θ-notation on the left-hand side applies to the variable k, but on the right-hand side, it applies to n. Such manipulations also apply to infinite convergent series.

Arithmetic series

The summation

$$\sum_{k=1}^{n}k = 1 + 2 + \cdots + n \ ,$$

is an *arithmetic series* and has the value

$$\sum_{k=1}^{n}k = \frac{n(n+1)}{2} \tag{A.1}$$

$$= \Theta(n^2) \ . \tag{A.2}$$

A *general arithmetic series* includes an additive constant $a \geq 0$ and a constant coefficient $b > 0$ in each term, but has the same total asymptotically:

$$\sum_{k=1}^{n}(a + bk) = \Theta(n^2) \ . \tag{A.3}$$

Sums of squares and cubes

The following formulas apply to summations of squares and cubes:

$$\sum_{k=0}^{n}k^2 = \frac{n(n+1)(2n+1)}{6} \ , \tag{A.4}$$

$$\sum_{k=0}^{n}k^3 = \frac{n^2(n+1)^2}{4} \ . \tag{A.5}$$

Geometric series

For real $x \neq 1$, the summation

$$\sum_{k=0}^{n} x^k = 1 + x + x^2 + \cdots + x^n$$

is a *geometric series* and has the value

$$\sum_{k=0}^{n} x^k = \frac{x^{n+1} - 1}{x - 1} . \tag{A.6}$$

The infinite decreasing geometric series occurs when the summation is infinite and $|x| < 1$:

$$\sum_{k=0}^{\infty} x^k = \frac{1}{1 - x} . \tag{A.7}$$

If we assume that $0^0 = 1$, these formulas apply even when $x = 0$.

Harmonic series

For positive integers n, the nth *harmonic number* is

$$
\begin{aligned}
H_n &= 1 + \frac{1}{2} + \frac{1}{3} + \frac{1}{4} + \cdots + \frac{1}{n} \\
&= \sum_{k=1}^{n} \frac{1}{k} \tag{A.8} \\
&= \ln n + O(1) . \tag{A.9}
\end{aligned}
$$

Inequalities (A.20) and (A.21) on page 1150 provide the stronger bounds

$$\ln(n + 1) \leq H_n \leq \ln n + 1 . \tag{A.10}$$

Integrating and differentiating series

Integrating or differentiating the formulas above yields additional formulas. For example, differentiating both sides of the infinite geometric series (A.7) and multiplying by x gives

$$\sum_{k=0}^{\infty} k x^k = \frac{x}{(1 - x)^2} \tag{A.11}$$

for $|x| < 1$.

Telescoping series

For any sequence $a_0, a_1, \ldots, a_n$,

$$\sum_{k=1}^{n}(a_k - a_{k-1}) = a_n - a_0 , \tag{A.12}$$

since each of the terms $a_1, a_2, \ldots, a_{n-1}$ is added in exactly once and subtracted out exactly once. We say that the sum *telescopes*. Similarly,

$$\sum_{k=0}^{n-1}(a_k - a_{k+1}) = a_0 - a_n .$$

As an example of a telescoping sum, consider the series

$$\sum_{k=1}^{n-1} \frac{1}{k(k + 1)} .$$

Rewriting each term as

$$\frac{1}{k(k + 1)} = \frac{1}{k} - \frac{1}{k + 1} ,$$

gives

$$\sum_{k=1}^{n-1} \frac{1}{k(k + 1)} = \sum_{k=1}^{n-1} \left(\frac{1}{k} - \frac{1}{k + 1} \right)$$
$$= 1 - \frac{1}{n} .$$

Reindexing summations

A series can sometimes be simplified by changing its index, often reversing the order of summation. Consider the series $\sum_{k=0}^{n} a_{n-k}$. Because the terms in this summation are $a_n, a_{n-1}, \ldots, a_0$, we can reverse the order of indices by letting $j = n - k$ and rewrite this summation as

$$\sum_{k=0}^{n} a_{n-k} = \sum_{j=0}^{n} a_j . \tag{A.13}$$

Generally, if the summation index appears in the body of the sum with a minus sign, it's worth thinking about reindexing.

As an example, consider the summation

$$\sum_{k=1}^{n} \frac{1}{n-k+1} .$$

The index k appears with a negative sign in $1/(n-k+1)$. And indeed, we can simplify this summation, this time setting $j = n - k + 1$, yielding

$$\sum_{k=1}^{n} \frac{1}{n-k+1} = \sum_{j=1}^{n} \frac{1}{j} , \tag{A.14}$$

which is just the harmonic series (A.8).

Products

The finite product $a_1 a_2 \cdots a_n$ can be expressed as

$$\prod_{k=1}^{n} a_k .$$

If $n = 0$, the value of the product is defined to be 1. You can convert a formula with a product to a formula with a summation by using the identity

$$\lg \left(\prod_{k=1}^{n} a_k \right) = \sum_{k=1}^{n} \lg a_k .$$

Exercises

A.1-1
Prove that $\sum_{k=1}^{n} O(f_k(i)) = O\left(\sum_{k=1}^{n} f_k(i) \right)$ by using the linearity property of summations.

A.1-2
Find a simple formula for $\sum_{k=1}^{n} (2k - 1)$.

A.1-3
Interpret the decimal number 111,111,111 in light of equation (A.6).

A.1-4
Evaluate the infinite series $1 - \frac{1}{2} + \frac{1}{4} - \frac{1}{8} + \frac{1}{16} - \cdots$.

A.1-5
Let $c \geq 0$ be a constant. Show that $\sum_{k=1}^{n} k^c = \Theta(n^{c+1})$.

A.1-6
Show that $\sum_{k=0}^{\infty} k^2 x^k = x(1+x)/(1-x)^3$ for $|x| < 1$.

A.1-7

Prove that $\sum_{k=1}^{n} \sqrt{k \lg k} = \Theta(n^{3/2} \lg^{1/2} n)$. (*Hint:* Show the asymptotic upper and lower bounds separately.)

★ ***A.1-8***

Show that $\sum_{k=1}^{n} 1/(2k - 1) = \ln(\sqrt{n}) + O(1)$ by manipulating the harmonic series.

★ ***A.1-9***

Show that $\sum_{k=0}^{\infty}(k - 1)/2^k = 0$.

★ ***A.1-10***

Evaluate the sum $\sum_{k=1}^{\infty}(2k + 1)x^{2k}$ for $|x| < 1$.

★ ***A.1-11***

Evaluate the product $\prod_{k=2}^{n}(1 - 1/k^2)$.

A.2 Bounding summations

You can choose from several techniques to bound the summations that describe the running times of algorithms. Here are some of the most frequently used methods.

Mathematical induction

The most basic way to evaluate a series is to use mathematical induction. As an example, let's prove that the arithmetic series $\sum_{k=1}^{n} k$ evaluates to $n(n + 1)/2$. For $n = 1$, we have that $n(n + 1)/2 = 1 \cdot 2/2 = 1$, which equals $\sum_{k=1}^{1} k$. With the inductive assumption that it holds for n, we prove that it holds for $n + 1$. We have

$$
\begin{aligned}
\sum_{k=1}^{n+1} k &= \sum_{k=1}^{n} k + (n + 1) \\
&= \frac{n(n + 1)}{2} + (n + 1) \\
&= \frac{n^2 + n + 2n + 2}{2} \\
&= \frac{(n + 1)(n + 2)}{2} .
\end{aligned}
$$

You don't always need to guess the exact value of a summation in order to use mathematical induction. Instead, you can use induction to prove an upper or lower bound on a summation. As an example, let's prove the asymptotic upper bound $\sum_{k=0}^{n} 3^k = O(3^n)$. More specifically, we'll prove that $\sum_{k=0}^{n} 3^k \leq c3^n$ for some constant c. For the initial condition $n = 0$, we have $\sum_{k=0}^{0} 3^k = 1 \leq c \cdot 1$ as long as $c \geq 1$. Assuming that the bound holds for n, we prove that it holds for $n + 1$. We have

$$
\begin{aligned}
\sum_{k=0}^{n+1} 3^k &= \sum_{k=0}^{n} 3^k + 3^{n+1} \\
&\leq c3^n + 3^{n+1} && \text{(by the inductive hypothesis)} \\
&= \left(\frac{1}{3} + \frac{1}{c} \right) c3^{n+1} \\
&\leq c3^{n+1}
\end{aligned}
$$

as long as $(1/3 + 1/c) \leq 1$ or, equivalently, $c \geq 3/2$. Thus, $\sum_{k=0}^{n} 3^k = O(3^n)$, as we wished to show.

You need to take care when using asymptotic notation to prove bounds by induction. Consider the following fallacious proof that $\sum_{k=1}^{n} k = O(n)$. Certainly, $\sum_{k=1}^{1} k = O(1)$. Assuming that the bound holds for n, we now prove it for $n + 1$:

$$
\begin{aligned}
\sum_{k=1}^{n+1} k &= \sum_{k=1}^{n} k + (n + 1) \\
&= O(n) + (n + 1) && \Longleftarrow \textit{wrong!} \\
&= O(n + 1) \, .
\end{aligned}
$$

The bug in the argument is that the "constant" hidden by the "big-oh" grows with n and thus is not constant. We have not shown that the same constant works for *all* n.

Bounding the terms

You can sometimes obtain a good upper bound on a series by bounding each term of the series, and it often suffices to use the largest term to bound the others. For example, a quick upper bound on the arithmetic series (A.1) is

$$
\begin{aligned}
\sum_{k=1}^{n} k &\leq \sum_{k=1}^{n} n \\
&= n^2 \, .
\end{aligned}
$$

In general, for a series $\sum_{k=1}^{n} a_k$, if we let $a_{max} = \max \{a_k : 1 \leq k \leq n\}$, then

$$
\sum_{k=1}^{n} a_k \leq n \cdot a_{max} \, .
$$

The technique of bounding each term in a series by the largest term is a weak method when the series can in fact be bounded by a geometric series. Given the series $\sum_{k=0}^{n} a_k$, suppose that $a_{k+1}/a_k \leq r$ for all $k \geq 0$, where $0 < r < 1$ is a constant. You can bound the sum by an infinite decreasing geometric series, since $a_k \leq a_0 r^k$, and thus

$$\sum_{k=0}^{n} a_k \leq \sum_{k=0}^{\infty} a_0 r^k$$

$$= a_0 \sum_{k=0}^{\infty} r^k \qquad\qquad (A.15)$$

$$= a_0 \frac{1}{1-r} . \qquad\qquad (A.16)$$

You can apply this method to bound the summation $\sum_{k=1}^{\infty} (k/3^k)$. In order to start the summation at $k = 0$, rewrite it as $\sum_{k=0}^{\infty} ((k+1)/3^{k+1})$. The first term ($a_0$) is $1/3$, and the ratio (r) of consecutive terms is

$$\frac{(k+2)/3^{k+2}}{(k+1)/3^{k+1}} = \frac{1}{3} \cdot \frac{k+2}{k+1}$$

$$\leq \frac{2}{3}$$

for all $k \geq 0$. Thus, we have

$$\sum_{k=1}^{\infty} \frac{k}{3^k} = \sum_{k=0}^{\infty} \frac{k+1}{3^{k+1}}$$

$$\leq \frac{1}{3} \cdot \frac{1}{1-2/3}$$

$$= 1 .$$

A common bug in applying this method is to show that the ratio of consecutive terms is less than 1 and then to assume that the summation is bounded by a geometric series. An example is the infinite harmonic series, which diverges since

$$\sum_{k=1}^{\infty} \frac{1}{k} = \lim_{n \to \infty} \sum_{k=1}^{n} \frac{1}{k}$$

$$= \lim_{n \to \infty} \Theta(\lg n)$$

$$= \infty .$$

The ratio of the $(k+1)$st and kth terms in this series is $k/(k+1) < 1$, but the series is not bounded by a decreasing geometric series. To bound a series by a geometric series, you need to show that there is an $r < 1$, which is a *constant*, such that the ratio of all pairs of consecutive terms never exceeds r. In the harmonic series, no such r exists because the ratio becomes arbitrarily close to 1.

Splitting summations

One way to obtain bounds on a difficult summation is to express the series as the sum of two or more series by partitioning the range of the index and then to bound each of the resulting series. For example, let's find a lower bound on the arithmetic series $\sum_{k=1}^{n} k$, which we have already seen has an upper bound of n^2. You might attempt to bound each term in the summation by the smallest term, but since that term is 1, you would get a lower bound of n for the summation—far off from the upper bound of n^2.

You can obtain a better lower bound by first splitting the summation. Assume for convenience that n is even, so that

$$
\begin{aligned}
\sum_{k=1}^{n} k &= \sum_{k=1}^{n/2} k + \sum_{k=n/2+1}^{n} k \\
&\geq \sum_{k=1}^{n/2} 0 + \sum_{k=n/2+1}^{n} \frac{n}{2} \\
&= \left(\frac{n}{2}\right)^2 \\
&= \Omega(n^2) \,,
\end{aligned}
$$

which is an asymptotically tight bound, since $\sum_{k=1}^{n} k = O(n^2)$.

For a summation arising from the analysis of an algorithm, you can sometimes split the summation and ignore a constant number of the initial terms. Generally, this technique applies when each term a_k in a summation $\sum_{k=0}^{n} a_k$ is independent of n. Then for any constant $k_0 > 0$, you can write

$$
\begin{aligned}
\sum_{k=0}^{n} a_k &= \sum_{k=0}^{k_0-1} a_k + \sum_{k=k_0}^{n} a_k \\
&= \Theta(1) + \sum_{k=k_0}^{n} a_k \,,
\end{aligned}
$$

since the initial terms of the summation are all constant and there are a constant number of them. You can then use other methods to bound $\sum_{k=k_0}^{n} a_k$. This technique applies to infinite summations as well. For example, let's find an asymptotic upper bound on $\sum_{k=0}^{\infty} k^2/2^k$. The ratio of consecutive terms is

$$\frac{(k+1)^2/2^{k+1}}{k^2/2^k} = \frac{(k+1)^2}{2k^2}$$
$$\leq 8/9$$

if $k \geq 3$. Thus, you can split the summation into

$$\sum_{k=0}^{\infty} \frac{k^2}{2^k} = \sum_{k=0}^{2} \frac{k^2}{2^k} + \sum_{k=3}^{\infty} \frac{k^2}{2^k}$$

$$= \sum_{k=0}^{2} \frac{k^2}{2^k} + \sum_{k=0}^{\infty} \frac{(k+3)^2}{2^{k+3}} \qquad \text{(by reindexing)}$$

$$\leq \sum_{k=0}^{2} \frac{k^2}{2^k} + \frac{9}{8} \sum_{k=0}^{\infty} \left(\frac{8}{9}\right)^k \qquad \text{(by inequality (A.15))}$$

$$= (0 + 1/2 + 1) + \frac{9/8}{1 - 8/9} \qquad \text{(by equation (A.16))}$$

$$= O(1) .$$

The technique of splitting summations can help determine asymptotic bounds in much more difficult situations. For example, here is one way to obtain a bound of $O(\lg n)$ on the harmonic series (A.9):

$$H_n = \sum_{k=1}^{n} \frac{1}{k} .$$

The idea is to split the range 1 to n into $\lfloor \lg n \rfloor + 1$ pieces and upper-bound the contribution of each piece by 1. For $i = 0, 1, \ldots, \lfloor \lg n \rfloor$, the ith piece consists of the terms starting at $1/2^i$ and going up to but not including $1/2^{i+1}$. The last piece might contain terms not in the original harmonic series, giving

$$\sum_{k=1}^{n} \frac{1}{k} \leq \sum_{i=0}^{\lfloor \lg n \rfloor} \sum_{j=0}^{2^i - 1} \frac{1}{2^i + j}$$

$$\leq \sum_{i=0}^{\lfloor \lg n \rfloor} \sum_{j=0}^{2^i - 1} \frac{1}{2^i}$$

$$= \sum_{i=0}^{\lfloor \lg n \rfloor} \left(2^i \cdot \frac{1}{2^i}\right)$$

$$= \sum_{i=0}^{\lfloor \lg n \rfloor} 1$$

$$\leq \lg n + 1 . \tag{A.17}$$

Approximation by integrals

When a summation has the form $\sum_{k=m}^{n} f(k)$, where $f(k)$ is a monotonically increasing function, you can approximate it by integrals:

$$\int_{m-1}^{n} f(x)\,dx \le \sum_{k=m}^{n} f(k) \le \int_{m}^{n+1} f(x)\,dx \;. \tag{A.18}$$

Figure A.1 justifies this approximation. The summation is represented as the area of the rectangles in the figure, and the integral is the blue region under the curve. When $f(k)$ is a monotonically decreasing function, you can use a similar method to provide the bounds

$$\int_{m}^{n+1} f(x)\,dx \le \sum_{k=m}^{n} f(k) \le \int_{m-1}^{n} f(x)\,dx \;. \tag{A.19}$$

The integral approximation (A.19) can be used to prove the tight bounds in inequality (A.10) for the nth harmonic number. The lower bound is

$$\sum_{k=1}^{n} \frac{1}{k} \ge \int_{1}^{n+1} \frac{dx}{x}$$

$$= \ln(n+1)\;, \tag{A.20}$$

For the upper bound, the integral approximation gives

$$\sum_{k=1}^{n} \frac{1}{k} = \sum_{k=2}^{n} \frac{1}{k} + 1$$

$$\le \int_{1}^{n} \frac{dx}{x} + 1$$

$$= \ln n + 1 \;. \tag{A.21}$$

Exercises

A.2-1
Show that $\sum_{k=1}^{n} 1/k^2$ is bounded above by a constant.

A.2-2
Find an asymptotic upper bound on the summation

$$\sum_{k=0}^{\lfloor \lg n \rfloor} \lceil n/2^k \rceil \;.$$

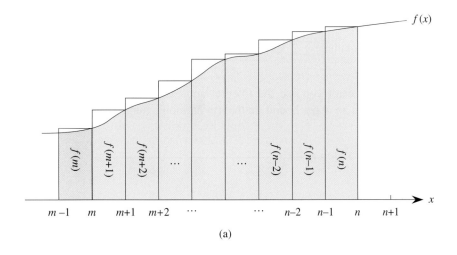

(a)

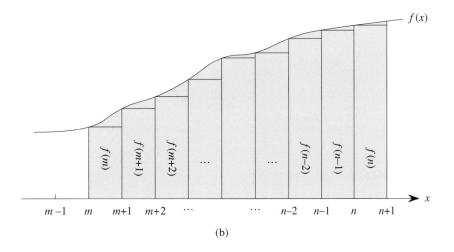

(b)

Figure A.1 Approximation of $\sum_{k=m}^{n} f(k)$ by integrals. The area of each rectangle is shown within the rectangle, and the total rectangle area represents the value of the summation. The integral is represented by the blue area under the curve. Comparing areas in **(a)** gives the lower bound $\int_{m-1}^{n} f(x)\,dx \leq \sum_{k=m}^{n} f(k)$. Shifting the rectangles one unit to the right gives the upper bound $\sum_{k=m}^{n} f(k) \leq \int_{m}^{n+1} f(x)\,dx$ in **(b)**.

A.2-3
Show that the nth harmonic number is $\Omega(\lg n)$ by splitting the summation.

A.2-4
Approximate $\sum_{k=1}^{n} k^3$ with an integral.

A.2-5
Why can't you use the integral approximation (A.19) directly on $\sum_{k=1}^{n} 1/k$ to obtain an upper bound on the nth harmonic number?

Problems

A-1   *Bounding summations*
Give asymptotically tight bounds on the following summations. Assume that $r \geq 0$ and $s \geq 0$ are constants.

a. $\displaystyle\sum_{k=1}^{n} k^r$.

b. $\displaystyle\sum_{k=1}^{n} \lg^s k$.

c. $\displaystyle\sum_{k=1}^{n} k^r \lg^s k$.

Appendix notes

Knuth [259] provides an excellent reference for the material presented here. You can find basic properties of series in any good calculus book, such as Apostol [19] or Thomas et al. [433].

B Sets, Etc.

Many chapters of this book touch on the elements of discrete mathematics. This appendix reviews the notations, definitions, and elementary properties of sets, relations, functions, graphs, and trees. If you are already well versed in this material, you can probably just skim this chapter.

B.1 Sets

A *set* is a collection of distinguishable objects, called its *members* or *elements*. If an object x is a member of a set S, we write $x \in S$ (read "x is a member of S" or, more briefly, "x belongs to S"). If x is not a member of S, we write $x \notin S$. To describe a set explicitly, write its members as a list inside braces. For example, to define a set S to contain precisely the numbers $1, 2$, and 3, write $S = \{1, 2, 3\}$. Since 2 belongs to the set S, we can write $2 \in S$, and since 4 is not a member, we can write $4 \notin S$. A set cannot contain the same object more than once,[1] and its elements are not ordered. Two sets A and B are *equal*, written $A = B$, if they contain the same elements. For example, $\{1, 2, 3, 1\} = \{1, 2, 3\} = \{3, 2, 1\}$.

We adopt special notations for frequently encountered sets:

- $\emptyset$ denotes the *empty set*, that is, the set containing no members.

- $\mathbb{Z}$ denotes the set of *integers*, that is, the set $\{\ldots, -2, -1, 0, 1, 2, \ldots\}$.

- $\mathbb{R}$ denotes the set of *real numbers*.

- $\mathbb{N}$ denotes the set of *natural numbers*, that is, the set $\{0, 1, 2, \ldots\}$.[2]

---

[1] A variation of a set, which can contain the same object more than once, is called a *multiset*.

[2] Some authors start the natural numbers with 1 instead of 0. The modern trend seems to be to start with 0.

If all the elements of a set A are contained in a set B, that is, if $x \in A$ implies $x \in B$, then we write $A \subseteq B$ and say that A is a *subset* of B. A set A is a *proper subset* of set B, written $A \subset B$, if $A \subseteq B$ but $A \neq B$. (Some authors use the symbol "$\subset$" to denote the ordinary subset relation, rather than the proper-subset relation.) Every set is a subset of itself: $A \subseteq A$ for any set A. For two sets A and B, we have $A = B$ if and only if $A \subseteq B$ and $B \subseteq A$. The subset relation is transitive (see page 1159): for any three sets A, B, and C, if $A \subseteq B$ and $B \subseteq C$, then $A \subseteq C$. The proper-subset relation is transitive as well. The empty set is a subset of all sets: for any set A, we have $\emptyset \subseteq A$.

Sets can be specified in terms of other sets. Given a set A, a set $B \subseteq A$ can be defined by stating a property that distinguishes the elements of B. For example, one way to define the set of even integers is $\{x : x \in \mathbb{Z} \text{ and } x/2 \text{ is an integer}\}$. The colon in this notation is read "such that." (Some authors use a vertical bar in place of the colon.)

Given two sets A and B, *set operations* define new sets:

- The *intersection* of sets A and B is the set

$$A \cap B = \{x : x \in A \text{ and } x \in B\} \ .$$

- The *union* of sets A and B is the set

$$A \cup B = \{x : x \in A \text{ or } x \in B\} \ .$$

- The *difference* between two sets A and B is the set

$$A - B = \{x : x \in A \text{ and } x \notin B\} \ .$$

Set operations obey the following laws:

Empty set laws:

$$A \cap \emptyset = \emptyset \ ,$$
$$A \cup \emptyset = A \ .$$

Idempotency laws:

$$A \cap A = A \ ,$$
$$A \cup A = A \ .$$

Commutative laws:

$$A \cap B = B \cap A \ ,$$
$$A \cup B = B \cup A \ .$$

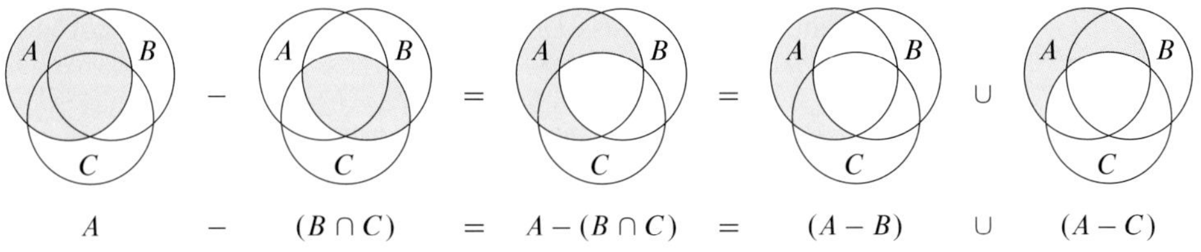

$$A \quad - \quad (B \cap C) \quad = \quad A - (B \cap C) \quad = \quad (A - B) \quad \cup \quad (A - C)$$

Figure B.1 A Venn diagram illustrating the first of DeMorgan's laws (B.2). Each of the sets A, B, and C is represented as a circle.

Associative laws:

$$A \cap (B \cap C) = (A \cap B) \cap C,$$
$$A \cup (B \cup C) = (A \cup B) \cup C.$$

Distributive laws:

$$A \cap (B \cup C) = (A \cap B) \cup (A \cap C),$$
$$A \cup (B \cap C) = (A \cup B) \cap (A \cup C).$$

(B.1)

Absorption laws:

$$A \cap (A \cup B) = A,$$
$$A \cup (A \cap B) = A.$$

DeMorgan's laws:

$$A - (B \cap C) = (A - B) \cup (A - C),$$
$$A - (B \cup C) = (A - B) \cap (A - C).$$

(B.2)

Figure B.1 illustrates the first of DeMorgan's laws, using a *Venn diagram*: a graphical picture in which sets are represented as regions of the plane.

Often, all the sets under consideration are subsets of some larger set U called the *universe*. For example, when considering various sets made up only of integers, the set $\mathbb{Z}$ of integers is an appropriate universe. Given a universe U, we define the *complement* of a set A as $\overline{A} = U - A = \{x : x \in U \text{ and } x \notin A\}$. For any set $A \subseteq U$, we have the following laws:

$$\overline{\overline{A}} = A,$$
$$A \cap \overline{A} = \emptyset,$$
$$A \cup \overline{A} = U.$$

An equivalent way to express DeMorgan's laws (B.2) uses set complements. For any two sets $B, C \subseteq U$, we have

$$\overline{B \cap C} = \overline{B} \cup \overline{C},$$
$$\overline{B \cup C} = \overline{B} \cap \overline{C}.$$

Two sets A and B are *disjoint* if they have no elements in common, that is, if $A \cap B = \emptyset$. A *collection* of sets $S_1, S_2, \ldots$, either finite or infinite, is a set of sets, in which each member is a set S_i. A collection $\mathcal{S} = \{S_i\}$ of nonempty sets forms a *partition* of a set S if

- the sets are *pairwise disjoint*, that is, $S_i, S_j \in \mathcal{S}$ and $i \neq j$ imply $S_i \cap S_j = \emptyset$, and

- their union is S, that is,

$$S = \bigcup_{S_i \in \mathcal{S}} S_i.$$

In other words, $\mathcal{S}$ forms a partition of S if each element of S appears in exactly one set $S_i \in \mathcal{S}$.

The number of elements in a set is the *cardinality* (or *size*) of the set, denoted $|S|$. Two sets have the same cardinality if their elements can be put into a one-to-one correspondence. The cardinality of the empty set is $|\emptyset| = 0$. If the cardinality of a set is a natural number, the set is *finite*, and otherwise, it is *infinite*. An infinite set that can be put into a one-to-one correspondence with the natural numbers $\mathbb{N}$ is *countably infinite*, and otherwise, it is *uncountable*. For example, the integers $\mathbb{Z}$ are countable, but the reals $\mathbb{R}$ are uncountable.

For any two finite sets A and B, we have the identity

$$|A \cup B| = |A| + |B| - |A \cap B|, \tag{B.3}$$

from which we can conclude that

$$|A \cup B| \leq |A| + |B|.$$

If A and B are disjoint, then $|A \cap B| = 0$ and thus $|A \cup B| = |A| + |B|$. If $A \subseteq B$, then $|A| \leq |B|$.

A finite set of n elements is sometimes called an *n-set*. A 1-set is called a *singleton*. A subset of k elements of a set is sometimes called a *k-subset*.

We denote the set of all subsets of a set S, including the empty set and S itself, by 2^S, called the *power set* of S. For example, $2^{\{a,b\}} = \{\emptyset, \{a\}, \{b\}, \{a, b\}\}$. The power set of a finite set S has cardinality $2^{|S|}$ (see Exercise B.1-5).

We sometimes care about setlike structures in which the elements are ordered. An *ordered pair* of two elements a and b is denoted (a, b) and is defined formally as the set $(a, b) = \{a, \{a, b\}\}$. Thus, the ordered pair (a, b) is *not* the same as the ordered pair (b, a).

The ***Cartesian product*** of two sets A and B, denoted $A \times B$, is the set of all ordered pairs such that the first element of the pair is an element of A and the second is an element of B. More formally,

$$A \times B = \{(a, b) : a \in A \text{ and } b \in B\} .$$

For example, $\{a, b\} \times \{a, b, c\} = \{(a, a), (a, b), (a, c), (b, a), (b, b), (b, c)\}$. When A and B are finite sets, the cardinality of their Cartesian product is

$$|A \times B| = |A| \cdot |B| . \tag{B.4}$$

The Cartesian product of n sets $A_1, A_2, \ldots, A_n$ is the set of ***n-tuples***

$$A_1 \times A_2 \times \cdots \times A_n = \{(a_1, a_2, \ldots, a_n) : a_i \in A_i \text{ for } i = 1, 2, \ldots, n\} ,$$

whose cardinality is

$$|A_1 \times A_2 \times \cdots \times A_n| = |A_1| \cdot |A_2| \cdots |A_n|$$

if all sets A_i are finite. We denote an n-fold Cartesian product over a single set A by the set

$$A^n = \underbrace{A \times A \times \cdots \times A}_{n \text{ times}} ,$$

whose cardinality is $|A^n| = |A|^n$ if A is finite. We can also view an n-tuple as a finite sequence of length n (see page 1162).

Intervals are continuous sets of real numbers. We denote them with parentheses and/or brackets. Given real numbers a and b, the ***closed interval*** $[a, b]$ is the set $\{x \in \mathbb{R} : a \leq x \leq b\}$ of reals between a and b, including both a and b. (If $a > b$, this definition implies that $[a, b] = \emptyset$.) The ***open interval*** $(a, b) = \{x \in \mathbb{R} : a < x < b\}$ omits both of the endpoints from the set. There are two ***half-open intervals*** $[a, b) = \{x \in \mathbb{R} : a \leq x < b\}$ and $(a, b] = \{x \in \mathbb{R} : a < x \leq b\}$, each of which excludes one endpoint.

Intervals can also be defined on the integers by replacing $\mathbb{R}$ in the these definitions by $\mathbb{Z}$. Whether the interval is defined over the reals or integers can usually be inferred from context.

Exercises

B.1-1
Draw Venn diagrams that illustrate the first of the distributive laws (B.1).

B.1-2

Prove the generalization of DeMorgan's laws to any finite collection of sets:

$$\overline{A_1 \cap A_2 \cap \cdots \cap A_n} = \overline{A_1} \cup \overline{A_2} \cup \cdots \cup \overline{A_n} \, ,$$
$$\overline{A_1 \cup A_2 \cup \cdots \cup A_n} = \overline{A_1} \cap \overline{A_2} \cap \cdots \cap \overline{A_n} \, .$$

★ **B.1-3**

Prove the generalization of equation (B.3), which is called the *principle of inclusion and exclusion*:

$$|A_1 \cup A_2 \cup \cdots \cup A_n| =$$
$$|A_1| + |A_2| + \cdots + |A_n|$$
$$- |A_1 \cap A_2| - |A_1 \cap A_3| - \cdots \qquad \text{(all pairs)}$$
$$+ |A_1 \cap A_2 \cap A_3| + \cdots \qquad \text{(all triples)}$$
$$\vdots$$
$$+ (-1)^{n-1} |A_1 \cap A_2 \cap \cdots \cap A_n| \, .$$

B.1-4

Show that the set of odd natural numbers is countable.

B.1-5

Show that for any finite set S, the power set 2^S has $2^{|S|}$ elements (that is, there are $2^{|S|}$ distinct subsets of S).

B.1-6

Give an inductive definition for an n-tuple by extending the set-theoretic definition for an ordered pair.

B.2   Relations

A *binary relation* R on two sets A and B is a subset of the Cartesian product $A \times B$. If $(a, b) \in R$, we sometimes write $a \, R \, b$. When we say that R is a binary relation on a set A, we mean that R is a subset of $A \times A$. For example, the "less than" relation on the natural numbers is the set $\{(a, b) : a, b \in \mathbb{N} \text{ and } a < b\}$. An n-ary relation on sets $A_1, A_2, \ldots, A_n$ is a subset of $A_1 \times A_2 \times \cdots \times A_n$.

A binary relation $R \subseteq A \times A$ is *reflexive* if

$$a \, R \, a$$

for all $a \in A$. For example, "$=$" and "$\leq$" are reflexive relations on $\mathbb{N}$, but "$<$" is not. The relation R is *symmetric* if

$$a \, R \, b \text{ implies } b \, R \, a$$

for all $a, b \in A$. For example, "$=$" is symmetric, but "$<$" and "$\leq$" are not. The relation R is *transitive* if

$$a \, R \, b \text{ and } b \, R \, c \text{ imply } a \, R \, c$$

for all $a, b, c \in A$. For example, the relations "$<$," "$\leq$," and "$=$" are transitive, but the relation $R = \{(a, b) : a, b \in \mathbb{N} \text{ and } a = b - 1\}$ is not, since $3 \, R \, 4$ and $4 \, R \, 5$ do not imply $3 \, R \, 5$.

A relation that is reflexive, symmetric, and transitive is an *equivalence relation*. For example, "$=$" is an equivalence relation on the natural numbers, but "$<$" is not. If R is an equivalence relation on a set A, then for $a \in A$, the *equivalence class* of a is the set $[a] = \{b \in A : a \, R \, b\}$, that is, the set of all elements equivalent to a. For example, if we define $R = \{(a, b) : a, b \in \mathbb{N} \text{ and } a + b \text{ is an even number}\}$, then R is an equivalence relation, since $a + a$ is even (reflexive), $a + b$ is even implies $b + a$ is even (symmetric), and $a + b$ is even and $b + c$ is even imply $a + c$ is even (transitive). The equivalence class of 4 is $[4] = \{0, 2, 4, 6, \ldots\}$, and the equivalence class of 3 is $[3] = \{1, 3, 5, 7, \ldots\}$. A basic theorem of equivalence classes is the following.

Theorem B.1 (An equivalence relation is the same as a partition)
The equivalence classes of any equivalence relation R on a set A form a partition of A, and any partition of A determines an equivalence relation on A for which the sets in the partition are the equivalence classes.

Proof For the first part of the proof, we must show that the equivalence classes of R are nonempty, pairwise-disjoint sets whose union is A. Because R is reflexive, $a \in [a]$, and so the equivalence classes are nonempty. Moreover, since every element $a \in A$ belongs to the equivalence class $[a]$, the union of the equivalence classes is A. It remains to show that the equivalence classes are pairwise disjoint, that is, if two equivalence classes $[a]$ and $[b]$ have an element c in common, then they are in fact the same set. Suppose that $a \, R \, c$ and $b \, R \, c$. Symmetry gives that $c \, R \, b$ and, by transitivity, $a \, R \, b$. Thus, we have $x \, R \, a$ for any arbitrary element $x \in [a]$ and, by transitivity, $x \, R \, b$, and thus $[a] \subseteq [b]$. Similarly, $[b] \subseteq [a]$, and thus $[a] = [b]$.

For the second part of the proof, let $\mathcal{A} = \{A_i\}$ be a partition of A, and define $R = \{(a, b) : \text{there exists } i \text{ such that } a \in A_i \text{ and } b \in A_i\}$. We claim that R is an equivalence relation on A. Reflexivity holds, since $a \in A_i$ implies $a \, R \, a$. Symmetry holds, because if $a \, R \, b$, then a and b belong to the same set A_i, and hence $b \, R \, a$. If $a \, R \, b$ and $b \, R \, c$, then all three elements are in the same set A_i, and thus $a \, R \, c$ and transitivity holds. To see that the sets in the partition are the equivalence classes of R, observe that if $a \in A_i$, then $x \in [a]$ implies $x \in A_i$, and $x \in A_i$ implies $x \in [a]$. ∎

A binary relation R on a set A is *antisymmetric* if

$$a \, R \, b \text{ and } b \, R \, a \text{ imply } a = b.$$

For example, the "$\leq$" relation on the natural numbers is antisymmetric, since $a \leq b$ and $b \leq a$ imply $a = b$. A relation that is reflexive, antisymmetric, and transitive is a *partial order*, and we call a set on which a partial order is defined a *partially ordered set*. For example, the relation "is a descendant of" is a partial order on the set of all people (if we view individuals as being their own descendants).

In a partially ordered set A, there may be no single "maximum" element a such that $b \, R \, a$ for all $b \in A$. Instead, the set may contain several *maximal* elements a such that for no $b \in A$, where $b \neq a$, is it the case that $a \, R \, b$. For example, a collection of different-sized boxes may contain several maximal boxes that don't fit inside any other box, yet it has no single "maximum" box into which any other box will fit.[3]

A relation R on a set A is a *total relation* if for all $a, b \in A$, we have $a \, R \, b$ or $b \, R \, a$ (or both), that is, if every pairing of elements of A is related by R. A partial order that is also a total relation is a *total order* or *linear order*. For example, the relation "$\leq$" is a total order on the natural numbers, but the "is a descendant of" relation is not a total order on the set of all people, since there are individuals neither of whom is descended from the other. A total relation that is transitive, but not necessarily either symmetric or antisymmetric, is a *total preorder*.

Exercises

B.2-1
Prove that the subset relation "$\subseteq$" on all subsets of $\mathbb{Z}$ is a partial order but not a total order.

B.2-2
Show that for any positive integer n, the relation "equivalent modulo n" is an equivalence relation on the integers. (We say that $a = b \pmod{n}$ if there exists an integer q such that $a - b = qn$.) Into what equivalence classes does this relation partition the integers?

---

[3] To be precise, in order for the "fit inside" relation to be a partial order, we need to view a box as fitting inside itself.

B.2-3
Give examples of relations that are

a. reflexive and symmetric but not transitive,

b. reflexive and transitive but not symmetric,

c. symmetric and transitive but not reflexive.

B.2-4
Let S be a finite set, and let R be an equivalence relation on $S \times S$. Show that if in addition R is antisymmetric, then the equivalence classes of S with respect to R are singletons.

B.2-5
Professor Narcissus claims that if a relation R is symmetric and transitive, then it is also reflexive. He offers the following proof. By symmetry, $a \, R \, b$ implies $b \, R \, a$. Transitivity, therefore, implies $a \, R \, a$. Is the professor correct?

B.3   Functions

Given two sets A and B, a *function* f is a binary relation on A and B such that for all $a \in A$, there exists precisely one $b \in B$ such that $(a, b) \in f$. The set A is called the *domain* of f, and the set B is called the *codomain* of f. We sometimes write $f : A \to B$, and if $(a, b) \in f$, we write $b = f(a)$, since the choice of a uniquely determines b.

Intuitively, the function f assigns an element of B to each element of A. No element of A is assigned two different elements of B, but the same element of B can be assigned to two different elements of A. For example, the binary relation

$$f = \{(a, b) : a, b \in \mathbb{N} \text{ and } b = a \bmod 2\}$$

is a function $f : \mathbb{N} \to \{0, 1\}$, since for each natural number a, there is exactly one value b in $\{0, 1\}$ such that $b = a \bmod 2$. For this example, $0 = f(0), 1 = f(1)$, $0 = f(2), 1 = f(3)$, etc. In contrast, the binary relation

$$g = \{(a, b) : a, b \in \mathbb{N} \text{ and } a + b \text{ is even}\}$$

is not a function, since $(1, 3)$ and $(1, 5)$ are both in g, and thus for the choice $a = 1$, there is not precisely one b such that $(a, b) \in g$.

Given a function $f : A \to B$, if $b = f(a)$, we say that a is the *argument* of f and that b is the *value* of f at a. We can define a function by stating its value for every element of its domain. For example, we might define $f(n) = 2n$ for $n \in \mathbb{N}$, which means $f = \{(n, 2n) : n \in \mathbb{N}\}$. Two functions f and g are *equal* if they have the same domain and codomain and if $f(a) = g(a)$ for all a in the domain.

A *finite sequence* of length n is a function f whose domain is the set of n integers $\{0, 1, \ldots, n-1\}$. We often denote a finite sequence by listing its values in angle brackets: $\langle f(0), f(1), \ldots, f(n-1) \rangle$. An *infinite sequence* is a function whose domain is the set $\mathbb{N}$ of natural numbers. For example, the Fibonacci sequence, defined by recurrence (3.31), is the infinite sequence $\langle 0, 1, 1, 2, 3, 5, 8, 13, 21, \ldots \rangle$.

When the domain of a function f is a Cartesian product, we often omit the extra parentheses surrounding the argument of f. For example, if we have a function $f : A_1 \times A_2 \times \cdots \times A_n \to B$, we write $b = f(a_1, a_2, \ldots, a_n)$ instead of writing $b = f((a_1, a_2, \ldots, a_n))$. We also call each a_i an *argument* to the function f, though technically f has just a single argument, which is the n-tuple $(a_1, a_2, \ldots, a_n)$.

If $f : A \to B$ is a function and $b = f(a)$, then we sometimes say that b is the *image* of a under f. The image of a set $A' \subseteq A$ under f is defined by

$$f(A') = \{b \in B : b = f(a) \text{ for some } a \in A'\} \ .$$

The *range* of f is the image of its domain, that is, $f(A)$. For example, the range of the function $f : \mathbb{N} \to \mathbb{N}$ defined by $f(n) = 2n$ is $f(\mathbb{N}) = \{m : m = 2n \text{ for some } n \in \mathbb{N}\}$, in other words, the set of nonnegative even integers.

A function is a *surjection* if its range is its codomain. For example, the function $f(n) = \lfloor n/2 \rfloor$ is a surjective function from $\mathbb{N}$ to $\mathbb{N}$, since every element in $\mathbb{N}$ appears as the value of f for some argument. In contrast, the function $f(n) = 2n$ is not a surjective function from $\mathbb{N}$ to $\mathbb{N}$, since no argument to f can produce any odd natural number as a value. The function $f(n) = 2n$ is, however, a surjective function from the natural numbers to the even numbers. A surjection $f : A \to B$ is sometimes described as mapping A *onto* B. When we say that f is onto, we mean that it is surjective.

A function $f : A \to B$ is an *injection* if distinct arguments to f produce distinct values, that is, if $a \neq a'$ implies $f(a) \neq f(a')$. For example, the function $f(n) = 2n$ is an injective function from $\mathbb{N}$ to $\mathbb{N}$, since each even number b is the image under f of at most one element of the domain, namely $b/2$. The function $f(n) = \lfloor n/2 \rfloor$ is not injective, since the value 1 is produced by two arguments: $f(2) = 1$ and $f(3) = 1$. An injection is sometimes called a *one-to-one* function.

A function $f : A \to B$ is a *bijection* if it is injective and surjective. For example, the function $f(n) = (-1)^n \lceil n/2 \rceil$ is a bijection from $\mathbb{N}$ to $\mathbb{Z}$:

$$0 \rightarrow \quad 0 \,,$$
$$1 \rightarrow -1 \,,$$
$$2 \rightarrow \quad 1 \,,$$
$$3 \rightarrow -2 \,,$$
$$4 \rightarrow \quad 2 \,,$$
$$\vdots$$

The function is injective, since no element of $\mathbb{Z}$ is the image of more than one element of $\mathbb{N}$. It is surjective, since every element of $\mathbb{Z}$ appears as the image of some element of $\mathbb{N}$. Hence, the function is bijective. A bijection is sometimes called a *one-to-one correspondence*, since it pairs elements in the domain and codomain. A bijection from a set A to itself is sometimes called a *permutation*.

When a function f is bijective, we define its *inverse* f^{-1} as

$$f^{-1}(b) = a \text{ if and only if } f(a) = b \,.$$

For example, the inverse of the function $f(n) = (-1)^n \lceil n/2 \rceil$ is

$$f^{-1}(m) = \begin{cases} 2m & \text{if } m \geq 0 \,, \\ -2m - 1 & \text{if } m < 0 \,. \end{cases}$$

Exercises

B.3-1
Let A and B be finite sets, and let $f : A \rightarrow B$ be a function. Show the following:

a. If f is injective, then $|A| \leq |B|$.

b. If f is surjective, then $|A| \geq |B|$.

B.3-2
Is the function $f(x) = x + 1$ bijective when the domain and the codomain are the set $\mathbb{N}$? Is it bijective when the domain and the codomain are the set $\mathbb{Z}$?

B.3-3
Give a natural definition for the inverse of a binary relation such that if a relation is in fact a bijective function, its relational inverse is its functional inverse.

★ B.3-4
Give a bijection from $\mathbb{Z}$ to $\mathbb{Z} \times \mathbb{Z}$.

B.4   Graphs

This section presents two kinds of graphs: directed and undirected. Certain definitions in the literature differ from those given here, but for the most part, the differences are slight. Section 20.1 shows how to represent graphs in computer memory.

A *directed graph* (or *digraph*) G is a pair (V, E), where V is a finite set and E is a binary relation on V. The set V is called the *vertex set* of G, and its elements are called *vertices* (singular: *vertex*). The set E is called the *edge set* of G, and its elements are called *edges*. Figure B.2(a) is a pictorial representation of a directed graph on the vertex set $\{1, 2, 3, 4, 5, 6\}$. Vertices are represented by circles in the figure, and edges are represented by arrows. *Self-loops*—edges from a vertex to itself—are possible.

In an *undirected graph* $G = (V, E)$, the edge set E consists of *unordered* pairs of vertices, rather than ordered pairs. That is, an edge is a set $\{u, v\}$, where $u, v \in V$ and $u \neq v$. By convention, we use the notation (u, v) for an edge, rather than the set notation $\{u, v\}$, and we consider (u, v) and (v, u) to be the same edge. In an undirected graph, self-loops are forbidden, so that every edge consists of two distinct vertices. Figure B.2(b) shows an undirected graph on the vertex set $\{1, 2, 3, 4, 5, 6\}$.

Many definitions for directed and undirected graphs are the same, although certain terms have slightly different meanings in the two contexts. If (u, v) is an edge in a directed graph $G = (V, E)$, we say that (u, v) is *incident from* or *leaves* vertex u and is *incident to* or *enters* vertex v. For example, the edges leaving vertex 2

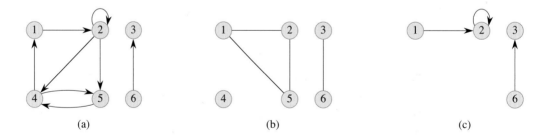

(a)   (b)   (c)

Figure B.2 Directed and undirected graphs. **(a)** A directed graph $G = (V, E)$, where $V = \{1, 2, 3, 4, 5, 6\}$ and $E = \{(1, 2), (2, 2), (2, 4), (2, 5), (4, 1), (4, 5), (5, 4), (6, 3)\}$. The edge $(2, 2)$ is a self-loop. **(b)** An undirected graph $G = (V, E)$, where $V = \{1, 2, 3, 4, 5, 6\}$ and $E = \{(1, 2), (1, 5), (2, 5), (3, 6)\}$. The vertex 4 is isolated. **(c)** The subgraph of the graph in part (a) induced by the vertex set $\{1, 2, 3, 6\}$.

in Figure B.2(a) are $(2, 2)$, $(2, 4)$, and $(2, 5)$. The edges entering vertex 2 are $(1, 2)$ and $(2, 2)$. If (u, v) is an edge in an undirected graph $G = (V, E)$, we say that (u, v) is *incident on* vertices u and v. In Figure B.2(b), the edges incident on vertex 2 are $(1, 2)$ and $(2, 5)$.

If (u, v) is an edge in a graph $G = (V, E)$, we say that vertex v is *adjacent* to vertex u. When the graph is undirected, the adjacency relation is symmetric. When the graph is directed, the adjacency relation is not necessarily symmetric. If v is adjacent to u in a directed graph, we can write $u \rightarrow v$. In parts (a) and (b) of Figure B.2, vertex 2 is adjacent to vertex 1, since the edge $(1, 2)$ belongs to both graphs. Vertex 1 is *not* adjacent to vertex 2 in Figure B.2(a), since the edge $(2, 1)$ is absent.

The *degree* of a vertex in an undirected graph is the number of edges incident on it. For example, vertex 2 in Figure B.2(b) has degree 2. A vertex whose degree is 0, such as vertex 4 in Figure B.2(b), is *isolated*. In a directed graph, the *out-degree* of a vertex is the number of edges leaving it, and the *in-degree* of a vertex is the number of edges entering it. The *degree* of a vertex in a directed graph is its in-degree plus its out-degree. Vertex 2 in Figure B.2(a) has in-degree 2, out-degree 3, and degree 5.

A *path* of *length* k from a vertex u to a vertex u' in a graph $G = (V, E)$ is a sequence $\langle v_0, v_1, v_2, \ldots, v_k \rangle$ of vertices such that $u = v_0$, $u' = v_k$, and $(v_{i-1}, v_i) \in E$ for $i = 1, 2, \ldots, k$. The length of the path is the number of edges in the path, which is 1 less than the number of vertices in the path. The path *contains* the vertices $v_0, v_1, \ldots, v_k$ and the edges $(v_0, v_1), (v_1, v_2), \ldots, (v_{k-1}, v_k)$. (There is always a 0-length path from u to u.) If there is a path p from u to u', we say that u' is *reachable* from u via p, which we can write as $u \overset{p}{\rightsquigarrow} u'$. A path is *simple*[4] if all vertices in the path are distinct. In Figure B.2(a), the path $\langle 1, 2, 5, 4 \rangle$ is a simple path of length 3. The path $\langle 2, 5, 4, 5 \rangle$ is not simple. A *subpath* of path $p = \langle v_0, v_1, \ldots, v_k \rangle$ is a contiguous subsequence of its vertices. That is, for any $0 \leq i \leq j \leq k$, the subsequence of vertices $\langle v_i, v_{i+1}, \ldots, v_j \rangle$ is a subpath of p.

In a directed graph, a path $\langle v_0, v_1, \ldots, v_k \rangle$ forms a *cycle* if $v_0 = v_k$ and the path contains at least one edge. The cycle is *simple* if, in addition, $v_1, v_2, \ldots, v_k$ are distinct. A cycle consisting of k vertices has *length* k. A self-loop is a cycle of length 1. Two paths $\langle v_0, v_1, v_2, \ldots, v_{k-1}, v_0 \rangle$ and $\langle v'_0, v'_1, v'_2, \ldots, v'_{k-1}, v'_0 \rangle$ form the same cycle if there exists an integer j such that $v'_i = v_{(i+j) \bmod k}$ for $i = 0, 1, \ldots, k-1$. In Figure B.2(a), the path $\langle 1, 2, 4, 1 \rangle$ forms the same cycle as the paths $\langle 2, 4, 1, 2 \rangle$ and $\langle 4, 1, 2, 4 \rangle$. This cycle is simple, but the cycle $\langle 1, 2, 4, 5, 4, 1 \rangle$ is not. The cycle $\langle 2, 2 \rangle$ formed by the edge $(2, 2)$ is a self-loop. A directed graph

---

[4] Some authors refer to what we call a path as a "walk" and to what we call a simple path as just a "path."

with no self-loops is *simple*. In an undirected graph, a path $\langle v_0, v_1, \ldots, v_k \rangle$ forms a *cycle* if $k > 0$, $v_0 = v_k$, and all edges on the path are distinct. The cycle is *simple* if $v_1, v_2, \ldots, v_k$ are distinct. For example, in Figure B.2(b), the path $\langle 1, 2, 5, 1 \rangle$ is a simple cycle. A graph with no simple cycles is *acyclic*.

An undirected graph is *connected* if every vertex is reachable from all other vertices. The *connected components* of an undirected graph are the equivalence classes of vertices under the "is reachable from" relation. The graph shown in Figure B.2(b) has three connected components: $\{1, 2, 5\}$, $\{3, 6\}$, and $\{4\}$. Every vertex in the connected component $\{1, 2, 5\}$ is reachable from every other vertex in $\{1, 2, 5\}$. An undirected graph is connected if it has exactly one connected component. The edges of a connected component are those that are incident on only the vertices of the component. In other words, edge (u, v) is an edge of a connected component only if both u and v are vertices of the component.

A directed graph is *strongly connected* if every two vertices are reachable from each other. The *strongly connected components* of a directed graph are the equivalence classes of vertices under the "are mutually reachable" relation. A directed graph is strongly connected if it has only one strongly connected component. The graph in Figure B.2(a) has three strongly connected components: $\{1, 2, 4, 5\}$, $\{3\}$, and $\{6\}$. All pairs of vertices in $\{1, 2, 4, 5\}$ are mutually reachable. The vertices $\{3, 6\}$ do not form a strongly connected component, since vertex 6 cannot be reached from vertex 3.

Two graphs $G = (V, E)$ and $G' = (V', E')$ are *isomorphic* if there exists a bijection $f : V \to V'$ such that $(u, v) \in E$ if and only if $(f(u), f(v)) \in E'$. In other words, G and G' are isomorphic if the vertices of G can be relabeled to be vertices of G', maintaining the corresponding edges in G and G'. Figure B.3(a) shows a pair of isomorphic graphs G and G' with respective vertex sets $V = \{1, 2, 3, 4, 5, 6\}$ and $V' = \{u, v, w, x, y, z\}$. The mapping from V to V' given by $f(1) = u$, $f(2) = v$, $f(3) = w$, $f(4) = x$, $f(5) = y$, $f(6) = z$ provides the required bijective function. The graphs in Figure B.3(b) are not isomorphic. Although both graphs have 5 vertices and 7 edges, the top graph has a vertex of degree 4 and the bottom graph does not.

We say that a graph $G' = (V', E')$ is a *subgraph* of $G = (V, E)$ if $V' \subseteq V$ and $E' \subseteq E$. Given a set $V' \subseteq V$, the subgraph of G *induced* by V' is the graph $G' = (V', E')$, where

$$E' = \{(u, v) \in E : u, v \in V'\} .$$

The subgraph induced by the vertex set $\{1, 2, 3, 6\}$ in Figure B.2(a) appears in Figure B.2(c) and has the edge set $\{(1, 2), (2, 2), (6, 3)\}$.

Given an undirected graph $G = (V, E)$, the *directed version* of G is the directed graph $G' = (V, E')$, where $(u, v) \in E'$ if and only if $(u, v) \in E$. That is, each undirected edge (u, v) in G turns into two directed edges, (u, v) and (v, u), in the

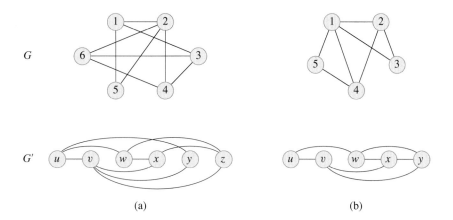

Figure B.3 **(a)** A pair of isomorphic graphs. The vertices of the top graph are mapped to the vertices of the bottom graph by $f(1) = u$, $f(2) = v$, $f(3) = w$, $f(4) = x$, $f(5) = y$, $f(6) = z$. **(b)** Two graphs that are not isomorphic. The top graph has a vertex of degree 4, and the bottom graph does not.

directed version. Given a directed graph $G = (V, E)$, the *undirected version* of G is the undirected graph $G' = (V, E')$, where $(u, v) \in E'$ if and only if $u \neq v$ and E contains at least one of the edges (u, v) and (v, u). That is, the undirected version contains the edges of G "with their directions removed" and with self-loops eliminated. (Since (u, v) and (v, u) are the same edge in an undirected graph, the undirected version of a directed graph contains it only once, even if the directed graph contains both edges (u, v) and (v, u).) In a directed graph $G = (V, E)$, a *neighbor* of a vertex u is any vertex that is adjacent to u in the undirected version of G. That is, v is a neighbor of u if $u \neq v$ and either $(u, v) \in E$ or $(v, u) \in E$. In an undirected graph, u and v are neighbors if they are adjacent.

Several kinds of graphs have special names. A *complete graph* is an undirected graph in which every pair of vertices is adjacent. An undirected graph $G = (V, E)$ is *bipartite* if V can be partitioned into two sets V_1 and V_2 such that $(u, v) \in E$ implies either $u \in V_1$ and $v \in V_2$ or $u \in V_2$ and $v \in V_1$. That is, all edges go between the two sets V_1 and V_2. An acyclic, undirected graph is a *forest*, and a connected, acyclic, undirected graph is a *(free) tree* (see Section B.5). We often take the first letters of "directed acyclic graph" and call such a graph a *dag*.

There are two variants of graphs that you may occasionally encounter. A *multigraph* is like an undirected graph, but it can have both multiple edges between vertices (such as two distinct edges (u, v) and (u, v)) and self-loops. A *hypergraph* is like an undirected graph, but each *hyperedge*, rather than connecting two vertices, connects an arbitrary subset of vertices. Many algorithms written for ordinary directed and undirected graphs can be adapted to run on these graphlike structures.

The *contraction* of an undirected graph $G = (V, E)$ by an edge $e = (u, v)$ is a graph $G' = (V', E')$, where $V' = V - \{u, v\} \cup \{x\}$ and x is a new vertex. The set of edges E' is formed from E by deleting the edge (u, v) and, for each vertex w adjacent to u or v, deleting whichever of (u, w) and (v, w) belongs to E and adding the new edge (x, w). In effect, u and v are "contracted" into a single vertex.

Exercises

B.4-1
Attendees of a faculty party shake hands to greet each other, with every pair of professors shaking hands one time. Each professor remembers the number of times he or she shook hands. At the end of the party, the department head asks the professors for their totals and adds them all up. Show that the result is even by proving the *handshaking lemma*: if $G = (V, E)$ is an undirected graph, then

$$\sum_{v \in V} \text{degree}(v) = 2 |E| \ .$$

B.4-2
Show that if a directed or undirected graph contains a path between two vertices u and v, then it contains a simple path between u and v. Show that if a directed graph contains a cycle, then it contains a simple cycle.

B.4-3
Show that any connected, undirected graph $G = (V, E)$ satisfies $|E| \geq |V| - 1$.

B.4-4
Verify that in an undirected graph, the "is reachable from" relation is an equivalence relation on the vertices of the graph. Which of the three properties of an equivalence relation hold in general for the "is reachable from" relation on the vertices of a directed graph?

B.4-5
What is the undirected version of the directed graph in Figure B.2(a)? What is the directed version of the undirected graph in Figure B.2(b)?

B.4-6
Show how a bipartite graph can represent a hypergraph by letting incidence in the hypergraph correspond to adjacency in the bipartite graph. (*Hint:* Let one set of

vertices in the bipartite graph correspond to vertices of the hypergraph, and let the other set of vertices of the bipartite graph correspond to hyperedges.)

B.5 Trees

As with graphs, there are many related, but slightly different, notions of trees. This section presents definitions and mathematical properties of several kinds of trees. Sections 10.3 and 20.1 describe how to represent trees in computer memory.

B.5.1 Free trees

As defined in Section B.4, a *free tree* is a connected, acyclic, undirected graph. We often omit the adjective "free" when we say that a graph is a tree. If an undirected graph is acyclic but possibly disconnected, it is a *forest*. Many algorithms that work for trees also work for forests. Figure B.4(a) shows a free tree, and Figure B.4(b) shows a forest. The forest in Figure B.4(b) is not a tree because it is not connected. The graph in Figure B.4(c) is connected but neither a tree nor a forest, because it contains a cycle.

The following theorem captures many important facts about free trees.

Theorem B.2 (Properties of free trees)
Let $G = (V, E)$ be an undirected graph. The following statements are equivalent.

1. G is a free tree.

2. Any two vertices in G are connected by a unique simple path.

3. G is connected, but if any edge is removed from E, the resulting graph is disconnected.

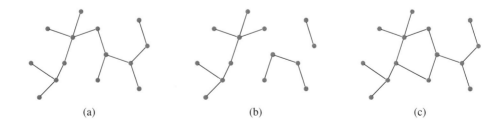

(a)   (b)   (c)

Figure B.4 **(a)** A free tree. **(b)** A forest. **(c)** A graph that contains a cycle and is therefore neither a tree nor a forest.

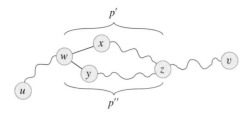

Figure B.5 A step in the proof of Theorem B.2: if (1) G is a free tree, then (2) any two vertices in G are connected by a unique simple path. Assume for the sake of contradiction that vertices u and v are connected by two distinct simple paths. These paths first diverge at vertex w, and they first reconverge at vertex z. The path p' concatenated with the reverse of the path p'' forms a cycle, which yields the contradiction.

4. G is connected, and $|E| = |V| - 1$.

5. G is acyclic, and $|E| = |V| - 1$.

6. G is acyclic, but if any edge is added to E, the resulting graph contains a cycle.

Proof (1) $\Rightarrow$ (2): Since a tree is connected, any two vertices in G are connected by at least one simple path. Suppose for the sake of contradiction that vertices u and v are connected by two distinct simple paths as shown in Figure B.5. Let w be the vertex at which the paths first diverge. That is, if we call the paths p_1 and p_2, then w is the first vertex on both p_1 and p_2 whose successor on p_1 is x and whose successor on p_2 is y, where $x \neq y$. Let z be the first vertex at which the paths reconverge, that is, z is the first vertex following w on p_1 that is also on p_2. Let $p' = w \rightarrow x \rightsquigarrow z$ be the subpath of p_1 from w through x to z, so that $p_1 = u \rightsquigarrow w \overset{p'}{\rightsquigarrow} z \rightsquigarrow v$, and let $p'' = w \rightarrow y \rightsquigarrow z$ be the subpath of p_2 from w through y to z, so that $p_2 = u \rightsquigarrow w \overset{p''}{\rightsquigarrow} z \rightsquigarrow v$. Paths p' and p'' share no vertices except their endpoints. Then, as Figure B.5 shows, the path obtained by concatenating p' and the reverse of p'' is a cycle, which contradicts our assumption that G is a tree. Thus, if G is a tree, there can be at most one simple path between two vertices.

(2) $\Rightarrow$ (3): If any two vertices in G are connected by a unique simple path, then G is connected. Let (u, v) be any edge in E. This edge is a path from u to v, and so it must be the unique path from u to v. If (u, v) were to be removed from G, there would be no path from u to v, and G would be disconnected.

(3) $\Rightarrow$ (4): By assumption, the graph G is connected, so Exercise B.4-3 gives that $|E| \geq |V| - 1$. We prove $|E| \leq |V| - 1$ by induction on $|V|$. The base cases are when $|V| = 1$ or $|V| = 2$, and in either case, $|E| = |V| - 1$. For the inductive step, suppose that $|V| \geq 3$ for graph G and that any graph $G' = (V', E')$, where

$|V'| < |V|$, that satisfies (3) also satisfies $|E'| \le |V'| - 1$. Removing an arbitrary edge from G separates the graph into $k \ge 2$ connected components (actually $k = 2$). Each component satisfies (3), or else G would not satisfy (3). Consider each connected component V_i, with edge set E_i, as a separate free tree. Then, because each connected component has fewer than $|V|$ vertices, the inductive hypothesis implies that $|E_i| \le |V_i| - 1$. Thus, the number of edges in all k connected components combined is at most $|V| - k \le |V| - 2$. Adding in the removed edge yields $|E| \le |V| - 1$.

(4) $\Rightarrow$ (5): Suppose that G is connected and that $|E| = |V| - 1$. We must show that G is acyclic. Suppose that G has a cycle containing k vertices $v_1, v_2, \ldots, v_k$, and without loss of generality assume that this cycle is simple. Let $G_k = (V_k, E_k)$ be the subgraph of G consisting of the cycle, so that $|V_k| = |E_k| = k$. If $k < |V|$, then because G is connected, there must be a vertex $v_{k+1} \in V - V_k$ that is adjacent to some vertex $v_i \in V_k$. Define $G_{k+1} = (V_{k+1}, E_{k+1})$ to be the subgraph of G with $V_{k+1} = V_k \cup \{v_{k+1}\}$ and $E_{k+1} = E_k \cup \{(v_i, v_{k+1})\}$. Note that $|V_{k+1}| = |E_{k+1}| = k + 1$. If $k + 1 < |V|$, then continue, defining G_{k+2} in the same manner, and so forth, until we obtain $G_n = (V_n, E_n)$, where $n = |V|$, $V_n = V$, and $|E_n| = |V_n| = |V|$. Since G_n is a subgraph of G, we have $E_n \subseteq E$, and hence $|E| \ge |E_n| = |V_n| = |V|$, which contradicts the assumption that $|E| = |V| - 1$. Thus, G is acyclic.

(5) $\Rightarrow$ (6): Suppose that G is acyclic and that $|E| = |V| - 1$. Let k be the number of connected components of G. Each connected component is a free tree by definition, and since (1) implies (5), the sum of all edges in all connected components of G is $|V| - k$. Consequently, k must equal 1, and G is in fact a tree. Since (1) implies (2), any two vertices in G are connected by a unique simple path. Thus, adding any edge to G creates a cycle.

(6) $\Rightarrow$ (1): Suppose that G is acyclic but that adding any edge to E creates a cycle. We must show that G is connected. Let u and v be arbitrary vertices in G. If u and v are not already adjacent, adding the edge (u, v) creates a cycle in which all edges but (u, v) belong to G. Thus, the cycle minus edge (u, v) must contain a path from u to v, and since u and v were chosen arbitrarily, G is connected.   ∎

B.5.2   Rooted and ordered trees

A *rooted tree* is a free tree in which one of the vertices is distinguished from the others. We call the distinguished vertex the *root* of the tree. We often refer to a

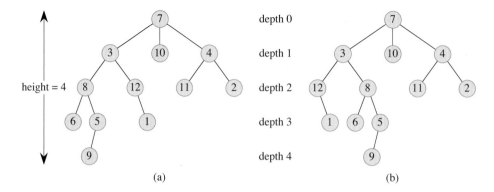

Figure B.6 Rooted and ordered trees. **(a)** A rooted tree with height 4. The tree is drawn in a standard way: the root (node 7) is at the top, its children (nodes with depth 1) are beneath it, their children (nodes with depth 2) are beneath them, and so forth. If the tree is ordered, the relative left-to-right order of the children of a node matters; otherwise, it doesn't. **(b)** Another rooted tree. As a rooted tree, it is identical to the tree in (a), but as an ordered tree it is different, since the children of node 3 appear in a different order.

vertex of a rooted tree as a *node*[5] of the tree. Figure B.6(a) shows a rooted tree on a set of 12 nodes with root 7.

Consider a node x in a rooted tree T with root r. We call any node y on the unique simple path from r to x an *ancestor* of x. If y is an ancestor of x, then x is a *descendant* of y. (Every node is both an ancestor and a descendant of itself.) If y is an ancestor of x and $x \neq y$, then y is a *proper ancestor* of x and x is a *proper descendant* of y. The *subtree rooted at* x is the tree induced by descendants of x, rooted at x. For example, the subtree rooted at node 8 in Figure B.6(a) contains nodes 8, 6, 5, and 9.

If the last edge on the simple path from the root r of a tree T to a node x is (y, x), then y is the *parent* of x, and x is a *child* of y. The root is the only node in T with no parent. If two nodes have the same parent, they are *siblings*. A node with no children is a *leaf* or *external node*. A nonleaf node is an *internal node*.

---

[5] The term "node" is often used in the graph theory literature as a synonym for "vertex." We reserve the term "node" to mean a vertex of a rooted tree.

The number of children of a node x in a rooted tree T is the *degree* of x.[6] The length of the simple path from the root r to a node x is the *depth* of x in T. A *level* of a tree consists of all nodes at the same depth. The *height* of a node in a tree is the number of edges on the longest simple downward path from the node to a leaf, and the height of a tree is the height of its root. The height of a tree is also equal to the largest depth of any node in the tree.

An *ordered tree* is a rooted tree in which the children of each node are ordered. That is, if a node has k children, then there is a first child, a second child, and so on, up to and including a kth child. The two trees in Figure B.6 are different when considered to be ordered trees, but the same when considered to be just rooted trees.

B.5.3   Binary and positional trees

We define binary trees recursively. A *binary tree* T is a structure defined on a finite set of nodes that either

- contains no nodes, or

- is composed of three disjoint sets of nodes: a *root* node, a binary tree called its *left subtree*, and a binary tree called its *right subtree*.

The binary tree that contains no nodes is called the *empty tree* or *null tree*, sometimes denoted NIL. If the left subtree is nonempty, its root is called the *left child* of the root of the entire tree. Likewise, the root of a nonnull right subtree is the *right child* of the root of the entire tree. If a subtree is the null tree NIL, we say that the child is *absent* or *missing*. Figure B.7(a) shows a binary tree.

A binary tree is not simply an ordered tree in which each node has degree at most 2. For example, in a binary tree, if a node has just one child, the position of the child—whether it is the *left child* or the *right child*—matters. In an ordered tree, there is no distinguishing a sole child as being either left or right. Figure B.7(b) shows a binary tree that differs from the tree in Figure B.7(a) because of the position of one node. Considered as ordered trees, however, the two trees are identical.

One way to represent the positioning information in a binary tree is by the internal nodes of an ordered tree, as shown in Figure B.7(c). The idea is to replace each missing child in the binary tree with a node having no children. These leaf nodes

---

[6] The degree of a node depends on whether we consider T to be a rooted tree or a free tree. The degree of a vertex in a free tree is, as in any undirected graph, the number of adjacent vertices. In a rooted tree, however, the degree is the number of children—the parent of a node does not count toward its degree.

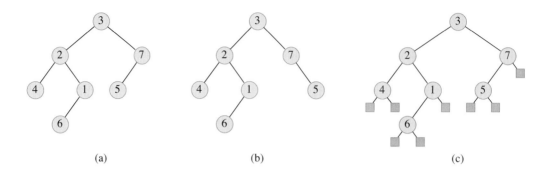

(a)   (b)   (c)

Figure B.7   Binary trees. **(a)** A binary tree drawn in a standard way. The left child of a node is drawn beneath the node and to the left. The right child is drawn beneath and to the right. **(b)** A binary tree different from the one in (a). In (a), the left child of node 7 is 5 and the right child is absent. In (b), the left child of node 7 is absent and the right child is 5. As ordered trees, these trees are the same, but as binary trees, they are distinct. **(c)** The binary tree in (a) represented by the internal nodes of a full binary tree: an ordered tree in which each internal node has degree 2. The leaves in the tree are shown as squares.

are drawn as squares in the figure. The tree that results is a *full binary tree*: each node is either a leaf or has degree exactly 2. No nodes have degree 1. Consequently, the order of the children of a node preserves the position information.

The positioning information that distinguishes binary trees from ordered trees extends to trees with more than two children per node. In a *positional tree*, the children of a node are labeled with distinct positive integers. The ith child of a node is *absent* if no child is labeled with integer i. A *k-ary* tree is a positional tree in which for every node, all children with labels greater than k are missing. Thus, a binary tree is a k-ary tree with $k = 2$.

A *complete k-ary tree* is a k-ary tree in which all leaves have the same depth and all internal nodes have degree k. Figure B.8 shows a complete binary tree of height 3. How many leaves does a complete k-ary tree of height h have? The root has k children at depth 1, each of which has k children at depth 2, etc. Thus, the number of nodes at depth d is k^d. In a complete k-ary tree with height h, the leaves are at depth h, so that there are k^h leaves. Consequently, the height of a complete k-ary tree with n leaves is $\log_k n$. A complete k-ary tree of height h has

$$1 + k + k^2 + \cdots + k^{h-1} = \sum_{d=0}^{h-1} k^d$$

$$= \frac{k^h - 1}{k - 1} \quad \text{(by equation (A.6) on page 1142)}$$

internal nodes. Thus, a complete binary tree has $2^h - 1$ internal nodes.

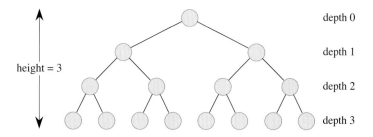

Figure B.8   A complete binary tree of height 3 with 8 leaves and 7 internal nodes.

Exercises

B.5-1
Draw all the free trees composed of the three vertices x, y, and z. Draw all the rooted trees with nodes x, y, and z with x as the root. Draw all the ordered trees with nodes x, y, and z with x as the root. Draw all the binary trees with nodes x, y, and z with x as the root.

B.5-2
Let $G = (V, E)$ be a directed acyclic graph in which there is a vertex $v_0 \in V$ such that there exists a unique path from v_0 to every vertex $v \in V$. Prove that the undirected version of G forms a tree.

B.5-3
Show by induction that the number of degree-2 nodes in any nonempty binary tree is one less than the number of leaves. Conclude that the number of internal nodes in a full binary tree is one less than the number of leaves.

B.5-4
Prove that for any integer $k \geq 1$, there is a full binary tree with k leaves.

B.5-5
Use induction to show that a nonempty binary tree with n nodes has height at least $\lfloor \lg n \rfloor$.

★ B.5-6
The *internal path length* of a full binary tree is the sum, taken over all internal nodes of the tree, of the depth of each node. Likewise, the *external path length* is the sum, taken over all leaves of the tree, of the depth of each leaf. Consider a full binary tree with n internal nodes, internal path length i, and external path length e. Prove that $e = i + 2n$.

★ **B.5-7**
Associate a "weight" $w(x) = 2^{-d}$ with each leaf x of depth d in a binary tree T, and let L be the set of leaves of T. Prove the ***Kraft inequality***: $\sum_{x \in L} w(x) \leq 1$.

★ **B.5-8**
Show that if $L \geq 2$, then every binary tree with L leaves contains a subtree having between $L/3$ and $2L/3$ leaves, inclusive.

Problems

B-1 *Graph coloring*
A *k-coloring* of undirected graph $G = (V, E)$ is a function $c : V \rightarrow \{1, 2, \ldots, k\}$ such that $c(u) \neq c(v)$ for every edge $(u, v) \in E$. In other words, the numbers $1, 2, \ldots, k$ represent the k colors, and adjacent vertices must have different colors.

a. Show that any tree is 2-colorable.

b. Show that the following are equivalent:

1. G is bipartite.
2. G is 2-colorable.
3. G has no cycles of odd length.

c. Let d be the maximum degree of any vertex in a graph G. Prove that G can be colored with $d + 1$ colors.

d. Show that if G has $O(|V|)$ edges, then G can be colored with $O(\sqrt{|V|})$ colors.

B-2 *Friendly graphs*
Reword each of the following statements as a theorem about undirected graphs, and then prove it. Assume that friendship is symmetric but not reflexive.

a. Any group of at least two people contains at least two people with the same number of friends in the group.

b. Every group of six people contains either at least three mutual friends or at least three mutual strangers.

c. Any group of people can be partitioned into two subgroups such that at least half the friends of each person belong to the subgroup of which that person is *not* a member.

d. If everyone in a group is the friend of at least half the people in the group, then the group can be seated around a table in such a way that everyone is seated between two friends.

B-3 Bisecting trees

Many divide-and-conquer algorithms that operate on graphs require that the graph be bisected into two nearly equal-sized subgraphs, which are induced by a partition of the vertices. This problem investigates bisections of trees formed by removing a small number of edges. We require that whenever two vertices end up in the same subtree after removing edges, then they must belong to the same partition.

a. Show that the vertices of any n-vertex binary tree can be partitioned into two sets A and B, such that $|A| \leq 3n/4$ and $|B| \leq 3n/4$, by removing a single edge.

b. Show that the constant $3/4$ in part (a) is optimal in the worst case by giving an example of a simple binary tree whose most evenly balanced partition upon removal of a single edge has $|A| = 3n/4$.

c. Show that by removing at most $O(\lg n)$ edges, we can partition the vertices of any n-vertex binary tree into two sets A and B such that $|A| = \lfloor n/2 \rfloor$ and $|B| = \lceil n/2 \rceil$.

Appendix notes

G. Boole pioneered the development of symbolic logic, and he introduced many of the basic set notations in a book published in 1854. Modern set theory was created by G. Cantor during the period 1874–1895. Cantor focused primarily on sets of infinite cardinality. The term "function" is attributed to G. W. Leibniz, who used it to refer to several kinds of mathematical formulas. His limited definition has been generalized many times. Graph theory originated in 1736, when L. Euler proved that it was impossible to cross each of the seven bridges in the city of Königsberg exactly once and return to the starting point.

The book by Harary [208] provides a useful compendium of many definitions and results from graph theory.

C   Counting and Probability

This appendix reviews elementary combinatorics and probability theory. If you have a good background in these areas, you may want to skim the beginning of this appendix lightly and concentrate on the later sections. Most of this book's chapters do not require probability, but for some chapters it is essential.

Section C.1 reviews elementary results in counting theory, including standard formulas for counting permutations and combinations. The axioms of probability and basic facts concerning probability distributions form Section C.2. Random variables are introduced in Section C.3, along with the properties of expectation and variance. Section C.4 investigates the geometric and binomial distributions that arise from studying Bernoulli trials. The study of the binomial distribution continues in Section C.5, an advanced discussion of the "tails" of the distribution.

C.1   Counting

Counting theory tries to answer the question "How many?" without actually enumerating all the choices. For example, you might ask, "How many different n-bit numbers are there?" or "How many orderings of n distinct elements are there?" This section reviews the elements of counting theory. Since some of the material assumes a basic understanding of sets, you might wish to start by reviewing the material in Section B.1.

Rules of sum and product

We can sometimes express a set of items that we wish to count as a union of disjoint sets or as a Cartesian product of sets.

The *rule of sum* says that the number of ways to choose one element from one of two *disjoint* sets is the sum of the cardinalities of the sets. That is, if A and B are two finite sets with no members in common, then $|A \cup B| = |A| + |B|$, which follows from equation (B.3) on page 1156. For example, if each position on a car's license plate is a letter or a digit, then the number of possibilities for each position is $26 + 10 = 36$, since there are 26 choices if it is a letter and 10 choices if it is a digit.

The *rule of product* says that the number of ways to choose an ordered pair is the number of ways to choose the first element times the number of ways to choose the second element. That is, if A and B are two finite sets, then $|A \times B| = |A| \cdot |B|$, which is simply equation (B.4) on page 1157. For example, if an ice-cream parlor offers 28 flavors of ice cream and four toppings, the number of possible sundaes with one scoop of ice cream and one topping is $28 \cdot 4 = 112$.

Strings

A *string* over a finite set S is a sequence of elements of S. For example, there are eight binary strings of length 3:

$$000, 001, 010, 011, 100, 101, 110, 111 \ .$$

(Here we use the shorthand of omitting the angle brackets when denoting a sequence.) We sometimes call a string of length k a *k-string*. A *substring* s' of a string s is an ordered sequence of consecutive elements of s. A *k-substring* of a string is a substring of length k. For example, 010 is a 3-substring of 01101001 (the 3-substring that begins in position 4), but 111 is not a substring of 01101001.

We can view a k-string over a set S as an element of the Cartesian product S^k of k-tuples, which means that there are $|S|^k$ strings of length k. For example, the number of binary k-strings is 2^k. Intuitively, to construct a k-string over an n-set, there are n ways to pick the first element; for each of these choices, there are n ways to pick the second element; and so forth k times. This construction leads to the k-fold product $\underbrace{n \cdot n \cdots n}_{n \text{ times}} = n^k$ as the number of k-strings.

Permutations

A *permutation* of a finite set S is an ordered sequence of all the elements of S, with each element appearing exactly once. For example, if $S = \{a, b, c\}$, then S has 6 permutations:

$$abc, acb, bac, bca, cab, cba \ .$$

(Again, we use the shorthand of omitting the angle brackets when denoting a sequence.) There are $n!$ permutations of a set of n elements, since there are n ways to choose the first element of the sequence, $n - 1$ ways for the second element, $n - 2$ ways for the third, and so on.

A *k-permutation* of S is an ordered sequence of k elements of S, with no element appearing more than once in the sequence. (Thus, an ordinary permutation is an n-permutation of an n-set.) Here are the 2-permutations of the set $\{a, b, c, d\}$:

$$ab, ac, ad, ba, bc, bd, ca, cb, cd, da, db, dc \;.$$

The number of k-permutations of an n-set is

$$n(n - 1)(n - 2) \cdots (n - k + 1) = \frac{n!}{(n - k)!} \;, \tag{C.1}$$

since there are n ways to choose the first element, $n - 1$ ways to choose the second element, and so on, until k elements are chosen, with the last element chosen from the remaining $n - k + 1$ elements. For the above example, with $n = 4$ and $k = 2$, the formula (C.1) evaluates to $4!/2! = 12$, matching the number of 2-permutations listed.

Combinations

A *k-combination* of an n-set S is simply a k-subset of S. For example, the 4-set $\{a, b, c, d\}$ has six 2-combinations:

$$ab, ac, ad, bc, bd, cd \;.$$

(Here we use the shorthand of omitting the braces around each subset.) To construct a k-combination of an n-set, choose k distinct (different) elements from the n-set. The order of selecting the elements does not matter.

We can express the number of k-combinations of an n-set in terms of the number of k-permutations of an n-set. Every k-combination has exactly $k!$ permutations of its elements, each of which is a distinct k-permutation of the n-set. Thus the number of k-combinations of an n-set is the number of k-permutations divided by $k!$. From equation (C.1), this quantity is

$$\frac{n!}{k! \, (n - k)!} \;. \tag{C.2}$$

For $k = 0$, this formula tells us that the number of ways to choose 0 elements from an n-set is 1 (not 0), since $0! = 1$.

Binomial coefficients

The notation $\binom{n}{k}$ (read "n choose k") denotes the number of k-combinations of an n-set. Equation (C.2) gives

$$\binom{n}{k} = \frac{n!}{k! \, (n - k)!} \;.$$

This formula is symmetric in k and $n - k$:

$$\binom{n}{k} = \binom{n}{n-k} .$$
(C.3)

These numbers are also known as *binomial coefficients*, due to their appearance in the *binomial theorem*:

$$(x + y)^n = \sum_{k=0}^{n} \binom{n}{k} x^k y^{n-k} ,$$
(C.4)

where $n \in \mathbb{N}$ and $x, y \in \mathbb{R}$. The right-hand side of equation (C.4) is called the *binomial expansion* of the left-hand side. A special case of the binomial theorem occurs when $x = y = 1$:

$$2^n = \sum_{k=0}^{n} \binom{n}{k} .$$

This formula corresponds to counting the 2^n binary n-strings by the number of 1s they contain: $\binom{n}{k}$ binary n-strings contain exactly k 1s, since there are $\binom{n}{k}$ ways to choose k out of the n positions in which to place the 1s.

Many identities involve binomial coefficients. The exercises at the end of this section give you the opportunity to prove a few.

Binomial bounds

You sometimes need to bound the size of a binomial coefficient. For $1 \leq k \leq n$, we have the lower bound

$$\binom{n}{k} = \frac{n(n-1) \cdots (n-k+1)}{k(k-1) \cdots 1}$$

$$= \left(\frac{n}{k} \right) \left(\frac{n-1}{k-1} \right) \cdots \left(\frac{n-k+1}{1} \right)$$

$$\geq \left(\frac{n}{k} \right)^k .$$
(C.5)

Taking advantage of the inequality $k! \geq (k/e)^k$ derived from Stirling's approximation (3.25) on page 67, we obtain the upper bounds

$$\binom{n}{k} = \frac{n(n-1) \cdots (n-k+1)}{k(k-1) \cdots 1}$$

$$\leq \frac{n^k}{k!}$$

$$\leq \left(\frac{en}{k} \right)^k .$$
(C.6)

For all integers k such that $0 \le k \le n$, you can use induction (see Exercise C.1-12) to prove the bound

$$\binom{n}{k} \le \frac{n^n}{k^k(n-k)^{n-k}} , \tag{C.7}$$

where for convenience we assume that $0^0 = 1$. For $k = \lambda n$, where $0 \le \lambda \le 1$, we can rewrite this bound as

$$\binom{n}{\lambda n} \le \frac{n^n}{(\lambda n)^{\lambda n}((1-\lambda)n)^{(1-\lambda)n}}$$

$$= \left(\left(\frac{1}{\lambda}\right)^{\lambda} \left(\frac{1}{1-\lambda}\right)^{1-\lambda} \right)^n$$

$$= 2^{n\,H(\lambda)} ,$$

where

$$H(\lambda) = -\lambda \lg \lambda - (1-\lambda) \lg(1-\lambda) \tag{C.8}$$

is the *(binary) entropy function* and where, for convenience, we assume that $0 \lg 0 = 0$, so that $H(0) = H(1) = 0$.

Exercises

C.1-1
How many k-substrings does an n-string have? (Consider identical k-substrings at different positions to be different.) How many substrings does an n-string have in total?

C.1-2
An n-input, m-output *boolean function* is a function from $\{0,1\}^n$ to $\{0,1\}^m$. How many n-input, 1-output boolean functions are there? How many n-input, m-output boolean functions are there?

C.1-3
In how many ways can n professors sit around a circular conference table? Consider two seatings to be the same if one can be rotated to form the other.

C.1-4
In how many ways is it possible to choose three distinct numbers from the set $\{1, 2, \dots, 99\}$ so that their sum is even?

C.1-5
Prove the identity

$$\binom{n}{k} = \frac{n}{k}\binom{n-1}{k-1} \tag{C.9}$$

for $0 < k \le n$.

C.1-6
Prove the identity

$$\binom{n}{k} = \frac{n}{n-k}\binom{n-1}{k}$$

for $0 \le k < n$.

C.1-7
To choose k objects from n, you can make one of the objects distinguished and consider whether the distinguished object is chosen. Use this approach to prove that

$$\binom{n}{k} = \binom{n-1}{k} + \binom{n-1}{k-1}.$$

C.1-8
Using the result of Exercise C.1-7, make a table for $n = 0, 1, \ldots, 6$ and $0 \le k \le n$ of the binomial coefficients $\binom{n}{k}$ with $\binom{0}{0}$ at the top, $\binom{1}{0}$ and $\binom{1}{1}$ on the next line, then $\binom{2}{0}$, $\binom{2}{1}$, and $\binom{2}{2}$, and so forth. Such a table of binomial coefficients is called *Pascal's triangle*.

C.1-9
Prove that

$$\sum_{i=1}^{n} i = \binom{n+1}{2}.$$

C.1-10
Show that for any integers $n \ge 0$ and $0 \le k \le n$, the expression $\binom{n}{k}$ achieves its maximum value when $k = \lfloor n/2 \rfloor$ or $k = \lceil n/2 \rceil$.

★ *C.1-11*

Argue that for any integers $n \geq 0$, $j \geq 0$, $k \geq 0$, and $j + k \leq n$,

$$\binom{n}{j+k} \leq \binom{n}{j}\binom{n-j}{k} . \tag{C.10}$$

Provide both an algebraic proof and an argument based on a method for choosing $j + k$ items out of n. Give an example in which equality does not hold.

★ *C.1-12*

Use induction on all integers k such that $0 \leq k \leq n/2$ to prove inequality (C.7), and use equation (C.3) to extend it to all integers k such that $0 \leq k \leq n$.

★ *C.1-13*

Use Stirling's approximation to prove that

$$\binom{2n}{n} = \frac{2^{2n}}{\sqrt{\pi n}}(1 + O(1/n)) . \tag{C.11}$$

★ *C.1-14*

By differentiating the entropy function $H(\lambda)$, show that it achieves its maximum value at $\lambda = 1/2$. What is $H(1/2)$?

★ *C.1-15*

Show that for any integer $n \geq 0$,

$$\sum_{k=0}^{n} \binom{n}{k} k = n \, 2^{n-1} . \tag{C.12}$$

★ *C.1-16*

Inequality (C.5) provides a lower bound on the binomial coefficient $\binom{n}{k}$. For small values of k, a stronger bound holds. Prove that

$$\binom{n}{k} \geq \frac{n^k}{4k!} \tag{C.13}$$

for $k \leq \sqrt{n}$.

C.2   Probability

Probability is an essential tool for the design and analysis of probabilistic and randomized algorithms. This section reviews basic probability theory.

We define probability in terms of a *sample space* S, which is a set whose elements are called *outcomes* or *elementary events*. Think of each outcome as a possible result of an experiment. For the experiment of flipping two distinguishable coins, with each individual flip resulting in a head (H) or a tail (T), you can view the sample space S as consisting of the set of all possible 2-strings over $\{H, T\}$:

$$S = \{HH, HT, TH, TT\} \ .$$

An *event* is a subset[1] of the sample space S. For example, in the experiment of flipping two coins, the event of obtaining one head and one tail is $\{HT, TH\}$. The event S is called the *certain event*, and the event $\emptyset$ is called the *null event*. We say that two events A and B are *mutually exclusive* if $A \cap B = \emptyset$. An outcome s also defines the event $\{s\}$, which we sometimes write as just s. By definition, all outcomes are mutually exclusive.

Axioms of probability

A *probability distribution* $\Pr\{\}$ on a sample space S is a mapping from events of S to real numbers satisfying the following *probability axioms*:

1. $\Pr\{A\} \geq 0$ for any event A.

2. $\Pr\{S\} = 1$.

3. $\Pr\{A \cup B\} = \Pr\{A\} + \Pr\{B\}$ for any two mutually exclusive events A and B. More generally, for any sequence of events $A_1, A_2, \ldots$ (finite or countably infinite) that are pairwise mutually exclusive,

$$\Pr\left\{\bigcup_i A_i\right\} = \sum_i \Pr\{A_i\} \ .$$

We call $\Pr\{A\}$ the *probability* of the event A. Axiom 2 is simply a normalization requirement: there is really nothing fundamental about choosing 1 as the probability of the certain event, except that it is natural and convenient.

Several results follow immediately from these axioms and basic set theory (see Section B.1). The null event $\emptyset$ has probability $\Pr\{\emptyset\} = 0$. If $A \subseteq B$, then

---

[1] For a general probability distribution, there may be some subsets of the sample space S that are not considered to be events. This situation usually arises when the sample space is uncountably infinite. The main requirement for what subsets are events is that the set of events of a sample space must be closed under the operations of taking the complement of an event, forming the union of a finite or countable number of events, and taking the intersection of a finite or countable number of events. Most of the probability distributions we see in this book are over finite or countable sample spaces, and we generally consider all subsets of a sample space to be events. A notable exception is the continuous uniform probability distribution, which we'll see shortly.

$\mathrm{Pr}\{A\} \leq \mathrm{Pr}\{B\}$. Using $\overline{A}$ to denote the event $S - A$ (the *complement* of A), we have $\mathrm{Pr}\{\overline{A}\} = 1 - \mathrm{Pr}\{A\}$. For any two events A and B,

$$\mathrm{Pr}\{A \cup B\} = \mathrm{Pr}\{A\} + \mathrm{Pr}\{B\} - \mathrm{Pr}\{A \cap B\} \tag{C.14}$$

$$\leq \mathrm{Pr}\{A\} + \mathrm{Pr}\{B\} \ . \tag{C.15}$$

In our coin-flipping example, suppose that each of the four outcomes has probability $1/4$. Then the probability of getting at least one head is

$$\mathrm{Pr}\{\mathrm{HH}, \mathrm{HT}, \mathrm{TH}\} = \mathrm{Pr}\{\mathrm{HH}\} + \mathrm{Pr}\{\mathrm{HT}\} + \mathrm{Pr}\{\mathrm{TH}\}$$

$$= 3/4 \ .$$

Another way to obtain the same result is to observe that since the probability of getting strictly less than one head is $\mathrm{Pr}\{\mathrm{TT}\} = 1/4$, the probability of getting at least one head is $1 - 1/4 = 3/4$.

Discrete probability distributions

A probability distribution is *discrete* if it is defined over a finite or countably infinite sample space. Let S be the sample space. Then for any event A,

$$\mathrm{Pr}\{A\} = \sum_{s \in A} \mathrm{Pr}\{s\} \ ,$$

since outcomes, specifically those in A, are mutually exclusive. If S is finite and every outcome $s \in S$ has probability $\mathrm{Pr}\{s\} = 1/|S|$, then we have the *uniform probability distribution* on S. In such a case the experiment is often described as "picking an element of S at random."

As an example, consider the process of flipping a *fair coin*, one for which the probability of obtaining a head is the same as the probability of obtaining a tail, that is, $1/2$. Flipping the coin n times gives the uniform probability distribution defined on the sample space $S = \{\mathrm{H}, \mathrm{T}\}^n$, a set of size 2^n. We can represent each outcome in S as a string of length n over $\{\mathrm{H}, \mathrm{T}\}$, with each string occurring with probability $1/2^n$. The event $A = \{\text{exactly } k \text{ heads and exactly } n - k \text{ tails occur}\}$ is a subset of S of size $|A| = \binom{n}{k}$, since $\binom{n}{k}$ strings of length n over $\{\mathrm{H}, \mathrm{T}\}$ contain exactly k H's. The probability of event A is thus $\mathrm{Pr}\{A\} = \binom{n}{k}/2^n$.

Continuous uniform probability distribution

The continuous uniform probability distribution is an example of a probability distribution in which not all subsets of the sample space are considered to be events. The continuous uniform probability distribution is defined over a closed interval $[a, b]$ of the reals, where $a < b$. The intuition is that each point in the interval $[a, b]$ should be "equally likely." Because there are an uncountable number of points, however, if all points had the same finite, positive probability, axioms 2 and 3 would not be simultaneously satisfied. For this reason, we'd like to associate a probability only with *some* of the subsets of S in such a way that the axioms are satisfied for these events.

For any closed interval $[c, d]$, where $a \le c \le d \le b$, the *continuous uniform probability distribution* defines the probability of the event $[c, d]$ to be

$$\Pr\{[c, d]\} = \frac{d - c}{b - a} \,.$$

Letting $c = d$ gives that the probability of a single point is 0. Removing the endpoints $[c, c]$ and $[d, d]$ of an interval $[c, d]$ results in the open interval (c, d). Since $[c, d] = [c, c] \cup (c, d) \cup [d, d]$, axiom 3 gives $\Pr\{[c, d]\} = \Pr\{(c, d)\}$. Generally, the set of events for the continuous uniform probability distribution contains any subset of the sample space $[a, b]$ that can be obtained by a finite or countable union of open and closed intervals, as well as certain more complicated sets.

Conditional probability and independence

Sometimes you have some prior partial knowledge about the outcome of an experiment. For example, suppose that a friend has flipped two fair coins and has told you that at least one of the coins showed a head. What is the probability that both coins are heads? The information given eliminates the possibility of two tails. The three remaining outcomes are equally likely, and so you infer that each occurs with probability 1/3. Since only one of these outcomes shows two heads, the answer is 1/3.

Conditional probability formalizes the notion of having prior partial knowledge of the outcome of an experiment. The *conditional probability* of an event A given that another event B occurs is defined to be

$$\Pr\{A \mid B\} = \frac{\Pr\{A \cap B\}}{\Pr\{B\}} \tag{C.16}$$

whenever $\Pr\{B\} \ne 0$. (Read "$\Pr\{A \mid B\}$" as "the probability of A given B.") The idea behind equation (C.16) is that since we are given that event B occurs, the event that A also occurs is $A \cap B$. That is, $A \cap B$ is the set of outcomes in which both A and B occur. Because the outcome is one of the elementary events in B, we normalize the probabilities of all the elementary events in B by dividing them by $\Pr\{B\}$, so that they sum to 1. The conditional probability of A given B is, therefore, the ratio of the probability of event $A \cap B$ to the probability of event B. In the example above, A is the event that both coins are heads, and B is the event that at least one coin is a head. Thus, $\Pr\{A \mid B\} = (1/4)/(3/4) = 1/3$.

Two events are *independent* if

$$\Pr\{A \cap B\} = \Pr\{A\} \Pr\{B\} \ , \tag{C.17}$$

which is equivalent, if $\Pr\{B\} \neq 0$, to the condition

$$\Pr\{A \mid B\} = \Pr\{A\} \ .$$

For example, suppose that you flip two fair coins and that the outcomes are independent. Then the probability of two heads is $(1/2)(1/2) = 1/4$. Now suppose that one event is that the first coin comes up heads and the other event is that the coins come up differently. Each of these events occurs with probability $1/2$, and the probability that both events occur is $1/4$. Thus, according to the definition of independence, the events are independent—even though you might think that both events depend on the first coin. Finally, suppose that the coins are welded together so that they both fall heads or both fall tails and that the two possibilities are equally likely. Then the probability that each coin comes up heads is $1/2$, but the probability that they both come up heads is $1/2 \neq (1/2)(1/2)$. Consequently, the event that one comes up heads and the event that the other comes up heads are not independent.

A collection $A_1, A_2, \ldots, A_n$ of events is said to be *pairwise independent* if

$$\Pr\{A_i \cap A_j\} = \Pr\{A_i\} \Pr\{A_j\}$$

for all $1 \leq i < j \leq n$. We say that the events of the collection are *(mutually) independent* if every k-subset $A_{i_1}, A_{i_2}, \ldots, A_{i_k}$ of the collection, where $2 \leq k \leq n$ and $1 \leq i_1 < i_2 < \cdots < i_k \leq n$, satisfies

$$\Pr\{A_{i_1} \cap A_{i_2} \cap \cdots \cap A_{i_k}\} = \Pr\{A_{i_1}\} \Pr\{A_{i_2}\} \cdots \Pr\{A_{i_k}\} \ .$$

For example, suppose that you flip two fair coins. Let A_1 be the event that the first coin is heads, let A_2 be the event that the second coin is heads, and let A_3 be the event that the two coins are different. Then,

$$
\begin{aligned}
\Pr\{A_1\} &= 1/2 \ , \\
\Pr\{A_2\} &= 1/2 \ , \\
\Pr\{A_3\} &= 1/2 \ , \\
\Pr\{A_1 \cap A_2\} &= 1/4 \ , \\
\Pr\{A_1 \cap A_3\} &= 1/4 \ , \\
\Pr\{A_2 \cap A_3\} &= 1/4 \ , \\
\Pr\{A_1 \cap A_2 \cap A_3\} &= 0 \ .
\end{aligned}
$$

Since for $1 \leq i < j \leq 3$, we have $\Pr\{A_i \cap A_j\} = \Pr\{A_i\} \Pr\{A_j\} = 1/4$, the events A_1, A_2, and A_3 are pairwise independent. The events are not mutually independent, however, because $\Pr\{A_1 \cap A_2 \cap A_3\} = 0$ and $\Pr\{A_1\} \Pr\{A_2\} \Pr\{A_3\} = 1/8 \neq 0$.

Bayes's theorem

From the definition (C.16) of conditional probability and the commutative law $A \cap B = B \cap A$, it follows that for two events A and B, each with nonzero probability,

$$\Pr\{A \cap B\} = \Pr\{B\}\Pr\{A \mid B\} \tag{C.18}$$
$$= \Pr\{A\}\Pr\{B \mid A\} .$$

Solving for $\Pr\{A \mid B\}$, we obtain

$$\Pr\{A \mid B\} = \frac{\Pr\{A\}\Pr\{B \mid A\}}{\Pr\{B\}} , \tag{C.19}$$

which is known as **Bayes's theorem**. The denominator $\Pr\{B\}$ is a normalizing constant, which we can reformulate as follows. Since $B = (B \cap A) \cup (B \cap \overline{A})$, and since $B \cap A$ and $B \cap \overline{A}$ are mutually exclusive events,

$$\Pr\{B\} = \Pr\{B \cap A\} + \Pr\{B \cap \overline{A}\}$$
$$= \Pr\{A\}\Pr\{B \mid A\} + \Pr\{\overline{A}\}\Pr\{B \mid \overline{A}\} .$$

Substituting into equation (C.19) produces an equivalent form of Bayes's theorem:

$$\Pr\{A \mid B\} = \frac{\Pr\{A\}\Pr\{B \mid A\}}{\Pr\{A\}\Pr\{B \mid A\} + \Pr\{\overline{A}\}\Pr\{B \mid \overline{A}\}} . \tag{C.20}$$

Bayes's theorem can simplify the computing of conditional probabilities. For example, suppose that you have a fair coin and a biased coin that always comes up heads. Run an experiment consisting of three independent events: choose one of the two coins at random, flip that coin once, and then flip it again. Suppose that the coin you have chosen comes up heads both times. What is the probability that it's the biased coin?

Bayes's theorem solves this problem. Let A be the event that you choose the biased coin, and let B be the event that the chosen coin comes up heads both times. We wish to determine $\Pr\{A \mid B\}$, knowing that $\Pr\{A\} = 1/2$, $\Pr\{B \mid A\} = 1$, $\Pr\{\overline{A}\} = 1/2$, and $\Pr\{B \mid \overline{A}\} = 1/4$. Thus we have

$$\Pr\{A \mid B\} = \frac{(1/2) \cdot 1}{(1/2) \cdot 1 + (1/2) \cdot (1/4)}$$
$$= 4/5 .$$

Exercises

C.2-1

Professor Rosencrantz flips a fair coin twice. Professor Guildenstern flips a fair coin once. What is the probability that Professor Rosencrantz obtains strictly more heads than Professor Guildenstern?

C.2-2

Prove *Boole's inequality*: For any finite or countably infinite sequence of events $A_1, A_2, \ldots$,

$$\Pr\{A_1 \cup A_2 \cup \cdots\} \leq \Pr\{A_1\} + \Pr\{A_2\} + \cdots . \tag{C.21}$$

C.2-3

You shuffle a deck of 10 cards, each bearing a distinct number from 1 to 10, in order to mix the cards thoroughly. You then remove three cards, one at a time, from the deck. What is the probability that the three cards you select are in sorted (increasing) order?

C.2-4

Prove that

$$\Pr\{A \mid B\} + \Pr\{\overline{A} \mid B\} = 1 .$$

C.2-5

Prove that for any collection of events $A_1, A_2, \ldots, A_n$,

$$\Pr\{A_1 \cap A_2 \cap \cdots \cap A_n\} = \Pr\{A_1\} \cdot \Pr\{A_2 \mid A_1\} \cdot \Pr\{A_3 \mid A_1 \cap A_2\} \cdots$$
$$\Pr\{A_n \mid A_1 \cap A_2 \cap \cdots \cap A_{n-1}\} . \tag{C.22}$$

★ *C.2-6*

Show how to construct a set of n events that are pairwise independent but such that no subset of $k > 2$ of them is mutually independent.

★ *C.2-7*

Two events A and B are *conditionally independent*, given C, if

$$\Pr\{A \cap B \mid C\} = \Pr\{A \mid C\} \cdot \Pr\{B \mid C\} .$$

Give a simple but nontrivial example of two events that are not independent but are conditionally independent given a third event.

★ *C.2-8*

Professor Gore teaches a music class on rhythm in which three students—Jeff, Tim, and Carmine—are in danger of failing. Professor Gore tells the three that one of them will pass the course and the other two will fail. Carmine asks Professor Gore privately which of Jeff and Tim will fail, arguing that since he already knows at least one of them will fail, the professor won't be revealing any information about Carmine's outcome. In a breach of privacy law, Professor Gore tells Carmine that Jeff will fail. Carmine feels somewhat relieved now, figuring that either he or Tim will pass, so that his probability of passing is now $1/2$. Is Carmine correct, or is his chance of passing still $1/3$? Explain.

C.3   Discrete random variables

A *(discrete) random variable* X is a function from a finite or countably infinite sample space S to the real numbers. It associates a real number with each possible outcome of an experiment, which allows us to work with the probability distribution induced on the resulting set of numbers. Random variables can also be defined for uncountably infinite sample spaces, but they raise technical issues that are unnecessary to address for our purposes. Therefore we'll assume that random variables are discrete.

For a random variable X and a real number x, we define the event $X = x$ to be $\{s \in S : X(s) = x\}$, and thus

$$\Pr\{X = x\} = \sum_{s \in S : X(s) = x} \Pr\{s\} \ .$$

The function

$$f(x) = \Pr\{X = x\}$$

is the *probability density function* of the random variable X. From the probability axioms, $\Pr\{X = x\} \geq 0$ and $\sum_x \Pr\{X = x\} = 1$.

As an example, consider the experiment of rolling a pair of ordinary, 6-sided dice. There are 36 possible outcomes in the sample space. Assume that the probability distribution is uniform, so that each outcome $s \in S$ is equally likely: $\Pr\{s\} = 1/36$. Define the random variable X to be the *maximum* of the two values showing on the dice. We have $\Pr\{X = 3\} = 5/36$, since X assigns a value of 3 to 5 of the 36 possible outcomes, namely, $(1, 3), (2, 3), (3, 3), (3, 2)$, and $(3, 1)$.

We can define several random variables on the same sample space. If X and Y are random variables, the function

$$f(x, y) = \Pr\{X = x \text{ and } Y = y\}$$

is the *joint probability density function* of X and Y. For a fixed value y,

$$\Pr\{Y = y\} = \sum_{x} \Pr\{X = x \text{ and } Y = y\} ,$$

and similarly, for a fixed value x,

$$\Pr\{X = x\} = \sum_{y} \Pr\{X = x \text{ and } Y = y\} .$$

Using the definition (C.16) of conditional probability on page 1187, we have

$$\Pr\{X = x \mid Y = y\} = \frac{\Pr\{X = x \text{ and } Y = y\}}{\Pr\{Y = y\}} .$$

We define two random variables X and Y to be *independent* if for all x and y, the events $X = x$ and $Y = y$ are independent or, equivalently, if for all x and y, we have $\Pr\{X = x \text{ and } Y = y\} = \Pr\{X = x\} \Pr\{Y = y\}$.

Given a set of random variables defined over the same sample space, we can define new random variables as sums, products, or other functions of the original variables.

Expected value of a random variable

The simplest, and often the most useful, summary of the distribution of a random variable is the "average" of the values it takes on. The *expected value* (or, synonymously, *expectation* or *mean*) of a discrete random variable X is

$$E[X] = \sum_{x} x \cdot \Pr\{X = x\} , \tag{C.23}$$

which is well defined if the sum is finite or converges absolutely. Sometimes the expectation of X is denoted by μ_X or, when the random variable is apparent from context, simply by μ.

Consider a game in which you flip two fair coins. You earn \$3 for each head but lose \$2 for each tail. The expected value of the random variable X representing your earnings is

$$
\begin{aligned}
E[X] &= 6 \cdot \Pr\{2 \text{ H's}\} + 1 \cdot \Pr\{1 \text{ H}, 1 \text{ T}\} - 4 \cdot \Pr\{2 \text{ T's}\} \\
&= 6 \cdot (1/4) + 1 \cdot (1/2) - 4 \cdot (1/4) \\
&= 1 .
\end{aligned}
$$

Linearity of expectation says that the expectation of the sum of two random variables is the sum of their expectations, that is,

$$E[X + Y] = E[X] + E[Y] , \tag{C.24}$$

whenever $\mathrm{E}[X]$ and $\mathrm{E}[Y]$ are defined. Linearity of expectation applies to a broad range of situations, holding even when X and Y are not independent. It also extends to finite and absolutely convergent summations of expectations. Linearity of expectation is the key property that enables us to perform probabilistic analyses by using indicator random variables (see Section 5.2).

If X is any random variable, any function $g(x)$ defines a new random variable $g(X)$. If the expectation of $g(X)$ is defined, then

$$\mathrm{E}[g(X)] = \sum_x g(x) \cdot \Pr\{X = x\} \ .$$

Letting $g(x) = ax$, we have for any constant a,

$$\mathrm{E}[aX] = a\mathrm{E}[X] \ . \tag{C.25}$$

Consequently, expectations are linear: for any two random variables X and Y and any constant a,

$$\mathrm{E}[aX + Y] = a\mathrm{E}[X] + \mathrm{E}[Y] \ . \tag{C.26}$$

When two random variables X and Y are independent and each has a defined expectation,

$$
\begin{aligned}
\mathrm{E}[XY] &= \sum_x \sum_y xy \cdot \Pr\{X = x \text{ and } Y = y\} \\
&= \sum_x \sum_y xy \cdot \Pr\{X = x\}\Pr\{Y = y\} \quad \text{(by independence of } X \text{ and } Y) \\
&= \left(\sum_x x \cdot \Pr\{X = x\}\right)\left(\sum_y y \cdot \Pr\{Y = y\}\right) \\
&= \mathrm{E}[X]\mathrm{E}[Y] \qquad\qquad\qquad\quad \text{(by equation (C.23))} \ .
\end{aligned}
$$

In general, when n random variables $X_1, X_2, \ldots, X_n$ are mutually independent,

$$\mathrm{E}[X_1 X_2 \cdots X_n] = \mathrm{E}[X_1]\mathrm{E}[X_2]\cdots\mathrm{E}[X_n] \ . \tag{C.27}$$

When a random variable X takes on values from the set of natural numbers $\mathbb{N} = \{0, 1, 2, \ldots\}$, we have a nice formula for its expectation:

$$
\begin{aligned}
\mathrm{E}[X] &= \sum_{i=0}^{\infty} i \cdot \Pr\{X = i\} \\
&= \sum_{i=0}^{\infty} i \cdot (\Pr\{X \geq i\} - \Pr\{X \geq i + 1\}) \\
&= \sum_{i=1}^{\infty} \Pr\{X \geq i\} \ , \tag{C.28}
\end{aligned}
$$

since each term $\Pr\{X \geq i\}$ is added in i times and subtracted out $i - 1$ times (except $\Pr\{X \geq 0\}$, which is added in 0 times and not subtracted out at all).

A function $f(x)$ is *convex* if

$$f(\lambda x + (1 - \lambda)y) \leq \lambda f(x) + (1 - \lambda)f(y) \tag{C.29}$$

for all x and y and for all $0 \leq \lambda \leq 1$. *Jensen's inequality* says that when a convex function $f(x)$ is applied to a random variable X,

$$\mathrm{E}[f(X)] \geq f(\mathrm{E}[X]), \tag{C.30}$$

provided that the expectations exist and are finite.

Variance and standard deviation

The expected value of a random variable does not express how "spread out" the variable's values are. For example, consider random variables X and Y for which $\Pr\{X = 1/4\} = \Pr\{X = 3/4\} = 1/2$ and $\Pr\{Y = 0\} = \Pr\{Y = 1\} = 1/2$. Then both $\mathrm{E}[X]$ and $\mathrm{E}[Y]$ are $1/2$, yet the actual values taken on by Y are further from the mean than the actual values taken on by X.

The notion of variance mathematically expresses how far from the mean a random variable's values are likely to be. The *variance* of a random variable X with mean $\mathrm{E}[X]$ is

$$
\begin{aligned}
\mathrm{Var}[X] &= \mathrm{E}\left[(X - \mathrm{E}[X])^2\right] \\
&= \mathrm{E}\left[X^2 - 2X\mathrm{E}[X] + \mathrm{E}^2[X]\right] \\
&= \mathrm{E}[X^2] - 2\mathrm{E}[X\mathrm{E}[X]] + \mathrm{E}^2[X] \\
&= \mathrm{E}[X^2] - 2\mathrm{E}^2[X] + \mathrm{E}^2[X] \\
&= \mathrm{E}[X^2] - \mathrm{E}^2[X] .
\end{aligned}
\tag{C.31}
$$

To justify the equation $\mathrm{E}[\mathrm{E}^2[X]] = \mathrm{E}^2[X]$, note that because $\mathrm{E}[X]$ is a real number and not a random variable, so is $\mathrm{E}^2[X]$. The equation $\mathrm{E}[X\mathrm{E}[X]] = \mathrm{E}^2[X]$ follows from equation (C.25), with $a = \mathrm{E}[X]$. Rewriting equation (C.31) yields an expression for the expectation of the square of a random variable:

$$\mathrm{E}[X^2] = \mathrm{Var}[X] + \mathrm{E}^2[X] . \tag{C.32}$$

The variance of a random variable X and the variance of aX are related (see Exercise C.3-10):

$$\mathrm{Var}[aX] = a^2\mathrm{Var}[X] .$$

When X and Y are independent random variables,

$$\mathrm{Var}[X + Y] = \mathrm{Var}[X] + \mathrm{Var}[Y] .$$

In general, if n random variables $X_1, X_2, \ldots, X_n$ are pairwise independent, then

$$\mathrm{Var}\left[\sum_{i=1}^{n} X_i\right] = \sum_{i=1}^{n} \mathrm{Var}[X_i] . \tag{C.33}$$

The *standard deviation* of a random variable X is the nonnegative square root of the variance of X. The standard deviation of a random variable X is sometimes denoted σ_X or simply σ when the random variable X is understood from context. With this notation, the variance of X is denoted σ^2.

Exercises

C.3-1
You roll two ordinary, 6-sided dice. What is the expectation of the sum of the two values showing? What is the expectation of the maximum of the two values showing?

C.3-2
An array $A[1:n]$ contains n distinct numbers that are randomly ordered, with each permutation of the n numbers being equally likely. What is the expectation of the index of the maximum element in the array? What is the expectation of the index of the minimum element in the array?

C.3-3
A carnival game consists of three dice in a cage. A player can bet a dollar on any of the numbers 1 through 6. The cage is shaken, and the payoff is as follows. If the player's number doesn't appear on any of the dice, the player loses the dollar. Otherwise, if the player's number appears on exactly k of the three dice, for $k = 1, 2, 3$, the player keeps the dollar and wins k more dollars. What is the expected gain from playing the carnival game once?

C.3-4
Argue that if X and Y are nonnegative random variables, then

$$E[\max\{X, Y\}] \leq E[X] + E[Y] .$$

★ *C.3-5*
Let X and Y be independent random variables. Prove that $f(X)$ and $g(Y)$ are independent for any choice of functions f and g.

★ **C.3-6**

Let X be a nonnegative random variable, and suppose that $E[X]$ is well defined. Prove *Markov's inequality*:

$$\Pr\{X \geq t\} \leq E[X]/t \tag{C.34}$$

for all $t > 0$.

★ **C.3-7**

Let S be a sample space, and let X and X' be random variables such that $X(s) \geq X'(s)$ for all $s \in S$. Prove that for any real constant t,

$$\Pr\{X \geq t\} \geq \Pr\{X' \geq t\} \ .$$

C.3-8

Which is larger: the expectation of the square of a random variable, or the square of its expectation?

C.3-9

Show that for any random variable X that takes on only the values 0 and 1, we have $\text{Var}[X] = E[X]E[1 - X]$.

C.3-10

Prove that $\text{Var}[aX] = a^2\text{Var}[X]$ from the definition (C.31) of variance.

C.4   The geometric and binomial distributions

A ***Bernoulli trial*** is an experiment with only two possible outcomes: ***success***, which occurs with probability p, and ***failure***, which occurs with probability $q = 1 - p$. A coin flip serves as an example where, depending on your point of view, heads equates to success and tails to failure. When we speak of ***Bernoulli trials*** collectively, we mean that the trials are mutually independent and, unless we specifically say otherwise, that each has the same probability p for success. Two important distributions arise from Bernoulli trials: the geometric distribution and the binomial distribution.

The geometric distribution

Consider a sequence of Bernoulli trials, each with a probability p of success and a probability $q = 1 - p$ of failure. How many trials occur before a success? Define the random variable X to be the number of trials needed to obtain a success. Then X has values in the range $\{1, 2, \ldots\}$, and for $k \geq 1$,

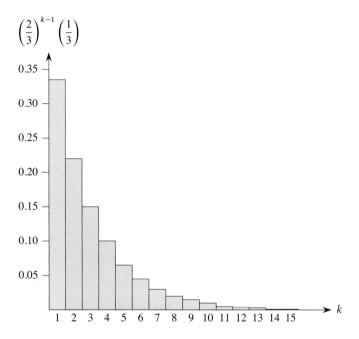

Figure C.1 A geometric distribution with probability $p = 1/3$ of success and a probability $q = 1 - p$ of failure. The expectation of the distribution is $1/p = 3$.

$$\Pr\{X = k\} = q^{k-1} p ,\qquad\qquad\text{(C.35)}$$

since $k - 1$ failures occur before the first success. A probability distribution satisfying equation (C.35) is said to be a *geometric distribution*. Figure C.1 illustrates such a distribution.

Assuming that $q < 1$, we can calculate the expectation of a geometric distribution:

$$
\begin{aligned}
\mathrm{E}[X] &= \sum_{k=1}^{\infty} k q^{k-1} p \\
&= \frac{p}{q} \sum_{k=0}^{\infty} k q^k \\
&= \frac{p}{q} \cdot \frac{q}{(1-q)^2} \quad \text{(by equation (A.11) on page 1142)} \\
&= \frac{p}{q} \cdot \frac{q}{p^2} \\
&= 1/p .
\end{aligned}
\qquad\qquad\text{(C.36)}
$$

Thus, on average, it takes $1/p$ trials before a success occurs, an intuitive result. As Exercise C.4-3 asks you to show, the variance is

$$\text{Var}\,[X] = q/p^2 \,. \tag{C.37}$$

As an example, suppose that you repeatedly roll two dice until you obtain either a seven or an eleven. Of the 36 possible outcomes, 6 yield a seven and 2 yield an eleven. Thus, the probability of success is $p = 8/36 = 2/9$, and you'd have to roll $1/p = 9/2 = 4.5$ times on average to obtain a seven or eleven.

The binomial distribution

How many successes occur during n Bernoulli trials, where a success occurs with probability p and a failure with probability $q = 1 - p$? Define the random variable X to be the number of successes in n trials. Then X has values in the range $\{0, 1, \ldots, n\}$, and for $k = 0, 1, \ldots, n$,

$$\Pr\{X = k\} = \binom{n}{k} p^k q^{n-k} \,, \tag{C.38}$$

since there are $\binom{n}{k}$ ways to pick which k of the n trials are successes, and the probability that each occurs is $p^k q^{n-k}$. A probability distribution satisfying equation (C.38) is said to be a *binomial distribution*. For convenience, we define the family of binomial distributions using the notation

$$b(k; n, p) = \binom{n}{k} p^k (1 - p)^{n-k} \,. \tag{C.39}$$

Figure C.2 illustrates a binomial distribution. The name "binomial" comes from the right-hand side of equation (C.38) being the kth term of the expansion of $(p + q)^n$. Consequently, since $p + q = 1$, equation (C.4) on page 1181 gives

$$\sum_{k=0}^{n} b(k; n, p) = 1 \,, \tag{C.40}$$

as axiom 2 of the probability axioms requires.

We can compute the expectation of a random variable having a binomial distribution from equations (C.9) and (C.40). Let X be a random variable that follows the binomial distribution $b(k; n, p)$, and let $q = 1 - p$. The definition of expectation gives

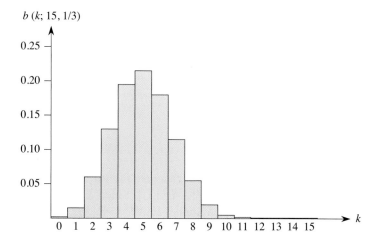

Figure C.2   The binomial distribution $b(k; 15, 1/3)$ resulting from $n = 15$ Bernoulli trials, each with probability $p = 1/3$ of success. The expectation of the distribution is $np = 5$.

$$
\begin{aligned}
\mathrm{E}[X] &= \sum_{k=0}^{n} k \cdot \mathrm{Pr}\{X = k\} \\
&= \sum_{k=0}^{n} k \cdot b(k; n, p) \\
&= \sum_{k=1}^{n} k \binom{n}{k} p^k q^{n-k} \\
&= np \sum_{k=1}^{n} \binom{n-1}{k-1} p^{k-1} q^{n-k} \quad \text{(by equation (C.9) on page 1183)} \\
&= np \sum_{k=0}^{n-1} \binom{n-1}{k} p^k q^{(n-1)-k} \\
&= np \sum_{k=0}^{n-1} b(k; n-1, p) \\
&= np \qquad\qquad\qquad\qquad\qquad \text{(by equation (C.40))} . \qquad\qquad\qquad \text{(C.41)}
\end{aligned}
$$

Linearity of expectation produces the same result with substantially less algebra. Let X_i be the random variable describing the number of successes in the ith trial. Then $\mathrm{E}[X_i] = p \cdot 1 + q \cdot 0 = p$, and the expected number of successes for n trials is

$$E[X] = E\left[\sum_{i=1}^{n} X_i\right]$$

$$= \sum_{i=1}^{n} E[X_i] \qquad \text{(by equation (C.24) on page 1192)}$$

$$= \sum_{i=1}^{n} p$$

$$= np . \tag{C.42}$$

We can use the same approach to calculate the variance of the distribution. By equation (C.31), $\text{Var}[X_i] = E[X_i^2] - E^2[X_i]$. Since X_i takes on only the values 0 and 1, we have $X_i^2 = X_i$, which implies $E[X_i^2] = E[X_i] = p$. Hence,

$$\text{Var}[X_i] = p - p^2 = p(1 - p) = pq . \tag{C.43}$$

To compute the variance of X, we take advantage of the independence of the n trials. By equation (C.33), we have

$$\text{Var}[X] = \text{Var}\left[\sum_{i=1}^{n} X_i\right]$$

$$= \sum_{i=1}^{n} \text{Var}[X_i]$$

$$= \sum_{i=1}^{n} pq$$

$$= npq . \tag{C.44}$$

As Figure C.2 shows, the binomial distribution $b(k; n, p)$ increases with k until it reaches the mean np, and then it decreases. To prove that the distribution always behaves in this manner, examine the ratio of successive terms:

$$\frac{b(k; n, p)}{b(k - 1; n, p)} = \frac{\binom{n}{k} p^k q^{n-k}}{\binom{n}{k-1} p^{k-1} q^{n-k+1}}$$

$$= \frac{n! (k - 1)! (n - k + 1)! p}{k! (n - k)! n! q}$$

$$= \frac{(n - k + 1) p}{kq} \tag{C.45}$$

$$= 1 + \frac{(n - k + 1) p - kq}{kq}$$

$$= 1 + \frac{(n - k + 1) p - k(1 - p)}{kq}$$

$$= 1 + \frac{(n+1)p - k}{kq} \; .$$

This ratio is greater than 1 precisely when $(n+1)p - k$ is positive. Consequently, $b(k;n,p) > b(k-1;n,p)$ for $k < (n+1)p$ (the distribution increases), and $b(k;n,p) < b(k-1;n,p)$ for $k > (n+1)p$ (the distribution decreases). If $(n+1)p$ is an integer, then for $k = (n+1)p$, the ratio $b(k;n,p)/b(k-1;n,p)$ equals 1, so that $b(k;n,p) = b(k-1;n,p)$. In this case, the distribution has two maxima: at $k = (n+1)p$ and at $k-1 = (n+1)p-1 = np-q$. Otherwise, it attains a maximum at the unique integer k that lies in the range $np - q < k < (n+1)p$.

The following lemma provides an upper bound on the binomial distribution.

Lemma C.1
Let $n \geq 0$, let $0 < p < 1$, let $q = 1 - p$, and let $0 \leq k \leq n$. Then

$$b(k;n,p) \leq \left(\frac{np}{k}\right)^{k} \left(\frac{nq}{n-k}\right)^{n-k} \; .$$

Proof   We have

$$b(k;n,p) = \binom{n}{k} p^{k} q^{n-k}$$

$$\leq \left(\frac{n}{k}\right)^{k} \left(\frac{n}{n-k}\right)^{n-k} p^{k} q^{n-k} \quad \text{(by inequality (C.7) on page 1182)}$$

$$= \left(\frac{np}{k}\right)^{k} \left(\frac{nq}{n-k}\right)^{n-k} \; .$$ ∎

Exercises

C.4-1
Verify axiom 2 of the probability axioms for the geometric distribution.

C.4-2
How many times on average do you need to flip six fair coins before obtaining three heads and three tails?

C.4-3
Show that the variance of the geometric distribution is q/p^2. (*Hint:* Use Exercise A.1-6 on page 1144.)

C.4-4
Show that $b(k;n,p) = b(n-k;n,q)$, where $q = 1 - p$.

C.4-5

Show that the value of the maximum of the binomial distribution $b(k; n, p)$ is approximately $1/\sqrt{2\pi npq}$, where $q = 1 - p$.

★ C.4-6

Show that the probability of no successes in n Bernoulli trials, each with probability $p = 1/n$ of success, is approximately $1/e$. Show that the probability of exactly one success is also approximately $1/e$.

★ C.4-7

Professor Rosencrantz flips a fair coin n times, and so does Professor Guildenstern. Show that the probability that they get the same number of heads is $\binom{2n}{n}/4^n$. (*Hint:* For Professor Rosencrantz, call a head a success, and for Professor Guildenstern, call a tail a success.) Use your argument to verify the identity

$$\sum_{k=0}^{n} \binom{n}{k}^2 = \binom{2n}{n}.$$

★ C.4-8

Show that for $0 \le k \le n$,

$$b(k; n, 1/2) \le 2^{n\, H(k/n) - n},$$

where $H(x)$ is the entropy function (C.8) on page 1182.

★ C.4-9

Consider n Bernoulli trials, where for $i = 1, 2, \ldots, n$, the ith trial has probability p_i of success, and let X be the random variable denoting the total number of successes. Let $p \ge p_i$ for all $i = 1, 2, \ldots, n$. Prove that for $1 \le k \le n$,

$$\Pr\{X < k\} \ge \sum_{i=0}^{k-1} b(i; n, p).$$

★ C.4-10

Let X be the random variable for the total number of successes in a set A of n Bernoulli trials, where the ith trial has a probability p_i of success, and let X' be the random variable for the total number of successes in a second set A' of n Bernoulli trials, where the ith trial has a probability $p_i' \ge p_i$ of success. Prove that for $0 \le k \le n$,

$$\Pr\{X' \ge k\} \ge \Pr\{X \ge k\}.$$

(*Hint:* Show how to obtain the Bernoulli trials in A' by an experiment involving the trials of A, and use the result of Exercise C.3-7.)

★ C.5   The tails of the binomial distribution

The probability of having at least, or at most, k successes in n Bernoulli trials, each with probability p of success, is often of more interest than the probability of having exactly k successes. In this section, we investigate the *tails* of the binomial distribution: the two regions of the distribution $b(k; n, p)$ that are far from the mean np. We'll prove several important bounds on (the sum of all terms in) a tail.

We first provide a bound on the right tail of the distribution $b(k; n, p)$. To determine bounds on the left tail, simply invert the roles of successes and failures.

Theorem C.2
Consider a sequence of n Bernoulli trials, where success occurs with probability p. Let X be the random variable denoting the total number of successes. Then for $0 \leq k \leq n$, the probability of at least k successes is

$$\Pr\{X \geq k\} = \sum_{i=k}^{n} b(i; n, p)$$

$$\leq \binom{n}{k} p^k \, .$$

Proof   For $S \subseteq \{1, 2, \ldots, n\}$, let A_S denote the event that the ith trial is a success for every $i \in S$. Since $\Pr\{A_S\} = p^k$, where $|S| = k$, we have

$$\Pr\{X \geq k\} = \Pr\{\text{there exists } S \subseteq \{1, 2, \ldots, n\} : |S| = k \text{ and } A_S\}$$

$$= \Pr\left\{ \bigcup_{S \subseteq \{1,2,\ldots,n\}:|S|=k} A_S \right\}$$

$$\leq \sum_{S \subseteq \{1,2,\ldots,n\}:|S|=k} \Pr\{A_S\} \qquad \text{(by inequality (C.21) on page 1190)}$$

$$= \binom{n}{k} p^k \, . \qquad \blacksquare$$

The following corollary restates the theorem for the left tail of the binomial distribution. In general, we'll leave it to you to adapt the proofs from one tail to the other.

Corollary C.3
Consider a sequence of n Bernoulli trials, where success occurs with probability p. If X is the random variable denoting the total number of successes, then for $0 \leq k \leq n$, the probability of at most k successes is

$$\Pr\{X \le k\} = \sum_{i=0}^{k} b(i;n,p)$$

$$\le \binom{n}{n-k}(1-p)^{n-k}$$

$$= \binom{n}{k}(1-p)^{n-k} \ . \qquad\blacksquare$$

Our next bound concerns the left tail of the binomial distribution. Its corollary shows that, far from the mean, the left tail diminishes exponentially.

Theorem C.4

Consider a sequence of n Bernoulli trials, where success occurs with probability p and failure with probability $q = 1 - p$. Let X be the random variable denoting the total number of successes. Then for $0 < k < np$, the probability of fewer than k successes is

$$\Pr\{X < k\} = \sum_{i=0}^{k-1} b(i;n,p)$$

$$< \frac{kq}{np-k}\, b(k;n,p) \ .$$

Proof   We bound the series $\sum_{i=0}^{k-1} b(i;n,p)$ by a geometric series using the technique from Section A.2, page 1147. For $i = 1, 2, \ldots, k$, equation (C.45) gives

$$\frac{b(i-1;n,p)}{b(i;n,p)} = \frac{iq}{(n-i+1)p}$$

$$< \frac{iq}{(n-i)p}$$

$$\le \frac{kq}{(n-k)p} \ .$$

If we let

$$x = \frac{kq}{(n-k)p}$$

$$< \frac{kq}{(n-np)p}$$

$$= \frac{kq}{nqp}$$

$$= \frac{k}{np}$$

$$< 1,$$

it follows that

$$b(i-1;n,p) < x\,b(i;n,p)$$

for $0 < i \le k$. Iteratively applying this inequality $k - i$ times gives

$$b(i;n,p) < x^{k-i}\,b(k;n,p)$$

for $0 \le i < k$, and hence

$$\sum_{i=0}^{k-1} b(i;n,p) < \sum_{i=0}^{k-1} x^{k-i} b(k;n,p)$$

$$< b(k;n,p) \sum_{i=1}^{\infty} x^i$$

$$= \frac{x}{1-x} b(k;n,p)$$

$$= \frac{kq/((n-k)p)}{((n-k)p - kq)/((n-k)p)} b(k;n,p)$$

$$= \frac{kq}{np - kp - kq} b(k;n,p)$$

$$= \frac{kq}{np - k} b(k;n,p). \qquad \blacksquare$$

Corollary C.5

Consider a sequence of n Bernoulli trials, where success occurs with probability p and failure with probability $q = 1 - p$. Then for $0 < k \le np/2$, the probability of fewer than k successes is less than half the probability of fewer than $k + 1$ successes.

Proof   Because $k \le np/2$, we have

$$\frac{kq}{np - k} \le \frac{(np/2)q}{np - (np/2)}$$

$$= \frac{(np/2)q}{np/2}$$

$$\le 1, \qquad\qquad\qquad\qquad\qquad\qquad (C.46)$$

since $q \le 1$. Letting X be the random variable denoting the number of successes, Theorem C.4 and inequality (C.46) imply that the probability of fewer than k successes is

$$\Pr\{X < k\} = \sum_{i=0}^{k-1} b(i;n,p) < b(k;n,p) \ .$$

Thus we have

$$\frac{\Pr\{X < k\}}{\Pr\{X < k+1\}} = \frac{\sum_{i=0}^{k-1} b(i;n,p)}{\sum_{i=0}^{k} b(i;n,p)}$$

$$= \frac{\sum_{i=0}^{k-1} b(i;n,p)}{\sum_{i=0}^{k-1} b(i;n,p) + b(k;n,p)}$$

$$< 1/2 \ ,$$

since $\sum_{i=0}^{k-1} b(i;n,p) < b(k;n,p)$.   ∎

Bounds on the right tail follow similarly. Exercise C.5-2 asks you to prove them.

Corollary C.6
Consider a sequence of n Bernoulli trials, where success occurs with probability p. Let X be the random variable denoting the total number of successes. Then for $np < k < n$, the probability of more than k successes is

$$\Pr\{X > k\} = \sum_{i=k+1}^{n} b(i;n,p)$$

$$< \frac{(n-k)p}{k - np} b(k;n,p) \ .$$ ∎

Corollary C.7
Consider a sequence of n Bernoulli trials, where success occurs with probability p and failure with probability $q = 1 - p$. Then for $(np + n)/2 < k < n$, the probability of more than k successes is less than half the probability of more than $k - 1$ successes.   ∎

The next theorem considers n Bernoulli trials, each with a probability p_i of success, for $i = 1, 2, \ldots, n$. As the subsequent corollary shows, we can use the theorem to provide a bound on the right tail of the binomial distribution by setting $p_i = p$ for each trial.

Theorem C.8
Consider a sequence of n Bernoulli trials, where in the ith trial, for $i = 1, 2, \ldots, n$, success occurs with probability p_i and failure occurs with probability $q_i = 1 - p_i$. Let X be the random variable describing the total number of successes, and let $\mu = \mathrm{E}[X]$. Then for $r > \mu$,

$$\Pr\{X - \mu \geq r\} \leq \left(\frac{\mu e}{r}\right)^r .$$

Proof   Since for any $\alpha > 0$, the function $e^{\alpha x}$ strictly increases in x,

$$\Pr\{X - \mu \geq r\} = \Pr\{e^{\alpha(X-\mu)} \geq e^{\alpha r}\} , \qquad (C.47)$$

where we will determine α later. Using Markov's inequality (C.34), we obtain

$$\Pr\{e^{\alpha(X-\mu)} \geq e^{\alpha r}\} \leq \mathrm{E}\left[e^{\alpha(X-\mu)}\right]e^{-\alpha r} . \qquad (C.48)$$

The bulk of the proof consists of bounding $\mathrm{E}\left[e^{\alpha(X-\mu)}\right]$ and substituting a suitable value for α in inequality (C.48). First, we evaluate $\mathrm{E}\left[e^{\alpha(X-\mu)}\right]$. Using the technique of indicator random variables (see Section 5.2), let $X_i = \mathrm{I}\{$the ith Bernoulli trial is a success$\}$ for $i = 1, 2, \ldots, n$. That is, X_i is the random variable that is 1 if the ith Bernoulli trial is a success and 0 if it is a failure. Thus, we have

$$X = \sum_{i=1}^{n} X_i ,$$

and by linearity of expectation,

$$\mu = \mathrm{E}[X] = \mathrm{E}\left[\sum_{i=1}^{n} X_i\right] = \sum_{i=1}^{n} \mathrm{E}[X_i] = \sum_{i=1}^{n} p_i ,$$

which implies

$$X - \mu = \sum_{i=1}^{n}(X_i - p_i) .$$

To evaluate $\mathrm{E}\left[e^{\alpha(X-\mu)}\right]$, we substitute for $X - \mu$, obtaining

$$
\begin{aligned}
\mathrm{E}\left[e^{\alpha(X-\mu)}\right] &= \mathrm{E}\left[e^{\alpha \sum_{i=1}^{n}(X_i - p_i)}\right] \\
&= \mathrm{E}\left[\prod_{i=1}^{n} e^{\alpha(X_i - p_i)}\right] \\
&= \prod_{i=1}^{n} \mathrm{E}\left[e^{\alpha(X_i - p_i)}\right] ,
\end{aligned}
$$

which follows from equation (C.27), since the mutual independence of the random variables X_i implies the mutual independence of the random variables $e^{\alpha(X_i - p_i)}$ (see Exercise C.3-5). By the definition of expectation,

$$\mathrm{E}\left[e^{\alpha(X_i - p_i)}\right] = e^{\alpha(1 - p_i)}p_i + e^{\alpha(0 - p_i)}q_i$$
$$= p_i e^{\alpha q_i} + q_i e^{-\alpha p_i}$$
$$\leq p_i e^{\alpha} + 1 \tag{C.49}$$
$$\leq \exp(p_i e^{\alpha}),$$

where $\exp(x)$ denotes the exponential function: $\exp(x) = e^x$. (Inequality (C.49) follows from the inequalities $\alpha > 0$, $q_i \leq 1$, $e^{\alpha q_i} \leq e^{\alpha}$, and $e^{-\alpha p_i} \leq 1$. The last line follows from inequality (3.14) on page 66.) Consequently,

$$\mathrm{E}\left[e^{\alpha(X - \mu)}\right] = \prod_{i=1}^{n} \mathrm{E}\left[e^{\alpha(X_i - p_i)}\right]$$
$$\leq \prod_{i=1}^{n} \exp(p_i e^{\alpha})$$
$$= \exp\left(\sum_{i=1}^{n} p_i e^{\alpha}\right)$$
$$= \exp(\mu e^{\alpha}), \tag{C.50}$$

since $\mu = \sum_{i=1}^{n} p_i$. Therefore, from equation (C.47) and inequalities (C.48) and (C.50), it follows that

$$\Pr\{X - \mu \geq r\} \leq \exp(\mu e^{\alpha} - \alpha r). \tag{C.51}$$

Choosing $\alpha = \ln(r/\mu)$ (see Exercise C.5-7), we obtain

$$\Pr\{X - \mu \geq r\} \leq \exp(\mu e^{\ln(r/\mu)} - r \ln(r/\mu))$$
$$= \exp(r - r \ln(r/\mu))$$
$$= \frac{e^r}{(r/\mu)^r}$$
$$= \left(\frac{\mu e}{r}\right)^r . \qquad \blacksquare$$

When applied to Bernoulli trials in which each trial has the same probability of success, Theorem C.8 yields the following corollary bounding the right tail of a binomial distribution.

Corollary C.9

Consider a sequence of n Bernoulli trials, where in each trial success occurs with probability p and failure occurs with probability $q = 1 - p$. Then for $r > np$,

$$\Pr\{X - np \geq r\} = \sum_{k=\lceil np+r \rceil}^{n} b(k;n,p)$$

$$\leq \left(\frac{npe}{r}\right)^r.$$

Proof   By equation (C.41), we have $\mu = \mathrm{E}[X] = np$.   ■

Exercises

★ *C.5-1*
Which is more likely: getting exactly n heads in $2n$ flips of a fair coin, or n heads in n flips of a fair coin?

★ *C.5-2*
Prove Corollaries C.6 and C.7.

★ *C.5-3*
Show that

$$\sum_{i=0}^{k-1} \binom{n}{i} a^i < (a+1)^n \frac{k}{na - k(a+1)} b(k;n,a/(a+1))$$

for all $a > 0$ and all k such that $0 < k < na/(a+1)$.

★ *C.5-4*
Prove that if $0 < k < np$, where $0 < p < 1$ and $q = 1 - p$, then

$$\sum_{i=0}^{k-1} p^i q^{n-i} < \frac{kq}{np-k} \left(\frac{np}{k}\right)^k \left(\frac{nq}{n-k}\right)^{n-k}.$$

★ *C.5-5*
Use Theorem C.8 to show that

$$\Pr\{\mu - X \geq r\} \leq \left(\frac{(n-\mu)e}{r}\right)^r$$

for $r > n - \mu$. Similarly, use Corollary C.9 to show that

$$\Pr\{np - X \geq r\} \leq \left(\frac{nqe}{r}\right)^r$$

for $r > n - np$.

★ **C.5-6**

Consider a sequence of n Bernoulli trials, where in the ith trial, for $i = 1, 2, \ldots, n$, success occurs with probability p_i and failure occurs with probability $q_i = 1 - p_i$. Let X be the random variable describing the total number of successes, and let $\mu = \mathrm{E}[X]$. Show that for $r \geq 0$,

$$\Pr\{X - \mu \geq r\} \leq e^{-r^2/2n} \ .$$

(*Hint:* Prove that $p_i e^{\alpha q_i} + q_i e^{-\alpha p_i} \leq e^{\alpha^2/2}$. Then follow the outline of the proof of Theorem C.8, using this inequality in place of inequality (C.49).)

★ **C.5-7**

Show that choosing $\alpha = \ln(r/\mu)$ minimizes the right-hand side of inequality (C.51).

Problems

C-1   The Monty Hall problem

Imagine that you are a contestant in the 1960s game show *Let's Make a Deal*, hosted by emcee Monty Hall. A valuable prize is hidden behind one of three doors and comparatively worthless prizes behind the other two doors. You will win the valuable prize, typically an automobile or other expensive product, if you select the correct door. After you have picked one door, but before the door has been opened, Monty, who knows which door hides the automobile, directs his assistant Carol Merrill to open one of the other doors, revealing a goat (not a valuable prize). He asks whether you would like to stick with your current choice or to switch to the other closed door. What should you do to maximize your chances of winning the automobile and not the other goat?

The answer to this question—stick or switch?—has been heavily debated, in part because the problem setup is ambiguous. We'll explore different subtle assumptions.

a. Suppose that your first pick is random, with probability $1/3$ of choosing the right door. Moreover, you know that Monty always gives every contestant (and will give you) the opportunity to switch. Prove that it is better to switch than stick. What is your probability of winning the automobile?

This answer is the one typically given, even though the original statement of the problem rarely mentions the assumption that Monty *always* offers the contestant the opportunity to switch. But, as the remainder of this problem will elucidate, your best strategy may be different if this unstated assumption does not hold. In fact, in the real game show, after a contestant picked a door, Monty sometimes simply asked Carol to open the door that the contestant had chosen.

Let's model the interactions between you and Monty as a probabilistic experiment, where you both employ randomized strategies. Specifically, after you pick a door, Monty offers you the opportunity to switch with probability p_{right} if you picked the right door and with probability p_{wrong} if you picked the wrong door. Given the opportunity to switch, you randomly choose to switch with probability p_{switch}. For example, if Monty always offers you the opportunity to switch, then his strategy is given by $p_{\text{right}} = p_{\text{wrong}} = 1$. If you always switch, then your strategy is given by $p_{\text{switch}} = 1$.

The game can now be viewed as an experiment consisting of five steps:

1. You pick a door at random, choosing the automobile (right) with probability $1/3$ or a goat (wrong) with probability $2/3$.

2. Carol opens one of the two closed doors, revealing a goat.

3. Monty offers you the opportunity to switch with probability p_{right} if your choice is right and with probability p_{wrong} if your choice is wrong.

4. If Monty makes you an offer in step 3, you switch with probability p_{switch}.

5. Carol opens the door you've chosen, revealing either an automobile (you win) or a goat (you lose).

Let's now analyze this game and understand how the choices of p_{right}, p_{wrong}, and p_{switch} influence the probability of winning.

b. What are the six outcomes in the sample space for this game? Which outcomes correspond to you winning the automobile? What are the probabilities in terms of p_{right}, p_{wrong}, and p_{switch} of each outcome? Organize your answers into a table.

c. Use the results of your table (or other means) to prove that the probability of winning the automobile is

$$\frac{1}{3}(2 p_{\text{wrong}} p_{\text{switch}} - p_{\text{right}} p_{\text{switch}} + 1) \,.$$

Suppose that Monty knows the probability p_{switch} that you switch, and his goal is to minimize your chance of winning.

d. If $p_{\text{switch}} > 0$ (you switch with a positive probability), what is Monty's best strategy, that is, his best choice for p_{right} and p_{wrong}?

e. If $p_{\text{switch}} = 0$ (you always stick), argue that all of Monty's possible strategies are optimal for him.

Suppose that now Monty's strategy is fixed, with particular values for p_{right} and p_{wrong}.

f. If you know p_{right} and p_{wrong}, what is your best strategy for choosing your probability p_{switch} of switching as a function of p_{right} and p_{wrong}?

g. If you don't know p_{right} and p_{wrong}, what choice of p_{switch} maximizes the minimum probability of winning over all the choices of p_{right} and p_{wrong}?

Let's return to the original problem as stated, where Monty has given you the option of switching, but you have no knowledge of Monty's possible motivations or strategies.

h. Argue that the conditional probability of winning the automobile given that Monty offers you the opportunity to switch is

$$\frac{p_{\text{right}} - p_{\text{right}} p_{\text{switch}} + 2 p_{\text{wrong}} p_{\text{switch}}}{p_{\text{right}} + 2 p_{\text{wrong}}} . \tag{C.52}$$

Explain why $p_{\text{right}} + 2 p_{\text{wrong}} \neq 0$.

i. What is the value of expression (C.52) when $p_{\text{switch}} = 1/2$? Show that choosing $p_{\text{switch}} < 1/2$ or $p_{\text{switch}} > 1/2$ allows Monty to select values for p_{right} and p_{wrong} that yield a lower value for expression (C.52) than choosing $p_{\text{switch}} = 1/2$.

j. Suppose that you don't know Monty's strategy. Explain why choosing to switch with probability $1/2$ is a good strategy for the original problem as stated. Summarize what you have learned overall from this problem.

C-2   Balls and bins

This problem investigates the effect of various assumptions on the number of ways of placing n balls into b distinct bins.

a. Suppose that the n balls are distinct and that their order within a bin does not matter. Argue that the number of ways of placing the balls in the bins is b^n.

b. Suppose that the balls are distinct and that the balls in each bin are ordered. Prove that there are exactly $(b + n - 1)!/(b - 1)!$ ways to place the balls in the bins. (*Hint:* Consider the number of ways of arranging n distinct balls and $b - 1$ indistinguishable sticks in a row.)

c. Suppose that the balls are identical, and hence their order within a bin does not matter. Show that the number of ways of placing the balls in the bins is $\binom{b+n-1}{n}$. (*Hint:* Of the arrangements in part (b), how many are repeated if the balls are made identical?)

d. Suppose that the balls are identical and that no bin may contain more than one ball, so that $n \le b$. Show that the number of ways of placing the balls is $\binom{b}{n}$.

e. Suppose that the balls are identical and that no bin may be left empty. Assuming that $n \ge b$, show that the number of ways of placing the balls is $\binom{n-1}{b-1}$.

Appendix notes

The first general methods for solving probability problems were discussed in a famous correspondence between B. Pascal and P. de Fermat, which began in 1654, and in a book by C. Huygens in 1657. Rigorous probability theory began with the work of J. Bernoulli in 1713 and A. De Moivre in 1730. Further developments of the theory were provided by P.-S. Laplace, S.-D. Poisson, and C. F. Gauss.

Sums of random variables were originally studied by P. L. Chebyshev and A. A. Markov. A. N. Kolmogorov axiomatized probability theory in 1933. Chernoff [91] and Hoeffding [222] provided bounds on the tails of distributions. Seminal work in random combinatorial structures was done by P. Erdős.

Knuth [259] and Liu [302] are good references for elementary combinatorics and counting. Standard textbooks such as Billingsley [56], Chung [93], Drake [125], Feller [139], and Rozanov [390] offer comprehensive introductions to probability.

D   Matrices

Matrices arise in numerous applications, including, but by no means limited to, scientific computing. If you have seen matrices before, much of the material in this appendix will be familiar to you, but some of it might be new. Section D.1 covers basic matrix definitions and operations, and Section D.2 presents some basic matrix properties.

D.1   Matrices and matrix operations

This section reviews some basic concepts of matrix theory and some fundamental properties of matrices.

Matrices and vectors

A *matrix* is a rectangular array of numbers. For example,

$$A = \begin{pmatrix} a_{11} & a_{12} & a_{13} \\ a_{21} & a_{22} & a_{23} \end{pmatrix}$$

$$= \begin{pmatrix} 1 & 2 & 3 \\ 4 & 5 & 6 \end{pmatrix} \tag{D.1}$$

is a 2×3 matrix $A = (a_{ij})$, where for $i = 1, 2$ and $j = 1, 2, 3$, the element of the matrix in row i and column j is denoted by a_{ij}. By convention, uppercase letters denote matrices and corresponding subscripted lowercase letters denote their elements. We denote the set of all $m \times n$ matrices with real-valued entries by $\mathbb{R}^{m \times n}$ and, in general, the set of $m \times n$ matrices with entries drawn from a set S by $S^{m \times n}$.

The *transpose* of a matrix A is the matrix A^{T} obtained by exchanging the rows and columns of A. For the matrix A of equation (D.1),

$$A^\mathrm{T} = \begin{pmatrix} 1 & 4 \\ 2 & 5 \\ 3 & 6 \end{pmatrix}.$$

A *vector* is a one-dimensional array of numbers. For example,

$$x = \begin{pmatrix} 2 \\ 3 \\ 5 \end{pmatrix}$$

is a vector of size 3. We sometimes call a vector of length n an *n-vector*. By convention, lowercase letters denote vectors, and the ith element of a size-n vector x is denoted by x_i, for $i = 1, 2, \ldots, n$. We take the standard form of a vector to be as a *column vector* equivalent to an $n \times 1$ matrix, whereas the corresponding *row vector* is obtained by taking the transpose:

$$x^\mathrm{T} = (2 \quad 3 \quad 5).$$

The *unit vector* e_i is the vector whose ith element is 1 and all of whose other elements are 0. Usually, the context makes the size of a unit vector clear.

A *zero matrix* is a matrix all of whose entries are 0. Such a matrix is often denoted 0, since the ambiguity between the number 0 and a matrix of 0s can usually be resolved from context. If a matrix of 0s is intended, then the size of the matrix also needs to be derived from the context.

Square matrices

Square $n \times n$ matrices arise frequently. Several special cases of square matrices are of particular interest:

1. A *diagonal matrix* has $a_{ij} = 0$ whenever $i \neq j$. Because all of the off-diagonal elements are 0, a succinct way to specify the matrix lists only the elements along the diagonal:

$$\mathrm{diag}(a_{11}, a_{22}, \ldots, a_{nn}) = \begin{pmatrix} a_{11} & 0 & \ldots & 0 \\ 0 & a_{22} & \ldots & 0 \\ \vdots & \vdots & \ddots & \vdots \\ 0 & 0 & \ldots & a_{nn} \end{pmatrix}.$$

2. The $n \times n$ *identity matrix* I_n is a diagonal matrix with 1s along the diagonal:

$$I_n = \mathrm{diag}(1, 1, \ldots, 1)$$
$$= \begin{pmatrix} 1 & 0 & \ldots & 0 \\ 0 & 1 & \ldots & 0 \\ \vdots & \vdots & \ddots & \vdots \\ 0 & 0 & \ldots & 1 \end{pmatrix}.$$

When I appears without a subscript, its size derives from the context. The ith column of an identity matrix is the unit vector e_i.

3. A **tridiagonal matrix** T is one for which $t_{ij} = 0$ if $|i - j| > 1$. Nonzero entries appear only on the main diagonal, immediately above the main diagonal ($t_{i,i+1}$ for $i = 1, 2, \ldots, n - 1$), or immediately below the main diagonal ($t_{i+1,i}$ for $i = 1, 2, \ldots, n - 1$):

$$T = \begin{pmatrix} t_{11} & t_{12} & 0 & 0 & \cdots & 0 & 0 & 0 \\ t_{21} & t_{22} & t_{23} & 0 & \cdots & 0 & 0 & 0 \\ 0 & t_{32} & t_{33} & t_{34} & \cdots & 0 & 0 & 0 \\ \vdots & \vdots & \vdots & \vdots & \ddots & \vdots & \vdots & \vdots \\ 0 & 0 & 0 & 0 & \cdots & t_{n-2,n-2} & t_{n-2,n-1} & 0 \\ 0 & 0 & 0 & 0 & \cdots & t_{n-1,n-2} & t_{n-1,n-1} & t_{n-1,n} \\ 0 & 0 & 0 & 0 & \cdots & 0 & t_{n,n-1} & t_{nn} \end{pmatrix}.$$

4. An **upper-triangular matrix** U is one for which $u_{ij} = 0$ if $i > j$. All entries below the diagonal are 0:

$$U = \begin{pmatrix} u_{11} & u_{12} & \cdots & u_{1n} \\ 0 & u_{22} & \cdots & u_{2n} \\ \vdots & \vdots & \ddots & \vdots \\ 0 & 0 & \cdots & u_{nn} \end{pmatrix}.$$

An upper-triangular matrix is **unit upper-triangular** if it has all 1s along the diagonal.

5. A **lower-triangular matrix** L is one for which $l_{ij} = 0$ if $i < j$. All entries above the diagonal are 0:

$$L = \begin{pmatrix} l_{11} & 0 & \cdots & 0 \\ l_{21} & l_{22} & \cdots & 0 \\ \vdots & \vdots & \ddots & \vdots \\ l_{n1} & l_{n2} & \cdots & l_{nn} \end{pmatrix}.$$

A lower-triangular matrix is **unit lower-triangular** if it has all 1s along the diagonal.

6. A *permutation matrix* P has exactly one 1 in each row or column, and 0s elsewhere. An example of a permutation matrix is

$$P = \begin{pmatrix} 0 & 1 & 0 & 0 & 0 \\ 0 & 0 & 0 & 1 & 0 \\ 1 & 0 & 0 & 0 & 0 \\ 0 & 0 & 0 & 0 & 1 \\ 0 & 0 & 1 & 0 & 0 \end{pmatrix}.$$

Such a matrix is called a permutation matrix because multiplying a vector x by a permutation matrix has the effect of permuting (rearranging) the elements of x. Exercise D.1-4 explores additional properties of permutation matrices.

7. A *symmetric matrix* A satisfies the condition $A = A^{\mathrm{T}}$. For example,

$$\begin{pmatrix} 1 & 2 & 3 \\ 2 & 6 & 4 \\ 3 & 4 & 5 \end{pmatrix}$$

is a symmetric matrix.

Basic matrix operations

The elements of a matrix or vector are *scalar numbers* from a number system, such as the real numbers, the complex numbers, or integers modulo a prime. The number system defines how to add and multiply scalars. These definitions extend to encompass addition and multiplication of matrices.

We define *matrix addition* as follows. If $A = (a_{ij})$ and $B = (b_{ij})$ are $m \times n$ matrices, then their matrix sum $C = (c_{ij}) = A + B$ is the $m \times n$ matrix defined by

$$c_{ij} = a_{ij} + b_{ij}$$

for $i = 1, 2, \ldots, m$ and $j = 1, 2, \ldots, n$. That is, matrix addition is performed componentwise. A zero matrix is the identity for matrix addition:

$$A + 0 = A = 0 + A .$$

If λ is a scalar number and $A = (a_{ij})$ is a matrix, then $\lambda A = (\lambda a_{ij})$ is the *scalar multiple* of A obtained by multiplying each of its elements by λ. As a special case, we define the *negative* of a matrix $A = (a_{ij})$ to be $-1 \cdot A = -A$, so that the ijth entry of $-A$ is $-a_{ij}$. Thus,

$$A + (-A) = 0 = (-A) + A .$$

The negative of a matrix defines *matrix subtraction*: $A - B = A + (-B)$.

We define *matrix multiplication* as follows. Start with two matrices A and B that are *compatible* in the sense that the number of columns of A equals the number of rows of B. (In general, an expression containing a matrix product AB is always assumed to imply that matrices A and B are compatible.) If $A = (a_{ik})$ is a $p \times q$ matrix and $B = (b_{kj})$ is a $q \times r$ matrix, then their matrix product $C = AB$ is the $p \times r$ matrix $C = (c_{ij})$, where

$$c_{ij} = \sum_{k=1}^{q} a_{ik} b_{kj} \tag{D.2}$$

for $i = 1, 2, \ldots, m$ and $j = 1, 2, \ldots, p$. The procedure RECTANGULAR-MATRIX-MULTIPLY on page 374 implements matrix multiplication in the straightforward manner based on equation (D.2), assuming that C is initialized to 0, using pqr multiplications and $p(q - 1)r$ additions for a running time of $\Theta(pqr)$. If the matrices are $n \times n$ square matrices, so that $n = p = q = r$, the pseudocode reduces to MATRIX-MULTIPLY on page 81, whose running time is $\Theta(n^3)$. (Section 4.2 describes an asymptotically faster $\Theta(n^{\lg 7})$-time algorithm due to V. Strassen.)

Matrices have many (but not all) of the algebraic properties typical of numbers. Identity matrices are identities for matrix multiplication:

$$I_m A = A I_n = A$$

for any $m \times n$ matrix A. Multiplying by a zero matrix gives a zero matrix:

$$A \cdot 0 = 0 .$$

Matrix multiplication is associative:

$$A(BC) = (AB)C$$

for compatible matrices A, B, and C. Matrix multiplication distributes over addition:

$$A(B + C) = AB + AC ,$$
$$(B + C)D = BD + CD .$$

For $n > 1$, multiplication of $n \times n$ matrices is not commutative. For example, if $A = \begin{pmatrix} 0 & 1 \\ 0 & 0 \end{pmatrix}$ and $B = \begin{pmatrix} 0 & 0 \\ 1 & 0 \end{pmatrix}$, then $AB = \begin{pmatrix} 1 & 0 \\ 0 & 0 \end{pmatrix}$ and $BA = \begin{pmatrix} 0 & 0 \\ 0 & 1 \end{pmatrix}$.

We define matrix-vector products or vector-vector products as if the vector were the equivalent $n \times 1$ matrix (or a $1 \times n$ matrix, in the case of a row vector). Thus, if A is an $m \times n$ matrix and x is an n-vector, then Ax is an m-vector. If x and y are n-vectors, then

$$x^\mathrm{T} y = \sum_{i=1}^{n} x_i y_i$$

is a scalar number (actually a 1×1 matrix) called the *inner product* of x and y. We also use the notation $\langle x, y \rangle$ to denote $x^\mathrm{T} y$. The inner-product operator is commutative: $\langle x, y \rangle = \langle y, x \rangle$. The matrix xy^T is an $n \times n$ matrix Z called the *outer product* of x and y, where $z_{ij} = x_i y_j$. The *(euclidean) norm* $\|x\|$ of an n-vector x is defined by

$$\begin{aligned} \|x\| &= (x_1^2 + x_2^2 + \cdots + x_n^2)^{1/2} \\ &= (x^\mathrm{T} x)^{1/2} \, . \end{aligned}$$

Thus, the norm of x is its length in n-dimensional euclidean space. A useful fact, which follows from the equality

$$\left((ax_1)^2 + (ax_2)^2 + \cdots + (ax_n)^2\right)^{1/2} = |a| \, (x_1^2 + x_2^2 + \cdots + x_n^2)^{1/2}$$

is that for any real number a and n-vector x,

$$\|ax\| = |a| \, \|x\| \, . \tag{D.3}$$

Exercises

D.1-1
Show that if A and B are symmetric $n \times n$ matrices, then so are $A + B$ and $A - B$.

D.1-2
Prove that $(AB)^\mathrm{T} = B^\mathrm{T} A^\mathrm{T}$ and that $A^\mathrm{T} A$ is always a symmetric matrix.

D.1-3
Prove that the product of two lower-triangular matrices is lower-triangular.

D.1-4
Prove that if P is an $n \times n$ permutation matrix and A is an $n \times n$ matrix, then the matrix product PA is A with its rows permuted, and the matrix product AP is A with its columns permuted. Prove that the product of two permutation matrices is a permutation matrix.

D.2   Basic matrix properties

We now define some basic properties pertaining to matrices: inverses, linear dependence and independence, rank, and determinants. We also define the class of positive-definite matrices.

Matrix inverses, ranks, and determinants

The *inverse* of an $n \times n$ matrix A is the $n \times n$ matrix, denoted A^{-1} (if it exists), such that $AA^{-1} = I_n = A^{-1}A$. For example,

$$\begin{pmatrix} 1 & 1 \\ 1 & 0 \end{pmatrix}^{-1} = \begin{pmatrix} 0 & 1 \\ 1 & -1 \end{pmatrix}.$$

Many nonzero $n \times n$ matrices do not have inverses. A matrix without an inverse is called *noninvertible*, or *singular*. An example of a nonzero singular matrix is

$$\begin{pmatrix} 1 & 0 \\ 1 & 0 \end{pmatrix}.$$

If a matrix has an inverse, it is called *invertible*, or *nonsingular*. Matrix inverses, when they exist, are unique. (See Exercise D.2-1.) If A and B are nonsingular $n \times n$ matrices, then

$$(BA)^{-1} = A^{-1}B^{-1}.$$

The inverse operation commutes with the transpose operation:

$$(A^{-1})^{\mathrm{T}} = (A^{\mathrm{T}})^{-1}.$$

The vectors $x_1, x_2, \ldots, x_n$ are *linearly dependent* if there exist coefficients $c_1, c_2, \ldots, c_n$, not all of which are 0, such that $c_1x_1 + c_2x_2 + \cdots + c_nx_n = 0$. The row vectors $x_1 = (1 \quad 2 \quad 3)$, $x_2 = (2 \quad 6 \quad 4)$, and $x_3 = (4 \quad 11 \quad 9)$ are linearly dependent, for example, since $2x_1 + 3x_2 - 2x_3 = 0$. If vectors are not linearly dependent, they are *linearly independent*. For example, the columns of an identity matrix are linearly independent.

The *column rank* of a nonzero $m \times n$ matrix A is the size of the largest set of linearly independent columns of A. Similarly, the *row rank* of A is the size of the largest set of linearly independent rows of A. A fundamental property of any matrix A is that its row rank always equals its column rank, so that we can simply refer to the *rank* of A. The rank of an $m \times n$ matrix is an integer between 0 and min $\{m, n\}$, inclusive. (The rank of a zero matrix is 0, and the rank of an $n \times n$ identity matrix is n.) An alternate, but equivalent and often more useful, definition is that the rank of a nonzero $m \times n$ matrix A is the smallest number r such that there exist matrices B and C of respective sizes $m \times r$ and $r \times n$ such that $A = BC$. A square $n \times n$ matrix has *full rank* if its rank is n. An $m \times n$ matrix has *full column rank* if its rank is n. The following theorem gives a fundamental property of ranks.

Theorem D.1
A square matrix has full rank if and only if it is nonsingular.   ∎

A *null vector* for a matrix A is a nonzero vector x such that $Ax = 0$. The following theorem (whose proof is left as Exercise D.2-7) and its corollary relate the notions of column rank and singularity to null vectors.

Theorem D.2
A matrix has full column rank if and only if it does not have a null vector. ∎

Corollary D.3
A square matrix is singular if and only if it has a null vector. ∎

The ijth *minor* of an $n \times n$ matrix A, for $n > 1$, is the $(n-1) \times (n-1)$ matrix $A_{[ij]}$ obtained by deleting the ith row and jth column of A. The *determinant* of an $n \times n$ matrix A is defined recursively in terms of its minors by

$$\det(A) = \begin{cases} a_{11} & \text{if } n = 1, \\ \displaystyle\sum_{j=1}^{n} (-1)^{1+j} a_{1j} \det(A_{[1j]}) & \text{if } n > 1. \end{cases}$$

The term $(-1)^{i+j} \det(A_{[ij]})$ is known as the *cofactor* of the element a_{ij}.

The following theorems, whose proofs are omitted, express fundamental properties of the determinant.

Theorem D.4 (Determinant properties)
The determinant of a square matrix A has the following properties:

- If any row or any column of A is zero, then $\det(A) = 0$.

- The determinant of A is multiplied by λ if the entries of any one row (or any one column) of A are all multiplied by λ.

- The determinant of A is unchanged if the entries in one row (respectively, column) are added to those in another row (respectively, column).

- The determinant of A equals the determinant of A^{T}.

- The determinant of A is multiplied by -1 if any two rows (or any two columns) are exchanged.

Also, for any square matrices A and B, we have $\det(AB) = \det(A) \det(B)$. ∎

Theorem D.5
An $n \times n$ matrix A is singular if and only if $\det(A) = 0$. ∎

Positive-definite matrices

Positive-definite matrices play an important role in many applications. An $n \times n$ matrix A is *positive-definite* if $x^T A x > 0$ for all n-vectors $x \neq 0$. For example, the identity matrix is positive-definite, since if $x = (\ x_1\ x_2\ \cdots\ x_n\ )^T$ is a nonzero vector, then

$$x^T I_n x = x^T x$$
$$= \sum_{i=1}^{n} x_i^2$$
$$> 0 \ .$$

Matrices that arise in applications are often positive-definite due to the following theorem.

Theorem D.6
For any matrix A with full column rank, the matrix $A^T A$ is positive-definite.

Proof We must show that $x^T (A^T A) x > 0$ for any nonzero vector x. For any vector x,

$$x^T (A^T A) x = (Ax)^T (Ax) \quad \text{(by Exercise D.1-2)}$$
$$= \| Ax \|^2 \ .$$

The value $\| Ax \|^2$ is just the sum of the squares of the elements of the vector Ax. Therefore, $\| Ax \|^2 \geq 0$. We'll show by contradiction that $\| Ax \|^2 > 0$. Suppose that $\| Ax \|^2 = 0$. Then, every element of Ax is 0, which is to say $Ax = 0$. Since A has full column rank, Theorem D.2 says that $x = 0$, which contradicts the requirement that x is nonzero. Hence, $A^T A$ is positive-definite. ∎

Section 28.3 explores other properties of positive-definite matrices. Section 33.3 uses a similar condition, known as positive-semidefinite. An $n \times n$ matrix A is *positive-semidefinite* if $x^T A x \geq 0$ for all n-vectors $x \neq 0$.

Exercises

D.2-1
Prove that matrix inverses are unique, that is, if B and C are inverses of A, then $B = C$.

D.2-2
Prove that the determinant of a lower-triangular or upper-triangular matrix is equal to the product of its diagonal elements. Prove that the inverse of a lower-triangular matrix, if it exists, is lower-triangular.

D.2-3
Prove that if P is a permutation matrix, then P is invertible, its inverse is P^{T}, and P^{T} is a permutation matrix.

D.2-4
Let A and B be $n \times n$ matrices such that $AB = I$. Prove that if A' is obtained from A by adding row j into row i, where $i \neq j$, then subtracting column i from column j of B yields the inverse B' of A'.

D.2-5
Let A be a nonsingular $n \times n$ matrix with complex entries. Show that every entry of A^{-1} is real if and only if every entry of A is real.

D.2-6
Show that if A is a nonsingular, symmetric, $n \times n$ matrix, then A^{-1} is symmetric. Show that if B is an arbitrary $m \times n$ matrix, then the $m \times m$ matrix given by the product BAB^{T} is symmetric.

D.2-7
Prove Theorem D.2. That is, show that a matrix A has full column rank if and only if $Ax = 0$ implies $x = 0$. (*Hint:* Express the linear dependence of one column on the others as a matrix-vector equation.)

D.2-8
Prove that for any two compatible matrices A and B,

$$\mathrm{rank}(AB) \leq \min\{\mathrm{rank}(A), \mathrm{rank}(B)\} \ ,$$

where equality holds if either A or B is a nonsingular square matrix. (*Hint:* Use the alternate definition of the rank of a matrix.)

Problems

D-1   *Vandermonde matrix*
Given numbers $x_0, x_1, \ldots, x_{n-1}$, prove that the determinant of the *Vandermonde matrix*

$$V(x_0, x_1, \ldots, x_{n-1}) = \begin{pmatrix} 1 & x_0 & x_0^2 & \cdots & x_0^{n-1} \\ 1 & x_1 & x_1^2 & \cdots & x_1^{n-1} \\ \vdots & \vdots & \vdots & \ddots & \vdots \\ 1 & x_{n-1} & x_{n-1}^2 & \cdots & x_{n-1}^{n-1} \end{pmatrix}$$

is

$$\det(V(x_0, x_1, \ldots, x_{n-1})) = \prod_{0 \le j < k \le n-1} (x_k - x_j) \,.$$

(*Hint:* Multiply column i by $-x_0$ and add it to column $i + 1$ for $i = n - 1$, $n - 2, \ldots, 1$, and then use induction.)

D-2   *Permutations defined by matrix-vector multiplication over GF(2)*

One class of permutations of the integers in the set $S_n = \{0, 1, 2, \ldots, 2^n - 1\}$ is defined by matrix multiplication over $GF(2)$, the Galois field of two elements. For each integer $x \in S_n$, we view its binary representation as an n-bit vector

$$\begin{pmatrix} x_0 \\ x_1 \\ x_2 \\ \vdots \\ x_{n-1} \end{pmatrix},$$

where $x = \sum_{i=0}^{n-1} x_i 2^i$. If A is an $n \times n$ matrix in which each entry is either 0 or 1, then we can define a permutation mapping each value $x \in S_n$ to the number whose binary representation is the matrix-vector product Ax. All this arithmetic is performed over $GF(2)$: all values are either 0 or 1, and with one exception, the usual rules of addition and multiplication apply. The exception is that $1 + 1 = 0$. You can think of arithmetic over $GF(2)$ as being just like regular integer arithmetic, except that you use only the least-significant bit.

As an example, for $S_2 = \{0, 1, 2, 3\}$, the matrix

$$A = \begin{pmatrix} 1 & 0 \\ 1 & 1 \end{pmatrix}$$

defines the following permutation π_A: $\pi_A(0) = 0$, $\pi_A(1) = 3$, $\pi_A(2) = 2$, $\pi_A(3) = 1$. To see why $\pi_A(3) = 1$, observe that, working in $GF(2)$,

$$\pi_A(3) = \begin{pmatrix} 1 & 0 \\ 1 & 1 \end{pmatrix}\begin{pmatrix} 1 \\ 1 \end{pmatrix}$$

$$= \begin{pmatrix} 1 \cdot 1 + 0 \cdot 1 \\ 1 \cdot 1 + 1 \cdot 1 \end{pmatrix}$$

$$= \begin{pmatrix} 1 \\ 0 \end{pmatrix},$$

which is the binary representation of 1.

For the remainder of this problem, we'll work over $GF(2)$, and all matrix and vector entries will be 0 or 1. Define the *rank* of a 0-1 matrix (a matrix for which each entry is either 0 or 1) over $GF(2)$ the same as for a regular matrix, but with all arithmetic that determines linear independence performed over $GF(2)$. We define the *range* of an $n \times n$ 0-1 matrix A by

$$R(A) = \{y : y = Ax \text{ for some } x \in S_n\} ,$$

so that $R(A)$ is the set of numbers in S_n that are produced by multiplying each value $x \in S_n$ by A.

a. If r is the rank of matrix A, prove that $|R(A)| = 2^r$. Conclude that A defines a permutation on S_n only if A has full rank.

For a given $n \times n$ matrix A and a given value $y \in R(A)$, we define the *preimage* of y by

$$P(A, y) = \{x : Ax = y\} ,$$

so that $P(A, y)$ is the set of values in S_n that map to y when multiplied by A.

b. If r is the rank of $n \times n$ matrix A and $y \in R(A)$, prove that $|P(A, y)| = 2^{n-r}$.

Let $0 \leq m \leq n$, and suppose that we partition the set S_n into blocks of consecutive numbers, where the ith block consists of the 2^m numbers $i2^m, i2^m + 1, i2^m + 2, \ldots, (i+1)2^m - 1$. For any subset $S \subseteq S_n$, define $B(S, m)$ to be the set of size-2^m blocks of S_n containing some element of S. As an example, when $n = 3$, $m = 1$, and $S = \{1, 4, 5\}$, then $B(S, m)$ consists of blocks 0 (since 1 is in the 0th block) and 2 (since both 4 and 5 belong to block 2).

c. Let r be the rank of the lower left $(n - m) \times m$ submatrix of A, that is, the matrix formed by taking the intersection of the bottom $n - m$ rows and the leftmost m columns of A. Let S be any size-2^m block of S_n, and let $S' = \{y : y = Ax \text{ for some } x \in S\}$. Prove that $|B(S', m)| = 2^r$ and that for each block in $B(S', m)$, exactly 2^{m-r} numbers in S map to that block.

Because multiplying the zero vector by any matrix yields a zero vector, the set of permutations of S_n defined by multiplying by $n \times n$ 0-1 matrices with full rank over $GF(2)$ cannot include all permutations of S_n. Let's extend the class of permutations defined by matrix-vector multiplication to include an additive term, so that $x \in S_n$ maps to $Ax + c$, where c is an n-bit vector and addition is performed over $GF(2)$. For example, when

$$A = \begin{pmatrix} 1 & 0 \\ 1 & 1 \end{pmatrix}$$

and

$$c = \begin{pmatrix} 0 \\ 1 \end{pmatrix},$$

we get the following permutation $\pi_{A,c}$: $\pi_{A,c}(0) = 2$, $\pi_{A,c}(1) = 1$, $\pi_{A,c}(2) = 0$, $\pi_{A,c}(3) = 3$. We call any permutation that maps $x \in S_n$ to $Ax + c$, for some $n \times n$ 0-1 matrix A with full rank and some n-bit vector c, a *linear permutation*.

> **d.** Use a counting argument to show that the number of linear permutations of S_n is much less than the number of permutations of S_n.

> **e.** Give an example of a value of n and a permutation of S_n that cannot be achieved by any linear permutation. (*Hint:* For a given permutation, think about how multiplying a matrix by a unit vector relates to the columns of the matrix.)

Appendix notes

Linear-algebra textbooks provide plenty of background information on matrices. The books by Strang [422, 423] are particularly good.

Bibliography

[1] Milton Abramowitz and Irene A. Stegun, editors. *Handbook of Mathematical Functions*. Dover, 1965.

[2] G. M. Adel'son-Vel'skiĭ and E. M. Landis. An algorithm for the organization of information. *Soviet Mathematics Doklady*, 3(5):1259–1263, 1962.

[3] Alok Aggarwal and Jeffrey Scott Vitter. The input/output complexity of sorting and related problems. *Communications of the ACM*, 31(9):1116–1127, 1988.

[4] Manindra Agrawal, Neeraj Kayal, and Nitin Saxena. PRIMES is in P. *Annals of Mathematics*, 160(2):781–793, 2004.

[5] Alfred V. Aho, John E. Hopcroft, and Jeffrey D. Ullman. *The Design and Analysis of Computer Algorithms*. Addison-Wesley, 1974.

[6] Alfred V. Aho, John E. Hopcroft, and Jeffrey D. Ullman. *Data Structures and Algorithms*. Addison-Wesley, 1983.

[7] Ravindra K. Ahuja, Thomas L. Magnanti, and James B. Orlin. *Network Flows: Theory, Algorithms, and Applications*. Prentice Hall, 1993.

[8] Ravindra K. Ahuja, Kurt Mehlhorn, James B. Orlin, and Robert E. Tarjan. Faster algorithms for the shortest path problem. *Journal of the ACM*, 37(2):213–223, 1990.

[9] Ravindra K. Ahuja and James B. Orlin. A fast and simple algorithm for the maximum flow problem. *Operations Research*, 37(5):748–759, 1989.

[10] Ravindra K. Ahuja, James B. Orlin, and Robert E. Tarjan. Improved time bounds for the maximum flow problem. *SIAM Journal on Computing*, 18(5):939–954, 1989.

[11] Miklós Ajtai, Nimrod Megiddo, and Orli Waarts. Improved algorithms and analysis for secretary problems and generalizations. *SIAM Journal on Discrete Mathematics*, 14(1):1–27, 2001.

[12] Selim G. Akl. *The Design and Analysis of Parallel Algorithms*. Prentice Hall, 1989.

[13] Mohamad Akra and Louay Bazzi. On the solution of linear recurrence equations. *Computational Optimization and Applications*, 10(2):195–210, 1998.

[14] Susanne Albers. Online algorithms: A survey. *Mathematical Programming*, 97(1-2):3–26, 2003.

[15] Noga Alon. Generating pseudo-random permutations and maximum flow algorithms. *Information Processing Letters*, 35:201–204, 1990.

[16] Arne Andersson. Balanced search trees made simple. In *Proceedings of the Third Workshop on Algorithms and Data Structures*, volume 709 of *Lecture Notes in Computer Science*, pages 60–71. Springer, 1993.

[17] Arne Andersson. Faster deterministic sorting and searching in linear space. In *Proceedings of the 37th Annual Symposium on Foundations of Computer Science*, pages 135–141, 1996.

[18] Arne Andersson, Torben Hagerup, Stefan Nilsson, and Rajeev Raman. Sorting in linear time? *Journal of Computer and System Sciences*, 57:74–93, 1998.

[19] Tom M. Apostol. *Calculus*, volume 1. Blaisdell Publishing Company, second edition, 1967.

[20] Nimar S. Arora, Robert D. Blumofe, and C. Greg Plaxton. Thread scheduling for multiprogrammed multiprocessors. *Theory of Computing Systems*, 34(2):115–144, 2001.

[21] Sanjeev Arora. *Probabilistic checking of proofs and the hardness of approximation problems*. PhD thesis, University of California, Berkeley, 1994.

[22] Sanjeev Arora. The approximability of NP-hard problems. In *Proceedings of the 30th Annual ACM Symposium on Theory of Computing*, pages 337–348, 1998.

[23] Sanjeev Arora. Polynomial time approximation schemes for euclidean traveling salesman and other geometric problems. *Journal of the ACM*, 45(5):753–782, 1998.

[24] Sanjeev Arora and Boaz Barak. *Computational Complexity: A Modern Approach*. Cambridge University Press, 2009.

[25] Sanjeev Arora, Elad Hazan, and Satyen Kale. The multiplicative weights update method: A meta-algorithm and applications. *Theory of Computing*, 8(1):121–164, 2012.

[26] Sanjeev Arora and Carsten Lund. Hardness of approximations. In Dorit S. Hochbaum, editor, *Approximation Algorithms for NP-Hard Problems*, pages 399–446. PWS Publishing Company, 1997.

[27] Mikhail J. Atallah and Marina Blanton, editors. *Algorithms and Theory of Computation Handbook*, volume 1. Chapman & Hall/CRC Press, second edition, 2009.

[28] Mikhail J. Atallah and Marina Blanton, editors. *Algorithms and Theory of Computation Handbook*, volume 2. Chapman & Hall/CRC Press, second edition, 2009.

[29] G. Ausiello, P. Crescenzi, G. Gambosi, V. Kann, A. Marchetti-Spaccamela, and M. Protasi. *Complexity and Approximation: Combinatorial Optimization Problems and Their Approximability Properties*. Springer, 1999.

[30] Shai Avidan and Ariel Shamir. Seam carving for content-aware image resizing. *ACM Transactions on Graphics*, 26(3), article 10, 2007.

[31] László Babai, Eugene M. Luks, and Ákos Seress. Fast management of permutation groups I. *SIAM Journal on Computing*, 26(5):1310–1342, 1997.

[32] Eric Bach. Private communication, 1989.

[33] Eric Bach. Number-theoretic algorithms. In *Annual Review of Computer Science*, volume 4, pages 119–172. Annual Reviews, Inc., 1990.

[34] Eric Bach and Jeffrey Shallit. *Algorithmic Number Theory—Volume I: Efficient Algorithms*. The MIT Press, 1996.

[35] Nikhil Bansal and Anupam Gupta. Potential-function proofs for first-order methods. *CoRR*, abs/1712.04581, 2017.

[36] Hannah Bast, Daniel Delling, Andrew V. Goldberg, Matthias Müller-Hannemann, Thomas Pajor, Peter Sanders, Dorothea Wagner, and Renato F. Werneck. Route planning in transportation networks. In *Algorithm Engineering - Selected Results and Surveys*, volume 9220 of *Lecture Notes in Computer Science*, pages 19–80. Springer, 2016.

[37] Surender Baswana, Ramesh Hariharan, and Sandeep Sen. Improved decremental algorithms for maintaining transitive closure and all-pairs shortest paths. *Journal of Algorithms*, 62(2):74–92, 2007.

[38] R. Bayer. Symmetric binary B-trees: Data structure and maintenance algorithms. *Acta Informatica*, 1(4):290–306, 1972.

[39] R. Bayer and E. M. McCreight. Organization and maintenance of large ordered indexes. *Acta Informatica*, 1(3):173–189, 1972.

[40] Pierre Beauchemin, Gilles Brassard, Claude Crépeau, Claude Goutier, and Carl Pomerance. The generation of random numbers that are probably prime. *Journal of Cryptology*, 1(1):53–64, 1988.

[41] L. A. Belady. A study of replacement algorithms for a virtual-storage computer. *IBM Systems Journal*, 5(2):78–101, 1966.

[42] Mihir Bellare, Joe Kilian, and Phillip Rogaway. The security of cipher block chaining message authentication code. *Journal of Computer and System Sciences*, 61(3):362–399, 2000.

[43] Mihir Bellare and Phillip Rogaway. Random oracles are practical: A paradigm for designing efficient protocols. In *CCS '93, Proceedings of the 1st ACM Conference on Computer and Communications Security*, pages 62–73, 1993.

[44] Richard Bellman. *Dynamic Programming*. Princeton University Press, 1957.

[45] Richard Bellman. On a routing problem. *Quarterly of Applied Mathematics*, 16(1):87–90, 1958.

[46] Michael Ben-Or. Lower bounds for algebraic computation trees. In *Proceedings of the Fifteenth Annual ACM Symposium on Theory of Computing*, pages 80–86, 1983.

[47] Michael A. Bender, Erik D. Demaine, and Martin Farach-Colton. Cache-oblivious B-trees. *SIAM Journal on Computing*, 35(2):341–358, 2005.

[48] Samuel W. Bent and John W. John. Finding the median requires $2n$ comparisons. In *Proceedings of the Seventeenth Annual ACM Symposium on Theory of Computing*, pages 213–216, 1985.

[49] Jon L. Bentley. *Writing Efficient Programs*. Prentice Hall, 1982.

[50] Jon L. Bentley. *More Programming Pearls: Confessions of a Coder*. Addison-Wesley, 1988.

[51] Jon L. Bentley. *Programming Pearls*. Addison-Wesley, second edition, 1999.

[52] Jon L. Bentley, Dorothea Haken, and James B. Saxe. A general method for solving divide-and-conquer recurrences. *SIGACT News*, 12(3):36–44, 1980.

[53] Claude Berge. Two theorems in graph theory. *Proceedings of the National Academy of Sciences*, 43(9):842–844, 1957.

[54] Aditya Y. Bhargava. *Grokking Algorithms: An Illustrated Guide For Programmers and Other Curious People*. Manning Publications, 2016.

[55] Daniel Bienstock and Benjamin McClosky. Tightening simplex mixed-integer sets with guaranteed bounds. *Optimization Online*, 2008.

[56] Patrick Billingsley. *Probability and Measure*. John Wiley & Sons, second edition, 1986.

[57] Guy E. Blelloch. *Scan Primitives and Parallel Vector Models*. PhD thesis, Department of Electrical Engineering and Computer Science, MIT, 1989. Available as MIT Laboratory for Computer Science Technical Report MIT/LCS/TR-463.

[58] Guy E. Blelloch. Programming parallel algorithms. *Communications of the ACM*, 39(3):85–97, 1996.

[59] Guy E. Blelloch, Jeremy T. Fineman, Phillip B. Gibbons, and Julian Shun. Internally deterministic parallel algorithms can be fast. In *17th ACM SIGPLAN Symposium on Principles and Practice of Parallel Programming*, pages 181–192, 2012.

[60] Guy E. Blelloch, Jeremy T. Fineman, Yan Gu, and Yihan Sun. Optimal parallel algorithms in the binary-forking model. In *Proceedings of the 32nd Annual ACM Symposium on Parallelism in Algorithms and Architectures*, pages 89–102, 2020.

[61] Guy E. Blelloch, Phillip B. Gibbons, and Yossi Matias. Provably efficient scheduling for languages with fine-grained parallelism. *Journal of the ACM*, 46(2):281–321, 1999.

[62] Manuel Blum, Robert W. Floyd, Vaughan Pratt, Ronald L. Rivest, and Robert E. Tarjan. Time bounds for selection. *Journal of Computer and System Sciences*, 7(4):448–461, 1973.

[63] Robert D. Blumofe and Charles E. Leiserson. Scheduling multithreaded computations by work stealing. *Journal of the ACM*, 46(5):720–748, 1999.

[64] Robert L Bocchino, Jr., Vikram S. Adve, Sarita V. Adve, and Marc Snir. Parallel programming must be deterministic by default. In *Proceedings of the First USENIX Conference on Hot Topics in Parallelism (HotPar)*, 2009.

[65] Béla Bollobás. *Random Graphs*. Academic Press, 1985.

[66] Leonardo Bonacci. *Liber Abaci*, 1202.

[67] J. A. Bondy and U. S. R. Murty. *Graph Theory with Applications*. American Elsevier, 1976.

[68] A. Borodin and R. El-Yaniv. *Online Computation and Competitive Analysis*. Cambridge University Press, 1998.

[69] Stephen P. Boyd and Lieven Vandenberghe. *Convex Optimization*. Cambridge University Press, 2004.

[70] Gilles Brassard and Paul Bratley. *Fundamentals of Algorithmics*. Prentice Hall, 1996.

[71] Richard P. Brent. The parallel evaluation of general arithmetic expressions. *Journal of the ACM*, 21(2):201–206, 1974.

[72] Gerth Stølting Brodal. A survey on priority queues. In Andrej Brodnik, Alejandro López-Ortiz, Venkatesh Raman, and Alfredo Viola, editors, *Space-Efficient Data Structures, Streams, and Algorithms: Papers in Honor of J. Ian Munro on the Occasion of His 66th Birthday*, volume 8066 of *Lecture Notes in Computer Science*, pages 150–163. Springer, 2013.

[73] Gerth Stølting Brodal, George Lagogiannis, and Robert E. Tarjan. Strict Fibonacci heaps. In *Proceedings of the 44th Annual ACM Symposium on Theory of Computing*, pages 1177–1184, 2012.

[74] George W. Brown. Some notes on computation of games solutions. *RAND Corporation Report*, P-78, 1949.

[75] Sébastien Bubeck. Convex optimization: Algorithms and complexity. *Foundations and Trends in Machine Learning*, 8(3-4):231–357, 2015.

[76] Niv Buchbinder and Joseph Naor. The design of competitive online algorithms via a primal-dual approach. *Foundations and Trends in Theoretical Computer Science*, 3(2–3):93–263, 2009.

[77] J. P. Buhler, H. W. Lenstra, Jr., and Carl Pomerance. Factoring integers with the number field sieve. In A. K. Lenstra and H. W. Lenstra, Jr., editors, *The Development of the Number Field Sieve*, volume 1554 of *Lecture Notes in Mathematics*, pages 50–94. Springer, 1993.

[78] M. Burrows and D. J. Wheeler. A block-sorting lossless data compression algorithm. SRC Research Report 124, Digital Equipment Corporation Systems Research Center, May 1994.

[79] Neville Campbell. Recurrences. Unpublished treatise available at https://nevillecampbell. com/Recurrences.pdf, 2020.

[80] J. Lawrence Carter and Mark N. Wegman. Universal classes of hash functions. *Journal of Computer and System Sciences*, 18(2):143–154, 1979.

[81] Barbara Chapman, Gabriele Jost, and Ruud van der Pas. *Using OpenMP: Portable Shared Memory Parallel Programming*. The MIT Press, 2007.

[82] Philippe Charles, Christian Grothoff, Vijay Saraswat, Christopher Donawa, Allan Kielstra, Kemal Ebcioglu, Christoph Von Praun, and Vivek Sarkar. X10: An object-oriented approach to non-uniform cluster computing. In *ACM SIGPLAN Conference on Object-oriented Programming, Systems, Languages, and Applications (OOPSLA)*, pages 519–538, 2005.

[83] Bernard Chazelle. A minimum spanning tree algorithm with inverse-Ackermann type complexity. *Journal of the ACM*, 47(6):1028–1047, 2000.

[84] Ke Chen and Adrian Dumitrescu. Selection algorithms with small groups. *International Journal of Foundations of Computer Science*, 31(3):355–369, 2020.

[85] Guang-Ien Cheng, Mingdong Feng, Charles E. Leiserson, Keith H. Randall, and Andrew F. Stark. Detecting data races in Cilk programs that use locks. In *Proceedings of the 10th Annual ACM Symposium on Parallel Algorithms and Architectures*, pages 298–309, 1998.

[86] Joseph Cheriyan and Torben Hagerup. A randomized maximum-flow algorithm. *SIAM Journal on Computing*, 24(2):203–226, 1995.

[87] Joseph Cheriyan and S. N. Maheshwari. Analysis of preflow push algorithms for maximum network flow. *SIAM Journal on Computing*, 18(6):1057–1086, 1989.

[88] Boris V. Cherkassky and Andrew V. Goldberg. On implementing the push-relabel method for the maximum flow problem. *Algorithmica*, 19(4):390–410, 1997.

[89] Boris V. Cherkassky, Andrew V. Goldberg, and Tomasz Radzik. Shortest paths algorithms: Theory and experimental evaluation. *Mathematical Programming*, 73(2):129–174, 1996.

[90] Boris V. Cherkassky, Andrew V. Goldberg, and Craig Silverstein. Buckets, heaps, lists and monotone priority queues. *SIAM Journal on Computing*, 28(4):1326–1346, 1999.

[91] H. Chernoff. A measure of asymptotic efficiency for tests of a hypothesis based on the sum of observations. *Annals of Mathematical Statistics*, 23(4):493–507, 1952.

[92] Brian Christian and Tom Griffiths. *Algorithms to Live By: The Computer Science of Human Decisions*. Picador, 2017.

[93] Kai Lai Chung. *Elementary Probability Theory with Stochastic Processes*. Springer, 1974.

[94] V. Chvátal. *Linear Programming*. W. H. Freeman and Company, 1983.

[95] V. Chvátal, D. A. Klarner, and D. E. Knuth. Selected combinatorial research problems. Technical Report STAN-CS-72-292, Computer Science Department, Stanford University, 1972.

[96] Alan Cobham. The intrinsic computational difficulty of functions. In *Proceedings of the 1964 Congress for Logic, Methodology, and the Philosophy of Science*, pages 24–30. North-Holland, 1964.

[97] H. Cohen and H. W. Lenstra, Jr. Primality testing and Jacobi sums. *Mathematics of Computation*, 42(165):297–330, 1984.

[98] Michael B. Cohen, Aleksander Madry, Piotr Sankowski, and Adrian Vladu. Negative-weight shortest paths and unit capacity minimum cost flow in $\widetilde{O}(m^{10/7} \log w)$ time (extended abstract). In *Proceedings of the 28th ACM-SIAM Symposium on Discrete Algorithms*, pages 752–771, 2017.

[99] Douglas Comer. The ubiquitous B-tree. *ACM Computing Surveys*, 11(2):121–137, 1979.

[100] Stephen Cook. The complexity of theorem proving procedures. In *Proceedings of the Third Annual ACM Symposium on Theory of Computing*, pages 151–158, 1971.

[101] James W. Cooley and John W. Tukey. An algorithm for the machine calculation of complex Fourier series. *Mathematics of Computation*, 19(90):297–301, 1965.

[102] Don Coppersmith. Modifications to the number field sieve. *Journal of Cryptology*, 6(3):169–180, 1993.

[103] Don Coppersmith and Shmuel Winograd. Matrix multiplication via arithmetic progression. *Journal of Symbolic Computation*, 9(3):251–280, 1990.

[104] Thomas H. Cormen. *Algorithms Unlocked*. The MIT Press, 2013.

[105] Thomas H. Cormen, Thomas Sundquist, and Leonard F. Wisniewski. Asymptotically tight bounds for performing BMMC permutations on parallel disk systems. *SIAM Journal on Computing*, 28(1):105–136, 1998.

[106] Don Dailey and Charles E. Leiserson. Using Cilk to write multiprocessor chess programs. In H. J. van den Herik and B. Monien, editors, *Advances in Computer Games*, volume 9, pages 25–52. University of Maastricht, Netherlands, 2001.

[107] Sanjoy Dasgupta, Christos Papadimitriou, and Umesh Vazirani. *Algorithms*. McGraw-Hill, 2008.

[108] Abraham de Moivre. De fractionibus algebraicis radicalitate immunibus ad fractiones simpliciores reducendis, deque summandis terminis quarundam serierum aequali intervallo a se distantibus. *Philosophical Transactions*, 32(373):162–168, 1722.

[109] Erik D. Demaine, Dion Harmon, John Iacono, and Mihai Pătraşcu. Dynamic optimality—almost. *SIAM Journal on Computing*, 37(1):240–251, 2007.

[110] Camil Demetrescu, David Eppstein, Zvi Galik, and Giuseppe F. Italiano. Dynamic graph algorithms. In Mikhail J. Attalah and Marina Blanton, editors, *Algorithms and Theory of Computation Handbook*, chapter 9, pages 9-1–9-28. Chapman & Hall/CRC, second edition, 2009.

[111] Camil Demetrescu and Giuseppe F. Italiano. Fully dynamic all pairs shortest paths with real edge weights. *Journal of Computer and System Sciences*, 72(5):813–837, 2006.

[112] Eric V. Denardo and Bennett L. Fox. Shortest-route methods: 1. Reaching, pruning, and buckets. *Operations Research*, 27(1):161–186, 1979.

[113] Martin Dietzfelbinger, Torben Hagerup, Jyrki Katajainen, and Martti Penttonen. A reliable randomized algorithm for the closest-pair problem. *Journal of Algorithms*, 25(1):19–51, 1997.

[114] Martin Dietzfelbinger, Anna Karlin, Kurt Mehlhorn, Friedhelm Meyer auf der Heide, Hans Rohnert, and Robert E. Tarjan. Dynamic perfect hashing: Upper and lower bounds. *SIAM Journal on Computing*, 23(4):738–761, 1994.

[115] Whitfield Diffie and Martin E. Hellman. New directions in cryptography. *IEEE Transactions on Information Theory*, IT-22(6):644–654, 1976.

[116] Edsger W. Dijkstra. A note on two problems in connexion with graphs. *Numerische Mathematik*, 1(1):269–271, 1959.

[117] Edsger W. Dijkstra. *A Discipline of Programming*. Prentice-Hall, 1976.

[118] Dimitar Dimitrov, Martin Vechev, and Vivek Sarkar. Race detection in two dimensions. *ACM Transactions on Parallel Computing*, 4(4):1–22, 2018.

[119] E. A. Dinic. Algorithm for solution of a problem of maximum flow in a network with power estimation. *Soviet Mathematics Doklady*, 11(5):1277–1280, 1970.

[120] Brandon Dixon, Monika Rauch, and Robert E. Tarjan. Verification and sensitivity analysis of minimum spanning trees in linear time. *SIAM Journal on Computing*, 21(6):1184–1192, 1992.

[121] John D. Dixon. Factorization and primality tests. *The American Mathematical Monthly*, 91(6):333–352, 1984.

[122] Dorit Dor, Johan Håstad, Staffan Ulfberg, and Uri Zwick. On lower bounds for selecting the median. *SIAM Journal on Discrete Mathematics*, 14(3):299–311, 2001.

[123] Dorit Dor and Uri Zwick. Selecting the median. *SIAM Journal on Computing*, 28(5):1722–1758, 1999.

[124] Dorit Dor and Uri Zwick. Median selection requires $(2 + \epsilon)n$ comparisons. *SIAM Journal on Discrete Mathematics*, 14(3):312–325, 2001.

[125] Alvin W. Drake. *Fundamentals of Applied Probability Theory*. McGraw-Hill, 1967.

[126] James R. Driscoll, Neil Sarnak, Daniel D. Sleator, and Robert E. Tarjan. Making data structures persistent. *Journal of Computer and System Sciences*, 38(1):86–124, 1989.

[127] Ran Duan, Seth Pettie, and Hsin-Hao Su. Scaling algorithms for weighted matching in general graphs. *ACM Transactions on Algorithms*, 14(1):8:1–8:35, 2018.

[128] Richard Durstenfeld. Algorithm 235 (RANDOM PERMUTATION). *Communications of the ACM*, 7(7):420, 1964.

[129] Derek L. Eager, John Zahorjan, and Edward D. Lazowska. Speedup versus efficiency in parallel systems. *IEEE Transactions on Computers*, 38(3):408–423, 1989.

[130] Jack Edmonds. Paths, trees, and flowers. *Canadian Journal of Mathematics*, 17:449–467, 1965.

[131] Jack Edmonds. Matroids and the greedy algorithm. *Mathematical Programming*, 1(1):127–136, 1971.

[132] Jack Edmonds and Richard M. Karp. Theoretical improvements in the algorithmic efficiency for network flow problems. *Journal of the ACM*, 19(2):248–264, 1972.

[133] Jeff Edmonds. *How To Think About Algorithms*. Cambridge University Press, 2008.

[134] Mourad Elloumi and Albert Y. Zomaya, editors. *Algorithms in Computational Molecular Biology: Techniques, Approaches and Applications*. John Wiley & Sons, 2011.

[135] Jeff Erickson. *Algorithms*. https://archive.org/details/Algorithms-Jeff-Erickson, 2019.

[136] Martin Erwig. *Once Upon an Algorithm: How Stories Explain Computing*. The MIT Press, 2017.

[137] Shimon Even. *Graph Algorithms*. Computer Science Press, 1979.

[138] Shimon Even and Yossi Shiloach. An on-line edge-deletion problem. *Journal of the ACM*, 28(1):1–4, 1981.

[139] William Feller. *An Introduction to Probability Theory and Its Applications*. John Wiley & Sons, third edition, 1968.

[140] Mingdong Feng and Charles E. Leiserson. Efficient detection of determinacy races in Cilk programs. In *Proceedings of the 9th Annual ACM Symposium on Parallel Algorithms and Architectures*, pages 1–11, 1997.

[141] Amos Fiat, Richard M. Karp, Michael Luby, Lyle A. McGeoch, Daniel Dominic Sleator, and Neal E. Young. Competitive paging algorithms. *Journal of Algorithms*, 12(4):685–699, 1991.

[142] Amos Fiat and Gerhard J. Woeginger, editors. *Online Algorithms, The State of the Art*, volume 1442 of *Lecture Notes in Computer Science*. Springer, 1998.

[143] Sir Ronald A. Fisher and Frank Yates. *Statistical Tables for Biological, Agricultural and Medical Research*. Hafner Publishing Company, fifth edition, 1957.

[144] Robert W. Floyd. Algorithm 97 (SHORTEST PATH). *Communications of the ACM*, 5(6):345, 1962.

[145] Robert W. Floyd. Algorithm 245 (TREESORT). *Communications of the ACM*, 7(12):701, 1964.

[146] Robert W. Floyd. Permuting information in idealized two-level storage. In Raymond E. Miller and James W. Thatcher, editors, *Complexity of Computer Computations*, pages 105–109. Plenum Press, 1972.

[147] Robert W. Floyd and Ronald L. Rivest. Expected time bounds for selection. *Communications of the ACM*, 18(3):165–172, 1975.

[148] L. R. Ford. *Network Flow Theory*. RAND Corporation, Santa Monica, CA, 1956.

[149] Lestor R. Ford, Jr. and D. R. Fulkerson. *Flows in Networks*. Princeton University Press, 1962.

[150] Lestor R. Ford, Jr. and Selmer M. Johnson. A tournament problem. *The American Mathematical Monthly*, 66(5):387–389, 1959.

[151] E. W. Forgy. Cluster analysis of multivariate efficiency versus interpretatbility of classifications. *Biometrics*, 21(3):768–769, 1965.

[152] Lance Fortnow. *The Golden Ticket: P, NP, and the Search for the Impossible.* Princeton University Press, 2013.

[153] Michael L. Fredman. New bounds on the complexity of the shortest path problem. *SIAM Journal on Computing*, 5(1):83–89, 1976.

[154] Michael L. Fredman, János Komlós, and Endre Szemerédi. Storing a sparse table with $O(1)$ worst case access time. *Journal of the ACM*, 31(3):538–544, 1984.

[155] Michael L. Fredman and Michael E. Saks. The cell probe complexity of dynamic data structures. In *Proceedings of the Twenty First Annual ACM Symposium on Theory of Computing*, pages 345–354, 1989.

[156] Michael L. Fredman and Robert E. Tarjan. Fibonacci heaps and their uses in improved network optimization algorithms. *Journal of the ACM*, 34(3):596–615, 1987.

[157] Michael L. Fredman and Dan E. Willard. Surpassing the information theoretic bound with fusion trees. *Journal of Computer and System Sciences*, 47(3):424–436, 1993.

[158] Michael L. Fredman and Dan E. Willard. Trans-dichotomous algorithms for minimum spanning trees and shortest paths. *Journal of Computer and System Sciences*, 48(3):533–551, 1994.

[159] Yoav Freund and Robert E. Schapire. A decision-theoretic generalization of on-line learning and an application to boosting. *Journal of Computer and System Sciences*, 55(1):119–139, 1997.

[160] Matteo Frigo, Pablo Halpern, Charles E. Leiserson, and Stephen Lewin-Berlin. Reducers and other Cilk++ hyperobjects. In *Proceedings of the 21st Annual ACM Symposium on Parallelism in Algorithms and Architectures*, pages 79–90, 2009.

[161] Matteo Frigo and Steven G. Johnson. The design and implementation of FFTW3. *Proceedings of the IEEE*, 93(2):216–231, 2005.

[162] Hannah Fry. *Hello World: Being Human in the Age of Algorithms.* W. W. Norton & Company, 2018.

[163] Harold N. Gabow. Path-based depth-first search for strong and biconnected components. *Information Processing Letters*, 74(3–4):107–114, 2000.

[164] Harold N. Gabow. The weighted matching approach to maximum cardinality matching. *Fundamenta Informaticae*, 154(1-4):109–130, 2017.

[165] Harold N. Gabow, Z. Galil, T. Spencer, and Robert E. Tarjan. Efficient algorithms for finding minimum spanning trees in undirected and directed graphs. *Combinatorica*, 6(2):109–122, 1986.

[166] Harold N. Gabow and Robert E. Tarjan. A linear-time algorithm for a special case of disjoint set union. *Journal of Computer and System Sciences*, 30(2):209–221, 1985.

[167] Harold N. Gabow and Robert E. Tarjan. Faster scaling algorithms for network problems. *SIAM Journal on Computing*, 18(5):1013–1036, 1989.

[168] Harold N. Gabow and Robert Endre Tarjan. Faster scaling algorithms for general graph-matching problems. *Journal of the ACM*, 38(4):815–853, 1991.

[169] D. Gale and L. S. Shapley. College admissions and the stability of marriage. *American Mathematical Monthly*, 69(1):9–15, 1962.

[170] Zvi Galil and Oded Margalit. All pairs shortest distances for graphs with small integer length edges. *Information and Computation*, 134(2):103–139, 1997.

[171] Zvi Galil and Oded Margalit. All pairs shortest paths for graphs with small integer length edges. *Journal of Computer and System Sciences*, 54(2):243–254, 1997.

[172] Zvi Galil and Kunsoo Park. Dynamic programming with convexity, concavity and sparsity. *Theoretical Computer Science*, 92(1):49–76, 1992.

[173] Zvi Galil and Joel Seiferas. Time-space-optimal string matching. *Journal of Computer and System Sciences*, 26(3):280–294, 1983.

[174] Igal Galperin and Ronald L. Rivest. Scapegoat trees. In *Proceedings of the 4th ACM-SIAM Symposium on Discrete Algorithms*, pages 165–174, 1993.

[175] Michael R. Garey, R. L. Graham, and J. D. Ullman. Worst-case analyis of memory allocation algorithms. In *Proceedings of the Fourth Annual ACM Symposium on Theory of Computing*, pages 143–150, 1972.

[176] Michael R. Garey and David S. Johnson. *Computers and Intractability: A Guide to the Theory of NP-Completeness*. W. H. Freeman, 1979.

[177] Naveen Garg and Jochen Könemann. Faster and simpler algorithms for multicommodity flow and other fractional packing problems. *SIAM Journal on Computing*, 37(2):630–652, 2007.

[178] Saul Gass. *Linear Programming: Methods and Applications*. International Thomson Publishing, fourth edition, 1975.

[179] Fănică Gavril. Algorithms for minimum coloring, maximum clique, minimum covering by cliques, and maximum independent set of a chordal graph. *SIAM Journal on Computing*, 1(2):180–187, 1972.

[180] Alan George and Joseph W-H Liu. *Computer Solution of Large Sparse Positive Definite Systems*. Prentice Hall, 1981.

[181] E. N. Gilbert and E. F. Moore. Variable-length binary encodings. *Bell System Technical Journal*, 38(4):933–967, 1959.

[182] Ashish Goel, Sanjeev Khanna, Daniel H. Larkin, and Rober E. Tarjan. Disjoint set union with randomized linking. In *Proceedings of the 25th ACM-SIAM Symposium on Discrete Algorithms*, pages 1005–1017, 2014.

[183] Michel X. Goemans and David P. Williamson. Improved approximation algorithms for maximum cut and satisfiability problems using semidefinite programming. *Journal of the ACM*, 42(6):1115–1145, 1995.

[184] Michel X. Goemans and David P. Williamson. The primal-dual method for approximation algorithms and its application to network design problems. In Dorit S. Hochbaum, editor, *Approximation Algorithms for NP-Hard Problems*, pages 144–191. PWS Publishing Company, 1997.

[185] Andrew V. Goldberg. *Efficient Graph Algorithms for Sequential and Parallel Computers*. PhD thesis, Department of Electrical Engineering and Computer Science, MIT, 1987.

[186] Andrew V. Goldberg. Scaling algorithms for the shortest paths problem. *SIAM Journal on Computing*, 24(3):494–504, 1995.

[187] Andrew V. Goldberg and Satish Rao. Beyond the flow decomposition barrier. *Journal of the ACM*, 45(5):783–797, 1998.

[188] Andrew V. Goldberg and Robert E. Tarjan. A new approach to the maximum flow problem. *Journal of the ACM*, 35(4):921–940, 1988.

[189] D. Goldfarb and M. J. Todd. Linear programming. In G. L. Nemhauser, A. H. G. Rinnooy-Kan, and M. J. Todd, editors, *Handbooks in Operations Research and Management Science, Vol. 1, Optimization*, pages 73–170. Elsevier Science Publishers, 1989.

[190] Shafi Goldwasser and Silvio Micali. Probabilistic encryption. *Journal of Computer and System Sciences*, 28(2):270–299, 1984.

[191] Shafi Goldwasser, Silvio Micali, and Ronald L. Rivest. A digital signature scheme secure against adaptive chosen-message attacks. *SIAM Journal on Computing*, 17(2):281–308, 1988.

[192] Gene H. Golub and Charles F. Van Loan. *Matrix Computations*. The Johns Hopkins University Press, third edition, 1996.

[193] G. H. Gonnet and R. Baeza-Yates. *Handbook of Algorithms and Data Structures in Pascal and C*. Addison-Wesley, second edition, 1991.

[194] Rafael C. Gonzalez and Richard E. Woods. *Digital Image Processing*. Addison-Wesley, 1992.

[195] Michael T. Goodrich and Roberto Tamassia. *Algorithm Design: Foundations, Analysis, and Internet Examples*. John Wiley & Sons, 2001.

[196] Michael T. Goodrich and Roberto Tamassia. *Data Structures and Algorithms in Java*. John Wiley & Sons, sixth edition, 2014.

[197] Ronald L. Graham. Bounds for certain multiprocessor anomalies. *Bell System Technical Journal*, 45(9):1563–1581, 1966.

[198] Ronald L. Graham and Pavol Hell. On the history of the minimum spanning tree problem. *Annals of the History of Computing*, 7(1):43–57, 1985.

[199] Ronald L. Graham, Donald E. Knuth, and Oren Patashnik. *Concrete Mathematics*. Addison-Wesley, second edition, 1994.

[200] David Gries. *The Science of Programming*. Springer, 1981.

[201] M. Grötschel, László Lovász, and Alexander Schrijver. *Geometric Algorithms and Combinatorial Optimization*. Springer, 1988.

[202] Leo J. Guibas and Robert Sedgewick. A dichromatic framework for balanced trees. In *Proceedings of the 19th Annual Symposium on Foundations of Computer Science*, pages 8–21, 1978.

[203] Dan Gusfield and Robert W. Irving. *The Stable Marriage Problem: Structure and Algorithms*. The MIT Press, 1989.

[204] Gregory Gutin and Abraham P. Punnen, editors. *The Traveling Salesman Problem and Its Variations*. Kluwer Academic Publishers, 2002.

[205] Torben Hagerup. Improved shortest paths on the word RAM. In *Procedings of 27th International Colloquium on Automata, Languages and Programming, ICALP 2000*, volume 1853 of *Lecture Notes in Computer Science*, pages 61–72. Springer, 2000.

[206] H. Halberstam and R. E. Ingram, editors. *The Mathematical Papers of Sir William Rowan Hamilton*, volume III (Algebra). Cambridge University Press, 1967.

[207] Yijie Han. Improved fast integer sorting in linear space. *Information and Computation*, 170(1):81–94, 2001.

[208] Frank Harary. *Graph Theory*. Addison-Wesley, 1969.

[209] Gregory C. Harfst and Edward M. Reingold. A potential-based amortized analysis of the union-find data structure. *SIGACT News*, 31(3):86–95, 2000.

[210] J. Hartmanis and R. E. Stearns. On the computational complexity of algorithms. *Transactions of the American Mathematical Society*, 117:285–306, 1965.

[211] Michael T. Heideman, Don H. Johnson, and C. Sidney Burrus. Gauss and the history of the Fast Fourier Transform. *IEEE ASSP Magazine*, 1(4):14–21, 1984.

[212] Monika R. Henzinger and Valerie King. Fully dynamic biconnectivity and transitive closure. In *Proceedings of the 36th Annual Symposium on Foundations of Computer Science*, pages 664–672, 1995.

[213] Monika R. Henzinger and Valerie King. Randomized fully dynamic graph algorithms with polylogarithmic time per operation. *Journal of the ACM*, 46(4):502–516, 1999.

[214] Monika R. Henzinger, Satish Rao, and Harold N. Gabow. Computing vertex connectivity: New bounds from old techniques. *Journal of Algorithms*, 34(2):222–250, 2000.

[215] Nicholas J. Higham. Exploiting fast matrix multiplication within the level 3 BLAS. *ACM Transactions on Mathematical Software*, 16(4):352–368, 1990.

[216] Nicholas J. Higham. *Accuracy and Stability of Numerical Algorithms*. SIAM, second edition, 2002.

[217] W. Daniel Hillis and Jr. Guy L. Steele. Data parallel algorithms. *Communications of the ACM*, 29(12):1170–1183, 1986.

[218] C. A. R. Hoare. Algorithm 63 (PARTITION) and algorithm 65 (FIND). *Communications of the ACM*, 4(7):321–322, 1961.

[219] C. A. R. Hoare. Quicksort. *The Computer Journal*, 5(1):10–15, 1962.

[220] Dorit S. Hochbaum. Efficient bounds for the stable set, vertex cover and set packing problems. *Discrete Applied Mathematics*, 6(3):243–254, 1983.

[221] Dorit S. Hochbaum, editor. *Approximation Algorithms for NP-Hard Problems*. PWS Publishing Company, 1997.

[222] W. Hoeffding. On the distribution of the number of successes in independent trials. *Annals of Mathematical Statistics*, 27(3):713–721, 1956.

[223] Micha Hofri. *Probabilistic Analysis of Algorithms*. Springer, 1987.

[224] John E. Hopcroft and Richard M. Karp. An $n^{5/2}$ algorithm for maximum matchings in bipartite graphs. *SIAM Journal on Computing*, 2(4):225–231, 1973.

[225] John E. Hopcroft, Rajeev Motwani, and Jeffrey D. Ullman. *Introduction to Automata Theory, Languages, and Computation*. Addison Wesley, third edition, 2006.

[226] John E. Hopcroft and Robert E. Tarjan. Efficient algorithms for graph manipulation. *Communications of the ACM*, 16(6):372–378, 1973.

[227] John E. Hopcroft and Jeffrey D. Ullman. Set merging algorithms. *SIAM Journal on Computing*, 2(4):294–303, 1973.

[228] John E. Hopcroft and Jeffrey D. Ullman. *Introduction to Automata Theory, Languages, and Computation*. Addison-Wesley, 1979.

[229] Juraj Hromkovič. *Algorithmics for Hard Problems: Introduction to Combinatorial Optimization, Randomization, Approximation, and Heuristics*. Springer-Verlag, 2001.

[230] T. C. Hu and M. T. Shing. Computation of matrix chain products. Part I. *SIAM Journal on Computing*, 11(2):362–373, 1982.

[231] T. C. Hu and M. T. Shing. Computation of matrix chain products. Part II. *SIAM Journal on Computing*, 13(2):228–251, 1984.

[232] T. C. Hu and A. C. Tucker. Optimal computer search trees and variable-length alphabetic codes. *SIAM Journal on Applied Mathematics*, 21(4):514–532, 1971.

[233] David A. Huffman. A method for the construction of minimum-redundancy codes. *Proceedings of the IRE*, 40(9):1098–1101, 1952.

[234] Oscar H. Ibarra and Chul E. Kim. Fast approximation algorithms for the knapsack and sum of subset problems. *Journal of the ACM*, 22(4):463–468, 1975.

[235] E. J. Isaac and R. C. Singleton. Sorting by address calculation. *Journal of the ACM*, 3(3):169–174, 1956.

[236] David S. Johnson. Approximation algorithms for combinatorial problems. *Journal of Computer and System Sciences*, 9(3):256–278, 1974.

[237] David S. Johnson. The NP-completeness column: An ongoing guide—The tale of the second prover. *Journal of Algorithms*, 13(3):502–524, 1992.

[238] Donald B. Johnson. Efficient algorithms for shortest paths in sparse networks. *Journal of the ACM*, 24(1):1–13, 1977.

[239] Richard Johnsonbaugh and Marcus Schaefer. *Algorithms*. Pearson Prentice Hall, 2004.

[240] Neil C. Jones and Pavel Pevzner. *An Introduction to Bioinformatics Algorithms*. The MIT Press, 2004.

[241] T. Kanungo, D. M. Mount, N. S. Netanyahu, C. D. Piatko, R. Silverman, and A. Y. Wu. A local search approximation algorithm for k-means clustering. *Computational Geometry*, 28:89–112, 2004.

[242] A. Karatsuba and Yu. Ofman. Multiplication of multidigit numbers on automata. *Soviet Physics—Doklady*, 7(7):595–596, 1963. Translation of an article in *Doklady Akademii Nauk SSSR*, 145(2), 1962.

[243] David R. Karger, Philip N. Klein, and Robert E. Tarjan. A randomized linear-time algorithm to find minimum spanning trees. *Journal of the ACM*, 42(2):321–328, 1995.

[244] David R. Karger, Daphne Koller, and Steven J. Phillips. Finding the hidden path: Time bounds for all-pairs shortest paths. *SIAM Journal on Computing*, 22(6):1199–1217, 1993.

[245] Juha Kärkkäinen, Peter Sanders, and Stefan Burkhardt. Linear work suffix array construction. *Journal of the ACM*, 53(6):918–936, 2006.

[246] Howard Karloff. *Linear Programming*. Birkhäuser, 1991.

[247] N. Karmarkar. A new polynomial-time algorithm for linear programming. *Combinatorica*, 4(4):373–395, 1984.

[248] Richard M. Karp. Reducibility among combinatorial problems. In Raymond E. Miller and James W. Thatcher, editors, *Complexity of Computer Computations*, pages 85–103. Plenum Press, 1972.

[249] Richard M. Karp. An introduction to randomized algorithms. *Discrete Applied Mathematics*, 34(1–3):165–201, 1991.

[250] Richard M. Karp and Michael O. Rabin. Efficient randomized pattern-matching algorithms. *IBM Journal of Research and Development*, 31(2):249–260, 1987.

[251] A. V. Karzanov. Determining the maximal flow in a network by the method of preflows. *Soviet Mathematics Doklady*, 15(2):434–437, 1974.

[252] Toru Kasai, Gunho Lee, Hiroki Arimura, Setsuo Arikawa, and Kunsoo Park. Linear-time longest-common-prefix computation in suffix arrays and its applications. In *Proceedings of the 12th Annual Symposium on Combinatorial Pattern Matching*, volume 2089, pages 181–192. Springer-Verlag, 2001.

[253] Jonathan Katz and Yehuda Lindell. *Introduction to Modern Cryptography*. CRC Press, second edition, 2015.

[254] Valerie King. A simpler minimum spanning tree verification algorithm. *Algorithmica*, 18(2):263–270, 1997.

[255] Valerie King, Satish Rao, and Robert E. Tarjan. A faster deterministic maximum flow algorithm. *Journal of Algorithms*, 17(3):447–474, 1994.

[256] Philip N. Klein and Neal E. Young. Approximation algorithms for NP-hard optimization problems. In *CRC Handbook on Algorithms*, pages 34-1–34-19. CRC Press, 1999.

[257] Jon Kleinberg and Éva Tardos. *Algorithm Design*. Addison-Wesley, 2006.

[258] Robert D. Kleinberg. A multiple-choice secretary algorithm with applications to online auctions. In *Proceedings of the 16th ACM-SIAM Symposium on Discrete Algorithms*, pages 630–631, 2005.

[259] Donald E. Knuth. *Fundamental Algorithms*, volume 1 of *The Art of Computer Programming*. Addison-Wesley, third edition, 1997.

[260] Donald E. Knuth. *Seminumerical Algorithms*, volume 2 of *The Art of Computer Programming*. Addison-Wesley, third edition, 1997.

[261] Donald E. Knuth. *Sorting and Searching*, volume 3 of *The Art of Computer Programming*. Addison-Wesley, second edition, 1998.

[262] Donald E. Knuth. *Combinatorial Algorithms*, volume 4A of *The Art of Computer Programming*. Addison-Wesley, 2011.

[263] Donald E. Knuth. *Satisfiability*, volume 4, fascicle 6 of *The Art of Computer Programming*. Addison-Wesley, 2015.

[264] Donald E. Knuth. Optimum binary search trees. *Acta Informatica*, 1(1):14–25, 1971.

[265] Donald E. Knuth. Big omicron and big omega and big theta. *SIGACT News*, 8(2):18–23, 1976.

[266] Donald E. Knuth. *Stable Marriage and Its Relation to Other Combinatorial Problems: An Introduction to the Mathematical Analysis of Algorithms*, volume 10 of *CRM Proceedings and Lecture Notes*. American Mathematical Society, 1997.

[267] Donald E. Knuth, James H. Morris, Jr., and Vaughan R. Pratt. Fast pattern matching in strings. *SIAM Journal on Computing*, 6(2):323–350, 1977.

[268] Mykel J. Kochenderfer and Tim A. Wheeler. *Algorithms for Optimization*. The MIT Press, 2019.

[269] J. Komlós. Linear verification for spanning trees. *Combinatorica*, 5(1):57–65, 1985.

[270] Dexter C. Kozen. *The Design and Analysis of Algorithms*. Springer, 1992.

[271] David W. Krumme, George Cybenko, and K. N. Venkataraman. Gossiping in minimal time. *SIAM Journal on Computing*, 21(1):111–139, 1992.

[272] Joseph B. Kruskal, Jr. On the shortest spanning subtree of a graph and the traveling salesman problem. *Proceedings of the American Mathematical Society*, 7(1):48–50, 1956.

[273] Harold W. Kuhn. The Hungarian method for the assignment problem. *Naval Research Logistics Quarterly*, 2:83–97, 1955.

[274] William Kuszmaul and Charles E. Leiserson. Floors and ceilings in divide-and-conquer recurrences. In *Proceedings of the 3rd SIAM Symposium on Simplicity in Algorithms*, pages 133–141, 2021.

[275] Leslie Lamport. How to make a multiprocessor computer that correctly executes multiprocess programs. *IEEE Transactions on Computers*, C-28(9):690–691, 1979.

[276] Eugene L. Lawler. *Combinatorial Optimization: Networks and Matroids*. Holt, Rinehart, and Winston, 1976.

[277] Eugene L. Lawler, J. K. Lenstra, A. H. G. Rinnooy Kan, and D. B. Shmoys, editors. *The Traveling Salesman Problem*. John Wiley & Sons, 1985.

[278] François Le Gall. Powers of tensors and fast matrix multiplication. In *Proceedings of the 2014 International Symposium on Symbolic and Algebraic Computation, (ISSAC)*, pages 296–303, 2014.

[279] Doug Lea. A Java fork/join framework. In *ACM 2000 Conference on Java Grande*, pages 36–43, 2000.

[280] C. Y. Lee. An algorithm for path connection and its applications. *IRE Transactions on Electronic Computers*, EC-10(3):346–365, 1961.

[281] Edward A. Lee. The problem with threads. *IEEE Computer*, 39(3):33–42, 2006.

[282] I-Ting Angelina Lee, Charles E. Leiserson, Tao B. Schardl, Zhunping Zhang, and Jim Sukha. On-the-fly pipeline parallelism. *ACM Transactions on Parallel Computing*, 2(3):17:1–17:42, 2015.

[283] I-Ting Angelina Lee and Tao B. Schardl. Efficient race detection for reducer hyperobjects. *ACM Transactions on Parallel Computing*, 4(4):1–40, 2018.

[284] Mun-Kyu Lee, Pierre Michaud, Jeong Seop Sim, and Daehun Nyang. A simple proof of optimality for the MIN cache replacement policy. *Information Processing Letters*, 116(2):168–170, 2016.

[285] Yin Tat Lee and Aaron Sidford. Path finding methods for linear programming: Solving linear programs in $\widetilde{O}(\sqrt{rank})$ iterations and faster algorithms for maximum flow. In *Proceedings of the 55th Annual Symposium on Foundations of Computer Science*, pages 424–433, 2014.

[286] Tom Leighton. Tight bounds on the complexity of parallel sorting. *IEEE Transactions on Computers*, C-34(4):344–354, 1985.

[287] Tom Leighton. Notes on better master theorems for divide-and-conquer recurrences. Class notes. Available at http://citeseerx.ist.psu.edu/viewdoc/summary?doi=10.1.1.39.1636, 1996.

[288] Tom Leighton and Satish Rao. Multicommodity max-flow min-cut theorems and their use in designing approximation algorithms. *Journal of the ACM*, 46(6):787–832, 1999.

[289] Daan Leijen and Judd Hall. Optimize managed code for multi-core machines. *MSDN Magazine*, 2007.

[290] Charles E. Leiserson. The Cilk++ concurrency platform. *Journal of Supercomputing*, 51(3):244–257, March 2010.

[291] Charles E. Leiserson. Cilk. In David Padua, editor, *Encyclopedia of Parallel Computing*, pages 273–288. Springer, 2011.

[292] Charles E. Leiserson, Tao B. Schardl, and Jim Sukha. Deterministic parallel random-number generation for dynamic-multithreading platforms. In *Proceddings of the 17th ACM SIGPLAN Symposium on Principles and Practice of Parallel Programming (PPoPP)*, pages 193–204, 2012.

[293] Charles E. Leiserson, Neil C. Thompson, Joel S. Emer, Bradley C. Kuszmaul, Butler W. Lampson, Daniel Sanchez, and Tao B. Schardl. There's plenty of room at the Top: What will drive computer performance after Moore's law? *Science*, 368(6495), 2020.

[294] Debra A. Lelewer and Daniel S. Hirschberg. Data compression. *ACM Computing Surveys*, 19(3):261–296, 1987.

[295] A. K. Lenstra, H. W. Lenstra, Jr., M. S. Manasse, and J. M. Pollard. The number field sieve. In A. K. Lenstra and H. W. Lenstra, Jr., editors, *The Development of the Number Field Sieve*, volume 1554 of *Lecture Notes in Mathematics*, pages 11–42. Springer, 1993.

[296] H. W. Lenstra, Jr. Factoring integers with elliptic curves. *Annals of Mathematics*, 126(3):649–673, 1987.

[297] L. A. Levin. Universal sequential search problems. *Problems of Information Transmission*, 9(3):265–266, 1973. Translated from the original Russian article in *Problemy Peredachi Informatsii* 9(3): 115–116, 1973.

[298] Anany Levitin. *Introduction to the Design & Analysis of Algorithms*. Addison-Wesley, third edition, 2011.

[299] Harry R. Lewis and Christos H. Papadimitriou. *Elements of the Theory of Computation*. Prentice Hall, second edition, 1998.

[300] Nick Littlestone. Learning quickly when irrelevant attributes abound: A new linear-threshold algorithm. *Machine Learning*, 2(4):285–318, 1988.

[301] Nick Littlestone and Manfred K. Warmuth. The weighted majority algorithm. *Information and Computation*, 108(2):212–261, 1994.

[302] C. L. Liu. *Introduction to Combinatorial Mathematics*. McGraw-Hill, 1968.

[303] Yang P. Liu and Aaron Sidford. Faster energy maximization for faster maximum flow. In *Proceedings of the 52nd Annual ACM Symposium on Theory of Computing*, pages 803–814, 2020.

[304] S. P. Lloyd. Least squares quantization in PCM. *IEEE Transactions on Information Theory*, 28(2):129–137, 1982.

[305] Panos Louridas. *Real-World Algorithms: A Beginner's Guide*. The MIT Press, 2017.

[306] László Lovász and Michael D. Plummer. *Matching Theory*, volume 121 of *Annals of Discrete Mathematics*. North Holland, 1986.

[307] John MacCormick. *9 Algorithms That Changed the Future: The Ingenious Ideas That Drive Today's Computers*. Princeton University Press, 2012.

[308] Aleksander Madry. Navigating central path with electrical flows: From flows to matchings, and back. In *Proceedings of the 54th Annual Symposium on Foundations of Computer Science*, pages 253–262, 2013.

[309] Bruce M. Maggs and Serge A. Plotkin. Minimum-cost spanning tree as a path-finding problem. *Information Processing Letters*, 26(6):291–293, 1988.

[310] M. Mahajan, P. Nimbhorkar, and K. Varadarajan. The planar k-means problem is NP-hard. In S. Das and R. Uehara, editors, *WALCOM 2009: Algorithms and Computation*, volume 5431 of *Lecture Notes in Computer Science*, pages 274–285. Springer, 2009.

[311] Michael Main. *Data Structures and Other Objects Using Java*. Addison-Wesley, 1999.

[312] Udi Manber and Gene Myers. Suffix arrays: A new method for on-line string searches. *SIAM Journal on Computing*, 22(5):935–948, 1993.

[313] David F. Manlove. *Algorithmics of Matching Under Preferences*, volume 2 of *Series on Theoretical Computer Science*. World Scientific, 2013.

[314] Giovanni Manzini. An analysis of the Burrows-Wheeler transform. *Journal of the ACM*, 48(3):407–430, 2001.

[315] Mario Andrea Marchisio, editor. *Computational Methods in Synthetic Biology*. Humana Press, 2015.

[316] William J. Masek and Michael S. Paterson. A faster algorithm computing string edit distances. *Journal of Computer and System Sciences*, 20(1):18–31, 1980.

[317] Yu. V. Matiyasevich. Real-time recognition of the inclusion relation. *Journal of Soviet Mathematics*, 1(1):64–70, 1973. Translated from the original Russian article in *Zapiski Nauchnykh Seminarov Leningradskogo Otdeleniya Matematicheskogo Institute im. V. A. Steklova Akademii Nauk SSSR* 20: 104–114, 1971.

[318] H. A. Maurer, Th. Ottmann, and H.-W. Six. Implementing dictionaries using binary trees of very small height. *Information Processing Letters*, 5(1):11–14, 1976.

[319] Ernst W. Mayr, Hans Jürgen Prömel, and Angelika Steger, editors. *Lectures on Proof Verification and Approximation Algorithms*, volume 1367 of *Lecture Notes in Computer Science*. Springer, 1998.

[320] Catherine C. McGeoch. All pairs shortest paths and the essential subgraph. *Algorithmica*, 13(5):426–441, 1995.

[321] Catherine C. McGeoch. *A Guide to Experimental Algorithmics*. Cambridge University Press, 2012.

[322] Andrew McGregor. Graph stream algorithms: A survey. *SIGMOD Record*, 43(1):9–20, 2014.

[323] M. D. McIlroy. A killer adversary for quicksort. *Software—Practice and Experience*, 29(4):341–344, 1999.

[324] Kurt Mehlhorn and Stefan Näher. *LEDA: A Platform for Combinatorial and Geometric Computing*. Cambridge University Press, 1999.

[325] Kurt Mehlhorn and Peter Sanders. *Algorithms and Data Structures: The Basic Toolbox*. Springer, 2008.

[326] Dinesh P. Mehta and Sartaj Sahni. *Handbook of Data Structures and Applications*. Chapman and Hall/CRC, second edition, 2018.

[327] Gary L. Miller. Riemann's hypothesis and tests for primality. *Journal of Computer and System Sciences*, 13(3):300–317, 1976.

[328] Marvin Minsky and Seymore A. Pappert. *Perceptrons*. The MIT Press, 1969.

[329] John C. Mitchell. *Foundations for Programming Languages*. The MIT Press, 1996.

[330] Joseph S. B. Mitchell. Guillotine subdivisions approximate polygonal subdivisions: A simple polynomial-time approximation scheme for geometric TSP, k-MST, and related problems. *SIAM Journal on Computing*, 28(4):1298–1309, 1999.

[331] Michael Mitzenmacher and Eli Upfal. *Probability and Computing*. Cambridge University Press, second edition, 2017.

[332] Louis Monier. *Algorithmes de Factorisation D'Entiers*. PhD thesis, L'Université Paris-Sud, 1980.

[333] Louis Monier. Evaluation and comparison of two efficient probabilistic primality testing algorithms. *Theoretical Computer Science*, 12(1):97–108, 1980.

[334] Edward F. Moore. The shortest path through a maze. In *Proceedings of the International Symposium on the Theory of Switching*, pages 285–292. Harvard University Press, 1959.

[335] Rajeev Motwani, Joseph (Seffi) Naor, and Prabhakar Raghavan. Randomized approximation algorithms in combinatorial optimization. In Dorit Hochbaum, editor, *Approximation Algorithms for NP-Hard Problems*, chapter 11, pages 447–481. PWS Publishing Company, 1997.

[336] Rajeev Motwani and Prabhakar Raghavan. *Randomized Algorithms*. Cambridge University Press, 1995.

[337] James Munkres. Algorithms for the assignment and transportation problems. *Journal of the Society for Industrial and Applied Mathematics*, 5(1):32–38, 1957.

[338] J. I. Munro and V. Raman. Fast stable in-place sorting with $O(n)$ data moves. *Algorithmica*, 16(2):151–160, 1996.

[339] Yoichi Muraoka and David J. Kuck. On the time required for a sequence of matrix products. *Communications of the ACM*, 16(1):22–26, 1973.

[340] Kevin P. Murphy. *Machine Learning: A Probabilistic Perspective*. MIT Press, 2012.

[341] S. Muthukrishnan. Data streams: Algorithms and applications. *Foundations and Trends in Theoretical Computer Science*, 1(2), 2005.

[342] Richard Neapolitan. *Foundations of Algorithms*. Jones & Bartlett Learning, fifth edition, 2014.

[343] Yurii Nesterov. *Introductory Lectures on Convex Optimization: A Basic Course*, volume 87 of *Applied Optimization*. Springer, 2004.

[344] J. Nievergelt and E. M. Reingold. Binary search trees of bounded balance. *SIAM Journal on Computing*, 2(1):33–43, 1973.

[345] Ivan Niven and Herbert S. Zuckerman. *An Introduction to the Theory of Numbers*. John Wiley & Sons, fourth edition, 1980.

[346] National Institute of Standards and Technology. Hash functions. https://csrc.nist.gov/projects/hash-functions, 2019.

[347] Alan V. Oppenheim and Ronald W. Schafer, with John R. Buck. *Discrete-Time Signal Processing*. Prentice Hall, second edition, 1998.

[348] Alan V. Oppenheim and Alan S. Willsky, with S. Hamid Nawab. *Signals and Systems*. Prentice Hall, second edition, 1997.

[349] James B. Orlin. A polynomial time primal network simplex algorithm for minimum cost flows. *Mathematical Programming*, 78(1):109–129, 1997.

[350] James B. Orlin. Max flows in $O(nm)$ time, or better. In *Proceedings of the 45th Annual ACM Symposium on Theory of Computing*, pages 765–774, 2013.

[351] Anna Pagh, Rasmus Pagh, and Milan Ruzic. Linear probing with constant independence. https://arxiv.org/abs/cs/0612055, 2006.

[352] Christos H. Papadimitriou. *Computational Complexity*. Addison-Wesley, 1994.

[353] Christos H. Papadimitriou and Kenneth Steiglitz. *Combinatorial Optimization: Algorithms and Complexity*. Prentice Hall, 1982.

[354] Michael S. Paterson. Progress in selection. In *Proceedings of the Fifth Scandinavian Workshop on Algorithm Theory*, pages 368–379, 1996.

[355] Seth Pettie. A new approach to all-pairs shortest paths on real-weighted graphs. *Theoretical Computer Science*, 312(1):47–74, 2004.

[356] Seth Pettie and Vijaya Ramachandran. An optimal minimum spanning tree algorithm. *Journal of the ACM*, 49(1):16–34, 2002.

[357] Seth Pettie and Vijaya Ramachandran. A shortest path algorithm for real-weighted undirected graphs. *SIAM Journal on Computing*, 34(6):1398–1431, 2005.

[358] Steven Phillips and Jeffery Westbrook. Online load balancing and network flow. *Algorithmica*, 21(3):245–261, 1998.

[359] Serge A. Plotkin, David. B. Shmoys, and Éva Tardos. Fast approximation algorithms for fractional packing and covering problems. *Mathematics of Operations Research*, 20:257–301, 1995.

[360] J. M. Pollard. Factoring with cubic integers. In A. K. Lenstra and H. W. Lenstra, Jr., editors, *The Development of the Number Field Sieve*, volume 1554 of *Lecture Notes in Mathematics*, pages 4–10. Springer, 1993.

[361] Carl Pomerance. On the distribution of pseudoprimes. *Mathematics of Computation*, 37(156):587–593, 1981.

[362] Carl Pomerance, editor. *Proceedings of the AMS Symposia in Applied Mathematics: Computational Number Theory and Cryptography*. American Mathematical Society, 1990.

[363] William K. Pratt. *Digital Image Processing*. John Wiley & Sons, fourth edition, 2007.

[364] Franco P. Preparata and Michael Ian Shamos. *Computational Geometry: An Introduction*. Springer, 1985.

[365] William H. Press, Saul A. Teukolsky, William T. Vetterling, and Brian P. Flannery. *Numerical Recipes in C++: The Art of Scientific Computing*. Cambridge University Press, second edition, 2002.

[366] William H. Press, Saul A. Teukolsky, William T. Vetterling, and Brian P. Flannery. *Numerical Recipes: The Art of Scientific Computing*. Cambridge University Press, third edition, 2007.

[367] R. C. Prim. Shortest connection networks and some generalizations. *Bell System Technical Journal*, 36(6):1389–1401, 1957.

[368] Robert L. Probert. On the additive complexity of matrix multiplication. *SIAM Journal on Computing*, 5(2):187–203, 1976.

[369] William Pugh. Skip lists: A probabilistic alternative to balanced trees. *Communications of the ACM*, 33(6):668–676, 1990.

[370] Simon J. Puglisi, W. F. Smyth, and Andrew H. Turpin. A taxonomy of suffix array construction algorithms. *ACM Computing Surveys*, 39(2), 2007.

[371] Paul W. Purdom, Jr. and Cynthia A. Brown. *The Analysis of Algorithms*. Holt, Rinehart, and Winston, 1985.

[372] Michael O. Rabin. Probabilistic algorithms. In J. F. Traub, editor, *Algorithms and Complexity: New Directions and Recent Results*, pages 21–39. Academic Press, 1976.

[373] Michael O. Rabin. Probabilistic algorithm for testing primality. *Journal of Number Theory*, 12(1):128–138, 1980.

[374] P. Raghavan and C. D. Thompson. Randomized rounding: A technique for provably good algorithms and algorithmic proofs. *Combinatorica*, 7(4):365–374, 1987.

[375] Rajeev Raman. Recent results on the single-source shortest paths problem. *SIGACT News*, 28(2):81–87, 1997.

[376] James Reinders. *Intel Threading Building Blocks: Outfitting C++ for Multi-core Processor Parallelism*. O'Reilly Media, Inc., 2007.

[377] Edward M. Reingold, Kenneth J. Urban, and David Gries. K-M-P string matching revisited. *Information Processing Letters*, 64(5):217–223, 1997.

[378] Hans Riesel. *Prime Numbers and Computer Methods for Factorization*, volume 126 of *Progress in Mathematics*. Birkhäuser, second edition, 1994.

[379] Ronald L. Rivest, M. J. B. Robshaw, R. Sidney, and Y. L. Yin. The RC6 block cipher. In *First Advanced Encryption Standard (AES) Conference*, 1998.

[380] Ronald L. Rivest, Adi Shamir, and Leonard M. Adleman. A method for obtaining digital signatures and public-key cryptosystems. *Communications of the ACM*, 21(2):120–126, 1978. See also U.S. Patent 4,405,829.

[381] Herbert Robbins. A remark on Stirling's formula. *American Mathematical Monthly*, 62(1):26–29, 1955.

[382] Julia Robinson. An iterative method of solving a game. *The Annals of Mathematics*, 54(2):296–301, 1951.

[383] Arch D. Robison and Charles E. Leiserson. Cilk Plus. In Pavan Balaji, editor, *Programming Models for Parallel Computing*, chapter 13, pages 323–352. The MIT Press, 2015.

[384] D. J. Rosenkrantz, R. E. Stearns, and P. M. Lewis. An analysis of several heuristics for the traveling salesman problem. *SIAM Journal on Computing*, 6(3):563–581, 1977.

[385] Tim Roughgarden. *Algorithms Illuminated, Part 1: The Basics*. Soundlikeyourself Publishing, 2017.

[386] Tim Roughgarden. *Algorithms Illuminated, Part 2: Graph Algorithms and Data Structures*. Soundlikeyourself Publishing, 2018.

[387] Tim Roughgarden. *Algorithms Illuminated, Part 3: Greedy Algorithms and Dynamic Programming*. Soundlikeyourself Publishing, 2019.

[388] Tim Roughgarden. *Algorithms Illuminated, Part 4: Algorithms for NP-Hard Problems*. Soundlikeyourself Publishing, 2020.

[389] Salvador Roura. Improved master theorems for divide-and-conquer recurrences. *Journal of the ACM*, 48(2):170–205, 2001.

[390] Y. A. Rozanov. *Probability Theory: A Concise Course*. Dover, 1969.

[391] Stuart Russell and Peter Norvig. *Artificial Intelligence: A Modern Approach*. Pearson, fourth edition, 2020.

[392] S. Sahni and T. Gonzalez. P-complete approximation problems. *Journal of the ACM*, 23(3):555–565, 1976.

[393] Peter Sanders, Kurt Mehlhorn, Martin Dietzfelbinger, and Roman Dementiev. *Sequential and Parallel Algorithms and Data Structures: The Basic Toolkit*. Springer, 2019.

[394] Piotr Sankowski. Shortest paths in matrix multiplication time. In *Proceedings of the 13th Annual European Symposium on Algorithms*, pages 770–778, 2005.

[395] Russel Schaffer and Robert Sedgewick. The analysis of heapsort. *Journal of Algorithms*, 15(1):76–100, 1993.

[396] Tao B. Schardl, I-Ting Angelina Lee, and Charles E. Leiserson. Brief announcement: Open Cilk. In *Proceedings of the 30th Annual ACM Symposium on Parallelism in Algorithms and Architectures*, pages 351–353, 2018.

[397] A. Schönhage, M. Paterson, and N. Pippenger. Finding the median. *Journal of Computer and System Sciences*, 13(2):184–199, 1976.

[398] Alexander Schrijver. *Theory of Linear and Integer Programming*. John Wiley & Sons, 1986.

[399] Alexander Schrijver. Paths and flows—A historical survey. *CWI Quarterly*, 6(3):169–183, 1993.

[400] Alexander Schrijver. On the history of the shortest paths problem. *Documenta Mathematica*, 17(1):155–167, 2012.

[401] Robert Sedgewick. Implementing quicksort programs. *Communications of the ACM*, 21(10):847–857, 1978.

[402] Robert Sedgewick and Kevin Wayne. *Algorithms*. Addison-Wesley, fourth edition, 2011.

[403] Raimund Seidel. On the all-pairs-shortest-path problem in unweighted undirected graphs. *Journal of Computer and System Sciences*, 51(3):400–403, 1995.

[404] Raimund Seidel and C. R. Aragon. Randomized search trees. *Algorithmica*, 16(4–5):464–497, 1996.

[405] João Setubal and João Meidanis. *Introduction to Computational Molecular Biology*. PWS Publishing Company, 1997.

[406] Clifford A. Shaffer. *A Practical Introduction to Data Structures and Algorithm Analysis*. Prentice Hall, second edition, 2001.

[407] Jeffrey Shallit. Origins of the analysis of the Euclidean algorithm. *Historia Mathematica*, 21(4):401–419, 1994.

[408] M. Sharir. A strong-connectivity algorithm and its applications in data flow analysis. *Computers and Mathematics with Applications*, 7(1):67–72, 1981.

[409] David B. Shmoys. Computing near-optimal solutions to combinatorial optimization problems. In William Cook, László Lovász, and Paul Seymour, editors, *Combinatorial Optimization*, volume 20 of *DIMACS Series in Discrete Mathematics and Theoretical Computer Science*. American Mathematical Society, 1995.

[410] Avi Shoshan and Uri Zwick. All pairs shortest paths in undirected graphs with integer weights. In *Proceedings of the 40th Annual Symposium on Foundations of Computer Science*, pages 605–614, 1999.

[411] Victor Shoup. *A Computational Introduction to Number Theory and Algebra*. Cambridge University Press, second edition, 2009.

[412] Julian Shun. *Shared-Memory Parallelism Can Be Simple, Fast, and Scalable*. Association for Computing Machinery and Morgan & Claypool, 2017.

[413] Michael Sipser. *Introduction to the Theory of Computation*. Cengage Learning, third edition, 2013.

[414] Steven S. Skiena. *The Algorithm Design Manual*. Springer, second edition, corrected printing, 2012.

[415] Daniel D. Sleator and Robert E. Tarjan. A data structure for dynamic trees. *Journal of Computer and System Sciences*, 26(3):362–391, 1983.

[416] Daniel D. Sleator and Robert E. Tarjan. Amortized efficiency of list update rules. In *Proceedings of the Sixteenth Annual ACM Symposium on Theory of Computing*, pages 488–492, 1984.

[417] Daniel D. Sleator and Robert E. Tarjan. Amortized efficiency of list update and paging rules. *Communications of the ACM*, 28(2):202–208, 1985.

[418] Daniel D. Sleator and Robert E. Tarjan. Self-adjusting binary search trees. *Journal of the ACM*, 32(3):652–686, 1985.

[419] Michael Soltys-Kulinicz. *An Introduction to the Analysis of Algorithms*. World Scientific, third edition, 2018.

[420] Joel Spencer. *Ten Lectures on the Probabilistic Method*, volume 64 of *CBMS-NSF Regional Conference Series in Applied Mathematics*. Society for Industrial and Applied Mathematics, 1993.

[421] Daniel A. Spielman and Shang-Hua Teng. Smoothed analysis of algorithms: Why the simplex algorithm usually takes polynomial time. *Journal of the ACM*, 51(3):385–463, 2004.

[422] Gilbert Strang. *Introduction to Applied Mathematics*. Wellesley-Cambridge Press, 1986.

[423] Gilbert Strang. *Linear Algebra and Its Applications*. Thomson Brooks/Cole, fourth edition, 2006.

[424] Volker Strassen. Gaussian elimination is not optimal. *Numerische Mathematik*, 14(3):354–356, 1969.

[425] T. G. Szymanski. A special case of the maximal common subsequence problem. Technical Report TR-170, Computer Science Laboratory, Princeton University, 1975.

[426] Robert E. Tarjan. Depth first search and linear graph algorithms. *SIAM Journal on Computing*, 1(2):146–160, 1972.

[427] Robert E. Tarjan. Efficiency of a good but not linear set union algorithm. *Journal of the ACM*, 22(2):215–225, 1975.

[428] Robert E. Tarjan. A class of algorithms which require nonlinear time to maintain disjoint sets. *Journal of Computer and System Sciences*, 18(2):110–127, 1979.

[429] Robert E. Tarjan. *Data Structures and Network Algorithms*. Society for Industrial and Applied Mathematics, 1983.

[430] Robert E. Tarjan. Amortized computational complexity. *SIAM Journal on Algebraic and Discrete Methods*, 6(2):306–318, 1985.

[431] Robert E. Tarjan. Class notes: Disjoint set union. COS 423, Princeton University, 1999. Available at https://www.cs.princeton.edu/courses/archive/spr00/cs423/handout3.pdf.

[432] Robert E. Tarjan and Jan van Leeuwen. Worst-case analysis of set union algorithms. *Journal of the ACM*, 31(2):245–281, 1984.

[433] George B. Thomas, Jr., Maurice D. Weir, Joel Hass, and Frank R. Giordano. *Thomas' Calculus*. Addison-Wesley, eleventh edition, 2005.

[434] Mikkel Thorup. Faster deterministic sorting and priority queues in linear space. In *Proceedings of the 9th ACM-SIAM Symposium on Discrete Algorithms*, pages 550–555, 1998.

[435] Mikkel Thorup. Undirected single-source shortest paths with positive integer weights in linear time. *Journal of the ACM*, 46(3):362–394, 1999.

[436] Mikkel Thorup. On RAM priority queues. *SIAM Journal on Computing*, 30(1):86–109, 2000.

[437] Mikkel Thorup. High speed hashing for integers and strings. http://arxiv.org/abs/1504.06804, 2015.

[438] Mikkel Thorup. Linear probing with 5-independent hashing. http://arxiv.org/abs/1509.04549, 2015.

[439] Richard Tolimieri, Myoung An, and Chao Lu. *Mathematics of Multidimensional Fourier Transform Algorithms*. Springer, second edition, 1997.

[440] P. van Emde Boas. Preserving order in a forest in less than logarithmic time and linear space. *Information Processing Letters*, 6(3):80–82, 1977.

[441] P. van Emde Boas, R. Kaas, and E. Zijlstra. Design and implementation of an efficient priority queue. *Mathematical Systems Theory*, 10(1):99–127, 1976.

[442] Charles Van Loan. *Computational Frameworks for the Fast Fourier Transform*. Society for Industrial and Applied Mathematics, 1992.

[443] Benjamin Van Roy. A short proof of optimality for the MIN cache replacement algorithm. *Information Processing Letters*, 102(2–3):72–73, 2007.

[444] Robert J. Vanderbei. *Linear Programming: Foundations and Extensions*. Kluwer Academic Publishers, 1996.

[445] Virginia Vassilevska Williams. Multiplying matrices faster than Coppersmith-Winograd. In *Proceedings of the 44th Annual ACM Symposium on Theory of Computing*, pages 887–898, 2012.

[446] Vijay V. Vazirani. *Approximation Algorithms*. Springer, 2001.

[447] Rakesh M. Verma. General techniques for analyzing recursive algorithms with applications. *SIAM Journal on Computing*, 26(2):568–581, 1997.

[448] Berthold Vöcking, Helmut Alt, Martin Dietzfelbinger, Rüdiger Reischuk, Christian Scheideler, Heribert Vollmer, and Dorothea Wager, editors. *Algorithms Unplugged*. Springer, 2011.

[449] Antony F. Ware. Fast approximate Fourier transforms for irregularly spaced data. *SIAM Review*, 40(4):838–856, 1998.

[450] Stephen Warshall. A theorem on boolean matrices. *Journal of the ACM*, 9(1):11–12, 1962.

[451] Mark Allen Weiss. *Data Structures and Problem Solving Using C++*. Addison-Wesley, second edition, 2000.

[452] Mark Allen Weiss. *Data Structures and Problem Solving Using Java*. Addison-Wesley, third edition, 2006.

[453] Mark Allen Weiss. *Data Structures and Algorithm Analysis in C++*. Addison-Wesley, third edition, 2007.

[454] Mark Allen Weiss. *Data Structures and Algorithm Analysis in Java*. Addison-Wesley, second edition, 2007.

[455] Herbert S. Wilf. *Algorithms and Complexity*. A K Peters, second edition, 2002.

[456] J. W. J. Williams. Algorithm 232 (HEAPSORT). *Communications of the ACM*, 7(6):347–348, 1964.

[457] Ryan Williams. Faster all-pairs shortest paths via circuit complexity. *SIAM Journal on Computing*, 47(5):1965–1985, 2018.

[458] David P. Williamson. *Network Flow Algorithms*. Cambridge University Press, 2019.

[459] David P. Williamson and David B. Shmoys. *The Design of Approximation Algorithms*. Cambridge University Press, 2011.

[460] Shmuel Winograd. On the algebraic complexity of functions. In *Actes du Congrès International des Mathématiciens*, volume 3, pages 283–288, 1970.

[461] Yifan Xu, I-Ting Angelina Lee, and Kunal Agrawal. Efficient parallel determinacy race detection for two-dimensional dags. In *Proceedings of the 23rd ACM SIGPLAN Symposium on Principles and Practice of Parallel Programming (PPoPP)*, pages 368–380, 2018.

[462] Chee Yap. A real elementary approach to the master recurrence and generalizations. In M. Ogihara and J. Tarui, editors, *Theory and Applications of Models of Computation. TAMC 2011*, volume 6648 of *Lecture Notes in Computer Science*, pages 14–26. Springer, 2011.

[463] Yinyu Ye. *Interior Point Algorithms: Theory and Analysis*. John Wiley & Sons, 1997.

[464] Neal E. Young. Online paging and caching. In *Encyclopedia of Algorithms*, pages 1457–1461. Springer, 2016.

[465] Raphael Yuster and Uri Zwick. Answering distance queries in directed graphs using fast matrix multiplication. In *Proceedings of the 46th Annual Symposium on Foundations of Computer Science*, pages 389–396, 2005.

[466] Jisheng Zhao and Vivek Sarkar. The design and implementation of the Habanero-Java parallel programming language. In *Symposium on Object-Oriented Programming, Systems, Languages and Applications (OOPSLA)*, pages 185–186, 2011.

[467] Uri Zwick. All pairs shortest paths using bridging sets and rectangular matrix multiplication. *Journal of the ACM*, 49(3):289–317, 2002.

[468] Daniel Zwillinger, editor. *CRC Standard Mathematical Tables and Formulae*. Chapman & Hall/CRC Press, 31st edition, 2003.

Index

This index uses the following conventions. Numbers are alphabetized as if spelled out; for example, "2-3-4 tree" is indexed as if it were "two-three-four tree." When an entry refers to a place other than the main text, the page number is followed by a tag: ex. for exercise, pr. for problem, fig. for figure, and n. for footnote. A tagged page number often indicates the first page of an exercise or problem, which is not necessarily the page on which the reference actually appears.